# THE ANCIENT MAYA

The corn god
from Late
Classic, Copan,
Honduras

# THE ANCIENT MAYA

## FIFTH EDITION

## ROBERT J. SHARER

Stanford University Press   Stanford, California

The first edition of this book, by Sylvanus G. Morley, was published in 1946; the second, with revisions by Morley, in 1947. The third edition, published in 1956, was prepared after Morley's death by George W. Brainerd, except for the final chapter, which was written after Brainerd's death by his editorial assistant, Betty Bell. The fourth edition, a revision of the third prepared by Robert J. Sharer and published in 1983, preserved much of the Morley-Brainerd text while adding the considerable results of research and reinterpretation then available (through ca. 1980). The present edition, also prepared by Robert J. Sharer, is a thoroughly rewritten and much expanded treatment based on the rapid advance in knowledge achieved in the dozen years since the fourth edition was prepared.

For the sources of the illustrations used in this volume, see the Illustration Credits.

Stanford University Press, Stanford, California
© 1946, 1947, 1956, 1983, 1994 by the Board of Trustees of the Leland Stanford Junior University

Printed in the United States of America

Fifth edition, 1994

CIP data appear at the end of the book

Original printing 1994

Last figure below indicates year of this printing:

05   04   03   02

# PREFACE

This book draws upon a number of disciplines, but the foundation of our knowledge about the ancient Maya is provided by archaeology, the science that reconstructs past societies from the study of their material remains. In recent decades, a variety of new techniques and technologies, better research designs, and more sophisticated theoretical frameworks, not to mention an explosive growth in the sheer numbers of Maya scholars and field studies, have all combined to make the results of archaeological investigation more precise and more complete than was previously possible. This unprecedented growth has fostered considerable advances in our understanding of the ancient Maya, but Maya archaeologists, like all scientists, realize that new discoveries will continue to change our perceptions in the years to come.

The archaeological foundation of our knowledge of the Maya is supplemented handsomely by ethnohistory, the discipline that reconstructs the history of non-Western societies. A wealth of information about Maya civilization that could never be recovered by archaeology alone is contained in written accounts by and about the Maya. A handful of pre-Columbian Maya books have survived, and many documents remain from the era of the Spanish Conquest. The nature of these written sources is summarized well by Sylvanus G. Morley, from his Preface to the first edition of this work:

During the century (1550–1650) following the Spanish Conquest, a number of native as well as Spanish writers carry on the story for us. Educated Maya who had been taught by the early Catholic missionaries to write their language in the characters of the Spanish alphabet in order to facilitate their instruction in the Catholic faith set down brief summaries of their own ancient history, probably copied directly from their then still surviving historical manuscripts in the Maya hieroglyphic writing. In addition to the foregoing native sources, several of the early Franciscan Fathers have left admirable accounts of the Maya as they were in the middle-sixteenth century, by far the most important being the contemporary narrative by Fray Diego de Landa, the second Bishop of Yucatán. His *Relación de las cosas de Yucatán*, written in 1566 . . . is [and remains today] unquestionably our leading authority on the ancient Maya.

But until the nineteenth century, most of the cities of the ancient Maya remained undiscovered, the spectacular achievements of their civilization largely unknown and the documents describing their society generally ignored. To continue with Morley's account:

During the next two centuries (1650–1840) very little was added to the Maya story, but in 1839–1841 John Lloyd Stephens, the American traveler, diplomat, and amateur archaeologist, accompanied by Frederick Catherwood, an English artist, visited the Maya area twice and embodied his impressions thereupon in two outstanding works: *Incidents of Travel in Central America, Chiapas, and Yucatan* (1841) and *Incidents of Travel in Yucatan* (1843). Both were illustrated by Catherwood's superb drawings; today, more than a hundred [now 150] years later, they still remain the most delightful books ever written about the Maya area.

Stephens' writings were chiefly responsible for bringing the great cities of the Maya civilization to the attention of the outside world. Before the publication of his two books, the very existence of these cities was unknown outside of Yucatan and northern Central America, but, after their appearance, knowledge of the Maya, who developed our greatest native American civilization, became general on both sides of the Atlantic. With Stephens also begins the period of the modern exploration of this region.

In the years that followed, a series of travelers explored the more accessible ruins of Maya civilization, and scholars began to rediscover many of the earlier accounts. The study of these documents provided the first useful information about the organization of ancient Maya society, about its customs, myths, and religion, and about its calendrical and writing systems. At length, during the final years of the nineteenth century and the early years of the twentieth century, the first formal archaeological investigations of Maya sites got under way. Quoting once again from Morley's original Preface:

Since Stephens' time many scientific institutions as well as individual students have been engaged in piecing together different parts of the Maya picture-puzzle. To mention all would expand this preface beyond reasonable limits, but the three most important should be noted: (1) the English archaeologist Sir Alfred P. Maudslay, the results of whose fifteen years of exploration in the Maya region (1881–1894) were published in the magnificent section on archaeology of the *Biología Centrali-Americana*, the first scientific publication about the Maya civilization; (2) the Peabody Museum of Archaeology and Ethnology of Harvard University, which, between 1888 and 1915, sent many expeditions to the Maya area under able leaders who have made many important contributions to our knowledge of the ancient Maya; (3) the Carnegie Institution of Washington, which [carried] on intensive studies in the

Maya field for [over] three decades. No fewer than twenty-five annual expeditions under trained archaeologists have been sent to different parts of the Maya area, and a vast amount of new material in many fields—archaeology, ethnology, anthropometry, history, linguistics, agriculture, botany, zoology, geography, medicine, and epidemiology—has been obtained.

Morley himself, one of the great pioneers in this era of Maya research, directed the Carnegie Institution's excavations at Chichen Itza (1924–40). On the strength of his years spent trekking through the lowland forests, discovering and recording scores of Maya monuments (in the course of which he published *The Inscriptions at Copan* and *The Inscriptions of the Peten*, both of them standard reference works for scholars to this day), he became the leading authority on Maya calendrical texts. Near the end of his career he wrote the first comprehensive account of Maya civilization, *The Ancient Maya*, published in 1946; a second edition appeared the following year. The second edition, based solidly on the evidence available at the time, quickly became a landmark in Maya studies. Nonetheless, the normal course of scientific progress and archaeological discovery soon rendered much of the work out-of-date. These new findings, arising most notably from the investigations at Mayapan, the excavation of the famous tomb beneath the Temple of the Inscriptions at Palenque, and the discovery of the Bonampak wall paintings, provided the basis for a posthumous revision of Morley's book by George W. Brainerd, University of California. This was published as the third edition of *The Ancient Maya*, in 1956.

As fate would have it, however, that very year marked the beginning of a veritable explosion of archaeological research in the Maya area. In 1956, the University Museum of the University of Pennsylvania initiated the Tikal Project, one of the largest and most comprehensive investigations of its kind ever undertaken by New World archaeologists. When the Penn program ended in 1970, its excavations continued, under the sponsorship of the Guatemalan Institute of Anthropology and History. And in the years following the mid-1950's, several dozen other archaeological research programs were undertaken throughout the Maya area, including large-scale projects at Altar de Sacrificios and Seibal, sponsored by the Peabody Museum of Harvard University, and at Dzibilchaltun, sponsored by the Middle American Research Institute of Tulane University. The results of this unprecedented era of investigation increased our store of information about the ancient Maya many times over. Not only did the volume of information increase, but beginning in the mid-1960's Maya archaeology also began to benefit, perhaps a bit belatedly, from the problem-oriented and more explicitly scientific research designs that were increasingly adopted by research projects elsewhere. These changes in the discipline of anthropological archaeology were part of the so-called "new archaeology," or "processual archaeology," the latter term being preferable by virtue of emphasizing an understanding of how ancient societies changed through time.

But perhaps the single most important advance in Maya studies in the past two decades sprang not from changes in the field of archaeology, but from rapid progress in deciphering Maya writing. Because this work gave archaeologists informed access to an ever-expanding corpus of hieroglyphic texts, the Maya of the Classic era in particular began emerging from the dim perspective of prehistory into the brighter light of recorded history. These advances, in both archaeology and decipherment, demonstrated by the mid-1970's that many of the basic premises we had held about ancient Maya subsistence, the organization of Maya society, and the course of Maya history were incorrect.

These obsolete notions about Maya civilization had formed the basis of the first three editions of *The Ancient Maya*, and the need for another, even more thorough, revision of Morley's original work became increasingly obvious. During the 1970's a great deal of new information was becoming available, not only about Maya civilization itself, but also about its origins and its geographical and temporal distribution and diversity. When the previous editions were written, most of the available data pertained to the Classic and Postclassic eras in the Maya lowlands, and there was a heavy emphasis on the Yucatecan ethnohistoric sources. The Preclassic period was little known, and there had been almost no consideration of the Maya of the southern highlands or the Pacific coast.

In 1980, work began on revising the third edition, and the result, the fourth edition, was published in 1983. Now, some twelve years after I began that task, the accelerating pace of research and the explosive growth in information have already rendered important sections of that edition woefully out-of-date. Furthermore, the field of archaeology has itself continued to change. Archaeology has always been allied to both anthropology and history, and processual archaeology, in particular, has always been closely allied to anthropology, often being pursued under the label of "anthropological archaeology." But in its studies of living societies, anthropology has developed *two* perspectives—a so-called "etic" view, which detaches the observer from the people being observed, with the goal of giving the study an unbiased, unintrusive, "scientific" perspective, and a so-called "emic" view, which unites the observer with the people being observed, with the goal of giving the study a more internal and intuitive perspective.

One of the most important recent trends in archaeology has in fact been to supplement the traditional etic, or external, scientific viewpoint of processual archaeology with a more emic perspective, one that seeks to develop a more internal understanding of past societies—to rediscover the view from within. (This development has been saddled with the unfortunate term "postprocessual archaeology," and some of its proponents believe their approach should replace processual archaeology.)

Of course anthropologists, conversing and participating with living people, and observing and recording their daily routines, can develop an emic perspective on a contemporary society, whereas archaeologists seeking an emic perspective on the past have yet to find a way to converse and participate with the dead, or observe their comings and goings. The most obvious corrective for this deficiency is history—the ability at least to read and understand the records written by those dead people about themselves. But that makes postprocessual archaeology almost totally dependent on written texts from the society being studied—and makes history, more than anthropology, its natural ally.

Although some archaeologists may maintain that pottery sherds speak to them, in truth, without being able to open the window of history afforded by written records, there is little chance that the scholar can ever achieve any sort of emic perspective on a society that is dead and gone. And processual archaeologists, for their part, must work with an incomplete inventory of material remains, knowing only that an unknowable number and range of products of human behavior have been lost to the processes of decay and destruction. In truth, both processual and postprocessual archaeology have their virtues, and both have their failings and their biases. Processual archaeology limits itself to making inferences from material remains, assuming that at a basic level, people and groups in all human societies behave in a more or less uniform manner. Thus a household rubbish pile, or a human burial accompanied by imported goods, reflects the same basic kinds of behavior whether it is found at a Maya site or at a site in Turkey. Postprocessual archaeology questions this assumption, and attempts to discover the particular, idiosyncratic behavior patterns of a vanished society. This is why written sources are so important, for they often reveal not only events, but also clues about attitudes, beliefs, and societal responses that would be impossible to glean from material remains alone. Still, as we all know, historical documents reflect the biases of their creators, and we are left inescapably with the problem of factoring out truth from propaganda.

Maya archaeologists are especially fortunate because, to a far greater degree than is true of any other pre-Columbian society, the ancient Maya left us not only the material remains eagerly sought by the processual archaeologists, but a sizable corpus of the written records—much of which can now be read—that furnishes the fodder for postprocessual study. Thus the ancient Maya provide us with an emic window, one that, to be sure, is restricted to only a portion of the long trajectory of Maya development and reflects almost exclusively the uppermost segment of society, but one that nonetheless offers a unique opportunity to supplement the scientific viewpoint with a more historical perspective. So long as we sustain a critical perspective—acknowledging that all our inferences about the past are but earnest approximations of what we know, and that all will be modified or rejected by tomorrow's discoveries—then we can combine the best of both worlds to useful effect. In fact, the combination of etic and emic perspectives is often found in the work of processual archaeologists who use *ethnoarchaeology*, basing their inferences about past human behavior on their own studies of behavior in living societies.

For the study of ancient Maya civilization, these two approaches are well-represented by two recently published works. Both appeared in 1990, and each is a kind of current summing up of what its approach can say about Maya civilization. *The New Archaeology and the Ancient Maya*, by Jeremy Sabloff, which represents the etic anthropological perspective, summarizes all the important progress made in understanding the ancient Maya by the application of increasingly sophisticated processual archaeological research. *A Forest of Kings*, by Linda Schele and David Freidel, which represents an emic and historical perspective, summarizes the important progress made in understanding the ancient Maya by some two decades of deciphering Maya inscriptions, including purely speculative reconstructions that often embellish the specific events recorded in the inscriptions.

There are scholars who believe that only one of these two avenues of investigation is valid. I take the position that both are valid, that although one may be preferable under certain circumstances, the best route to an understanding of the past is to combine the resources of the two, especially when one can be used to check or amplify the other. This book thus incorporates both the findings and interpretations of rigorously scientific archaeology and the readings and insights from emic historical decipherment. Because the historical texts record little or nothing about certain topics, some of the discussions—about Maya subsistence, for example—will be based primarily on the results of old-fashioned processual archaeology. But elsewhere—in Classic-period political history, for example—the texts provide a great deal of information. To be sure, much of that information is propagandistic, but by cross-checking one text against another, or checking the historical accounts *against the evidence from dirt archaeology*, we can often determine the reliability of these accounts. Still, even the propaganda is important, for it tells us something about the basis of power for Maya rulers and how they manipulated events to suit their own purposes. We will on occasion, therefore, report accounts that are almost surely elaborations, if not outright fabrications, in order to gain some insight into the problems faced by individual Maya rulers, and how they attempted to solve those problems.

It is thus not only the new field discoveries and the recent technical and quantitative advances in our understanding of the ancient Maya, but also the development of a more diverse range of perspectives on the Maya past, that have compelled me to return to the word processor to produce the present fifth edition of *The Ancient Maya*. (And even as I worked, important new discoveries were made at Caracol, Copan, and Dos Pilas, among others.)

The fifth edition, as did the fourth, attempts to retain and expand the scope and balance of Morley's original endeavor, while presenting a synthesis of as much of the old and new information about the ancient Maya as can reasonably be assembled in a single volume. To accomplish this, a number of passages and illustrations in the preceding edition have been dropped, many have been rewritten and moved, a vast amount of new information and a great many new illustrations have been incorporated (the text is now more than one-fourth longer), and virtually every paragraph, figure legend, and table has been revised, modestly or substantially.

The text is now organized into an Introduction, fifteen core chapters, and an Epilogue. The Introduction contemplates the Maya peoples and their fate across time and urges an end to the widespread desecration of remote sites by thieves and vandals. Chapter 1 describes the environmental setting of the Maya area. Chapters 2 through 7 offer completely revised and expanded discussions of the cultural history of the ancient Maya, incorporating descriptions of an expanded inventory of individual sites (previous editions treated that inventory in the chapter on architecture). A much more detailed treatment of the Classic era necessitated dividing its discussion in two, as Chapter 4 (Early Classic) and Chapter 5 (Late Classic). Chapter 8 covers ancient subsistence systems; Chapter 9, trade and external contact. Chapter 10, on Maya social and political organization, combines former Chapters 8 and 9; it has been revised to make use of important new data. Chapter 11, on ideology and cosmology, and Chapter 12, on arithmetic, calendrics, and astronomy, have been revised extensively. Chapter 13, on language and writing, has been revised with additions of considerable new information. Chapter 14 is reorganized to consider architecture and its associated sculpture and painting together. The main text closes with Chapter 15, a reorganized discussion of artifacts, and an Epilogue briefly recounting the Spanish Conquest. A short Appendix explains how Maya and Gregorian (modern) chronologies are converted, one to the other. The reader should note that, as with the fourth edition, all citations to relevant source materials are to be found, not in the text, but in chapter-by-chapter Bibliographic Summaries. The Bibliography proper, which follows the Summaries, furnishes full references for all the sources cited in the Summaries and elsewhere. The Index is both entirely new and greatly expanded.

As was the case with the fourth edition, the present work could not have been completed without the invaluable assistance of colleagues, friends, and family. My professional colleagues have continued to share generously with me the results of their work and their thoughts about the ancient Maya. Though it is impossible to mention all who have helped me, I will try to mention as many as I can of those who have provided direct and vital assistance.

Several colleagues kindly agreed to take the time to read and comment on large portions of the final draft of the text, and I want to thank personally professors E. Wyllys Andrews of Tulane University and Joyce Marcus of the University of Michigan for taking on this task; both offered many important suggestions that have considerably improved the present work. Other scholars have been equally generous in sharing their expertise with me, and have thus enriched the material covered here; included among them are Lic. Ricardo Agurcia F. (Asociación de Estudios

Precolombinos Copán), professors Richard E. W. Adams (University of Texas at San Antonio), Wendy Ashmore (University of Pennsylvania), Anthony Aveni (Colgate University), Diane Chase and Arlen Chase (both of the University of Central Florida), T. Patrick Culbert (University of Arizona), Arthur Demarest (Vanderbilt University), William Fash (Northern Illinois University), David Freidel (Southern Methodist University), David C. Grove (University of Illinois), Richard Hansen (UCLA), Stephen Houston (Vanderbilt), Richard Leventhal (UCLA), John Lucy (University of Pennsylvania), Peter Mathews (University of Calgary), Mary Miller (Yale University), Prudence Rice and Don Rice (both of Southern Illinois University), Jeremy Sabloff (University of Pittsburgh), Linda Schele (University of Texas), Edward Schortman and Patricia Urban (both of Kenyon College), David Stuart (Vanderbilt), and Gordon R. Willey (Harvard University).

Many of the illustrations in this book were provided by my colleagues. Though they are too numerous to be mentioned by name here (see Illustration Credits, just preceding the Index), I want to express my appreciation to all of them. I wish to acknowledge also the contributions made by several scholars to the fourth edition that have been retained in varying degrees here: Ian Graham (Harvard University) and professors Lyle Campbell (SUNY Albany), William R. Coe (University of Pennsylvania, emeritus), Arthur G. Miller (University of Maryland), and especially James A. Fox (Stanford University). A number of readers of the fourth edition have also written me with suggestions, and several found errors in the calendrical data (Chapter 16 and Appendix of that edition). I thank these people for their efforts, which have, I hope, led to improvements in the accuracy of the present edition. If any errors remain in these materials, or elsewhere in this book, they are my responsibility.

My colleagues at The University Museum, University of Pennsylvania, especially Christopher Jones, Peter Furst, and David Sedat, gave me valuable assistance. Julia C. Miller, while a graduate student in the Department of Anthropology at Penn, converted the entire text of the fourth edition to an electronic format (Microsoft Word); her work, which was supported by a much-appreciated grant from Stanford University Press, provided the vital starting point for the preparation of the fifth edition. She also handled the difficult but essential task of checking the Bibliographic Summaries against the Bibliography.

Finally, I am once again especially grateful to my editors at Stanford University Press: Ellen F. Smith, who guided this book through the final stages of its production, and in particular Bill Carver, who saw to the needs of the fourth edition and supported or augmented all my proposals for revision in both editions.

*Yax Ca'an Ha*                                                                    R.J.S.
East Jordan, Michigan

# CONTENTS

# TABLES

# FIGURES

## Introduction

## Chapter 1: The Setting

## Chapter 2: The Origins of Maya Civilization

## Chapter 3: The Preclassic Maya

## Chapter 4: The Early Classic and the Rise of Tikal

## Chapter 5: The Late Classic and the Expansion of the Lowland States

## Chapter 6: The Terminal Classic

## Chapter 7: The Postclassic

## Chapter 12: Arithmetic, Calendrics, and Astronomy

## Chapter 13: Language and Writing

## Chapter 14: Architecture, Sculpture, and Painting

## Chapter 15: Artifacts

# A NOTE ON NAMES, PRONUNCIATION, AND CONVENTIONS

The term "Maya" is used throughout this book as both a noun, in reference to the Maya people, as in "the Maya," and as an adjective, as in "Maya books," "Maya writing," etc. When referring specifically to the language *family*, however, it is customary to use the term "Mayan," as both a noun and an adjective, as in "the Mayan languages," "Proto-Mayan," "Yucatec Mayan," etc.

The names of some of the ancient Maya centers were recorded in the early colonial chronicles of Yucatan and the southern highlands. It would appear from these that Chichen Itza and Mayapan, for example, are original Maya names retained from the Postclassic era. But apart from exceptions like these, the original Maya names for most sites have been lost, and the names used today are in most cases those that were applied at the time the sites were discovered: Palenque, for example, was named after a nearby town with a Spanish name (*palenque*, or palisade), and Copan was named for a local chieftain shortly after the Conquest. Many centers have been given Spanish or Maya names that commemorate some outstanding attribute; examples include Piedras Negras ("black stones"), Uaxactun ("eight stone"), Coba ("wind-stirred water"), Tulum ("rampart"), and El Chayal (from "obsidian"). In the highlands, where the Spanish conquerors were accompanied by military allies from Central Mexico, most of the Maya site names were translated into Nahuatl (the language of the Mexica, or Aztecs) and are known by these terms to this day (the Quiche Maya capital of Gumarcaaj is known as Utatlan, its Nahuatl name). In some cases, for example Tikal and Quirigua, the origins and meanings of site names remain obscure (though it would appear that Quirigua is from a non-Mayan language that preceded Mayan in that area).

The orthography for the various Mayan and other indigenous Mesoamerican languages was first worked out by Spanish scholars of the colonial period. Thus transcribed, Mayan vowels are pronounced as in Spanish; rough English equivalents for the vowels of Yucatec Mayan are:

| | |
|---|---|
| *a* as in f*a*ther | *u* as in r*u*le |
| *e* as in l*e*t | (except before |
| *i* as in mach*i*ne | another vowel, then |
| *o* as in f*o*rty | as an English *w*) |

Consonants are also pronounced as in Spanish. Some, however, need special mention here:

| | |
|---|---|
| *c* (hard) as in *c*aught | *x* as *sh* in *sh*e |
| *ch* as in *ch*ur*ch* | *h* as in *h*is |
| *tz* as *ts* in nigh*ts* | |

Also, in Mayan languages there is a significant distinction between *glottalized* and plain consonants (see Chapter 13). The glottalized consonants have no English or Spanish equivalents.

Stress is usually regular in Mayan languages and is consequently not marked. In Yucatec, for example, it is on the final syllable, whereas it generally occurs on the next-to-last syllable in Spanish and Nahuatl. Though Yucatec does have distinctive pitch accents, or tones, these were usually not marked by colonial lexicographers and are omitted here, as are accents on indigenous words generally, following the usage of Ian Graham, *Corpus of Maya Hieroglyphic Inscriptions* (1975: 11).

The sound *tl* so often seen in words derived from Nahuatl is known as a lateral affricate. It is pronounced with the tongue in position for a *t* but with the release of air at the sides rather than over the tongue.

Archaeologists often use arbitrary terms derived from geographical names, indigenous words, and the like to designate time periods or assemblages of artifacts—for example the names of "ceramic complexes," which are blocks of time during which distinctive pottery types were made and used. Because the sheer numbers of such terms can be daunting to the nonspecialist, in this book we will limit the number of references to such terminology to only the most essential examples.

A fair number of unfamiliar terms—English, Mayan, Nahuatl (Aztec), and otherwise—are employed in the text. We have tried to see that only the more useful and more established of such terms are employed and that each is defined on first occurrence. For those English terms not defined in the text, see a standard desk dictionary.

This book employs the metric system, and does not offer English-measure equivalents, for the metric system is the standard both in science, internationally, and in the Latin American countries where the Maya still live, and will one day be standard in the United States as well. For those who wish to use English measures, the following conversions can be used: 1 centimeter (cm) = 0.39 inch; 1 meter (m) = 39.37 inches, or 3.28 feet; 1 kilometer (km) = 0.62 mile; 1 hectare = 2.47 acres; 1 square kilometer (km²) = 0.38 square mile; and 1 kilogram = 2.2 pounds.

# THE ANCIENT MAYA

# INTRODUCTION

This is the account of how all was in suspense, all calm, in silence; all
motionless, still, and the expanse of the sky was empty. . . . There was
nothing standing; only the calm water, the placid sea, alone and
tranquil. . . . Then came the word. Tepeu and Gucumatz came together in
the darkness, in the night, and Tepeu and Gucumatz talked together. They
talked then, discussing and deliberating; they agreed, they united their
words and their thoughts.

—*Popol Vuh* (Recinos 1950: 81–82)

**D**eep in the tropical forest of Guatemala lie the remains of one of the great
centers of Maya civilization, one of the foremost archaeological sites in all the
world. Hundreds of finely crafted masonry structures, evidently unknown to the
Spanish conquistadores and first seen by outsiders only in the mid-nineteenth century, are still in evidence at Tikal today. There are magnificent temples rising more
than 70 meters (230 feet) above the ground, grand complexes of palaces and administrative buildings, sculptured monuments bearing intricate hieroglyphs and the
portraits of powerful rulers and their gods. And there are reservoirs, causeways, and
a host of lesser constructions. The elite of Tikal society presided over an elaborate
hierarchy of nobles, priests, merchants, artisans, warriors, farmers, and servants,
and reaped the wealth of a network of commerce that extended from Central America to Central Mexico. The priestly elite had mastered many of the intricacies of
mathematics and had accurately calculated the movements of sun, moon, and
planets, and they interceded regularly with their gods in matters of noble destiny,
military or agricultural success, and long-term prosperity. Some 100,000 people
lived in and around Tikal during its prime, twelve hundred years ago. But Tikal was
not alone: the course of Maya history saw the rise and fall of a score or more of
cities that approached Tikal in size and power. And there were hundreds of smaller
towns and villages scattered across the Maya area, from the seacoasts to the rocky
highlands.

Just as Troy and Samarkand, Timbuktu and Rome, in the Old World, so also
the great Maya cities rose and fell, over a span of some two thousand years. During
that span, the cities of Nakbe, El Mirador, Tikal, Copan, Uxmal, Chichen Itza,
Mayapan, and a host of others enjoyed careers of expansion and prosperity, and
eventually declined, each in its time. By the time of the Spanish Conquest in the

The principal buildings of Tikal, rising above the tropical forest of lowland Guatemala (see also Fig. 4.6).

The centers of Maya civilization, often set deep in the tropical forest, have evoked feelings of mystery for centuries (Temple IV, the tallest structure at Tikal; see Fig. 4.6).

sixteenth century, Tulum, Tayasal, Utatlan, and Iximche had come to be among the most prominent of Maya powers. But these and the remaining Maya centers were crushed in a protracted, traumatic subjugation that consumed thousands of lives, of soldiers and non-soldiers alike. It was a scourge marked by appalling brutality, the determined mediation of the Church, and catastrophic epidemic disease. Thus did Maya civilization, along with the other indigenous societies of the New World, succumb at the hands of Europeans.

Ever since the remains of this brilliant civilization were first brought to light in the eighteenth and nineteenth centuries, the ancient Maya have attracted widespread interest and profound admiration. Part of this fascination undoubtedly derives from the romantic image of a "lost civilization" and the seeming mysteries evoked by the discovery of scores of ruined cities deep in the jungles of Mexico and Central America. But many of the questions posed by these discoveries were more genuine, and more obvious. Where had this civilization come from? How could the Maya have sustained themselves so successfully in such a supposedly inhospitable environment? What catastrophes had overwhelmed their abandoned cities? Today, scientific research, in a variety of disciplines, has made considerable progress in answering such questions. The mysteries are being solved, and basic misconceptions about the Maya are being corrected.

Still, the allure of the ancient Maya persists. The more we learn of them, the more profound is our respect. For as the record shows, these were a people of astonishing achievement: in mathematics, astronomy, calendrics, and writing systems; in technology, political organization, and commerce; in sculpture, painting, architecture, and the other arts. For the first time we are beginning to understand the origins of the civilization and the reasons for its growth and prosperity, as well as its setbacks. With this increasing knowledge we can recognize in the rise and decline of Maya civilization the same processes that underlie all human achievement, all human history. And although the ancient Maya may still seem somewhat alien from our point of view, their story is our story, a central event in the saga of human cultural development.

The story of the development of Western civilization is familiar to most of us—heirs, as we are, to a cultural tradition with its roots in the ancient cultures of the Near East (Egypt, Mesopotamia) and in the Classic world of Greek and Roman civilization. We are aware, too, of the great and enduring civilizations of the Far East (China, Japan, India). We are less well acquainted, perhaps, with a distinct cultural tradition that gave rise to another series of spectacular civilizations, including that of the Maya. This tradition was unknown to the peoples of the Old World until, five hundred years ago, their explorers suddenly encountered a vast New World, one inhabited by a variety of cultures, including sophisticated peoples living in cities as large as or larger than those of Europe, who practiced the arts of

The seeming mysteries of the ancient
Maya are receding in the face of
evidence gathered by modern research:
(*right*) archaeologists Aubrey Trik and
(in the foreground) Froelich Rainey
excavating beneath Temple II, Tikal,
Guatemala; (*below*) art historian
Arthur Miller and (at left)
archaeologist George Stuart at Tancah,
Quintana Roo, Mexico.

writing, metallurgy, architecture, and sculpture. These discoveries shocked and amazed the Spanish, who were intrigued by the civilizations of Mexico and Peru even as they were destroying them. One of the soldiers in the army of Cortés that marched into the Valley of Mexico in 1519, Bernal Díaz del Castillo, described the moment when Europeans caught their first view of the Mexica (Aztec) capital of Tenochtitlan from the mountain pass overlooking the sprawling city:

and when we saw so many cities and villages built in the water and other great towns on dry land and that straight and level causeway going towards Mexico, we were amazed and said that it was like the enchantments they tell of in the legend of Amadis, on account of the great towers . . . and buildings rising from the water, and all built of masonry. And some of our soldiers even asked whether the things we saw were not a dream. . . . I do not know how to describe it seeing things as we did that had never been heard of or seen before, not even dreamed about. (1963: 190–91)

To the Europeans of the sixteenth century, secure in the knowledge that they alone represented civilized life on earth, the discovery of the Mexica, the Inca, and the Maya came as a rude surprise. The situation may have been not unlike the one that would confront us today if, content that ours is the only known civilized planet in our Milky Way galaxy, we were suddenly to discover another planet inhabited not only by life, but by a civilization at least as sophisticated as our own. How would we react? Would we establish a peaceful dialogue, and learn from each other? Or would we seize the advantage and destroy that new world as the Spaniards did? The peoples of the New World, though capable of their own brutalities, were innocent of the ways of total, genocidal warfare as practiced by the Europeans, and in their vulnerability they were ultimately crushed by the conquistadores.

The Old World of the sixteenth century was not content merely to destroy the Mexica, Inca, and Maya civilizations. Their achievements had to be belittled, and their "pagan" religious rites, especially the mass human sacrifices of the Mexica, were held up as horrors justifying the Conquest. But lest we too easily decry such practices—they persisted for centuries among the ancient Maya too (see Chapter 11)—we should remember that Europeans of just four hundred years ago burned people alive in the name of religion and submitted their prisoners or heretics to an array of carefully perfected methods of torture and protracted executions. None of these peculiar Old World practices is known to have occurred in the New World prior to European colonization. Genocide, too, is a horror not of the New World, but of the Old, reaching new levels of efficiency and scale during World War II in Europe and East Asia, and even more recently in the killing fields of Cambodia.

But the greater part of the genocide unleashed upon the New World in the sixteenth century was accidental—for as far as we know, no one intentionally introduced the European diseases that dispatched millions of indigenous souls. There can be no arguing, however, that the destruction of the cultural and social fabric of these peoples was deliberate, the result of forced resettlement, religious conversion, and other coercive policies. And as the ultimate disparagement, Europeans even sought to deny the New World peoples their cultural heritage. When the new masters of the land tried to explain how civilization could have risen among the "savages," the answer was clear: the impetus had to have come from the Old World, the known birthplace of all such enlightenment. Thus the Mexica, Inca, and Maya were seen as the survivors of forgotten colonists from the Old World civilizations. Egypt was perhaps the most commonly attributed source, but Greece, Carthage, Phoenicia, Israel, Mesopotamia, Rome, Africa, India, China, Japan, and others have all been invoked for this shabby purpose at one time or another. In the first published description of the important Maya site of Palenque, in Chiapas, Mexico (written at the end of the eighteenth century), we find the following explanation for these mysterious ruins:

The conclusion drawn from thence must be, that the ancient inhabitants of these structures lived in extreme darkness, for, in their fabulous superstitions, we seem to view the ideology of the Phoenicians, the Greeks, the Romans and other primitive nations most strongly portrayed. On this account it may reasonably be conjectured, that some one of these nations pursued their conquests even to this country, where it is probable they only remained long enough to enable the Indian tribes to imitate their ideas and adapt, in a rude and awkward manner, such arts as their invaders thought fit to inculcate. (del Rio 1822: 19)

This idea, which either explicitly or implicitly asserts that the peoples of the New World were incapable of shaping their own destiny or of developing sophisticated cultures independently of Old World influence, is still popular in some quarters.

But this is but one more popular myth devoid of fact, for the evidence points unmistakably toward the evolution of civilization in the New World independently of developments in the Old World. After more than a century of gathering and analyzing archaeological evidence, we have discovered nothing to support the idea of intervention by peoples from the Old World. Rather, the evidence points consistently to an indigenous cultural development in the New World long after the original migrations populated North and South America from Asia via the Bering land bridge, over twelve thousand years ago.

And even while archaeology was in its infancy, in the nineteenth century, there were scholars who held that the Maya and other New World peoples reached their peak of development independently of influences from the Old World. One of the major figures in the discovery of Maya civilization, John Lloyd Stephens, anticipated the present-day consensus for indigenous development: "We are not warranted in going back to any ancient nation of the Old World for the builders of these cities. . . . There are strong reasons to believe them the creations of the same races who inhabited the country at the time of the Spanish Conquest, or of some not-very-distant progenitors" (1841, Vol. II: 455).

This is not to say that accidental contacts between Old and New World peoples could not have occurred before the age of European exploration. And it is just as likely that lost fishermen or merchants from the New World landed on the shores of Asia or Africa as vice versa (though this possibility is seldom, if ever, mentioned in such discussions). Still, the archaeological or archival evidence to demonstrate such contact, with one notable exception, has thus far failed to materialize. If firm evidence of early contact *is* discovered in years to come, it will be significant only if it can be demonstrated that the meeting affected the cultural development of one or both societies. Obviously, the contact initiated in 1492 has been significant for the changes it wrought in both the Old World and the New thereafter. But there are numerous accounts of earlier voyages to "lands across the sea" and contacts with unknown peoples. The Vikings, for example, recorded apparent New World landings by Leif Eriksson in 1001, and by Thorfinn Karlsefni eight years later, and their accounts have been supported by archaeological discoveries at L'Anse aux Meadows in Newfoundland, Canada. But these contacts apparently had no lasting effect on either society, the usual consequence of such limited encounters.

On the basis of the available evidence, then, the courses of cultural development in the New and Old Worlds seem clearly independent of each other and devoid of significant contact until 1492. This book assumes that we can understand the ancient Maya on their own terms, that the most brilliant of the New World civilizations was shaped by a combination of internal cultural processes, interactions with adjacent peoples of Mexico and Central America, and, to a lesser degree, stimuli from more distant societies as far away as North and South America. As such, the ancient Maya are to be "explained" not as a product of transplanted Old World civilization, but as the result of the processes that underlie the growth of any culture, including those that develop the kind of complexity we call civilization.

Our story will conclude with the Spanish Conquest, for the destruction wrought by this violent subjugation irretrievably transformed the developmental course of Maya civilization. The wars of the Conquest accounted for much of the immediate destruction, for the Maya resisted the loss of their independence with great tenacity. The prolonged conflict also disrupted agricultural production and commerce, and the resulting famines took a terrible toll. But the greatest loss of life is attributable to the diseases unwittingly introduced by the Europeans, against which the Maya had no immune defenses. In the face of all these destructive agencies, the institutions that had governed Maya society were swept away and replaced by a civil and religious colonial administration that was an integral part of the Spanish Empire. The Maya elite class—rulers, priests, military leaders, and even craftsmen and merchants—was decimated, and its survivors were stripped of their wealth and power. Religious conversion was a fundamental policy of the new authority, and a variety of coercive measures, including the Inquisition, were brought to bear in attempts to crush the vestiges of Maya ritual and belief. In the course of these changes, many of the intellectual achievements of the ancient Maya were lost or sorely attenuated. The native books (codices) were burned, and the use of Maya script soon ceased. As a result, a considerable body of knowledge and beliefs—essential information about the ancient calendar, cosmology, deities, ritual, medicine, and history—was lost forever. Many of the traditional arts—painting, sculpture, metallurgy, lapidary work, and featherwork—also expired, along with their practitioners.

The Maya economic system, too, was drastically altered. The best lands were seized, and plantations were established for the new masters. New products (such as coffee and sugarcane) soon replaced the goods that were fundamental to ancient commerce (cacao, obsidian, jadeite, feathers, etc.), and new markets and methods of transport replaced much of the complex network of trade routes that had linked the many cities and outposts of the Maya area. Not all the changes were violent or forcible: for the most part the Maya readily accepted the new European technology, and iron and steel tools, for example, quickly replaced those of flint and obsidian.

Yet, in the face of these profound changes, much of the ancient Maya culture survived. Although most of its hallmarks were stripped away with the Conquest, the very heart of Maya society—the agricultural family and community—clung tenaciously to its traditions and preserved many of its lifeways. For the most part the Spanish administrators did not or could not reach the agricultural villages, except in areas where forced resettlement was instituted; and as long as the required tax and labor obligations were met, these communities continued largely to govern their own affairs. The social institutions of marriage and kinship that governed family life continued with little change.

Weaving with the back-strap loom is an ancient craft still practiced in Maya communities today (mother and daughter, San Pedro Necta, Huehuetenango, Guatemala).

After the Conquest, the Maya family continued to subsist by its own efforts, deriving from the newly arrived steel tools more efficient agricultural production. Traditional crafts oriented to household consumption—weaving, basketry, pottery making—continued essentially unchanged. Local agricultural and manufactured products, together with those essentials in scarce supply (salt, tools, etc.), were exchanged in community markets that persisted long after the Conquest; native commerce survived, albeit on a more limited scale. In some cases the new masters of the land actually encouraged the indigenous economy, by ordering and using pottery cooking or storage vessels or other Maya products. But because these items were usually made to European specification, their production introduced still another avenue for altering ancient traditions.

The most enduring elements of Maya culture have been ideology and language, elements that lie at the heart of all cultures. The traditions of Maya ideology and language permeated and reinforced all facets of family and community life, and today continue to be most resistant to change. Despite the vigorous efforts by missionaries to convert the Maya to Christianity, the traditional beliefs governing family life and the agricultural cycle have managed to survive even while accommodating the new religion. The Mayan languages, too, continued in the new setting. A secondary knowledge of Spanish is obviously useful in dealing with the wider world—for civil and economic interaction, for example—but the Mayan tongues have persisted as the first-learned and sometimes only languages in traditional family life.

Centralized markets, another activity persisting from ancient times, are found in many Maya communities today (market at Chichicastenango, El Quiché, Guatemala).

The direct heirs to these Maya traditions continue to this day to live in the area once occupied by the great civilization of their ancestors. Although often isolated by their many related dialects and languages, there are today at least four million Mayan-speaking people in Mexico, Belize, and Guatemala. Obviously, to the extent that traditional social organization, agricultural practices, technology, and belief systems (including vestiges of the ancient calendar) survive, the study of contemporary Maya communities offers an important source of information for the reconstruction of the ancient Maya civilization. The work of anthropologists who have studied these communities, including the research of several Maya scholars, has preserved information that has been invaluable to our understanding of past and present.

Today, however, the traditional culture of these people, already altered by Conquest decrees and subsequent colonial policies, is changing at an unprecedented rate. The insidious influences of the modern world seem capable of changing profoundly what the Spanish could only partially disturb. Today, in Maya communities from Yucatan to Guatemala, store-bought clothing has replaced handwoven textiles, plastic containers are often more common than traditional pottery vessels, and satellite television bombards the Maya with alien languages, images, and ideologies that accelerate the process of "westernization." As a result, the younger generations in formerly isolated communities are turning away from the traditions that once assured the survival of Maya culture.

But the traditional culture of the Maya people is not the only heritage of Maya civilization that is disappearing in today's world. The physical embodiment of the Maya past is also facing destruction, as the archaeological remains of hundreds of ancient Maya sites are being pillaged by looters searching for jade, painted pottery, and sculpture that can be sold on the thriving antiquities market. Examples of Classic-period Maya "art" fetch the highest prices, so that many ruined cities never seen by the Spanish conquistadores, sites that have lain undisturbed for a thousand years, have been utterly destroyed for a few objects that have commercial value. Today, as sad as it may seem, archaeologists acknowledge that just about every Maya site has been pillaged—and most of them will probably never be scientifically investigated.

As we shall see, the studies of Maya sites by archaeologists, decipherers, and other scholars have produced considerable advances in our understanding of the ancient Maya. The key to this knowledge is archaeological evidence, the careful discovery and recording of the remains of buildings and artifacts which, like pieces of a jigsaw puzzle, reveal a picture only when all are found and put properly into place. The recent advances in deciphering Maya writing and reconstructing dynastic histories at many Maya centers have been possible only because the sources of information were known to come from specific sites and to be associated there with

The Lacandon are a Maya group dwelling in the lowland forest of Chiapas, Mexico: (*above*) a small girl holding a peccary she has tamed; (*right*) a young man in front of Stela 1 at the Classic Maya site of Bonampak; (*below*) a family with their dugout canoe.

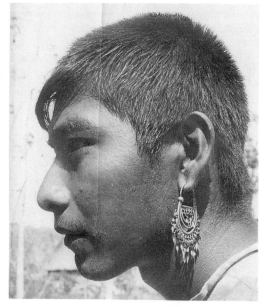

The Yucatec Maya inhabit the vast northern lowlands of the Yucatan peninsula: (*above*) a family in Tixcacal, Quintana Roo, Mexico; (*left*) the wife of the headman of Tixcacal; (*below*) Juan Bautista Poot, a minor official in Tixcacal.

The Maya constitute numerous linguistic groups: (*upper row*) Yucatec Maya from the northern lowlands, Yucatan, Mexico; (*middle row*) Quiche Maya from the highlands of Guatemala; (*lower left*) Mam Maya officials from the highland community of San Pedro Necta, Huehuetenango, Guatemala, holding staffs of office, traditional symbols of authority.

Tzotzil Maya from the highlands of Chiapas, Mexico: (*upper right*) youth from Chamula; (*middle right*) young girl from Izapa; (*lower right*) young man from Chamula; (*below*) man from Zinacantan.

other kinds of evidence, such as texts from within a tomb or from a specific building. Without this kind of contextual information, these advances in knowledge cannot be made. Thus, when tombs are plundered for their jade and pottery, or sculptures are torn from buildings or sawed off of stelae (stone monuments), their full meaning is destroyed.

The destruction wrought by archaeological looting is a complex and controversial topic, and the solution to the problem is by no means clear. But make no mistake, any archaeological object sold without documentary proof that it was legally acquired and exported from its country of origin was almost certainly found by looting. Some collectors of Maya "art"—including, sad to say, even some with scholarly standing—have defended the pillage of ancient sites by claiming that the fragments of sculpture and the painted pots that are sold on the market are at least

The destruction of archaeological sites by illegal looting robs the Maya of their cultural heritage: here a looter's trench leads to a plundered tomb at the site of Naachtun, Guatemala; the trench, photographed in 1976, is strewn with broken plain pottery destroyed in the search for a few prized polychrome vessels to be sold on the "art" market.

Another common form of desecration from illegal looting: (*above*) Stela 1 at the site of Jimbal, Guatemala, photographed after its discovery in 1965 by archaeologists from the Tikal project; (*below*) the same stela a few years later, after looters failed in an attempt to saw off the sculptured front surface, utterly destroying the upper part of the carving.

being saved from decay or neglect. According to this argument, the looting that feeds the flourishing market in stolen archaeological artifacts is done by humble peasants who happened to come upon buried pots and carved monuments. Though it is true that some peasant farmers add to their meager living by digging up antiquities, only a small fraction of the archaeological plunder can be accounted for from such sources. In reality, the purchasers of plundered artifacts support an elaborate black market employing thousands of thieves and middlemen. This illicit network begins with looters who are more often than not skilled specialists and continues with local buyers, smugglers, "restorers," and dealers. In some cases, looting expeditions that target a specific site or region are planned and financed by the dealers and collectors. And for every pot or sculptured stela that is "preserved" by this activity, dozens or even hundreds of objects are destroyed by frenzied digging aimed only at finding the very rare, well-preserved, and marketable items. As for the few objects deemed valuable enough for the art market, it is true that these will be physically preserved, but their meaning for archaeological interpretation will have been altered or destroyed. This is not to deny that in some cases there is information that can be gleaned from looted objects—the best example probably being the hieroglyphic texts inscribed on artifacts, which can often be deciphered. But even in the best-case example, the information obtained from such a text would be far more complete and meaningful if we knew exactly where the object came from, what it was found with, and the other kinds of contextual data that archaeologists record and looters ignore or kick aside.

Looted artifacts can also present scholars with another problem: many objects destined for the black market are "restored" to increase their value. Such restoration often alters the original piece, by "improving" painted scenes or hieroglyphic texts, or it may even add a text where originally there was none. In fact, the black market is infected with complete forgeries, some so skillful that they go undetected. Thus all attempts to gain legitimate archaeological data from undocumented objects run the risk of accepting distorted or even completely bogus information.

Does art collecting preserve objects that would otherwise be lost? There is no denying that the physical remains of the past will inevitably decay—but this is true whether they are still in the ground, or in the hands of a professional archaeologist, or on the shelf of a private collector. But the *knowledge* that can be gained from an archaeological site by modern archaeological methods will never decay. And once an archaeological site has been pillaged to recover a few marketable objects, humanity has irretrievably lost much of the information that archaeologists might have assembled from that site. The loss of this kind of data is irreversible; once a building is torn apart to loot a single pottery vessel, all the evidence that had accompanied that artifact is also destroyed. The remains of the past, including those of ancient Maya civilization, in a very real sense are a *nonrenewable resource* representing knowledge about a vanished society. With every site that is plundered, we lose another portion of that knowledge *forever*.

What can be done to halt this destruction? There may be no slowing the cultural changes wrought by progress on traditional Maya communities, but most countries do have laws against archaeological looting. In Mexico, Guatemala, Belize, Honduras, and El Salvador, it is illegal to plunder Maya sites. It is also illegal to import looted materials into the United States and many other countries. Still, no country has the money or the manpower to police all of its archaeological sites, or to prevent all antiquity smuggling. And lest we criticize those nations that have custody of the ancient Maya sites, we should recognize that every year dozens of prehistoric and historic sites are looted and destroyed in the United States as well.

The ultimate answer to this worldwide problem is economic. Sites are looted for one reason: some people will pay astounding prices for certain antiquities. Art collecting is a respectable and rewarding hobby or business, as long as it trades in paintings, sculptures, and other art that has been produced by artists, past or present, for our enjoyment. But the buying and selling of artifacts fresh from an archaeological site is not art collecting; a Classic Maya vase does not come from an artist's studio, but from a looted tomb. Since nothing can be done to replace the information lost by an already-looted object, the buying and selling of items already known to be in private collections can do no further harm. But the art market that supports ongoing looting continues to take an increasing toll of humanity's archaeological resources. The only solution to this expanding destruction is to decrease the demand for new objects. Collectors and dealers know something about the origins of objects being offered for sale, and they can usually recognize newly looted artifacts, *so if they refuse to buy these objects, the pillaging will decline.* It would be ironic if today's world, responsible for the interest and research that has done so much to recover the lost glories of Maya civilization, should also be responsible for the final destruction of the physical remains of the ancient civilization and the severing of the last living links—cultural, ideological, linguistic—that bind the modern Maya to their own heritage.

What we do know about the once enigmatic ancestors of the modern Maya is prodigious, and as the chapters that follow will demonstrate, their tale is at once fascinating and astonishing. There remains much to study—provided the opportunities are not denied us—and how much more we will learn in the years ahead depends in large measure on how much of the archaeological record can be preserved from destruction.

# THE SETTING

There is the white sea, and there is a red sea. They say that there is a sea
like milk. . . . Because they say that there is just water under the earth.
And over the water we are floating. Because they say that where the edge
of the world remains . . . there is just water . . . there they join, the edge
of the world and the sky.

—Contemporary Chorti Maya view of their world
  (after Fought 1972: 373)

The broad expanse of territory occupied by the Maya in the centuries before the Conquest—we shall call it the Maya area—is defined both by the distribution of ancient ruins of Maya civilization and by the known distribution of
peoples still speaking Mayan languages. These criteria bound an area of some
324,000 km², a region roughly the size of the State of New Mexico. The area embraces the southeastern extremity of Mexico, including the whole of the Yucatan
Peninsula and most of the modern states of Chiapas and Tabasco, to the west, and
much of northwestern Central America, to the east, including the nations of Guatemala and Belize and the western parts of Honduras and El Salvador (Fig. 1.1).
Firm geographic boundaries to the Maya area exist only to the south (the Pacific
Ocean) and to the north (the Gulf of Mexico and the Caribbean Sea). To the southwest and southeast, boundaries are more difficult to fix, since they correspond not
to discrete geographic features but to zones of cultural transition between Maya
and non-Maya peoples. Still, on the west, the Isthmus of Tehuantepec, a narrowing
of the Mexican landmass to just under 200 km wide, provides a convenient and
fairly accurate boundary between the Maya and non-Maya areas of southern Mexico. And on the east, the zone of transition falls roughly along a line from the lower
Río Lempa in central El Salvador northward to Lago de Yojoa and thence along
the Río Ulúa to the Gulf of Honduras in the Caribbean Sea.

The diffuse nature of these cultural boundaries reminds us that Maya civilization cannot be seen as an isolated development. Beyond sharing common roots
in language and tradition, the ancient Maya were very much a part of a larger cultural area that has come to be called Mesoamerica.

•    The Mesoamerican culture area extends from northern Mexico into Central America as far as Costa Rica. Like the Andean culture area of South America, Mesoamerica is often referred to as a "nuclear area," for during the last several millennia prior to European colonization it was host to a series of crucial cultural developments. These included the origins of permanently settled villages, the development of agriculture (based on maize, beans, squashes, and other crops), and the emergence of complex societies with urban or semi-urban centers, monumental architecture, calendrical systems, writing, and similar cultural features that are collectively and conveniently referred to as *civilization*. Thus, as part of Mesoamerica, the ancient Maya were influenced by, and in turn influenced, their neighboring cultures, such as the Olmec to the northwest, on the Gulf coastal plain, the Zapotec and Mixtec of Oaxaca (west of the isthmus), the cultures centered in Teotihuacan and Tula (to the north, in Central Mexico), and the less well known societies to the southeast in Central America.

## Natural and Cultural Subdivisions of the Maya Area

Traditionally, scholars have divided the Maya area into two broad zones, the highlands in the south and the lowlands in the north (Fig. 1.1). According to this somewhat oversimplified view, the highland zone was seen to be both ecologically diverse and rich in a variety of resources, whereas the lowlands were often viewed as ecologically uniform and poor in resources. This distinction was often extended to cultural development in the highland and lowland Maya zones, the view being that the lowland environment was inhospitable or even hostile to human utilization. Thus the ancient lowland Maya were seen as an enigma, an exception to the geographer's traditional "rule" that brilliant civilizations could not develop in marginal tropical-lowland environments.

Recent, more thorough studies have laid these preconceptions to rest. It is now known, for example, that the Maya lowlands are not deficient in resources and that, far from being ecologically uniform, they display considerable variation. More important, recent ecological and archaeological investigations demonstrate that both the environment of the Maya area and the cultural development it supported are far too diversified to be subsumed under a simple highland/lowland dichotomy.

For its size, the Maya area represents one of the most varied environments on earth. There are contrasts in landform from rugged, almost inaccessible terrain to vast, level plains. Differences in altitude produce differences in climate: cool, temperate conditions prevail in most highland valleys and plateaus, and hot, tropical conditions prevail at many of the lower elevations (Figs. 1.2 and 1.3). The climatic subdivisions traditionally employed in works on the Maya area reflect these altitude differences: *tierra caliente* (hot country), from sea level to about 800 m; *tierra templada* (temperate country), from 800 m to about 2,000 m; and *tierra fría* (cold

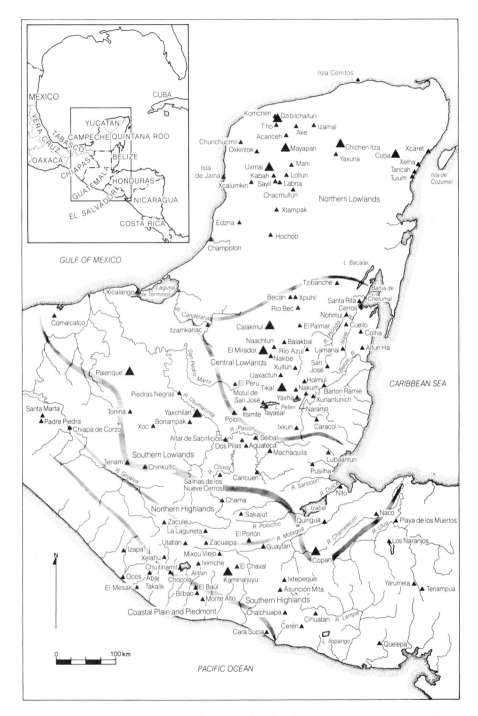

Fig. 1.1. Map of the Maya area, showing principal archaeological sites, major rivers, and generalized environmental-cultural subdivisions (owing to density of settlement, not all sites mentioned in the text appear on this map).

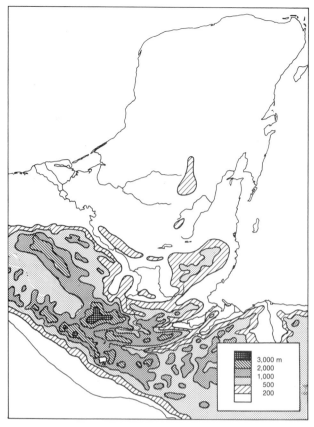

Fig. 1.2. Surface elevations above mean sea level in the Maya area; the highlands lie entirely to the south.

| | |
|---|---|
| | 3,000 m |
| | 2,000 |
| | 1,000 |
| | 500 |
| | 200 |

Fig. 1.3. Mean annual temperatures in the Maya area; the pattern more or less follows elevation.

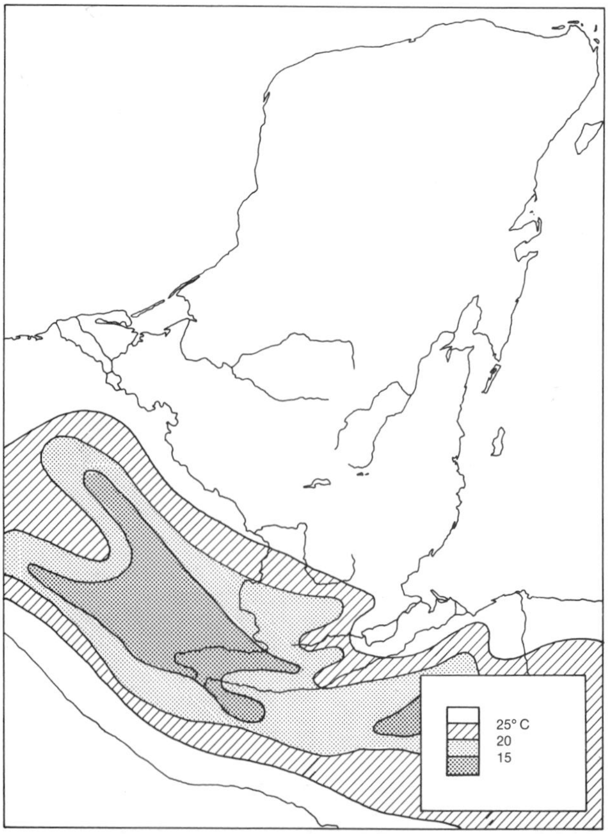

| | |
|---|---|
| | 25° C |
| | 20 |
| | 15 |

country), above 2,000 m. But altitude is not the sole determinant of climate. Variations in the amount and timing of rainfall create contrasts across the full range of elevation (Fig. 1.4): dry, almost desertlike environments are found in certain zones of both highlands and lowlands; and elsewhere, at almost any altitude, a superabundance of moisture can produce zones of tropical rain forest. Water is often readily available in free-flowing rivers; elsewhere it may be found only in caverns deep beneath the surface, and all but inaccessible. In some areas, deep alluvial or volcanic soils support highly productive agriculture; in others, thin, poor soils support little except thorn and scrub forest.

The southern reaches of the Maya area are extremely active geologically. Here, where three continental plates converge, volcanic eruptions and earthquakes have repeatedly produced local and regional disasters—some of which have been detected archaeologically.

In order to assess the impact of this varied environment on the ancient Maya, modern investigators often attempt to reconstruct the natural conditions that obtained in the past. The starting point for such studies combines a description of the present environment with the available archaeological evidence bearing on the ancient environment. By comparing evidence from both past and present, scholars attempt to determine how similar the ancient conditions were to those found today, and to what degree human interference or natural processes may have altered the environment. In a general sense, the findings from such studies indicate that during

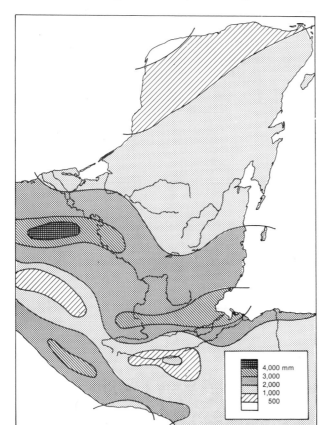

Fig. 1.4. Mean annual rainfall in the Maya area; the pattern is quite complex in the highlands to the south, but as one moves north, moderately dry shades steadily into very dry.

4,000 mm
3,000
2,000
1,000
500

the past several thousand years the environment of the Maya area has been rather uniform, especially as regards landform and climatic factors. Some changes have occurred, however; there is evidence, for example, of a general trend toward diminishing rainfall in some areas of the Maya lowlands, which may mean that the number and size of the lakes in the lowlands were greater in the past than they are today, and that the drying up of these lakes may have played a role in the shifting patterns of human occupation seen in the archaeological record of the lowlands. There are also indications that short-term variations in seasonal rainfall patterns may have affected living conditions in the past, especially in lowland areas such as the Yucatan Peninsula. And in many highland areas the basic form of the landscape has been altered by volcanic deposits and erosion. But the most drastic changes, in the highlands and elsewhere, are to be seen in the areas of heaviest recent occupation, where agricultural over-exploitation has resulted in deforestation, erosion, and soil exhaustion.

In general, the Maya area can be looked upon as constituting three basic environmental, or ecological, zones, each of which may be further divided. From south to north the environmental zones of the Maya area are: (1) the Pacific coastal plain and piedmont, or foothills; (2) the highlands, subdivided into the volcanic, or southern, highlands, and the metamorphic, or northern, highlands; and (3) the lowlands, subdivided into the transitional, or southern, lowlands, the Peten, or central, lowlands, and the Yucatecan, or northern, lowlands (Fig. 1.1). The boundaries of these zones and subdivisions are of course to a large extent arbitrary, since each actually is bordered by subtle transitions to adjacent zones or subdivisions. Furthermore, because none of the subdivisions is itself uniform, the description of each must also be generalized.

Because of limitations of space, it has been impossible to include all Maya site names and all geographic features on Fig. 1.1. For a larger-format map with far more information, the reader should consult the map titled *The Ancient World of the Maya*, published by the National Geographic Society.

## The Pacific Coastal Plain and Piedmont

A broad, fertile plain composed of Recent (Quaternary) sediments stretches along the Pacific coast from the Isthmus of Tehuantepec, across southern Guatemala, and into western El Salvador. This plain has long provided rich resources for human existence and an avenue for both migration and commerce. Some of the earliest traces of permanent settlement in Mesoamerica have been found along the margins of the mangrove swamps, coastal lagoons, and meandering river mouths that lie just behind the Pacific beaches (Fig. 1.5). Extending inland from the sea lies the gently rising coastal plain proper, known for its rich alluvial and volcanic soils, but long denuded of most of its original forest cover.

Fig. 1.5. Pacific coastal plain: mangrove growth in a coastal lagoon, Guatemala.

The plain is transected by a series of relatively short, swiftly flowing rivers that drain the piedmont and upper slopes of the chain of volcanoes that parallels the coast some 50 to 70 km inland. The only major river cutting the plain is the Río Lempa in El Salvador, which is also the traditional southeastern boundary of the Maya area.

For far longer than any other peoples of the Maya area, those of the Pacific plain have had to contend with waves of foreign migrants and invaders. The earliest of these appear to have been related to the Olmec tradition centered in the Gulf coastal region, to the northwest. Later on, a succession of peoples from Central Mexico settled the plain, and today, in the aftermath of the Spanish Conquest, various peoples of European descent are also among the inhabitants of the area.

Before the Conquest, the coastal plain was well known among Mesoamerican peoples for its extensive cacao (chocolate) plantations. Today, the best lands are given over to the cultivation of sugarcane and cotton and to cattle ranches, and the higher slopes support vast coffee plantations.

The climate of the plain is tropical (*tierra caliente*), with mean annual temperatures in the 25°–35°C range (77°–95°F), becoming somewhat cooler with the increasing altitude of the piedmont. There is a relatively dry period from January to April, the hottest days being those at the end of the dry season, and heavy rains fall from May to December. These rains are produced as the warm westerly winds from the Pacific Ocean rise and cool against the slopes of the volcanic highlands. The result is one of the highest rainfall rates in the Maya area: an average of over 3,000 mm of rain per year falls on the Pacific slopes of the State of Chiapas, in Mexico, and on western Guatemala, and over 2,000 mm of rainfall is typical for most of the rest of these coastal areas (Fig. 1.4).

In the zones of higher precipitation, relic stands of the original rain forest still exist, usually at altitudes between 150 m and 800 m. The tallest trees here may reach 30–40 m in height, and a lower canopy averages 20 m above the ground. Beneath this cover a variety of palms, ferns, shrubs, and small trees, including cacao (the chocolate tree), may be found. As one moves into higher elevations, the rain forest gives way to seasonal growth of the mixed oak and pine woodland typical of the highlands.

Although much of the original animal life of the south coast has been disturbed or destroyed by modern settlement and plantation agriculture, many species remain. The sea and coastal lagoons still abound with fish, shellfish, amphibians, and sea birds. Aquatic reptiles like the sea turtle, water moccasin, and caiman (a relative of the alligator) are still found. Inland, iguanas and various smaller lizards, small mammals, and birds of all sorts are typical, along with rarer species such as the python. And the Pacific coast especially teems with mosquitoes, biting flies, and other insect pests.

The Pacific shoreline and lagoons were exploited throughout the pre-Columbian era, for not only is this environment rich in food resources, but the extraction of salt from seawater by evaporation provided a lucrative product for trade. Further inland, a series of sites grew to importance as centers of marketing, ceremonial, and political activity. Early centers such as Izapa, Abaj Takalik, El Baúl, and Chocola represent the first flowering of Maya civilization, and appear to have prospered from the production of cacao and the control of important trade routes that transect this region. The successors of these centers were still thriving over a thousand years later, at the time of the Spanish Conquest, but many centuries earlier the heartland of Maya civilization had already begun shifting to the lowlands, to the north. Thereafter, the Pacific plain was clearly peripheral to developments farther north.

## The Highlands

The greatest concentration of environmental diversity in the Maya area is found in the highlands, an area generally above 800 m in elevation and characterized by both *tierra templada* and *tierra fría* climates. Owing to its diversity, many subdivisions can be defined within this zone. Lowland areas, for example, penetrate deep into the highlands, as canyons carved by the rivers that flow toward the coasts. But for our purposes, distinguishing just two major highland areas will be sufficient: one to the south, highly populated and dominated by recent volcanic activity, and the other to the north, less disturbed and characterized by older, metamorphic formations.

## *The Volcanic, or Southern, Highlands*

The southern highlands lie in an east-west band between, on the south, the belt of volcanic cones that parallels the Pacific coast and, on the north, the great rift-valley system (Fig. 1.1). This rift system marks, at least in part, the junction of two continental plates. As a consequence, this highland area experiences frequent tectonic activity, in the form of earthquakes and volcanic eruptions, and a nearly continuous line of young volcanoes forms the continental divide from the border of Chiapas, Mexico, through Guatemala, and into Central America (Fig. 1.6). From west to east the major cones are Tacana, Tajumulco, Santa María, Zunil, San Pedro, Atitlan, Toliman, Acatenango, Fuego, Agua, and Pacaya, all in Guatemala, and Santa Ana, Izalco, and San Salvador, in El Salvador. The highest is Tajumulco at 4,410 m. In recent years, Santa María, Fuego, and Pacaya have been especially active; and Izalco, the youngest volcano, has erupted almost continuously from its birth in 1770 until quite recently.

North of the belt of active volcanoes are the rugged, older volcanic highlands, capped by thick deposits of lava and ash. In many areas, river and stream action

Fig. 1.6. Southern highlands: Agua volcano, 3,766 meters tall, with Antigua, the capital of Guatemala during the Spanish Colonial era, in the foreground.

•    has dissected these deposits to form deep, steep-sided gullies, or *barrancas*. Within these older highlands the fertile volcanic soils of the valleys and basins have supported large human populations for thousands of years. The largest of these basins is the Valley of Guatemala, the location of modern Guatemala City. Others include the Valley of Quetzaltenango, in western Guatemala, and the Ahuachapan and Zapotitan basins, both in western El Salvador. Many of the highland basins and volcanic calderas of the region contain lakes of significant size. One of these is Lago Amatitlan, in the southern part of the Valley of Guatemala. The most famous, owing to its extraordinary beauty, is Lago Atitlan, in central Guatemala. Lago Ilopango, near the city of San Salvador, was formed in the caldera left by a violent eruption in about A.D. 200.

Some of these basins are characterized by interior drainage, but the principal rivers of the southern highlands flow northward as tributaries of the Río Motagua, which then follows the continental rift eastward to the Gulf of Honduras in the Caribbean, or as tributaries of the Río Grijalva, which flows westward through the central depression of Chiapas and on into the Gulf of Mexico.

The volcanic highlands have long provided important resources for their inhabitants. The ancient Maya quarried obsidian (volcanic glass, important as a source for sharp cutting tools) at several locations, the most favored being El Chayal, on the upland flanks of the Motagua Valley, northeast of the Valley of Guatemala, and Ixtepeque, some 85 km to the southeast. Another basic necessity was their grinding stones (manos and metates), which they fashioned from basaltic rocks such as andesite, available throughout most of the southern highlands. Although the steel cutting tools introduced by the Europeans quickly displaced the ancient reliance on obsidian, the traditional mano and metate may still be found as the favored means for grinding maize and other foods.

The climate of the southern highlands is predominantly temperate (*tierra templada*), with mean annual temperatures usually between 15°C and 25°C (59°–77°F). On the sparsely occupied upper slopes of the higher volcanoes, above 3,000 m, much cooler temperatures (*tierra fría*) prevail, with frequent frosts and occasional snow accumulations during the winter. Throughout the region a well-defined dry season extends from January to April, followed by a May-to-December wet season. Although the wet season may bring periods of steady rainfall lasting for several days, the usual pattern sees clear skies in the mornings followed by showers or thunderstorms in the afternoons or evenings. Rainfall totals are generally less than in the wetter areas of the Pacific coast, averaging 2,000–3,000 mm annually in most areas. Rainfall is much less in areas sheltered from the prevailing easterly trade winds. In the interior of the Motagua Valley, for example, and in the central Chiapas depression, annual rainfall is typically less than 1,000 mm.

Today the rich valleys and basins of the southern highlands support the greatest population concentrations in the entire Maya area. The fertile volcanic soils and nearly ideal ("springlike") climate have lured settlers from both near and far for at least the past 3,000 years. Yet, the earthquakes and volcanic eruptions would seem to belie the rich promise. Some 1,800 years ago a catastrophic eruption of Ilopango appears to have destroyed all life within 20–30 km, and the widespread ash fall rendered a larger zone (within a radius of 100 km from the volcano) uninhabitable for perhaps 200 years. But even small-scale volcanic eruptions endanger life and livelihood—as witness the recently excavated settlement of farmhouses and adjacent agricultural fields that had been instantaneously buried under (and dramatically preserved by) several meters of ash released by a nearby volcanic vent at Cerén, El Salvador, sometime around A.D. 600 (Fig. 1.7). So-called minor eruptions, bring-

Fig. 1.7. Southern highlands: archaeological excavations at Cerén, El Salvador, have revealed portions of a village covered by a sudden and very localized volcanic eruption; here, the remains of an adobe house (Classic period, ca. A.D. 650).

- ing more modest ash falls and occasional lava flows, continue to disrupt people's lives today.

Earthquakes have probably taken an even larger toll in lives and property. Historical accounts beginning with the Spanish Conquest document a long series of major quakes. The first to be recorded occurred in the southern highlands during the campaign of Pedro de Alvarado in 1526 (see the Epilogue). According to the account written by Bernal Díaz del Castillo, "the next day [we] came upon this valley . . . where now this city of Guatemala is settled. At that time it was altogether hostile, and we found many barricades and pits, and we fought with the natives to force a passage; and I remember that as we were descending a slope the earth began to tremble so that many soldiers fell to the ground, for the earthquake continued a long time." Among the most significant of these earthquakes is the cluster that destroyed the colonial capital of Antigua in the eighteenth century, the one in 1918 that all but destroyed Guatemala City, and the rupture of the Motagua fault in 1976, which took more than 24,000 lives.

In many highland areas the effect of long-term, high-density human settlement has been to alter or destroy the original flora and fauna. Except in a few remote areas, the populations of many animal species (see the following section) have been reduced or extirpated. Much of the original flora of the highlands appears to have been a mixed evergreen-and-deciduous forest. Although deforestation has advanced into all but the most remote lands and higher elevations, stands containing various oaks, laurels, sweetgum, dogwood, and many kinds of pine may still be found. At higher elevations, pines often predominate, sometimes mixed with cypress or juniper.

Beginning with the Spanish colonial era, wasteful agricultural methods and overgrazing by cattle and sheep have led to increased rates of erosion, eventually rendering entire landscapes almost uninhabitable. Efforts have been made recently to halt or even reverse this process, and reforestation has been successful in some areas. Such efforts seek to ensure that the southern highlands can continue to support sizable populations.

## The Metamorphic, or Northern, Highlands

North of the continental rift marked by the Motagua and Grijalva valleys lies a second vast belt of highlands (Figs. 1.1 and 1.2). The highest peaks—those in the south, which exceed 3,000 m—are composed mostly of metamorphic deposits and range in age from the Paleozoic to the Cenozoic. Further north are the beginnings of Cenozoic sedimentary formations. To the west are the Chiapas highlands of Mexico and the Altos Cuchumatanes of northwestern Guatemala and eastern Chiapas, followed by the Sierra de Chuacús in central Guatemala and the Sierra de las Minas that extends eastward almost to the Caribbean. The rich mineral deposits in these highlands have been mined for centuries. Perhaps the most important are

Fig. 1.8. Northern highlands: the Salama Valley, Guatemala, where excavations have revealed evidence of occupation spanning most of the pre-Columbian era.

the jadeite and serpentine deposits found along the southern flanks of the Sierra de las Minas, in the middle Motagua Valley, which were quarried extensively by the ancient Maya.

As one proceeds north, the rugged metamorphic mountains give way to limestone formations, such as those north of the Río Grijalva in Chiapas and in the Alta Verapaz of Guatemala. In this region of spectacular karst topography typified by "haystack" hills and beautiful underground caverns, waterfalls spring from the sides of mountains, and rivers disappear beneath the porous hills only to reappear miles away.

Although many of the slopes of the northern highlands are ill-suited to agriculture, richer alluvial soils have accumulated in many of the valleys and basins, such as the Rabinal and Salama Valleys (Fig. 1.8) north of the Sierra de Chuacús. Farther north, good soils, plentiful rainfall, and cool temperatures make the basins of the Alta Verapaz a prime choice for modern coffee cultivation.

Much of the northern highland area is drained by the tributaries of the Río Usumacinta, which in turn flows northwest into the southern lowlands and on into the Gulf of Mexico. Beginning in the west, the first of these tributaries is the Río Jatate, which flows out of the limestone highlands of Chiapas and joins the Río Lacantun, which in turn originates along the eastern flank of the Altos Cuchumatanes. The main tributary of the Usumacinta, called the Río Chixoy (or Negro or

Salinas), drains most of the modern Department of El Quiché, the central portion of the northern highlands. The other major tributary, the Río Pasión, originates farther east, in the Alta Verapaz, and the eastern flank of the northern highlands is drained by the Río Polochic, which flows though a lush, steep-sided valley into Lago Izabal, in the lowlands of the Caribbean coast. Izabal's outlet to the sea is via the spectacular gorge of the Río Dulce.

The climate of the northern highlands ranges from annual means below 15°C (59°F) in the *tierra fría* of the Altos Cuchumatanes, the highest mountains of the region, to the tropical *tierra caliente* typical of the low-lying margins found to the west, north, and east. Several of the plateaus of the Cuchumatanes support the highest and coldest modern communities in Guatemala: San Mateo Ixtatan and Santa Eulalia, which lie above timberline at elevations over 2,500 m. Yet most of the inhabited valleys lie between 750 m and 2,000 m, in typical *tierra templada* climates. These areas support a varied semitropical vegetation, whereas the mountain slopes, where rainfall is sufficient, are covered with pine and oak forests.

For the most part, rainfall in the northern highlands follows the same pattern as in the southern highlands, but the intensity and length of the wet season tend to increase toward the north. On the northern fringes of the highlands in both Chiapas, Mexico, and the Alta Verapaz of Guatemala, rainfall totals average over 3,000 mm per year. The Alta Verapaz is famed for its highland rain forest, the traditional preserve of the rare and prized quetzal. The quetzal, now the national bird of Guatemala, was of special importance to the ancient Maya, whose ruling elite used its long, slender, brilliant-green plumes in their headdresses.

Because human disturbance has been less severe in the north than in the areas to the south, the northern highlands retain more vestiges of the original plant and animal life. Here one can still find both howler and spider monkeys, kinkajous, coatimundis, weasels, foxes, peccaries, armadillos, opossums, bats, owls, hawks, vultures, parrots, and, as mentioned, the rare quetzal. But modern development in the form of highways, logging operations, petroleum exploitation, and hydroelectric power plants now threatens this once remote and beautiful area.

## The Pattern of Power in the Highlands

The development of pre-Columbian settlement in the Maya highlands generally parallels that of the Pacific plain, although many traces of early occupation no doubt lie undiscovered beneath deep volcanic and alluvial deposits and may predate the settlements on the Pacific plain. But whatever the effects of those deposits, the northern highlands seem never to have been as densely occupied as the highlands to the south, and the southern highlands would seem to share with the Pacific plain the early growth of Maya civilization. During much of the pre-Columbian era the major population centers were located in the midst of the largest and richest highland valleys. Kaminaljuyu, situated in the Valley of Guatemala, dominated the entire southern highlands during the early development of Maya civilization. Adjacent regions were dominated by such important, but less powerful, centers as Chiapa de Corzo, in the central depression of Chiapas to the west, El Portón in the Salama Valley to the north, and Chalchuapa to the southeast on the periphery of the Maya area. Later, during the peaking of lowland Maya civilization, cultural influences from the north penetrated the northern highlands, as at Chama in the Alta Verapaz, and at Asunción Mita in the southern highlands. One of the major lowland Maya centers of the Classic period, Copan, stands on the eastern margin of the southern highlands.

After the Classic period, highland settlements began to shift away from the valley floors toward higher ground until, shortly before the Conquest, most major centers had come to be located in more secure settings, such as hilltops or plateaus surrounded by ravines. Here the Spanish encountered the capitals of the dominant southern Maya highland kingdoms, such as Zaculeu, Utatlan, Iximche, and Mixcu Viejo.

## The Lowlands

The greater part of the Maya area, to the north of the two belts of highlands, lies below 800 m in elevation and is characterized by a *tierra caliente* climate. But this lowland zone is far from uniform, for many of the factors creating the diversity of the highlands operate here as well. Variations in elevation, rainfall, drainage, soils, and other factors create considerable diversity in the lowland environment, although these variations are usually less dramatic than those in the highlands. In the drier areas of Yucatan to the north the forest is stunted or reduced to scrub, but farther south, precipitation increases, and true tropical rain forest, which still covers the vast undisturbed portions of the zone, is in fact the most conspicuous feature of the lowlands. These forests are evergreen, or nearly so, with only very brief periods of occasional leaf fall. Rain forests flourish in areas of consistently high rainfall and are characterized by a great diversity of plant species—many of them unfamiliar to those of us living in nontropical zones—that form multi-story canopies. The uppermost canopy, some 40–70 m above the ground, is dominated by such giant trees as mahogany and ceiba (a cottonwood, a tree sacred to the Maya). Beneath this, often 25–50 m in height, are found the American fig (amate), sapodilla, bari, Spanish cedar, and many other species. A lower story, usually 15–25 m in height, includes the ramon, or breadnut tree, rubber and allspice trees, avocado trees, and a profusion of palms such as the cohune and escoba. Many trees support other plants, including strangler vines, lianas, bromeliads, and orchids. In the deep shade beneath the canopy are ferns, young trees, and many large-leaved plants.

Many of these plants were of course used by the ancient Maya. Ramon and avocado trees furnished food, the vanilla vine and the allspice tree provided condiments, and the palms contributed thatch and many other products. (The roles that these and other plants played in ancient Maya subsistence will be considered in Chapter 8.)

The lowland forest is host to a great variety of animal life, including most of the species already mentioned as inhabitants of the highlands and Pacific coastal plain. In addition there are anteaters, agoutis, pacas (large, edible rodents), and other food animals such as tapirs, brocket deer, and cottontail rabbits. There are also primates (howler and spider monkeys) and carnivores (the ocelot, the jaguarundi, and the largest New World cat, the jaguar). The ancient Maya held the jaguar in high esteem, especially for its pelt, which was symbolic of elite and ceremonial status. Bird life abounds: doves, parrots, woodpeckers, and toucans; and game birds, including quail, curassows, chachalacas, and the prized ocellated turkey. But the quetzal, most prized of all, is found only in the highland rain forests. Reptiles and amphibians are also abundant: many species of toads, tree frogs, turtles, lizards, and snakes, including boas, racers, coral snakes, rattlesnakes, and the deadly pit viper, the fer-de-lance. The emergence of the primitive *Uo* frog each year from its underground habitat continues to signal the onset of the rainy season, just as it did for the ancient Maya. The rivers and lakes of the region provide edible snails (*jute*) and fish such as the mojarra and catfish. Lago Izabal is famed for its tarpon, as well as robalo (snook) and snapper. The lowland coasts abound with shellfish—shrimp, spiny lobsters, crabs—and sea turtles, which in ancient times were probably the single most important source of food from the sea. The manatee, or sea cow, is also native to the southern coasts, and evidence from coastal Belize, supported by the sixteenth-century narrative of Bishop Diego de Landa, indicates that this large mammal also was used by the Maya.

Of course the most common forms of terrestrial animal life in the lowlands are the invertebrates, including a host of spiders, scorpions, and insects. Most remain little known, but one commonly sees dragonflies, myriad butterflies (including the famous blue morpho), leafcutting and army ants, termites, and a variety of beetles and bugs. More often felt than seen are mosquitoes, gnats, fleas, ticks, chiggers, biting flies, wasps, and other stinging insects. The ancient Maya raised stingless bees as a source of honey, and their descendants continue to keep hives today. Less beneficial are species that transmit serious diseases: sand flies that carry American leishmaniasis, assassin bugs that carry trypanosomiasis (Chagas's disease), and the malaria mosquito. Many of these, however, did not plague the ancient Maya; malaria and a host of other diseases were unknown in the New World until they were introduced from the Old World after the Conquest.

The lowlands are usually divided into at least three major subzones (Fig. 1.1): the transitional (or southern) lowlands, the Peten (or central lowlands), and the Yucatecan (or northern) lowlands. Each of these comprises further localized subareas, but our purposes will be served by confining our discussion to the three major sub-zones.

## The Transitional, or Southern, Lowlands

The transition between the highlands and the lowlands is often gradual. Thus the rain forest that begins in the karst region of the northern highlands continues without interruption into the lower elevations to the north. A convenient, albeit arbitrary, distinction is the equally gradual transition from *tierra templada* to *tierra caliente* climates, generally marked by the 800–1,000 m elevation contours, which run from northern Chiapas, in Mexico, through the northern portions of the departments of Huehuetenango, El Quiché, Alta Verapaz, and Izabal, in Guatemala.

This subzone comprises the southern lowlands, an area adjacent to and partly within the rugged, broken karst terrain to the south. The southern lowlands, composed mostly of Mesozoic and Cenozoic limestone formations, are typified by high rainfall and good surface drainage. Large rivers flowing out of the adjacent highland regions afford year-round access to water and canoe transport, and much of the southern lowlands possesses deep, rich soils and a high proportion of rain forest. Within this area are found the middle drainage basins of the Río Usumacinta (Fig. 1.9) and its tributaries (the Jatate, Lacantun, Chixoy, and Pasión), the Río Sarstoon (which forms the southern boundary of the nation of Belize), Lago Izabal, the Río

Fig. 1.9. Southern lowlands: the Río Usumacinta, a major artery, here near the site of Yaxchilan, Chiapas, Mexico.

Dulce, and the great alluvial valley of the lower Motagua, as well as the adjacent floodplains and coastal areas of northwestern Honduras (Río Chamelecon and Río Ulúa).

In this region of high precipitation, 2,000–3,000 mm of rain fall each year (Fig. 1.4). Temperatures are also very high, averaging in the 25°–35°C (77°–95°F) range typical of *tierra caliente* climates (Fig. 1.3). In several areas of highest rainfall the dry season may be limited to only a month or two (usually between March and May), and rain may occur even during these periods.

Mangrove and other swamp flora predominate in the low-lying and coastal regions on the edges of this zone, but throughout the rest of the region conditions are often ideal for the growth of true tropical rain-forest species.

## *The Peten, or Central Lowlands*

As one proceeds north from the Usumacinta drainage basin, rainfall rates begin to diminish and the landscape becomes less rugged, although still characterized by low, generally east-west ridges of folded and faulted Cenozoic limestone. Within this region is a diverse range of soil and forest types, of lakes and low seasonal swamps (*bajos*). There is less surface drainage, the rivers are smaller, and, except near lakes, water may not be readily available throughout the year. These features help define the overall environment of the vast central lowland region of northern Guatemala, often referred to as El Peten.

Near the heart of the Peten is an interior drainage basin, some 100 km long from east to west and about 30 km wide. Along the base of the hills that form the northern side of this basin is a chain of about fourteen lakes, several of which are interconnected during the rainy season. The largest, Lago Peten Itza, is situated about midway within the basin (Fig. 1.10); today, it is some 32 km long and 5 km wide. South of the basin lies a great, irregularly shaped savanna (Fig. 1.11). Few trees grow on this grassy plain, and the soil is a compact red clay, apparently not well suited to cultivation. Together with the relative sparsity of remains of ancient occupation, soil of that sort suggests that this savanna was not heavily populated in the past, but recent research indicates that at least some Peten savanna lands were occupied in ancient times. The average elevation of the savanna is about 150 m, above which the karst ridges rise to an average of 300 m.

The few streams rising in the central savanna find their way south and west into the Río Pasión. To the east, along the border with southern Belize, are the jagged Maya Mountains, an outcrop of underlying metamorphic formations (Fig. 1.2) reaching its highest elevation at Cockscomb Peak, at a little over 1,100 m. The narrow coastal plain east of the Maya Mountains is watered by a number of short streams flowing into the Caribbean. And on the western (Gulf) coast is a broad alluvial plain, comprising most of the Mexican states of Tabasco and southern Campeche, that is for the most part a low-lying and often swampy region of lagoons

Fig. 1.10. Central lowlands: Lago Peten Itza and the island town of Flores, capital of the Department of the Peten, Guatemala, and the site of Tayasal, the last independent Maya capital (see Epilogue).

Fig. 1.11. Central lowlands: savanna landscape near Lago Peten Itza, Guatemala.

• and islands, homeland of the Chontal Maya and their canoe-borne commerce (see Chapter 7).

In the low ranges northwest, north, and northeast of the interior drainage basin, six rivers have their origin. Two of these, the Candelaria and the Mamantel, flowing generally west and north, empty into the great Laguna de Términos on the Gulf of Mexico, on the west coast of the Yucatan Peninsula. Farther south, the San Pedro Mártir generally parallels the Río Usumacinta. The remaining three, the Hondo, the New, and the Belize, flow generally northeast and discharge into the Caribbean on the east coast of the Peninsula; of these, the first two flow into Bahía de Chetumal, the largest bay on the coast of the Yucatan Peninsula.

The ranges of hills surrounding the savanna lands are covered with a dense tropical forest that includes all the plant species found in the transitional lowlands to the south. The southern slopes of the Peten hills are unusually sharp, whereas the northern slopes drop almost imperceptibly from each crest to the next watercourse. The vegetation of the Peten is usually classified as seasonal rain forest, since the more irregular distribution of rainfall throughout the year results in extensive dry periods. The variations are subtle, however, and to the untrained eye the forest cover in the central lowlands appears little different from the true rain forests to the south (Fig. 1.12). The tallest trees rise to 50 m above the forest floor, but for the most part these towering examples of ceiba, American fig, or mahogany do not form a continuous canopy. The dense forest canopy, usually lower, is composed of ramon, sapodilla, fig, and numerous other species. A lower story, averaging 10 m in height, often includes custard apple, allspice, palms, and other species. The shaded forest floor supports a relatively sparse distribution of young trees, ferns, and other broad-leaved plants.

Here and there this tropical forest is interrupted by grassland areas, or by seasonal swamps called *bajos* (*akalche* in Yucatec Mayan) that are covered with low scrub and thorn growth. North of the interior drainage basin, the *bajos* become more common, forming a zone of mixed forest and *bajo* growth. Today, the *bajos* of the Peten become swampy or water-filled only during the rainy season, but in the past these depressions may have held permanent water, forming an area pocked by shallow lakes (see Chapter 8).

Rainfall tends to be somewhat less in the Peten lowlands than in the transitional lowlands to the south, although temperatures differ little (Figs. 1.3 and 1.4). The rainy season extends from May through January, the dry season from February to May (although showers are not infrequent during these months). In most areas annual rainfall averages about 2,000 mm. Water never freezes, although cold "northers" in the winter frequently drive temperatures into the uncomfortably cool range. Averages are in the *tierra caliente* range (25°–30°C; 77°–86°F), although dry-season daytime temperatures often rise above 38°C (100°F).

Fig. 1.12. Central lowlands: tropical-forest undergrowth at Tikal, Guatemala.

Although those living in temperate climates tend to assume that this tropical environment is unproductive and even dangerous, the adaptations fashioned by the ancient Maya made it both productive and hospitable. Where extensive areas of good soils could be found, they were cultivated, using a variety of methods. Rich plant and animal resources supplied food, clothing, and medicine in great abundance. The local limestone made a fine building material; not only was it easily quarried with stone tools (the Maya had no metal tools), but it hardens on exposure to the elements. When burned, it reduces to lime, which the Maya employed as plaster for buildings and paving. Throughout the region there are beds of friable granular limestone, which the Maya used, as we use sand and gravel, to make lime mortar. And in several areas the limestone bedrock holds deposits of chert, or flint, which the Maya chipped into a variety of cutting, chopping, and scraping tools.

It is in these central lowlands that the earliest known centers of Classic Maya civilization have been discovered. From this heartland the achievements of the ancient Maya spread throughout the lowlands and reached their apex during the so-called Golden Age, from the third to the ninth centuries A.D.

### The Yucatecan, or Northern, Lowlands

Another subtle transition marks the beginning of the northernmost lowland subdivision. This broad region, which corresponds roughly to the northern half of the Yucatan Peninsula (Fig. 1.1), is characterized by a general lack of surface drainage, so that access to water becomes an increasingly critical factor in the location of settlements. Except for a wet pocket in the northeastern corner of the Peninsula, rainfall is far less than in the south (Fig. 1.4). Overall, the terrain is quite flat, except for a few ranges of low hills.

Almost imperceptibly, the high forest of the Peten becomes the bush of the northern Yucatan Peninsula. As one goes north, the giant mahoganies, sapodillas, Spanish cedars, and ceibas give way to lower trees and a much thicker undergrowth (Fig. 1.13). Palmetto grows in abundance along the east coast of the Peninsula. Farther inland and extending into the somewhat wetter northeastern corner of Yucatan is a long, fingerlike extension of the southern rain forest containing mahogany, Spanish cedar, sapodilla, and other hardwoods. The fauna of the northern lowlands is essentially the same as that in the regions to the south, except that species adapted to drier habitats increasingly predominate.

Immediately north of the Peten is the Río Bec–Chenes area, which is geographically and culturally transitional between the central and northern lowlands. As we

Fig. 1.13. Northern lowlands: low forest and bush in the dry season of Yucatan, Mexico.

Fig. 1.14. Northern lowlands: a *serranía*, or low range of hills (Mayan, *puuc*), Yucatan, Mexico.

shall see, the development of the Maya centers in the Río Bec–Chenes area initially paralleled the development of the centers to the south in the Peten, but later followed the course charted by the Maya of northern Yucatan.

Northern Yucatan is low and flat; the humus is usually not more than a few centimeters in depth, in contrast to the Peten soil, which may be up to a meter deep. There are extensive outcroppings of porous Cenozoic limestone (Tertiary and Recent), and, owing to the underground drainage of rainfall, there are almost no surface streams. A range of low hills, generally not exceeding 100 m in height, begins at Champoton on the west coast of the Peninsula, runs as far north as the city of Campeche, turns northeast to the town of Maxcanu, and then extends southeastward beyond Tzucacab in central southern Yucatan. This range is known locally as the *serranía*, or Puuc hills (Fig. 1.14).

Only a few lakes and rivers are to be found in northern Yucatan, and the rivers are little more than creeks. The largest body of water, Laguna de Bacalar in southeastern Quintana Roo, is about 56 km long and only 10 to 11 km wide. There are several smaller lakes, such as those around the site of Coba in northeastern Yucatan, and three small rivers, little more than shallow arms of the sea. On the east coast are two large, shallow bays, Asunción and Espíritu Santo.

The northern lowlands are unusually dry, owing to both low rainfall and extensive underground drainage. Rainfall averages less than 2,000 mm annually in most areas, most of it coming during a well-defined wet season (June–December), and the driest areas of northwestern Yucatan receive less than 500 mm in a given year. Temperatures are typical of the *tierra caliente*. The only surface water, barring the few lakes and small brackish streams near the coast, is that afforded by cenotes (from the Yucatec Mayan *dz'onot*). These large, natural wells are found throughout the area, especially in the extreme north. Cenotes are natural formations, places where the surface limestone has collapsed and exposed the subterranean water table (Fig. 1.15). Some of these natural wells are up to 100 m in diameter, and their depth varies according to the local water-table level: near the north coast the subterranean water is less than 5 m below ground level, but as one proceeds southward the depth of the cenotes increases to more than 30 m.

In country as devoid of surface water as northern Yucatan, cenotes are the principal sources of water today, and they must have been equally important in determining the location of ancient settlements. Where there is a cenote, there one can expect to find traces of human occupation.

Fig. 1.15. Northern lowlands: a cenote, or natural sinkhole, at Valladolid, Yucatan, Mexico.

## The Pattern of Power in the Lowlands

Recent archaeological discoveries indicate that the Caribbean coastal margins of the lowlands were exploited long before settled village life emerged. Some of the earliest known Maya villages appeared in this same region, and agricultural settlements seem to have spread into the interior along the rivers of the southern and central lowlands. The earliest centers of lowland Maya civilization appear in the interior of the Peten, as at Nakbe, El Mirador, and Tikal, and the central lowlands were long dominated by Tikal and a series of adjacent centers. Other important sites arose in the southern lowlands. These included those in the upper and middle Usumacinta drainage (Seibal, Yaxchilan, Piedras Negras, and Palenque) and others far to the southeast at Copan and Quirigua. Concurrent with these were large centers in the northern lowlands, at Coba and Dzibilchaltun, but after the southern and central lowland centers declined, the northern, or Yucatecan, region rose to prominence, dominated in succession by the centers at Uxmal, Chichen Itza, and, finally, Mayapan.

Differences in elevation, amount of rainfall, availability of water, temperature, distribution of plant and animal life, and location of natural resources combine in the Maya area to produce one of the most diverse environments for its size found anywhere in the world. But in characterizing this diversity by describing a series of different ecological subdivisions, we must bear in mind that the variations within each may sometimes be as great as those that distinguish one subdivision from another.

# 2
.. THE ORIGINS OF
MAYA CIVILIZATION

> This is the history of the world in those times, because it has been written
> down, because the time has not yet ended for making these books, these
> many explanations, so that Maya men may be asked if they know how
> they were born in this country, when the land was founded.
> —*The Book of Chilam Balam of Chumayel* (Roys 1967: 98)

**W**ho preceded the Maya, and what shaped the development of Maya culture? In seeking answers to these questions, we will do well to remember that the ancient Maya civilization originated and prospered, not in isolation, but in the context of conditions and events scattered across the breadth of Mesoamerica and, ultimately, the entire New World. We will be well advised, then, before considering the origins of the Maya themselves, to set the stage by outlining the chronology that orders these developments.

## The Chronological Framework

New World prehistorians have traditionally used a five-stage chronological scheme to span the time from the earliest known peoples to the arrival of European colonists in the sixteenth century. Today, however, these stages are generally called *periods*, for they have come to denote spans of time more than developmental stages. The initial period, called the Lithic, began with the earliest migrations of peoples from Asia across the Bering land bridge during the last ice age, beginning at least 12,000 years ago (some would date its beginning twenty or even forty thousand years ago, but the evidence remains uncertain), and concludes at roughly 6000 B.C. During this period small bands roamed over much of the New World, hunting and gathering food and relying on simple chipped-stone tools. But these early bands were not unchanging, and archaeologists can discern an increasing reliance on a few particular food resources as the bands in each region became more specialized. This reliance on the seasonal growth cycles of food plants or the availability of food animals was the first step toward two fundamental changes, the establishment of permanent villages and, eventually, the domestication of certain food plants and animals.

The development of settled communities identifies the next period, the Archaic (ca. 6000–2000 B.C.). The earliest known villages appeared along the seacoasts, such as those along the Caribbean and the Pacific, where the rich food resources of the shore and lagoon could support year-round settled life. Thus a rich environment, combined with an efficient food-collecting technology, gave rise to the first known villages in the New World. Recent evidence from the site of Monte Verde in Chile suggests that the origins of settled communities in coastal environments may have been far earlier, perhaps as early as 12,500 years ago. But regardless of their antiquity, the process of settling down was followed by increasing reliance on a few food plants—especially species that could be easily stored and those with genetic makeups and other characteristics that would allow people to improve upon their natural yields. In other words, human manipulation of plants, as for example in selecting only the largest seeds for planting each year, or in cross-breeding one plant with another to produce hybrids, gradually led to the domestication of a variety of species, including maize (corn), squash, beans, and other plants in highland Mesoamerica, and manioc, potatoes, and a variety of other crops in South America. Generally speaking, this process resulted in an increased and more reliable food supply. This stability in food supply also led to the establishment of permanent village life in areas previously occupied by migratory bands. Over the centuries the consequences of all these developments were ever larger population concentrations that came to be the foundations of all the civilizations of the New World.

For the remaining three periods, or epochs, we will follow the names and dates as they are used in Mesoamerica (see Table 2.1; different terms and dates are used by archaeologists working in other New World areas). The Preclassic (ca. 2000 B.C. to A.D. 250), which follows the Archaic, is usually subdivided into three eras, an Early Preclassic (ca. 2000–1000 B.C.), a Middle Preclassic (ca. 1000–400 B.C.), and a Late Preclassic (ca. 400 B.C. to A.D. 250). Generally speaking, the first New World societies sufficiently complex and sophisticated to be called civilization have their origins in the Early Preclassic. These include cultures in the Gulf coast lowlands of Mexico (the Olmec) and in highland basins such as the Valley of Mexico and the Valley of Oaxaca. Similar developments have been traced to about this same time in Andean South America, with the Chavin and other complex early societies. These initial civilizations develop their full character during the Middle Preclassic, having by then begun to exhibit evidence for social stratification (minimal distinctions between elite and non-elite segments, often corresponding to kin groups such as lineages), sophisticated religious and economic institutions, and, in these institutions, the basis of authority for hereditary leaders, or *chiefs*. These initial chiefdoms established a basic cultural pattern that most later societies in both Mesoamerica and the Andes came to follow. In Mesoamerica we can see the continued evolution of

TABLE 2.1

Principal Epochs of Maya Cultural Development

| General cultural eras | Chronology | Area | | |
|---|---|---|---|---|
| | | Pacific plain and highlands | Southern and central lowlands | Northern lowlands |
| Colonial | | Spanish Conquest | Conquest of Tayasal Itza | Spanish Conquest |
| Late Postclassic | A.D. 1500 | Highland conquest states (Quiche, Cakchiquel) | Cortés expedition visits Tayasal and Nito | Political fragmentation; Fall of Mayapan |
| Early Postclassic | | Quiche warrior elites' entry into highlands from Gulf coast | Itza occupation of Lago Peten Itza region | Domination by Mayapan; Chichen Itza abandoned |
| Terminal Classic | A.D. 1000 | Initial occupation of hilltop and fortified sites; Cotzumalhuapa sculptural style along coast | Population loss and eventual abandonment of many centers; Putun Maya expansion; decline at many centers; Peak of population and size at most lowland centers | Domination by Chichen Itza; Reoccupation of Chichen Itza by Itza; Putun Maya expansion; rise of Puuc centers; Growth in size and population of many centers; ties to central lowlands |
| Late Classic | | Renewed development at Kaminaljuyu with economic and political ties to lowlands | Increasing competition and warfare among polities; Expansion of Maya elite culture to peripheries of central lowlands | Initial sculptured stone monuments with hieroglyphic texts and dates; development of dynastic rule (origins of state systems) |
| Early Classic | A.D. 500 | Eruption of Ilopango volcano; Peak of population and size at many southern sites | Initial sculptured stone monuments with hieroglyphic texts and dates; development of dynastic rule | |
| Protoclassic | 0 | | | |

| Period | Date | Events |
|---|---|---|
| Late Preclassic | 500 B.C. | Sculptured stone monuments (early Maya and Izapan styles), some with hieroglyphic texts and dates; probable development of dynastic rule (origins of state systems) — Monumental architecture, including vaulted tombs, stucco-decorated façades, etc. (origins of state systems) — Monumental architecture (development of complex social, political, and economic systems) |
| Middle Preclassic | 1000 B.C. | Interaction with adjacent groups (Mixe-Zoquean, Olmec, etc.); initial monumental sculpture and architecture (origins of complex social, political, and economic systems) — Initial monumental architecture (origins of complex economic, social, and political institutions) — Expansion of settlement into nonriverine areas — Initial architecture (origins of economic, social, and political institutions) |
| | 1500 B.C. | Expansion of settlement along rivers into central lowlands |
| Early Preclassic | 1500 B.C. | Early sedentism along the Pacific coast (origins of village life?) |
| | 2000 B.C. | |

Scale markers (right side, A.D.): 500, 1000, 1500, 2000

civilization during the Late Preclassic, the period when the first examples of writing appear in the archaeological record, and in which the origins for many other developments of the Classic period can be traced.

[The subsequent Classic period (ca. A.D. 250–900) is also usually subdivided into three eras, the Early Classic (ca. A.D. 250–600), the Late Classic (ca. 600–800), and the Terminal Classic (ca. 800–1000). Generally speaking, it is during this span that a series of civilizations expanded in both Mesoamerica and South America, civilizations that involved a more complex political organization, the preindustrial state. States, which have large populations and often see the development of cities, are also characterized by full-time craft specializations, complex social stratification ("classes"), and powerful sanctions (armies and palace guards, for example) to support a centralized political authority. Early states emerged during the Classic period in both highland and lowland Mesoamerica. The best documented highland examples are Teotihuacan, in the Valley of Mexico, and Monte Alban, in the Valley of Oaxaca. The best known lowland example is the Maya, who developed their own unique style of civilization, one that was distinct in many ways from the more urbanized states of Mexico and South America.

The Terminal Classic overlaps with the Postclassic (ca. A.D. 900–1500), usually subdivided into just two eras, the Early Postclassic (ca. 900–1200) and the Late Postclassic (ca. 1200–1500). The Postclassic is marked by further population growth, expansion in the number of cities, an increase in militarism, and the development of the most complex and powerful states in the New World prior to European colonization, including the well-known Toltec and the later Mexica, or Aztec, states in Mesoamerica, and the Chimu and Inca empires in Andean South America.

## The Developmental Stages of Maya Civilization

In this book we will follow the growth of Maya civilization within the framework of the chronological periods and eras just defined, for this scheme remains the most widely used for dating and comparing archaeological remains. But we should be aware that this scheme carries with it some biases that may hinder a fuller understanding of Maya civilization. One of these is the assumption that each of these chronological boundaries corresponds to sharp and profound changes. None does. The changes that are visible in the archaeological record are almost always gradual, and the chronological dividing lines, such as A.D. 250, which marks the end of the Preclassic and the beginning of the Classic, are therefore in every case arbitrary. They simply define conveniently segregated blocks in the flow of time. As we have seen, there is no reason to expect, given the considerable diversity within the Maya area, that changes occurred everywhere at the same time or at the same rate. Thus, when we are considering the process of development that occurred during the

course of Maya civilization, we should always think of these chronological boundaries not as fixed dates, but as approximations of transitions that actually extended
over a significant span of time (and space), usually corresponding to one or more
centuries.

Another problem presented by this chronological scheme derives from its original usage: its inventors associated Maya civilization with the Classic period, and
viewed the time periods that preceded and followed as lesser stages of a Classic
culmination or florescence. Thus, the Preclassic (or "Formative") was often seen as
a necessary precursor to civilization, but not a time characterized by the attributes
of civilization in its own right; and the Postclassic was seen as a time of decline for
the great civilization of the Classic, a period "after the fall" marked by decadence,
rather than an era of continued evolution of Maya civilization.

Today Maya scholars tend to take a much broader view, one based on vastly
more data than were available a few years ago; they define episodes within a civilization that was expressed over a far longer span of time than just the Classic period. Most scholars see Maya civilization in far wider spatial terms as well—
whereas formerly it was thought to be confined to the lowlands, today Maya civilization is seen as a far more diverse expression spread throughout the broader
Maya area.

One Maya scholar, Jeremy Sabloff, has proposed a very useful developmental
framework (as opposed to a chronological scheme) to account for this changed perception of Maya civilization. Sabloff's proposal would simply refer to three developmental episodes: Early, Middle, and Late Maya civilization. There need be no
fixed limits in time or space for each of these stages, but, rather, each is seen as
marked by a pulse of activity and growth leading to profound changes that set the
stage for the next. New evidence that has come to light since Sabloff made his proposal only emphasizes the virtues of a flexible scheme of this sort.

Adapting Sabloff's scheme today would see his Early Maya Civilization, as the
label implies, referring to the first expressions of cultural complexity associated
with the rise of the first polities, roughly corresponding to the Middle and Late Preclassic periods. His Middle Maya Civilization would refer to the growth of state-
level organizations, an episode marked by sporadic growth in the size and complexity of such organizations, along with periodic failures, and ending with the
breakup of the last of the large polities in about 1200. As we shall see, there was
an important change in political organization during this middle period—best expressed, perhaps, as a shift from the concentration of authority in one individual
to the sharing of authority among a council of many. In chronological terms Middle
Maya Civilization corresponds roughly to the Classic and Early Postclassic periods.
Sabloff's Late Maya Civilization, which was marked by subsequent political fragmentation and corresponds roughly to the Late Postclassic, should be viewed not
as a decline, but as the commencement of a new stage cut short abruptly by external

• •  events—namely the Spanish Conquest, which began shortly after 1500. Without this outside intervention, which destroyed most of its native institutions, Late Maya Civilization would have continued its own evolutionary course.

Sabloff's scheme has much to recommend it. Still, for convenience, we will organize the presentation of Maya culture history within the traditional cultural periods and eras. But as we follow the ebb and flow of Maya civilization through these blocks of time, the reader should keep the *continuities* of this durable tradition in mind. For we will be tracing the course of a civilization that was gradually and continuously evolving in a range of diverse settings across a span of over two thousand years.

## The Origins of Highland and Coastal Cultural Traditions

We begin tracing this development with the origins of sedentary life. Two broad traditions of settled village life, one in the highlands, the other along the coasts, developed in Mesoamerica during the Archaic and Early Preclassic periods. The places where these two traditions emerged overlapped, in part, the larger area ultimately occupied by the ancient Maya.

The most complete record of the development both of village life and of agriculture in highland Mesoamerica comes from outside the Maya area, in the Oaxaca and Tehuacan valleys of Mexico. In their studies of the Valley of Oaxaca, Kent Flannery, Joyce Marcus, and their colleagues have documented a sequence of human occupation of some 10,000 years, spanning the transition from nomadic hunting and gathering to the rise of civilization. In the Tehuacan valley, located southeast of the Valley of Mexico, archaeological investigations conducted by Richard MacNeish and his colleagues traced a similar 10,000-year sequence. In this semi-arid highland valley (presumably along with other locales that remain undocumented), conditions were right for the gradual domestication of wild maize and other food plants. But the development of highland agriculture was a long, slow process, extending over several thousand years. It took a great deal of time to perfect agricultural methods that could support a group of people year-round. Thus permanent village life emerged slowly, by about 2000 B.C. in the Valley of Oaxaca (about the same time as in the Valley of Mexico), and it was not until about 1500 B.C. that firm evidence of permanent settlements appears in the more marginal Tehuacan valley.

There is less evidence for early human occupation in the Maya highlands. Refuse from Santa Marta cave, in Chiapas, Mexico, reveals that occupation by hunters and gatherers ended by about 3500 B.C. Unfortunately, there is a gap in the cave sequence after this date until around 1300 B.C., when the cave was reoccupied by people who relied exclusively on farming for subsistence. Research in the Quiche basin of the southern highlands of Guatemala has located over a hundred preagricultural sites, marked by chipped-stone tools made from basalt. These early hunting and gathering sites have been tentatively dated to a span from about 11,000 B.C. to 1200 B.C. However, the evidence for the transition to the beginnings of village life in this area, as in Chiapas, remains elusive.

This dearth of information appears to be due largely to environmental conditions that have destroyed or obscured archaeological remains. Volcanic activity has deposited deep layers of ash over many areas of the highlands, and the heavy rains of the region have redeposited volcanic materials and other soil on valley floors, deeply burying whatever might remain from the earliest settlers. As a result we can only speculate, on the basis of the evidence from other highland areas such as the Tehuacan valley, that the earliest peoples in the Maya highlands also followed a long, slow path to village life, adapting agricultural methods to a variety of local conditions. Though the environment of the Tehuacan valley is quite different from that of most of the Maya highlands (the middle Motagua Valley and a few other areas in Guatemala have a similar semi-arid climate), a comparable general process probably took place. Yet because of the variety of soil types, rainfall rates, and terrain, it is likely that it took centuries for human groups to adapt successfully to the diversity of the Maya highlands.

In any case, we do not encounter firm evidence of settled village life in the Maya highlands until well into the Preclassic era. Current theories favor the idea that these first agriculturists were migrants from outside the highlands, probably from adjacent coastal regions, but it remains possible that they represented an indigenous tradition of highland agricultural development, like that seen in the Tehuacan valley.

The best-known village development has been found on the Pacific coast at several sites in southern Chiapas (Mexico), Guatemala, and western El Salvador. The earliest of these settlements is associated with Early Preclassic pottery of the Barra Ceramic Complex (ca. 1700–1500 B.C.), followed by a more elaborate and diverse pottery tradition, the Ocos Ceramic Complex (ca. 1500–1200 B.C.). Subsistence for these early coastal villagers was based on seashore and lagoon gathering, possibly supplemented by agriculture. By Ocos times, population had increased, occupation had spread inland (at least as far as the Grijalva river valley in central Chiapas), and livelihood was clearly dependent on agriculture. Recent excavations at sites on the coast of eastern Guatemala and western El Salvador have disclosed evidence of this same pattern of development (Fig. 2.1). It has been suggested that the earliest Pacific coast villagers cultivated manioc, a root crop, but at least some reliance on maize is also probable.

Archaeological research along the Caribbean coast of Belize, also directed by MacNeish, has reconstructed a long sequence of human exploitation of this shoreline environment. These finds come from surface surveys and are not yet firmly dated or verified by excavation. Nonetheless, MacNeish is able to report that

Fig. 2.1. Early Preclassic occupational levels at the site of El Mesak, on the Pacific coast of Guatemala (ca. 1600 B.C.); pottery excavated from this site is of the Ocos ceramic tradition.

Archaic-period hunting and gathering appeared here before about 9000 B.C. He also reports very early evidence of settled village life in this coastal area, estimated at about 4200 B.C. to 3300 B.C. Although these data must be interpreted with caution, owing to the fragmentary nature of the record and the dearth of well-dated remains, it appears that these early coastal villagers may have supplemented their diet with agricultural products. Still, it seems, as on the Pacific coast, that basic subsistence depended on gathering the plentiful resources of the sea, lagoons, rivers, and adjacent land—resources that included fish, shellfish, turtles, sea birds, reptiles, and a variety of other animals (as evidenced by the recovered remains of these species). Once again, in a pattern similar to that seen on the Pacific coast, the concentration and year-round availability of these food sources probably enabled people to live in permanent villages, rather than having to move from place to place to find adequate food supplies. Indeed, this pattern of coastal subsistence supports small villages along some of these same coasts today.

It is equally difficult to pinpoint the transition from hunting and gathering to agricultural village life in the Caribbean coastal lowlands, but it may have been by the beginning of the Early Preclassic. Yet the earliest evidence of *inland* pottery-producing settlements (Fig. 2.2) does not appear until the subsequent Middle Preclassic, about the same time as elsewhere in the Maya lowlands (see Chapter 3). The Swasey Ceramic Complex of northern Belize, formerly dated to the Early Preclassic, has been revised by a new series of radiocarbon dates to roughly 1000–500 B.C., which is equivalent to the timing of other lowland Maya Middle Preclassic pottery traditions.

Fig. 2.2. Middle Preclassic platforms at Cuello, Belize: (*above*) Feature 262, a very low plastered platform with postholes from an apparently perishable building with an interior clay-lined hearth; (*below*) Feature 250, a slightly higher plastered platform, with rounded sides and a low frontal step, that overlay Feature 262 (the rectangular pit to the right in both photos is a later grave shaft intruded from above).

• •    Excavations in northern Yucatan at Mani and the cave of Loltun have recovered pottery seemingly as old as the Swasey ceramics; and the finding of mammoth bones associated with stone tools in occupation levels beneath the earliest pottery in the cave of Loltun raises the possibility of far earlier hunting groups in Yucatan.

The Pacific and Caribbean coastal villagers were culturally precocious, in the sense that they manifested the first indications of part-time craft specialties, social-status distinctions, and even long-distance trade networks. But neither of these coastal village traditions appears to have been related directly to highland developments. Whereas the earliest pottery from the Tehuacan valley appears to have copied the forms of still earlier stone-container prototypes, no immediate ancestors for the earliest Pacific coast Barra ceramics have been discovered.

The diversity and sophistication of these early coastal pottery traditions argue for yet undiscovered origins, either local or in some distant region. The lack of known prototypes has led some to postulate migrations from, or other contacts with, northern South America, the only New World area with a documented, earlier, pottery-making coastal village tradition. At Puerto Hormiga, Colombia, early village life is dated by radiocarbon methods to at least 3000 B.C. Radiocarbon dating puts similar coastal villages on the Pacific coast of Ecuador, near Valdivia, at the same time, if not earlier. The fact that manioc, a cultigen postulated to be part of the early Pacific coast village tradition in Mesoamerica, originated in South America may be indicative of Archaic-period contacts between these two areas. And the evidence of maize, domesticated in Mesoamerica but found in South America at about the same time, would appear to strengthen the arguments for contact. At present, however, only fragmentary evidence exists for these postulated connections, and only further archaeological exploration and research, especially in the intermediate areas of lower Central America, can hope to resolve this problem.

## Preclassic Antecedents and Contemporaries

Initially, the developmental course of the Maya lowlands lagged behind the Mesoamerican highland and lowland areas reviewed thus far, all of which supported the emergence of settled communities by the Early Preclassic. In contrast, there is no evidence of substantial Early Preclassic occupation in the Maya lowlands. Current evidence indicates that this area was not colonized until the Middle Preclassic, at which time there must have been fairly rapid population growth and sociopolitical development. The latter would indicate that this process was accelerated as a result of contacts with other regions, including both the southern Maya area and adjacent regions of Mesoamerica. Here, we will summarize the crucial Preclassic developments from the non-Maya areas of Mesoamerica (comparable developments in the Maya area will be traced in Chapter 3).

The Pacific coastal village tradition in the southern Maya area is related to a similar early sedentary development found to the north, across the Isthmus of Tehuantepec, along the Mexican Gulf coast. In this humid, lowland jungle setting, one of the earliest civilizations in Mesoamerica, the Olmec, rose and fell during the Early and Middle Preclassic. Although we cannot treat the accomplishments of the Olmec at length here, it is important that we consider their development, for in adapting to a similar tropical-lowland environment, the Olmec established a cultural pattern that in many ways paralleled the longer career enjoyed by Maya civilization.

Of particular concern is tracing the origins and development of ruling elites and their basis of power, so as to gain an insight into the origins of civilization itself. For the essential fabric of what we refer to as "Maya civilization" corresponds to the institutions and culture of the ruling elite class. In this sense especially, the Maya developed as part of a wider political context that included much of Mesoamerica.

Archaeological investigations at two key Olmec sites, La Venta and San Lorenzo, indicate that Olmec civilization had its roots in an early coastal village tradition much like that seen on the Pacific shores of the Maya area. These two sites were to become major Olmec religious and economic centers in the Middle Preclassic. Although other Olmec sites are known, most remain uninvestigated. La Venta, the first Olmec site to be studied archaeologically, lies on a salt dome or "island" surrounded by lowland swamp. New archaeological research at La Venta, the first settlement study at a major Olmec site, provides the first direct evidence that the organization of Olmec society was more complex than had been described by traditional models. It is clear now that in the specific adaptations to a lowland riverine environment, in the size of populations, and in the complexity of sociopolitical organization, the Olmec more closely resembled Classic Maya society than had previously been acknowledged.

These new data fully document for the first time the existence of river-levee settlement in the swampy terrain surrounding the La Venta island (Fig. 2.3), along with a sequence of local environmental changes, beginning in the Early Preclassic and continuing through the Middle Preclassic (ca. 2200–500 B.C.). The evidence indicates that populations increased substantially during this span, supported by a combination of coastal fishing and gathering, hunting, and highly productive river-levee agriculture (maize being the staple crop). Also for the first time, evidence of domestic occupation adjacent to the civic-ceremonial core has been found, contradicting the traditional "vacant ceremonial center" organizational model that had often been applied to Olmec society. The new data support the development of a hierarchy of three site levels, reflecting economic, sociopolitical, and ritual distinctions, a hierarchy that was in place by the time La Venta reached its Middle Preclassic apogee (ca. 800–500 B.C.). This site hierarchy was headed by La Venta itself,

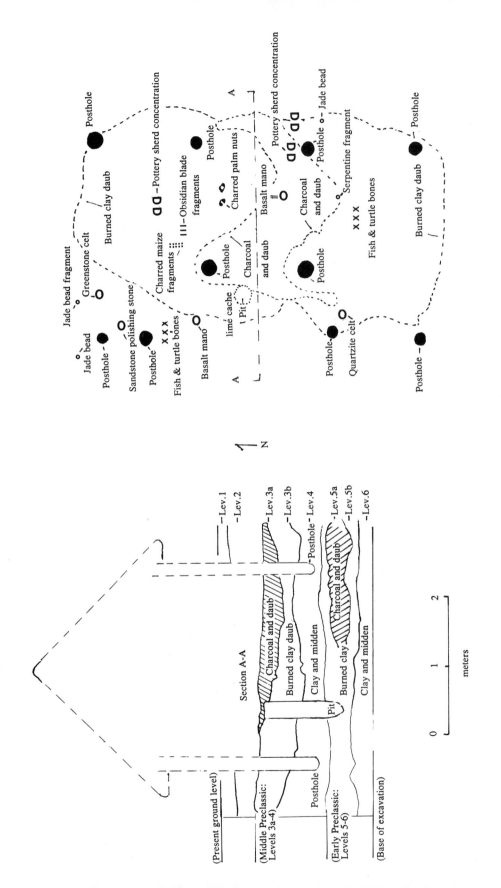

Fig. 2.3. Middle Preclassic house platform at La Venta, Tabasco, Mexico (ca. 1000–400 B.C.): (*left*) section showing postholes and underlying Early Preclassic levels; (*right*) plan of house with postholes and associated artifacts and food remains.

a fully developed "temple town" containing the well-known monumental earthen platforms and sculpture, supported by a population that resided on the island. The second and third levels comprised two types of settlements in the surrounding riverine settings, one with large platform constructions that used a broader array of resources, the other without such constructions and with fewer resources. This evidence, in turn, allows the reconstruction of a concentrated settlement at La Venta of considerable size and complexity, including some degree of economic and social stratification.

At San Lorenzo, a low-hilltop ceremonial center overlooking the Río Coatzacoalcos and its tributaries, the earliest remains of occupation (before ca. 1200 B.C.) include pottery related to the Ocos Ceramic Complex of the Pacific coast. This period is followed by a "proto-Olmec" period (ca. 1250–1150 B.C.), during which some Olmec-style motifs, such as incised designs on pottery and hollow, baby-faced ceramic figurines, first appear. Then, during the period about 1150–900 B.C., San Lorenzo was apparently transformed into a major center: in a mammoth construction project that required probably hundreds of laborers, the hilltop was leveled and shaped, and surmounted by monuments and building platforms. Although none of the structures approaches those at La Venta in size, the stone monuments are certainly equivalent to those at La Venta, the most famous being the colossal carved stone heads.

Evidence of this kind indicates that by around 1200 B.C. the Olmec had developed a *theocratic* chiefdom. In this system a complex society is managed by an elite class under one ultimate authority, the chief, whose power derives principally from the stewardship of religion and wealth. We infer that Olmec chiefs were bestowed a religious power derived from the belief that they would provide security for the populace, through rituals to "ensure" proper conditions for agriculture and other essential activities, while reinforcing the authority of their elite kinsmen. We can perhaps also infer that the chief's economic power had its base in the management of agricultural and other food-producing activities, and in concomitant rights to receive food tribute. Economic power also derived from the control of trade networks; direct archaeological evidence demonstrates that these networks provided the Olmec with a variety of exotic products, including jadeite, serpentine, and magnetite, that were used as symbols of the ruling elite's prestige and authority.

Olmec contacts were established at major centers in the central-Mexican highlands (the most important being the famous Chalcatzingo site) and along the Pacific coast as far as Chalchuapa in western El Salvador (Fig. 2.4). Obsidian was imported from Central Mexico and from the Maya highlands, to be manufactured into cutting tools. Other exotic items, many apparently reserved for elite use, included jade from the middle Motagua Valley in Guatemala, magnetite (used to fashion ceremonial mirrors) possibly from the Valley of Oaxaca in southern Mexico, and fine kaolin clay (used to make a distinctive whiteware pottery) mined near

Chalcatzingo. Perishable commodities were undoubtedly traded also; although no direct evidence has survived, the Olmec likely imported cacao (the seeds of which are the source of chocolate) from the Pacific coast of the Maya area and quetzal feathers from the Maya highlands, as well as textiles and other products from a variety of sources. These pan-Mesoamerican economic networks provided avenues for social, political, and religious interaction as well, and in the process would have tended to facilitate communication, and thus accelerated cultural development, throughout Mesoamerica.

Although the traditional view that the Olmec were the source of all subsequent civilization in Mesoamerica has been swept away by a tide of evidence for equivalent complex societies elsewhere in Preclassic Mesoamerica, it remains obvious that developments on the Gulf coast were among the most significant precursors to Maya elite institutions. Monumental Olmec sculpture appears by the end of the Early Preclassic and is well developed within the Middle Preclassic. Motifs include portraits of rulers with their insignia and paraphernalia (such as mirrors and scepters) that are prototypes of objects used by later Maya kings. Although the colossal

Fig. 2.4. Monument 12 at Chalchuapa, El Salvador: rubbing of an Olmec-style boulder sculpture (Middle Preclassic, ca. 1000–400 B.C.).

portrait heads are unique to the Olmec, the inventory of Olmec monuments includes two basic types—upright stones with standing portraits and rectangular stones with seated portraits—that parallel common Maya forms ("stelae" and "altars"). The iconography of these sculptures also anticipates themes in later Maya art, as for example in the well-known portrait of the ruler seated in the cave (or jaws) at the entrance to the underworld. And, as David Grove has pointed out, some of these Olmec rulers are identified by symbols, or *glyphs*, that could have served as emblems for names or titles, and even the custom of defacing or breaking of monuments, presumably done after a given ruler's death in order to negate the residual supernatural power within the stone, anticipates similar treatment accorded Classic Maya stelae.

The timing of developments in the Mexican highlands paralleled that on the Gulf coast. Interaction with the Gulf coast Olmec played a role in these processes in both the Valley of Mexico and at Chalcatzingo, where Olmec links are most explicitly apparent in the famous sculptures. But recent work at Chalcatzingo and in the Valley of Mexico demonstrates simultaneous local sociopolitical development that was *not* Olmec-directed or -derived. One of the best-documented cases of this independent process lies in the evolutionary sequence from the Valley of Oaxaca, where the first glimmerings of social stratification appear near the end of the Early Preclassic. By the Middle Preclassic (ca. 700–500 B.C.) the Valley appears to have been apportioned among a series of rival polities, each polity ruled by an elite group who occupied residences that were closely associated with ceremonial structures and distinct from those of the remainder of society. Middle Preclassic Oaxacan pottery bears motifs usually labeled "Olmec," including the "fire serpent" and "were-jaguar," but similar designs appear throughout Mesoamerica (as far away as Trujillo on the north coast of Honduras). It now seems clear that, rather than being Olmec motifs per se, these designs were used by peoples in many parts of Mesoamerica for their own purposes, such as emblems for local lineages. The first carved monuments also appear during this era (ca. 700–500 B.C). These monuments use simple glyphs to record calendrical dates or personal names (Fig. 2.5). But the motifs on these upright stones—the display of captives and sacrifices—are completely distinct from those of the Olmec. Whereas the Middle Preclassic Olmec rulers reinforced their authority with personal portraits that linked them to the powers of the cosmos (earth and sky), the early Oaxacan rulers asserted their authority with records of their successes in leading raids and taking captives. As we shall see, both themes were utilized by Maya kings in their public displays of power.

An interpretation by Kent Flannery, based on data from the Valley of Oaxaca, provides an example of trade with the Gulf coast—and of the *effects* of that trade—that was probably typical of long-distance interaction during the Middle Preclassic. Flannery infers that the Olmec treated the Oaxacans as equal trading partners, acquiring Oaxacan products in exchange not only for material goods but also for both esoteric and practical knowledge. Thus, the Oaxacan elite seem to have sought

Fig. 2.5. Monument 3 at San José Mogote, Oaxaca, Mexico, a Middle Preclassic monument depicting a sacrificed captive with two glyphs (at lower right) reading "One Earthquake," probably a name or date associated with the captive/sacrifice event.

out, in the Olmec religion, concepts that would better unify their own society, and may have adopted from the Olmec better mechanisms of economic and political organization, as well. Of course any such relationship is a two-way street: the Olmec ruling elite, for its part, not only secured exotic items that helped to maintain their status and authority, but their contacts with the Oaxacans (and other evolving societies in Mesoamerica) exposed them, as well, to new ideas—some of which undoubtedly helped change the developmental course of their own society.

Many centuries later the power of the Olmec waned, for reasons unknown, and ultimately they lost access to the exotic resources carried by the trade routes that linked much of Mesoamerica. These Early and Middle Preclassic economic networks furnished a web of interaction within which, throughout Mesoamerica, regional civilizations emerged. The wealth of ideas, as well as goods, that flowed along these routes spurred further developments. Access to new crops and agricultural techniques increased food supplies and allowed populations to increase. Access to new natural resources, crafts, and markets increased prosperity and created a host of production specialists and middlemen. And as societies grew larger and more complex, the ruling elites consolidated their control with new economic, political, and religious institutions. These developing Preclassic institutions were the foundations for the further growth and elaboration of Mesoamerican civilization during the subsequent Classic era. Located at a crossroads between Mesoamerica and Central America, and situated within a rich and diverse environment, the Preclassic Maya nurtured the first flowering of their ancient culture, the New World's most brilliant civilization.

## Factors Underlying the Rise of Maya Civilization

By the beginning of the Middle Preclassic, most of the villagers and town dwellers in the Maya area subsisted by coastal gathering, swidden (slash-and-burn) agriculture, or a combination of the two, and produced a variety of products. These early Maya, already deeply in touch with their own environment, learned much from contact with other Mesoamerican groups, from their nearest neighbors to the distant peoples of the Gulf coast, Oaxaca, Central Mexico, and Central America. There were many reasons for the meteoric rise of the Maya, and archaeologists have by no means uncovered all of them. But recent research has tended to emphasize the search for "causes," and we can now identify many of the more important forces in the development of Maya civilization. The most significant of these factors—ecological adaptation, temporal and spatial diversity, unity of elite subculture, networks of interaction, competition, and ideology—merit some examination. They did not operate in isolation, of course, but rather in concert, to shape this remarkable civilization.

### Ecological Adaptation

Ecological adaptation comprises the interrelated factors of environment, subsistence, and population growth. These are obviously important to an understanding of any human society, for environmental conditions and the means used to produce food largely determine the characteristics of a human population, including its health and nutritional status and whether or not it can sustain growth in size, density, or organizational complexity. The Maya experience is in many ways an excellent illustration of these relationships, for the Maya area presented its inhabitants with an extremely diverse environment, one that is rich in resources and blessed with a variety of opportunities for developing means to obtain food, and the Maya, for much of their history at least, made the most of their environmental opportunities. The earliest means of human subsistence, hunting and gathering, was greatly facilitated in this environment. Rich in food resources, the area in time came to support permanent villages in the most productive coastal environments and connecting river valleys. Throughout Maya prehistory, in fact, hunting and gathering continued to provide essential protein. Later refinements may have included the development of artificial ponds for the raising of fish, such as those that have been identified along the west coast of the Yucatan Peninsula.

One of the earliest forms of cultivation in the Maya area was undoubtedly swidden agriculture, whereby fields were cleared, burned off, and planted with a variety of food crops, including maize, beans, squash, chilis, and such root crops as manioc and sweet potatoes. But whatever the crop, tropical soils become exhausted after several years of cultivation, and new fields must be cleared and planted while the old lie fallow. Swidden agriculture is nonetheless adaptable to a wide range of environments, from highland valleys and mountain slopes to lowland jungle and scrub forest. For the modern Maya farmer, in fact, it remains the most common method of cultivation, and it is still practiced from the highlands of Guatemala to the lowlands of Yucatan.

Swidden cultivation is an example of *extensive* agriculture: large areas are needed to produce rather low yields per unit area, since a large proportion of land must remain fallow at any given time. More *intensive* agricultural methods usually require some means of replenishing the soils. Under certain favorable circumstances, such as the periodic flooding that revives alluvial river valleys, the replenishment is the gift of nature. But in their household gardens, the Maya did their own replenishing, using what is probably the oldest intensive method of cultivation: a plot of land adjacent to the family dwelling is fertilized by household refuse. Household gardens are still in use in many Maya communities today. Important garden cultigens include tree crops such as avocado, cacao, guava, papaya, hog plum, palm, and ramon (breadnut), and some small plots are given over to the many crops grown in the swidden fields. Such crops, however, were not confined to the household gardens of the ancient Maya; those with commercial value, such as cotton, cacao, and probably oil palm may well have been grown in large stands located in favorable areas like (in the case of cacao) the Pacific coast, the lower Motagua Valley, and the Caribbean coast.

Other intensive methods, techniques found rarely or not at all in this area today, included agricultural terracing and raised fields. Evidence for ancient terracing has been found in parts of the Maya highlands and in hilly portions of the lowlands. Raised fields, similar to the *chinampas* ("floating gardens") of Central Mexico, allowed productive use of swampy or poorly drained land. Crops were grown on parallel or intersecting ridges of well-drained, fertile soil built up from the swamp floor. The canals between the raised fields provided drainage and served as a source for rich soil that was periodically scooped up to renew the growing areas. The canals may also have been used for raising fish and other aquatic life. These raised fields could support a variety of crops, including nonfood items such as cotton and tobacco for local consumption or, more importantly, commercial production for export to other areas. It has been suggested that many of the raised fields whose remains have been found in northern Belize were used for growing cacao as well as maize. Relic raised-field systems have also been identified in the western lowlands, along the lower Río Usumacinta and Río Candelaria, in the eastern lowlands, and possibly in the *bajos* (seasonal swamps) of the central Peten.

How do these subsistence adaptations help us to understand the development of Maya civilization? To begin with, given the diversity of the environment within the Maya area, it follows that there would have been a corresponding variety in the subsistence modes and resources available from one locale to the next and, consequently, a diversity of potentials for growth and for exchanges with neighboring areas. Although each of the subsistence methods we have outlined had its own, distinct origins—some at an early date, others much later—all undoubtedly followed a similar pattern of development. As a given area was colonized, its environmental potentials led to a sequence of cultural responses: initial experimentation with known resource-acquisition methods, followed either by acceptance (with or without modification), if they proved successful, or by rejection and renewed experimentation with new methods. Ultimately, areas suitable for increased food production and rich in other resources supported population growth and expanded settlements, which in turn produced powerful incentives for still more intensified agriculture.

## Temporal and Spatial Diversity

Classic Maya civilization, once viewed as a uniform, monolithic entity, confined to a period of some six hundred years (the Classic), is now seen as evolving and changing over a span of more than two thousand years (from the Middle Preclassic through the Postclassic). This temporal diversity is to be expected, given such an extensive time depth and a spatial setting that saw a whole mosaic of independent Preclassic centers developing across contrasting lowland, highland, and coastal environments.

The spatial and cultural diversity of Classic Maya civilization originated in and was maintained by boundaries that were set by both natural and cultural factors. Many of the qualities of diversity within Maya civilization no doubt derive primarily from environmental limits, reinforced and perpetuated by social boundaries. Ascribing cultural diversity to environmental diversity and limits is particularly justified in the much more broken topography of the Maya highlands, but, although the impact of the environment is less dramatic in the lowlands (and was, until recently, often ignored), it was important there as well. Still, social boundaries in the lowlands stemmed chiefly from a pattern that saw multiple groups expanding and settling the landscape and, in the process, creating social and political groups that discouraged both fissioning from within and incursions from without.

One important consequence of environmental and cultural boundaries may be

• •  found in the Maya political structure. *It seems clear that the Maya were never politically unified*; from beginning to end, their society was fragmented into scores of independent polities. The basis of this organizational and political diversity has been sought from several perspectives, often by drawing upon analogies from non-Maya ethnographic or historical sources. These include models of Classic Maya sociopolitical organization as a "chiefdom-like" ranked society integrated by vertical patron-client obligations (these based on ethnographic analogies with East African or similar preindustrial kingdoms) or as a feudal system with a more stratified organization integrated by both vertical obligations and horizontal marriage alliances (these derived from analogies with a variety of societies, including medieval Western Europe, feudal Japan, and contemporary East Africa). And more recently, Jeremy Sabloff has viewed the Classic Maya as a system of peer polities, or a cluster of independent petty states where proximity and competition checked the growth of any single polity and discouraged political unification. In contrast to these models, which tend to see political power as deriving from control over production, David Freidel has proposed a more dispersed and subtle system of political authority maintained by control over distribution (he draws his model from analogies of pilgrimages and market fairs). Although all these models offer useful insights, we must base our understanding of Maya sociopolitical organization on analogies drawn directly from Maya archaeological, historical, and ethnographic data, as well.

One difficulty of all such models derived from analogies with other societies is that they often portray Classic Maya sociopolitical organization as uniform in character, right across the lowlands. The available archaeological and ethnohistorical data from the Maya themselves, however, clearly indicate that the independent Maya polities varied in their organizational structure and changed through time.

This should come as no surprise, since the success of any given polity (archaeologically measured by its duration, by the size of its architecture, and by its breadth of settlement) was determined by a variety of factors, including favorability of location, environmental potential, local and regional economic conditions, organizational efficiency, prestige, military success, and the individual careers of rulers—especially as regards their leadership capabilities and length of reign. We can glimpse reflections of the operation of these factors in the more obvious distinctions between centers (size, architectural complexity, etc.) but also from differences in their evolutionary careers (the timing of their rise and fall, their duration, the breadth of land occupied, etc.). Maya polities appear to have been mostly small-scale localized states, and we are just beginning to address questions concerning the organizational diversity among these polities, and the delineation of their individual developmental trajectories. Important integrative factors—forces tending to link polities rather than divide them—also operated throughout the course of Maya civilization. Some of these were economic or ideological. Others involved political aggrandizement—brought about either by marriage alliances or by conquest and military alliances—although expansions of this sort appear to have been relatively fragile and short-lived. In general, these and other integrative factors produced a degree of mutual interdependence among the lowland polities (yielding what has come to be called "a system of states") that helps to explain the less-than-random pattern visible in several episodes of growth and decline. At many (but not all) of the sites in the central Maya lowlands we can actually see two or three cycles of this synchronized process.

The element of sociocultural diversity within Maya civilization is in fact seldom emphasized, owing mostly to the difficulty in detecting this kind of variability in the archaeological record. But we must keep in mind that at a very basic level the Maya represent a diverse social and linguistic assemblage. Studies of contemporary language distributions in the Maya highlands, coupled with theories of language change, have yielded reasonable reconstructions of the probable time depth of these linguistic subdivisions. Farther north, Cholan languages are often assumed to have been the tongues spoken during much of the Classic period, although given the extent of Postclassic depopulation over much of the central and southern Maya lowlands, reconstructed linguistic distributions in this area have been more elusive. Recent successes in the decipherment of Classic Maya texts, however, have allowed linguists to identify the particular languages spoken at several lowland Maya centers—and in the process to raise the possibility that Yucatec Mayan was spoken more extensively than previously believed. But however successful the linguists may be with these specific language identifications, it is becoming increasingly clear that what we define as Classic Maya civilization was sustained by a population that spoke more than one language.

The possibilities for more profound ethnic or cultural distinctions have been investigated from several perspectives. Interaction between adjacent ethnic groups seems to have stimulated several key episodes of development. It seems likely, for example, that some of the Preclassic inhabitants of the southern Maya area were non-Maya (Mixe-Zoquean speakers being the most likely "foreign" group)—at a time when many of the elements of later Maya writing and sculptural style were apparently crystallizing in this very area. The southeastern periphery of the Maya area also saw considerable ebb and flow of Maya and non-Maya populations, and Edward Schortman has recently postulated a plausible reconstruction of dynamic interaction between Maya and non-Maya inhabitants of the Motagua Valley during the Classic period.

Thus, far from being a monolithic entity, Maya civilization was a vast and diverse manifestation, flowering over a varied geographical area and across an extensive temporal span. Though the Classic period is traditionally defined as ca. A.D. 250–900, many characteristics of Maya civilization originated during the previous 800 or so years of the Middle and Late Preclassic, and persisted for more than 600

•  •  years beyond the Classic, through the Postclassic. During this long span of time the character of Maya civilization constantly changed. But at no point in time can we recognize a unified system, for what we term Maya civilization always comprised many linguistic, social, and political groupings.

## The Unity of the Elite Subculture

This underlying diversity conflicts with the very basis for our definition of Maya civilization: the general homogeneity seen in the inventory of material culture throughout the lowlands. Since it is material culture that provides the basis of archaeological inquiry, it is not surprising that for many years descriptions of Classic Maya civilization emphasized its essential, almost monolithic, unity. The homogeneity of Maya civilization as reflected in the archaeological record is most apparent in those aspects of material culture that reflect high sociopolitical status or ideological concerns—those aspects, that is, that represent the elite subculture. Thus, the basic unity that underlies our definition of Maya civilization rests on the traits and activities of this dominant but numerically minor stratum within society. These include consistent preferences for particular exotic materials (jade, certain marine products, quetzal feathers, etc.), particular art styles (painting and sculpture), and particular writing and calendrical systems, clothing, symbols of office, architecture, and site planning. In other words, the apparent unity of Classic Maya society derives from above, not from below. The considerable indications of *diversity* in the culture generally reflect the traits and activities of the non-elite, the bulk of lowland Maya populations.

Thus our definition of Maya civilization rests heavily on the material manifestations of the elite subculture, the class within each Maya polity that managed and directed the course of that polity. And to the degree that these polities formed an interdependent system of states (or peer polities), the economic, social, and ideological ties that created this network were maintained by the elite. Seen in a dynamic perspective, it was these elite-directed activities, both within and between the independent Maya polities, that fueled the evolutionary course of Maya civilization. Elites sponsored the innovations—recognizable in the archaeological record—that stimulated the cycles of growth and decline we can see throughout the course of Maya civilization. These range from the intensification of agriculture to more efficient political institutions. During the Classic period, authority centered on the position of the Maya king, or *ahau*, who ruled in each of the major lowland polities. The *ahau*'s power was legitimized by a synthesis of preexisting and innovative forms, including the erection of monuments for the display of genealogies and momentous events, the hereditary transmission of power within the ruling lineage, and the construction of a monumental funerary temple dedicated to veneration of the ruler's divinity. Smaller or less-successful centers may never have adopted all these Classic-period mechanisms of political authority, and their perpetuation of older

(Preclassic) elite institutions, and the evolution of new institutions of political power after the Classic period, would then have contributed to the contrasting organizational diversity of Maya civilization.

## Networks of Interaction

As we have seen, the Maya were not isolated, but were active participants in a network of interconnections with the rest of Mesoamerica to the west, and Central America to the east. These networks moved principally people and goods, but they were also the conduits for the interchange of ideas. Of course trade, the exchange of goods, is the activity most apparent in the archaeological record. Trade among the ancient Maya embraced a complex of economic activity involving the acquisition and transport of goods and the exchange of goods and services (often in centralized markets). Although no conclusive physical evidence of ancient markets exists, trade centers were noted by the Spaniards at the time of the Conquest, and their antiquity is assumed. But direct archaeological evidence for trade itself, in a variety of commodities, does exist.

A distinction is often made between *localized* trade, that *within* a single environmental zone, such as a highland valley, and *long-distance* trade, that *between* environmental zones. The ancient Maya were a crucial part of a system of long-distance trade routes that ran the length and breadth of Mesoamerica and beyond. The primary long-distance trade routes in the Maya area were those that connected Central Mexico (to the northwest of the Maya) with Central America (to the southeast of the Maya). There were three primary route systems: the southern route, running along the Pacific coastal plain; the central route, running across the Peten; and the northern route, following the Yucatan coast. Secondary routes connected the highlands with adjacent areas to the west, via the Pasión and other river valleys that lead to the Usumacinta or the central Peten. North-south trade routes tied together the Maya area, connecting northern Yucatan and its plentiful salt resources, for instance, with the highland and coastal regions to the south. As intermediaries between Mexico and Central America, and as producers of highly desirable resources (jadeite, obsidian, salt, quetzal feathers, and much more), the Maya were inescapably the middlemen and the masters of much of the Mesoamerican economic system.

The development of centralized markets was undoubtedly a crucial factor in the growth of Maya society. Because goods could be exchanged in a single, central location, a village could engage in specialized production (of textiles or pottery, for example, according to its environmental potential), take its products to the market center, and exchange them for other necessities from other villages. The result was an economic unity and interdependence focused on the market center, and each such market was linked to others by means of long-distance trade, as well. The long-distance trade networks also furnished exotic goods that were often reserved for limited segments of society, the most important being the items that furnished wealth and symbols of status for the elite class.

Together, these economic factors were a powerful stimulus for social organization and development. The market centers, to which the villages were tied, were controlled by the emerging elite class, and the resulting economic power accorded the elites became a crucial foundation for their local status and authority. Those centers in locations favorable to acquiring essential goods or controlling important trade routes were in a more advantageous position, and in most cases developed the organizations necessary to consolidate their control of the acquisition, transport, and distribution of trade goods. As the managers of these organizations, the elite increased their wealth, prestige, and power throughout much of the history of Maya civilization.

### Competition and Conflict

Even in the initial, expansive colonization of the Maya area, competition for land and other resources could have been expected to ensue as soon as areas suitable for agriculture and settlement began to be scarce. Though more intensive methods of cultivation, developed in response to population growth and increasing scarcity, served to contain local competition somewhat, another form emerged, that of competition between centers. The initial competition may well have been economic or religious, as market and ceremonial centers attempted to gain control over larger territories by winning the allegiance of groups of villagers. By the Middle Preclassic, the Maya had begun raiding neighboring groups to take captives, which they used for labor and for ritualized sacrifices. These sporadic conflicts expressed and maintained the dominance of one polity over another and increased the prestige of the victorious leaders—while often eliminating the vanquished leaders as sacrifices. Eventually, the ultimate competitive option was taken up: open military conflict between polities, with the goal of expanding the victor's control over people, land, and resources.

But military activity necessarily involves certain developmental consequences. In the first place, it creates the need for a new specialty, ultimately a new occupational class, the warrior. In time, the Maya warrior class seems to have become part of the "middle class," between farmer and elite, that had initially consisted of craftsmen, merchants, and bureaucrats. In the second place, conflict between centers creates new demands on social organization; and centralized authority is usually the most efficient means of directing a society and its military forces, in either an aggressive or a defensive situation. Thus, for the Maya, as with all societies, competition and conflict were a major factor in the development of a more complex society and an increase in centralized authority.

Another consequence of war, for an area as environmentally diverse as the Maya, was that those centers already holding an advantage in population size and organizational efficiency tended to expand at the expense of the less powerful centers. In such an unstable situation, an expansive power may continue to capture territory from its neighbors until it reaches the limits of its own organization and resources, or until it is checked by an alliance of lesser powers.

## Ideology and Cosmology

The ancient Maya made no distinction between the natural and supernatural worlds, as we do, and there can be no doubt that their ideology—their belief system, which explained the character and order of the world—was a significant factor in the development of their civilization. But the difficulties in reconstructing the beliefs of a long-vanished society are formidable, since so little of any ideological system leaves tangible traces for archaeologists to recover. Yet there are clues, and the Maya, through their elaborate calendrical and writing systems and their extensive inventory of sculpture and other art forms, have left a rich symbolic legacy of their ideas and concepts. By combining what we know about contemporary Maya ideology with the knowledge recorded at the time of the Spanish Conquest and the recent advances in deciphering Maya writing, much of this legacy can be reconstructed.

But the farther one ventures into the past, searching for the origins of various concepts, the less evidence there is to work with. Thus, whereas some symbols of ancient Maya ideology are available for study, others are likely to remain forever shrouded in mystery. And, of course, some crucial concepts may never have been codified in symbols—they may have existed only in the minds of the ancient Maya.

That said, we can nonetheless perceive the role of ideology in the development of ancient Maya civilization. It is difficult to separate ideology from any other aspect of Maya culture. The supernatural guided all aspects of life, even the daily activities of individual people and the ways by which food and other resources were acquired. Economic transactions, political events, and social relationships, including family and village life, were seen to be subject to supernatural control. Thus ideology was embedded in ecological adaptation and in the organization of society, trade, and competition, the very factors considered crucial underpinnings of social evolution.

The structure of Maya society was defined and sanctioned by an elaborate cosmological system. The Maya cosmos was an animate, living system in which invisible powers governed all aspects of the visible world—all that was to be seen in the earth and the sky—and even the underworld hidden beneath. Each individual and social group had its role to play in this system, and the whole elaborate hierarchy of social classes, surmounted by the elite and ruling lords, existed simply to maintain this cosmological order. The ultimate sanction, then, was the threat of supernatural retaliation, a sanction that helped to preserve the structure of society—for any individual, from farmer to king, who deviated from an appointed task

• •  or failed in an obligation to the supernatural powers, would be punished by misfortune, illness, or even death. There were, of course, supernatural specialists, intermediaries between humans and the supernatural world, who could intervene to gain favor, or to discover the meaning of events and what the future would hold (this pursuit is called *divination*).

The earliest supernatural intermediaries were village shamans, part-time specialists who cured illness and divined the future. But as Maya society grew and elaborated, an elite class with priestly powers emerged: full-time specialists with both supernatural and political authority, conferring on themselves the prerogatives of mediating between the supernatural and the rest of society. In essence, the Maya ruler was the supreme shaman for the society he governed, and as such was responsible for the prosperity, health, and security of all his subjects. In ancient Maya society, therefore, kings were both political leaders and priests, and the ruling elite thereby came to direct *all* community activities—the giving of tribute, the building of temples and palaces, the maintenance of long-distance trade, the launching of military expeditions, and the performance of the complex of rituals that nourish and placate the gods—all as ordained by the cosmological order.

Within such a system, success bred success, for with each bumper crop of maize, or with each victory over a rival power, the allegiance to the ruler by the ruled was strengthened, and the morale of the entire society was bolstered. But although successes increased the power and prestige of the ruler, failures did not necessarily diminish them; for minor failures could be explained away, laid against other factors, rather than be taken as signs of supernatural disfavor toward the ruler. Thus, as long as the belief in the ruler's supernatural connections remained intact, the system would not be threatened. Sudden catastrophes, of course, such as the capture of the ruler by a rival power, or long-term disasters, such as repeated crop failures, could—and often did—shake belief in the ruler's powers and place the entire system in jeopardy.

Each of the factors we have discussed here—ecological adaptation, temporal and spatial diversity, unity of elite subculture, interaction networks, competition and conflict, and ideology—was instrumental in determining the character of ancient Maya civilization. The next five chapters trace the growth of that civilization through time, from its earliest manifestations in the Middle Preclassic to the close of the Postclassic, which came to its shattering end with the arrival of the Spaniards in the sixteenth century. Throughout these chapters we will find ourselves returning to various aspects of these determining factors, and in the four chapters that follow those, we shall discuss, specifically and in detail, ancient Maya ecological relationships and subsistence, trade and external interaction, social and political organization, and ideology and cosmology.

# THE PRECLASSIC MAYA

The Lords governed the town, settling disputes, ordering and settling the
affairs of their domain, all of which they did by the hands of the leading
men, who were very well obeyed and highly esteemed.
—*Landa's relación de las cosas de Yucatán* (Tozzer 1941:87)

**W**e have seen how the early inhabitants of the Pacific coast established
some of the first settled communities in the Maya area. Archaeological evidence
from the coastal and adjacent highland region indicates that these people, the ancestors of the later inhabitants of the southern Maya area, built an important foundation for what was to become Maya civilization. The peoples of the southern area
were blessed with a rich supply of natural resources, especially an abundance of
food from both the sea and the forest and a wealth of minerals such as obsidian,
basalt, jadeite, and serpentine. As if to compound that good fortune, their lands lay
along the most direct land routes between Mexico and Central America, giving
ready access to the benefits of long-distance trade.

We can in fact trace the origins and early development of Preclassic Maya civilization within two broadly defined areas: that same southern Maya region (Pacific
coast and highlands) and the Peten, or central lowlands, to the north. Although
these two areas were separated by the southern lowlands and by stark environmental differences, the interaction between the two was crucial to the rise of civilization.
And as we shall see, in developing formal systems of writing, the southern area
seems to have contributed one of the key ingredients around which civilization in
the Classic Maya lowlands crystallized.

The Preclassic period is usually divided into four eras. The Early Preclassic (ca.
2000–1000 B.C.) saw the origins of agriculture and settled communities, chiefly
along the Pacific coast. The Middle Preclassic era (ca. 1000–400 B.C.) was marked
by the first indications of social and political complexity and by evidence of interaction with the Olmec and other Mesoamerican groups. The subsequent Late Preclassic (ca. 400 B.C. to A.D. 100) saw the emergence of Maya civilization, in both

• • •  south and north; many of the institutions characteristic of later Classic-period civilization in the lowlands (Chapters 4–6) actually arose during the Late Preclassic.
Finally, the end of the Preclassic, often referred to as the Terminal Preclassic or Protoclassic (ca. A.D. 100–250), marks the apparent decline of the southern Maya at
the very time the lowland Maya to the north began to ascend the heights of their
development. (This interval is an extra refinement of the sequence defined in Chapter 2.)

## The Emergence of Complex Societies in the Maya Area

The genesis of Maya civilization has been a major concern of archaeological
research for a number of years. Several traditional theories, each of them based on
a simple, unilinear model, have attempted to explain the phenomenon. The best-
known of these theories propose that lowland Maya civilization evolved in isolation; that lowland civilization was produced by a "cultural transplant" from the
Maya highlands; and that the Olmec were the direct ancestors of Maya civilization
(the "cultura madre" theory). Today, most scholars agree that none of these single-
cause theories accounts adequately for the complexity of the evolutionary process
that led to civilization, either in the Maya area or elsewhere in Mesoamerica.

Although we still cannot claim to have found the solution to this problem, it is
now clear that Maya civilization was the product of a complex, multicausal process
within a broad temporal and spatial framework. The relevant time frame probably
includes the entire Preclassic period, ca. 2000 B.C. to A.D. 250, though the latter
half of this period (Middle, Late, and Terminal Preclassic) was undoubtedly the
most crucial (the known Early Preclassic developments were covered in Chapter 2).
The relevant spatial distribution is a broad array of environmental zones and cultural regions, including both the lowland heartland of Classic Maya civilization and
a far more vast "periphery." In fact, one of the most important developments of the
past few decades of Maya research has been the recognition that this so-called periphery—including, to the north, Yucatan, and, to the south, a broad highland and
coastal region from Chiapas to El Salvador and Honduras—played a crucial role
in the evolution of Maya civilization.

It is now clear that certain symbols manifested consistently in the artifactual
record constitute crucial evidence of complex sociopolitical evolution in the southern Maya area. These symbols began to be seen during the Middle Preclassic on a
variety of portable and fixed sculpture, including those pieces usually labeled "Olmec" in style; and Late Preclassic carved stelae in the same area exhibit obvious
Maya stylistic characteristics—including initial examples of Maya writing. Recent
research has documented these and related diagnostics of precocious Preclassic cultural development in the Guatemalan highlands, on the Pacific coast and piedmont,
in western El Salvador, and in western Honduras. As we shall see, interaction

among several complex regional Preclassic societies in the southern area was clearly instrumental in the evolution of Classic Maya civilization in the north.

But as if to balance this perspective, a similar amount of recent evidence bearing on the issue of the origins of Maya civilization comes from the lowland heartland area itself. Excavations have revealed important new indications of Preclassic development at such lowland sites as Komchen, in Yucatan, and Cerros, Cuello, and Lamanai, all in the eastern lowlands of Belize. The most dramatic findings, however, come from the very core of the heartland, at Nakbe, and at the immense site of its probable successor, El Mirador. The Nakbe and El Mirador evidence (discussed below, on pp. 82–84 and 110–17), especially when combined with data from Preclassic sites in Belize and other lowland areas, indicates that the levels of Preclassic populations and organizational complexity in the lowlands were far greater than previously suspected.

Archaeologists often equate early complex societies, such as those of Preclassic Mesoamerica, with the chiefdoms that are documented in the chronicles of the Conquest and other ethnographic and ethnohistoric literature. Chiefdoms are characterized by enduring distinctions in social and political status, such as social ranking and occupational specialization, but as in less complex tribal societies, the organization of chiefdoms is also based on kinship. That is, social and political status is usually determined by birth: a person born into a high-ranking lineage tends to receive the status commensurate with his or her birthright.

In such organizations, the leader of the highest-ranking lineage usually assumes the role of chief, the personage possessing the highest status and authority within the society. The *role* of the chief derives from birth, but the *power* of the chief derives from supernatural sanctions and economic control: as leader of the highest-ranking lineage, he inherits the supernatural support of the deities and his own illustrious ancestors; and, typically, the chief also receives the largest share of tribute (goods and services) from the economic surpluses produced by others. Still, the chief's authority is often limited to what can be accomplished by persuasion or by gaining and maintaining the allegiance of other lineages through the sponsoring of key rituals and feasts, and by the bestowal of favors and gifts, often from collected tribute.

## The Pacific Coastal Plain in the Middle Preclassic

By the Middle Preclassic, a series of complex societies with many of the attributes of chiefdoms had emerged throughout Mesoamerica. It is now apparent that there were equivalent and related developments of this sort both in the southern Maya area and in the central Maya lowlands. As we have seen, one of these Middle Preclassic civilizations, the Gulf coast Olmec, appears to have had a close relationship with peoples of the southern Maya area, especially those along the expanse of

• • •   Pacific coastal plain stretching from Chiapas to Honduras and El Salvador. These contacts were almost certainly the result of long-distance trading relationships. Materials uncovered at Olmec sites of the Gulf coast, for example, include obsidian that had to have come from sources in the southern Maya highlands, and jadeite, serpentine, hematite, feathers, and other highland products were probably also traded to the Olmec heartland. These south-coast trade routes were part of an even larger economic network that connected Mexico with southeastern Central America. Although the fragile and perishable evidence of cacao cultivation (from seeds, pollen, or other plant remains) has not survived, the peoples of the southern Maya area were quite likely involved in the production and distribution of cacao, since, as later times attest, the Pacific coastal plain was a prime growing area for this prized crop.

Evidence for the evolution of complex societies in the southern Maya area and for interaction with other Mesoamerican regions is provided by a chain of Preclassic archaeological sites along the south coastal plain. Their rise has been traced via increasing numbers of sites, the expansion of territories occupied by settled communities, and increases in the size of individual sites, along the south coast and in the piedmont. Much of the archaeological research in these areas has by necessity concentrated on the larger, more visible sites, for the smaller sites are usually invisible, owing to erosion or other destructive forces or to burial by alluvium. Thus we do not have a good picture of the full extent and range of Preclassic occupation in this region, or a sense of the hierarchy among the sites, all of which could tell us a good deal about ancient social and political complexity.

The investigations by Barbara Voorhies in the Soconusco region indicate a Middle Preclassic expansion inland from the Early Preclassic coastal sites. Farther east, in the Escuintla region of Guatemala, Frederick Bove has identified a string of five piedmont sites, spaced about 10 km apart and dating to about 800–600 B.C., that occupy a single environmental zone paralleling the coast. All lie between the coast and the highlands, at elevations of between 120 and 125 m, at an average of 35 km from the sea, within a zone of especially fertile soils and favorable rainfall. By the later Middle Preclassic (ca. 600–400 B.C.) the number of sites in Bove's survey zone more than double, to twelve, and there are indications of a more complex site hierarchy. Site locations show that although two-thirds of the occupation continued to be at elevations above 100 m, the remaining third had expanded back toward the coast (below 100 m). Voorhies's study area in the Soconusco shows a similar pattern of expansion of occupation over time.

These sites possess large-scale earthen platforms, and many are associated with monumental sculptures, the latter often using Middle Preclassic carving styles and motifs, some with Olmec affiliations, to depict important personages. These stone monuments are distributed from Chiapas through southern Guatemala as far east as western El Salvador, in a pattern that suggests a lowland trade and communication network connecting the Pacific coast with the Gulf coast via the Isthmus of

Tehuantepec. The spatial pattern of the monuments may also reflect occupation by a closely related population speaking a language ancestral to Mixe-Zoquean. Thus, this region on the western border of the Maya area appears to have been the locus of an emerging regional tradition produced by early Mixe-Zoquean peoples who might have had ethnic links with Gulf coast Olmec populations. The ethnic affiliation of the Olmec has long been debated, but early Mixe-Zoquean has become the leading candidate; later in this chapter we shall discuss the relationships between the Mixe-Zoqueans and their Maya neighbors.

The portraits on these Middle Preclassic southern monuments seem to represent elite leaders, probably local chiefs who derived at least part of their authority from prestigious and profitable trading relationships. Although we should not expect to find that the diagnostics of the Classic Maya ruling elite were the same as those of the Preclassic—at a time when political institutions were developing and changing—we *can* trace to that earlier time many of the characteristics that reflect the evolution of social and political complexity. Thus, Preclassic architectural remains—elaborated residences, tombs, and shrines—provide clues to the development of social stratification. Preclassic artifacts and monuments bearing portraits, insignia, and texts are especially important in tracing the origins of Maya political institutions. In fact, there are good indications that to reinforce their authority, the emerging ruling elites at these southern centers adopted particular motifs from the general inventory of Mesoamerican political and religious symbols.

What, then, is the basis for the suggestion of Olmec presence or influence in these southern lands? At Padre Piedra, in the central depression of Chiapas, there is an Olmec-style monument along with figurines and other artifacts similar to those found at the Olmec sites on the Gulf coast, and some of the best-known of these Olmec-style sculptures are found along or adjacent to the Pacific coastal plain, from Chiapas to El Salvador. A series of rock carvings at Pijijiapan, Chiapas, depicts several groups of figures with elaborate headdresses and costumes. Farther east, at Abaj Takalik, Guatemala, a large boulder sculpture depicts an Olmec-style personage (Fig. 3.1). Nearby, the excavations directed by John Graham have uncovered a series of small monuments carved in typical Olmec style. Farthest to the southeast, the Las Victorias boulder at Chalchuapa, El Salvador (Fig. 2.4), displays four carved figures; the two larger ones clearly depict important personages with Olmec-style paraphernalia, although some of their specific attributes, such as the "winged capes," seem more closely related to the bas-reliefs at the central-Mexican highland site of Chalcatzingo. Excavations in the El Trapiche group at Chalchuapa have revealed a large, conical earthen mound 22 m high that was built during the Middle Preclassic (ca. 600–700 B.C.). The only similar Mesoamerican construction known from this time period is the famed conical "pyramid" at La Venta, the Olmec site on the Gulf coast, which has been interpreted as representing a volcano (in both cases there is a small, conical volcano nearby), although this interpretation is not widely accepted.

Fig. 3.1. Monument 1 at Abaj Takalik, Guatemala, a boulder sculpture probably of Middle Pre-classic age (ca. 1000–400 B.C.).

## The Highlands in the Middle Preclassic

The Pacific coastal plain was not the only area of Middle Preclassic development. In the highlands there is a similar pattern of development, accompanied by evidence of external contacts, although here there are far fewer indications of direct contact with the Gulf coast. In this period Kaminaljuyu, a major center in the Valley of Guatemala, began to emerge as a dominant power, outgrowing the smaller-scale Early Preclassic settlements there (the Kaminaljuyu site will be discussed in our treatment of the Late Preclassic). Some of the best evidence for the local evolution of Middle Preclassic ruling elites comes from the Salama Valley (Fig. 1.8), in the Guatemalan highlands.

### THE SALAMA VALLEY

This fertile valley, immediately north of the Río Motagua, is drained by a tributary of the Río Chixoy, and thus enjoyed good natural connections to both the southern highlands and the lowlands to the north. Research in the valley has documented occupation spanning most of the pre-Columbian era, from the Early Preclassic through the Postclassic. Fourteen sites with evidence of Preclassic occupation have been identified. The chronological distribution of these sites indicates population growth only through the Late Preclassic, however, with a decline during the Terminal Preclassic.

Of particular interest here is the Middle Preclassic, wherein temple platforms, distinct and elaborated elite residences, and specialized mortuary complexes appear, between about 800 and 500 B.C. At Los Mangales, a small mortuary site dating to this era, the first clear evidence of elite status in the valley is provided by an elaborate burial of an adult male, possibly a village headman or even a chief, in a stone-lined crypt within a specialized mortuary platform (Fig. 3.2). The man was accompanied by objects of jade and shell, and by three trophy heads; around the crypt, at least twelve others, probably retainers, were buried, amid indications of sacrifice and dismemberment. This elite interment culminates an earlier series of low, apparently residential, platforms, one of which contained a single, unaccompanied burial beneath a small adobe "altar."

About 500 B.C. there was a shift in the pattern of settlement in the Salama Valley. A previously undifferentiated valley-center settlement, El Portón, was transformed by a series of new earthen terrace and platform constructions into the focus of political and religious activity—the latter indicated by a series of paired stelae (upright stone shafts) and altars. The most prominent of these was Monument 1, a large schist stela (Fig. 3.3) carved with a now-eroded central scene and a partially preserved column of glyphs (individual writing elements) and numerals along its right margin. Its erection has been placed at around 400 B.C., on the basis of a single associated radiocarbon date. Because the glyphs appear to be ancestral to later

Fig. 3.2. Los Mangales, Salama Valley, Guatemala: a Middle Preclassic chambered tomb (ca. 800–500 B.C.) surrounded by the remains of sacrificed attendants visible on the near side of the stone burial crypt.

Fig. 3.3. El Portón, Guatemala: excavations in Str. J7-4 exposing a monumental basin "altar" (foreground) and Monument 1 (background), the latter a partially preserved carved stela with an early glyphic text (Middle Preclassic, ca. 400 B.C.).

• • •   Maya forms, El Portón Monument 1 may be one of the earliest examples of Maya writing thus far discovered. This was the first in a series of constructions and plain monuments erected at this location in a pattern similar to, but probably older than, the Late Preclassic monument assemblages in the southern highland and Pacific coastal areas. The best-known carved stela traditions with glyphic inscriptions that predate El Portón Monument 1 are outside the Maya area in the Valley of Oaxaca (see Fig. 2.5). The even earlier examples of carved monuments, on the Gulf and Pacific coasts and at Chalcatzingo in Central Mexico, lack texts.

These sculptures, monumental constructions (for example the conical platform at Chalchuapa), tombs bearing indications of status distinctions (including sacrifices), and the presence of similar, specialized pottery wares in different locations all indicate that the complex chiefdom-level societies that emerged in the southern Maya area had maintained contacts within a broad area of southern Mesoamerica at least as early as the Middle Preclassic.

## The Lowlands in the Middle Preclassic

In the lowlands to the north, the Middle Preclassic saw the beginnings of colonization, followed by relatively rapid population growth and the development of sociopolitical complexity. The colonizers seem to have originated in a variety of locales to the south, and probably included non-Maya as well as early Mayan-speaking groups. These first lowland communities were situated on or near seacoasts, rivers, or lakes that would have provided stable sources of water and easy routes of communication. The most cogent reconstruction of this era has been presented by E. Wyllys Andrews V, on the basis of available ceramic and other archaeological data, chronologically controlled by radiocarbon dates. His conclusions, though surely subject to further testing, see at least two separate groups of agricultural colonists, associated with the two best-known early ceramic traditions in the lowlands. These are the Xe Ceramic Complex of the Usumacinta drainage (ca. 900–700 B.C.) and the Swasey Complex of northern Belize (ca. 1000–500 B.C.). The Xe colonization can be tentatively associated with Mixe-Zoquean peoples originating in the isthmian area of Chiapas to the southwest. This tradition, which grew out of the earliest coastal settlements on both the Pacific and Gulf coasts, is usually associated, in the Middle Preclassic, with the rise of complex societies in these same areas (as discussed earlier in this chapter). The Swasey (and other, possibly related, early ceramic traditions, such as the Eb Ceramic Complex, found at Tikal in the central Peten) can be tentatively associated with Mayan speakers ultimately deriving from the Maya highlands to the south and southeast.

Regardless of their origins, during the later Middle Preclassic the new lowland populations grew, the number of villages increased, and settlement expanded beyond the confines of riverine environments and into the interior forested regions. This expansion was seemingly dependent on several innovations, including new agricultural techniques suited to the heavily forested inland areas, and on the construction of water-storage facilities to ensure adequate supplies during the dry season. The expansion was also accompanied by a gradual merging of differences in ceramic and other material items, until by sometime between 700 and 600 B.C. a new tradition, the Mamom Ceramic Complex (ca. 700–400 B.C.), is recognized across most of the southern and central lowlands.

Compared to the southern area, there is relatively little evidence, thus far, of interaction between the Gulf coast and the Maya lowlands. At Seibal an Olmec-style implement described as a "bloodletter" was excavated from a cross-shaped cache. Because this implement is much like those found at the heartland Olmec site of La Venta, it seems to demonstrate links across the lowlands to the Gulf coast. Farther to the west, at the site of Xoc in the southern lowlands of Chiapas, a spectacularly sculptured Olmec-style personage or deity carrying a maize plant was discovered on a rock outcrop. Tragically, the entire Xoc sculpture was destroyed in the early 1970's by looters attempting to remove it for illegal sale.

Until recently, the available archaeological evidence pointed to an egalitarian (non-chiefdom) agricultural society living in villages scattered throughout the lowlands during these Middle Preclassic times. The research of Norman Hammond and his associates revealed a portion of one such village at Cuello, dated by a series of associated radiocarbon dates to the first millennium B.C. The finds at Cuello include low house platforms (Fig. 2.2) coated with lime plaster and containing postholes (presumably once supporting pole-and-thatch houses), hearths, human burials, food remains, and a full assemblage of stone tools and pottery. The earliest pottery at Cuello, assigned to the Swasey Ceramic Complex (ca. 1000–500 B.C.) forms a ceramic assemblage similar to other Middle Preclassic traditions in the Maya area and beyond. Also of interest is the discovery in the earliest levels of at least one mano and one metate fragment (stone implements used jointly to grind grain) and of other evidence for maize agriculture.

Here and elsewhere in the lowlands, pottery and other artifacts such as chipped-stone tools generally lack the kind of diversity that would indicate the presence of occupational specialists or social-class distinctions. The meager sample of Middle Preclassic architectural remains seems to reflect a simple division between domestic structures and a few, slightly larger public platforms, the latter perhaps used for community festivals or ceremonies. One of these, at Altar de Sacrificios, is a platform 4 m high facing a plaza area; another, at Cuello, is a similar lime-plastered platform built of boulders. The Cuello platform was surmounted by a small building with rough, stone-rubble walls faced with plaster; its roof must have been thatched.

• • •

NAKBE

This modest picture has changed with recent discoveries of far larger structures at Nakbe. This site is located in northern Guatemala, in the department of El Petén, about 13 km southeast of the even larger center of El Mirador (which will be discussed below, in the treatment of the Late Preclassic). Nakbe and El Mirador, both reported in an aerial survey of the Maya lowlands in 1930, are connected by a causeway. Nakbe was surveyed and mapped by Ian Graham in 1962, and since 1989 the site has been investigated by a project from UCLA led by Richard Hansen.

Nakbe's civic-ceremonial core (Fig. 3.4), like El Mirador's, is divided into an eastern and a western group, although Nakbe's area of monumental construction covers a smaller area (ca. 0.9 km east-west). The largest platform of Nakbe's eastern group is 32 m high, and the largest in the western group is 45 m high. Fragments of an extraordinary, newly discovered carved monument, Stela 1, were discovered in the main plaza of the eastern group, in front of a small platform, Str. 52. This monument has been reconstructed, and although there are no signs that it was ever inscribed with hieroglyphs, it is an outstanding example of Preclassic sculpture depicting two facing figures (Fig. 3.5). Additional fragments of monuments carved with an early and unusual style have also been recovered from the site, but until more complete examples are found, their significance remains unknown.

The excavations continue, but the results thus far indicate that a major period of construction and occupation at Nakbe dates to the Middle Preclassic. This conclusion is based on both radiocarbon dates and ceramics. Nineteen uncorrected radiocarbon assessments date between 1200 and 450 B.C., and the overwhelming majority of pottery sherds associated with construction and occupation belong to the Mamom Complex. Nakbe is the first known Middle Preclassic lowland Maya site with evidence of such monumental construction. This evidence has revolutionized our concepts of the early development of Maya civilization, and even more recently additional examples of comparable early buildings have been found at a few other central-lowland sites. But the sequence of early architectural development remains better documented at Nakbe, and Nakbe provides our best evidence for the beginnings of monumental civic-ceremonial construction thus far found in the Maya lowlands. In the first half of the Middle Preclassic, ca. 1000–600 B.C., Nakbe's architecture—small structures and low walls, apparently distributed throughout the site—was similar to that of other Mamom-period sites. But a major transformation took place in the latter half of the Middle Preclassic, ca. 600–400 B.C., with the construction of a massive basal platform and a series of individual terraced structures ranging between 4 and 13 m tall—the largest may well have been some 18 m high. Construction activity continued to expand during the first part of the Late Preclassic, ca. 400–200 B.C., when four of Nakbe's largest structures were built (see below).

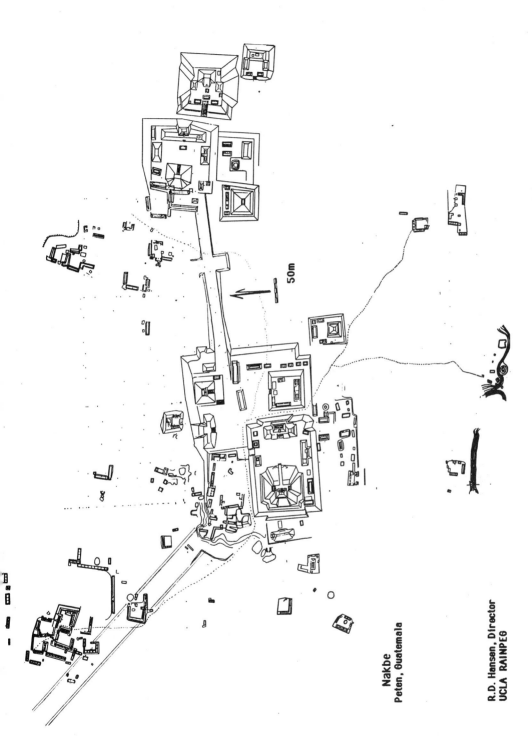

**Nakbe**
Peten, Guatemala

R.D. Hansen, Director
UCLA RAINPEG

50m

Fig. 3.4. Map of Nakbe, Guatemala: the core of the site is a series of monumental Preclassic platforms, some (as at lower left) exhibiting the triadic form typical of this era.

Fig. 3.5. Stela 1, Nakbe, Guatemala: (*left*) the reassembled monument; (*right*) drawing showing the facing pair of carved figures (Late Preclassic, ca. 400 B.C.–A.D. 100).

The beginning of the Middle Preclassic (ca. 1000 B.C.) apparently witnessed the very origins of settlement of the Maya lowlands. Yet, the relatively swift emergence of a major center at Nakbe occurred seemingly within a few centuries of the initial colonization of the central lowlands, and the rapid emergence of sociopolitical complexity apparent from the planning and size of its civic-ceremonial architecture may have been due in part to interaction with external areas. Although adjacent regions of Mesoamerica cannot be ruled out as the origins of this outside influence, the most likely stimulus would be from within the Maya area itself—most probably from the highlands and the Pacific coastal plain to the south. And because our sample of Middle Preclassic sites in the Maya lowlands is still so limited, we may yet find that local evolution was responsible for the cultural development seen at Nakbe.

## Late Preclassic Maya Civilization and the Origins of Writing

The period between ca. 400 B.C. and A.D. 250, embracing the Late and Terminal Preclassic, saw the emergence of civilization throughout much of the Maya area. Archaeological investigations indicate a rapid growth in population and in the development of stratified organizations, as demonstrated by elaborate funerary remains, massive ceremonial structures housing the artifacts of a variety of ritual activities, and the crystallization of a sophisticated art style, all recognized as typically Maya. One regional distinction does seem to hold, however: the earliest examples of Maya hieroglyphic writing are found at Late Preclassic southern Maya centers, whereas writing in the lowlands appears to begin somewhat later.

The most distinctive characteristic of Late Preclassic and Classic Maya civilization was the development of hieroglyphic writing and a distinct sculptural-art style. Writing in Mesoamerica seems to have originated outside the Maya area, however, in the Middle Preclassic period. Although there is at least one example of a carved monument with a glyphic text in the Maya area that may date as early as the Middle Preclassic (see El Portón Monument 1, above), there is a sizable corpus of monuments with hieroglyphic writing in the Valley of Oaxaca beginning in the Middle Preclassic. The earliest known of these, at San José Mogote (Fig. 2.5), has a numeral and "earthquake" glyph that may represent either a date or a personal name (probably the name of the captive portrayed on the stone). At Monte Albán, in Oaxaca, some of the glyphic notations appearing on stelae (upright stone shafts) may represent the names or titles of individuals, place names, or calendric notations. The Oaxacan numbers are represented by the common Mesoamerican bar-and-dot numerals (a dot equals one and a bar equals five). Two of the Monte Albán stelae (nos. 12 and 13) may have been carved as early as 500–400 b.c., although this date is only an estimate. Both have bar-and-dot numerals and what appear to be calendric and noncalendric glyphs. There are also apparent glyphs on some Gulf coast monuments that may date to about the same era.

Given the presence of these earlier Mesoamerican writing traditions, it is logical to assume that the knowledge of writing came to the Maya area from the Oaxacan and Gulf coast centers, by way of well-established trade routes, via the Pacific coastal centers. One cannot altogether rule out in situ evolution, however, for the first known texts carved on stone are fully developed, implying origins in more modestly developed forms in earlier time periods (perhaps on perishable media such as bark paper). But regardless of origins, the durable evidence of stone inscriptions indicates that writing knowledge was quickly adapted by the peoples of the southern Maya area to their own uses. Some "foreign" glyphs may have been borrowed from neighboring systems, and others developed in situ, to create eventually the most complex writing system in the pre-Columbian New World (see Chapter 13).

The issue of the origins of Maya writing, then, is by no means simple or resolved, and involves several different languages and ethnic groups along the way. Moreover, the ethnic identity of the Preclassic populations in the southern Maya area is not entirely clear, since correlating linguistic groups with archaeological remains is extremely difficult. Clues are available from what linguists know about the

• • •    distribution and development of Mesoamerican languages (see Chapter 13), and this evidence has been used to propose that the Preclassic peoples of the southern area spoke early forms of Mayan languages such as Chol, Mam, or Pocomam, while others (see p. 65, above) spoke a non-Mayan language such as ancestral Mixe-Zoquean. Thus, the same two major groups of peoples who apparently participated in the original settlement of the Maya lowlands were involved in the origins of Preclassic writing systems. The two groups, at about the same time during the Late Preclassic, developed writing and calendric systems that shared many characteristics, and the arena that saw the development of these two writing traditions was the lowland zone that stretched from the Gulf coast, across the Isthmus of Tehuantepec, to the Pacific coastal plain of Chiapas and Guatemala. There were apparently no clear-cut boundaries between the two ethnic and language groups, and there was probably a great deal of movement and mixing (a geographically disjunct area occupied by a Mayan-language group, the Huastec, is today isolated on the northern limit of this lowland zone). Nonetheless, most of the remains associated with the Mixe-Zoquean tradition are in the western portion of this zone (the Gulf coast and Chiapas), whereas those associated with the Maya tradition tend to be in the eastern portion (Guatemala and El Salvador).

## The Late Preclassic Mixe-Zoquean Tradition

Over the past few decades scholars led by Gareth Lowe have in fact defined a Mixe-Zoquean tradition in the Late Preclassic archaeological record of Chiapas (and some archaeologists and linguists have proposed that the Olmec were ancestral Mixe-Zoqueans). Yet the existence of a distinct, non-Maya writing system in this area, most likely associated with Mixe-Zoquean, has been recognized only recently, owing to the relatively small number of preserved examples. The potential for a breakthrough in understanding this writing tradition is presented by the discovery of a magnificent monument, Stela 1 at La Mojarra (Fig. 3.6), a Gulf coast site located along the Río Acula, approximately halfway between the "Olmec" sites of Tres Zapotes and Cerro de las Mesas in the state of Veracruz. This stela has the longest and most complete text of any known in this script. Another, far briefer, example can be seen on a portable effigy known as the Tuxtla Statuette (Fig. 3.7), found in the same area some years ago.

The most significant intellectual achievement stemming from the evolution of these two writing systems was the invention of a calendrical system with a fixed-zero date, known as the Long Count or Initial Series (see Chapter 12), that was used to record specific events. Long Count dates were often sculptured on stone stelae that served as durable memorials to rulers and other elite personages. As such, they appear to have become objects of ancestor worship, as well as symbols of political legitimacy. Written records very likely were also kept on perishable ma-

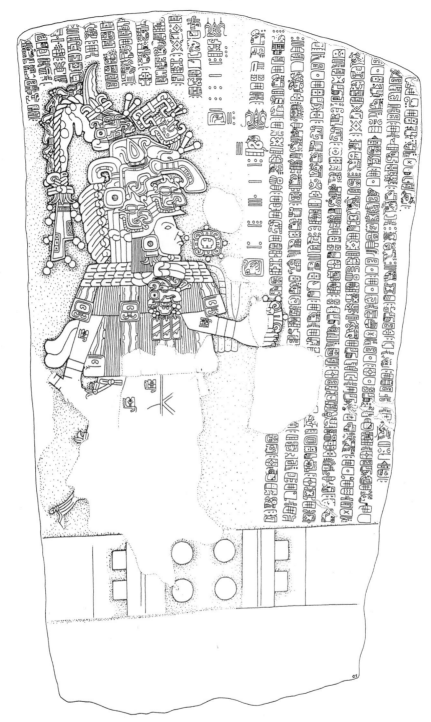

Fig. 3.6. Stela 1, La Mojarra, Veracruz, Mexico: the carved scene depicts an elaborately costumed Late Preclassic ruler, and the lengthy hieroglyphic text, apparently rendered in the Mixe-Zoquean writing system, includes two bar-and-dot dates, probably corresponding to A.D. 143 and 156.

• • •    Fig. 3.7. Tuxtla Statuette, San Andres Tuxtla, Veracruz, Mexico, inscribed with glyphs in the Mixe-Zoquean tradition; the incised bar-and-dot date on the front appears to be equivalent to A.D. 162.

terials such as bark paper, like that used in later times. The best evidence for this practice is that the basic Mayan word for "to write," according to one interpretation, is based on the root for "to paint (with a fine brush)." Portable records in the form of painted tallies and messages could have been used for tribute lists or inventories of trade goods, which would have accorded the southern Maya an obvious advantage in their economic competition with other regions.

Long Count dates apparently associated with the Mixe-Zoquean tradition used a single vertical column of bar-and-dot numerals. The earliest known example is Stela C at the site of Tres Zapotes, Veracruz, which bears a simple bar-and-dot inscription and sculptured elements (Fig. 3.8). If the Tres Zapotes inscription was based on the same zero date as was later used by the Classic Maya, as seems likely, then the Stela C date corresponds to 31 B.C. (of course, if a different zero date was used on the Gulf coast, the Maya correlation could not be used to convert the Tres Zapotes inscription to a Gregorian date). If we assume that the two cultures did employ the same zero date, then the two Long Count dates on La Mojarra Stela 1 equate to A.D. 143 and 156, and the single date on the Tuxtla Statuette would be A.D. 162. Another date probably associated with the Mixe-Zoquean tradition is found on Stela 2 at Chiapa de Corzo, in Chiapas. Although incomplete, the most plausible reconstruction would be 7.16.3.2.13, or 36 B.C.

One of the most important centers associated with the Mixe-Zoquean tradition is the site of Izapa, on the Pacific coastal plain of Chiapas.

### IZAPA

Investigations by the New World Archaeological Foundation indicate that
Izapa was occupied throughout the Preclassic, and beyond into the Classic and Postclassic periods. Suzanna Ekholm's excavation of Mound 30a revealed it to be an
important early example of monumental architecture, dating to the Middle Preclassic "Duende" period (ca. 800–500 B.C.). Settlement and construction increased
during the subsequent "Frontera" period (ca. 500–300 B.C.). But most of the visible
mounds in the main group date to the Late Preclassic "Guillen" period (ca. 300–
50 B.C.). These are typically earthen-fill platforms faced with unmodified river cob-
bles and plastered with adobe or clay, arranged around level plaza areas (Fig. 3.9).
Most of Izapa's well-known carved stelae and altars are associated with these constructions, and the excavators conclude that they were carved and set in place dur-

Fig. 3.8. Fragment of Stela C, Tres Zapotes, Veracruz, Mexico; the recently
discovered upper portion of this monument bears the initial bar-and-dot
number seven, verifying an apparent date equivalent to 31 B.C.

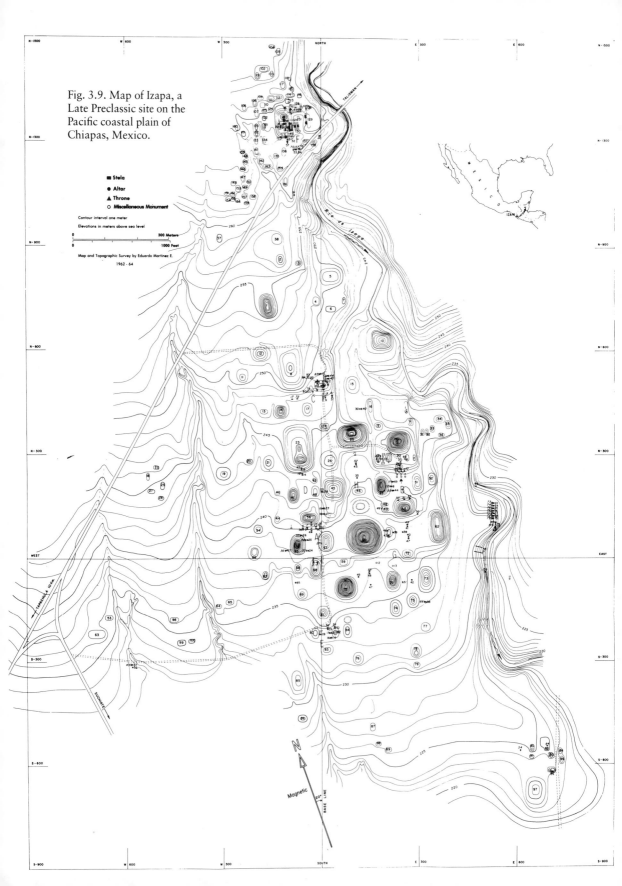

Fig. 3.9. Map of Izapa, a
Late Preclassic site on the
Pacific coastal plain of
Chiapas, Mexico.

■ Stela
● Altar
▲ Throne
○ Miscellaneous Monument

Contour interval one meter
Elevations in meters above sea level

0                    300 Meters
0                    1000 Feet

Map and Topographic Survey by Eduardo Martinez E.
1962 - 64

ing the Guillen period. The "Hato" period (ca. 50 B.C. to A.D. 100) then marks a shift to the northern Group F, although the central site area continued to be used for rituals and burials.

Eighty-nine stelae have been catalogued at Izapa. Less than half of these (38) are carved; the remainder, along with the vast majority of the "altars," are plain stones. The focus of the Guillen-period carved monuments was apparently Group A, where a formalized arrangement of stelae and altars is associated with four platforms, one on each side of a plaza. The eleven monuments found in front of the northern platform (Str. 56) include six carved stelae (five of these are paired with altars, and two are carved). Three carved stelae (two paired with carved altars) front the southern Str. 58. A single carved stela was placed on the frontal axis of the eastern Str. 57, and four plain stelae/altar pairs are associated with the western Str. 55.

These and the other carved monuments at the site define the basic characteristics of Izapa sculpture. The themes appear to be both historical and mythical events, carved in low relief (Fig. 3.10). In the words of Garth Norman, who has studied and published the entire Izapa corpus, these monuments employ "a highly narrative style [with] a wealth of ideographic symbols often interwoven in complex relationships." These carved scenes are almost always framed on top by a sky or celestial band, and on the bottom by an Earth or underworld motif. Although at least some of the figures probably represent historical personages—probably rulers, priests, or other authorities—none thus far has been discovered with texts or calendric dates. If we assume that Izapa represents an aspect of Mixe-Zoquean development, as advocated by Gareth Lowe, then its lack of hieroglyphs and dates indicates that, as with the Maya, there was significant diversity within this neighboring Preclassic tradition.

Izapa was one of the most important centers of Late Preclassic sculpture, and because it represents a distinctive and elaborate stylistic development, this aspect of a presumed Mixe-Zoquean tradition is often referred to as "Izapan." It has even been proposed that Izapan sculpture marks the transition between Olmec and Maya styles. Now, however, with a far larger inventory of carved monuments to study, distributed throughout much of the southern Maya area, most scholars recognize that the transition between Middle and Late Preclassic sculptural traditions was too diverse and complex to be explained by events at a single site.

## The Southern Maya in the Late Preclassic

The trends toward expanding populations and greater social complexity seen in the Middle Preclassic continue during the Late Preclassic, both on the Pacific coastal plain and in the highlands. During the next few centuries many southern Maya centers reached a peak of development and prosperity, and some seem to have emerged as independent mercantile powers. Of these, the largest and most powerful

Fig. 3.10. Stela 21, Izapa, Chiapas, Mexico: rubbing showing a decapitation scene and an elite personage being borne in an elaborate sedan chair; the Late Preclassic sculptural style known as Izapan takes its name from monuments like this one.

was the highland center of Kaminaljuyu, which, like a series of smaller sites in the highlands and on the coastal plain, seems to have been the capital of a prosperous regional chiefdom and a center for ceremonial, political, and economic activities. The role of these sites as ceremonial centers is attested by the considerable investment in construction of large temple platforms and adjacent plazas for the assembly of large numbers of people. Their political functions are reflected in carved monuments bearing portraits of rulers, and in the lavishly furnished tombs for these elite leaders. Their economic functions included the nearby cultivation and distribution of cacao and other crops, as well as commerce both in highland minerals and in commodities from Central America. Most of these goods seem to have been borne by human carriers along the trails that followed the natural overland routes of the area. One of these, the highland route northwestward from Kaminaljuyu, followed the central depression of Chiapas to Chiapa de Corzo (an important site probably associated with Mixe-Zoquean occupation) and on from there to the Gulf coast. Kaminaljuyu was also a crossroads for north-south routes connecting the Pacific plain to the northern highlands (a prime source for quetzal feathers). But the most important route ran along the Pacific coast from Central America, via the string of Preclassic centers stretching from El Salvador all the way to the Isthmus of Tehuantepec, and ultimately north to the great centers on the Gulf coast and beyond in Mexico. Thus the extensive trade network first consolidated in the Middle Preclassic appears to have continued to prosper and grow under the ruling elites that controlled the separate regional centers along these routes.

### KAMINALJUYU

The growth of Late Preclassic Maya civilization was first recognized from archaeological excavations conducted at Kaminaljuyu, the largest and most powerful highland Maya site known. The first modern investigations at the site were conducted by the Carnegie Institution of Washington, most notably by A. V. Kidder and Edwin Shook, beginning in 1935 and continuing after World War II. After work in several individual mounds, such as the excavation of Mound D-III-13 by Heinrich Berlin, investigations at the site and in the surrounding Valley of Guatemala were resumed by a rescue project in the 1960's, directed by William T. Sanders of the Pennsylvania State University in response to the rapid destruction caused by the expansion of nearby Guatemala City (Fig. 3.11).

The site of Kaminaljuyu ("Place of the Ancient Ones") is located in the Valley of Guatemala (elevation ca. 1,500 m), on a flat and fertile plateau that straddles the divide between the Pacific and Atlantic (Caribbean) watersheds. There are numerous sites in the valley, many or all being satellites of Kaminaljuyu at one time

Fig. 3.11. Kaminaljuyu, Guatemala: the huge earthen mounds in one small part of this once-extensive highland site remain relatively undisturbed by the encroachment from nearby Guatemala City (upper right).

Fig. 3.12. Drawing of Stela 10, Kaminaljuyu, Guatemala: this Late Preclassic fragment shows a masked (?) figure (upper left) holding aloft a chipped-stone decapitator (center), a grotesque mask (upper right), and a secondary figure (below); in the upper-left corner is a finely incised hiero-glyphic text (above the masked head) to the right of a *tzolkin* (260-day calendar) date, and in the lower center is the more complete inscription to the right of another *tzolkin* date, the lower in-scription apparently beginning with a count of 300 days (fifteen *uinals*, or periods of twenty days).

or another. At the time of the Carnegie work the site covered about 5 km² and contained over 200 earthen mounds ranging from 1 to 20 m in height. As at most southern-area sites, these represent the remnants of adobe-plastered earthen platforms that once supported buildings of wood, plaster, and thatch (basalt and other volcanic stones of the southern areas being used primarily for artifacts such as grinding stones and monuments—and occasionally for drains, steps, and other architectural elements). Most of these platforms were arranged in groups, often in a linear north-south trend, but others apparently stood in isolation. The site is laid out around a shallow lagoon or lake that probably served as a reservoir.

The Carnegie investigations indicated that about half of the constructions at Kaminaljuyu, including many of the largest, were Preclassic. Occupation began by the end of the Early Preclassic, and the development of monumental architecture and other signs of sociopolitical stratification, such as carved monuments, is detectable by the Middle Preclassic. Kaminaljuyu reached its peak of development in the Late Preclassic (its "Miraflores" period), as measured by its overall size, the number and size of its constructions, its vast assemblage of carved monuments (including examples with hieroglyphic texts, such as Stela 10; see Fig. 3.12), the extent of its external (trade) contacts, and the wealth and power held by its rulers. In the Early Classic ("Esperanza" period) the site saw a revitalization marked by strong contacts with Teotihuacan, as seen in the arrays of pottery, other artifacts, and architecture exhibiting links to Central Mexico. A new civic-ceremonial complex was constructed in the talud-tablero architectural style seen at Teotihuacan. Occupation continued into the Postclassic, but the site was apparently abandoned by the time of the Spanish Conquest.

Although no single center dominated the entire southern area in the Late Preclassic, Kaminaljuyu, in the largest basin of the southern Maya highlands, appears to have been the most powerful. Its direct control of one of the most important obsidian quarries in the highlands, at El Chayal (20 km to the northeast), made it the center of a trade network that distributed this prized commodity throughout the Pacific coast, the western highlands, and northward into the lowlands. The power and wealth that accrued to the Late Preclassic chiefs of Kaminaljuyu is vividly demonstrated by the two spectacular tombs excavated by Kidder and Shook. Both were found within the huge earthen mound of Str. E-III-3, which probably served as the platform for the ancestral shrines that were built over the tombs of these powerful chiefs (Fig. 3.13).

### CHALCHUAPA

A similar, albeit smaller-scale, Preclassic development has been revealed by archaeological research at the site of Chalchuapa, located in a setting transitional between highlands and coastal plain, to the southeast of Kaminaljuyu. Initial investigations carried out between 1920 and 1950, by Jorge Larde and John Longyear, culminated in the extensive excavation and restoration of two large Classic-period structures (in the Tazumal Group; see below) by Stanley Boggs. Systematic survey and excavations of the entire site, including the production of the first detailed site map, were carried out by a project directed by Robert Sharer, of the University Museum, University of Pennsylvania, from 1966 to 1970.

Located in the southeastern periphery of the Maya area, on the frontiers of Central America in what is now western El Salvador, Chalchuapa is about 120 km from Kaminaljuyu. The site is at an altitude of 700 m in the drainage of the Río Paz, which flows south to the Pacific. The mapped area of the site covers 3 km² within

Fig. 3.13. Plan of a tomb in Str. E-III-3, Kaminaljuyu, Guatemala, showing the remains of a Late Preclassic ruler (center) and three young sacrificial companions; the numbered items refer to various grave offerings, including jade beads, a jade mask or headdress, obsidian blades, stingray spines, stuccoed gourds, quartz crystals (most of which were clustered at the feet and along the right side of the ruler), and 157 pottery vessels (the circular objects).

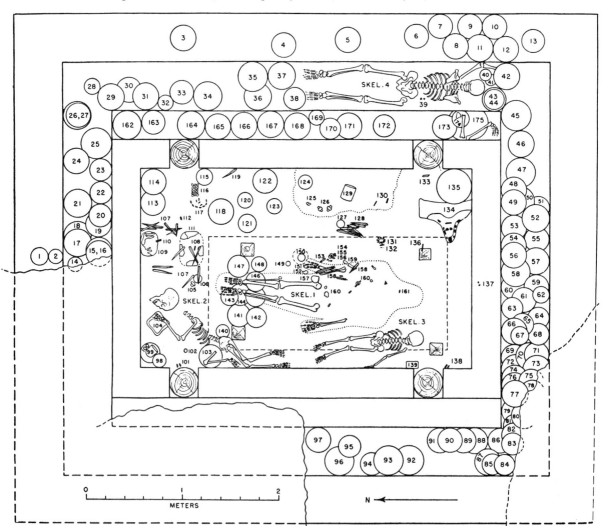

which 58 large earthen/adobe mounds and at least 87 smaller "house platforms" have survived on terrain sloping gradually to the north that was apparently leveled by a series of artificial terraces. Most of the mounds are arranged in groups around open plaza areas, the largest of which have been given names (Tazumal, Casa Blanca, Pampe, and El Trapiche). There are other activity areas without mounds, such as Las Victorias (Olmec-style boulder sculptures on Monument 12; see Fig. 2.4); and two volcanic depressions that formed shallow lakes (Laguna Cuzcachapa and Laguna Seca) were foci of ancient occupation and ritual activity. Stratified middens on the shores of these depressions were excavated and have been shown to provide good chronological control for the sequence of occupation.

Chalchuapa appears to have been settled near the end of the Early Preclassic, probably by colonists moving into the highlands from the Pacific coast. As at other southern sites in the Middle Preclassic, there is evidence of sociopolitical stratification and extensive external contacts, most explicitly with the Gulf coast, as exemplified by the monumental Olmec-style carvings and the construction of a massive conical earthen structure (E3-1, 22 m high) at the northern apex of the site in the El Trapiche Group. As at Kaminaljuyu, the Late Preclassic witnessed a peak of development at Chalchuapa. Pottery and a variety of other remains link Kaminaljuyu during its "Miraflores" period to Chalchuapa during this era. A fragment of a battered carved stela, known as Monument 1, was excavated from the base of Late Preclassic constructions that refurbished the earlier Str. E3-1 at El Trapiche. This stela contains traces of an extensive hieroglyphic text that incorporates several recognizable glyphs, including bar-and-dot numerals and Maya calendric symbols (such as a uinal, or 20-day month sign; Fig. 3.14).

Monument 1 and all other remains of the Late Preclassic florescence were buried under ash deposits from Ilopango, which erupted at the end of the Preclassic period (ca. A.D. 250). Recovery from this natural disaster was slow at Chalchuapa, but by the Late Classic an important civic-ceremonial complex was in use at Tazumal, in the southern sector of the site. Occupation continued through the Postclassic to the time of the Spanish Conquest, when Chalchuapa was known as a Pokomam Mayan-speaking town.

### ABAJ TAKALIK

The site of Abaj Takalik is situated on the volcanic slopes of the Pacific piedmont in Guatemala, about 45 km from the Mexican border, near the southwestern periphery of the southern Maya area. Portions of the site were formerly known by two other names, Santa Margarita and San Isidro Piedra Parada. Studies of carved monuments from these "sites" began in the 1920's with work by Walter Lehman, and continued with the accounts by J. Eric Thompson, in 1943, and later work by Susanna Miles, Lee Parsons, and Edwin Shook. From 1976 to 1980, excavations directed by John Graham, sponsored by the University of California (Berkeley),

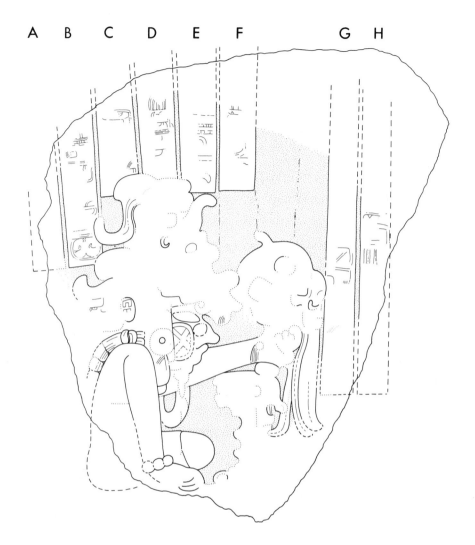

Fig. 3.14. Monument 1, Chalchuapa, El Salvador: drawing of a badly battered sculpture rendered in early southern Maya style, showing a seated ruler (?) holding a trophy head (?) below eight columns of hieroglyphic text (the bottom symbol in Column B is a *uinal*, or Maya 20-day unit glyph).

were conducted at Abaj Takalik, the Maya name later given to what was realized to be a large, single site. Since that time, archaeologists from the Instituto de Antropología e Historia (IDAEH) of Guatemala, led by Miguel Orrego, have continued the investigations.

The mapped core of the site covers about 1 km² lying across a much steeper gradient than that at Chalchuapa. In consequence of that gradient, a series of large terraces steps down from north to south, and the site is roughly 2 km north-south by 0.5 km east-west. Within this area is a series of earthen platforms arranged around open courts or plazas, the settings for an array of carved monuments. According to Graham's analysis, these monuments represent at least three stylistic traditions: Olmec, Izapan, and early Maya. But as is frequently the case, most of these monuments are not in their original settings, having been moved and reset during later periods of activity at the site. For example, a row of four monuments was found on a plaza in front of a low platform apparently constructed at the close of the Classic period. Yet at least two of the four stones are of Preclassic age—Altar 12, carved in early Maya style (Late Preclassic), and Monument 23, an Olmec-style colossal head subsequently recarved to form a figure seated in a niche (probably originally Middle Preclassic).

The dating of these and most other monuments at Abaj Takalik is dependent on stylistic comparisons. But there are several examples, at the site, of stelae carved in early Maya style and inscribed with hieroglyphic texts that include Long Count dates, fixing them within the Late Preclassic. A partially preserved date on Stela 2 (Fig. 3.15) has at least three possible readings, the latest of which equates to the first century B.C. (probably 7.16.?.?.?). The much-better-preserved Stela 5 bears

Fig. 3.15. Stela 2, Abaj Takalik, Guatemala, carved in the early southern Maya style, showing a partially preserved Long Count date probably equivalent to the first century B.C., flanked by two human figures (only their headdresses are now visible).

Fig. 3.16. Stela 5, Abaj Takalik, Guatemala: two personages rendered in the early southern Maya style flanking a hieroglyphic inscription with two Long Count dates, the later of the two equivalent to A.D. 126.

two Long Count dates—8.3?.2.10.5 and 8.4.5.17.11, the latter corresponding to A.D. 126 (Fig. 3.16). Graham sees these monuments as well-developed examples of the early Maya style, ancestral to the later Classic style of the Maya lowlands. And to judge from the bits and pieces of carved monuments lacking inscribed dates, which can be placed in time only by stylistic analysis, the ultimate origins of Maya style must lie even earlier in the Preclassic.

## Other Southern Maya Sites in the Late Preclassic

Evidence of similar monuments and constructions have been found at other Late Preclassic highland and coastal centers, such as Chocola (Fig. 3.17). The ceramics from these centers (which correspond to the Miraflores Ceramic Complex at Kaminaljuyu), the adobe architectural style, and the particular characteristics of site planning give evidence of common traditions that may reflect economic or even, in some cases, political connections with Kaminaljuyu. For instance, burials and caches containing pottery nearly identical to the Miraflores assemblage found in the Str. E-III-3 tombs have been found at many southern Maya sites, including El Baúl (on the Pacific plain), El Portón (in the highlands to the north in the Salama Valley), and Chalchuapa (in El Salvador). One diagnostic type of pottery within this assemblage, Usulutan ware, is distinctively decorated with swirling "resist" lines, usually in cream against an orange background (Fig. 15.5). Usulutan pottery,

Fig. 3.17. Fragmentary Late Preclassic sculpture executed in the early southern Maya style; Chocola, Guatemala, a site on the Pacific coastal plain.

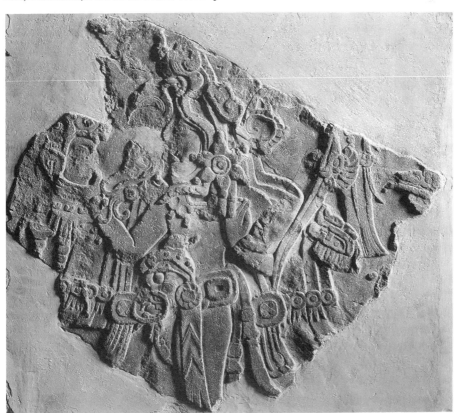

• • •   its antecedents distributed throughout the Middle Preclassic at Chalchuapa and other sites of the southeast region, apparently developed in the southeastern Maya area. By Late Preclassic times it was probably manufactured at several southern centers, including Kaminaljuyu, Chalchuapa, and Quelepa (eastern El Salvador), and it was traded throughout the southern Maya area. Usulutan pottery has been found in many of the elite tombs of the important Chiapa de Corzo site in Chiapas, in the lowlands to the north, as at El Mirador and Tikal, and in Central America as far east as Costa Rica.

Most early calendric inscriptions have been found in the southern Maya area, and it is telling that these southern monuments were sculptured in an early version of a distinctive Maya style. These calendric notations consist of simple bar-and-dot symbols carved in the fashion of the lowland inscriptions of the earliest Classic period but often without the accompanying day-unit glyphs. We have already seen, at Abaj Takalik, several fine examples of such early Maya-style monuments with Long Count dates. And Stela 1, at El Baúl, on the Pacific coast, has both a partially destroyed but readable date (7.19.15.7.12) equivalent to A.D. 36 and a sculptured personage rendered in early Maya style (Fig. 3.18). Many other Late Preclassic sculptured monuments, lacking calendrical notations, are known from the southern Maya area. Executed with considerable artistic skill, they demonstrate the ceremonial and political authority vested in the chiefs. The great southern highland center of Kaminaljuyu erected a series of Late Preclassic monuments; of these, the magnificently sculptured fragment of Stela 10 (see Fig. 3.12) is perhaps the most significant, for it contains a rather long (noncalendric) hieroglyphic text. And as mentioned above, another sizable text, badly damaged, was found on the fragmentary Late Preclassic Monument 1 at Chalchuapa (Fig. 3.14).

Farther north, at the site of La Lagunita, in the Guatemalan department of El Quiché, Alain Ichon and his colleagues excavated the remains of Preclassic construction and a series of broken and reused carved monuments. Although one fragmentary carved-profile human head, Sculpture 12, may be related to the Middle Preclassic Olmec style, there are at least seven examples that can be dated to the Late Preclassic by their affiliations with the Izapa and Kaminaljuyu traditions. East of La Lagunita, in the Salama Valley, the carved-monument tradition continued during the Late Preclassic, as represented by four redeposited stelae. Like the La Lagunita examples, these four Salama Valley monuments bear elaborately carved human figures, but show no trace of glyphic texts (Fig. 3.19). Although these monuments show stylistic affinities to sculptural traditions employed at Kaminaljuyu and Izapa in the same time frame, they also manifest an apparent localized development, termed the Verapaz Sculptural Style, that unites them with the larger corpus of carvings at La Lagunita. Significantly, both of these centers of highland Late Preclassic sculpture are located along important trade routes.

Another distinctive component of this southern Late Preclassic sculptural tra-

Fig. 3.18. Stela 1, El Baúl, Guatemala, showing a personage carved in the early southern Maya style carrying a staff, with a partially destroyed hieroglyphic inscription that includes a bar-and-dot Long Count date equivalent to A.D. 36.

Fig. 3.19. Monument 16, Salama Valley, Guatemala, rendered in the Late Preclassic style of the northern Maya highlands, showing a kneeling personage with glyph-like elements to the left of his head and in the upper and lower panels.

dition is the so-called "pot-bellied" figure (Fig. 3.20). These are obese human figures, often monumental in size, that are carved in the round from boulders. Well-preserved examples are known from Kaminaljuyu and many Pacific coast sites, including Abaj Takalik, Bilbao, El Baúl, and Monte Alto, and there are also smaller, "portable" versions, including one found at Tikal in the Maya lowlands. The dating

Fig. 3.20. Late Preclassic "pot-belly" sculptures provide one of the links between the southern Maya area and the lowlands to the north: (*above*) example from Chocola, southwestern Guatemala; (*right*) Monument 40, Abaj Takalik, also southwestern Guatemala; (*below*) drawings of a miniature example excavated at Tikal, in the central Maya lowlands.

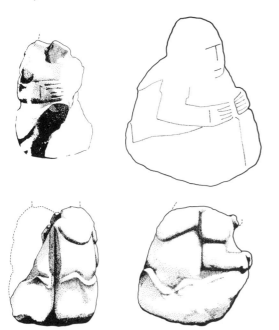

of these sculptures remains controversial, although most scholars accept a Middle Preclassic date for the earliest versions, and a Late to Terminal Preclassic date for most examples. A small figure carved in this style, dating perhaps from the Middle Preclassic, was excavated from beneath the construction levels of Late Preclassic Str. E3-1 at Chalchuapa. Several large and especially obese pot-bellied sculptures were found set into a Late Preclassic terrace at the nearby site of Santa Leticia, El Salvador.

The best indications of affiliations between Preclassic highland sites and later Classic Maya civilization are found in attributes reflecting elite political and religious institutions. Architecturally, we can look to distinct and elaborated residences, as well as to funerary shrines associated with tombs of rulers. Some of the shrines, for example Str. E-III-3 at Kaminaljuyu, are truly monumental in size. But because not all Late Preclassic monumental structures can be assigned a mortuary function, we remain unsure of the degree to which public works were dedicated to individual rulers. Still, those that have been excavated do furnish evidence of the prestige and exalted status enjoyed by these personages. The E-III-3 tombs (Fig. 3.13) were filled with hundreds of ceramic offering vessels and other goods, including stingray spines, indicating that blood sacrifices may have been carried out by these Preclassic rulers, as in Classic and Postclassic times.

The contents of excavated southern Maya tombs also provide graphic evidence that captives and sacrifice were associated with the mortuary rites for rulers. The earliest crypt burial at Los Mangales (ca. 400 B.C.) in the Salama Valley (Fig. 3.2) was surrounded by a dozen sacrificed individuals, some of whom had been dismembered or beheaded. The elite male interred in this burial was accompanied by a large jade object, 22 cm long, that can only be described as a scepter—perhaps a symbol of office. One of his sacrificed companions—perhaps a captured rival ruler sacrificed for the occasion—took along a similar jade scepter. Another such Late Preclassic burial, surrounded by mutilated sacrifices, was excavated at Chalchuapa. The buried rulers in the much more elaborate tombs at Kaminaljuyu also included sacrificed companions: the tall elite male buried there in E-III-3 Tomb 2, wearing a jade mask or headdress, was accompanied by three unadorned individuals (two children and a young adult) who had been placed face-down in the chamber (Fig. 3.13). The burials of two Late Preclassic elite males at Los Mangales contained, in addition to other grave goods, human skulls (probably trophy heads).

The most direct evidence of antecedents to Classic Maya political organization is furnished by the rich corpus of Preclassic carved monuments found in the southern Maya area. As mentioned above, the southwestern peripheral Izapan tradition has been seen as transitional between Olmec and Maya, but its themes could also be seen as combining the prevailing Oaxacan captive-sacrifice motif and the Olmec ruler portrait associated with cosmological symbols. As with a more recently defined tradition of Late Preclassic carved monuments found in the northern high-

• • •   lands (at La Lagunita and in the Salama Valley), the Izapan monuments usually lack texts.

The first monuments to unite extensive texts with iconography—combining the narrative and visual representations of events—are those rendered in the early Maya style associated with a Preclassic southern Maya tradition (Figs. 3.12, 3.14–3.18). The earliest example, although its central scene is largely destroyed, may well be El Portón Monument 1 (Fig. 3.3), dated at ca. 400 B.C. Among the best Late Preclassic examples in the southern Maya area are Kaminaljuyu Stela 10 and Chalchuapa Monument 1; both are fragments but both bear remnants of extensive inscriptions that include calendrical references (without surviving Long Count dates). Although little progress has been made in deciphering the archaic forms of glyphs in these Preclassic texts (other than their calendrical references), the ruler portraits do allow a degree of interpretation. The prevalent themes appear to be either warfare-sacrifice or the succession of political offices. Warfare themes are indicated by weapons or trophy heads, as on Kaminaljuyu Stela 10 and on a fragment in the same style from the south-coastal site of Chocola, Guatemala. Chalchuapa Monument 1 depicts a single seated personage with an elaborate headdress, presenting what appears to be a trophy head, although the theme could be seen as political (especially if the figure originally faced a now-vanished second figure). The single figure on El Baúl Stela 1 stands before a two-column hieroglyphic text, holding a spear/scepter. At Abaj Takalik, stelae 2 and 5 each depict two standing figures with elaborate headdresses facing each other, separated by texts opening with one or two Long Count dates, which may commemorate the transfer of power from one ruler to his successor. As we have seen, the twin-facing-figure motif is found on what may be the earliest lowland Maya monument discovered thus far, Nakbe Stela 1, a monument devoid of glyphic text.

In sum, it is clear that the Late Preclassic southern Maya were fully literate and employed a fully developed hieroglyphic writing system that included zero-date calendrical notation. And since these early dates do not correspond to the ends of calendrical cycles ("period-ending dates"), these Late Preclassic stelae are undoubtedly part of a Maya tradition of commemorating specific historical events and individual rulers. This inference is supported by the prevalence of defaced or broken stelae, since destruction of this sort was usually a concomitant of rituals held after the death of the honoree, as an expression of Maya ancestor worship (see Chapter 11).

Most significantly, the archaeological evidence shows that the southern Maya area was the setting for the emergence of civilization during the Late Preclassic. Networks of economic, political, and ideological interaction integrated this varied region, and apparently fostered the growth of an increasingly complex society. The clustering of the same characteristics at site after site, as seen in artifacts (especially ceramics and trade goods), architecture, sculpture, and writing, indicates that the period was characterized by continued interaction between centers.

The elite-associated characteristics that define Preclassic southern Maya civilization—in architectural elements, sculpture, writing, and the calendrical system—are all prototypes of those that later blossomed in the lowlands during the Classic period. Thus the cultural development of the southern Maya can only be seen as directly ancestral to Classic Maya civilization.

## Highland-Lowland Interaction in the Preclassic

Maya scholars have long recognized the linguistic and cultural relationships between highland and lowland Maya peoples. With the initial discoveries of Preclassic remains in the lowlands (at Uaxactun in the 1930's) and in the highlands (at Kaminaljuyu in the 1940's) came recognition of general similarities in pottery, figurines, and other artifacts. From such evidence it was assumed that contact between the highlands and the lowlands began during the Preclassic period. Thus, despite the sparseness of direct archaeological evidence, as early as 1940 A. V. Kidder pointed to the Verapaz region of the northern highlands (see Fig. 1.1), located astride the most direct north-south routes, as the logical intermediate locus for trade and other interaction between highlands and lowlands.

Archaeological evidence indicates that sedentary populations occupied the northern Maya highlands throughout the Preclassic, beginning the region's colonization as early as the Early Preclassic, sometime between about 1200 and 800 B.C. The dating and distributional pattern of this evidence suggests population growth throughout the remainder of the Preclassic, with a probable decline during the Terminal Preclassic. We have already mentioned the full sequence of Preclassic occupation in the Salama Valley. Farther north, occupation dating to the Early and Middle Preclassic has been identified at three sites in the Alta Verapaz. Two of these, Sulin, some 6 km east of Purulhá, and Carchá I, on the Río Cahabón, are located along major river courses. The third site, Sakajut, is situated above a small tributary of the upper Río Cahabón, along a still-used north-south overland trade route. Research by Charlotte Arnauld identified seven additional sites in the Alta Verapaz with occupation dating to the Late or Terminal Preclassic. Six of these sites are within the upper drainage basin of the Río Cahabón or its tributaries; the seventh takes its name from the Río Chichen, 8 km southwest of Sakajut.

West of the Verapaz region, in El Quiché, Ledyard Smith's survey located two Preclassic sites in the headwaters of the Río Chixoy. The more recent work of the French Archaeological Mission identified at least twelve sites with Preclassic occupation farther east along the Río Chixoy, and another eleven sites with Preclassic occupation in two adjacent regions south of the river. Five of these sites have yielded pottery dating to the Early or Middle Preclassic, as well as later types. The remaining twenty sites show occupation dating to the Late or Terminal Preclassic.

Preclassic sites in the northern highlands tend to cluster in two regions, a west-

• • • ern group (middle Chixoy valley and adjacent areas of El Quiché) and an eastern group (the Baja and Alta Verapaz). Neither cluster was isolated, and both were in fact involved in widespread communication with other regions of the Maya area—highland and lowland alike. A model based on data from the Salama Valley allows for the reconstruction of the regional systems that emerged in the larger valleys of the Maya highlands during the Middle Preclassic, each system dominated by a single organizational center that eventually controlled a range of activities including resource acquisition, local and long-distance exchange, political leadership, and ceremonialism. The best known of these, and the most powerful Preclassic highland center, was Kaminaljuyu (discussed above). These regional systems grew in size and importance through the Late Preclassic, until suffering an apparent decline in the Terminal Preclassic. As we shall see, similar regional centers arose in the Maya lowlands, where emerging political leaders controlled their own hinterlands and maintained communication networks that spanned much of the Maya area.

The northern Maya highlands provided critical developmental links in the communication networks between the southern highlands and the lowlands to the north. These valleys and their regional centers (such as El Portón) signal the importance of interregional interaction within the overall evolution of Maya civilization. But these northern highland valleys were not simply trading links within a larger system; both the middle Chixoy valley and the Salama Valley, for example, participated in the development of key aspects of ancient Maya culture, including sociopolitical complexity, ceremonialism, and both writing and sculptural traditions. Data from the northern Maya highlands reinforces, therefore, the perception of the ancient Maya world as a mosaic of interrelated but diverse regions and traditions, each of which contributed in varying degrees to the origins and growth of Maya civilization.

## The Central Lowlands in the Late Preclassic

In the lowlands, the transition from the Middle Preclassic to the Late Preclassic, the latter corresponding to the Chicanel Ceramic Complex (ca. 400 B.C. to A.D. 100), was marked by the emergence of larger and more complex social units. Sites founded in earlier times appear to have greatly increased in size; and many new centers began, as evidenced by the widespread findings of Chicanel-period pottery throughout the lowlands, perhaps a reflection of better communication between centers. Clear evidence of class distinctions is present in the artifactual remains. Specialized pottery forms became common, and some were used for ceremonial offerings (in caches) or as burial gifts. Other artifacts show the increasing differentiation associated with the presence of a wealthy ruling class. The tombs of these elites contain a varied inventory of imported luxury goods: jadeite, seashells, and pottery, including the prized highland Usulutan ware. Stingray spines, used for ritual bloodletting by the ruling class, are also found. Besides reflecting class and status differences, these goods indicate increased trade contacts with coastal regions, the southern Maya area, and beyond.

The architectural remains demonstrate the same trends. The oldest lowland buildings of monumental size date from the Middle Preclassic. By the Late Preclassic these compare in size and energy expenditure with any constructed in Mesoamerica. A platform some 33 m high was built at Lamanai (Fig. 3.21), and one nearly as large (22 m high) was constructed at Cerros, both in the eastern part of the central lowlands. At Tikal, the Lost World Pyramid (Str. 5C-54) of this period measures some 80 m square at the base and over 20 m high. The oldest ceremonial precinct at Tikal, the North Acropolis, built of cut-stone masonry, was begun in the Late Preclassic. Within this old complex several Late Preclassic tombs have been excavated; one consisted of a masonry chamber representing the earliest known example of a Maya corbeled vault. Again at Tikal, wall paintings (Fig. 3.22) were executed in a manner closely related to the southern Maya style, especially that of the Miraflores period at Kaminaljuyu. This link to the south, also evidenced by certain ceramic and other artifactual similarities, may represent the beginning of important economic and political connections with Kaminaljuyu.

As we have seen, the early part of the Late Preclassic (ca. 400–200 B.C.) saw the construction of the largest buildings at Nakbe, known as strs. 1, 13, 27, and

Fig. 3.21. Restoration drawing of Str. N10-43, Lamanai, Belize, a large Late Preclassic terraced platform with a height of some 33 meters.

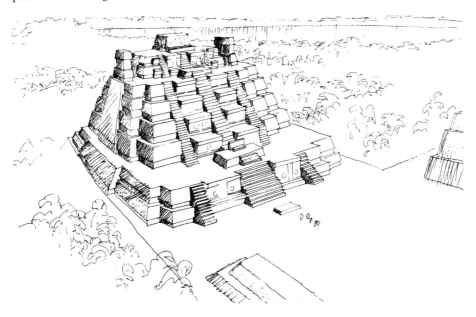

Fig. 3.22. Murals from Str. 5D-Sub-10-1st, Tikal, Guatemala, a Late Preclassic building found buried beneath the North Acropolis: *(left)* drawing of one of the painted figures on the wall of the tomb beneath the platform; *(center and right)* drawing of the partially preserved murals on the front façade of the building.

59, and similarly massive buildings have been identified by Richard Hansen's research at two other sites in the region. At one of these sites, moreover, known as Guiro, Hansen's excavations have documented a series of Late Preclassic elite tombs, probably belonging to the site's Late Preclassic rulers. We may never be quite sure of the importance of these tombs, however, because they were discovered and pillaged by looters before the site was investigated by archaeologists. At the other site in the region, Tintal, Hansen's excavations have identified monumental buildings, stelae, and jade caches attributable to the Late Preclassic. But the most impressive constructions are at El Mirador, the largest known Late Preclassic center in the Maya area. As we shall see, a key to understanding the origins and significance of the southern Maya connection may be found at this huge lowland center, north of Tikal, which possesses sculpture executed in a style related to that found in the southern Maya area and which appears to have reached its apogee at the end of the Preclassic. Far to the north, a sculptured relief in the cave of Loltun in Yucatan, probably dating to the end of the Preclassic era (Fig. 3.23), demonstrates obvious affinities to the same southern Maya tradition.

## EL MIRADOR

The massive site of El Mirador is located in Guatemala, north of Tikal, some 7 km south of the Mexican border. El Mirador was first reported in 1926, and in 1930 its forest-covered temples were photographed from the air by Percy Madeira,

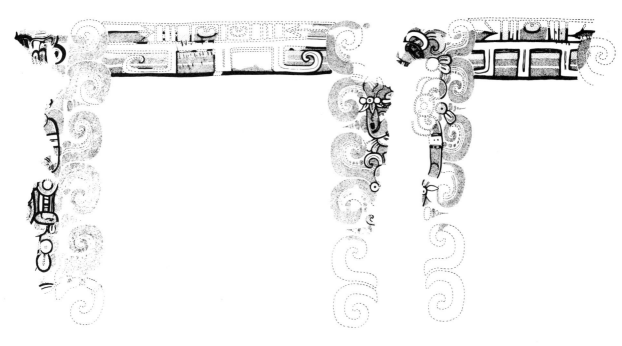

Jr., as part of his aerial reconnaissance of Maya sites. In 1962 Ian Graham surveyed and mapped the central core of the site and, on the basis of observed sherd material and sculpture fragments, tentatively dated the site to the Late Preclassic era. Few, if any, Maya scholars accepted this evaluation at the time, since the size of the constructions at the site contradicted the prevailing assessments of lowland Maya development prior to the Classic period. But Graham's estimate has been verified by a series of more recent investigations, including those during the 1980's directed by Bruce Dahlin, Ray Matheny, and Arthur Demarest and Robert Sharer. Excavations were renewed in 1990, under the direction of Richard Hansen.

El Mirador is situated at the hub of a series of radiating causeways that connect it to an extensive (but as yet undefined) hinterland. The known extent of the civic and ceremonial core covers an area some 2 km from east to west, about the same as that of central Tikal. But within this area is a series of architectural complexes and individual constructions that dwarf anything built by the Maya in later times (Fig. 3.24). The most distinctive of these monumental structures is the triadic pyramid (a central structure flanked by two smaller constructions, the three integrated on a single basal platform). The largest mapped and investigated triadic pyramid, El Tigre (Fig. 3.25), covers a surface area six times larger than Temple IV at Tikal, the greatest building at that mammoth Classic site.

El Tigre dominates a complex of structures on the western edge of the main, or western, group of monumental architecture at El Mirador. Test excavations within the Tigre pyramid itself indicate construction during the Late Preclassic, although even earlier building phases may underlie the bulk of the untested platform. Test excavations directed by Demarest and Sharer in 1982, in the plaza fronting the

Fig. 3.23. Cave of Loltun, Yucatan, Mexico: rubbing of a sculptured figure rendered in a Late Preclassic style closely related to that of the southern Maya area.

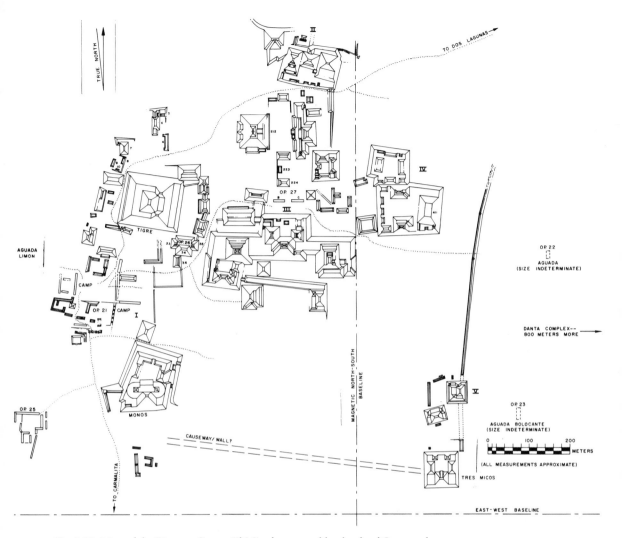

Fig. 3.24. Map of the Western Group, El Mirador, central lowlands of Guatemala.

Tigre pyramid to its east, revealed a series of superimposed floors all dating to the Late Preclassic. One Sierra Red sherd recovered from the redeposited trash sealed beneath these floors was incised with a design very similar to carved motifs from Late Preclassic monuments in the southern Maya area (as at Abaj Takalik, Kaminal-juyu, and El Portón). Terminal activity at this locus may be represented by the filling of a *chultun*, or storage pit, in the El Tigre plaza, for the trash from this feature dates to the Protoclassic era.

A relatively small triadic platform on the south side of the Tigre complex, Str. 34 (Fig. 3.26), excavated by Richard Hansen, is the most thoroughly investigated building at El Mirador. Debris from roof collapse sealed Late Preclassic material on the floor of the central temple building, and a pit in the top step of the central stairway, intruded after the partial collapse of the building walls, provided a carbon

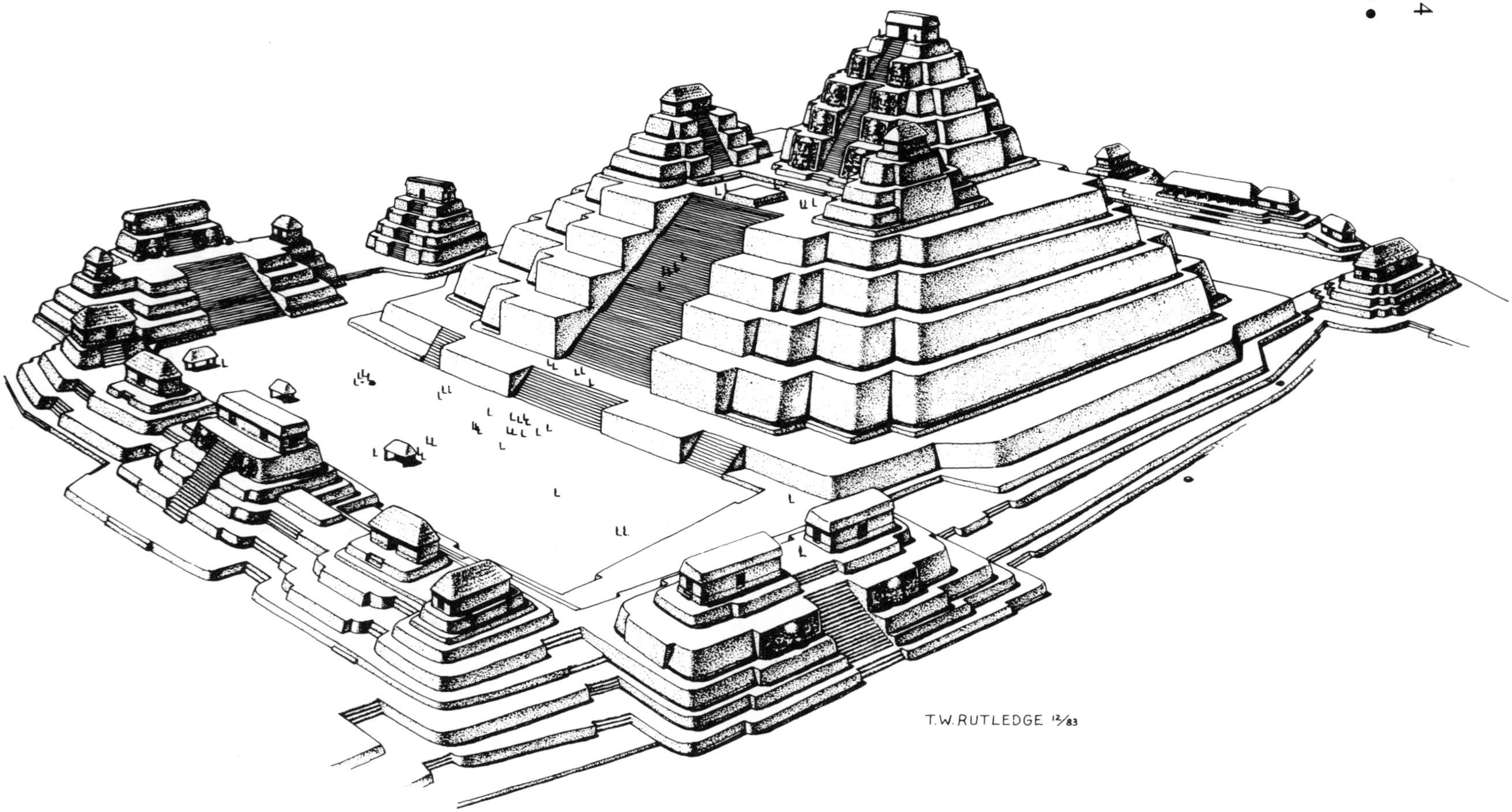

Fig. 3.25. El Tigre Group, the largest complex in the Western Group at El Mirador, Guatemala, named after its largest platform; typically, this platform as well as the smaller Str. 34 (upper left), is surmounted by a triadic temple arrangement.

T.W.RUTLEDGE 12/83

Fig. 3.26. The Late Preclassic Str. 34, El Mirador, Guatemala, a relatively small platform located immediately southeast of the El Tigre platform (Fig. 3.25): (*above*) the south (rear) façade rises some 20 meters to the original cornice; (*below*) a stucco-modeled mask (lower left, partially destroyed) detailed with a jaguar-paw ear flare, flanking the plastered stairway (compare Figs. 3.29, 3.30, 3.31).

• • •    sample dated at ca. 130 B.C. The staircase was flanked by the remains of monumental stucco masks (Fig. 3.26) like those found on Late Preclassic platforms at
other lowland sites, including Cerros, Tikal, and Uaxactun (discussed below).

Test excavations were conducted within the Central Acropolis, immediately
east of the Tigre complex, near the plaza containing the shattered remains of a few
sculpted stelae showing apparent stylistic affinities to Terminal Preclassic monuments of the southern Maya area. The series of buildings on the Central Acropolis
includes at least one large complex identified as an elite residence and dated by
Matheny to the Late Preclassic. Construction of the Central Acropolis appears to
have begun during the Middle Preclassic, although the bulk of it was constructed
in the Late Preclassic. As in many other precincts of the site, there is evidence here
of overlaid construction and occupation during the Classic period.

The western group is bounded on its east side by a north-south masonry wall
joining it to a little-known complex to the southeast known as Tres Micos. In 1982,
excavations in this boundary wall indicated that it dates to the Late Preclassic. The
excavations also revealed a sculptured monument or lintel fragment (reused as a
wall stone) that appears to be the broken top portion of a Preclassic stela.

An east-west causeway links a portal in this wall to the largest single architectural complex at El Mirador, known as Danta. (Its vast bulk is not all structure,
however, for it includes the modification, by terracing, of a low natural hill.) A plain
stela and altar have been found at the base of this complex, near the termination of
the causeway. The Danta Complex rises above a basal terrace in three stages. The
lowest platform, measuring about 300 m on each side and about 7 m high, supports
a series of buildings including, in its southwest quadrant, a monumental triadic pyramid 11 m high, named Pava. The second, smaller platform rises about another 7
m, and in turn supports a third platform some 21 m high. Crowning this third platform, at its eastern apex, is another triadic pyramid, known as Danta. This third-
level pyramid is about the same size as Tigre in basal area, but its summit is some
15 m higher, rising to about 70 m above the forest floor at its eastern base. Excavations in the Pava pyramid supervised by Wayne Howell indicate construction during the Late Preclassic; charcoal from burning at the base of its principal stairway—
apparently representing terminal use of the structure—furnished a date of ca. A.D.
180. Although the Danta pyramid has not been adequately tested by excavation,
its triadic plan and method of construction are consistent with the other monumental Late Preclassic platforms at the site (Tigre, Pava, and Str. 34).

The archaeological evidence from the monumental core of El Mirador clearly
favors a Late Preclassic date for the bulk of construction activity. In order to test
this Preclassic date further, Demarest and Sharer conducted a pilot settlement-
research program at the site in 1982, aimed at locating, mapping, testing, and dating the remains of domestic activity at El Mirador. Prior to this work, there was
simply no information about the location, size, or antiquity of the settlement re-

mains at the site. Quite obviously, determining the age of the occupational remains at El Mirador would be instrumental in verifying the date of the site.

This program succeeded in locating a series of residential groups in areas immediately peripheral to the civic and ceremonial core. These remains possessed the usual characteristics of lowland Maya "house platforms"—typically low, elongated mounds arranged in orthogonal patterns, three or four such mounds typically enclosing a central plaza space. Test excavations in a sample of these groups recovered occupational debris from both constructional and midden contexts. Debris from both of these contexts yielded evidence of domestic occupation dating to the Late Preclassic. The midden material comprised typical debris from household activities. Of particular interest were Late Preclassic sherds reflecting direct contacts with the southern Maya area, including Usulutan decorated trade wares probably imported from the Maya highlands. Earlier Mamom Complex pottery, found in smaller quantities, usually mixed with later Chicanel Complex sherds in construction fills, indicates that the origins of occupation at the site date at least as early as the Middle Preclassic. Excavations also documented subsequent residential activity in the Late Classic, but settlement this late seems clearly to represent a reoccupation after a long period of severe decline or near-abandonment (Classic remains are often perched on top of Preclassic monumental platforms such as the Danta Complex).

It seems clear, therefore, that El Mirador represents a significant Late Preclassic development—the largest known site for its time in the Maya area. Beyond that distinction, El Mirador is also part of a widespread emergence of sociopolitical complexity in the Maya area during the Late Preclassic. The scale of architecture at El Mirador indicates the development of a level of social and political complexity that is on a par with any elsewhere in Mesoamerica at that time. Old models for the origins of Classic sociopolitical organization have been modified in light of the El Mirador evidence, especially given its rapid growth and the unprecedented size of its constructions. But more research is needed, for it is obvious that to better understand the origins and nature of Maya civilization we need to know still more about El Mirador.

Despite the rapid growth of the lowland centers in the Late Preclassic, there are few known examples of Maya hieroglyphic writing or calendrical notations from this period outside of the southern area. That lack could be due to poor preservation—Richard Hansen has recently detected the faint traces of several incised glyphs on one of the Late Preclassic-style El Mirador monuments discovered by Ian Graham (Fig. 3.27), and in Belize a newly discovered text might refer to a calendrical date in the second century A.D. Moreover, results of archaeological investigations at lowland centers, such as Colha and Cerros, in northern Belize, have been interpreted as showing a pattern of evolution of lowland economic and political institutions quite comparable to that seen in the southern area. As an example of these developments, we will look at the case of Cerros.

• • • Fig. 3.27. Stela 2, El Mirador, Guatemala: an eroded Late Preclassic monument, showing faintly incised glyphs in the upper-right panel.

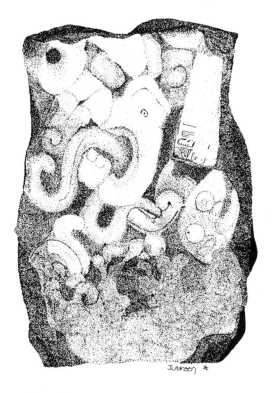

## CERROS

In its final form, Cerros was a small Preclassic center situated on a blunt peninsula that juts north into the Bahía de Chetumal. The landward side of the center was defined by a semicircular canal, within which were raised fields, houses, ballcourts, and shrines. But most of the major temples and elite buildings were clustered on a series of elevated platforms on the northern tip of the peninsula (Fig. 3.28). Cerros and Komchen (in Yucatan; to be discussed later) are the only thoroughly investigated Preclassic centers not partially obscured by later (Classic or Postclassic) overburden. In describing the development of Cerros we will follow the reconstruction offered by David Freidel, the director of its excavation.

Like many other communities in the Maya lowlands, Cerros began life as a Preclassic village. But unlike most such communities, it enjoyed a strategic location that gave its inhabitants—farmers, fishermen, and traders—ready access to the sea and its resources, as well as to the products that moved by canoe up and down the east coast of Yucatan. And because Cerros is of such modest size, the archaeological research conducted by Freidel and his colleagues gives us a relatively complete picture of the transformation of this village into a small regal center, via the same process that probably produced even the largest of Maya cities. For beginning about 50 B.C. the small original settlement was buried under a series of monumental platforms and buildings. Cerros was thus transformed, either by the will of the community or by imposition from outside. Because of its all but ideal location, it would obviously have been appealing to an elite lineage from another lowland center,

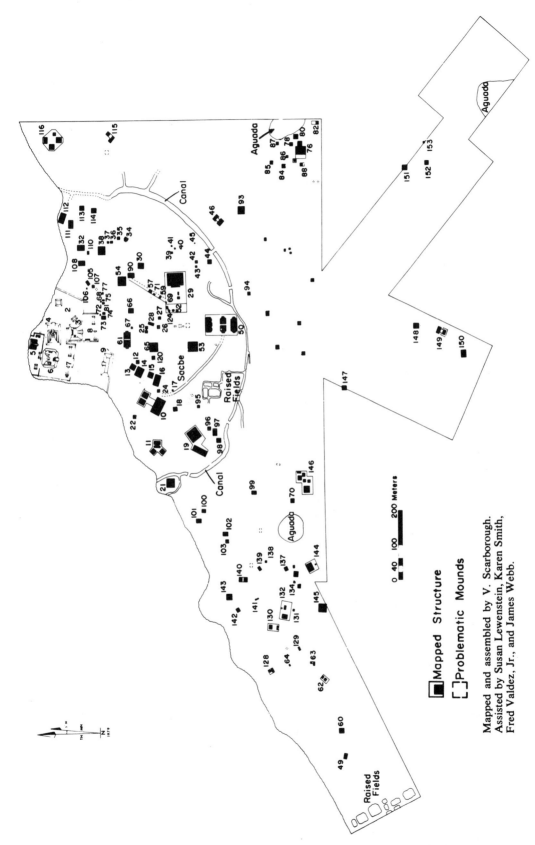

Fig. 3.28. Map of Cerros, Belize, on the south shore of Chetumal Bay, its central civic-ceremonial precinct defined by a shallow canal.

Mapped and assembled by V. Scarborough.
Assisted by Susan Lewenstein, Karen Smith,
Fred Valdez, Jr., and James Webb.

■ Mapped Structure
[ ] Problematic Mounds

0  40  100        200 Meters

• • •    which might have wrested control by installing a son there as its new ruler. The most logical candidate for such a hypothetical origin would be the site of Lamanai, the closest major Preclassic center (see Fig. 3.21).

In any case, the first step in the redefinition of the settlement was the construction of a new temple, known to archaeologists as Str. 5C-2nd (Fig. 3.29). This temple, with its back at the edge of the bay and its front facing the entire settlement to the south, marked the northern point of a sacred north-south axis that ran through the new center, ending with a ballcourt at its southern termination (a second ballcourt is located about halfway along this axis). In Maya cosmology, north is the direction of the sky, the celestial domain of the gods, and south is the direction of the underworld. This placement of the first royal structure thus allied the new ruler physically and symbolically with the celestial domain, and confirmed his exalted status within the cosmos.

As befits the size of the community, Str. 5C-2nd was a modest temple, not anything like the soaring pyramids of El Mirador or the other major Preclassic centers. A two-terraced platform was surmounted by an unvaulted building, presumably the setting for private rituals involving the ruler and the cosmological forces that guided his destiny. But the temple was situated and designed so as to command the attention of the entire community. The temple stairway, which extended far to the south, incorporated two broad landings, one midway from the bottom and another in front of the broad doorway leading into the temple building. The result was a highly visible setting for the public rituals presumably performed by the ruler himself, both on the landings and during his ascent to the summit. And as the ruler made his ascent, he would have been flanked on either side by huge, painted plaster masks of the primary forces of the cosmos. On the eastern side of the lower terrace was the rising sun, complemented on the west by the setting sun. On the eastern side of the upper terrace was Venus, the morning star, complemented on the west, again, by Venus, the evening star. Thus by ascending the stairway, the new ruler was placed at the center of these forces, the daily cycle of birth (rising) and death (setting) of the sun and its companion (Venus, as morning star, "leads" the sun in its rising, and, as evening star, "follows" the sun in its setting). The upper masks along the stairway wear the triadic headband of the king, or *ahau*, while the lower masks bear the *kin* (sun) sign on their cheeks. Other associations with Maya mythology (Chapter 11) are possible: the *ahau* headband may in fact mark the elder Hero Twin, Hun-Ahau, and the *kin* sign may mark his younger brother, Yax-Balam; in the mythology, these Hero Twins are often seen as the first Maya rulers and as representing the basis of all subsequent kingly power.

Each subsequent ruler of Cerros may have sponsored the construction of a new temple, each temple associated with masks and other trappings symbolizing the power of the ruler and his place within the cosmos. Because four such buildings have been identified (apart from the reconstruction of the original versions, such as

Fig. 3.29. Late Preclassic Str. 5C-2nd, Cerros, Belize: (*above*) excavation of the elaborately decorated, terraced platform; (*below*) one of the painted, stucco-modeled masks flanking the axial stairway.

• • •    Str. 5C-1st, which may have been sponsored by the same ruler), then even in the
absence of a historical record, it may reasonably be proposed that a dynasty of at
least five rulers reigned at Cerros during the Late Preclassic. The second temple,
known as Str. 6, was larger than the first, and is located on the west side of the north-
south axis; like Str. 5C, it faces south. But whereas the first temple stood alone, the
second temple marks the establishment of a triadic pattern followed by all subsequent examples at Cerros—a main temple flanked by two smaller buildings, all elevated on a broad platform. As we have seen, this triadic plan, three temples sharing
a single platform, was a hallmark at such major Preclassic centers as Nakbe and El
Mirador. It is also found much closer to Cerros, at the larger site of Lamanai (Str.
N10-43). It would appear, then, that by emulating this architectural plan, the
*ahauob*, or rulers, of Cerros intended to further reinforce a basic triadic cosmological principle underlying their power.

The third temple at Cerros, Str. 4, was the largest construction at the site. Located on the east side of the axis, opposite the second temple, it faced east and the
reborn rising sun. Its change of orientation evidently signaled a shift in the primary
association between the royal temple and the ruler, probably because it was intended to be a funerary shrine (its tomb chamber was empty when found, for reasons unknown). The fourth temple, Str. 29C, faced west. It marks yet another
change, for it was built outside the original northern sacred precinct in the southern
area of the site, forming the western apex of a triangle otherwise delineated by the
two ballcourts. It also is the clearest expression of the Preclassic triadic temple plan
at the site. The builders of the fifth, and final, temple returned it to the northern
precinct and the south-facing orientation of the earliest temples. But it is of shoddy
construction, signaling perhaps that the power of the elite rulers at Cerros was already in decline; and for reasons unknown, Cerros was later abandoned as an elite
center. We know that other Late Preclassic centers, including the great El Mirador,
also experienced difficulties at about this time, and whatever shifts in economic and
political fortune brought on the downfall of El Mirador may also have been felt at
Cerros. The cosmological order that governed Maya life may have played a part in
these changes as well. Regardless of cause, when the elite abandoned Cerros, termination rituals, involving the burning and smashing of ritual articles, seem to have
been performed at the royal temples. And for a time, Cerros returned to its days as
a simple community, before being abandoned forever.

## The Style of Power in Late Preclassic Maya Civilization

As at other lowland sites, there are no Preclassic inscriptions at Cerros. And as
was the case with its contemporaries—such centers as Uaxactun (Str. E-VII-sub;
Figs. 3.30 and 3.31), El Mirador (Str. 34; Fig. 3.26), and Tikal (Str. 5C-54)—the
Preclassic architecture at Cerros included large, plastered masonry platforms dec-

Fig. 3.30. Str. E-VII, Uaxactun, central lowlands of Guatemala: (*above*) remains of the Classic-period platform before excavation; (*below*) the well-preserved Late Preclassic Str. E-VII-sub after excavation, with its stuccoed and masked façade.

Fig. 3.31. Str. E-VII-sub, Uaxactun, Guatemala: details of Late Preclassic stucco-modeled masks after excavation.

orated with huge painted plaster masks (Fig. 3.29). Individual glyphic elements are also present, though these are not elements of discrete texts, but rather are incorporated into the masks and other building decorations.

The director of the Cerros research, David Freidel, interprets this kind of architectural, artistic, and symbolic unity as reflecting a centralization of religious and civil authority in the Late Preclassic lowlands. That is, the representations of both religious and political power were fused together and presented architecturally. In the southern Maya area, by contrast, the use of free-standing stone stelae, which originated there, combined text and image depicting the ruler as warrior-sacrificer, and as transmitter of power to his successor. This southern custom apparently separated royal political and religious symbols from architecture, but we must bear in mind that the poor preservation of adobe construction in the highland and Pacific coastal areas may be preventing us from seeing elaborate architectural masks and other decorations like those found in the lowlands.

But even if this distinction between a lowland pattern of embellished architecture and a southern pattern of carved stelae is valid, its meaning is not yet clear. It could reflect different functions for monumental architecture: the large masked temple platforms in the lowlands may have been stages for public rituals (as with

Cerros Str. 5), and the elevated temples in the southern area may have been primarily nonpublic funerary shrines (as with Kaminaljuyu Str. E-III-3). The distinction could also mean that there was less centralized authority among the southern
Maya, or merely that there was a different tradition of expressing the symbols of
authority. What is clear is that when the southern custom of erecting stelae that
combined text and image was fully adopted throughout the lowlands, it allowed
a new means for recording the activities, ideological symbols, calendrical dates,
and historical texts that would reinforce a preexisting, centralized, civic and religious authority. Notwithstanding, the tradition of using massive architectural
sculpture for the same purposes continued in the lowlands throughout the Classic
period.

If we look at what is known about Late Preclassic burial practices we can see
further support for positing differences in the institution of rulership as it evolved
in the two areas. The North Acropolis tombs of Tikal's Late Preclassic rulers are
big enough only for a single interment and a small inventory of offerings. To date
no Late Preclassic tomb found in the lowlands has been of a size comparable to
those at Kaminaljuyu (though such tombs may yet be found, perhaps at Nakbe or
El Mirador). Although there is evidence of mass human sacrifice in Late Preclassic
Belize, in the eastern lowlands, it is not clear whether or not these sacrifices are
associated with the burials of rulers. In general, Late Preclassic lowland burials do
not seem to be accompanied by the sacrifices found in the southern area (although,
again, these may be expected in some of the larger Late Preclassic centers, and such
sacrifices *are* found in some later Classic lowland royal tombs). There are also similarities, of course, between lowland and southern practices, beginning with the
most obvious—the association of burial crypts or tombs beneath shrine structures
on elevated platforms, which undoubtedly served as the focus of veneration for the
dead ruler. But as we have seen, the initial architectural emphasis in the lowlands
seems to have been the monumental temple dedicated to the cosmological forces
that supported the *institution* of rulership, rather than personal association with a
specific ruler or his tomb. In contrast, the Late Preclassic rulers in the southern area
were commemorated by both portrait stelae and monumental funerary shrines built
over their tombs.

Several fragmentary lowland stelae are certainly Preclassic in style, but among
those discovered thus far, none has either the textual information or the securely
early dates found on the southern monuments. This is not to say that the Late Preclassic lowland elite did not use writing, even on monuments (see Fig. 3.27), and
glyphs also occur on both architecture and portable objects, such as the Kichpanha
bloodletter and Pomona flare (Fig. 3.32). But thus far the evidence indicates that
the origins of the Classic-period custom of using stelae combining text and image
to commemorate rulership lie in the southern Maya area. The earliest securely dated
lowland monument bearing a ruler portrait and a Long Count date remains Tikal
Stela 29 (A.D. 292), although one famous looted monument, the so-called Hauburg

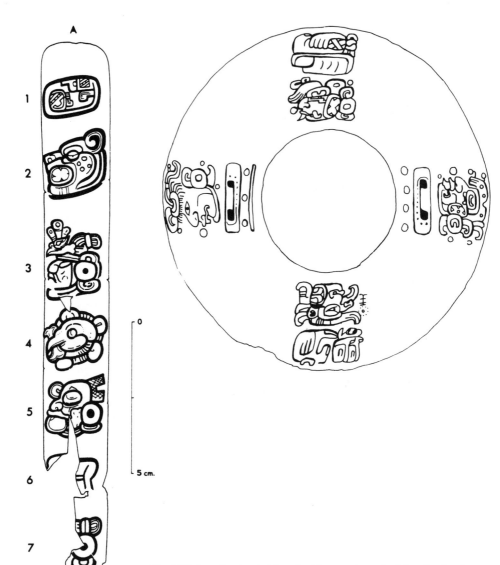

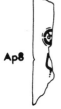

Fig. 3.32. Late Preclassic hieroglyphic texts from the Maya lowlands: (*left*), drawing of the text on a bone "bloodletter" from Kichpanha, Belize; (*right*) drawing of the text on a jade earflare from Pomona, Belize.

Stela, original site unknown, bears a date almost a century earlier (Fig. 3.33). Incidentally, the ruler on Tikal Stela 29, and the rulers in other early lowland portraits (such as the Leyden Plaque; see Chapter 4) often include apparent trophy heads among their paraphernalia, another ruler-associated southern custom that extends as far back as the Middle Preclassic.

The question then becomes, where and when do these two traditions of rulership commemoration merge in the lowlands? Although recent excavations have revealed important Late Preclassic developments at such sites as Cerros, Cuello, and Lamanai, all located in the eastern lowlands of Belize, the findings from the lowland core at Nakbe and El Mirador provide the only Middle and Late Preclassic sites, respectively, that exhibit both massive architecture and carved stelae. Nakbe

Fig. 3.33. Drawing of a miniature carved stela now known as the "Hauburg Stela," looted from an unknown Maya site but probably dating from the end of the Preclassic period. To the left is a hieroglyphic text; to the right is a standing figure holding in his arms a serpent that supports four small deities, while a probable ancestor or "spirit companion" (*way*, see Ch. 13) emerges from its mouth above.

• • •    Stela 1 (Fig. 3.5), with its two elaborately costumed and masked figures facing each other, is similar in theme to Stela 5 at Abaj Takalik in the south (Fig. 3.16). Although Nakbe Stela 1 conceivably dates as early as the later Middle Preclassic, it may well be of Late Preclassic origin. There are also fragments of several carved stelae in the Late Preclassic style at El Mirador. Though the carved monuments at both sites are clearly Preclassic, only one of those discovered thus far has glyphs, and all lack Long Count dates.

Taking all the available evidence into consideration, it seems probable that these different traditions of rulership commemoration, as presented on architecture and stelae, were established in the lowlands as a two-stage process. The first stage involved the association of the abstract power of rulership with the cosmos as represented by temples, and probably originated in the core of the lowland area at such sites as El Mirador and Nakbe. It may also have been in this original heartland of lowland rulership that carved scenes, probably cosmological in theme rather than personifications of individual kings (such as are seen in the south), were first carved onto stone stelae. The second stage, probably during the Protoclassic (see below), saw the emergence of power manifest in individual rulers signaled by adopting the southern practice of combining the image of the king with calendric and other textual information on carved stelae. This innovation was apparently first adopted by the early rulers of emerging powers such as Tikal that followed in the wake of the decline of the "old-order" lowland powers such as El Mirador.

Apart from the issue of the origins of individually commemorated rulership, the archaeological evidence from Nakbe and El Mirador now indicates that Preclassic populations and organizational complexity were far greater, and reached far earlier, than has previously been suspected, especially when corroborated by the data from Preclassic sites in Belize and other lowland areas. By the Late Preclassic many of the distinctive material traits that characterize the elite subculture of the Classic period had begun to emerge or were already present. There can be little doubt that the scale of architectural planning and execution at El Mirador signals the presence of a powerful elite that controlled its own destiny. At the same time, the disparity in sheer size between El Mirador and other Late Preclassic sites may reflect the organizational diversity within the elite segment of society—at a minimum it would seem to reflect relative differences in the power that the sites derived from control over human and natural resources.

It is now apparent that a hierarchy of sites, scaled by size, had emerged in the lowlands by the Late Preclassic. El Mirador would occupy the uppermost position in such a hierarchy, sites such as Late Preclassic Tikal and Lamanai might be second-order centers, sites like Cerros might be third-order centers, and sites like Kichpanha (not discussed) might be fourth-order centers. Although we cannot yet describe the structure of this hierarchy in any detail, it seems reasonable to assume that the relationships between these Late Preclassic polities were antecedent to the system of small-scale independent states of the Classic era.

## The Northern Lowlands in the Late Preclassic

Recent research has provided a much clearer picture of cultural developments in Yucatan than was available just a few years ago. It now appears that the origins of settlement in the northern lowlands date to the Middle Preclassic (ca. 700–650 B.C.), almost certainly as part of the same expansion of farming populations that saw much of the lowlands to the south first colonized by Mayan-speakers. The best evidence for this process is that these initial Yucatecan populations made and used pottery clearly within the same Mamom tradition seen in the south, as revealed by the work of E. Wyllys Andrews V in his research at the Preclassic site of Komchen. Andrews's research at Komchen has also given us the best picture we have of the further development of Preclassic civilization in Yucatan during the Late Preclassic era.

### KOMCHEN

This site is situated in the northwestern corner of Yucatan, only 20 km from the seacoast and adjacent to the later and much larger Classic-period center of Dzibilchaltun (see Chapter 6). The location of Komchen near the salt-producing shores of the Caribbean may indicate that one of its ancient roles involved the exploitation of salt (see Chapter 9). Because the site is only some 5 m above sea level, within one of the driest portions of the northern lowlands, its water supplies had to have been furnished by wells excavated by its inhabitants, as well as by the natural cenotes that dot this region of Yucatan.

Completed archaeological research at both Komchen and Dzibilchaltun reveals that local occupation of this area spanned about two thousand years. The earliest remains, identified by Middle Preclassic Mamom Complex pottery, are of structures begun by ca. 700–650 B.C. There is no known masonry architecture at Komchen itself during this initial period, but a Mamom settlement with masonry platforms has been identified at a small, nearby center named the Mirador Group (Fig. 3.34), which included the earliest known example of a Maya sweat bath. Local population grew during the subsequent centuries, and several ceremonial complexes dating to the Late Preclassic have been found.

Komchen was excavated by the Middle American Research Institute of Tulane University, the most recent work being in 1980, under the direction of E. Wyllys Andrews V. Although the site has been heavily looted for stone building materials, this research revealed that Komchen is composed of roughly one thousand residential platforms concentrated within an area of 2 km². There is a roughly concentric pattern of buildings, with size of platforms tending to increase inward from the site periphery. At the core of the site are five large platforms surrounding a central plaza, the largest of the platforms being some 8 m high. A stone *sacbe*, or causeway, running 235 m northeast to another large structure, is the earliest causeway thus far identified in Yucatan.

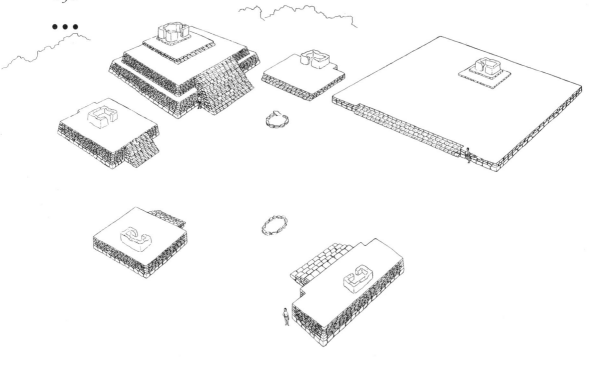

Fig. 3.34. Dzibilchaltun, Yucatan, Mexico: platforms in the Mirador Group, which date from the Middle to Late Preclassic (the summit buildings were added in the Late Classic, and the two oval house platforms in the plaza are post-Conquest).

In the Middle Preclassic, Komchen was probably an agricultural village, for occupation in that era seems to have been limited to perishable family residences. The first substantial platforms (Figs. 3.35 and 3.36), built around the central plaza at the end of the Middle Preclassic and the beginning of the Late Preclassic (ca. 450–350 B.C.), are associated with a new ceramic inventory that may reflect an intrusion of peoples from the Puuc area to the south. During the peak of constructional activity (ca. 350–150 B.C.), the largest masonry platforms at the site were built. The final centuries of the Preclassic were marked by a sharp decrease in constructional activity and probably a reduction in population (ca. 150 B.C. to A.D. 250), and by the latter date the site had been abandoned. Portions of Komchen were reoccupied during the Late Classic heyday of the nearby center of Dzibilchaltun.

## The Protoclassic and the Decline of the Southern Maya

In the closing years of the Preclassic, an era known as the Protoclassic (ca. A.D. 100–250), the precocious southern Maya fell into sudden decline, seemingly in the midst of their prosperity. There are exceptions: the northern highland site of La

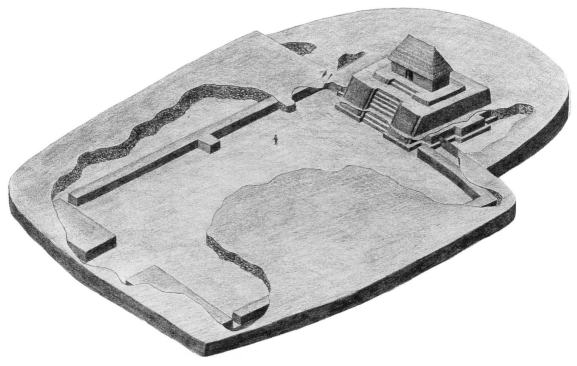

Fig. 3.35. Str. 450, Komchen, Yucatan, Mexico, built during the Middle and Late Preclassic; this structure is connected to Str. 500 (Fig. 3.36) by a 250-meter-long sacbe (causeway).

Fig. 3.36. Str. 500, Komchen, Yucatan, Mexico: excavations revealed construction from the Middle through the Late Preclassic; the ramp and short stairway along the near side date from the Middle Preclassic.

• • •    Lagunita seems to have reached its apogee at this time. But in general, there appears to have been a decline throughout the area. And although the effects of the Proto-classic decline were much more devastating in the southern area—the old custom of erecting carved stelae with hieroglyphic texts ceased, and many sites were completely abandoned—the impact of the decline was not confined to the south: in the lowlands many Chicanel-period centers underwent a setback at the same time; El Mirador declined dramatically; and a few centers, like Cerros, appear to have been abandoned completely.

For years, scholars have debated the causes for the demise of the southern Maya. Archaeological research in El Salvador has provided a promising answer to this vexing question. The downfall of the southern Maya now seems due to two related causes, one natural and the other economic. The major natural cause was the catastrophic eruption of Ilopango volcano (Fig. 3.37), in central El Salvador. This eruption was first recognized in the archaeological record at Chalchuapa, for in the subsequent years the site there suffered a major decline. Continuing research directed by Payson Sheets and his colleagues in the nearby Zapotitan valley has placed the timing of this disaster at about A.D. 200–250 and has demonstrated, from both surveys and excavations, that the eruption brought about staggering declines in both population and agricultural production, over a wide area. One consequence was that massive ash falls rendered the area within a 100-km radius of Ilopango uninhabitable for up to 200 years. These investigations indicate that a

Fig. 3.37. View of the lake-filled caldera of Ilopango, all that remains of the volcano after its catastrophic eruption at the end of the Preclassic (in the foreground, San Salvador, capital of El Salvador).

vast zone within the southeastern Maya area became depopulated—for whether through death or emigration, its inhabitants vanished. Although much of the Pacific coastal agricultural region appears to have escaped really heavy damage, ash falls certainly reduced production at least temporarily. It has also been proposed that torrential rainfalls spawned by Ilopango's ash cloud may have led to disastrous flooding over much of the Maya area, and that far-reaching ash falls could have reduced the aquatic food resources harvested from rivers and coastal areas.

The economic component of the southern Maya downfall lay in a chain of events following on the heels of the natural disaster. An overall decline in agricultural production would have affected the immediate ashfall zone. This would have caused population decline, even the complete abandonment of the center of the disaster area, and the old coastal trade routes, no longer maintainable without their sustaining population, would have been severed. The consequent loss of trade connections through the area would have produced a far broader economic disaster, one affecting even those southern Maya populations not directly impacted by the volcanic eruption. And the decline in trade along the Pacific coast may also have led to an increase in commerce farther north, such as along the trans-Peten routes, thus boosting the fortunes of centers able to take advantage of the changing trade patterns.

After the decline of the southern area, in any case, opportunities would certainly have opened up for other emerging powers in this area. Ultimately, the power that may have been best positioned to take advantage of the situation was the central-Mexican Teotihuacan state, far to the northwest. This great center (Fig. 3.38) rose to preeminence in the Valley of Mexico during the last few centuries of the Preclassic period. Seemingly filling the power vacuum following the decline of the southern Maya area, Teotihuacan does appear to have entered the Pacific coastal region early in the Classic period, probably in an effort to reestablish (and control) the area's former strength in agricultural production and trade. And as the region's population and production of such resources as cacao recovered, Teotihuacan seems to have established a close alliance with Kaminaljuyu, perhaps including the establishment of a trading enclave there. Although the idea is entirely hypothetical, some have proposed the motive to have been an attempt to monopolize trade and the distribution of products from the southern Maya area—especially obsidian, but possibly also cacao and jadeite.

## Summary: Reconstructing the Maya Preclassic

The foregoing review of available evidence permits us a summary of the pattern of Preclassic development in the Maya area. Although sporadic traces of preagricultural hunters and gatherers have been found in several regions of the Maya area, the earliest known permanent settlements were in lowland zones along the Pacific

• • • coast, and all subsisted by specialized gathering and cultivation on rich alluvial soils. During this Early Preclassic, total human population here was very small, and confined to small scattered villages, hamlets, fishing camps, and similar settlements. There is little to indicate any kind of social or political differences among the inhabitants, other than those based on age and sex. We know little or nothing about the ideology of these early villagers, but supernatural affairs were probably the responsibility of part-time shamans, much as they are in many Maya villages today. We know that critical items such as obsidian were exchanged over long distances (probably along with commodities that cannot be traced in the archaeological record, such as salt). Even in early times, these people were in contact with other areas of Mesoamerica.

Because the southern Maya area lay along the principal trade routes between Mexico and Central America, and because it enjoyed prime agricultural lands—supporting both subsistence crops and crops for export such as cacao—it became especially important during the Preclassic. These favorable conditions attracted a succession of outsiders to the area, including perhaps traders from the Olmec home-

Fig. 3.38. Teotihuacan, Valley of Mexico: the "Pyramid of the Sun," constructed over a cave and sacred spring during the rise to power of this important central-Mexican urban state. During the Early Classic several important Maya polities, such as Kaminaljuyu, Copan, and Tikal, maintained trade and other connections with Teotihuacan.

land on the Gulf coast and other distant lands. By the Middle Preclassic, various populations now recognized as early Maya and Mixe-Zoquean groups began to colonize the lowlands to the north, following riverine routes and establishing the first settled communities in these tropical northern forests. From this point onward, networks of commerce and innovation linked the two major zones of the Maya area, one of many factors that stimulated the development of greater social and political complexity both in the lowlands and in the southern Maya area.

Many regions of the Maya area encouraged the expansion of human settlements and populations: as long as new lands were available and population continued to increase, excess people could have moved into virgin areas, clearing new fields and establishing new communities, thus continuing the cycle. Accordingly, population could grow without an increase in density, as farming villages dispersed over the landscape. Eventually, however, expansion of this sort had to slow and, ultimately, stop, as new lands became scarce or unavailable. And, of course, because not all lands were suitable for swidden agriculture, new methods, such as terracing and raised fields, had to be developed, under constant pressure from the need to feed more and more people.

Areas with prime soil and favorable rainfall, locations that permitted control of critical resources, or even sacred places that were believed to possess special powers could attract and support more people than could less-favored locations. It was in these more-favored areas that the first complex societies appear, societies characterized by growing social distinctions between elite and non-elite segments of the population. The earliest of these were the initial chiefdoms that emerged in the Middle Preclassic. The first ceremonial centers seem to have grown around the residences of chiefs and an allied elite class that commanded both religious and economic status. Each of these centers functioned as a chief's power base and as the setting for religious, funerary, and economic activities that bound the elite class to the non-elites, who farmed the land or extracted the resources destined for trade. The power of the chief and the elite class relied on a reciprocal alliance with the people in the surrounding villages: the chiefs, as war leaders and religious specialists, aided by general belief in their alliance with supernatural forces and their links to sacred ancestors, provided security and the necessities of life, in return for tribute in labor or food. The ceremonial precincts, then, provided a measure of well-being, and adjacent markets may have furnished ready access to a variety of food, goods, and services, as well as loci for the exchange of household products. Direct archaeological evidence of markets is difficult to obtain, but on the basis of analogies with later Mesoamerican societies, we can presume both their existence and the likelihood that their control was an important source of elite power. Moreover, control over craft production and long-distance trade would have been both a source of wealth for the elite and a stimulus for the development of the efficient organizations to procure and transport both mundane and high-status goods to and from

• • • faraway lands. But it was probably access to the supernatural forces believed to control the cosmos that provided the essential foundation for the power of the emerging elite rulers and their kin.

In the Middle and Late Preclassic of both the highlands and the lowlands we are beginning to see the results of these processes, as inferred from the often rapid development of major population centers and their monumental temple and funerary constructions. Growth on this scale probably led these Maya chiefdoms into direct competition, and perhaps even into armed conflict, in their attempts to gain control over ever larger territories, populations, and trade routes. In some cases the competitive edge went to sites that controlled scarce but vital raw materials and specialized in processing and exporting the products made from these materials. Kaminaljuyu, controlling highland products such as obsidian and jade, became the dominant Preclassic center of the southern area. Other regional centers located along major routes of communication seem to have specialized in the transport, exchange, and redistribution of products. Thus Nakbe, situated so as to control the portages between riverine routes across the base of the Yucatan peninsula, was perhaps the first major site to emerge in the lowlands. By the Late Preclassic, Nakbe's role seems to have been usurped by El Mirador, but other lowland sites evidently continued to profit by controlling local resources (as for example Colha, with chert, and Komchen, with salt) or by controlling the transport and transshipment of goods (as for example Cerros, situated on Bahía de Chetumal). In the southern area we see similar developments along trade routes, as at Abaj Takalik, El Baúl, and Chalchuapa. Of course such developments were not due simply to location and economic control—social, political, and religious functions surely were also instrumental in the evolution of these Preclassic regional systems, although, once again, the archaeological evidence for such factors is difficult to secure.

Although in the lowlands the Mixe-Zoquean groups were eventually absorbed or displaced by Maya populations, in the highlands and on the Pacific coastal plain they developed related cultural traditions, culminating in the Late Preclassic with the first stable, authoritarian political institutions—hereditary rulers who were commemorated on sculptured monuments displaying calendric dates and hieroglyphic texts. A similar process occurred in the lowlands, although here the basis for the power of these early rulers was seemingly commemorated in architecture—in settings for elaborate ritual, decorated with the symbols of the cosmological order. Eventually, these two traditions would merge, initially at the first great Preclassic centers of Nakbe and El Mirador, and later in conjunction with the rise of the great Classic states at Tikal and elsewhere across the lowlands.

The close of the Preclassic saw major disturbances and changes in the economic and political landscape. Old centers declined, or were abandoned altogether, and new powers began to assert themselves. The causes for the decline may never be fully known, but were surely complex. In the southern Maya area at least some of these changes were due to a rather sudden shift in population and trade routes, seemingly caused by a catastrophic eruption of Ilopango volcano in the southeastern highlands. These events could well have had repercussions in the lowlands, for the loss of commerce in the south could have led to an increase in traffic along the northern trade routes (and some population movements could have reached the lowlands as well), leading to a stimulus to development in some regions, and to decline in others. But internal processes, beginning with the relatively sudden rise of a major center such as Nakbe in the Middle Preclassic, followed by the even greater power manifested in the huge center at El Mirador, indicate that social and political evolution was already transforming the lowland landscape, ultimately leading to the domination of the lowlands by a series of powerful polities.

The term "civilization" can mean many things. But if we use the term to refer, as it often does, to societies composed of large populations with complex economic, social, and political organizations, and marked by sophisticated intellectual development and ideology, we can no longer restrict the label "Maya civilization" to the Classic period. Maya civilization had emerged by the Late Preclassic. What lies beyond—in the remarkable developments of the Classic and Postclassic periods—are essentially elaborations upon, and changes in, the basic pattern set in the Preclassic.

# 4
....

# THE EARLY CLASSIC AND THE RISE OF TIKAL

In due measure did they recite the good prayers; in due measure they
sought the lucky days, until they saw the good stars enter into their reign;
then they kept watch while the reign of the good stars began. Then
everything was good.

—*The Book of Chilam Balam of Chumayel* (Roys 1967:83)

**T**raditional examinations of the Classic period of the ancient Maya (ca.
A.D. 250–900) tended to focus almost exclusively on the southern and central lowlands, and it is indeed within these areas that the lowland Maya rose to prominence
and established the hallmarks recognized as the flowering of Maya civilization. But
in recent years scholars have taken a more holistic view, recognizing that Classic
Maya civilization was more extensive than that, more diverse, and that it embraced,
as well, the northern lowlands and even the southern Maya area. Necessarily, however, we will concentrate on the areas that saw the most vigorous development during the Classic period, the southern and central lowlands.

As with the Preclassic, archaeologists have established certain chronological
divisions as points of reference in discussing the period, beginning with the Protoclassic (or Terminal Preclassic, ca. 100–250), which was at once the closing years
of the Preclassic and the transition to the Classic. This was followed by the Early
Classic (ca. 250–600), the era when state-level political organizations developed
and expanded in the Maya area, especially in the southern and central lowlands.
The subsequent Late Classic (ca. 600–800) saw the rise of important new polities
and the peaking of population and cultural development in the southern and central
lowlands. Finally, the Terminal Classic (ca. 800–900) witnessed the decline of the
southern and central lowlands and the ascent of the northern lowlands. Traditionally, archaeologists have identified the time of transition from the Early Classic
(dominance of Tikal) to the Late Classic (rise of new states) as the Middle Classic
Hiatus (dated as A.D. 534 to 593 but lasting as late as 692 at Tikal). This chapter
concludes, and the following chapter begins, with arguments for the causes and
effects of the so-called "hiatus."

## The Emergence of States in the Maya Area

Implicit in our discussion of the Classic period is the notion that during this time the lowland Maya were organized at a state level of social complexity. As we have seen, some of the characteristics of state organizations originated during the Preclassic; there was no sudden transformation of society at the outset of the Classic. But it is during the Classic that we see the widest distribution of most or all of the features that signal the level of social and organizational complexity typical of archaic or preindustrial states. Archaic states are stratified into a series of classes including full-time occupational specialists, and are topped by a highly centralized, hierarchical government that rules a territory with more or less defined boundaries. These social and economic divisions are reflected in the archaeological record by distinctions in the housing, artifacts, and burials associated with each class. Archaeologically, it is often possible to recognize a settlement hierarchy that corresponds to the administrative structure of the state. This hierarchy, typically comprising four tiers, is reflected in the size, functional complexity, and patterning of sites, beginning with the "capital" and working down through progressively smaller settlements.

States characteristically develop and utilize true political power, in addition to the authority they derive from economic, social, and religious sanctions. Political authority must of course be backed by the means to carry out governmental policies and decisions: the implicit or explicit use of force by the state. All of these sanctions are augmented by a stable, well-organized administrative hierarchy of full-time specialists in the management of the state.

In archaic or preindustrial states, political power is monopolized by the uppermost social stratum—an elite class that is separated from the remainder of society by birth, privilege, and other distinctions. The elite class is usually defined by kinship criteria such as membership in a descent group whose real or mythical origins set it apart from the remainder of society. This distinction is usually maintained, from one generation to the next, by endogamy (marriage within the group). The most powerful member of the elite class is the ruler or "king" (both terms will be used here to designate the supreme political authority in ancient Maya society). In addition to his social standing, the ruler possesses considerable power, by virtue of his position as head of the administrative hierarchy and its institutions of enforcement. Power is also based on economic and religious sanctions, such as the right of tribute collection, and the belief that their supernatural origins give the king and his family the divine right to rule. Political stability is further assured if there is a uniform rule of succession to the rulership, as in father to eldest son (primogeniture). Orderly succession by primogeniture or other means usually yields ruling dynasties like those found in most preindustrial states (ancient Egypt, China, medieval Europe, and so forth). But the continuity of the system may be in jeopardy

•••• when there is no uniform rule of succession, or when a dying ruler leaves no clear heir. Periods of uncertainty and even chaos are often the result (even some modern industrial states may experience such traumas if they lack an established rule of succession).

In the case of the ancient Maya, we can see the emergence of most of these features in the Preclassic and their full flowering in the Classic. These include the appearance of a four-level settlement hierarchy and the construction of elaborate masonry palace architecture, the residences of rulers and their immediate kin. Evidence for full-time craft specialists, as well as administrative specialists, is also detectable. But the most dramatic change was in the exalted status of the "king" and the elite class, signaled by wealth, privilege, and supernatural associations. There is evidence that Classic Maya rulers claimed a kind of divine right to rule, taking on the sort of supernatural identity enjoyed by god-kings in many preindustrial states of the Old World. But since the Classic Maya were never unified into a single political unit or polity, at any given time there were numerous Maya "kings," each ruling over his own polity.

During the Classic period, the highest Maya political authority in a particular polity was given the title *ahau*, which can be translated as "lord" or "noble." As we have seen (Chapter 3), this title originated in the Preclassic. But as the political system evolved during the Classic, and the hierarchy of authority grew, the use of the title "*ahau*" expanded until apparently it could be used to refer to any member of the ruling elite. Still, as we shall see, the paramount *ahau*, the personage we label the ruler, or "king," in each polity, can usually be identified in the inscriptions, typically by simple frequency of occurrence but also by his other royal titles. The most diagnostic of these royal titles is the so-called emblem glyph, first identified by Heinrich Berlin, in 1958.

Each emblem glyph includes a principal element, or main sign, unique to one site (Figs. 4.1 and 4.2). Accompanying this main sign are two essential affixes, one called the "ben-ich," the other called the "water group." The "ben-ich" prefix, which translates as *ah po* ("lord of the mat"), is a ruling title used in the Maya highlands, and probably then adopted in the lowlands from the southern area, where Maya writing appears to have originated. In any case, there is secure evidence that the *ah po* affix was read in the lowlands as *ahau*. The second affix, the "water

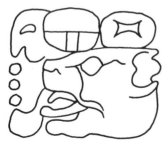

Fig. 4.1. Maya emblem glyph from Str. 1B-1 (A.D. 810) at Quirigua, east-central Guatemala: in this case the variable main sign is composed of a dog-head (which symbolizes an unidentified site) with the "water group" prefix to the left and the "ben-ich" prefix above, the whole translated as *k'ul ahau*, or "divine lord."

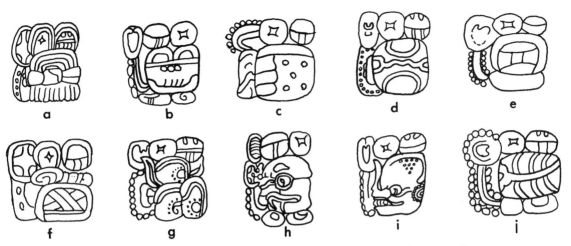

Fig. 4.2. Maya emblem glyphs: (*a*) Tikal; (*b*) Yaxchilan; (*c*) Piedras Negras; (*d*) Palenque; (*e*) Naranjo; (*f*) Tonina; (*g*) Seibal; (*h*) Calakmul; (*i*) Copan; (*j*) Quirigua.

group," has been translated as *k'u* or *k'ul* ("holy" or "divine"). The meaning of the main signs is still debated; they may refer either to ruling-lineage (dynastic) names or to place names, or both. In a few cases, a main sign has been read phonetically, as for example *Yaxha* ("clear" or "blue-green water"), the appropriate name of a central lowland site (and lake) that still carries this name. But regardless of precise meaning, each main sign functions to identify the place where the named *k'ul ahau* held power. Thus, a plausible reading of the emblem glyph associated with the kings of the Tikal site would be "Divine Tikal Lord" (Tikal *k'ul ahau*).

The presence and continuity of emblem glyphs in the lowland texts dealing with the political history of a given site may be seen as prima facie evidence that the polity in question possessed a state-level organization. This supposition is supported by additional epigraphic evidence, resulting largely from the pioneering work of Tatiana Proskouriakoff, that led to the partial decipherment of texts dealing with the succession of individual rulers at several lowland sites, and subsequent research has greatly expanded the list of identified rulers. The glyphs referring to a particular ruler, or *k'ul ahau*, seem to be composed of both personal names and titles. Mayan words have been proposed as readings for some of these; one example is Pacal ("shield"), a prominent ruler of Palenque. But in most cases modern researchers have simply assigned to the individual rulers nicknames, typically from English or Mayan, that are suggested by the appearance of the glyphs. (Because many of these names are so well established in the scholarly literature, further linguistic and epigraphic research is not likely to change them.)

As we have seen, by the Late Preclassic era, in the southern Maya area, there is evidence for the use of carved monuments to commemorate the achievements and dates associated with individual rulers (Chapter 3). But it is in the lowlands to the north where recent advances in the decipherment of Classic-period hieroglyphic texts provide the most secure evidence for sequences of such rulers—which invokes the principle of dynastic rule. Texts at each of several sites trace a succession of rulers from the same family or lineage, and since for the Maya the dominant rule

•••• of descent followed the male line, these were undoubtedly patrilineages (see Chapter 10). At several sites a "founder" title has been identified, designating a past ruler recognized or claimed as the first member of the site's royal family or lineage. Subsequent kings often counted their place in the succession from the founder by the use of the *hel* ("change") glyph. Thus a text referring to a particular ruler might include the title "16 hel," meaning that the king counted himself as the sixteenth successor to the dynastic founder.

Kinship glyphs in the Classic inscriptions, which have also been identified, suggest that the basic rule of succession was indeed primogeniture, although there are cases of succession among brothers (from older to younger). In a few cases there are hints of problems in the selection of a new ruler, and there are examples of shifts from one ruling patrilineage to another—a dynastic shift probably brought on by the lack of a male heir to the throne. In such cases the previous king's daughter, married to a man from another elite lineage (or even the royal lineage of another polity), might produce a son who would become king. But the new king would break the patrilineal succession, for he would belong to the lineage of his father, not that of the previous king, his maternal grandfather. Under such circumstances, as we shall see, the texts point to individual women as royal power brokers. In a few cases the inscriptions refer to women actually assuming the throne as ruler.

There is epigraphic and ethnohistoric evidence that a measure of power was delegated to other officials, each with a specific function and title. These offices were probably held by members of the ruling lineage—brothers, sons, and other relatives of the ruler—or by members of other elite lineages. Other lines of evidence indicate that the structure of Classic Maya political organization varied in time and space, and scholars remain divided on the issue of the size of the territory controlled by particular Classic lowland polities. One position sees the emblem glyph as indicating sovereignty, so that a site with texts referring to a particular *k'ul ahau* defines an independent polity. Because there are so many sites, so densely distributed, this proposition would mean that the Maya lowlands were subdivided into at least several dozen small-scale polities. The other position sees much larger, regional states, in which the largest sites controlled hierarchies of smaller sites, including neighbors that were themselves ruled by *k'ul ahauob* ("-*ob*" renders "*ahau*" plural). This would allow for a maximum of less than a dozen independent polities in the Maya lowlands. We will consider this question later, in Chapter 10, but these two alternatives need not be mutually exclusive, since as Joyce Marcus has correctly emphasized, using a dynamic model, it is evident that the size and power of individual polities expanded and contracted over the course of the Classic period. Thus, there were undoubtedly periods of time when the lowland political landscape was fractured into dozens of individual polities (like eighteenth-century Germany) and other times when formerly independent polities were consolidated into larger political units (like nineteenth-century Germany). It is also true that political unity is a relative concept, and in considering factors such as economic interdependence, distances between sites, and differences in site size and power, there were undoubtedly varying degrees of sovereignty as well.

## Competition and Warfare in the Maya Area

In Chapter 2 we considered the role of competition in the development of complex societies. For the ancient Maya, warfare played an important role, one that was associated with the origins of complexity during the Preclassic, and, perhaps more important, was a determinant of the relative power and prestige enjoyed by individual polities during the Classic period. Pointing to the presence of several fortified Maya cities, such as Becan, some scholars, David Webster for one, have argued that militarism aimed at conquest of territory and resources was instrumental in the establishment and perpetuation of the ruling elite and in the rise of centralized political authority, beginning in the later Preclassic. Certainly success in taking captives was important for the prestige of the victor, and therefore contributed to the growth of royal power. But most Maya centers, including all those of the Preclassic and all but a few Classic cities, developed without fortifications, which indicates that for most of their history, the ancient Maya did not practice large-scale warfare for conquest or other political ends, but instead limited conflict among polities, both in scale and in scope. But as the Classic period wore on, conflict certainly grew in intensity as competition for land, resources, prestige, and power increased, and it became even more frequent in the Late Classic, when we can see the beginning of "endemic warfare" that was to become even more common in the Postclassic. Still, for most of the Classic period, the primary objective of conflict was the demonstration of dominance by the taking of tribute and sacrificial captives from neighboring polities. Sacrificial captives were especially important for the sanctifying of certain events, such as the inauguration of a new ruler or the dedication of a new temple. Thus successful raiding was important in increasing the prestige of rulers and their dynasties, especially in establishing the power of new dynasties as the number of Maya polities grew. In fact, these raids seem to have been reenacted in ritual ball games, held in the victorious city, in which the leaders of the losing side (the captives) would be sacrificed after playing out the preordained scenario. The timing of these rituals and raids was often fixed to coincide with important anniversaries of past events, or with auspicious positions of the planets (especially Venus), in keeping with Maya beliefs in predestiny and the cyclical nature of time.

Although, as we shall see, some Maya polities did occasionally engage in limited conquests, or established new polities by breaking away from one another, the prevailing mode of warfare was a ritualized conflict or raiding without intent to gain territory, a practice common in Mesoamerican societies. To ensure success, of course, the targets were usually the smaller centers, rather than the capitals of other

•••• major polities. Since the primary purpose of such warfare was to gain tribute and take captives, and thus assert the prestige of one ruler and his polity as against another, these aggressions usually did not seek to kill as many enemy warriors as possible, or to annex their kingdom. Non-elite captives, judging from later Postclassic accounts, were in fact often used as servants, or even adopted into needy families, by the victors. The loser would pay tribute to the winner, but usually not lose sovereignty. The higher the rank of the captive, however, the more prestige would redound to the captor—and the more likely it would be that the unfortunate person would be sacrificed.

Of course the greatest coup was for one ruler to capture and sacrifice another king, an event, although relatively rare, that would be glorified by both text and image on the monuments of the victor. In such cases for which we have historical accounts, the event would have profound effects on the fortunes of victor and vanquished alike. When the previously subordinate ruler of Quirigua captured and sacrificed the great king of powerful Copan, probably by turning the tables when the latter sallied forth to gain a few easy captives for one of his rituals, Quirigua was able to assert its independence and prosper as a result. Yet, aside from losing a former vassal state and a source of wealth, the consequences for defeated Copan were short-term and relatively minor. But when the ruler of the newly emerging power of Caracol claimed to capture the great king of Tikal, not only did Caracol benefit dramatically, but Tikal seems to have been plunged into a depression that lasted more than a century. Obviously, the loss of a ruler was a severe blow to any polity, for to the ancient Maya he was the living link between this world and the supernatural, and thus was necessary to the continuance of normal existence. Until a new king was on the throne, his polity would be in a state of suspended animation, and a successor could not assume power until the former king died. Thus it appears that the ruler of Tonina deliberately kept the captured Palenque ruler alive for years in order to further weaken his now powerless kingdom.

## The Protoclassic as Transition to the Classic

The period of one to two hundred years immediately preceding the beginning of the Classic period is traditionally known as the Protoclassic, because it saw the first known traces of certain traits seen as typical of the Classic. The most diagnostic feature of this era has been the appearance of polychrome pottery (vessels decorated by three or more colors), since polychrome ceramics are one of the hallmarks of the Classic period in the archaeological record. More significantly, it would appear that the first lowland stelae (free-standing monuments) bearing inscriptions date to this period, although the evidence for this is very fragmentary and incomplete. This development may signal the final step in the emergence of the distinctive pattern of

Classic Maya elite subculture, especially the political structure headed by the *k'ul ahau,* or "king."

Although there are other markers of the Protoclassic, including architecture and, at some sites, apparent dramatic increases in population, these changes are for the most part local or regional in scope. Even the trait that was first seen as defining this era, the appearance of typical Protoclassic pottery, including the first true polychromes, seems to have been concentrated in the eastern lowlands. As we have seen, recent research has shown that many of the significant developments leading to the Classic period have their origins earlier than the Protoclassic, as far back as the Late or even Middle Preclassic.

The significance of the changes seen in the Protoclassic has been the subject of at least two different traditional interpretations. One of these postulates that the development seen in the Protoclassic was indigenous, resulting in the emergence of Classic lowland civilization without significant influence from outside areas. This internal pattern of development may be most apparent in the very center of the lowlands, such as at Tikal, where the evidence reflects a steady progression both in population growth and in the elaboration of architecture and other material remains.

The other interpretation sees the Protoclassic as a result of interaction between indigenous growth and outside influence. The best evidence for this view comes from sites in the eastern lowlands—Holmul, Barton Ramie, and Nohmul. At these sites the archaeological record is marked by rather sudden changes during the Protoclassic: evidence of rapid population increase, new stone tools such as bark beaters (probably used to make paper or for other tasks), and the appearance of a new ceramic inventory (including diagnostic Usulutan and polychrome decoration, and vessels, each with four bulbous supports, known as mammiform tetrapods). These changes have been best documented at Barton Ramie, where it was found that twice as many house platforms were occupied during the Protoclassic as in the preceding era. This evidence suggests an influx of new peoples into the eastern lowlands during the Protoclassic, and the homeland of these migrants has been postulated to have been the southeastern periphery of the Maya area. Archaeological research at Chalchuapa and other sites in El Salvador has discovered that material traits present in the lowland Protoclassic, especially Usulutan pottery traditions, do appear to have originated in this southeastern region. The most probable cause for the apparent migration northward was the same volcanic disaster that devastated southern Maya society around A.D. 200–250 (see Chapter 3).

This interpretation of the Protoclassic thus sees the expansion of lowland populations and the elaboration of lowland culture as having been triggered by the arrival of new peoples from the southern Maya area. In this way many of the institutions already present among the southern Maya could have been introduced into

•••• the lowlands—for example, "kingship" and its royal title (recalling that this originated as *ah po*, a highland term), the association of kingship with carved stelae recording the king's activities in text and image (involving a distinctive art style and Long Count calendrical notation), and various economic systems (including possibly the production of cash crops such as cacao).

But the development of any society, including the lowland Maya, cannot be explained by the simple imposition of a new order originating from an outside group. It is clear that important trade contacts and even political ties existed between the southern and lowland Maya before the Protoclassic era. It is also clear, as we have seen (Chapter 3), that the process of lowland Maya development was well under way at Preclassic sites such as Nakbe and El Mirador. So that rather than postulate a Protoclassic migration as the cause of the sudden surge in the development of lowland society, it is more reasonable to assume that the contact between the two areas complemented a process already inherent in lowland Maya society. It is the fusion of these two cultural traditions that is reflected in what we call the Protoclassic, not a sudden change in the direction of development.

The key to the process of cultural development in the Protoclassic probably lies in the vast Late Preclassic site of El Mirador, which reached its zenith during this era. El Mirador may even have been the focal point for southern Maya economic and political contact with the lowlands prior to the Protoclassic. The location of this great center was certainly conducive to securing control of trans-lowland trade and the connections to the south.

El Mirador may have seen the first introduction of a southern-Maya-style ruling dynasty, either by the direct imposition of a southern Maya ruler or by marriage between ruling lineages. This is speculation, but the southern-style sculptured monuments at the site do suggest the possibility. Whatever its origins, the institution of the *k'ul ahau* and dynastic rule dominated the political fortunes of the lowlands for the next six hundred years. El Mirador, by virtue of its precocious size alone, seems to have been the principal power in the lowlands prior to the Classic. It is undoubtedly significant—though for reasons yet unknown—that with its decline the Classic period began.

## The Southern Maya Area in the Classic

Compared to the amount of archaeological research that has been done in the lowlands, the investigation of the southern Maya area during the Classic period has been rather meager. Although archaeological surveys in many highland areas have been quite extensive, actual excavations have been less frequent, and those conducted at Kaminaljuyu (see Chapter 3) remain the principal referent for the highland Classic period. Important Classic-period occupation has also been revealed by excavations at several other centers, most notably Zaculeu, near Huehuetenango;

Chuitinamit-Atitlan, near Lago de Atitlan; and Zacualpa, Los Cimientos–
Sajcabaja, La Lagunita, and Chitinamit, in the Quiche Maya area to the north. On
the Pacific coastal plain, Bilbao and Abaj Takalik remain the most thoroughly investigated sites that include Classic-period occupation.

The most conspicuous external involvement we know of was the impact on
some areas along the Pacific coast from Central Mexico, especially the city of Teotihuacan, the dominant central-Mexican power during the Early Classic. Teotihuacan apparently was also involved with the major highland power of the Early
Classic, Kaminaljuyu. Part of the civic and ceremonial core of this site was rebuilt
at that time in the talud-tablero style of Central Mexico. Excavation has revealed
that some of these structures covered elaborate tombs, thus probably serving as
funerary shrines for Kaminaljuyu's rulers.

The nature of central-Mexican influence in the southern area is still debated,
but it seemingly included a process of increasing economic and political alliance—
perhaps even the establishment of a Teotihuacan enclave at Kaminaljuyu that could
have included intermarriage between ruling families. But aside from the widespread
occurrence of artifacts associated with Central Mexico (especially diagnostic cylindrical tripod pottery, often used as offering vessels in tombs and burials), this
external linkage is not well documented in the archaeological record of other highland Maya sites.

Kaminaljuyu seems to have declined during the Late Classic, owing in part,
perhaps, to the apparent withdrawal of contacts with Teotihuacan by about A.D.
600 (about the time this central-Mexican power apparently fell on hard times itself,
in due course to be essentially abandoned). There are in any case no known Late
Classic highland centers of a size to rival the great powers of the Maya lowlands
during this era. The most common indications point to economic contacts with the
lowlands to the north, as evidenced by imported polychrome pottery vessels and
other goods. Predictably, highland products, especially obsidian and jadeite, were
extensively traded into the lowlands. These and other highland products from the
Classic period are usually common at the southern Maya sites, reflecting a well-
developed regional trading network.

Many portions of the southern Maya area seem not to have been densely occupied during the Classic period. In part, this may have been due to the slow recovery from the disruptions that ended the Preclassic florescence there (see Chapter
3); but the area did remain a rich and valuable source for a variety of products that
were traded locally and sought by outside powers. Thus the production of cacao on
the Pacific coast probably attracted, for a time at least, the attention even of Teotihuacan. During the same period the southern highland center of Kaminaljuyu provided access to the El Chayal obsidian source and to the sources of other local products. The lowland Maya centers we shall examine also continued to have access to
highland resources by using the principal river systems, especially to the south via

•••• the upper Usumacinta–Río Chixoy system and its tributaries, and to the Caribbean by way of the Motagua Valley. A series of these lowland centers rose to prominence during the Late Classic; significantly, they were the ones situated such that they could control trade along these routes to and from the highlands.

## The Lowlands in the Early Classic

The Early Classic (ca A.D. 250–600) witnessed the apparent domination of the central lowlands by Tikal, the best-known and most enduring polity in the region. Although we have a larger, richer body of evidence from Tikal than from other lowland centers of this time, which may bias our understanding of this development, it does appear that Tikal's sociopolitical development was more accelerated than that of most other Early Classic sites. Furthermore, it seems likely that in its rise to power Tikal was able to eclipse other centers that had been prominent during earlier periods, and a realignment of power in the Early Classic is clearly indicated by the fact that many Preclassic centers (including the formerly dominant center of El Mirador) declined or disappeared during the first several centuries A.D. In some cases, as for example the recently investigated Late Preclassic center of Cerros (see Chapter 3), previously important sites were completely abandoned by the time of the Early Classic.

The reconstruction of the history of the central lowlands, then, is anchored by what we know of Tikal, the largest site of the region, and among the largest of all Maya sites. Our understanding of the history of Tikal is based primarily on two complementary kinds of information: the results of archaeological investigations and the recent advances in hieroglyphic decipherment. The excavation of Tikal's North Acropolis, which unveiled the most protracted sequence of monumental construction known in the Maya area, is especially significant to our understanding of this site's Early Classic history (Figs. 4.3 and 4.4). As mentioned in Chapter 3, the origins of Tikal as a polity center lie in the Late Preclassic, with the establishment of a permanent, ruling elite class, as indicated by the tombs and funerary shrines in the deepest levels under the North Acropolis, and in the construction of the monumental "Lost World" pyramid nearby. Tikal and other early lowland centers of development, such as nearby Uaxactun, may have been under the domination of El Mirador during this era, but with the latter's decline at the end of the Preclassic, the stage was evidently set for the expansion of the first major polity of the Classic period.

We will begin with a description of Tikal, as background for our discussion of the Classic-period history of the central lowlands. Later on we will examine the other sites of this region, some of which become major factors in the history of the central lowlands. And along the way, we will find it necessary to keep returning to Tikal and its shifting fortunes.

TIKAL

The largest known Maya center, Tikal (Fig. 4.5), has been subjected to one of the most comprehensive archaeological investigations of any Maya site. Tikal, far from any modern settlement and isolated by thick jungle growth, remained unknown to the outside world for centuries following the Conquest, despite the fact that Cortés and his soldiers must have come very close to the ruins in 1525 during their march from Mexico to Honduras (see the Epilogue). The official discovery was made by a Guatemalan government expedition led by Modesto Mendez and Ambrosio Tut, which reached Tikal in 1848 and recorded some of its ruins. Later in

Fig. 4.3. Tikal, Guatemala: base of the North Acropolis trench, looking south, during excavations that revealed an exceptionally long and complex constructional sequence.

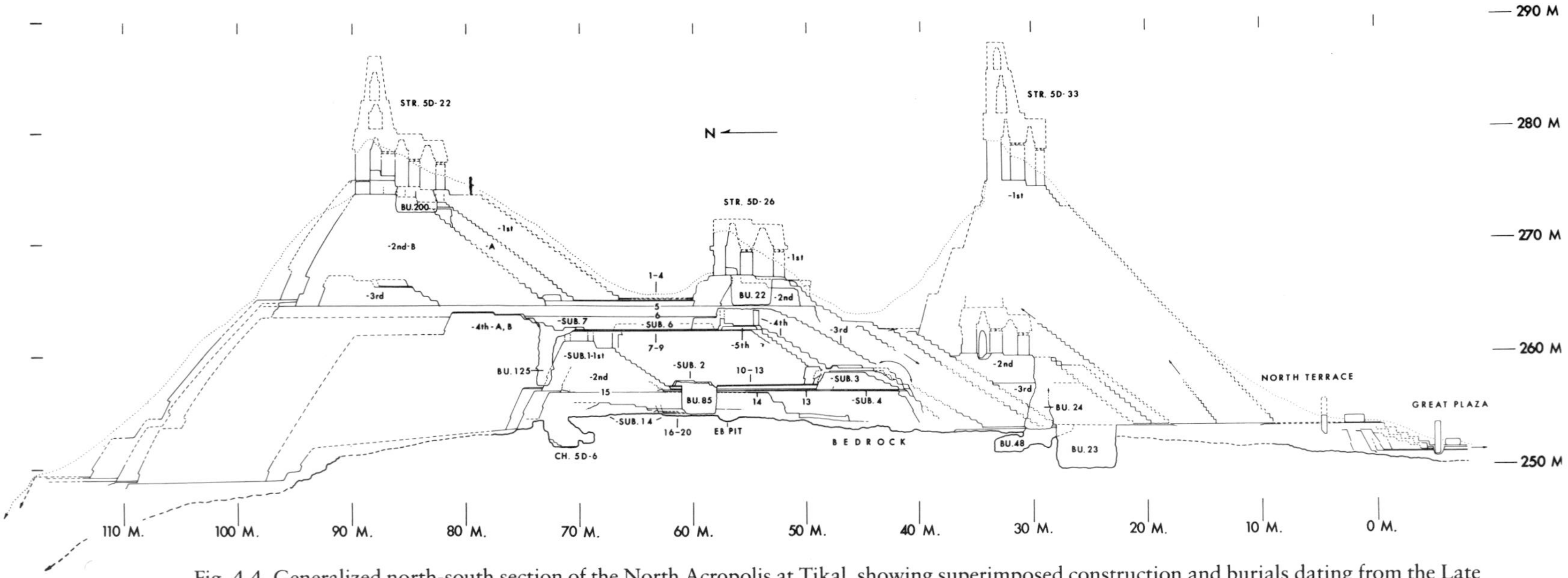

Fig. 4.4. Generalized north-south section of the North Acropolis at Tikal, showing superimposed construction and burials dating from the Late Preclassic to the beginning of the Late Classic; Burial 48 lies beneath Str. 5D33-2nd, and Stela 31 is interred in the rear room of this buried building (see Figs. 4.9 and 4.10).

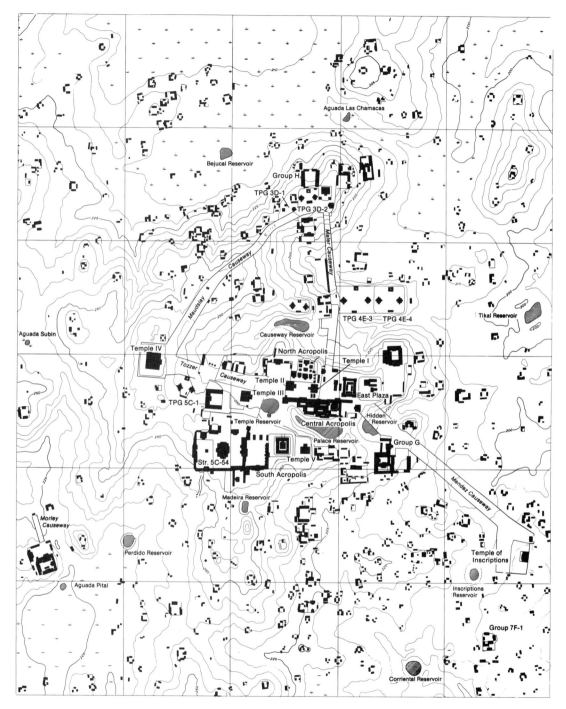

Fig. 4.5. Map of the central portion of Tikal, Guatemala, showing some of the site's principal buildings and groups (TPG = Twin Pyramid Group); the grid is in 500-meter squares; elevations are in meters.

•••• the nineteenth century several of the magnificently carved wooden lintels from Temples I and IV were removed to the Museum für Völkerkunde in Basel, Switzerland, by an expedition led by Gustav Bernoulli. Alfred Maudslay's visits in 1881 and 1882 were the first to photographically record the sculpture and architecture at Tikal, and in 1885 and 1904, Teobert Maler continued this work, as part of his efforts to record Maya sites for the Peabody Museum of Harvard University. Maler's work at Tikal was finished by Alfred Tozzer and R. E. Merwin, both of the Peabody Museum, who successfully completed the first map of the site (published in 1911). The monuments and inscriptions at Tikal were systematically recorded by Sylvanus Morley as part of his pioneering study of Maya hieroglyphic texts, after visits in 1914, 1921, 1922, and 1928. During the first year of the Carnegie Institution of Washington's excavations at nearby Uaxactun (see below), Edwin Shook visited Tikal and discovered a previously overlooked building complex, Group H, and two new causeways (now named after Maler and Maudslay). At this time Shook began to formulate plans for a full-scale archaeological investigation of Tikal—plans that were realized nearly twenty years later.

During these years Tikal could be reached only by an arduous journey on foot or muleback using the trails blazed by the chicleros, collectors of raw chewing gum. But in 1951 the Guatemalan Air Force cleared a dirt airstrip out of the jungle, adjacent to the ruins. This airstrip made possible the large-scale movement of people and supplies into Tikal, and as a result an archaeological research program became feasible. In 1956, after several years of planning, the University Museum of the University of Pennsylvania initiated the Tikal Project, which it was to continue for the next fifteen years. Shook served as the first field director for this research, and William Coe directed the project during its last seven years. Judged by almost any standard, the scale of the Tikal Project was unprecedented for Maya archaeology. By its final year, in 1970, its professional staff had over the years totaled 113 archaeologists. The final results of the project's research are being published in a corpus that has so far seen 10 preliminary reports, a site map, and some seventeen out of a projected total of 37 final reports. In addition, well over a hundred scholarly articles and other publications based on data gathered at Tikal have appeared.

With the close of the University of Pennsylvania's project in 1970, excavations of the buildings and their consolidation (reinforcement) continued under the auspices of the Instituto de Antropología e Historia (IDAEH) of Guatemala. Under the direction of two expert Guatemalan archaeologists, Carlos Rudy Larios and Miguel Orrego, this work has concentrated on Group G, a large palace complex southeast of the Great Plaza. A new and expanded program of IDAEH investigations at Tikal, concentrating on the Mundo Perdido (Lost World) Group, was initiated in 1980, under the direction of Juan Pedro Laporte.

The core area of Tikal is strategically situated on a series of low ridges (average elevation 250 m) that rise about 50 m above two swampy depressions (bajos) lying

Fig. 4.6. Aerial view of Tikal, looking northwest to the major buildings towering above the tropical forest: Temple IV (upper left), Temple V (lower left), Temple III (center left), and (to the right), Temples I and II facing the Great Plaza, with the North Acropolis beyond and the palaces of the Central Acropolis in the foreground (see figures on p. 2 in Introduction).

to the east and west. Most of the great buildings presently visible (Fig. 4.6), which are clustered on the high ground of the site core, date from the Late Classic, the time of Tikal's greatest power and most pronounced construction activity. Although excavations revealed that many earlier buildings lie encased within Late Classic structures, the North Acropolis (Fig. 4.4) remained largely free from renovation, and its buildings are mostly from the Early Classic era. Another example of early construction is the Lost World Pyramid (Str. 5C-54), a massive Late Preclassic platform unaffected by later building activity.

The major building complexes of the site core were interconnected by a series of monumental causeways (*sacbeob*) that radiate from the heart of the site, the Great Plaza and its adjacent buildings (Fig. 4.5). Leading southeast to Temple VI is the Mendez Causeway; leading west to Temple IV is the Tozzer Causeway; and leading north to Group H is the Maler Causeway. The Maudslay Causeway directly connects the latter two complexes. Beyond the site core a series of outlying groups of structures lies scattered over an area of residential occupation covering some 60 km², mostly on the higher and better-drained terrain. A system of earthworks, consisting of a shallow moat below an interior rubble wall, connects the two swampy depressions (which may once have been shallow lakes), to protect Tikal from both the north and the south. The area within these defensible boundaries totals some 123 km².

The most intensive excavations of the Tikal Project took place in the North Acropolis, which lies immediately north of the Great Plaza. The North Acropolis is essentially a huge platform, measuring 100 by 80 m, that supports numerous rebuildings and expansions ultimately constituting a symmetrical arrangement of eight funerary temples (Fig. 4.7) constructed over a 300-year period (ca. A.D. 250–550). Older buildings lie buried beneath this platform, as revealed by extensive

Fig. 4.7. Str. 5D-22, Tikal, one of the funerary temples of the North Acropolis; the terraces of this Early Classic platform are decorated with plaster masks (above and below the man at work in the center) flanking the axial stairway (at far right) and overlapping upper zones, or "apron" moldings, on the terraces.

trenching and tunneling (Fig. 4.3). The earliest of these buildings appears to have been built during the Late Preclassic (ca. 200 B.C.). Four additional temples, each elevated by a high terraced platform, were later constructed, one by one, along the southern edge of the acropolis. Their stairways once led southward toward the Great Plaza below. Once constructed, these structures effectively screened off the North Acropolis from easy access during the final centuries of Tikal's occupation. Three smaller shrines flank the southeastern corner of the platform.

The North Acropolis excavations revealed not only a complex sequence of construction, but a succession of richly furnished tombs, indicating that this precinct of Tikal served as a royal necropolis, the burial place for Tikal's rulers from the Late Preclassic through the Early Classic. Our knowledge of the dynastic history of Tikal spans the entire Classic period; a minimum of 39 rulers counted their succession from the founder of the royal lineage, who probably lived in the third century A.D., and the last known ruler was inaugurated in 768. This dynastic reconstruction is based on deciphered inscriptions from Tikal's monuments and lintels and from evidence excavated from the tombs of a number of rulers. Several of these tombs in the North Acropolis have been identified as those of particular Early Classic rulers.

The earliest royal tombs in the North Acropolis date to the Late Preclassic. Fragmentary wall paintings found in two of these tombs, Burials 166 and 167, conform closely to the style and iconography of the southern Maya area (see Chapter 3). As we have seen, there is certainly evidence of contact between these two areas, including trade in obsidian, jadeite, and other products. One of the Late Preclassic funerary shrines excavated above these tombs, Str. 5D-Sub-10-1st, was also decorated by wall paintings, including one fragmentary portrait of what is probably an early Tikal ruler, flanked by smoke scrolls. This example, along with very similar Late Preclassic portraits discovered at Uaxactun (see below), indicates that there were explicit associations between rulers and buildings some years before the southern Maya custom of erecting stelae in front of structures was adopted by the Classic lowland Maya. The earliest known dynastic monument in the Maya lowlands—Tikal Stela 29 (A.D. 292), with its portrayal of a standing profile figure accompanied by a historical Long Count date (Fig. 4.8)—reflects the adoption of the earlier sculptural heritage found in the south.

The earliest known North Acropolis tomb from the Classic period was discovered under Str. 5D-26 (Burial 22). It is dated to the Early Classic, probably the late fourth century A.D. Unfortunately, it appears to have been opened and looted during the Late Classic, but on the basis of what remained at the time of its excavation it has been tentatively proposed that the tomb originally contained the burial of the ninth ruler in the Tikal dynasty, Great Jaguar Paw. Str. 5D-34, on the west front of the North Acropolis, covers a deeply buried tomb (Burial 10) that is most likely that of the next ruler, Curl Nose. The largest building of the North Acropolis,

Fig. 4.8. Tikal Stela 29 with the earliest Long Count date yet known from the Maya lowlands: (*above*) drawing and photo of the front, showing the carved portrait of the early Tikal ruler Scroll Ahau Jaguar carrying a two-headed ceremonial bar; (*below*) the back, showing the Long Count date 8.12.14.8.15 (A.D. 292).

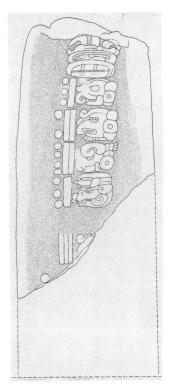

Str. 5D-33-1st, was built during the early years of the Late Classic era, but had been so badly preserved that it was disassembled by excavation to reveal the earlier structures buried beneath. The first of these, Str. 5D-33-3rd, was built over the tomb (Burial 48; Fig. 4.9) of Tikal's greatest Early Classic ruler, Stormy Sky, probably as his mortuary shrine. Not long after, this building was replaced by another (Str. 5D-33-2nd), possibly to commemorate an important anniversary of Stormy Sky's

Fig. 4.9. Chamber of Tikal Burial 48 beneath Str. 5D-33 in the North Acropolis (see Fig. 4.4), after excavation and removal of its contents; the Long Count date seen here painted on the wall of the tomb is the presumed death date of the ruler "Stormy Sky," 9.1.1.10.10 (A.D. 456).

Fig. 4.10. Tikal Stela 31 (see Fig. 4.4): (*left*) drawing of the frontal carved portrait of Stormy Sky thrusting aloft a masked headdress, holding a head topped by the "bundle" main sign of the Tikal emblem glyph, and wearing his name glyph in his headdress; (*center*) side view of the stela, after its excavation in Str. 5D-33-2nd, with carved warrior figure carrying a shield adorned with the Mexican rain god Tlaloc; (*right*) drawing of the extensive hieroglyphic text on the back of the stela, which recounts the history of Tikal.

Fig. 4.11. Tikal Temple II, on the west side of the Great Plaza, seen here shortly after its excavation and consolidation.

death. Finally, the great ruler of Late Classic Tikal, Ah Cacau (also known as Ruler A), seems to have marked an anniversary of his illustrious ancestor's death by dedicating 5D-33-1st. But before this latest building was constructed, Stormy Sky's magnificent monument, Stela 31 (Fig. 4.10), which had probably stood in front of his mortuary temple, was carried up the stairway and reset within the rear room of 5D-33-2nd, almost directly over his tomb (which had been concealed long before, soon after his death). There, after rituals that left smashed incensarios strewn about the room and the broken base of the monument burned, the stela was carefully encased in rubble fill, and the partially dismantled building was buried beneath the new shrine. Here Stela 31 was found during the excavations of the Tikal Project, just as the Maya had left it.

Immediately south of the North Acropolis is the Great Plaza, flanked by two magnificent structures, Temple I on the east and Temple II on the west. Both were built in the Late Classic period, although Temple II takes the form of an enlarged version of Tikal's typical Early Classic architectural style (Fig. 4.11). The wooden lintel of Temple II seems to portray a woman, and may have commemorated the wife of Ah Cacau (Fig. 4.12). Temple I, rising some 47 m above the plaza, is innovative in its location outside the traditional necropolis (Fig. 4.13), breaking a centuries-old royal funerary tradition. From this time onward Tikal's rulers would be buried outside of the North Acropolis. Temple I also departed from architectural tradition: its proportions and nine stepped terraces stress its height, as contrasted with earlier platforms, which used but two or three terraces. It may have been modeled after the slightly earlier Str. 5D-33-1st, the last North Acropolis shrine, which was probably built by Ah Cacau to honor Stormy Sky, and thus may have been symbolic of the thirteen-katun link between the two reigns. Temple I, the funerary shrine of Ah Cacau, was built after his death, probably under instructions he gave

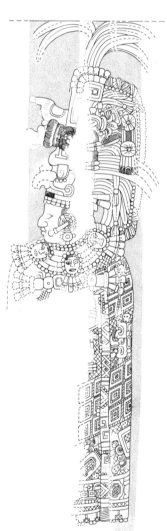

Fig. 4.12. Tikal Temple II: drawing of the carved wooden lintel from inside the temple, showing the portrait of a woman, presumably the wife of the ruler Ah Cacau.

Fig. 4.13. Tikal Temple I, on the east side of the Great Plaza, facing west opposite Temple II, showing the stairway leading to the funerary temple on the summit, and the seated portrait of the ruler
Ah Cacau on the roof comb above.

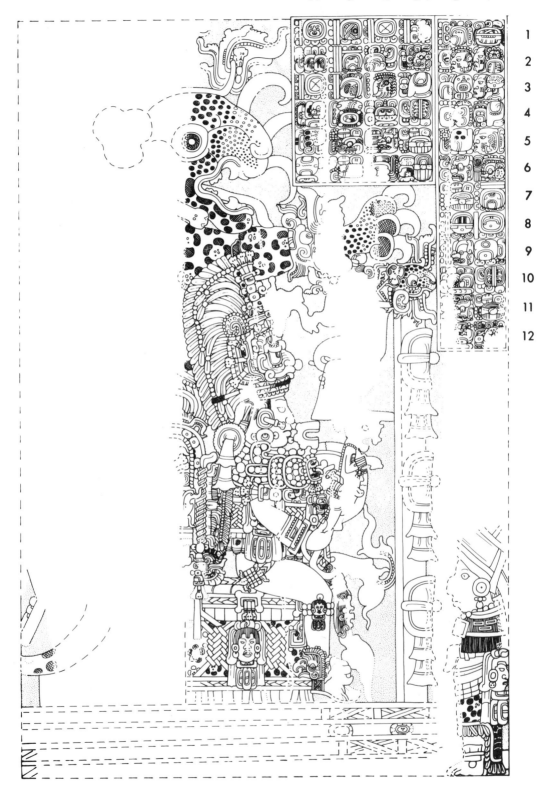

to his son and successor, Yax Kin Caan Chac. Ah Cacau's tomb was discovered underneath the shrine, north of the centerline of the pyramid. On its summit is a three-room temple surmounted by a huge roof comb portraying the ruler seated on his throne; this temple undoubtedly served as his mortuary shrine. A carved wooden lintel inside the shrine (Fig. 4.14) depicts Ah Cacau seated before an immense jaguar-protector deity, and records his inauguration.

His tomb (Burial 116) consists of a large vaulted sepulcher constructed within an excavation nearly 7 m deep, over which Temple I was then built (Fig. 4.15). The chamber, measuring some 5 by 2.5 m and over 4 m high, was mostly taken up by a masonry bench. On the bench were found the skeletal remains of Ah Cacau, lying on what had once been a woven mat (*pop*, a symbol of rulership) bordered by ornaments of oyster shell and jadeite (Fig. 4.16). Gathered about the remains was an array of offerings, including polychrome ceramic vessels, shells, pearls, and jade.

Fig. 4.14 (*opposite*). Tikal Temple I: drawing of the carved wooden lintel from inside the temple, showing the ruler Ah Cacau seated on a throne and a giant jaguar "protector" looming behind.

Fig. 4.15. Tikal Temple I: sectional drawing of the western base of the temple platform, showing the vaulted tomb of Ah Cacau (Burial 116) carved from the bedrock beneath (see Fig. 4.16).

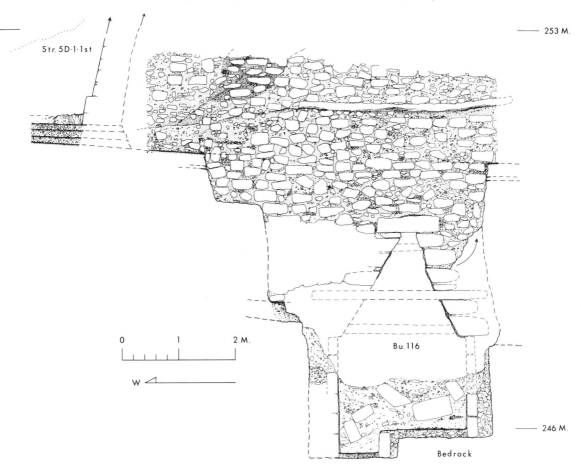

Ah Cacau himself was adorned by a massive jadeite necklace made of large round beads, like that depicted around his neck in his sculptured portraits on Stelae 16 and 30. Among the more than 16 pounds of jadeite in the tomb was a jade-mosaic cylindrical vase with a cover bearing Ah Cacau's hieroglyphic name and possibly a miniature portrait of his head (Fig. 15.40). A bundle of carved human bones lay nearby. When cleaned, 37 of the bones were found to include finely incised hieroglyphic inscriptions, including Ah Cacau's name glyphs and passages seemingly referring to events of his life and his journey to the underworld after his death. The underworld journey is depicted as having been in a canoe borne by animal deities.

South of the Great Plaza lie several massive architectural complexes and the adjacent Central Acropolis, consisting of a maze of multiroom and multistory residential structures arranged around a series of internal courtyards (Fig. 4.17). This area surely housed Tikal's ruling dynasty and their retainers during much of the

Fig. 4.16. Tikal Temple I: the tomb of Ah Cacau, as found by archaeologists who entered the chamber through the roof vault; the skeletal remains of the ruler, encrusted with jade, shell, and other ornaments, lay on a stone bench, surrounded by pottery vessels.

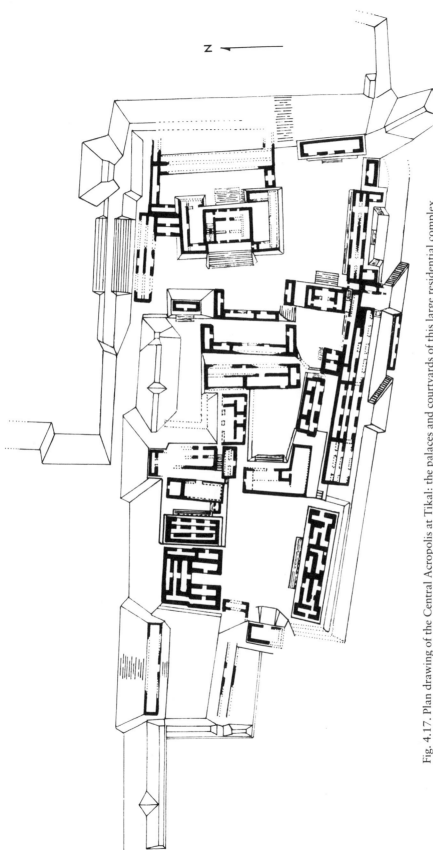

Z

Fig. 4.17. Plan drawing of the Central Acropolis at Tikal: the palaces and courtyards of this large residential complex were used by the Classic-period rulers.

••••   Classic period. Farther to the south, across one of the reservoirs constructed to ensure a constant supply of water during dry seasons, lies Temple V, the apparent mortuary shrine to an unknown ruler (Fig. 4.6). This structure, some 57 m high, is the
second tallest of Tikal's temples (after Temple IV). West of Temple V is the massive
South Acropolis and the Plaza of the Seven Temples, the latter named after a row
of nearly identical shrines on its east side. This plaza is also notable for the unique
triple ballcourt on its northern edge. Still farther west lies a large, enclosed plaza
in the center of which stands the huge Late Preclassic Lost World Pyramid, which
was seemingly associated with Tikal's early history and was maintained, because
of its importance, throughout the center's occupation. The recent excavations directed by Juan Pedro Laporte in this group have found important new evidence of
Tikal's Early Classic development, including Stela 39. This fragmentary monument
was found in Str. 5D-86, a four-stairwayed platform on the west side of a plaza,
facing three smaller platforms to the east that mark the positions of the solar cycle
(see Fig. 4.25, below, and the discussion under Uaxactun Group E, below).

Immediately north of the Central Acropolis, and just behind Temple I, lies the
East Plaza. Its most conspicuous feature is a large, rectangular assemblage of multiroom buildings (Strs. 5E-32 to 5E-36) that may have served as Tikal's major market. Just to the west of the East Plaza is Tikal's largest ballcourt. The plaza provides
an intersection for two sacbeob—the Maler Causeway, leading northward to
Group H, and the Mendez Causeway, leading southeast to Temple VI (Temple of
the Inscriptions). The Mendez Causeway also provides an avenue to Group G, a
major palace complex nearly as large as the Central Acropolis. Recent excavations
in Group G have revealed a buried building under Str. 5E-55; its rooms were unusually well preserved because of the obvious care with which rubble fill was packed
into them before construction covered them. The interior walls of several of these
rooms were decorated with a variety of incised and painted graffiti, including several short, finely executed, hieroglyphic texts and a gruesome human-sacrificial
scene. A red sun symbol, found painted on the vault of the central room, is reminiscent of the same sort of sign painted on the vault of Ah Cacau's tomb under
Temple I. The walls of an adjoining room were covered with handprints of red paint
and mud slurry; the mud-slurry prints depict *ahau* glyphs, one of them formed by
three handprints, all done at the time the rooms were being filled and abandoned.

The reign of Ah Cacau was marked by the construction of the first of two dated
twin-pyramid groups. The twin-pyramid group is a symmetrical architectural assemblage originating in Early Classic Tikal (only one example is known from another site; see Yaxha, below). The assemblage consists of two flat-topped, four-
stairwayed pyramids flanking the east and west sides of a plaza (Fig. 4.18). On the
south side is a single building with nine doorways; on the north, a walled enclosure
containing a stela and an altar (Fig. 4.19). Twin-pyramid groups were constructed

Fig. 4.18. Tikal Twin Pyramid Group 4E-4: restoration showing the eastern and western four-stairwayed platforms, the southern nine-doorwayed building (at lower right), and the northern enclosure holding Stela 22 and Altar 10 (see Fig. 4.22).

Fig. 4.19. Tikal Stela 16 from Twin Pyramid Group 5D-1, portraying the ruler Ah Cacau (9.14.0.0.0, or A.D. 711).

for the rituals commemorating the passage of each katun (see Chapter 12), a period
of twenty 360-day years.

The Tozzer Causeway leads west from the rear of Temple II to the massive Temple IV, the largest structure at Tikal, towering some 70 m high (Fig. 4.6). Temple IV appears to mark the reign of Ah Cacau's son and successor, Yax Kin Caan Chac. The two carved wooden lintels (Fig. 4.20) over the wide doorway leading into the narrow-roomed shrine on its summit record the date 9.15.10.0.0 (A.D. 741). The inauguration of Yax Kin (also known as Ruler B) was commemorated on Stela 21, which stands at the base of Temple VI, far to the southeast. Temple VI, also built during or immediately after Yax Kin's reign, is notable for the extensive hieroglyphic text on the sides and back of its roof comb, which is dated 9.16.15.0.0 (A.D. 766) and records much of the dynastic history of Tikal. Yax Kin marked the end of the first katun of his reign with Twin Pyramid Group 3D-2, at the northern terminus of the Maler Causeway in Group H, the setting for Stela 20 and its fine portrait of Tikal's 27th ruler (Fig. 4.21).

The tomb of Yax Kin has not been positively identified. Several scholars have suggested that it is probably located either in Temple IV or in Temple VI, both of them likely candidates for mortuary shrines. During the Tikal Project excavations, however, a richly furnished tomb (Burial 196) was found beneath a small pyramid, Str. 5D-73, immediately south of Temple II in the Great Plaza. This building is unusual in having no masonry structure on its summit. But the contents of the tomb were fully as sumptuous as those of Ah Cacau's Burial 116. In fact, as William Coe has pointed out, the contents and organization of Burial 196 duplicated those of Burial 116 in many ways. The most striking parallel was the presence of a cylindrical jadeite mosaic vessel in each tomb (see Fig. 15.40). Although there are no hieroglyphic texts from Burial 196 to identify its occupant, its contents included a carved bone bearing the date 9.16.3.0.0, or around 766, not long before the time of Yax Kin's death. Thus, Yax Kin's tomb has probably already been found, and his mortuary shrine seems to have been built apart from his final resting place.

The latest twin-pyramid groups are associated with the last identified ruler of Tikal, known as Chitam (Ruler C). The first of these, and the largest at Tikal, is Twin Pyramid Group 4E-4 (Fig. 4.18), located east of the Maler Causeway, halfway between the East Plaza and Group H. It is the setting for Stela 22 and Altar 10 (Fig. 4.22). The other, Twin Pyramid Group 4E-3, built next to 4E-4, includes Stela 19 and Altar 6.

The latest of Tikal's Late Classic pyramid temples, Temple III, may have served as Chitam's mortuary shrine, or it might be associated with a subsequent, and still unidentified, ruler. Temple III is located west of the Great Plaza, and its summit shrine contains a carved wooden lintel depicting a corpulent ruler dressed in a jaguar skin (Fig. 4.23). At its base is a pair of monuments, Stela 24 and Altar 7, which

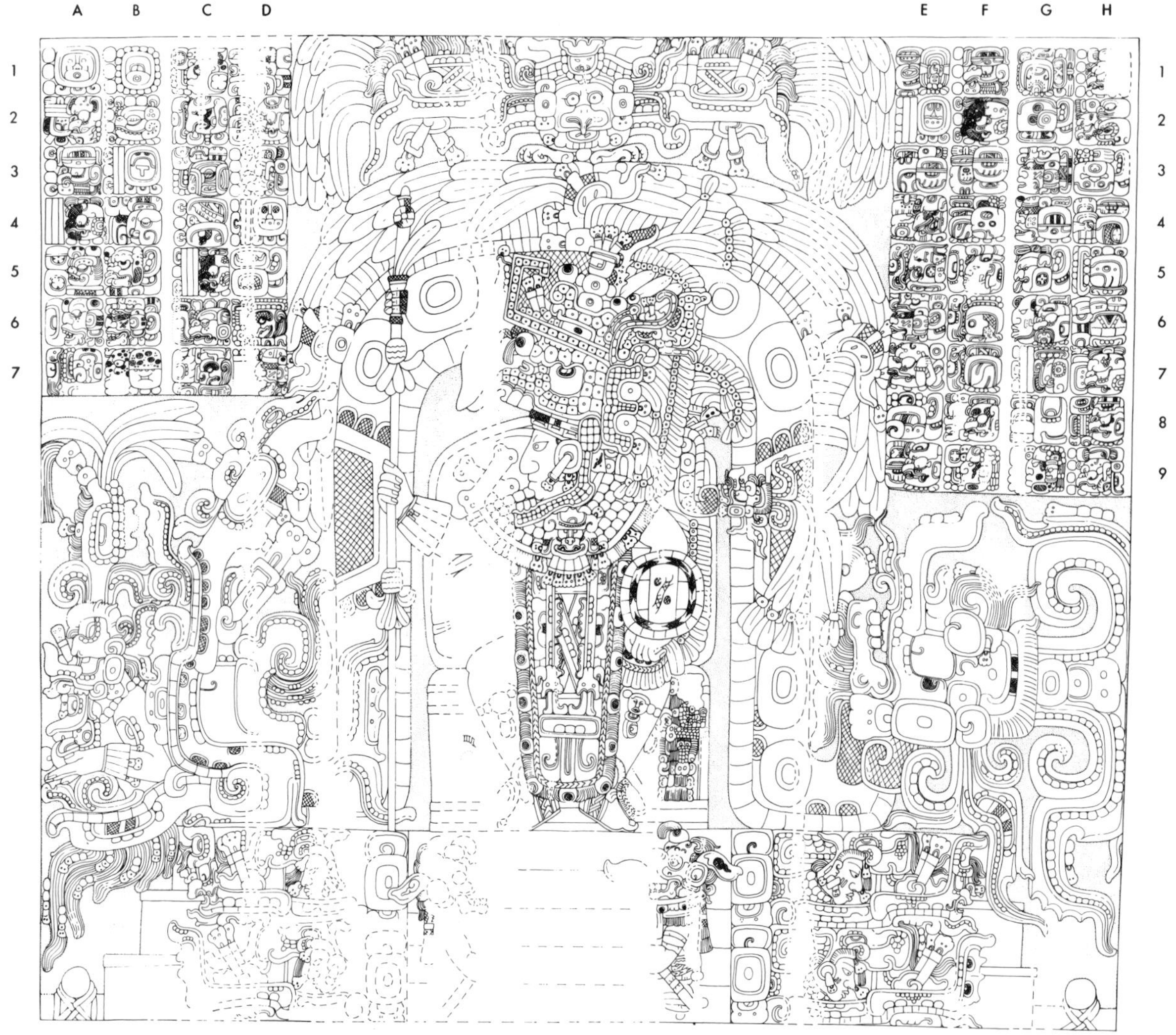

Fig. 4.20. Tikal Temple IV: drawing of the carved wooden lintels from inside the temple, showing (*above*) the ruler Yax Kin seated on his throne, enveloped by a giant double-headed serpent, symbol of the Maya universe, and (*facing page*) Yax Kin holding a manikin scepter, symbol of rulership, and seated in front of a giant "protector" figure.

have been dated to 810 (9.19.0.0.0). Only one monument at Tikal, Stela 11 in the Great Plaza, bears a later date, 10.2.0.0.0 (869). This date may commemorate yet another ruler, but by this time construction activity had long since ceased, and the center was rapidly losing population. By the end of the tenth century, its days of power and glory past, Tikal seems to have been totally abandoned.

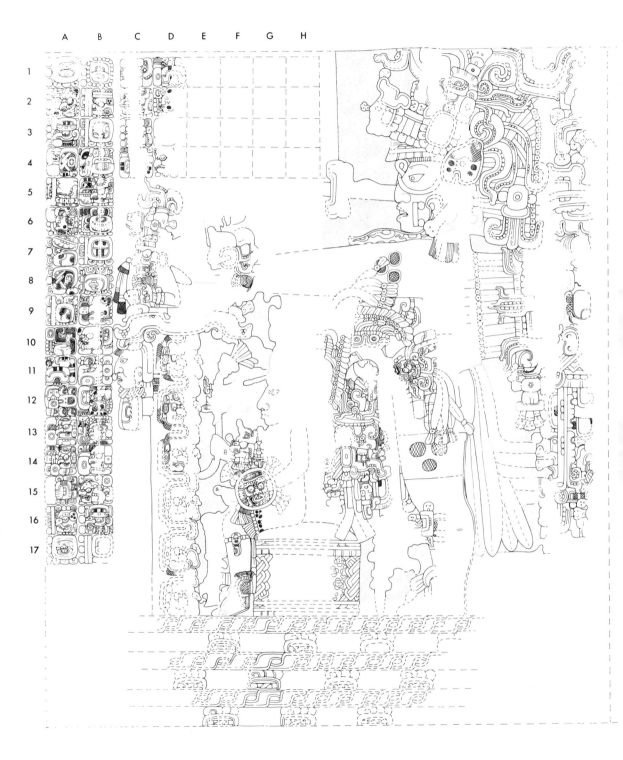

1
2
3
4
5
6
7
8
9

Fig. 4.21. Tikal Stela 20 from Twin Pyramid Group 3D-2, portraying the ruler Yax Kin standing in front of a jaguar throne, holding a staff armed with three celts (axe blades).

Fig. 4.22. Tikal Stela 22 and Altar 10, inside the northern enclosure of Twin Pyramid Group 4E-4 (Fig. 4.18); the carved portrait of the ruler Chitam is visible on Stela 22 (9.17.0.0.0, or A.D. 771; see Fig. 13.14 for a reading of the Stela 22 text).

Fig. 4.23. Tikal Temple III: drawing of the carved wooden lintel from inside the temple, showing the portrait of a corpulent ruler (possibly Chitam) dressed in a jaguar pelt.

TABLE 4.1
Dynastic Chronology of Early Classic Tikal

| Ruler (with *hel* position) | Long Count date | Date A.D. | Event |
|---|---|---|---|
| Yax Moch Xoc | | | "Founder" |
| Scroll Ahau Jaguar | 8.12.14.1.15 | 292 | Unknown Event |
| Great Jaguar Paw I (?) | 8.14.0.0.0 | 317 | |
| Moon Zero Bird | 8.14.3.1.12 | 320 | Accession |
| Great Jaguar Paw II (9) | 8.17.0.0.0 | 376 | Celebrated katun ending |
| | 8.17.1.4.12 | 378 | Smoking Frog at Uaxactun |
| Curl Nose (10) | 8.17.2.16.17 | 379 | Accession |
| | | ca. 392 | Conquest (?) of Río Azul |
| | 8.18.0.0.0 | 396 | Celebrated katun ending |
| Stormy Sky (11) | 8.18.15.11.0 | 411 | Accession (?) |
| | 9.0.10.0.0 | 445 | Dedicated Stela 31 |
| | 9.1.1.10.10 | 457 | Death (?) |
| Kan Boar (12) | 9.2.0.0.0 | 475 | Celebrated katun ending |
| Mahkina Chan (13)? | — | | |
| Jaguar Paw Skull (14) | 9.2.13.0.0 | 488 | |
| (Rulers 15–18) | 9.3.2.0.0 | 497 | |
| | 9.4.0.0.0 | 514 | |
| | 9.4.3.0.0 | 517 | |
| Curl Head (19) | 9.4.13.0.0 | 527 | |
| | 9.5.4.5.16 | 538 | |
| (Ruler 20) | — | | |
| Double Bird (21) | 9.5.3.9.15 | 537 | |
| | 9.6.2.1.1 | 556 | Conflict with Caracol |
| | 9.6.8.4.2 | 562 | Capture and sacrifice by Caracol (?) |

## Tikal as a Major Power in the Early Classic

We can see the makings of Tikal's emergence as a major power in the wake of El Mirador's demise. Later rulers at Tikal recorded their succession from a man given the name Yax Moch Xoc. Though he was clearly not the first ruler at Tikal, as attested by the earlier tombs in the North Acropolis, he was considered the founder of Tikal's royal dynasty by his successors (Table 4.1). Yax Moch Xoc probably earned the retrospective title of dynastic founder by his actions, perhaps as an outstanding war leader or for being the first to proclaim Tikal's political independence. But since no monuments from his reign are known to survive, there is no record of his rule, except in later references. The best estimate we have, based on research by Peter Mathews and Christopher Jones projecting back from the known historical record, would place the reign of Yax Moch Xoc in the third century, probably sometime between A.D. 219 and 238. These scholars have contributed much to the reconstruction of Tikal's dynastic history, which was first worked out by Clemency Coggins by combining textual and archaeological data. Other important glyphic readings have been made by Linda Schele.

In the actual archaeological record, the hallmark of Tikal's first attaining the

••••  status of capital of an independent polity is the dedication of the earliest known lowland monument, Stela 29 (Fig. 4.8). This is the upper fragment of a stela, and on its back is carved an almost complete Long Count date of 8.12.14.8.15 (A.D. 292). On the front it bears the partial portrait of a Tikal *ahau*, given the name Scroll Ahau Jaguar, who is wearing the regalia of a ruler and holding a double-headed serpent bar, one of the two most important emblems of Maya kings. Above him is the head of a down-gazing ancestor, possibly the dynastic founder or his father. Scroll Ahau Jaguar wears a head on his belt and holds another in his hand. The latter wears the king's name glyphs, while the belt head and the front head of the serpent bar are both crowned with the main sign of the Tikal emblem glyph. The appearance of this emblem, a symbol that was to endure for some six hundred years, is perhaps the best evidence of Tikal's status as the center of an independent polity, ruled by its own royal lineage. Unfortunately, the stela bears no hel-glyph notation (an indication of place in the lineage); Scroll Ahau Jaguar probably ruled before this custom was instituted, and although he must have been one of the first few successors of Yax Moch Xoc, we do not know his exact place in the dynastic sequence.

The next Tikal ruler, known as Moon Zero Bird, also does not record his dynastic placement. But the famous artifact associated with his reign, the Leyden Plaque (Fig. 4.24), bears the date 8.14.3.1.12 (320) followed by a brief text that tells us this is the date of his "seating" as ruler. On the front of this plaque (actually an incised jade *celt*) is the portrait of Moon Zero Bird, dressed in full royal costume, holding the double-headed serpent bar, and wearing the royal belt with its god heads and dangling chain (rear) and celts (front). In fact, the Leyden Plaque itself may well be one of the actual objects shown dangling from Moon Zero Bird's royal belt. Incidentally, the Leyden Plaque (named after its current location) was not found at Tikal, but was discovered in the nineteenth century near the mouth of the Río Motagua. It may have come from Moon Zero Bird's tomb, which was looted in ancient times, and perhaps carried or traded to the southeast before being lost. On the celt, the king is standing over the prone figure of a captive, probably the sacrifice used to sanctify his inauguration. As we have seen (Chapter 3), captive sacrifice was an ancient custom, associated with the southern Maya rulers, that originated well back into the Preclassic. Now we see the same tradition—undertaken for royal rituals and portrayed to dramatize the power and prestige of the victor—associated with the earliest lowland rulers, in the Classic.

The first Tikal ruler whose place in the dynastic sequence is identified is Great Jaguar Paw I, recorded as the ninth successor of Yax Moch Xoc. The lower portion of one of his monuments, Stela 39, was discovered in the excavation of Str. 5D-86-6 in the Lost World Group. The excavator, Juan Pedro Laporte, has concluded that the Lost World Complex was built during Great Jaguar Paw's reign. Stela 39 marks the ceremonies ending the seventeenth katun (8.17.0.0.0, or A.D. 376), which prob-

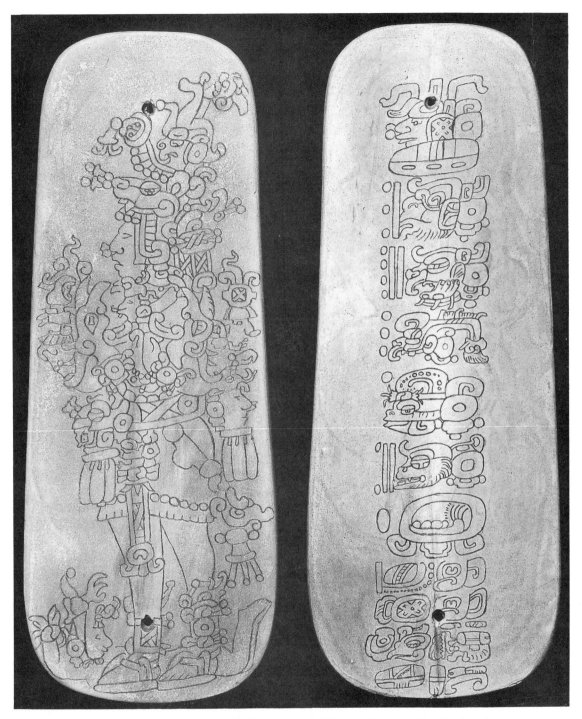

Fig. 4.24. The Leyden Plaque, an incised jadeite celt, probably originally from Tikal but found near the delta of the Río Motagua in the nineteenth century: (*left*) the front bears a portrait of a ruler identified as Moon Zero Bird (note the celts hanging from his belt) standing over a bound captive; (*right*) the back is inscribed with a Long Count date of 8.14.3.1.12 (A.D. 320).

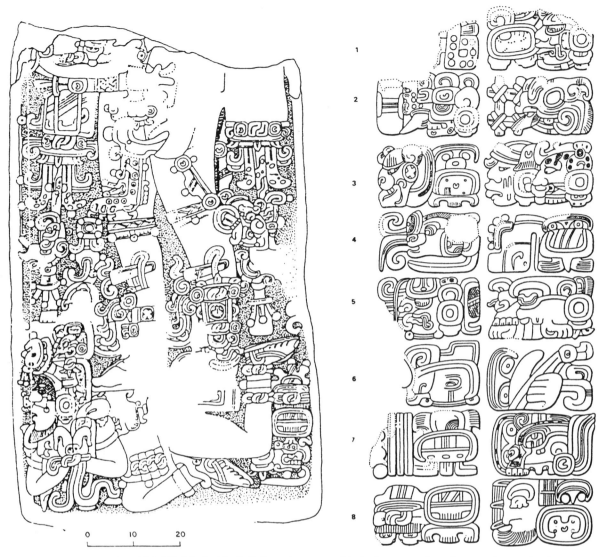

Fig. 4.25. Tikal Stela 39: (*left*) front fragment with the lower portion of a carved portrait of a ruler, presumably Great Jaguar Paw, carrying an axe shaped as a jaguar paw and standing on a bound captive; (*right*) the back, bearing the glyphs for Great Jaguar Paw (at the left of row two) and for Yax Moch Xoc, the Tikal dynastic founder (at the right of row two).

ably took place at this location. It shows Great Jaguar Paw wearing the royal belt and standing over a bound captive—an elite personage, to judge from his headdress and other regalia—while holding an axe decorated with jaguar markings that was undoubtedly used as the sacrificial instrument (Fig. 4.25).

The house of Great Jaguar Paw, Str. 5D-46 in the Central Acropolis, has been identified from a cached vessel excavated from beneath its west stairway. The text on this vessel identifies its use as part of the dedication rituals for the *k'ul na* (sacred house) of Great Jaguar Paw. Peter Harrison's research on the architectural history of the Central Acropolis has shown how later residences in this complex were located by reference to previous buildings, including 5D-46, and how several early buildings were preserved by later generations of rulers, owing probably to their associations with important kings.

Before continuing our account of Tikal's Early Classic development, we will follow briefly the events at some of the neighboring centers during this time.

## Some Neighboring Centers in the Central Lowlands

Other central-lowland centers asserted their independence and importance by erecting monuments during the eighth baktun, which corresponds to the initial portion of the Early Classic, although none is known to possess an emblem as early as Tikal's. Balakbal erected a single stela in 406 (8.18.10.0.0), and four other centers near Tikal have monuments datable to this same span: Uolantun, Stela 2; El Zapote, stelae 1, 4, and 7; Xultun, Stela 12; and Yaxha, Stela 5 (we will discuss Yaxha a bit later in this chapter). The nearby site of Uaxactun commemorated its early political history with a series of six monuments dated between 328 and 416 (8.14.10.13.15 and 8.19.0.0.0). The earliest of these, Stela 9 (Fig. 4.26), is badly eroded, but the standing figure on its front was undoubtedly an early Uaxactun ruler. Stela 19, dated at 8.16.0.0.0 (357), and the eroded Stela 18 are the earliest

Fig. 4.26. Stela 9 at Uaxactun, central lowlands of Guatemala, the earliest known monument from the site: (*left*) the front, with a badly eroded portrait of an unidentified ruler; (*right*) the back, with eroded text and a Long Count date of 8.14.10.13.15 (A.D. 328).

• • • •   known monuments dedicated to katun endings (a period of approximately twenty
years probably occasioned by large-scale community ceremonies, as in later times;
see Chapter 11). The figure on Stela 19 is also clearly that of a Uaxactun king, standing over a kneeling (and bound?) captive, in the prevailing motif employed to dramatize royal authority and prestige.

Major polities were also emerging in other regions of the lowlands, and we will
turn to some of these later in this chapter. But for the time being, we should bear
in mind that centers such as Calakmul (another major Classic city, north of Tikal,
that expanded in the vacuum left by El Mirador) were destined to grow in size and
power, ultimately rivaling Tikal. And to the southeast, secure in the uplands of the
Maya Mountains of Belize, the city of Caracol was developing into another major
power, one that would confront and claim to defeat Tikal during a series of conflicts
later in the Classic. Other polities emerging during this period that were to gain
great power and prestige over the course of the Classic period include Yaxchilan,
on the Río Usumacinta, and Copan, on the southeastern edge of the Maya area (we
will take up both of these centers in Chapter 5).

Still, most of the lowland centers possessing the earliest known Long Count
dates are located in the heart of the Peten. And their being for the most part evenly
spaced throughout the region suggests that, at least initially, they were political
equals, independent of and competitive with each other. But it also appears that
Tikal soon began to assert its power over its nearest neighbors: the fact that most
of these sites ceased to erect monuments shortly after they had adopted the custom
is mute testimony to Tikal's dominance. The means by which Tikal asserted control
is not clear, however, although conflict—in which the defeated ruler was sacrificed
or acknowledged the supremacy of the Tikal ruler—is the likeliest possibility. The
best evidence of this development comes from Tikal's unsuccessful rival Uaxactun,
and before considering these events, we will briefly describe Uaxactun.

### UAXACTUN

Uaxactun is located some 40 km north of Tikal. Meaning "eight stone," the
name was coined by archaeologists in recognition of the site's Stela 9 (Fig. 4.26),
which dates from the eighth baktun. Although Uaxactun is substantially smaller
than Tikal, its span of occupation seems to have been about the same, with origins
in the Middle Preclassic and abandonment by the Early Postclassic.

The first comprehensive archaeological investigations in the central lowlands,
even before those at Tikal, were conducted at Uaxactun by the Carnegie Institution
of Washington over twelve years (1926–37). The pioneering research of the participating scholars, who included Franz Blom, Oliver Ricketson, Edwin Shook, A.
Ledyard Smith, Robert Smith, and Robert Wauchope, produced a series of landmark precedents in lowland Maya archaeology. The project established, for example, the basic cultural chronology for the central lowlands, used as the starting
point for almost all other chronological sequences in the region. It was founded on

Uaxactun's available calendrical inscriptions, pottery sequence, and architectural development. As a case in point, the chronology of pottery forms and types at Tikal, owing to their similarities to those at Uaxactun, is founded on the work done by the original Carnegie research.

Uaxactun, mapped during the Carnegie investigations, consists of a series of architectural groups situated on five low hills or ridges, surrounded by the remains of house platforms. The house-mound survey at Uaxactun, directed by Ricketson, discovered an apparent density of occupation far higher than a swidden-subsistence system would have allowed, and thus yielded one of the first suggestions that Maya agriculture must have been more productive than contemporary theories had held (see Chapter 8). Although no consolidation or restoration was undertaken by the Carnegie project, Shook, years later, returned to the site to direct the consolidation of Str. E-VII-sub (see below), ensuring the preservation of this important example of early Maya architecture. More recently, the Instituto de Antropología e Historia completed a program of excavation and consolidation, directed by Juan Antonio Valdés, that included important discoveries in Group H.

The excavations in Group E at Uaxactun revealed the first known Maya architectural assemblage aligned so as to function as an astronomical observatory. In the years since, similar building alignments have been found at a number of other Classic-period centers, including the example in the Lost World Complex at Tikal. These alignments seem to have been used to commemorate the positions of the equinoxes and solstices. On the west side of a court at Uaxactun, facing due east, was a pyramid (Fig. 4.27). On the opposite side, on a terrace, were three temples with façades running north and south, and arranged so as to establish lines of sight when observed from the stairway of the pyramid on the west side. From this observation point, the sun, on its way north, rose directly behind the middle temple (Str. E-II in the figure) on March 21, the vernal equinox; behind the northernmost front corner of the north temple (Str. E-I) on June 21, the summer solstice; behind the middle temple again on its way back south on September 23, the autumnal equinox; and behind the southernmost front corner of the south temple (Str. E-III) on December 21, the winter solstice. This assemblage of buildings thus marked the longest and shortest days of the year, as well as the two intermediate positions, when day and night are of equal length.

Excavation of the badly ruined Str. E-VII revealed a well-preserved earlier platform underneath, thereafter dubbed E-VII-sub. This substructure dates from the Late Preclassic era, and at the time of its discovery it was the earliest building known from the Maya lowlands. The terraced surfaces of E-VII-sub were completely covered with lime-based plaster, as were its four stairways and sixteen side masks, two at each side of each stairway (Figs. 3.30 and 3.31). These masks seem to depict cosmological themes similar to those found on Str. 5C-2nd at Cerros, in Belize, a center that reached its apogee in the Late Preclassic (see Chapter 3). But unlike the latter building, the summit of E-VII-sub apparently never supported a masonry

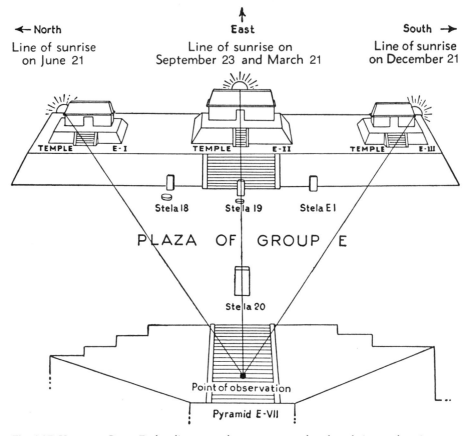

Fig. 4.27. Uaxactun Group E: the alignments shown correspond to the solstices and equinoxes.

building. Four postholes found in the plaster floor probably supported the corner posts for a thatched-roof structure. Since E-VII-sub's discovery, several buildings of the same age have been excavated, including the larger Lost World Pyramid at Tikal and Str. 5C-2nd at Cerros.

Recent excavations directed by the Guatemalan archaeologist Juan Antonio Valdés in Uaxactun's Group H, located northeast of Group E, revealed a major complex of Late Preclassic architecture buried beneath later Early Classic construction. The focus of this complex is the South Plaza, a low, elevated platform surmounted by building platforms on its east, north, and south sides. The six buildings on the eastern platform were decorated by an extraordinary assemblage of Late Preclassic plaster masks (Fig. 4.28). The western façade of the principal eastern platform, Str. H-Sub-3, supported two superimposed masks on either side of a central stairway, in the typical Late Preclassic pattern. In this case, the masks depict the Maya "sacred mountain" (*witz* in Mayan), and incorporate motifs representing the earth (both land and sea). As such, these masks identify Str. H-Sub-3, along with other Maya temples, as a sacred mountain. In Maya cosmology, caves in mountainsides were the entrances to the underworld (Xibalba). Thus temples were often identified as sacred mountains, and their entrances were equated with caves that gave entry to Xibalba, providing the setting for royal rituals performed to communicate with the supernatural realm. More specific connections with Uaxactun's earliest rulers are found in the plaster decorations of Str. H-Sub-10, a smaller building directly west of H-Sub-3 that served as a gateway to the eastern platform. The low, twin eastern and western stairways of H-Sub-10 were flanked by *ahau* masks, and the walls of the building were decorated by figures representing the king, standing on throne symbols and surrounded by smoke scrolls, like those found painted on the walls of Tikal Str. 5D-Sub 10. Alternating with these portraits were panels of woven mats— the *ahau pop*, one of the most enduring symbols of Maya kingship, found in both the highlands and the lowlands.

The earlier Carnegie investigations had also conducted excavations in Uaxactun's Group A, a complex of temples, palaces, and monuments. A *sacbe* (causeway) leads north from Group A, past an ancient water reservoir, to Group B. There, in the excavation of Str. B-XIII, was a mural dating to the end of the Early Classic (Fig. 4.29). The painting, which has since perished (fortunately after it was accu-

Fig. 4.28. Uaxactun Group H: drawing of a stucco *witz* (mountain) mask on Str. H-Sub-3, probably identifying this building as a "sacred mountain."

Fig. 4.29. Uaxactun Group B: drawing of a mural in Str. B-XIII dating to the end of the Early Classic era: (*above*) left portion; (*below*) right portion; the left portion aligns with the lower part of the right portion.

rately copied by Antonio Tejeda), depicts a flat-roofed building within which are seated three women. Just outside is a black-painted male, with one arm across his chest in the sign of greeting. He faces another man, dressed in Mexican attire, who holds an atlatl (spearthrower). These figures, together with the more than twenty others depicted, are accompanied by hieroglyphic texts. The scene appears to represent a meeting or ceremony between local elites and a foreign representative, perhaps from Kaminaljuyu or even Teotihuacan (the atlatl is a central-Mexican weapon, and the word itself is Nahuatl, not Mayan).

Although eventually overshadowed by its neighbor Tikal, Uaxactun is an impressive site, important especially in the early development of Classic Maya political institutions. In fact, the destinies of Uaxactun and Tikal were closely intertwined for some one thousand years, from their Middle Preclassic origins, Late Preclassic growth, and Early Classic emergence as rival powers right through the Classic. But given their proximity it was only a matter of time before rivalry would be translated into conflict and one power would succeed in dominating the other.

## Tikal Consolidates Its Position

It now seems clear that Uaxactun lost its independence to Tikal during the final years of Great Jaguar Paw's reign. The key date of this event (8.17.1.4.12, or A.D. 378) is recorded on at least two monuments at both sites. On the basis of his own research, Peter Mathews has concluded that this date commemorates a bloodletting ritual that marked Tikal's assumption of control over Uaxactun by placing a member of the Tikal royal family, a man with the intriguing name Smoking Frog, on the throne at Uaxactun. The most reasonable means by which this could have occurred was by either a royal marriage or conquest. Although Mathews leaves open both possibilities, two other scholars, Linda Schele and David Freidel, have concluded that Smoking Frog, as leader of the Tikal forces, undertook a war against Uaxactun, conquered the city and was installed on the throne. Their conclusion is based on warfare motifs associated with Smoking Frog, such as his portrait on Uaxactun Stela 5 (Fig. 4.30), where he is carrying both an atlatl and a warclub inset with obsidian blades. It is also supported by their interpretations of texts referring to the event, such as the retroactive reference on the famous Tikal Stela 31 that identifies Smoking Frog as the one who "demolished and threw down the buildings of Uaxactun." (Schele and Freidel, it should be noted, acknowledge that the meaning of this text is not completely understood.)

That there was at least the potential for conflict between these centers is indicated by the construction of earthworks along the northern boundary of Tikal (facing Uaxactun), which had apparently been constructed by this time. But the most dramatic, albeit circumstantial, evidence for a violent consequence of Tikal's takeover is the multiple burials found in a tomb under Uaxactun Str. B-VIII, excavated

Fig. 4.30. Uaxactun Stela 5: eroded portrait of a warrior identified as Smoking Frog, who led the takeover of Uaxactun and may have been from Tikal, shown carrying a warclub in his right hand and an atlatl (spearthrower) in his left (8.17.1.4.12, or A.D. 378).

by Ledyard Smith during the Carnegie project. The tomb, formed by a deep shaft extending from beneath the temple floor to bedrock, held five bodies, two adult women (one was pregnant), a child, and an infant, all of whom seem to have been killed. Stela 5, the monument recording Tikal's takeover of Uaxactun by Smoking Frog, was placed at the foot of the stairway at the time the temple and tomb were constructed. From this evidence, Schele and Freidel conclude that the stela and Str. B-VIII constitute Tikal's victory monument at Uaxactun, and that the burials are the slaughtered family of Uaxactun's defeated king (who was presumably taken to Tikal and sacrificed). If all this is correct, therefore, Smoking Frog's conquest not only was the first time known to us that one polity conquered another in the Maya lowlands, but was also a clear example of the extermination of a ruling family and its replacement by another—in this case, apparently, by a branch of the Tikal royal lineage.

The texts (in particular Uaxactun Stela 5) identify Smoking Frog as an *ahau* of Tikal, and Schele and Freidel postulate that he was a younger brother of the Tikal king, Great Jaguar Paw, and served his brother as war leader. Following the take-over, Smoking Frog presumably ruled at Uaxactun under the aegis of Great Jaguar Paw, at least initially. But the Tikal king must have died within two years, for the Tikal texts record an event associated with a new Tikal ruler, Curl Nose, on 8.17.2.16.17 (379). If Schele and Freidel are correct, then, Curl Nose was Smoking Frog's nephew, the son of Great Jaguar Paw. In any case, a retroactive reference to Curl Nose on the most important historical monument at Tikal, Stela 31, mentions that he "displayed the royal scepter in the land of (*u cabi*) Smoking Frog." It would appear, therefore, that with Great Jaguar Paw's death the Uaxactun ruler became the senior authority in the combined kingdom, and the new king at Tikal was sub-ordinated to Smoking Frog.

On the next katun ending (8.18.0.0.0, or 396), Smoking Frog dedicated a Ua-xactun monument, Stela 4, which he erected next to Stela 5. The importance of the Uaxactun takeover is attested by continued reference to the event on the later monuments of both sites. We have already mentioned the citations on the later Stela 31 at Tikal, and the text on a carved ballcourt marker refers not only to the same date, 8.17.1.4.12, that had been associated with Tikal's takeover of Uaxactun, but also to Smoking Frog. The marker was discovered in a residential compound south of the Lost World complex, and its text also records the accession of the fourth *ahau* of an elite, but nonroyal, lineage, presumably the headman of the kin group who lived in the compound.

This ballcourt marker is unusual in that its shape is in the tradition of Central Mexico rather than that of the lowland Maya. Much of the architecture of the Lost World Group is in fact modeled after that of the central-Mexican power, Teotihua-can, and central-Mexican influences peak at Tikal during this period. Schele and Freidel go so far as to postulate that the institution and regalia of conquest warfare

Fig. 4.31. Tikal Stela 4, recording the accession of the ruler Curl Nose in A.D. 378: (*right*) the front of the monument; (*below*) drawings of the front and back.

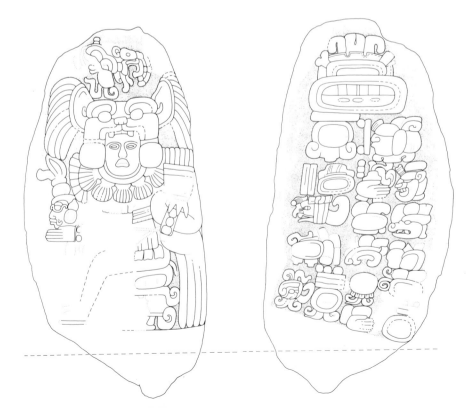

carried out by Tikal against Uaxactun were borrowed from Teotihuacan. This they label Tlaloc-Venus warfare, after the central-Mexican deity (Tlaloc) and the fact that the dates chosen for such warfare events correlated strongly with certain positions of Venus, especially Venus as Evening Star. When subsequent Maya rulers went to war they used versions of the same regalia first associated with Smoking Frog. And many of these aggressions were timed to coincide with what were believed to be favorable positions of Venus and other celestial bodies. In fact, as Mathews and others have pointed out, later texts often refer to warfare between polities by superimposing the "shell-star" glyph (which invokes Venus) over the main sign of the target polity.

Central-Mexican themes continue at Tikal during the reigns of Curl Nose and his son, Stormy Sky. Stela 4 (Fig. 4.31) portrays the tenth ruler in the Tikal succession, Curl Nose, who is named after his presumed name glyph. Its date—probably the same date recorded on his son's monument, Stela 31, associated with the royal scepter display, 8.17.2.16.17, A.D. 379—seems to refer to Curl Nose's inauguration. The style of Stela 4, and the regalia worn by the sculptured portrait of Curl Nose, especially his shell necklace, recall Teotihuacan traditions. In contrast to the style of earlier Tikal monuments, on which portrait figures stand in profile, Stela 4 depicts Curl Nose seated and facing front. The protector figure over Curl Nose's head is the Maya deity Bolon Tza'cab (God K), the patron of royalty (the Maya gods and religious customs are discussed in Chapter 11). Like Smoking Frog, in the earlier portrait on Uaxactun Stela 5, Curl Nose holds a spearthrower in his left arm. According to Clemency Coggins, the God K patron was eventually combined with the central-Mexican weapon, the spearthrower, to form the "manikin scepter," the symbol of lowland Maya dynastic rulership (an image of God K mounted on a shaft with a curved butt like that on a spearthrower; see Fig. 11.8).

A later monument dedicated during Curl Nose's reign, Stela 18 of 396 (8.18.0.0.0), commemorates the katun ending. Both Stela 4 and Stela 18 are near the front of Str. 5D-34, which covers a tomb (Burial 10), most likely that of Curl Nose, who died about 425, after being in power for some 47 years. The tomb contained the skeletal remains of the ruler and a variety of offerings that demonstrate close connections with the Early Classic elite tombs of Kaminaljuyu. As we saw in Chapter 3, during this era Kaminaljuyu was closely linked to Teotihuacan, and these connections are also apparent in Curl Nose's tomb. Burial 10 contained a variety of pottery vessels having southern Maya associations, including several with stucco-painted decoration executed in central-Mexican style, a grotesque ceramic effigy of the "old god" (a deity of great importance in the southern area), and animal offerings (turtle carapaces, a crocodile skeleton, and bird remains), all reminiscent of the contents of contemporary tombs at Kaminaljuyu. Finally, a small curved jadeite head from Burial 10 has been interpreted as a representation of the ruler's name glyph. From this evidence it has been concluded that Curl Nose maintained

• • • •    or intensified the southern Maya connections seen in the Late Preclassic (see Chapter 3).

These ties continued during the reign of the eleventh ruler in the succession, recorded on Stela 31 as Curl Nose's son, Stormy Sky. This magnificent monument (Fig. 4.10), discovered enshrined and buried in the temple built over his tomb, was dedicated in 435 (9.0.10.0.0). Stela 31 portrays Stormy Sky in traditional Maya regalia, with his name glyph attached to a headdress he is holding aloft. Above him, proclaiming his right to rule, is his father, Curl Nose, as his celestial protector and ancestor. In the crook of his left arm he carries a head having Sun Jaguar attributes and bearing the Tikal emblem glyph. On both sides of the monument are standing figures identified as mirror-image portraits of his father, Curl Nose, dressed in central-Mexican-style military garb, carrying shields, spearthrowers, and feathered darts. Coggins characterizes Stormy Sky's reign as a time of synthesis of lowland Maya tradition and Teotihuacan-Kaminaljuyu economic and political institutions. Symbolic of this synthesis, Stormy Sky is portrayed on Stela 31 standing in profile, according to the old Maya fashion, displaying the insignia of traditional Maya rulers; but dramatically, the flanking figures show his father dressed in foreign military regalia.

The base of the text of Stela 31 has been destroyed, and passages in the preserved portion remain difficult to decipher, but it is clear that the sequence of dates, personages, and events recorded in the lengthy hieroglyphic inscription on the back trace nothing less than the early dynastic history of Tikal, including references to the dynastic founder (Yax Moch Xoc), the Stela 29 ruler (Scroll Aḥau Jaguar), the Leyden Plaque ruler (Moon Zero Bird), and, as we have seen, mention of the principals in the Uaxactun drama, his grandfather Great Jaguar Paw and Smoking Frog. This history is brought up to Stormy Sky's era with a record of the reign of his father, Curl Nose (including the reference mentioned above, to his displaying the scepter in 379 "in the land of" Smoking Frog), and, apparently, the date of his own inauguration. Although the event glyph associated with this date (8.18.15.11.0, A.D. 411) is lost in the damaged portion of the text, Frederico Fahsen has made a convincing case that this refers to Stormy Sky's accession as ruler.

Stormy Sky's tomb, known as Burial 48 (Fig. 4.9), was found deep beneath the tall central North Acropolis temple (33 m high), Str. 5D-33-1st. This tomb also contained materials linked to both Teotihuacan and Kaminaljuyu, including a vessel painted with the butterfly motifs closely tied to central-Mexican art. On the plastered walls of the tomb is a painted Long Count date of 9.1.1.10.10 (A.D. 456), which occurs after the events of his reign mentioned on Stela 31 and is probably the date of Stormy Sky's death.

During Stormy Sky's reign, Tikal's influence appears to have reached its greatest extent. Tikal appears to have been involved in the affairs of Yaxchilan, in the southwest region, by about 475 (9.2.0.0.0), as indicated by the presence of Tikal's emblem on Lintel 37 (dated at ca. 504) in Str. 12 there, and by the persistence of a

Tikal sculptural style at Yaxchilan as late as 524 (Stela 14, 9.4.10.0.0). Thereby Tikal may have secured a foothold on the strategic Río Usumacinta route that connects the northern highlands with the Gulf coast.

Even farther afield, Tikal seems to have established its influence at Quirigua and possibly Copan, both of which are in the southeastern periphery of the Maya area. Copan Stela 35 has no surviving glyphs, but its standing figures closely resemble those on several Late Preclassic sculptures in the southern Maya style, as well as the earliest lowland portraits. Copan's earliest glyphic inscriptions indicate that the full calendrical and sculptural tradition of the central lowlands had expanded to this southeastern center by the fourth century. A more specific sculptural tie to Tikal is provided by Monument 26 at Quirigua (Fig. 5.53). This sculpture preserves an apparent date of 9.2.18.?.? (493), and seems to be clearly in the stylistic tradition of the Tikal-Uaxactun region. Later Quirigua monuments appear to have continued this stylistic link to the north.

With a presence in the southeast, then, Tikal could have gained access to the gateway to Central America, and to the Motagua Valley route between the highlands and the Caribbean. Copan and Quirigua, moreover, were situated so as to control access to several valuable resources, such as jadeite from the middle Motagua Valley and obsidian from the Ixtepeque source, and Tikal may have skirted the obsidian monopoly held by Kaminaljuyu and its presumed central-Mexican allies, which controlled the prime source at nearby El Chayal.

## Some Other Centers in the Central Lowlands

Tikal seems also to have forged ties closer to home, especially to the north and east, probably to secure control over the trade in cacao and other products that moved by river from the Caribbean coast. There is a series of important sites in this adjacent region, two of which (Yaxha and Nakum) we will briefly describe here. Farther to the north are two more sites that emerged in the Early Classic as powers in the wake of El Mirador's fall. The larger of these was Calakmul, a city that rivaled Tikal in size and power throughout the Classic period. We will describe Calakmul and the recent discovery of an important Early Classic tomb there in this chapter, but we will take up its Late Classic political relationships in our next chapter. The second northern site is Becan, notable for its huge defensive works probably built to withstand threats from its larger southern neighbors, Calakmul and even Tikal. But we will begin with Río Azul, located some 80 km to the northeast, since it has perhaps the best-documented Early Classic links to Tikal.

### RÍO AZUL

Located in the northeast corner of Guatemala, the site of Río Azul was discovered by Trinidad Pech in 1962. The results of an initial survey of Río Azul and other sites in this region were published by Richard Adams and John Gatling two

•••• years later. No subsequent work was done and the site fell prey to looters who discovered and plundered a series of elaborate and richly furnished tombs over the next two decades. When word of this activity reached Ian Graham in 1981, he journeyed to Río Azul to assess and report the damage to the Guatemalan government. As a result, guards were stationed at the site. Graham also contacted Adams, who then organized a program of investigation that began work in 1983.

The results of this research reveal that Río Azul covered an area of about 1.3 km², the densest concentration of large buildings (350) being in the central 0.5 km² area (Fig. 4.32). The site is on a low, leveled ridge on the banks of the Río Azul, which forms a northern and western boundary. The earliest traces of occupation date to the Middle Preclassic, with pronounced growth, including the construction of at least two temple platforms, occurring in the Late Preclassic (the largest platform, Str. G-103, is 15 m high). Four other Late Preclassic platforms have been detected in the BA-20 Group several kilometers to the northeast. Between ca. 390 and 540 the BA-20 Group was abandoned and Río Azul appears to have reached its maximum growth in constructional activity and population size (estimated at ca. 3,500) during that same span. Decline at Río Azul, or even its abandonment, is indicated at the end of the Early Classic (ca. 530–600), followed by a Late Classic (ca. 680–830) resettlement of the site and the surrounding area. But this resettlement appears to have been primarily residential occupation, with little major new construction, pursued probably under the aegis of the Late Classic administrative center of Kinal, located 12 km to the south of Río Azul.

What is known about Río Azul's political history from its scant texts supports the notion of dominance by Tikal during the Early Classic. Three round altars estimated to date from ca. 385 depict the execution of eight or more elite individuals. These depictions, together with references to at least two Tikal rulers in later Río Azul texts, may indicate that the capture and sacrifice of its elite leaders placed Río Azul under the authority of Tikal. If so, this takeover, presumably by or during the reign of Curl Nose at Tikal, followed on the heels of the putative conquest of Uaxactun by Smoking Frog. It may be significant, therefore, that both of these *ahauob* appear to be mentioned in the texts of Río Azul.

Stela 1, dated to 392, mentions a local ruler who has been identified and named Zac Balam by Federico Fahsen, and may also mention the name Smoking Frog. A looted greenstone mask from Río Azul is inscribed with Zac Balam's name and the so-called Río Azul emblem glyph (an attenuated form of the usual emblem glyph that may refer to Río Azul's status as a subsidiary to Tikal). A slightly later text, painted on the walls of Río Azul Tomb 12, refers to Curl Nose of Tikal. It is important to note that residues found in several Río Azul pots have been identified as cacao, verifying David Stuart's reading of the hieroglyphs on one such vessel as labeling it a "cacao pot." This evidence suggests that at least one commodity traded through this region was cacao, and that it was probably one motive for Tikal's interest in Río Azul.

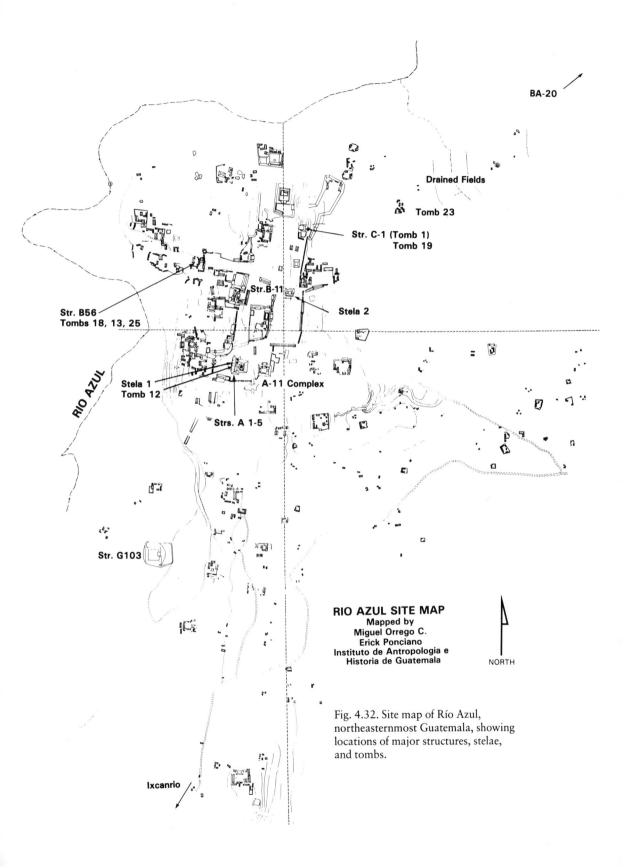

BA-20

Drained Fields

Tomb 23

Str. C-1 (Tomb 1)
Tomb 19

Str. B-11

Str. B56
Tombs 18, 13, 25

Stela 2

RÍO AZUL

Stela 1
Tomb 12

A-11 Complex

Strs. A 1-5

Str. G103

**RÍO AZUL SITE MAP**
Mapped by
Miguel Orrego C.
Erick Ponciano
Instituto de Antropologia e
Historia de Guatemala

NORTH

Fig. 4.32. Site map of Río Azul,
northeasternmost Guatemala, showing
locations of major structures, stelae,
and tombs.

Ixcanrio

••••    The three Early Classic altars at Río Azul were buried under a large temple complex (Str. A-3), which was also the setting for Zac Balam's Stela 1. Like most of the buildings at the site, this complex was constructed during the heydey of Río Azul (390–530) that followed its apparent takeover by Tikal. A series of tomb chambers with painted walls was discovered in the A-3 complex by looters. Although most of the contents of these chambers was stolen, the painted walls include hieroglyphic texts that impart some valuable information. The text from Tomb 12, for example, contains a reference to a personage named Six Sky, the Río Azul emblem, and a death or burial date corresponding to 450. Tomb 1 in Str. C-1, also looted but containing the most elaborate of any known Early Classic wall paintings (Fig. 4.33), includes a Long Count birth date of 8.19.1.9.13 (417) and huge medallion glyphs of Six Sky's father, Stormy Sky, and mother, Bird Claw, of Tikal. This same tomb contains the already mentioned reference to Curl Nose, Stormy Sky's father. The Tomb 12 texts indicate that a presumed ruler of Río Azul, born in 417, was the son of the Tikal ruler and probably acted on his father's behalf.

Adams reports evidence that there was deliberate destruction at Río Azul, followed by near or complete abandonment for nearly a century (ca. 530–600). This span of years corresponds to what is recognized as a period of decline at Tikal. Thus, it would appear that the demise or even violent end of Early Classic Río Azul was related to far larger events involving the great central lowlands power of the Early Classic, Tikal.

### YAXHA

This site, located on the north shore of Lago Yaxha, is much closer to Tikal, about 30 km to the southeast. First reported by Teobert Maler after his visit in 1904, Yaxha was mapped during the 1930's by the Carnegie Institution of Washington, and in the early 1970's further mapping and test excavations were conducted at the site core under the direction of Nicholas Helmuth. David Stuart has deciphered its emblem glyph phonetically, to read *Yaxha*; at least in this case, then, there is good evidence of an ancient site name (as well as the name of the lake) being preserved to the present day. The architectural core of Yaxha consists of a series of plazas and acropolis groups, and three sacbeob provide access to several outlying groups and the lakeshore. At Yaxha there is an architectural alignment similar to that of Group E at Uaxactun (see p. 181) and the only twin-pyramid group identified outside of Tikal. The sculptured monuments indicate elite occupation from the Early to Late Classic (8.16.0.0.0 to 9.18.3.0.0, or 357 to 793).

### NAKUM

Another neighbor of Tikal, located only 25 km to the east near the headwaters of the Río Holmul, was Nakum, which probably once served as an important trade link between Tikal and the Caribbean coast. Nakum was made known to the outside world by the explorations of Maurice de Perigny in 1905–6. A preliminary study and partial site map, by Alfred Tozzer, were published in 1913. Additional mapping was done by Nicholas Helmuth in 1973, but no overall settlement map has been prepared. These maps reveal that the core of the Nakum site comprises two large architectural complexes connected by a *sacbe* (the Perigny Causeway). Like Yaxha, the southern complex contains a Group-E astronomical alignment. Temple A, on the east side of this group, is noteworthy in having two unusual corbel-vaulted doorways flanking a central, wooden-linteled doorway. To the south is a large acropolis, comparable to the Central Acropolis at Tikal, that supports a series of apparently residential structures and courts. Near its center is a higher platform surmounted by four buildings facing an inner court, possibly the residence of Nakum's ruling family. Unfortunately, the site has been heavily looted, and some of its buildings are threatened with collapse. Of the some fifteen stelae known from the site, three are dated, with dates corresponding to 771, 810, and 849.

### CALAKMUL

Calakmul, one of the largest and most important of all lowland Maya sites, is in southeastern Campeche, Mexico, north of El Mirador and some 35 km from the Guatemalan border. Situated on high ground about 35 m above the eastern edge of a large bajo, or marsh, the core area of monumental architecture covers nearly

Fig. 4.33. Río Azul Str. C-1: this Long Count date of 8.19.1.9.13 (A.D. 417) is the central element of the mural on this wall of Tomb 1.

•••• 2 km² and contains about one thousand structures (Fig. 4.34). Beyond this area, the mapped extent of smaller residential remains covers well over 20 km². Some 6,250 structures have been located and mapped within this area. A network of canals and reservoirs surrounds much of the site. Both in extent and estimated maximum population (ca. 50,000), Calakmul is on a par with Tikal, and to judge from the new map, the density of constructions at Calakmul appears to be greater. A newly discovered defensive wall at Calakmul suggests that this powerful polity was a major adversary of Tikal as well.

Calakmul was first reported by Cyrus Lundell in 1931. In the following year Lundell informed Sylvanus Morley, then working at Chichen Itza, of the new site and his count of over 60 stelae there. Morley was resolutely dedicated to recording dated monuments, and he soon organized the first Carnegie Institution of Washington expeditions to the site in April 1932. These were followed by three additional surveys, the last concluding in 1938, that resulted in the mapping of the core area of the site (by J.S. Bolles) and the recording of 103 stelae. Investigations at Calakmul then ceased for more than 40 years; in 1982 it became the focus of a new research project undertaken by the Universidad Autónoma de Campeche, directed by William J. Folan. This work has produced a new settlement map of the site, the discovery of more monuments, and a series of excavations. Joyce Marcus, project epigrapher, has assumed the task of analyzing the inscriptions at Calakmul, including those from the recently discovered Early Classic tomb described below.

Calakmul has always been known for the great quantity of its monuments, and it is unique for its paired sets of stelae with male-female portraits, the depictions of rulers and their wives. The count of stelae stands at 113, the largest total for any Maya site, most of them being carved (and badly eroded). A few of the newly discovered stelae are in outlying areas, but most of the monuments have been found in the site core. The Central Plaza and its associated buildings are the setting for many of these; most of the remaining stelae are in the adjacent West Group, in the Northeast Group, and associated with the giant strs. I and II to the south. The smaller East Group lacks monuments and seems to have functioned as a palace complex, probably for the ruling family. The larger West Group probably served more public functions, given its more open plazas, a ballcourt, and its monuments, including a sculptured rock outcrop depicting seven bound captives.

Str. II, the largest architectural feature at Calakmul, rests on a massive basal platform (ca. 125 by 140 m) bearing a series of Classic monuments along its northern face. This platform supports a triadic pyramid that recalls the Preclassic temple architecture of El Mirador and other sites. As Folan has suggested, this arrangement

Fig. 4.34 (*opposite*). Map of Calakmul, Campeche, Mexico, showing reservoirs (upper left) and surrounding canals that may have aided in the defense of the city; the large black platform in the center is Str. II, the largest building at the site, and the smaller platform southeast of Str. II is Str. I. The map indicates that Calakmul was at least as large as Tikal (see Fig. 4.5), and a defensive wall (not shown) suggests that Calakmul was probably a major adversary of Tikal as well.

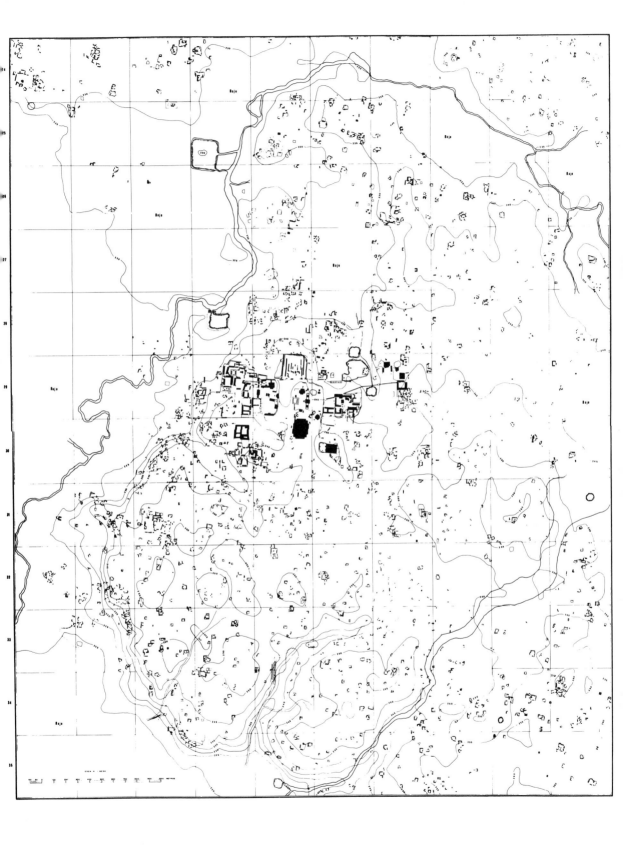

•••• may indicate that Calakmul, too, was an important Preclassic center, one that, unlike its great neighbor to the south, survived the upheavals at the outset of the Classic period and continued on to become a major power. To the southeast of Str. II is Str. I, ca. 85 by 95 m at its base, and the highest point at the site, sitting, as it does, on the crest of a low (6 m) hill. A series of monuments on its frontal (western) terrace includes Stela 51 (Fig. 4.35), portraying Ruler 7. When Morley recorded it, this was the best-preserved of Calakmul's sculptures, but in more recent times it was sawed into small blocks by looters. Fortunately, the blocks were recovered, and the restored monument is today in the Museo Nacional de Antropología in Mexico City. A worse fate has befallen other monuments: Stela 89, for example, once stood at the top of the Str. I stairway, but only a few discarded blocks remain there now, the rest having been hauled off to parts unknown to be sold.

Str. III, a smaller platform located east of Str. II, is the setting for an important tomb, probably that of one of Calakmul's Early Classic rulers. When Folan discovered the tomb, beneath Room 6 of the palace-type superstructure, it contained the skeletal remains of a male, at least 30 years old, lying fully extended on his back. Beneath him were five pottery dishes. Fragments of textiles and stucco, all impregnated with red pigment, were found with the bones.

Among the numerous offerings in the chamber, which included a stingray spine, two pearls, thousands of shell beads, and nine elaborately painted pottery vessels, was an unusually large number of jade items. These include 32 beads, a ring, six earflares, and three mosaic masks. One of the jade masks, of some 170 mosaic pieces, was worn over the buried man's face; another, of 120 pieces, was on his chest; and the third, of 92 pieces, was on his belt. There were also three bluish-colored jade celts, originally suspended from one of the masks, each inscribed with an incised pair of glyphs. Joyce Marcus has been able to read the name and title on one of these glyphs: she gives them as "Long-Lipped Jawbone" and "*caan na*" (sky house?), which probably identified the tomb's occupant.

The pottery vessels date the tomb to a time before the earliest known historical reference to a Calakmul ruler on the site's monuments (the ruler identified on Stela 43, which was dedicated in A.D. 514). Thus, until further Early Classic texts are discovered, we cannot verify that "Long-Lipped Jawbone" was a ruler (and not some other important elite figure) or determine his potential place in the dynastic sequence.

A sequence of the known monuments, based on the procedure established by Tatiana Proskouriakoff, has been worked out by Joyce Marcus. As a result, we have the outline of a sequence of Calakmul rulers and a tentative chronology for those structures associated with the dated monuments. Marcus's analysis provides the basis for a research design for excavations that will test and refine the architectural sequence (and hopefully define the functions of particular buildings). In the meantime, we can summarize the sequence of known rulers.

Fig. 4.35. Calakmul Stela 51, with its portrait of Ruler 7, was originally from the western terrace of Str. I; it is shown here reassembled after being sawed into small blocks by looters.

••••    Though there are earlier dated stelae at smaller sites in the surrounding region, most notably Stela 5 at Balakbal, to the southeast (8.18.9.17.18, or A.D. 406), the first known date at Calakmul, and the only known date associated with Ruler 1 in the Calakmul sequence, is on Stela 43 at 9.4.0.0.0 (514), which was probably reset in front of Str. II. After this, there is a gap of over a century in the local historic record, ending with Ruler 2, who is associated with two monuments at 9.9.10.0.0 (623). These two, the first twin portraits of a ruler (Stela 29) and his wife (Stela 28), were placed in front of Str. V on the south side of the Central Plaza.

Marcus associates nine stelae with the succeeding Ruler 3, dating between 9.11.5.0.0 (?) and 9.12.0.0.0 (657 and 672), all located in the Central Plaza area. Ruler 4 may have commissioned the largest number (ten) of surviving stelae of any Calakmul ruler, all of them found outside the Central Plaza, most of them (six) in the West Group. Together, the ten span one katun, from 9.12.0.0.0 to 9.13.0.0.0 (672–692). Ruler 4 appears to be the same unfortunate Jaguar Paw who, as we will relate in the next chapter, began his career under the protection of Dos Pilas Ruler 1 and ended his reign as the captive of Tikal's Ah Cacau in 695.

The first known monument associated with Ruler 5 (Stela 24) is paired with Stela 23, which portrays his wife; both monuments were on the west side of the Central Plaza, and both date to 9.13.10.0.0 (702). Three more stelae of the same date are in front of Str. II. Ruler 6 is associated with four stelae, spanning the years 711 to 721. His successor, Ruler 7, is associated with seven monuments (see Fig. 4.35), all in front of Str. I, which may be his funerary temple; the looted Stela 89, originally on the summit of Str. I, dates to 9.15.0.0.14 (731). Ruler 8 is known from six monuments in the western sector of the Central Plaza, beginning at 9.15.5.0.0 (736) and ending at 9.16.0.0.0 (751). Ruler 9 is associated with three stelae in the West Group dating to the katun endings of 9.17.0.0.0 (771) and 9.18.0.0.0 (790). The last known ruler may be associated with the West Group carved outcrop at 9.18.0.0.0 (800) and seven stelae, including several with 9.19.0.0.0 (810) dates.

Archaeological work at Calakmul is expected to continue, and in time we should have a more complete picture of this giant site's development and of its role in the events of the Classic Maya lowlands. But it is already apparent that, given its immense size, the number of its monuments, and its formidable defenses, Calakmul was one of the most important of Maya polities and probably Tikal's principal rival for supremacy in the central lowlands throughout much of the Classic period.

### BECAN

Situated far to the north, some 150 km from Tikal, Becan lies within the heart of the Yucatan Peninsula. The site was discovered in 1934 by two archaeologists, Karl Ruppert and John Denison, who named it after its most conspicuous feature, an encircling moat and rampart (*becan*: "ditch filled with water"). Three seasons of archaeological investigations in the Río Bec region, much of the work focused on Becan, were carried out from 1969 to 1971. The project was sponsored by Tulane University and the National Geographic Society, and conducted under the overall direction of E. Wyllys Andrews IV. The research also examined the settlement and subsistence activities around Becan and investigated the nearby, unfortified, elite center of Chicanna.

The core of Becan is defined by the moat and rampart, which enclose an oval-shaped area of about 114 hectares (Fig. 4.36). Excavations revealed that the moat was originally some 5 m deep and about 16 m wide, its interior rampart rising another 5 m. Access to the site was by seven narrow, solid causeways across the moat, formed by leaving strips of the limestone bedrock intact. The rampart was built of the underlying soft-limestone rubble (*sascab*). There is no evidence of a parapet and interior walkway, as was found at the smaller, later fortifications of Mayapan and Tulum. Construction of the moat and rampart is dated to the first part of the Early Classic, or possibly even slightly earlier.

Ceramic evidence indicates that Becan and its surrounding region were first settled near the end of the Middle Preclassic (by ca. 550 B.C.). Rapid population growth seems to have occurred throughout the Late Preclassic, when an elite center first emerged. Str. IV-sub, some 15 m high, was built during this era. A combination

Fig. 4.36. Becan, Campeche, Mexico: aerial view showing the surrounding protective ditch and earthen rampart, with an access ramp at the left.

•••• of good agricultural potential and a strategic position along trade routes appears to have stimulated Becan's expansion. The defensive facilities were probably constructed to maintain Becan's political and economic control over the region.

But Becan's population seems to have declined shortly after the moat-and-rampart system was constructed, and the decline seems to have continued through the end of the Early Classic, for reasons unknown, although Tikal's or Calakmul's success in monopolizing the trans-Peten trade network may have brought hard times to Becan. Nonetheless, trade contacts between Becan and Teotihuacan are indicated by the presence of central-Mexican obsidian and by a famous cache of a slab-leg cylindrical vessel (with Maya style decoration) containing a hollow Teotihuacan figurine, excavated from Str. XIV (see Fig. 15.11, lower illustration).

To close out the known story of this site, Becan was revitalized in the Late Classic: the population increased dramatically and vigorous building activity resumed. Most of the civic structures at the site, and at the nearby centers of Chicanna and Xpuhil, reflect the Chenes and Río Bec architectural styles that developed during

Fig. 4.37. Chicanna, Campeche, Mexico: the excavated and consolidated Str. II, with its central doorway framed by a giant earth-monster mask, provides an excellent example of the Chenes regional architectural style.

Fig. 4.38. Xpuhil, Campeche, Mexico, drawing by Tatiana Proskouriakoff of Str. 1: with its solid (false) towers modeled after the high temple platforms of Tikal and other central-lowland sites, Xpuhil is an excellent example of the Río Bec regional architectural style.

this era (Figs. 4.37 and 4.38). The building activity of the Late Classic ceased by ca. 830, and changes in the ceramic inventory indicate that peoples from northern Yucatan settled at Becan during the ninth century. Thereafter, however, Becan and its surrounding region saw the beginning of a steady population decline, and the elite centers of the Río Bec region were soon abandoned.

## The Successors of Stormy Sky at Tikal

We return now to Tikal, where the available evidence allows us to outline the remainder of this center's Early Classic history. After an illustrious reign, Stormy Sky was succeeded by a ruler known as Kan Boar, who was inaugurated as the twelfth successor of Yax Moch Xoc, probably in A.D. 475. Kan Boar's portraits on Stelae 9 and 13 abandon the war-and-captive motifs used by his ancestors. Instead, he is depicted in a simple, traditional, standing-profile posture, holding a staff (Fig.

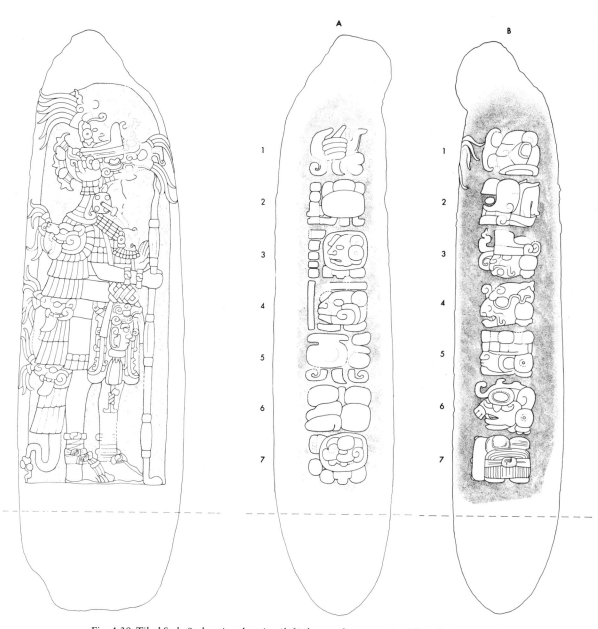

Fig. 4.39. Tikal Stela 9: drawing showing (*left*) the standing portrait of the ruler Kan Boar, holding a staff; the text (*center and right*), inscribed on both narrow sides of the monument, ends with Kan Boar's name glyph and the Tikal emblem glyph.

4.39). Few monuments have survived from this era, and, compared to his immediate predecessors, we know relatively little about Kan Boar's successors, except that their reigns were relatively short (ten rulers in a period of about 60 years). But on the basis of the archaeological record, we know that this was a period of continued growth and prosperity at Tikal. New buildings were constructed on the

North Acropolis, beginning with the splendid shrine built over Stormy Sky's tomb, Str. 5D-33-2nd. As we have seen elsewhere (see the discussion of Uaxactun Str. H-Sub-3, above), the *witz* masks adorning the façade of the platform and superstructure identify this as a sacred mountain, the place of entry to Xibalba, the underworld. As mentioned above (p. 159), Stela 31 was probably placed in front of this building originally; years later it was reset inside the temple, prior to the entire edifice's being covered by Str. 5D-33-1st.

Kan Boar seems to have been followed by a little-known ruler named Mahkina Chan. The fourteenth ruler, Jaguar Paw Skull, came to power by 488 (9.2.13.0.0) and was portrayed on Stela 7 holding a staff in the style of Kan Boar's monuments. He also dedicated Stela 26, once a magnificent sculpture showing Jaguar Paw Skull in a full frontal portrait with, at the sides, hieroglyphic texts naming his ancestors, Great Jaguar Paw, Stormy Sky, and Curl Nose. But this monument was deliberately smashed, and only the basal portion remains (Fig. 4.40), discovered buried inside a North Acropolis temple (Str. 5D-34-1st), as was Stela 31. Beyond this point the dynastic record is obscure, owing to the severe erosion and deliberate destruction of many monuments, such as Stela 26. An exception is Stela 23 (Fig. 4.41) found in an elite residential complex on the southeastern edge of Tikal; this monument depicts a woman, and gives her date of birth and her name, Woman of Tikal. She was the first of many Maya women portrayed on stelae, in both primary and secondary roles. Though her identity and role in Tikal's dynastic history are unclear, William Haviland has identified this residential complex and its tombs with Woman of Tikal and her elite lineage.

The nineteenth ruler in the Tikal succession, associated with stelae 10 and 12 (ca. 527), has been named Curl Head. He must have been followed by an unknown ruler, for the accession of the 21st ruler, Double Bird, in 537 (9.5.3.9.15) is documented on Stela 17 (Fig. 4.42). A parentage statement in this inscription is badly eroded, but the mother's name appears to be Woman of Tikal, and the father's name may be Jaguar Paw Skull. If so, this might explain the interval of numerous short reigns as being a time when the uncles and brothers of Double Bird ruled. Regardless, Stela 17 and Double Bird mark the end of the Early Classic era at Tikal. For the next century and a half, Tikal was eclipsed by events that are just now being understood.

## The Basis of Tikal's Power in the Early Classic

As we have seen, the Early Classic Maya of the lowlands developed a complex society characterized by an elite ruling class and a non-elite class of farmers, craft specialists, and other laborers. Yet, according to an analysis by William Rathje, there appears to have been considerable social mobility during this period. Individuals seem to have been able to earn higher social rank by acquiring wealth and power; and two prime means for gaining wealth were colonizing new lands or

Fig. 4.40. Tikal Stela 26, a shattered monument found interred inside North Acropolis Str. 5S-34-1st: drawing of the lower portion, showing (*left*) a remnant portrait of the ruler Jaguar Paw Skull and (*right*) the remnant text, with references to Stormy Sky, Kan Boar, and Jaguar Paw Skull and ending with the Tikal emblem glyph.

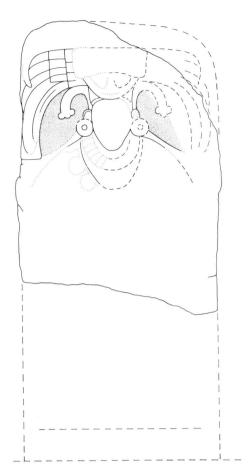

Fig. 4.41. Tikal Stela 23: drawing of a badly eroded fragment that records the birth of "Woman of Tikal."

peoples and controlling valuable resources or trade routes. Moreover, those who succeeded in these economic ventures very likely formed the basis for a new elite class that ruled over a series of newly emerging centers.

How did Early Classic Tikal achieve such spectacular success in economically and politically dominating the central lowlands? How did it rise above the precocious dominance of El Mirador and emerge as the primary center in the lowlands during this era? Although our answers are still incomplete, several known factors must have contributed to Tikal's success.

The first of these is location. Tikal is situated on a series of low hills that form part of the divide between the Caribbean and Gulf of Mexico drainage systems. These hills contain chert, or flint, which for the lowland Maya was a valuable resource for the making of chipped-stone tools, and from the center's very beginnings, the people of Tikal thus controlled a critical natural resource. To the east and west of Tikal lie two large seasonal swamps (once, perhaps, shallow lakes) that might have been exploited for intensive agriculture. At least portions of these depressions were apparently modified by raised-field systems, providing Tikal with a productive

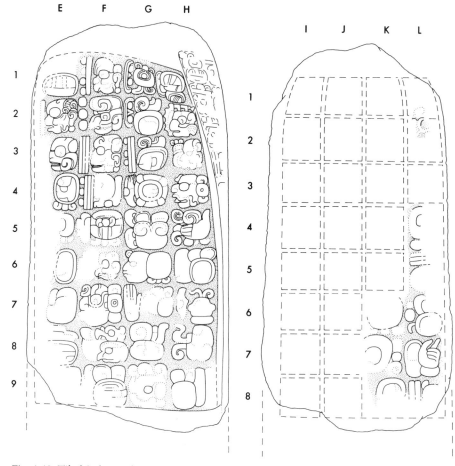

Fig. 4.42. Tikal Stela 17: drawing of the broken monument of the ruler Double Bird, showing his eroded portrait on the front and the text that covers the other three sides; the text includes his apparent accession on 9.5.3.9.15 (A.D. 537; glyphs F1–F3, far left) and his position as the 21st successor of the dynastic founder (glyphs G1, H1, far left).

local agricultural resource. Beyond affording Tikal this rich subsistence base, each of the shallow lakes is ultimately connected to a major river system, one flowing northeast to the Caribbean, the other flowing west to the Gulf.

Much of Tikal's prosperity must have derived from the trade that followed these river systems through its territory. As postulated by Christopher Jones, these rivers would have provided a primary avenue of canoe-borne commerce between the Caribbean and the Gulf of Mexico. And because Tikal was situated on a critical portage between these two drainage systems, it would have controlled one of the major east-west trade routes passing across the Maya lowlands. As we have seen, Tikal's apparent control of Río Azul may have been motivated by an ambition to control commerce in this area, including trade in cacao. For a time, Tikal may have controlled an even wider sphere of central-lowland commerce, perhaps acting as

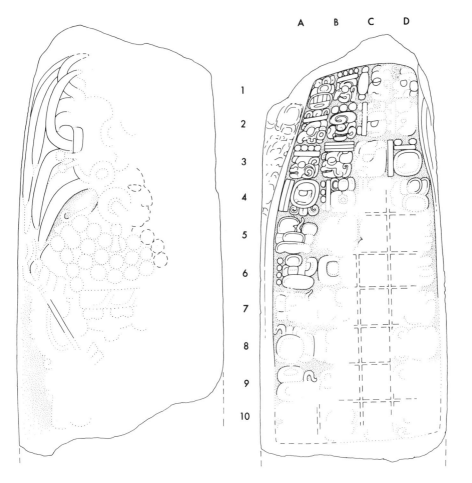

the central redistribution point both for lowland goods destined for other regions and for foreign commodities (such as obsidian) entering the lowlands. Tikal's links to Kaminaljuyu and Central Mexico were probably due, at least in part, to its strategic location, and Tikal may in fact have been the principal trading partner of Kaminaljuyu (and even Teotihuacan) for the lowlands.

Tikal also occupied a strategic defensive position, such that in times of conflict it could be effectively defended against attack. The swamps (or lakes) to the east and west effectively eliminated threats from those directions. Approaches from either the north or the south were defended by a ditch and rampart that may have been constructed during the apparently turbulent Protoclassic or Early Classic, perhaps during Tikal's confrontation with Uaxactun. The smaller center of Becan, farther north of Tikal, may also have constructed a massive defensive ditch and earthwork around its civic core during this period, and Tikal's rival, Calakmul, was defended by a wall as well.

Tikal certainly became an important lowland religious center, as well, and probably a shrine for pilgrimages. Ultimately, it symbolized the supernatural as-

•••• sociations that empowered and sanctioned the political and social order, for it was the seat of the oldest dynasty, and the first to embark successfully on a program of expansion at the expense of neighboring polities. As the focus of the fusion of Maya and central-Mexican religious, political, and military institutions, Tikal possessed both the prestige and the supernatural associations necessary to a position of power in the Early Classic lowlands. Even while new dynasties were establishing themselves, and new polities were emerging at Calakmul, Caracol, Yaxchilan, Copan, and elsewhere, Tikal probably continued to be seen as the source of the supernatural power that had established, and had for so long preserved, lowland society. In a sense, Tikal may have been, for a time, the Rome, "the eternal city," of the lowland Maya.

## The Middle Classic "Hiatus" and the Decline of Tikal

In the sixth century, however, Tikal's economic prosperity and political domination suffered a setback, at the time of the so-called Middle Classic Hiatus, which is traditionally dated from about A.D. 534 to 593 (9.5.0.0.0 to 9.8.0.0.0), but at Tikal lasted as late as 692 (9.13.0.0.0). Many years ago, archaeologists defined the onset of the hiatus by the halt in the erection of monuments at Tikal, and by a similar decline at several other lowland sites. At Tikal, the furnishings in the burials and tombs of this time, even in tombs obviously belonging to members of the ruling elite, have been characterized as "impoverished" when compared to the sumptuous offerings of earlier or later times.

In the next chapter we shall see how new evidence uncovered by archaeological research at the site of Caracol has pointed to a possible cause for the hiatus at Tikal. This evidence suggests that the seeds sown by Tikal during its expansion bore bitter fruit indeed, for the text of a newly discovered monument records the capture of Double Bird, ruler of Tikal, by the ruler of Caracol. Writing in the early days of the Tikal Project in 1957, its director, Edwin Shook, suggested that the destruction of many of Tikal's monuments may have been the result of violence that was "responsible for the end of the Early Classic . . . and the hiatus in the known sequence of inscriptions at Tikal." It now appears possible that the violence and destruction were carried out in the wake of Tikal's confrontation with Caracol. But as archaeologists such as William Haviland have pointed out, not all the evidence at Tikal can be explained by a Caracol victory. It is probable, therefore, that the events surrounding Tikal's downfall were complex and that there was an even more powerful agent behind these events, most likely Calakmul. Regardless of the causes, it seems clear that Tikal's change in fortunes not only upset the established lowland order, but ushered in a whole new era in the political development of the Maya lowlands.

# THE LATE CLASSIC AND THE EXPANSION OF THE LOWLAND STATES

It was here where they multiplied . . . here they were, too, when the sun, the moon, and the stars appeared, when it dawned and the face of the earth and the whole world was lighted.
—*Popol Vuh* (Recinos 1950: 189)

**A**lthough Tikal appears to have dominated much of the Maya lowlands during the Early Classic, the era also saw the rise of a number of vigorous, competitive new polities. The subsequent decline of Tikal thus ushered in profound changes in the lowland order, leaving in its wake a kind of power vacuum that would be filled by a series of these rapidly expanding Maya cities. Confronted by unprecedented opportunity, they began to compete actively for the leadership role that Tikal had played in a variety of arenas—economic, political, military, and religious.

## The New Order in the Late Classic

This new age in the Maya lowlands corresponds to the Late Classic (ca. A.D. 600–800), a relatively brief span of unprecedented expansion and vigor that has long been regarded as the apex of Maya civilization. The details of the events that characterized and drove this era, illuminated by expanded archaeological research and the decipherment of ever greater numbers of Maya inscriptions, are just beginning to come to light.

In this chapter we will describe Late Classic developments at the major centers of Late Classic power, beginning with Caracol, the polity that seems to have kindled the fires of change with its confrontation with Tikal.

### CARACOL

Caracol is situated on the Vaca plateau at an altitude of 500 m adjacent to the Maya Mountains, in south-central Belize. Its location provided ready access to the resources of the area, especially a crystalline rock well suited to the fashioning of grinding stones. Caracol's command of these resources and its relatively secure setting undoubtedly contributed to its development and prosperity. Faced with a lack of accessible water sources, its inhabitants constructed artificial reservoirs for the capture of rainwater.

Discovered in 1938, the site was initially investigated during two field seasons, in 1951 and 1953, by an expedition from the University Museum, University of Pennsylvania, under the direction of Linton Satterthwaite. The principal objective of this work was to record and preserve the recently discovered sculptured monuments and to map the site. Clearing and excavations undertaken to locate additional monuments uncovered four new stelae and a series of elite tombs associated with the stelae. In 1956 and 1958, excavations conducted by A. H. Anderson, Archaeological Commissioner of Belize, resulted in the discovery of more burials and an additional stela. A larger, long-term investigation was initiated at Caracol in 1985, under the direction of Arlen and Diane Chase of the University of Central Florida. The principal objective of this work, which has included settlement survey, the creation of an expanded site map, and excavations in a variety of contexts, has been the linking of archaeological data with the historical record available from the texts carved on Caracol's monuments and painted on its tomb walls.

These investigations have revealed that Caracol was an extensive site (Fig. 5.1), covering between 28 and 50 km², with high densities of construction (and, by inference, population) in the core area of the site (Fig. 5.2). One mapped and excavated sample of the core area contains 677 structures arranged in 128 plaza groups within 2.26 km². Seven *sacbeob*, or causeways, extend outward from the site center. Two of these, each less than a kilometer long, terminate in elite residential complexes; two others, 3 km long, end in plaza complexes equivalent in size to the central group; and the longest extends 8 km to the main plaza of the subordinate site of Cahal Pichik (Fig. 5.1).

Excavations indicate that Caracol was founded in the Late Preclassic, and during the Early Classic, while it was still a relatively small site, its rulers commissioned an "E Group" like those found at Uaxactun and Tikal. Dramatic increases in construction activity and population are detectable during the century or so following Caracol's confrontation with Tikal. Population expanded rapidly, probably tripling or quadrupling, to reach levels equivalent to those of Tikal at its peak: between 30,000 and 60,000 in the site proper and a minimum of 100,000 within the entire Caracol polity. The causeway system provided communication and transport throughout the city, and extensive systems of agricultural terraces boosted food production to feed the burgeoning population.

Fig. 5.1 (*opposite*). Map of Caracol, Belize: (*above*) the extensive network of causeways (sacbeob) that radiate from the central Caana Group; (*below*) the Caana Group, named after the major complex in its northeastern corner (see Fig. 5.2).

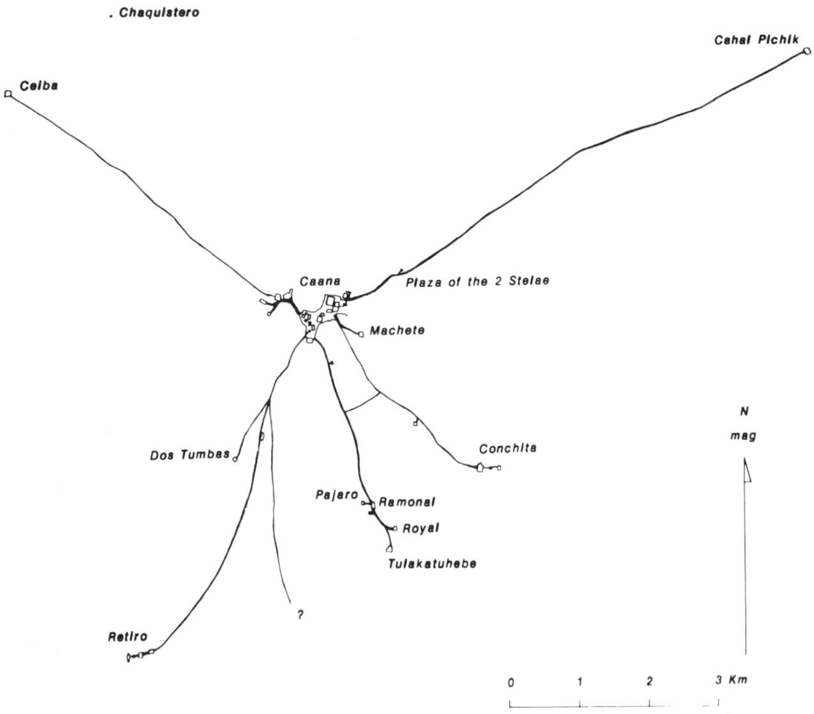

Chaquistero

Cahal Pichik

Ceiba

Caana    Plaza of the 2 Stelae

Machete

N
mag

Dos Tumbas

Conchita

Pajaro  Ramonal

Royal

Tulakatuhebe

?

Retiro

0    1    2    3 Km

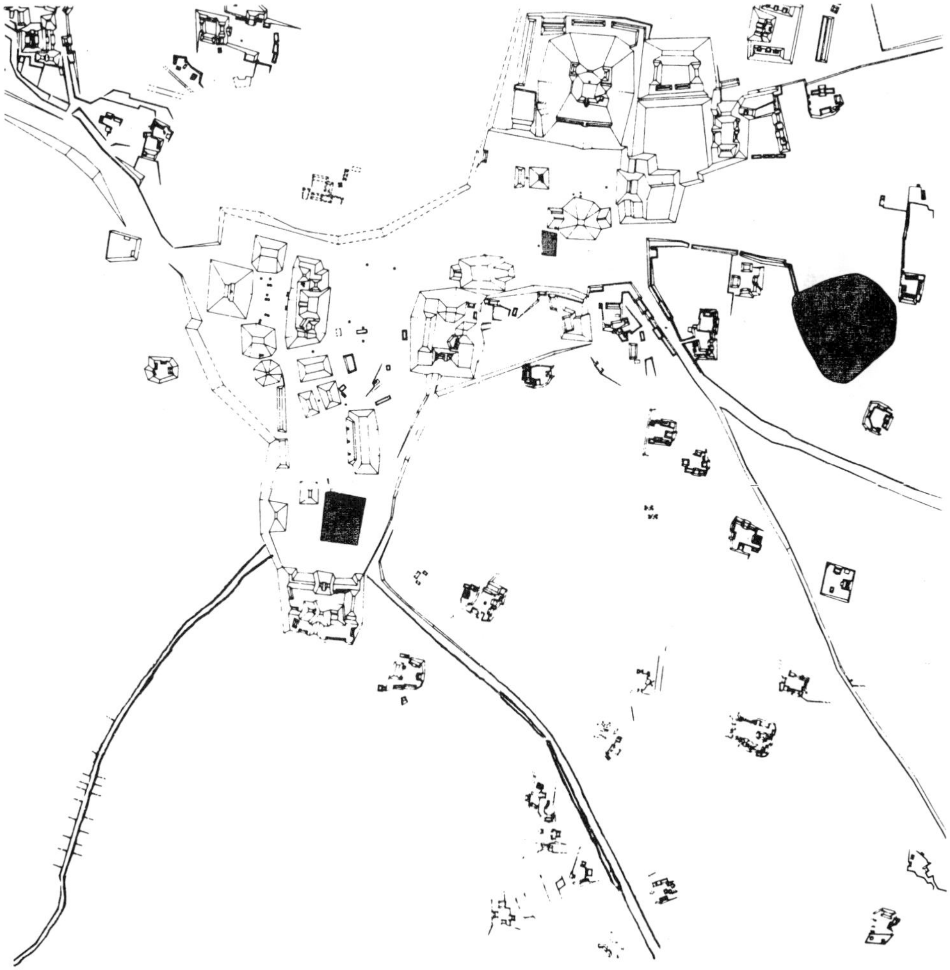

Fig. 5.2. Monumental architecture in the site core at Caracol, Belize: the Caana platform complex from the southeast, during excavation.

## The Decline of Tikal and the Rise of the New Polities

Over 40 monuments, spanning most of the Classic period, are now known from Caracol. This record has allowed the reconstruction of much of the city's dynastic sequence, through work done originally by Carl Beetz on the basis of Satterthwaite's record, and supplemented, but not seriously modified, by more recent research. The most crucial addition has been Altar 21 (Fig. 5.3), which was discovered during the excavation of the playing alley of the Group A Ballcourt. Al-

Fig. 5.3. Caracol Altar 21, which records the birth of the ruler Lord Kan (A, B), the accession of his father, Lord Water (K, L), and two conflicts with Tikal (O, P and Q, R); note the central giant *ahau* (day) glyph, a characteristic of Caracol altars.

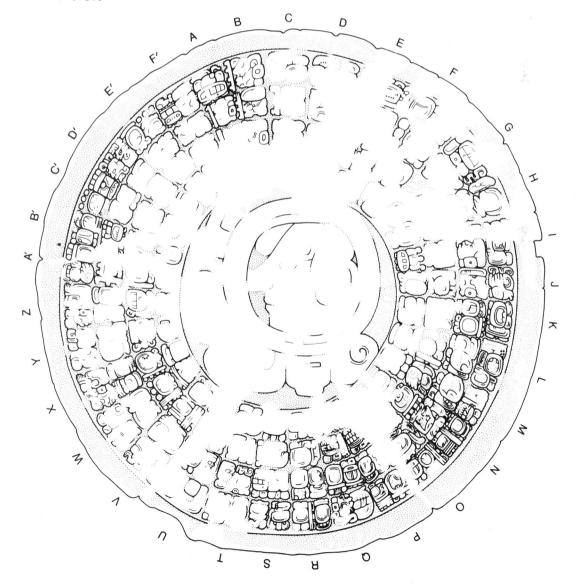

though originally designated an "altar," this circular carved stone (diameter 1.28 m) was undoubtedly the central marker in the Maya ballgame, which, as we have already seen, had important associations with warfare and ritual sacrifice. In the center of the stone is the diagnostic feature of Caracol altars, a giant glyph of the day sign *ahau*. The surrounding text comprises 160 glyphs, some of them damaged or completely eroded. The readable portion of the text has been deciphered by Stephen Houston. It records the birth of the ruler who commissioned the stone, Lord Kan II, in 9.7.14.10.8 (588) and the accession of his father, Lord Water, in 9.5.19.1.2 (553). It then records an "axe event" that took place "in the territory of" the ruler of Tikal in 9.6.2.1.11 (556). Although the latter's name is eroded, the date given is shortly before Double Bird erected Tikal Stela 17 (557).

This event has usually been interpreted as the moment when Caracol opened hostilities against Tikal. Since Tikal Stela 17 indicates that Double Bird was still on the throne after this event, and since Caracol Altar 21 records that the axe event (or sacrifice) took place in Tikal's territory, it would appear that the Caracol text is referring to the capture and sacrifice by the Tikal ruler of someone from Caracol—and thus that this was the event that triggered the hostilities against Tikal recorded in Caracol's texts. In any case, the axe event date is followed by a "shell-star" over Tikal event in 9.6.8.4.2 (562), which marks the claim of a successful war waged by the Caracol ruler Lord Water, which (as Arlen and Diane Chase originally suggested) may help explain both the dramatic increase in the size and prosperity of Caracol and the equally profound but opposite changes seen in the archaeological and historical record of Tikal.

If we assume that these events recorded at Caracol are accurate, then it is very likely that the defeat of Tikal resulted in the capture and sacrifice of Double Bird. It also appears to explain the destruction of many of the monuments of Tikal's rulers then on display in the Great Plaza. For although Tikal's ancient dynasty was presumably allowed to continue, it may have done so under tribute obligations to Caracol. It has been shown that of the several royal tombs in Tikal's North Acropolis dating to this interval that have been excavated, none is as elaborate as those from before and after Tikal's downfall. The rulers of Tikal during this Mid-Classic Hiatus, the 22nd through the 25th in the dynastic succession, may in fact have been prohibited from erecting monuments, and we may presume that much of the wealth formerly accumulated by Tikal's rulers was diverted as tribute to Caracol. If we follow this scenario further, we can postulate that Tikal's prestige and fortunes may have been suppressed for as long as 150 years, perhaps first by the successes of Caracol, then by competition from such other rising powers as the Petexbatun polity (discussed below). Regardless, the archaeological record at Tikal shows that population growth ground to a standstill during the Hiatus, and many of the households in the outlying areas resettled closer to the core of the site, presumably for greater security.

In the meantime, Lord Water ruled at Caracol for another 37 years, overseeing the initial stages of explosive growth that his city's newfound prosperity and power nourished. Lord Water was succeeded in 599 by his son Lord Kan I, who apparently continued his father's policies at home for some 19 years. He was followed on the throne by his brother, Lord Kan II, in 618. Caracol apparently continued to prosper, but Lord Kan II nonetheless chose to return to the aggressive policies of his father, Lord Water. In fact he exceeded them, and one of his first acts involved the huge polity to the north, Calakmul.

## Further Caracol Conflicts

On Caracol Stela 3, Lord Kan II recorded that in 619 he had performed an unidentified event "in the land of" a Calakmul *ahau*. The event was probably some sort of ritual that sealed an alliance with Calakmul, very likely to counter any threat that Calakmul, or even Tikal, might pose to the plans Caracol was contemplating. For shortly afterward, in 626, the Caracol texts record another external involvement, this time with a series of actions directed against a smaller polity, Naranjo (discussed further below). This site was probably an ally of, or subordinate to, Calakmul, for in 546, many years previously, the ruler of Naranjo had celebrated an important event "in the land of" the Calakmul ruler. Thus the event performed by Lord Kan II associated with Calakmul in 619 may have assured him of having a free hand to deal with Naranjo.

The record of Lord Kan II's actions is found both on Caracol Stela 3 and in the hieroglyphic text on a stairway erected at Naranjo by the Caracol king. The first move resulted in the apparent capture of an unidentified person from Naranjo, probably a high-status lord. A year later Lord Kan II recorded a ballgame at Caracol involving this captured lord, who was eventually to be sacrificed. And in 631 both Stela 3 and the Naranjo hieroglyphic stairway record the ominous "shell-star" over Naranjo glyphs, indicating defeat at the hands of Caracol and the sacrifice of at least one captive, presumably the Naranjo ruler. Although Naranjo was apparently reeling by this time, Lord Kan II let five years pass before delivering the final attack on his hapless victim. This "shell-star" war resulted in Lord Kan II's claim of taking another elite captive, named 18 Rabbit, who also was undoubtedly dispatched according to custom.

The details of the later history of Caracol are still being pieced together, but on the basis of their archaeological investigations, Diane and Arlen Chase report a decline at Caracol in the Late Classic, accompanied by the destruction of monuments. It would seem, then, that the successors of Lord Kan II eventually reaped the fruit of the violent policies they had for so long sown. Still, at the close of the Classic period Caracol apparently saw a resurgence of its external adventures, for a newly discovered inscription at the site claims success in the capture of a late Tikal king.

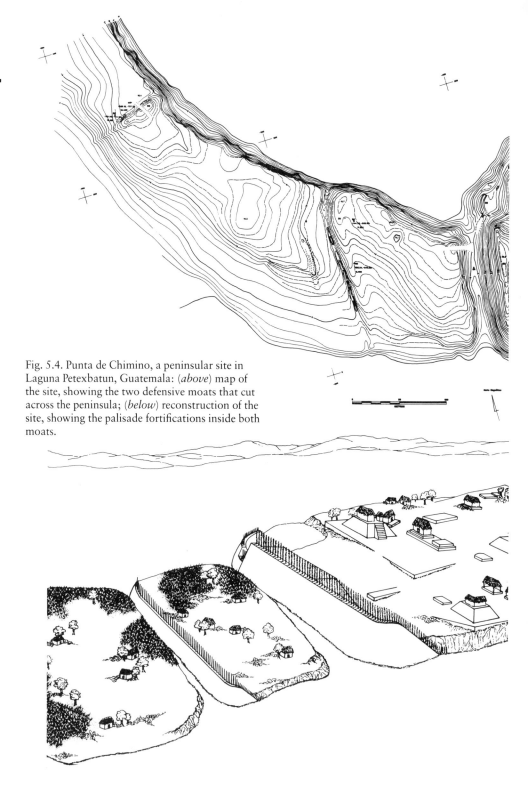

Fig. 5.4. Punta de Chimino, a peninsular site in Laguna Petexbatun, Guatemala: (*above*) map of the site, showing the two defensive moats that cut across the peninsula; (*below*) reconstruction of the site, showing the palisade fortifications inside both moats.

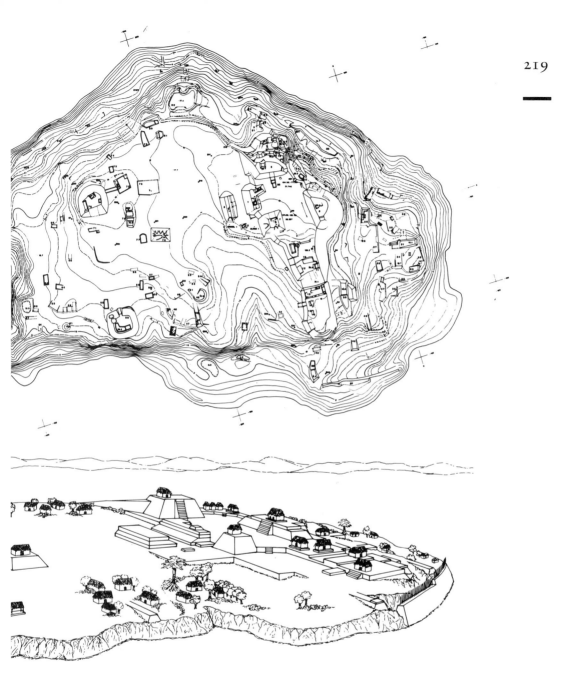

## The Rise of the Petexbatun

Recently available evidence indicates that another power, situated far to the south in the rain forests of the Petexbatun region, emerged in the Maya lowlands in the wake of Tikal's downfall. The Petexbatun region is part of a larger zone defined by the drainage of the Río Pasión, a tributary of the Usumacinta. The Pasión Zone is defined by particular varieties of ceramics and architecture and other distinctive characteristics. Peter Mathews and Gordon Willey have identified some 25 sites within the zone, and at least a dozen of these possessed their own emblem glyphs. Elsewhere in this book we will treat two of these: Altar de Sacrificios, on the margin between the Pasión and Usumacinta zones (see below), and Seibal, the largest site in the area (see Chapter 6), which enjoyed its peak of success somewhat later, in the Terminal Classic.

The Petexbatun region, so called after the lake of the same name, lies in the heart of the Pasión Zone. Lago Petexbatun drains northward to the Río Pasión. A peninsula jutting from the western shore of the lake is the setting for Punta de Chimino, a site heavily fortified by a series of moatlike ditches that were cut across the base of the peninsula in Late Classic times (Fig. 5.4). To the west of the lake basin a steep escarpment rises 60 to 80 m. Along this escarpment, from north to south, are three additional sites—Tamarindito, El Excavado, and Aguateca—and the important site of Dos Pilas is situated some 10 km to the west of Tamarindito.

The Petexbatun region has been the subject of a major investigation conducted under the direction of Arthur Demarest and a large team of archaeologists, epigraphers, and other specialists from Vanderbilt University and Guatemala. Much of our understanding of regional developments is due to this research, to the prior studies by Stephen Houston, Kevin Johnston, and Peter Mathews, and to the even earlier work by the Harvard University Seibal Project.

It was in this region that refugees from the royal lineage of Tikal, probably escaping the domination of Caracol, established a new polity in the Late Classic. The evidence for this deduction lies in their emblem glyph, which uses a bundle main sign essentially identical to that of Tikal, thus probably indicating descent from the same lineage. The texts indicate that the newly established royal lineage, while doubtless drawing on the traditional prestige of Tikal, embarked on an independent and aggressive course, playing an active role in lowland history by consolidating its local base of power, expanding its realm, and involving itself with the older polities to the north. In their career, the *ahauob* of the Petexbatun dynasty resided in at least two capitals in the Pasión Zone, first Dos Pilas and later Aguateca.

### THE PETEXBATUN CAPITALS: DOS PILAS AND AGUATECA

Dos Pilas (Fig. 5.5) consists of two clusters of monumental architecture, the Main and El Duende groups, within an area of little more than 1 km². The Main

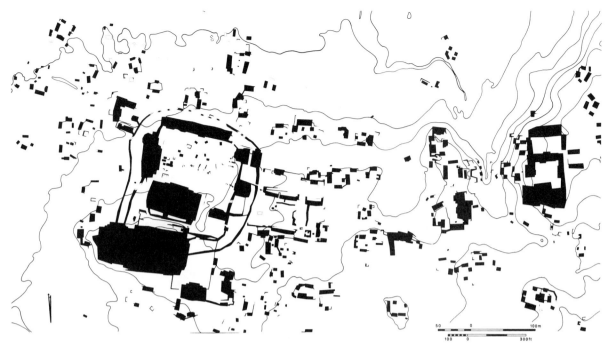

Fig. 5.5. Map of Dos Pilas, Guatemala; the Main Group is at the left, with the remains of the fortifications built during the site's final phase shown ringing the complex.

Group contains a large, open monument plaza bordered on all four sides by platforms and temples, at least two of which were reached by hieroglyphic stairways. Most of the known carved monuments at Dos Pilas are in this complex. South of this plaza is a series of smaller, elevated plazas flanked by palace-type buildings, these most likely the residential complex for the ruling dynasty. Another hieroglyphic stairway adorns the southeasternmost of these buildings. Smaller plazas and platforms surround the Main Group and fill at least a portion of the intervening area to the east, where the El Duende Group is located. Dominating El Duende is a monumental platform that crowns a natural hill and is flanked by terraces and smaller buildings. More carved stelae have been found in this complex. A series of concentric walls (Fig. 5.6) built at the very end of Dos Pilas's span as capital of the Petexbatun polity (and constructed with a rubble base and upper wooden palisade) surrounds both the Main Group and the El Duende Group.

The second Petexbatun "capital," Aguateca (Fig. 5.7), covers about half as much area as does Dos Pilas, but occupies one of the most spectacular settings of any lowland Maya site. It was constructed along the limestone escarpment, overlooking a shallow, swampy basin to the east (once perhaps part of a larger Lago Petexbatun, which is now several kilometers to the northeast of Aguateca). A chasm formed by a fault that runs some 100 m west of and parallel to the escarpment splits Aguateca into two areas. In the area west of the chasm is a large plaza surrounded by platforms and buildings, two of which (those on the western and southern sides)

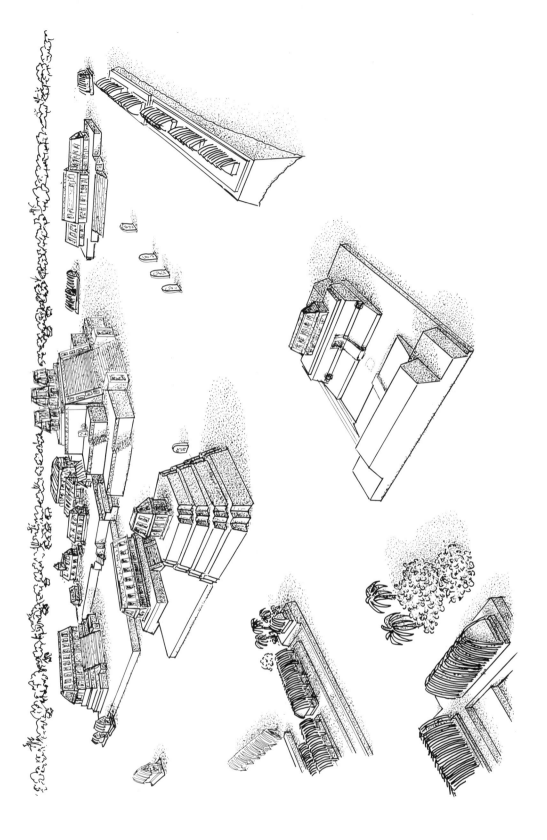

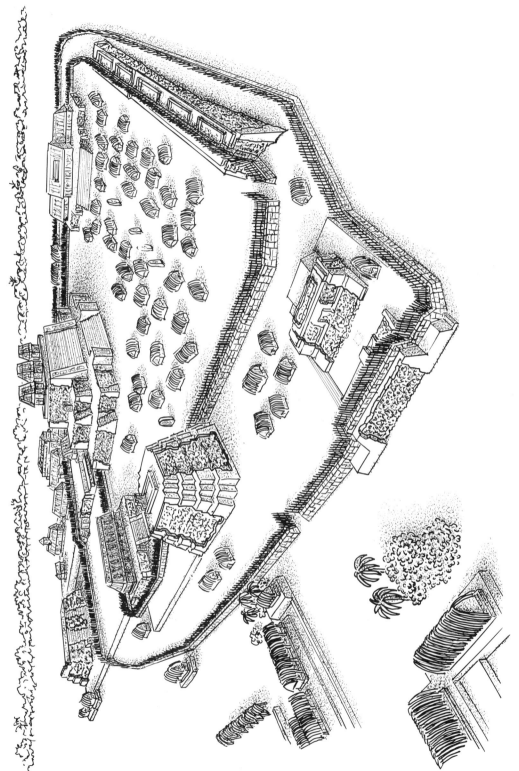

Fig. 5.6. Dos Pilas, Guatemala: (*above*) the Main Group from the northeast (note the ballcourt in the foreground); (*below*) the Main Group after construction of the rubble wall and palisaded fortifications, which used stone salvaged from the site's major structures.

Fig. 5.7. Map of Aguateca, Guatemala, a site situated along a spectacular escarpment: short hachures indicate the deep chasm separating the open plaza area to the west from the palace complex to the east; black lines indicate the remains of rubble walls and palisaded fortifications.

are the largest at the site. A natural limestone bridge over the fault connects this plaza to the eastern area, which is composed of a series of connecting plazas that spread to the north. The northernmost of these is an enclosed compound of palace-type buildings that was undoubtedly the residence of the ruling dynasty. The escarpment and its parallel chasm provide natural defensive barriers for this eastern complex, and a series of stone-based palisades apparently protected the more open western reaches of the site. As at Dos Pilas, Aguateca is surrounded by a series of walls built during the final period of the site's occupation (Fig. 5.8).

## The Petexbatun Expansion

There is hieroglyphic evidence of a local Early Classic ruling lineage in the Petexbatun region, with its capital at Tamarindito. The first known ruler from this family, Ruler A, was in power by 9.3.19.0.0 (A.D. 513). He was followed by at least two successors (Rulers B and C), the latter reigning until at least 9.9.0.0.0 (613). But in the Late Classic era this small polity fell prey to a new power that established itself at Dos Pilas.

The founder of the new polity, known as Ruler 1 (or "Flint Sky"), appears to have been inaugurated at Dos Pilas shortly before A.D. 647. As we have mentioned, the emblem glyph of this new ruling lineage is essentially that of Tikal, indicating that the lineage derived from that old and prestigious dynasty, probably after its mid-Classic setbacks. In any case, after investing the first katun of his reign consolidating his new kingdom, Ruler 1 would seem to have pursued higher ambitions, becoming one of the leading political figures in the Maya lowlands. He began these machinations by marrying a woman from Itzan, a center located on a tributary of the Río Pasión, about 25 km northwest of Dos Pilas. He also dispatched one of his daughters to Naranjo to revive that fallen polity (as we shall see below), and sent off another woman from his family to marry the ruler of El Chorro, a small center located on a minor tributary of the Usumacinta some 35 km northwest of Dos Pilas, presumably to secure an alliance with that polity as well.

A hieroglyphic stairway discovered at Dos Pilas in 1990 provides the most complete record of Ruler 1's external activity known thus far (Fig. 5.9). The texts left to us previously had allowed us to surmise that his conquests were local, involving smaller centers within the Petexbatun region, and that he may thereby have added some territory to his kingdom. But in the newest inscriptions is the claim that Dos Pilas was involved in a whole series of hostilities with Tikal, seemingly just as that ancient polity was recovering from its confrontation with Caracol. The text closes with the apparent culmination of the Tikal conflicts by recording claims for the capture and sacrifice of Shield Skull, the 26th ruler of Tikal, in 679. This new historical record affords us a whole new perspective on the origins of the Petexbatun dynasty and its Tikal connections, and opens the possibility that some of the de-

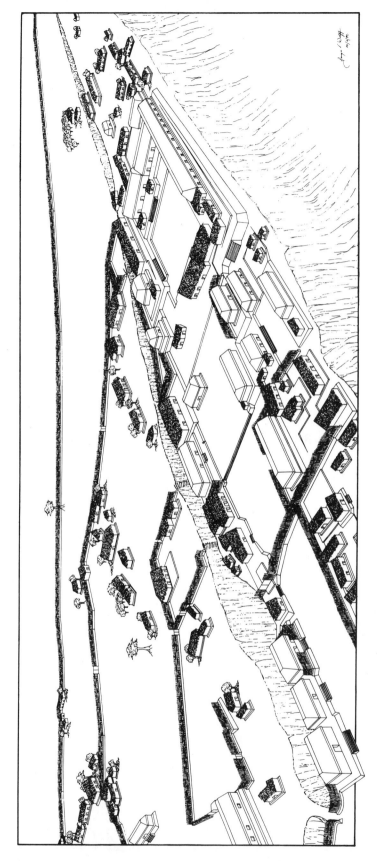

Fig. 5.8. Aguateca: (*above*) the palace complex from the southeast, showing the natural defenses formed by the escarpment and chasm, supplemented by rubble walls and palisaded fortifications; (*below*) the western group, across the chasm, showing the defensive palisades that restrict access via the natural bridges over the chasm.

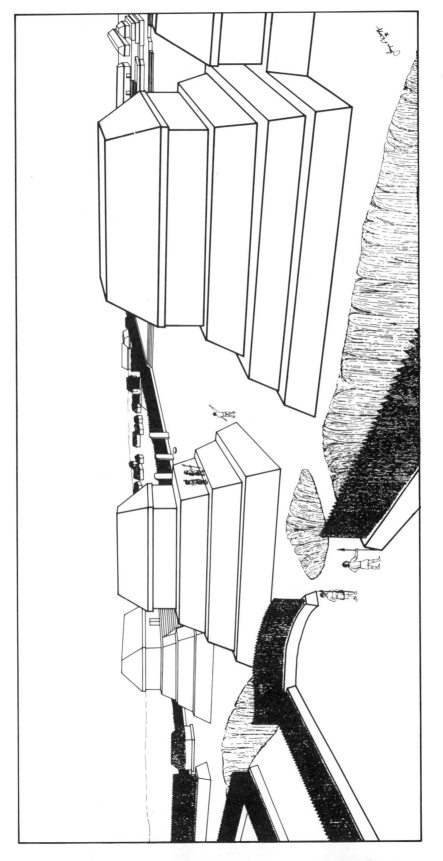

Fig. 5.9. Dos Pilas, Guatemala: excavation of the hieroglyphic stairway discovered in 1990; its text relates the conquests of Petexbatun Ruler 1, including his claim to have captured and sacrificed Shield Skull, the 26th ruler of Tikal.

struction of monuments at Tikal during the Hiatus period, especially those of Shield Skull, may have been promoted by Dos Pilas Ruler 1.

By allying himself with Jaguar Paw, the future ruler of the much larger and more powerful Calakmul polity, located far to the north, Ruler 1 was probably able to move beyond the Petexbatun sphere to challenge Tikal. The looted panels from the Dos Pilas hieroglyphic stairs mention Jaguar Paw several times, in one instance noting his birth (in 649) and in at least two others citing later rituals he conducted with Ruler 1 that may have cemented their alliance. The first ritual was at the city of Yaxha, and the second (in 683) was at Dos Pilas. Dos Pilas Ruler 1 was the older of the two, and already in power, and he appears to have held the superior position in the relationship, serving perhaps as a kind of ritual guardian or "sponsor," as is probably depicted on a looted pot that shows Jaguar Paw kneeling before the enthroned Dos Pilas ruler. When the 15-year-old Jaguar Paw was inaugurated as *k'ul ahau* of Calakmul in 666, Ruler 1 was apparently there to witness the event (as recorded on Dos Pilas Stela 13). This alliance apparently also involved a third polity, El Perú (located in the western lowlands, about midway between Dos Pilas and

Calakmul). Two looted monuments from El Perú record the accession of Jaguar Paw, and assert that the new Calakmul king witnessed the displaying of the manikin scepter by the El Perú ruler, Mahkina Balam.

In 698, Dos Pilas Ruler 1 was succeeded by his son, Ruler 2 ("Shield God K"), who began a series of campaigns that was to see the Petexbatun kingdom become the dominant military power in the southwestern lowlands. The wealth and prestige that accrued is reflected in the rapid expansion of Dos Pilas itself. Ruler 2 apparently sponsored the construction of the massive El Duende complex, and his successor, Ruler 3, who came to power in 727, continued the practice of employing both conquest and marriage alliances to further expand the polity's domain. Ruler 3 recorded that in 735 the ruler of Seibal (which is located to the east, on the banks of the Pasión) was captured and brought back to Dos Pilas for sacrifice. The Seibal king is portrayed beneath the feet of the victorious Petexbatun ruler on Aguateca Stela 2. A crucial alliance with the strategic site of Cancuen, located up the Pasión near the foothills of the highlands, some 55 km to the south, was sealed by Ruler 3's marriage to a woman from the Cancuen ruling family. This may have added a vast new territory to the Petexbatun polity, and almost certainly consolidated its control of the lucrative trade from the highlands.

Research at Dos Pilas in 1990 identified the palace, throne, and well-furnished tomb of Ruler 3's wife. A newly discovered carved panel from this palace depicts Ruler 3 and his wife witnessing a ritual bloodletting performed on their son and designated heir (the future Ruler 4). Also witnessing the event is an elite personage from Calakmul, presumably Ruler 4's "ritual guardian" (apparently a reciprocal arrangement, recalling the earlier "sponsorship" of Calakmul's ruler Jaguar Paw by Dos Pilas Ruler 1).

Ruler 4 came to the throne in 741. Evidence gathered thus far from both archaeological and textual sources indicates that the Petexbatun polity reached its maximum extent during his reign, controlling much of the territory between the Pasión and the Chixoy (the two major tributaries of the Usumacinta), an area estimated at some 4,000 km². But at its height, this powerful, expansionist state was suddenly brought to its knees. The inscriptions tell us that in 761 Ruler 4 was captured and sacrificed by his subordinates at Tamarindito. Excavations at Dos Pilas demonstrate that the concentric palisaded walls surrounding both the Main and El Duende groups were constructed at this same time, and that these defenses were hastily erected over the very symbols of the power of Dos Pilas (even over one of the hieroglyphic stairways recording the history and conquests of the Petexbatun dynasty), using stone ripped from its greatest buildings, including the royal palaces (Fig. 5.10). In the monument plaza inside the Main Group defenses, archaeologists have found the remnants and domestic debris of houses, dating to the same time period, that probably constituted the village occupied by the last defenders of Dos Pilas. Although further research remains to be done, a likely scenario would see

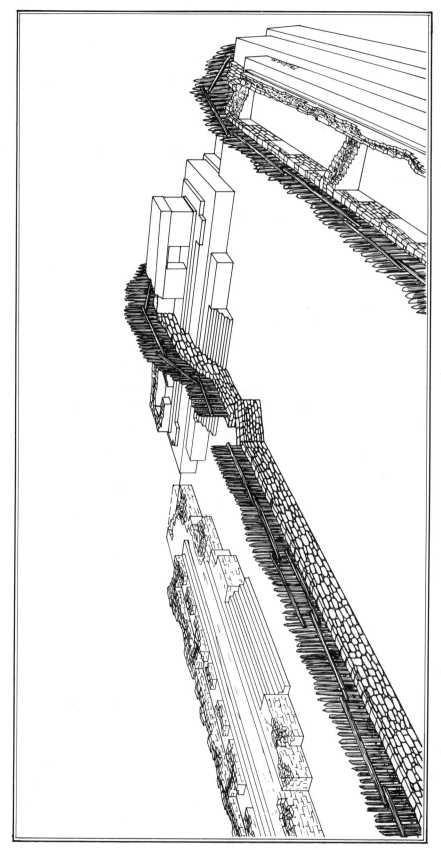

Fig. 5.10. Dos Pilas: reconstruction of the palisades in the Main Group, showing how buildings were partially demolished to provide stone for the defensive walls.

Ruler 4's sudden capture and demise leading to a widespread revolt by his former vassals, including the lords of Tamarindito, culminating in the siege of the royal capital. There was apparently time for the defenders to transform both the Main and El Duende groups into citadels by building a series of palisades, and for a time they may have held out against their attackers. Archaeologists have found several dozen chert spearheads in the area between the double walls. The concentric palisades that surround both groups (see Fig. 5.6) seem to have been constructed so as to concentrate and trap attackers in the area between the walls, leaving them easy targets for defenders stationed behind the inner palisade. Excavations have also found the buried skulls of decapitated young adult males in pits outside the walls—presumably sacrificed captives from the forces that attacked Dos Pilas. Despite such measures, it would appear that Dos Pilas was ultimately overrun and its defenders defeated. The lack of evidence of later occupation, especially the virtual absence of the Fine Orange pottery that is a signature of the years after ca. 800, indicates that Dos Pilas was abandoned after the siege.

After 761 the scene shifts to Aguateca, where there is evidence from both artifacts (including the presence of Fine Orange pottery) and hieroglyphic texts to indicate continued and even intensified occupation. Although the date of Aguateca's founding is not yet established, it was controlled by Dos Pilas before Ruler 4's downfall, as several stelae dedicated by Rulers 2 and 3 testify. But after the fall of Dos Pilas, it is reasonably certain that the Aguateca site, strategically placed and well defended, became the principal capital of the Petexbatun polity. The later monuments of Aguateca record the succession of Ruler 5, and indicate that the Petexbatun dynasty held out for at least another 40 years from their fortified capital. But it would appear that at some point during these years following the defeat of Dos Pilas, the former Petexbatun polity came to be divided among several competing and warlike ruling lineages, each established in a well-defended site.

The final decades of the Late Classic era were a time of ever-increasing warfare in the Petexbatun region, during which besieged populations attempted to defend their settlements and fields against rival polities—and, perhaps, from groups from the Gulf coast who were destined ultimately to dominate this and other areas during the subsequent Terminal Classic (see Chapter 6). In any case, over 4.5 km of palisades have been discovered in and around Aguateca, clearly constructed to defend the capital and its access to both water and prime agricultural areas. Extensive areas along the escarpment that runs north of Aguateca above the west side of Lago Petexbatun were fortified by walls, presumably to defend areas of terraced fields and thus to secure food supplies for the beleaguered population. Other fortified sites, ranging from walled agricultural villages to massive hilltop fortresses, have also been found in the region. Not surprisingly, excavations indicate a sharp decline in the standard of living for the people who lived in these besieged settlements.

The most dramatic example of these late-period defensive strongholds is Punta de Chimino. Excavations by the Vanderbilt project have dated the massive defensive constructions that isolate this Lago Petexbatun peninsula site from the mainland to the period after 761. Three parallel ditch-and-wall barriers defend the site from access by land. The innermost revetment is over 140 m long, with a ditch excavated some 15 m into bedrock to allow the waters of Lago Petexbatun to cut off the peninsula and transform Punta de Chimino into an island fortress (Fig. 5.4). On the east side of the island archaeologists have found a fortified installation that seems to be a canoe-landing area, along with adjacent deposits of imported obsidian and pottery. This evidence may reflect one reason for the huge investment of labor in Punta de Chimino's defense—control of canoe-borne commerce. Of course in times of siege, commerce was undoubtedly replaced by canoe-borne defense, and this too may explain the fortified landing area.

Evidence has been found of at least one attack against the ramparts of Punta de Chimino. The excavation of an area at the bottom of the innermost and deepest moat defined a large, burned area littered with both broken and intact chert spearheads. It is not yet clear if this attack succeeded, or for how long Punta de Chimino was able to hold out and remain secure behind its formidable defenses. But it would appear that this was the last stronghold of the old Petexbatun polity. After Punta de Chimino finally fell, probably shortly after A.D. 800, a new polity was established, with its capital at Seibal, presumably by those who ultimately emerged the victors in the long and violent struggle to control this region. The transition ushered in a new era in the Petexbatun and elsewhere in the Maya lowlands—a subject we will discuss in our next chapter.

## Resurgence in the Central Lowlands

Elsewhere in the lowlands the Late Classic saw an expansion of new polities, as well as the resurgence of former powers. One of these resurgent polities was Naranjo, a site whose inscriptions afford us far more information than have the results of archaeological investigations there.

### NARANJO

The site of Naranjo is about 12 km northeast of Laguna Yaxha in the eastern Peten, and about the same distance west of the Guatemalan-Belize border. The site was reported by Teobert Maler following his explorations in 1905. Later, Sylvanus Morley worked at the site, as part of his effort to record lowland Maya inscriptions. Our knowledge of the site today includes the results of a more recent survey led by Ian Graham. Naranjo contains impressive carved monuments and architectural remains. The main group, composed of several courtyard groups and an elevated northern group situated on a hilltop, lies along the western shore of an extensive *bajo* that still contains water today, at least in the rainy season. Naranjo's rather numerous carved monuments include 40 stelae, one altar, one lintel, and a hieroglyphic stairway. The dates on these monuments span the Late Classic period (9.8.0.0.0 to 9.19.10.0.0), and their texts record the achievements of a succession of rulers, including their interactions with other major lowland powers.

The available evidence indicates that, in 682, while Dos Pilas Ruler 1 was securing his alliance with Calakmul (and perhaps indirectly with El Perú), his daughter, Lady Wac Chanil Ahau ("Six Celestial Lord"), was sent to Naranjo to marry an unnamed local lord. It should be noted that this woman was originally identified by Tatiana Proskouriakoff as coming from Tikal, because of the bundle emblem glyph associated with her name in the Naranjo texts (an identification followed by subsequent scholars). But more recent research by Peter Mathews has identified the name of Lady Wac Chanil Ahau's father in these same texts as Ruler 1 of Dos Pilas (and has him sharing the same bundle emblem with Tikal). Though this identification warrants further testing, it allows the following provisional interpretation of events in the central lowlands.

The consequence of this arrival event apparently was so important in Naranjo's history that it was recorded repeatedly on later monuments. A ritual performed on this occasion, involving the dedication of a new temple at Naranjo, may have celebrated the symbolic revival of the royal lineage, the "ruling house of Naranjo," after its disastrous encounters with Caracol a half century earlier. These same later texts record the birth date (688) of Smoking Squirrel, who was destined to become ruler of Naranjo at the ripe old age of five (in 693). A series of monuments—most of which were erected in the plaza of Group C, a complex built on the eastern edge of the civic-ceremonial core of Naranjo—records the successes of Smoking Squirrel's reign, and each of these records was accompanied by a monument portraying Lady Wac Chanil Ahau. Thus, although Smoking Squirrel never mentions his parents, it is reasonable to accept Proskouriakoff's original conclusion that Lady Wac Chanil Ahau was his mother. This series of monuments pays homage both to her and to her royal pedigree from Dos Pilas and, more distantly, Tikal, thereby reinforcing Smoking Squirrel's own right to rule.

One uinal (a Maya "month" of 20 days) after the inauguration of Smoking Squirrel, a captive was taken in a raid against the site of Ucanal, perhaps as part of the rituals surrounding the accession of the new king. On the later Naranjo Stela 24, Lady Wac Chanil Ahau is shown standing on the body of the captive, named Kinich Cab (Fig. 5.11*a*). Five Maya months later another raid produced an Ucanal *ahau* named Shield Jaguar. And some nine years later this important captive is shown kneeling at the feet of an enthroned Smoking Squirrel on Stela 22 (Fig. 5.11*b*), the twin of Stela 24 (both were dedicated in 702). It was probably no ac-

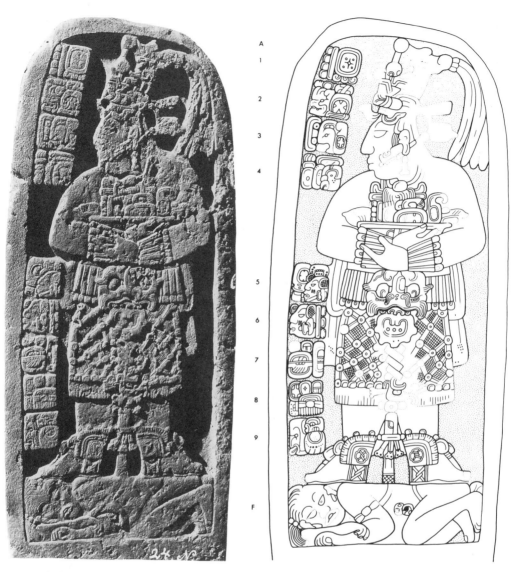

Fig. 5.11. Naranjo, Guatemala: Fig. 5.11a (*above*) photo and drawing of Stela 24, showing Lady Wac Chanil Ahau standing on the crumpled body of the captive Kinich Cab; Fig. 5.11b (*facing page*) Stela 22, showing the ruler Smoking Squirrel seated on an elaborate masked throne and holding a two-headed ceremonial bar, with Shield Jaguar, his captive, kneeling at his feet (both A.D. 702).

cident that Naranjo chose Ucanal as the place to reassert its power and prestige, for this site is situated to the south, immediately west of Caracol, and was probably an economic, if not political, ally of Naranjo's former nemesis. Significantly, the hieroglyphic stairway that Caracol erected at Naranjo after its victory was disassembled when Naranjo was revived under Lady Wac Chanil Ahau and Smoking

Squirrel. And one of these blocks was transported all the way to Ucanal and placed in that site's ballcourt (where it was discovered by Ian Graham), presumably as a fitting seal on the reversal of Naranjo's fortunes.

Once Smoking Squirrel reached adulthood, he embarked on a series of battles on his own, raiding sites in the Yaxha region in 710 and 711, as recorded on Stela 23. In 9.14.1.3.19 (713) he dedicated the last of the twin monuments to himself and Lady Wac Chanil Ahau, commemorating the first-katun anniversary of his inauguration and recalling yet again the date of his presumed mother's arrival, the event that marked the beginning of Naranjo's restoration. The success of the restoration is attested by the fact that a new dynastic continuity was established by Smoking Squirrel, for he was apparently able to ensure the succession of his son, Smoking Batab, in 755.

## The Expansion of Polities on the Usumacinta

To the west of the expansionist Petexbatun region, another string of important polities developed into vigorous and competing powers during the Late Classic. The centers of this region are arranged along the great Río Usumacinta and its tributaries, one of the most important trade and communication routes between the Maya highlands and lowlands. The Usumacinta rises in the western highlands, where it is known as the Río Negro or Río Chixoy. Flowing east, the Chixoy makes a great bend to the north, forming a great gorge through the ridges of the northern highlands as it makes its way toward the lowlands. There, joined by the Río Pasión, it becomes the Usumacinta for the rest of its northwesterly course to the Gulf of Mexico.

### ALTAR DE SACRIFICIOS

We begin with a center situated at the key junction of the Río Pasión and the Usumacinta. Sitting at this favorable location, the Classic-period rulers of Altar de Sacrificios must have enjoyed considerable benefits from the commerce that flowed up and down the two river systems, connecting southward to the highlands and northwestward to the Gulf coast. But they also lived in a dangerous world, and had to struggle to maintain their independence from their neighbors, among them the powerful polity that arose downriver at Yaxchilan, and then, even closer at hand, the aggressive Petexbatun state to the east.

From 1958 through 1963, Altar de Sacrificios was the subject of an archaeological research program from the Peabody Museum, Harvard University, led by A. Ledyard Smith and Gordon Willey. The Peabody excavations revealed a long sequence of occupation at the site, beginning with some of the earliest known settlement in the lowlands, established prior to that at Tikal and most other central-lowland centers. The evidence for the site's antiquity was provided by Xe pottery, probably associated with Mixe-Zoquean colonists from the west (see Chapter 3). Later in the Preclassic, there is evidence that Mayan-speaking peoples settled at Altar de Sacrificios. The site reached its peak of development in the Late Classic era, and although it was by then a fairly commanding polity, its architectural remains are neither large nor extensive. The dated monuments from Altar de Sacrificios span much of the Classic era, from 9.10.0.0.0 (A.D. 455) to 10.1.0.0.0 (849), although most are poorly preserved. The famous Altar Vase, discovered during the excavation of Str. A-III, commemorates a specific event in the center's dynastic history (see Chapter 15 and Fig. 15.19). Ceramic evidence indicates that outsiders, probably Putun Maya groups, occupied the site during the Terminal Classic, at about the time they also took control of Seibal (see Chapter 6).

### YAXCHILAN

This large and important center (Fig. 5.12) is located in the Usumacinta region about 80 km downriver from Altar de Sacrificios. Yaxchilan is well situated, occupying the southern bank of the Usumacinta, on the Mexican side of the river, at the top of a nearly closed loop. It is thus defended from landward approaches by a natural moat on all sides, except for a narrow waist of land to the south. From this secure base the kings of Yaxchilan ruled a powerful and independent polity, one that prospered throughout the Classic era.

Yaxchilan came to the attention of the outside world through the explorations of Désiré Charnay, who called the site "Lorillard City," and soon afterward through the surveys and recordings made by Alfred Maudslay and Teobert Maler. Maudslay referred to the site as Menché, but Maler later named it Yaxchilan. In more recent years Yaxchilan has been investigated by archaeologists from the Instituto Nacional de Antropología e Historia (INAH) of Mexico. This work has succeeded in consolidating and preserving at least the central portion of the site.

The site possesses impressive architectural remains. A great plaza bordered by palaces and temples extends along a terrace above the river. Above the plaza, a series of important buildings surmounts the higher terraces and hills to the south, overlooking both the river and the endless green expanse of lowland forest beyond. The exteriors of many of these buildings are elaborately decorated, but ever since Maudslay's first forays, the beautifully carved stone lintels above their doorways have been what made Yaxchilan justifiably famous. In fact, these sculptured lintels (Fig. 5.13), together with the carved stelae set in front of major buildings (Fig. 5.14), provide the primary record, in both text and image, for the full dynastic history of Yaxchilan. This history, first worked out by Proskouriakoff, has been extended in recent years by the studies pursued by Peter Mathews and other epigraphers and art historians. The most important sources for the early dynastic history are the inscriptions of Hieroglyphic Stairs 1 and a new lintel discovered in 1983 by the Mexican archaeologist Roberto Moll Garcia.

As at many other lowland sites, the texts commemorated by the later kings trace the origins of the royal dynasty—in Yaxchilan's case to a founding lord who ruled in the Early Classic (see Table 5.1). That lord, a ruler named Yat Balam ("Penis Jaguar"), was credited with founding the dynasty in 8.14.2.17.6 (A.D. 320), a date first recognized by David Stuart. Peter Mathews's research has outlined a succession of some ten rulers during the first three centuries following the accession of Yat

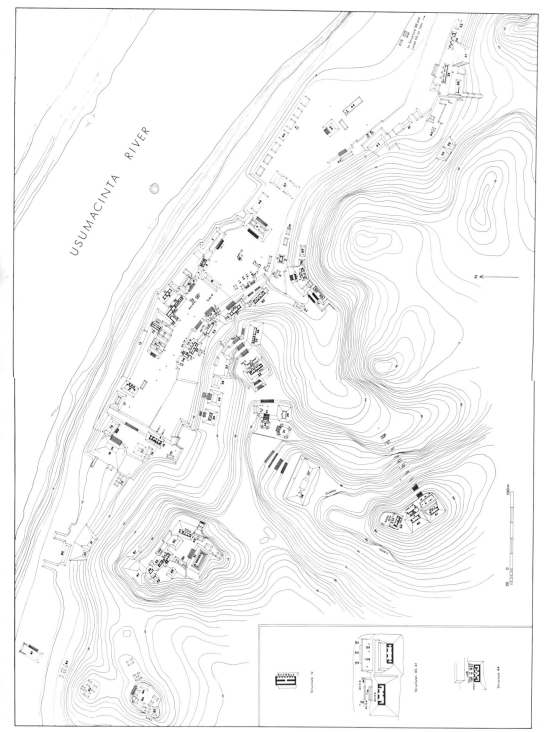

Fig. 5.12. Map of Yaxchilan, Chiapas, Mexico: the plazas and buildings of the site core are constructed on the terraces along the southern bank of the Río Usumacinta.

Balam. But as at other sites, Yaxchilan's early dynastic history is obscured by an incomplete historical record. Records of at least one of these early kings, the seventh successor, named Moon Skull, were preserved by a later ruler, Bird Jaguar III (the third and eighth successors had the same name glyphs), when a new building incorporated four of Moon Skull's carved lintels.

Yaxchilan prospered during the Early Classic. Though it grew slowly, it eventually became a major power in the Maya world, undoubtedly dominating the Usumacinta region, and forging important and lasting alliances with the ruling houses of its neighbors. The most significant of these alliances was with Piedras Negras (see below). The earliest known event in this relationship was a royal visit by the ninth Yaxchilan ruler, Knot Jaguar, to Piedras Negras, as recorded on Piedras Negras Lintel 12 (ca. 9.4.3.0.17, or A.D. 517). During the Early Classic, Yaxchilan also received royal visitors, both from Piedras Negras and from other polities, ranging from the mighty kingdom of Tikal to the much smaller center of Bonampak (see below). The tenth successor, named Tah Skull, apparently took the throne in 9.4.11.8.16 (526), but after his reign the record of numbered successors of Yat Balam becomes obscure.

The era of Yaxchilan's greatness becomes far clearer in the Late Classic, beginning with 6 Tun Bird Jaguar, who seems to have come to the throne in about 630, and who ruled until the accession of his son, Shield Jaguar II, in 681 (the second successor bore the same name). During the reign of 6 Tun Bird Jaguar, Yaxchilan seems to have been involved in a conflict with Palenque. An inscription on the steps of House C of the Palenque Palace refers to the *ahau* Pacal's capture in 654 of one Balam Te Chac, a Yaxchilan noble who was apparently Shield Jaguar's brother. At the time of this event Shield Jaguar was still a boy, although as Schele and Friedel have argued, the mention of Shield Jaguar in the Palenque text indicates that he was already an important figure, perhaps because he had been made the designated heir to the throne by this time.

It was during the reign of Shield Jaguar II and in that of his son, Bird Jaguar III, that Yaxchilan reached the peak of its power and prestige. Success in this case, like the success we have seen at other Maya sites, was due to a combination of longevity and aggressive policies toward neighboring polities. Covering an extraordinary reign recorded to have lasted some 61 years, Shield Jaguar II's monuments preserve a long list of captives taken in battle. Although we have no record of his birth date, Proskouriakoff's estimate of about 647 for this event would mean that Shield Jaguar II was in his nineties at his death in 9.15.10.17.14 (742). Near the end of his reign, when he would have been in his eighties, a new structure, Temple

Fig. 5.13 (*next three pages*). Drawings of the carved lintels from Yaxchilan Temple 23 (A.D. 726): Fig. 5.13*a* (*p. 240*) Lintel 24, showing the ruler Shield Jaguar and his wife, Lady Xoc, conducting a bloodletting ritual; Fig. 5.13*b* (*p. 241*) Lintel 25, showing Lady Xoc before the dynastic founder Yat Balam, who appears from the jaws of a two-headed serpent; Fig. 5.13*c* (*p. 242*) Lintel 26, showing the ruler Shield Jaguar preparing for battle, assisted by Lady Xoc.

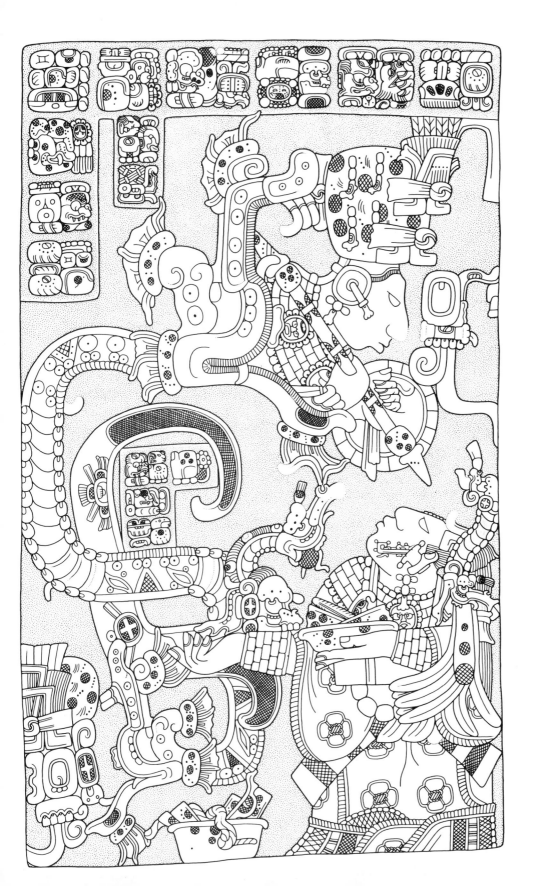

Fig. 5.14. Yaxchilan Stela 11: the ruler Bird Jaguar, wearing an elaborate deity mask, stands over three of his captives, probably before their sacrifice to sanctify his accession in A.D. 752; the figures in the upper register have been identified as his parents, Shield Jaguar and Lady Evening Star.

TABLE 5.1
Dynastic Chronology of Classic Yaxchilan

| Ruler (with *hel* position) | Long Count date | Date A.D. | Event |
|---|---|---|---|
| Penis Jaguar | 8.14.2.17.6? | 320 | Accession |
| Shield Jaguar I (2) | — | | |
| Bird Jaguar I (3) | 8.17.1.17.16 | 378 | Accession |
| Yax Antler Skull (4) | 8.17.13.3.8? | 389 | Accession |
| ? (5) | — | | |
| Tah Skull I (6) | — | | (Bird Jaguar of Bonampak acts at Yaxchilan) |
| Moon Skull (7) | 9.0.19.2.4 | 454 | "Palace event" |
| Bird Jaguar II (8) | — | | |
| Knot Jaguar (9) | 9.3.0.14.13 | 495 | |
| | 9.3.3.16.4 | 498 | |
| | 9.3.13.12.19 | 508 | Ah Balam, *ahau* of Jaguar Paw Skull of Tikal, acts at Yaxchilan |
| | 9.4.8.14.9 | 523 | Fish Fin of Bonampak acts at Yaxchilan |
| Tah Skull II (10) | 9.4.11.8.16 | 526 | Accession |
| | 9.5.2.10.6 | 537 | Event associated with Site Q |
| 6 Tun Bird Jaguar | 9.9.16.10.13 | 629 | Accession |
| | 9.10.14.13.0 | 647 | Capture of unidentified lord |
| | 9.11.16.2.8 | 668 | Celebrates ballgame |
| Shield Jaguar II | 9.11.18.15.1 | 671 | "Palace event" |
| | 9.12.8.14.1 | 680 | Capture of Ah Ahaua |
| | 9.12.9.8.1 | 681 | Accession |
| | 9.12.17.12.0 | 689 | Capture of Ah Zac |
| | 9.13.9.14.14 | 701 | |
| | 9.14.1.17.14 | 713 | Capture of Ah Kan |
| | 9.14.14.8.1 | 726 | Celebrates 25-tun anniversary |
| | 9.14.17.15.11 | 729 | Capture of Ah Chuen |
| | 9.15.0.12.0 | 732 | Capture of Na Cauac Manik |
| | 9.15.9.17.16 | 741 | Staff event |
| | 9.15.10.17.14 | 742 | Death |
| Bird Jaguar III | 9.16.0.13.17 | 752 | Captures Chac Cib Tok |
| | 9.16.0.14.5 | 752 | Birth of heir |
| | 9.16.1.0.0 | 752 | Accession |
| | 9.16.1.0.9 | 752 | |
| | 9.16.1.2.0 | 752 | |
| | 9.16.1.8.6 | 752 | Celebrates rituals |
| | 9.16.4.1.1 | 755 | Captures Jeweled Skull |
| | 9.16.6.0.0 | 757 | Celebrates 5-tun anniversary with heir |
| | 9.16.15.0.0 | 766 | |
| | 9.16.15.18.9 | 767 | Sacrifices Ek' Chan |
| | 9.16.16.1.6 | 767 | Celebrates rituals |
| Shield Jaguar III | 9.18.6.4.19 | 796 | |
| | 9.18.6.5.11 | 796 | |
| | 9.18.7.6.0 | 798 | Captures lords |
| | 9.18.7.16.9 | 798 | |
| | 9.18.8.10.12 | 799 | Celebrates rituals |
| | 9.18.9.9.14 | 800 | Captures a lord |
| | 9.18.9.10.10 | 800 | Captures Ahpo Pah |
| Tah Skull III | 9.18.17.12.6 | 808 | Captures Turtle Bat |
| | 9.18.17.13.10 | 808 | |
| | 9.18.17.13.14 | 808 | Celebrates rituals |

44, was dedicated to his prowess as a warrior and a taker of captives, although one might suppose that by this time his subordinates were shouldering most of that burden.

Shield Jaguar's career as a warrior began early, for there are several references to his capture of an important neighboring lord named Ah Ahau in 9.12.8.14.1 (680). This event, which occurred just before Shield Jaguar took the throne in 681, was probably undertaken to supply the customary human sacrifice to sanctify the new king's rites of accession. Years later this and other crucial events in his life were recalled in the famous lintels above the three doorways of Temple 23. This building, dedicated during the 45th year of Shield Jaguar's reign, in 9.14.14.13.17 (726), is located along the southern side of the great plaza that parallels and overlooks the Usumacinta. Lintel 24, over the left doorway, commemorates the birth of his son, Bird Jaguar III, in 9.13.17.12.10 (709) and shows Shield Jaguar II holding a great staff over his kneeling wife, Lady Xoc (also known as Lady Fist Fish), who is engaged in a ritual bloodletting by passing a thorned cord through her tongue (Fig. 5.13a). Lintel 25, above the central doorway, portrays Lady Xoc performing another ritual involving the materialization of an ancestral figure, probably the dynastic founder Yat Balam, from the jaws of a great serpent (Fig. 5.13b). Lintel 26, over the right doorway, depicts Shield Jaguar, dressed as a warrior and holding a large knife, as he prepares to venture forth to take captives for sacrifice, assisted by Lady Xoc (Fig. 5.13c).

Although Temple 23 prominently honors a noble lady, and although the lady was certainly Lady Xoc, Shield Jaguar's son and heir was not her son: on Stela 10 the new ruler, Bird Jaguar III, refers to his father as Shield Jaguar, but names his mother as Lady Evening Star, a royal woman from a foreign site, probably Calakmul. We can only presume that Shield Jaguar designated Bird Jaguar III as the royal heir either because his first wife, Lady Xoc, had no surviving sons, or because he needed to solidify an alliance with the foreign power that Lady Evening Star represented. Alternatively, there may have been a rival candidate, perhaps even a son of Lady Xoc, but since unsuccessful claimants to the throne are almost never mentioned in royal histories, it is not surprising that no record mentioning such a hypothetical personage survives. What we do have is a series of sculptures and texts that advance the case for Bird Jaguar III, as well as the record of an apparent hiatus of some ten years between the death of Shield Jaguar in 9.15.10.17.14 (742) and the accession of his son in 9.16.1.0.0 (752). From these facts we can surmise both an apparent need to document Bird Jaguar's legitimacy and the possibility of a power struggle following Shield Jaguar's death.

The available evidence indicates that Bird Jaguar spent the decade after his father's death consolidating his position. He led numerous raids from Yaxchilan, taking many captives, as is duly claimed on his later monuments. He married an important Yaxchilan woman, Lady Great Skull, and thereby undoubtedly gained the support of her elite lineage. Their marriage produced a son, born shortly before Bird Jaguar took the throne, who would ultimately become the next ruler of Yaxchilan.

Bird Jaguar III advertised his legitimacy as royal heir in both text and image on Stela 11 (Fig. 5.14). The text records his accession to the throne in 752, and the carved scene on one side of the monument shows Bird Jaguar standing over three captives he has taken for sacrifice. Above him are shown his deified parents, Shield Jaguar and Lady Evening Star. The other side of the stela depicts Bird Jaguar assisting his father in the performance of an important ritual, one that was apparently associated with the summer solstice, in 9.15.9.17.16 (741), a year before his father's death. Shield Jaguar had commemorated the same solstice rituals earlier in his reign by dedicating both Stela 16 and Temple 41 on the highest hilltop at Yaxchilan; Bird Jaguar placed his Stela 11 in front of a twin building, Temple 40, on the same hilltop, thus emphasizing the association and continuity between father and son.

Another example of this theme of continuity can be seen on a newly discovered stela found during the recent INAH investigations at Yaxchilan. It shows Bird Jaguar's mother, Lady Evening Star, performing the same tongue bloodletting ritual that Lady Xoc had conducted on Lintel 24 in Temple 23. This new stela was found in Temple 21, which Bird Jaguar constructed adjacent to Temple 23 and decorated with Lintels 15, 16, and 17. These lintels directly emulate the scenes his father had carved on the lintels of Temple 23. Temple 21 Lintel 17 depicts Bird Jaguar seated in front of one of his other wives, who performs the same tongue bloodletting ritual shown on Lintel 24 in Temple 23. Lintel 15 shows another of his wives in the same ancestral ritual as Lady Xoc performs on Lintel 25. (It should be pointed out that Houston and Stuart have identified the serpent on this lintel and similar serpents at Yaxchilan and elsewhere as *wayab*, or depictions of spirit companions; see Chapter 13). Lintel 16 parallels the warfare theme of Lintel 26, except that Bird Jaguar is shown with his captive, identified as Chac Cib Tok, who was undoubtedly destined to be sacrificed at the accession rituals.

Temple 21, one of at least six buildings flanking the great plaza paralleling the Río Usumacinta, was constructed by Bird Jaguar to proclaim the legitimacy of his right to rule at Yaxchilan. One of the most important of the other buildings is Temple 33; clearing its steps in 1974, archaeologists found that they were carved in a series of ballgame scenes, showing Bird Jaguar III with several of his illustrious captives bound into the form of the large ball used in the ballgame sacrifice ritual. One of these helpless victims is an enemy lord named Jeweled Skull. Above these carved steps on Temple 33 is Lintel 1, which shows Bird Jaguar at his accession dressed in the full regalia of a Maya king, displaying the manikin scepter, accompanied by his first wife, Lady Great Skull (Fig. 5.15a). The other two lintels in this building emphasize the other concerns of Bird Jaguar's reign: ensuring the succession of his son and securing the loyalty of the heads of secondary elite lineages, who are given the

Fig. 5.15. Drawings of the carved lintels from Yaxchilan Temple 33 (A.D. 756): Fig. 5.15*a* (*above*) Lintel 1, accession of the ruler Bird Jaguar, holding his manikin scepter, with his wife, Lady Great Skull, carrying a bundle; Fig. 5.15*b* (*p. 248*) Lintel 2, Bird Jaguar and his son and heir Chel Te (at left), both holding cross-shaped scepters decorated with birds; Fig. 5.15*c* (*p. 249*) Bird Jaguar with one of his subordinate lords, Ah Mac Kin Mo', both holding manikin scepters.

title *cahalob* (sing. *cahal*). Lintel 2 shows the king accompanied by his son and heir, Chel Te, who is assisting Bird Jaguar in a royal ritual (Fig. 5.15*b*). Lintel 3 shows Bird Jaguar holding the manikin scepter in still another ritual, this time assisted by one of his *cahalob*, who also was privileged to display a manikin scepter (Fig. 5.15*c*). In both cases, the figure of the king is larger and dominates the scene, but the depiction of the royal heir and a loyal subordinate, both of them alongside Bird

Jaguar, was obviously intended to increase the prestige of these individuals. Bird Jaguar's objective seems clear: to leave no doubt about who the next ruler will be and to flatter one of his *cahalob* and thereby cement his allegiance.

These twin concerns of course are related, for loyalty to the king also meant supporting his choice of successor. Thus, the later buildings of Bird Jaguar's reign repeat the themes first seen in Temple 33, in both text and image. These include Temple 1, located on a terrace at the base of a hill on the southeast side of the Great Plaza, and Temple 42, built on a hilltop to the west of the same plaza. Temple 1 was the setting for Lintel 8, a famous scene depicting Bird Jaguar in the act of capturing Jeweled Skull (Fig. 5.16). But in this sculpture he once again flatters one of his important subordinates, the *cahal* Kan Toc, by allowing him to be shown taking a captive alongside Bird Jaguar's own. The allegiance of another of his *cahalob*, in this case the ruler of the secondary center of La Pasadita (on the opposite bank of the Usumacinta, north of Yaxchilan), was commemorated by lintels that have been found at that site. On La Pasadita Lintel 1 we see the *cahal*, named Tilot, presiding with Bird Jaguar over a captive. On Lintel 2 Tilot is shown assisting Bird Jaguar as the latter conducts a scattering ritual on the 9.16.15.0.0 period ending (766). Finally, Lintel 3 depicts Tilot paying homage to Chel Te, the royal heir at Yaxchilan, who is seated on a royal throne.

As if to ensure the issue of his son's succession, Bird Jaguar used the same means to secure the loyalty of the lineage of his first wife, Lady Great Skull. On the last known sculpture of his reign, on Lintel 9 of Temple 2 (located adjacent to Temple 1), Bird Jaguar conducted the same solstice ritual commemorated on his accession monument, Stela 11. But this time, on the 27th anniversary of the celebration conducted with his father in 741, Bird Jaguar shared the event with his wife's brother, who, as the uncle of Chel Te, probably oversaw the accession of the royal heir after Bird Jaguar's death.

All in all, it would appear that in his efforts to proclaim his own legitimacy, to secure the royal succession for his son, and to strengthen the loyalty of his elite subordinates, Bird Jaguar sponsored the most ambitious building program in Yaxchilan's history. Not only did he reconstruct much of the central area of the site, but he expanded his capital upriver (to the southeast) with several new temples. In temples 54 and 55 his lintels portray Bird Jaguar, his wife, Lady Great Skull, and their son, Chel Te. In one of these depictions, on Lintel 52 of Temple 55, Bird Jaguar and his son appear together, both of them holding the symbol of royal office, the manikin scepter.

Bird Jaguar's prestige beyond the borders of Yaxchilan is attested by his participation in an important event at the site of Piedras Negras. A famous and beau-

tiful sculpture at Piedras Negras, Wall Panel 3 (Fig. 5.17), commemorates the ceremony held by Ruler 4 in 9.16.6.9.16 (757) in which he designated his son as royal heir. The scene shows Piedras Negras Ruler 4 seated on the royal throne above a group of *cahalob* seated below. To the right of the king stand an adult and three youths, one of which is the royal heir. To the left of the king stand three men, identified in the accompanying text as Yaxchilan lords, including the ruler Bird Jaguar. The Yaxchilan lords probably came to Piedras Negras to witness this crucial ritual precisely to ensure the orderly transmission of power, thus lending their prestige to what was almost surely a reciprocal obligation among the rulers of allied or friendly polities.

Fig. 5.16. Drawing of Yaxchilan Lintel 8 from Temple 1: the ruler Bird Jaguar captures the enemy lord Jeweled Skull, whose name glyph appears on his thigh; to the left, Bird Jaguar's subordinate lord Kan Toc takes another captive (A.D. 755).

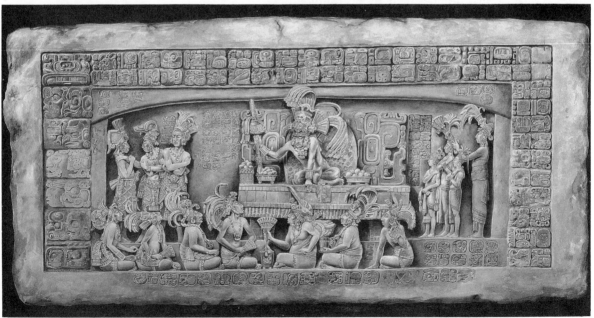

Fig. 5.17. Wall Panel 3 at Piedras Negras, northwesternmost Guatemala, commemorating the designation of the royal heir by Ruler 4 (shown seated on his throne) in A.D. 757; one of the three visiting lords on the left is probably Bird Jaguar of Yaxchilan; original (*above*) and restoration drawing by M. Louise Baker (*below*).

Bird Jaguar's efforts appear to have been successful, not only abroad but at home. For after Bird Jaguar's death, his son Chel Te, now referred to as Shield Jaguar III, took the throne, and the reign of Shield Jaguar III is marked by a continued emphasis on the histories of the Late Classic Yaxchilan rulers—references to a series of captures and ritual events. The last known ruler of Yaxchilan, Tah Skull III, seems to have come to the throne shortly after 800, but the record of his reign is brief, and the absence of texts beyond these references seems to be mute testimony to the downfall of the Yaxchilan ruling house early in the ninth century.

### BONAMPAK

This small center is situated on the east side of the valley of the Río Lacanha, about 30 km south of Yaxchilan. The site and its celebrated murals were reported to the outside world by Giles Healey in 1946. A subsequent reconnaissance conducted by the Carnegie Institution of Washington recorded the murals and other features of the site. The murals were photographed, and excellent color copies were painted by Antonio Tejeda and Agustín Villagra. Subsequent work conducted by INAH cleared the site and attempted to conserve the building and the murals within. The success of these efforts is yet to be determined, although there have been warnings that unless a concerted effort is made, both the buildings and the murals may disintegrate in the near future.

On the basis of the known dated inscriptions, there are only hints of Early Classic elite activity at Bonampak, a center that was undoubtedly heavily influenced by nearby Yaxchilan. Peter Mathews has identified, in the inscriptions of Yaxchilan, several early rulers of Bonampak: a Bird Jaguar of Bonampak is recorded in association with the sixth ruler of Yaxchilan, and a ruler designated Fish Fin is associated with Yaxchilan's ninth successor. This relationship between the two polities continued into the Late Classic. Mary Miller has pointed to the discovery of a sacbe leading from Bonampak to the northeast. Though its destination is unknown, it may lead to Yaxchilan. Knot-eye Jaguar, the father of the Bonampak ruler who commissioned the great murals, has been identified by Peter Mathews on a wall panel at the site of Lacanha, located on the western side of the river. (The Bonampak murals are further described and illustrated in Chapter 14).

The architectural core of Bonampak is composed of a massive acropolis, built over a natural ridge, that overlooks a large plaza flanked by smaller platforms and buildings (Fig. 5.18). Stelae 1 and 4 were set in the plaza, and stelae 2 and 3 are set flanking the acropolis stairway. Three of these (stelae 1–3) pertain to Chan Muan, the ruler identified as the protagonist in the murals. The remainder of the site is yet to be mapped, though there are reports of additional platforms in the surrounding forest and on the opposite side of the river. The murals are in Str. 1, a three-roomed building on the first terrace of the acropolis (Fig. 5.19).

The exterior of Str. 1 was decorated with stucco figures and reliefs, these now

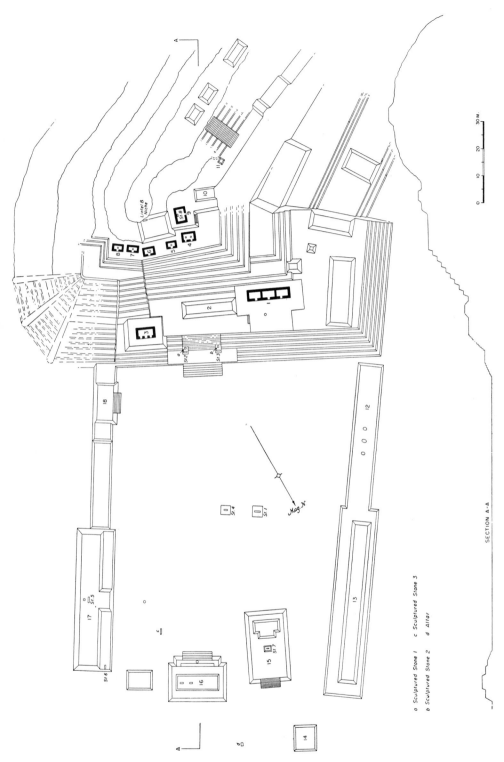

Fig. 5.18. Map of Bonampak, Chiapas, Mexico, showing the location of Str. 1, its three rooms decorated by the famous murals.

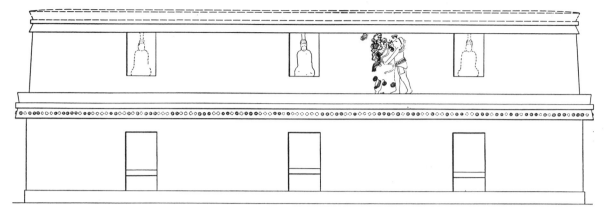

Fig. 5.19. Bonampak Str. 1: elevation drawing of the building façade.

largely gone. Lintels carved with texts and scenes of captive taking, depicted in a style similar to that employed at Yaxchilan, are set in each of the three doorways. According to the readings by Mathews, the earliest date (9.15.9.3.14; A.D. 740) is on Lintel 3, which names Chan Muan's father, Knot-eye Jaguar; Chan Muan seems to have come to power at Bonampak in 9.17.5.8.9 (776). Lintel 2 dates to later in Chan Muan's reign (9.17.16.3.8, or 787) and refers to someone from Yaxchilan, probably the ruler Shield Jaguar II; and the date on Lintel 1 is four days later.

The walls of all three rooms are covered with murals rendered in a vivid and skillful manner (Figs. 5.20–5.22). They record the designation of the heir to the throne, one of the most important royal rituals of the Maya. The heir commemorated in this case is Chan Muan's young son; and related events, which took place over a two-year period (790–792), are also shown. Although scholars have disagreed on the proper chronological sequence of the murals, the depicted events seem to flow from Room 1 through rooms 2 and 3. Low benches occupy most of the floor space in each room, and the murals were probably intended to be viewed from the vantage point of these benches.

The narrative begins in Room 1 (Fig. 5.20) with a Long Count date and hieroglyphic text that divide the upper and lower registers of the murals, the registers corresponding to the surfaces of vault and wall, respectively. The text is only partially preserved and has been only partially deciphered. The best reading for the Long Count date appears to be 9.18.0.3.4 (790), as originally read by Eric Thompson. This date probably refers to the initial event depicted in the upper register, the presentation of the royal heir to the assembled court, fourteen lords dressed in long white mantles. The first scene is within a palace, although its location cannot be determined. Two seated figures, probably Chan Muan and his wife, the mother of the heir, watch from a large throne or dais (west wall).

A second date in the text probably refers to an event 336 days later. Three lords are shown preparing for this ceremony; one of them, the frontally portrayed figure wearing the largest feathered headdress, is also probably Chan Muan (north wall, upper register). The culminating ceremonial procession is displayed on the lower register of the room, complete with elaborately costumed members of the court and nine musicians playing gourd rattles, a wooden drum, and turtleshells. The same three lords are shown dancing in the center of the procession (south wall). Many of the other attending lords are identified by the title of *cahal* (or *sahal*), which connotes their position as secondary rulers.

Room 2 (Fig. 5.21) is filled with one of the true masterpieces of Maya art, a vivid and dynamic battle scene that covers the walls and vaults of all but the north side of the room. The confusion and horror of hand-to-hand combat is brilliantly depicted, although the scene has suffered damage that obscures many of the details. Spears are thrust and thrown, one penetrates the forehead of a warrior, prisoners are pulled down by their hair, and pairs of victors combine to overwhelm single enemy warriors. At the focus of the scene stands the war leader, standing full front and grasping a captive by the hair while holding in his other hand a thrusting spear decorated by a jaguar pelt (south wall, upper register). This figure, identified as Chan Muan, is accompanied by another elite warrior who may be an allied ruler (possibly Shield Jaguar II from Yaxchilan?); both wear jaguar tunics and elaborate headdresses, and each is protected by an entourage of elite warriors.

The aftermath of the battle is presented on the north wall. Here the full-front figure holding his jaguar-pelted spear—again probably Chan Muan, accompanied by his warrior allies and his entourage, along with two women at the far right—stands on the summit of a platform to preside over the captives taken in the battle. The principal captive sits at Chan Muan's feet, while the rest of the prisoners are displayed on the six steps of the platform, where they are tortured and bled from their fingernails, all the while held and guarded by additional victorious warriors. These are the captives who will be sacrificed to sanctify the heir-designation rituals; one sprawled figure may already be dead, and the severed head of another defeated warrior has already been placed on the steps.

The murals in Room 3 (Fig. 5.22) have suffered the most damage. Nonetheless, it is clear that they depict a great ceremony, probably the one that culminates the sequence of events commemorated in rooms 1 and 2. The ceremony seems to be divided into two parts. The first is a display of elaborately costumed royalty on a stepped pyramid with a procession of dancers and musicians below. The second, in a more private setting inside a palace, includes the ruler Chan Muan, standing with his noble entourage, and the royal family, seated on a dais like that seen in Room 1. In this last scene the royal family performs a bloodletting ritual to complete and seal the heir-designation ritual cycle.

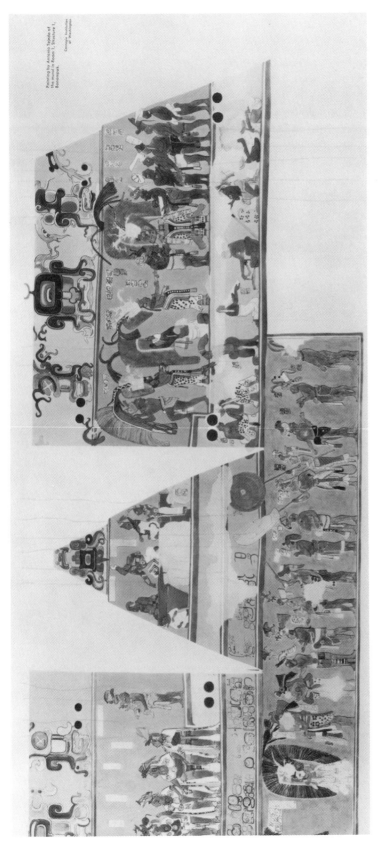

Painting by Antonio Tejeda of
the mural in Room 1, Structure 1,
Bonampak

Carnegie Institution
of Washington

Fig. 5.20. Bonampak Str. 1, Room 1 murals: rituals celebrating the designation of the royal heir of the ruler Chan Muan (restoration drawing by Antonio Tejeda).

Fig. 5.21. Bonampak Str. 1, Room 2 murals: the battle scene (*above*) followed by the presentation of the captives (*below*) to ruler Chan Muan (restoration drawing by Antonio Tejeda; see also Fig. 14.30).

Fig. 5.22. Bonampak Str. 1, Room 3 murals: final rituals and dances (*above*) and (*below*) the royal family seated on a dais (restoration drawing by Antonio Tejeda).

## PIEDRAS NEGRAS

Piedras Negras, located on the north bank of the Usumacinta some 40 km downriver from Yaxchilan, was investigated by an archaeological project from the University Museum of the University of Pennsylvania from 1931 to 1939, under the direction of J. Alden Mason and Linton Satterthwaite. Their findings revealed vital new information about variation in Maya architecture, including the fact that many of its often badly deteriorated structures were built without masonry vaults and were probably roofed by beam and thatch. But Piedras Negras is perhaps best known, and justly so, for its excellent sculpture, which culminated, in the opinion of most, in Wall Panel 3 from Temple O-13 (see Fig. 5.17).

Piedras Negras enjoyed a long history of independent rule over its surrounding polity. The beautifully sculptured inscriptions and monuments detailing the political history of its rulers provided the key evidence in the discovery that Maya texts dealt with political history. From 9.8.15.0.0 to 9.19.0.0.0 (608 to 810), each of the 22 consecutive hotun (1,800-day) period endings was celebrated by the erection of a sculptured monument, and every monument has survived. This unbroken series of stelae was the foundation for the breakthrough made by Tatiana Proskouriakoff. She noted that the sequence of dated stelae formed at least six groups, each of which began with a monument depicting a male figure seated in an elevated niche, usually with an older female figure below (Fig. 5.23). This motif was associated with a date and an event glyph that could be read as "accession to power." Thus, Proskouriakoff concluded, the text paralleled the scene on these initial monuments, recording both the inauguration of the new ruler and the participation of the female line in the ceremony, so as to ensure the dynastic succession. The later monuments in each group usually commemorated the successive five-tun (five-year) periods of the ruler's reign. Proskouriakoff identified other "event" glyphs in the Piedras Negras inscriptions as well, including those for birth and death. The span of any one of the monument groups does not exceed a normal human lifetime, and the sequence of Piedras Negras rulers worked out by Proskouriakoff represents reigns of 35, 47, 42, 28, 5, and 17 years.

The early dynastic history at Piedras Negras is poorly known. The earliest dated monument is Lintel 12 at 9.3.19.12.12 (A.D. 514), and there is prior reference to the Piedras Negras emblem glyph's being associated with the seventh ruler at Yaxchilan. Matters are a bit more clear in the Late Classic, and the sequence of numbered ruling lords first worked out by Proskouriakoff is still felt to be generally valid, although a seventh ruler has been identified. Ruler 1 took the throne in 603 (9.8.10.6.16) and commemorated a series of events until his death in 639 (9.10.6.2.1). Ruler 2 was born in 626 (9.9.13.4.1) and acceded to power 39 days after Ruler 1's death. Ruler 2, who celebrated a long and active reign with a series of monuments that record at least two wars with unidentified enemies, died in 686 (9.12.14.10.14) and was succeeded by Ruler 3 in 687 (9.12.14.13.1). Ruler 3, who

Fig. 5.23. Series of niched stelae that commemorate ruler accession at Piedras Negras, Guatemala: (*upper left*) Stela 25 (Ruler 1), A.D. 603; (*lower left*) Stela 6 (Ruler 3), A.D. 687; (*above left*) Stela 11 (Ruler 4), A.D. 729; (*above right*) Stela 14 (Ruler 5), A.D. 758 (note the portrait of the maternal figure below the niche).

was born in 665 (9.11.12.7.2), also lived a long life, celebrating his 3-katun anniversary in 724 (9.14.12.7.2), although he must have died about five years later. Ruler 4 was born in 701 (9.13.9.14.15) and took the throne in 729 (9.14.18.3.13).

As we have seen, the designation of the royal heir of Ruler 4 at Piedras Negras appears to have been witnessed by a ceremonial visit from Yaxchilan in 757; the ritual that Bird Jaguar III and his entourage apparently participated in is commemorated by the beautiful Wall Panel 3 (Fig. 5.17). Piedras Negras Ruler 4 died 40 days later (9.16.6.11.17), and the heir-designate, Ruler 5, took the throne in 758 (9.16.6.17.17). We do not know much about his short reign, or even his date of death. Ruler 6 acceded to the throne in 763 (9.16.12.10.8), but the rest of his reign, too, is unknown, as is the date his successor came to the throne. Ruler 7, however, did mark several warfare events, including one at 9.17.9.5.1 (780), and a successful campaign against the smaller site of Pomona in 787 (9.17.16.14.19). The final dates in the Piedras Negras dynastic sequence belong to Ruler 7's reign: his 46th-tun anniversary, in 795 (9.18.4.16.7), and the last known date at the 9.18.5.0.0 period ending (795).

## The Revitalization of Tikal

Now that we have reviewed events in the southwest, we can return to the central Peten and trace Tikal's rising fortunes in the Late Classic era. We have seen how Tikal's fortunes were dashed in the years following Caracol's claims of victory over Double Bird, the 21st successor of Tikal's founder, Yax Moch Xoc (Table 5.2). There is relatively little archaeological trace of the succeeding four rulers, and practically no historical record of their reigns, since, evidently, they were unable to erect monuments. These Tikal rulers did sponsor limited construction during this hiatus, in both the North Acropolis and the East Court. Str. 5D-34-1st was built over the tomb of Double Bird's successor (Burial 195). Two tombs were intruded into Str. 5D-33-3rd, the funerary shrine of Stormy Sky, Tikal's greatest Early Classic ruler, and a splendid new version of this building, Str. 5D-33-2nd, decorated by fantastic *witz* (sacred mountain) masks, was constructed (see Chapter 4). The first of these tombs, Burial 23, was identified by Clemency Coggins as containing the remains of the 25th successor, named Shield Skull. Linda Schele has pointed out that the painted ceramic dishes from the other tomb, Burial 24, seem to provide the name of both Shield Skull's father, the presumed 24th ruler, and grandfather, apparently the 23rd. No other trace of the 23rd ruler has been found.

But Tikal's fortunes rose dramatically after the accession of the 26th ruler, originally designated Ruler A and now often named Ah Cacau, which occurred in 682 (9.12.9.17.16). Christopher Jones has pointed out that the long inscription on one of the wooden lintels of Temple I, as well as the texts on the carved bones from the tomb of Ah Cacau, name his father as Shield Skull, whose position as prior ruler

TABLE 5.2
Dynastic Chronology of Classic Tikal

| Ruler (with *hel* position) | Long Count date | Date A.D. | Event |
|---|---|---|---|
| Yax Moch Xoc | | | "Founder" |
| Scroll Ahau Jaguar | 8.12.14.1.15 | 292 | Unknown event |
| Great Jaguar Paw I (?) | 8.14.0.0.0 | 317 | |
| Moon Zero Bird | 8.14.3.1.12 | 320 | Accession |
| Great Jaguar Paw II (9) | 8.17.0.0.0 | 376 | Celebrated katun ending |
| | 8.17.1.4.12 | 378 | Smoking Frog at Uaxactun |
| Curl Nose (10) | 8.17.2.16.17 | 379 | Accession |
| | | ca. 392 | Conquest (?) of Río Azul |
| | 8.18.0.0.0 | 396 | Celebrated katun ending |
| Stormy Sky (11) | 8.18.15.11.0 | 411 | Accession (?) |
| | 9.0.10.0.0 | 445 | Dedicated Stela 31 |
| | 9.1.1.10.10 | 457 | Death (?) |
| Kan Boar (12) | 9.2.0.0.0 | 475 | Celebrated katun ending |
| Mahkina Chan (13)? | — | | |
| Jaguar Paw Skull (14) | 9.2.13.0.0 | 488 | |
| (Rulers 15–18) | 9.3.2.0.0 | 497 | |
| | 9.4.0.0.0 | 514 | |
| | 9.4.3.0.0 | 517 | |
| Curl Head (19) | 9.4.13.0.0 | 527 | |
| | 9.5.4.5.16 | 538 | |
| (Ruler 20) | — | | |
| Double Bird (21) | 9.5.3.9.15 | 537 | |
| | 9.6.2.1.1 | 556 | Conflict with Caracol |
| | 9.6.8.4.2 | 562 | Capture and sacrifice by Caracol (?) |
| (Rulers 22–24) | — | | |
| Shield Skull (25) | — | | Conflict with Dos Pilas |
| | — | (679) | Capture and sacrifice by Dos Pilas |
| Ah Cacau (26) | 9.12.9.17.16 | 682 | Accession |
| | 9.13.0.0.0 | 692 | Celebrated katun ending |
| | 9.13.3.7.18 | 695 | Capture of Jaguar Paw of Calakmul |
| | 9.14.0.0.0 | 711 | Celebrated katun ending |
| | 9.14.11.17.3 | 723 | Death (?) |
| Yax Kin (27) | 9.15.3.6.8 | 734 | Accession |
| | 9.15.10.0.0 | 741 | Dedication of Temple I |
| | 9.16.0.0.0 | 751 | Celebrated katun ending |
| (Ruler 28) | — | | |
| Chitam (29) | 9.16.17.16.4 | 768 | Accession |
| | 9.17.0.0.0 | 771 | Celebrated katun ending |
| | 9.18.0.0.0 | 790 | Celebrated katun ending |
| (Latest rulers) | 9.19.0.0.0 | 810 | |
| | 10.2.0.0.0 | 869 | |
| | 10.3.0.0.0 | 889 | |

of Tikal is shown by the use of the Tikal emblem glyph. Coggins has proposed that the date of Ah Cacau's inauguration was chosen so as to occur precisely thirteen katuns (256 years) after the succession of Stormy Sky, and thus to commemorate the completion of one round of katuns and the beginning of a new era of prosperity for the polity. Throughout his reign, Ah Cacau's efforts to renew Tikal's prestige and power seem consciously associated with his illustrious ancestor and the first great period of Tikal's history. This phenomenon is known as cultural revitalization, whereby the lagging fortunes of a society are rebuilt by efforts to recall and duplicate past glories.

The most explicit example of Ah Cacau's homage to Stormy Sky was the construction of Str. 5D-33-1st, which covered and sealed both versions of his ancestor's great funerary temple and his great monument, Stela 31. As we have seen, it probably also sealed the tomb of Ah Cacau's father, Shield Skull, and perhaps that of his grandfather as well. In any case, before the new temple was constructed, Stela 31 was carefully placed inside the rear room of Str. 5D-33-2nd together with offerings that were probably used in the termination rituals for both the temple and the monument. The architecture for the new temple was innovative and probably served as a prototype for Ah Cacau's own funerary shrine, Temple I, as demonstrated by its great height and its use of multiple terraces. Unfortunately, the temple was poorly constructed, probably in response to efforts to hasten its completion and ensure its timely dedication. Ah Cacau also apparently directed the reburial of the shattered remains of Stela 26, which had been dedicated by another of his ancestors, Jaguar Paw Skull, within a new bench placed inside Temple 5D-34-1st, the funerary shrine of Curl Nose.

The new temple built by Ah Cacau, 5D-33-1st, was positioned in the very center of the south face of the North Acropolis, thus blocking the former entrances to the complex and effectively sealing off and terminating this traditional necropolis of Tikal's rulers. Thus, Ah Cacau's efforts in the North Acropolis not only paid homage to his ancestors, but also paved the way for a new beginning for himself and the future of Tikal.

Ah Cacau's program of revitalization also included a return to the traditional ceremonies associated with katun endings, ceremonies that had regularly punctuated the reigns of Stormy Sky and Tikal's other Early Classic rulers. This reversion is manifested by the construction of twin-pyramid groups dedicated to the commemoration of katun endings. A study by Chris Jones indicates that three such groups were built before Ah Cacau's reign. But it was during Ah Cacau's rule and thereafter that the twin-pyramid groups were used as settings for carved katun-ending monuments. According to Coggins, the public katun-ending rituals held in these groups reflected the heritage of the Tikal dynasty.

The first katun ending of Ah Cacau's rule was marked by Twin Pyramid Group 3D-1, situated in Group H, 1 km north of the Great Plaza. Group 3D-1 was razed by later construction, but its monuments have survived. Stela 30 retains its portrait of Ah Cacau, rendered in the traditional profile style; apparently modeled after the portrait of Double Bird on Stela 17 (Fig. 4.42), this depiction of Ah Cacau wears a necklace of large spherical jade beads and holds an elaborate staff in the crook of his arm (Fig. 5.24a). The companion Altar 14 bears a giant 8-*ahau* glyph (Fig. 5.24b), naming the current katun, and a Long Count date of 9.13.0.0.0, corre-

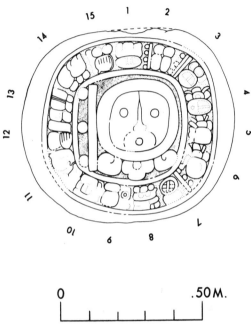

Fig. 5.24. Monuments from the razed Twin Pyramid Group 3D-1 at Tikal (A.D. 692): Fig. 5.24a (*left*) Stela 30, showing the ruler Ah Cacau holding an elaborate staff; Fig. 5.24b (*right*) its companion Altar 14, with a central giant *ahau* (day) glyph in the style associated with Caracol (see Fig. 5.3).

sponding to March 18, A.D. 692, nearly ten years after his accession to power. It is interesting to note that the giant *ahau* on Altar 14 is rendered in the Caracol style (see the discussion of Caracol Altar 21, above). It would appear that Ah Cacau was sufficiently confident of his own destiny to have his first monuments pair the traditions of Tikal's sculpture with those of its nemesis.

Having restored the destiny of his dynasty by renewed construction and new monuments, Ah Cacau next moved to reestablish the prestige and power of Tikal in a wider arena. The traditional means to accomplish this was to strike at another polity to secure captives; in this case, the captives would have been used for the dedication of his new monuments. But Ah Cacau took an especially bold step, one that left no doubt that Tikal was reclaiming its paramount position. If the record reflects actual events and not propaganda, his move must have sent shock waves throughout the Maya world, for the carved wooden lintels of Temple I declare that in 695 (9.13.3.7.18) Ah Cacau raided the powerful state of Calakmul and took its ruler, Jaguar Paw, captive. The date of this event was apparently not fixed by the usual celestial portents, but chosen as another link between Ah Cacau's destiny and that of Stormy Sky, for the action against Calakmul falls on the thirteenth katun anniversary of the last date on Stormy Sky's Stela 31 (which may also have been associated with a war event).

The captives from this battle with Calakmul were displayed at Tikal, according to the remains of a modeled stucco rendering of the event (Fig. 5.25) excavated from Str. 5D-57 in the Central Acropolis, Tikal's royal residential and administrative complex. The rendering shows Ah Cacau dressed in his war costume, holding one of the seated captives, named Ah Bolon Bakin, by the rope that binds his arms behind his back. The accompanying text dates the display at "13 days after" (the capture) and describes the captive as "being adorned" (for sacrifice). The Temple I lintels record a dedication held two uinals (40 days) after the battle, at which we can presume Jaguar Paw and Ah Bolon Bakin were sacrificed. Although these records do not identify what was dedicated, it is likely that it was Temple 5D-33-1st, the centerpiece of Ah Cacau's revitalization plan.

Given that it seems likely Calakmul was Tikal's greatest rival, this triumph was the key to Ah Cacau's newfound success. Alliance with, and support from, Calakmul would certainly help explain how smaller polities such as Caracol and the Petexbatun capitals were able to successfully challenge and even defeat Tikal in the first place. Thus, Ah Cacau's victory over Calakmul probably served to revenge these earlier humiliations and restored Tikal's prestige and power.

The next katun ending, 9.14.0.0.0 (711), was commemorated by Twin Pyramid Group 5D-1, located to the west of the Great Plaza, adjacent to the Tozzer Causeway and near the base of Temple IV. In the remains of the enclosure are Stela 16, bearing its portrait of Ah Cacau (Fig. 4.19), and Altar 5, whose text and sculptured scene may refer to the death of his wife or another important woman from the ruling dynasty.

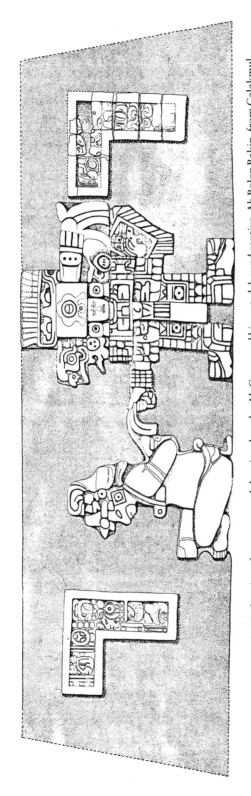

Fig. 5.25. Tikal Str. 5D-57: drawing of a stucco panel showing the ruler Ah Cacau and his seated, bound captive, Ah Bolon Bakin, from Calakmul. The defeat of Calakmul, undoubtedly Tikal's most powerful adversary, may have sparked the revitalization of Tikal's fortunes during the reign of Ah Cacau.

The carved wooden lintels of Temple IV, dated at 9.15.10.0.0 (741), offer elaborate portraits of the ruler (Fig. 4.20), and bear the name glyphs of both the ruler and his father, who is noted as having lived into his fourth katun (and was thus between 60 and 80 years old). The exact date of Ah Cacau's death is not known, but it was apparently between 721 and 734. One of the carved bones in his tomb bears the date 9.14.11.17.3 (723), which may refer to his death.

The tomb of Ah Cacau, over which was built his spectacular funerary shrine, Temple I (Figs. 4.13 and 4.15), was sumptuously furnished with jadeite, shell, pottery, and beautiful works of art, all of these testimony to Tikal's renewed vigor and prosperity (Fig. 4.16). Jade ornaments, dominated by a huge necklace of large spherical beads just as we see in his carved portraits, once covered his body. Included in the burial offerings were an exquisite jade mosaic vase (see Fig. 15.40) and a set of beautifully engraved and carved bones, one of which carries inscribed references to the emblems of Copan, Palenque, and two other centers. There are also references to further raids conducted during Ah Cacau's reign, for another of these carved bones is adorned with the famous portrait of a noble captive named Ox Ha Te Ixil. There are also scenes of Ah Cacau in the company of the gods of Xibalba, being conducted by canoe to the watery underworld (Fig. 11.6). Other bones give Ah Cacau's name glyphs and repeat his parentage statements.

After a reign of some 50 years, Ah Cacau was succeeded by his son, Yax Kin (Ruler B), who was inaugurated in 734 (9.15.3.6.8). This date is commemorated on Stela 21, which stands at the base of Temple VI. Yax Kin continued, or more likely exceeded, his father's efforts to transform Tikal into one of the most impressive and powerful centers of the Late Classic Maya world. He began with the construction of Temple I, which covered and sealed his father's tomb and provided the shrine to his ancestral memory. But Temple I had probably been planned by Ah Cacau, who also oversaw the carving of the beautiful wooden lintels that would later adorn his funerary shrine on the temple's summit. This structure and its tomb broke the long funerary tradition of the North Acropolis, and this too had undoubtedly been planned by Ah Cacau, ever since he constructed the temple (Str. 5D-33-1st) that had terminated Tikal's traditional royal necropolis.

Yax Kin marked the end of the first katun of his reign with the construction of Twin Pyramid Group 3D-2, at the northern terminus of the Maler Causeway in Group H. Its enclosure contains Stela 20 (Fig. 4.21) and Altar 8, both dedicated to the katun ending 9.16.0.0.0 (751).

It was probably Yax Kin who ordered the construction of what is today the largest temple pyramid at Tikal, Temple IV, which marks the western boundary of Tikal's civic and ceremonial core (see Fig. 4.6), although the structure may have been erected after his death as his funerary shrine. The great causeway avenues that interconnect the major architectural complexes of Tikal were probably also built during this period; one of these leads to the Temple of the Inscriptions (Temple VI), which was built, either during Yax Kin's reign or by a little-known successor, to mark Tikal's eastern perimeter. The roof comb of this temple contains a giant hieroglyphic inscription that evidently records principal events in the history of Tikal. The earliest date on the roof comb corresponds either to a mythical founding date for Tikal, at 5.0.0.0.0 (1139 B.C.), or, as Jones has suggested, to a long-remembered historical event of the Olmec era, since it is contemporary with the heyday of the early Gulf coast sites (see Chapter 2). The next date, 6.14.16.9.16 (457 B.C.), almost certainly records a historical event, perhaps a founding date, since it corresponds to the time Tikal was emerging as a Preclassic lowland center. The third date, 7.10.0.0.0 (156 B.C.), harks back to the era of the first North Acropolis structures, or about the time of Tikal's earliest rulers, as represented by the initial tombs in the North Acropolis. Several dates in the Early Classic follow, and the remaining text seems to refer only to the reign of Yax Kin.

Yax Kin died in about A.D. 768. As discussed earlier, his tomb has been identified as Burial 196, located within a relatively small structure on the south side of the Great Plaza (see Chapter 4). He was succeeded by a little-known ruler, the 28th successor. The next ruler of Tikal, named Chitam, was the 29th and last known member of Tikal's long and illustrious dynastic line. Chitam seems to have attempted to carry on his forefathers' programs. He marked two katun endings with twin-pyramid groups, each of them almost double the size of any of the earlier examples. The first of these, Twin Pyramid Group 4E-4, was dedicated in 9.17.0.0.0 (771) and contains Stela 22 and Altar 10 (Figs. 4.18 and 4.22). The stela, bearing a portrait of Chitam, records the date of his accession to power, 9.16.17.16.4 (768). One katun later (9.18.0.0.0, or 790), Twin Pyramid Group 4E-3 was built next to 4E-4; it includes Stela 19 and Altar 6.

But Tikal's prosperity and power were by now already in decline. Two rulers succeeding Chitam may have been commemorated by Stela 24 (9.19.0.0.0; 810) and Stela 11 (10.2.0.0.0; 869). The latest known monument from the vicinity of Tikal records the date 889 (10.3.0.0.0), but by this time the history and fate of Tikal and its ruling dynasty have receded into obscurity.

## Sites in the Eastern Lowlands

To the east of Tikal, in present-day Belize, there is a series of sites whose polities reached their apogees in the Late Classic. Although the details of their alliances and relationships with other centers are not yet established, to a greater or lesser degree these smaller polities certainly played a role in the affairs of the Late Classic lowlands. We will briefly examine three of them, all of which have received archaeological investigation.

## ALTUN HA

This site is located in northern Belize, near the Caribbean coast. It was named Altun Ha, or "place of stone water," after the adjacent town of Rockstone Pond. Archaeological investigations directed by David Pendergast, and sponsored by the Royal Ontario Museum, were undertaken at Altun Ha between 1964 and 1970. These investigations revealed that this center had been occupied since the Early Pre-classic (ca. 1000 B.C.), but the currently visible construction results largely from expansion during the Classic period. Population probably peaked at about 3,000 during that time.

The core of the site is clustered around two plazas, one of them (Group A; Fig. 5.26) to the north and the other (Group B) to the south. The excavation of Str. B-4 (Fig. 5.27), on the east side of Plaza B, revealed a richly furnished tomb, probably that of one of Altun Ha's rulers. Among its contents was the largest Maya jadeite sculpture yet found (Fig. 5.28), a representation of Kinich Ahau, the sun deity (God G), weighing 4.42 kg. Another tomb (Fig. 5.29), discovered in Str. A-1, contained some 300 jadeite objects and the decomposed residue of a codex, or Maya book. All this is evidence that the rulers of Altun Ha held considerable wealth and power, an unexpected finding in what had previously been thought to be a minor and un-important center on the eastern fringe of the lowlands. But the evidence excavated from Altun Ha indicates that this center participated in, and reaped the benefits from, a trade network—probably dominated by Tikal—that connected the Carib-bean coast with the core of the central lowlands.

Fig. 5.26. Altun Ha, Belize: Group A, after the excavation and consolidation of its structures.

Fig. 5.27 (*above*). Altun Ha, Belize: Str. B-4, where excavation uncovered the jade carving of Kinich Ahau, the sun deity (see Fig. 5.28).

Fig. 5.28 (*left*). Altun Ha, Belize: The carved head of Kinich Ahau from Str. B-4, the largest known Maya jade carving, weighing 4.42 kilograms (9.7 pounds).

Fig. 5.29. Altun Ha, Belize: the inside of the Str. A-1 tomb, showing the grave goods as found.

## XUNANTUNICH

This small site, also known as Benque Viejo, sits near the headwaters of the Río Belize, just east of the Guatemala-Belize border. Teobert Maler visited Xunantunich in 1905, and several investigators, including J. Eric Thompson (1938) and Linton Satterthwaite (1951), conducted brief archaeological work at the site before an expedition from the Museum of Archaeology and Ethnology, Cambridge University, excavated and consolidated portions of the site core, in 1959–60. This work revealed evidence of structural damage caused by an earthquake near the end of the Classic-period occupation of Xunantunich, and that finding led to the development of the now-abandoned theory that earthquakes may have caused the Classic Maya "collapse" (see Chapter 6). More recent work in this region has been conducted by

Joseph Ball. One result of his research has been the proposition that Xunantunich was a specialized palace complex, perhaps founded by a refugee elite lineage at the end of the Classic period. Research now under way under the direction of Richard Leventhal and Wendy Ashmore promises to add new information—and preliminary results already indicate a possible relationship with the larger site of Naranjo. Xunantunich is dominated by Str. A-6, a large building complex that rises to a height of some 40 m and contains an elaborate stucco-and-stone mosaic façade. The site has only one known dated monument, from the Terminal Classic (10.1.0.0.0, or A.D. 849).

### LUBAANTUN

Lubaantun is a small Late Classic center located in the dense rain forest of southern Belize, well within the southern lowlands. The site is situated close to the Río Grande, a small river that affords access to the Caribbean, only 30 km to the southeast. The ruins, discovered in 1903 by Thomas Gann, were sporadically investigated by Gann and others, including R. E. Merwin, whose explorations for the Peabody Museum of Harvard University brought him to Lubaantun in 1915. In 1926 and 1927, T. A. Joyce led a British Museum expedition that began to excavate the site, but in 1928 the project was abandoned in favor of surveying the newly discovered site of Pusilha, about 32 km to the southwest. (Pusilha provoked more interest at the time, since unlike Lubaantun it contained sculptured stelae with hieroglyphic inscriptions.)

The investigation of Lubaantun was resumed in 1970 by a project jointly sponsored by Cambridge and Harvard universities and directed by Norman Hammond. This research produced a new map of the site core and verified earlier conclusions that Lubaantun had been occupied relatively briefly, only from about A.D. 700 to 870. Thus, Lubaantun seems to have been the result of a Late Classic colonization of the Río Grande region, and the recent research suggests that this was done to administer the production of the principal export item of the region, cacao.

The site does not display the two hallmarks of Classic lowland Maya centers: vaulted buildings and sculptured monuments. The Lubaantun core is essentially a single acropolis unit constructed on a low ridge between two streams. There is a ballcourt to the south, and two high, terraced platforms near its center. To the north is another ballcourt, directly west of a large plaza. The plainness and monumentality of many of Lubaantun's masonry terraces, especially in the use of large stone blocks, recalls the final architectural phase of Quirigua, to the south (see below).

## The Expansion of Polities in the Southwest Lowlands

Throughout the pre-Columbian era, the western region of the Maya lowlands was the setting for interaction with non-Maya groups occupying the Gulf coast and the highland regions of Chiapas. Evidence of Preclassic contacts between Olmec and Maya populations is likely to be found here, for the now-destroyed Olmec-style relief at Xoc is located within the area later occupied by the Classic Maya. There are also reports of large Preclassic sites in the lowlands of what is now the Mexican state of Tabasco. It is likely that much of the western lowlands was colonized by expanding Maya groups, but the timing and pattern of this process is yet to be determined. Apart from investigations at several of the better-known Classic Maya centers (Palenque, Tonina, Comalcalco), relatively little work has been done in this region, and the delineation of the origins and development of civilization in this area is incomplete.

During the Late Classic, Palenque was the dominant Classic Maya city of the western lowlands. Our knowledge of the site derives primarily from studies of its texts, architecture, and pictorial images. In fact, the historical records of Palenque were the primary resources used by scholars for the decipherment breakthroughs they achieved in the 1970's. As a result we now know that much of this record deals with creation myth and dynastic succession, and the record offers more detail than is available at any other Classic Maya site. Thus, Palenque provides us with a unique perspective on Maya cosmology, and on how both myth and history were manipulated by Maya rulers for political purposes. There is a paradox in this situation, however. For whereas the information base we have for sites such as Tikal or Copan is vast, at Palenque relatively little archaeological excavation has been conducted, and we have very little hard data against which to correlate or test the conclusions from these historical sources. This is not to say that the historical record is any the less important, for it still stands as the richest and most detailed of any known Maya city, but if we could combine this information with the results from a comprehensive archaeological investigation, we would undoubtedly be able to produce a more complete reconstruction of political development at Palenque than we have been able to assemble for any other Maya site. Indeed, such a record for Palenque would probably tell us a good deal more about *all* of Maya cosmology and history.

Palenque was one of the first lowland centers to gain prominence in the wake of the upheavals and changes of the Middle Classic Hiatus. Prior to the Hiatus, during the Early Classic, Palenque was a minor center, as the archaeological investigations of Robert Rands and his colleagues have demonstrated.

### PALENQUE

The site of Palenque sits dramatically at the foot of the northernmost hills of the Chiapas highlands (Fig. 5.30), overlooking the vast, once-forested Gulf coast plain. It occupies a position on the southwestern periphery of the Maya area, in one of the wettest and most lush environments of the Maya lowlands. El Tortuguero, an apparently subsidiary center, and Comalcalco are the only sizable Maya centers located farther west.

Fig. 5.30. Palenque, Chiapas, Mexico, at the foot of the northern highlands: the multi-doorwayed Temple of the Inscriptions is at the right (see Fig. 5.31); the Palace, with its restored tower, is in the left foreground; and beyond are the Temples of the Cross, the Foliated Cross, and the Sun.

Palenque has been well known to the outside world since the eighteenth century, when a succession of explorers, including Antonio del Río, reported the site. In the nineteenth century, Palenque became the most studied of all Maya sites, owing to the efforts and publications of William Dupaix, Frederick Waldeck, John Lloyd Stephens, Arthur Morley, Désiré Charnay, and others. Alfred Maudslay's superb photographic record remains a valuable resource for scholars studying Palenque and the other sites he visited. Many of these nineteenth-century scholars recorded Palenque's famous stucco relief panels in both drawings and photographs. Because these fragile panels have suffered further disintegration in the intervening years, these early records have proved to be invaluable.

Investigations at Palenque continued in the early twentieth century, with further studies by Edward Seler, Sylvanus Morley, Franz Blom, and Oliver LaFarge. Prior to World War II, the Mexican government began a program of conservation and restoration at the site that has continued to the present day. Although Palenque is yet to be made the subject of comprehensive archaeological research, limited excavations have been undertaken in conjunction with the restoration program. The most notable of these were directed by Alberto Ruz Lhuillier, primarily in the Temple of the Inscriptions, but they also included the Palace and several smaller temples. Archaeological investigations of the surrounding area, directed by Robert Rands of Southern Illinois University, focused on an innovative study of pottery-manufacturing zones; this work has provided valuable chronological data as well as information on the development of settlement in the Palenque region. As already mentioned, pioneering epigraphic studies by a series of scholars, led by Floyd Lounsbury, David Kelley, Linda Schele, and Peter Mathews, have focused on the texts from Palenque, reconstructing in detail various aspects of Maya cosmology and the center's dynastic history. In recent years INAH has continued work, including excavations directed by Arnoldo González in the Temple of the Cross (see below) that have revealed a series of caches and tombs.

Today, as in the past, the visitor cannot help but be captivated by the beauty of Palenque's temples and palaces, placed like finely wrought jewels in a vivid tropical-green setting. To a visitor entering from the west, two of the site's most impressive structures instantly invite exploration: the Temple of the Inscriptions, with its unusual five doorways, and the multiroom Palace, with its unique four-story tower (Fig. 5.30). To the north of the Palace and its platform stairway is a plaza with a small ballcourt on its east side, the ballcourt now nearly invisible. The north side of the plaza is bounded by a series of small temples. One of these is the Temple of the Count, named after Count Frederick Waldeck, who reportedly lived there for several years while studying the ruins of Palenque in the early nineteenth century. The tomb of the archaeologist who made the greatest discoveries at Palenque, Alberto Ruz Lhuillier, is situated opposite the stairway leading to the summit of the Temple of the Inscriptions.

Palenque's distinctive architectural style is immediately apparent. Despite its use of the block masonry and corbel-vaulted rooms typical of most Classic-period lowland sites, the multiple doorways, sloping upper façades, and low, open-work roof combs—all decorated with stucco relief panels—give Palenque's architecture a delicate and serene character. By contrast with the vertical thrust of the lofty, dominating temples at Tikal, Palenque's structures are in harmony with the green hills that rise behind them like a backdrop.

One remarkable feature of Palenque is the absence of freestanding sculptured monuments. Rather than appearing on stelae or altars, the portraits of Palenque's rulers were either carved on stone panels or modeled in plaster, and then placed on the walls of buildings. Most of these portraits (see Fig. 14.25) are now fragmentary, but both stone and stucco work were once brightly painted, and many interior walls show traces of these modeled and painted decorations. Fortunately, some of the portraits and most of the hieroglyphic texts carved on stone panels remain largely intact, and these (or skillful casts) can be seen inside several of the site's most prominent buildings.

The Temple Olvidado, located in the western portion of the site, is the oldest building known to have been associated with Pacal, Palenque's greatest ruler. In many ways it served as a prototype for the distinctive architectural style that characterizes Palenque. During Pacal's reign portions of the famous Palace still visible today were built (see below), as was the Temple of the Count, north of the Palace complex. But the culmination of Pacal's construction efforts was the Temple of the Inscriptions, rising some 25 m on a rectangular, terraced platform (Fig. 5.31). This temple was erected to serve as his mortuary shrine and tomb, and the tomb was hidden deep inside the pyramid supporting the temple.

The tomb lay undetected during more than a century of explorations that failed to discover the obvious clues to its existence. It was finally discovered in the mid-twentieth century during the archaeological investigations of Ruz Lhuillier, when he noted that the inner walls of the temple did not end at their junction with the floor, but continued below it. This observation, together with his deduction that

Fig. 5.31. Palenque, Chiapas, Mexico: drawing of the Temple of the Inscriptions, showing the vaulted staircase that leads from the temple floor, deep beneath the platform, to the vaulted tomb chamber below (see also Fig. 5.32, 5.33, 5.34).

the unusual holes in one large floor slab were in fact lifting holds, led him to the conclusion that something important lay beneath the temple. This was confirmed when the slab was lifted, revealing a corbel-vaulted staircase filled with rubble. It took some three years to clear the rubble, but in 1952 the end of the staircase was reached, deep beneath the temple floor, and outside the huge stone door leading to the burial chamber was found a stone box that contained the bones of five sacrifices, four men and a woman. Upon opening the door, the archaeologists found a large tomb chamber (Fig. 5.32) about 10 by 4 m in size, with a vaulted ceiling over 7 m high. The walls are decorated by nine stucco figures (Fig. 5.32, upper right illustration) representing the nine lords of the underworld, the Bolontiku (see Chapter 11). Most of the chamber was filled by a mammoth limestone sarcophagus, its sides carved with portraits and hieroglyphs (Fig. 5.33). Inside lay a single male skeleton covered with jade beads, a disintegrated jade mosaic mask, and other offerings.

But the most stunning object in the tomb was the magnificently carved sarcophagus lid (Fig. 5.34). Its scene shows Pacal at the moment of death, falling like the sun at sunset into Xibalba. The association is clear, for Pacal is reclining on the mask of the sun god, the mask part skeletal so as to mark the transition from life to death, and together they are consumed by the open jaws of the earth. The implication of this association is also clear, for like the sun, Pacal will master the forces of Xibalba and be reborn as a deity, just as the sun is reborn each day at sunrise. The pathway of their descent is marked by the world tree, shown sprouting from behind Pacal. In its jeweled branches rests the double-headed serpent bar, the cosmic symbol of Maya rulership, and on its crown sits the celestial bird. The entire scene is framed by a skyband containing the symbols of the most important celestial deities, including the sun, the moon, and Venus.

The figures and hieroglyphs on the sides of the sarcophagus record Pacal's ancestors, and the text on the edge of the lid records the kings of Palenque and their death dates. These and other inscriptions at Palenque give Pacal's birth date as 603 (9.8.9.13.0) and his death as 683 (9.12.11.5.18). The texts record his accession to power in 615 (9.9.2.4.8), when he was just 12 years old. The epigraphic data indicate, therefore, that Pacal ruled for over 68 years and lived to be well over 80. Ruz Lhuillier has pointed out, however, that an examination of Pacal's bones indicates that he lived to be no more than about 40, and the apparent contradiction is yet to be resolved.

A lengthy text carved on three panels on the walls of the funerary shrine, far above the tomb, records Palenque's dynastic history up to the inauguration of Pacal's first-born son, Chan Bahlum. This text is the longest intact Maya inscription known (Copan's hieroglyphic stairway is longer, but most of its text has been badly jumbled by the collapse of the steps). Included is a remarkable reference to Pacal's royal predecessor, his mother Lady Zac Kuk ("White Macaw"), who had taken the throne in 612 (9.8.19.7.18): her name is written not matter-of-factly, but with the

Fig. 5.32. Interior of the tomb beneath the Temple of the Inscriptions, Palenque: (*above left*) entry, with stone door removed; (*above right*) stucco figures on the wall of the tomb; (*below left*) the carved sarcophagus lid, as seen looking toward the entrance; (*below right*) the interior, as seen from the entrance.

Fig. 5.33. Tomb beneath the Temple of the Inscriptions, Palenque: (*above*) the sarcophagus lid removed, revealing the remains of the ruler identified as Pacal, with jade and other adornments; (*below*) detail of the sculptured relief on the side of the sarcophagus.

Fig. 5.34. Tomb beneath the Temple of the Inscriptions, Palenque: rubbing of the sculptured sarcophagus lid, depicting Pacal falling in death into the open jaws of the underworld, along the axis mundi, and the cross-shaped tree of life that supports the heavens, which are represented by the two-headed serpent and the celestial bird.

glyph for the First Mother deity, the mother of the gods. Via this device, and by calendrically linking his date of birth in 603 to the mythical birth date of the First Mother, Pacal seems to have been asserting a kind of divine right to rule, claiming himself to be literally a child of the gods.

The new king, Chan Bahlum, is shown on the outer piers of the temple, which were modeled in stucco relief, being presented as heir to the throne—a child in the arms of his ancestors. (Chan Bahlum can be identified by the extra toe on one of his feet, a deformity shown on his adult portraits later on.) He, too, is depicted as divine, in this case as the living incarnation of Bolon Tza'cab (God K), the patron of rulers, for one of his legs ends in a serpent head and he has a smoking axe in his forehead. Both of these are characteristics of God K.

The major Palenque shrines dating from Chan Bahlum's reign are the three smaller structures known as the Temples of the Sun, Cross, and Foliated Cross. These are located on a large, elevated plaza along the eastern side of the site. The Temple of the Sun sits on a low, terraced platform on the west side of the elevated plaza (Fig. 5.35). Opposite the Temple of the Sun is the Temple of the Foliated Cross, its platform incorporating part of the hill behind; its front room is now collapsed. And on the north side of the plaza is the Temple of the Cross, supported by the highest platform of the group, in keeping with the celestial associations that north commands in Maya cosmology. In all, the arrangement and orientation of this group recall the two earliest and most important templates in Maya architecture: the Preclassic triadic arrangement, seen at Nakbe and El Mirador, and the placement of the tallest building at the north, seen in the North Acropolis at Tikal and in the initial temple at Cerros. The tomb of Chan Bahlum has not been found, but one good possibility for its location would be beneath the northern Temple of the Cross.

Each of these three buildings is architecturally similar to the others, with the façade above the doors and a roof comb that was once decorated with stucco modeling. The preserved façade of the Temple of the Cross depicts *witz* masks, demonstrating once again that temples such as these were conceived as sacred mountains. Three doorways lead to a front room, and a central rear room is flanked by two small side rooms. The outer doorways into the front room are framed by hieroglyphic texts (on the end piers) and stucco panels (on the central piers). The central rear room contains a roofed shrine chamber (Fig. 5.36)—a room within a room—that is called the *pib na* (the "underworld house" within the "sacred mountain"). In each of the three buildings, the doorjamb texts give the name for the building, apparently derived from the central motif that decorates the extraordinary carved panel on the inside back wall of each *pib na*. It is the principal attributes of these motifs that have given the three temples their popular names (Fig. 5.37). Additional panels were set on the front wall of each building, on both sides of the doorway, and the doorjambs were inscribed with further texts.

Fig. 5.35. Palenque, Chiapas, Mexico: the Temple of the Sun, the most intact of the three shrines dedicated by the ruler Chan Bahlum, before its consolidation.

Fig. 5.36. Temple of the Cross, Palenque: drawing of the interior shrine, the *pib na*, or "underworld house" (see also Fig. 5.37); the carved figures on the exterior represent God L (at right) and the ruler Chan Bahlum (at left); the central motif on the carved tablet within the shrine, in this case the cross-shaped tree of life, provides the inspiration for the building's popular name.

The motif on the back panel of the *pib na* in the Temple of the Sun (the western building, called the "*mah kina cab*") is associated with the setting sun and death; it commemorates warfare, captive sacrifice, and the underworld's jaguar patron. Here the central element of the motif is a shield adorned with the jaguar sun, supported by crossed spears resting on a throne decorated with heads of jaguars and serpents, supported in turn by two gods of Xibalba (the underworld) in the pose of captives. The central motif of the Temple of the Cross (the northern building, or "*wakah chan*," associated with the celestial realm), is the World Tree at the center of the world that supports the heavens, rising from the mask of the great earth monster. The twin branches of the tree (thus its superficial resemblance to a cross) supports the double-headed serpent bar, one of the primary symbols of kingship, and the Celestial Bird is perched on top (Fig. 5.37). The motif in the Temple of the Foliated Cross (the "*na te kan*"), commemorates the earthly realm, in keeping with its location on the east, the life-giving direction of the rising sun. This motif depicts the maize plant, the sustainer of life, from which sprout human heads (in the creation myth of the *Popol Vuh*, human beings were fashioned by the gods from maize dough).

Fig. 5.37. Temple of the Cross, Palenque: the carved tablet within the *pib na*, depicting the cross-shaped tree of life and the two-headed serpent surmounted by the celestial bird (compare Fig. 5.34), flanked by Chan Bahlum at his accession (at right), and witnessed by his dead father, Pacal (at left).

The composition flanking these central motifs inside the *pib na* in each case is similar in character; each depicts the deceased Pacal facing a larger portrait of the new ruler, Chan Bahlum, who is receiving the symbols of his kingship from his father in Xibalba. These figures are flanked in turn by extensive hieroglyphic texts. The panels on the front inside wall of each *pib na* depict Chan Bahlum in this world, after receiving his power from his father; he is wearing the royal costume and insignia as the new ruler of Palenque. The texts tell us that the child Chan Bahlum was designated as royal heir by a ritual held in 641 (9.10.8.9.3) that ended on the summer solstice, when he "became the sun" (this is the scene portrayed on the end piers of the Temple of the Inscriptions). Chan Bahlum's inauguration as ruler is recorded as having taken place in 684 (9.12.11.12.10), 132 days after Pacal's death.

The left-hand columns of text on all three panels record aspects of the Maya creation myth, the births of the First Mother and First Father and their three children, the three gods who were so closely linked to the power wielded by Maya rulers (these three gods—GI, GII, and GIII—first identified here by Heinrich Berlin, are sometimes known as the Palenque Triad). The Temple of the Cross texts open this mythical chronology by recording the births of the First Father (3122 B.C.) and the First Mother (3121 B.C.); both of these events occurred before the current world began. The creation of the present world, the beginning of the current baktun cycle of the Maya calendar, is recorded next (August 14, 3114 B.C.), after which, in 3112 B.C., the First Father "raised up the sky" (*wakah chan*, also the name of this temple). This was followed by the birth of the first of the gods of this world, the Venus deity, GI or Hunahpu (as he is known elsewhere), in 2360 B.C. The birth of the second deity, the Jaguar Sun god, Ahau Kin or GIII, is recorded in the Temple of the Sun text as happening four days later. The birth of the third deity, the god of royal dynasties, Bolon Tza'cab (God K) or GII, is recorded in the Temple of the Foliated Cross text as happening sixteen days later. The Temple of the Cross also records the accession of the First Mother at the young age of 815 (in 2305 B.C.). According to the Temple of the Foliated Cross inscriptions, she then celebrated the end of the second katun of the current world by being the first to let blood, initiating the core ritual offering made by royalty thenceforth.

The right-hand columns of the panel texts record the ceremonies performed to dedicate these beautiful temples, over a period of four days during July, 690 (beginning on 9.12.18.5.1). The final inscriptions refer to rites Chan Bahlum himself conducted in 692 (9.12.19.14.12), the eighth anniversary of his inauguration as Palenque's ruler.

Palenque's central building complex, its largest, is the aptly named Great Palace (Fig. 5.30). These buildings, situated on a large platform 10 m high and 100 by 80 m in extent, undoubtedly served as the residence for most, if not all, of Palenque's historically identified rulers. The main entrance was by way of a wide stairway on the northern side of the platform. Carved stone and stucco reliefs decorate the exteriors of most buildings. Even the vaults are elaborated, and each major building is marked by a different style of vaulting. The buildings comprise a series of galleries and rooms arranged around several interior courts or patios. In the southwest court are a steam bath and three latrines, as well as Palenque's famous four-story tower. The interiors of the rooms, too, were decorated with modeled stucco masks.

The earliest still-visible buildings in the Great Palace most likely originated during the reign of Pacal, but earlier structures lie buried beneath the Palace's platform. Pacal's accession to power is commemorated on the Oval Palace Tablet; on this beautiful carved panel, he is being handed his crown by his mother, Lady Zac Kuk. Subsequent rulers rebuilt and expanded the Palace complex, particularly its northern part (Houses A, D, and AD), which is associated with Palenque's later rulers, notably Chan Bahlum and his younger brother and successor, Kan Xul.

## The Early Rulers of Palenque

The decipherment of Palenque's texts allows us to reconstruct its sequence of rulers, one that is unusually complete. The kings of Palenque held power by the same means as those of Tikal and other Maya polities: they arrayed themselves in the same trappings of power, claimed affinity to the gods, performed the same rituals to ensure the continuance of the world order, led raids against their neighbors, took and sacrificed captives, and accumulated the prestige and wealth that not only set them apart from the rest of society while they lived, but also, in their elaborate tombs, continued these distinctions even after death. But although the later rulers of Palenque acknowledge a founding king, as do those of many other polities, they apparently did not use the customary hel glyph notation to count themselves in the sequence of succession from the founder. That they did not is presumably because the royal lineage of the founder was not perpetuated throughout Palenque's history. Rather, the record of royal succession was interrupted twice by shifts that saw new patrilineages assume the status of royal family. In both instances the shift was occasioned by an unusual event in Maya political history, the taking of the throne by a woman who, in each case, then passed the right to rule on to a son who was a member—not of her own patrilineage, but of his father's, thus breaking the line of patrilineal succession.

The inscriptions at Palenque record the lives and reigns of its earliest rulers seemingly as a mixture of history and legend (see Table 5.3). The first, named Kin Chan, is certainly a mythical founder. He is claimed to have been inaugurated as Palenque's first ruler over a thousand years before the Classic period began (on a date corresponding to 967 B.C.). The texts then record the likely historical founder of a ruling lineage, someone named Bahlum Kuk ("Jaguar Macaw") who was born

TABLE 5.3

Dynastic Chronology of Classic Palenque

| Ruler | Long Count date | Date A.D. | Event |
|---|---|---|---|
| Balam Kuk | 8.19.15.3.4 | 431 | Accession |
| Casper | 8.19.19.11.17 | 435 | Accession |
| Manik | 9.2.12.6.18 | 487 | Accession |
| Chaacal I | 9.3.6.7.13 | 501 | Accession |
| | 9.4.10.4.17 | 524 | Death |
| Kan Xul I | 9.4.14.0.4 | 529 | Accession |
| | 9.6.11.0.16 | 565 | Death |
| Chaacal II | 9.6.11.5.1 | 565 | Accession |
| | 9.6.16.10.7 | 570 | Death |
| Chan Bahlum I | 9.6.18.5.12 | 572 | Accession |
| | 9.7.9.5.5 | 583 | Death |
| Lady Kanal Ikal | 9.7.10.3.8 | 583 | Accession |
| | 9.8.11.6.12 | 604 | Death |
| Ac Kan | 9.8.11.9.0 | 605 | Accession |
| | 9.8.18.14.11 | 612 | Death of Pacal I |
| | 9.8.19.4.6 | 612 | Death |
| Lady Zac Kuk | 9.8.19.7.18 | 612 | Accession |
| | 9.10.7.13.5 | 640 | Death |
| Pacal | 9.9.2.4.8 | 615 | Accession |
| | 9.9.6.10.19 | 619 | Palace event (House C) |
| | 9.9.13.0.17 | 626 | Wife (Lady Ahpo Hel) takes title |
| | 9.10.8.9.3 | 641 | Chan Bahlum II made heir |
| | 9.10.10.1.6 | 642 | Death of father (Kan Bahlum Mo') |
| | 9.11.2.1.11 | 654 | Palace event (House E) |
| | 9.11.6.16.11 | 659 | Warfare with Yaxchilan |
| | 9.12.0.6.8 | 672 | Death of Lady Ahpo Hel |
| | 9.12.3.6.6 | 675 | Bloodletting ritual |
| | 9.12.11.5.18 | 683 | Death |
| Chan Bahlum II | 9.12.11.12.10 | 684 | Accession |
| | 9.12.18.5.16ff | 690 | Dedications of Cross Group |
| | 9.13.10.1.5 | 702 | Death |
| Kan Xul II | 9.13.10.6.8 | 702 | Accession |
| | 9.13.19.13.3 | 711 | Captured by Ruler 3 of Tonina (eventually sacrificed) |
| Xoc ("regent") | 9.14.8.14.15 | 720 | Assumes office |
| Chaacal III | 9.14.10.4.2 | 722 | Accession |
| | 9.14.11.12.14 | 723 | Chac Zutz inaugurated as Cahal |
| | 9.14.11.17.6 | 723 | Capture of Knot Manik (Chac Zutz) |
| | 9.14.13.11.2 | 725 | Warfare event (Chac Zutz) |
| | 9.14.17.12.18 | 729 | Warfare event (Chac Zutz) |
| Kuk | 9.16.13.0.7 | 764 | Accession |
| 6 Cimi Pacal | 9.18.9.4.4 | 799 | Accession |

in 397 A.D. (8.18.0.13.6) and became ruler of Palenque in 431 (8.19.15.3.4) at the age of 34. It should be noted, however, that unlike what we know of Tikal, Copan, and several other polities, the historical veracity of the reigns of the earlier rulers of Palenque is yet to be supported either by archaeological research at the site or by the discovery elsewhere of contemporaneous glyphic records of their reigns.

According to the later (retrospective) accounts, the succeeding six Palenque rulers were members of Bahlum Kuk's patrilineage, beginning with Bahlum Kuk's son, nicknamed Casper, born in 422 (8.19.6.8.8) and inaugurated as a 13-year-old king four years after his father's death, in 435 (8.19.19.11.17). Casper ruled for 52 years, second in length of reign only to Pacal the Great at Palenque, and was succeeded by his two sons. The first of these, Manik, born in 459 (9.1.4.5.0), took the throne in 487 (9.2.12.6.18) at the age of 28. At his death 14 years later, his younger brother Chaacal I, who was born in 465 (9.1.10.0.0), was inaugurated, at the age of 35 in 501 (9.3.6.7.13). After a reign of 23 years, Chaacal I died, in 524 (9.4.10.4.17), at the age of 59. He was succeeded by his 39-year-old son, Kan Xul I, born in 490 (9.2.15.3.8), who came to the throne in 529 (9.4.14.0.4) and died after a reign of 35 years, at the age of 74 in 565 (9.6.11.0.16). His son, Chaacal II, whose birth is recorded as occurring in 523 (9.4.9.9.4), was inaugurated in 565 (9.6.11.5.1) at the age of 41, but he reigned for only five years (his recorded death was in 570). He was succeeded by his 47-year-old brother Chan Bahlum I, who had been born in 524 (9.4.10.1.5) and became ruler in 572 (9.6.18.5.12). Upon his death in 583 (9.7.9.5.5), the throne passed to Chan Bahlum I's daughter, Lady Kanal Ikal, presumably because neither he nor his brother had any male heirs. The texts do not record Lady Kanal Ikal's age, only that she became the first woman ruler of Palenque in 583 (9.7.10.3.8) and reigned for twenty years, until her death in 604 (9.8.11.6.12). Lady Kanal Ikal was the last member of Bahlum Kuk's lineage to rule at Palenque, for with the accession of her son, Ac Kan, a new patrilineage controlled the throne (the name of Ac Kan's father is not recorded).

Ac Kan took the throne in 605 (9.8.11.9.0), and reigned until his death in 612 (9.8.19.4.6). Normally, he would have been succeeded by either his son or his brother, but apparently the only potential heir had been a younger brother, named Pacal, who had died earlier that same year (9.8.18.14.11). Thus the throne apparently passed to Pacal's daughter, Lady Zac Kuk, in 612 (9.8.19.7.18). Lady Zac Kuk married a man named Kan Bahlum Mo', whom we can only presume was of noble birth, but evidently of a different, nonroyal patrilineage. Lady Zac Kuk ruled for three years, until her son Pacal, at age 12, was considered old enough to assume the throne. With this event Pacal brought the patrilineage of his father, Kan Bahlum Mo', to the royal succession, marking the second shift in ruling lineage in Palenque's political history. As we have seen, Pacal's own records claim a reign of 67 years, until his death in 683.

The archaeological and historical evidence comes to the forefront with Pacal's reign, and from all indications Palenque became a major power during this time, dominating the southwestern region of the Maya lowlands and expanding its authority over the surrounding region. The first known use of Palenque's emblem glyph is recorded at the beginning of Pacal's rule. In 633, an apparent marriage between a woman from the Palenque ruling class and the ruler of the neighboring site of El Tortuguero cemented an alliance between these two centers, although seemingly subordinating this smaller polity to the will of Palenque. The growth of Palenque's power and prestige was probably due at least in part to the political stability engendered by Pacal's long and successful reign. At Tikal, too, under Ah Cacau, and in several like cases in other Maya polities, prosperity was linked to external successes and political longevity.

## The Supernatural Basis of Power in Maya Cosmology

From the decipherment of the records left by Pacal and his successors we can not only reconstruct a sequence of mythical and historical kings, but gain a unique insight into the supernatural world of the ancient Maya and how this belief system was invoked to maintain the status and power of their rulers. Beginning with Pacal, the Palenque texts contain far more details about Maya creation mythology and cosmology than do those of most other Maya sites. Why Pacal, in particular, should be so preoccupied with such arcane matters is clear from a reconstruction of his inheritance. Pacal inherited the throne from his mother, Lady Zac Kuk, in direct violation of the patrilineal pattern of succession that had governed this and all other Maya positions of power. Whereas his father's lineage could make no claim to the throne, his mother had inherited the right to rule patrilineally, via her father to her paternal uncle (Chan Bahlum I), her predecessor on the throne. Pacal's son and successor, Chan Bahlum II, also belonged to Pacal's patrilineage and therefore inherited the same problem. The justification for Pacal's right to rule, set forth initially in the texts and portraits of his sarcophagus and in the Temple of the Inscriptions, was later elaborated upon by Chan Bahlum in his great triadic enterprise, the Temples of the Sun, the Cross, and the Foliated Cross.

In essence, Pacal and his son based the justification for their rule on two precedents, both deriving from the fact that succession through the female line had happened before. The first precedent was apparently historical: Lady Zac Kuk's uncle, Ac Kan, had succeeded his mother as ruler, thus producing a prior shift in the royal lineages of Palenque. The second precedent was clearly supernatural; it was also much more audacious, for Pacal and his heirs claimed to be a living replication of the mythological events surrounding the creation of the present world. In this Maya creation myth the Palenque Triad, the special patron gods of Maya rulers, had inherited their powers from the First Mother, who was born in the previous creation, and went on to create a new order, the present world. In granting divinity to Lady Zac Kuk (born of the preceding royal lineage) by identifying her with the First Mother, Pacal and his son not only inherited a divine right to rule, but also replicated, thereby, the creation of a new order, like that manifested by the Palenque Triad.

The beginnings of these claims can be seen on Pacal's sarcophagus, where his ancestry is traced back through both the female and male lines to Chacaal I, representing the original dynasty of the founder, Bahlum Kuk. But his most important ancestors, starting with his mother and father, are each depicted twice. That the only other ancestor shown twice is his great-grandmother Lady Kanal Ikal emphasizes the precedent for the shift in the royal patrilineage brought on by Pacal's succession from his mother. As we have already seen, in the royal records on the Temple of the Inscriptions, Pacal makes the case for his mother's divinity by associating her with the First Mother. The same building proclaims the divinity of his son, Chan Bahlum, who appears as a manifestation of Bolon Tza'cab on the scenes recording the heir-designation ceremonies.

Pacal was succeeded some 132 days after his death by his 48-year-old son Chan Bahlum. During a reign of just over eighteen years, Chan Bahlum significantly expanded the Palenque site. His most famous monuments are the three beautiful buildings to the east of his father's funerary temple. In these famous temples Chan Bahlum elaborated the justifications that reinforced his right to rule, beginning with the claim of his father's divinity demonstrated by linking the date of his birth with that of the First Mother. The texts in Chan Bahlum's temples record the events of the Maya creation, and show how they were replicated by Palenque's dynastic succession from the old order to the new. The ceremonies performed by Chan Bahlum himself, including his inauguration as ruler and his dedication of his three temples, are recorded in these texts as reenactments of the creation of the present world by the gods, his ancestors. Other linkages include recording the birth of the first two gods of the present creation as the children of the First Mother, to parallel the birth of Pacal as the child of Lady Zac Kuk, while associating the birth of the third god, the same Bolon Tza'cab manifested in Chan Bahlum's presentation scenes on the Temple of the Inscriptions, with the birth of the First Father. Thus did Chan Bahlum establish the claim that he was to his father as Bolon Tza'cab was to the First Father.

## The Later Rulers of Palenque

Chan Bahlum died in 702 (9.13.10.1.5), and his younger brother, Kan Xul II, then 57 years old, succeeded him 53 days later. During the reign of Kan Xul II, Palenque's realm appears to have reached its maximum extent—and to have suffered its greatest setback. Early in his reign, he ordered that Temple 14 be built on the northwest corner of his brother's great triadic temple complex. A broken tablet from within this building appears to commemorate Chan Bahlum's apotheosis (or "deification") in 705 (9.13.13.1.5).

Palenque's later rulers continued to enlarge their splendid residence, the Great

Palace, in particular raising the famed and unique four-story tower. Although evidence for its construction date is yet to be found, Linda Schele has hypothesized that it was built by Kan Xul II in veneration of his father, Pacal. When viewed from the top of the Great Palace tower on the winter solstice, the sun sets directly behind the Temple of the Inscriptions, appearing to enter the underworld through Pacal's tomb. Kan Xul II also began the construction of the northern building of the Palace. Excavations conducted by Albert Ruz Lhuillier there uncovered a stone panel carved with an extensive hieroglyphic text and an accession scene. The text reviews the preceding reigns and appears to depict Kan Xul at his inauguration, attended by his mother. But it also contains an ominous clue to a disaster that befell Palenque's ruling house.

Although no record of the event has been found at Palenque, Kan Xul II apparently led a raid on the neighboring site of Tonina in order to secure the captive sacrifices necessary to the dedication of his new palace. But fate dictated otherwise: at Tonina archaeologists have discovered a record of Kan Xul's capture by Ruler 3 of Tonina. That Kan Xul II had been taken captive and was apparently held for a long period before eventually being sacrificed must have plunged the Palenque polity into despair, for the tablet at Palenque's Great Palace records that the new building was completed and dedicated by a man named Xoc, not as ruler but apparently as a stand-in during this interregnum. It would appear that a new king could not assume the throne while the old king still lived, notwithstanding that the royal captive at Tonina could no longer exercise rule.

## TONINA

Tonina sits in a transitional lowland-highland setting at an elevation of 800–900 m about 50 km south of Palenque in the Ocosingo valley. The site was investigated during the 1970's by the French Archaeological Mission in Mexico, under the direction of Pierre Becquelin and Claude Baudez. The dynastic sequence at Tonina has been worked out from the site's inscriptions by Peter Mathews.

Tonina is known best for its monuments, which are considered, stylistically, the least typical of all Classic Maya sculpture. The sixteen known monuments are all small when compared to the average 2.5–3 m height of those at other Maya centers; most of the Tonina stelae are less than about 2 m tall. They also differ, significantly, in being carved fully in the round, like statuary (Fig. 5.38). The dated monuments reportedly span most of the Classic period, from 9.3.0.0.0 to 10.4.0.0.0 (A.D. 495 to 909), although the earliest surely dated inscription (on Monument 106) is 9.8.0.0.0 (593). The recently discovered Monument 101 bears the latest Long Count date of any Maya stela, 10.4.0.0.0 (909).

The first known ruler at Tonina celebrated the 9.8.0.0.0 period ending (593), and may also be mentioned on Monument 74, which dates to 9.9.2.4.18 (615). The

Fig. 5.38. Tonina, Chiapas, Mexico: Stela 12, dated to 9.12.0.0.0 (A.D. 672), with its portrait of Ruler 2 carved in the round like most other monuments from this site.

Fig. 5.39. Tonina Monument 122: drawing of the carved figure of a bound captive, Palenque ruler Kan Xul, identified by the name glyph and Palenque emblem-glyph main sign on his thigh, with reference to the capture event ("star over Palenque") at the right (A.D. 711).

better-documented reign of Ruler 2 begins with his accession in 668 (9.11.16.0.1). He is shown on Monument 113, and he celebrated a period ending in 682 (9.12.10.0.0) with a presentation of captives. Ruler 3, who took the throne in 688 (9.12.16.3.12), climaxed his rule with the capture of Kan Xul II of Palenque in 711 (9.13.19.12.3). This event is depicted in low relief on Monument 122 (Fig. 5.39), a clear exception to the prevailing style of Tonina's full-round sculptural style. The monument shows a reclining figure identified by three glyphs incised on his right thigh. These read, "Kan Xul Ahau of Palenque." The date carved along the right-hand edge of the stone probably records the date of his capture by Tonina Ruler 3. Linda Schele has proposed that the carving style of Monument 122, in the tradition of Palenque rather than that of Tonina, may be evidence of the tribute paid to the victorious polity by Palenque—a master stone sculptor dispatched to Tonina to carve the monument commemorating the defeat of his former king. A more recent discovery at Tonina settles the issue of Kan Xul's fate—a sculptural panel depicts the Palenque ruler's severed head.

Ruler 3 at Tonina must have died soon thereafter, for the next two period endings (9.14.5.0.0 and 9.14.10.0.0) were celebrated by his successor, Ruler 4. Ruler 5 marked a series of events between 9.14.15.0.0 and 9.14.17.9.0, and died in 734 (9.15.3.7.5). The 9.15.5.0.0 period ending was celebrated by Ruler 6, but we know little else about him or his successor, Ruler 7, except that the latter died in 775 (9.17.4.12.5). A series of events between 9.17.18.13.9 (789) and 9.18.15.15.0 (805) mark the reign of Ruler 8, and a single event in 837 (10.0.7.9.0) is associated with his successor, Ruler 9. A century later the last period ending known to have been celebrated at this or any other Maya site, 10.4.0.0.0 (909), was commemorated by the last known Tonina *ahau*, Ruler 10.

## Recovery and Decline at Palenque

With the sacrifice of Kan Xul II, after a protracted captivity, Palenque could restore its destiny with a new king. The new ruler, Chaacal III, was inaugurated in 722 (9.14.10.4.2). Very likely he was Kan Xul's younger brother, since he was 43 when he came to the throne. One of two carved tablets found flanking the tower stairs, the "Orator Tablet," appears to depict Chaacal III. His reign is also recorded on a series of constructions including Str. 18, located south of the Temple of the Foliated Cross, and Temple 21, situated south of the Temple of the Sun. Temple 18A, adjacent to Temple 18 and apparently built by Chaacal III, was constructed over an earlier, deeply buried crypt excavated in 1957 by Ruz Lhuillier. This crypt appears to have been the tomb of an Early Classic ruler, perhaps Chaacal I or II, but although it contains artifacts indicative of a royal interment, the identity of its occupant remains unknown. During the reign of Chaacal III one of his subordinate lords, a man named Chac Zutz, rose to prominence within the Palenque political hierarchy. Chac Zutz appears to be depicted on the Tablet of the Slaves, found in Group IV, a smaller palace located west of the main site that probably served as his residential compound. Excavations in this group directed by Robert Rands revealed it to contain a cemetery area.

The length of Chaacal III's reign is not known, and it may be that centralized authority at Palenque was eroding, just as it would at Copan (see below). After another interregnum (or perhaps simply a gap in the historical record) of about 33 years, the son of Chaacal III, Kuk, took the throne in 764 (9.16.13.0.7). But by this time Palenque's power seems to have waned considerably, and in 771 (9.17.0.0.0) Pomona, a former dependency of Palenque, appears to have achieved its independence, displaying its own emblem for the first time.

The historical record at Palenque essentially ends with the reign of Kuk. An inscribed pottery vessel records the accession of an apparent ruler with the name of 6 Cimi Pacal in 799 (9.18.9.4.4), but we know nothing else about this man or the ultimate fate of Palenque's dynasty or polity.

## The Expansion of Polities in the Southeast Lowlands

The southeastern region is probably the most diverse of any Maya lowland area. Located in a transitional lowland-highland zone on the frontiers of Central America, this region is adjacent to valuable resources (jade and obsidian) and enjoyed ready access both to these products and to the connections to surrounding regions provided by natural transportation corridors (Lago de Izabal, the Río Dulce, the Motagua Valley) and the Caribbean Sea. The environment is favorable for human settlement, with plentiful rainfall and fertile volcanic or alluvial soils.

Copan, in western Honduras, is the southeasternmost major Classic Maya site. Copan and, for a time, Quirigua, in the adjacent lower Motagua Valley, were the dominant powers on the borderlands with Central America. We will turn to Quirigua a bit later.

### COPAN

During the Classic period Copan was the capital of a powerful polity that dominated the southeastern Maya region, the frontier with Central America. Although classified by archaeologists as a lowland center, its setting in a fertile valley at an average elevation of 700 m, surrounded by mountains, is certainly transitional to a highland environment (Fig. 5.40). Justly famed for its splendid sculptural and architectural style, Copan represents a distinctive variation within the lowland Maya tradition; in fact, the exuberant sculpture found on its buildings and monuments vividly emphasizes Maya traditions in a setting nearly surrounded by non-Maya groups, as is so often the case along cultural frontiers.

More than a century of research at Copan has demonstrated an unbroken sequence of more than two thousand years of pre-Columbian occupation (Early Preclassic to Postclassic). The city reached the maximum extent of its occupation during the Classic period (ca. 250–900), by which time it had come to manifest the economic, social, political, and ideological dimensions of a complex state organization. Copan's historical record, well-developed but still growing, now spans most of the Classic period, and is being steadily integrated with archaeological data.

Current investigation employs archaeological, epigraphic, and iconographic research in a cross-cutting, self-correcting strategy aimed at reconstructing the sociopolitical history of Copan. The effort is anchored by a wide range of archaeological research, including study of valley settlement and population, local and regional ecology, and excavations in the full range of activity areas, from the humblest dwellings to the palaces and temples of Copan's kings, all directed toward the refinement and improvement of our understanding of the ancient polity.

Copan has been known since shortly after the Spanish Conquest, and was described by Don Diego Garcia de Palacios in 1576. In the nineteenth century, the site was brought to the attention of the outside world through the descriptions and illustrations of John Lloyd Stephens and Frederick Catherwood. Later, Alfred Maudslay's excavations and photographic record of Copan's sculptures rekindled interest in the site, and from 1891 to 1894 the Peabody Museum, Harvard University, conducted investigations at Copan under the direction of George Gordon. For several years, beginning in 1935, this work was followed by a program of excavations and restoration conducted by the Carnegie Institution of Washington.

One of the most important archaeological features of Copan is the *corte*, or cross section of the Acropolis exposed by the Río Copan (Fig. 5.41). The corte, one of the largest archaeological cross sections in the world, clearly exposes the sequence of Acropolis construction. It was produced after the city was abandoned, when the river changed its course and cut away a great portion of the eastern base of the Acropolis, exposing a vertical face some 37 m high at the highest point and 300 m long at the base. (Unfortunately, before the Carnegie work got under way,

Fig. 5.40. Copan, Honduras: aerial view from the north, with most of the Acropolis obscured beneath the dark trees in the center, the diverted course of the Río Copan to the left, and the old course and the river cut (*corte*) visible immediately to the left of the trees.

Fig. 5.41. The section of the east side of the Copan Acropolis that was exposed by the Río Copan before it was diverted, as seen from the southeast: the pyramidal shape of Str. 16 is in the center of the Acropolis at the far left; several walls and plaza floors belonging to earlier stages of Acropolis construction are visible in the river cut.

several buildings recorded by research in the nineteenth century, strs. 10L-19, 20, 20A, and 21, were undercut and tumbled into the river.) Reconstruction was an important part of the Carnegie work at Copan. Most significantly, a diversion re-channeled the river, so that the Acropolis is no longer threatened with destruction. In addition, more than a dozen fallen and broken monuments were repaired and re-erected. Strs. 10L-11, 21A, 22, and 26 and the Ballcourt (strs. 9 and 10) were excavated and repaired, and several tunnels were driven through the Acropolis to find earlier constructions.

The modern era of archaeological research at Copan was initiated in 1975, when a team from the Peabody Museum, under the direction of Gordon Willey, returned to Copan to investigate the distribution of Classic-period settlement in the valley region surrounding the site's Principal Group. The investigation spawned a series of research projects that has continued to the present day and represents the longest and largest archaeological program being conducted at any Maya site. Willey's Copan Valley Project (1975–77) defined the basic settlement patterns in the surrounding valley and excavated the first sample of residential compounds, including one in the Sepulturas Group, an elite suburb of Copan. The Instituto Hondureño de Antropología e Historia (IHAH) then began sponsorship of the Copan work, beginning with the first phase of the Copan Archaeological Project (PAC I), directed by Claude Baudez from 1977 to 1980, which conducted further valley settlement work and opened excavations in the Principal Group. The second phase of this investigation (PAC II), directed by William Sanders from 1980 to 1985, continued these programs with more valley settlement work, including the dating of occupation by obsidian-hydration studies, and further excavations in the Sepulturas Group. Since 1985, research at Copan has continued under a variety of programs coordinated by IHAH. These include further valley settlement investigations, directed by Sanders and David Webster, between 1986 and 1989; the excavation of elite complexes represented by the North Group, directed by Wendy Ashmore, in 1988 and 1989, and of those represented by Group 8N-11, directed by David Webster, in 1990; and beginning in 1985 the Copan Mosaics Project, directed by William and Barbara Fash, which seeks to identify the huge corpus of fallen sculptural façades at the site. The most extensive efforts still under way at Copan are the several programs of the Copan Acropolis Archaeological Project (PAAC), directed by William Fash, which began with the excavation of Str. 10L-26, the Temple of the Hieroglyphic Stairway, in 1985. This project also includes the Early Copan Acropolis Program, directed by Robert Sharer, which began in 1989 to document the architectural history of the Acropolis. Also part of the PAAC are the excavation of Str. 10L-16, directed by Ricardo Agurcia, which started in 1989, and the excavation of the Cemetery Group immediately south of the Acropolis, directed by E. Wyllys Andrews V, which began in 1990.

The site core of Copan, covering an area about 600 by 300 m, is composed of a massive elevated complex on the south, the Acropolis, and a series of connecting plazas and smaller structures to the north (Fig. 5.42) that includes the Court of the Hieroglyphic Stairway (flanked by the famous Ballcourt) and the Monument Plaza, the setting for the greatest grouping of Copan's stelae and altars. The Court and the Plaza are separated by Str. 10L-4, a platform with four stairways. South of the Acropolis is a series of smaller plazas and buildings, the Cemetery Group, that consists mostly of Late Classic elite residential structures. A sacbe leads northeast to another series of Late Classic elite residences in the Sepulturas Group, the site of excavations that have seen the discovery of activity areas, burials and tombs, and several sculptured benches bearing hieroglyphic inscriptions. Farther north, set on the first terraces of the valley, are several Late Classic compounds known as the

Fig. 5.42 (*opposite*). Map of the Principal Group of Copan, Honduras: at the top is the Great Plaza; in the center is the Ballcourt and Str. 26, with its hieroglyphic stairway; at the bottom is the Acropolis, with its West and East courts and the river cut on its east side (strs. 20 and 21 depicted here were destroyed by the Río Copan before its diversion).

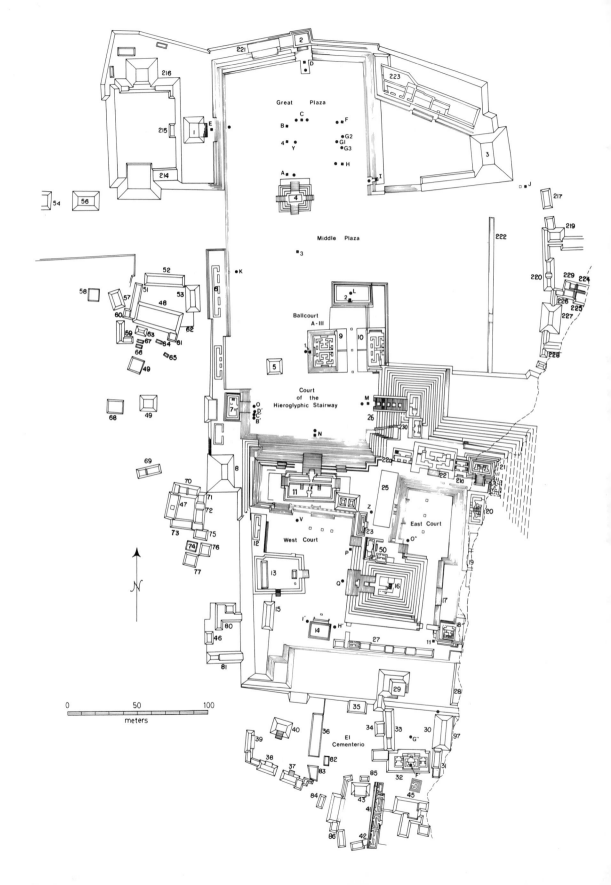

North Group. Work here has discovered fallen façades decorated with hieroglyphic and sculptural motifs, and several elite tombs.

The Acropolis is crowned by a series of elevated structures arranged around two plazas, the East and West courts (Fig. 5.42). The north side of the West Court is formed by Str. 10L-11, apparently the residence of the last Copan ruler Yax Pac, but built over several earlier structures. It is reached by a broad monumental stairway on its north side. The highest point on the Acropolis is the summit of Str. 10L-16, facing the West Court on its eastern side, and also associated with Yax Pac. Perhaps the most famous Acropolis building is Str. 10L-22, which appears to have served as a residence and dates to the reign of 18 Rabbit (A.D. 771). This structure faces south from its position high on the north side of the East Court (Fig. 5.43, above). It houses an inner doorway framed by a magnificent sculptured relief and corner masks, and an outer doorway framed by a giant mask, in the style of the Chenes architecture of Yucatan (see Chapter 6). To its west is Str. 10L-22A, and to its east is the smaller Str. 21A and a vestige of the fallen Str. 10L-21, once the tallest building on the northern edge of the East Court. The west side of the court is bounded by a stairway flanked by upright striding jaguars (Fig. 5.43, below).

Str. 10L-18 is located on the southeastern corner of the Acropolis, its eastern edge long ago swept away by the old course of the Río Copan. Its excavation revealed a building elaborately decorated with sculptured reliefs (Fig. 5.44). On 10L-18's rear (southern) side is a flight of stairs, also discovered by excavation, that leads down to a sepulcher roofed by a four-sided vault (a corbeled "dome"). In its floor the excavators found a sunken burial chamber. This tomb, probably that of Copan's last identified ruler, Yax Pac, was probably looted not long after it was sealed, for when it was found it was virtually empty.

Str. 10L-26, dating to A.D. 756, forms a northern projection of the Acropolis. It is reached from the west by the Hieroglyphic Stairway, which rises from the court below (Fig. 5.45). A large figure sits at the midpoint of every twelfth step; although eroded, the figures apparently represent the major rulers of Copan's dynasty. The faces of the steps are sculptured with some 2,200 individual glyphs, the longest inscription in Maya hieroglyphic writing; unfortunately, however, the steps were largely jumbled by the collapse of the stairway, and only the lowest portion is in its original position. From the Hieroglyphic Stairway one has a magnificent view of the famed Ballcourt and Great Plaza beyond (Fig. 5.46).

## Archaeology and History at Copan

The earliest traces of human occupation in the Copan Valley date to the very end of the Early Preclassic (ca. 1000 B.C.). Although remaining small in scale, populations increased through the Middle Preclassic, when archaeological evidence of social stratification first appears. The most dramatic evidence of stratification is a

Fig. 5.43. The Acropolis East Court, Copan: (*above*) Str. 10L-22, dated to the reign of the thirteenth ruler, 18 Rabbit; (*below*) the Jaguar Stairway on the west side of the court (striding jaguar at left), the initial version of which was built over a well-preserved royal tomb dated to the midsixth century.

Fig. 5.44. Remains of Copan Str. 10L-18 at the southern entrance to the East Court: (*right*) sculptured doorjamb with warrior figure identified as the sixteenth ruler, Yax Pac; (*below*) doorway and carved interior bench.

Fig. 5.45. The Hieroglyphic Stairway, Str. 10L-26, at Copan, completed in the reign of the fifteenth ruler, Smoke Shell; the text carved on the steps records the history of the Copan polity. (Stela M is at the base of the stairs to the left.)

Fig. 5.46. The Great Ballcourt, Copan: apparently dedicated during the reign of the ruler 18 Rabbit, this is the latest of a series of earlier ballcourts revealed by excavation; beyond is Str. 10L-4, with its four stairways, and the Great Plaza.

Middle Preclassic elite cemetery excavated by William Fash beneath the plaza of a much later (Late Classic) residential/administrative complex in the Sepulturas Group. For reasons unknown, populations declined in the Late Preclassic.

The occupation of the Copan Valley began to revive during the early portion of the Classic (ca. 250–400). Settlement research indicates that populations began to be nucleated (concentrated) in the Copan pocket in the fourth century A.D., if not earlier. Nucleation began modestly and then accelerated during the mid-Classic (ca. 400–600), still concentrated in the alluvial bottomlands adjacent to the Principal Group but beginning to expand to the foothills. By this time there were also significant settlements outside of the valley bottomlands. A maximum population for this period might be on the order of 8,000–10,000. Occupation continued to expand thereafter, and peak population in the Copan Valley during the Late Classic (ca. 600–800) is estimated at ca. 18,000–25,000.

The dated monuments of Copan span the entire Classic period. A stela fragment found broken and relegated to the rubble of Str. 10L-4, in the Monument Plaza, lacks a hieroglyphic inscription. But the style of the sculptured portrait of the lower part of a human figure is very early—reminiscent, in fact, of the monuments from the southern Maya area—and its age is therefore certainly equivalent to the oldest known lowland stela. Several later texts refer to important dates apparently falling at the very beginning of the Copan polity, perhaps with the establishment of the site's first Maya rulers. Stela I retrospectively records the period-ending date of 8.6.0.0.0 (A.D. 159), then counts forward 208 days (to July 13, 160) to refer to an unidentified event occurring at Copan, perhaps the installment of an early ruler. But later kings counted their order in the dynastic succession from a ruler named Yax Kuk Mo', who is often associated in these texts with a title that apparently means lineage "founder." The dynastic sequence of the successors of Yax Kuk Mo' has been worked out (Table 5.4), although the reigns of several of the early rulers are still unclear, owing to disturbances to both the historical record and the constructional record by later activity.

The key historical evidence for Yax Kuk Mo', and for the Copan dynasty he is credited with founding, is provided by Altar Q (Fig. 5.47), a rectangular stone dedicated by the last ruler, Yax Pac, and placed at the base of the Str. 10L-16 stairway in the West Court. The four sides of this extraordinary monument display the carved portraits of the sixteen rulers in the dynasty, each seated on his name glyph, which serves as a throne. The sequence begins and ends on the west side, where the founder, Yax Kuk Mo', seated left of center and wearing his name glyph in his headdress (he is seated on an *ahau* glyph), is facing Yax Pac, the sixteenth ruler, and handing him the scepter of office. Behind Yax Kuk Mo' sits his successor, the second ruler of Copan, followed by the next four rulers on the north side of the monument, the seventh through the tenth rulers on the east side, and the eleventh through the fourteenth rulers on the south side. The fifteenth ruler, Smoke Shell, is seated im-

TABLE 5.4

Dynastic Chronology of Classic Copan

| Ruler (with hel position) | Long Count date | Date A.D. | Event |
|---|---|---|---|
| ? | 8.6.0.0.0 | 159 | Unknown event |
| | 8.6.0.10.8 | 160 | Unknown event |
| Yax Kuk Mo' (1) | — | | Founder |
| | 8.19.10.10.17 | 426 | Displayed manikin scepter |
| | 8.19.10.11.0 | 426 | Unknown event |
| | 9.0.0.0.0 | 435 | Celebrated katun ending (?) |
| | 9.0.2.0.0? | 437 | Death or burial |
| ? (2) | — | | |
| ? (3) | — | | Dedicated Stela 63 in Papagayo Str. |
| Cu Ix (4) | 9.2.18.0.0? | 493 | (References to Copan rulers 3 and 4 on Quirigua Monument 26?) |
| | — | | Dedicated hieroglyphic step in Papagayo Str. |
| ? (5) | — | | |
| ? (6) | — | | |
| Waterlily Jaguar (7) | | | Dedicated "House of Mah Kina Yax Kuk Mo'" (under Str. 10L-11) |
| ? (8) | — | | |
| ? (9) | — | | |
| Moon Jaguar (10) | 9.5.19.3.0 | 553 | Accession |
| | 9.7.4.17.4 | 578 | Death |
| Butz Chan (11) | 9.7.5.0.8 | 578 | Accession |
| | | | Action at Los Higos (Stela P)? |
| | 9.9.14.16.9 | 628 | Death |
| Smoke Imix (12) | 9.9.14.17.5 | 628 | Accession |
| | 9.11.0.0.0 | 652 | Celebrated katun ending with stelae on east and west edges of Copan Valley |
| | 9.11.0.11.11 | 653 | Action at Quirigua |
| | 9.13.3.5.7 | 695 | Death |
| 18 Rabbit (13) | 9.13.3.6.8 | 695 | Accession |
| | 9.14.13.14.17 | 725 | Inauguration of Cauac Sky of Quirigua "in land of" Copan |
| | 9.15.0.0.0 | 731 | Celebrated katun ending; Copan as one of four great polities of Maya world (Stela A) |
| | 9.15.3.2.0 | 734 | Cauac Sky as k'ul ahau of Quirigua |
| | 9.15.6.8.13 | 738 | Dedicated Great Ballcourt |
| | 9.15.6.14.6 | 738 | Captured/sacrificed by Cauac Sky of Quirigua |
| Smoke Monkey (14) | 9.15.6.16.5 | 738 | Accession |
| | 9.15.15.0.0? | 746 | Dedicated Str. 10L-22A (popul na)? |
| | 9.15.17.12.16 | 749 | Death |
| Smoke Shell (15) | 9.15.17.13.10 | 749 | Accession |
| | | | Dedication of Str. 10L-22 (Hieroglyphic Stairway) |
| Yax Pac (16) | 9.16.12.5.17 | 763 | Accession |
| | | 769 | Dedicated West Court "Reviewing Stand" |
| | | 773 | Dedicated Str. 10L-11 |
| | 9.17.5.0.0 | 775 | Dedicated Altar Q ("Yax Kuk Mo' throne stone") |
| | 9.17.12.5.17 | 783 | Celebrated first katun of reign |
| | 9.18.10.17.18 | 801 | Dedicated Str. 10L-18 |
| | 9.19.0.0.0 | 810 | Celebrated katun ending with Jade Sky of Quirigua |
| | 9.19.10.0.0 | 820 | Apotheosis? (posthumous reference on Stela 11) |
| U Cit Tok (?) | 9.19.11.14.5 | 822 | Attempted accession? (Altar L) |

Fig. 5.47. Copan dynastic monuments: (*above*) the west side of Altar Q, depicting the dynastic founder, Yax Kuk Mo' (near left) handing his scepter to his sixteenth successor, Yax Pac (near right), as well as the intervening rulers in the dynastic sequence, beginning with the second successor at the far left, followed by the third through the fourteenth successors on the other three sides, and the fifteenth at the far right; (*below*) Stela 63 on its side, as found interred in the "Founder's Temple" beneath Str. 10L-26, its Long Count date marking the period ending 9.0.0.0.0 (A.D. 435).

mediately behind Yax Pac on the west side. On its upper surface Altar Q records two dated events associated with Yax Kuk Mo', beginning with his display of the manikin scepter on 8.19.10.10.17 and then his "arrival" or, perhaps, "founding," three days later (September 6 and 9, 426). A slightly earlier date, 8.19.0.0.0 (February 1, 426), in a reference to the same founder, is recorded on Stela 15, which was dedicated by the seventh ruler a century later.

As is true of most sites, no monument actually dedicated by the founder is known to survive. But a monument found in 1989, Stela 63 (Fig. 5.47) bears a Long Count date of 9.0.0.0.0, and is the earliest discovered thus far at Copan. It was found during excavations into the platform of Str. 10L-26 (the final phase of which bears the Hieroglyphic Stairway), and the excavations have revealed a number of earlier buildings that can be tied directly into the overall Acropolis sequence (see below). One of these buildings, known as Papagayo, constructed during the initial Acropolis period (ca. A.D. 400–500), was the original setting for Stela 63. The upper section of the stela was found against the south side of the room, but its broken base was still in place against the back (east) wall. It had been erected inside this building, probably by the second or third ruler, as part of a shrine to honor the founder of the Copan dynasty. Stela 63's text, which refers to Ruler 2 as the son of Yax Kuk Mo', may recall an important event or ceremony performed by the dynastic founder on the period-ending date 9.0.0.0.0 (A.D. 435). That this date and his name also occur on several Late Classic monuments indicates that this event continued to be considered important long after its initial recording on Stela 63. About the time of the fourth ruler, Cu Ix, a new floor was placed inside Papagayo and a hieroglyphic step was commemorated at the base of Stela 63.

Current excavations by the Early Copan Acropolis Program provide the basis for what we know of the timing and scale of activities of the earliest of Copan's rulers. Over 2 km of tunnels have been excavated from the well-defined architectural stratigraphy revealed in the corte face; these tunnels document the construction sequence underlying the entire East Court (Str. 10L-22 and adjacent buildings). This sequence has been extended to adjacent excavations under Str. 10L-16 (directed by Ricardo Agurcia) and under Str. 10L-26 (directed by William Fash). Archaeologists are securing temporal control of Copan history from stratigraphy, various dating techniques, ceramics and other artifacts, and newly discovered inscriptions bearing Long Count calendrical dates. It is now apparent, from a reconciling of all these resources, that the Acropolis began to take shape before A.D. 400 with the construction of a series of monumental platforms. A major expansion with new buildings appears to coincide chronologically with the historical founding of the dynasty by Yax Kuk Mo'. These early Acropolis constructions clearly represent the first royal administrative, residential, and ritual complex at this locus, as indicated by the scale and elaboration of their architecture and the history recorded by the associated epigraphic and iconographic features.

By ca. A.D. 400–500 the early Acropolis appears to have covered about the same area as all subsequent configurations (ca. 500–800). The size and elaboration of the structures in this early Acropolis complex reflect the initiation of political power at Copan during the very period said by the later inscriptions to have seen the founding of the royal dynasty and the reigns of the first kings.

A dramatic discovery in the spring of 1993 (as this book neared completion) may provide one of the most significant links between archaeology and history ever found in the Maya area—actual buildings used by a founder. Tunnels excavated by the Early Copan Acropolis Program discovered a large vaulted chamber (ca. 1.5m by 4.2m) within the earliest known masonry platform, called Margarita, deep beneath the Acropolis. A large stone with a carved text rests in the southern wall of the chamber. The text includes a date, probably corresponding to A.D. 437, associated with the name of the second successor. Yax Kuk Mo' 's name is at the end of the text. This text is evidence that the chamber holds the remains of the dynastic founder, Yax Kuk Mo' himself, or his successor; the date may refer to a dedication or another event associated with the tomb. These and related issues can only be clarified by the careful excavation of the chamber, and it is estimated that two more years will be required for this task.

The early Acropolis (ca. 400–500) consisted of a huge platform that occupied the bulk of the southeastern quadrant of the later, fully developed Acropolis (its full eastward extent may never be known, owing to destruction by the Río Copan). To the north a lower platform supported a large complex of multiroomed (unvaulted) masonry administrative/residential buildings, all underlying the later buildings of the northeastern quadrant of the Acropolis. Excavation has revealed that these structures were arranged around an east-west alignment of three courts. The exteriors of these northern buildings were decorated with elaborately modeled and painted stucco reliefs (now destroyed) and the first interior painted hieroglyphic text ever found at Copan (heavily damaged when the building was partially dismantled and buried by subsequent construction).

Almost nothing is known about the two rulers who succeeded Cu Ix. But the archaeological record indicates that their reigns were marked by building activity little different from that of their predecessors. Individual structures enjoyed almost continuous rebuilding and refurbishment, and much of the Acropolis was transformed by at least two major renewal/construction projects between ca. 500 and 650, a time corresponding roughly to the reigns of the fifth through the eleventh rulers. Significant structures dated to this period include a major two-tiered platform on the eastern side of the East Court, decorated on all four sides with large plaster and painted masks (Fig. 5.48). On its summit the platform supported a vaulted building also decorated with elaborate stucco reliefs.

The platform is designated Ante Structure. Among a series of caches excavated beneath its east-west axis was one, found beneath the stairway, that contained a

Fig. 5.48. Excavation of Ante Structure in the East Court of the Copan Acropolis, the penultimate version of Str. 10L-20 (now destroyed): (*above*) elaborate stucco mask from the west side of the Ante platform; (*below*) jade figurine nested in a spondylus shell, found cached beneath the Ante stairway.

carved jade figurine within a spiny oyster shell covered with red pigment (Fig. 5.48). A hieroglyphic text discovered on one of the steps in the stairway leading to its summit indicates that this building may have been associated with the seventh ruler, Waterlily Jaguar (ca. 504–544). This king apparently built his palace under Str. 10L-11 on the south side of the Great Plaza, and named it the "House of Mah Kina Yax Kuk Mo'," according to David Stuart's reading of the building's hieroglyphic step.

Beneath a stairway directly across the court from Ante Structure is a well-preserved tomb, found in 1992, that dates to this same era. It contains the bones of a young adult male who had been placed on an elevated stone platform. On the floor beneath the platform were the remains of funerary offerings, including some two dozen pottery vessels, several of which were brilliantly painted in stucco with polychrome motifs. The pottery and stratigraphic position of the tomb date it to the mid-sixth century, indicating that the bones may be those of Waterlily Jaguar or either of his two little-known successors, both of whom had exceptionally short reigns in the years between ca. A.D. 544 and 553. The tomb could even be that of the tenth ruler, Moon Jaguar, about whom we have a bit more information. Moon Jaguar was inaugurated on May 26, 553, and died on October 26, 578, after a reign of 25 years.

Although Ante Structure was partially demolished by the final phase of construction in the East Court (ca. 650–800), another building belonging to the middle span of the Acropolis sequence has been discovered sealed beneath the final-phase Str. 10L-16, a large temple that is being excavated by Ricardo Agurcia. This earlier building, known as Rosalila (Fig. 5.49), was a two-story, multiroomed structure. Its entire façade was decorated with elaborate stucco masks, once painted in brilliant colors. Rosalila was obviously an especially venerated building, for not only was it maintained and used for an exceptionally long time, but when it was finally abandoned it was carefully preserved and buried intact, unlike most Copan buildings, which were at least partially demolished before being covered by new construction. Inside the buried rooms of Rosalila, Agurcia's excavations have found several termination caches, the most spectacular being a horde of nine beautifully worked eccentric flints (Fig. 15.31).

The eleventh ruler, Butz Chan, had the third-longest reign of any known Copan king: some 50 years, from November 19, 578, to his death on January 23, 628. During this time he appears to have initiated the expansion of the Copan polity, for the text on one of his two known monuments, Stela P (Fig. 5.50), appears to refer to Los Higos, a smaller site located in the La Venta valley to the east of Copan, which could indicate that Copan extended its control into this neighboring region during this time. Butz Chan's successor, Smoke Imix, the twelfth in the dynasty, reigned longer than any other known ruler at Copan, from 628 to 695 (67 years). During this long and stable segment of Copan's political history, he saw the polity

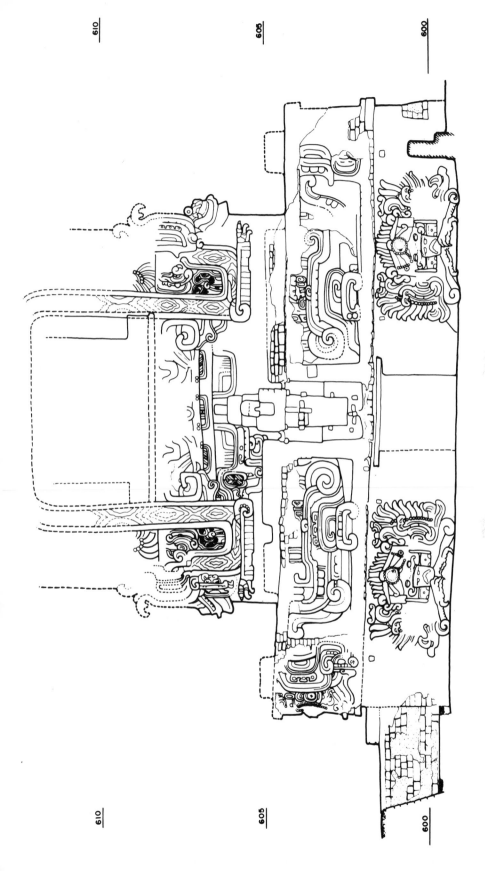

Fig. 5.49. Rosalila Structure, Copan, Honduras: (*above*) Str. 10L-16 from the west, showing the carefully interred Rosalila structure under its northern side (Stela P, shown in Fig. 5.50, stands in the West Court in front of Rosalila's buried doorway); (*below*) the elaborate western façade of Rosalila, representing a giant deity mask (partially reconstructed composite based on excavation as of 1991). A tomb discovered in an earlier platform directly beneath Rosalila may be that of the founding ruler, Yax Kuk Mo', or his successor, Ruler 2.

Fig. 5.50. Copan Stela P, with its portrait of the eleventh ruler, Butz Chan: this stela, dated at 9.9.10.0.0 (A.D. 623), stands in the West Court; in the background is the northern side of Str. 10L-16 (see Fig. 5.49).

reach its maximum extent in area, power, and prestige. His dominion apparently included Quirigua and, from that base, much of the lower Motagua Valley, with its fertile agricultural resources and its strategic hold over the jade route that followed this river from the mineral sources upstream to Lago de Izabal and the Caribbean. David Stuart first identified the name glyphs on Quirigua Monument 12 (Altar 12) as those of Smoke Imix. The text on the monument dates an event that may have been the joining or annexing of Quirigua to the Copan polity, in 9.11.0.11.11 (A.D. 653). Back at the capital, Smoke Imix commemorated the 9.11.0.0.0 (652) period ending with a series of monuments at the eastern and western entrances to the Copan Valley. Stelae 12, 13, and 23 were erected on the eastern approaches, and stelae 10 and 19 were similarly placed on the western approaches.

A tomb discovered beneath Str. 10L-26, within a previous architectural stage designated Chorcha, can be dated to this interval. If not the ruler Smoke Imix himself, the tomb's occupant appears to have been a close relative of the king, perhaps a brother or son, who may have been a royal scribe.

Upon Smoke Imix's death, in 695, the ruler known as 18 Rabbit took the throne. The agenda of this thirteenth successor, which concentrated on constructions and monuments in the site center, contrasts with that of his predecessor. Although the final major renewals of the Copan Acropolis may have been initiated by Smoke Imix, much of the present arrangement of this complex originated during 18 Rabbit's reign. The still-visible East and West courts were probably laid out at this time, and the edifice that dominates the East Court from its northern side, Str. 10L-22, was built as 18 Rabbit's palace and sanctuary. This structure is the last in a series of such buildings built by his predecessors at this location as "sacred mountains," identified as such by their *witz* corner masks. One of the major architectural changes introduced about this time at Copan was the use of carved stone for building decoration, replacing the previous tradition of modeled plaster. Although originally covered with plaster and paint, the underlying stone sculpture provided a much more durable foundation for architectural decoration.

A refurbishment of the Great Plaza north of the Acropolis, which took place during 18 Rabbit's reign, served as the setting for his portrait monuments, the greatest assemblage of such monuments ever created at Copan, and the culmination of the Copan sculptural tradition. These include, in chronological order, stelae C, F, 4, H, A, B, and D; all are carved in a florid, deep relief. Stela H (Fig. 5.51a) is probably the best preserved stela at Copan, while Stela A (Fig. 5.51b) is famous for its text proclaiming that 18 Rabbit's kingdom of Copan ranked with three others—Tikal, Palenque, and Calakmul—as one of the four greatest polities of the Maya world at the period ending of 9.15.0.0.0 (A.D. 731).

A series of ballcourts had been constructed and used during the Classic period at Copan, and the last project of 18 Rabbit's reign may have been the building of the final version, the Great Ballcourt. Located southwest of Str. 10L-26, the Great Ballcourt constituted a transition between the public space of the Great Plaza to the north and the forbidden temples and palaces of Copan's rulers in the Acropolis to the south. The date of its dedication is recorded on the eastern structure, and has been read as 9.15.6.8.13, which Linda Schele and David Freidel note is only 113 days before 18 Rabbit's capture and execution by Cauac Sky of Quirigua (9.15.6.14.6), thus suggesting the plausible scenario that the Copan king had been raiding the northern borders of his realm to secure captives for the dedication of his new ballcourt when he fell victim to his erstwhile vassal at Quirigua.

## QUIRIGUA

Quirigua (Fig. 5.52) is a small center situated along the lower Río Motagua in the southeastern lowlands, within the most extensive alluvial valley in the Maya area. Its location was strategically sound, lying, as it did, between the sources of jadeite and obsidian farther up the Motagua and the trade connections the river provided to the Caribbean coast, the central lowlands, and Central America beyond.

Fig. 5.51. Stelae of Copan ruler 18 Rabbit in the Great Plaza: Fig. 5.51a (*left*) Stela H, 9.14.19.5.0 (A.D. 730); Fig. 5.51b (*right*) Stela A, 9.15.0.3.0 (A.D. 731), with text mentioning Copan and three other great cities of the Late Classic Maya world, Tikal, Palenque, and Calakmul (compare Fig. 6.3).

In the nineteenth century, after a visit to the ruins by Frederick Catherwood, John Lloyd Stephens reported Quirigua's existence to the outside world. Alfred Maudslay spent several seasons there, photographing the famous monumental sculptures and sponsoring the first excavations at the site. In the early twentieth century, the Archaeological Institute of America conducted excavations under the direction of Edgar Lee Hewett and Sylvanus Morley, and further work by the Carnegie Institution of Washington followed. From 1974 to 1979 the University Museum, University of Pennsylvania, conducted a comprehensive program to investigate the site core, its surrounding settlement, and contemporaneous sites within the lower Motagua Valley under the direction of Robert Sharer. The Pennsylvania project also worked with the Guatemalan government, through the Instituto de Antropología e Historia, to conserve the site's monuments and consolidate its major buildings.

Fig. 5.52. Quirigua, Guatemala: aerial view of the Motagua Valley, showing the main group of Quirigua in the forested area in the center of the photograph, the Sierra de las Minas in the background.

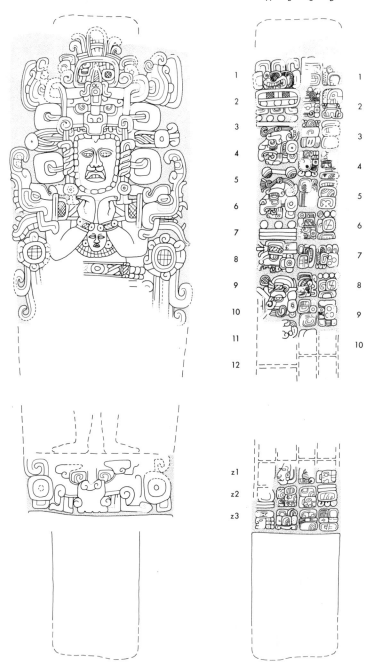

Fig. 5.53. Drawing of Quirigua Monument 26, upper fragment: (*left*) front, with a lord (perhaps the fourth ruler of Copan, Cu Ix, or his Quirigua subordinate) holding a two-headed serpent bar; (*right*) back, with Long Count date 9.2.18.0.0? (ca. A.D. 493) and apparent references to the third Copan ruler (glyphs C6, D6), and the fourth Copan ruler (glyphs C8, D8).

These more recent investigations combined archaeological and historical research by integrating excavation with studies of Quirigua's hieroglyphic inscriptions. The effort revealed that Quirigua was founded during the Early Classic era, probably by elite colonists from the central lowlands, possibly from Tikal. Settlement and construction seem to have begun during this era at Group A, high on a hilltop overlooking the valley, and on the floodplain itself, along the banks of the Motagua (all remains of this early settlement on the floodplain are now covered by deep deposits of alluvium). The period is marked by at least two fifth-century monuments: one, Monument 21, from Group A, dedicated in 9.2.3.8.0 (478); the other, Monument 26, from an early precinct on the floodplain north of the main group, dedicated in 9.2.18.0.0? (493). Together, these are among the earliest stelae outside the central lowlands to combine portraiture and dated hieroglyphic texts (Fig. 5.53). The text on the back of Monument 26 refers to two rulers, their names linked to 3 hel and 4 hel titles that identify them as the third and fourth rulers in a dynastic succession. Thus, Monument 26 may portray Quirigua's fourth ruler, and may refer both to him and to his predecessor. An alternative reading has recently been suggested by Linda Schele, who sees the inscription referring to the third and fourth rulers, not of Quirigua, but of Copan (see below).

The main group at Quirigua (Figs. 5.52 and 5.54), comprising the structures and monuments visible today, is largely the product of a flurry of building activity in the Late Classic and Terminal Classic eras. Under the soils of the floodplain are the remains of most of the domestic settlement of Quirigua, and of several larger compounds built as elite residences or for other specialized purposes. The only examples of the latter still visible are the East Group and the South Group. Further traces of settlement have been found on the terraces above the floodplain. Quirigua actually developed along the north bank of the Motagua, but today, after changing its ancient course, the riverbed is about 1 km south of the main group. The main group can be divided into three areas, the Great Plaza on the north, the Acropolis on the south, and the Ballcourt Plaza between.

The Acropolis is a quadrangle of structures around a central court: residential and administrative buildings on the north, west, and south sides of the court, and a series of smaller shrines on the east side of the court, the whole reflecting an ancient residential pattern found also at Tikal. The shrines on the east side of the court probably served as the focus for rituals venerating the ancestors of Quirigua's ruling lineage. The oldest of the shrines, dating from the middle of the Classic period, covered a deeply buried crypt in which were found the remains of a single male adult, possibly the ancestral founder of the residential complex. Under the west side of the Acropolis, excavations and tunnels uncovered a completely buried ballcourt dating from the outset of the Late Classic. Str. 1B-2, in the southwestern corner of the Acropolis, was a small residence, nearly buried by later construction. This building, elaborately decorated with sculptured masonry reliefs, probably served as the initial

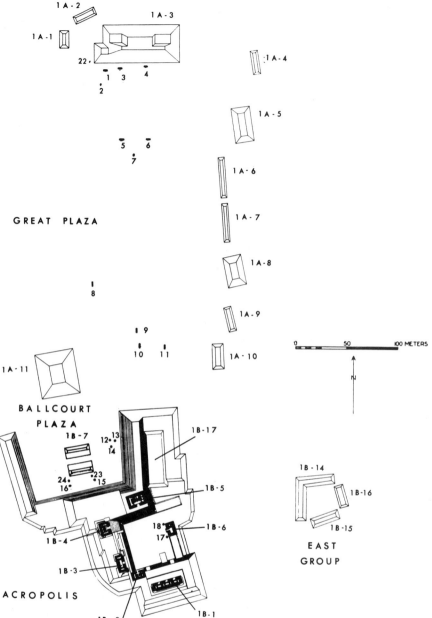

1A-2

1A-1

1A-3

22.

1 3

2

1A-4

1A-5

5 6

7

1A-6

GREAT PLAZA

1A-7

1A-8

8

1A-9

9

1A-11

10 11

1A-10

BALLCOURT
PLAZA

1B-7

1B-17

12 13
14

24 23
16 15

1B-5

1B-4

18
17

1B-6

1B-3

ACROPOLIS

1B-2

1B-1

0        50        100 METERS

N

1B-14

1B-16

1B-15

EAST
GROUP

Fig. 5.54. Map of Quirigua, Guatemala:
the Late Classic layout of the site, executed
by the ruler Cauac Sky following his
vanquishing of 18 Rabbit, the ruler of
Copan, was apparently patterned after
that of Copan (see Fig. 5.42), but on a
much more modest scale (except for the
far larger Great Plaza, the setting for the
largest stelae in the Maya area).

SOUTH
GROUP

1B-8

1B-9

1B-11

1B-10

1B-12

1B-13

residence of Quirigua's greatest ruler, Cauac Sky, in the mid-eighth century. The two largest structures, 1B-1 on the south side (Fig. 5.55) and 1B-5 on the north, were constructed during the reign of Quirigua's last historically recorded ruler, Jade Sky, whose portrait appears on Monument 11 (Stela K). An earlier wall, decorated with the sculptured mosaic head of Kinich Ahau, the Maya sun deity (God G), was discovered in 1975 along the west side of the Acropolis (Fig. 5.56), from which it must once have overlooked the Río Motagua.

North of the Acropolis is the Ballcourt Plaza, enclosed on three sides by stepped "reviewing stands," in the center of which is a small, later ballcourt. Monument 12 (Altar L), with its reference to Smoke Imix, ruler of Copan (see above), was originally found in this court, together with Monument 13 (Altar M); Monument 13 bears the earliest known reference to Quirigua's emblem glyph (9.15.3.2.0, or 734). But the most famous sculptures in the Ballcourt Plaza are the two giant carved boulders (Fig. 5.57), or "zoomorphs" (monuments 15 and 16), each paired with a beautiful altar "throne" (Fig. 5.58) bearing carvings over its upper surface (monuments 23 and 24), all four of them dedicated by the ruler Sky Xul. The Ballcourt Plaza is bounded on the north by a badly ruined, terraced pyramid, and on the west by a deep basin, now silted in but once perhaps providing facilities for Quirigua's river port.

North of the Acropolis and the Ballcourt Plaza lies the Great Plaza, the setting for the most extensive array of monuments in the Maya area. Here, eleven of the

Fig. 5.55. The Acropolis at Quirigua, Guatemala, showing Str. 1B-1, built during the reign of Jade Sky and containing the latest known Quirigua date, 9.19.0.0.0 (A.D. 810), and Str. 1B-2 (at lower right), an earlier building that may have been the palace of Cauac Sky.

Fig. 5.56. Quirigua, Guatemala: Late Classic carved-mosaic mask of Kinich Ahau, the sun deity, part of a west-facing decorated wall between Acropolis strs. 1B-3 and 1B-4 that was discovered during excavations in 1975.

Fig. 5.57. Quirigua Monument 16 (or Zoomorph P): one of a pair of so-called "zoomorphs" in the Ballcourt Plaza, and one of the most spectacular of all Maya carved monuments, Monument 16 depicts a young ruler (Jade Sky?) seated in the open maw of the underworld, holding a manikin scepter (at left) and a shield adorned with the face of the sun deity; 9.18.5.0.0 (A.D. 795).

largest Maya sculptures known (Fig. 5.59) are located. All but two of these sculptures pertain to the long reign of Cauac Sky (see Fig. 5.60), who was inaugurated in A.D. 724, and one of these (Zoomorph G) marks the date of his death in 784. Cauac Sky's portrait adorns most of the monuments in the plaza (stelae A, C, D, E, F, H, and J). Most of the terraces and stairways at Quirigua are monumental in size but devoid of embellishment. Architectural sculpture seems to have been reserved for the vaulted buildings, where it took the form either of masonry (as in Str. 1B-2

Fig. 5.58. Quirigua Monument 23: drawing of one of a pair of altars in the Ballcourt Plaza, showing a figure wearing a jaguar mask dancing in the coils of a serpent; reign of Jade Sky, 9.18.0.0.0 (A.D. 790).

Fig. 5.59. Quirigua: the Great Plaza, looking south toward the Acropolis, with several of the ruler Cauac Sky's great monuments visible between the trees: Monument 4 (Stela D) at the far right and, in the middle distance, Monument 7 (Zoomorph G) between monuments 5 (Stela E, right) and 6 (Stela F, left).

and the mosaic-decorated wall) or of stucco-façade reliefs (found as ruined fragments in structural debris).

Most of this construction occurred after 738, the year the Quirigua inscriptions record that Cauac Sky captured 18 Rabbit, ruler of Copan. The expansion of Quirigua, lasting for about a century during the reigns of Cauac Sky and his successors, appears to have been directly stimulated by the newfound wealth and power deriving from the city's gaining independence from Copan, then wresting control of the Motagua Valley resources and commerce.

## A Tale of Two Cities

Some 35 years into his reign, 18 Rabbit presided over the accession of a new *ahau* at Quirigua, which was Copan's principal dependency and controlled the lucrative Motagua jade route. On his later monuments, the new *ahau*, Cauac Sky, recorded this inauguration event ("taking the manikin scepter in hand") as having taken place "in the land of" (*u cab*) 18 Rabbit of Copan in 725 (9.14.13.14.17). As we have mentioned, an earlier Quirigua monument, Altar L, indicates that Quirigua had been subordinated to Copan during the reign of 18 Rabbit's predecessor, Smoke Imix, and the history of Quirigua's domination by Copan may be even older than this. The reinterpretation of the text on the second-earliest dated stela at Quirigua (Monument 26) argues that, rather than naming the third and fourth rulers

Fig. 5.60. Quirigua Monument 5 (Stela E), the largest known stela in the Maya area, bearing the portrait of the ruler Cauac Sky (9.17.0.0.0, or A.D. 771).

of Quirigua, as had been originally assumed, the inscription refers to the third and fourth kings of Copan (Ruler 3 and Cu Ix, respectively). This raises the intriguing possibility that Copan controlled a vast Early Classic realm from the earliest days of Quirigua's political history, rather than as a result of the later expansionism led by Smoke Imix.

Regardless, shortly after becoming ruler of Quirigua, Cauac Sky adopted his own emblem glyph, claiming the title of *k'ul ahau* on his earliest known monument, the modest Altar M. This date appears to refer to an unknown event in 9.15.3.2.0 (734), which may have signaled a bid for Quirigua's independence from Copan. If so, Cauac Sky's ambitions, probably motivated by a desire to control the lucrative trade that flowed through Copan's precincts, appear to have led to conflict with Copan.

Matters came to a head in 738 (9.15.6.14.6), a date repeatedly given prominence on Quirigua's monuments, when Cauac Sky captured and sacrificed 18 Rabbit. The event broke Copan's ancient hegemony over the southeastern region, and the twenty-year gap in Copan's inscriptions may reflect the political and economic turmoil that would have followed.

Though the date of the end of 18 Rabbit's reign understandably occurs repeatedly on Quirigua's monuments, it is mentioned only once at Copan (in the historical chronicle on the Hieroglyphic Stairway). At Copan there were undoubtedly two important consequences of this defeat. In the first place, although Quirigua may not have conquered Copan, it had certainly broken away from Copan's control and gained its independence. This had to have been a severe economic blow to Copan, which lost not only its primary dependent power but also its control over the rich trade flowing along the Motagua route and along the most direct route north to the central lowlands. In the second place, as in other cases where a polity lost its ruler to capture and sacrifice, the defeat dealt the great city a crushing blow, resulting in the loss of prestige and morale. For those at Copan, the gods had obviously withdrawn their blessings on the city's king and its destiny.

At Quirigua a major rebuilding effort, pursued for the remainder of Cauac Sky's 60-year reign, transformed the entire site, as vivid evidence of the newly won wealth and prestige that followed Copan's defeat. Though the Quirigua inscriptions name Cauac Sky the fourteenth ruler (14 hel), this designation may refer, not to a local dynastic succession, but rather, as Berthold Riese has suggested, to Cauac Sky's claim to have been the successor to 18 Rabbit, the thirteenth ruler at Copan. Cauac Sky's victory seems to have blunted the power and prestige of Copan for a time, but it is not clear whether Copan heeded any claim he might have made to be the fourteenth successor of Yax Kuk Mo'. Because no known monuments were erected during this period at Copan, what little we know about 18 Rabbit's successor, named Smoke Monkey, rests in references by later rulers, as on Altar Q. These later references record the succession of Smoke Monkey as fourteenth ruler at Copan, 39 days after 18 Rabbit's death (9.15.6.16.5). It remains possible, however, that Cauac Sky did manage to control Copan during this period, and that Smoke Monkey was installed as his subordinate. Thus Smoke Monkey, if he existed at all, may have been accorded Copan's fourteenth rulership only in the retrospective accounts of later rulers, who would have sought to gloss over the humiliation following 18 Rabbit's defeat and sacrifice. Regardless of events at Copan, it is clear that Cauac Sky made the most of his victory in bolstering his own prestige at home. The string of titles linked to his name on his monuments at Quirigua often includes the *zotz* glyph, the head of the leaf-nosed bat, which served as the main sign of the Copan emblem glyph.

The damage to Copan's power and prestige is evident in the years following 18 Rabbit's death. It is evident not only in the lack of carved monuments from this period, but also in the slowdown in construction. Most significantly, we see evidence for internal political changes at Copan following the disastrous loss of 18 Rabbit. It seems likely that authority was maintained during this critical period by an unprecedented degree of power sharing among the leaders of the highest-ranking elite lineages. Excavations directed by Barbara and William Fash in 1989 in Str. 10L-22A, the only building known to have been built during this ten-year period (Fig. 5.61), provided the evidence.

This structure, which stands immediately west of 18 Rabbit's great building, Str. 10L-22, has been identified as a council house by the careful work of specialists in archaeology, architectural restoration, art, and epigraphy, who were able to expose, identify, and re-articulate the sculptures and glyphs that had fallen from this building. These adornments include ten large mat designs that identify the structure as the *popol na* ("council house"). The building is also adorned by "9 Ahau" glyphs that probably date it to the period ending 9.15.15.0.0 9 Ahau 18 Xul (A.D. 746); by *ahaulil* glyphs ("governance," or "act of governing"); by nine large hieroglyphs, on the corners and three sides of the building, that seemingly refer to the names or emblems of Copan's leading elite lineages; and by cross-legged, seated human figures, seated in niches above the hieroglyphs, bearing distinctive chest and headdress adornments. These seated figures were probably portraits of the elite lineage heads in the Copan Valley who had gained a voice in the political deliberations that took place in the council house.

Excavations directed by David Webster in Group 8N-11, part of the suburban Sepulturas Group, have yielded further clues to the nature of Str. 10L-22A. Barbara Fash has reconstructed the upper body of a large carved figure from the eastern structure of Group 8N-11, and shown that its chest adornment is identical to that of a figure on the west side of the Str. 10L-22A council house. From this and other iconographic information, it has been proposed that the personage who once lived in Group 8N-11 was a war captain and one of the lineage heads who took part in the governing of the Copan polity during this critical period in its history.

Fig. 5.61. Copan, Honduras: the front of Str. 10L-22A, the *popol na*, or "house of the mat" (note the mat motifs above the doorways); 10L-22A, constructed during the reign of the fourteenth ruler, Smoke Monkey, stands immediately west of Str. 10L-22 (Fig. 5.43).

## The Revitalization of Copan

It would seem that the new leadership at Copan set about quietly but determinedly to restore the city's economic foundations. The loss of Quirigua effectively weakened or even severed Copan's trade and tribute from the north, and its apparent response was to build and expand the economic networks to the south and east, into Central America. The contemporary archaeological record in these areas, ranging from the Late Classic sites in El Salvador (to the south) to the sites of the Río Ulua and other regions in Honduras (to the east), shows evidence of pronounced increases in trade and influences that originated at Copan.

William Fash's excavation of Str. 10L-26 (see Fig. 5.45) also indicates that the construction of this greatest of all of Copan's monuments was begun during this same period. The structure may have been planned under the aegis of the ruling council, or even of the mysterious Smoke Monkey, but it is clear that it was completed and dedicated by the fifteenth ruler, Smoke Shell. Regardless, the significance of Str. 10L-26 and its unprecedented Hieroglyphic Stairway is based on its sacred location, as a new temple built over the original shrine to the dynastic founder, Yax Kuk Mo'. Its stairway was carved with the longest known Maya inscription, some 2,200 glyphs, and was embellished at regular intervals with statues of warrior-kings (these have been identified by Linda Schele as Moon Jaguar, Butz Chan, Smoke Imix, 18 Rabbit, and Smoke Shell). Although these specified identifications are uncertain, what *is* certain, as William Fash has shown, is that the Temple of the Hieroglyphic Stairway, in presenting the full and glorious history of Copan in both text and image, was the means used by the successors of 18 Rabbit to wipe away the humiliation of Quirigua's victory and restore the prestige of Copan and its ancient ruling dynasty. The message of this magnificent monument is clear: the cosmic order has been reestablished by the restoration of Copan to its former place of prominence in the Maya world.

The death of Smoke Monkey is later recorded as having happened in 749, and the accession of the fifteenth successor, Smoke Shell, took place fourteen days later in the same year (9.15.17.13.10). It was by Smoke Shell's efforts that the prestige of Copan was fully restored. Not only did he dedicate the Temple of the Hieroglyphic Stairway to proclaim this fact for all to see, but he succeeded in forging an alliance with one of the most important Late Classic cities, Palenque. He accomplished all this in the established manner by marrying a woman from Palenque's royal family. This marriage, which sealed the longest-distance alliance of any known from Maya history, was successful in the sense that it produced a son, Yax Pac, who would be the next ruler of Copan. But although Copan's prestige had been largely restored, it would appear that its later kings would never recover from the weakening of central authority that followed in the wake of 18 Rabbit's defeat.

The date of Smoke Shell's death is not known, but Copan's texts do record the inauguration of Yax Pac (also known as "Sun-at-Horizon" or "Madrugada") in 763. Destined to be the sixteenth and last known ruler in Copan's dynastic succession, Yax Pac inherited both the prestige and the problems of his predecessors. He did carry out an ambitious construction program, which produced at least two of the major buildings that still dominate the Acropolis, Strs. 10L-11 and 10L-16, as well as the much smaller Str. 10L-21A. The construction of Str. 10L-11, which was clearly one of Yax Pac's most important undertakings, began with the erection of a reviewing-stand stairway, dedicated in 769, on the north side of the West Court. Mary Miller has shown how the iconography of this stairway, in conjunction with the three markers set in the plaza below, identifies the West Court with Xibalba, with its watery motifs (shells and caimans), where the Hero Twins played ball with the gods of the underworld—altogether an appropriate setting for captive-sacrifice rituals.

Above the reviewing stand, with doorways facing in all four directions, Yax

Pac built his "sacred mountain." Str. 10L-11 is a two-story building—dedicated four years later, in 773—that seems to have served both as his residence and as a place of ritual. Str. 10L-16, his principal temple, also facing the West Court, is replete with war imagery. In front of this building, as we have seen, Yax Pac placed the most important monument of his reign, Altar Q, which he dedicated in 9.17.5.0.0. A stone throne adorned with his royal ancestors, Altar Q may actually have been where Yax Pac sat while overseeing the rituals held in the West Court. Excavations behind this monument in 1988 revealed that the dedication of the altar was sanctified by an unusual ceremony in which at least fifteen jaguars—each perhaps symbolizing the ancestral spirit of one of Yax Pac's predecessors—were sacrificed, then buried beneath the altar.

But Yax Pac's problems, too, are visible in these buildings, for none was constructed or decorated with the skill and durability of Copan's earlier architecture. He seems to have attempted to hold his kingdom together by rewarding his nobles and officials with greater status and increasing wealth, but in the process they amassed more power as well. Each of these men was the head of a lineage; each was also a state official or councilor of the *popol na*, or council house; and the authority they exercised was proclaimed on the carved benches in their residences from which they presided—like lesser versions of the great king himself. Several of these benches, dating to the reign of Yax Pac, have been found in their residential compounds in the Sepulturas Group.

One of the most powerful of these men, to judge from the size of his compound and the opulence of his house, was the royal scribe who lived in Group 9N-8, a primary focus of excavations directed by William Sanders during the PAC II research at Copan. The house of the royal scribe is the largest and tallest building on the southern side of his compound, and portraits of him adorn the building. In each case he holds the tools of his trade, the scribe's brush and shell (probably used to contain paint). His bench, found in the central room of Str. 9N-82, was carved in the most ornate style, using full-figure glyphs to represent the cosmos and to record not only his name, Mak Chanil, but also that of his father, Kuk Kawil, who probably held the same office before him, and the name of his king, Yax Pac. In the complex that Mak Chanil commanded were houses for his lineage, his servants, and his workshops, and even accommodations for a group of non-Maya people, probably from the Ulua valley, who seem to have produced pottery or other goods under his patronage.

Two of Yax Pac's brothers seem to have held even more important posts in Copan's political hierarchy. One of these men, Yahau Chan, appears to have governed the western district of the valley from a secondary administrative center now covered by the modern town of Copan. Linda Schele has shown that a monument (Altar T) placed at this locus by Yax Pac on the first-katun anniversary of his succession in 9.17.12.5.17 also honored his brother. When Yahau Chan later dedicated his own monument (Altar U) nearby, he saw that it gave his parentage: the monument names his mother, Lady Chac Ahau Xoc, as the mother of the Copan ruler (Yax Pac, who may have had a different father). From several texts in the Principal Group, David Stuart has identified Yax Pac's other brother. His name or title is Yax K'amlay, which has been translated as "First Steward." A carved text found during Wyllys Andrews's 1990 excavations of the cemetery group (the administrative and residential compound located at the entrance immediately south of the Acropolis) seems to identify Yax K'amlay as the occupant of this compound during Yax Pac's reign.

Another important official during the reign of Yax Pac apparently lived in the North Group, two large rectangular compounds on the terraces commanding the valley. The northern location of these compounds suggests associations with the supernatural and the heavens. Two seasons of test excavations in 1988 and 1989, directed by Wendy Ashmore, offer vital clues to their function and show that both of them date from the Late Classic. The southern compound (Group 8L-12) appears to have been the principal residence for an elite lineage, and the elite appear to have been served by attendants who lived in the surrounding structures (at least nineteen ancillary platforms), in a pattern like that found in the major residential compounds of the Sepulturas Group. And after the fashion of other known elite compounds, the architectural decorations here are individual portraits, each presumably identifying an occupant's status and role within the Copan hierarchy. In contrast, the higher northern compound (Group 8L-10) is devoid of such ancillary structures, and the fallen façade sculpture does not portray or identify individuals. For example, the fallen carved stones from one building façade in the northern compound present themes of ritual, sacrifice, and the heavens, and those from its companion building include the name of the fallen ruler 18 Rabbit, and a calendar-round date (8 Lamat 6 Tzec) that probably refers to 9.15.6.14.8 (May 3, 738, two days after 18 Rabbit's capture and sacrifice). Further excavations are in order, but these clues suggest that the elite residents of Group 8L-12 administered an adjacent ceremonial complex, Group 8L-10, that venerated the deceased Copan ruler 18 Rabbit. The complex may be a shrine to his apotheosis (or deification), following his sacrifice.

The final building erected during Yax Pac's reign is Str. 10L-18 (see Fig. 5.44), which was dedicated in 801 (9.18.10.17.18). The building is located on a platform at the southern end of the East Court, immediately east of a portal arch that once marked the entrance to the court. It faces north, toward the East Court, commanded by buildings on its northern edge, the *popol na* (10L-22A), 18 Rabbit's sacred mountain (10L-22), and strs. 10L-21A and 10L-21 (now destroyed). The carved doorjambs of 10L-18 show Yax Pac and a companion, probably one of his brothers, as warriors, holding spears and shields and adorned with trophy heads and ropes for binding captives. This is the only known example of active-warfare motifs at Copan, which perhaps testifies to the increasing conflicts that probably plagued the last years of Yax Pac's rule.

Yax Pac's last years are not recorded on major monuments. His final public monument, dedicated in 9.18.10.0.0 (800), was Altar G1, the last of three elaborate altars set among the stelae of his ancestor 18 Rabbit in the Great Plaza. He commemorated his second katun of rule, not on a stela or altar, but on a small carved-stone incense burner. The katun ending of 9.19.0.0.0 (810) is marked not at Copan, but rather on Str. 1B-1 at Quirigua, where Yax Pac is recorded as performing a ritual with Quirigua's last ruler, Jade Sky. Because a ruler's performing such a ritual outside his own capital is an unusual occasion, it has been suggested that Yax Pac may have been a refugee from his home city by this time. We do not know his death date, but Stela 11, dedicated in 9.19.10.0.0 (820), depicts an aged and deceased Yax Pac standing in Xibalba, in the manifestation of God K. This stela was placed on the platform of Str. 10L-18, and because of the death associations of this monument, it seems likely that the anciently looted Str. 10L-18 tomb may once have been Yax Pac's place of burial.

The end of centralized rule at Copan is told on its last known monument, Altar L (Fig. 5.62), dated at 9.19.11.14.5 (822), which was placed on the north platform overlooking the Great Ballcourt. Altar L, a rather pathetic imitation of Altar Q, shows Yax Pac seated opposite U Cit Tok, the man who attempted to succeed him as the seventeenth ruler of Copan. His failure to do so, and the end of the dynastic succession, are inferred from the fact that Altar L was never finished. The glyph blocks on the opposite side of the stone were never carved, and the other two sides are blank. Like the intended purpose of Altar L, the power that had sustained the kings of Copan for so long had vanished.

## The Last Days of Quirigua

For a full century after they defeated Copan and gained their own independence, the rulers of Quirigua appear to have reigned supreme over the lower Motagua Valley and its adjacent lands, controlling the jade route between the highlands to the west and the Caribbean to the east. After establishing the blueprint for his new polity's success, Cauac Sky died, in 784, and he was succeeded 78 days later by his presumed son, Sky Xul, who seems to have ruled for about eleven years.

Sky Xul was followed by the last identified Quirigua ruler, Jade Sky, who took the throne about 800, and Quirigua's power appears to have peaked during his reign. Jade Sky launched another massive construction program, rebuilding much of the Acropolis compound. (Curiously, throughout more than a century of construction activity in Quirigua's Acropolis, a small but elaborately decorated building [Str. 1B-2] that has been identified as Cauac Sky's original palace remained untouched, and was probably venerated by his successors.) In 810 the last known date recorded at Quirigua was inscribed on the façade of Str. 1B-1, one of Jade Sky's new Acropolis buildings (Fig. 5.55). The texts from this building include the rather mysterious reference to Yax Pac, ruler of Copan, who apparently visited Quirigua expressly to perform a ritual associated with the dedication of this building.

A few years later Jade Sky's presumed palace, the largest building at Quirigua (Str. 1B-5), was completed, but although construction elsewhere at the site continued thereafter, the historical record ceases at this point. Quirigua was unquestionably occupied in the years following Jade Sky's reign, which probably ended sometime in the mid-ninth century, but the occupants seem to have included intruders from the Caribbean coast, to the north, who probably settled in to control the center and its commercial interests. Construction also continued in the Acropolis: relatively flimsy rooms were added to Str. 1B-1, some adobe buildings were raised, and a massive new platform buried the Kinich Ahau masks overlooking the Motagua river. But no more Classic-style monuments were erected. Within a century or so of the end of Jade Sky's reign, Quirigua seems to have been completely abandoned.

Fig. 5.62. Copan Altar L, the end of the royal dynasty: here, the carved south side, the only finished portion of the monument, showing (at right) the sixteenth ruler, Yax Pac, opposite (at left) U Cit Tok, his possible successor (9.19.11.14.5, or A.D. 822).

## The Development of the Maya Lowlands in the Late Classic

During the Late Classic era the lowland Maya world continued to expand in population, area, and complexity. In earlier times a series of single powers seems to have enjoyed a measure of supremacy, dominating the lowland stage by a combination of economic and political power that was reinforced by the sheer prestige of being the center of the Maya world. Thus Nakbe was succeeded by El Mirador, which in turn was succeeded by Tikal. But in time, with dramatic growth in population and the proliferation of elite lineages commanding both seats of power and subject populations, the pattern of lowland society began to change. Thus the older, established powers came to be challenged by an expanding host of lesser centers all jockeying for positions of advantage. Some of these were allied to more powerful polities, others sought to remain unaligned or were defeated and absorbed into the realms of larger centers, and still others seized their own independence when the opportunity arose.

As a result, the Late Classic lowland polities not only expanded but also diversified, both economically and politically, by dividing sovereignty among a greater number of centers. Yet the surprising uniformity found in so many aspects of culture and artifacts throughout the Late Classic indicates frequent communication and even strong alliances between centers. A number of years ago Tatiana Proskouriakoff noted that the stylistic and iconographic variations typical of many Early Classic monuments were in time replaced by a more uniform tradition. Today, most scholars also define regional styles, such as the narrative compositions seen across the Usumacinta area. Artifacts such as ceramics, at least in the elaborately decorated pottery styles, also tend to be very similar within particular regions. Significantly, artifacts of this sort are associated with the elite class, and their similarity reflects considerable communication and cooperation among the ruling classes of most lowland centers. Further evidence of linkage is to be found in inscriptions detailing marriage exchanges and even military alliances, as well as in indications that certain centers were evidently seen to be, across whole regions, of great religious importance.

Joyce Marcus has in fact proposed that certain polities enjoyed a special ceremonial status during the Late Classic, as is suggested by an inscription from Stela A at Copan (Fig. 5.51), dated at 731 (9.15.0.0.0), which records the emblem glyphs of Tikal, Copan, Palenque, and possibly Calakmul. Each of these centers is associated in Stela A's text with one of the four cardinal direction glyphs. The same quadripartite principle may have been honored at least 150 years later, as can be seen in a similar inscription at Seibal, although two new centers had by then replaced Copan and Palenque on the roster.

Yet it should be reemphasized that despite all the intersite linkages and possible hierarchical rankings in status and prestige, there is no evidence that the Late Classic Maya were unified politically or even economically. The political landscape of the Late Classic Maya consisted, rather, of a series of independent polities. Still, although the use of emblem glyphs in the texts of these polities may have signalled a measure of political independence, there were certainly differences in size and power among them, and in any case the regional power and prestige of each sovereign polity waxed and waned throughout the Classic era. Thus we can see now how a city like Tikal, which once dominated much of the central lowlands, could fall prey to an alliance between its ancient rival Calakmul and the ambitious new power Caracol, only to be revitalized under the dynamic leadership of Ah Cacau and his successors. Similarly, an emerging power like Dos Pilas could establish itself by claims to royal connections to the ancient prestige of Tikal, and by blatant military expansionism, only to fall victim to the same forces of violence it had unleashed. And a well-established polity like Copan could suffer crushing defeat at the hands of its former vassal Quirigua, a defeat that split its ancient realm in two, sorely threatened its prestige and confidence, and changed forever some of its basic political institutions.

Modern archaeological and historical research are combining their techniques and insights to sort out these sequences of events, and we see now that the processes of expansion and diversification were fueled by increasing competition over lowland resources, as the rulers of polities each sought to control as much land, trade, people, power, allegiance, and prestige as possible. At the same time, concomitant increases in population and environmental exploitation brought the ecological balance to the critical edge of vulnerability, and during the subsequent Terminal Classic, therefore, the lowland landscape would undergo profound changes.

# 6

# THE TERMINAL CLASSIC

There were no more lucky days for us; we had no sound judgment. At the end of our loss of vision, and of our shame, everything shall be revealed.
—*The Book of Chilam Balam of Chumayel* (Roys 1967: 83)

**W**ith few exceptions, Maya centers throughout the southern and central lowlands suffered a seemingly dramatic decline during the Terminal Classic era. Over a span corresponding roughly to the ninth century (A.D. 790 to 889, or 9.18.0.0.0 to 10.3.0.0.0 in the Maya calendar), a slowdown and then cessation in intellectual and cultural activities are reflected in the archaeological record over much of the area that had seen so many great achievements during the Early and Late Classic. By the end of the Terminal Classic the construction of major administrative, residential, and ceremonial structures had ceased at most central and southern lowland sites. No new dynastic monuments were erected, and Long Count calendrical dates were no longer recorded (the last known Long Count date on a stela is 10.4.0.0.0 [909], on Tonina Monument 101). The manufacture and distribution of the elaborate traditional luxury and ritual goods made of pottery, jade, wood, bone, and shell all but disappeared. From this kind of evidence, it can be inferred that the decline of the Classic lowland Maya involved in particular the ruling elite, the social class that had sponsored and directed most of the activities that disappear from the archaeological record.

At the same time, many centers to the north, in the Yucatan Peninsula, were reaching their greatest levels of power and prosperity even as the cities to the south waned. But even among the newly emerging powers of the northern lowlands there were signs of profound political change. Long Count dates, for so long used to chronicle the achievements of the supreme rulers of the Classic Maya city-states, were no longer being recorded in the north *or* in the south. Throughout the Maya area the focus on the single ruler and his reign all but vanishes from both the inscriptions and the portraits carved after the last recorded Long Count date (Tonina's

909). This groundswell of political change is perhaps best characterized by the shifting trends seen in Maya sculpture and paintings. Portraits of individual rulers with all the trappings of supernatural and secular power, alone and aloof except for their downtrodden captives, typify most Classic-period stelae. But in the Late Classic the ruler begins to share center stage, as subordinate elite increasingly appear on monuments, holding prestigious titles or offices, taking captives, and living in larger and more elaborate residences. During the Terminal Classic the depiction of the individual ruler often disappears completely, replaced by multiple portraits of elite personages of apparently equally high status, usually carved on lintels or painted on buildings, rather than on free-standing monuments.

## The Decline of Dynastic Rule

Recent research at Copan offers us one of the best glimpses we have of the political changes that began to take shape within the elite ruling organization. As we saw in the preceding chapter, centralized dynastic rule at Copan suffered a setback in the eighth century. The causes for this decline in authority lay not so much in a particular event—in this case the loss of a single powerful ruler, 18 Rabbit—as in, very likely, the power-sharing and title-sharing that his successors began to institute in their determined attempts to recover from this setback. The process continued and even increased under Yax Pac, and the wider problems faced by the ruling elite at other Maya centers were much the same in character as the pressures brought to bear on Copan's final kings. Certainly the combination of overpopulation, environmental degradation, and the concomitant intensification of warfare, with all of its destructive effects, destabilized authority and severely disrupted Maya society in many areas of the lowlands. But at Copan, at least, the effects of warfare seem not to have been crucial. Rather, policies aimed specifically at recovering a wounded dynasty's prestige and power, particularly when combined with the more general problems of overpopulation and deforestation, played the key role in the destabilization of the political system and the final collapse of centralized authority.

Within the Copan polity this process culminated in the demise of the dynastic ruler as supreme political and religious authority. This is not to say that there may not have been disorder with the breakdown of traditional centralized authority, including violence against the old ruling elite and their symbols of power. Andrews's recent excavations in the elite compound south of Copan's Acropolis show that at least one major building was destroyed by fire. And the looting of several elite tombs, including the plundering of the presumed burial chamber of the sixteenth ruler (Yax Pac) under Str. 10L-18, may have occurred during this time. In any event, the dynastic demise can be traced roughly to an unfinished inscription on Altar L, which portrays the purported accession of a successor to Copan's sixteenth ruler, Yax Pac, in A.D. 822. But the new *ahau* apparently never managed to gain the support of his elite confederates, let alone the loyalty of his non-elite subjects. In his stead the second tier of authority, the heads of the various elite lineages in the Copan Valley, continued their hold on authority for most of the Terminal Classic. That they did so is clear from the archaeological investigations in the Copan Valley, which show that the ongoing political changes and environmental degradation in the valley did not result in its immediate abandonment. Many of the major elite administrative and residential compounds throughout the valley continued to be occupied after the fall of the last ruler at Copan. Thus it seems that even after the population peaked, in the first half of the ninth century, there was still enough productive, arable land in the surrounding region for occupation to continue—if in slowly declining numbers and in progressively less nucleated communities—for several centuries thereafter. To judge from the obsidian-hydration dates obtained from valley settlements, the final abandonment of the Copan Valley did not occur until ca. 1100–1200, three to four centuries later.

Current research at Copan has reinforced the notion that the pattern of decline is not the same everywhere in the lowlands. In contrast to the endemic violence that brought down dynasties and entire polities in the Petexbatun region, the end at Copan seems far more gradual and far less violent. The pattern at Copan was a three-stage process involving, first, the weakening and decentralization of political and religious power in the eighth century, second, the demise of centralized authority in the ninth century, and third—following persistent occupation of the Copan Valley for several centuries thereafter under a decentralized elite authority—the eventual abandonment of the valley. In the centuries following the political collapse, the population slowly declined in numbers and redistributed itself across the landscape. This same pattern of political change and declining centralized authority—accompanied and followed, across centuries, by a delayed demographic decline—has been seen at other sites in the Maya lowlands, and the "Classic collapse" so often cited in the literature should in fact be viewed as a protracted process, not as a sudden catastrophe.

## The Collapse Issue

For years, one of the most popular and most persistent issues in Maya research has been the "collapse" of Classic civilization. That the practice of erecting monuments bearing Long Count dates had been abandoned was taken as evidence for a sudden and dramatic end to the great city-states of the Classic lowlands, but it is now apparent that the abandonment of the practice is only one symptom of a widespread process of change that operated over several centuries. These changes were due to a variety of processes, ranging from endemic warfare in some regions, such as the Petexbatun, to more long-term political and economic changes, such as those seen at Copan. Although no single event or process was responsible for all of the changes seen at the close of the Classic period, and although the actual sequence of contributing events surely varied from place to place, the process seen at Copan was similar to that almost certainly at work in other Maya centers as well. After all, the fortunes of the Classic Maya polities were linked in a variety of ways—economically, politically, and socially—and trouble in one polity was therefore likely to affect others as well.

The spatial pattern of these fundamental shifts indicates that the failure was earlier and more complete in the heartlands of the southern and central lowlands than it was to the north (in Yucatan) or the east (in Belize). Occupation continued in these outlying regions, and in Yucatan actually increased. But in the great central-lowland sites, such as Tikal, the archaeological record reflects a profound dispersal and decrease in population. And although the region continued to be occupied for several centuries, ultimately, at some point several hundred years prior to the arrival of the Spaniards, the population centers throughout the central lowlands—except for a few settlements around the lakes of the central Peten—were abandoned to the rain forest. In drawing such conclusions, however, it must be remembered that vast areas of the lowlands are yet to be investigated, and future research could certainly alter our present view of the Terminal Classic even here.

Maya civilization thus did not come to an end with the close of the Classic period. In fact it now appears that there was considerable overlap between the decline of the Classic centers in the central lowlands and the rise of a series of enterprising new centers in Yucatan to the north. In fact, subsequent Postclassic Maya polities were concentrated in two distinct regions outside the central and southern lowlands, the northern half of the Yucatan Peninsula and the far-removed southern highlands of Guatemala. The focus of interest in the Terminal Classic has been, in almost all cases, a search for the causes of the decline in Classic society, but the related and equally important issue of the causes and character of the growth in the northern-lowland and Guatemalan-highland polities has in consequence been very poorly addressed. Fortunately, recent research in the northern lowlands has begun to rectify this disparity.

In the remainder of this chapter we will examine both topics, beginning with a survey of the various theories traditionally advanced for the demise of the Classic lowland Maya, and closing with a discussion of the rise of the new northern polities.

## Investigations into the Classic Decline

What brought on the demise of the Classic lowland Maya? The question began to be asked as soon as many of the great Classic centers were rediscovered in the lowland rain forest, during the eighteenth and nineteenth centuries. The early answers all stressed sudden catastrophe—a seemingly obvious conclusion, given the stark contrast between the silent, jungle-covered ruins and what was recognized as a once-populous and highly developed civilization. To the European mind, a great civilization set in the depths of what seemed to them an inhospitable rain forest was a contradiction in terms. It seemed only logical, therefore, to assume that the Maya failed because of the constraints of their environment. And that they had succeeded so brilliantly for a time was viewed, sometimes even to this day, as something of a "mystery." To early scholars, therefore, the question of the Maya "failure" was often not as important as the question of Maya origins. And that question was initially answered, of course, by recourse to theories of migrations from a host of known civilizations in the Old World, which for the early scholars "explained" the mystery of a complex civilization buried in the jungle.

With the more recent general acceptance of the idea that the Maya represented a wholly indigenous New World development, attention has turned to the reasons for the abandonment of the great lowland cities. Over the past century, dozens of theories have been advanced. The popularity of individual explanations has waxed and waned, but in recent years two general trends can be discerned. First, there has been a shift away from theories that propose a single cause, toward theories that advance multiple factors. Second, as we have seen, there has been a shift away from sudden and dramatic catastrophe, as the engine of change, toward more gradual, long-term processes. More important, the newer theories allow for both regional variation and the interdependence of the lowland economic and political systems. This means that while there may have been different causes for decline in individual polities, their interdependence meant that the demise of one affected others, creating a domino effect that accelerated the process of change throughout the lowlands.

A better understanding of the Classic Maya demise has been achieved through an increase in knowledge about ancient Maya society. The results of recent research have in fact challenged and overthrown many traditional concepts about ancient Maya economic, social, and political organization. Maya archaeology (like the archaeology of many other complex societies) was long dominated by investigations of the largest sites and, within those sites, of the most elaborate or impressive buildings. As a result, there has been a heavy bias toward the elite class, the ancient occupants of palaces, temples, and tombs. A more balanced sampling of archaeological data, including surface surveys of the countryside, has begun to produce a better picture of all aspects of ancient Maya society, and of its environment. As the older concepts of the ancient Maya are modified or replaced by new information and new theories, so too is our understanding of the end of the Classic Maya, and any evaluation of this issue must be considered with this perspective in mind.

The theories concerned with the demise of Maya civilization in the central and southern lowlands emphasize either *internal* factors or *external* factors. Theories emphasizing internal factors view the Classic Maya decline as generally isolated from developments occurring in the wider context of Mesoamerica. Theories emphasizing external factors propose that the demise was due largely to developments beyond the immediate Maya area.

## Theories Emphasizing Internal Factors

Most of the earliest theories attributed the end of Classic Maya civilization to internal events, but several recent proposals have also emphasized these factors. The themes of the three most useful of these theories are natural catastrophes, ecological degradation leading to disaster, and sociopolitical breakdown and disintegration.

Several kinds of natural catastrophes have been advanced as possibly triggering the demise of Maya civilization. Earlier we explored the well-grounded hypothesis that volcanism—exemplified most dramatically by the violent eruption of Ilopango—played a role in the decline of Preclassic society in the southern Maya area (Chapter 3), but volcanism could not have wreaked much havoc elsewhere in the Maya area.

Though most of the Maya lowlands is not geologically active, earthquakes do occur. Using the evidence of unrepaired structural damage to a major palace at the site of Xunantunich in the central lowlands, an area of low tectonic activity, it has been proposed that one or more catastrophic earthquakes may have contributed to the downfall and abandonment of various lowland sites.

But only the southern fringes of the lowlands are seriously vulnerable to tectonic activity. Recent excavations at Quirigua, far to the south of Xunantunich, leave no doubt that major earthquakes did indeed plague the inhabitants of the southeastern Maya lowlands. Quirigua was built directly on the Motagua fault, the same one whose rupture in 1976 caused a disastrous earthquake in Guatemala, clearly revealing the fault trace. Evidence of ancient damaged and collapsed construction there, as well as massive secondary buttressing of masonry buildings, testifies to ancient tectonic activity. But although earthquakes may have affected certain areas, including particularly Quirigua but perhaps also Xunantunich, there is no evidence and little likelihood that tectonic catastrophes devastated the entire Maya lowlands.

Other natural disasters have been proposed as culprits in the Classic Maya downfall. The Maya lowlands are frequently visited by Caribbean hurricanes, and a major storm of this kind can easily destroy agricultural production over a wide area. Still, the idea that the transient and relatively localized effects of hurricanes could trigger the failure of a whole civilization is difficult to swallow. The destruction of a forest in a hurricane's path might even prove to be beneficial, for a major effect of the destruction is likely to be the clearing of new lands for agricultural exploitation.

Epidemic diseases could have produced catastrophic depopulation of the Maya lowlands. Yellow fever has been among the most often suggested of such culprits. The disastrous effect of the epidemic diseases introduced among the New World populations at the time of the Spanish Conquest is tragically documented. Malaria, smallpox, and other Old World diseases had monumental consequences. Yellow fever is also considered an Old World disease by most authorities, but its discovery among New World primates (especially howler monkeys) indicates that it may be indigenous to Central and South America as well. The historically documented bubonic plague that ravaged medieval Europe obviously did not affect the Maya directly, but it does illustrate the social consequences of sudden and severe, disease-induced depopulation, and offers an analogue for the lowland decline—though we have no evidence that such a catastrophe befell the Maya, there is no reason it could not have. That the ancient Maya were vulnerable to epidemic disease is indicated by skeletal studies at Tikal, Altar de Sacrificios, and Copan. These studies demonstrate progressive nutritional deficiencies and increasing disease potentials in lowland populations toward the end of the Classic period, owing probably to food shortages, crowding, and overpopulation.

A variety of ecological disasters has been proposed to explain the Maya demise. The earliest pointed to the harmful consequences of swidden agriculture, which is believed to have been the basis of lowland subsistence at one time. Its arguably destructive long-term effects on soil fertility and in turn the gradual conversion of forested areas into savanna grasslands have been used to explain the failure of Classic Maya civilization. Since the Maya had no tools with which to cultivate the grasslands, so this argument goes, farmers would eventually have been forced to abandon the central lowlands. Other supposed effects of swidden cultivation in combination with the heavy tropical rainfall of the lowlands were severe erosion and the deposition of soil into what would formerly have been shallow lakes, yielding the swampy depressions (*bajos*) found in many areas of the lowlands today. The question whether or not all these depressions were originally shallow lakes, at least within the span of Maya civilization, is yet to be resolved. In any event, the ecological-disaster theories based on swidden cultivation can no longer be supported, given the recent evidence that the agriculture practiced by the ancient Maya was both diversified and intensive (see Chapter 8).

Some investigators, however, never accepted the idea that the ancient Maya relied on swidden agriculture, proposing that only intensive agriculture could have supported the peak populations of the lowlands. Still, accepting the idea that the ancient Maya pursued intensive agriculture does not necessarily mean ruling out ecological disaster as a cause of the Classic decline. Most Maya scholars now agree that the documented intensification and increasing sophistication of Maya agriculture was a response to increasing population and its attendant ecological pressures. Thus, the original ecological-failure proposals have been redrafted to allow for the possibility that lowland population levels eventually expanded beyond the food-production capabilities of an overexploited environment. Furthermore, although the evidence is somewhat contradictory, the critical balance between increasing population and a subsistence system stretched to its limits may have been tipped by either temporary or long-term climatic changes, such as declines in rainfall.

The third of the three basic themes underlying internal-collapse theories, which attributes the decline to social and political failures, is based, either implicitly or explicitly, on supposed weaknesses inherent in Classic Maya society. These theories assume that in one way or another the prestige and authority of the ruling elite came to be eroded or even eliminated, the most dramatic variant involving violent revolts by the non-elite classes, and that as a result, Classic society collapsed and the lowland centers were abandoned.

The idea of a revolt has been extremely popular. Several investigators have suggested that the increasing size of the ruling class, combined with its abuses of power, led to a popular revolution. The most prominent advocate of the revolution theory was J. Eric Thompson. His "peasant revolt" theory was widely acknowledged among Maya scholars and often even accepted. (It should be noted, however, that although this notion often turns up in Thompson's popular writings, it seldom appears in his scholarly publications.) The thesis holds that a combination of factors, including agricultural difficulties, malnutrition or disease, and perhaps even natural disasters—all bespeaking a chronic failure of the elite to intercede with the gods—culminated in widespread disillusionment among the Maya peasant class and a loss of confidence in the rulers. The situation was exacerbated, so the argument goes, by an increasing dissociation from the concerns of the populace by a theocratically organized elite, who turned increasingly to esoteric matters rather than to practical approaches to the mounting crisis. The proposed result was a violent revolt by the peasants and the destruction of the ruling class.

An economic variation on this theme holds that the elite-controlled trade network of the central lowlands (the core area) was eventually cut off from access to critical commodities by the rise of trading centers on the peripheries. As a result, the core area collapsed, followed thereafter by the peripheries, which were left with no trading customers. Archaeological evidence indicates, however, that many sites located in the peripheries declined long before those in the core area, quite the opposite of what this theory projects.

Another variation of the sociopolitical-failure thesis (actually one based on external conditions) attributes the Terminal Classic demise to a changing economic and political environment, specifically to competition from rival Mexican states. This thesis holds that more efficient means of mobilizing food resources, manpower, and wealth were introduced from the highland states of Mexico and placed the Maya in a vulnerable position. Specifically, so the argument goes, the traditional ruling elite could not or would not institute the changes necessary to confront the competition and ensure the survival of the Classic Maya civilization. Yet changes seen in the archaeological record during the Late Classic might well be interpreted precisely as attempts by the ruling elite to adapt to such crisis conditions. For example, the increasing investment in intensive agricultural systems may well have been managed by the ruling elite. Although of little practical benefit (except perhaps as a mechanism of psychological reassurance), even the apparent acceleration in the construction of monumental architecture during this era could be argued to have been an attempt to appease the supernatural powers believed to control Maya destiny, and thus to improve conditions and encourage confidence.

The Maya's own concept of cyclical history—especially its emphasis on fatalistic prophecies associated with a round of thirteen katuns (approximately 256 years; see Chapters 11 and 12)—is clearly relevant to the demise issue. Each katun in the cycle was numbered and had its own distinctive set of prophecies; and the Maya believed that the recurrence of a particular, numbered katun every 256 years would bring with it the reenactment of corresponding events and conditions from the past. Research has revealed indications that this cyclical concept of history guided the elite rulers at Late Classic Tikal, leading them for example to associate themselves deliberately and publicly with katuns representing earlier periods of prosperity (Chapter 5). This, in turn, has led to hypotheses that the Late Classic rulers at Tikal were in the midst of attempting a cultural revitalization aimed at reestablishing past glories, in part by invoking the katun cycle, and that their failure to realize the revitalization may have coincided with the decline of their polity.

On the basis of such reasoning, the late Dennis Puleston proposed that the Maya concept of cyclical history contributed actively to the decline. Prophecies of fundamental political and religious change associated with specific katuns are known from the ethnohistorical record. For example, the Spanish conquest of the last bastion of Maya independence at the site of Tayasal in 1697 was probably hastened by the approach of a new katun cycle that augured momentous changes (see the Epilogue). The earliest signs of trouble in the Maya lowlands began with the onset of a new katun cycle, in A.D. 790; the beginning of the preceding cycle (A.D. 534) corresponded with the series of changes associated with the decline of Tikal and the rise of new aggressive powers such as Caracol; and counting back an additional katun cycle, to A.D. 278, brings us to a time eerily close to the beginnings of the era of lowland Maya ascendancy that followed the eruption of Ilopango and the demise of the southern Maya's prosperity (Chapter 3). Some scholars conclude from these apparent regularities that as the Late Classic katun cycle approached its end, the fatalistic Maya may have failed to resist the forces of change that were sweeping away the old order out of a conviction that it would be futile to challenge prophecies that foretold fundamental changes in their society—particularly when the signs of decline were already there for all to see.

The final internal-factor theory considers accelerating civil warfare to have been a factor contributing to sociopolitical disintegration. This thesis ascribes the Terminal Classic disruption to an ever-expanding cycle of wars of conquest undertaken by one or more of the major Classic centers—a situation analogous to the Peloponnesian wars that debilitated Greece in the fifth century B.C. As we have seen, the traditional forms of ritualized raiding for tribute and captives were indeed transformed in the Classic, presumably as the result of increasing competition for land, labor, trade routes, and prestige. Powers such as Dos Pilas resorted to outright wars of conquest, and, at least initially, were successful. The new evidence from the Petexbatun region testifies to the consequences of conquest warfare: massive defensive installations and the eventual siege and destruction of the former capital of the conquest state, Dos Pilas. This research has proposed that the need to concentrate populations for defensive purposes put additional strains on an already overextended agricultural system. But although the disruptions caused by such endemic warfare may have been profound in regions like the Petexbatun, there is thus far no evidence that military conflict and its consequences approached the same intensity in other areas of the lowlands. Still, although warfare on a scale sufficient to bring ruin upon the entire Maya lowlands is yet to be demonstrated, as mentioned previously the interdependence of Maya polities meant that endemic conflicts in one region could have contributed to the destabilization of economic, social, political, and related systems far beyond their area of direct impact.

### Theories Emphasizing External Factors

Explanations for the demise of the Classic Maya that include external factors have gained increasing favor in recent years, since it no longer seems sensible to ignore the context of the larger issues and conditions that obtained throughout Mesoamerica.

Foreign invasion of the Maya lowlands has been proposed by several scholars. The evidence from Altar de Sacrificios, provided primarily by a rather complete shift in the pottery inventory, indicates that the site was invaded and conquered at the close of the Classic period. A similar event, suggested by changes seen in the architectural and sculptural records, as well as in the pottery, has been reconstructed at the site of Seibal, in the Petexbatun region. There would seem to be little doubt, in fact, that Seibal was occupied by a new ruling group at the end of the Classic period. In both cases, the identity of the homeland of the invaders remains in doubt, but stylistic evidence and the portraits of individual rulers on the postconquest monuments at Seibal suggest that they were foreigners sharing at least some cultural traditions with the lowland Maya. As we shall see, these invaders, who rose to power in the Terminal Classic, have been identified as Putun Maya, a Chontal-speaking group from the Gulf coast of Tabasco, Mexico, an area peripheral to Classic Maya civilization. As we have already suggested, these invaders, taking advantage of the chaos attending endemic warfare in the Petexbatun region, seemingly emerged as the ultimate victors in the area.

As is posited by the internal endemic-warfare theorists, proponents of the foreign-invasion thesis hold that the resulting disruptions in lowland Maya society were sufficient to bring about its demise. But the lack of evidence for invasion or conflict at most centers other than Seibal and Altar de Sacrificios casts considerable doubt on the cause-and-effect relationship between invasion and collapse. Arguably, invasion was more an *effect* than a *cause*—made possible, in fact, only by the already weakened condition of Maya society. At Tikal, Quirigua, and several other centers, there is little indication of invasion or any other kind of incursion from outside until well after these sites were in decline.

The economic relationships between the lowland Maya and the other peoples of Mesoamerica suggest another theory for the demise. The changes in Mesoamerican long-distance trade networks that mark the Terminal Classic may have isolated the southern- and central-lowland Maya from the economic and political powers that came to dominate the Postclassic. As we shall see, during this period the Putun Maya appear to have monopolized the seacoast trade routes, which had become increasingly important by the end of the Classic period. The investigation of a Postclassic trading center on Isla de Cozumel, off the northeast coast of Yucatan, related the demise to the failure of the traditional lowland elite to recognize the importance of the new sea trade around the Peninsula. As a result, the land routes were largely abandoned, and the lowland Maya were increasingly left out of the trade network and became isolated economically. A case for the rise of Tikal can be built around the site's position of control over trans-lowland canoe routes; conversely, a case can be made that it was when these routes diminished in importance that Tikal and other sites dependent on the trans-Peten connections appear to have fallen on hard times, eventually to be abandoned.

## The Emergence of New Power Brokers

Perhaps the most profound change of the Terminal Classic is associated with the rise of a new group, the Putun (or Chontal) Maya, whose homeland appears to have been along the Gulf coast in the lowlands of what is today the Mexican state of Tabasco. The Putun were not a single Maya "nation," but comprised several independent groups. They appear to have been unified only in language (Chontal Mayan; see Chapter 13) and in cultural traditions, which were heavily Mexicanized, especially among the ruling elite. The political and religious institutions of the Putun in fact reflected many characteristics typical of Central Mexico, and at least some Putun groups seem to have been allied with the Toltec, the major power of Early Postclassic Mexico.

The Putun Maya were both warriors and merchants, and their aggressive undertakings during the Postclassic seem often to have been motivated by a desire to seize and control important resources and trade routes. Initially, they seem to have been concerned with maintaining several of the old riverine and overland routes in the central and southern lowlands that had flourished during the Classic period. Eventually, however, they came to control the seacoast trade around the Yucatan Peninsula, which connected the east and west coasts, and, ultimately, the commerce between Gulf-coast Mexico and Central America. Most of the series of ports in this sea-trading network included colonies of resident Putun merchants: for example Xicalango, in the Putun heartland along the Gulf coast; Isla de Cozumel, off north-eastern Yucatan; Isla Cerritos, off northern Yucatan; and Nito, on the Gulf of Honduras at the base of the east coast of the Peninsula.

The Yucatec Maya chronicles, such as the *Books of Chilam Balam*, speak of an important group known as the Itza, who may be one of the Putun groups. The Itza were a famous, historically identified Maya group whose destiny was central to the fortunes of Postclassic Yucatan, as we shall see. Given our uncertainties about the ethnic identity of all these peoples in the archaeological record, the term Putun will be used here to refer to the generalized Mexicanized Maya (including the Itza) who clearly seem to have expanded their commercial and political power during the Postclassic. A clearer picture emerges at the time of the Spanish Conquest, when the Putun homeland on the Gulf coast of the Yucatan Peninsula was known as Acalan, or "land of canoes." The capital of this region, known as Itzamkanac, was described by the Spanish as a substantial and prosperous center. At the time of Cortés's visit in 1524, the ruler of Acalan was both the leading merchant of Itzamkanac and the holder of the ancient title of *ahau*, or supreme ruling lord.

## Intervention in the Southern Lowlands

Evidence of Putun movements can be detected as early as the Terminal Classic, when they made significant penetrations into the central and southern Maya lowlands. The ceramics at Becan, Tikal, and several other sites change during this era in ways that suggest outside influence, perhaps that of the Putun. But the principal thrust of at least one Putun group, at least initially, was up the Río Usumacinta, the major trade route between the Gulf coast and the region of the southern lowlands and the adjacent highlands. Here, on the Río Pasión, a strategic tributary of the Usumacinta, is the site of Seibal, a relatively minor center during the Late Classic, when it was defeated and dominated by the aggressive Petexbatun polity, only to rise again in the Terminal Classic, apparently under Putun Maya leadership.

### SEIBAL

This center, the largest in the Pasión region, is situated on the bluffs overlooking the Río Pasión, in the southern lowland rain forest, about 60 km east of Altar de Sacrificios. The site was reported and photographed by Teobert Maler in the early twentieth century. From 1963 to 1968 Seibal was the subject of a comprehensive archaeological investigation conducted by the Peabody Museum of Harvard University under the overall direction of Gordon Willey; the project's excavations were directed by A. Ledyard Smith.

The three major groups of the site (groups A, C, and D) are arranged on adjacent hilltops, interconnected by causeways (Fig. 6.1). Most of the core of Seibal (Group A) is arranged around two small plazas. The northern plaza contains a ballcourt on its west side. Four stairways on the southern plaza grace a central platform (Str. A-3). A stela (Fig. 6.2) stands at the base of each side of the platform, and inside the summit structure is a fifth stela. All were dedicated to the 10.1.0.0.0 katun ending by a ruler named Ah Bolon Tun.

Never a major Classic-period center, Seibal reached an apogee in the Late Preclassic, then declined in the Early Classic. As we saw in Chapter 5, one of its rulers was captured in 735 by Dos Pilas Ruler 3, who apparently incorporated Seibal into the Petexbatun realm. A hieroglyphic stairway dedicated at Seibal by Dos Pilas Ruler 4 in 9.16.0.0.0 commemorates this event. But following the destruction of Dos Pilas and the breakup of its conquest state, Seibal must have regained its independence. In any case, the Peabody research at Seibal indicates that the site reached its zenith in the Terminal Classic during the time when it apparently was taken over by a powerful outside group, now identified as the Putun Maya. The architectural and ceramic remains reflect this foreign heritage, and some of Seibal's late buildings have strong architectural ties to the northern lowlands, which also links it to the Putun expansion. Perhaps the best example of this linkage is a round masonry platform reached by a sacbe east and south of Group A. Still, a series of well-executed carved monuments dating from 10.1.0.0.0 to 10.3.0.0.0 provide the most vivid evidence for Seibal's nontraditional Maya heritage in the Terminal Classic. These monuments depict rulers whose manner and costuming combine Classic Maya and foreign elements. The first of these is associated with Str. A-3 and Ah Bolon Tun, who was apparently the first of the new Seibal rulers. The magnificent Stela 10 (849) depicts Ah Bolon Tun dressed in very Late Classic Maya regalia, holding a double-headed ceremonial bar, but his mustached face appears distinctly non-Maya (see Fig. 6.3). Even more alien-appearing are stelae 2, 14, and 19, all dating to approximately 870. Stela 14, for example, portrays an impersonator of the Mexican wind deity, Ehecatl. Several of the portraits of Seibal's apparent Putun rulers during the Terminal Classic strongly resemble in style the painted figures on the recently discovered murals at Cacaxtla, in Central Mexico (see below).

Thus, beginning about A.D. 830 and continuing through the remainder of the ninth century, Seibal was significantly transformed into a new and major center. And though the new buildings and monuments erected at this time show many nontraditional characteristics, the sculptured portraits of Seibal's new rulers show that they had adopted many conventions of the traditional Classic Maya elite. The most dramatic evidence for their acculturation is in the text of Stela 10, where, as Joyce Marcus has pointed out, we see the emblem glyphs of Seibal and three other lowland

Fig. 6.1. Map of Seibal, located on the west bank of the Río Pasión, in Guatemala; sacbeob connect major groups in the site core.

Fig. 6.2. Seibal Str. A-3, a Terminal Classic platform with four stairways: (*above*) before excavation; (*below*) after excavation and consolidation, with one of its four monuments, Stela 10, standing at its base.

polities: Tikal, Calakmul (?), and Motul de San José (?). In her interpretation, these emblems refer to the four polities acknowledged as being paramount at the time, recalling a similar passage on Copan Stela A (Chapter 5). David Stuart has since construed the verb in this passage as indicating that these emblems refer to visits from these centers to witness the katun-ending ceremonies commemorated by the monument. By either interpretation, Stela 10 offers testimony to the authority and prestige claimed by Seibal's new rulers. Thus, although Ah Bolon Tun and his successors may have been Putun Maya, they quickly adopted the conventional lowland political institutions, and were apparently accepted by the traditional ruling houses of the neighboring great powers of the times.

The archaeological evidence indicates that shortly after 900 the city of Seibal was abandoned, for reasons unknown. Perhaps when the old trans-Peten trade routes broke down, Seibal lost much of its strategic commercial advantage. There are also indications that renewed invasions, probably by competing Putun groups from the Gulf coast, may have brought about the end of Seibal's Putun dynasty.

Fig. 6.3. Seibal Stela 10: the ruler Ah Bolon Tun holds a traditional symbol of rulership, the double-headed serpent bar; the text at the lower left records the emblem glyphs of Seibal and three other Maya cities, Tikal, Calakmul, and possibly Motul de San José (compare Fig. 5.51; 10.1.0.0.0, or A.D. 849; see also Fig. 6.2).

## Putun Connections to Yucatan and Central Mexico

The Yucatecan chronicles describe the history of this period: "There were thirteen folds of katuns when they established their houses at Chakanputun. . . . For thirteen folds of katuns they had dwelt in their houses at Chakanputun. This was always the katun when the Itza went beneath the trees, beneath the bushes, beneath the vines, to their misfortune." As originally suggested by Joseph Ball, it is quite possible that Chakanputun is Seibal, deep in the southern rain forest ("beneath the trees . . . beneath the vines"), and that the foreigners who took over Seibal were Putun Maya from Tabasco.

During this period Chichen Itza, destined to become the dominant center of the Maya world, was founded as a new political and economic capital. We will describe this great city and follow its fortunes in our next chapter, but the famous wall paintings in the Temple of the Jaguars, above the Great Ball Court at Chichen Itza, are worth noting here, for they may depict scenes from the history of the Putun Maya, and one series of these scenes was clearly set in the rain forest of the southern lowlands. These might have been intended as a representation of Seibal and the period of Putun domination over portions of the southern lowlands. The other group of murals depicts a highland setting similar to the environment of Central Mexico. This setting, together with the theme of the murals themselves—the confrontation between two war leaders and their forces—recalls connections even farther afield, and implies that the Putun Maya were closely involved in the commercial and even political affairs of Central Mexico.

This implication is supported by evidence at several sites in Central Mexico, and it now seems likely that Putun Maya groups penetrated westward as far as the Valley of Puebla, perhaps to secure trade networks during a period of disorganization between the fall of Teotihuacan and the rise of Tula, capital of the Early Postclassic Toltec state. The evidence for this conclusion begins with the long-known Maya-style architectural reliefs at the site of Xochicalco, in the state of Morelos. Further support for Putun expansion lies in the Valley of Puebla, at Cacaxtla, where spectacular, newly discovered murals depict a great battle between opposing forces, both led by war captains who display combined Maya and Mexican characteristics. Finally, pottery employed in the Valley of Puebla during this era includes Plumbate and Fine Orange types that are usually associated with Putun Maya.

## Reconstructing the Classic Decline

It is now clear that the rise of the Putun or Chontal Maya was closely linked to both the decline of the traditional powers of the Classic Maya lowlands and the rise of the new polities of the Terminal Classic, especially in the northern lowlands. Before considering these northern heirs to the traditions of Maya civilization, we shall summarize what we know of the process of change that ended the Classic period.

On the basis of what we now know, it is obvious that the decline of the Classic lowland Maya was a complex, gradual, and far-ranging process. No single site or region can supply the causes for all these changes. A variety of factors combined to exacerbate the stresses within Classic Maya society, and although we may never know the details, it would seem that these factors created problems that ultimately could be solved, if at all, only by drastic population displacements and massive re-formulations of lowland Maya economic, social, and political systems.

Though the most obvious expressions of the decline are identified with the elite class, the process surely involved and affected all levels of Maya society. And the lowland elite, for their part, worked ceaselessly to promote widely shared training, beliefs, symbols of prestige, and lines of authority, all reinforced by increasingly elaborate ceremonialism, to encourage the scores of polities to cooperate in the maintenance of political alliances and the control of trade. All the while, however, the ruling elites were relying increasingly on warfare to strengthen their individual bases of power. As we have seen (in Chapter 5), these conflicting goals created an interdependent but highly intercompetitive relationship among the lowland states, which then promoted sudden, violent swings of fortune in a number of individual polities, and saw the downfall of several powerful ruling lineages and their polities. The many swings of fortune of individual Maya polities created several apparent cycles of prosperity and decline through the course of Maya civilization. These include a peak in the Late Preclassic, a decline at the end of the Preclassic, another peak in the Early Classic, a decline in the mid-Classic, and the greatest peaking of prosperity in the Late Classic. In a sense, therefore, the demise of Classic lowland civilization can be seen as another downswing in this cyclic process, one that endured longer than—and affected far more than—any seen previously.

The self-serving, even self-deifying activities of the upper class also served to increase the social distance between the elite and the various non-elite classes. The demands of a growing nobility for more, larger, and increasingly elaborate palaces, along with the other trappings of elite wealth and power, widened the gap between the privileged and unprivileged classes. At the same time, crushing failures in warfare, in food production, or in any other enterprise, by the very rulers who were seen as the gods' agents on earth, must have been interpreted as signs of supernatural disfavor. Within such a belief system, the psychological effects of the mounting tally of failures must have been devastating, especially against a background of resentment over the ever-increasing privileges of the elite. Reinforced by fatalistic belief in prophecies—in particular that katun endings would usher in chaotic change—resentment and failure produced a decline in confidence and popular support. All this was translated into loss of power and prestige, which led ultimately to the downfall of the traditional institutions of rulership, whether by endemic warfare, revolt, or more subtle changes in the structure of the political system.

Continued population growth during the Classic intensified the pressures on an increasingly complex and vulnerable subsistence system even as the incidence of malnutrition and disease increased and productivity decreased. The expansion of the elite and other specialist groups also meant that, proportionally, the numbers of privileged nonproducers increased at the expense of the beleaguered, non-elite farmers. The elite's probable responses to these crisis conditions—accelerated investments in intensive agricultural systems and in the construction of ever larger ceremonial structures—would also have exacerbated the situation, by placing heavier labor demands on the populace and in turn compounding the problems of food production and distribution.

The stresses brought about by population growth and increasing agricultural intensification all had their most direct impact on the natural environment. Evidence of soil erosion and deforestation demonstrates overexploitation of the increasingly vulnerable lowland environment, and pressures to produce more food were met by decreasing fallow times and other measures that led, rather, to a decline in productivity. As forests disappeared, so did supplies of firewood essential for both cooking and the production of lime plaster for construction. These are not sudden turns of events, of course, and populations tended to decrease in overexploited areas as people moved and resettled in areas offering better soils and more extensive supplies of wood. (The same trends can be seen today, as for example in the movement of Kekchi Maya groups from the northern highland regions into the southern lowlands.) But seen over the full span of the Terminal Classic, these trends resulted in the abandonment of much of the central lowlands, as well as steady increases in populations in the surrounding regions of the highlands and Yucatan. We still do not know if these long-term processes were sufficient to produce the demonstrated demographic shifts. Nor do we know whether climatic change may have played a part; although the evidence is not conclusive, it is quite possible that long-term trends of decreasing rainfall, or even short-term declines in rainfall at the most crucial times, may have intensified the problem.

At the same time, the traditional long-distance trade networks, via land and river canoe, diminished in importance with the increase in seacoast trade around the Yucatan Peninsula. The failure of the established elite to adapt to these changing economic patterns led to a further loss of wealth, prestige, and power. Although several southern-lowland centers, including Altar de Sacrificios, Seibal, and Quirigua, seemingly were occupied and refurbished by the members of the new mercantile elite, eventually they too declined in importance and had to be abandoned.

The combination of these factors brought about a shift in the structure of economic and political power in the lowlands, from the traditional ruling lineages in the old inland Classic centers to a newer mercantile elite—the Putun Maya—who occupied the old centers or founded competing centers of power. As suggested above, much of the population that had occupied the central lowlands during the Classic period, including those members of the elite class able to adapt to new conditions, gradually moved to the new power centers in areas controlled by the prosperous new states in northern Yucatan and portions of the highlands, and—as we shall see—to the new mercantile elite centers along the Gulf and Caribbean coasts.

However these factors are ultimately sorted out, it no longer seems profitable to look for single, dramatic causes for the decline of the Classic Maya. Thus the issue has shifted from finding causes for a dramatic "Classic collapse" to reexamining the very concept of protracted cultural decline. The traditional term "collapse" now clearly seems inappropriate, for the Classic Maya appear not to have suddenly disintegrated; rather, both internal and external processes—multiple, subtle, and simultaneous—yielded a gradual transformation of the social, political, economic, and even ideological foundations of Maya society. During the Terminal Classic these processes produced a reoriented culture based in areas outside the central lowlands—on the coasts, in portions of the highlands, and in Yucatan—a culture that would prosper during the Postclassic era and then suffer the ravages of the Spanish Conquest. The most important center of this reorientation process was in the Terminal Classic northern lowlands, at the very time most of the traditional Late Classic polities to the south were declining.

## The Rise of the Northern Polities

Both rainfall and soil cover diminish as one proceeds north through the Yucatan Peninsula (see Chapter 1), and population growth in the northern lowlands had to have been constrained by the limited agricultural potential of the region. Yet, as we have seen, despite these limitations the archaeological evidence clearly establishes that a series of populous and prosperous Maya centers developed in the Peninsula, beginning in the Preclassic with centers like Komchen (see Chapter 3).

In large measure, these centers owed their existence to valuable local goods, especially sea resources (fish and salt), production of plant fibers (cotton and sisal), fruit, honey, and animal products. Control over the production and export of these or other commodities was undoubtedly the foundation of the prosperity seen in the archaeological record of the Peninsula. Several large northern centers, such as those located in areas of very thin soils near the coastal salt sources, were probably at least partially dependent on food imports to sustain their populations.

The Early Classic era remains poorly known in much of the northern lowlands. No single major center seems to have dominated the political and economic life of the era, although several important sites (such as Ake, Acanceh, and Izamal) that might be able to furnish data about this timespan are known but essentially uninvestigated. Hieroglyphic texts from the Classic period are also rather scarce in

Yucatan. The scattering of dated Early Classic monuments that does exist in the area includes Lintel 1 at Oxkintok (Fig. 6.4) from 475 (9.2.0.0.0) and Stela 1 at Tulum (found there but undoubtedly moved from elsewhere) from 564 (9.6.10.0.0). But these are isolated occurrences, since long sequences of dynastic monuments are not typical of most northern lowland Classic sites.

Several northern centers appear to have risen to prominence during the Late Classic. Dzibilchaltun, located immediately north of the modern city of Mérida, expanded rapidly during the Late and Terminal Classic eras, ultimately becoming, in its time, one of the largest northern centers. Its growth and prosperity were probably bolstered by control over the production and export of local salt resources, and its strength clearly made it heir to the prominence enjoyed by Komchen during the Late Preclassic. Although no hieroglyphic texts have survived, the presence of sculptured stelae indicates that this center was ruled by an elite dynasty. The prosperity of Chunchucmil, located some 100 km southwest of Dzibilchaltun, also seems to have reached its apogee in this era. Given its location in one of the driest areas of Yucatan, its prosperity also might have been founded on salt and other nonagricultural commerce.

### DZIBILCHALTUN

Dzibilchaltun is an extensive, important site situated in the far northwestern corner of Yucatan, only 20 km from the coast. Its location, so near the salt-

Fig. 6.4. Oxkintok, Yucatan, Mexico: Lintel 1, with the earliest known Long Count date in the northern lowlands (9.2.0.0.0, or A.D. 475).

producing shores of the Caribbean, certainly suggests that one of its ancient roles involved the salt trade (see Chapter 9). The site, only some 5 m above sea level, is within one of the driest stretches of the northern lowlands. Its water supplies were furnished by the Xlacah Cenote, located in the southwestern corner of the site's main plaza.

A major program of archaeological investigation at Dzibilchaltun began in 1956 and continued for the next ten years. This research was directed by E. Wyllys Andrews IV, who along with George Brainerd had reported the site in 1941, after its discovery by Alfredo Barrera Vásquez. The Dzibilchaltun Project was sponsored by the Middle American Research Institute of Tulane University.

These investigations revealed that in ancient times the entire region surrounding the site was densely settled (see Komchen, Chapter 3). In fact, the near-continuous extent of settlement remains made it difficult to determine the boundaries of the site. The mapped area of Dzibilchaltun covers more than 19 km² and includes over 8,000 identified structures, most of which are apparently house platforms that probably once supported pole-and-thatch dwellings. About 2,000 platforms preserve the remains of low stone walls enclosing either one or two rooms, which undoubtedly were once covered by thatched roofs. The central 0.5 km² of the site contains close to a hundred masonry structures, including vaulted buildings on low platforms and terraced pyramids clustered around several plaza areas (Fig. 6.5). Many of these core-area buildings seem to have housed the ruling elite of Dzibilchaltun (Fig. 6.6).

A series of sacbeob, or causeways, connects nearby and outlying groups with the central area. The zone surrounding the central area, 3 km² in extent, contains smaller clusters of structures, some with masonry vaults, often distributed continuously or linked by sacbeob. Beyond this zone lies an area of some 13 km² that contains scattered groups of ruins, some including vaulted buildings. Outside this area, and stretching over some 100 km², are the remains of the bulk of the house platforms, spotted amid plentiful open areas that probably served as the ancient agricultural sustaining area for Dzibilchaltun's population.

From a near-abandonment of the area during the Early Classic, Dzibilchaltun grew to its maximum extent during the Late and Terminal Classic eras, reaching a population of 25,000 or more by A.D. 800. During this time of expansion nearly all the masonry-vaulted buildings were constructed, and some 90 percent of all residential structures appear to have been occupied. During this time, too, most if not all of the more than 25 monuments known from the site were erected. One period-ending date (probably 10.1.0.0.0, or 849) survives, on Stela 9. The front of Stela 19 depicts a ruler holding a manikin scepter, the symbol of high office at most Classic lowland Maya sites.

Masonry buildings constructed during the Late Classic were built in typical lowland style, using stone blocks and true corbeled vaulting. But during the Ter-

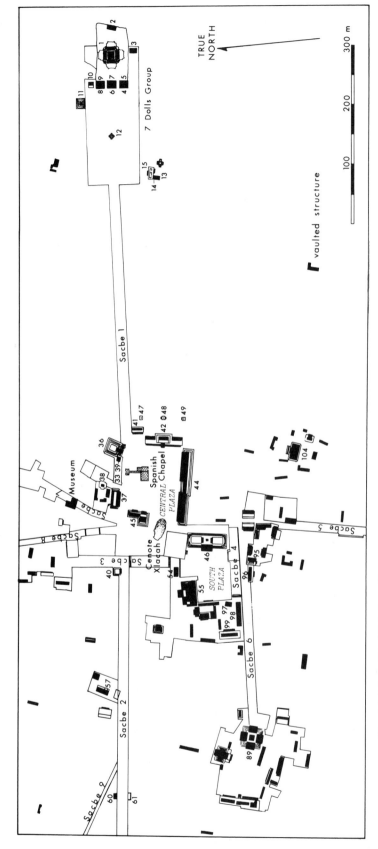

Fig. 6.5. Map of Dzibilchaltun, Yucatan, Mexico; a system of sacbeob connects the site core with outlying groups (many small structures have been deleted from this map, which is adapted from the detailed site map).

360

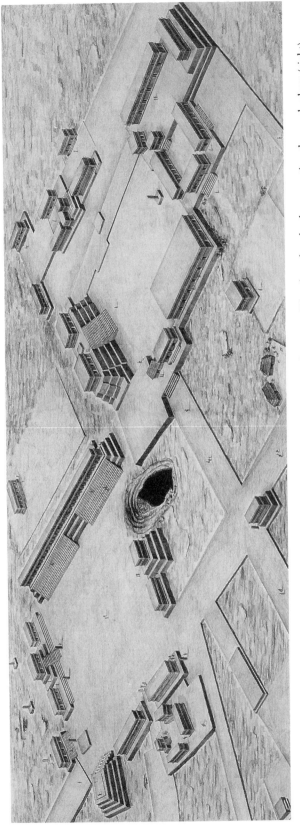

Fig. 6.6. Dzibilchaltun, Yucatan: the site core looking southeast, showing the cenote Xlacah and sacbeob connecting the south plaza (right), central plaza (left), and other architectural groups.

minal Classic era, the distinctive Puuc architectural style appeared at Dzibilchaltun. This style is represented by veneer masonry and carved-mosaic façade decoration instead of the earlier stucco, and reflects links to the sites to the south that expanded rapidly during this era. The presence of this architectural style may indicate that the site and the northwest region of the Peninsula participated in the last-gasp prosperity that marked the Puuc florescence (see below). Total population at Dzibilchaltun during the Terminal Classic may have fallen slightly, but the concentration of buildings at the site core seems to have increased.

In the Early Postclassic, or after about 1000, the population declined rapidly and building activity ceased for a time. A modest revival occurred around 1200, when several new buildings were constructed of reused masonry. A small population continued to dwell at Dzibilchaltun during the Late Postclassic, reusing earlier buildings as residences and shrines, before the site was ultimately abandoned.

One of the most notable buildings at Dzibilchaltun is the Temple of the Seven Dolls, which is architecturally important in several respects (Fig. 6.7). Built about 700, it is one of the earliest vaulted buildings at the site, a square temple on the summit of a platform served by four stairways. Four wide doorways lead into a continuously vaulted corridor that surrounds a central room, and the central room is surmounted by a high four-sided vault that forms a low tower above the roof. Rectangular windows flank the eastern and western doorways. The upper exterior façades were decorated with elaborate but apparently unpainted stucco masks. Before the end of the Classic period the temple and its platform were completely encased in a much larger four-stairway pyramid. Centuries later, during the Late Postclassic, when the pyramid was in ruins, its west side was dug into and the long-buried Temple of the Seven Dolls was reopened and used as a shrine. An altar was erected inside the temple, and painted with four successive hieroglyphic medallions during the years it was in use. Seven crudely fashioned clay figurines, after which the temple was given its present name, were placed in the floor as an offering, in front of the altar.

### EDZNA

The site of Edzna is located to the south of Dzibilchaltun, inland from the Gulf coast. Unlike Dzibilchaltun and other northern sites, it is known for its long sequence of monuments, extending from A.D. 633 to 810 (9.10.0.0.0 to 9.19.0.0.0). The sculptural, architectural, and ceramic affiliations at Edzna indicate that it was allied to the major Classic centers to the south. These cultural ties probably reflect a commercial network uniting Edzna and western Yucatan with the southern Classic centers, perhaps as an inland collection point for cotton, salt, and other important northern products. The capital of a powerful but still little-known polity, Edzna directed the construction of one of the most ambitious hydraulic projects ever attempted by the Maya. A radiating system of canals was connected to a moatlike circular canal surrounding a major portion of the site. These features seem to have fulfilled several functions—husbanding water in the dry season, draining water during the rainy season, and also, probably, providing a measure of defense (Fig. 8.4).

Edzna was also a transitional site for subsequent developments to the north, and many of its buildings show characteristics that are antecedent to the Puuc architectural style that emerged in the Terminal Classic (Fig. 6.8; see below).

Fig. 6.7. Seven Dolls Group at Dzibilchaltun: (*above*) from the southwest, as it appeared about A.D. 700–750; (*below*) the excavated and consolidated Temple of the Seven Dolls (note the remains of the overlying structure at the right side).

Fig. 6.8. Edzna, Campeche, Mexico: the excavated and consolidated Palace, combining the architecture of the terraced temple platform with that of the multi-roomed palace.

## COBA AND YAXUNA

A similar picture emerges at Coba, the capital of the largest Late Classic polity in the northern lowlands. Coba is a mammoth site situated in northeastern Yucatan amid five small, shallow lakes, a rare physiographic feature in this area (Fig. 6.9). The site is in the wettest region of the northern lowlands, and shows some of the closest affinities to the great centers of the Peten, or central lowlands. First surveyed by the Carnegie Institution of Washington, the center and its outlying dependencies were investigated more recently under a program sponsored by the Instituto Nacional de Antropología e Historia of Mexico (INAH), under the direction of William Folan.

The site is known for its great length of occupation. The earliest known stela dates to A.D. 623 (9.9.10.0.0), and Coba was occupied, at least intermittently, until late Postclassic times, around the fourteenth or fifteenth centuries. Coba possesses more Classic-era stelae—32 (23 of them sculptured)—than any other northern Yucatan center. One of the best preserved of these monuments is Stela 20, which bears a date of 9.12.12.0.5 (684). It was found near the base of Str. 1, the great Nohoch

Mul pyramid (Fig. 6.10), northeast of the main group. Str. 1 is a Late Classic construction, some 24 m in height, that is capped by the addition of a Late Postclassic building similar in style to those of Tulum (see Chapter 7).

The main group at Coba, located between lakes Coba and Macanxoc, is dominated by the Castillo, another pyramid 24 m high. A series of sacbeob radiates in five directions from this group to other areas of the site, connecting the central section with its outlying groups. Coba is famed for these raised roads, of which sixteen are known.

The word *sacbe* (pl. *sacbeob*) means "white road" in Mayan (*sac*, "white"; *be*, "road"). These limestone roads (Fig. 6.11) are often about 4.5 m wide and rise between 0.5 and 2.5 m above ground level. The sides are built of roughly dressed stone, and the tops are covered with a natural lime cement called *sascab*, which hardens under wetting and pressure. The sacbeob of Coba, the shortest being a little less than a kilometer in length, run in straight lines between major architectural groups, and include two causeways that intersect each other just south of the isthmus between the two largest lakes at the site.

Fig. 6.9. Coba, Quintana Roo, Mexico: aerial view of the forest-covered city set amid several small lakes in the northeastern lowlands; the traces of two crossing sacbeob are dimly visible as a large "X" in the center of the photograph.

Fig. 6.10. Coba, Quintana Roo, Mexico: the large Late Classic temple known as Nohoch Mul, as reused in the Late Postclassic when the building seen on the summit was constructed.

The longest causeway runs over 100 km generally westward from Coba to Yaxuna. Except for a few slight deviations, this great sacbe is straight, the first six of the seven changes in direction occurring within 32 km of Coba, apparently in order to pass through smaller dependent settlements. The fact that the causeway connects Coba with Yaxuna indicates that when it was constructed—probably in the Late or Terminal Classic—Coba controlled this important city in the center of Yucatan, along with the largest territory of any contemporary Maya polity. In fact, it is hypothesized that Coba secured control of Yaxuna as a strategic outpost on the western border of its territory, probably in response to the worrisome expansion of a series of new polities to the west, in the Puuc region of Yucatan. David Freidel's recent investigations at Yaxuna indicate that several building complexes were rebuilt and reoriented to face the terminus of the great sacbe from Coba. But at some point Coba's control of Yaxuna may have been directly challenged by one of its rivals, for there is at least one major architectural group at Yaxuna rendered in Puuc style.

Fig. 6.11. Sacbe connecting the cities of Coba (Quintana Roo) and Yaxuna (Yucatan): masonry construction at the causeway's highest point.

## The Puuc and Related Regional Traditions

Centered within the only hilly region of the northern lowlands, the Puuc region (*puuc* is Mayan for hills) is the best known of several Late and Terminal Classic regional developments in Yucatan. The Río Bec tradition, centered at the base of the Yucatan Peninsula and including the sites of Becan, Xpuhil, and Río Bec, displays architectural and ceramic traits that combine the styles of the central and northern lowlands. In architecture, for instance, Río Bec is noted for the use of high, terraced towers incorporating false steps, façades, and doors, and crowned by non-functional "temples"—the whole thought to imitate the great pyramid temples of the Classic centers in the Peten region, most notably at Tikal. This southern characteristic was combined with elaborate building façades decorated with mosaic masks, features typical of Yucatecan architecture (Fig. 4.38).

Farther to the north, Xtampak and several other Maya sites display an architectural style similar to Río Bec, except for the absence of the "false" pyramid towers. This architecture, which emphasizes elaborate mosaic façades and doorways framed by ornate "monster masks," has been labeled the Chenes style (Fig. 4.37). But Chenes clearly is a close relative of the same regional cultural tradition seen at Río Bec.

Developed in northwestern Yucatan, the famous Puuc architectural style gave rise to some of the most beautiful and appealing of all Maya buildings. The characteristic finely fitted veneer masonry covers a self-supporting structural fill held together by lime-based concrete. Typically, the plain lower zones of Puuc buildings contrast with their upper zones, which are decorated with intricate mosaic designs. The earliest examples of this style seem to be those at Edzna (Fig. 6.8), Xcalumkin, and Oxkintok, built during the Classic period, but its finest examples are found at sites that reached their zenith during the Yucatecan Terminal Classic (ca. A.D. 800–1000). The available epigraphic evidence from Uxmal, the largest of these sites (Fig. 6.12), indicates that a ruling lineage was in power during this time. Apparently Uxmal and its neighbors—Kabah, Sayil, Labna, and others—were founded, grew, and prospered during this relatively brief interval. Settlement of the Puuc region seems to have been stimulated by northward population displacements and other changes brought on by the decline of the Classic cities in the central lowlands. There is little doubt that these new cities were the direct outgrowth of movements of peoples from the south, especially from the Río Bec and Chenes regions, not as a single mass migration but as a gradual shift in population distributed over a century or more. Prior to the Terminal Classic the Puuc was sparsely settled, probably because the lack of either surface water or cenotes made it difficult to secure water during the long dry season. The fact that the soils of this hilly region are among the best in the Yucatan Peninsula was sufficient motivation to encourage the investment in manpower and organization necessary to the construction of artificial water-storage facilities (*chultunes*, or cisterns), and the Puuc became densely settled during the Terminal Classic.

A high density of settlement combined with the unusually close spacing between Puuc cities might suggest a competitive social environment. Yet there are few indications that warfare plagued this region. At least one site, Uxmal, does have a low surrounding wall, but the wall does not seem to have been sufficient for defense. Nor do the surviving sculptures and murals depict warriors or captives. The impression given, especially in contrast to the increasing martial themes evident from much of the Late Classic and Terminal Classic lowlands to the south, is that the new cities of the Puuc managed to develop a political order with less emphasis on warfare, at least for a time. But because of the paucity of hieroglyphic texts and images of the ruling elite, we still know relatively little about the political organization of these cities. Perhaps the Puuc sites were ruled by elite lineages that maintained an effective, cooperative relationship (such as a confederation) by marriage or even by political alliances. Or perhaps one site managed to dominate the entire region, enforcing a relatively tranquil order for most of the Terminal Classic era. If so, the best candidate for that dominant power would be the largest city of the region, Uxmal.

### UXMAL

Uxmal is situated in western Yucatan, about 80 km south of Dzibilchaltun. To judge from its location and size (Fig. 6.12), it was an important political and economic center, and it is especially impressive for its superb assemblage of buildings, most of which were constructed in the Puuc architectural style. Unfortunately, however, little in the way of systematic archaeological excavation has been done at Uxmal to date, although INAH has conducted a series of investigations in conjunction with the consolidation of major architecture. A series of undated stelae at Uxmal (Fig. 6.13) can be stylistically dated to the Terminal Classic (ca. A.D. 800–1000), and the predominance of Puuc architecture at the site indicates that Uxmal reached its apogee during this span, but the length of occupation before and after this era is undocumented. The lack of later architectural styles points to a probable decline at the outset of the Postclassic.

The core of the site is dominated by extensive, complex multiroom structures, undoubtedly the residences of the ruling elite (Fig. 6.14). In the largest of these palace-type complexes, the badly ruined South Group, three palace quadrangles were built on a series of ascending terraces, the tallest and southernmost of the quadrangles constructed around a pyramid. Just to the east is the Great Pyramid, and beyond that is the Governor's Palace (Fig. 6.15), which is the largest single structure of its kind at Uxmal and often considered the finest example of Puuc architecture extant. A comprehensive study of this building by Jeffrey Kowalski concludes that it was built in the final phase of occupation and was probably sponsored

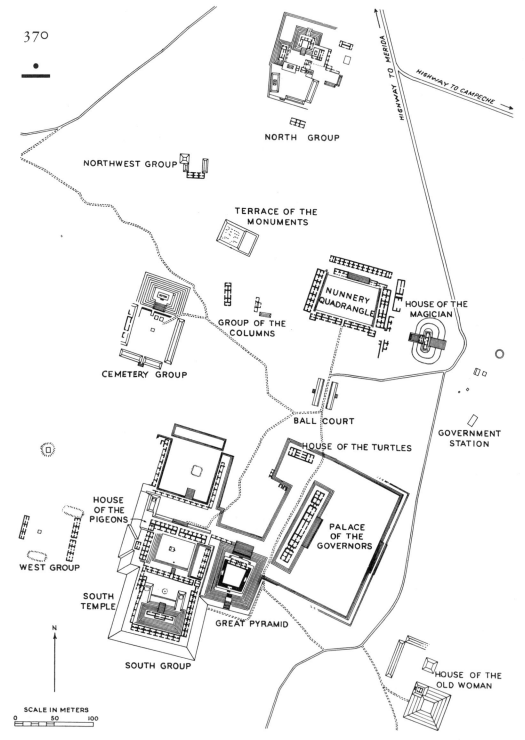

NORTH GROUP

NORTHWEST GROUP

HIGHWAY TO MERIDA

HIGHWAY TO CAMPECHE

TERRACE OF THE
MONUMENTS

NUNNERY
QUADRANGLE

HOUSE OF THE
MAGICIAN

GROUP OF THE
COLUMNS

CEMETERY GROUP

BALL COURT

GOVERNMENT
STATION

HOUSE OF THE TURTLES

HOUSE
OF THE
PIGEONS

PALACE
OF THE
GOVERNORS

WEST GROUP

SOUTH
TEMPLE

GREAT PYRAMID

N

SOUTH GROUP

HOUSE OF THE
OLD WOMAN

SCALE IN METERS
0    50    100

Fig. 6.12. Map of Uxmal, Yucatan, Mexico: the site core with its major buildings.

Fig. 6.13. Uxmal Stela 14, one of the few surviving carved
stelae from the site, which may portray the ruler Lord Chac.

Fig. 6.14. Uxmal: aerial view toward the northwest, showing the buildings in the site core, including the Governor's Palace (lower center), the Nunnery Quadrangle (middle right), and the House of the Magician (right).

by the only identified Uxmal ruler, Lord Chac (see below). It surmounts a triple terrace 15 m high and covering 2 hectares of ground; the palace itself is nearly 100 m long, 12 m wide, and 8 m tall and contains 24 chambers. The elaborate mosaics decorating its four façades comprise some twenty thousand elements. The prevalent mat motifs in these designs may identify the function of the Governor's Palace as a *popol na* (or ruling council house). A recent probe near the northeastern corner has revealed the existence of an earlier, Chenes-style palace beneath the building. Southeast of the Governor's Palace lies another pyramid, the House of the Old Woman.

On the northwestern corner of the terrace is a smaller palace, a small gem of Puuc architecture known as the House of the Turtles because of the decorations on its upper façade. From this vantage point there is a spectacular view to the north, past a ballcourt toward the most celebrated residential complex at Uxmal, the so-called Nunnery Quadrangle (Fig. 6.16), and immediately to the east is a high, round-cornered platform supporting two temples that is known as the Adivino (House of the Diviner, or Magician). The two carved rings from the ballcourt have been dated at 10.3.15.16.14 and 10.3.15.16.15 (A.D. 905).

The magnificent Nunnery Quadrangle consists of four buildings, each with a sculptured façade, arranged around the sides of a court measuring 76 by 61 m. This court is entered through a central corbeled arcade in the building on the court's south side. The structure on the north side surmounts a terrace 5.5 m high and is reached by a stairway 27.5 m wide. A repaired monument (Stela 17) with an eroded hieroglyphic text is set in the midst of the stairway. Architecturally, the northern structure is the most important unit on the quadrangle, though the two flanking units, the East and West buildings (Fig. 6.16), are scarcely less impressive. The mosaic façade of the western building, for instance, includes feathered-serpent motifs, models of thatched-roof houses, and a central throned pavilion that may once have held the sculptured portrait of an elite personage. Several painted capstones from this palace complex bear partial calendrical dates that are best reconstructed to the Terminal Classic era. The capstone from the eastern building dates to 10.3.17.12.1 (906), and another from Str. Y, to 10.3.18.9.12 (907); both dates (determined by Eric Thompson) are consistent with a radiocarbon date obtained from the northern building of this palace complex.

The Adivino seems to have been built in at least four stages, each stage incorporating the earlier buildings within its mass. The penultimate construction is represented by a Chenes-style temple that crowns the first terrace of the platform. This terrace is reached from the west by a steep stairway (Fig. 6.17) that affords access

Fig. 6.15. Uxmal, Yucatan, Mexico: the Governor's Palace, with its mosaic upper façade, is one of the finest examples of the Puuc architectural style.

Fig. 6.16. Uxmal, the Nunnery Quadrangle, after consolidation: (*above*) the east wing; (*below*) the west wing.

Fig. 6.17 (*opposite*). Uxmal: west-side stairway and Chenes-style lower temple of the Adivino, or House of the Magician, after its consolidation.

•

to the temple, which is elaborately decorated to represent a giant monster mask, its mouth forming the west-facing doorway. The uppermost temple, in Puuc style, faces a higher stairway on the east.

West of the Nunnery is another quadrangle, known as the Cemetery Group, that faces a pyramid on its north side. Farther to the north is a large platform supporting the bulk of the stelae from Uxmal, and beyond that is another ruined complex, the North Group.

Uxmal possesses a quantity of phallic sculpture, a feature quite unusual among Maya sites. There are phallic motifs on the rear façade of the Nunnery Quadrangle's north building and on the front façade of the west building. There is a collection of phallic sculpture east of the platform supporting the Governors' Palace, and this motif also adorns the façade of the aptly named Temple of the Phallus, located farther to the south.

Kowalski's studies have yielded the tentative identification of Uxmal's emblem glyph and the names of several prominent personages. One of the most productive historical texts is on a small cylindrical altar found just south of the Governor's Palace. This monument appears to record the name of the most prominent Uxmal leader, Lord Chac, and his probable parents, Chac Uinal Kan and Lady Bone. Lord Chac may also be named on Stela 14 (Fig. 6.13); its portrait of a richly clad lord standing on a double-headed jaguar throne is much like that found sculptured in stone on the platform east of the Governor's Palace. These monuments lack identifiable dates, but stylistically belong to the Terminal Classic; their location suggests that both the Governor's Palace and the Nunnery Quadrangle were associated with Lord Chac's reign at Uxmal.

### KABAH

A sacbe about 18 km long connects Uxmal with the smaller Puuc site of Kabah to the south. Another tie to Uxmal is suggested by a hieroglyphic text on a carved altar on the terrace in front of the Palace of the Masks (Fig. 6.18). This text records two emblem glyphs: one may be that of Kabah; the other has been tentatively identified as that of Uxmal. The latter glyph is associated with the name glyph of Lord Chac of Uxmal, which probably indicates that Kabah was subordinate to its larger neighbor.

The Palace of the Masks, 46 m long, is the best-known of Kabah's buildings. It contains ten chambers arranged in two rows of five each. The chambers of each pair are built one directly behind the other, with a single doorway to the outside, including one with a carved doorjamb (Fig. 6.19). Though the exteriors of most Puuc-style buildings are devoid of sculptural decoration below the medial molding, the entire façade of the Palace of the Masks is covered by intricate mosaics. The building stands on a low platform, the face of which is decorated with a single row of mask panels; above this is a carved molding that is surmounted by the lower half

Fig. 6.18. Kabah, Yucatan, Mexico: Str. 2C-6, or Palace of the Masks, named for the repetitive mask motif covering its façade.

Fig. 6.19. Kabah: carved doorjambs of Str. 2C-6, showing elite warriors and the taking of captives.

of the façade, which is in turn composed of three rows of mask panels running across the front of the building. Above an elaborate medial molding are, again, three rows of mask panels, the topmost being surmounted by a terminal molding.

Another unique feature of Kabah is its stone corbeled arch (Fig. 6.20). Standing apart from any other building, at the head of the sacbe leading to Uxmal, it spans nearly 5 m as now restored. It probably marked a formal boundary between the elite and non-elite areas of the site and the entrance to the civic core of Kabah.

### SAYIL

This beautiful site is located 7 km south of Kabah, within a shallow basin between several series of low but steep-sided hills. The mapped extent of its buildings covers an area of about 4.5 km², generally following a north-south alignment defined by an intrasite causeway system (Fig. 6.21). These buildings range from elaborate masonry palaces to the remains of humble, perishable houses, most of which are associated with one or more *chultunes*.

The northern terminus of the causeway is the Great Palace (Fig. 6.22), the largest and most celebrated of Sayil's buildings. Usually described as a three-storied building, it is actually composed of a two-terraced platform with multiple rooms arranged along all four sides of each terrace. The upper terrace is surmounted by a long building with a single row of rooms. A central stairway on the south side gives

Fig. 6.20. Kabah, Yucatan, Mexico: entrance arch on the sacbe from Uxmal, before reconstruction.

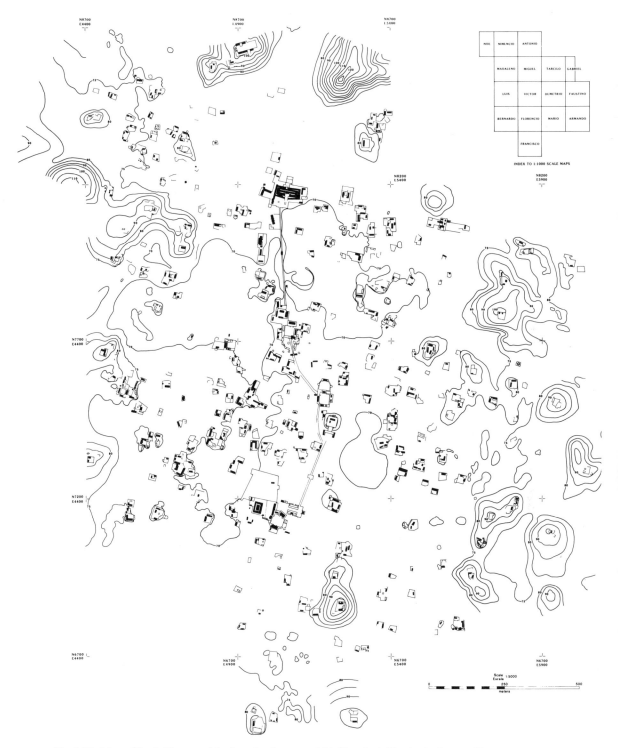

Fig. 6.21. Map of Sayil, Yucatan, Mexico: the site core of this Terminal Classic site is served by a sacbe terminating in the north at the Great Palace.

Fig. 6.22. The Great Palace at Sayil, a multi-terraced structure with a central stairway.

access to the second and third "stories." The palace is not symmetrical, and was constructed in several stages over an unknown span of time in the Terminal Classic.

One of the causeways connects the palace with another complex of multi-roomed buildings about 350 m to the south. This group includes a badly ruined south-facing temple-type structure known as the Mirador, and near the group is a rather famous phallic sculpture of unknown date. Another causeway leads to a complex of buildings some 200 m to the southeast, before continuing on for another 350 m to the southernmost major group, which includes a ballcourt and several palaces. Near the midpoint of this extension of the causeway is a small platform where the remains of eight stelae and seven plain altars were found (at least 30 more plain altars have been reported from the site). Although the monuments are broken and badly eroded, Tatiana Proskouriakoff suggested approximate dates for three of them, placing Stela 6 at about 9.19.0.0.0 (810) and stelae 3 and 5 a little later in the ninth century.

Numerous other buildings are situated along the causeway system, largely to the east and west. A few are notable for their decorations. An interior doorway in Str. 3B1 is framed by a band of carved hieroglyphs. In the central doorway of Str. 4B1 are two carved columns, each supporting carved capitals and three carved lintels. To the north, perched on the summit of a hill overlooking the rest of the site, is another palace group.

From 1983 to 1988 Sayil was the subject of an important archaeological investigation conducted under the direction of Jeremy Sabloff and Gair Tourtellot. By examining a major Puuc center the investigation sought to gain an understanding both of the critical Terminal Classic era and a pivotal region that had never been comprehensively investigated. The focus of the research was the settlement history of the site, and the research included detailed mapping and both surface collections and excavations within a range of residential structures (Fig. 6.23). Results indicate that Sayil's occupation corresponds to the Terminal Classic (ca. 800–1000), and that its occupants were probably Yucatec Maya (as opposed to Chontal or Putun Maya) perhaps from the Chenes region to the south. Sayil was a city with a clearly bounded urban core within which once lived some 10,000 people. Another 7,000 people occupied the surrounding, less densely settled "suburbs." These population levels, reached by ca. A.D. 900, represent about the maximum sustainable by the agricultural potential of the local soils. Crops were grown even among and between the residential compounds. The reasons for Sayil's abandonment around 1000, like those at other Puuc cities, remain unclear, but the abandonment appears to have been relatively rapid and may have been due to outside intervention, a topic we shall consider further when we deal with Chichen Itza in our next chapter.

### LABNA

Labna is situated about 8 km to the southeast of Sayil. Its two-terrace palace, similar in style to the Sayil example, is connected by a short sacbe to another architectural group that includes a pyramid capped by a partially fallen temple. Atop

Fig. 6.23. Sayil: excavation and consolidation of the foundations of a domestic structure, the remainder of which was constructed of perishable materials.

●

the temple is a high façade or frontal roof comb, and adjacent to the pyramid is a small palace group entered by way of a famous archway (Fig. 6.24), one of the most beautiful examples of Puuc architecture. Labna was briefly investigated by Edward Thompson in the late nineteenth century, and its principal buildings have been partially restored.

## The Emergence of a New Order in the Northern Lowlands

As we have seen, the Terminal Classic in the Yucatan Peninsula was marked by an unprecedented leap in both population and prosperity, linked in large measure directly to the decline of the traditional powers to the south. Most of the centers in the central lowlands were losing population, and most were eventually abandoned. And all the while, increasing numbers of people were resettling in areas outside the central and southern lowlands, including northwestern Yucatan, triggering the spectacular rise of the new cities in the Puuc region. Some of the older Yucatecan polities such as Coba not only were able to survive the challenges of this era, but probably *gained* population, from the peoples who were migrating northward. But perhaps the most important change of the Terminal Classic is associated with the

Fig. 6.24. Labna, Yucatan, Mexico: the palace arch, leading to an inner courtyard of this Puuc-style building.

arrival of the Putun (or Chontal) Maya in Yucatan. The aim of the Putun warriors and merchants was to seize control of important resources and trade routes, as they had done in the southern lowlands, and eventually they monopolized the seacoast trade around the Yucatan Peninsula.

By the tenth century the Putun seem to have developed large seagoing canoes, and the use of these craft was to change the fortunes of much of Yucatan. Areas formerly peripheral to the loci of power, such as the northeastern coast, began to attract the sizable populations necessary to maintain port facilities and connecting inland routes, and to consolidate their position the Putun Maya established new coastal trading centers, such as the island port of Isla Cerritos just off the north coast of Yucatan. But with the founding of a new land-based political and religious capital, the Putun Maya opened a new era in the history of Maya civilization, an era that—more than any other—had far-reaching consequences throughout Mesoamerica. Their new capital, still known by its original name, Chichen Itza, would come to dominate the Maya lowlands for more than two centuries.

# 7 THE POSTCLASSIC

:.

> 6 Ahau was when the discovery of Chichen Itza occurred. 13 Ahau was
> when the mat of the katun was counted in order. 8 Ahau was when
> Chichen Itza was abandoned. There were thirteen folds of katuns when
> they established their houses at Chakanputun.
>
> —*The Book of Chilam Balam of Chumayel* (Roys 1967: 135–36)

Archaeologists usually place the Postclassic period at ca. A.D. 900–1500, often overlapping the Terminal Classic. The Postclassic has long been characterized as a time of decline following the cultural florescence of the Classic period, and it is usually divided into two eras, the Early Postclassic (ca. 900–1200, dominance of Chichen Itza) and the Late Postclassic (ca. 1200–1500, dominance of Mayapan). Traditionally, the era has been defined by three prominent characteristics: militarism, secularism, and urbanism. But in fact these criteria were not new to the Postclassic. Some writers have used the term "decadent" to describe the Late Postclassic, either to typify an observable shift in the standards of artistic expression or to characterize other aspects of life in these later times. But such judgments reflect an application of our own standards to Maya society, and we do better to view the developmental course of Maya civilization in its own terms.

The Postclassic Maya emerged from the transition that characterized the Terminal Classic with a new political orientation, one epitomized in the northern lowlands by the regional state controlled from Chichen Itza. (This great center spans both the Terminal Classic and the Early Postclassic, and we have somewhat arbitrarily chosen to treat it in this chapter.) Possibly the largest and most powerful of all Maya polities, Chichen Itza was certainly the most cosmopolitan. For the Postclassic was above all else a time when the distinctions between traditional regional cultures became less clearly defined. Populations continued to increase in many areas during this era, and commerce, alliances, group migrations, and military conquests led to more numerous, more widespread, and more frequent interregional contacts.

The increases in population and contacts enlarged the sphere of groups that came to share common Mesoamerican cultural traditions. The Postclassic has long been recognized in the Maya area as a period of "Mexicanization," a time when cultural traits from Central Mexico and other regions were increasingly incorporated into Maya art, architecture, ceramics, and the other products of culture recovered by archaeologists. The active agents of these changes were the Itza and allied Putun Maya groups from the southwest periphery of the Maya area. These Maya peoples were heavily influenced by the Mexican cultures across the isthmus, along the Gulf coast and beyond, and their expansion into both the Yucatan Peninsula and the highlands far to the south brought the heartland Maya into contact with new political ideas, military tactics, and religious practices, all of which induced further changes in their society. There were important cultural continuities as well—in technology, agriculture, architecture, economy, social organization, language, religion, and cosmology—but aspects of almost all these areas were also changed, especially for the elite members of Maya society.

Thus, for the Maya, the Postclassic period was a time of complex and profound changes. In many ways, the cultural traditions that took form in the Preclassic and developed throughout the Classic were permanently altered. The Yucatecan Maya saw their traditional way of life as a time when "they adhered to their reason. . . . At that time the course of humanity was orderly." But like all peoples they resisted change, and they saw the Putun Maya as bringing about their misfortune, by ushering in an era of political instability marked by "the origin of the two-day throne, the two-day reign. . . . There were no more lucky days for us; we had no sound judgment."

The extant Postclassic Maya chronicles, such as *The Book of Chilam Balam* from which we quote, understandably reflect the Maya's own view of their past. This view is not so much history, in our sense of the word, as it is the reconciliation of actual events with prophecy. As a result, the chronology of particular events in Maya writings may be distorted, compressed, or expanded, at times even presented in contradictory terms. To further the difficulty, the results of archaeological research do not always accord with the chronicles and the other available ethnohistorical accounts. But although our knowledge of the Postclassic era is imperfect, we can nonetheless outline the main sequence of events.

Whereas the focus of major developments during the Classic period was the central and southern lowland areas, the Postclassic saw the almost uninterrupted development of the northern lowlands of Yucatan (Table 7.1) reach its climax, as well as a return to prominence of the southern area, especially in the highlands. We will consider events in Yucatan first, then briefly review Postclassic developments in the southern Maya area before returning to Yucatan to trace the final pre-Conquest years of the ancient Maya.

··
‒‒

| Date | | Event |
|---|---|---|
| Maya period-ending | A.D. (approximate) | |
| 10.1.0.0.0 | 849 | Itza Maya abandon Chakanputun and occupy Chichen Itza, beginning the era of dominance of that site in the north. |
| 10.8.0.0.0 | 987 | Mayapan founded (?). |
| 10.9.0.0.0 | 1007 | Xiu Maya reoccupy Uxmal (?). |
| 11.0.0.0.0 | 1224 | Conquest of Chichen Itza led by Hunac Ceel, ruler of Mayapan; Itza driven from Chichen Itza (ca. 1221); era of Mayapan dominance in the north begins. |
| 11.11.0.0.0 | 1441 | Revolt led by Ah Xupan Xiu; Mayapan and its Cocom leaders (save one) destroyed. |
| 11.13.0.0.0 | 1480 | Civil wars rage between northern centers (ca. 1496). |
| 11.14.0.0.0 | 1500 | Spaniards first seen (1511). |
| 11.15.0.0.0 | 1520 | First two attempts at conquest by the Spanish are defeated (1527–35). Ah Dzun Xiu and party massacred by order of Nachi Cocom (1536), thus avenging the Xiu-led revolt against Mayapan. |
| 11.16.0.0.0 | 1539 | Spanish Conquest of the Yucatan (1540–46; see the Epilogue). |

## The Dominance of Chichen Itza

As we saw in Chapter 6, many of the political and social changes wrought in the Terminal Classic are associated with the expansion of the Putun Maya. The critical penetration of the Putun into Yucatan is dated to the late ninth and the tenth centuries, probably beginning about 850. During this period a Putun Maya group, in the later Yucatecan chronicles called the Itza, or people "who speak our language brokenly" (probably with reference to their Chontal Mayan dialects) invaded the northern lowlands, apparently exploiting the "no man's land" of the central boundary region between the powerful polity of Coba to the east and the more numerous states in both the Puuc region and the Dzibilchaltun region to the west.

The Putun's first strategic foothold was apparently an island port on the northern coast at a site known as Isla Cerritos, along with an adjacent mainland site known as Paso del Cerro. Isla Cerritos, a little over 200 m in diameter, stands about 500 m offshore (Fig. 7.1). The remains of a sea wall with two narrow entrances, some 60 m from the island's south shore, define an ancient harbor suitable for

Fig. 7.1. Isla Cerritos, Yucatan, Mexico: aerial view of the island port off the northern coast, with the remains of a protective sea wall visible at the left, circling behind the island.

coastal trading canoes. Traces of stone piers have been detected all around the island. Low platforms and large quantities of sherds cover the surface of the site. Survey and excavations directed by Anthony Andrews and his colleagues have provided firm support for the hypothesis that this site later served as the chief port for Chichen Itza; although it was occupied from at least Late Preclassic times, its major period of activity coincides with the ascendancy of Chichen Itza. The majority of the sherds at Isla Cerritos, which belong to a group known technically as the Sotuta Ceramic Sphere, are diagnostic of this period, and trade types from both the Gulf and Caribbean coasts are plentiful. The port was ultimately abandoned at the time of the fall of Chichen Itza.

There is also evidence of Itza occupation of other sites in the central region of Yucatan. Apart from Chichen Itza, perhaps the most important of these is Izamal, a major site that has yet to receive thorough investigation. But there is no doubt that the dominant political, economic, and religious center of central Yucatan was Chichen Itza (Fig. 7.2). The later Yucatecan chronicles relate that the Itza established a new capital at this site. Although the dating of the founding has always remained in dispute, recent findings, based on investigations at the site, new chronological assessments for Sotuta ceramics, and reevaluations of the few Maya dates recorded at Chichen Itza, place the founding of the city in the Terminal Classic, probably by about 850. From their new inland capital, the Itza appear to have expanded their dominion by a variety of means, whether trade, marriage alliances, or, especially, military conquests, to control most of the northern lowlands during the subsequent Early Postclassic era.

## CHICHEN ITZA

This famous site, located in north-central Yucatan and much favored by tourists, is one of the largest centers in the northern lowlands, its known extent covering an area of at least 5 km² of relatively dense architectural ruins (Fig. 7.3). Beyond this core there are remains of occupation—house platforms and other, smaller structures—that extend for an unknown distance. The pre-Columbian name Chichen Itza, recorded by Bishop Landa (see below and Chapter 13), means "opening of the wells of the Itza," a reference to the two large cenotes at the site. The city also appears to have been named Uucyabnal, "seven great rulers," and was probably one of the mythical Tollans or "great cities" referred to in later epics (as discussed further below).

The first large-scale archaeological investigations by the Carnegie Institution of Washington were undertaken at Chichen Itza, under the direction of Sylvanus Morley. This work, which commenced in 1924 and continued for two decades, concentrated on the excavation and restoration of the site's major buildings, but in the process several nearly intact structures were discovered beneath subsequent

Fig. 7.2. Chichen Itza, Yucatan, Mexico: aerial view from the south, with El Castillo near the center of the photo, the Great Ball Court to its left, and the Temple of the Warriors to its right.

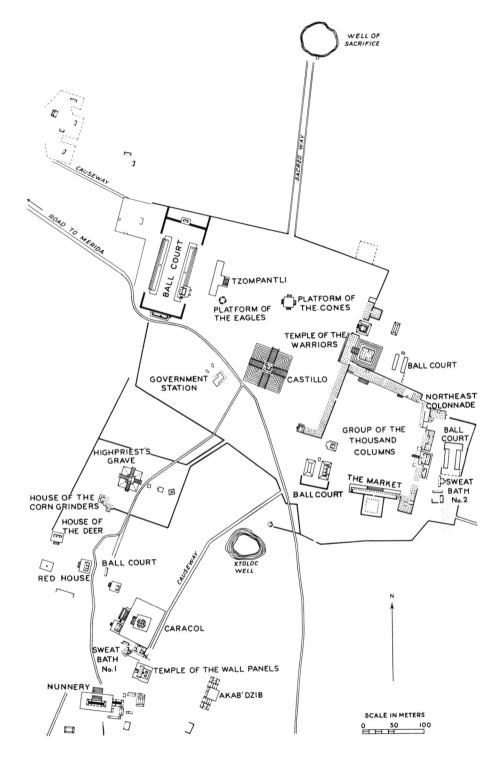

Fig. 7.3. Chichen Itza, Yucatan, Mexico: map of the central area.

•• ••

constructions. Much valuable work was done in architectural recording, but the site still lacks some critical information of the kind obtained from modern archaeological research, including data about population size, settlement patterns, and building functions. A basic chronological scheme for the site also remains a problem in some respects, but a majority of scholars now accepts a recently advanced proposal that has the traditionally defined two periods of the site's history overlapping substantially.

On the basis of the Carnegie-period research, most of the visible structures at Chichen Itza were assigned to one of two architectural periods: the "florescent" (Terminal Classic), associated with an indigenous Puuc style, and the "modified florescent" (Early Postclassic), associated with the addition of certain Mexican architectural traits to a Maya masonry tradition. This twofold architectural chronology was linked to a proposed pottery sequence, with Terminal Classic Cehpech ceramics predating Early Postclassic Sotuta ceramics. In light of current findings, however, neither of these chronological divisions can be supported. There is now sufficient evidence for substantial overlap between Cehpech and Sotuta ceramics, the latter in fact associated with Chichen Itza from its Terminal Classic beginnings through its Early Postclassic demise. There is similar evidence for an overlap between the two architectural styles at Chichen Itza, as well as for the association of some "modified florescent" buildings and sculpture with carved Maya dates belonging to the Terminal Classic, as first pointed out by Tatiana Proskouriakoff.

The Puuc-style buildings at Chichen Itza, concentrated in the southern part of the site, were constructed with the typical mosaic-decorated upper façades, but usually have block-masonry walls rather than the fine veneer work of the Puuc heartland farther to the west. This block masonry can be seen in the terrace supporting the Caracol, in the House of the Deer, and in the Red House. The Puuc style also appears in a series of nonelevated palace structures, including the original buildings in the Nunnery Group (Monjas, Annex, and Iglesia; Fig. 7.4) and in the Akabtzib. Radiocarbon dates obtained from the wooden beams in the Red House and Iglesia are about A.D. 600–780, but these may reflect the growth period of the wood (or the wood may be reused), rather than the later building construction. The later additions to the Akabtzib (which means "dark," or "hidden," "writing") have been dated from a sculptured inscription over one of its inner doorways as either 10.2.0.0.0 or 10.3.0.0.0 (869 or 889).

In the southern portion of the site there are several buildings with inscribed texts, but only one of these, on a lintel in the Temple of the Initial Series, has a Long Count date, 10.2.9.1.9 (878). Several others—the Temple of the Three Lintels, the Temple of the Four Lintels, and Las Monjas—utilize period-ending dates that designate the Calendar Round, the tun, and an Ahau day marking the end of a katun (see Chapter 12). These all fall within about three years of the Temple of the Initial Series date. Texts associated with a badly ruined temple known as the "High Priest's

Fig. 7.4. Chichen Itza: the "florescent" (Puuc-style) buildings in Las Monjas Group include this example with the decorated lower façade and masked doorway typical of the Chenes style (see also Fig. 14.3). Note the rubble wall hearting visible to the left of the doorway where the veneer of masonry has fallen away.

Grave" include a date assigned to 10.8.10.11.0 (998), the latest known at Chichen Itza. But the style of this structure indicates that it may be an earlier prototype of the much larger El Castillo (see below), and the natural cave beneath the platform suggests that it may have served as a kind of "founder's temple" commemorating an original sacred entrance to the underworld, in the manner of the famous cave beneath the Temple of the Sun at Teotihuacan. If so, then this building's period-ending date may be far earlier—other positions that fit are 10.3.5.3.0 (894) or 10.0.12.8.0 (842), the latter being especially appropriate for a founding date.

The Caracol (see Fig. 7.5) is a distinctive round structure crowning two super-imposed rectangular platforms. It is something of an architectural mismatch, characterized by J. Eric Thompson as "a two-decker wedding cake on the square carton in which it came." The round superstructure appears to be of somewhat later vintage than are its supporting platforms, and seems to have been refurbished during the Early Postclassic era. The Carnegie excavations found that the upper platform of the Caracol was associated with a stela that has been dated by David Kelley to 10.3.17.0.0 (906).

In Central Mexico, round structures were often temples associated with Ehe-catl, the wind-deity aspect of the god Quetzalcoatl (or Kukulcan in Mayan), and it is possible to assume that the Caracol fulfilled this kind of function at Chichen Itza. Some 12.5 m high, its central core of masonry conceals a spiral staircase that winds up to a small chamber near the top of the building. The Spanish name for such a stairway is *caracol*, because of its fancied resemblance to the convolutions of a snail shell. The window-like openings through the thick walls of the chambers (Fig. 7.6) seem to provide certain astronomically important lines of sight. For example, one line of sight through the west wall bisects the setting sun on March 21, the vernal equinox; and other lines coincide with moonset on this same date.

The northern part of Chichen Itza is dominated by El Castillo, a large four-stairway pyramid supporting a flat-topped temple (Fig. 7.7). Like several Late Clas-sic Maya pyramids, El Castillo has nine terraces (compare Temple I at Tikal), and its stairway design recalls the platforms in Tikal's Twin Pyramid groups. The temple of El Castillo has four doorways, but the wider northern doorway is divided by two feathered-serpent columns. Similar columns are known from six other buildings at the site. Inside the buried temple of an older structure encased within El Castillo, Carnegie archaeologists found a chacmool (see innovation number 9, below) and a red-painted jaguar "throne," which has fangs of chert, jadeite eyes, and, to rep-resent its spots, inlaid jadeite disks (Fig. 7.8).

To the west is the Great Ball Court, which incorporates an earlier building (the Lower Temple of the Jaguars, with its prized murals) under its southeastern corner

Fig. 7.5. The Caracol, Chichen Itza, a round temple constructed on a series of platforms; a stela from the upper platform has been dated at 10.3.17.0.0 (A.D. 906).

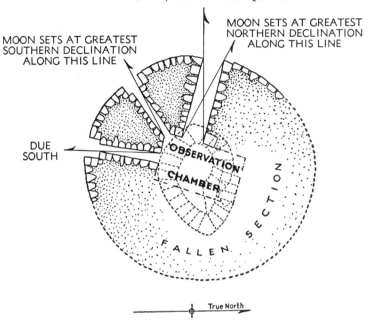

DUE WEST
SUN SETS ALONG THIS LINE ON
MARCH 21, THE VERNAL EQUINOX

MOON SETS AT GREATEST
SOUTHERN DECLINATION
ALONG THIS LINE

MOON SETS AT GREATEST
NORTHERN DECLINATION
ALONG THIS LINE

DUE
SOUTH

OBSERVATION CHAMBER

FALLEN SECTION

True North

Fig. 7.6. Plan of the Caracol, Chichen Itza, showing the astronomical alignments of its upper windows.

Fig. 7.7. El Castillo, Chichen Itza, the largest temple at the site, has a nine-terraced platform and four stairways.

(Fig. 7.9). The Upper Temple of the Jaguars, corresponding to the last construction stage of the Great Ball Court, sits above the same corner; its murals may depict episodes in the history of the Putun Maya (see Chapter 6). The Great Ball Court is the largest in Mesoamerica, measuring 166 by 68 m overall, with a playing alley 146 by 36 m. The vertical playing surfaces, with their single stone ring set midway in each, contrast with the long, sloping zones typical of earlier courts at Copan and other Classic lowland sites, indicating perhaps that the game in Yucatan at this time differed from the earlier contest. A greater number of ballcourts (thirteen) are known at Chichen Itza than at any other Maya center. The object of the game played here was to drive the ball through one of the rings, the openings of which required a trajectory parallel to the ground.

The balls used in these games were of solid rubber, and the description of them given by the early Spanish historians marks the first European notice of rubber. According to these accounts, the ball could not be thrown by the hand but had to be struck by the elbow, wrist, or hip, and leather pads were fastened to these parts of the body for the purpose. The winning stroke was made so rarely that when it did occur, the spectators had to forfeit to the lucky player all their clothing and jewelry. The moment the ball was driven through the ring, of course, the spectators fled, to avoid paying the forfeit, and the friends of the lucky player ran after them to exact it.

Fig. 7.8. The Red Jaguar Throne, from the interior of the temple buried beneath El Castillo at Chichen Itza.

Fig. 7.9. Great Ball Court and Temple of the Jaguars, Chichen Itza: (*above*) the playing alley of the Ball Court, looking south, with the Temple of the Jaguars at upper left; (*below*) Temple of the Jaguars, with its feathered-serpent columns.

•  •

The relief sculptures along the basal terrace of the Great Ball Court's walls, which depict a more gruesome outcome, probably represent at least one version of the ballgame that was played here—the ritual reenactment of warfare culminating in the sacrifice of captives. On the left stands an apparently victorious ballplayer or warrior with a knife in one hand and the head of his vanquished foe in the other. The decapitated foe, with streams of blood transformed into serpents spurting from his neck, kneels to the right of a disk, or shield, bearing a death's head. A recently discovered carved monument known as the Great Ball Court Stone bears a lengthy, eroded inscription that includes a date almost certainly equivalent to A.D. 864, making it one of the earliest dates at Chichen Itza.

To the north of El Castillo is a vast plaza supporting two small platforms (Fig. 7.10) and a *tzompantli* (skull rack; see below and Fig. 7.11). On the east side of this plaza sits the Temple of the Warriors (Fig. 7.12). Although larger and more finely built, its architecture reflects that of Pyramid B at Tula, the site that has been identified as the Toltec capital, north of Mexico City. The staircase leading to the large summit structure, the roof of which disappeared long ago, was reached by passing through a spacious colonnaded building. These colonnaded halls, which extend to the south and east of the Temple of the Warriors, were once roofed with beam and mortar, and may have been used as council halls. Colonnades completely surround the Court of the Thousand Columns, a great open plaza of 1.8 hectares, composed of a series of structures, including one known as El Mercado, or "The Market" (Fig. 7.13). The most imposing colonnaded building of the ancient city,

Fig. 7.10. Platform of the Cones, Chichen Itza, with its Mexican-style sloping lower wall and inset-paneled vertical upper zone (talud-tablero style).

Fig. 7.11. The *tzompantli* (skull rack) at Chichen Itza, identified by its shallow reliefs depicting human skulls impaled on poles.

this structure incorporates the tallest columns ever erected by the Maya. Despite its popular name, it may have been the seat of the city's government (see below).

An earlier building was found during the excavations under the Temple of the Warriors. Known as the Temple of the Chacmool, it bore murals apparently presenting both Yucatec Maya and Putun Maya elites. Beneath the floor of this temple, the investigators discovered a cache containing a mosaic disk made of turquoise, a substance not found in the Maya area but usually imported from Central Mexico (Fig. 7.14).

Within the site at Chichen Itza are two large natural wells, or cenotes, which contributed greatly to the importance of the city and no doubt determined its location. The centrally located Xtoloc Cenote was the water supply for the center's populace. A sacbe leads north from El Castillo to the edge of the second well, the Cenote of Sacrifice (Fig. 7.15), which fulfilled a different function. During Chichen Itza's ascendancy, and even after its downfall in the Late Postclassic, pilgrimages were made to this sacred cenote from all parts of the Maya area and beyond, so that offerings might be cast into its depths. Dredging of the cenote has produced carved

Fig. 7.12. Temple of the Warriors, Chichen Itza: (*above*) from the west, showing the basal colonnades, once roofed with timber and plaster, along the front and southern sides; (*below*) entrance to the summit temple with its feathered-serpent columns that once supported a massive wooden lintel.

jade, gold jewelry, pottery, human bone, and other items; but contrary to popular belief, there is no evidence that virgins were sacrificed in this way (see Chapter 11).

Chichen Itza, its art and architecture inspired by both traditional Maya and non-Maya styles, was a truly splendid capital. The Maya traditions most prominently represented are from the Puuc region, while the most obvious non-Maya parallels reflect origins in Tula, the Toltec capital. But all in all, Chichen Itza's buildings are a vigorous affirmation of Yucatecan Maya architecture. They are finely built, using veneer-masonry techniques, vaults, and mosaic façades, and in most cases the Maya-built masonry at Chichen Itza is far finer than the masonry at Tula. But the Itza capital was not simply an assemblage of borrowings; much of its architecture and sculpture is innovative. The major characteristics of the site's architecture and sculpture, including its innovations, are as follows:

1. Colonnades, either within or adjacent to buildings (Fig. 7.12), formed of columns either square or round in section, each column built up as a series of stone drums, often sculptured in low relief. The form of the colonnades varies widely. A series of columns, often in rows, may be found at the base of a pyramid that bears a temple on its summit (Temple of the Warriors, Temple of the Wall Panels). Large interior rooms were sometimes roofed on rows of columns (Temple of the Warriors). Colonnades also stand alone, backed by a solid wall and sometimes terminated by end walls as well (South Temple of the Great Ball Court); or such a colonnade may

Fig. 7.13. El Mercado, or The Market, Chichen Itza: interior court with its columns, the tallest at the site.

Fig. 7.14. Chichen Itza: (*above*) turquoise mosaic disk found cached in the Temple of the Chacmool, an earlier building beneath the Temple of the Warriors; (*below*) the limestone vessel that contained the disk.

be backed by a courtyard surrounded by another colonnade (El Mercado; Fig. 7.13). Where colonnades are furnished with backing walls, accessory structures such as benches or a dais are often attached to the rear wall. Above the colonnades may be either beam-and-mortar roofing (Temple of the Warriors), wood or thatch roofing (El Mercado), or Maya corbeled vaulting (the majority of structures). Beam-and-mortar roofs are typical of Mexican architecture. Where vaulted roofs are employed, the column-lintel arrangement is substituted for the continuous masonry walls of Classic Maya buildings, and the roofs are supported on exceedingly long wooden lintels.

2. Round temples, which occurred from early times on the Mexican mainland but are rare in the Maya area and may first appear at Chichen Itza (the Caracol; Fig. 7.5).

3. Wide doorways interrupted by two stone columns carved in the form of feathered serpents; the head is on the floor surface, the body is vertical, and the tail runs forward and up to support a wooden lintel. Feathered serpents also appear frequently as ornaments on balustrades, panels, and other architectural elements.

Fig. 7.15. Sacred Cenote (or "Well of Sacrifice"), Chichen Itza, where offerings were made to the watery underworld.

4. A battered basal zone on the exterior faces of most pyramids and building walls. This zone, usually standing about a meter tall at an angle of about 75 degrees, contrasts with the characteristically vertical Maya walls.

5. Bas-relief carvings of prowling jaguars, full-frontal Tlaloc figures, vultures in profile (each holding a human heart in its talons), and reclining human figures holding long, diagonally placed spears. The expressions of these motifs at Chichen Itza are nearly identical to those at Tula. Maya deities, most often the crucially important Chac (lightning or rain god), are often featured alongside Mexican deities.

6. The *tzompantli* (Fig. 7.11): a low platform walled in stone and covered with human skulls sculptured in relief (or used to display actual trophy heads from sacrifice or warfare).

7. Atlantean figures: men with hands upraised to support a dais or door lintel, sculptured in full round.

8. Warrior figures in a variety of sculptural treatments, but always wearing characteristic clothing, ornaments, and insignia. They are found in processions on altars, or singly on square columns, or as caryatids sculptured in full round, as at Tula. Insignias include butterfly-shaped gorgets and headdress ornaments; headgear, of various styles, includes those types related to the later Mexica (Aztec) military orders of Eagles and Jaguars. Many figures carry an atlatl, or spearthrower (another implement of Mexican origin).

9. Chacmools: in-the-round figures lying on their backs, their knees and heads raised, their heads turned to the side to gaze at the onlooker, their hands surrounding a carved, bowl-shaped depression at about the position of the navel (probably used to receive offerings).

10. Standard bearers: sculptured standing figures with hands held together in front of the body. A perforation between the hands was seemingly designed to hold a pole, which likely bore a banner at its top.

## The Organization of the Itza State

Chichen Itza dominated Yucatan for the next two hundred years, but its murals and sculptured reliefs show that this hegemony was not always peaceful. By sheer force of arms and new tactics, the Putun, perhaps reinforced by contingents of Toltec or other Mexican mercenaries, subdued all resistance summoned up by the Yucatec Maya, and their enduring dominance appears to have ended the old order, under which most of Yucatan had been divided between Coba, the Puuc states, and perhaps Dzibilchaltun and other polities of the northwestern reaches of the peninsula.

The Putun invasion of central Yucatan and the establishment of the new capital at Chichen Itza were undoubtedly greeted with hostility by the old masters of the land, especially those at Coba. To connect their powerful eastern-Maya capital with the central boundary city of Yaxuna, the Coba rulers constructed the greatest of all Maya causeways, as we saw in Chapter 6. Their purpose in undertaking such a massive project was most likely to consolidate this broad area under Coba's control and to block further penetration into central Yucatan by the newcomers. Whatever their motivation, recent research at Yaxuna directed by David Freidel suggests that this outpost of the Coba realm ultimately fell victim to conquest by Chichen Itza, notwithstanding the virtues of the causeway. The best evidence for this turn of events lies in findings of unused masonry blocks still at the base of incomplete platforms, and of various signs of destruction, such as carved panels torn from their buildings, all of which speaks to a sudden abandonment of the site.

The fate of the other polities of the northern lowlands remains unclear, although all seem to have declined in the wake of Chichen Itza's expansion. The recent discoveries of Sotuta pottery sherds in the latest occupation levels at Uxmal may reflect the eventual takeover of that key Puuc site by Chichen Itza as well. But the most compelling sign of Chichen Itza's dominance is the fall from prominence seen at most of the other centers in Yucatan during the Early Postclassic. Even Coba, the most powerful and most distant of Chichen Itza's rivals, seems to have slipped into an inexorable decline. Gradually cut off from its former economic and political allies in Yucatan and bypassed by the new coastal trade routes, it was ultimately abandoned.

Chichen Itza's success in expanding its power base and dominating the northern lowlands was undoubtedly due to a combination of factors. As was the case with other successful Maya polities, these certainly included control of trade, and Chichen Itza, in the tradition of Putun Maya coastal commerce, enjoyed economic advantages of a new sort from its seaport at Isla Cerritos. Military prowess, as attested by the prominent depictions of warriors, captives, and human sacrifices, was clearly a major factor, both in securing the Itza's initial foothold on the peninsula in the Terminal Classic and in the political and territorial expansion of the Itza state. And belief systems must have played a major role also, for Chichen Itza, with its temples and, especially, its sacred cenote, was such an important religious center that it continued to be a focus for religious pilgrimages long after it was abandoned. But to these factors we can add a new ingredient: an innovative, flexible, and stable form of government, one that proved to be much more successful in administering a conquest state than the traditional Maya political organization had been.

Our evidence for the political organization of the Chichen Itza state is less direct than that for the lowland polities of the Classic period, for in contrast to the latter, one of the most obviously distinctive characteristics of the new political order in Yucatan is the virtual absence of historical texts, Long Count dates, and grand depictions of the *ahau* or supreme ruler. Instead, the carved and painted images at Chichen Itza present a multitude of elite figures, perhaps playing a variety of roles, such as warriors, priests, and ballplayers, but no single, identifiable ruler. As suggested by David Kelley, and reinforced by the readings made by Ruth Krochock and others, the inscribed lintels serve to dedicate buildings rather than to record the reigns of rulers. Though the texts are sparse, they do mention names, and epigraphers have identified at least eight prominent individuals, three women and five men, but these people are not associated with glyphs that indicate a line of descent within a ruling lineage, as was the case in most Classic-period Maya texts. Rather, the Chichen Itza inscriptions use the sibling glyph (*yitah*) to express relationships among the luminaries portrayed (at least three of the men are named as "brothers"). The information in the inscriptions is amazingly consistent with the later account by Bishop Landa, who spoke of the political leadership of Chichen Itza in the following passage:

> It is said that it was ruled by three lords who were brothers who came into that country from the west, who were very devout, and so they built very beautiful temples and they lived very chastely without wives, and one of them died or went away, upon which the others acted unjustly and indecently and for this they were put to death. . . .

The combined weight of evidence indicates that political authority at Chichen Itza, rather than concentrating power in a single ruler, resided in a group of elite individuals, perhaps literally brothers, but more likely "brothers" in the sense of being members of the same elite lineage. The picture is of rule by supreme council, the members of which probably held specific offices and/or may have administered specific territorial divisions within the Itza state. The noted ethnohistorian Ralph Roys documented such a form of government at Mayapan, the successor to Chichen Itza (see below), and some Yucatecan polities still operated under this system at the time of the Conquest, when it was called *multepal* (*mul* meaning "together," *tepal* meaning "to govern"). In this later period, colonnaded structures, one of the most distinctive of Chichen Itza's architectural innovations, were still being built for use as civic and ritual assembly areas and often as meeting places for ruling councils. This finding argues strongly for the existence of a multepal system at heavily colonnaded Chichen Itza, convening perhaps in one of the major structures in the Group of the Thousand Columns, such as the so-called El Mercado.

Of course this kind of political organization is not entirely new in the Maya area, for, as we have mentioned, a trend toward the dispersal of power among elite lineage heads can be discerned in the Late Classic at several major lowland cities, such as Copan. The multepal system, then, should be looked upon not as a sudden innovation, but as the culmination of a long evolutionary trend in political organization. It seems to have crystallized at Chichen Itza, affording this polity one of several advantages in the highly competitive environment of the Terminal Classic and Early Postclassic eras, and it continued to evolve at Mayapan and in several of the last Maya polities remaining independent prior to the Spanish Conquest.

Such a system would have had several advantages over the single-ruler form of government. Most significantly, perhaps, a multepal system removed Chichen Itza from the direst vulnerability of the traditional form of rulership, whereby the capture and sacrifice of a ruling *ahau* could paralyze a defeated polity. Decision-making by a ruling council also precludes relying on the abilities or irrationalities of a single individual whose leadership qualities may be good or bad. (This sharing of wisdom within a ruling council is of course a virtue only if the council has the means to arrive at clear-cut decisions, failing which another form of paralysis could seize the government.) Finally, the use of the multepal system could be of great advantage to the dominant power: Mayapan, as we shall see, maintained control over captured territory by requiring that members of the defeated ruling families live in the capital, as a kind of hostage insurance against revolts. And although the chronicles indicate that some local Maya kings continued to rule over their own provinces, provided they paid proper tribute and allegiance to the rulers at Chichen Itza, we must assume that Chichen Itza, too, knew very well how to employ such coercive means in the control of its conquered polities.

Suppressive measures of some sort may in fact explain some of the rather uncomplimentary references to the period of Chichen Itza's hegemony in the later Yucatecan Maya chronicles: "They brought shameful things when they came. They lost their innocence in carnal sin. . . . There was no great teacher, no great speaker, no supreme priest when the change of rulers occurred at their arrival. Lewd were the priests when they came to be settled here by the foreigners. Furthermore, they left their descendants here at Mayapan. These then received the misfortunes, after the affliction of these foreigners. These, they say, were the Itza."

But the judgments of history are often inconsistent. As we have seen, Bishop Landa's characterization in the *Relación de las cosas de Yucatán* describes the rulers of Chichen Itza as "very devout." A native Maya book, the *Chilam Balam of Mani,* describes the Itzas as "holy men."

One of the "brothers" who ruled at Chichen Itza seems to have held a supreme religious office, a post distinct from the workings of the council. The Postclassic chronicles relate that there was a high priest presiding over all of Yucatan, one who received no allotment of servants from the reigning lords but was supported by gifts. He held himself apart from political allegiances and from most sacrifices, and although shorn of direct political power, he was nonetheless influential and respected. He appointed all priests (second sons of ruling lords were usually trained as priests), and his advice on matters of learning was much respected by the ruling lords. His duties included the performance of calendric and related ceremonies, the pronouncement of divinations and prophecies, and the dispensing of cures for diseases. The office of supreme priest was hereditary, and might even have derived from the post of ruler or principal lord in the old Classic Maya system. The memory of this religious office is found in Landa's post-Conquest account: "It is believed among the Indians that with the Itzas who occupied Chichen Itza there reigned a great lord, named Kukulcan, and that the principal building, which is called Kukulcan, shows this to be true. They say that he arrived from the west; but they differ among themselves as to whether he arrived before or after the Itzas or with them."

The ruling political groups in Yucatan at the time of the Spanish Conquest prided themselves on their "Mexican" ancestry, but what they were probably referring to was the mixed heritage fostered by the Putun Maya. To ensure that no Yucatec Maya impostors had crept into their ranks, the Putun leaders periodically conducted a kind of ritual interrogation of officials, using what was called the language of Zuyua in the *Chilam Balam of Chumayel* to ferret out the pretenders. (Zuyua, a mythical place associated with Mexica origins, is considered to be the birthplace of Kukulcan.) This "language" of Zuyua must have been passed down from father to son among the ruling elite. But despite its claim to rely on esoteric Mexican lore, the language is studded with Maya calendrical and religious references, undoubtedly the result of the blending of Maya and Mexican cultures characteristic of the Putun heritage.

In later times, political dynasties throughout Mesoamerica claimed descent from the rulers of a city called Tollan, or Tulan, a name usually identified with the archaeological site of Tula, the great center of the Toltec nation in Central Mexico. But the old idea of a Toltec invasion and takeover at Chichen Itza has been displaced by the weight of additional information, including archaeological evidence showing that many Mexican elements were already in Yucatan by the Terminal Classic, and perhaps earlier. It has been further argued that, in contrast to the remains in Yucatan, Tula reveals no prototypes for some of the architectural features at Chichen Itza described earlier; and certainly Chichen Itza is the better-constructed center. These pieces of information suggest that Tula may have been an outpost of Mexicanized Maya expansion, *the reverse of the traditional theory*, and that references to the fabled city of Tollan in later times may refer to Chichen Itza.

## External Connections of the Itza State

As we have seen, beginning in the Terminal Classic there were many incursions into the Maya area of peoples bearing a Mexicanized Maya culture. These incursions are identifiable in Yucatan (Chichen Itza), in the southern Maya lowlands (Seibal), in the highlands (discussed below), on the Pacific coast (Cotzumalhuapa), and even in Central Mexico (at sites such as Xochicalco and Cacaxtla). When we take into account not only the architecture, but the art styles, pottery, and other artifacts, the archaeological evidence indicates that Chichen Itza was the center of a powerful state that manifested a hybrid mix of Maya and Mexican cultural elements during the Terminal Classic and Early Postclassic eras. It is this hybrid culture that has been most often associated with the Putun Maya. Assuming that the bearers of the culture were indeed the Putun Maya groups, we can suggest the following reconstruction of events.

The Putun were successful merchants, warriors, and opportunists. By taking advantage of the power vacuums left in the wake of the decline of the Classic states of Mexico and the Maya lowlands, they succeeded in capturing the critical resources and trade routes formerly controlled by these Classic-period powers (certainly control over the lucrative salt trade was one prime objective). Because the Putun groups were not politically unified, they established a series of regional capitals in various areas of Mesoamerica, apparently integrated into a loose commercial confederation. The best archaeological evidence for the existence of this economic network is provided by certain trade goods, such as Fine Orange and Plumbate pottery, that are found throughout Mesoamerica.

Chichen Itza was the greatest of the centers reflecting the Putun associations that began to appear in the Terminal Classic and continued during the Early Postclassic. Its relationship with Tula and the Toltecs of Central Mexico remains unclear, though it is now apparent that Chichen Itza was not a Toltec colonial outpost (as suggested above, the reverse of this traditional scenario can now be entertained). But regardless of their respective origins and relative dominance, it is very likely that the two centers maintained close commercial ties, as well as military and diplomatic alliances.

The spread of the Putun Maya–controlled sea-trade network during this period can be traced via its trail of ceramics. Fine Orange pottery—more than a dozen whole vessels and numerous fragments—has been found at Chichen Itza. This pottery, among the best of any made in Mesoamerica, was manufactured on the Gulf coast (see Chapter 15); it must have been shipped by canoe along the coast, a distance of over 1,000 km, then by land perhaps another 120 km. The effects of this pottery tradition on the local artisans are clearly evident: Yucatecan pottery of all sorts, except for cooking pots, shows an imitation of Gulf coast shapes, but the copies are usually inaccurate because of the retention of the old Yucatecan forming techniques; the designs on the Yucatecan pieces, also copied, capture little of the verve and precision of the imported pieces; and the designs were incised before the application of the slip, a native Yucatecan practice not found in the fashioning of Fine Orange pottery.

Smaller quantities of pottery from elsewhere in Mexico have also been found at Chichen Itza. A long, fragile clay pipe seems to have been brought from far west of Mexico City to Chichen Itza. Vessels of Plumbate pottery came from the south coast of Guatemala. Trade in luxury goods included gold in some quantity from Panama, turquoise from Mexico, and jadeite from the Maya highlands.

Architectural remains also provide evidence of the spread of Chichen Itza's influence. At Nohmul in northern Belize, on the eastern coast of Yucatan, archaeological work has uncovered two buildings reminiscent of those at Chichen Itza. One

.. .

is a round structural platform, the other a courtyard building similar to the typical residential structures at Chichen Itza. Farther south, at the Classic center of Quirigua, Postclassic occupation has been revealed by ceramic refuse that includes pottery imported from the eastern coast of Yucatan. Significantly, a sculptured stone chacmool found at Quirigua in the nineteenth century may indicate a direct link to Chichen Itza (see p. 402).

## The Dominance of Mayapan

According to the chronicles, in A.D. 1221 the hegemony of Chichen Itza was broken. Mayapan, the new dominant center, was built after the fall of Chichen Itza, and sixteenth-century documents report that it had been abandoned before the Spanish Conquest, about A.D. 1450. The precise circumstances under which Mayapan replaced Chichen Itza are unclear in the chronicles. Political intrigue played a part, as did the kidnapping, by the ruler of Izamal, of the wife of the Chichen Itza ruler. In the ensuing war, Hunac Ceel, ruler of Mayapan, was said to have conquered Chichen Itza, and there is supporting archaeological evidence that Chichen Itza was sacked. Excavations in the Temple of the Warriors indicate that sculptures were intentionally thrown down, and cached offerings seem to have been looted at about that time. There is both archaeological and documentary evidence of contacts with Mexico in the political affairs of Yucatan in these times: Hunac Ceel is said to have employed mercenaries against Chichen Itza; and the later Cocom rulers of Mayapan twice brought in warriors from garrisons in Tabasco.

Archaeological excavations at Mayapan have provided a chronological sequence that generally parallels the events recorded in the Yucatecan chronicles. Two consecutive architectural eras, the earlier at Chichen Itza, the later at Mayapan, have been worked out. Associated with the buildings at Chichen Itza is an assemblage of recognizable artifacts and Sotuta ceramics, including Plumbate and other pottery trade wares. Pottery of a later assemblage, almost entirely postdating these structures, is also found, and this same pottery assemblage is found in the lower levels of Mayapan as well, mixed with the later pottery characteristic of that site.

Shortly before the abandonment of Chichen Itza (about 1200), a new tempering material was introduced in the pottery-making craft, and its use spread rapidly through the Peninsula. Then, not long after the establishment of Mayapan, a new slip color appeared, one that has continued in use in Yucatan until the present day. Using these changes as time markers suggests that Chichen Itza was depopulated gradually, despite the apparently violent end that struck the site center. The ceramic evidence also raises the possibility of a time lapse between the abandonment of Chichen Itza and the founding of Mayapan. The ritual sanctity of Chichen Itza, however, persisted until the Spanish Conquest and beyond, and there is abundant evidence, both archaeological and documentary, of pilgrimages to the site across that span of time.

## MAYAPAN

The ruins of Mayapan, a city far smaller than Chichen Itza, lie about 100 km to the west, at almost the same latitude. Landa described Mayapan in the following terms:

Kukulcan established another city after arranging with the native lords of the country that he and they should live there and that all their affairs and business should be brought there; and for this purpose they chose a very good situation, eight leagues farther in the interior than Mérida is now, and fifteen or sixteen leagues from the sea. They surrounded it with a very broad stone wall, laid dry, of about an eighth of a league, leaving in it only two narrow gates. The wall was not very high and in the midst of this enclosure they built their temples, and the largest, which is like that of Chichen Itza, they called Kukulcan, and they built another building of a round form with four doors, entirely different from all the others in that land, as well as a great number of others round about joined together. In this enclosure they built houses for the lords only, dividing all the land among them, giving towns to each one, according to the antiquity of his lineage and his personal value. And Kukulcan gave a name to this city—not his own as the Ah Itzas had done in Chichen Itza, which means the well of Ah Itzas, but he called it Mayapan, which means "the standard of the Maya," because they called the language of the country Maya, and the Indians [say] "Ichpa" which means "within the enclosure." This Kukulcan lived with the lords in that city for several years; and leaving them in great peace and friendship, he returned by the same way to Mexico, and on the way he stopped at Champoton, and in memory of him and of his departure, he erected a fine building in the sea like that of Chichen Itza, a long stone's throw from the shore. And thus Kukulcan left a perpetual remembrance in Yucatan.

The temple described by Landa is identifiable today, its four-stairway platform and flat-topped temple obvious copies of those at the much larger and better-built El Castillo at Chichen Itza (see Fig. 7.17).

Intensive archaeological excavations conducted by the Carnegie Institution at Mayapan over some five years produced a variety of information about domestic and religious architecture. Like some other Maya cities built in earlier and later times, it was walled (Fig. 7.16), but the patterning of settlement at Mayapan is a dramatic departure from that of earlier Maya cities. Whereas house platforms at almost all Maya sites are dispersed sufficiently to permit the working of garden plots in the intervening spaces, the remains of residences within the 4 km² area of Mayapan's walls are far more densely packed, and the four gateways of the surrounding wall demonstrate careful planning against military attack.

Thirty-five hundred buildings have been counted within the walls of Mayapan, and the population must have totaled over 15,000. The major buildings are near the center of the city (Fig. 7.17), just as Landa had described them, but the low, secondary wall said to have surrounded this precinct has not been located. Within

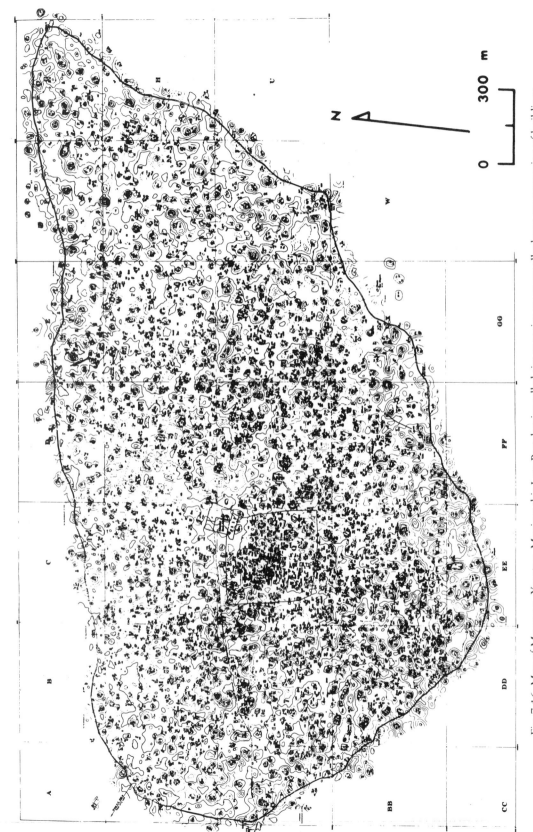

Fig. 7.16. Map of Mayapan, Yucatan, Mexico: this Late Postclassic walled site contains an unusually dense concentration of buildings.

this central area is a cenote, and grouped around the temples are rectangular buildings, with frontal colonnades and solid rear walls, that are most likely elite residences facing a series of paved plazas. Mayapan's buildings, unlike those at Chichen Itza, were made of crudely shaped blocks set in mud or plaster mortar. Not a vaulted roof of this period remains standing and the sculpture is equally slipshod.

The remaining area is covered by densely but irregularly spaced houses, most of which were at least partially of masonry construction. When available, slightly elevated ground was chosen, for better drainage. Low, dry-stone property walls surround these houses, enclosing irregularly shaped yards that average about a quarter of an acre. Meandering among the haphazardly placed houses are lanes or pathways, their irregular boundaries fixed by low property walls. It would seem that the Maya, even in these densely settled conditions, retained the plans of their rural farmsteads wherever possible, and there is still room to keep bees and raise fruit and a few other crops in kitchen gardens. Although Mayapan was described as

Fig. 7.17. Mayapan: El Castillo, a four-stairwayed temple modeled after the larger building of the same name at Chichen Itza.

being dependent on tribute from other parts of the country for subsistence, and thus may not be a typical settlement, it fits the description of native towns given by the early Spaniards. In Landa's words,

Before the Spaniards had conquered that country, the natives lived together in towns in a very civilized fashion. They kept the land well cleared and free from weeds, and planted very good trees. Their dwelling place was as follows: in the middle of the town were their temples with beautiful plazas, and all around the temples stood the houses of the lords and the priests, and then of the most important people. Thus came the houses of the richest and of those who were held in the highest estimation nearest to these, and at the outskirts of the town were the houses of the lower class. And the wells, if there were but few of them, were near the houses of the lords; and they had their improved lands planted with wine trees and they sowed cotton, pepper and maize, and they lived thus close together for fear of their enemies, who took them captive, and it was owing to the wars of the Spaniards that they scattered in the woods.

The pottery found at Mayapan demonstrates that the influence of the Gulf coast shapes continued; the sizes and forms of vessels are reminiscent of the Late Postclassic Mexica, with a few identical details, and another style of Fine Orange ware, of poorer quality, was imported in some quantity from the nearby Campeche coast. New vessel forms were introduced at some time late in the history of Mayapan. Since these seem to have had western origins, they may have arrived with the mercenary warriors, and the introduction of a new cooking pot, the cauldron, suggests that women came with the mercenaries. Elaborate figurine incensarios (incense burners), which also appeared at this time, are similar in detail to those of a very wide area, stretching from southern Veracruz through Belize and inland as far as Lago Peten Itza. Figurine incensarios have been found over this whole area, on the surfaces of more ancient Maya ruins as well as near temples of their own time period, notwithstanding that the Spaniards destroyed such "idols" in large numbers during the first years of the Conquest.

The Yucatecan chronicles record that the Cocom lineage, descendants of Hunac Ceel, destroyer of Chichen Itza, was the most prestigious family at Mayapan. The Cocom were an elite Itza lineage that had probably been well established in the political organization of Chichen Itza, to judge from at least two occurrences of the name Cocom in the hieroglyphic texts of the first Itza capital. Mayapan became the successor capital state for the Itza, its architecture and *multepal* government apparently modeled after those of its larger and more splendid predecessor. The chronicles tell us that Mayapan managed to hold sway over a fairly unified Yucatan for nearly 250 years, by a combination of marriage alliances with the other noble lineages of the area, and by the seemingly simple means of keeping the heads of each of these local ruling families resident at Mayapan, and thus under their direct control. Just to be sure, the Cocom also employed contingents of foreign mercenaries known as the Ah Canul. But of course we do not know the limits of Mayapan's domain, or the degree to which the chronicles simply perpetuate propaganda designed to impress the reader with Mayapan's power and importance.

## The East Coast of Yucatan

The best-preserved architectural remains of the period dominated by Mayapan are those at Tulum and at other sites on or near the east coast of Yucatan. Others are off the east coast on Isla de Cozumel (close to the mainland) and Isla de Mujeres (farther offshore), and shrines of this period have been identified at nearby Coba, indicating that this large Classic center was reoccupied during the Late Postclassic. Cozumel has been seen as one of the major Putun trading centers along the sea routes reaching around the Yucatan Peninsula. Mayapan-style figurine incensarios and pottery found in these east-coast ruins testify to their external connections.

Beautifully executed murals from Santa Rita Corozal, farther down the east coast (see below and Fig. 7.18), show close similarities to the less well-preserved paintings on the Tulum temples (Fig. 7.20) and at the nearby site of Tancah (see Fig. 14.37). Though the Tancah murals show stylistic links to the Late Postclassic Maya codices, those of Tulum and Santa Rita show striking similarities to the designs of pre-Conquest Mixtec codices from the Mexican highlands and to murals at Mitla, in Oaxaca, all rendered in a Late Postclassic tradition known as the Mixteca-Puebla style. The presence of these murals at Tulum and Santa Rita attests to the economic prosperity of the east-coast sites during this period, for the murals appear to be the work of expert foreign artists commissioned by the local elite. These murals indicate, moreover, that the Maya rulers of these east-coast centers were part of a widespread network—involving both trade and marriage alliances—that linked the elite classes of many different ethnic groups throughout Mesoamerica.

But concerning the east coast of Yucatan, the documentary record is frustratingly sketchy. The *Books of Chilam Balam*, though they mention the names of east-

Fig. 7.18. Santa Rita Corozal, Belize: drawing of a Late Postclassic mural of about 1440 or later.

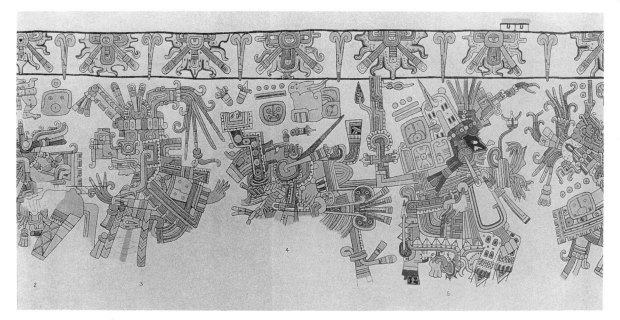

• •

ern towns and give an impression of friendly relations with them, do not tell us about their political affiliations. Tulum, the most spectacular archaeological site of the area, is still a landmark to mariners along the east coast. Occupied until Conquest times, it was probably the Maya center sighted and compared to Seville in an early account of Spanish voyages (see the Epilogue).

### TULUM

The dramatic ruins of Tulum stand on the sea cliffs overlooking the Caribbean on the east coast of the Yucatan Peninsula (Fig. 7.19), just south of the channel between Isla de Cozumel and the mainland. The site appears to have been occupied at the time of the Spanish Conquest, and was probably sighted by Juan de Grijalva during his reconnaissance of the coast in 1518. During their visit to Tulum, John Lloyd Stephens and Frederick Catherwood discovered the fragments of a reused Early Classic stela at the site. In the early twentieth century the buildings were mapped and investigated by Samuel Lothrop. Later studies of the region's settlement area were conducted by William Sanders. Recently, Arthur Miller directed a

Fig. 7.19. Tulum, Quintana Roo, Mexico: the Late Postclassic walled city as seen from the north, showing El Castillo, or major temple, overlooking the sea, and the canoe-landing beach below.

program of archaeological and art-historical research focused on the mural paintings at Tulum and Tancah.

These investigations reveal that Tulum was first occupied in the Late Postclassic, beginning about A.D. 1200. Its principal structures show several parallels with the earlier Modified-Florescent period at Chichen Itza and the later buildings of Mayapan, though Tulum's architecture was executed on a much reduced scale. One motivation for its founding, very likely, was to establish a trading center on Yucatan's east coast, probably by a Putun Maya group allied to the rulers of Mayapan.

The site is bounded on its landward sides by a stone wall that was once equipped with a walkway and parapet and averages some 6 m thick and 3–5 m high. In all, the wall circumscribes a roughly rectangular area measuring about 385 m from north to south and 165 m from east to west. Approach from the east is protected by sea cliffs averaging some 12 m in height, and the wall on the landward side is broken only by five narrow gateways, one on the west side and two each on the north and south. Small structures ("watchtowers") mark the landward corners. A small cenote near the northern wall provided a source of water within Tulum's walls. A small building (Str. 35) is perched on the limestone ledge overhanging this water source.

Within the wall lies a series of masonry platforms and buildings, including colonnaded palaces and elevated temples. In general, Tulum's masonry is very crude and often covered with thick coatings of plaster. Traces of at least one "street" can be detected by a north-south alignment of structures just inside the western gate.

The largest palace-type buildings, strs. 21 and 25, lie along this alignment. Both have colonnades and once had beam-and-mortar roofs. Just to the south of Str. 21 is the Temple of the Frescoes (Str. 16), which consists of a small lower gallery, opened to the west by a colonnade, and an even smaller second-story temple. On the inner wall of the lower gallery are frescoes dating, according to Miller's analyses, to some time later than 1450 (Fig. 7.20). The style of these murals is similar to the designs of the Paris Codex, one of the few surviving Maya books (see Chapter 13). The façade of Str. 16 is decorated with stucco reliefs, including niched figures of the "diving god" identified as representations of Xux Ek, the Maya "wasp star," or Venus deity.

To the east is a central precinct defined by a low masonry wall. Its principal building, the Castillo (Str. 1), is a platform 7.5 m high supporting a small, vaulted two-room temple, which is reached on its western side by a stairway with a wide balustrade. On the west side of the temple building is a single doorway supported by two circular columns. Later modification transformed these into feathered-serpent columns similar to those employed so frequently at Chichen Itza. The Castillo platform was built over an earlier colonnaded palace with a beam-and-mortar roof, and the wings of this earlier palace extend north and south from beneath the platform (Fig. 7.21).

Fig. 7.20. Tulum: part of the murals on the interior walls of Str. 16, rendered in a Late Postclassic style (ca. 1450 or later).

Immediately north of the Castillo is a tiny elevated structure, also reached by a stairway on its western side, known as the Temple of the Diving God, or Str. 5 (Fig. 7.22). Its walls have a pronounced negative batter, and traces of a splendid mural painting on its interior (eastern) wall can still be discerned (Fig. 7.23). Its single doorway is on its west side, and above the doorway is the structure's namesake, a stucco figure of the diving god.

Str. 45, to the north of the central precinct, is dramatically situated on a promontory above the sea (Fig. 7.24). Resting on a circular platform, it contains an altar that was still being used by the local Maya when Lothrop conducted his research at Tulum in 1924. A small shrine in front of Str. 45 appears to have been used as a beacon for seagoing canoes. There is a break in the offshore barrier reef, opposite the site, and canoes seeking to make port at Tulum could have used such beacons to guide their safe passage through the reef. Between the Castillo and Str. 45 a gap in the sea cliff forms a cove and landing beach where the great Maya trading canoes could be hauled out. Tulum undoubtedly served as a major port and trading center during the Late Postclassic and was occupied until the time of the Spanish Conquest.

## The Fall of Mayapan and the Rise of Petty States

Shortly before 1450, Ah Xupan, a noble lord of the Xiu lineage at Mayapan, organized and led a successful revolt against the Cocom. All members of the Cocom lineage were killed, except one who was away on a trading mission. The Xiu, like the Cocom, claimed descent from Tollan, and thus could brandish a prestigious and legitimate claim to power. The great center of Uxmal lies within the region the Xiu ruled, but despite the claims in the Xiu histories (see Figs. 10.9 and 10.10), the Xiu lords appear to have come to the area too late to have ruled during the Terminal Classic apogee of that center. By the time they would have arrived, the city was already in ruins.

Following the revolt against the Cocom, Mayapan was sacked and abandoned, an event again verified by archaeology. Excavations have revealed evidence of burned buildings, ancient looting, and even the skeletal remains of people who may have been killed during the revolt.

Landa, in describing the calamities that befell Yucatan during the century between the fall of Mayapan and the Spanish Conquest, fixed the time of the fall at

Fig. 7.21. Tulum: El Castillo, as depicted by Frederick Catherwood in the mid-nineteenth century.

Fig. 7.22. Tulum: looking north from the front of El Castillo, with Str. 5 in the center and part of the defensive wall in the distance (note the corner tower at left).

1441. Four of the five native chronicles, as well as the two leading early Spanish authorities—Cogolludo, writing in 1656, and Villagutierre Soto-Mayor, in 1700—support this dating. Taking the year of his writing, 1566, as his point of departure, Landa says: "Since the last plague, more than fifty years have now passed, the pestilence of the swelling was sixteen years before the wars, and the hurricane another sixteen years before that, and twenty-two or twenty-three years after the destruction of the city of Mayapan. Thus according to this count it has been 125 years since its overthrow within which the people of this country have passed through the calamities described."

This reckoning fixes the date of the plague at 1516 or 1515, the date of the mortality from the wars at 1496, the date of the pestilence at 1480, the date of the hurricane at 1464, and, again, the date of the destruction of Mayapan at 1441. The chronicle from *The Book of Chilam Balam of Tizimin* and the first and second chronicles from *The Chilam Balam of Chumayel* record that there was pestilence in Katun 4 Ahau (1480–1550), which Landa indeed dated to the very beginning of this katun. The first chronicle from *The Book of Chilam Balam of Chumayel* describes an epidemic of smallpox as having taken place in Katun 2 Ahau (1500–1520); this seems to be Landa's plague "with great pustules that rotted the body," which he reckoned to have occurred in 1515 or 1516. Small though these two items of confirmation may be, they suggest a high degree of reliability in the native chronicles, at least for this timespan.

After the fall of Mayapan, all the larger cities of the region fell into decline, and many were soon abandoned. In the wake of the fall, various noble lineages reestablished themselves elsewhere. The Chels, a prominent noble family of Mayapan, left after the fall of the city and established their principal new settlement at Tecoh. The

Fig. 7.23. Tulum: part of the murals on the interior wall of Str. 5, rendered in a Late Postclassic style (see also Fig. 7.20).

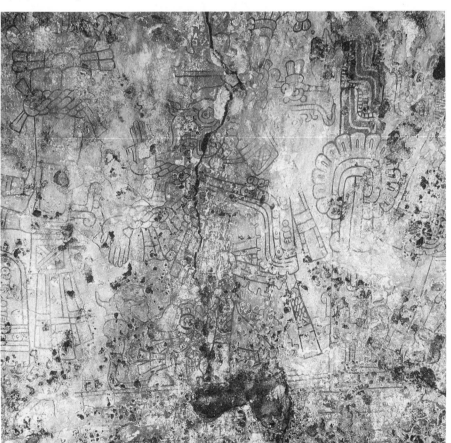

Fig. 7.24. Tulum: the rear of Str. 5, with Str. 45 on the promontory beyond the landing beach.

only surviving son of the slain Cocom ruler, the one who had been away on business, gathered his remaining people about him and established his rule at Tibolon, near Sotuta. The victors, the Tutul Xiu, also founded a new capital, which they called Mani, meaning, in Mayan, "It is passed."

The southernmost of these Late Postclassic realms, far to the south of Tulum, was known as Chetumal. Its capital, or chief town, also known as Chetumal, was recorded by the Spanish in the sixteenth century as being sizable and prosperous. The available evidence indicates that the ethnohistorically recorded town of Chetumal corresponds to the archaeological site known as Santa Rita Corozal. Though the site had been occupied continuously for more than 2,000 years, it clearly came under new and vigorous rule in the years following the fall of Mayapan.

### SANTA RITA COROZAL

This site is situated on a bluff overlooking Chetumal Bay, midway between the Hondo and New rivers, in northern Belize. (As a former British colony, Belize retains a number of English spellings; to others in the area, the bay is Bahía de Chetumal, and the Hondo is the Río Hondo.) The archaeological site of Santa Rita Corozal continues to be occupied today by the town of Corozal. Today, there are no remains of large platforms or temples at the site, and the remains of the ancient Maya town are inconspicuous. Fishing and sea-coast trading would have been important for its original inhabitants, however, and it may be that few monumental structures were ever built, though it is obvious that modern occupation has produced significant destruction at the site.

Excavations directed by Thomas Gann at the turn of the century uncovered the famous Late Postclassic murals mentioned previously (Fig. 7.18). In the interim, tragically, these murals have been destroyed. Further research was conducted at the site by several archaeologists in the 1970's, and the most comprehensive investigation, instigated by the Corozal Postclassic Project directed by Diane and Arlen Chase, undertook mapping, surface collection, and excavations during four field seasons between 1979 and 1985.

This recent research revealed an occupational history as long as any known from a Maya lowland site, extending from the end of the Early Preclassic (ca. 1000–1200 B.C.) to the Spanish Conquest some 2,500 years later. Initially, Santa Rita Corozal was a very small settlement, its population probably only a few hundred, but from the Late Preclassic onward it had an estimated population ranging between 1,000 and 2,000 people. Ultimately, during the final two centuries before the Spanish Conquest, the site tripled in size (to ca. 7,000 people), probably as a consequence of its status as the political capital of the Late Postclassic Chetumal state.

One goal of the Corozal research was to define and test the whole range of building types at the site, most of which were invisible from the surface, so as to reconstruct the social and religious life of its ancient inhabitants. Some of the most interesting results of this work shed light on ritual activities, especially during the Late Postclassic, for archaeological evidence from that era can be evaluated against ethnohistoric descriptions. The patterning and contents of the ritual deposits (caches) associated with various buildings have been linked with Bishop Landa's description of the Maya New Year ceremonies conducted during the five "unlucky" Uayeb days at the end of the solar year (see Chapter 12). There are also indications that high-status personages conducted bloodletting in these and other rituals, not only in the Late Postclassic, but in earlier times as well. High-status males in burial sites have often been found with stingray spines in the pelvic area. The most vivid evidence for this practice comes from a series of cached pottery figurines depicting genital bloodletting. Taken altogether, the Santa Rita research demonstrates a degree of continuity in Maya ritual activities over an extraordinarily long span of occupation, despite the changing economic and political conditions during this span.

## The Final Days of Maya Independence

The last important event in the pre-Conquest history of Yucatan was the ill-fated pilgrimage of the Xiu ruler and his court to offer human sacrifice in the Cenote of Sacrifice at Chichen Itza in 1536. At the time, not a Spaniard remained in Yucatan. After unsuccessful attempts to subjugate the Maya in 1527–28 and 1531–35, the Spaniards had been forced to withdraw completely from the peninsula (see the Epilogue). And at the time they began their final assault, later in the sixteenth century, there were some eighteen independent states in the northern lowlands.

Ah Dzun Xiu, ruler of the Tutul Xiu at their new capital of Mani, thought the moment propitious for undertaking a pilgrimage to appease the Maya gods, who for so many years had afflicted the land with calamities. Because his great-grandfather, Ah Xupan Xiu, had played a major role in the slaying of Nachi Cocom's great-grandfather, the last ruler of Mayapan, Ah Dzun Xiu took precautions. No doubt fearing reprisals, he applied for safe-conduct passage from Nachi Cocom, the ruler of Sotuta, through whose province the pilgrims would have to pass.

Nachi Cocom had not forgotten the murder of his great-grandfather, indeed held Xiu treachery responsible for it, and he welcomed the Xiu request as an opportunity for revenge. The fact that the Xiu had offered to submit to the Spaniards, in the second phase of the Conquest (1531–35), when the Cocom had resisted, probably added fuel to the Cocom's ancient hatred of the Xiu and provided an added motive for revenge. The safe conduct was in any case promptly granted, and a pilgrimage headed by Ah Dzun Xiu, his son Ah Ziyah Xiu, and 40 other leaders of the Xiu nation set out for Chichen Itza via the province of Sotuta. Nachi Cocom, with a large delegation of his people, met them at Otzmal, 8 km southeast of the Cocom capital. The Xiu pilgrims were royally entertained for four days, but at a banquet on the evening of the fourth day the Cocom attacked their guests and killed them all. This act of treachery split the warring Maya anew, and pitted the two most powerful ruling houses in the northern peninsula against each other.

The Otzmal massacre, coming so shortly before the final phase of the Spanish Conquest, sealed the fate of the northern Maya by reviving old hatreds and effectively preventing a united stand against the Spaniards, who returned to Yucatan in 1540 determined to subdue the countryside. Exhausted by civil war, betrayed by some of their own leading lineages, and decimated by disease, the Maya were ultimately unable to defeat the better-armed Spaniards and finally were subjugated by the invaders' superior forces.

But the final chapter in the history of the ancient Yucatecan Maya would not be completed for another 150 years. The Yucatecan chronicles relate that around 1221 the survivors of the final destruction of Chichen Itza had moved southward, back "beneath the trees . . . beneath the vines" into the Peten rain forests still remembered from the Putun sojourn to Chakanputun centuries earlier. There, on a series of islands in one of the lakes of the central Peten lowlands, the Itza built a new capital, which they named Tayasal. Long after the Spaniards had conquered most other areas of Mesoamerica, in the early sixteenth century, Tayasal remained independent. Isolated and insulated by the dense rain forest, Tayasal remained beyond the reach of Spanish power until it was finally captured, sacked, and abandoned in 1697 (see the Epilogue). Most scholars have set the location of Tayasal in Lago Peten Itza, on the island of Flores. Certainly Late Postclassic remains exist on Flores, but the archaeological evidence is obscured by the modern capital of the Peten (see Fig. 1.10). Most of the ruins on the adjacent Tayasal peninsula date to the Classic period, although recent excavations have revealed Postclassic domestic occupational remains (Fig. 7.25). Another Late Postclassic center, known as To-

Fig. 7.25. Tayasal, on the shores of Lago Peten Itza in Guatemala: excavations at this Classic-period central-lowland site have discovered evidence of Postclassic domestic occupation along the lakeshore associated with the Late Postclassic city of Tayasal located on an island in the lake, visible above the trees (see Fig. 1.10).

poxte, stands to the east, on the islands of Lago Yaxha. The ruins of Topoxte appear to have been occupied during the same interval, and the site must have been related in some way to the Itza occupation of the central Peten. As recent research has shown, the Peten region remained an important if vestigial outpost of Maya independence, even as most other areas of Mesoamerica came to be subdued and colonized by the Spanish.

## The Southern Maya Area in the Postclassic

The rich resources of ethnohistoric information about the Postclassic Maya highlands include the unique chronicle of the Quiche Maya, the *Popol Vuh*, and other native documents. But as in Yucatan, these accounts do not always agree with the available archaeological evidence. Archaeological investigation in the southern Maya area has so far been less extensive than that in the lowlands, and further work may resolve many of the apparent discrepancies. In the meantime, only a tentative outline of Postclassic events in the southern area can be offered.

The history of the Postclassic peoples in the southern Maya area seems to generally accord with events in the northern lowlands. The ethnohistoric accounts mention the conquest of Maya highland areas by outsiders who claimed descent from Tollan, just as in Yucatan. In fact, the *Popol Vuh* relates that three Quiche Maya princes traveled to their former homeland to seek the authority and symbols of their legitimate right to rule the highlands. This visit to Tollan may in fact have been a visit to Chichen Itza, since the *Popol Vuh* records that their journey was initially to the east, after which "they crossed the sea." Seemingly, their route had taken them eastward down the Motagua Valley to the Caribbean, thence northward by boat along the coast of the peninsula. Furthermore, the *Popol Vuh* identifies the ruler of Tollan at the time as Nacxit, and the Yucatecan documents record Nacxit-Xuchit as the founder of Chichen Itza. The same Yucatecan chronicles also mention gifts sent to Chichen Itza from Guatemala, probably in deference to the prominence of Chichen Itza during the Early Postclassic era. Dennis Tedlock has offered an interesting alternative interpretation: that the Quiche princes traveled east to the much nearer lowland polity of Copan to receive their symbols of authority and rulership. Regardless of the actual location of this external contact, it seems clear that the southern Maya area was affected by the same expansion of Mexicanized Putun Maya groups that dominated the fortunes of Yucatan throughout much of the Postclassic.

In the southern Maya area the earliest evidence of contact with Mexicanized outsiders seems to date to the Terminal Classic. On the Pacific coast this influence is demonstrated by a monumental sculptural tradition of combined Maya and Mexican elements known as the Cotzumalhuapa style (Fig. 7.26). The chronological

Fig. 7.26. Rubbing of
Monument 3, Bilbao,
Guatemala: an example of the
Cotzumalhuapa sculptural style,
reflecting influences from
Mexico that began to appear in
the Maya area during the
Terminal Classic.

position of the Cotzumalhuapa style is a subject of debate, and some scholars associate it with a mid-Classic Teotihuacan colonization of the Pacific coast (see Chapter 4). But it seems better linked to the Terminal Classic and may in fact be related to the expansion of the Gulf coast Chontal Maya. In any case, both ethnohistorical and linguistic evidence indicates that by Postclassic times many areas of the Pacific coast were occupied by migrants from Central Mexico who spoke a Nahua language (Pipil). Only further archaeological research can establish the proper dating for the Cotzumalhuapa development.

As we have seen (in Chapter 6), the expansion by the Putun up the Río Usumacinta drainage appears to have given them control over several southern-lowland centers, such as Altar de Sacrificios and Seibal. These movements were probably also responsible for the first expressions of Mexicanized site planning, architecture, and artifacts (including, reportedly, Gulf coast Fine Orange pottery) that are known in the northern highlands. That is, the Chontal colonists and traders may have penetrated all the way into the northern highlands, by way of the upper Usumacinta (Río Chixoy and its tributaries).

Significantly, the archaeological record indicates a sudden change in highland society around 800: some sites were abruptly abandoned; others were rebuilt and expanded. And both the rebuilt centers and a series of apparently newly founded Terminal Classic highland centers were often larger than the older Classic sites had been.

The subsequent Early Postclassic era was marked by a dramatic shift in settlement pattern. The earlier sites, situated for the most part in open-valley settings, were largely abandoned, to be replaced by centers constructed in easily defended locations, usually on hilltops or promontories surrounded by steep-sided ravines. Ditch-and-wall fortifications often supplemented the natural defenses. This shift in site location has been correlated with a second wave of intruders, one contemporary with Chichen Itza's ascendancy in Yucatan. As in the northern lowlands, the highland documentary sources speak of conquests by warriors who established new ruling lineages and married into the local population. The recorded names of several of the new highland ruling families strongly suggest Mexican and Yucatecan affinities: Kumatz ("serpent"), for example, and Xiuj Toltecat (as we have just seen, "Toltec Xiu" is a name associated with a Yucatecan ruling lineage). Thus the Early Postclassic newcomers in the highlands may be seen as secondary waves of the people who established hegemony over Yucatan from their capital at Chichen Itza—Mexicanized Putun Maya warrior groups from the Gulf coast lowlands.

In several cases archaeological excavations support this connection. For instance, the remains from Early Postclassic highland sites often include a sculptural motif nearly identical to one associated with the Putun expansion in the coastal lowlands—an open-mouthed, feathered-serpent head from which human (warrior?) heads protrude. A serpent frieze excavated at Chuitinamit-Atitlan, on the south shore of Lago de Atitlan, matches a similar motif at Chichen Itza. Architectural parallels are also common. A platform that may be a *tzompantli* (see p. 402) has been noted from at least one highland site, at Chalchitan near the headwaters of the Río Chixoy. It should be acknowledged, however, that in some cases, as in the recent excavations at Chitinamit, northeast of Utatlan, no evidence of Mexicanized sculptural or architectural forms has been found.

Assuming that a new wave of Mexicanized Maya warriors established these fortified Early Postclassic centers, their routes into the highlands seem to have been via both the upper Usumacinta and the Motagua. Studies have identified a series of Early Postclassic sites situated throughout the upper drainage basins of these rivers and their tributaries. While the Usumacinta gave direct access to the hinterlands from the Putun homeland in the Gulf coast lowlands, the Motagua would have provided a route from the Caribbean coast to the east. And it may be recalled that there were indeed ties with the Putun along the Caribbean coast. Quirigua, in the lower Motagua Valley, seems to have been occupied during the Early Postclassic by peoples closely linked to Yucatan's east coast and Chichen Itza. This link may reflect Putun Maya control over the circum-Yucatan coastal trade network, including the Motagua Valley commerce between the highlands and the Caribbean. In this way, the Motagua seems to have provided a secondary avenue for Putun penetration into the Maya highlands.

Though the situation in the Early Postclassic remains somewhat murky, the picture for the Late Postclassic is clearer. The various ethnohistoric sources agree on the prominence of a series of highland Maya groups and their major population centers, many of which were encountered and described by the Spaniards early in the sixteenth century. These centers, all located in easily defended positions as were their Early Postclassic precursors, included several powerful regional capitals and many secondary centers, all of which competed for control over the people, products, and trade routes within their regions. Warfare was the usual mechanism for settling disputes, and several of these highland groups, notably the Quiche and Cakchiquel Maya, extended their spheres of control at the expense of neighboring societies. Both of these groups also expanded into the Pacific coastal plain, undoubtedly to gain control over cacao and the coast's other resources.

The major highland centers at the time of the Conquest dominated regions populated by the historically identified linguistic groups who are still to be found in the area today (see Chapter 13). These included centers in the Pokomam area (such as Mixcu Viejo, Fig. 7.27; and Chinautla Viejo), Atitlan (the major settlement of the Tzutuhil peoples living around the lake of the same name), Zaculeu (in the Mam area; Fig. 7.28), Utatlan (the principal center of the Quiche; Figs. 7.29 and 7.30), and Iximche (capital of the Cakchiquel; Fig. 7.31). Major archaeological investigations have been undertaken at Zaculeu, Mixcu Viejo, Iximche, and Utatlan, as well as at several secondary centers such as Zacualpa.

Fig. 7.27. Mixcu Viejo, Guatemala: a Late Postclassic site in the Maya highlands, situated on a series of small, defensible plateaus surrounded by ravines, a landscape typical of this era.

Fig. 7.28. Zaculeu, Guatemala: a Late Postclassic site in the Mam Maya region of the highlands; the restored structures are seen here against the Altos Cuchumatanes.

Fig. 7.29. Map of Utatlan, Guatemala, the Late Postclassic capital of the Quiche Maya state: identification of the major buildings is postulated (after Carmack 1981) as (a) Temple of Tohil, the Quiche sun deity; (b) Temple of Awilix, the moon deity; (c) Temple of Jakawitz, the sky deity; (d) Temple of Gucumatz, the feathered serpent deity; (e) ballcourt; (f) palace, possibly of the Cawek ruling lineage.

429

Fig. 7.30. Utatlan: unexcavated ruins of the building identified as the Temple of Awilix, the Quiche moon deity, on the east side of the main plaza.

Fig. 7.31. Iximche, Guatemala, the Late Postclassic capital of the Cakchiquel Maya state: view toward the east, showing the partially restored Str. 3 facing two small platforms in Plaza A, with the remains of the major palace complex in the background.

TABLE 7.2

Dynastic Chronology of the Postclassic Quiche Maya

| Ruler | Approximate dates[a] | Chief accomplishments or events |
|---|---|---|
| Balam Quitze | 1225–1250 | Leads migration into northern highlands. |
| Cocoja | 1250–1275 | |
| Tziquin and E | 1275–1300 | Leads conquest of Pokomam Maya to the east (Rabinal). |
| Ahcan | 1300–1325 | |
| C'ocaib | 1325–1350 | Returns to the east (Tollan?) to gain title of *ahpop*. |
| Conache | 1350–1375 | Founds new capital at Ismachi. |
| Cotuja | 1375–1400 | Expands Quiche territory. |
| Gucumatz | 1400–1425 | Utatlan (Gumarcaaj) founded as final Quiche capital. |
| Quicab | 1425–1475 | Quiche conquests reach maximum extent. |
| Vahxaqui-Caam | 1475–1500 | Cakchiquel revolt; independent capital at Iximche established. |
| Oxib-Queh | 1500–1524 | Killed by Spanish after conquest of Utatlan (see the Epilogue). |

[a]Estimated by allowing about 25 years per generation (see Wauchope 1949; Carmack 1981).

On the basis of later ethnohistoric accounts, it seems likely that the ancestors of the warrior elite groups that eventually forged the Quiche and Cakchiquel states entered the highlands from the Gulf coastal lowlands shortly after 1200. These warrior groups were probably a new wave of Mexicanized Putun Maya, as evidenced by their own claims of descent from Tollan and by their religion, which combined Maya and Mexican elements. Although these warrior elites came as conquerors, they seem eventually to have lost their native tongue, in the course of adopting the Quiche, Cakchiquel, and other Mayan languages of the highland peoples they subjugated. But throughout their history they carefully maintained their elite status and traditions and set themselves apart from the indigenous population. The line of Quiche rulers, as reconstructed by Robert Wauchope and Robert Carmack from the *Popol Vuh* and other accounts, is presented in Table 7.2.

Initially, the invading warrior groups occupied mountain strongholds. From these, they mounted raids, and eventually they subjugated the local populace. Their first capital, known then as Jakawitz, has been identified as the archaeological site called Chitinamit today. It was during this period that the three new Quiche princes returned to their homeland seeking authority to rule over their expanded domains. According to the accounts, one of the returning princes, C'ocaib, appears to have been the first to hold the title of *ahpop* ("he of the mat"), the paramount political office of the Quiche state (see Chapter 10).

By about 1350 the Quiche had consolidated their control over the central highland region, between the headwaters of the Río Chixoy and the upper Motagua.

.. ⸻

There they founded a new capital, Ismachi, on a narrow plateau between two steep-sided ravines. Here, during the reign of *ahpop* Cotuja, an unsuccessful revolt was waged against the Quiche. According to the *Popol Vuh* the would-be usurpers "were sacrificed before the gods, and this was the punishment for their sins by order of the king Cotuja. Many also fell into slavery and servitude. . . . The destruction and ruin of the Quiche race and their ruler was what they wished, but they did not succeed."

Early in the fifteenth century, during the reign of Gucumatz ("feathered serpent"), a new capital was founded. Situated on another plateau surrounded by ravines, immediately north of Ismachi, it was named Gumarcaaj ("place of the rotten reeds"), or, as it is now known, Utatlan.

Gucumatz, Utatlan's first ruler, was glorified in the chronicles, for he extended the power of the Quiche to the north and west of their home region: "The nature of this king was truly marvelous, and all the other lords were filled with terror before him. Tidings of the wonderful nature of the king were spread and all the lords of the towns heard it. And this was the beginning of the grandeur of the Quiche, when King Gucumatz gave these signs of his power. His sons and his grandsons never forgot him." His successor, Quicab, expanded the Quiche domain through further conquests in the western highlands and southward to the Pacific coast: "He made war on them and certainly conquered and destroyed the fields and towns of the people of Rabinal, the Cakchiquel, and the people of Zaculeu; he came and conquered all the towns, and the soldiers of Quicab carried his arms to distant parts. One or two tribes did not bring tribute, and then he fell upon all the towns and they were forced to bring tribute."

But the Quiche state suffered a severe setback in the late fifteenth century, during the reign of Vahxaqui-Caam. About 1470 the Cakchiquel Maya, who had submitted to the Quiche as subjects and allies during the conquests of Gucumatz and Quicab, rebelled against their masters and established an independent state in the region south and east of Utatlan. The Cakchiquel founded a new capital, Iximche ("ramon tree," the breadnut), which was also defended by surrounding ravines. From Iximche the Cakchiquel began their own new cycle of conquests, subjugating areas formerly controlled by the Quiche. On a number of occasions the Quiche attempted to reconquer the Cakchiquel, but in vain. In one major battle, recounted in the highland document *Annals of the Cakchiquels*, the attacking army from Utatlan was annihilated; thousands of Quiche warriors were slaughtered, and their leaders were captured and sacrificed. As always, of course, such claims must be seen to some degree as the propaganda of the victors, but regardless, the Cakchiquel seem to have been still expanding their domain in the early sixteenth century, when their rise to power was arrested by the Spanish conquerors.

And so there remained only Tayasal, founded deep in the interior of the Peten by the survivors of Chichen Itza, which would hold out for another 150 years.

## Summary: The Evolution of Maya Civilization

The archaeological and historical reconstruction of the growth of ancient Maya civilization, though still incomplete, nonetheless presents a coherent picture of successive regional development, prosperity, and decline across the entire Maya area during a span of some 2,000 years. Using the developmental framework proposed by Jeremy Sabloff and introduced in Chapter 2, we can summarize this complex evolutionary process in three major episodes. Underlying the first, Early Maya civilization, were the foundations laid by the region's first settled agricultural societies.

The prelude to Early Maya civilization lies of course even deeper in the past, in the wandering hunters and gatherers of the Lithic period. In time, the productivity of maize and other plants, along with increasing specialization in the subsistence activities and lifeways of these peoples, led to the emergence of settled life and agriculture. The earliest known villages, which emerged along the coastal margins of the Maya area during the Archaic period, established the basis of the farming family and community that underlay all subsequent growth in Maya society. The stage was thus set, during the Preclassic period, for the emergence of civilization, beginning with the first signs of cultural and social complexity, during the Middle Preclassic.

Early Maya civilization appears to have developed simultaneously both in the southern area—along the Pacific coastal plain and in the adjacent highlands—and in the central lowlands. It is in these regions that the archaeological record first affords us the signs of sociopolitical complexity. But although even in these early times these southern and northern areas were linked by trade and other sorts of contacts, each also appears to have evolved some distinct features of its own. In the southern Maya area, the most obvious of these hallmarks, arising in the Middle Preclassic and expanding in the Late Preclassic, are the sculptured stone monuments commemorating dynastic rule, each monument bearing depictions of rulers, Long Count dates, and hieroglyphic texts. Concurrently, the central lowlands saw the rise of the first great cities, Nakbe and El Mirador, which featured such hallmarks as monumental masonry constructions (including both acropoli and terraced temple platforms decorated by giant deity masks), vast paved plazas, and both intrasite and intersite sacbeob, or causeways.

The second evolutionary stage, Middle Maya civilization, emerges from these foundations. It was a time marked by the decline of most of the major centers that had dominated Early Maya civilization. The decline seems to have been more complete in the southern area, where the tradition of erecting dated monuments and, by extension, of dynastic rule as well, seems to have ended. In the lowlands, the demise of the greatest city of the Early Maya world, El Mirador, was followed by the rise of Tikal, the first major city of Middle Maya civilization. With Tikal the thread of history begins to supplement archaeological evidence, and our understanding of the developmental course of Maya civilization becomes much more complete. It was during the Classic period that the southern and central lowlands became the setting for the florescence of Maya art, architecture, and intellectual achievement. But from a developmental perspective, the onset of Middle Maya civilization is defined not by architecture, but by the emergence and expansion of dynastic political systems among the lowland polities, each centered on the "cult of personality" of an individual ruler. By the same token, the decline of this political system marks the end of Middle Maya civilization. The causes for the decline are seen to be a complex mixture of environmental degradation, overpopulation, increasingly destructive warfare, changing trade networks, and fatalistic beliefs in prophecy that undermined both authority and morale. The transition to a new economic and political order fell in the Terminal Classic, a time when the old order enjoyed a last moment of success with the Puuc florescence in the northern lowlands, even as the great cities to the south declined and were ultimately abandoned.

The final evolutionary stage, Late Maya civilization, then, emerged from the failures and decline of the traditional political order. The prime movers of the new order were a mercantile and warrior elite from the western periphery of the lowlands, who successfully adopted both Maya and Mexican traditions and expanded into the vacuum left in the wake of Middle Maya civilization. Collectively known as the Putun Maya, these elites adopted a political system more suited to consolidating and maintaining economic and military control. The heart of the new system appears to have been collective rule by council. Ironically enough, this innovation has also tended to reduce the information available to us, for the demise of individualized dynastic rule spelled the end to the rich historical and iconographic record it had fostered. We do know—from the archaeological record, supplemented by indigenous texts and later retrospective histories—that the centers of power in Late Maya civilization developed in two disjunct areas, the northern lowlands and the southern highlands. In the northern lowlands a Putun group known as the Itza established a new capital at Chichen Itza and parlayed great seagoing canoes into a commanding marine trading system. From this base, the Itza replaced the old powers in Yucatan (principally Coba and the Puuc centers) and dominated most of the peninsula for several centuries. When Chichen Itza was destroyed, apparently by armed intervention, a new center, Mayapan, was founded. The new center would reign supreme in the northern lowlands until shortly before the Conquest, when centralized authority was fragmented into a series of independent, petty states. Having also suffered plague, pestilence, and hurricanes, these squabbling duchies were wholly unprepared for the shock of Spanish arms. A similar course was charted in the southern highlands, where the aggressive Quiche Maya, whose ruling elite derived from the same Putun Maya heritage, gradually consolidated a handful of small polities. The Quiche and their chief rivals, the rapidly rising Cakchiquel state, jockeyed violently for political and military supremacy until events there, too, were cut short by the Conquest.

# SUBSISTENCE SYSTEMS

And the greatest number were cultivators and men who apply themselves
to harvesting the maize and other grains, which they keep in fine
underground palaces and granaries, so as to be able to sell at the proper
time.
—*Landa's relación de las cosas de Yucatán* (Tozzer 1941: 96)

**A**rchaeology attempts to understand how past human societies develop
through time. Underlying the growth of Maya society, just as that of other ancient
civilizations, archaeological research has identified several critical factors, beginning with the subsistence systems, which sustained population growth; the trade
systems, which secured both goods and ideas; the systems of sociopolitical organization, which saw to the management of society; and the ideological systems,
which guided and inspired the destiny of all aspects of society. In the next few chapters we will discuss how each of these factors was involved in the growth of Maya
civilization, through the cycles of expansion and contraction that characterized ancient Maya society during its history and across the breadth of its settled area. We
begin by examining ancient Maya subsistence systems, which, as in all societies,
provided the energy that fueled the development of civilization.

## The Traditional View

For many years the ancient Maya were thought to have relied for their food
resources almost solely on swidden agriculture, a system that makes use of an extensive land area by alternately burning off each individual field, cultivating it, and
allowing it to remain fallow for a period at least as long as the time of cultivation
before once again burning it off. In most cases, replenishment of the soil's nutrients
requires at least two years of fallow for each year of cultivation. Thus, no more than
a third of the available farmland is actually growing crops in any given year; the
bulk lies fallow. Swidden agriculture therefore requires extensive land area relative
to its levels of food production, and it cannot support large or dense concentrations
of people.

### ● ● ●

It has long been known that most ancient civilizations, in both the Old World and the New, relied on subsistence systems that were far more intensive and productive (using less land with few or no fallow periods) than is swidden agriculture. Thus the ancient Maya were seen as an anomaly: a brilliant civilization whose subsistence relied on "primitive" agricultural practice. But doubts soon arose, and scholars began to question the assumption that the ancient Maya were dependent on this one system of agriculture.

The traditional assumption had derived from the observation that the present-day Maya practice swidden techniques to produce most of their food. The Spaniards, who first conquered and colonized the peoples of Central Mexico, homeland of the Mexica (Aztecs), helped spread the use of the Nahuatl or Aztec word for maize field, *milpa*, by using it to denote maize fields in other parts of Mesoamerica as well. (The Yucatecan Mayan word for maize field is *col*, and in other Mayan languages the word for it is similar.) Shortly after the Conquest, Bishop Diego de Landa described the cultivation of maize by the Yucatec Maya in terms that sound like swidden agriculture:

They plant in many places, so that if one fails the others will suffice. In cultivating the land they do nothing more than clear the brush, and burn it in order to sow it afterward, and from the middle of January to April they work it and then when the rains come they plant it, which they do by carrying a small sack on the shoulders, and with a pointed stick, they make a hole in the ground, dropping in it five or six grains, covering them with the same stick. And when it rains, it is marvelous to see how it grows. (Fig. 8.1.)

But it should be noted that Landa's account does not necessarily describe a shifting pattern of cultivation, only one in which each farmer planted many milpas to be assured of the success of at least some of them. That seems to be a sensible practice where the climate is dry and the soil is marginal, as is the case in northern Yucatan. Even if we assume that Landa did observe a true swidden system in the sixteenth

Fig. 8.1. Sowing maize with the Maya planting stick; from the Madrid Codex, p. 36.

century, such a system need not have been typical of all Maya agriculture at that time *or* in the more distant past. Other techniques could well have been used in different environments and in earlier times.

Today, the swidden agriculture used by the Maya relies on steel tools, especially the machete, sometimes supplemented by the axe. The machete allows the farmer to clear overgrown (fallow) fields with relative ease, and the axe greatly eases the task of clearing new lands of large trees (Fig. 8.2). But the ancient Maya did not have steel tools, only stone axes and blades of obsidian or flint. Without steel cutting tools, the clearing of new forest or second growth in fallow areas requires considerably more energy and time. Although experiments indicate that stone axes can adequately fell large trees, no known ancient Maya tool would be capable of dealing efficiently with the dense stands of second growth blanketing milpas after only one or two years of fallow. We assume that once the time and effort had been invested in wresting a new field from the forest, it would be maintained for as long as possible by constant weeding. This practice, which prevents the growth of competitors to the food plants, would not have required sharp cutting tools, since the weeding can be done by hand.

But all this is only an assumption. In most circumstances, the traces of an ancient swidden system cannot be detected today. Extraordinary circumstances, however, have preserved Classic-era fields for maize and other crops. These fields, buried by volcanic ash, were excavated recently at Ceren, El Salvador. Exacting work by Payson Sheets and his colleagues revealed carefully tilled rows for the plants, separated by furrows that would have facilitated drainage (Fig. 8.3). These fields, adjacent to houses, storage facilities, and other domestic buildings, were carefully tended, and in some cases were protected by fences. The evidence indicates that these fields were under continuous cultivation, and were probably kept fertile by crop rotation and the use of household refuse for fertilizer. To reveal the form and identity of the crops, the casts or hollow spaces left in the ash deposit by the decayed plants have been filled with dental plaster. This evidence shows that maize, manioc, and several other crops, in different fields, were being grown at the moment disaster struck.

Several lines of archaeological research indicate that ancient Maya populations and population densities were far above the levels that swidden agriculture is known to be able to support. And a final blow to the assumption of swidden practice has been the discovery and recognition of actual traces of far more complex and productive agricultural methods in the Maya lowlands. Today, most Maya scholars agree that the ancient Maya developed and perfected, over a span of hundreds or even thousands of years, a variety of subsistence methods. The environmental differences found throughout the Maya area allowed—or required—the Maya to rely on an array of combinations of these methods, each suited to the particular conditions of a given locale.

Fig. 8.2. A Lacandon Maya man felling a tree, using a modern steel axe (the platform is made necessary by the great thickness of the tree base), Chiapas, Mexico.

We now know the ancient Maya to have been capable of supporting far greater populations than would have been possible using swidden agriculture alone. As a result, some of the "mystery" of how the ancient Maya sustained a vast and complex civilization in a supposedly "hostile" environment has been resolved. Of course each of the various environmental settings has its limits for agricultural exploitation, and as we have seen (Chapter 6), overpopulation and overexploitation in the southern and central lowlands probably contributed to the demise of Classic Maya civilization in these regions. The various subsistence resources used by the ancient Maya follow, as presently understood. But a multitude of unanswered questions remains, enough to keep Maya scholars busy for decades to come.

## Subsistence Systems Available to the Ancient Maya

The ancient Maya relied on a complex array of resources for their subsistence, and the precise combination of ways they acquired or produced food differed from place to place and from time to time. Although only tentatively understood, their

Fig. 8.3. Ceren, El Salvador: rows and furrows of a Late Classic maize field preserved under volcanic ash; a string tag has been placed in the small hole left by each maize plant (the size of the holes indicates that the ash fall occurred in the spring, when the plants were young).

subsistence system can be broadly outlined by dividing it into three major areas, according to source and technology: hunting and gathering (wild-food subsistence), animal husbandry, and agriculture. The actual procurement of food undoubtedly incorporated both direct access and exchange. Direct access describes the practices of a farming family that grows food for its own needs. Exchange uses barter or payment to acquire food from others, possibly specialized producers. Although the vast majority of ancient Maya households produced much of their own food, most of them probably obtained at least some food from centralized markets, much like those described by the Spanish in the sixteenth century and used today (see Chapter 9).

With time, as populations grew and increased the pressures on the subsistence system, the ancient Maya probably relied more and more on the marketplace for acquiring both staples and exotic foods. Some evidence suggests that certain lowland areas were cultivated for large-scale food production; their harvests were then evidently transported to the major population centers.

The same basic technology might have extracted important nonfood resources from forest, field, and sea. From the forest came firewood, one of the most crucial of all resources, essential as fuel for cooking, firing pottery, making lime plaster, and other purposes. Proper maintenance of forest areas also ensured supplies of wood and thatch for buildings, and a multitude of fibers for baskets, rope, and bark cloth. Cotton was cultivated, spun into thread, dyed with a rich array of vegetable and mineral colors, and woven into garments and textiles (Chapter 15). Animal bone, teeth, and pelts were manufactured into a variety of adornments and ritual objects, as were coral and seashells.

### Hunting and Gathering

The ancient Maya, like all pre-Columbian peoples, relied in part on wild food resources. Lacking a varied inventory of domesticated animals, they supplemented their dietary needs for protein by fishing and hunting (see Table 8.1). Deer, tapir, agoutis, rabbits, peccaries, monkeys, and other animals were hunted or trapped for food. One ancient source illustrates the use of a snare to trap deer. Interestingly, some foraging species, such as deer, may actually have experienced an increase in population concurrent with that of the ancient human residents. Archaeological evidence in the form of skeletal remains found at Tikal indicates that the Maya consumed an increasing proportion of deer meat through time. Perhaps the greater availability of deer was due to the expansion of agricultural areas in the lowlands, which in turn would have provided greater expanses of cleared fields well suited to the browsing needs of a growing deer population, as well as to a decrease in predators.

Apart from snares and traps, weapons like the blowgun were apparently used to hunt birds, monkeys, kinkajous, and other arboreal animals. Small, hard clay pellets found in archaeological remains may have been used as the projectiles.

TABLE 8.1

Common Wild-Animal Resources Available to the Ancient Lowland Maya[a]

| | | | |
|---|---|---|---|
| Birds | Chachalaca (*Ortalis vetula*) | Edentates | Armadillo (*Dasypus novemcinctus*) |
| | Crested guan (*Penelope purpurascens*) | | Tamandua (*Tamandua tetradactyla*) |
| | Curassow (*Crax rubra*) | Lagomorph | Forest rabbit (*Sylvilagus brasiliensis*) |
| | Ocellated turkey (*Agriocharis ocellata*) | Marsupial | Opossum (*Didelphis marsupialis*) |
| | Scarlet macaw (*Ara macao*) | | |
| Artiodactyls | Brocket deer (*Mazama americana*) | Perissodactyls | Collared peccary (*Tayassu tajacu*) |
| | White-tailed deer (*Odocoileus virginianus*) | | White-lipped peccary (*Tayassu pecari*) |
| Carnivores | Cacomistle (*Bassariscus sumichrasti*) | | Tapir (*Tapirus bairdii*) |
| | Coati (*Nasua narica*) | Pinniped | Manatee (*Trichechus manatus*) |
| | Cougar (*Felis concolor*) | Primates | Howler monkey (*Alouatta villosa*) |
| | Gray fox (*Urocyon cinereoargenteus*) | | Spider monkey (*Ateles geofroyi*) |
| | Jaguar (*Felis onca*) | Rodents | Agouti (*Dasyprocta* ssp.) |
| | Jaguarundi (*Felis jaguarondi*) | | Paca (*Agouti paca*) |
| | Kinkajou (*Potos flavus*) | | Porcupine (*Coendou mexicanus*) |
| | Margay (*Felis wiedii*) | | Squirrel (*Sciurus yucatanensis*) |
| | Ocelot (*Felis pardalis*) | | |
| | Raccoon (*Procyon lotor*) | | |

[a] After Wiseman (1978).

Aquatic resources also made an important contribution to the ancient Maya diet. Archaeologists have found fired-clay net weights and bone fishhooks, as well as artistic representations of dugout canoes, that reflect the technology the Maya used to collect food resources from the sea, the lakes, and the rivers. Both fish and shellfish provided a steady diet for people living along the coasts, and it is likely that dried fish were traded far inland, just as is done today throughout the Maya area. The freshwater lakes and rivers of the highlands and the southern and central lowlands provided a variety of fish and shellfish, and the importance of fish is indicated by their frequent representation in Maya art. Evidence from the lakes region of the central lowlands indicates that the consumption of freshwater mollusks decreased over a period of nearly a thousand years (Middle Preclassic to the Late Classic) before suddenly increasing again at the end of the Classic period. The decrease may have reflected the expansion of agriculture, for the accelerated clearing of forested areas would have led to increased sedimentation in the lakes, which would have reduced the mollusk populations (which rebounded after a decrease in population and sedimentation).

Wild plants of all sorts abound in the Maya area, and the present-day collection of many of these for food, medicines, and other uses undoubtedly continues an ancient practice. Common wild food plants include species of papaya, *Annona*, sapodilla, cherimoya, and coyol, as well as condiments like allspice, vanilla, and oregano. Many of these trees and plants, though not fully domesticated, were probably tended and cultivated in household gardens (see below).

### Animal Husbandry

Though the ancient Maya did domesticate a few animals, these were not a prime source of food. One was the dog, which was descended from strains that accompanied the first peoples to enter the New World via the Bering Land Bridge and was a guardian of the household and a companion in hunting, as it is today. Other domesticated species seemed to have included the dove, the turkey, and the Muscovy duck, though the duck, a South American native, may not have been known to the Maya until after the Conquest. The Maya may also have tended or managed certain wild animals, possibly for food, and it is possible that certain varieties of dog were fattened and eaten, as was the custom in ancient Central Mexico.

The Maya today often raise a variety of wild animals as pets, including parrots and other birds, monkeys, coatis, kinkajous, and the like. Landa notes that the sixteenth-century Maya of the Yucatan did likewise: "Some people raise doves as tame as ours and they multiply rapidly . . . there is an animal which they call *chic* [the coatimundi, and] the women raise them and they leave nothing which they do not root over and turn upside down. . . ." Animals like these were probably raised for food before the Conquest, and several scholars have suggested that the ancient Maya raised herds of deer for food in large penned areas. Landa reported that women "raise other domestic animals, and let the deer suck their breasts, by which means they raise them and make them so tame that they will never go into the woods, although they take them and carry them through the woods and raise them there." The artificial channels discovered along the Río Candelaria in the central lowlands (see below) raise the possibility that fish were raised there or in artificial ponds. Supporting archaeological and ethnohistorical evidence suggests that the ancient Maya may have had a far greater potential for exploiting sources of dietary protein than can currently be demonstrated.

### Agriculture: Fallow Systems

There can be little doubt that agriculture (Table 8.2) provided the major source of ancient Maya subsistence, and two millennia of development and environmental adaptation yielded a complex combination of cultivation methods. For convenience we describe these methods under two categories: fallow systems, in which fields are cultivated several years and then allowed to lie fallow, or "rest," for a time before cultivation is renewed; and intensive systems, in which fields are cultivated all but continuously, the fallow periods altogether lacking or lasting less than a year for each year of cultivation.

In areas of good soil and rainfall, short-term swidden agriculture can be prac-

TABLE 8.2
Common Plant Cultigens Available to the Ancient Lowland Maya[a]

| Cultigen | Month planted | Month harvested | Yield[b] |
|---|---|---|---|
| Amaranth (*Amaranthus*) | | | |
| Avocado (*Persea americana*) | | | |
| Ayote (squash) (*Cucurbita pepo*) | Feb.–May | Oct. | 9,557* |
| Bean, common (*Phaseolus vulgaris*) | June–Aug. | Nov. | 24,013 |
| Breadnut (*Brosimum alicastrum*) | | Dry season | 1,100–2,700[c] |
| Cacao (*Theobroma cacao*) | | | |
| Cassava (*Manihot esculenta*) | | Jan.–Mar. | 2,600 |
| Chili (*Capsicum annuum*) | Mar. | June | |
| Guava (*Psidium guajava*) | | | |
| Maize (*Zea mays*) (first-year milpa) | Apr.–May | Nov.–Jan. | 1,600 |
| (second-year milpa) | | | 1,134 |
| (third-year milpa) | | | 468 |
| Mombin (*Spondias mombin*) | | | |
| Nance (*Byrsonima crassifolia*) | | | |
| Papaya (*Carica papaya*) | | | |
| Pineapple (*Ananas comosus*) | June | Any | 7,718* |
| Sapodilla (*Achras zapota*) | | | |
| Soursop (*Annona* sp.) | | | |
| Sweet potato (*Ipomoea batatas*) | May | Dec. | 22,469 |
| Vanilla (*Vanilla fragrans*) | | | |
| Yautia (*Xanthosoma violaceum*) | | | 40,909 |
| Yucca (*Yucca elephantipes*) | | | |

[a]After Wiseman (1978), with additions.
[b]Given in kg/hectare, except those marked by an asterisk (*), which are given in fruits/hectare.
[c]Lower figure given in Wiseman, the higher figure in Puleston (1978).

ticed with fallow periods generally running from one to three years for each year of cultivation. In more marginal environments long-term swidden agriculture generally requires three to six years for each year of cultivation. For the ancient Maya, both methods probably involved the arduous task of clearing fields with stone tools and allowing the cut vegetation to dry, after which it would be burned and the field planted. Large trees and other plant species that provided wild foods were probably allowed to grow within the stands of maize, beans, squashes, manioc, and other planted species. Each field would have been planted and harvested for several successive seasons, depending on local conditions of rainfall, soil quality, and so forth. But once a field became unproductive, owing to competition from weeds and to soil depletion, it would have been abandoned to lie fallow while new or long-fallowed fields were cleared for cultivation.

Long-term swidden methods are probably among the oldest forms of agriculture in the Maya area. Maya scholars believe that the original colonization of forested areas was made possible by agriculturists practicing long-term swidden cultivation. Because of its reliance on low maintenance and long periods of fallow, this method gives relatively low overall yields while requiring large expanses of land,

and is therefore best suited for small, scattered populations. As populations increased and more efficient methods developed, long-term swidden cultivation diminished in importance until, in time, it was confined to marginal environments.

Short-term swidden agriculture necessitates increased maintenance of the fields, both by periodic weeding and by intercropping (growing a variety of complementary species together). These techniques reduce competition for the food plants, diminish the rate of soil depletion (or even replenish nutrients if the proper crops are used for intercropping), and thereby reduce the need for longer fallow periods. In areas of moderate soil quality and good rainfall, short-term fallow systems can be highly productive. Although the ancient Maya apparently lacked efficient means for clearing dense stands of second growth from fallow fields, which would have made swidden methods increasingly difficult to maintain, they might well have been helped by their climate. For in areas with long dry seasons, such as northern Yucatan, the underbrush usually becomes sufficiently combustible to allow its clearing by burning alone, without the need for extensive prior cutting by stone tools.

No direct evidence exists for the use of either kind of swidden agriculture by the ancient Maya. Indirect evidence lies in the analyses of pollen samples embedded in sediment cores taken from the beds of several lakes in the central lowlands; these samples demonstrate that the Middle Preclassic settlers of that region grew maize, and swidden techniques are indicated by remnants of ash fallout in the cores, possibly from field burning. More direct evidence lies in the discovery of relic field systems, chiefly in the northern lowlands. It may well be that these systems, consisting of stone boundary walls and water-flow deflectors, were cultivated by short-term swidden methods.

The modification of sloped landscape by terracing has also been identified in several areas within or adjacent to the central lowlands. The largest arrays of terracing seem to be in the Río Bec region, on the northern margin of the central lowlands, where estimates based on ground surveys indicate that some 150,000 hectares of agricultural land were modified by constructed terraces. Another zone has been found in the Maya Mountains of Belize, in the Caracol region on the eastern margin of the central lowlands, where at least 40,000 hectares of terraced land have been identified. Archaeological excavations in both areas reveal that these terraces were constructed during the Classic period, and the heavy investment of labor they represent implies that they may have been used for more intensive agricultural methods. The Maya, as farmers elsewhere, seem to have used hillside terracing to help retain water in the soil and thus to increase productivity.

## Agriculture: Intensive Systems

The intensive agricultural methods known or suspected to have been used by the ancient Maya include continuous field cultivation, household gardens, arboriculture, and hydraulic modifications.

In continuous field cultivation, crops are grown with fallow periods of sufficiently short duration that the fields do not become overgrown, a method that requires constant labor to weed out the competitors of the food crops. At least in areas with well-drained, fertile soils and plentiful rainfall, the ancient Maya could have practiced this method of cultivation. Prime candidates for this method would have been the alluvial valleys, like those found in various parts of the southern and coastal lowlands. There, on the natural river levees and on the older terraces (of former riverbeds) found above the localized or extensive floodplains of such rivers as the Usumacinta, the Motagua, the Belize, and their tributaries, continuous field cultivation could have been very productive; periodic flooding in these areas would have replenished soil fertility by depositing new alluvial soils. The lowest portions of active floodplains (backswamps) are often too wet for too much of the year to allow cultivation without hydraulic modifications (see below). Where older alluvial soils were no longer being replenished by flood deposits, their nutrient depletion could have been controlled by proper intercropping.

As with swidden agriculture, little direct evidence for ancient continuous cultivation has been found, although the wonderfully preserved fields at Ceren, El Salvador, discussed earlier, seem to represent this kind of agricultural system. Today, local areas of rich soils—the volcanic basins of the southern highlands and along the Pacific coastal plain, the deeper soil pockets of the northern highlands and southern lowlands, and the floodplains—support continuous or near-continuous cultivation. Intensive weeding or frequent intercropping are not needed in these areas today, even after centuries of agricultural exploitation, and conditions in the past should have been at least equally productive. It seems likely that some of the relic agricultural features, such as the bounded fields and the vast expanses of terraces mentioned above, could have been used for continuous cultivation. Present knowledge about the peak sizes and densities of Classic-period Maya populations in the central lowlands suggests that some form of continuous cultivation may have been an essential component of the ancient system. Given the nutritive potential of the alluvial plains in the southern lowlands, and of similarly fertile areas elsewhere, continuous cultivation could have transformed them into "breadbaskets" supplying large amounts of surplus staples for trade with the great population centers.

Household gardens, as the name implies, are cultivated patches in the open spaces adjacent to and between family residences. Some of the agricultural remains found immediately adjacent to the farmhouses at Ceren, El Salvador, were probably of this type. In the tropics, household gardens may contain a great variety of food plants: annual root crops, maize, beans, and other field species; and perennial shrubs, vines, and trees. The potential of this kind of intensive cultivation is made possible by the great array of food plants native to the area and still grown in Maya household gardens today. Per unit of land, household gardens supply continuously high yields of a variety of foods and condiments. The necessary care, mostly weeding, is minimal, and the rate of soil depletion is low, owing to the replenishment of nutrients afforded by intercropping; thus nutrients from the residues of the cultivated plants, augmented by human and animal wastes originating in and around the household, continuously and conveniently nourish the soil.

From the sixteenth-century Spanish accounts and from contemporary practice, we know that the Maya employed household gardens. This form of cultivation may well have been practiced in earlier times as well, and indirect but persuasive evidence is provided by botanical and settlement-pattern studies. At many archaeological sites in the lowlands, investigators have long noted disproportionately heavy stands of such food-producing trees as the ramon, or breadnut. And at such sites as Tikal and Coba, settlement studies show a near-uniform spacing of residential clusters throughout the settlement area. The spaces between these residential compounds, not large enough for efficient field agriculture, are comparable to those found today in tropical settlements where household gardens are cultivated.

Arboriculture is the cultivation of tree crops (like the ramon mentioned above) in extensive stands, rather than in household gardens. The variety of productive tree species available to the ancient Maya included the ramon, cacao, sapodilla, and avocado. Studies of the potential harvests from ramon production indicate that orchards of these trees can produce ten times the amount of food per unit of land that maize does. Ramon is a starchy food that can be processed and used like maize to make tortillas or tamales, although people familiar with this food today consider it much less desirable than maize. Many tree crops require much less labor than does maize; weeding is not necessary, and the fruit or nuts of some species, including the ramon, may be collected from the ground as they fall. Ramon or cacao might have been grown in monocrop plantations, just as coffee and bananas (imported Old World species) are cultivated in the Maya area today. But the most efficient method available to the ancients would likely have been a form of intercropping, producing what is sometimes called an artificial rain forest by cutting out the unwanted species in the forest and planting a mixture of desirable species in the free spaces. The mingling of different kinds of food trees in a single stand discourages the pests or diseases that favor a single tree species, thus greatly reducing the risk of their spreading throughout the stand. Intercropping in field cultivation offers the same advantages it does in household gardens, of course, and in the tropics today, monocrop plantation agriculture is made possible only through the heavy use of chemical pesticides.

Although occasional food remains and ethnohistorical accounts indicate that tree crops were once important to the Maya, direct archaeological evidence is again difficult to obtain. Cacao was unquestionably one of the prime tree crops grown in suitable lowland environments, but because its pollen is extremely perishable, we may find that traces of ancient cultivation are impossible to detect. Ceramic images of cacao pods, found at Copan, Quirigua, Lubaantun, and other Maya sites, do indicate that the surrounding valleys were important areas of cacao production. But any direct evidence that the Classic Maya maintained great artificial rain-forest plantations has long ago been absorbed into the natural forest of the lowlands.

Hydraulic modification of the landscape serves either to irrigate crops or to drain excess water from saturated soils so as to encourage better growth. There is evidence that the ancient Maya constructed irrigation networks, but on a scale much smaller than that of the notable examples elsewhere in the New World, along the Pacific coast of Peru and in the southwestern United States.

Evidence of an ancient irrigation system has been found at Edzna, in the drier transitional zone between the central and northern lowlands. Investigations there, directed by Ray Matheny, revealed an impressive canal and reservoir system capable of serving a minimum of 450 hectares of cultivated land (Fig. 8.4). The archaeo-

Fig. 8.4. Edzna, Campeche, Mexico: aerial view showing the remains of an ancient canal system (dark lines) used for drainage, irrigation, and possibly defense (note the enclosed group at lower right center); Edzna's site core is in the lighter area (upper center), at the apex of several radiating canals.

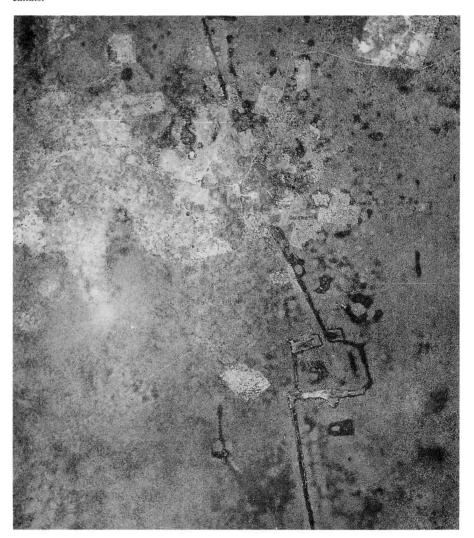

logical evidence from these excavations indicates that the Edzna hydraulic system was constructed, not late in Maya history, as one might suppose, but during the Late Preclassic era (ca. 300–50 B.C.).

A growing body of evidence shows that the Maya also built raised fields in low-lying areas such as *bajos* or seasonal swamps to provide fertile, yet well-drained, growing conditions for a variety of crops. Raised fields are constructed by digging narrow drainage channels in water-saturated soils and heaping the earth dug from the channels into continuous mounds, thus forming ridges on which the crops may be grown. Raised fields permit continuous cultivation, since periodic hand-dredging of muck from the drainage channels brings fresh soil and organic debris to the cultivated ridge (Fig. 8.5). These channels may also have been used as sources for the harvest of fish, mollusks, and other aquatic life, or may even have been stocked. (Cultivation and stocking of this sort are employed in many areas of the world today.)

Raised fields can be used to grow a variety of crops, and we possess some direct evidence from ancient Maya times. Excavations at Pulltrouser Swamp, Belize, have revealed clear remnants of raised fields dating from the Classic period (Fig. 8.6). From the plant remains recovered by this work, it appears that the Maya used these particular fields to grow maize, amaranth, cotton, and possibly cacao.

Fig. 8.5. Pulltrouser Swamp, Belize: ground view of relic raised fields; shallow standing water fills the silted-in drainage canals during the rainy season.

Fig. 8.6. Dry-season excavations at Pulltrouser Swamp: the far test pit is on the shore of the *bajo* (swamp), with the line of excavations descending into a relic canal and up onto a raised field (foreground); the excavator is cutting into the artificial fill used to elevate the field plot above the ancient water level.

Fortunately, the distinctive ridged pattern of ancient raised fields is durable and can in many cases be detected by aerial photography (Fig. 8.7). The first to be recognized in the Maya area, those on the floodplain of the Río Candelaria in southern Campeche, Mexico, covered an area estimated at some 2 km² (Fig. 8.8). A larger zone of raised fields (estimated to cover an area of about 85 km²) has been found on the opposite side of the Yucatan Peninsula, in the valleys of the Hondo and New rivers in northern Belize. North of this region, studies of aerial photographs have tentatively identified a series of raised-field systems in the *bajos* of southern Quintana Roo, Mexico, covering an area of over 200 km². An aerial survey using a NASA radar-mapping system has revealed additional evidence of networks of drainage canals in the Maya lowlands.

## Reconstructing the Patterns of Maya Subsistence

It is very likely that all of the subsistence alternatives reviewed here, and perhaps other systems not yet recognized, were used by the ancient Maya. Research on this subject is still too incomplete for us to reconstruct in any detail how these

Fig. 8.7. Aerial view of Pulltrouser Swamp, showing relic raised fields (dark) and canals (light) along the southern edge of the *bajo*.

Fig. 8.8. Río Candelaria, Campeche, Mexico: aerial view of relic raised fields (the regular clumps of higher vegetation) and canals in the back swamps along the river.

various methods were developed and recombined within the variety of environments in the Maya area. We can, however, suggest some logical steps that may represent how things in fact took place.

The development of ancient Maya subsistence involved two complementary processes: expansion and intensification. Expansion increases the land (or water) areas being exploited for food; as Maya populations grew, the food supply could be increased simply by colonizing new regions, to tap larger areas for food. Intensification increases crop yields without increasing the land (or water) areas exploited for subsistence; since there were real limits to the expansion of the subsistence system, continued population increases eventually could be accommodated only through intensification—by increasing the amount of food produced from a given land or water area.

Environmental differences guarantee that there was no single original Maya subsistence method. We know that prior to the Preclassic period, agricultural techniques were added to the far older inventory of hunting-and-gathering methods. As populations grew, new areas were opened for agricultural exploitation, and the initial expansion and colonization of most new areas probably led to a subsistence strategy that supplemented hunting and gathering with long-term swidden cultivation. Raised fields were built in several river valleys on the margins of the central Maya lowlands. The need for an intensification of agriculture seems to have led to progressively shorter fallow periods within a swidden system, to the development of household gardens, and ultimately to continuous field cultivation, arboriculture, and the spread of raised fields into new environments, such as lowland *bajos*. At the same time, an intensification of hunting and gathering led to new capabilities in animal husbandry, such as the raising or penning of wild animals or, in combination with raised fields in the wetter lowlands, the raising of aquatic species.

This scenario appears logical, but only through further archaeological research into ancient Maya subsistence methods can we hope to improve our currently imperfect understanding.

# 9
....

# TRADE AND EXTERNAL CONTACT

The occupation to which they had the greatest inclination was trade,
carrying salt and cloth and slaves to the lands of the Ulua and Tabasco,
exchanging all they had for cacao and stone beads which were their
money.

—*Landa's relación de las cosas de Yucatán* (Tozzer 1941: 94–95)

In this chapter we will consider trade and external contact, the second
basic factor that underlay the evolution of Maya civilization through time. To identify the true role of trade in the development of Maya civilization, we must widen
our focus well beyond the Maya area itself and include all of Mesoamerica, for trade
provided the principal means by which the ancient Maya maintained contact with
their neighbors. We must also remember that trade networks were a conduit not
only for goods, but also for people and ideas, throughout Mesoamerica, and therefore affected all aspects of Maya society—and even the ebb and flow in the fortunes
of the major centers.

## Prehistoric Trade in Mesoamerica

In contrast to the Andean area of South America, which was eventually integrated by the highly centralized political power of the Inca, Mesoamerica was never
united under a single political system. But if Mesoamerica was never politically integrated, it was to varying degrees unified by commerce. Both archaeological evidence and ethnohistorical data (such as surviving native tribute lists and Spanish
accounts) describe a complex system of exchange networks and trade relationships,
ranging from simple barter to large-scale redistribution through centralized markets, that provided economic ties linking together regions and even broader areas
within (and beyond) Mesoamerica.

Mesoamerica possesses a wealth of environmental contrasts and diversity, and
even in prehistoric times its inhabitants were afforded opportunities to develop a

multitude of local economic specializations, which in turn fostered the development of exchange networks, so that specialized resources, goods, and services might find broad distribution.

For archaeologists, *regional trade* is exchange *within* a major environmental area; the so-called central-Mexican Symbiotic Zone in the Valley of Mexico is a widely accepted example. *Long-distance trade* is exchange *between* major environmental areas; in this larger sense, all of prehistoric Mesoamerica, from what is now the U.S. Southwest to northernmost Central America, can be seen as a single symbiotic area, integrated by long-distance trade.

It is convenient to distinguish two other broad classes of trade, as well: exchange either of utilitarian goods (food and tools) or of nonutilitarian goods (ritual, exotic, and status items). But whereas the regional trade networks that arose throughout Mesoamerica certainly provided the conduits for both, the long-distance trade networks appear to have been devoted primarily to the exchange of nonutilitarian items. There were exceptions, of course, and some critical utilitarian resources with limited and specific sources, such as obsidian, used to make incredibly sharp cutting blades and well suited for a variety of cutting tasks, enjoyed wide distribution throughout ancient Mesoamerica. Note, however, that obsidian knives were also used for nonutilitarian purposes, such as ritual bloodletting.

William Rathje postulated that the exchange of utilitarian goods (typically salt, obsidian, and grinding stones) played a central role in the origins of Mesoamerican civilization. His thesis holds that in certain resource-deficient regions, such as the Gulf coast and the central Maya lowlands, prehistoric populations developed complex organizations expressly to manage the acquisition and redistribution of utilitarian goods; this development ultimately led to social stratification and a permanent ruling elite (two characteristics of chiefdoms and, ultimately, of state organizations). Other scholars, in contrast, see trade in nonutilitarian goods as the crucial factor in the emergence of social stratification and ruling elites. For them, the control of such items as jadeite, magnetite, and feathers by the elite segments of society marked and reinforced their elevated status. Although neither model has been rigorously tested by archaeological research, Rathje's scheme fails in light of the broad inventory of locally produced utilitarian items recovered in the Maya lowlands beginning during the Preclassic era, especially from the dominant center Tikal, and the long-overdue recognition of the true diversity and economic potential of the Maya lowland environment. Salt, for instance, was readily available in the southern lowlands at Salinas de los Nueve Cerros. And beginning as early as Middle Preclassic times, jade and other nonutilitarian items were traded into the Maya lowlands from sources in the highlands to the south. But regardless of particular theories, it may be concluded that long-distance trade, comprising both utilitarian and nonutilitarian exchange, was vital to the development and integration of all pre-

•••• historic Mesoamerican civilizations, including the Maya. And archaeological and ethnohistorical evidence certainly testifies to the importance and persistence of both regional and long-distance trade among the Maya.

Two factors made the ancient Maya prominent in Mesoamerican long-distance trade networks. First, the Maya occupied a strategic position astride the routes that connected Mexico in the northwest to Central America in the southeast. Because

TABLE 9.1

Principal Trade Goods from the Maya Area

| Type of goods | Principal place of origin | Type of goods | Principal place of origin |
|---|---|---|---|
| | | PRIMARILY UTILITARIAN | |
| Agricultural products | Various | Obsidian | Southern highlands (specifically, El Chayal, Ixtepeque, and Jilotepeque) |
| Balsam | Pacific coast | | |
| Bark cloth | Pacific coast, lowlands | | |
| Basketry | Various | Ocote or pitch pine | Highlands |
| Condiments | Various | | |
| Cotton | Lowlands, Pacific coast, Yucatan | Pottery | Various |
| | | Salt | Northern (coastal) lowlands (lesser sources in southern lowlands, highlands, and Pacific coast) |
| Dyes and pigments | Various | | |
| Fish and sea products | Coastal areas, lakes | | |
| Flint (chert) | Lowlands (for example, Colha) | Sugar (honey and wax) | Caribbean coast, Isla de Cozumel |
| Game | Various | Textiles | Various, especially northern lowlands |
| Henequen (maguey) | Northern lowlands | | |
| Lime | Lowlands | Tobacco | Lowlands |
| Manos, metates (grinding stones) | Southern highlands | Tortoise shell | Coastal areas, especially Gulf coast |
| | | Volcanic ash | Highlands |
| | | PRIMARILY NONUTILITARIAN | |
| Amber | Chiapas | Jadeite | Northern highlands (middle Motagua valley) |
| Cacao | Lowlands, especially Caribbean, Gulf, and Pacific coasts | | |
| | | Jaguar pelts, teeth, etc. | Southern and central lowlands |
| Cinnabar | Southern highlands | | |
| Copal (*pom*) | Lowlands | Pyrite | Highlands |
| Feathers | Highlands, lowlands, and Bay Islands | Serpentine, albite, diorite | Highlands |
| Feathers, quetzal | Northern highlands (Verapaz) | Shark teeth | Coastal areas |
| | | Shell, coral, etc. | Coastal areas |
| Hematite | Southern highlands | Stingray spines | Coastal areas |

TABLE 9.2
Goods Traded to or through the Maya Area

| Goods from Mexico | | Goods from Central America | |
|---|---|---|---|
| Kaolin (?) | Pottery | Chalcedony (?) | Pottery |
| Magnetite (?) | Textiles | Cotton | Rubber |
| Metals (especially | Turquoise | Feathers | Slaves |
| copper) | | Metals (gold, silver, | |
| Pelts (especially rabbit) | | copper, and alloys) | |

trade to supply the populous Mexican states with goods originating in Central America and beyond had to pass through the Maya area, the ancient Maya were able to control this commerce as "middlemen." Second, the Maya area was blessed with a variety of resources that were prized not only by the local inhabitants (see Chapter 1), but by peoples in foreign lands, such as the highland valleys of Mexico. Among the most important exports from the Maya area were jadeite, serpentine, obsidian, salt, cacao, honey, animal pelts, and quetzal feathers (see Table 9.1).

## Goods and Mechanisms in Long-Distance Trade

The extant archaeological records and ethnohistorical literature demonstrate that the key variables of long-distance trade in prehistoric Mesoamerica were the most frequently exchanged and most valued items, the primary sources for these items, the means of transport, the primary routes, the methods of exchange, and the control centers.

The basic goods that originated in the Maya area and were exported by long-distance trade are listed in Table 9.1. Products traded through the Maya area from outside sources are listed in Table 9.2. Whether on land or water, the principal means of transport in prehistoric Mesoamerica relied on manpower; burdens secured with tumplines about the head or chest were carried on the backs of porters, often organized into human caravans, or packed into man-powered dugout canoes, for shipment along both riverine and sea-coastal routes. Although the ancient people of Mesoamerica knew the principle of the wheel (and used it to make wheeled toys), the wheel was not used for transport, owing mainly to the lack of suitable draft animals and to an environment that was (and in some areas remains today) far better suited for foot or boat travel than for travel by wheeled vehicles.

Ancient Maya trade was in the hands of several groups of merchants. The majority were probably members of a non-elite "middle class," and these people seem to have handled the bulk of the local trade within the Maya area. These non-elite merchants included professional peddlers and itinerant traders (still traversing the countryside today) who bought and sold a variety of goods, either in markets or in dealings with individual producers and consumers. Many other members of society

••••  engaged in trading activities on a part-time basis; these were the people who manufactured and sold their own goods—farmers, potters, weavers, knappers (makers
of chipped-stone tools), and other craftsmen. But it was a smaller cadre of wealthy
merchants, members of the elite class, who possessed the means to organize and
maintain long-distance trade operations, and indeed the means to control most of
the movement of goods that passed through the Maya area.

The most important economic institution in ancient Mesoamerica was the centralized market. In Guatemala and Yucatan today, markets still provide the principal means for the exchange of food and other goods. Held on scheduled days each
week (often on Sundays in rural communities) or daily in the large urban centers,
markets provide a central meeting ground for direct dealings between producer and
consumer. The same patterns probably dominated exchange in prehistoric times,
although direct archaeological evidence is scant. Markets in the past, as today, were
seldom associated with permanent structures; most were undoubtedly disposed in
open plazas, with only pole-and-thatch stands for shelter. At Tikal, an enclosed
rectangular arrangement of multi-doorway structures in the East Plaza (Fig. 4.5)
has been identified as the probable central market for this largest of Classic Maya
centers. Yet, the evidence is too sparse to allow us to rule out other functions for
these structures.

At the time of the Conquest, centralized markets were prospering in Central
Mexico, Yucatan, the Maya highlands, and elsewhere. The largest and most spectacular market described by the Spaniards was that in Tlatelolco, adjacent to Tenochtitlan, capital of the Mexica (Aztecs) in the Valley of Mexico (the site of
present-day Mexico City). The market square in Tlatelolco was surrounded by an
arcade, and the stalls were arranged along a grid of "streets" around a central elevated platform used for public announcements and the execution of thieves. On
one corner stood the court of the market officials, where disputes were settled. At
Tlatelolco, one could find goods from all over Mesoamerica, including a variety of
food and drink, jewelry made from precious metals (gold or silver) and stones (jadeite or turquoise), medicines, clothing, rubber, paper, building materials, baskets,
mats, pottery, grinding stones, and obsidian blades and other tools. One could also
find stalls for the purchase of slaves and prostitutes.

The descriptions of markets in the Maya area are similar, although none was
as elaborate as Tlatelolco. Postclassic centers such as Iximche, in the highlands, set
aside a permanent plaza area for the market, and installed government officials to
enforce rules, settle disputes, and collect taxes. The larger markets even maintained
facilities to house foreign merchants. Like those at Tlatelolco, the markets were well
organized, with designated areas for particular commodities.

During the Postclassic period long-distance trade for the Mexica was handled
by a government-sanctioned guild of merchants, the *pochteca*. The Maya had no
comparable organization, since long-distance trade was in the hands of rulers or

other elite-class entrepreneurs, and since the *pochteca* were known to act as military spies for the Mexica, they were usually not welcome in Maya centers. It has been suggested that periodic meetings held in intermediate areas such as Soconusco (on the Pacific coast of Chiapas) allowed the elite Maya merchants and the *pochteca* to carry out their commercial exchanges free of such concerns.

As in many Maya towns today, special days for combining ritual and even recreational activities with commerce may have existed during earlier times, and may have provided a primary means for peaceful interaction between the Classic-period Maya centers. These occasions may have been scheduled according to the events of the ritual calendar, and they probably coincided with pilgrimages to locally important religious shrines. In Postclassic times the shrines on Isla de Cozumel, the important trading center off the Yucatan coast, attracted great numbers of pilgrims.

At various times during the prehistoric era in Mesoamerica, long-distance trade was dominated by specific regional powers. In some periods, dominance resided in the establishment of foreign trade colonies, and in others in the establishment of trading alliances with foreign powers. The Olmec, centered in the Gulf coast lowlands, were one of several Middle Preclassic regional powers that appear to have created the first integrated long-distance trade network in Mesoamerica. Competition from former allied regions, including highland Mexico and south-coastal Guatemala, appears to have contributed to the eventual decline of the Olmec. In the Early Classic the Teotihuacan state of Central Mexico reestablished the economic integration of Mesoamerica through long-distance trade, and seemingly exerted a centralized control over this network until its own demise at the beginning of the Late Classic. Competition from new centers in Central Mexico—Cholula, El Tajin, Xochicalco, and others that emerged along the long-distance trade routes—and the rise of the Putun Maya probably contributed to Teotihuacan's downfall. In the decades that followed and until the Spanish Conquest, a succession of centers, beginning in the Terminal Classic with the rise of Chichen Itza, followed in the Early Postclassic by the Toltec capital of Tula, and then in the Late Postclassic by the Mexica capital of Tenochtitlan, dominated much of the long-distance trade in Mesoamerica.

The primary long-distance routes in Mesoamerica ran east-west, to the major consuming power centers in Mexico from the major source regions in the Maya area, and beyond. Specifically, the earliest routes, associated with the Middle Preclassic regional powers, appear to have been primarily land-based, radiating from the Gulf coast, Oaxaca, the Mexican highlands, the Maya highlands, and along the Pacific coastal plain, to tap resources within Mesoamerica and beyond in Central America. The Classic routes may have extended more directly eastward through the Maya lowlands, using both land and river-canoe transport, again to tap resources in the Maya highlands (via the Usumacinta drainage) and beyond (via the Caribbean) into Central America. The old Preclassic land route across the southern

•••• coastal plain appears to have been reduced to secondary importance during this
period. Beginning in the Terminal Classic the Putun Maya, operating from a number of sites, including their greatest capital at Chichen Itza, maintained a diverse
network of long-distance commerce. Their network included sea trade operating
larger and more efficient canoes that expanded the water routes well around the
Yucatan Peninsula. Of the many land routes that continued to thrive, the most important was the old south-coast access to the Maya highlands and Central America.

In addition to these generally east-west routes, an important north-south trading axis connected the southern Maya area and its resources with the lowland areas
to the north. Evidence for interaction along this highland-lowland axis can be seen
as early as the Middle Preclassic. The rise of Nakbe and El Mirador, followed by
the relationship between Kaminaljuyu and Tikal, which can be seen in the archaeological record from the Late Preclassic and Early Classic eras (see Chapters 3 and
4) probably reflected the importance of continued economic interaction between
the southern highlands and the central lowlands.

## Preclassic Trade

As we have seen, the origins of Maya civilization were marked by social stratification, monumental architecture, and the recording of calendrical and dynastic
hieroglyphic texts in the distinctive "Maya style," on upright sculptured monuments within ceremonial centers (see Chapter 3). These developments were focused
in both the southern Maya area (coastal plain and highlands) and the lowlands to
the north. Not incidentally, both areas were important for the acquisition and exchange of goods. The Pacific coastal plain, the primary east-west avenue between
Mexico and Central America, was a major growing area for cacao and other important crops. The highlands were the source of many valued mineral resources,
especially obsidian and jade, and provided the connecting links between the northern and southern reaches of the Maya area. The lowlands furnished a variety of
tropical forest products and furnished both the riverine and the overland routes that
connected the Caribbean with the Gulf of Mexico.

The growing prosperity of the southern Maya was cut short at the end of the
Preclassic era. Several theories have been advanced to explain this sudden demise,
but the eruption of Ilopango volcano (ca. A.D. 250) was apparently of sufficient
magnitude to disrupt the structure of southern Maya society (see Chapter 3). Agricultural activities and population levels throughout the ashfall area were severely
diminished for a considerable period, perhaps for several generations, and the impact of such a disruption on the existing trade networks in the southeastern Maya
area—the exchange links in central El Salvador must have been totally extirpated—
would have been equally devastating. Thus, the explosion would have led to the
weakening or severing of the ancient Pacific coast trade route to Central America.

Because of the extent and duration of depopulation in much of this region, the route could have been disrupted for several centuries. Though ash-free areas of the Pacific coast may have remained an important resource zone for cacao, the loss of the trade link to Central America would certainly have had a significant and lasting effect on the future of the entire Maya area, and all of Mesoamerica.

Recent research by David Freidel and others has revealed evidence of a Late Preclassic coastal trade network to the north during this era, one that followed the margins of the Yucatan Peninsula. To judge from excavations at Cerros, near the Caribbean coast in northern Belize (Fig. 3.28), and investigations of northern Yucatec Maya coastal sites and the rise of the salt trade (Fig. 9.1), it is apparent that by the Late Preclassic period, circumpeninsular canoe trade provided an important means for both communication and economic exchange. Although modest in scale compared to that of later times (as we shall see), this formative coastal trade network seems to have brought prosperity to Komchen and other Yucatan sites (see Chapter 3), which in exchange for salt received jadeite and other nonutilitarian goods from the south. The rapid growth of Cerros in the Late Preclassic, together with the evidence of its ties to regions both north and south, testifies to the importance of the coastal Caribbean route by this time. Sites along this route obviously

Fig. 9.1. Dzemul, Yucatan, Mexico: aerial view of the Xtampu salt-evaporation pans on the Caribbean coast, of the type used in pre-Columbian times; archaeological evidence indicates that this area was an important salt source from the Late Preclassic onward.

•••• 

prospered, and some may have been able to adapt to the changes that marked the Classic era. But Cerros appears to have been unable to survive these changes, most notably an apparent realignment of trade routes in the Maya area, for the site was abandoned at the close of the Preclassic period.

The dominant Maya lowland center in the Late Preclassic was undoubtedly El Mirador, presumably the heir of its earlier prototype at nearby Nakbe. Although the economic role of this precocious power is only beginning to be documented, it appears that El Mirador served as a major redistribution node and probably controlled trans-Peten commerce in its heyday, especially the trans-peninsula trade between the Caribbean and Gulf coasts and exchange with the major highland power, Kaminaljuyu.

From all indications, then, long-distance trade was well established in the Maya area during the Preclassic. Two primary axes can be inferred: an east-west axis in the south, connecting Mexico with the resources of the Maya highlands and Central America by way of the Pacific coastal plain; and a north-south axis, connecting Yucatan and its salt supplies to the markets and resources to the south by way of both the Gulf and Caribbean coasts.

## Classic Trade

The Classic period saw two developments that profoundly affected not only long-distance trade in Mesoamerica but also the developmental course of Maya civilization. The first of these was a shift in the bulk of east-west commerce from the ancient Preclassic trade routes along the Pacific coastal plain and the coast of Yucatan to central-Maya routes through the highlands and, more important, along the rivers that crossed the lowlands. The second was the emergence of a new power at Teotihuacan, which was apparently able to integrate much of the Mesoamerican long-distance trade network during the Early Classic period.

During its prime (ca. 100 B.C. to A.D. 700; see Fig. 3.38), Teotihuacan was one of the greatest cities of the ancient world. By A.D. 400 this new power appears to have gained control over much of the long-distance trade between the Maya area and Central Mexico. Among Teotihuacan's alliances in the Maya area, the most notable was apparently with Kaminaljuyu, where a central precinct of the site was rebuilt in a style duplicating the civic architecture of Teotihuacan. Alliances with several centers on the Pacific coastal plain south and west of Kaminaljuyu may have provided access to cacao production. At least one ceramic manufacturing center in this region also produced elaborate Teotihuacan ritual vessels and incensarios. Teotihuacan products were imported throughout much of the Maya area, and even pottery and other locally produced items often emulated central-Mexican styles.

The southern Maya area provided Teotihuacan and other Mesoamerican centers with several critical commodities. The El Chayal quarry near Kaminaljuyu and several other sources in the highlands provided obsidian. The northern-highlands jade and other minerals were exported from the middle Motagua Valley and adjacent regions. The northern highlands also furnished the quetzal feathers that were so prized by the ruling elites of Mesoamerica. From the south coast a bounty of marine and agricultural products, the latter including the much valued cacao, was exported to a variety of regions throughout Mesoamerica.

As we have seen, the first centers to rise to prominence in the central lowlands were situated on the portages between river systems flowing east to the Caribbean and west to the Gulf of Mexico. Thus, centers such as Nakbe and El Mirador were in a position, throughout the Preclassic, to control the east-west commerce that crossed the base of the Yucatan Peninsula. With Ilopango's disruption of the Pacific-coast connection to Central America, these lowland routes took on new importance. Before long, a powerful new lowland polity was established at Copan with its dependency, Quirigua. These centers could tap the Central American trade that bypassed the devastated southeastern zone, for the new routes from Central America probably lay to the north, overland through western Honduras or along the Caribbean coast. From there, products could be transported by canoe up the coast of Belize and then west across the lowlands by river. Concurrently, the east coast of the lowlands appears to have become a major cacao production area; southern Maya refugees from the Ilopango disaster may have helped to establish this traditional south-coast cash crop in the eastern lowlands. These speculations are supported by indications of increased contacts from the southeast at this time in this region, as at Barton Ramie, in the Belize River valley. One market for much of this lowland cacao lay in Mexico, and the same riverine routes across the lowlands must have been used to transport the crop westward. And the crucial link in the east-west connection between the Maya lowlands and Central Mexico was provided by the Chontal (or Putun) Maya, who eventually would ride their commercial prowess to political and military dominance in Postclassic Mesoamerica.

El Mirador seems to have been the first lowland center to have reaped the benefits of this trans-Peten commerce. The period of its greatest prosperity corresponds to the Late and Terminal Preclassic, after which this great polity seems to have declined rapidly. Thereafter, another site astride the lowland portages, Tikal, became the dominant power in the lowlands. It is tempting to conclude that El Mirador and Tikal were commercial rivals, and that the decline of the former was related to the rise of the latter. One could suggest that Tikal's location farther south gave it an advantage, or that El Mirador was vanquished in a time of conflict. But at this point we know too little about El Mirador to support a discussion about rivalry in either economic or political terms. Calakmul, destined to be Tikal's chief Classic-period rival, was an even more obvious successor to El Mirador's power, given its adjacent location, but once again we need to know more about the development of this great city.

During the Early Classic a series of new lowland centers was established, all in locations suitable for controlling the principal lowland trade routes. Some may have

•••• been founded by elite colonists from Tikal, or may have been allied to Tikal by marriages between ruling families. We have already mentioned Copan and Quirigua, in the southeastern area, which secured the Central American trade connections; Quirigua also controlled the important Motagua Valley jade route to the Caribbean. Other centers, such as Yaxchilan, would have secured the valuable Usumacinta route between the highlands and the Gulf coast. Far to the northeast, Coba may have been established to control resources and monitor trade in northern Yucatan.

The mid-Classic decline of Tikal profoundly changed the economic and political landscape of the lowland Maya. But other lowland Maya centers, including Tikal's former allies, along with her enemies, appear to have gained new prosperity and power in the wake of these developments—Caracol and Dos Pilas being prime examples. In the southwestern lowlands, Palenque seemingly gained ascendancy over land-based commerce between Mexico and the interior lowlands. By this time the southeastern area had been resettled, and the Pacific coastal route to Central America was undoubtedly reestablished. Copan appears to have maintained control over much of this commerce, and Copan's subordinate, Quirigua, probably still controlled the Motagua jade route. Yaxchilan and its allies maintained dominance of the Usumacinta routes.

Thus although power in the lowlands was reoriented in the Late Classic, and although the new powers were increasingly competitive, the overall pattern of long-distance trade that had developed during the Early Classic appears not to have changed significantly.

## Postclassic Trade

A crucial change did begin to occur, however, by the Terminal Classic (ca. A.D. 800–1000). By this time a group of seacoast traders, the Putun (or Chontal) Maya, from the Gulf coast region of Tabasco, were increasing their hold over commerce along the coasts (see Chapter 6). The Putun Maya established themselves at Xicalango, a major port on Laguna de Términos, and there, as documented by Spanish colonial sources, the land-based merchants from Central Mexico traded a variety of products with the Putun sea merchants, who brought their goods from as far away as lower Central America. The source of the Putun Maya's prosperity and power lay both in their strategic location on the Gulf coast and in an apparent technological breakthrough, the development of large oceangoing canoes capable of transporting huge loads of goods at costs lower than the former methods would have allowed.

Waterborne commerce was undoubtedly an ancient tradition among the Maya, extending back at least as far as the Late Preclassic. Besides plying the riverine routes across the southern and central lowlands, the smaller canoes of this time seem to have begun to exploit the islands off the east coast of Belize and the other coastal margins of the Yucatan Peninsula. But it appears that by the Postclassic, much larger vessels had been developed. A single large seagoing canoe could carry more goods with less manpower than could land-based porters or even river craft (during portage, the latter, too, required considerable manpower).

Using these great sea-trading vessels, the Putun Maya soon extended their trade routes all the way around the Yucatan Peninsula, establishing their own ports at several strategic points. During the Postclassic period, Isla de Cozumel, off the northeastern coast, was perhaps the most important port of trade for the new sea-borne commerce. Other Putun colonies were established at Champoton on the west coast of Yucatan, at Isla Cerritos on the north coast of Yucatan (Fig. 7.1), and at Nito on the mouth of the Río Dulce, on the east coast of the Peninsula near its base.

Although almost any product could be transported by sea, this mode of travel especially favored the heavier and bulkier products, such as salt, grinding stones, cacao, and so forth. A famous encounter with a Maya trading canoe off the north coast of Honduras near Islas de la Bahía (Bay Islands), recorded by Columbus on his fourth voyage, is our best eyewitness account. The canoe, described as being as long as a Spanish galley and 2.5 m wide, had a cabin amidships and a crew of some two dozen men, plus its captain and a number of women and children. It carried a cargo of cacao, metal products (copper bells and axes), pottery (including crucibles to melt metal), cotton clothing, and *macanas* (Mexican-style wooden swords set with obsidian blades).

As one would expect, the dominance of sea trade in the Postclassic produced a shift in human settlement toward the seacoasts of the Yucatan Peninsula. This reorientation in long-distance trade routes might well have precipitated the decline of Classic lowland society, for the demise of Classic Maya civilization seems to be defined by the decline of the older lowland centers, especially those like Tikal that were located far inland and were dependent on the older trans-Peten trade routes (Chapter 6). Yet the opposite can also be argued—that is, that the chaos resulting from the breakdown of Classic lowland society disrupted the older riverine and land-based trade routes, thus necessitating the growth of seacoast commerce and inspiring the design of the large seagoing canoes.

Notwithstanding the critical role of sea trade during this period, porter-borne overland trade in Yucatan and throughout the Maya area remained important during the Postclassic period, and even into the early colonial era—in the sixteenth and seventeenth centuries, unconquered Maya groups such as the Tayasal Itza (Chapter 7) continued to maintain a vestigial overland trade network through the central and southern lowlands. But in ways that were sometimes abrupt and sometimes much more subtle, the ancient technology of Mesoamerican production and distribution, and the patterns of the region's trade networks, were changed forever by the arrival of Europeans.

# 10

## THE ORGANIZATION OF SOCIETY

Before the Spanish had conquered that country, the natives lived together in towns in a very civilized fashion . . . [and] in the middle of the town were their temples with beautiful plazas, and all around the temples stood the houses of the lords and priests, and then the most important people. Thus came the houses of the richest and of those who were held in the highest estimation nearest to these, and at the outskirts of the town were the houses of the lower class.

—*Landa's relación de las cosas de Yucatán* (Tozzer 1941: 62)

We turn now to consideration of another in our inventory of basic factors underlying Maya civilization, namely the ways by which the Maya organized themselves, both socially and politically. Our understanding of ancient Maya social and political organization is based on several complementary forms of research: archaeology, epigraphy (decipherment), human ecology, ethnohistory (often supplemented by ethnography), history, and art history. The archaeological approach centers on the form and spatial distribution of the remains of ancient occupation, from the smallest hearth or trash pit to the largest building complex or city—the basic strategy of what is usually called settlement archaeology. The distribution and patterning of these settlement remains are taken to reflect not only ancient social and political relationships, but also the residents' interaction with their environment, agricultural and otherwise. In the Maya area, this kind of settlement research has been complemented by epigraphic studies that have enabled scholars to read references to elite-class marriage and kin-based relationships and even to reconstruct dynastic histories and the form of elite hierarchies for several Classic-period sites (see Chapters 4 and 5).

Ethnohistoric research is based on a variety of surviving documents from the time of the Spanish Conquest and the early Colonial years. Among other things, these documents describe the organization and daily-life patterns of ancient Maya society during its final era. The anthropological descriptions of present-day Maya communities (ethnography) have also been used in the reconstruction of ancient Maya social and political organization.

Although these various approaches build on different sources of information, as we shall see in reviewing what is currently known and surmised about the organization of ancient Maya society, the results obtained from one source may be used to amplify or test the conclusions derived from others. The first half of the chapter will consider the social structure of ancient Maya society; the second half, the political structure.

## RECONSTRUCTING THE SOCIAL LANDSCAPE

There was no single form of social organization that describes all Maya society in the pre-Columbian past. As with other aspects of the ancient Maya, variation rather than uniformity was the norm. Differences in time, space, ethnicity, language, and social complexity all contributed to gradients and contrasts in organizational forms. The same is true today in contemporary Maya social organization. Although the most complete reconstructions of the ancient Maya world are assembled from an interdisciplinary approach, the task of describing the variations in ancient Maya social organization is fundamentally an archaeological problem. And although historical sources, whether deciphered Classic texts or retrospectively applied ethnohistoric documents, are very helpful, archaeological data and interpretation remain the core of reconstructions of ancient social organization. The approach of archaeology is to draw inferences from a series of overlapping data sources—artifact patterning, burials, architecture, settlement patterning, and much more. In most cases, archaeological studies of Maya social organization have been heavily weighted toward the elite, although a recent increase in the investigation of non-elite domestic remains is slowly providing a more balanced perspective.

Historical and ethnohistorical studies confront the same problem. Contemporaneous Classic texts deal mostly with politics and ritual, and even the specific kinship and marriage information they record is restricted to the elite class—the vast majority of the population, the non-elite, is not even mentioned. Classic-period sculpture, painting, and other iconographic evidence can greatly assist our understanding of social relationships, but once again the information yielded pertains almost solely to the Maya elite. The rich ethnohistoric sources provide far more complete information about Maya social organization, including data on the non-elite, but are most useful for Postclassic studies. These sources of course become less reliable the farther back in time one proceeds; they are less useful in dealing with the Classic period and particularly unhelpful in dealing with the Preclassic.

Nonetheless, we know a great deal about ancient Maya social patterns and organization. In this half of the chapter, we will begin with a review of Maya settlement studies and population reconstructions, then turn to the individual life cycle, marriage and the family, descent groups, and social stratification.

=    ## Evidence from Settlement Studies

The patterning of sites and other remains that archaeologists use to reconstruct the organization of ancient Maya society is obviously affected by environmental conditions—availability of water and good agricultural soils, access to other necessary resources—and settlement studies are in fact used to reconstruct ecological relationships. But more important here, settlement patterns can be used to reconstruct ancient social and political organization. For instance, the content and distribution of the archaeological remains within a single household (cooking vessels, tools, hearth, burials, refuse, and the remains of the house structure itself) may reflect male and female work areas and other activities that once took place there, and perhaps something about the size and organization of the family.

On a larger (and statistically more significant) scale, the patterning of all such household remains within a single site may reflect the social and political ties that once defined a functioning community. A pattern that reveals a series of clusters of individual houses may indicate that the ancient society was organized according to multi-family groupings such as lineages. Differences within a class of residential structures, for example in size, elaborateness, or type of construction, may speak to social or economic class structure. And the pattern of residential structures in relation to architecture with nonresidential functions—temples, storage facilities, courts and plazas, administrative structures, and so forth—may permit the reconstruction of political organization.

In order to undertake such reconstructions, the archaeologist must be able to identify the kinds of activities that took place; that is, it is necessary to determine the function of ancient buildings from their remains and their spatial orientation. Obviously, the most crucial functional identification is that of the ancient residence itself—the building associated with the basic family activities (eating, sleeping, reproduction, child rearing). Of course it cannot be assumed that there was always a one-to-one correspondence between a single building and a single family unit: in some cases, families might have shared a building; or a single family might have utilized several buildings—one for sleeping, another for a kitchen, and still others for storage or such specialized tasks as tool and pottery manufacturing.

According to the ethnohistoric sources, the typical family slept in one room. Landa wrote, in this connection:

And then they build a wall in the middle dividing the house lengthwise, and in this wall they leave several doors into the half which they call the back of the house, where they have their beds, and the other half they whitened very nicely with lime [this outer room would seem to have been a sort of porch open at the front and sides] . . . and they have beds made of small rods [saplings] and on the top a mat on which they sleep, covering themselves with their mantas [cloths/cloaks, or *patis*] of cotton. In summer they usually sleep in the whitened part of the house [the porch], on one side of those mats, especially the men.

A seventeenth-century writer, in discussing a house in the lowlands of the Río Usumacinta, described a bed that took the form of a crude wooden framework sufficiently large to hold four persons. Today the Maya in the lowland regions often use hammocks, but it seems almost certain that had they been in general use at the time of the Conquest, Landa would have mentioned them. He states explicitly, however, that the Maya had "beds made of small rods." In the highlands, the traditional mat is often still used for a bed, and the hammock, in fact, was probably imported from the Caribbean region, sometime in recent centuries.

Other activities were undoubtedly pursued in the open space around such buildings. Here we will use the term *residence* (or residential unit; see below) to refer to the dwelling space (buildings and adjacent grounds) presumably occupied by a single family. In practice, except for the masonry "palaces" of the elite, the vast majority of such residences in the Maya area are detected archaeologically as low earthen or rubble platforms. Originally, the typical platform supported a single building made of pole and thatch (inferred from patterns of postholes), sometimes with more durable stone foundations or walls (Fig. 10.1).

But in defining ancient residences, the archaeologist must be able to ascertain which of the activity areas were mutually contemporaneous. Although identifying function may at times be difficult, it is usually not so difficult as determining the concurrent use of archaeological remains. The issue of contemporaneity is crucial, since in order to reconstruct the organization of ancient society, the archaeologist must have some assurance that the activity areas being studied were all elements of the same functioning system. For instance, a cluster of family residences might represent a lineage system if they were all occupied at the same time. But if they were occupied at *different* times, they might represent a series of houses occupied sequentially by a single family.

Most methods used by archaeologists to furnish the necessary chronological control—radiocarbon dating, pottery-style analysis, and other techniques—are rarely accurate enough to define time spans of less than about a hundred years. So far as Classic Maya sites are concerned, an exception occurs when a structure can be associated with a Maya calendrical date, but most inscriptions of this kind are limited to the elite areas of sites. Thus, for the majority of cases, concurrency in the occupation of structures is assumed no more precisely than within periods averaging about a hundred years in length, which at that time was equivalent to approximately four human generations.

## Population Reconstructions

The problem of chronological accuracy relates directly to the problem of reconstructing the size of ancient populations. If we could be sure that all of the residences originally in use at a given site are extant as remains today, and that all were

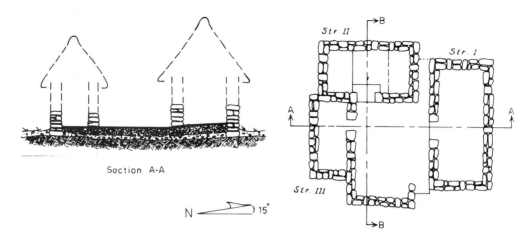

Section A-A

N ⟩ 15°

Str. II

Str. I

A — A

Str. III

B

occupied at the same time, then we would have only to count the number of houses and multiply by the number of people in an average family (which raises another problem, discussed below) to produce a total population for that site. But of course we cannot make that assumption; all Maya sites were occupied for more than a generation. Thus where possible, periods of occupation of residences are assigned on the basis of associated datable materials, usually pottery samples, sometimes supplemented by other means such as radiocarbon dating or, in the case of Copan, obsidian dating. In the final analysis, this means that population estimates must be based on occupation spans of more than one generation at the very least, and for several centuries at most (basic chronological time periods are usually adjusted to account for the expectation that not all residential units were occupied simultaneously; the most thorough compilation of population-size studies for the ancient lowland Maya uses 150 years as the average occupational span for any given residential unit).

In recent studies of population size the actual archaeological features being counted have varied, depending on circumstances. Typically, studies have focused on the traditional residential platform, but some have relied on numbers of individual rooms in buildings. But regardless of the feature being counted, there will at any site be an unknown proportion of residences that the count missed, either because they lacked platforms, have been completely destroyed, or are so deeply buried as to be undetectable. At Tikal, for example, it was estimated that the actual number of ancient residences was 10 percent greater than the mapped total of residence platforms. At Copan this factor was higher (between 39 and 50 percent), and at the badly disturbed site of Santa Rita Corozal, it was much greater (between 50 and 100 percent). In an innovative study at Sayil, population was estimated on the basis of the number of *chultunes* and their water capacity, but this technique can be applied only to sites that employed such artificial water-storage features.

Although the problems of reconstructing ancient population size from archaeological remains are formidable, the results of settlement studies give us a good foundation at least for comparing the numbers and densities of structures from one

Section B-B

0  1  2  3
Meters

Fig. 10.1. Ancient Maya residential group east of Xpuhil, Campeche, Mexico: section and plan views of typical ancient Maya houses with reconstructed view at the right.

site to the next. The results for a sample of Maya lowland sites are presented in Table 10.1. These give central Copan the greatest construction density of any Maya site (1,449 structures per km²), due in part at least to the unusually close confinement of the Copan Valley. Most Classic Maya sites range from 200 to 450 structures per km², although both Quirigua (129) and Uaxactun (124) are well below this range.

TABLE 10.1
Density of Structures at Selected Lowland Sites[a]

| Site | Site area | Area surveyed (km²) | Structures/km² |
|------|-----------|---------------------|----------------|
| Becan | Central and periphery | 3.0 | 389[e] |
| Caracol | Central | 2.26 | 300 |
| Chunchucmil | Central and periphery | 6.0 | 400 |
| Copan | Central | 0.6 | 1,449 |
| | Central and periphery | 24.6 | 143 |
| Dzibilchaltun | Central and periphery | 19.0 | 442 |
| Mayapan | Central and periphery | 4.2 | 986 |
| Nohmul | Central | 4.0 | 58 |
| | Periphery | 18.0 | 12 |
| Quirigua | Central | 3.0 | 130 |
| Sayil | Central | 2.4 | 220 |
| Seibal | Central | 1.6 | 436[e] |
| | Periphery | 0.7 | 244[e] |
| Tikal | Central | 9.0 | 294[e] |
| | Periphery[b] | 7.0 | 307[e] |
| | Periphery (transect sample)[c] | 8.5 | 194[e] |
| | Rural (transect sample)[d] | 11.5 | 98[e] |
| Uaxactun | Central | 2.0 | 124[e] |
| | Periphery | 2.25 | 53[e] |

[a] After Rice and Culbert (1990), Table 1.1.
[b] Adjacent to central area.
[c] Inside site boundaries.
[d] Outside site boundaries.
[e] Corrected by subtracting uninhabitable land area (*bajo*, savannah, steep slopes).

Late Postclassic Mayapan shows the second-highest density (996 structures per km²), an artifact of concentrating many buildings behind a defensive wall. If we restrict our attention to the Late Classic, the time when most lowland sites reached their population peaks (see below), we find that the same general pattern holds, although for most sites (Table 10.2) the density range is somewhat lower.

For estimates based on some form of residential unit counts, the next step is to determine the conversion factor—the size of the family unit. Most studies use one of several ethnohistoric or ethnographic accounts. The former give census figures for several Maya communities shortly after the Conquest. These generally vary from 4.9 people per nuclear family (Isla de Cozumel) to 10 people per nuclear family (in the Peten). Ethnographic estimates of the average size of modern Maya families living in traditional communities, in terms of people per nuclear family, include 4.9 (the average of a Yucatecan sample), 5.6 (Chan Kom, Yucatan), and 6.1 (X-Cacal, Quintana Roo).

Applying these conversion factors to the residential unit counts by time period affords us a means for making population estimates. The figures for a sample of lowland sites at their population peaks are given in Table 10.3 (the larger sites are divided into central and peripheral areas). The table shows us that Tikal was the largest single site for which we have population estimates, with a Late Classic peak of some 62,000 people within the site proper (defined by the 120 km² that are bounded on the north and south by earthworks, on the east and west by *bajos*). The rural hinterland, defined by an area within a radius of 10 km, was occupied by an estimated 30,000 additional people, giving "greater Tikal" an estimated population of 92,000 during the Late Classic. For comparison, "greater Copan," defined by the occupied areas of the Copan Valley, was about one-fourth the size of Tikal,

TABLE 10.2

Late Classic Densities of Structures at Selected Lowland Sites and Rural Areas[a]

| Site | Site centers | | Site peripheries | | Rural areas |
| | Area surveyed (km²) | strs/km² | Area surveyed (km²) | strs/km² | strs/km² |
|---|---|---|---|---|---|
| Becan | 3.0 | 171 | | | |
| Caracol | 2.2 | 300 | | | |
| Copan | 0.6 | 1,449 | 23.7 | 84 | 15 |
| Dzibilchaltun | 19.0 | 398 | | | |
| Nohmul | 4.0 | 58 | | | 12 |
| Quirigua | 3.0 | 145 | | | |
| Sayil | 2.4 | 220 | | | 220 |
| Seibal | 1.6 | 222 | 13.6 | 116 | |
| Tikal | 9.0 | 235 | 111.0 | 116 | 39 |
| Uaxactun | 16.0 | 106 | | | 30 |
| Belize Valley | | | | | 116 |
| Central Peten Lakes | | | | | 49 |
| Tikal-Yaxha transect | | | | | 60 |

[a]After Rice and Culbert (1990), Table 1.2.

TABLE 10.3

Population Estimates at Selected Lowland Sites and Rural Areas, in Various Eras[a]

| Site | Site area | Area (km²) | Estimated population | Period |
|---|---|---|---|---|
| Copan | Central | 0.6 | 6,000–9,000 | Late Classic |
| | Periphery | 23.4 | 9,000–12,000 | Late Classic |
| | Rural | 476.0 | 3,000–4,000 | Late Classic |
| | Total (Copan Valley) | 500.0 | 18,000–25,000 | Late Classic |
| Komchen | Total | 2.0 | 2,500–3,000 | Late Preclassic |
| Nohmul | Total | 22.0 | 3,300 | Late/Terminal Classic |
| Quirigua | Central | 3.0 | 1,200–1,600 | Late Classic |
| Santa Rita | Total | 5.0 | 5,000–8,700 | Late Postclassic |
| Sayil | Total | 3.5 | 8,000–10,000[b] | Terminal Classic |
| | | | 5,000–10,000[c] | Terminal Classic |
| Seibal | Central | 1.6 | 1,600 | Late Preclassic |
| | Periphery | 13.6 | 8,000 | Late Preclassic |
| | Total | 15.2 | 9,600 | Late Preclassic |
| Tayasal | Total | 90.0 | 22,000–32,000 | Late Classic |
| Tikal | Central | 9.0 | 11,300[d] | Late Classic |
| | Periphery | 111.0 | 50,700 | Late Classic |
| | Total (inside boundary) | 120.0 | 62,000 | Late Classic |
| | Rural | 194.0 | 30,000 | Late Classic |
| | Total | 314.0 | 92,000 | Late Classic |
| Yaxha | Total | 237.0 | 42,000 | Late Classic |

[a] After Rice and Culbert (1990), Table 1.3.
[b] Estimate based on structure count.
[c] Estimate based on chultun count.
[d] Estimate includes ca. 3,000 living in masonry (palace) structures.

with an estimated maximum population of between 19,000 and 25,000 people in this same period. It should be kept in mind that these are population estimates for sites, not polities, and since there is no clear agreement about the size of sovereign political territories (as we shall see), there is no way to estimate the number of people who would have been subjects of the rulers of Tikal, Copan, or any other Classic-period Maya center.

The most surprising result of a recent study of lowland population size was the high density of rural settlement in inter-site areas. Investigations of several such areas in the central lowlands, including a transect between Tikal and Yaxha, and a series of transects in the central lake region of the Peten, concluded that this area supported about 190 people per km² during the Late Classic. This estimate places the central Maya lowlands among the most densely populated preindustrial societies of the world, comparable to pre-twentieth-century China and Java. This level of population density certainly exerted pressure on the environment, and makes it all the more likely that population pressure and environmental stresses were critical factors in the decline seen in this region at the end of the Classic period.

Finally, these reconstructions allow us a glimpse of the patterns of population growth and decline through time. Some of these trends can be seen in data from a sample of lowland sites (Table 10.4) and rural areas (Table 10.5) that show relative

TABLE 10.4

Relative Population Sizes, by Eras, as Percentages
of Maximum Population Estimates, at Selected Lowland Sites[a]

| | | | | Sites | | | |
|---|---|---|---|---|---|---|---|
| Era | Becan | Dzibilchaltun | Komchen | Seibal | Santa Rita | Central Tikal | Peripheral Tikal |
| Late Postclassic | | 6 | 6 | | 100 | | |
| | | | | | 11 | | |
| Early Postclassic | 29 | 5 | 1 | 14 | 40 | 4 | 1 |
| Terminal Classic | 59 | | | 85 | | 14 | 20 |
| | | 100 | 71 | | 54 | | |
| Late Classic | 100 | | | 85 | | 100 | 64 |
| | 74 | | | — | | 95 | 67 |
| Early Classic | 94 | 5 | — | 34 | 23 | 78 | 100 |
| | | | | | 11 | | |
| Late Preclassic | 94 | | 58 | 100 | 34 | 19 | 14 |
| | | 29 | 100 | | | 24 | 1 |
| | | | | | | 20 | |
| Middle Preclassic | 9 | | 6 | 28 | 6 | 4 | 1 |
| | | | | 14 | | | 1 |
| | | | | | 3 | | |

[a] After Rice and Culbert (1990), Table 1.4.

TABLE 10.5

Relative Population Sizes, by Eras, as Percentages
of Maximum Population Estimates, in Selected Rural Areas[a]

| | | Region | | | |
|---|---|---|---|---|---|
| | | Central Peten lakes | | | |
| Era | Tikal-Yaxha | Macanche/Salpeten | Quexil/Petenxil | Yaxha/Sacnab | Belize Valley |
| Late Postclassic | — | 10 | — | — | |
| Early Postclassic | — | 19 | 2 | 8 | 21 |
| Terminal Classic | 92 | 29 | 29 | 11 | 50 |
| Late Classic | 100 | 100 | 100 | 100 | 100 |
| Early Classic | 84 | 8 | 5 | 46 | 50 |
| Late Preclassic | 100 | 18 | 10 | 29 | 93 |
| Middle Preclassic | 41 | 25 | 34 | 13 | 52 |

[a] After Rice and Culbert (1990), Table 1.4.

population-size estimates at each major time period as a percentage of the maximum population reached by that site or rural area. These data support what most archaeologists have concluded on the basis of other lines of evidence, namely that the highest levels of population were reached at two points in time, during the Late Preclassic and the Late Classic (the second of these population peaks was no doubt by far the greater of the two). Two sites and one rural area in the sample (Komchen, Seibal, and the Tikal-Yaxha transect) appear to have peaked in population size during the Late Preclassic, and two sites and two rural areas peaked in the Late Classic. Both peaks are followed by population declines, with the drop following the Late Classic being the most precipitous. The Early Classic population decline is moderate at Santa Rita Corozal and in most rural areas, severe at Seibal, and total at Komchen. At Becan there is no appreciable change between the Late Preclassic and Early Classic population levels. The Terminal Classic population decline is moderate at Becan, peripheral Tikal, and the Tikal-Yaxha transect, and severe at central Tikal and in the central-Peten lake region. At Seibal there is essentially no change in Late and Terminal Classic population levels. At least some occupation continued in the Early Postclassic in most areas before final abandonment in the Late Postclassic. One site, Santa Rita Corozal, reached its peak population at the close of the Late Postclassic.

## Settlement Units in the Maya Lowlands

As we have seen, the Maya area in which settlement has been most thoroughly studied is the lowland zone, including sites in the central and northern lowlands. For this reason, the conclusions about archaeological settlement units made herein are based on lowland data from the Classic period although, with allowances for regional cultural and environmental differences, they can be considered generally applicable to other regions and, to a lesser extent, to other time periods. The settlement units identified by archaeologists generally reflect the hierarchy of unit categories used by the Maya themselves, as seen in their languages. In Yucatec Mayan, *na* means a single house, *nalil* refers to a group of houses, *china* means a cluster of house groups that compose a ward or barrio, and *cah* is an entire town or city.

The *na* corresponds to the minimal settlement feature, or *residential unit*, that we defined earlier in this chapter. This unit is usually a low earthen or rubble platform that supported oblong or rectangular structures of one or more rooms with stone walls roofed by pole and thatch (Fig. 10.1), or built entirely of perishable materials. The minimum size of these structures appears to be about 20 m² of roofed space. Structures built without platforms are much more difficult to detect archaeologically, their only trace usually being corner postholes. In some cases residential units had walls built of adobe or mud blocks; or only the lower portion of the walls was built of durable materials, either adobe or, on occasion, masonry blocks, leaving the upper walls and roof to be constructed of perishable materials. In the highest-status residential units, the structures were often bigger, placed on larger, higher, masonry-faced platforms, and built completely of dressed stone, including their vaulted roofs.

Items found in association with residential units include burials under the floors, burned areas or hearths, workshop areas where chipped-stone tools and various other products were made, storage pits for food or water (*chultunes*), and debris such as pottery sherds, broken grinding stones (manos and metates), worn-out flint or obsidian tools, and even food remains. Evidence of this kind indicates that these structures were indeed residential in function, probably housing nuclear families (husband, wife, and children). Still, an unknown percentage of structures that might reasonably be labeled residential units could have served specialized functions as storage sheds, detached kitchens, or household shrines. Occasionally, a flood, volcanic eruption, or other sudden catastrophe overwhelmed a household, preserving both the building and the tools and other furnishings just as they were disposed at the moment of the disaster. An example of this kind of event has been discovered at the Classic site of Cerén, El Salvador, where several adobe houses, along with work and storage areas, household articles, and adjacent agricultural fields, were suddenly buried and sealed under a thick blanket of volcanic ash (Figs. 1.7 and 8.3).

A *nalil*, two or more residential units found in proximity, defines a *residential group* (Fig. 10.2a). Commonly averaging two to six units, groupings of this kind are assumed to have been occupied by an extended family, that is, two or more nuclear families related by close kinship ties. Extended family groupings may be generational (grandparents, parents, and married children maintaining separate but proximate residences), collateral (siblings or cousins doing the same), or both. Craft specializations such as stoneworking or potterymaking seem to have been associated with some residential groupings, and we might conclude that certain occupations followed family lines in ancient Maya society. Specialized non-residential structures have also been found within residential groups. In some cases the presence of a leader or headman of an extended family may be indicated by a single larger or more elaborate residential structure within a residential group. In some groups, the units are arranged around a central open space, or patio (Fig. 10.2b). A particular residential-group pattern found repeatedly at Tikal, for example, called "Plaza Plan 2," consists of a rectangular central patio bordered on three sides by residential units and by a smaller but often higher-platform structure on the east side. This special building has been seen as the household shrine for the extended family, where ancestral rituals were performed above the burial place of the family's founder.

The ward or barrio (*china*) was an important subdivision in Maya settlements. The *china* may correspond to larger aggregates of structures that have been detected from settlement-pattern studies. A *cluster* consists of two or more residential groups separated by open space from other such clusters (Fig. 10.2c, d), and one cluster usually embraces five to twelve groups; one group, or one structure, moreover, is often larger or more elaborate than the others (Fig. 10.2e, f). If these residential clusters were occupied by larger kin groups, such as whole lineages, we assume that the lineage head and his extended family lived in the largest residential group within a given cluster, and that his residential group may have included a

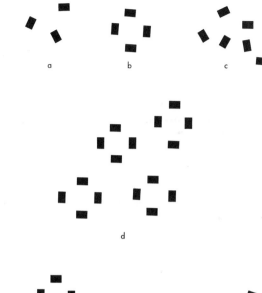

Fig. 10.2. Schematic plans of typical Maya settlement units: (*a*) informal residential group; (*b*) residential patio group; (*c*) informal residential cluster; (*d*) homogeneous patio cluster; (*e*) structure-focused patio cluster; (*f*) group-focused patio cluster, each probably corresponding to Maya social units.

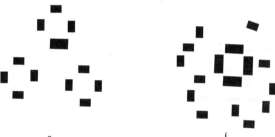

lineage shrine in the largest ceremonial structure in the cluster. The other residential groups within a cluster presumably would have been occupied by the remaining extended families of the lineage, although some scholars have suggested a slightly different interpretation of clusters, postulating that the surrounding smaller residential groups housed the retainers, servants, and such who were dependent on the larger, more elaborate residential group. Both views may in fact be correct.

Beyond the residential level, Maya sites are dominated by central concentrations of special-purpose structures, including platforms, causeways, temples, ballcourts, palaces, plain or sculptured stone monuments, and occasionally fortifications. These are the items that define most of the familiar Maya archaeological sites, and the neutral term *center* is now often preferred to former labels such as "ceremonial center" whose functional implications are too restrictive. These centers, appropriately named because they are usually spatially central to the residential groupings that surround them, must have served a variety of functions: there are areas for public gatherings, ceremonies, ballgames, and markets, and facilities for political and administrative activities like receiving visitors, collecting tribute, and hearing grievances. It is usually possible to discern the functions of these various areas, and the distinction between public and restricted areas is often especially clear. Many centers, such as Lubaantun and Quirigua, consisted of two definable areas: one open, spacious, and public; the other closed in, restricted, and private. Larger centers like Tikal include many such contrasting areas. Certainly the largest and most elaborate residences were in or near these centers, and were usually constructed so as to restrict access to and maintain privacy for the courtly and domestic activities of the ruling families and their rituals.

In a very real sense, however, even the largest of Maya centers were simply larger and more complex versions of the smaller residential clusters. In fact, some scholars have viewed Maya sites as the residences (palaces) for the most wealthy and powerful elite lineages, those of the ruling family and other important political and religious offices, with temple pyramids representing simply the ancestral shrines of the elites. In other views Maya centers were more complex, the setting not only for the royal court, but for all the functions usually found in any preindustrial city.

But regardless of the varying emphases given to different functional aspects of Maya sites, each settlement, from the smallest village to the largest city, defined the remains of an ancient social unit, the *cah*, or what anthropologists define as the *community*. The *cah* provided the setting for the organizational networks that gave Maya society its basic structure. Many of these networks were based on kinship: the nuclear family, extended family, and lineage bonds that were the foundations of Maya society. Others were based on economic, political, or even religious ties. Although a good deal of this organization is archaeologically invisible, we can describe much of it from ethnohistorical and ethnographic sources.

## The Individual in Maya Society

The best sources of information about life among the ancient Maya are the descriptions of sixteenth-century Maya society written immediately after the Spanish Conquest. These accounts are often usefully supplemented by archaeological discoveries, as well as by ethnographic descriptions of customs surviving from the past and still practiced today. After discussing personal appearance, we shall follow the individual in Maya society through birth, childhood, puberty, marriage and the family, and death, stage by stage, before closing with consideration of the larger social units—descent groups and classes.

### Personal Appearance

The principal male garment was the loincloth, called *ex* in Yucatec Mayan. It was a band of cotton cloth, five fingers wide and long enough to be wound around the waist several times and passed between the legs. These loincloths were woven on hand looms, and the ends were often elaborately embroidered with feathers:

"They wore the *mastil* [probably a corruption of *maxtli*, the Mexican word for the same garment] between their legs, which was a large strip of woven *manta*, which, tying it on the abdomen and giving it a turn below, covered their private parts, the two long points having on them much plumage hanging before and behind." The *ex* is represented everywhere in Maya graphic arts, from the gorgeously decorated loincloths worn by the rulers and other elite men to the simple, unadorned versions of the non-elite (Fig. 10.3).

Fig. 10.3. Ancient Maya clothing: examples of loincloths, or *ex*, from Classic-period monuments.

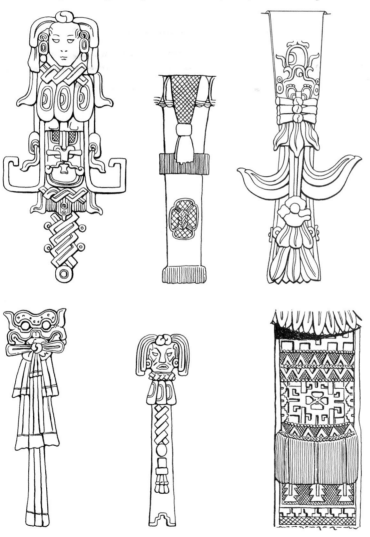

In addition to the *ex*, the men sometimes wore a large, square cotton cloth called the *pati*, knotted around the shoulders. Decorated according to the station of the wearer, this garment also served the commoners as a covering for their beds at night.

Sandals made of untanned deer hide and tied with hemp cords completed the costume of the non-elite man. On sculptured monuments of the Classic period, the sandals worn by elite men are exceedingly elaborate. One difference between these ancient sandals and those now in use is that formerly the sandals were bound to the feet by two thongs, one passing between the first and second toes, the other between the third and fourth toes, whereas today, from the highlands of Guatemala to northern Yucatan, only the first of these thongs is used (Fig. 10.4).

Except for a bare spot burned on the top of the head, the men wore their hair long. The hair was braided and wound around the head like a coronet, with a queue falling behind. Warriors painted themselves black and red, prisoners were painted in black and white stripes, and the priests were painted blue. The priests and sacrificial victim depicted in a fresco from the Temple of the Warriors at Chichen Itza are painted blue from head to foot (Fig. 11.1*f*). Many of the balls of *pom* (copal)

Fig. 10.4. Ancient Maya clothing: examples of sandals, or *xanab*: (*a–f*) from Classic-period monuments; (*g-j*) from Postclassic monuments; (*k*) ancient binding with two cords; (*l*) modern binding with one cord.

incense found in the Cenote of Sacrifice at Chichen Itza were also painted a bright turquoise blue. Blue was the color associated with sacrifice among the late Pre-classic Maya, just as it was among the Mexicans.

Paint was also used in tattooing: "Those who do the work, first painted the part which they wish with color, and afterwards they delicately cut in the paintings, and so with blood and coloring-matter the marks remained on the body. This work is done a little at a time on account of the extreme pain, and afterwards also they were quite sick with it, since the designs festered and matter formed. In spite of all this they made fun of those who were not tattooed."

There are several accounts of the principal garment worn by Maya women. Landa's account says, "The women of the coast and of the Provinces of Bacalar and of Campeche are more modest in their dress, for, besides the covering which they wore from the waist down [a kind of skirt], they covered their breasts, tying a folded *manta* [*pati*] underneath their armpits. All the others did not wear more than one garment like a long and wide sack, opened on both sides, and drawn in as far as the hips, where they fastened it together, with the same width as before." The official Spanish historian Herrera writes, "They wore a dress like a sack, long and wide, open on both sides and sewn as far as the hips." A cotton kerchief was worn over the head, "open like a short cowl, which also served to cover their breasts."

Today the principal woman's garment is known as the *huipil*, a Mexica (Nahuatl) word (Fig. 10.5). In the highlands of Guatemala the *huipil* is a blouse, worn with a wraparound skirt. The *huipil* worn in each Maya highland community preserves a design unique to that community. In Yucatan the *huipil* is a white, loose-fitting cotton dress, of the same width from top to bottom and sewn at the sides, with holes for the arms and a square opening for the head. The armholes, neck opening, and bottom hem of the garment are beautifully embroidered in cross-stitch. This garment, with its unusual embroidery, almost certainly survives from ancient times (Fig. 10.5, lower illustrations).

Underneath is worn a full, long petticoat (Maya, *pic*), which hangs below the *huipil*. This petticoat is sometimes embroidered around the hem, always in white. A Maya woman never leaves her house without her shawl (Maya, *booch*), a scarf draped around her neck or thrown over her head; this may be a survival of the cotton kerchief mentioned above. Today, the women wear slippers of European style, but formerly they no doubt used sandals for festive occasions.

Women and girls wore their hair long and took great care of it. The hair was arranged in various ways, the style for married women differing from that for the young girls. The women, like their husbands, anointed themselves with a sweet-smelling red ointment, the odor of which lasted for many days. They tattooed themselves from the waist up, except for their breasts, with designs more delicate than those tattooed on the men.

The costume of the rulers, so much in evidence on monuments and in wall paintings, was imbued with the symbols of the supernatural basis of their power.

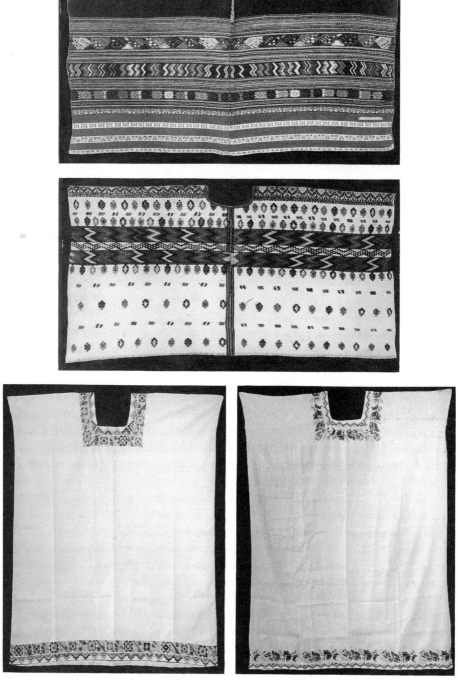

Fig. 10.5. Modern Maya huipils: (*top*) from Comalpa, Guatemala; (*center*) from San Pedro Sacatepequez, Guatemala; (*lower left*) from Tixcacal, Quintana Roo, Mexico; (*lower right*) from Mérida, Yucatan, Mexico.

Yet these articles of dress, though elaborately decorated, were basically the same as the garments of the common man—loincloth, cape, and sandals, with the addition of a headdress. The belt holding the elaborated loincloth was adorned with jade masks (often these can be seen as representations of the *ahau* glyph), from which jade plaques, or celts, were suspended. In earlier versions especially, a chain, suspending a small supernatural image, dangled behind. A god mask was often worn as a pectoral (on the chest), along with necklaces of jade beads. The simple square cotton *pati* of the common man became a magnificent cape of embroidered cotton stuff, jaguar skin, or even brilliantly colored feathers. The beautiful, iridescent tail feathers of the quetzal were reserved for the elite.

It is in the headdresses, however, where we see the most magnificent displays. The framework was probably of wicker or wood, carved to represent the head of a jaguar, a serpent, a bird, or, most typically, a composite animal representing an important supernatural being. These frames were covered with jaguar skin, feather mosaics, and carved jades, and were surmounted by lofty panaches of plumes. Always the most striking part of the costume, the panache indicated the rank and social class of the wearer. Specialized headdresses, including the "balloon headdress" associated with warfare, can also be seen. In early representations, the ruler wears a headband with a trilobed frontal element, sometimes personified by three heads of the so-called "jester god."

Collars, necklaces, wristlets, anklets, and knee bands served as costume accessories. These were made of feathers, jade beads, shells, jaguar teeth and claws, crocodile teeth, or, in later times, gold or copper. Other kinds of jewelry were nose ornaments, earrings, and lip plugs of jade, stone, obsidian, or less valuable materials. Ornaments of the lower classes were confined largely to simple nose plugs, lip plugs, and earrings of bone, wood, shell, or stone.

## Birth and Early Childhood

In ancient times the life cycle and behavior of each individual were set by custom and governed by religious beliefs, much as they are today among traditional Maya families. The ritual obligations of each individual were determined by the 260-day sacred almanac (Chapter 12). Where in this almanac a person's date of birth fell controlled the person's temperament and destiny, because that determined which gods were well disposed to the person and which were hostile. Each of the 260 days was accorded a name, and among many highland Maya peoples, such as the Cakchiquel, all given names were made the same as the day of birth. This practice, if ever present among the Yucatec Maya, had disappeared in the northern area by the time of the Spanish Conquest. There the young child was carried to a priest, who performed a divining ceremony and therein determined the child's given name. Each Yucatec Maya individual had in fact three or four different names: (1) *paal kaba*, the given name; (2) the father's family name; (3) *naal kaba*, the father's and mother's family names combined; and (4) *coco kaba*, the nickname.

The Maya of today love their children deeply and usually treat them with a great deal of indulgence. The same was undoubtedly true in ancient times. Children were greatly desired, and women even "asked them of the idols with gifts and prayers." In order to induce pregnancy, a woman placed under her bed an image of Ix Chel, goddess of childbirth.

Flattened foreheads, considered a mark of beauty among the ancient Maya, were achieved by binding the heads of babies between a pair of flat boards, one at the back of the head, the other against the forehead. These boards were left in place for several days, after which the head remained flattened for life. Maya representations of the human head in profile show that this practice must have been almost universal among the elite class.

Another mark of distinction was crossed eyes, which mothers tried to bring about by hanging little balls of resin to the hairs falling between their children's eyes. Persistent focusing on these pellets tended to cross their eyes. The ears, lips, and septum of the nose were pierced to hold ornaments.

The *hetzmek*, marking the first time a baby is carried astride the hip, is a ceremony performed among the modern Maya of Yucatan that may have survived from ancient times. This is done at three months for girls, and at four months for boys. The two differ, it is said, because the Maya hearth, symbolic of woman's activities, has three stones; and the maize field, symbolic of man's activities, has four corners. Usually two godparents, a husband and wife, participate in this ceremony. Nine objects symbolic of the child's later life are placed on a table. The father hands the baby to the godfather, who sets the child astride his left hip and makes nine circuits of the table, each time selecting one of the nine objects and putting it into the child's hand, reciting instructions on the object's use. He then turns the child over to the godmother, who repeats the procedure and returns the child to the godfather. While handing the child back to the father, the godfather says, "We have made the *hetzmek* for your child." The parents then kneel before the godparents in a sign of gratitude, and an assistant distributes food, rum, boiled fowl, and tortillas to those present.

Until the age of three or four, children were brought up almost exclusively by their mothers. When a boy was about four or five, a small white bead was fastened to the hair on the top of his head, and his father began the training of his son. When a girl reached the same age, a string was tied around her waist, and a red shell, a symbol of virginity, was hung from the string. To remove either of these before the puberty ceremony was thought to be highly improper.

## Puberty

Once a year, those boys and girls in the community deemed eligible for marriage would be assembled for a puberty ceremony. According to Bishop Landa, the day for the ceremony was carefully selected to ensure that it would not be an unlucky day. An elder man of the town was chosen by the families as sponsor to assist the priest during the ceremony and to furnish the feast. Four honorable old men were selected as *chacs*, to assist the priest and sponsor in conducting the ceremony. On the appointed day, all assembled at the courtyard of the sponsor's house, which had been newly swept and strewn with fresh leaves. Then the priest purified the dwelling and conducted a ceremony to expel evil spirits.

When the spirits had been driven from the premises, the court was swept out again, fresh leaves were scattered about, and mats were spread on the floor. The priest, dressed in a handsome jacket and miter-like headdress of colored feathers, sprinkled sacred water from rattlesnake tails hanging from a finely worked short stick. The *chacs* then approached the children and placed pieces of white cloth on their heads. The older children were asked if they had committed "any sin or obscene act," as Landa put it. If they had, they were separated from the others (Landa does not say whether they were allowed to continue in the rite). The priest next ordered everyone to be seated and to maintain absolute silence, and after pronouncing a prayer for the children, he sat down. The sponsor of the ceremony, using a bone given him by the priest, tapped each child nine times on the forehead, moistening the forehead, the face, and the spaces between the fingers and toes with water.

With the anointing completed, the priest removed the white cloths from the children's heads. The children then gave the *chacs* feathers and cacao beans that they had brought as gifts. The priest next cut the white beads from the boys' heads. The attendants carried pipes, which they smoked from time to time, giving each child a puff of smoke. Gifts of food, brought by the mothers, were distributed to the children, and a wine offering was made to the gods; this offering had to be drunk at one draught by a specially appointed official.

The girls were then dismissed, each mother removing from her daughter the red shell she had worn as a symbol of purity. With this, the girls were considered of marriageable age. The young men were dismissed next. When they had left, their parents distributed pieces of cotton cloth among the spectators and officials as gifts. The ceremony, called "the descent of the gods," closed with feasting and heavy drinking.

As they grew older, young unmarried men of the community began to live in a house set apart for them. They gathered there for their diversions and usually slept there until marriage. They painted themselves black until they were married, but were not supposed to tattoo themselves before that time. From an early age boys helped their fathers work the family maize field. Wrote Landa, "In all other things they always accompanied their fathers, and thus they became as great idolators as they, and served them very well in their labors."

After the puberty ceremony, the young women, by way of preparation for marriage, were taught to be modest: whenever they met a man they turned their backs to him, stepping aside to allow him to pass; when giving a man a drink of water, they lowered their eyes. Mothers taught their daughters how to make tortillas, an occupation that consumed a great part of every woman's time. The women were the housekeepers, cooks, weavers, and spinners. They raised fowl and went to the market to buy and sell the articles they produced. When need arose, they carried burdens alongside their menfolk and assisted them in sowing and cultivating.

## Life and Death

When ill, a person summoned a religious specialist, or shaman. This curer of ills used a combination of prayers, ceremonies, and administration of herbs to cure his patients. Many medicinal herbs and plants are to be found in the Maya area, and an extensive pharmacopoeia was at the disposal of these shamans. Several seventeenth-century Maya manuscripts, listing many ills and their corresponding cures, have come down to us, and some remedies contain chemicals that produce the desired effects. Others smack of medieval European superstition mixed with Maya magic, as in this remedy for toothache: "You take the bill of a woodpecker and bleed the gums a little with it; if a man, thirteen times; if a woman, nine times. [The gum] shall be slightly pierced by the bill of the woodpecker. Thus also a piece of a tree struck by lightning is to be grated with a fish-skin and wrapped in cotton-wool. Then you apply it to the tooth. He will recover by this means." This sort of bleeding of the gums might alleviate some kinds of toothache, but the thirteen times for a man and the nine times for a woman are surely ritualistic survivals from the ancient Maya, the former corresponding to the thirteen levels of the Upper World and the latter to the nine levels of the Lower World.

By contrast, some of the native plants, for example the *kanlol* (*Tecoma stans*), which grows in northern Yucatan, undoubtedly possess medicinal properties. A dose of an extract made from this plant, two to ten drops taken hourly, acts as a strong diuretic and probably a mild stimulant as well.

We learn from Landa that, "There were also surgeons, or better said, sorcerers, who cured with herbs and many superstitious rites. . . . The sorcerers and physicians performed their cures by bleedings of the parts which gave pain to the sick man . . . [the Maya] believed that death, sickness and afflictions came to them for their wrongdoing and their sin; they had a custom of confessing themselves, when they were already sick."

Landa states also that the Maya had great fear of death, and when it took friends or kin, their grief was profound and enduring:

This people had a great and excessive fear of death and they showed this in that all the services, which they made to their gods, were for no other end, nor for any other purpose than that they [the gods] should give them health, life and sustenance. But when, in time, they came to die, it was indeed a thing to see the sorrow and the cries which they made for their dead, and the great grief it caused them. During the day they wept for them in silence; and at night with loud and very sad cries, so that it was pitiful to hear them. And they passed many days in deep sorrow. They made abstinences and fasts for the dead, especially the husband or wife; and they said that the devil had taken him away since they thought that all evils came to them from him [the devil], and especially death.

The body was wrapped in a shroud, and the mouth filled with ground maize and one or more jadeite beads, "which they use for money, so that they should not be without something to eat in the other life." In many archaeologically recovered burials, jade beads still lie between the jaws of the skull. The common people were buried under the floors or behind their houses; and the houses were usually then abandoned. Into the grave were placed idols of clay, wood, or stone, and objects indicating the profession or trade of the deceased. These customs, too, are reflected in the archaeological record.

As we have seen, the burials of the ruling classes were more elaborate. Landa says that the bodies of the nobles and other persons of high esteem were burned, their ashes placed in great urns, and temples built above them. The construction of funerary shrines over burials and tombs has been amply confirmed by archaeological excavation (Fig. 4.13). Burials range from those under small shrines associated with residential groups (often on the east side) to the great tombs of powerful rulers, such as Pacal's final resting place at Palenque (Figs. 5.31 and 5.32). Cremation must have been instituted late, however, for the remains of elite individuals uncovered in excavations of Classic-period structures were not burned (Fig. 10.6).

Graves of important persons (again, not cremated) have also been found in small, stone-lined burial vaults, with corbel-arched roofs, that were built under plaza floor levels at Chichen Itza, Palenque, Uaxactun, and Copan. Most of these pyramid and plaza subfloor burials were accompanied by elaborate mortuary furniture, exquisitely painted pottery and vessels, carved jadeite beads and pendants, and ornately chipped objects of flint and obsidian.

Landa described another late burial custom among the elite of northern Yucatan. A hollow wooden or pottery statue was made to look like the dead man. Ashes from a part of the cremated body were placed in a hollow at the back of the statue's head; the rest of the ashes were buried. These statues and crematory urns were venerated among the family idols.

The Cocom, the ruling lineage of Mayapan, had their own burial custom. According to Landa, the bodies of dead lords were boiled until the fleshy parts could be completely removed from the bones. The back half of the skull was then sawed off, leaving the front half intact. A new face was built up with resin and kept in the household shrines with the family idols. These heads were held in great veneration, and so that the lords would lack nothing in their afterlife, offerings of food were made to them on feast days.

There is good support for Landa's account. During a dredging of the Cenote of Sacrifice at Chichen Itza a skull with its crown cut away was recovered. The eye sockets were filled with wooden plugs, and on the front were the remains of painted plaster. Excavation in the Department of El Quiche, Guatemala, uncovered the front part of a human skull covered with a thick coat of lime plaster modeled to represent a human face.

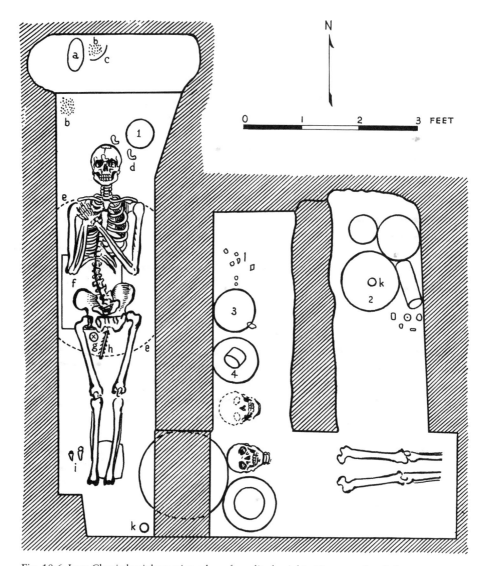

Fig. 10.6. Late Classic burial practice: plan of an elite burial in Uaxactun Str. A-1.

## Marriage and the Family

Among the contemporary Maya the life of every individual is intimately intertwined with his or her immediate family and kin group, the community, and the supernatural. The life cycle—birth, acquisition of names, puberty, marriage, and death—are all marked by ritual, as they were in Bishop Landa's day. And through marriage, each individual establishes ties with another family group.

Bishop Landa says that formerly the Maya married when they were 20 years old, but that in his time they married when they were 12 to 14. In the eighteenth and early nineteenth centuries, young men in Yucatan married at about 17 or 18, and young women at about 14 or 15. Today in the villages of the northern reaches of the Peninsula the average age of men at marriage is 21, and that of women is nearly 17.

The fathers took great care to find suitable wives for their sons, preferably young women of the same social class and of the same village. Certain relationship taboos operated: it was considered incestuous to marry a girl who had the same surname (patronym), or for a widower to marry his stepmother, the sister of his deceased wife, the widow of his brother, or his maternal aunt, though first-cousin marriages were not forbidden.

The custom of employing a professional matchmaker (*ah atanzah*) has survived in rural districts in northern Yucatan. The matchmaker having been selected, the ceremony would then be discussed and the amount of the dowry agreed upon. This usually consisted of dresses and other articles, for which the young man's father paid. At the same time his mother made ready some clothing for her son and pro-spective daughter-in-law. Today, in northern Yucatan, the groom or his family de-frays all expenses of the wedding, even the bride's trousseau.

When the day of the ceremony arrived, the relatives and guests assembled at the house of the bride's father. As soon as the priest entered the house, the fathers of the couple presented the young people to him. The priest then made a speech setting forth the details of the marriage agreement. That completed, he perfumed the house and blessed the bridal pair, and the company sat down to the feast that concluded the ceremony.

In the sixteenth century, marriages were often arranged between families while the boy and girl were still very young; the arrangement was then manifested when they came of age. Monogamy was, and remains, the rule. But polygyny was per-mitted, and was probably much more widespread among the Classic elite than among the non-elite; today, in traditional Maya communities, it is often determined by the wealth of the individual.

Cross-cousin marriages were allowed, and in fact have been proposed as an ancestral form of preferential marriage.

Divorce, consisting of little more than a simple repudiation, was easy, and oc-curred often, as an early Spanish witness indicates: "They left her for trifling rea-sons, and married another, and there were men who married ten and twelve times; and the women had the same liberty to leave their husbands and take another, but the first time they got married it was by a priest." Custom decreed that widowers and widows should remain single for at least a year after the death of their previous mates. They could then remarry, without ceremony; the man simply went to the house of the woman of his choice, and to indicate her acceptance, she simply gave him something to eat.

The son-in-law lived and worked in the house of his wife's parents (uxorilocal residence) for six or seven years. His mother-in-law saw to it that her daughter gave the young husband food and drink as a token of the parental recognition of the marriage, but if the young man failed to work, he could be put out of the house. The uxorilocal period was followed by patrilocal residence, the son now establishing a new nuclear household adjacent to that of his father. Patrilocal residence tends to form generationally extended family residential groups, which is probably what is reflected in the patio clusters of housemounds at lowland sites. In fact, a study of settlement at Seibal offers some cautious support for a Classic pattern of patrilocal residence.

## Descent Groups

*Descent*, the transmission of social-group membership from generation to generation, is distinguished from related systems of *inheritance* (the "descent" of property) and of *succession* (the "descent" of power, usually effected through political and religious offices). Historical and ethnohistorical sources agree that patrilineal (father and children) descent was a basic organizational principle among the Classic Maya. Ethnohistorically, the primary source has always been Landa's description of the Yucatec Maya. A long line of investigators has concluded that Landa's account is most consistent with a system of exogamous, patrilineal clans or lineages. In this sort of social group, membership is based on the sharing of a common surname, and while they did not live in a distinct area, these kin groups seem to have been identified both with patron deities and with various social obligations. The determination of patrilineal organization is supported by analysis of Maya kinship terminology, other Conquest-period accounts (such as Las Casas's description of the Verapaz region of Guatemala), and ethnographic data from the Lacandon and other Maya groups. The inheritance of wealth seems also to have been patrilineal.

There is, of course, good support at many lowland Maya sites for the claim that patrilineal descent groups predominated within specific ruling families during the Late Classic. Deciphered texts in these cases document the succession of rulers through time, often specified as from father to son, forming what can only be termed ruling lineages or dynasties. At Palenque, texts relate a sequence of rulers that passed through three patrilineages over time. At Copan, Altar Q offers a dramatic iconographic summary of that site's dynasty; the inscriptions and depictions on the altar include the portraits and name glyphs of sixteen male rulers spanning some 400 years, the sequence being completed by the sixteenth ruler, Yax Pac, who is shown seated, facing the dynastic founder, Yax Kuk Mo', from whom he is receiving his emblems of office (see Fig. 5.47).

Evidence for regional variation in the pattern of dynastic rule and succession is abundant in the Classic-period inscriptions. At some sites, for example Palenque, accounts stress succession of rule through both the male line and the female line, whereas at other sites, for example Tikal and Copan, the male line is emphasized. At Piedras Negras, Coba, Yaxchilan, Bonampak, and Palenque there are prominent portraits of elite women in association with rulership, and at Calakmul and El Perú there are paired male/female portraits. At still other sites, including Tikal, Quirigua, and Copan, depictions of women are rare or nonexistent. Though there is no evidence that women ever ruled at these three sites, there are accounts of women rulers at Palenque and at several of the smaller Usumacinta sites. This pattern of variation within the uppermost echelons of elite society is consistent with other evidence for diversity in Classic Maya social organization.

In determining the lines of succession for Maya rulers, flexibility may have had advantages, for the availability of options for succession often allows for a more successful transmission of power and may help avoid potentially disastrous power struggles. Still, there is no compelling evidence for anything other than patrilineal descent among the ruling houses of the Classic Maya lowlands, or among the great mass of non-elites.

Of course, in working with the deciphered accounts of ruling genealogies, archaeologists seek independent evidence to separate fact from fiction, as they do with all such examples of historical texts. Where there are citations of founders and other early members of ruling dynasties *in much later inscriptions* there is often reason to suspect retrospective "creative history" on the part of Late Classic rulers. But there are several cases—Tikal, Quirigua, and Copan, for example—where a little digging has produced hard evidence to support and/or refine these later claims. At Copan, excavations in Str. 26 and the adjacent Acropolis have produced architectural, sculptural, and textual evidence contemporary with the reign of Yax Kuk Mo', including the earliest dated stela known at the site, apparently dedicated to the illustrious founder Yax Kuk Mo' by his son and successor.

But even though we have documented specific cases by combining historical and archaeological evidence, we must bear in mind that within each polity the ruling lineage represented only one elite family among many. And beyond the elite level, among the non-elite, the archaeological evidence for the existence of particular forms of descent groups is indirect at best. In the later ethnohistoric record (and among some contemporary Maya groups) the case for patrilineal descent groups is highly suggestive, but when working solely from the archaeological record the case is difficult to document.

## Social Stratification

On the strength of an overwhelming assemblage of evidence from archaeological, art-historical, epigraphic, and ethnohistoric sources, modern scholars are in near-universal agreement that Classic Maya society was stratified into two basic classes—termed here the elite and the non-elite. And the great wealth of data from related Mesoamerican societies provides a useful supplement to the Maya sources.

Archaeologists usually define stratification on the basis of differential access to basic resources, and the differences in access are usually determined by social factors of inheritance, marriage, and rank. Most agree that the archaeological data reflect these broad distinctions between Maya elite and non-elite. Burial data may show a shift in the pattern of inheritance from achieved (earned) status during the Early Classic to ascribed (inherited) status during the Late Classic, but apart from a few examples of this sort, it is often difficult to discern actual patterns of inheritance, marriage, and rank in the archaeological record.

The usual indicator of these distinctions is wealth. But definitions of wealth and distinctions of wealth in preindustrial societies have been another issue for debate. Obviously, we cannot use our own concepts of wealth to define those recognized by the ancient Maya. And in fact the gradations within archaeological remains suggest that the distinction between elite and non-elite is more a continuum than a well-defined division, a finding that probably reflects internal ranking gradations within the elite class. In their efforts to define an elite/non-elite distinction, archaeologists most commonly utilize data from burials and architecture. But even here the situation is seldom clear-cut. A study of lowland Maya residential architecture at Seibal, for example, contradicts the traditional assumption that size of dwelling necessarily reflects wealth or status. On the whole, the Seibal data show that residences exhibit no clear dichotomy, except between those built with stone walls and those built without stone walls.

Concerning the question whether elites and non-elites were similarly organized, two views have been advanced. Some contend that both classes were internally ranked, while others see an elite ordered by rank and a non-elite lacking such internal social distinctions. The epigraphic evidence and Conquest-period ethnohistoric accounts in both Yucatan and the Maya highlands indicate that the Late Classic Maya elite were ranked, a finding corroborated by the gradations in the architectural and burial data. But the most direct support for ranking comes from a series of official titles recently deciphered from Classic texts. Although individual rulers usually monopolized the inventory of these titles, aggregating them all to themselves, by the Late Classic a case can be made for at least three ranks within the ruling hierarchy, as we shall see.

Thus we have only begun to ferret out the true nature of the variability between and within the two basic classes of ancient Maya society, and we have altogether too little knowledge about the lowest strata of Maya society. New research is needed to define social variability, and to secure a deeper understanding of the non-elite class.

# RECONSTRUCTING THE POLITICAL LANDSCAPE

We have seen how social ties formed a network that bound Maya society together, from the individual and the immediate family to the community and the class system. But there were other levels of organization that transcended kinship ties, including economic and religious systems that attracted people from all levels of society to the centers to participate in ceremonies and to exchange goods and services. And in time, the typical center took on increasingly political functions as it became the headquarters for a centralized administrative organization, structured as a hierarchy of hereditary offices such as those held by lineage heads. Given the existence of governing councils composed of such officials in the Postclassic, it seems likely that this form of political authority (the *multepal*, which we shall discuss) was an ancient institution, with roots as far back as the Preclassic. It is also possible that such ruling councils continued to wield power in smaller communities lacking a single supreme leader. And the emerging authority of the *k'ul ahau* (supreme or sacred ruler) probably entailed the persistence of some form of elite council that advised or assisted the ruler in his duties. Such a structure can be seen as early as the Late Preclassic, with the emergence of the position of *ahau*, or ruler. During the Classic, heads of state took on the title of *k'ul ahau*. Classic rulers also accumulated titles honoring their achievements in battle ("captor of . . ."), their age ("four-katun lord"), and their identification with supernatural powers ("he of the sun," or "sun-faced one"). At the same time, the expansion of the elite class, and the increase in the number of political offices it controlled, seems to have led to a broadening of the use of the *ahau* title, until it came to refer to any important elite officeholder or lineage head. The hierarchy of power continued to expand with the use of new subordinate titles, such as *cahal* (also translated as *sahal*) or "subordinate ruler."

As we have seen, these trends, together with the other forces at work late in the Classic period, led to the downfall of the practice of vesting political power in the hands of single supreme rulers, and in turn led to the growth of alternative forms of government, including a far greater role for the multepal system associated with the *popol na* or council house. A precursor of this trend has been reconstructed from the archaeological, epigraphic, and iconographic evidence at Copan.

These are examples of the clues to reconstructing Maya political systems, and their growth over time, that emerge from our ability to read many of the Classic-period inscriptions. But although obviously crucial to such an understanding, historical sources can provide only a part of the picture. Other information about ancient Maya political organization comes from archaeology, especially in studies of the location, size, and patterning of the major sites that were the centers of political power. In the remainder of this chapter, after considering the evidence gleaned from archaeological research, we will turn to the ethnohistoric record to examine Maya political organization, both in Yucatan and in the Maya highlands, on the eve of the Spanish Conquest.

## Location and Power

In general, the founding location and prosperity of Maya sites were undoubtedly determined, as they are for all human settlements, by access to essential resources such as water and food. Other factors, such as strategic positions along trade routes, or locations that could be defended in times of conflict, were clearly important as well in some cases. A number of Maya sites indeed seem to have been located to take advantage of such special circumstances, and at least some of these apparently enjoyed considerable prosperity as a result. In the southern lowlands, many important centers—Yaxchilan, Piedras Negras, and Quirigua, to name just three—are situated along major rivers that served as important routes of communication and trade, besides providing productive alluvial soils for agriculture. In the central lowlands several sites—El Mirador, Tikal, and Uaxactun, for example—are on high ground at or near the divide between major drainage basins, which afforded them command of the portages for canoe transport across the Peten. Most centers in this region are also associated with *bajos*, the shallow lakes or swamps that provided water and probably yielded rich harvests when modified as raised fields (Chapter 8). The needs of seacoast trade seem to have determined the location of many other Maya sites, from the Preclassic onward; for example, along the Caribbean littoral of the east coast of the Yucatan Peninsula, we find sites such as Cerros (Preclassic), Lamanai (Preclassic through Postclassic), and Tulum (Late Postclassic).

Single resources in widespread demand seem to have been major factors in the location and prosperity of several centers. Examples are Dzibilchaltun, in northern Yucatan (access to coastal salt); Colha, in Belize (good-quality flint); Salinas de los Nueve Cerros, in the southern lowlands (salt); Guaytan, in the middle Motagua Valley (jadeite); and Kaminaljuyu, in the southern highlands (obsidian).

These environmental and economic factors have long dominated the discussion of site location. But in recent years it has become increasingly apparent that ideological considerations were important to both the location and the planning of ancient Maya settlements (see Chapter 11). Some Maya cities, such as Dos Pilas, are situated above extensive caverns, which were seen as important links to the underworld. Important temples and ceremonial groups were often placed on high promontories—sometimes, as with Group A at Quirigua, which is located on a hill north of the later main group, these can be identified as the founding locus for an entire center. Intrasite planning was dependent on certain principles, such as the threefold layering of the universe, and the fourfold cardinal directions. Archaeologists Wendy Ashmore and Joyce Marcus and art historians Clemency Coggins and Mary Miller have been in the forefront of showing how Maya cosmological principles help explain the way Maya sites were organized and how they grew through time. Thanks to their efforts, we can see the ideological dimension as a complement to environmental and economic factors in shaping site layout and planning.

## Size and Power

Maya centers varied considerably in size, configuration, and architectural style. The smallest may cover less than a square kilometer, whereas others were far larger: Tikal, the largest known Maya site, extended over an area of some 123 km². A center's size, together with the elaborateness of its buildings, the quantity of its monuments and hieroglyphic inscriptions, and its other characteristics, undoubtedly reflected its relative political and economic power. Scholars have long recognized variations in configuration and architectural style from one site to another, and have often used the differences between them to divide the Maya area into regions—though whether such divisions accord with ancient social and political geography is often debatable.

The dramatic differences in site size and complexity support the conclusion that some Maya centers exerted political dominance over others (see Chapters 4–6). Many larger centers certainly employed economic, social, and political alliances to exert control over smaller centers. The evidence also suggests that dominant centers like Tikal sponsored the founding of colonial, or satellite, centers in outlying regions. Military raids or even open warfare certainly seem to have been used by some polities to dominate others. The distances between the larger Maya sites average 20–30 km, whereas a whole range of smaller centers is found at lesser intervals. Yet ranking sites according to their size and complexity has proved difficult, even when both subjective and objective criteria are applied, and bears no assurance that the rankings accurately assess political power. Epigraphic evidence, however, when combined with criteria of size and location, seems to offer important clues for the reconstruction of ancient intersite political relationships; this kind of evidence indicates for example that a conflict between the small center of Quirigua and the much larger center of Copan resulted in Copan's defeat and the breakaway of Quirigua as an independent polity.

The distribution of Maya sacbe (causeway) systems has also been used to infer the pattern and extent of political realms in the past. The earliest known example is found in the Late Preclassic, in the radiating causeway system that may define the El Mirador polity (Chapter 3). A similar system has recently been mapped at the Classic center of Caracol (Chapter 5). Most applications of this sort of inference have been made in Yucatan, where the remains of sacbeob are relatively easy to spot and trace. At Coba, for example, an extensive network of roadways connects the site core with a series of outlying sites, clearly reflecting its ancient centralized authority.

## Number and Size of Lowland Polities

The reconstruction of ancient Maya political realms and relationships has been approached from several directions. One technique for inferring the extent of territory for a given center is the use of maps to construct Thiessen polygons, in which boundaries around neighboring sites are drawn through the midpoints between them (Fig. 10.7). But this approach assumes that each center was politically independent, and thus does not accommodate territorial variance owing to differences in power held by neighboring centers.

A more promising technique is based on the distribution of emblem glyphs in the inscriptions of the centers. Emblem glyphs appear to represent the seats of sovereign political authority, and each center's glyph was distinctive (see Chapter 13). A study by Peter Mathews, based on the use of emblem glyphs as indicators of sovereignty, shows the growth in the number of independent polities through the Classic period, and finds that the greatest number was reached late in the eighth century (Fig. 10.8). Mathews used Thiessen polygons to define the territories of each of these polities, but as noted above, this technique fails to discriminate between different degrees of power and territorial control. But the use of emblem glyphs does discriminate between centers claiming sovereignty and those that do not, as noted originally by Joyce Marcus. In other words, evidence for the use of an emblem glyph can be taken as at least a *claim* for a polity's sovereignty, even if we cannot be certain about the degree of independence that polity was able to maintain. Mathews's study results in a reconstructed political landscape populated by numerous small-scale polities (a maximum of about 60) in the Late Classic Maya lowlands (in a pattern similar to the city-state model postulated a number of years ago by J. Eric Thompson).

At the other end of the spectrum is a method of ranking lowland Maya sites on architectural criteria (for example by number of courtyard groups). This proposal

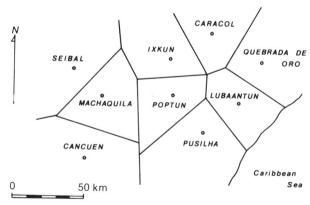

Fig. 10.7. Thiessen polygons drawn around a series of sites in the southern lowlands of Belize to define, arbitrarily, approximate boundaries between centers.

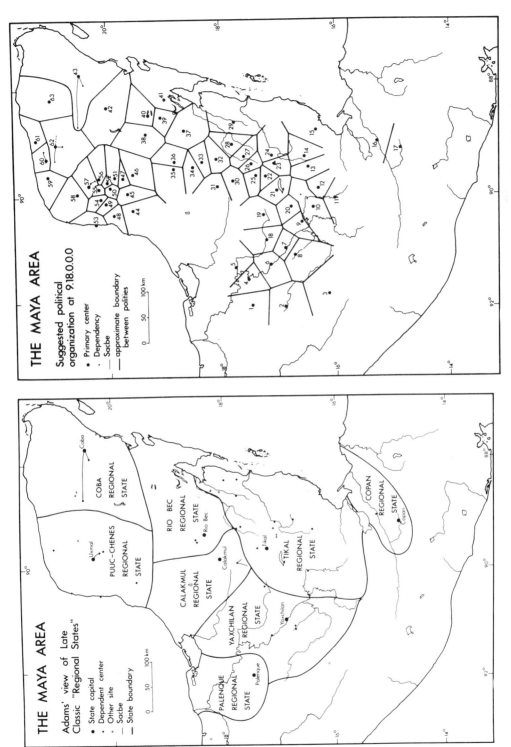

Fig. 10.8. Two interpretations of Late Classic Maya polities: (*left*) regional states; (*right*) small-scale states defined by emblem glyphs (at A.D. 790). The first implies a few large polities in the lowlands; the second, many smaller polities.

TABLE 10.6
Example of a Lowland-Site Hierarchy Based on Number of
Architectural Plaza Units (Tikal Region)[a]

| Site | Number of plaza units | Site | Number of plaza units | Site | Number of plaza units |
|---|---|---|---|---|---|
| Tikal | 85 | Ucanal | 11 | Hatzcab Ceel | 5 |
| Naranjo | 42+ | Tayasal | 10 | Holmul | 5 |
| Uaxactun | 23 | Chochkitam | 8 | Ixlu | 5 |
| Kinal | 20 | Ikkun | 8 | Cahal Pichik | 4 |
| Yaxha | 20 | Xultun | 7 | Itsimte | 4 |
| Caracol | 17 | Xunantunich | 5 | Río Azul | 4 |
| La Honradez | 16 | Chunhuitz | 5 | Motul de San José | 3 |
| Nakum | 16 | San Clemente | 5 | Uolantun | 1 |

[a] After Adams and Jones (1981).

has led to an ordering of sites (Table 10.6) that suggests political and economic hierarchies within much larger "regional states." Using this technique leads to the definition of far fewer polities, perhaps no more than six to eight, within the Late Classic lowland landscape, each polity being far greater in extent than those defined by emblem-glyph distributions (Fig. 10.8).

The disadvantages of the size-hierarchy method are obvious, on several grounds. Size does not always correlate with the relative regional power of political capitals of preindustrial (or even modern) states; Winchester, the capital of the largest Saxon kingdom at the time of the Norman conquest of England, was far smaller than London. The size-hierarchy method is also insufficiently sensitive to changes in the political landscape over time, because most of the architectural units being compared cannot be accurately dated. Because the number and distribution of emblem glyphs can usually be dated by inscriptions, this approach does reveal patterns of change in the number and distribution of polities over time, but at the same time it does not provide for differences in *degree* of sovereignty and power. It also assumes that every claim of independence was valid, and we know from documented historical cases that claims of sovereignty do not always correspond to reality.

Sovereignty is of course relative, and it seems reasonable to expect that the Classic lowland political landscape resembled that revealed by studies of emblem-glyph distributions. But the picture cannot have been that simple. Like the landscape of historically documented Conquest-period Yucatan (see below), the Classic lowlands were undoubtedly populated by a diverse array of polities. Some were obviously larger and more powerful than others, and we would expect to find that they controlled larger territories and exercised at least a degree of dominance over their smaller neighbors. For example, in the Early Classic Tikal seems to have exerted at least some authority over Río Azul. At the same time those smaller centers that displayed their own emblem glyphs, like Río Azul, probably maintained at least a degree of sovereignty. We also know that some formerly subordinate sites, like Quirigua, broke away and asserted their own independence, about the same time they displayed their own emblem glyph for the first time. Of course in other cases, especially powerful polities expanded their realms through conquest: Early Classic Tikal apparently annexed Uaxactun (Chapter 4), and the Petexbatun state pursued an aggressive policy of territorial expansion during the Late Classic (Chapter 5).

These examples point to another crucial dimension of the lowland political landscape, namely that it was constantly changing. In Chapters 3–6 we traced the individual fortunes of some of the more prominent lowland polities, each of which enjoyed one or more cycles of growth and prosperity followed by decline and stagnation. As Joyce Marcus has pointed out, these shifting fortunes can be seen, collectively, as fluctuations between times of political consolidation (fewer and larger polities) and times of political fragmentation (more and smaller polities). Prosperity for the great centers tended to mean decline for the lesser centers, and vice versa.

At certain times, however, these cycles were more or less synchronized, so that we see periods marked by peaks of prosperity over widespread areas, such as those of the Late Preclassic and Late Classic in the central and southern lowlands. These peaks were followed by widespread declines over the same area in the Early and Terminal Classic (the first of these episodic declines was followed by recovery; the second was not). But as the Terminal Classic polities to the south fell into final decline, many cities in the northern lowlands experienced their greatest episode of growth and prosperity. That episode led to a period of political consolidation dominated by the best-documented regional state, that of the Putun Maya, with their capital at Chichen Itza. Following the Postclassic demise of this polity, a successor state emerged with the founding of a new capital at Mayapan. And when Mayapan, in turn, fell, Yucatan entered a period of political fragmentation and instability—right on the eve of the Spanish Conquest. In the highlands, other expansionist states were beginning to emerge when these developments, too, were cut short by the Conquest.

## Evidence from Ethnohistoric Studies

The ethnohistoric approach to reconstructing ancient Maya political organization draws on the rich resource of documents describing Maya society at the time of the Conquest, and on additional information from more recent studies of ongoing traditional Maya communities. Both sources have inherent limitations. First and most obvious, the accounts of the sixteenth century must be projected back in time for at least seven to eight hundred years if they are to be used to reconstruct Classic-period Maya society. Obviously, such an enterprise must be undertaken with caution, for there is good reason to believe that major organizational changes would have occurred across eight centuries. By attempting to isolate correspondences between the ethnohistorical accounts and the archaeological data, we can more accurately extend our projections into the past. A second weakness of the ethnohistoric approach derives from the biases of the accounts themselves. Some accounts were written by Maya individuals; others, by Spanish soldiers, priests, and administrators. Each writer would have had his own axe to grind, and distortions surely resulted. Many of the documents have been recopied and translated several times, which would itself have resulted in numerous errors, omissions, and additions after the fact. Fortunately, cross-checking within the ethnohistorical record, and detailed comparison with the archaeological evidence, can often minimize these difficulties.

The ethnohistoric approach is most effective in regions that are well documented and thoroughly researched. There are two. The first is the Postclassic Maya area of northern Yucatan, known best from the excellent accounts written by Bishop Diego de Landa in the sixteenth century and from a series of native chronicles known as the *Books of Chilam Balam*. The second is the Postclassic Quiche Maya area of the central Guatemalan highlands, well-known from the most remarkable of all native Maya books, the *Popol Vuh*, and other highland Maya chronicles. We shall examine both. It should be noted, however, that by Postclassic times the Maya of both areas had come to be heavily influenced by other Mesoamerican cultures, and in some cases it is difficult to separate those aspects of society that were Maya in origin from those that were imported from non-Maya areas of Mexico or other external realms.

## The Postclassic Yucatan Maya

We have argued that ancient Maya society was characteristically composed of two classes, the elite and the non-elite. But according to Bishop Landa, Yucatecan society was divided into more than two categories—the *almehenob* (nobles), *ah-kinob* (priests), *ah chembal uinicob* (commoners), and *p'entacob* (slaves).

Studies by ethnohistorian Ralph Roys show that at the time of the Conquest there were three basic forms of political organization in Yucatan. These were the loose confederation of allied cities ruled by related lineages; the *multepal*, or rule by a council of elite lineage leaders; and rule by a single individual. The third of these was the most common—in at least nine of the eighteen Yucatecan polities, rule was by a single leader, or *halach uinic* ("true man")—although there were important variations in political organization from one of these petty states to another. The *halach uinic* system merits examination in some detail, for it seems to have descended from the most common Classic-period political system.

The position of ruler in this system was hereditary. Landa, describing Late Postclassic conditions, states that the lords were succeeded by their oldest sons:

If the lord died, although his oldest son succeeded him, the other children were always very much respected and assisted and regarded as lords themselves; . . . if, when the lord died, there were no sons [old enough] to reign, and he [the deceased lord] had brothers, the oldest of the brothers, or the best qualified, reigned, and they taught the heir their customs and feasts against the time he should become a man; and these brothers [paternal uncles of the heir], although the heir was [ready] to reign, commanded all their lives; and if he [the deceased lord] had no brothers, the priests and principal people elected a man proper for the position.

The *halach uinic* was also called *ahau*, a word the sixteenth-century Maya manuscript-dictionaries define as "king, emperor, monarch, prince, or great lord." This was the title used by the Maya of the colonial period in referring to the King of Spain. As we have seen, *ahau* (or its equivalent *k'ul ahau*) was probably the title held previously by the rulers of the great Classic centers of the Maya lowlands. The powers enjoyed by the *halach uinic* were broad. He probably formulated foreign and domestic policies with the aid of a council of the leading chiefs, priests, and town councillors (*ah cuch cabob*). He appointed the town and village chiefs (*batabob*), who stood in a subordinate relation to him, and the most important of whom were no doubt close blood relatives (younger brothers, nephews, and cousins).

In addition to being the highest administrative and executive officer of the state, the *halach uinic* was most likely the highest ecclesiastical authority as well. It has even been suggested that Classic-period government was theocratic, the highest civil and religious powers being combined in the person of the *ahau*, who perhaps even then was called the *halach uinic*.

Below the *halach uinic* stood the *batabob*, or lesser lords or rulers. These were the local magistrates and executives who administered the affairs of the towns and villages. In the Postclassic and probably in the Classic era as well, they were appointed from among the members of the hereditary nobility, the *almehenob*. The *batabob* exercised executive and judicial authority in their communities, and although in times of war all served under one supreme military chief, each *batab* personally commanded his own soldiers. He presided over the local council and saw to it that the houses were kept in repair and that the people cut, burned, and planted their fields at the proper times. In his capacity as judge he sentenced criminals and decided civil suits. If these suits were of unusual importance he consulted the *halach uinic* before passing judgment. No tribute was paid directly to the *batab*, but he was nonetheless supported by the people. One of his principal duties was in fact to see that his town or village paid its tribute promptly to the *halach uinic*.

The *batab* title has been translated from glyph T1030, one element of which is an axe (*baat*). This glyph appears in many Classic lowland texts in association with the names of rulers. In major centers the *batab* title appears to have been held by the supreme ruler (the *ahau*), who was the political and military leader of the center, but in tributary towns under the jurisdiction of the *ahau*, it was held by lesser leaders. At the time of the Conquest the highest authorities in several Yucatec states held the *batab* title.

There were two kinds of war captains: one was hereditary, presumably the *batab*; the other, the *nacom*, held office for a period of three years. From Landa again,

This one, called the *nacom*, could not, during these three years, have relations with any woman, even his own wife, nor eat red meat. They held him in great veneration and gave him fish and iguanas, which are like lizards, to eat. In this time [his tenure of office] he did not get drunk, and he kept separate in his house the utensils and other objects which he used, and no women served him and he had but little communication with the people. At the end of these three years [all was] as before. These two captains [the *nacom* and *batab*] discussed the affairs of war and put them in order. . . . They bore them [the *nacom*] in great pomp, perfuming him as if he were an idol, to the temple where they seated him and burned incense to him as to an idol.

It would seem that the *nacom* formulated the strategy of war, whereas the *batabob*, the hereditary leaders, led their respective contingents into battle. That distinction seems to make the *nacom* the more important of the two, where war is concerned.

Next below the *batab* were the town councillors, the *ah cuch cabob*, two or three in number in the typical polity. Each had a vote in the town government, and their assent was required for all major decisions. Each stood at the head of a subdivision of the town, and they were likened by Spanish writers of the sixteenth century to the *regidores* in Spanish town governments.

The *ah kulelob*, or deputies, usually two or three of them, were the assistants who carried out the *batab's* orders; they accompanied him wherever he went.

The duties of the *ah holpopob*, meaning in Yucatecan Mayan "those at the head of the mat," are not so clear. These officials are said to have assisted the lords in the government of their towns and to have served as intermediaries through whom the townspeople might approach the lords. At least two towns in Late Postclassic Yucatan were ruled by a *holpop*; and as we shall see, the holder of this title was the supreme ruler of the sixteenth-century Quiche Maya, in the highlands. But in Yucatan the *holpopob* were the advisers of the lords on matters of foreign policy, and masters of the *popol na*, the house where the town council met to discuss public affairs and to learn the dances for the town festivals. It would seem, therefore, that the elite council could either exist alongside the *halach uinic* as a kind of advisory body or, in a polity not beholden to a single ruler, act as the supreme authority—the *multepal*. After being stripped of much of their power by the Spaniards during the Colonial era; the *ah holpopob* continued to be the chief singers and chanters in charge of the dances and musical instruments.

Finally, the *tupiles*, or town constables, were responsible for enforcing the laws and keeping the peace.

In describing arrangements in the Late Postclassic, Landa says that both political and religious offices were hereditary and were derived from the nobility: "They taught the sons of the other priests and the second sons of the lords who [were] brought them from their infancy, if they saw that they had an inclination for this profession; . . . and [the high priest's] sons or his nearest relatives succeeded him in office." A. Herrera, the official historian of the Indies for the Crown of Spain, writes, "For the matters concerning the worship of their gods they had one who was the high-priest, whose sons succeeded him in the priesthood." There is little doubt that both the highest civil and religious offices were hereditary, being filled in each state from the members of one or several elite families.

Landa says that in Late Postclassic times the high priest was called Ahaucan Mai. This term, however, seems to be a combination of the title *ahaucan* and the family name Mai, which is common in the Yucatan. The high priest may have been called simply the *ahaucan*, since this word means "the Lord Serpent" in Mayan. In affixing the surname Mai, Landa was doubtless invoking a specific family in which the office seems to have been hereditary. Landa says further that

He was very much respected by the lords and had [no Indians specially set aside for his personal service], but besides the offerings, the lords made him presents and all the priests of the town brought contributions to him. . . . In him was the key of their learning and it was to these matters that they [the high priests] mostly dedicated themselves; and they gave advice to the lords and replied to their questions. They seldom dealt with matters pertaining to the sacrifices except at the time of the principal feasts, or very important matters of business. They provided priests for the towns when they were needed, examining them in the sciences and ceremonies and committing to them the duties of their office, and set good example to people and provided them with books and sent them forth. And they employed themselves in the duties of the temples and in teaching their sciences as well as writing books about them. . . .

The sciences which they taught were the computation of the years, months and days, the festivals and ceremonies, the administration of the sacraments, the fateful days and seasons, their methods of divination and their prophecies, events and the cures for diseases and their antiquities [history] and how to read and write with their letters and characters [hieroglyphics] with which they wrote, and [to make] drawings which illustrate the meaning of the writings.

Another category of priests was the *chilanes*, or "speakers," whose duty it was to report to the people the replies of the gods. The *chilanes* were held in such high respect that the people carried them on their shoulders when they appeared in public.

Still another priest was the *nacom* (not to be confused with the war chief of the same title), who was appointed for life. He was the functionary who slit open the breasts of the sacrificial victims and plucked out their hearts, and according to Landa he was held in little esteem:

At this time came the executioner, the *nacom*, with a knife of stone, and with much skill and cruelty struck him [the sacrificial victim] with the knife between the ribs of his left side under the nipple, and at once plunged his hand in there and seized the heart like a raging tiger, tearing it out alive, and having placed it on a plate, he gave it to the priest, who went quickly and anointed the face of the idols with that fresh blood.

The *nacom* was assisted in the ceremony of human sacrifice by four aides called *chacs*, respectable old men chosen anew on each occasion. Wrote Landa, "The *chacs* seized the poor man whom they were going to sacrifice, and with great haste placed him on his back upon that stone and all four held him by the legs and arms so that they divided him in the middle." The *chacs* also assisted at the puberty ceremony, kindled the new fire at the beginning of the Maya New Year, and fasted and anointed idols with blood in the month of Mol, which was dedicated to the making of new idols.

*Ahkin* was the general name for "priest" in Mayan. The word means literally "he of the sun." Some of the *ahkins* had specialized duties, for example, as prophets of the thirteen differently numbered katuns (see Chapter 12). At a sanctuary on Isla de Cozumel and at the sacred Cenote of Sacrifice at Chichen Itza, an *ahkin* served as the oracle. It was also an *ahkin* who received the hearts of the sacrificial victims from the hands of the *nacom* and offered them to the idols of the Maya gods.

When the modern Maya of northern Yucatan practice the ancient ceremonies that have survived among them, they employ the services of a shaman or *ahmen*, he "who understands." The *ahmen* is a diviner and, at times, can be the inflicter as well as the healer of diseases.

The great mass of the people in Postclassic times were humble maize farmers, whose toil supported not only themselves but also their supreme ruler, their local lords, and the priesthood. And they were the builders of the great, complex ceremonial centers and the raised stone highways (sacbeob) that connected the principal cities.

Other obligations of the lower class were to pay tribute to the *halach uinic*, to present gifts to their local lords, and to make offerings to the gods, through the priests. In all three, what was offered consisted of food (all kinds of vegetable produce, domesticated fowl, salt, dried fish, and all kinds of game and birds), a kind of woven cotton cloth called *pati*, or more precious items (cacao, *pom* [copal] for incense, honey and beeswax, strings of jade and coral beads, and shells). The lands of the lower class were held and tilled in common, probably on the basis of lineage ownership. Landa says:

The common people at their own expense made the houses of the lords. . . . Beyond the house, all the people did their sowing for the lord, cared for his fields and harvested what was necessary for him and his household; and when there was hunting or fishing, or when it was time to get their salt, they always gave the lord his share, since these things they always did as a community. . . . They also joined together for hunting in companies of fifty, more or less, and they roast the flesh of the deer on grills, so that it shall not be wasted [spoil], and having reached the town, they make presents to their lord and distribute [them] as among friends. And they do the same in their fishing.

The common people lived on the outskirts of the towns and villages, and the relative distance of a man's house from the central plaza may have reflected his ranking in the social scale.

We do not know what term described the common people in ancient times, though sixteenth-century Maya dictionaries give *ah chembal uinicob*, *memba uinicob*, and *yalba uinicob* as meaning "the common people, the plebeians"; literally, these Yucatec Mayan terms mean "the inferior or lower men." At the time of the Conquest the common people were called *mazehualob*, a Nahuatl (not Mayan) word that means the lower classes, as contrasted with the elite. That term is still used in northern Yucatan, but it now carries a distinct connotation of social inferiority.

At the bottom of the social scale were the slaves, the *p'entacob*. Slavery may have existed in both the Classic and Postclassic eras. Landa's assertion to the contrary—that it was introduced in Late Postclassic times by one of the Cocom rulers of Mayapan—is difficult to believe in view of the frequent representations of "captive figures" on Classic Maya monuments. Although the high-status captives were usually sacrificed, the lower-status prisoners more likely were made servants and slaves of a sort, assigned to labor and other menial tasks.

In Postclassic times, for which we have documentary evidence, slaves were created in a variety of ways: by being born to the calling; as punishment for stealing; by being taken prisoner in war; by being orphaned; or through purchase or trade. Provision was made by law and custom for the redemption of children born into slavery. If a person was caught stealing, he was bound over to the person he had robbed and remained a slave for life or until he was able to make restitution for the stolen articles. Prisoners of war were always enslaved; those of high rank were sacrificed immediately, but those of lower rank became the property of the soldier who had captured them. In mural paintings from the Temple of the Warriors at Chichen Itza, captives are portrayed naked, their bodies painted with black and white stripes.

Orphans were acquired for sacrifice either by purchase or by kidnaping. The purchase price of a small boy varied from five to ten stone beads. Orphans who had been brought up by rich lords were frequently sacrificed, especially if they had been the children of slave women. Finally, slaves could be acquired; Landa, in enumerating what he referred to as the vices of the Maya, mentions "idolatries and repudiation of their wives and orgies of public drunkenness and buying and selling slaves . . . they were accustomed to buy slaves or other beads because they were fine and good."

At the time of the Conquest, the five leading ruling lineages of the Peninsula were the Xiu, or Tutul Xiu, with their capital at Mani; the Cocom, with their capital at Sotuta; the Canek, with their capital at Tayasal in central Peten; the Chel, with their capital at Tecoh; and the Pech, with their capital at Motul.

The foremost of these were the Xiu, perhaps because this family had taken the leading role in the successful revolt against Mayapan in 1441. The Peabody Museum of Archaeology and Ethnology at Harvard University holds the documents claiming the nobility of the Xiu family that were accumulated during the Spanish colonial period. The three earliest—a map, a land treaty, and a genealogical tree—date from 1557, only 15 years after the Spanish Conquest.

The map (Fig. 10.9) shows the province of the Xiu with its capital, Mani, at the center. The symbol for each town and village is a Catholic church with a tower surmounted by a cross; for the smaller villages there are only crosses. The symbol for the archaeological site of Uxmal, which was abandoned by the middle of the fifteenth century, is a representation of a Maya temple.

The treaty of the Maya lords, which accompanies the map and bears the same date, is the earliest known document to be written in Spanish script in Yucatec Mayan. It describes the boundaries between the Xiu state and the adjoining provinces.

The genealogical tree (Fig. 10.10) shows Hun Uitzil Chac Tutul Xiu seated at its base, holding a fan. Because its handle terminates in the head of a serpent, the fan is thought to be a Late Postclassic form of the manikin scepter. At Hun Uitzil Chac's right side kneels his wife; she points to their joint achievement—the spreading Xiu family tree. It is to be noted, however, that the tree rises from *his* loins and not from hers, a graphic insistence on patrilineal descent. The purpose of the tree was to lay claim, before the Spanish Crown, to the descent of the Conquest-period Xiu from their purported former capital at Uxmal; thus the "founder" of Uxmal, Hun Uitzil Chac, appears as the progenitor of the lineage.

Other documents carry the Xiu story down to the time of Mexican Independence in 1821, and from members of the family, who live today at Ticul, in Yucatan, it has been possible to continue their history to the present day.

## The Postclassic Quiche Maya

On the eve of the Spanish Conquest, the Maya of the central Guatemalan highlands were organized in much the same fashion as was Postclassic Yucatan. The best-documented Postclassic highland society is that of the Quiche Maya, who like the Yucatec Maya were heavily influenced by non-Maya Mexican cultures.

At the time of the Conquest, the Quiche were organized into several social categories. The *ahauab* were the nobility, descended from the original, founding Quiche conquerors, who were probably Putun Maya from the Gulf coastal lowlands, and who in turn claimed their origins from the mythical city of Tollan (Chapter 6). The *ahauab*—the political rulers and their officials, priests, and military leaders—were considered sacred, controlled most of the polity's wealth by collection of tribute, and lived in masonry palaces located in fortified centers.

A less well-defined middle class was composed of merchants (*ahbeyom*), professional warriors (*achij*), estate managers (*uytzam chinamital*), bureaucrats,

Fig. 10.9. Colonial-period map of the province of Mani, Yucatan, Mexico.

Fig. 10.10. Colonial-period genealogical tree of the Xiu lineage of Mani, Yucatan, Mexico.

artisans, and other specialists. Farmers and laborers made up the bulk of the lower class, or commoners (*al c'ahol*). The commoners were not associated with the sacred origins of the *ahauab*, produced the food and tribute for the nobility, and lived outside the fortified centers in thatched wattle-and-daub houses. The *al c'ahol* worked their own land, which was held in common by their lineage, and lived there or on land rented from the *ahauab*. A group of landless peasants, the *nimak achi*, worked the fields of the elite and were inherited along with the land. At the bottom of the social scale were the *munib*, slaves owned by the nobility. The *munib* consisted of commoners captured in war, sentenced criminals, and impoverished souls sold into slavery by their families. Slaves were usually sacrificed when their masters died, so that they could continue in their service.

All Quiche society, regardless of class, was based on patrilineal descent groups, that is, on lineages in which children belonged to the same group as did their fathers. Marriage was exogamous—an individual married outside his or her patrilineage. At the time of the Conquest the *ahauab* of Utatlan, the most important Quiche center, were organized into 24 lineages, each lineage a branch of the four original patrilineal descent groups: the Cawek (nine lineages), Nihaib (nine lineages), Ahau Quiche (four lineages), and Sakic (two lineages). The *ahauab* lineages held rights to one or more *chinamits*. The *chinamit* territorial and residential units, consisting of the principal administrative structure, or "big house" (*nimha*), parcels of land, and their *nimak achi* and resident *al c'ahol*, formed the basis of the organization that bound Quiche society together.

Each *ahauab* lineage was associated with specific political, military, or religious offices. One lineage, named Yagui Winak, furnished many of the priestly offices. Priests (*chalamicat*), although highly esteemed, held little secular power. Their chief duties, apart from conducting the specialized and often bloody sacrificial rituals, lay in their role as caretakers of the sacred codices that recorded the ritual calendar and divination tables that foretold future events.

The head of each noble lineage occupied the principal office of that lineage, and held ultimate authority over its members. At the same time, the *ahauab* lineage heads, together with other specialists, including several high priests, formed a council that advised the ruler and helped formulate policy for all Quiche society. Thus an elite lineage head functioned in two capacities: as leader of his kinsmen and as part of the highest-ranking body of state officials.

The *ahauab* lineages were not all of equal status, but, rather, were ranked according to differing degrees of authority and prestige. At Utatlan, it appears that three descent groups, the Cawek, the Nihaib, and the Ahau Quiche, held a higher status than the others. Each seems to have been associated with one of the Quiche deities: the Cawek patron was Tohil, the male sun deity; for the Nihaib, Awilix, the female moon deity; for the Ahau Quiche, Jakawitz, the male sky deity. The heads of the three lineages held the most powerful offices in the polity. The *ahpop* ("lord of the mat") was head of the Cawek and, at the time of the Conquest, supreme ruler of Utatlan and all Quiche society. Besides possessing the power to make political appointments and leading the religious rituals held for the well-being of the population, the *ahpop* was the head of the army and the most important speaker in the ruling council. The *ahpop* was a hereditary office, usually succeeded by whichever son of the ruler held the office of *nima rahpop achij* ("great military captain"). Another Cawek official, the *ahpop c'amha* ("he of the mat of the receiving house"), received visiting officials in the name of the ruler, and may have served as interim ruler upon the death of the *ahpop* until the new ruler took office. According to the *Popol Vuh*, there were nine Cawek offices, one for the headman of each Cawek lineage.

The other high officials were the *k'alel* ("courtier"), head of the Nihaib, who served as a judge and counselor, and the *atzij winak* ("speaker"), head of the Ahau Quiche. There were nine Nihaib offices, four Ahau Quiche offices, and two Sakic offices, again one for the head of each constituent lineage.

Adjacent to Utatlan were two other Quiche centers, Chisalin and Ismachi, each with its own ruling elite lineages and populations organized according to the same social categories. Owing to Utatlan's marriage alliances with these lineages and the military supremacy exercised by the *ahpop* in Utatlan, Quiche society functioned as a fairly unified kingdom at the time of the Conquest. Yet Quiche society had a built-in structural weakness: a secondary lineage and its leader could marshal sufficient military strength to challenge the power of the *ahpop*. This did indeed happen on several occasions, and culminated in the revolt of the Cakchiquel and their subsequent establishment of an independent state that was centered at Iximche (see Chapter 7).

At the time of the Conquest, the Maya highlands were occupied by a series of other Maya groups who appear to have been organized in a manner similar to that of the Quiche. Some of these Maya peoples, such as the neighboring Cakchiquel and Tzutuhil, were often at war with the Quiche. Although the Quiche were able to expand their authority to the north and to both the east and west of Utatlan, extending their power over the Mam of Zaculeu and other polities, the Cakchiquel successfully resisted Quiche attempts at conquest. Despite these hostilities, Utatlan maintained mutually amicable relationships with its neighbors through peaceful commerce, religious pilgrimages, gift exchanges, and marriage alliances among the nobility. Thus, although far from being politically unified, the polities of the Postclassic Maya highlands were tied together by economic, religious, and kinship bonds.

## The Evolution of Social Systems

Thus far we have described aspects of ancient Maya social and political organization. We will close with a summary of the foundations of Maya society, and a broad evolutionary sequence of its organizational forms as they correspond to the overall developmental sequence of Maya civilization (see Chapter 2).

As in many human societies, the nuclear family most likely formed the elementary nexus of organization for the ancient Maya. As we have seen, this assumption is supported by the archaeological evidence, including the prevalence of residential structures of a size suitable to house a single married couple and their children. The same conclusion may be drawn from the ethnohistorical record; indeed, contemporary Maya societies invariably are built around the nuclear family. In this kind of family organization today, the father or eldest male member is the authority figure for the family, and the same can be assumed for the past. This does not mean that women are or were without status in Maya society; in fact, the domestic authority of the mother or eldest female member of the family is an important factor in the Maya social system today. Both the male and the female lines of descent were apparently considered important in ancient Maya society.

Larger kin groups were composed of many nuclear families. We have reviewed the archaeological and ethnohistorical evidence, which argues both for the presence of extended-family residential groups and for the existence of patrilineal descent groups in ancient Maya society. These descent groups, important in Postclassic time in both Yucatan and highland Guatemala, remain discernible in many contemporary Maya communities. Corporate groups defined by patrilineal descent (patrilineages) were strongly developed by the Quiche Maya, for instance, and are still found in several highland areas, most notably in Chiapas. If patrilineal descent is combined with patrilocal residence (married sons continuing to reside near their father), then the lineage becomes a residential group. This may have been the case in ancient times; the residential clusters seen at many Maya sites could represent occupation by patrilineal descent groups.

In the Early Preclassic, prior to the emergence of civilization, Maya society was basically egalitarian. As ethnographic studies of the Chiapas highlands have shown, contemporary Maya communities usually are organized along similar lines. The community of Zinacantan, for instance, is organized around an egalitarian *cargo* system, whereby the positions of political and religious authority are held for one-year terms by male officeholders accompanied by their wives (who also share duties), and the officeholders rotate from one position to another. By taking office once every few years, each individual advances in the community hierarchy with age, and the positions of highest authority are thus held by the elders of society. In such a system all levels of power are shared, and there is no permanent ruling class. A similar system may have operated among the ancient Maya, perhaps during the earliest time periods, perhaps also as a basic organizational framework for small communities in later centuries. In either case, one may assume that beyond the basic lineage organization, people in rural residential clusters held rotating political and religious offices in the local agricultural villages.

With the beginnings of stratified society in the Middle Preclassic, we find the first nonegalitarian organizational structures in the Maya area. In the oldest and most basic of these, the two-tiered system, the outlying residential clusters were settled by peasant agriculturalists, while the centers were occupied by a small but permanent and powerful class of elites along with their servants and retainers. The peasantry supported the ruling class by providing labor for the construction and maintenance of the temples, palaces, and other facilities in the centers and by supplying food, goods, and services. In return, the elite class provided the peasantry the leadership, direction, and security that derived from their knowledge of calendrics and supernatural prophecy. That knowledge allowed the rulers to determine the proper times to plant and harvest crops, thus ensuring agricultural success for the common good of society. Such a system, which seems to underlie Early Maya Civilization (see Chapter 2), corresponds to the first stages of social complexity seen in the Preclassic of the southern Maya area and the lowlands. That system is also compatible with what we know of at least some of Late Maya Civilization, for example Postclassic Yucatan.

A third, and the most complex, version of ancient Maya society, termed the multitiered model, seems to have originated in the Late Preclassic, and was probably associated with all of what we have termed Middle Maya Civilization. This organizational model suggests that Maya centers were populated by concentrations of nonagricultural specialists representing many occupational groups and social classes, and by large numbers of agriculturists as well. In this sense, the Maya centers functioned as cities, albeit not marked by the degree of population concentration and orderly layout associated with Teotihuacan and other pre-Columbian cities in Central Mexico. Nonetheless, this model sees Maya centers occupied by far more than the ruling classes, and thus as performing far more functions than called for in the previous schemes. Maya society then can be seen as having been composed of a ruling elite class, a non-elite class, and an emerging intermediate group composed of prosperous commoners and the lower ranks of the elite.

Except, perhaps, for the service personnel needed by the ruling class, the nonelite inhabited the most humble dwellings, those generally located on the periphery of the centers, and probably included servants, bearers, and maintenance workers, in addition to full-time agriculturists. The middle ranks of Maya society were composed of such full-time occupational groups as bureaucrats, merchants, warriors, craftsmen, architects, and artists who probably lived closer to the civic and religious core. The core, of course, was inhabited by the ruling class: the ruler, his family, and other members of allied or related elite lineages that presumably held the major positions in the political, religious, and economic institutions.

## The Lowland Maya as Galactic Polities

In this chapter we have considered the archaeological evidence bearing on the number, size, and form of lowland polities, especially in the Classic period. Epigraphic and ethnohistoric evidence informs the description of the types of organizations typical of the lowland states. Another approach often useful in supplementing such internal sources of evidence is the application of models derived from more complete historical or ethnographic descriptions of distinct but apparently similar systems, as analogies to assist in describing the less well-known ancient Maya political systems. Such an approach does not imply that the Maya were organized in the fashion of other societies, but rather that the analogies provide points of comparison that can be tested by further research, as well as offering insights to understanding what otherwise might be missed.

Over the years, scholars have offered a series of such analogies to help understand the ancient Maya. These models have ranged from descriptions of medieval feudal Europe to recent chiefdoms in West Africa. The example that seems to have been the most productive, in the sense of offering both insight and opportunities for further testing, has been the galactic polity model of the historical kingdoms of Southeast Asia, which is based on both archaeological and documentary sources. The most vocal advocate of the application of a Southeast Asian galactic polity model to the ancient Maya has been Arthur Demarest, who has tested the expectations from the model in his field project in the Petexbatun region of the Maya lowlands.

Galactic polities are a variant of what are often referred to as "segmentary states" or "peer polities." In such systems authority is determined by birth and heredity, such that specific offices are determined by lineage membership, just as we have seen in the Quiche Maya example. These elite lineages were ranked, the highest-ranking lineage furnishing the supreme ruler and various subordinate elite lineages filling the other offices in the political and religious hierarchy. The galactic variant emphasizes the importance of ideology and attempts to centralize power through ritual, rather than political, mechanisms. The result is a political landscape populated with unstable, competitive kingdoms, all of which shared a common set of cultural values and identity by virtue of sharing a religious ideology, along with common subsistence, demographic, and economic systems (we will discuss the role of ideology among the ancient Maya in Chapter 11).

In such a system each polity consisted of a loose array of subordinate centers surrounding a principal center, or capital, the residence of the ruling lineage, thus the term "galactic." The system saw a degree of duplication of functions between the capital center and its dependencies, in contrast to a specialized economic or political hierarchy. But we must keep in mind that not all functions and services were duplicated at all levels in the Maya site hierarchy. This was especially true for economic functions, for, as we have seen, there were sites that specialized in trade, the extraction of salt, the mining of jade and other minerals, or the manufacture of tools (Colha being the prime example). On the other hand, there may have been more replication of administrative functions from site to site within each polity. This kind of duplication led to political instability, as the generally self-sufficient subordinate centers attempted to break free, or to shift their alliances to other centers. At the same time, some capitals attempted to expand and/or centralize their power and control, which created further instability in the overall system. Political power in such a system was heavily dependent on the personal performance of the ruler in warfare, on his ability to establish alliances, and on his success in conducting rituals. It was also dependent on his control over his subordinates, rather than on control of land or economic systems. Thus the expansion and prosperity of a given polity would have been due largely to the charismatic leadership qualities of an individual ruler.

Such a model does recall much of what we have seen among the Classic lowland Maya. The inherent weaknesses of such systems also bring to mind the processes apparently at work in the Terminal Classic period. The new political order that emerged out of that period of change, led by the mercantile Putun Maya, may have succeeded because of a new and distinctive organizational style, one based on specialized, nonredundant economic and political systems, which produced a stronger and more centralized structure of power.

It does seem that the most effectual and powerful of the new lowland states, Chichen Itza, was for a time able to control far more territory and resources than had its Classic-period predecessors. Of course, Chichen Itza was succeeded by a new capital at Mayapan, but when this last attempt at centralized authority was destroyed, the northern-lowland political landscape fragmented into the many small, diverse polities that the Spaniards encountered. It would seem, therefore, that the galactic-polity model does not describe the dynamic quality seen in the long-term evolution of Maya states (nor does it describe the diversity of political organization in operation at any one time). As we have seen, a long-term perspective reveals a diverse and changing political environment that shifted between periods of fragmentation and periods of consolidation. The galactic-polity model may better describe the less centralized polities that characterized times of fragmentation, rather than the more centralized polities that dominated times of consolidation.

How would the Maya political landscape have evolved had it not been so brutally and suddenly truncated by outsiders? Obviously, there can be no answer to this question. But on the basis of the record of some 2,000 years of political evolution, we might expect that further changes in the institutions of power would have continued to share time with episodes of political consolidation and political fragmentation. If we turn to the specific political organizations extant at the time of the Conquest, we can see variations on the recurrent themes apparent in the evolution of the Maya political landscape. On the whole, these are systems based on the concentration of power in the hands of individual rulers, and on the dispersal of power among multiple offices.

# IDEOLOGY AND COSMOLOGY

You are God our Father. You are our master in the Sky. Sun, Sun, you shed
your light on us. Never can we pay for your blessings which you give to us.
Everything is the sun; there is no way we can pay you.
—Contemporary Chorti Maya prayer (Fought 1972: 489)

They had a very great number of idols and temples, which were
magnificent in their own fashion. And besides the community temples, the
lords, priests and the leading men had also oratories and idols in their
houses, where they made their prayers and offerings in private.
—*Landa's relación de las cosas de Yucatán* (Tozzer 1941: 108)

In this chapter we come to the last of the major factors underlying the
cycles of growth and decline that marked the course of Maya civilization—religion
and ideology. Each human society holds, more or less, to a particular ideology, a
body of concepts that provide order and explain the unknown. In our Western view,
religion is a kind of ideology, one based on belief in the supernatural, the use of
ritual to communicate with the supernatural, and an explanation of the world and
the universe (cosmology) that includes the supernatural, all of which tends to reinforce human values and guide human behavior. But these categorical distinctions
are not so clear-cut when we begin to consider the ideology of the ancient Maya.
The Maya of today continue to maintain the vestiges of an ancient ideology quite
unlike our Western concepts of life and the universe. We conceive of our world as
being composed of two discrete components, the natural realm and the supernatural realm. The natural world corresponds to that which is observable, and is divided into an animate (living) realm of creatures on this earth (including us) and an
inanimate (nonliving) realm of objects on the earth and beyond, organized into the
solar system, our galaxy, and the entire universe. We reserve the unobservable realm
to something we call the supernatural, be it concepts like ghosts and luck and superstition or the codified philosophy, beliefs, and faith at the core of religion.

Although the ideological concepts of the ancient Maya were severely rent by
the trauma of the Spanish Conquest, and then by subsequent events, much has endured, and we can reconstruct some aspects of the ancient belief system from what
we know of present-day Maya culture, from the ethnohistorical accounts set down
around the time of the Conquest, and from an analysis of the archaeological evidence. The resulting picture, although imperfect, is reasonably complete and coherent.

The world of the ancient Maya, so different from our own, was governed by a cosmological order that transcended our distinction between the natural and supernatural realms. All things, whether animate or inanimate, were imbued with an unseen power. In some cases—especially the "spirits" inhabiting rocks, trees, and other objects (a concept we call animism)—the invisible power was amorphous. In other cases the unseen power was embodied in a "deity" perceived to take animal-like (zoomorphic) or humanlike (anthropomorphic) form. This fusion of the observable and the unobservable is best expressed by the Maya concept of *cuxolalob*, the knowledge of that which is both rational and supernatural.

In its normal state the world was seen as an ordered place. Order, the foundation of the Maya world, stemmed from the predictable movements of the "sky wanderers," the sun, moon, planets, and stars that marked the passage of time. Each of these celestial bodies was animate, a deity by our definition. Human destiny was linked with these celestial beings, and when cataclysmic events overwhelmed the Maya world, as they did from time to time, the sky wanderers and the calendar-based books of prophecy would be consulted to find portents of change. Once found and recorded, such portents explained the disorder that had fallen upon the world and thus allowed the world order to be restored.

The basic unit of order was the day, the kin, marked by the sun rising out of the underworld at dawn and crossing the sky, only to be swallowed once again by the underworld at dusk. A succession of twenty kins, each of which was represented by its own anthropomorphic deity, collectively formed a uinal, which was also represented by an anthropomorphic deity. (See below for a discussion of Maya time deities.) The central importance of time in the world order is indicated by the fact that *uinic* means "man" in Yucatec Mayan, perhaps because it was men who "knew the rhythm of the days in themselves," as recorded in *The Book of Chilam Balam of Chumayel*. Thus in the ancient Maya scheme of things, time itself was animate, and the *cuxolalob* of time provided the fundamental order for the universe (the Maya calendar is described in Chapter 12).

## The Origins of Maya Ideology

The origins of these and other Maya ideological concepts undoubtedly lie in the distant past, even as far back as the hunters and gatherers, who first entered the New World from Asia, and who needed to be intimately acquainted with their total environment to assure themselves of adequate shelter and food and to survive its dangers. Under such conditions, animistic concepts help explain a world that inspires both security and fear. The discovery of order in one's surroundings, perhaps especially in the predictable movements of the sun and moon, increases understanding and reduces insecurity. An ideology based on these fundamental and observable phenomena requires no specialists, and was probably typical of early human cultures the world over. Each family head was probably responsible for ensuring that the animistic forces in the environment were satisfied, so as to guard against accident, illness, or other disasters.

But as any society grows and increases in complexity, occupational specialists begin to emerge. One kind of specialist, the shaman, intervenes in relationships between humans and the surrounding animistic forces. In the Maya area shamanism was probably well developed before the Preclassic, and may also have its roots in the first migrations into the New World. The shaman's medicinal substances, knowledge of illness, and appeals to unseen forces were used to cure the sick, and his ability to communicate with these forces by divination provided a measure of power over the other members of society. The earliest Maya shamans probably also developed the beginnings of the calendrical system, and were therefore charged with maintaining the world order by keeping track of the various cycles reckoned by the movements of the "sky wanderers." The most practical benefit of this knowledge was the ability to predict the coming of the seasons, and thereby to choose the proper times to hunt and gather wild food and, later on, plant and harvest crops.

By the Preclassic period, as society increased in size and complexity, full-time specialists and leaders began to establish themselves, and the management of unseen forces became a fundamental concern of the ruling elite, who saw to such matters both to reinforce and support their own elevated status and to ensure prosperity. Those aspects of shamanism involved with societal matters—the management of the calendar so as to maintain the world order, the performance of public divination ceremonies and other rituals to ensure success and prosperity—soon became the responsibility of an increasingly full-time priesthood that became an intrinsic part of the ruling class.

The Maya priesthood became an institution both self-contained, at the heart of the elite class, and self-perpetuated, through the recruitment and training of acolytes. By the beginning of the Classic period, Maya priests had developed a substantial body of esoteric knowledge, probably codified and recorded by a written system in books (codices; see Chapter 13). This body of knowledge—records of myth, history, ritual, calendrical cycles, and astronomical observations—was used primarily to develop and maintain an increasingly complex calendrical system whose principal purpose seems to have been astrological—by divining the predilections and intentions of the unseen forces, the priests could predict events and determine the destiny of the world.

The priesthood performed a variety of often spectacular public ceremonies to inspire awe and obedience in the populace. Such ceremonies usually involved music, dancing, the burning of incense, and offerings, which often included the blood of priests and, on certain occasions, human sacrifices. In a very important sense, the Maya ruler served as chief priest and shaman for his subjects, protecting them from disease and misfortune, divining the future and the will of the gods, performing rituals to ensure the success of the state, and maintaining the cosmos through his own blood sacrifices. In this way the functions of political and religious leadership were fused in the person of the Maya ruler.

## Transformations by Outsiders

Later Maya writings and the accounts by the Spanish observers often refer to the introduction of Postclassic-period religious changes by outsiders, either Mexican peoples or Mayan-speaking groups influenced by Mexican customs. The principal changes seem to be greater emphasis on the worship of the images of deities ("idolatry") and increased human sacrifice, as recorded in the *Relación de Quinacama* (1581):

The old men of these provinces [Yucatan] say that anciently, near to eight hundred years ago, idolatry was not practiced, and afterwards when the Mexicans entered it and took possession of it, a captain, who was called Quetzalquat [Quetzalcoatl] in the Mexican language, which is to say in ours, plumage of the serpent . . . introduced idolatry into this land and the use of idols for gods, which he had made of wood, of clay and of stone. And he made them [the Maya] worship these idols and they offered many things of the hunt, of merchandise and above all the blood of their nostrils and ears, and the hearts of those whom they sacrificed in his service. . . . They say that the first inhabitants of Chichenyza [Chichen Itza] were not idolators, until a Mexican captain Ku Kalcan [Kukulcan] entered into these parts, who taught idolatry, and the necessity, so they say, to teach and practice it.

Herrera, the official historian of the Indies for the Crown of Spain, leaves no doubt about this point, stating bluntly that "the number of people sacrificed was great. And this custom was introduced into Yucatan by the Mexicans."

But it should be borne in mind that both of these practices were known to the Maya long before they were "introduced" by foreigners. Pottery incensarios adorned with masks or images of deities are frequently found in archaeological remains dating from both the Preclassic and Classic periods. Representations of human sacrifice are found on Classic monuments, polychrome pottery, and the graffiti inscribed on building walls (Fig. 11.1). Raiding and the taking of "trophy heads" appear to have had ritualistic associations during the Preclassic and Classic periods; one such trophy is depicted on the Bonampak murals. A spectacular example of early mass human sacrifice has been excavated from beneath a Late Preclassic platform at Chalchuapa, in the southern Maya area; 33 individuals, mostly young males (probably captives), were buried together, many with unmistakable signs of sacrifice and mutilation (decapitation, and severing of limbs). A Late Preclassic monument from Izapa (Stela 21) depicts a decapitated person (Fig. 3.10).

Maya ideology in any case underwent its greatest transformation at the hands of the Spaniards, when Christianity was imposed, sometimes forcibly, upon the native population. The most profound change was the disappearance of the esoteric

Fig. 11.1. Scenes of human sacrifice. From the Classic period: (*a*) Piedras Negras Stela 11; (*b*) Piedras Negras Stela 14. From the Postclassic period: (*c*) Dresden Codex; (*d*) Madrid Codex; (*e*) Chichen Itza Temple of the Jaguars; (*f*) Chichen Itza Temple of the Warriors.

cult perpetuated by the Maya priesthood, for this was the most visible aspect of "paganism" as Europeans defined it, and therefore most vulnerable to elimination by the Spaniards' program of conversion. Public shrines and their "idols" were destroyed, books were burned, and the priests themselves were either forcibly converted or executed. And along with the formal and public aspects of Maya religion went much of Maya learning, including the writing system. Fortunately, some native accounts survived, preserving a partial record of ancient Maya ideology.

The less public elements of the Maya belief system often escaped detection and have been perpetuated within Maya family and village life down to the present. In areas where the Spanish pressure for conversion was most intense—in colonized regions of northern Yucatan and in the southern highlands, for example—Maya beliefs and rituals often went underground, held apart from Christianity. Although baptized and thus officially "converted," many Maya people learned to accept the new religion in its public setting, the church, while continuing the old family rituals in the house and the agricultural rituals in the fields. Of course when elements of Christianity happened to correspond to aspects of native ideology, the Maya could "accommodate" their conquerors by seeming to accept the Christian concepts, all the while maintaining their old beliefs under a new guise. For instance, because the cross had been a Maya symbol for the "tree of life," the sacred ceiba supporting the heavens, the Maya could readily accept the Christian cross, though they often worshiped it for its ancient Maya connotation.

In northern Yucatan, when evidence for the secret continuance of Maya beliefs was discovered, the Inquisition was brought in to extinguish all vestiges of "paganism." The Maya response was often to flee, and a series of refugee settlements arose deep in the bush of southeastern Yucatan, where the traditional way of life could be pursued free of interference from the Spanish authorities. A fierce tradition of Maya nativism and independence flourished in these areas of Quintana Roo, and at the heart of this nativistic Maya tradition was a cult centered around the worship of a "talking cross," a wooden image that served as an oracle. Efforts in the nineteenth century by the newly independent government of Mexico to assert its control over the region resulted in a protracted conflict, the War of the Castes, and until well into the twentieth century many villages in Quintana Roo remained isolated and independent of outside control.

The Lacandon Maya of the southern lowlands have remained relatively untouched by Western contact until the present century. Much of the ancient Maya ideology survives in the Lacandon belief system, albeit in greatly attenuated form. At least until recently, for instance, the Lacandon still manufactured and used pottery incensarios that were similar in form to some of those used during the Classic era. Rituals are still held in sacred caves and even in the Classic-period ruins found in the area (Fig. 11.2).

In other regions, however, including the Alta Verapaz in the highlands of Gua-

Fig. 11.2. Ritual burning of *pom* (copal) incense by the Lacandon Maya at the site of Yaxchilan; the man holds a prayer board with small lumps of *pom* to be burned as offerings inside the ancient temples.

temala, Christianity was introduced peacefully, owing to the efforts of Father Bartolomé de Las Casas. In the absence of coercion, Maya and Christian ideologies tended to blend into a single system that is neither indigenous nor Western. In many highland Maya communities, isolated until recently from outside interference, the ideological system has in fact been controlled by native shamans. These religious specialists assumed control of public ceremonies, such as baptisms and masses held in churches, as well as divining and curing rituals undertaken on behalf of individuals. In several of these highland communities the Maya shamans have maintained elements of the ancient calendrical system, such as the 260-day almanac, still used to determine the birthday names of infants and the proper days for ceremonies (see Chapter 12).

In Yucatecan cosmology, the archangel Gabriel and other Christian saints become the Pauahtuns of ancient Maya mythology, the guardians of the four cardinal points; the archangel Michael leads the Chacs, the four rain gods. In Belize it is St. Vincent who is the patron of rain, and St. Joseph the guiding spirit of the cornfields.

The cosmological order in the Maya highlands links Kinich Ahau (see below) with the Christian God, called "Our Father Sun" or sometimes "Our Father Rain." A female counterpart, equated with the Virgin Mary, is "Our Mother Moon" or "Our Mother Maize." Christ is identified with Hunapu, a familiar figure from the *Popol Vuh*, and the cross, worshiped as a deity, is sometimes associated with the deity of the Maya day Ahau. Other anthropomorphized powers, directly descended from ancient Maya counterparts, dwell in the physical world (mountains, volcanoes, caves, lakes) and in animals and other forms of life.

## Cosmology

The ancient Maya believed that there had been several worlds before the present one, and that each had been destroyed by a deluge. Bishop Diego de Landa records this tradition but fails to state the number of worlds thus destroyed:

Among the multitude of gods which this people adored, they worshipped four, each of whom was called Bacab. They said they were four brothers whom God [Hunab Ku], when he created the world, placed at the four points of it, to hold up the sky, so that it should not fall. They also said of these Bacabs, that they escaped when the world was destroyed by the deluge. They gave to each one of them other names and [thus] designated by them the part of the world where God placed [each one] to bear up the heavens.

This tradition, the end of the world by a deluge, is depicted on the last page of the Dresden Codex (Fig. 11.3), according to one interpretation. Across the sky stretches the Milky Way, a serpentlike creature; symbols of the constellations are on its side, and signs for solar and lunar eclipses hang from its belly. From its open jaws, and from the two eclipse signs, a flood of water pours earthward. Below the heavenly serpent, the Old Woman Goddess—the patroness of death and destruction, with long talonlike fingernails and toenails—holds an inverted bowl from which also gushes a devastating flood. At the bottom the Muan bird of evil omen rests on the head of the black war-and-death deity (see below under "Other Deities"). In his right hand he holds two javelins and in his left a long staff, all pointing downward.

The modern Maya of northern Yucatan believe that there have been three worlds previous to this one. The first world was inhabited by dwarfs, the *saiyam uinicob* or "adjuster men," who are thought to have built the great ruined cities. Their work was done in darkness, for the sun had not yet been created, and when the sun rose for the first time, the dwarfs were turned to stone. That first world was ended by a universal deluge, the *haiyococab*, or "water over the earth." The second

Fig. 11.3. Destruction of the Maya world by water; from the Dresden Codex.

world, inhabited by people called the *dzolob*, or "offenders," was ended by the second flood. The third world was populated by the Maya themselves, the common people or *mazehualob*; this world was ended by the third flood, called the *hunyecil* or *bulkabal*, which means the "immersing." This last deluge was followed by the present or fourth world, peopled by a mixture of all the previous inhabitants of the Peninsula, and this world too will eventually be destroyed, by a fourth flood.

## The Creation Myth

The most complete and most literate version of the Maya creation myth is preserved in the extraordinary book of the highland Quiche Maya, the *Popol Vuh*. We have quoted the opening passage from this account at the outset of the Introduction of this book. The *Popol Vuh* goes on to recount how there had been multiple creations before the present world. It then relates the saga of the first humans, the Hero Twins, known in Quiche Mayan as Hunapu and Xbalanque, names that refer to the sun (celestial/life) and jaguar (underworld/death) associations (Hun Ahau and Yax Balam, respectively, in Yucatec Mayan).

The fathers of the Hero Twins, also twins, had been ballplayers who had been sacrificed by the gods of death, lords of the underworld (Xibalba). One father was buried under the Xibalba ballcourt; the other was decapitated, his head hung from a calabash tree. From this tree the head had spit into the hand of one of the daughters of the death gods, which impregnated her. Fleeing her angry father, the pregnant girl came to earth and was sheltered by the grandmother of the dead twins. There she gave birth to the Hero Twins, who grew up, found their father's ballgame equipment, and followed in the footsteps of their father and uncle, becoming such expert ballplayers that they too were invited to Xibalba.

In Xibalba the Hero Twins soon demonstrated that they were a better match for the gods of death. Their adversaries subjected them to a series of daily ballgames and nightly trials, but the twins outwitted the death gods at every turn. Finally the twins arranged for their own demise, sacrificing themselves by fire. The death gods ground their bones and threw the powder into a river. But in the river the twins were reborn, and eventually they returned to Xibalba. This time they took their revenge, demonstrating for the death gods an amazing trick by which one twin decapitated the other, then brought him back to life. The death gods were amazed at this and demanded that the Hero Twins perform the trick on them. This they did, of course, decapitating the gods of death, but then did not bring them back to life. The reborn Hero Twins became the primary celestial bodies, the sun and Venus, destined to reenact forever both their descent into Xibalba each evening and their escape each dawn (Venus as either evening or morning star).

The myth of the Hero Twins was one of the central axioms of ancient Maya life and ritual. It demonstrated how extraordinary humans could enter Xibalba, outwit the gods of death, and return, and thus was a metaphor for the greatest life force in the cosmos, the sun, which emerges from Xibalba every morning (see below). The myth also demonstrated that rebirth is possible only through sacrifice (the twins were reborn after sacrifice by both fire and decapitation), and thus was a metaphor for life after death. Sacrifice and rebirth was a theme specifically celebrated by the Maya ritual of human sacrifice (see below), and in the Maya centers the ballcourt was seen as the threshold between this world and Xibalba, the arena for confrontation; the ritualized ballgame played therein reenacted the original contest between the Hero Twins and the gods of death.

The myth of the Hero Twins highlights another axiom in Maya ideology, the strongly dualistic theme seen in the eternal struggle—between the powers of good and the powers of evil—over the destiny of many. The benevolent forces, bringing thunder, lightning, and rain, set the corn to fruit and ensure plenty. The malevolent powers, bringing drought, hurricanes, and war, ruin the corn and bring famine, misery, death, and destruction. This contest is depicted in the codices, where Chac, the rain deity, is shown caring for a young tree; behind him follows the death god, who breaks the tree in two (Fig. 11.4).

## The Maya Universe

Certain numbers were especially sacred to the ancient Maya, and were imbued with special powers (though with a good deal less conviction, we accord such powers to our "lucky" number seven, or "unlucky" number thirteen). The number three was especially important, reflecting as it does the threefold layers of the universe composed of the visible earth and two invisible worlds, the celestial realm of the sky, above, and Xibalba, below. The earth was the back of a huge reptile, sometimes represented as a caiman, sometimes as a turtle, that swam in the primordial sea. At the center of the world stood the great sacred tree, a giant ceiba, which supported the sky (see Fig. 5.34). The celestial realm was conceived of as having thirteen layers; over each presided one of the Thirteen Gods of the Upper World, or Oxlahuntiku (in Yucatec Mayan, *oxlahun*, "thirteen"; *ti*, "of"; and *ku* "god"). Xibalba had nine layers; over each presided one of the Bolontiku, the Nine Gods of the Lower World (*bolon*, "nine"). The three domains were not bounded but, rather, formed a continuum. This, then, is another example of the Maya's not recognizing the clear distinction we see between the natural and supernatural realms.

The various domains of the Maya universe were connected by both visible and invisible manifestations of supernatural power. The salient visible manifestations were the wanderers of the celestial realm, the sun, moon, planets, and stars (see Chapter 12), the movements of which defined the universe in time and space. As a complement to the sacred number three, the number four, representing the cardinal directions, was also especially important to the ancient Maya. East was the direction of the reborn sun, emerging from Xibalba each morning. The zenith (conflated by the Maya with north) was the sun in the fullness of life, each day at noon. West was the direction of the dying sun, journeying back to Xibalba, the domain of death. The nadir (conflated with south) was the dead sun at midnight, battling the lords of Xibalba in order to be reborn, as had the Hero Twins. The sky, or more specifically the Milky Way, was often depicted as another reptile, the great two-headed serpent, one head associated with life, the other with death (see Itzamna,

Fig. 11.4. Maya deities first nourish a tree, then break it; from the Madrid Codex.

•
══

below). It is this representation of the cosmos, the double-headed serpent bar (Figs. 4.8, 4.20, 5.53, and 6.3), that many of the Classic-period rulers depicted on monuments bear in their arms.

Caves are found in many parts of the Maya area. For the Maya, openings in the surface of the earth were the entrances to Xibalba, and therefore especially sacred and dangerous places. The Maya conducted rituals and buried their dead in caves. Their great temples were seen as manifestations of *witz*, or the sacred mountain, and the temple entrances were caves allowing ruler and priest to enter and communicate with the lords of Xibalba. The rulers were of course associated with the Hero Twins, men with the power not only to enter Xibalba, but to confront the death gods, play the sacred ballgame, and perform human sacrifice. It was only fitting, therefore, that when one Maya ruler was defeated by another, he should be sacrificed by decapitation, to be born again in the sky, like the Hero Twins.

The places where the Maya lived, from the smallest house to the largest city, were conceived of as symbolic representations of their universe. The arrangements of ritual structures reveal this symbolism most clearly. Clemency Coggins has shown how the Twin Pyramid Groups at Tikal, built to host katun-ending ceremonies (see below), were representations of the Maya cosmos (Fig. 4.18). As such, these architectural groups simultaneously symbolized the threefold and fourfold aspects of the universe. The pyramids on the east and west represent the earthly plane and mark the cycles of time, specifically the birth and death of the sun. The nine-doorwayed building on the south represents the nine-layered underworld. And the walled enclosure on the north, open to the sky, represents the celestial domain, a fitting place for the stela and "throne stone" of the sponsoring ruler to reside (Fig. 4.22).

Maya cities, like those of many preindustrial civilizations, were also conceived of as symbolizing the Maya cosmos. From such associations, their inhabitants reaped the security and benefits of living in a sacred and properly ordered place, under the protection of a favored and powerful ruler. This is not to say that Maya sites were laid out all at one time according to a single master plan. Obviously, each city grew over time, thus often obscuring the positions of buildings that had been properly aligned with the cosmos, or simply burying the old under the new. Peter Harrison has demonstrated how the sequence of palaces in Tikal's Central Acropolis, the complex occupied by the ruling dynasty, were constructed by aligning new buildings so as to be in proper harmony with those already in place. On an even larger scale, as Wendy Ashmore has shown, we can still see vestiges of cosmic templates in the layout of entire Maya cities, especially in the smaller, shorter-termed centers, such as Cerros and Quirigua.

In these cosmograms, the associations with the primary directions of the Maya world, especially the three-layered view of the universe, are the most obvious. The earthly realm at the center of the cosmos is often represented by the palaces of the living ruler at or near the center of the site. North, associated with the celestial realm and the dead rulers, who after their apotheosis dwell in the sky, is usually the setting for the funerary shrines and tombs. These buildings are often physically located to the north of the palaces, or on a higher setting, or both. The intervening threshold between this world and the next is the ballcourt, where the ritual ballgame and sacrifices celebrating the creation myth were conducted. The ballcourts are often located between the palaces of the earthly realm and the funerary shrines of the celestial realm.

We can see this general pattern as early as the Late Preclassic at Cerros (Fig. 3.28), and again in the Late Classic at Quirigua (Fig. 5.54). It is also apparent at Tikal, where the central Palace complex and the funerary shrines of the North Acropolis are separated by a ballcourt (Fig. 4.5). Research by Ashmore, in excavations conducted in the North Group at Copan to test the aspects of cosmological directionality in the Late Classic architectural layout of the city (see Chapter 5), revealed celestial, life-after-death associations for this group (Fig. 5.42) in a large complex of buildings decorated with the name of the dead Copan ruler 18 Rabbit, and a date associated with his sacrifice by decapitation at the hands of Cauac Sky, ruler of Quirigua. This seems to indicate that the North Group was dedicated in part to commemorate the apotheosis of the defeated and sacrificed Copan ruler.

## The Afterlife

The *Popol Vuh* creation myth relates the Maya concept of an afterlife in Xibalba. According to Landa, the future was divided into a place of suffering and a place of rest. The Maya paradise was described as a place of delights, offering an abundance of food and drink and freedom from pain and suffering. There grew the *yaxche*, sacred tree of the Maya (the ceiba), in the shade of which they could rest forever from labor. Those who had led evil lives descended into the ninth, or lowest, underworld, Mitnal, the Maya hell. There devils tormented them with hunger, cold, weariness, and grief, although there is some suspicion of European influence in such accounts.

People who committed suicide by hanging or who were sacrificed, warriors killed in battle, women who died in childbirth, priests, and rulers went directly to the Maya paradise: "They also said and held it as absolutely certain that those who hanged themselves went to this heaven of theirs; and thus there were many who on slight occasions of sorrows, troubles or sicknesses, hanged themselves in order to escape these things and to go and rest in their heaven, where they said that the Goddess of the Gallows, whom they called Ixtab, came to fetch them."

What we know from the circumstances discovered in the excavations of rulers' tombs at Palenque, Tikal, and other Classic-period centers suggests that these most powerful of individuals were believed to have been transformed into supernatural beings upon death. In a sense, they became deities, and their passage to this status seems to have been commemorated in both funeral and later apotheosis rituals. The trappings of funeral rituals are often found in the offerings placed in tombs. Apotheosis rituals were sometimes recorded in the texts associated with funerary shrines or temples, as at Palenque (see Chapter 5). The deification of deceased rulers, and their veneration in funerary shrines, was an elaborated expression of ancestor worship, a theme that probably permeated ancient Maya religion. Several sculptures associated with the death of rulers, such as the sarcophagus lid from Pacal's tomb at Palenque (Fig. 5.34), and Monument 24 at Quirigua (Fig. 11.5), depict rulers at the moment of death and deification falling into the underworld, usually depicted by jaguar symbolism. Jaguars seem to have been both lords of the underworld and protectors of rulers during their reigns (see Fig. 4.14). In Ah Cacau's tomb at Tikal, several beautifully incised bones show the dead ruler being transported to Xibalba in a canoe propelled by the "paddler gods" and other supernaturals (Fig. 11.6).

## Maya Deities

To the ancient Maya, the cosmos represented both unity and diversity, simultaneously. The power inherent in all things, whether natural or supernatural in our terms, could be manifested in supernatural beings we label "deities." Inasmuch as all Maya deities were aspects of the same power, the Maya supernatural realm can be viewed as monotheistic. But inasmuch as each aspect can be represented in a distinct manner, and defined as an individual deity, the Maya supernatural realm can also be viewed as polytheistic.

The diverse aspects of the Maya supernatural may be characterized by a variety of criteria, including function (a war deity, as opposed to a sun deity), sex (male or female), direction (commonly east and west, but also north, south, and center), age, color, and so forth. The quality of multiple aspects is one of the most basic features of the Maya supernatural realm. This quality can be seen in many representations of fantastic creatures in Maya art, beginning with Preclassic sculptures, such as those at Kaminaljuyu (see Fig. 3.12). It is their frequent combining of the attributes of several animals that identifies these creatures as supernatural beings. Several of the Classic "zoomorphs" at Quirigua (Fig. 5.57) combine reptilian (or amphibian) and jaguar characteristics, confounding attempts to impose our (Western) standards on Maya concepts, thus to identify these sculptures with a single animal. Maya supernaturals also combine animal and human characteristics. Examples of such anthropomorphic ("human-form") supernaturals can also be found in Maya art, of all periods (see, for example, the anthropomorphic "protector figure" behind the ruler Yax Kin in Fig. 4.20, right).

The diffuse quality of sacredness inherent in this supernatural realm has inevitably led to confusion in attempts to identify individual deities. A series of studies

Fig. 11.5. Quirigua Monument 24: scene of a jaguar-masked ruler apparently falling backward into the underworld, clutching an elaborate double-headed serpent (9.18.5.0.0, or A.D. 795).

undertaken to classify and describe specific deities drew upon the Maya codices, wherein the portraits and associated glyphs representing particular anthropomorphic deities are most clearly represented. But although there is general consensus about the identity of a dozen or so of these deities, not surprisingly there is confusion about the remainder, and even disagreement over the total number of "separate deities." In large measure, this confusion stems from our Westernized attempts to classify what is a fluid concept of supernatural power into our own ordered and demarcated categories. In what follows, you will find that this fluidity of concept is occasionally reflected in a fluidity of names, as well.

Since the Maya codices date from the Postclassic period, and since some of the attributes of the deity portraits they contain can be linked to non-Maya (Mexican) supernatural beings, it can be argued that the deities in the codices derive in some measure from the belief systems of ancient Mexico. This position seems to be supported by the relative rarity of comparable representations of anthropomorphic deities in Maya materials created prior to the Postclassic era. Thus the seemingly ordered polytheistic character of Maya ideology apparent from the studies of the Postclassic codices may reflect, at least in part, the incorporation of non-Maya beliefs, rather than indigenous Maya ideological concepts.

Several studies of Maya ideology have explored the painted scenes on Classic pottery vessels. Most of the scenes are difficult to interpret, but they appear to represent aspects of ancient Maya myth and ritual, occasionally depicting anthropomorphic deities, such as God N (see below under "Other Deities"), in settings that suggest myth. More often, they depict humans engaged in apparent ritual, sometimes wearing costumes, masks, and headdresses to impersonate deities. These studies contribute to our understanding of Maya ideology, but their usefulness is limited by the fact that most of the vessels upon which their interpretations are based have been looted from Maya sites, and whatever we would like to have known about how, where, and with what they were found is lost forever. However intriguing, then, the interpretations of the scenes on these vessels remain limited and unverified (see the Introduction for a discussion of the physical and analytical destruction wrought by the continued looting of Maya archaeological sites).

With these qualifications in mind, we can briefly consider the principal anthropomorphic deities represented in the codices (Fig. 11.7), in approximately decreasing order of frequency of appearance. The letter designations proposed by Paul Schellhas at the beginning of the twentieth century, and still in general use with some modifications, are noted here for convenience.

### Itzamna, a Reptilian Deity (God D)

Itzamna, the all-pervasive reptilian deity of the ancient Maya, embodies well the monotheistic-polytheistic duality of the Maya supernatural. "Itzamna" means

Fig. 11.6. Drawing of a scene on an incised bone from the tomb of Ah Cacau, depicting the Tikal ruler (center) being borne in a canoe into the watery underworld by the "paddler gods" and animal deities.

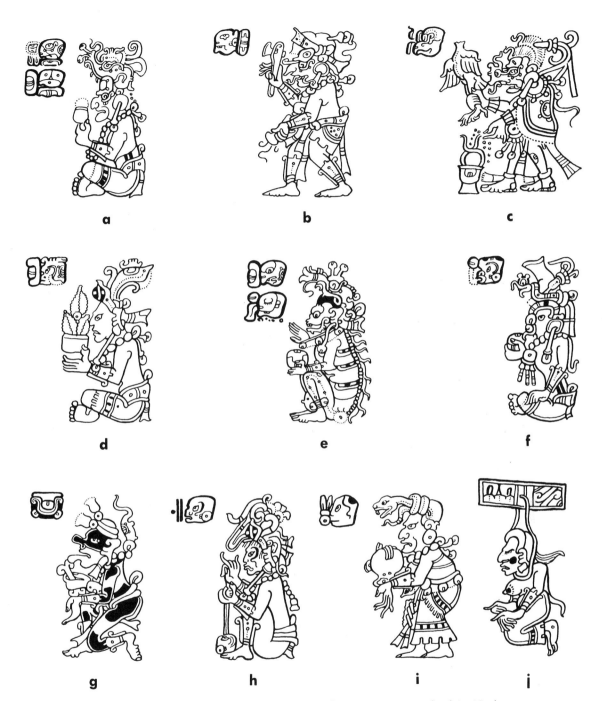

Fig. 11.7. Maya deities, as represented in the Postclassic codices: (*a*) Itzamna, a sky deity (God D); (*b*) Chac, a rain deity (God B); (*c*) Bolon Tza'cab, a ruling-lineage deity (God K); (*d*) Yum Kaax, a maize deity (God E); (*e*) Yum Cimil, a death deity (God A); (*f*) Ah Chicum Ek, a North Star deity (God C); (*g*) Ek Chuah, a merchant deity (God M); (*h*) Buluc Chabtan, a war and human-sacrifice deity (God F); (*i*) Ix Chel, a rainbow deity (Goddess I); (*j*) Ixtab, a suicide deity. Kinich Ahau (God G) is not shown.

in Yucatec Mayan "reptile (or iguana) house," which alludes, it would seem, to the fact that both earth and sky were reptilian in Maya cosmology, and indeed Itzamna had both terrestrial and celestial aspects. In perhaps its most fundamental aspect, Itzamna was Hunab Ku, the creator of the universe. "They worshiped a single god who was named Hunab and Zamana, which is to say one only god." "Hunab Ku" means precisely that in Yucatec Mayan (*hun*, "one"; *ab*, "state of being"; *ku*, "god"). Itzamna's role as creator was so remote from everyday affairs, however, that Hunab Ku seems to have figured little in the life of the ancient Maya, and no representations of Hunab Ku have been identified in the codices or elsewhere. In the *Popol Vuh*, the sacred book of the highland Quiche Maya, the creator fashioned humankind out of maize.

In the codices, Itzamna is represented as an old man with toothless jaws and sunken cheeks (Fig. 11.7*a*). He has two name glyphs: one may be a conventionalized representation of his head; the other contains as its main element the day-sign Ahau. Since *ahau* meant "king, monarch, prince, or great lord," Itzamna's name glyph verifies his supernatural primacy. He was patron of the day Ahau, the last and most important of the twenty Maya days.

Itzamna was considered lord of the heavens, and lord of day and night. He is credited with inventing books and writing, and is said to have named the places in Yucatan and to have divided its lands.

As early as the Late Preclassic (as on Stela 19 at Kaminaljuyu), the central element of the night sky, the Milky Way, was depicted as a two-headed serpent, and representations of that sort continued on the sculpture of the Classic and Postclassic periods. In this sense, the celestial serpent is probably another manifestation of Itzamna, his body representing the Milky Way or sky; his front (right-hand) head faces east, symbolizing the rising sun, the morning star (Venus), and life itself; his rear (left-hand) head representing the west, the setting sun, and death, usually depicted by a fleshless lower jaw (see Fig. 4.20, left). The so-called ceremonial bar, held by rulers in the sculptured portraits on many Classic Maya stelae such as those at Copan, is clearly a representation of this two-headed, celestial-serpent aspect of Itzamna.

Itzamna appears to be associated with the ruling lineages of Maya centers, probably as their chief patron. This is especially apparent from the identification of rulers with Kinich Ahau (also called Ah Kinchil and God G), the sun aspect of Itzamna in his role as lord of the day (see below). The Temple of the Cross at Palenque, the building supposedly dedicated to the birth of the gods and the origins of that center's three patrons (known as the Palenque Triad; see Chapter 5 and Fig. 5.37), appears to have been associated with Itzamna. The inscriptions in this building record a mythical date (1.18.5.3.2 9 Ik 15 Ceh) that may refer to his birth. The two companion temples are linked to the other members of the Palenque Triad and seem to record similar, though later, mythical dates for these deities.

Another reptilian deity, the feathered serpent Kukulcan, may be but another aspect of Itzamna. Kukulcan was especially prominent in the Postclassic period, in keeping with his strong associations with Mexican ideology. In Mexico the feathered serpent, known by his Nahuatl name Quetzalcoatl, was the supernatural patron of rulers. Study has shown that part of the birth date recorded in Palenque's Temple of the Cross, 9 Ik, corresponds to an alternative name for Quetzalcoatl, 9 Wind. It has also been suggested that there are twin aspects of Kukulcan/ Quetzalcoatl, one associated with good omens, the other with evil omens. The duality manifest in the good/evil aspects of Quetzalcoatl parallels the life/death aspects of Itzamna symbolized in his two-headed, celestial-spirit representation.

During the important ceremonies in connection with the Maya New Year, Itzamna was especially invoked to avert calamities. In the month of Uo, at a ceremony in honor of his manifestation as the sun god, the priests consulted the sacred books to learn the auguries for the coming year. In the month of Zip he was invoked as the god of medicine, together with Ix Chel. In the month of Mac he was worshiped by the old men in a ceremony with the four aspects of Chac (see Chac, below). In these ceremonies Itzamna was benevolent, never linked with destruction or disaster; in the codices he never appears with the symbols of death.

### Kinich Ahau (Ah Kinchil), a Sun Deity (God G)

Although Kinich Ahau, or Ah Kinchil, "the sun-faced one," has been considered a distinct figure, he seems clearly to have been the day aspect of Itzamna. As such, symbolizing the sun's life in its daily journey across the sky, and hence all life, this aspect of Itzamna was closely associated with Maya rulers. The rulers of several Maya centers appear to have assumed an identity with Kinich Ahau, either because they wanted to associate themselves with their powerful supernatural patron or because they wanted to foster the belief that they were manifestations of the sun god.

### Chac, a Rain Deity (God B)

The figure identified as Chac, the Maya rain deity, is represented in the codices with a reptilian face, a long, often down-curling snout, and two curved fangs projecting downward from the mouth (Fig. 11.7b). Although the portraits of God B in the codices have also been identified as Kukulcan and Itzamna, it seems more likely that God B represents Chac, his reptilian appearance simply indicating a close relationship to Itzamna or perhaps a manifestation of him. God B's name glyph in the Madrid Codex has a T-shaped eye, probably reflecting an association with Tlaloc, the Mexican rain god, who is recognized by this attribute.

Chac had four principal aspects, each linked to a cardinal direction and each associated with its own color: Chac Xib Chac, the Red Chac of the East; Sac Xib Chac, the White Chac of the North; Ek Xib Chac, the Black Chac of the West; and Kan Xib Chac, the Yellow Chac of the South. Chac Xib Chac has been identified as part of the imagery associated with rulers, specifically as the figurine that often dangles from the belt chain on Early Classic portraits.

In the months of Chen or Yax a great festival, called *ocna*, meaning "enter the house," was held in honor of the Chacs. The four gods known as the Bacabs, who were closely associated with the Chacs, were consulted to determine a propitious day for the ceremony, which was devoted to renovation of the Temple of the Chacs. During this annual ceremony, the idols and incense burners were renewed, and if necessary, the temple itself was rebuilt. A tablet commemorating the event was set into the temple wall.

The rain god, like Itzamna a benevolent god, was associated with creation and life. For the ordinary Maya farmer whose paramount interest was his maize field, Chac was the all-important deity, and his friendly intervention was sought more frequently than that of all the other gods combined. The mask panels with long curling noses found throughout the Maya area, but especially in Puuc architecture, are probably representations of the head of this god (Fig. 14.4).

### Bolon Tza'cab, a Ruling-Lineage Deity (God K)

Bolon Tza'cab is also portrayed in the codices with a reptilian face. His long snout is more elaborate than that of God B, and usually upturned (Fig. 11.7*c*). In Classic-period representations, he is usually depicted with an axe or smoking cigar in his forehead. As might be expected, God K is associated with both Itzamna (God D) and Chac (God B), and thus can also be viewed as a manifestation of Itzamna. Bolon Tza'cab, "he of nine (many) generations," is mentioned in the *Books of Chilam Balam*, and his name glyph (recognizable from the codices) appears as a title or name for rulers in the texts from several Classic-period Maya sites.

God K is the image portrayed on the manikin scepter (Fig. 11.8), often held as a symbol of office by the rulers depicted on the sculptured stelae of the Classic period (Fig. 11.8*b*). In fact, the act of acquiring the manikin scepter is usually seen as the equivalent to inauguration for ancient Maya rulers. The first known representations of God K on the manikin scepter appear at Tikal, where the figure appears to be related to Tlaloc, the Mexican rain deity. It has been suggested that this symbol of rulership developed from images of Tlaloc or from the emblem associated with the dynasty that assumed power at Tikal during the Early Classic (see Chapter 4). The manikin scepter itself seems to have been derived from the atlatl carried by militant rulers at Tikal and elsewhere. The role of God K as patron-protector of ruling families is supported by the association with Itzamna and by the procreative role reflected in the name Bolon Tza'cab, with its implications for the continuity of the dynasty (also known as Kawil in Classic texts).

At Palenque, God K is linked closely to the Temple of the Foliated Cross, where his (mythical) birth date (1.18.5.4.0 1 Ahau 13 Mac) is recorded. This temple commemorates the origins and reign of Palenque's ruling lineage.

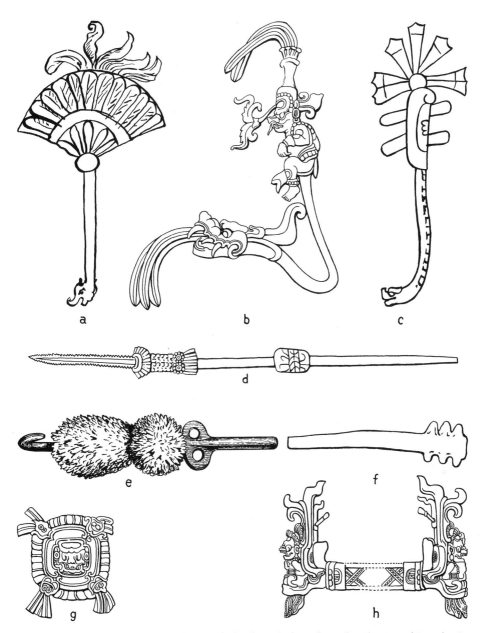

Fig. 11.8. Manikin scepters and other symbols of royal power from the Classic and Postclassic periods: (*a*) representation of a Late Postclassic manikin scepter from the colonial-period Xiu genealogical tree (see Fig. 10.10); (*b*) Late Classic manikin scepter from Monument 16, Quirigua (see Fig. 5.57); (*c*) Early Postclassic manikin scepter from a fresco in the Temple of the Warriors, Chichen Itza; (*d*) spear; (*e*) atlatl (spear-thrower); (*f*) war club; (*g*) small Classic ceremonial shield; (*h*) double-headed Classic-period ceremonial bar, the cosmic symbol of supreme authority.

## Yum Kaax, a Maize Deity (God E)

God E, associated with agriculture (especially maize), is always represented as a youth (see frontispiece), sometimes with an ear of corn as his headdress (Fig. 11.7*d*). Occasionally the corn is shown sprouting from the glyph for the day Kan, which is itself the symbol for corn in the codices (God E was the patron of this day). Of all the deities represented in the codices, God E shows the greatest extent of head deformation. His name glyph is his own head, which merges at the top into a highly conventionalized ear of corn, surmounted by leaves.

God E, as patron of husbandry, is shown engaged in a variety of agricultural pursuits. In Classic-period sculpture, rulers are occasionally depicted in the guise of God E, scattering grains of maize (or drops of blood). Like the maize he typified, he had many enemies, and his destiny was controlled by the gods of rain, wind, drought, famine, and death. In one place he is shown under the protection of the rain god and in another in combat with a death god.

Although the specific name for a maize deity is unknown, in later Postclassic times his identity seems to have merged with that of a more general agricultural deity known as Yum Kaax. Like one aspect of Itzamna and Chac, he was benevolent, representing life, prosperity, and abundance.

## Yum Cimil, a Death Deity (God A)

God A, identified as Yum Cimil (as he is known in Yucatan), has a skull for a head, bare ribs, and spiny vertebral projections; if his body is clothed with flesh, it is bloated and marked with black circles, suggesting decomposition (Fig. 11.7*e*). The principal accessories of the death deity, his "sleigh-bell" ornaments, sometimes appear fastened in his hair or to bands around his forearms or legs, but more often they are attached to a stiff, rufflike collar. Such bells, of all sizes and made of copper or sometimes gold, were found in quantity during the dredging of the Cenote of Sacrifice at Chichen Itza, where they may have been thrown with sacrificial victims (Figs. 15.41*d–f*).

Only Itzamna and God A, his antithesis, have two name glyphs. The first glyph of God A represents the head of a corpse, its eyes closed in death; the second is the head of the god himself, with truncated nose, fleshless jaws, and a flint sacrificial knife as a prefix. A sign frequently associated with God A is not unlike our own percentage sign. God A was the patron deity of the day Cimi, which means "death" in Mayan.

God A appears to have had several manifestations, one of which presided over the lowest of the nine Maya underworlds, Mitnal. God A is frequently associated with the god of war and human sacrifice (God F; see below), and his companions include the Muan bird and the owl, both considered creatures of evil omen and death. Today the Yucatecan Maya believe that Yum Cimil continues to prowl around the houses of the sick, looking for prospective prey.

## Ah Chicum Ek, a North Star Deity (God C)

God C has been identified as Ah Chicum Ek, "the guiding star." He is always portrayed with a snub-nosed face and peculiar black markings on his head (Fig. 11.7*f*). He has only one name glyph, which has been likened to the head of a monkey. This head, with a different prefix than that of his own name glyph, is also the hieroglyph for the direction north, thus tending to confirm his association with the North Star. The circumstances of the occurrences of his name glyph in the manuscripts also indicate that he must have personified some important heavenly body.

In one place the North Star is spoken of as the guide of merchants—which is appropriate, because the North Star is the only star in the latitudes of the Peten and Yucatan that does not change its position radically through the year. Merchants are also said to have offered *pom* incense (a resin from the copal tree) to him at altars along roadsides. He was benevolent, and is found in association with the rain god; he was probably the patron of the day Chuen.

## Ek Chuah, a Merchant Deity (God M)

God M has a large, drooping lower lip; he is usually shown painted black (Fig. 11.7*g*); and his name glyph is an eye rimmed in black. God M is usually identified as Ek Chuah, "black scorpion," the black deity of merchants. He appears with a bundle of merchandise on his back like an itinerant merchant, and in one place he is shown with the head of God C, the North Star deity and guide of merchants. Ek Chuah was also the patron of cacao, one of the most important products traded by Maya merchants. Those who owned cacao plantations held a ceremony in his honor in the month of Muan.

## Buluc Chabtan, a War and Human-Sacrifice Deity (God F)

In the codices, portraits of God F occur in connection with death. His constant characteristic is a black line partly encircling his eye and extending down his cheek (Fig. 11.7*h*). His own head, with the number eleven in front of it, is his name glyph. God F has been identified as Buluc Chabtan, "eleven faster," although other manifestations (or separate deities) with similar functions (and different names) appear to have existed. God F seems to have been the patron of the Maya day Manik, the sign for which is the grasping hand. He is sometimes shown in company with God A at scenes of human sacrifice. A war god in his own right, he is often shown burning houses with a torch in one hand while he demolishes them with a spear in the other. The concept of a war god, a god of death by violence and human sacrifice, seems to be embodied in God F.

## Ix Chel, a Rainbow Deity (Goddess I)

Goddess I is often associated with serpents and destruction, perhaps because of her association with the black war deity (God L). But her identification as Ix

Chel, "she of the rainbow," implies the more benevolent side: healing, childbirth, and divination (Fig. 11.7*i*). In the Postclassic period the focal point for the veneration of Ix Chel was Isla de Cozumel, off the east coast of Yucatan.

## Other Deities Portrayed in the Codices

A variety of additional deities are portrayed in the codices, and although some have been classified and described, few enjoy a clear consensus on their identity.

God L, the black war-and-death deity, is often linked or confused with God M, the black deity of merchants, and with at least two additional black-painted deities. God L, identified as the third member of the Palenque Triad and apparently dedicated to warfare and the underworld, is associated with the Temple of the Sun at Palenque. God L's probable (mythical) birth date is recorded in this building as 1.18.5.3.6 13 Cimi 19 Ceh (note again that Cimi means "death").

God N, too, often has underworld associations, and has been identified as Mam, a highland Maya earth deity, and as Pauahtun, a lowland Maya deity with unknown functions. Often depicted as an old man, God N has been identified on several painted Classic vessels, sometimes accompanied by a retinue of young and beautiful women.

Goddess O, probably named Ix Chebel Yax, seems to have been the patroness of weaving. Other, less well-defined female deities also appear in the codices. One of these, often confused with Ix Chel, seems to have been associated with the moon. Ixtab, the suicide deity, is depicted in the Dresden Codex (Fig. 11.7*j*) hanging from the sky by a halter looped around her neck; her eyes are closed in death, and a black circle, representing decomposition, appears on her cheek.

## The Thirteen Deities of the Upper World and the Nine Deities of the Lower World

As we have seen, the ancient Maya conceived of their deities as both single and composite entities. Although the Oxlahuntiku, or Thirteen Gods of the Upper World, were regarded collectively as a single deity, they were also considered to be thirteen separate gods; and the Bolontiku, or Nine Gods of the Lower World, were similarly regarded.

Certain myths preserved in *The Book of Chilam Balam of Chumayel* clearly set forth the idea of unity and the composite character of the Oxlahuntiku and Bolontiku, whereas in the inscriptions of the Classic period the multiple conception of the Bolontiku is repeatedly emphasized. Each of the nine Bolontiku (Fig. 11.9) was, in turn, the patron of a day of the Maya calendar, and it was believed that these nine gods followed each other in endless succession throughout time. Thus, if God X were patron of the first day, he would again be patron of the tenth day, the nineteenth day, and so forth; if God Y were patron of the second day, he would again be patron of the eleventh, the twentieth, etc.

First  Second  Third

Fig. 11.9. Glyphs representing the nine deities of the underworld (or "lords of the night").

Fourth  Fifth  Sixth

Seventh  Eighth  Ninth

We do not know the name glyphs for the thirteen Oxlahuntiku, although together with the Bolontiku they must have constituted one of the most important groups of Maya deities. It has been suggested that thirteen of the head-variant numerals of the Maya arithmetical system (all but zero) represent the heads of these gods.

## The Thirteen Deities of the Katuns

Each of the thirteen different katuns, or twenty-year periods, had its special patron. Although the names and name glyphs of these gods are unknown, they seem to be shown in the fragmentary Paris Codex, one side of which presents a succession of katuns with their corresponding patron deities. Some of these, such as the rain god and the wind god in the representation of Katun 7 Ahau (Fig. 11.10), seem to be recognizable.

## Other Calendrical Deities

Each of the calendrical units (Chapter 12) was also a deity. For example, the deities and the corresponding name glyphs of the nineteen Maya months have been identified (Fig. 11.11). Some of these are signs of heavenly bodies, others are the heads of animals or birds. In addition to the Bolontiku patrons for the Maya days, each day was presided over by a particular deity. God D was the patron of each day called Ahau, the last and most important day in the twenty-day uinal; God B, of the Ik days; God E, of the Kan days; God A, of the Cimi days; God C, of the Chuen days; God F, of the Manik days; and Kinich Ahau, of the Muluc days. The remaining thirteen days doubtless had their own patron deities, which have not yet been identified.

Fig. 11.10. Ceremony celebrating the end of the twenty-year period of Katun 7 Ahau (perhaps A.D. 1323–1342); from the Paris Codex, p. 6.

Fig. 11.11. Glyphs representing the deities of the nineteen Maya months.

| | | | |
|---|---|---|---|
| Pop | Uo | Zip | Zotz |
| Jaguar | God of Number 7 (?) | | Bat |

| | | | | |
|---|---|---|---|---|
| Tzec | Xul | Yaxkin | Mol | Chen |
| | | Sun | | Moon |

| | | | | |
|---|---|---|---|---|
| Yax | Zac | Ceh | Mac | Kankin |
| Venus | Toad | New Fire Symbol | | |

| | | | | |
|---|---|---|---|---|
| Muan | Pax | Kayab | Cumku | Uayeb |
| | | | | North Star (?) |

*The Deities of the Numerals 0–13*

Another important series of gods included the patrons of numerals, depicted as the heads of deities, each associated with a number. God A was the patron of the number ten, which is depicted as the fleshless skull of the god himself. God G was the patron of the number four, and God B, the patron of the number thirteen. The heads of the numbers one to thirteen inclusive, as already suggested, may be those of the thirteen Oxlahuntiku.

## Rituals and Ceremonies

The Maya, like all human societies, performed rituals and ceremonies to communicate with the forces that governed their lives. To the ancient Maya, the main purpose of ritual was the procuring of life, health, and sustenance. A number of early authorities express this idea: "They worship idols . . . in order to petition [the gods] for health and good seasons"; or, in prayer, "All powerful god, these sacrifices we make to thee and we offer these hearts so that thou mayest give us life and temporal goods." Sacrifices were made "in order to buy food from the gods so that they [the people] might have much to eat."

The gods were invoked and placated by a number of different offices. The rulers of Maya centers performed sacrifices of their own blood, presumably symbolizing the blood of the ruling lineage, to assure the continuity of the cosmos. Classic sculptures sometimes depict rulers with an implement identified as a bloodletter, used to draw blood from the foreskin of the penis, a ritual of seemingly obvious symbolic meaning for human fertility. Although Landa reports that only men practiced bloodletting, several Classic scenes show elite women drawing blood, often from the tongue (Fig. 5.13*a*). The blood was apparently absorbed by bark-paper strips contained in pottery vessels, and burned as offerings. At Copan, a cache excavated at the base of the Hieroglyphic Stairway contained a spondylus shell with a residue identified by chemical tests as human blood. The Madrid Codex shows both a man and a woman in the act of drawing blood from their ears (Fig. 11.12). In Postclassic times the blood thus obtained, and that from human and animal sacrificial victims, was liberally sprinkled over idols placed in temples.

Fig. 11.12. Bloodletting rituals; from the Madrid Codex, p. 95.

They make sacrifices of their own blood, sometimes cutting the edges [of their ears] in pieces, and thus they left them as a sign [of their devotion]. Other times they pierced their cheeks, other times the lower lips; again they scarify parts of the body; or again they perforate their tongues in a slanting direction from side to side, passing pieces of straw through the holes, with horrible suffering; and yet again they slit the superfluous part of the virile member [the foreskin], leaving it like their ears, which deceived the general historian of the Indies [Oviedo] into saying that they practiced circumcision. . . . The women do not practice these blood-lettings, although they were very devout; furthermore, of all things that they have, whether it be birds of the sky, animals of the earth, or fish of the sea, they always anointed the face of the demon [their idols] with the blood of these.

Rulers and other members of the elite seem to have performed these and other rituals in which they impersonated, or perhaps actually assumed the identity of, supernatural powers. A case in point is preserved in the scene depicted on a sculptured panel from Palenque, which is directly comparable to a portion of the Madrid Codex. In the Palenque scene, a human figure, probably a ruler, wears a maize headdress and holds an axe. In the Madrid Codex a figure is portrayed representing the maize deity (God E); he too holds an axe. Similar hieroglyphic inscriptions accompany both scenes and include the same verbal glyphs.

According to Landa, almost all important ceremonies began with fasts and other abstinences. They were scrupulously observed, and to break one's fast was considered a great sin. These preparatory purifications, which also included sexual continence, were mandatory for the priests and those who assisted directly in the ceremonies, and voluntary for others. In their fasting, they observed restrictions on flesh foods and the seasonings salt and chili pepper.

Sacrifices were an important part of Maya worship; they ranged from simple offerings of food, to the presentation of all kinds of ornaments and valuables, to the practice of human sacrifice. The offerings varied according to the urgency of the occasion. If the sacrifice was to cure a sickness or to avert some minor trouble, offerings of food or ornaments might be made. In times of great common need, human victims were sacrificed, especially in order to bring rain to such dry areas as northern Yucatan.

The burning of incense formed an indispensable part of every ceremony. It was made principally of copal (*pom*), a resin extracted from the copal tree (*Protium copal*) and less frequently of rubber, chicle, or another resin called *puk ak* in Mayan. The trees that produced these resins were grown on special plantations. The incense, highly prized for personal use and as an article of trade, was made into small cakes decorated with cross-hatching and painted a bright turquoise blue. Scores of such cakes were recovered in the dredging of the Cenote of Sacrifice at Chichen Itza. The priest's assistants prepared balls of fresh incense, laying them out on small boards made for the purpose, as the Lacandon Maya of Chiapas still do today. The incense was then burned in specially shaped pottery vessels on the outside of which the head or figure of some deity had been modeled.

*Pom* burns with a fragrant odor. If the hearts of large animals were not available for offerings, Landa says, imitation hearts were sometimes molded out of *pom* incense. "And if they were not able to have large animals like tigers [jaguars], lions [pumas], or crocodiles [alligators or caimans], they fashioned hearts out of their incense." Landa's statement has been corroborated by the discovery of a human-shaped heart, made of some vegetable substance, in the center of one of the incense cakes recovered from the Cenote of Sacrifice. Faint memories of the ancient beliefs and the holy places linger among modern Maya in remote regions. Until recently the Lacandon still burned *pom* incense in typical Maya incense burners in the principal temple at the ruins of Yaxchilan (Fig. 11.2), and the Maya of eastern Yucatan offered incense in the ruins of Tulum on the east coast of the Peninsula.

Another religious observance was dancing. There were many kinds, varying with the different ceremonies, but social dancing was entirely unknown. Each sex had its own dances, and only rarely did men and women dance together. In one of their war dances some 800 dancers took part: "There is another dance [*holcan okot*] in which eight hundred Indians, more or less, dance with small banners, taking long war-steps to the beat [of a drum], and among them there is not one who is out of step." In another dance, great skill was shown in catching reeds with a little stick:

One is a game of reeds, and thus they call it *colomche*, which means that. In order to play it, they form a large circle of dancers, whom the music accompanies, and two of them enter the circle in time to the music, one with a handful of reeds with which he dances holding himself upright; the other dancer crouches, both of them always inside the circle. And he with the reeds throws them with all his strength at the other, who with great skill, catches them, by means of a small stick. Having finished throwing, they return in time to their places in the circle, and others go out to do the same thing.

Another sixteenth-century writer wrote, "There were many other dances of which there would be more than one thousand kinds, and they considered this as an extremely important thing and so great a number of people assemble to see it that more than fifteen thousand Indians would gather, and they came from more than thirty leagues [120 km] to see it, because, as I say, they considered it an extremely important affair."

There were many ceremonies for individual or group needs, but a pattern runs through all of them. All were preceded by fasting and abstinence, which are symbolic of spiritual purification, and priestly divination always determined the most auspicious day for the rite. The ceremonies themselves also shared common features: expulsion of the evil spirit from the worshipers; incensing of the idols; prayers; and the sacrifice, if possible, of some living thing, animal or human. In the Postclassic era, after the sacrifice the victim's blood was smeared on the idol of the god in whose honor the ceremony was being held. The priests themselves were also smeared with blood, their hair becoming clotted, gory mops. Most of the ceremonies closed with feasting and general drunkenness—according to Spanish sources an inevitable conclusion to every Maya ceremony.

Blood sacrifice, the burning of copal, and ritual drinking and dancing all survive as central elements in the traditional rituals conducted in Maya communities today. But human blood has been replaced by that from sacrificed animals, almost always chickens.

### Divination and Altered Consciousness

The drunkenness reported by the Spanish (see below) was undoubtedly related to an aspect of Maya ritual not well described in the ethnohistorical documents: divination, or ritual acts designed to communicate directly with supernatural powers. Divination is used to foretell future events and to determine causes for events otherwise not understood—the reasons for illness, misfortune, and so forth. A variety of divinatory rituals is still practiced by highland Maya shamans today. These include the interpretation of repetitions in the 260-day calendar and, in Mam Maya communities, the casting of *mech*, the sacred red beans (in which an odd count may mean a positive answer, and an even count a negative one). The ancient 365-day Maya calendar certainly served to foretell events (see Chapter 12). And the Classic-period sculptures that show rulers "sowing maize" may depict divination analogous to the *mech* ritual of present-day highland Maya shamans.

But the ancient Maya also seem to have used substances that altered the individual's normal state of consciousness, almost certainly as a part of divinatory ritual. Thus the ingestion of narcotics, hallucinogens, and other psychotropic substances was seen as a way to transform existence and to meet or communicate with unseen powers. These experiences could then be interpreted to answer specific questions and determine future events. Psychotropic substances may have been used for other ritual purposes, but divination seems to have been the most important.

The Maya, like most Mesoamerican peoples, made fermented alcoholic beverages, using maize and agave (pulque); especially favored for ritual purposes was the drink balche, made from fermented honey and the bark of the balche tree (*Lonchocarpus longistylis*). Leaves from the wild tobacco plant (*Nicotiana rustica*), much more potent than today's domestic varieties, and other species were rolled into cigars and smoked, inducing a trancelike state. Cigar-smoking is shown in a variety of ways in Classic-period contexts from the Maya area.

The Maya area includes the natural habitats for several mushroom species containing hallucinogens. Stone figures of mushrooms are found in the southern Maya area as early as the Late Preclassic era, for example in the Kaminaljuyu tombs (Fig. 3.13). Dictionaries of highland languages compiled immediately after the Spanish Conquest mention several mushroom varieties whose names clearly indicate their use. One type was called *xibalbaj okox*, "underworld mushroom," in reference to the belief that one would be transported to a supernatural realm. It was also named *k'aizalah okox*, "lost-judgment mushroom."

Other hallucinogenic substances were certainly available to the ancient Maya for divinatory rituals, although their use is not securely documented. These include peyote (a cactus), the morning glory, the poison gland of tropical toads (*Bufo marinus*), and perhaps other undocumented substances such as the water lily.

Landa recorded that alcoholic beverages were drunk at every ritual occasion. In the seventeenth century, Thomas Gage reported that the highland Pokomam added tobacco or toads to their fermented beverages to strengthen the result. In earlier times, some of these substances were probably consumed as part of specialized divinatory rituals. During the Classic period at least, these substances were not always administered orally. Several painted pottery vessels graphically depict the use of an enema apparatus in apparently ritual settings; the direct introduction of alcoholic or hallucinogenic substances into the colon results in immediate absorption by the body, thereby hastening the effect.

## Human Sacrifice

As we have seen, one of the aims of warfare was to secure captives; while low-status prisoners might simply have been enslaved, elite captives were prized for sacrifices. These sacrifices were apparently essential to the sanctifying of important rituals, such as the inauguration of a new ruler, the designation of a new heir to the throne, or the dedication of a new building. Of course the most prized of all elite captives was another ruler. Ruler sacrifice, while relatively rare, seems to have called for a special ritual decapitation, and is usually rendered in the Classic texts by the appropriately named "axe event" glyph. The decapitation of a captured ruler was probably performed as the climax of a ritual ballgame, both as a reenactment of the military victory that made the defeated ruler captive and as a commemoration of the Hero Twins' defeat of the lords of Xibalba in the Maya creation myth.

Apart from decapitation, human-sacrifice rituals were performed in several ways; the most common manner in the Postclassic period, adopted from the Mexican culture, was the removal of the heart (Fig. 11.1*c–f*). Women and children were sacrificed as frequently as men. The intended victim—stripped, painted blue (the sacrificial color), and wearing a special peaked headdress—was led to the place of sacrifice, usually either the temple courtyard or the summit of the pyramid supporting the temple. When the evil spirits had been expelled, the altar, usually a convex stone that curved the victim's breast upward, was smeared with the sacred blue paint. The four *chacs* (see Chapter 10), also painted blue, next grasped the victim by the arms and legs and stretched him on his back over the altar. The *nacom* (again, see Chapter 10) advanced with the sacrificial flint knife and plunged it into the victim's ribs just below the left breast. Thrusting his hand into the opening, he pulled out the still-beating heart and handed it to the *chilan*, or officiating priest, who smeared blood on the idol to whom the sacrifice was being made. If the victim had been sacrificed on the summit of a pyramid, the *chacs* threw the corpse to the courtyard below, where priests of lower rank skinned the body, except for the hands and feet. The *chilan*, having removed his sacrificial vestments, arrayed himself in the skin of the victim and solemnly danced with the spectators. If the sacrificial victim had been a valiant and brave soldier, his body was sometimes divided and eaten by the nobles and other spectators. The hands and feet were reserved for the *chilan*, and, if the victim was a prisoner of war, his captor wore certain of his bones as a mark of prowess.

Archaeological corroboration of this ceremony was found several times in the wall paintings at Chichen Itza (Fig. 11.1*e*, *f*). One such scene portrays a human sacrifice to Kukulcan, the feathered serpent, patron deity of the center. A lower coil of the serpent-god's body forms the sacrificial altar, while the upper coils and the head rise in front of the doorway of his temple. Only two *chacs* are shown, perhaps because of the difficulty of drawing one figure directly behind another. The *chilan* stands between the altar and the god, his upraised hand holding the sacrificial knife. Several of these knives have been recovered from the Cenote of Sacrifice. One has a blade of finely chipped flint and a handle of wood, carved in the likeness of two intertwined serpents, their bodies overlaid with gold (Fig. 11.13).

In other representations of human sacrifice the victim's breast is shown already opened. Rising out of it is a portrayal of the dead man's soul, conceived in one case as a tree ascending toward the heavens, a bird perched on its branches (Fig. 11.1*c*).

A bow and arrow were also used in human sacrifice:

If he [the victim] was to be sacrificed by arrows, they stripped him naked and anointed his body with a blue color, and put a pointed cap on his head. When they had reached the victim, all of them, armed with bows and arrows, made a solemn dance with him around the stake, and while dancing they put him up on it and bound him to it, all of them keeping on dancing and looking at him. The foul priest in vestments went up and wounded the victim in the parts of shame, whether it were a man or woman, and drew blood and came down and anointed the face of the idol with it. And making a certain sign to the dancers, as they passed rapidly before [the prisoner] still dancing, they began one after another to shoot at his heart, which had been marked beforehand with a white sign. And in this manner they made his whole chest one point like a hedgehog of arrows.

This type of sacrifice is depicted in an incised drawing from the walls of Temple II at Tikal (Fig. 11.14), most likely scratched there after the center had been abandoned. Probably imported from Central Mexico in late Postclassic times, this ceremony is also shown in the Mexican codices.

But human sacrifice was clearly practiced during the Classic period as well, as evidenced by sculptured scenes and other depictions. An example of autosacrifice by cutting the throat is depicted on a ceramic vessel recovered by archaeological excavations at Altar de Sacrificios (Fig. 15.19). The significance of the sacrificial scene in the funeral ritual can be interpreted by results of careful excavation (see Chapter 15 for a résumé of this interpretation).

A glimpse of a most gruesome form of human sacrifice was recently discovered

Fig. 11.13. Sacrificial knife recovered from the Sacred Cenote, Chichen Itza.

in the excavations of Group G at Tikal. There in a building buried by later construction, well-preserved graffiti dating from the Late Classic era were revealed. These graffiti include finely executed black-painted glyphs and motifs incised in the plaster walls. One scene vividly depicts a man who, his hands tied to a post behind his head, has been disemboweled.

As mentioned, human sacrifice was practiced in the Cenote of Sacrifice at Chichen Itza during the Postclassic, and perhaps in earlier periods as well. In times of famine, epidemic, or prolonged drought, victims were hurled into this great pocket in the limestone. More or less oval in shape, the Cenote of Sacrifice (see Fig. 7.15) averages about 50 m wide and the surface of the water is some 20 m below ground level. The depth of the water averages another 20 m, and the sides of the well are either vertical or undercut. Pilgrimages were made from great distances to attend these sacrifices, and valuables were hurled into the well with the living victims in order to appease the angry rain gods. The Cenote is connected with El Castillo, the principal temple dedicated to Kukulcan, by a stone causeway 300 m long and 6 m wide, varying in height from 1 to 4.5 m above ground level. Wrote Landa,

Into this well they have had, and then [middle-sixteenth century] had, the custom of throwing men alive, as a sacrifice to the gods in times of drought, and they believed they did not die though they never saw them again. They also threw into it many other things, like precious stones and things that they prized. And so if this country had had gold, it would be

Fig. 11.14. Graffiti from Tikal Temple II, showing the sacrifice of a bound captive by an arrow or spear.

this well that would have the greater part of it, so great was the devotion which the Indians showed for it.

This prediction has been confirmed by archaeology of a sort. In 1905–8 the Peabody Museum of Archaeology and Ethnology of Harvard University carried on dredging operations in the Cenote of Sacrifice, bringing to the surface a quantity of sacrificial offerings. These articles include masks, cups, saucers, gold and copper repoussé plates, and gold jewelry. Many copper sacrificial bells of different sizes were found, and small ceremonial axes. There were numbers of polished jade beads, as well as carved jade ornaments, sacrificial knives, and several atlatls. Fragments of cotton textiles were found, and ornaments of carved bone and shell. There were also about 50 human crania and numerous human long bones. Some of the bones were carved, perhaps for use as trophies of war. Most numerous of all were the cakes of *pom* incense, usually found in the bottoms of crude pottery vessels and painted a bright turquoise blue. Study of the gold and copper objects found in the Cenote of Sacrifice indicates that they were brought to Chichen Itza from points as far distant as Colombia and Panama to the south and from as far north as Oaxaca and the Valley of Mexico.

In addition to appealing to the gods by these offerings and human sacrifice, worshipers extracted a prognosticative element from these ceremonies. The victims, especially children, their hands and feet unbound, were thrown into the Cenote by their masters at daybreak. If any survived the plunge, a rope was lowered at midday to haul them out, and the children were asked by the lords what manner of year the gods had in store for them. If a child did not survive the ordeal, "all that lord's people [that is, the retainers of the child's master] as well as the lord himself threw large stones into the water and with great hue and cry took flight from there."

## The Thirteen Katun Endings

One of the oldest and most important ceremonies worked the end of each katun, or 7,200-day period. Each of the thirteen differently named katuns had its own patron deity and its special rites. Although this ceremony started as a katun-ending rite during the Early Classic at some central lowland sites, such as at Uaxactun in 357 (8.16.0.0.0), it soon came to be celebrated twice each katun, with the dedication of a monument at the halfway point (the *lahuntun*, or 3,600-day-period ending) and at the end of the katun. In a few centers, notably Quirigua and Piedras Negras, during the Classic, the quarter-katun endings (the *hotun*, or 1,800-day-period endings) were also commemorated. But by the late Postclassic, a time when a number of contemporary sources made references to this ceremony, it was celebrated only on the katun endings.

One of the most constant features of the ceremony, and one which persisted for most of the Classic and Postclassic periods, was the erection of a monument, usually inscribed with hieroglyphics giving the date of the katun ending and additional historical information. The most elaborate version of the katun ceremony was celebrated at Tikal during the Classic period. A series of katuns were marked at that site not only by the construction of sculptured monuments, but by an entire architectural complex, the Twin Pyramid Group, constructed especially for the occasion (see Chapter 5).

The Late Postclassic version of the ceremony was spelled out by Landa. Katun 7 Ahau, for example, possibly represented on page 6 of the Paris Codex (Fig. 11.10) ran from 1323 to 1342. During the first half of this 7,200-day period (1323–32), the idol of Katun 7 Ahau ruled alone in the temple, after having been a guest there for the ten years preceding his actual rule. During the second half (1332–42) the idol of the following katun, 5 Ahau (who was to rule from 1342 to 1362), was placed in the same temple as a guest and was shown respect as the successor. In 1342, when the rule of 7 Ahau came to an end, his idol was removed and the idol of 5 Ahau was left to rule for ten years (1342–52). Thus the idol of each katun was worshiped for 30 years: the first decade as the guest of his predecessor, the second when he ruled alone, and the third when he shared the rule with his successor.

## New Year Ceremonies

Another important group of ceremonies centered around the Maya New Year. At the time of the Spanish Conquest the Maya year-bearers, the days upon which a New Year could begin, were Kan, Muluc, Ix, and Cauac (in earlier times, other sets of days had been year-bearers; see Chapter 12). Each was associated with one of the cardinal points: Kan years with the east, Muluc with the north, Ix with the west, and Cauac with the south. The New Year ceremonies began in the closing five days of the preceding year; the five days of the last month, Uayeb, were unlucky days, when everyone stayed at home lest misfortune befall. The celebrations corresponding to the four kinds of Maya New Years, although differing in details, follow the same general pattern. (For a résumé of the ceremonies and dance of the Maya year, see Table 11.1.)

As a result of her excavations at Santa Rita Corozal, the apparent capital of the Late Postclassic kingdom of Chetumal (see Chapter 7), Diane Chase was able to correlate ritual caches with the New Year ceremonies described by Landa. A résumé of these, as recorded in sixteenth-century Yucatan, follows.

The New Year ceremonies for Kan years began during the five closing days of the preceding, or Cauac, year. A pottery idol of the god Kan U Uayeb was set up temporarily on a pile of stones at the south entrance to the town, because south was the cardinal point of the dying Cauac year. A lord was chosen at whose house all the feasts connected with the ceremony were to be held, and there the idol of Bolon

TABLE 11.1

Yucatecan Maya Ceremonies of the Postclassic Period, After Bishop Landa

| Month | Patron of month | Name of ceremony | Patron god or gods | Object of ceremony | Group or groups participating in ceremony | Kind of dance |
|---|---|---|---|---|---|---|
| Pop | Jaguar | | All gods | New Year rites and renewing all utensils | General | |
| Uo | God of Number 7 | *Pocam* | Itzamna | Ascertaining prognostications for the year | Priests, physicians, sorcerers, hunters, fishermen | *Okot uil* |
| | | | Ix Chel, Itzamna, Cit Bolon Tun, Ahau Chamahes | Appealing to these gods of medicine for their help | Physicians, sorcerers | *Chan tuniah* |
| Zip | A serpent god | | Acanum, Suhui Dzipitabai | Appealing to these gods of the hunt for successful hunting | Hunters | |
| | | | Ah Kak Nexoy, Ah Pua, Ah Cit, Dzamal Cum | Appealing to these gods of fishing for successful fishing | Fishermen | *Chohom* |
| Zotz | Bat | No special ceremonies reported; devoted to preparation for that of the following month | | | | |
| Tzec | God of the Day Caban (?) | | Four Bacabs, but especially Hobnil, Bacab of Kan years | Appealing to the god of bees for an abundance of honey | Owners of beehives | |
| Xul | Unknown | *Chic kaban* | Kukulcan | Blessing of the idols | General | |
| Yaxkin | Sun | *Olob zab kamyax* | No special ceremonies reported; devoted to preparation for that of the following month | | | |
| | | | All gods | Anointing all utensils with sacred blue ointment | General | |
| Mol | An old god (?) | | Four Acantuns | Flowers for the bees | Owners of beehives | |
| | | | | Making new idols of the gods | Individual having new idols made for him | |

| Month | Patron of month | Name of ceremony | Patron god or gods | Object of ceremony | Group or groups participating in ceremony | Kind of dance |
|---|---|---|---|---|---|---|
| Chen | Moon | Idol-making ceremonies continued | | | General | |
| Yax | Venus | Ocna | Chacs | Renovating the Temple of Chac | General | |
| Zac | God of the uinal (twenty-day time period) | | Acanum, Suhui Dzipitabai | Appeasing the gods of the hunt for having shed blood in the chase | Hunters | |
| Ceh | New fire | No special ceremony reported | | | | |
| Mac | A young god (?) | Tup' kak | Chacs, Itzamna | Securing rains for the corn and a good year | Old men | |
| Kankin | Unknown | No special ceremony reported | | | | |
| Muan | A young god (?) | | Ek Chuah, Hobnil | Ensuring a successful year for the cacao plants | Owners of cacao plantations | |
| Pax | A god with a Roman nose | Pacum chac | Cit Chac Coh | Obtaining victory in war | Warriors | Holcan okot |
| Kayab } Cumku | A young god (?) | Sabacil than | | Pleasure and diversion | General | Unknown |
| Uayeb | Unknown | | Chac (red) U Uayeb, Sac (white) U Uayeb, Ek (black) U Uayeb, Kan (yellow) U Uayeb | Preparing for the New Year ceremonies, one for each of the four kinds of years: Kan, Muluc, Ix, and Cauac | General | |

Tza'cab (God K), who was to be patron of the new Kan year, was erected. Next the whole community went to the south entrance, where the idol of Kan U Uayeb had been set up, and there the priest offered it an incense mixture of ground corn and *pom*; cutting off the head of a turkey, he offered the fowl to the idol. The idol, amid rejoicing and dancing, was then carried to the house of the lord who was donor of the feast. Here the idol of Kan U Uayeb was placed in front of that of Bolon Tza'cab, and many gifts of food and drink were offered to them. Afterward these offerings were distributed among those present, and the officiating priest was given a haunch of venison. The devout drew blood from their ears and smeared the idols with it, offering heart-shaped loaves of cornmeal and squash seeds to the idol of the New Year.

The two idols were kept at the lord's house for the five days of Uayeb (it was incensed regularly during this period because it was believed that failure to do so would be followed by the special sicknesses that afflicted humankind during Kan years). As soon as the five Uayeb days had passed, the idol of Bolon Tza'cab, patron of the Kan year, was taken to the temple; that of Kan U Uayeb was set up at the east gate, east being the cardinal point associated with Kan years. Here the idol of Kan U Uayeb stood until the end of the Kan year. Kan years were considered good ones "because the Bacab Hobnil who ruled with the sign Kan, they said, had never sinned as had his brothers [especially the two who presided over the Ix and Cauac years], and it was on this account that no calamity came to them in it [a Kan year]."

Later in the year, if misfortunes began to ensue, the priests ordered another idol to be made and erected to Itzamna (God D). This too was placed in the temple; three balls of rubber were burned before it, and a dog, or if possible a human, was sacrificed to it—by being hurled from the summit of the pyramid onto a pile of stones in the court below. The heart of the victim was removed and offered to the new idol, together with gifts of food. This second ceremony closed with a dance given by the old women of the community, dressed in special garments. Landa says that this was the only occasion when women could be present at a ceremony celebrated in a temple.

In Muluc years, which followed Kan years, the idol Chac U Uayeb was taken to the east entrance, where the idol of Kan U Uayeb had been left the year before. The same ceremonies were repeated, but in Muluc years the idol set up in the house of the lord chosen to give the feast was that of Kinich Ahau, the sun deity (God G). The same dances were performed, offerings of food and incense were made, and when the five unlucky days were over, the idol of Chac U Uayeb was carried to the north entrance and set up on one of two piles of stone.

Muluc years were thought to be good years, because the Bacab who presided over them was believed to be "the best and greatest of the Bacab gods." If a Muluc year turned out badly, however, the priests turned to the god Yax Cocay Mut, "the green firefly pheasant," whose image was made and worshiped, and old women performed a special dance on high stilts and offered pottery dogs bearing food on their backs.

In Ix years the idol Sac U Uayeb was erected at the north entrance of the town and a statue of Itzamna, the patron of the Ix year (God D), was set up in the house of the lord selected to give the feast. The same series of rites was performed; at the end of a Muluc year the idol of Itzamna was carried to the temple and that of Sac U Uayeb to one of the piles of stone at the west gate. Ix years were considered unfavorable: people were especially prone to fainting fits and eye troubles; and there were supposedly more hot suns, drought, famine, thefts, discord, changes of rulers, wars, and plagues of locusts. If any of these calamities occurred, the priests ordered an idol made to Kinich Ahau and again old women executed a special dance.

In Cauac years an idol called Ek U Uayeb was made and carried to the west entrance of the town, and another of Uac Mitun Ahau was placed in the house of the lord who was giving the New Year's feast; the same ceremonies followed. Uac Mitun Ahau was lord of the sixth hell of the underworld. When the ceremonies had been performed, the idol of Uac Mitun Ahau was carried to the south entrance of the town, where it was installed for the coming year.

Cauac years were considered the most dangerous of all; heavy mortality and hot suns were to be expected, as well as flocks of birds and swarms of ants that would devour the young seed. But again the priests came forward with their remedy. This time the people had to make idols of four gods—Chic Chac Chob, Ek Balam Chac, Ah Canuol Cab, and Ah Buluc Balam—which were then installed in the temple; one ceremony required burning a huge pile of sticks and dancing among the embers on bare feet.

Throughout the year, in traditionally designated months, other ceremonies were celebrated to propitiate various gods, in order to procure rain or good harvests and to ensure success in hunting, trading, war, and other activities. Most of these have long since been forgotten, but a few of the most important are discussed in what follows.

## Celebrations of the Nineteen Months

In Postclassic Yucatan there were ceremonies associated with the months of the solar year (Chapter 12). On the Maya New Year's Day, the first day of the month of Pop, which fell on July 16 of the year 1556 in the Julian calendar (July 26 of the Gregorian calendar), all the household articles in daily use were replaced during a solemn renovation ceremony. Houses were swept clean and old utensils were thrown out on the town refuse pile. The four *chacs* who were to serve the priest for the ensuing year were chosen, and the priest himself prepared the balls of incense for the New Year ceremony.

During Uo, the second month, the priests, physicians, sorcerers, hunters, and fishermen celebrated festivals in honor of their respective patron gods. A priest consulted the sacred books to learn the auguries for the coming year, and after feasting and drinking, the festivities closed with a dance in honor of the month. The special ceremonies of these five vocations were continued into the third month, Zip.

During the fourth month, Zotz, the owners of beehives began to prepare for their feast, which was held in the fifth month, Tzec. Their divine intercessors were the four Bacabs, and Hobnil, the Bacab who was patron of the Kan years, was their special friend. Incense was burned and pictures were painted on the incense boards, using honey as paint. The object of the feast was to increase the yield of honey, and the owners of hives contributed an abundance of it, from which a wine was brewed with the bark of the balche tree; heavy drinking of this beverage concluded the ceremony.

On the sixteenth day of Xul, the sixth month, one of the most important festivals of the Maya year was celebrated, in honor of Kukulcan. This ceremony was formerly observed all over Yucatan, but after the fall of Mayapan in 1341 it was held only at the Xiu capital of Mani. Other provinces sent gifts, among them the magnificent banners of featherwork used in the rite.

People from the surrounding towns and villages assembled at Mani on the day of the feast, called *chic kaban*, having prepared for it by fasting and abstinences. At evening a great procession of lords, priests, common people, and jesters (a special feature of the celebration) set out from the house of the lord who was giving the feast and proceeded to the Temple of Kukulcan. The exorcisms and prayers were made, the feather banners were broken out from the summit of the temple pyramid, and the participants spread out their personal idols of wood and clay in the court in front of the temple. A new fire was kindled, incense was burned, and offerings were made of food, cooked without salt or chili pepper, and of a beverage composed of ground beans and squash seeds.

The lords and all those who had fasted stayed at the temple for the remaining five days and nights of the month, making offerings to their idols, praying, and performing sacred dances. During these five days the jesters passed among the houses of the well-to-do, playing their comedies and collecting gifts, which were divided among the lords, priests, and dancers. The banners and idols were then gathered up and taken to the house of the donor lord; from there each participant departed for his or her own home. It was believed that Kukulcan himself descended from heaven on the last day of the feast to receive the offerings of the worshipers.

During the seventh month, Yaxkin, preparations were made for another general ceremony in honor of all the gods, which was celebrated in Mol, the eighth month, on a day fixed by the priests. It was called, according to Landa, *olob zab kamyax*, which is probably a corruption of the Mayan phrase *yolob u dzab kamyax*, meaning "they wish to administer the receiving of the blue color." After the people had assembled at the temple and the exorcism and incensing had been carried out, the principal object of the ceremony, which was to anoint everything with the sacred blue ointment, was begun. All utensils and even the doorjambs of the houses were smeared with blue ointment. The boys and girls of the town were assembled, and the backs of their hands were struck nine times to make them skillful in the occupations of their parents. An old woman, called the *ixmol*, or "conductress," did this for the girls, and a priest did it for the boys. The beekeepers celebrated a second festival in the month of Mol so that the gods might provide flowers for the bees.

Another important ceremony was held in Mol (or in some other month if the priests found that the omens of Mol were not propitious). Called "making gods," it was the occasion for making the wooden idols. The sculptors who carved these idols were fearful of their own art, since it was thought very dangerous to make representations of the gods. They consented to do it with great reluctance, fearing that some member of their families might fall ill or die. As soon as the sculptor who was to make the idols had been selected, the priest, the four *chacs*, and the sculptor began to fast. A man was selected to build a thatched hut in the forest, cut the wood from which the idols were to be carved, and install a covered pottery urn so that the finished idols could be kept decently under cover. This same individual would eventually receive and keep the new idols.

The wood used was always the same—cedar, the most easily carved of all native woods. The Mayan word for cedar is *kuche*, which means "god tree," perhaps because such idols were made from it. Incense taken to the hut was offered to images of four gods, called Acantuns, each of whom presided over one of the cardinal points.

The priest, the *chacs*, and the sculptor were shut up in the hut and went to work, first cutting their ears and smearing the images of the Acantuns with blood, then incensing and praying. They continued thus until the idols were finished. Complete sexual abstinence was required of all, and no outsider was allowed to approach the place.

By the ninth month, Chen, the idols were finished. The priest, the *chacs*, and the sculptor were paid with gifts of food and beads, and the idols taken to an arbor in the new owner's yard. Here the priest and the sculptor cleaned themselves, and the priest blessed the idols with prayers. The evil spirits having been exorcised and incense burned, the idols were wrapped in cloth, placed in a basket, and turned over to the owner, who received them with great devotion and reverence. The ceremony, as usual, closed with feasting and drinking.

A renovation ceremony, already described in connection with the rain god, Chac (God B), was celebrated in Yax, the tenth month. Clay idols and incense burners were replaced probably with ceremonies similar to those described in connection with the making of wooden idols.

During Zac, the eleventh month, the hunters again celebrated a festival like the one in the month of Zip, to make amends to the gods for any blood they might have shed in the chase. Any bloodshed, except in sacrifice, was believed to be an abomination for which atonement had to be made.

No special ceremony is described for the twelfth month, Ceh, but in the thirteenth month, Mac, the old men celebrated a feast in honor of the four Chacs and Itzamna (God D). This was called *tup' kak*, or "the killing of the fire." A great hunt was organized, and many animals and birds were run down or trapped. On the day of the ceremony these were brought to the courtyard of the temple, where a great fire was made. After the usual exorcisms and incensing, the animals and birds were sacrificed and their hearts thrown into the fire. When the hearts were consumed, the *chacs* extinguished the fire and the ceremony proper began. For this feast only the lord who gave it was obliged to fast. All assembled in the court of the temple, where a stone altar had been built near the temple stairway. When the altar had been ceremonially purified, mud was smeared on the bottom step and the sacred blue ointment on the other steps. Incense was burned, and the Chacs (the four rain gods) and Itzamna (God D) were invoked with prayers and offerings; eating and drinking closed the ceremony. The month Mac fell in the latter part of March and early April, not long before the beginning of the rainy season, and it was thought that the *tup' kak* ceremony would ensure plentiful rain for the corn.

No special ceremony is reported for the fourteenth month, Kankin, but in the fifteenth month, Muan, a festival in honor of Ek Chuah (the merchant and cacao deity, God M) and Hobnil (the Bacab of the Kan years) was celebrated by owners of cacao plantations. A dog with cacao-colored spots was sacrificed on one of the plantations, incense was burned, blue iguanas, blue feathers, and game were offered to the idols of these gods, and the long pods of the cacao beans were given to each official who participated in the rite. When the offerings and prayers were over, the ceremony closed with the usual feasting and drinking, this time without drunkenness. Landa says, "there were three drinks of wine for each one and no more."

In Pax, the sixteenth month, there was a ceremony called *pacum Chac*, "the recompensing of Chac," in honor of the god Cit Chac Coh, "Father Red Puma." Judging from the nature of the ceremony, we suppose this god to be a patron of warriors. The lords and priests of the smaller towns and villages went to the larger centers, where the celebration was held, in the Temple of Cit Chac Coh. Sometime before the fifth day preceding the festival, everyone went to the house of the war captain, the elected *nacom* of the great center, and with great pomp bore him in a palanquin to the temple, where he was seated and incensed. The next five days were spent in offering prayers, gifts, and incense at the temple and in feasting, drinking, and dancing the *holcan okot*, or dance of the warriors. Then the ceremony proper began, and since it was a rite to secure victory in war, it was celebrated with great solemnity.

The ceremony proper opened with the same sacrifices by fire as practiced in the month of Mac, and the sacrifices were followed by prayers, offerings, and incensing.

The lords carried the *nacom* around the temple in his palanquin, on their shoulders, incensing him as they went. A dog was sacrificed and its heart offered to the idol of Cit Chac Coh. When the *chacs* opened a large jar of wine, the festival at the temple was over. The other celebrants escorted the *nacom* back to his home, where everybody but the *nacom* himself got ceremoniously drunk. The next day the *nacom* distributed quantities of incense among the participants in the feast, and urged them to observe all the festivals of the coming year with diligence and fidelity in order that the year should be prosperous.

The strenuous schedule of religious ceremonies in the first sixteen Maya months dictated a need for some relaxation before the exacting rites of the New Year began again. The lighter festivities, held during the last three months—Kayab, Cumku, and Uayeb—were called the *sabacil than* and were celebrated in this manner:

They sought in the town among those who were the richest for someone who would be willing to give this festival, and advised him of the day, in order that these three months that remained before the New Year should have more diversion. And what they did was to assemble in the house of him who gave the festival, and there they performed the ceremonies of driving out the evil spirit, and burned copal [*pom*] and made offerings with rejoicings and dances, and they made wine-skins of themselves, and this was the inevitable conclusion. And so great was the excess which there was in the festivals during these three months that it was a great pity to see them, for some went about covered with scratches, others bruised, others with their eyes enflamed from much drunkenness, and all the while with such a passion for wine that they were lost because of it.

In judging Landa's constant complaints about the drunkenness of Maya ceremonies, it must be remembered that every observance of the ancient religion was anathema to him. The bishop's observations about the drunken orgies—with which, he says, these ceremonies always concluded—should probably be taken with a grain of salt.

# 12

## ARITHMETIC, CALENDRICS, AND ASTRONOMY

> The sciences they taught were the computation of the years, months, and days, the festivals and ceremonies, the administration of the sacraments, the fateful days and seasons, their methods of divination, and their prophecies.
>
> —*Landa's relación de las cosas de Yucatán* (Tozzer 1941: 27)

**K**nowledge of arithmetical, calendrical, and astronomical matters was seemingly more highly developed by the ancient Maya than by any other New World peoples. Like the medieval alchemists of our own Western tradition, the Maya pursued these realms for both mystical and practical purposes. Numbers, time, and the cosmos were ruled by supernatural forces (see Chapter 11), and by discovering and recording the regularities in these realms the Maya believed they were in a position to better understand trends and events—and even to predict them. These regularities were expressed in the various cycles of the calendar; and to the ancient Maya each passing cycle brought with it the possibility of repeated destiny—and an opportunity to interpret earthly events as confirmations of the idea of cyclical history. Of course, the calendrical system was also used simply to record the chronology of events, the reigns and conquests of rulers, and other historical matters, but it was chiefly as proprietors of cosmic knowledge and prophecy that the rulers of the Maya world were held in such esteem and awe by the bulk of the non-elite population. Although the inscriptions and writings dealing with these matters have been largely understood since the nineteenth century, much progress has been made in the twentieth.

## Arithmetic

It now appears that by the Late Preclassic the Maya had begun to use a system of numeration by position—one, that is, much like our own, involving the use of the mathematical concept of zero, a notable intellectual accomplishment and apparently the earliest known instance of this concept in the world. The ancient Maya settled on the vigesimal system of counting, which is based on a position shift at twenty (rather than, for example, at ten, where our decimal system makes the shift).

In writing their numbers, the Maya commonly used a bar-and-dot notation. In this system, the dot (•) has a numerical value of one, and the bar (━) a numerical value of five (in the page margins of this book we have used this system to indicate chapter numbers). A shell (⬯) has the value of "completion" (our zero performs the same function). Combinations of the bar and dot symbols represent the numbers one to nineteen (see Fig. 12.1). The numbers above nineteen are indicated on the basis of position (see Fig. 12.2), just as the numbers above nine are in our system. This system is just as useful as our own decimal-place system. Besides being base twenty instead of base ten, it differs from ours in using combinations of just three symbols, the shell, bar, and dot, whereas we use unique symbols for each of the values one to nine, as well as for zero.

Maya bar-and-dot notation was simpler and far more efficient for mathematical calculations than was the contemporary Roman system used in the Old World (the Arabic system we use was adopted by Europeans only in the thirteenth century). Instead of three symbols, the Roman system required seven (I, V, X, L, C, D, and M), and in combining these, a symbol *following* one of equal or greater value *adds* to its value (LXXVI = 76), whereas a symbol *preceding* one of greater value *subtracts* from its value (XC = 90). In order to write the same numbers in Maya bar-and-dot notation, one employs fewer symbols and only one arithmetical process, addition. Moreover, the concept of regular position shifts—the foundation of the

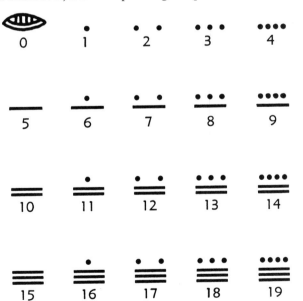

Fig. 12.1. Glyphs for completion ("zero") and for the numbers one to nineteen.

vigesimal and decimal systems—is wholly lacking in Roman notation, and a seemingly simple number like 1984 thus becomes CMLXXXIV in Roman.

In our decimal system, the positions to the left of the decimal point increase by powers of ten (1, 10, 100, etc.). In Maya mathematical calculations the values of the positions increase by powers of twenty, and from bottom to top (as shown in Fig. 12.2), not from right to left. This form of the place-notational system was not often used in calendrical inscriptions, however; in such cases the usual order is from top to bottom (as we shall see). Another exception was made in counting calendrical time, for, as will be explained later (see the right side of Fig. 12.2), the third time unit (the *tun*) was obtained by multiplying the value of the second position by eighteen (obtaining 360) rather than (as vigesimal counting would have it) by twenty.

To illustrate the Maya vigesimal mathematical system at work (Fig. 12.2), the number twenty is indicated by a single dot in the second order ("20's") and a shell is given in the first order, to symbolize zero units in that position (and to ensure that the position of the single dot will not be misread). Examples of other numbers recorded in this system are also shown, and the illustration shows, as well, the ease of adding Maya numbers: 10,951, the sum of the numbers in the two preceding columns, is found simply by combining the bars and dots of 806 and 10,145 to arrive at this total. Though at first glance the Maya system might seem very different, it is quite analogous to our own.

According to Bishop Diego de Landa, the Maya vigesimal system was used by merchants to keep track of their commercial dealings. Maya merchants used counters, often cacao beans, to make their computations, laying them out in proper placement on the ground or any other available flat surface.

On some of their calendrical inscriptions the ancient Maya used an alternative

Fig. 12.2. Examples of positional mathematics.

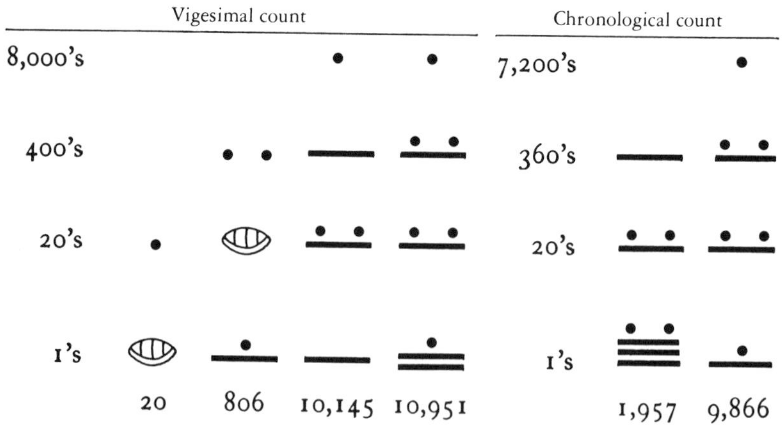

| Vigesimal count | | | | | Chronological count | | |
|---|---|---|---|---|---|---|---|
| 8,000's | | | • | • | 7,200's | | • |
| 400's | | •  • | — | •• • | 360's | — | •• • |
| 20's | | • | ⟨Ⅱ⟩ | •• • | •• • | 20's | •• • | •• • |
| 1's | ⟨Ⅱ⟩ | • | — | • | 1's | ≡ •• | • |
| | 20 | 806 | 10,145 | 10,951 | | 1,957 | 9,866 |

notational system to record numbers. This less commonly used method, known as the *head-variant system*, relied on a series of distinctive anthropomorphic-deity head glyphs (written characters drawn in the form of humanlike heads) to represent zero and the numbers one to thirteen (see Fig. 12.3, below). The head-variant system is thus more comparable to our Arabic notation, wherein ten unique symbols represent zero and the numbers one to nine. In this alternative Maya system the head-variant glyph for ten is a skull, and in forming the head variants for the numbers fourteen to nineteen the Maya used, in each case, a fleshless lower jaw to represent the value of ten. For example, if the fleshless jaw is attached to the head glyph that designates six (which is characterized by crossed elements in each eye), the resulting complete head symbolizes sixteen. It has been suggested that the heads representing the numbers one to thirteen are those of the Oxlahuntiku, the Thirteen Deities of the Upper World (see Chapter 11).

## The Calendar

The Maya calendar was far more complex than ours, for it served a variety of purposes, both practical (such as determining times to plant maize) and esoteric (such as plumbing the mysteries of astrological divination). The full knowledge of the Maya calendar must have been guarded jealously by the ruling elite, since it was undoubtedly a source of great power—demonstrating to the populace, as it must have, that the rulers held close communion with the supernatural forces that governed the cosmos. One might assume, however, that even the poorest farmer had some knowledge of the basic system, by which to guide his family's daily life.

In their calendrical system, the Maya kept records of a series of recurring cycles of time based on the movements of celestial deities (sun, moon, and the planet Venus being the most prominent). In this system any given date would recur at cyclic intervals, just as a date like January 1 in our calendar recurs after every solar revolution, or 365 days. As we shall see, these cycles were compounded into much greater cycles, and by counting from a single beginning date in the remote past, the Maya could use the system for establishing absolute chronology (in an absolute chronological system, any given date is unique, as July 4, 1776, is in our system).

### Basic Units and Cycles

The unit of the Maya calendar was the day, or kin. The second order of units, composed of twenty kins, was the uinal, roughly the equivalent of our month (nothing like a week was recognized). In a perfect vigesimal system (the *arithmetic* of the Maya *was* such a system), the third order would be 400 kins ($20 \times 20 \times 1$; see Fig. 12.2), but for their calendrical reckoning the Maya introduced a variation at this point: the third order, the tun, an especially important unit of time in ancient Maya reckoning, was composed, not of twenty uinals, but of eighteen, or 360 (instead of

400) kins. This was done, apparently, to create a closer approximation to the length of the solar year, though the Maya knew very well that the actual solar year was 365+ days.

Above the third order the unit of progression was again uniformly twenty, as is seen in the numerical values of all nine orders of time periods:

|  |  |  |
|---:|:---:|:---|
|  |  | 1 kin, or 1 day |
| 20 kins | = | 1 uinal, or 20 days |
| 18 uinals | = | 1 tun, or 360 days |
| 20 tuns | = | 1 katun, or 7,200 days |
| 20 katuns | = | 1 baktun, or 144,000 days |
| 20 baktuns | = | 1 pictun, or 2,880,000 days |
| 20 pictuns | = | 1 calabtun, or 57,600,000 days |
| 20 calabtuns | = | 1 kinchiltun, or 1,152,000,000 days |
| 20 kinchiltuns | = | 1 alautun, or 23,040,000,000 days |

(The period of the fifth order was originally called the "cycle" by investigators; "baktun," which may have been the ancient name, is the term now in use among Maya scholars.) The normal and head-variant glyphs for these time periods are given in Fig. 12.3 (normal glyphs on the left; head variants, if known, on the right); how the head variants function is discussed under Arithmetic, above.

The three cyclic counts most frequently used by the ancient Maya—the 260-day sacred almanac, the 365-day vague year, and the 52-year calendar round—are very old concepts, shared by all Mesoamerican peoples. But the ancient Maya also had many other ways of grouping days to reckon cycles that were important to their way of understanding the universe. For example, there was a count of 819 days associated with each of the four quadrants of the universe, each quadrant ruled over by one of the four color and directional aspects of God K (see Chapter 11); thus the red aspect was paired with the east, black with the west, white with the north, and yellow with the south. We will not examine these other cycles. We *will* consider each of the three basic calendrical cycles, then turn to a description of a chronological system unique to the Maya: the Long Count (or Initial Series) and its derivatives—distance number dating, period-ending dating, and short-count dating. The Long Count operated independently of the 260-day and 365-day cycles; it functioned as an absolute chronology, by tracking the number of days elapsed from a zero date, deep in the past, to reach a given day recorded by these two basic calendrical cycles.

## The Sacred Almanac of 260 Days

The *sacred almanac* of 260 days, or "count of days," determined the pattern of Maya ceremonial life and provided a basis for prophecy. The fact that this span approximates the human gestation period may explain the significance of this number of days for the sacred almanac, but among scholars there is no agreement on either the origin of the 260-day almanac or the meaning of its length. Perhaps sig-

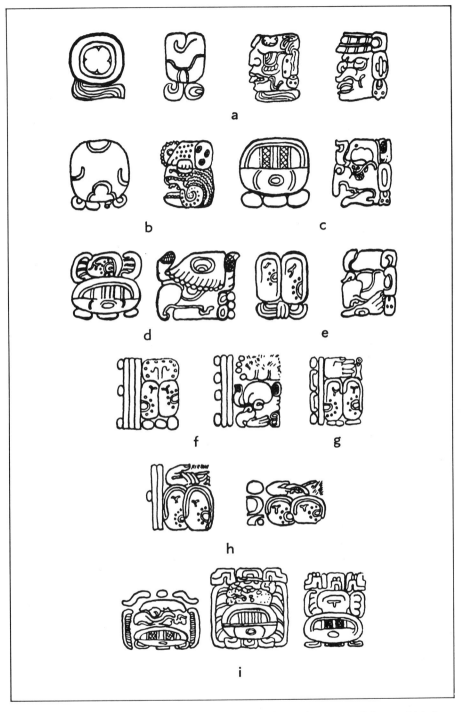

Fig. 12.3. Glyphs for the Maya time periods: (*a*) kin; (*b*) uinal; (*c*) tun; (*d*) katun; (*e*) baktun; (*f*) pictun; (*g*) calabtun; (*h*) kinchiltun; (*i*) alautun, or Long Count introductory glyph.

nificantly, birth dates were recorded by this almanac, and the patron deity of the particular day of a person's birth became closely associated with that person's destiny. Among the Cakchiquel Maya of the Guatemalan highlands, where the 260-day almanac is still used, parents still assign their children given names from their birth dates (see Chapter 10).

The sacred almanac was not divided into months, but was, rather, a single succession of 260 days, each day uniquely designated by prefixing a number from one to thirteen before one of the twenty Maya day names. The Yucatec Mayan forms of the day names are given below, and their corresponding hieroglyphs are shown in Fig. 12.4 (the day names proceed down the first column, then down the second column, and so forth).

| | | | |
|---|---|---|---|
| Akbal | Lamat | Ben | Etz'nab |
| Kan | Muluc | Ix | Cauac |
| Chicchan | Oc | Men | Ahau |
| Cimi | Chuen | Cib | Imix |
| Manik | Eb | Caban | Ik |

Again, each day name was prefixed by a number from one to thirteen, and the calendar thus began: 1 Akbal, 2 Kan, 3 Chicchan, 4 Cimi, and so on. The fourteenth day name, Cib, at this point bore the number one that Akbal had borne the first time around; next came 2 Caban; and so on to 7 Ik. Following 7 Ik was 8 Akbal, for the second time through this sequence of day names, the first of them, Akbal, would receive the number eight, the next in number sequence. Not until every one of the thirteen numbers (wheel B in Fig. 12.6) had been attached in turn to every one of the twenty day names (wheel A) was an almanac cycle complete, and since 13 and 20 have no common factor, 260 days had to elapse before 1 Akbal recurred and a new 260-day cycle began. The combining of the numbers one to thirteen with the twenty day names is represented by the meshing of wheels A and B ("Ceh" in wheel C is one of the nineteen Maya months, as we will see next).

## The Vague Year of 365 Days

The *vague year*, or *haab*, was composed of nineteen months—eighteen months (uinals) of twenty days each and a closing month, called Uayeb, of five days, making a total of 365 day positions in the calendar year. The vague year only approximates the solar year, which is of course slightly longer than 365 days, yielding leap-year corrections in our calendar. The nineteen monthly divisions in Yucatec Mayan are given below, and their corresponding hieroglyphs are shown in Fig. 12.5.

| | | | |
|---|---|---|---|
| Pop | Xul | Zac | Pax |
| Uo | Yaxkin | Ceh | Kayab |
| Zip | Mol | Mac | Cumku |
| Zotz | Chen | Kankin | Uayeb (five days) |
| Tzec | Yax | Muan | |

Fig. 12.4. Glyphs for the twenty Maya days: (*a*) Imix; (*b*) Ik; (*c*) Aknal; (*d*) Kan; (*e*) Chicchan; (*f*) Cimi; (*g*) Manik; (*h*) Lamat; (*i*) Muluc; (*j*) Oc; (*k*) Chuen; (*l*) Eb; (*m*) Ben; (*n*) Ix; (*o*) Men; (*p*) Cib; (*q*) Caban; (*r*) Etz'nab; (*s*) Cauac; (*t*) Ahau.

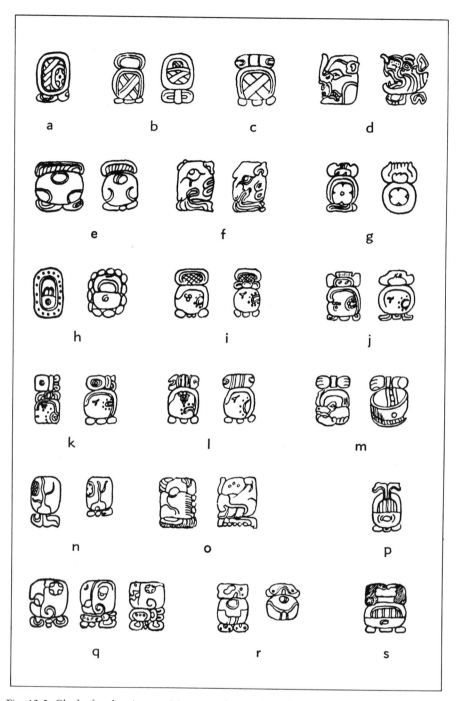

Fig. 12.5. Glyphs for the nineteen Maya months: (*a*) Pop; (*b*) Uo; (*c*) Zip; (*d*) Zotz; (*e*) Tzec; (*f*) Xul; (*g*) Yaxkin; (*h*) Mol; (*i*) Chen; (*j*) Yax; (*k*) Zac; (*l*) Ceh; (*m*) Mac; (*n*) Kankin; (*o*) Muan; (*p*) Pax; (*q*) Kayab; (*r*) Cumku; (*s*) Uayeb.

In order to show how the Maya combined the 260 days of the sacred almanac with the 365 positions of the haab, we will return to the graphic representation of interacting cogwheels (Fig. 12.6). But before the two wheels are joined, we must know two additional facts about the ancient Maya calendar. First, although the Maya New Year's Day was written 1 Pop, the preceding day (often referred to as "the seating of Pop") was expressed as 0 Pop, because in the Maya concept of time this was the day the influence of Pop began to be felt. This inclusion of a "0" day in the twenty-day month means that the last day of Pop (similarly, of each other twenty-day month) is recorded as 19 Pop (not 20 Pop), and the final day of Uayeb, the lone five-day month, is 4 Uayeb (not 5 Uayeb).

Second, because of the mathematical permutations of the combined 260-day and 365-day cycles, only four of the thirteen day names of the sacred almanac could ever align with the first position of the 365-day haab. In Classic times these were the days Akbal, Lamat, Ben, and Etz'nab, and they were known as *year-bearers*. Since each of these four day names had the numbers one to thirteen prefixed to them in turn (just as all other day names did), only 52 (4 × 13) days of the 260-day sacred almanac could begin the 365-day haab or any of its months. These 52 year-bearer possibilities fell in the following pattern (note that the pattern begins to recycle in the fifth column, with 1 Akbal):

| | | | | |
|---|---|---|---|---|
| 1 Akbal | 1 Lamat | 1 Ben | 1 Etz'nab | 1 Akbal |
| 2 Lamat | 2 Ben | 2 Etz'nab | 2 Akbal | 2 Lamat |
| 3 Ben | 3 Etz'nab | 3 Akbal | 3 Lamat | etc. |
| 4 Etz'nab | 4 Akbal | 4 Lamat | 4 Ben | |
| 5 Akbal | 5 Lamat | 5 Ben | 5 Etz'nab | |
| 6 Lamat | 6 Ben | 6 Etz'nab | 6 Akbal | |
| 7 Ben | 7 Etz'nab | 7 Akbal | 7 Lamat | |
| 8 Etz'nab | 8 Akbal | 8 Lamat | 8 Ben | |
| 9 Akbal | 9 Lamat | 9 Ben | 9 Etz'nab | |
| 10 Lamat | 10 Ben | 10 Etz'nab | 10 Akbal | |
| 11 Ben | 11 Etz'nab | 11 Akbal | 11 Lamat | |
| 12 Etz'nab | 12 Akbal | 12 Lamat | 12 Ben | |
| 13 Akbal | 13 Lamat | 13 Ben | 13 Etz'nab | |

By the time of the Spanish Conquest, the Maya year-bearers in Yucatan had been shifted forward, for reasons unknown, to the days named Kan, Muluc, Ix, and Cauac, but in many traditional highland Maya communities that still maintain the sacred almanac the old, Classic year-bearer pattern continues to hold. Today, and presumably in the past, the year-bearers help influence the destiny of the entire year.

## The Calendar Round

The complete designation of any day in the Maya calendar included the day positions in both the 260-day almanac and the 365-day haab. Thus, when the two wheels are meshed (Fig. 12.6), the position on the almanac wheel representing 8

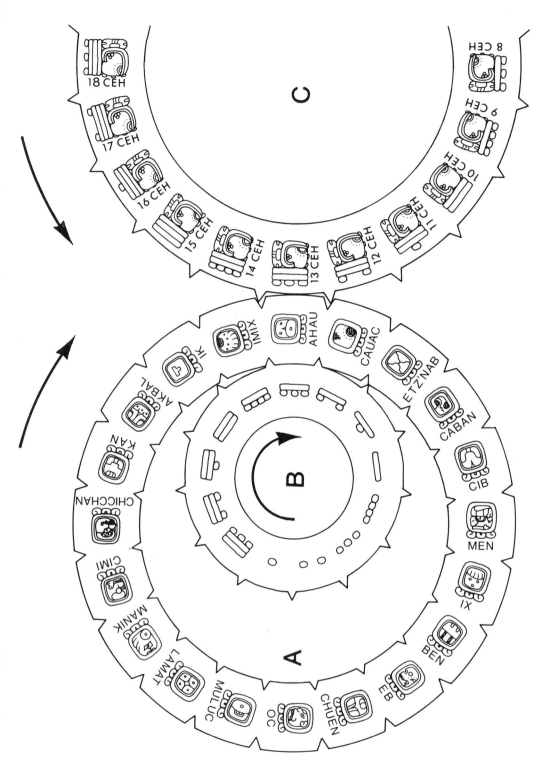

Fig. 12.6. Diagram illustrating the meshing of the 260-day almanac (left) with the 365-day year (right), the latter represented here by a wheel for just one of the Maya months (Ceh). (Note that wheel C should in reality be one that includes *all* of the Maya months, thus a wheel that would dwarf wheel A and extend far beyond the confines of the page.)

Ahau aligns with the position of the haab month wheel representing 13 Ceh, giving the full designation of this day as 8 Ahau 13 Ceh. Now our problem is to find how much time will elapse before 8 Ahau will again coincide with 13 Ceh. To discover that, we must first determine the least common denominator of 260 and 365. Both numbers are in fact divisible by 5; 260 yields a quotient of 52, and 365 yields a quotient of 73. The least common *multiple* of 260 and 365 is thus $5 \times 52 \times 73$, or 18,980. Therefore, 18,980 days, or 52 vague (365-day) years, will have elapsed before this (or any other) particular date recurs.

Once every 52 years, then, the calendar repeated itself. We do not know the ancient Maya name or hieroglyph for this 52-year period, but modern students of the Maya calendar designate it the *calendar round*.

None of the other peoples of Mesoamerica made use of time periods longer than this 18,980-day period. The Mexica (Aztecs), for example, conceived time as an endless succession of these 52-year periods and gave to them the name *xiuhmol-pilli*, meaning "year bundle." They had two special glyphs for this period, the first a knot indicating that the bundle of 52 years had been tied up, the second a stick and drill for kindling the Sacred Fire (Fig. 12.7). The Mexica believed that the world would come to an end at the close of one of these 52-year periods, and on the last night of each *xiuhmolpilli*, the population of Tenochtitlan (Mexico City) withdrew to the hills surrounding the city to await the dawn. When the sun rose the next morning, there was general rejoicing, the Sacred Fire was rekindled, the houses were cleaned and set in order, and the business of life resumed. The gods had given hu-mankind another 52-year lease on life. We do not know, however, whether the Maya shared this belief.

## The Long Count, or Initial Series

Most peoples have realized the advantage of having a fixed point in the past from which to count their chronological records, and thus to give each day in the long span of time a unique designation, but the ancient Maya seem to have been among the first in the world to put this basic concept to use.

The events selected by different societies as starting points for their chronologies have been either specific or hypothetical. The most familiar chronology of the specific type is our present (Gregorian) calendar, which begins with the birth of Christ; the Greeks reckoned time by four-year periods called olympiads, beginning with the date of the earliest olympic festival for which the winner's name was

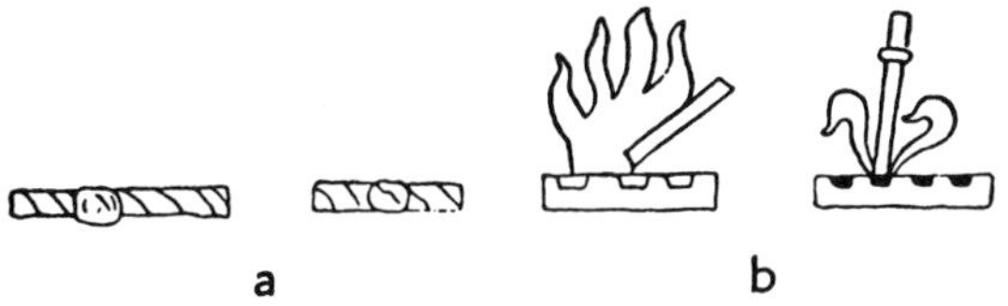

a                                b

Fig. 12.7. Mexica (central-Mexican) glyphs for the *xiuhmolpilli*, or 52-year period: (*a*) two examples of the knot; (*b*) two examples of the stick drill used to kindle the sacred fire.

known, which in our calendar was a day in the year 776 B.C. Other chronologies begin with hypothetical starting points, for example the supposed date of the creation of the world: the era of Constantinople, the chronological system used by the Greek Church, begins with a creation date corresponding to 5509 B.C., and the Jewish calendar begins with a creation date corresponding to 3761 B.C.

The ancient Maya may have believed that the world came to an end, and was recreated afresh, at the close of each *great cycle* of thirteen baktuns, a period of approximately 5,128 solar years, and they reckoned the chronology of their current world from a fixed point corresponding to the end of the preceding great cycle. The beginning date of the current great cycle, 13.0.0.0.0 4 Ahau 8 Cumku (corresponding to a day in 3114 B.C.), evidently refers to the creation of the current world in the Maya cosmology, but may represent some other important event in the past. That date in any case precedes the earliest known Maya-area Long Count date (on Stela 2 at Chiapa de Corzo; see Chapter 3) by over 3,000 years. According to the generally accepted calendrical correlation (see below), the current great cycle—and our current world—will end on December 21, 2012 (see the Appendix).

Because great-cycle dates open most Classic Maya inscriptions, Alfred Maudslay, in the nineteenth century, named them the *Initial Series*. But because, more significantly, Initial Series dates were reckoned from a fixed point in the distant past, this form of chronology came in time to be known as the *Long Count*, the term employed in all current archaeological research and writing. Long Count dates first appear on Late Preclassic monuments in the southern Maya area, and are found later, during the Classic period, throughout the Maya lowlands, providing dedicatory dates for monuments and other inscribed or painted surfaces.

The Long Count date fixes a given calendar-round day within the great cycle of thirteen baktuns (1,872,000 days). On the ancient monuments it is preceded by a standardized, oversized glyph, usually four times as large as the following hieroglyphs, that is known today as the *introductory glyph* (Fig. 12.8). The only part of this introductory glyph that varies is the central element. The various forms of this variable element correspond to the nineteen months of the haab, or vague year, and the actual glyph employed in each case is probably the name glyph for the patron deity of that haab month.

The five glyph blocks that follow the introductory glyph record the numbers of baktuns, katuns, tuns, uinals, and kins that have elapsed since the beginning of the current great cycle. Bear in mind here that the Maya used their vigesimal system to record twenty units of each order of the Long Count, with one exception: for uinals they counted only eighteen units (360 kins). The first part of the calendar-round date, the sacred almanac designation (here 13 Ahau), follows the introductory glyph, and after a series of intervening glyphs (discussed below) the second part of the calendar-round date, the haab designation (here 18 Cumku), closes the Long Count. The system can be better understood by closer examination.

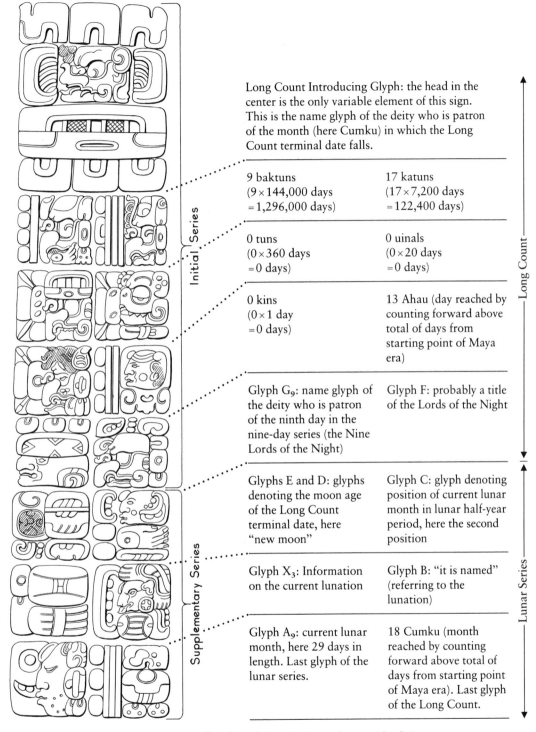

Long Count Introducing Glyph: the head in the center is the only variable element of this sign. This is the name glyph of the deity who is patron of the month (here Cumku) in which the Long Count terminal date falls.

| | |
|---|---|
| 9 baktuns (9 × 144,000 days = 1,296,000 days) | 17 katuns (17 × 7,200 days = 122,400 days) |
| 0 tuns (0 × 360 days = 0 days) | 0 uinals (0 × 20 days = 0 days) |
| 0 kins (0 × 1 day = 0 days) | 13 Ahau (day reached by counting forward above total of days from starting point of Maya era) |
| Glyph G₉: name glyph of the deity who is patron of the ninth day in the nine-day series (the Nine Lords of the Night) | Glyph F: probably a title of the Lords of the Night |
| Glyphs E and D: glyphs denoting the moon age of the Long Count terminal date, here "new moon" | Glyph C: glyph denoting position of current lunar month in lunar half-year period, here the second position |
| Glyph X₃: Information on the current lunation | Glyph B: "it is named" (referring to the lunation) |
| Glyph A₉: current lunar month, here 29 days in length. Last glyph of the lunar series. | 18 Cumku (month reached by counting forward above total of days from starting point of Maya era). Last glyph of the Long Count. |

Labels on the drawing: Initial Series; Supplementary Series; Long Count; Lunar Series

Fig. 12.8. Example of a Maya Long Count date, from the inscription on the east side of Monument 6, Quirigua, Guatemala.

The basic unit of the Long Count is the day (kin), whereas that of our chronology is the year, but the two systems are similar in their methods of recording. When we write the date Friday, January 1, 1995, we mean that one period of one thousand years, nine periods of one hundred years, nine periods of ten years, and five periods of one year—as well as zero months and zero days—have elapsed since the beginning point in our chronology (the birth of Christ) to reach the day Friday, January 1, 1995. When the ancient Maya recorded a Long Count date that we would indicate in Arabic notation as 9.17.0.0.0 13 Ahau 18 Cumku, the first five places corresponded to nine periods of 144,000 days (nine baktuns), seventeen periods of 7,200 days (seventeen katuns), zero periods of 360 days (zero tuns), zero periods of twenty days (zero uinals), and zero periods of one day (zero kins) that had elapsed since the beginning point in their chronology to reach the day recorded as 13 Ahau 18 Cumku. (Note that 9.17.0.0.0 specifies a particular *day*; 13 Ahau 18 Cumku is simply the *name* of that day.) A date like 9.17.0.0.0, commemorating as it does the conclusion of a katun (thus zeros in the three terminal positions) is called a *katun-ending date* (see Period-Ending Dates, below); dates of this sort occur frequently on ancient Maya monuments.

In the Long Count, the glyph for the calendar-round day in the sacred 260-day almanac, in this case 13 Ahau, is usually found in the sixth position after the introductory glyph, immediately following the kin notation (see the right-hand glyph of the fourth row in Fig. 12.8).

Glyph G (in the next row), which takes one of nine possible forms, follows the almanac day in the seventh position after the introductory glyph. Each of the nine variants for Glyph G corresponds to one of the Bolontiku, or Nine Gods of the Night (Underworld; see Chapter 11), and represents the particular deity who was the patron of the day recorded by the Long Count. In this particular example, that was the sun deity, patron of the ninth day. Following Glyph G is Glyph F, perhaps a title referring to the Bolontiku as "lords of the night."

Between Glyph F and the haab date there is usually a group of six glyphs (the first two appear as one) designated the *lunar series*. These six glyphs give information about the age of the moon on the date recorded, the length of the lunar month in which the Long Count date fell, the number of the particular lunation in the lunar half-year period, and references to a possible lunar calendar. The haab day and month glyphs, here 18 Cumku, follow and close the Long Count calendrical inscription.

## Distance-Number Dates

As we have just seen, the Long Count method of dating was accurate but cumbersome—to express a single day, ten different glyphs were necessary—and its full repetition for any additional date in an inscription would be superfluous; for if one date in an inscription, typically the initial dedicatory date, was fixed (the "base date"), other dates could be calculated from it. These derived dates are based on distance numbers, or the number of days to be counted forward or backward from the base date to arrive at the new calendar-round position. The distance numbers are usually in ascending order (kins, uinals, tuns, and so forth), rather than in the descending order of the Long Count. For example, a Long Count date of 9.16.0.0.0 2 Ahau 13 Tzec might be followed, somewhere later in the inscription, by a distance number of eleven kins and eight uinals (a total of 171 days), and the calendar-round date of 4 Chuen 4 Kan. This distance number yields a count of 171 days (forward in this case), which places the date at 9.16.0.8.11 4 Chuen 4 Kan.

Distance-number dates were once thought to be a calendar-correction formula, somewhat like our leap-year correction, but the known instances of distance-number dates on monuments span intervals as short as one day and perhaps as long as hundreds of millions of years. Thus distance numbers served a variety of purposes, but in many cases these dates seem to refer to cyclical antecedents used by lords to legitimize their royal ancestry and their right to rule. In some cases, in fact, these inscriptions refer to dates deep in the mythical past. For example, on two monuments at Quirigua, several extremely long calculations into the past, presumably to probe the mythological mists of time, have been proposed from distance-number dates. Monument 6 (Stela F) at Quirigua records a date of 1 Ahau 13 Yaxkin, calculated as 91,683,930 tuns (over 90 million years) earlier than the Long Count date of 9.16.10.0.0 1 Ahau 3 Zip (A.D. 761). But this is nothing compared to a distance-number date on Monument 4 (Stela D), calculated to be 411,863,930 tuns (over 400 million years) before the monument's Long Count date of 9.16.15.0.0 7 Ahau 18 Pop (A.D. 766).

## Period-Ending Dates and the Short Count

By the middle of the Late Classic era, Long Count dating began to pass out of use for commemorations of katun endings, to be replaced by an abbreviated system termed *period-ending dating*. By this method the inscriptions record only a particular katun (or 7,200-day period) and the name of the day that katun ended; thus the ten glyphs needed to express the Long Count katun-ending date 9.16.0.0.0 2 Ahau 13 Tzec are reduced to three, namely Katun 16 2 Ahau 13 Tzec (Fig. 12.9; see also the opening of the Tikal Stela 22 text in Fig. 13.14). Though not computed over such a long period as the Long Count great cycle, a given period-ending date was nevertheless exact to a day within a cyclic period of nearly 19,000 years.

By Late Postclassic times the Maya chronological system had undergone still further abbreviation for katun endings, now reduced to accuracy within a period of only 260 tuns (about 256 years). This new system, recorded in the *u kahlay katunob*, or "count of the katuns," is called by Maya students the *Short Count*. In our previous example, the Long Count date 9.16.0.0.0 2 Ahau 13 Tzec, the katun ending of the Long Count (the day upon which this katun ended) was 2 Ahau. In the *u kahlay katunob* everything was eliminated *except* this ending day; all other time periods of the Long Count were suppressed. This particular katun was known simply as Katun 2 Ahau.

For any given day Ahau, this method of dating needed only one glyph for its expression, with the understanding that the day in question ended some katun of the Long Count. Since there were only thirteen differently designated katuns in this method of dating (1 Ahau, 2 Ahau, 3 Ahau, etc.), a katun of any given designation would return after a lapse of thirteen katuns; thus since each katun equals 19.71 of our years, the cycle would repeat in $13 \times 19.71$ years, or $256\frac{1}{4}$ years. If a Katun 2 Ahau ended in 751, another Katun 2 Ahau ended in 1007, and another in 1263.

Each katun in the *u kahlay katunob* was named after its last day, but the day numbers of successive katun-ending dates did not follow each other in ascending numerical sequence. It follows from the arithmetic ($7,200 \div 13 = 553$ with a remainder of 11) that the number of the day Ahau that concluded each successive katun was two less ($13 - 11$) than that of the last day of the preceding katun: Katun 13 Ahau, Katun 11 Ahau, etc. (see the Appendix). This round of the katuns was represented graphically by the ancient Maya as a wheel, the periphery of which was divided into sections, one for each of the thirteen differently numbered katuns. Landa describes and illustrates one of these katun wheels (Fig. 12.10):

> Not only did the Indians have a count for the year and months, as has been said and previously set out, but they also had a certain method of counting time and their affairs by their ages, which they counted by twenty-year periods, counting thirteen twenties, with one of the twenty signs of their months, which they call Ahau, not in order, but going backward as appears in the following circular design. In their language they call these [periods] katuns, and with these they make a calculation of their ages that is marvelous, thus it was easy for the old man of whom I spoke in the first chapter [of Landa's original manuscript] to recall events that had taken place three hundred years before. Had I not known of these calculations, I should not have believed it possible to recall thus after such a period.

The direction of movement is counterclockwise, in order that the katuns (written with Roman numerals) pass the cross at the top in the proper sequence, the days Ahau decreasing by two in each section of the wheel. The words in the center of Landa's wheel read, "They call this count in their language *wazlazon katam* [more

Fig. 12.9. A period-ending date: (*a*) Katun 16; (*b*) 2 Ahau; (*c*) 13 Tzec, marking the end of Katun 16, which fell on the day called 2 Ahau 13 Tzec (9.16.0.0.0 2 Ahau 13 Tzec in the Long Count).

a          b          c

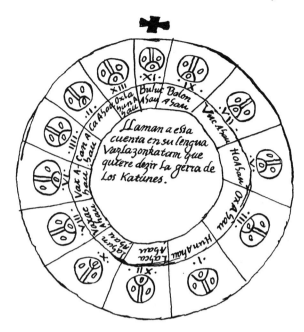

Fig. 12.10. The round of the katuns represented as a wheel, from Bishop Landa's *Relación de las cosas de Yucatán.*

properly *wazaklom katun*], which means the round [or return] of the epochs [katuns]."

The katun from which this round was counted seems to have been a Katun 8 Ahau. The repetition of the whole sequence began after each Katun 8 Ahau was completed, and these repeated katuns were called *uudz katunob*, "the katuns that are doubled back."

Each of the thirteen katuns had its patron deity, its prophecies, and its special ceremonies. A series of eleven katuns, part of the *u kahlay katunob*, is presented in the Paris Codex, beginning with a Katun 4 Ahau (perhaps A.D. 1224–44) and closing with a Katun 10 Ahau (perhaps 1421–41). One of the intermediate katuns, a Katun 7 Ahau (perhaps 1323–42) has been reproduced in part in Fig. 11.10.

The *u kahlay katunob*, or Short Count, was a kind of historical synopsis presented in a succession of approximately twenty-year periods, and so long as the sequences remained unbroken it was accurate enough for ordinary purposes. At the time of the Spanish Conquest, this record, if we can trust its ordering, stretched back through 62 katuns, to 9.0.0.0.0 (A.D. 435), a period of eleven centuries.

## Correlating the Maya and European Calendars

As we have seen, the Maya calendar was based on the basic Mesoamerican 52-year cycle, or calendar round, which was determined by the permutation of the 260-day sacred almanac and the 365-day vague year. The combination of the numbers

≡  

one to thirteen and the twenty named days produced the 260-day almanac ($13 \times 20 = 260$); the 365-day vague year comprised eighteen named months, each composed of twenty days (numbered zero to nineteen), and a final five-day month (numbered zero to four) named Uayeb.

The Long Count system used by the ancient Maya was developed during the Late Preclassic and is found on monuments of the Classic era throughout the lowlands. It recorded calendar-round dates within a great cycle of thirteen baktuns (1,872,000 days, or some 5,128 years), thus fixing any given day within the current great cycle, which began in 3114 B.C. To accomplish this precision, a modified vigesimal numerical system was used to record (in reverse order) the numbers of kins (days), uinals (twenty kins), tuns (eighteen uinals, or 360 days), katuns (twenty tuns, or 7,200 days), and baktuns (twenty katuns, or 144,000 days) elapsed from the beginning of the current great cycle or zero date. The series of glyphs recording a given Long Count date is readily expressed in our Arabic numerals, as for example 9.15.10.0.0, which constitutes nine baktuns (1,296,000 days), fifteen katuns (108,000 days), ten tuns (3,600 days), zero uinals, and zero kins and designates the calendar-round date 3 Ahau 3 Mol (June 30, A.D. 741).

Once a given calendrical inscription established a Long Count date, any other date within that inscription could be recorded by giving the number of days (distance numbers) needed to count forward or backward from the Long Count position to the second date. As we have seen, some Classic texts recorded abbreviated or period-ending dates, which consisted simply of the katun number and the calendar-round date. Thus, the previously given Long Count date could also be recorded simply as Katun 15 3 Ahau 3 Mol. And the Late Postclassic saw the even briefer Short Count, which recorded only the day on which the katun ended, in this case Katun 3 Ahau.

Because the Long Count system was no longer in use by the time of the Spanish Conquest, the Maya Long Count cannot be directly correlated with the European calendar. We do have correlations with the Short Count system then in use, however, because sixteenth-century documents record *u kahlay katunob* dates corresponding to days in the Julian calendar then in use in Europe (see the Appendix). These include the founding of the city of Mérida, in Yucatan, on January 6, 1542. By comparing dates like these, scholars have concluded that a Katun 13 Ahau of the Short Count ended sometime during the Julian year 1539. Assuming continuity with the old Long Count, the problem becomes one of determining which Katun 13 Ahau Long Count position (out of several possibilities) might correspond to the recorded Short Count Katun 13 Ahau. In other words, the correlation problem becomes a question of integrating the Postclassic Short Count with the earlier Long Count system, then relating that date to the Julian calendar and converting the Julian date to the modern Gregorian calendar.

The generally accepted correlation, and the one followed throughout this book, is Goodman-Martinez-Thompson (the GMT correlation), which places the Long

Count katun ending of 11.16.0.0.0 13 Ahau 8 Xul on the Gregorian date of November 12, 1539 (just how this is all accomplished is explained in the Appendix). The GMT correlation is in best accord with chronological evidence from both archaeological and historical sources, but numerous other correlations have been proposed. One of these, the Spinden correlation, also generally satisfies the documentary evidence, and although in some ways it is in better accord (than GMT) with the archaeological data from the northern lowlands, it is less in agreement with the evidence from archaeology in the rest of the Maya area. The Spinden correlation would require all Maya dates to be placed about 256 years (one Short Count cycle) earlier than the GMT correlation, since it establishes the Katun 13 Ahau Short Count date at 12.9.0.0.0 in the Long Count. Another correlation, advanced by George Vaillant, places Katun 13 Ahau at 11.3.0.0.0; this would *add* some 256 years to the dates given by the GMT correlation, placing the end of the Classic period at about 1150 and greatly compressing the Postclassic era. Though most scholars advocate the 11.16.0.0.0 (GMT) correlation, some do not rule out Vaillant's 11.3 correlation. Additional correlations, based on astronomical criteria such as the lunar tables in the Dresden Codex, tend to lack support from archaeological or historical sources.

The advent of radiocarbon dating afforded archaeologists a new opportunity to test these various correlations. Although not infallible, radiocarbon dating can increase the certainty of archaeological results. The tests were run with sapodilla-wood samples from the dated lintels preserved at Tikal (minute samples of the wood are all that were needed). The earliest tests, run before the radiocarbon method was perfected, seemed to favor the Spinden correlation. A much larger sample, however, was tested later, using an improved radiocarbon procedure. In one of these later tests, twelve samples were dated from Temple IV. Of these, ten were consistent with the age span predicted by the GMT correlation (A.D. 741–51), and only one fell within the span based on the Spinden correlation (A.D. 481–91). This and the one remaining sample (which fell halfway between these two spans) were probably from older beams reused in Temple IV. This test, along with those based on samples from other Tikal temples, offers strong support for the GMT correlation.

The Long Count katun and half-katun endings from 8.0.0.0.0 to 13.0.0.0.0, calculated on the basis of the GMT correlation, are given in the Appendix of this book, and the Appendix includes detailed instructions on how to convert Maya Long Count dates to our calendar and vice versa. All Gregorian conversions of Long Count dates in the preceding text employ the GMT correlation.

## Astronomy

Most of our knowledge of ancient Maya astronomical calculations, which provided the basis not only for their complex calendar but also for many of their cosmological beliefs (see Chapter 11), comes from the texts carved on monuments or written in the surviving codices. Moreover, archaeological remains indicate that some of the structures built by the Maya are linked to astronomical events. Examples include preserved monumental and architectural alignments, such as stelae 10 and 12 at Copan (Fig. 12.11), and the more complex Group E assemblage at Uaxactun, which are aligned to mark the solstices and equinoxes (Fig. 4.27). The

Fig. 12.11. An astronomical alignment composed of stelae 10 and 12 at Copan, Honduras.

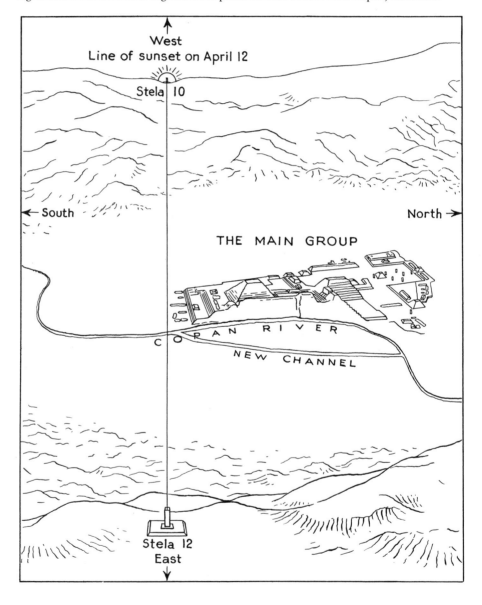

Caracol at Chichen Itza (Fig. 7.6) may preserve similar astronomical alignments. Although the simple sighting devices that the Maya apparently used, presumably fashioned of wood, have not survived, there can be little doubt that architectural alignments preserve some of the means by which ancient astronomical observations were made.

## The Sun and the Moon

As we have seen, the Maya had a fixed calendar year of 365 days with which to measure an astronomical phenomenon that actually requires, according to modern measurements, 365.2422 days to complete. The Maya probably realized the discrepancy between their vague year and the true solar year, and probably corrected for it; but although earlier theories credited the Maya with fixing the length of the year more accurately than does our Gregorian calendar, there is no evidence to support this idea at present.

We do have evidence that the Maya made advances in measuring the exact length of the lunar-month cycle, a period that modern astronomy puts at a little over 29.53059 days. But since Maya arithmetic had no fractions (or decimal points), how did their priests measure a fraction as complex as 53,059/100,000 of a day? The solution to their lunar-month problem was accomplished much as we keep our own calendar year in harmony with the true solar year by the use of the leap-year correction. We have three years of 365 days each, followed by a fourth that is 366 days long. We make a further correction at the end of certain centuries: those that are divisible by 400 (for example, A.D. 400, 800, 1200) are leap years; the other century endings, which otherwise would be leap years, are not (see the Appendix). Our process thus gives a slight overcorrection every four years, compensated for by a slight undercorrection in three out of four centuries. This system of successive adjustments keeps our calendar closely in harmony with the natural year.

The Maya probably worked out their lunar corrections in the following way. We can assume they began with a 30-day lunar cycle, but they would soon have seen that the actual new moons were falling short of this periodicity. Next, they may have allowed 29 days for a lunation, only to discover that the moons were exceeding 29 days in length. They may then have tried alternating lunations of 29 and 30 days.

But even this correction would have failed, if more slowly. Every two lunations reckoned this way would give an average lunation of 29.5 days, but the actual figure is a little longer. This kind of lunar calendar would gain on the actual phenomenon at the rate of 3,059+/100,000 of a day every lunation, an error that would reach an entire day every two and two-thirds years. It would appear that, in time, the Maya determined that 4,400 days equaled 149 moons, corresponding to a lunation value (29.53020) that was certainly close enough to the actual period to minimize further discrepancies.

Pages 51–58 of the Dresden Codex present 405 consecutive lunations (about 32¾ years), arranged in 69 groups. Sixty of these groups are composed of six lunations each, the other nine of five each. In the 60 six-lunation groups, each totals either 178 or 177 days, depending on whether three or four 30-day months have been used, giving $30+29+30+29+30+30=178$ days, or $30+29+30+29+30+29=177$ days. Each of the nine five-lunation groups totals 148 days, or $30+29+30+29+30=148$. These pages of the Dresden Codex are in fact a solar-eclipse table, since the closing days of each of these groups are days upon which, under certain conditions, a solar eclipse would be visible somewhere on the earth. The extra 30-day lunar months are so skillfully interpolated that nowhere throughout these 405 successive lunations does the discrepancy between the calendar placement and the actual appearance of new moons amount to one day.

### Venus

Recall (from Chapter 11) that in the Maya creation myth, Venus and the sun represent the Hero Twins. For the ancient Maya astronomers, therefore, Venus was one of the most important "stars" they observed. There seem to have been at least two names for it: Noh ek, "the great star," and Xux ek, "the wasp star." Landa mentions Venus as the morning star, but gives no specific name for it: "They used the Pleiades and Gemini as guides by night, so as to know the hour of the Morning Star."

The planet Venus makes one full synodical cycle (the time it takes to reappear at the same given point on the horizon) in almost exactly 583.92 days. (The individual cycles run in series of five—of approximately 580, 587, 583, 583, and 587 days each—but any five consecutive cycles average about the same length.) The Maya called this period 584 days, but they knew that this value was a bit too high.

The synodical cycle of Venus is divided into four phases: (1) after inferior conjunction it is the morning star for about 240 days; (2) it then disappears for about 90 days during superior conjunction; (3) it reappears as the evening star for another 240 days; and (4) it then disappears again for 14 days during inferior conjunction. The Maya assigned slightly different day counts to these four phases, although the total number of days in one cycle remained, for them, always 584. According to Maya calculations, Venus was the morning star for 236 days; invisible during superior conjunction for 90 days; the evening star for 250 days; and invisible during inferior conjunction for 8 days. It has been suggested that the Maya arbitrarily fixed the lengths of these four Venus phases to agree with lunations.

Ascribing 584 days to one synodical cycle of Venus made the cycle too long by 8/100 of a day. The Maya were aware of this error and knew how to correct it. One of their important ceremonial periods was the time unit composed of five synodical cycles of Venus ($5 \times 584 = 2,920$ days), for the Maya had also discovered that this period was equal to eight of their calendar years ($8 \times 365 = 2,920$ days), a coincidence that they found useful. It combined eight earth years with five Venus years and supplied a convenient period for correcting their Venus calendar, which was falling behind the apparent Venus year at the rate of two-fifths of a day every eight calendar years.

As recorded in the Dresden Codex, the Maya Venus calendar is really three distinct calendars, each composed of 65 synodical cycles of the planet. Each of the three Venus calendars is equal to 104 earth years, but there is an overlap between the first and second, and another overlap between the second and the third. At these points, at which the accumulated calendar Venus-years of 584 days had overrun the synodical Venus-years, the Maya inserted their corrections. By the end of the 57th Venus-solar period of the first calendar, the accumulated error had reached eight days. By dropping back eight days from this date, the zero date of the second calendar was reached. At the end of the 61st Venus-solar period of the *second* calendar, an error of four days had accumulated, and by dropping back four days from this point in the second calendar, the zero date of the third calendar was reached. By the use of this table the calculated Venus-solar period was kept in harmony with the visible movements of the planet for 384 years before the accumulated error began to render the table useless.

## Other Planets, the Stars, and the Constellations

There is some evidence that the ancient Maya observed and recorded the movements of other planets. Mars has a synodical cycle of about 780 days, and some scholars have pointed to the tables in the Dresden Codex dealing with multiples of 78 as being reckonings for the movements of Mars. The other planets readily visible to the naked eye, Mercury and Jupiter, were also of interest to the ancient Maya astronomers. Floyd Lounsbury has shown how several important dynastic events at Palenque (Chapter 5) were fixed to coincide with positions of Jupiter as it was observed by the Maya in the night sky. James Fox and John Justeson have also demonstrated a reference to Saturn on a Classic Maya inscription (Dumbarton Oaks Relief Panel 1).

The North Star was of great importance to the Maya. Its apparent immobility and the orderly procession of the other constellations around it made it a dependable beacon. Regularities have been observed in the alignments of many Maya structures, and there can be little doubt that the North Star and other celestial bodies were used to guide the orientation of buildings and entire sites (see Chapter 11).

In Yucatec Mayan the Pleiades were called *tzab*, the word for the rattles of a rattlesnake, perhaps because of their fancied resemblance. Gemini was *aac*, "the tortoise."

The ancient Maya may have had a kind of zodiac, composed of thirteen houses, and it may be what is represented on pages 23 and 24 of the Paris Codex. If so, the first three signs, or houses, seem to have been Scorpion, Tortoise, and Rattlesnake.

These are the first three figures shown hanging from a constellation band in the middle section of page 24 of the codex (Fig. 13.3).

### Astronomical Observatories

It may be asked how the ancient Maya achieved such a high degree of astronomical accuracy without the instruments upon which modern astronomers depend. But if the lines of sight are sufficiently long, accuracy to within less than a day's error across a span of a year or more may be reached in fixing the synodical cycle or apparent revolution of many of the heavenly bodies. Most Maya temples are sufficiently high to obtain clear lines of sight from their summits to distant points on the horizon, and a pair of crossed sticks or similar sighting devices were probably set up on top of these buildings for that purpose. From one of these, as a fixed observation point, the particular place where the sun, the moon, or a planet rose or set could have been noted with reference to some natural feature on the horizon. When the heavenly body under observation rose or set behind this same point a second time, the duration of one synodical cycle would have been established.

Although the known Maya codices contain no representations of observatories, pictures of them are found in the central-Mexican codices (Fig. 12.12). In the Nuttall Codex, in the doorway of a temple, is a pair of crossed sticks, and looking out through them is the head of a man. In the Selden Codex, an eye appears in the notch made by a pair of crossed sticks in the temple doorway. Another Mexican codex, the Bodleian, shows an eye between two crossed sticks, a star descending into a notch, and two observers. With such simple instruments the ancient Maya, too, probably predicted eclipses and the risings and settings of the morning and evening stars.

The ancient Maya thus accumulated and recorded a considerable body of astronomical knowledge, including the cycles of the moon and Venus. Their solar-eclipse tables appear to have allowed them to make accurate predictions of eclipse phenomena. And they seem to have observed and recorded other planetary cycles

Fig. 12.12. Representations of astronomical observations in the Postclassic Mexican codices: (*left*) from the Nuttall Codex; (*center*) from the Selden Codex; (*right*) from the Bodleian Codex.

and astronomical phenomena, though the evidence for this knowledge is sometimes a matter of dispute among scholars. To the ancient Maya, of course, these celestial objects represented deities, not planets or stars. Their observations and calculations were undertaken, and in due course refined, so as to better predict the events on earth that these deities were believed to control. There is no evidence that the ancient Maya understood these movements as Kepler and Copernicus did.

# 13 LANGUAGE AND WRITING

America, say historians, was peopled by savages; but savages never reared these structures, savages never carved these stones . . . standing as they do in the depths of a tropical forest, silent and solemn, strange in design, excellent in sculpture, rich in ornament . . . their whole history so entirely unknown, with hieroglyphics explaining all, but perfectly unintelligible. . . . No Champollion has yet brought to them the energies of his inquiring mind. Who shall read them?

—*Incidents of Travel in Central America, Chiapas, and Yucatan* (Stephens 1841, Vol. I: 104, 148, 160)

**T**here are today about 4 million speakers of 28 Mayan languages. Except for the Huastecs of Veracruz and San Luis Potosí, Mexico, they occupy a compact area embracing the Mexican states of Chiapas, Tabasco, Campeche, Yucatan, and Quintana Roo, most of Guatemala, and parts of Belize, Honduras, and El Salvador (Fig. 13.1). Many are at least minimally bilingual in Spanish, and by now all Mayan languages have been influenced by (and have influenced) the Spanish spoken in the Maya area. Nevertheless, a Mayan language is still the language of the home for most of the indigenous peoples of this area. Despite the Conquest and centuries of social change, the Mayan languages have survived well: although at least two are extinct and a few others are nearly so, others (for example, Kekchi) are actually expanding in territory and number of speakers.

Studies of the modern Mayan languages and their colonial antecedents, in conjunction with modern theories of how languages change over time, provide a rich source for historical inferences about the languages and cultures of the ancient Maya. Most directly, they provide crucial tools for the decipherment of Maya writing. They provide much more, of course, but these are the aspects we emphasize here.

## History of the Mayan Languages

The Mayan language family takes its name from a language of Yucatan, once called Maya but now commonly referred to by scholars as Yucatec. For linguists, the grouping of languages into families is often a matter of dispute, but the Mayan languages are so similar to one another (and so different from the languages to the

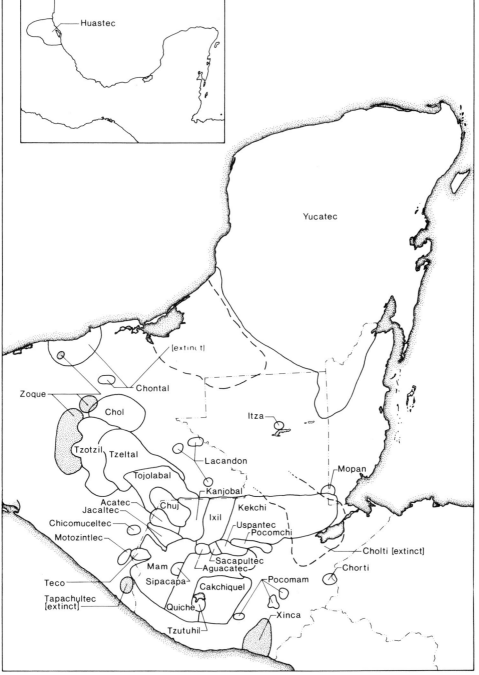

Fig. 13.1. Map of the geographical distribution of the Mayan languages: areas of non-Mayan languages are stippled; dashed boundaries indicate approximate extent of extinct languages; dash-double-dotted lines are national boundaries.

west and east) that the propriety of grouping them as a language family is readily apparent, and was recognized in colonial times. Recent research by the linguist Joseph Greenberg suggests that all New World languages belong to just three major families, each of which represents a separate migration from Asia across the Bering land bridge, a broad expanse, otherwise of seafloor, exposed during major periods of glaciation. The Mayan family, along with the majority of other New World languages, belongs to the earliest and most widespread of these three major families, known to linguists as Amerind.

As their geography suggests, the 28 known Mayan languages (except Huastec, as noted above) have been in contact with each other for many centuries, and in many cases grade into each other just as the environmental zones of the area do (Chapter 1). Changes have spread from one language to another in different degrees of penetration according to the social and political factors that pertained at various times. It is therefore impossible to assign all Mayan languages, unequivocally, to particular places on a family tree; this is so partly because not enough is known of their linguistic history, but also because no family tree would adequately represent their complex relationships. It *is* possible, however, to construct a generalized subgrouping (Fig. 13.2) that permits some historical inferences.

Linguists generally recognize three major subgroups of Mayan: Huastecan, Yucatecan, and the rest of Mayan (which we may call "Southern Mayan"). It is commonly supposed that Proto-Mayan (the hypothetical ancestor of *all* Mayan languages) first diverged into Huastecan and the ancestor of all the other Mayan languages, and that the latter then diverged into Yucatecan and Southern Mayan. On first inspection, it seems obvious that Huastecan is the most remote subgroup; it certainly is separate spatially, which is consistent with the relatively small amount of vocabulary that Huastecan shares with other Mayan languages. Indeed, Huastecan was the last major subgroup to be recognized as a part of the Mayan family by linguists. Recently, however, several linguists have pointed out that Huastecan shares many phonological innovations with the Tzeltalan-Cholan subgroup of Mayan, and this occasions some hesitation in accepting the antiquity of Huastecan. Such a radical revision of its position would imply that its sharply divergent vocabulary is due to an intense, recent influence from non-Mayan languages.

But assuming a Proto-Mayan speech community that became differentiated through migration or some other social disruption, and assuming also that the resulting communities (say, the antecedents of Huastecan and the rest of Mayan) themselves eventually diverged, whether according to a neat family tree or not, how can such periods of differentiation be dated, and where were these early communities situated geographically? Where no direct historical evidence is available, the first question is usually answered impressionistically, by an intuitive comparison of the amount of change to be accounted for, across a given amount of time, with the amount of change that has occurred in language families for which there *is* such evidence, for example Romance or Germanic.

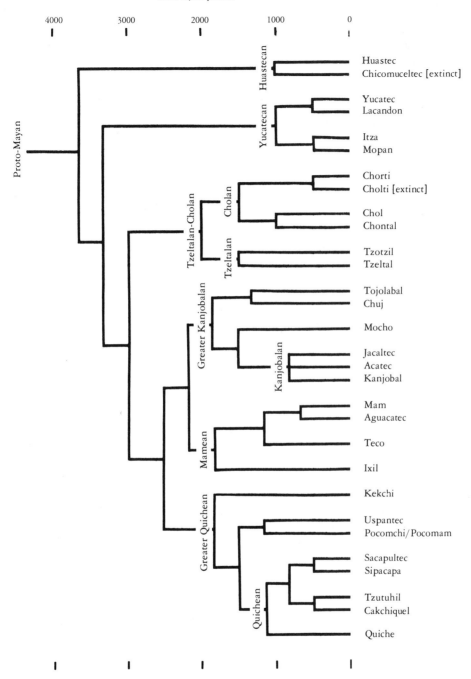

Fig. 13.2. Diagram of proposed interrelationships, subgroupings, and time depth of the Mayan languages.

Since the 1950's, however, attempts have been made to quantify both the amount and rate of linguistic change in a given language family. In one technique, known as *glottochronology*, it is posited that an original basic vocabulary that is relatively immune to borrowing (that is, body-part terms, kin terms, numerals, pronouns, etc.) will tend to be replaced in the original meanings by new words at a constant and universal rate (derived from the average rate of change in some dozen languages, mostly of Indo-European stock); at the postulated rate of change, roughly 20 percent of this basic vocabulary will change each thousand years. The degree of separation of languages can therefore be given an absolute time depth by collecting the relevant words from each language, noting the percentage of shared cognates, and computing the time span of change (in years) using the retention rate in a simple formula.

Though the assumptions thus entertained are vulnerable to many criticisms, and though the results are at best only approximations, such calculations can be highly suggestive, at the least, and the several studies that have carried them out for Mayan tend to be in agreement on an important point: all the major Mayan subgroups (i.e., Huastecan, Yucatecan, Tzeltalan-Cholan, Greater Kanjobalan, Mamean, and Greater Quichean) appear to have become mutually distinct between about 2000 B.C. and A.D. 100, that is, during the Preclassic era (see Chapter 3). Lesser distinctions (for example among the Cholan languages) arose later.

The location of the Proto-Mayan homeland has also been the subject of some inquiry, and the conclusions here are just as speculative. According to the principles pioneered by the renowned American linguist Edward Sapir, more than a half-century ago, the greater the degree of differentiation present, the longer the period of time we should assume for the development of that differentiation, other factors remaining equal. The geographical center of gravity is determined by postulating a homeland requiring the least possible number and distance of migrations to get the major divisions to their current locations. As we noted above, however, problems persist in the determination of Mayan subgrouping. Generally, Mayanists remain convinced that the homeland was in the Guatemala-Chiapas highlands. This conclusion is based on the relative lack of linguistic differentiation in Yucatecan, given its large area, and on the comparatively greater differentiation in the highlands. But in this case other factors are pertinent; the greater differentiation in the highlands may also be due to terrain barriers (compare Fig. 13.1 with the physical map, Fig. 1.1), and, conversely, the linguistic homogeneity of Yucatan may be partly due to the more passable terrain there.

The homeland issue has in some cases (for example, Indo-European) been addressed through comparison of the reconstructed vocabulary of the hypothetical protolanguage with the natural environment it would have been responding to, insofar as that can also be reconstructed. If one can demonstrate that ancestral words referred to natural items whose ancient ranges were quite limited (for example, a particular kind of tree), an area may then be indicated within which the speech community must have resided or with which it had other very close contact. Using such techniques it is easy to show that the ancient Maya inhabited an area in Mesoamerica, but that determination is of course obvious and trivial. A more precise location is sought, but for the ancient Maya it is quite difficult to obtain, for several reasons. In addition to the usual problems of determining the ancient meanings of words and the composition of natural environments, we are faced with the distinctive geography of southern Mesoamerica. Its flora and fauna are associated not so much with particular areas as with particular elevations, and the Maya speech communities, well adapted as they were to this situation, tended to inhabit several ecological zones within a relatively small horizontal area, or to engage in intense trade back and forth across those elevational zones, so that all are likely to have been familiar with words for natural objects that were themselves narrowly delimited.

The few cases that have been made also point to the highlands as the Proto-Mayan homeland, but these arguments are not without their weaknesses. At the end of the nineteenth century Karl Sapper used the Proto-Mayan word *tyax, for which he reconstructed the meaning "pine," to rule out the Yucatan lowlands as a part of the Proto-Mayan homeland (the asterisk designates a word not attested in any known language, but, rather, postulated by a linguist for reconstructional purposes). According to Sapper, the pine (several species of which have a high resin content, and are used throughout the highlands for tinder and torches) does not, and very likely did not, occur in Yucatan. Yucatec Mayan does have a descendant (or *reflex*) of the ancestral word, namely *tah*, "torch"; Sapper explained this as a natural consequence of the Yucatec migration, which left the Yucatecs with no referent for *tah* other than what was originally only one of many in its semantic range. The weakness, even if one accepts Sapper's opinion concerning the ancient range of the pine, is that the highland meanings could as easily have been extensions from "torch" in a migration going the other way. More evidence is needed before this approach can be said to implicate one area conclusively. Other studies have shown some promise for establishing more precise dating of linguistic innovations by correlating loan-words with the archaeologically verified introduction of the objects designated by the words.

Mary Haas has characterized a reconstructed protolanguage as a "glorious artifact"; for the purposes of cultural as well as geographical inference, this characterization holds especially well for the reconstructed vocabulary. The meanings of the reconstructed words tell us much about early society and culture, and much of this information is not amenable to archaeological investigation (used with caution, then, reconstructed vocabularies become another resource for the archaeologist). Not unexpectedly, the Proto-Mayan speech community had a rich vocabulary for maize agriculture, with separate words for generic maize, the green ear, the mature ear, the cob, maize flour, maize dough, the tortilla, a toasted maize drink, the grindstone, and for the first, second, and third (increasingly fine) grindings of maize. The earliest word for slaked lime (used in softening maize and giving consistency to the dough, as well as for processing other foods) was closely related to the word for ashes, suggesting that ashes may have preceded slaked lime in this function. Alternatively, since limestone is not found in many highland areas, this may be additional evidence of a highland origin for Mayan. Expectably, the reconstructed vocabulary also included a complex array of weaving terms (to weave, the spindle, cotton, etc.).

Most of the cognates that provide the evidence for reconstructing the maize complex in Proto-Mayan vocabulary are shared by most Mayan languages, and have obviously not been readily replaced through borrowing or other processes. Other strong cognate sets also seem to indicate culturally important items: salt, chili, bean, squash, sweet potato, sweet manioc, avocado, tobacco, honey, etc. Finally, terms reflecting material culture and social structure are well represented: sling, blowgun, hammock, bridge/ladder, sharpening stone, fireplace stone (trivet), plate, varnish worm (crushed insect used for lacquer), bench, mat, sandal, comb, to write, book, mother's brother, sister's son, etc.

Since 1861, when E. G. Squier first suggested that Zoque is related to Yucatec, it has become clear that Mayan and the adjacent Mixe-Zoquean family (Mixe, Sayula Popoluca, Sierra Popoluca, Zoque, and Tapachultec; for the last two, see Fig. 13.1) jointly form a higher-order linguistic family. Though some scholars still believe that the striking similarities between the two are due entirely to borrowing, many of the cognates and correspondences now proposed are not likely to have been due simply to contact. In particular, there is deep grammatical evidence for the relationship, including several Mayan kinship and body-part terms that contain archaic pronominal prefixes identical to the reconstructed pronouns of Mixe-Zoquean. This is not to say there was no borrowing between these groups, for there certainly was. Much like the impact of Norman French on English, the borrowing was between related languages; consequently, arguments for either common descent or borrowing must take into account both possibilities. But the genetic classification of Mayan with Mixe-Zoquean is of only marginal relevance to our understanding of the ancient Maya, for the divergence between these ancient families must have been great even by the Early Preclassic. The borrowing between the two groups almost certainly took place in the Preclassic, and reflects the extraordinary cultural influence of the Mixe-Zoquean on the Maya (see Chapter 2), since most of the borrowing was in that direction. Terrence Kaufman has noted the close correspondence between the current distribution of Mixe-Zoquean languages and the distribution of Olmec archaeological sites, and has proposed that the Olmec were speakers of a Mixe-Zoquean language. The identification of the archaeological Olmec with early Mixe-Zoquean speech communities would certainly explain the influence of Mixe-Zoquean on Mayan, for archaeology has indicated mutual influence between Olmec and Maya culture (see Chapter 2).

Most Mayan languages also have at least a small number of loanwords taken from Nahuatl (the language of the Mexica, or Aztecs) and closely related central-Mexican languages; these loanwords presumably reflect the rising prominence of the central-Mexican states from the Late Preclassic on (here we see archaeology as a resource for the comparative linguist).

The early Maya were not just *receivers* of cultural influence, however. Lyle Campbell has shown that Xinca, a nearly extinct non-Mayan language of south-eastern Guatemala, has a fairly large number of loanwords from Mayan, reflecting a cultural influence of the Maya on the Xinca comparable to that of the Mixe-Zoqueans on the Maya.

The same techniques used in the dating and geographical location of early Mayan have been applied, with considerably more reliability, to the issue of the linguistic identity of the Classic Maya. Until recently, the former heartland of Classic lowland Maya civilization—the central Peten and upper Usumacinta drainage—had been largely depopulated, because of the massive extermination and forced re-settlement of the Acalan Chontal, the western and eastern Chol, and various Yucatecan-speaking groups in late colonial times, which effectively removed what small population had remained after the Classic period. Now the Itza, Lacandon, and Mopan, who are thought to have entered the Peten long after the Classic, and who in some measure escaped the colonial depopulation, have been joined by scattered settlements of Kekchi and Spanish speakers, and the area is enjoying a vigorous in-migration. But what were the languages of their predecessors in this region?

Hyacinthe de Charencey, Karl Sapper, and William Gates independently established the close relationship of modern Chorti, Chol, and Chontal in a Cholan subgroup of Mayan that may well have begun to diversify in Classic times. Sapper and, independently, J. Eric Thompson concluded that the modern distribution of the Cholan languages, and the large number of Cholan loanwords in Kekchi (which absorbed some colonial Cholan resettlements and is today expanding into the Peten), indicates the former existence of a belt of Cholan speakers from the Laguna de Términos on the Gulf coast through the Usumacinta and Pasión drainages to the Golfo Dulce on Guatemala's Caribbean coast, as well as the area around Copan still occupied by the Chorti. This belt of Cholan speakers was confirmed with Gates's discovery of a colonial manuscript dictionary from the now-lost village of Delores, generally supposed to have been somewhere near the Lacantun and Ixcan rivers in southwestern Peten (that is, in the middle of the belt). This dictionary was of the now-extinct Cholti language, which was virtually a dialectal variant of Chorti, as the names suggest.

It seemed justified, therefore, to infer that Cholan, perhaps already dialectally differentiated, was the language of the Classic Maya heartland. John Justeson and James Fox have recently proposed, from the inscriptional evidence, that Cholan was indeed the language spoken at several sites (Palenque, Dos Pilas, Aguateca, Copan) along the southern edge of the proposed belt, but they also show that Yucatecan was being used much farther south than had been anticipated, namely, in Piedras Negras, Bonampak, Yaxchilan, Seibal, and Naranjo. Tzeltalan, too, is at least geographically implicated as a language that may have been used at highland Chiapas sites, but it has not yet been possible to distinguish it hieroglyphically. Inscriptional evidence is the only hope for such precise definition of ancient language borders, since most place names in the depopulated area are new and thus give no evidence of the language of the earlier inhabitants.

Notwithstanding our subgrouping of Mayan (Fig. 13.2), in which Yucatecan is shown as only distantly related to Cholan and Tzeltalan, these language families have been geographically adjacent to one another for a long time, during which their speakers shared the cultural advancements of Classic Maya civilization. In particular, Cholan and Yucatecan share some important features not found in Tzeltalan. But because the three families influenced each other so substantially, especially in loanwords and writing, they may be treated as a cultural subgroup, which may be termed Greater Lowland Mayan.

## The Structure of Mayan Languages

Although the study of Mayan linguistic structures is relevant to many disciplines, including theoretical linguistics, we are here concerned mostly with those aspects that have been directly applicable to the decipherment of Maya writing. The focus, therefore, will be on the structures of the Greater Lowland Mayan languages, and upon those features of linguistic structure that are most relevant to decipherment. In so restricting ourselves we miss much, but unavoidably; the field is large, and even the most cursory general summary would require a volume in its own right.

The sound systems of the Mayan languages, like other aspects of their structure, show close similarities. We are perhaps best served by the example of Yucatec, since so many Yucatec words have become traditional in Maya scholarship. The Modern Yucatec sound system (Table 13.1) includes five vowels, each of which may be either short or long. Yucatec is also a "tone" language: its long vowels carry distinctive pitch, which may be either rising-falling or low-level, the two marked with acute and grave accents, respectively.

Yucatec has eighteen consonants, some of which involve a feature that is not unusual in languages of the world as a whole, but is unfamiliar to English speakers: the "glottalized" consonants. These are made like their nonglottalized ("plain") counterparts, except that simultaneously, or nearly so, the vocal cords of the larynx are closed at the moment of articulation. All Mayan languages have series of plain and glottalized consonants, though some have more than others. Mayan languages also have a "glottal stop," which is simply the closing and opening of the vocal cords

TABLE 13.1

Yucatec Mayan Sounds and Transcriptions

| Consonants | Labial | Dental | Palatal | Velar | Glottal |
|---|---|---|---|---|---|
| Plain stops | p | t | | c | ʔ (doubled vowel) |
| Plain affricates | | tz | ch | | |
| Glottalized stops | p' (pp) | t' (th) | | k | |
| | b | | | | |
| Glottalized affricates | | tz' (dz) | ch' | | |
| Spirants | | s | x | | h |
| Nasals | m | n | | | |
| Lateral | | l | | | |
| Semiconsonants | w (u) | | y | | |

| Vowels | Front | Central | Back | Modifications | | |
|---|---|---|---|---|---|---|
| High | i | | u | Length | V: | (not marked in traditional |
| Mid | | e | o | High pitch | V́ | transcription) |
| Low | | a | | Low Pitch | V̀ | |

NOTE: Unlike some phonetic alphabets, this Spanish-based traditional orthography sometimes uses more than one letter for a single distinctive sound. Sounds used only in Spanish loanwords are omitted from this table. Yucatec Mayan has two glottalized stops in the labial position; these differ in the type of glottalization (explosion versus implosion). The symbol "V" (not itself used in transcriptions) here represents simply any of the five vowels of Yucatec. Colonial Yucatec had the velar spirant *j* as well as *h*, but they were not differentiated in transcription; modern Yucatec has only *h*. Where colonial orthography differed from the transcription used here (as in the old use of both *s* and *z* for our *s*), the most common versions are placed here in parentheses following the modern symbol. See also "A Note on Names and Pronunciation" in the front matter.

without accompanying oral articulation (English has this same sound; it is the "constricted" sound in the middle of expressions like "uh-uh" and "oh-oh"). The Cholan languages have essentially the same sounds as Yucatec, though they do not employ distinctive pitch. Chorti also has the consonant *r*, which is lacking in Yucatec (except in Spanish loanwords and, in some dialects, as a predictable alternant, or allophone, of *l*).

One of the main tasks of the early colonial friars, who became fluent in Yucatec and other Mayan languages, was to devise an orthography that would allow these languages to be written down in dictionaries, sermons, catechisms, legal documents, etc., without recourse to the seemingly cumbersome (and dying) indigenous writing. The systems they developed were based on Spanish spelling, augmented by a few new letters and various small modifying marks, or "diacritics," attached to the old letters. These systems ignored some distinctions in the native languages (notably, in Yucatec, distinctive pitch), but were effectively (if sometimes inconsistently) used and survive today in scholarly works as traditional spellings of Mayan words. They have been modified for use with modern type fonts, but the modern forms are essentially direct descendants of the colonial versions. A traditional orthography is used in this book, except in representing sounds not distinguished by traditional spelling (see Table 13.1 and "A Note on Names, Pronunciation, and Conventions" in the front matter).

The root morphemes (that is, the root elements of words) of Mayan are of interest from the points of view of both theoretical linguistics and decipherment. They are generally regular in their sound structure, consisting predominantly of three sounds, namely a consonant ($c_1$) followed by a vowel (v), followed by a consonant ($c_2$); that is, they have the shape $c_1vc_2$. There are statistical tendencies governing the consonants that co-occur within the same morpheme. As we will see, the cvc structure of Mayan root morphemes presented some challenges to the ancient inventors of the original written Maya syllabary.

Mayan languages are polysynthetic; that is, there is a high ratio of morphemes per word, such that one complex word may often express what we know in English as a complete sentence.

Typical Mayan word order, reflected in both written pre-Columbian texts and spoken language, is verb-object-subject in transitive sentences, verb-subject in intransitive sentences. Mayan verbs are accompanied by pronominal markers of subject and object, even if there are separate nouns serving these functions. In most Mayan languages the pronominal markers are of two basic types, the *ergative*, used for possession and the subject of transitive verbs, and the *absolutive*, used for the object of transitive verbs and the subject of intransitive verbs. Their use contrasts with that of English pronouns, which group subjects (whether transitive or intransitive) under the nominative, mark objects with the accusative, and have separate genitive (possessive) forms, without regard to the nature of the verb. The term ergative is used to refer to such constructions where there is a formal parallel between the object of a transitive verb and the subject of an intransitive verb. It is as if one were to say, in a pseudo-English version of Mayan, "He hit him" (transitive) and "slept him" (intransitive). The formal parallel in this case is indicated by both the form and the position of the pronoun "him."

Mayan languages thus distinguish between actors in transitive events and actors in intransitive events, and treat transitive verbs and possessive constructions similarly. This ergative structure is quite common in the languages of the world, though its specific mode of expression (through pronouns, case, etc.) may vary. Several Mayan languages are ergative only in some grammatical constructions and are "accusative" (that is, English-like) in others. From the point of view of decipherment, the importance of Mayan ergativity lies in the probability that it will be observable in the ancient texts, and indeed, the hieroglyph for the third-person pronominal prefix *u*, which can serve as an ergative marker, has been identified.

Given the Maya preoccupation with calculations, it is important to understand Mayan numeral systems, which were among the most interesting and rarest types in the world. We describe here the systems as they were recorded in colonial times; they have since become more like Spanish. The colonial numeral systems were *vigesimal* (base twenty) rather than *decimal* (base ten); that is, the Maya counted by twenties, four hundreds, eight thousands, etc. (see Chapter 12), rather than by tens, hundreds, and thousands, and their numeral expressions reflect this. In English, we find new words (ten, hundred, thousand, etc.) at the appropriate decimal multiples, with combinations of these and the numerals below ten filling in the intervening counts (except for eleven and twelve, which are archaic forms from former expressions meaning "one left over" and "two left over"). In Mayan languages, we find the new words at the vigesimal multiples (twenty, four hundred, eight thousand, etc.). The Mayan numerals one through nineteen, however, were quite like our own, with unique numerals up to and including ten, and the "teens" produced as combinations of one through nine with ten. The use of a lesser base for lower numerals in a high-base system like a vigesimal one is common in world systems, and obviously functional, since it reduces the number of unique lower numerals needed. The Greater Lowland Mayan languages had unique numerals through twelve, just like English; the etymology of their "eleven" is obscure, but their "twelve" differed from the structure of thirteen through nineteen only in employing an archaic morpheme order.

What was rare about the Mayan systems was not their vigesimal base or subordinate decimal base, but their use of an *anticipatory* method of counting above twenty. This is best explained by example. Instead of saying the Mayan equivalent of "twenty-one" (21), "twenty-sixteen" (36), or "two-twenty-nineteen" (59), as we might expect by analogy with our own system, the Maya used numeral phrases equivalent to "one going on one-twenty" (21), "sixteen going on two-twenty" (36), and "nineteen going on three-twenty" (59).

The Mayan system was capable of an efficient expression of very large numbers, and one might hope to find it in the hieroglyphic texts, except that the Maya adopted a written notation that was even more efficient, and used a modified vigesimal base in calendrical records. With only two exceptions (both in the Dresden Codex), Mayan numerals have not been found "spelled out" in the pre-Columbian texts.

Another feature of the grammar of both colonial and modern Mayan numerical expressions is a large class of words termed *numeral classifiers*. One of these classifiers is inserted between a numeral (or other quantifier, such as "many," "some," etc.) and the thing numbered. This word encodes information about the shape, position, or size of the enumerated object(s); a pseudo-English equivalent would be something like "four arranged-in-a-straight-line stone," where our hyphenated phrase stands for a single Mayan numeral classifier. Such classifiers are obligatory, though there are several general classifiers that can be used when the speaker does not wish to be so precise. The few numeral classifiers that have been identified in Maya writing seem to be of the generic, or less discriminating, type.

Mayan languages also have some distinctive verb conjugations. There are conjugations for *positional* verbs, that is, a class of verbs that refer to various ways of taking position, for example Chorti *a-cha-wan* "he-lies-down" (*wan* being a dependent modifier of the verb to indicate the state of lying down). The positional suffix -*wan* in our example has been identified in the hieroglyphic texts. In addition, Mayan languages employ demonstrative pronouns and adjectives that make fine distinctions in the distance and direction of movement of their referents. Such grammatical treatment of the semantics of space is not uncommon in the languages of the world, though it perhaps strikes us as unusual. We may infer that this particular sort of spatial information was and is important in the culture of the speakers, whether Classic Maya or not; and recent studies have shown a special sensitivity to the cardinal directions in Mayan languages.

Finally, Mayan languages in colonial times had well-developed systems for personal names and titles, including two morphemes (the masculine and feminine *proclitics*, also found in modern Mayan languages) that began male and female names, hereditary and occupational titles, and titles of place of origin. They were also found, usually in a diminutive sense, as the first morphemes of many animal and plant names. Both proclitics have been identified in the inscriptions. Mayan languages did not distinguish gender in the pronouns, as does English, but they did so in such titular expressions, in kinship terms, and in other terms defining social role relationships.

Dictionaries of Mayan languages, some of them highly specialized, appear frequently, and all of them attest to the richness of the modern vocabularies. But some of the earliest colonial dictionaries were also the most comprehensive, and these are invaluable in decipherment, since they reflect language a good deal closer to the actual time the hieroglyphic texts were written, and preserve terms and constructions that have been lost in the spoken languages during the colonial era. Mayan vocabularies have been subjected to intensive investigation, especially with an eye to making cultural and cognitive inferences about the speakers. For example, there are comprehensive treatises on the botanical and zoological nomenclatures of several Mayan languages, as well as specialized works on numeral classifiers, color terminology, and kinship terminology. Studies of colonial dictionaries have achieved considerable success in reconstructing culture through vocabulary, and much of this work has been of great value in the decipherment and interpretation of Classic Maya texts.

The Mayan languages today are parts of sophisticated local repertoires of verbal and nonverbal communication systems, and some studies now emerging promise to elucidate these matters in a way that will also benefit research into ancient Maya civilization. In many areas the Maya still use poetic and ritual language reminiscent of the discourse structure of the pre-Columbian codices. John Fought has recently demonstrated how the structure of modern Chorti folklore follows many of the ancient poetic conventions found in the *Popol Vuh* (see below). We are learning more about Maya discourse, especially in the Tzeltalan area, site of the productive Chicago and Harvard Chiapas projects. There are monographs on Tzotzil folklore, tales, dreams, gossip, and humor, and growing collections of tales, dreams, and ritual discourse in many other Maya areas. John Du Bois has studied gestural systems among the modern Maya of highland Guatemala, and these have already suggested hypotheses for the meanings of some of the glyphs representing hands in various positions.

It must be emphasized that most of these studies, from phonological to ethnographic, were not made for the sole or even major purpose of learning more about the ancient Maya and their writing system. Even if they had been, it would obviously be a grave error to expect studies of the modern or colonial Maya to give all the necessary keys to the ancient, any more than, say, modern Rumanian could be expected to do that for Latin; we are sure that the modern/colonial and ancient will be shown, indeed have been shown, to be different in important respects. Nevertheless, the methods of linguistic reconstruction are rigorous and have already afforded valuable insights into the language and culture of the pre-Columbian Maya.

## Maya Documents of the Colonial Period

One of the first concerns of the Spanish friars after the Conquest was to teach the Maya to write their own languages, using the letters of the Spanish alphabet with a few innovations. The Maya were supposed to use this new writing only for Christian purposes, but they managed to record in it a considerable number of native prophecies, myths, rituals, current events, synopses of their own history, and petitions to the Crown.

Many of these native manuscripts were written during the century following the Conquest, in Yucatan. The most important were the *Books of Chilam Balam*. The *Chilan* (the final *n* changed to *m* before a following labial consonant like *b*) were native seers, a class of priests or shamans. *Balam*, meaning literally "jaguar," was an honored personal name as well as a title in pre-Columbian and colonial Yucatan. Ralph Roys believed that Chilam Balam was an individual seer whose fame was so great (because he prophesied the coming of the white man) that many local communities named their accounts after him. These books, kept by local religious leaders, were (and are) distinguished from each other by the addition of the name of the town where each was written. Only a few of them have survived or been revealed to scholars. The most important are the *Books of Chilam Balam* of Mani, Tizimin, Chumayel, Kaua, Ixil, and Tusik, and the Codex Pérez, which is a nineteenth-century compilation of rescripts copied down from others that are now lost.

For history, the most significant sections of the *Books of Chilam Balam* are the *u kahlay katunob* (see Chapter 12), the "count of the katuns" (the katun equals 360 days) or native chronicles, which briefly set forth the leading events of the Yucatec past in the context of a belief in the cyclical nature of history. Five such historical accounts are preserved: one in the Mani, one in the Tizimin, and three in the Chumayel *Books of Chilam Balam*. The astrological and numerological almanacs found in the *Books of Chilam Balam* strongly resemble those in the pre-Columbian books (see below), and we have little doubt that these colonial manuscripts are at least partly translations of pre-Columbian sources, the originals of which were presumably destroyed by the Spaniards. However, it is also clear that there is much purely colonial influence in the *Books of Chilam Balam*, including Spanish loanwords and concepts. Moreover, each account was influenced by the political motives of the rulers of the respective towns. In short, the interpretation of the *Books of Chilam Balam* is subject to the usual historiographical concerns of cultural and personal bias, and the same is true of the other colonial (and pre-Columbian) documents.

There was also a rich colonial literary tradition among the Quichean peoples of the highlands of Guatemala. The *Popol Vuh* ("book of the mat") of the Quiche state is not only the single most outstanding Maya literary work, it is one of the truly great products of all Native American literature and oral tradition. A brilliant poem of over 9,000 lines, the *Popol Vuh* preserves a coherent cosmogony, mythology, and traditional history of the Quiche, one of the most powerful peoples of the Guatemalan highlands (see Chapter 7). The elegance of both the language and the literary style of the *Popol Vuh* emphasizes the loss we and the Quiche have suffered in the annihilation of the Quiche learning during the colonial period. The poetic structure of the *Popol Vuh* is essentially semantic and grammatical rather than phonetic. Little use is made of rhyming, alliteration, or meter; rather, elaborate couplets, triplets, etc., are built up of semantically and grammatically parallel lines. The mythology of the *Popol Vuh* has been used as a key to the interpretation of Classic Maya cosmology (see Chapter 11).

The *Popol Vuh* was evidently written in sixteenth-century Utatlan, the Quiche capital, by a Spanish-trained native Quiche, very probably using a combination of oral and written (pre-Columbian) sources. The manuscript, which shows some evidence of colonial Spanish influence, was evidently copied several times; the original was lost by the mid-1800's. We owe the discovery of our copy of this manuscript, which is now in the Newberry Library in Chicago, to a keen and enthusiastic nineteenth-century student of Mesoamerican prehistory, the Flemish Abbé Charles Brasseur de Bourbourg, one-time parish priest of Rabinal, Guatemala. If Brasseur had given us only the *Popol Vuh* his fame would have been secure, but we are also indebted to him (as we shall see) for the discovery of (to name only the most significant) the *Annals of the Cakchiquels* (a short but otherwise *Popul Vuh*–like history of the Cakchiquel state); the *Rabinal Achi* (a Quiche dance-drama that Brasseur learned was still known by the people of his parish; he paid out of his own pocket for a last performance, during which he wrote detailed notes, later published); the Tro portion of the Madrid Codex; the only surviving copy of Bishop

Diego de Landa's *Relación de las cosas de Yucatán*; and the *Diccionario de Motul*, an enormous colonial Yucatec dictionary. These works, together with other fragmentary colonial documents from both the highlands and the Yucatan Peninsula, provide a priceless source of information about Postclassic Maya language, history, social and political institutions, religion, and other facets of past Maya culture.

## Ancient Maya Writing

Scholars have traditionally considered the use of writing to be one of the hallmarks of civilization, and the ancient Maya writing system is often and justly hailed as one of the most significant achievements of the pre-Columbian New World. By allowing its users to keep relatively permanent records, writing greatly increases the efficiency of the transmission and accumulation of knowledge from generation to generation. The ancient Maya, in particular, were able to record seasonal and astronomical information over long periods of time, and these records contributed to the development of accurate calendars and to impressive breakthroughs in their understanding of astronomical events and mathematics.

The Maya developed writing to an extraordinary peak, but theirs was not the only Native American writing system. The Postclassic Mixtec and Mexica (Aztec) states recorded a large body of historical and commercial information using essentially pictographic writing systems far less tied to their spoken languages than the Maya system was to theirs, and these scripts, like that of the Maya, were but the latest in a long tradition of writing going back to the Mesoamerican Preclassic. In fact, the Mixtec and Mexica systems had the advantage (over a more language-bound one like that of the Maya) that they could be read by speakers of different languages, once a few basic orthographic conventions were understood. This is precisely the advantage of modern Chinese writing over phonetic systems. The latter, of course, have their own advantages (including ease of learning and efficiency), but it is important to realize that the interethnic flexibility of the Mixtec and Mexica systems made them more efficient for handling the trade and tribute records of these expanding states. Similarly, the Inca *quipu* system, which many scholars consider to have been at best a marginal form of writing, was well adapted for the bookkeeping functions of a state that was more centralized than any other in pre-Columbian America.

In fact, the most eminent scholars of the mid-twentieth century believed until recently that the surviving Maya texts were devoted entirely to astronomy, astrology, and calendrics, in spite of colonial accounts that spoke of pre-Columbian Maya histories, genealogies, medical texts, treatises on plants and animals, and maps. As recently as 1950, J. Eric Thompson could assert that the Maya did not record history on their stone monuments, and could describe the Maya as "excelling in the impractical, yet failing in the practical." Sylvanus Morley was generally so unconcerned with noncalendrical glyphs that he did not draw them in his records of inscriptions. Nonetheless, the general view expressed earlier in the nineteenth and early twentieth century was that the texts did indeed contain undeciphered historical records. In Herbert Spinden's words, written in 1917, which have proved remarkably accurate, "We may expect to find in the Mayan inscriptions some hieroglyphs that give the names of individuals, cities, and political divisions and others that represent feasts, sacrifices, tribute, and common objects of trade as well as signs referring to birth, death, establishment, conquest, destruction, and other fundamentals of individual and social existence." Later scholars, however, understandably swept up in the rapid progress being made in deciphering the astronomical and calendrical parts of the inscriptions, became more and more inclined to the view that what remained to be deciphered would prove to be simply more of the same nature. And traditional scholarship was still rejecting early colonial assertions that there was a phonetic component in Maya writing.

All that is changed now. With recent advances in the decipherment of Maya hieroglyphs, it can be stated with certainty that the suppositions of the earlier scholars, which were based partly on colonial accounts, were correct. Many ancient Maya texts, especially those from the Classic period, deal with historical events in addition to calendrical and other esoteric matters. Like the records of ancient Egypt, Sumer, and other early states, the Maya texts deal with the histories of specific centers, with the reigns and political fortunes of their rulers, and with genealogy, marriages, alliances, and conflicts. Recognizing the historical information in this material has significantly altered our understanding of Maya civilization.

We now know, too, that Maya writing had a phonetic component, and that the relative importance of phoneticism increased with time. Thus, Maya writing was not static, and great progress has been made in elucidating its principles and their origins. Our increased understanding of the nature of Maya writing, notably the phonetic component, offers a crucial foundation for future decipherment, and a new approach to understanding the history of several Mayan languages—the first for which we have significant pre-Columbian documentation. In both the sociocultural and linguistic senses, then, advances in decipherment have begun to move the study of the ancient Maya from the realm of prehistory into that of history. Studies of the ancient Maya from this new perspective require the critical assessment of Maya hieroglyphic texts, using comparisons between texts and archaeology whenever possible, to test the veracity of Maya inscriptions.

## Pre-Columbian Maya Texts

Knowledge of Maya writing did not long survive the Spanish Conquest, owing to the diligence of church and government officials who rooted out all manifestations of this visible symbol of "paganism." Landa, in a passage that ironically accompanies his invaluable eyewitness description of Maya writing, described his own role in its suppression: "We found a large number of books in these characters and, as they contained nothing in which there were not to be seen superstition and lies of the devil, we burned them all, which they regretted to an amazing degree, and which caused them much affliction." Of course far older books dating to the Classic or even Preclassic have all apparently succumbed to the ravages of time.

By extraordinary good fortune, however, the early colonists sent a few books to officials and friends in Europe. Three of these pre-Columbian Maya books, dated to the Postclassic, have survived to the present day. They are now known as the Dresden, Madrid, and Paris codices (a codex is an important manuscript volume), named for the cities in which they now reside. The Maya codices, of which there were once whole libraries, were made of paper manufactured from the inner bark of several species of the *amate* (Yucatec *kopo*; the native fig tree, *Ficus cotonifolia, F. padifolia*) pounded into a pulp and held together with natural gums as a bonding substance. This paper was also used for costumes, and as a receptacle for blood in bloodletting rites. Ancient stone bark beaters—hand-sized, oblong tools with closely spaced parallel grooves (see Fig. 15.29)—have been found in great numbers in Maya archaeological sites. Bark beaters of wood, still used among the Jicaque Indians of Honduras, may also have been used (though they would not have survived).

Each sheet of book paper was made in a long strip and folded like a screen. The individual leaves of the Madrid Codex average about 23 cm high by 9 cm wide; those of the Paris Codex about 22 cm by 12.5 cm. The Dresden Codex is a little smaller and more regular, with leaves about 20.4 cm by 9 cm. A coating of fine white lime was applied to both sides of the paper sheet, and on the smooth finish thus obtained were painted a number of columns of glyphs and, often in bright colors, various pictures of gods, animals, and other objects evidently involved in ceremonies or other activities. The pages were divided into horizontal sections by red lines, and the order of reading was usually from left to right, top to bottom, remaining in the same horizontal section through one to as many as eight folds, then descending to the next section. The books were thus organized into chapter-like sections, and since they were painted on both sides, were read all the way along one side of the strip, then turned and read along the reverse. They were bound between decorated boards, and when completely opened were quite long. The Madrid Codex is the longest, at 6.7 m with 56 leaves (112 pages); the Dresden Codex is 3.5 m long and has 39 leaves (78 pages, four of them blank); and the Paris Codex, which is only a fragment, is 1.45 m long and has 11 leaves (22 pages). Several facsimile editions of each codex have been published.

The Dresden Codex was bought for the Dresdener Bibliothek in 1739 by its director, Johann Christian Götze, who found it in a private library in Vienna. Its earlier history is unknown. Since it was obtained in Vienna, and since Austria and Spain had a common sovereign at the time of the Conquest, the book may well have been sent back to the emperor Charles V by some priest or soldier (we know that Cortés himself sent examples of Mesoamerican books to Charles V in 1519). Charles V's residence was in Vienna; much of the Moctezuma treasure (originally gifts to Cortés) and the five letters from Cortés to Charles V were eventually discovered there. By the early 1800's, the Dresden Codex had fallen into three parts, leading to early confusion in pagination. Now in the Sächsische Landesbibliothek in Dresden, Germany, it suffered some water damage as a result of bombing during World War II, but has been restored. A sample page is shown in Fig. 11.3.

The Paris Codex was rediscovered by León de Rosny in the Bibliothèque Nationale in Paris in 1859, in a basket of old papers in a chimney corner, its existence apparently forgotten after earlier discoveries in the 1830's and in 1855. It was wrapped in a piece of torn paper with the word "Pérez" written on it, which led to its earlier name, Codex Peresianus (now changed to prevent confusion with the Codex Pérez described above, which is also owned by the Bibliothèque Nationale). The Paris Codex, which is only a small fragment of the original book, is in much worse condition than are the other two codices. The lime coating has eroded away at the page margins, taking with it all the pictures and glyphs except those in the middle of the pages. A sample page is shown in Fig. 13.3.

The Madrid Codex, divided into two unequal parts, was found in Spain in the 1860's. Although the two parts were found at different places, León de Rosny discovered early in the 1880's that they were parts of the same original manuscript. The larger section, found in 1866 by Brasseur de Bourbourg in the possession of Professor Juan de Tro y Ortolano, of Madrid, was given to Brasseur for publication and for some time went under the name of Manuscrit Troano, or Codex Tro. The smaller part belonged to José Ignacio Miro, who had acquired it from Juan Palacios. Miro sold it in 1875 to the Museo Arqueológico in Madrid, which now owns both parts. The second part was supposed to have come from the Spanish province of Extremadura and was first called the Codex Cortesianus under the assumption that it had been brought there by Cortés. But the conqueror of Yucatan, Francisco de Montejo, and many of his soldiers were from Extremadura, and one of these men may have brought the whole codex from Yucatan. The combined sections, for some time known as the Codex Tro-Cortesianus, are now known as the Madrid Codex. A page is shown in Fig. 13.4.

The Dresden Codex can be characterized as a treatise on divination and astronomy. The Madrid Codex, likewise, is devoted to horoscopes and almanacs used by Maya priests in their divinations and ceremonies, but it contains fewer astronomical tables. What we have of the Paris Codex is also ritualistic, one side being completely devoted to a katun sequence and its patron deities and ceremonies; it also contains a depiction of the still poorly interpreted Maya zodiac (Fig. 13.3). Thus all three codices are of a similar nature, and contain little if any history.

Internal evidence from the codices points to origins in Yucatan. According to J. Eric Thompson, most of the glyphic and iconographic associations in the Dresden

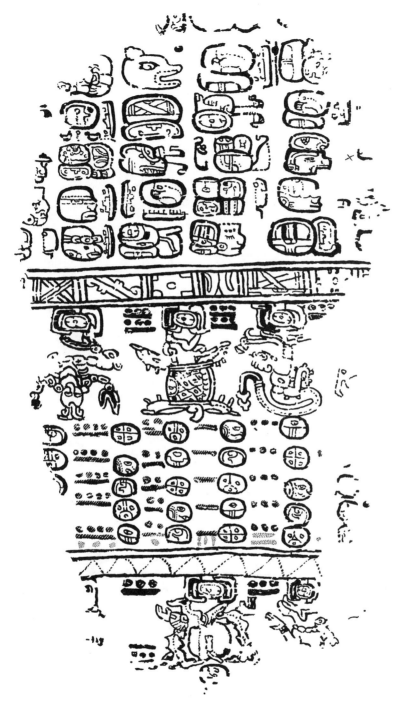

Fig. 13.3. Portion of the Maya "zodiac" from the Paris Codex, p. 4: of the seven zodiacal animals originally depicted on this page (there were thirteen such animals in all), the scorpion, turtle, rattle-snake (middle section), and bat (lower section) are still visible; note the right-facing glyphic heads in the text above, a rare example of right-to-left reading order.

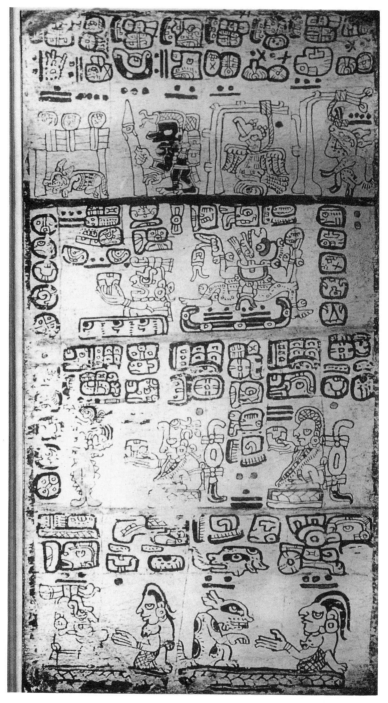

Fig. 13.4. Various almanacs from the Madrid Codex, p. 91: the bird hanging from a noose in a tree in the top section is an ocellated turkey; its glyphic name (reading *cutz*; see text) appears above the tree branch.

Codex are with central and eastern Yucatan, especially Chichen Itza, which he considered the most likely point of origin. He believed the book to be a product of the early thirteenth century, though it, like the other two, was probably at least partly copied from earlier books. Günter Zimmermann found evidence for the work of eight different scribes in the Dresden Codex.

Both the Paris and Madrid codices show stylistic associations with the murals of Tulum and those at Tancah, both on the east coast of Yucatan, indicating possible origins in those areas. However, the year-bearers (the days on which Maya years could begin; see Chapter 12) of the Madrid Codex are shifted one day forward (from Akbal, Lamat, Ben, and Etz'nab to Kan, Muluc, Ix, and Cauac) from those prevalent in Classic times and in the other two codices. This shift is traceable to western Yucatan, which persuaded Thompson that the codex probably originated there; the Postclassic east-coast year-bearers are not known, however, and it remains possible that the Madrid Codex is of east-coast origin. Thompson assigned both the Madrid and the Paris codices to the period 1250–1450, that is, later than the Dresden Codex.

None of these codices was found through archaeological excavations; the climate in most of the Maya area is so moist, and the mildew so destructive, as to virtually preclude the survival of a buried book. Nevertheless, fragments have been found in several Classic-period tombs, including those at Uaxactun, Altun Ha, and Guaytan in the Maya area and at Mirador, Chiapas, in an area of uncertain ancient linguistic affiliation. Except for the Mirador Codex, all of these buried books were found in a nearly disintegrated state, and were not recoverable. The Mirador Codex, much smaller in format than the intact Maya codices, today lies unopened in the Museo Nacional de Antropología in Mexico City. Exposed to pressure and water percolation, the paper of the book had long since rotted away, and the lime page coatings (on which the painting had been imposed) had coalesced into a solid block. Experiments on minor fragments revealed intact painting inside, but were not so successful as to allow risking the main block.

An intact fragment of another possible pre-Columbian Maya book (the Grolier Codex, named after the Grolier Club in New York City, where it was first placed on public display) appeared in a private collection. Although tests indicate that the paper is pre-Columbian, the authenticity of the Grolier Codex is doubted by some scholars, who feel that the style of the pictures is incorrect, and who point out that caches of blank pre-Columbian paper have been found in dry Mexican caves and are presumably available to forgers. Whether authentic or not, the Grolier Codex deals entirely with Venus almanacs in a simplistic fashion, adding almost no new information to the sophisticated treatment of Venus in the Dresden Codex. Scholars remain hopeful that more Mayan books will yet be found in recoverable condition, but we obviously cannot expect to find libraries like the clay-brick archives of the ancient Near East.

In contrast to what has been discovered in or from the Maya area, over four hundred native Mixtec-Mexica manuscripts have come down to us, of which about thirteen are of pre-Columbian origin. Some of these are made of deerskin, others of cotton or paper. If materials other than bark paper were ever the primary ones used in a Maya book, no examples have survived, nor does Landa mention them. The remains of an animal-hide binding, connecting separate sections of the paper strip, have been found in the Dresden Codex, but it is not known whether this was the original binding or the remains of a subsequent repair. Colonial texts claim that maps were made with a cotton backing, but no pre-colonial Maya maps have come down to us.

Fortunately, a large number of Maya texts on more permanent media have survived both time and neglect and the Spaniards' destructive efforts, though they are faring less well at the hands of modern looters and smugglers of pre-Columbian art. All the earliest known texts from the Late Preclassic were carved on stone, as parts of free-standing monuments, that is, stelae and altars. Most of the texts, too, surviving from the Classic were carved on such monuments, or on parts of masonry buildings (lintels, wall panels, etc.). At Tikal and a few other sites, wooden lintels bearing carved texts have survived. Other Classic texts were incised on portable artifacts made of bone, stone, or pottery, or were fashioned on the stucco façades of buildings. In other cases they were painted on walls and on elaborately decorated ceramic vessels. Many texts have not been published, however, and most of those that have been are scattered through an almost hopeless tangle of out-of-print literature. Recently Ian Graham and his associates at Harvard University's Peabody Museum have begun the formidable task of assembling photographs and drawings of all the known pre-Columbian monument inscriptions in a single set of publications, the *Corpus of Maya Hieroglyphic Inscriptions*, which will run to some 50 volumes. Roll-out photographs and drawings of the beautiful renderings on polychrome ceramic vessels have also begun to appear, but for these there is still no prospect for a published set of the magnitude of the *Corpus*. It is important to note that most of these vessels were looted and are without archaeological context. Their texts must therefore be used with caution, since some examples have been revealed as modern fakes.

## Deciphering Maya Writing

The decipherment of Maya writing has been a popular and long-enduring subject of study. We begin our account with a brief introduction both to the basic typological dimensions used in classifying and explaining writing systems and to the basic elements and structure of Maya writing.

Traditionally, writing systems have been classified into several different major types: *pictographic, ideographic, logographic, syllabic,* and *alphabetic.* These types have often been seen as successively more sophisticated stages of the evolutionary development of all writing systems (particular cases, of course, do not always obey that judgment). Essentially, these major types include two different dimensions of classification: the type of unit that an element of the writing system represents—whether a sound, a syllable, an idea, or whatever—and the mode of representation the system employs—whether through signs that resemble or otherwise make clear what their own meanings are, or through signs whose shapes bear no current relationship to their meanings. Alphabetic units represent the individual distinctive sounds, or phonemes, of language, and syllabic units represent whole syllables; both of these types are *phonetic*. Logographic units (*logograms*) represent whole morphemes or words. Pictographic scripts are intended to represent words, ideas, or groups of words or ideas by means of elements that visually portray their associated meanings (for example, a box for a house, or a stick figure for a human being), whereas ideographic scripts do so by means of elements whose relationships to their meanings are less or not at all obvious. Most scripts are actually combinations of these (for example, ancient Sumerian is *logosyllabic*), and the historical development of scripts is much more complicated than this classification might suggest, though it is true that even individual phonetic signs, like those in the roman alphabet, are typically descended from logograms, and across time the relentless trend toward simplification drives the signs from the pictographic to the (seemingly) arbitrary.

Maya writing is built on a system of individual elements, or *glyphs*, that are themselves generally grouped into *glyph groups*, each group typically having a squared or oval shape (see Fig. 13.5). Commonly, Mayanists refer to both glyphs and glyph groups as glyphs; proposals have been made to make usage more precise, but none has won acceptance. The individual glyphs, like Maya art generally, appear quite elaborate to Western eyes. Some are obviously "pictures" of some natural object, but many others seem strictly arbitrary in appearance, though of course they may not have been so to the Maya. According to their size and normal position within glyph groups, Maya glyphs have been classified as *main signs* (the largest and more central glyphs within a group) and *affixes*, which are joined to the main sign and are themselves subclassified into *prefixes*, *superfixes*, *subfixes*, and *postfixes*, according to whether they are positioned to the left of, over, below, or to the right of the main sign. (Both prefixes and superfixes are usually referred to as prefixes, and subfixes and postfixes as postfixes.) Affixes can also be fused within the main sign, in which case they are known as *infixes*. And main signs, finally, can themselves be compounded of two or more main signs. The reading order of glyphs within a glyph group is typically in the order prefix, superfix, main sign, subfix, and postfix, though factors such as the way the affixes are attached, scribal variation, artistic license, etc., can affect the normal order.

There are about 800 known Maya glyphs, including affixes; they have been

Fig. 13.5. Structure of the accession (*a–d*) and "was born" (*e–g*) glyphs: (*a*) prefix T59 *ti/ta* "at"; (*b*) superfix T168 *ahpo* (see text); (*c*) main sign T684b, a vulture with a knotted band (or "toothache" glyph); (*d*) subfix T188; (*e*) main sign T740 (or "upended frog" glyph); (*f*) subfix T126 *ih*; (*g*) postfix T181 *ah*, a verbal suffix (or "lunar postfix").

catalogued, and they are referred to by their catalogue numbers (usually in J. Eric Thompson's system, in which their numbers are preceded by "T") or by nicknames based on appearance or supposed significance; for example T740, the main sign in Fig. 13.5, is sometimes called "upended frog."

A text normally consists of several such glyph groups organized into rows and/ or columns. Glyph groups within a single text are read from left to right in the row and top to bottom in the column. In even numbers of columns, the groups are read in pairs of columns:

| | | | | |
|---|---|---|---|---|
| 1 | 2 | 7 | 8 | |
| 3 | 4 | 9 | 10 | |
| 5 | 6 | 11 | 12 | etc. |

For odd numbers of columns, the order is usually either

| | | | | | | | |
|---|---|---|---|---|---|---|---|
| 1 | 4 | 5 | | | 1 | 2 | 7 |
| 2 | 6 | 7 | | or | 3 | 4 | 8 |
| 3 | 8 | 9 | etc. | | 5 | 6 | 9 | etc. |

Frequently one column is longer than others, especially when an inscription wraps around a carved figure on a monument; these long columns are finished before the text moves on to the next set of columns:

| | | | | | |
|---|---|---|---|---|---|
| 1 | 2 | 10 | 11 | 16 | 17 |
| 3 | 4 | 12 | 13 | 18 | 19 |
| 5 | 6 | 14 | 15 | 20 | 21 |
| 7 | | | | | 22 |
| 8 | | | | | 23 |
| 9 | | | | | 24 |

For easy reference to a particular glyph group in a text, the text is often given a set of coordinates, with letters for columns and numbers for rows, so that any group has a unique coordinate identity (for example, A1, B1, A2, etc.):

| | A | B | C | D |
|---|---|---|---|---|
| 1 | (A1) | (B1) | (C1) | (D1) |
| 2 | (A2) | (B2) | (C2) | (D2) |
| 3 | (A3) | (B3) | (C3) | (D3) |

The most common variation from the normal reading order is right-to-left (for example, on pp. 23–24 of the Paris Codex; see Fig. 13.3); in such cases, those glyphs depicting recognizable faces (for example an animal or a human) or having particular orientations are found to be faced in the opposite direction (switched, that is, from left-facing to right-facing), though the influence of normal order on the scribes can often be seen in orientation errors in these cases.

Until the 1950's, most experts on the subject were convinced that Maya writing was logographic, differing from other Mesoamerican scripts only in the size of its vocabulary, in its heavy representation of grammatical affixes and particles as well as the usual nouns and verbs, and in its supposedly greater use of the "rebus" principle (using a logogram to stand for a similar-sounding word, the only phoneticism then believed to have been characteristic of the system). The roughly 800 glyphs in the Maya script far exceeded the maximum number needed for a phonetic alphabet (about 30 in the Mayan case) or even a syllabary (about 125), and its failure to reach the proportions of well-known logographic scripts like Chinese, which employs thousands of characters, was attributed to its evidently limited range of use, that is, in little more than calendrical and astronomical matters. But the number of different Maya glyphs is in fact quite comparable to that of known mixed scripts.

The groundwork for Maya decipherment was laid by the Franciscan friar and Bishop of Yucatan, Diego de Landa, who included significant information about Maya writing in his *Relación de las cosas de Yucatán*, a detailed history and description of the Maya of Yucatan written about 1566. Landa based much of his account on interviews with learned Maya informants. There is also evidence that part of his account was literally translated from at least one source written in Yucatec, presumably in Spanish characters. From Landa we have our most important account of the Maya calendar, together with the Maya signs for the twenty days, the eighteen twenty-day uinals, and a "Maya alphabet." After Landa's death, in 1573, his original manuscript was kept in the Franciscan convent at Mérida, in Yucatan, and is now lost. The present edition stems from an abridged copy made in the early seventeenth century. This copy was discovered in 1863 by Brasseur de Bourbourg in the library of the Academía de Historia in Madrid, and first published in 1864. From Landa's death until the discovery of this abridged copy the study of Maya hieroglyphic writing was practically dormant, though a growing interest in the ancient Maya encouraged travelers and explorers to undertake the documentation of the inscriptions that would prove crucial to later scholars. Among these early explorers we are especially indebted to John Lloyd Stephens and his talented artist companion, Frederick Catherwood (see Fig. 7.21), who recorded many Maya inscriptions in the rugged frontiers of Guatemala and Mexico in the 1830's and 1840's.

Brasseur also discovered the Tro portion of the Madrid Codex in 1866 and, familiar as he was with the Landa manuscript, recognized that the characters were so similar to Landa's that the Codex had to be a Maya book, the first that was so identified. In 1869–70 Brasseur published the Tro along with his own interpretation, which he based on the Landa manuscript. Although he was able to recognize Landa's day signs, the sign for "sun" or "day," and the bar-dot numeric notation, Brasseur's conclusions regarding the supposed phonetic signs were almost completely in error; the major exception was his reading of Landa's *u* as the Yucatec third-person pronoun. Though these contributions were important, Brasseur's claims to be able to translate line after line of the Codex were decidedly premature; we now know that he was reading the Codex backwards! Other early scholars, such as León de Rosny and Cyrus Thomas, would keep trying to apply the Landa "alphabet" to achieve phonetic solutions to the puzzle of Maya writing, but these attempts all foundered on three problems: (1) difficulty in recognizing the poorly drawn glyphs in the Landa copy; (2) ignorance of what constituted the critical features of a glyph, and hence its range of variation in the renderings of the Maya scribes; and (3) failure to consider counter-evidence. By the turn of the century, understanding of the astronomical and calendrical portions of Maya texts had progressed so far, and the phonetic readings were so uncertain, that the whole phonetic approach to Maya writing was repudiated, even by some of its own previous adherents.

Although Brasseur and Rosny had some early success in the calendrical and astronomical interpretations (in 1876, Rosny deciphered the four directional glyphs north, south, east, and west), the scholar to whom most credit is due for the success of this approach was Ernst Förstemann, head librarian of the Dresdener Bibliothek and an accomplished Germanic philologist. Förstemann began in 1880 (in his late fifties) a study of the Dresden Codex and other Maya texts that would occupy him for the rest of his life. Within a few years, he had published an insightful commentary on the Codex and many articles, in which he identified Landa's month signs, correctly interpreted the signs for "zero" and "twenty," explained the abbreviated almanacs in the codices, and interpreted Maya vigesimal and positional notation, the Venus tables of the Dresden Codex, the Long Count, the zero date of the Long Count at 4 Ahau 8 Cumku (see Chapter 12), the basic reading order of texts (independently discovered by others, including Cyrus Thomas), the signs for time periods and their head variants (see below), and the workings of the inscriptional distance numbers (see Chapter 12 for calendrical details).

Förstemann's work partly overlapped that of J. Thomas Goodman (once owner and editor of the Virginia City, Nevada, newspaper, *The Territorial Enterprise*, and a lifelong friend of Mark Twain; Goodman gave Twain his first job as a journalist). Goodman scorned the decipherment efforts of the scholars of his day, and published (in 1897) an important volume in which many of Förstemann's discoveries are stated as if they had been made independently by Goodman. We are still unsure of the extent of Goodman's knowledge of Förstemann's accomplishments, but it is clear, at least, that Goodman made several important discoveries on his own, including the head variants for the Maya numbers (see Chapter 12) and, in 1905, the correlation for the Maya and Western calendars that today is the most widely accepted (the Goodman-Martinez-Thompson, or GMT, correlation; Martinez and Thompson made minor modifications).

By this time Eduard Seler had deciphered the color glyphs, Paul Schellhas had catalogued the deities pictured in the codices and linked them with their glyphic names (see Chapter 11), and Daniel Brinton had produced the first summary of what was known about Maya writing in *A Primer of Maya Hieroglyphs* (1885). Knowledge of the inscriptions had begun to accumulate, owing largely to the efforts of two indefatigable Maya explorers, Alfred P. Maudslay and Teobert Maler. In the 1880's, Maudslay recorded hundreds of inscriptions with both photographs and plaster casts, and published the photographs along with good drawings (by Annie Hunter) at great difficulty. In the early 1900's, Maler, who had fought in the emperor Maximilian's army in Mexico, published several volumes of excellent photographs of many of the less accessible sites.

By the early years of the twentieth century, epigraphers were emphasizing calendrical and astronomical decipherment, and had gone beyond their earlier preoccupation with the codices to the now increasingly accessible carved inscriptions of the Classic period. Many refinements were made in the understanding of the calendar, and with them came better site chronologies. The explorations undertaken by Sylvanus Morley throughout the Maya lowlands resulted in the discovery and recording of a greatly expanded corpus of Classic texts. Morley also produced a more complete summary of Maya writing, *An Introduction to the Study of Maya*

*Hieroglyphs* (1914). John Teeple deciphered much of the "supplementary series" (now "lunar series") that followed Long Count dates in many Classic-period inscriptions, showing its relationship to a lost lunar calendar. Hermann Beyer established that the "variable element" in the introductory glyph for Long Count dates represents the deity for the then-current "month" in the 365-day calendar (see Chapter 12).

By the mid-twentieth century, great progress had been made in establishing the critical features of the Maya glyphs and in assembling them in catalogues and concordances. This work was led by Thompson, whose monumental *Maya Hieroglyphic Writing: An Introduction* (1950) became the most widely used summary of Maya writing. Günter Zimmermann produced the first good catalogue of the glyphs that appear in the codices, but this was soon all but superseded by Thompson's *A Catalog of Maya Hieroglyphs* (1962), which encompassed both the codices and the carved inscriptions and proposed the referencing system still used by many Maya scholars. Thompson also identified the glyphs for several grammatical morphemes, including numeral classifiers. Largely because of his and Morley's influence, scholarly opinion on Maya writing had crystallized by the 1950's into the erroneous view that the system was logographic and contained no historical information. But by systematizing the identities, ranges of variation, and locations of Maya glyphs, Thompson succeeded in opening the study of Maya writing to new scholars as no one before him had.

The modern era of decipherment was opened by two major developments in the late 1950's: the discoveries by Heinrich Berlin and Tatiana Proskouriakoff of historical content in the Classic inscriptions, and the first convincing demonstration of phoneticism in Maya writing by Yurii V. Knorozov.

Berlin, a German-Mexican, had noticed that a certain type of glyph group (see Fig. 13.6), characterized by a consistent set of prefixes but with a highly variable main sign, was not randomly distributed at Maya sites. Several major sites exhibited such glyph groups, and in each case the main sign was found to be practically unique to that site. This distribution led him to the conclusion, published in 1958, that these groups actually constitute expressions identifying particular sites, and he called them *emblem glyphs*. Subsequent work by Berlin and other scholars has confirmed the pattern at site after site.

Berlin was not sure whether the emblem glyph was a place name or perhaps the name of a ruling dynasty or lineage; he inclined to the latter view. The emblem glyphs of some sites do appear at other sites, but these cases have been explained as evidence of various sorts of relationships between one site and another (see Chapter 10). At a few sites (Tikal, Yaxchilan, and Palenque) more than one main sign for the emblem glyph occurs, which may indicate that the rulership at a particular site was in some way linked to two lineages; the best hypothesis seems to be that they represent a founding lineage firmly associated with a particular site.

Fig. 13.6. Emblem-glyph affixes (*a–c*) and main signs (*d–m*): (*a*) prefix T36 with kan cross *k'ul*; (*b*) superfix T168 *ahpo*; (*c*) subfix 130 *wa* (phonetic complement; see text); (*d*) main sign T756, a bat (Copan); (*e*) main sign T559, a cacao tree with pod (?) (Quirigua); (*f*) main sign T562 "cleft sky" (Yaxchilan); (*g*) main sign T569, a bundle (Tikal); (*h*) main sign T585 "Quincunx" (Piedras Negras); (*i*) main sign T570, a bone (Palenque); (*j*) main sign T1040, a skull (also Palenque); (*k*) tripled main sign T528, Cauac (Seibal); (*l*) main sign T553, crossed sky bands (Naranjo); (*m*) main sign T716, bundle (Petexbatun).

The identification of the emblem glyph, hailed immediately as an important breakthrough, constituted the first demonstration that the Classic inscriptions contain anything as mundane as a local, completely noncalendrical name, and it seemed to make the Maya inscriptions resemble their Old World counterparts more than had been supposed. This impression was soon confirmed in another significant breakthrough. Proskouriakoff, a Russian-American scholar and an expert on Maya art, had been studying the inscriptions of Piedras Negras and found that they exhibit a singular pattern with a compelling historical interpretation. At the site are several stelae with glyphic texts surrounding carved scenes of a person seated within a niche formed of the body of the "celestial dragon" (see Fig. 5.23). Proskouriakoff noticed that each monument of this type was the first to be erected in a given location, and that monuments grouped with it, each bearing other motifs, had been set up every five tuns (that is, every five 360-day years), until, at length, another group of monuments was started at another temple at that site. Within each group of monuments is recorded not only the erection date of each but also two earlier dates. One, which she termed the "inaugural date," precedes the date of the first stela in the group by only a short time, and is nearly always followed immediately by a glyph group whose most prominent main sign is T684 (dubbed "toothache" by Thompson, because its main characteristic is a cloth wrapped around the jaw of a vulture and tied off on top of the head; see Fig. 13.7). The other, which she termed the "initial date," was in this case anywhere from 12 to 31 years prior to the inaugural date, and is usually followed by a glyph group with the main sign T740, the "upended frog" (see Figs. 13.5 and 13.7). Both of these dates are referred to in later texts at the same site (in effect, as "anniversaries"). In Proskouriakoff's words, published in 1959,

Doubtless there are various events in history that are paired this way, but surely the most common is the birth of some person who in his mature years acquires great prestige or political power. But if the "upended frog" date is a birth date, the fact that it was celebrated for only a limited period suggests that the period was the person's lifetime, and effectively refutes my original notion that the "toothache glyph" expresses the human sacrifice shown on "niche" stelae. More likely, these stelae portray the accession of a new ruler, the "seating on high of the Lord," as the Maya books put it.

Proskouriakoff discovered that the time covered by any single group of inscriptions in no case exceeded 60 years, a normal human lifetime (a conclusion also reached by Charles Bowditch in 1901 and Morley in 1914, both of whom had correctly guessed the nature of Piedras Negras Stela 1 but never followed up on it). In a series of logical conclusions based on her brilliant original insight, Proskouriakoff went on to propose that each group of inscriptions documents the life of the then ruling lord of Piedras Negras; that the initial date is his birth date or the record of his accession to power; that the inaugural date is various; that anniversaries of these dates were celebrated later; that the male figure dominating the front of a monument is a depiction of the ruler; that the female figures on a monument depict the ruler's wife or mother or, in one case with two female figures, his wife and daughter; that rulers' names and titles follow the glyph groups for the ruler's birth and inauguration; and that female names are prefixed by a glyph that resembles a woman's face, with a characteristic lock of hair (see Fig. 13.7).

It is difficult now to imagine the shock engendered by Proskouriakoff's work. The dominating male figures on the monuments usually had been thought to be gods, and the females usually had been thought to be males in priestly garb. The various secondary dates in the texts had been thought to be corrections for the difference between the 365-day year and the slightly longer true solar year. Now the texts were seen to be historical, and there was even the prospect that the associated buildings had been built by or for these rulers (in some cases, as shrines and to secure their tombs).

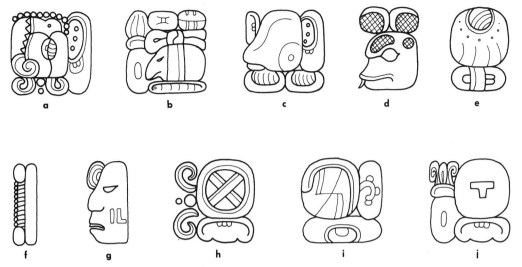

Fig. 13.7. Various glyphs with historical and sociopolitical implications: (*a*) "was born"; (*b*) accession; (*c*) capture; (*d*) captor; (*e*) captive; (*f*) male prefix; (*g*) female prefix; (*h*) wife; (*i*) "hel," or count of rulers; (*j*) death.

Proskouriakoff's evidence included similar texts from other sites. After the publication of her initial discoveries, she went on to a detailed study of the inscriptions of Yaxchilan, in which she was able to demonstrate the decipherment of glyphs for death, capture, and captor (see Fig. 13.7), and to show the relevance of her interpretations to inter-site relationships. Thompson accepted her conclusions enthusiastically, and today they are accepted as the basis for current progress in historical decipherment.

It will be noticed that Proskouriakoff's decipherments did not involve actual *readings* of Mayan words; instead, she was able to *interpret* glyphs without positing the actual phonetic identity or particular word involved. This distinction between semantic or grammatical interpretations and phonetic readings is important, and it is clear that the latter would not readily be forthcoming if the Maya script were strictly logographic. It is also evident that the discovery of any sort of phonetic system in the script would aid greatly in semantic interpretation, and vice versa. As recently as 1972, however, no less a scholar than Thompson could confidently state as his first "rule" of decipherment, "Maya writing is not syllabic or alphabetic in part or in whole. Some early students, bemused by Landa's so-called alphabet, supposed that they had found an alphabetic-syllabic system in the Maya glyphs, but such ideas were soon abandoned as untenable, only to be revived in recent years amid strident claims to have read the Maya glyphs."

Except for the brief advocacy of Benjamin Whorf in the 1930's and 1940's, the last real try for a phonetic breakthrough had ended with Cyrus Thomas's admitted failure near the turn of the century. Thomas had actually hit upon what we now know to have been a few nearly correct solutions, but they were couched in an alphabetic hypothesis that, along with his faulty standards of glyph recognition and proof (see above), turned him in the wrong direction. Whorf, an American linguist with a considerable reputation in other circles, wrote a series of papers in which he claimed to be able to read whole passages from the codices phonetically, but his readings met strong and mostly deserved criticism from Thompson. Nevertheless, Whorf had made one advance over Thomas's earlier work by pointing out that the Maya phonetic system was likely to have involved a syllabary rather than an alphabet.

The "recent strident claims" referred to by Thompson were those of Knorozov, the Russian linguist who, using a "Marxist-Leninist" approach, began the other revolution of the 1950's. This revolution would be slower to develop, partly because Knorozov's arguments (published in 1952 and subsequent years) were not nearly as careful as Proskouriakoff's. Knorozov tried to demonstrate how a system of signs for cv syllables could have been used for writing a language with predominantly cvc word roots. The basic problem is: How is the final consonant to be represented, given that in a cv writing system there are no signs for single consonants? Knorozov proposed that the final consonant was written with a second cv sign that agreed with the vowel of the first, in a principle he called *synharmony*; thus the Mayan word *cutz*, "turkey," would be spelled in the cv system, *cu-tz(u)*.

Knorozov, using the Landa "alphabet" as his key, proceeded in the grand tradition of Whorf, Thomas, and Brasseur to bury his key insights in a veritable mountain of incorrect identifications, assumptions, and decipherments, affording Thompson ample opportunity to demolish his arguments, as he had done with Whorf's before. But Knorozov had succeeded, we now know, in deciphering several glyphs correctly, and, perhaps even more important, he had succeeded in convincing a few scholars that he was on the right track. Among these was David Kelley, who defended Knorozov's principles and some of his decipherments in a series of papers that culminated in his 1976 summary of the state of the art, *Deciphering the Maya Script*. Kelley took Knorozov's insights and constructed a more conservative argument for the existence of a Maya syllabary, only a small part of which was claimed to have been ascertained. Kelley also added a few new syllabic signs to the list.

We can appreciate the logic of the phonetic argument if we construct a chain of hypotheses somewhat similar to those encountered in the solution of an ordinary cryptogram. Obviously, the Maya texts are not really enciphered in a secret system; but the method of decipherment in the two cases is similar. We begin with a glyph group from the codices whose semantic interpretation is well known and beyond dispute, namely the one for "turkey" (it regularly accompanies depictions of turkeys in both the Dresden and Madrid codices; see Fig. 13.4, top section, where the glyph group accompanies a turkey shown hanging from a noose). The glyph group involves two main signs compounded, read here in left-to-right order:

We have several hypotheses to begin with: (1) that the codices are twelfth- to fourteenth-century Yucatec; (2) that the sixteenth-century Yucatec word for turkey might well be the same as the earlier one; and (3) that the compound is a phonetic construction written according to Knorozov's principle of synharmony. We also have a fact: a sixteenth-century Yucatec word for turkey was *cutz*, according to contemporary colonial dictionaries.

We can now use Landa's "alphabet" (Fig. 13.8). Notice that Landa frequently matched more than one glyph with each letter of his alphabet, and that in some cases the letters of the alphabet are accompanied by vowels; let us assume that these pairs (consonant-plus-vowel) are syllables. Noting that our first glyph in the compound for turkey is similar to the glyph over Landa's *cu* (within each, for example,

Fig. 13.8. The Landa "alphabet," the key to the phonetic code within Maya writing, as recorded in the *Relación de las cosas de Yucatán*.

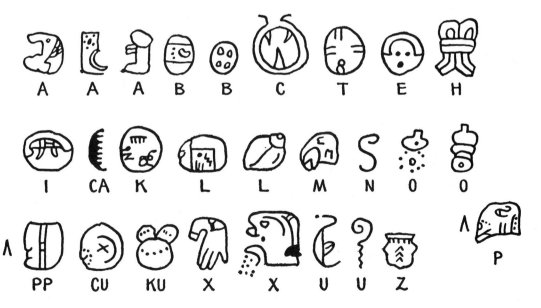

is the X-shape), we hypothesize that this glyph is the syllabic sign for *cu*, and the word being spelled in the codices is *cutz*. This generates a second hypothesis, that the second glyph in our compound is the synharmonic syllabic sign *tz(u)*, for a spelling in which the second vowel is only conventional, not real phonetically. This can be tested by finding *independent* uses of the two glyphs for which our values provide successful analyses.

For example, our *cu* glyph is also found in the following glyph group (the first glyph is eroded):

This group can be found on p. 19 of the Dresden Codex, where the *cu* glyph is third in reading order (the eroded glyph is first, and the other glyph is second). We know the meaning of this glyph group; it is one of the two numbers that are actually spelled out rather than entered in bar-and-dot notation in the Dresden Codex. And because of the mathematical structure of the almanac it is in, we can calculate which number it ought to be, namely eleven. The colonial Yucatec word for eleven was *buluc*. By Knorozov's principle, then, our three glyphs should read *bu*[eroded]-*lu-c(u)*; in other words, the placement of *cu* in the third position (again, as a synharmonic sign) is predicted by our hypotheses. And we have generated yet another hypothesis: that the second glyph is *lu*. In fact, the glyphic compound *tzu-l(u)* occurs frequently in the codices:

Its meaning too has long been known: it is the domestic dog. If all our hypotheses so far are correct, there should have been a word *tzul* meaning domestic dog in Yucatec, and there was indeed just such a word.

In this way one can proceed from hypothesis to hypothesis, each one generating the next in a logical chain, continuously refining earlier hypotheses, with results that would very unlikely be due to chance. It is this type of argument that persuaded many modern researchers of the essential correctness of the principles employed. So why did this not convince Thompson? Why was Knorozov unable to proceed directly to a correct and complete syllabary? And why did not Landa's "alphabet" prove as effective in Maya decipherment as the Rosetta stone had for Egyptian?

Essentially, the answer is that Maya writing turns out to be a mixed system, usually much more complex than the words above, with their purely phonetic and neatly synharmonic spellings, would suggest. Even in the codices, which are generally more phonetic than are the Classic inscriptions, many words are only partially phonetic, and many are purely logographic. Moreover, phonetic spellings are often nonsynharmonic (as with the phonetic rendering *ku-ch(i)* for *kuch*, "vulture"). And because the script was in use for at least 1,500 years, it is no surprise that we find (as in English) archaic spellings, that is, spellings that were once phonetically or pictographically representative, but which have lost this characteristic through language change, or through borrowing of written forms from one language to another. Small wonder, then, that Thomas, Whorf, and Knorozov were unable to leap from their initial insights to the overall phonetic breakthrough they sought. To experts who firmly believed the system was logographic, it was only too easy to demolish the overblown claims, misidentifications, and other errors, rejecting the good with the bad. Yet Knorozov's insights were an advance over those of Thomas or Whorf, and he won a following that they had not. Today almost all specialists in Maya writing agree that the system was logosyllabic, and that it displayed increasing phoneticism over time.

## Recent Advances in Decipherment

Proceeding along the lines of the chained hypotheses above, several scholars have added convincing readings of specific glyphs as well as new insights into the nature of the Maya script. In 1973, when Floyd Lounsbury deciphered the compound prefix T168, long suspected of being a personal title, as *ahau*, "lord" (Fig. 13.5; see also Fig. 13.6, which shows T168 as a constant prefix on emblem glyphs), he was able to demonstrate his reading by an ingenious argument that set a standard for later work. Lounsbury showed that the individual elements of the prefix were to be read *AH* (logograms, as opposed to syllabic signs, are transcribed in capitals) and *po*, respectively, for an archaic title of *ahpo* that apparently survived only in colonial Quichean, where it meant "lord"; whether this title was simply a variant of colonial Quichean *ahpop* (see Chapter 10) or a completely separate title has not been determined. Lounsbury then showed that this title was often accompanied by a suffixed T130, which he read as the syllable *wa*. The Classic lowland Maya, he argued, had adopted the archaic written title *ahpo*, probably from a highland language, but substituted their own term *ahau* for it, and indicated this pronunciation with the suffix *wa* as a phonetic complement. Since Lounsbury's publication, the validity of these syllabic readings has been repeatedly confirmed. But their real significance does not lie in the specific values one might assign to syllables or glyphs; rather, Lounsbury showed how phonetic signs, such as *wa*, could be used to partially indicate the reading of a logogram when the word was not fully spelled phonetically (that is, as a phonetic *complement*), and he showed not only that a historical explanation for an archaic spelling was necessary, but that it could also implicate other languages in the history of the script.

Lounsbury's breakthrough application of the phonetic principle was soon reinforced by other discoveries, most notably when he joined forces with Linda Schele and Peter Mathews. This team began to reconstruct the dynastic sequence of Palenque, identifying the names of specific kings, beginning with the dual representation of Pacal by both a logogram and a phonetic rendering. Schele, Mathews, Lounsbury, and a few others continued to tackle the Palenque texts, puzzling out the complexities of dates, rituals, and references to ancestors and deities, until an astonishingly detailed chronicle of Palenque's mythical and historical past was revealed (some of the high points of the results have been related in Chapter 5).

Since then the pace of progress in the decipherment of Maya texts has been steadily accelerating. There are now dozens of dedicated professional specialists, and many more expert amateurs, involved in this work. Several annual workshops and conferences are devoted to hieroglyphic decipherment, and there are even specialized publications to report the results, including *Research Reports on Ancient Maya Writing*, published by the Center for Maya Research, and *The Copan Notes*, dedicated to disseminating the decipherments of texts and related discoveries resulting from research at Copan, Honduras.

Among the many advances, we can note only a sample. Peter Mathews began an entire chain of decipherments by his 1979 reading of glyphs on a jade ear spool excavated at Altun Ha, Belize. Mathews's reading, *u tup*, "his ear spool," revealed for the first time writing on personal objects that identified possession by the original owner, a custom he labeled "name tagging." David Stuart followed by reading glyphs of the incised bones from Ah Cacau's tomb at Tikal as *u bak*, "his bone." Since then Stephen Houston, Karl Taube, and others have shown that this custom extended to ceramics, expressed as *u lak*, "his bowl or plate," in texts that were accompanied by names and titles of historically known rulers at several sites. David Stuart has identified the ownership phrase of a carved bowl in the Dumbarton Oaks collection as belonging to "Casper," one of the early quasi-mythical rulers of Palenque. He has also identified the signature of the artist on a Late Classic polychrome bowl that was looted from an unknown site. The signature reads in part "the son of the Naranjo ruler and the Lady of Yaxha." A well-known vessel from the Tomb of Yax Kin, ruler of Tikal, is name-tagged with the owner's name, and shows him seated on a throne. To his front is a small pot displaying the Naranjo emblem glyph, which seemingly identified the source of the tribute presented to the Tikal ruler. Finally, name-tagging has been shown to include the function of the object, as well; a pot from Río Azul is painted with glyphs identifying it as a container for chocolate (*kakaw*).

Emblem glyphs have been another focus of decipherment. The work of Peter Mathews has proposed that these refer, not specifically to centers, but to polities (as we saw in Chapter 10; see Fig. 10.8). David Stuart has shown that the phonetic reading of the Yaxha emblem glyph is *Yax ha*, the first indication that an ancient name has survived to the present day. Stephen Houston has shown that there are locative glyphs for places within polities, as in the name for the site we call Aguateca (within the Petexbatun kingdom; see Chapter 5). The glyph for this site in Mayan was *k'inich witz*, or "sun-faced hill." The hill glyph in the expression is split, reflecting the deep fissure that divides the summit of the escarpment on which Aguateca is located. Place names within sites, including what are apparently the names of individual buildings, have been identified at Palenque and Tikal. The texts from Tikal seem to contain more such references than do those of any other known site. The glyphs for what archaeologists call a stela have been deciphered as "tree stone" and those for altar have been deciphered as "throne stone."

In a breakthrough that offers one of the most important insights for understanding ancient Maya belief systems, Stephen Houston and David Stuart have deciphered T539, a glyph depicting an *ahau* face half covered with a jaguar pelt, with a phonetic reading of *way*. In a variety of Mayan languages, the word *way* refers to the supernatural spirit companion or "co-essence" possessed by living things (see Chapter 11). The concept of the supernatural companion has long been recognized in contemporary Maya belief systems, and is widely distributed throughout Mesoamerica (also known by the Nahua word *nagual*). The *way* glyph is fairly common in Classic period texts, on both stone and pottery, and thus contributes immediately to our understanding of a variety of associated images. For instance, the passages on the famous Altar Vase (Fig. 15.19) identify the dancing figures on this vessel as spirit companions. It is now apparent that many of the figures on painted pottery vessels, previously identified as gods, dead rulers, or underworld lords, are in fact depictions of *wayab*, or supernatural companions. On Yaxchilan Lintel 14, a serpent named *kaanal chak bay kan* is referred to as the *way* of the woman it is wound around, Lady Chak Skull (the same *way* is shown on Lintel 13). Another Yaxchilan sculpture, Lintel 25, shows a serpent named *na chan* that is identified as the *way* of the important Maya deity God K (Chapter 11). The same *way* of God K may be depicted on Lintel 3 of Tikal Temple IV (Fig. 14.23).

## The Mayan Syllabary

On the strength of the work of many scholars, we now have at least the rough outlines of a Mayan syllabary (Fig. 13.9), along with a considerable understanding of its associated orthographic rules and the origins of individual meanings. James Fox and John Justeson, in several coauthored papers, have added a large number of glyphs to the known Mayan syllabary, but their work too has had implications beyond their specific decipherments. They show that glyphs that are phonetically equivalent can be used in alternative spellings of the same word, and that this was

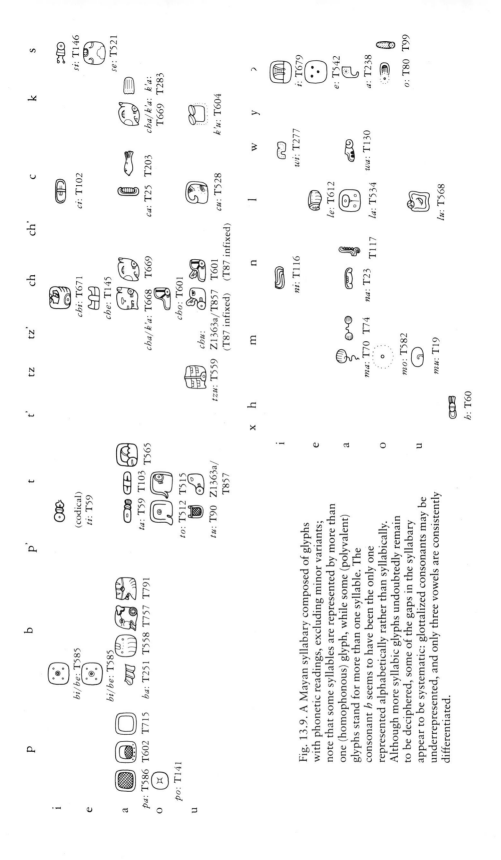

Fig. 13.9. A Mayan syllabary composed of glyphs with phonetic readings, excluding minor variants; note that some syllables are represented by more than one (homophonous) glyph, while some (polyvalent) glyphs stand for more than one syllable. The consonant *h* seems to have been the only one represented alphabetically rather than syllabically. Although more syllabic glyphs undoubtedly remain to be deciphered, some of the gaps in the syllabary appear to be systematic: glottalized consonants may be underrepresented, and only three vowels are consistently differentiated.

done in the codices for aesthetic effect. Perhaps most important, they were able to resolve what had been for many a major stumbling block in accepting syllabic meanings for Mayan signs: they demonstrated that a large number of Mayan glyphs were *polyvalent* (had two or more meanings), and explained the development of polyvalence for each sign historically by specific changes in the language or in the script, or by borrowings from one written language to another, doing for individual glyphs what Lounsbury had done for glyph groups. In separate work, Justeson has made significant advances in our understanding of the aesthetic conventions of Maya writing and of Maya literacy and scribal practice generally.

And now we can solve the riddle of the Landa "alphabet." A number of signs in the Landa manuscript resemble some in the emerging syllabary. In each case, a simple hypothesis concerning Landa's actual procedure demonstrates that the letter value he assigned is actually in accord with the accepted syllabic meaning he was asking his informant to write, not the glyphs for the sounds of Yucatec, nor even the glyphs for the sounds of Spanish, but the glyphs for the sounds of the *names of the letters* in the Spanish alphabet! These are, of course, mostly one-syllable words, as in English, but the words that name the letters are not the same as the phonetic values of the letters; and some are of more than one syllable, such as *f* (*efe*) and *h* (*hache*). Landa's informant responded with the glyphs corresponding to the most prominent syllables he heard. For example, Landa's *cu* (hard *c*) falls where the letter *q* (pronounced *cu*) occurs in alphabetical order, and the associated glyph is now known to have had the syllabic value *cu* along with several logographic values. For Landa's *h* the informant responded with the syllabic sign *che*, the second syllable of the Spanish word *hache*. This is a fairly simple procedure, and one wonders whether Landa could have been that naive. Perhaps so—confusion of sounds with letters was even more common in his day than in ours—but we are still not sure what Landa's intentions were. In the text he implies that he was teaching the Maya to write with their own characters according to Spanish (alphabetic) rules. Was he describing the pre-Columbian system, or a now-lost Mayan-Spanish hybrid?

## The Origins of Maya Writing

Some glyph meanings and archaic glyph groups clearly had their immediate origins among Cholan writers, even though they were used by Yucatecans. The Cholan syllabic sign *chi*, for example, was also used as a logogram for "deer" (Yucatec *ceh*) and the Yucatec day Manik. The sign was therefore polyvalent in Yucatec, but the values were nearly equivalent in Cholan, where the words for "deer" and the Manik day sign were both *chih*. Many of the glyph groups signifying the month names (see Figs. 13.10 and 12.5) are easy to explain on the basis of Cholan origins. For example, the glyph group for the Yucatec month Kankin is a logogram followed usually by the phonetic complement *wa*, occasionally by *ni* and *wa*, leading us to expect a month name ending in *-niw* or *-new*. This does not fit the Yucatec

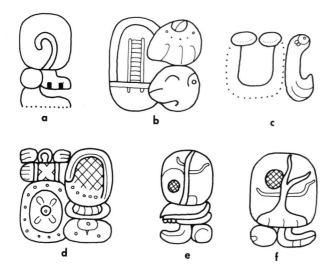

Fig. 13.10. Examples of syllabic spellings and complementations: (*a*) the month Muan, spelled *mu-an-n(e)*; (*b*) the glyph for armadillo, Yucatec *ibach*, spelled *i-ba-ch(e)*; (*c*) the glyph for vulture, Yucatec *kuch*, spelled *ku-ch(i)*; (*d*) Pacal, ruler of Palenque, represented by a shield (pacal) glyph complemented by the syllables *pa-ca-l(a)*; (*e*) the Cholan month *uniw* or *onew*, represented by a tree glyph (see Fig. 13.6*e*) plus the phonetic complement *ne-w(a)*; (*f*) the month *uniw* with only one phonetic complement, *w(a)*.

name, but it does fit the Cholan *uniw*. Similarly, the Yucatec month Tzec, spelled with a prefixed *se* and suffixed *ca* in the codices, is spelled *ca-se-w(a)* in the Classic texts, and the Cholan name for the month was *caseu*. In the Landa versions of the Yucatec month spellings, syllabic signs are added to the fossilized traditional spellings to give the current Yucatec pronunciations of the names. For example, the Landa spelling for the Yucatec month Zip, traditionally spelled with the logograms *IK* and *KAT* (the Cholan name for this month was *ik kat*, "black cross"), has a prefixed phonetic complement *si* in Landa's spelling.

The ultimate origins of Maya writing, however, are still obscure. The earliest known lowland Maya text is on Tikal Stela 29, dated at 292 B.C. (there are of course

Fig. 13.11. The direction and color glyphs: (*a*) west (Yucatec Mayan *chikin*) and its associated color, black (Yucatec *ek*); (*b*) east (Yucatec *likin*, earlier *lakin*) and its associated color, red (Yucatec *chac*); (*c*) north/up (Yucatec *xaman*) and its associated color, white (Yucatec *sac*); (*d*) south/down (Yucatec *nohol*) and its associated color, yellow (Yucatec *kan*); (*e*) the colors blue and green (Yucatec *yax*), associated with the center.

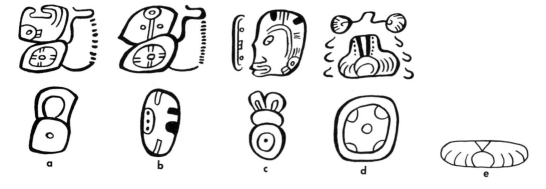

earlier Maya monuments without writing). Scholars usually agree that the ancestors of lowland Maya writing can be found at Preclassic sites, especially those in highland Guatemala, along the Pacific piedmont of Guatemala, in the Isthmus of Tehuantepec, and in Oaxaca, but its development is hard to trace in detail because of the paucity of glyphic texts from this period. Of these, perhaps the most clearly Maya in nature is the famous Late Preclassic inscription on Kaminaljuyu Stela 10 (Fig. 3.12), which seems to begin with a time count of 14 uinals (or 280 days), and to contain the Maya "capture" compound. Inscriptions at sites such as El Baúl, Abaj Takalik, Chiapa de Corzo, and Tres Zapotes have Maya Long Count dates and the predecessors of some Maya (and central-Mexican) glyphs, but some of these areas were not Mayan-speaking in colonial times, and we cannot yet ascertain their pre-Columbian linguistic affiliations. Internal evidence from the script itself (for example, Lounsbury's reference to Quichean), may eventually implicate some non-Greater Lowland Mayan languages in the origins of glyph meanings, but that evidence is still insufficient.

## The Status of Decipherment

What, then, of Maya writing can be read now? We have the syllabary, still incomplete, and we can interpret and actually read a great many glyphs and glyph groups. Apart from the calendrical and astronomical glyphs (see Chapter 12), we have the glyphs for the colors and directions (Fig. 13.11), which are associated in the Maya texts and in Mesoamerican cultures generally in the following manner: east/red, north/white, west/black, south/yellow, center/blue-and-green (Mayan languages did not distinguish blue from green as abstract colors). Glyphs for many deities (see Chapter 11 and Fig. 11.7), animals, plants, and other objects have been identified through their phonetics and context; some of these (Fig. 13.12) clearly

Fig. 13.12. Examples of glyphs depicting recognizable animal heads: (*a, b*) variants of a glyph for fish (T738a, T738c); (*c*) macaw (T744b); (*d*) vulture (T747a); (*e*) jaguar (T751b); (*f*) dog (T752); (*g*) leaf-nosed bat (T556a); (*h*) gopher (T757).

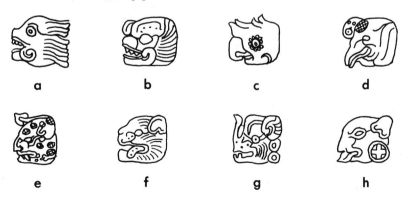

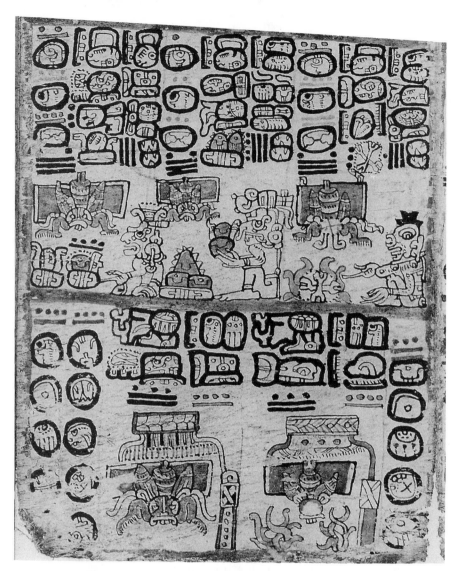

TEXT 1

| 7 | | a | b |
| Cib | | | |
| 8 | | c | d |
| Caban | | | |
| 9 | | e | f |
| Etz'nab | | | |
| 17 | | g | h |

ILLUSTRATION 1

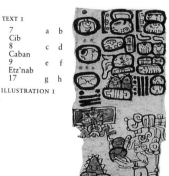

TEXT 2

| 1 | | a | b |
| Cib | | | |
| 2 | | c | d |
| Caban | | | |
| 3 | | e | f |
| Etz'nab | | | |
| 17 | | g | h |

ILLUSTRATION 2

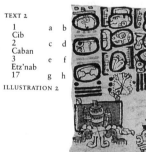

TEXT 3

| 8 | | a | b |
| Cib | | | |
| 9 | | c | d |
| Caban | | | |
| 10 | | e | f |
| Etz'nab | | | |
| 17 | | g | h |

ILLUSTRATION 3

Fig. 13.13 (*facing page*). From the Madrid Codex, p. 103, part of a section on beekeeping. The illustrations and glyphic texts of the top half are separated and analyzed below the figure as an aid to understanding the explanation below; both the schematization and the translations are by James A. Fox. Successive stations in the calendrical framework give auguries and ritual information, but the complex interpretations necessary to understand them are not given here. Syllabic signs are transliterated in lowercase italics, logographic signs in italic small capitals; when the English meaning for a sign is known, but the exact Yucatec Mayan word is not, the meaning is given in small capitals.

*Illustration 1.* Bee descending from hive over seated god Itzamna and offerings of an unidentified animal and some sort of maize (toasted?). The number 9 above the maize probably counts the number of items to be offered.

| *Text 1* | a | b | c | d |
|---|---|---|---|---|
| Glyphs | *u-pa-cha* | *u-pa-cha* | ITZAMNA-*na* | AHAU-IL-IL |
| Yucatec | *u-pach* | *u-pach* | *itzam na* | *ahau-l-il* |
| Meaning | he takes | he takes | Itzamna | lord |

| | e | f | g | h |
|---|---|---|---|---|
| Glyphs | 3-*oc-wa* | *h*-HA?-IL | [offering] | 15-[offering] |
| Yucatec | *noh-oc-wah* | *ha?-il* | ? | 15 ? |
| Meaning | big feast | rain | [offering] | 15 [offering] |

Translation: "Lord Itzamna takes his honey; big feast [and] rain [are the auguries]; [?] and 15 [?] [are the offerings]."

In glyph group *b*, *u-pa-cha* is almost certainly a scribal error for *u-*CÀ:B-*ba* ("his honey"), as in Texts 2 and 3. In Yucatec, 3 and 9 are used metaphorically for "big, many"; see group *e* for an example.

*Illustration 2.* Bee descending, seated god Chac, offerings of maize in hand and maize with superimposed iguana symbol in dish.

| *Text 2* | a | b | c | d |
|---|---|---|---|---|
| Glyphs | *u-pa-cha* | *u-*CÀ:B-*ba* | *cha-ci* | ?-WATER-MAIZE |
| Yucatec | *u-pach* | *u-cà:b* | *chac* | ? *ha?-kan* |
| Meaning | he takes | his honey | Chac [the rain god] | ? water, maize |

| | e | f | g | h |
|---|---|---|---|---|
| Glyphs | *tu-?-na* | *ah-po* / AHAU-*le* | MAIZE, IGUANA | 19-[offering] |
| Yucatec | *t-u-?* | *ahau-le?* | *kan, hù:h* | 19 ? |
| Meaning | in his ? | noose? | maize, iguana | 19 [offering] |

Translation: "Chac takes his honey; ? water [and] maize, in his ? [the] noose [are the auguries]; maize, iguana, and 19 [?] [are the offerings]."

The glyph for the day Kan is used for maize throughout the codices, as it is here in groups *d* and *g*; it is often (but not here) suffixed with T130 (*wa*), perhaps for *kan wah*, "yellow food," presumably a metaphor for maize (*ixim*).

*Illustration 3.* Bee (headless) descending, etc., seated death god before burning crossed bones.

| *Text 3* | a | b | c | d |
|---|---|---|---|---|
| Glyphs | *u-pa-cha* | *u-*CÀ:B-*ba* | DEATH GOD | *tu*-DEATH |
| Yucatec | *u-pach* | *u-cà:b* | *cisin* | *t-u-*[*cim-il*?] |
| Meaning | he takes | his honey | Cisin | in his death |

| | e | f | g | h |
|---|---|---|---|---|
| Glyphs | *u*-MUC | *h*-HA? / CHANGE-IL | 3-BURNING BONES | 16-[offering] |
| Yucatec | *u-muc* | *ha?-il* / CHANGE | 3 ?? | 16 ? |
| Meaning | its omen | change [from?] rain | 3 (or many) burning bones | 16 [offering] |

Translation: "Cisin takes his honey; death [is] its omen; rain [stops?]; many burning bones [and] 16 [?] [are the offerings]."

The rain glyph has an infixed swastika-like sign (the *hel* glyph, meaning change).

A  B

1
2
3
4
5
6

7
8
9
10
11
12

Fig. 13.14. Translation of Tikal Stela 22 (*facing page*; see also Fig. 4.22), by Christopher Jones. Some English words have been interpolated to make the cryptic Maya text more understandable.

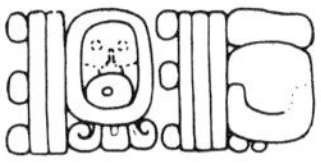

The day 13 Ahau
Eighteenth day of the month, Cumku,

End of the seventeenth katun.
The completion of its period.

[Part of the ruler's name?]
Chitam

In the dynastic line, lord of Tikal,
[A title]

The ninth plus twenty,
In the count of the rulers

[Successor to?]
His lord father,

Yax Kin Caan Chac
[A probable title,]

In the dynastic line, lord of Tikal,
In his fourth katun,

The leader [*batab*]
Sixteen days plus one period of twenty days,

Plus two tuns [back to],
The day 11 Kan,

Twelfth day of the month of the parrot, Kayab,
He took the throne,

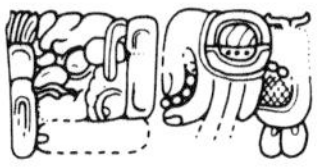

At the place of leadership,
He who scatters blessings.

represent their meanings pictographically (for example, turkey, vulture, leaf-nosed bat, dog, armadillo, and gopher), though they may be found spelled phonetically as well.

Glyphs corresponding to various parts of speech—verbs, nouns, adjectives, and particles—have been identified, as well as glyphs for various grammatical prefixes and suffixes. Generally, the main signs in Maya writing represent logograms, and the affixes represent either phonetic complements or (logographic or phonetic) grammatical affixes, but this generalization, too, has many exceptions. The ordering of glyphs in Maya texts reflects the grammatical structure of the languages (the Yucatec codices, for example, are ordered verb-object-subject, which corresponds to Yucatec usage), but the glyphic texts can be highly abbreviated, sometimes almost telegraphic or mnemonic.

Many glyphic identifications are being made as a direct result of advances in understanding the scenes accompanying the inscriptions. Whorf pioneered using the iconography of such scenes to provide crucial clues to the content of the texts. In many cases individual elements (such as implements, items of clothing, etc.) first identified through extensive comparison of such scenes have eventually turned out to be depicted or represented by individual glyphs.

More glyphs of social or historical importance have been identified. To the emblem glyphs and glyphs for birth, accession, death, titles, capture, and captor deciphered by Berlin and Proskouriakoff have been added more emblem glyphs and titles, a glyph for captive, glyphs for marriage, and a glyph for numerical position in the dynastic line. Personal names and titles have also been identified, and many of these can be read phonetically. Pacal, for example, the ruler of Palenque mentioned above, has in his name glyphs a shield (*pacal*) that is often accompanied by the phonetic spelling *pa-ca-l(a)*. Texts naming rulers also name their predecessors, and the associated genealogical relations are explicitly stated with kinship glyphs. Schele, Mathews, and Lounsbury have together been instrumental in establishing the genealogical nature of these expressions, and have proposed that the actual meanings include "child of man," "child of woman," and "child of parent (sex unspecified)," distinctions that are common in Mayan languages. They have also proposed that the line of succession in the Maya states was from father to son, as is reflected in interpretations elsewhere in this book.

We are not sure how many more syllabic signs we can expect to decipher, and the number of texts available to us is limited. Nor can we foresee how many equivalent and polyvalent signs there may have been. And syllabaries do not always, or even usually, list separate signs for every possible syllable. For example, the Mayan syllabary appears to be lacking in signs for several of the glottalized consonants, though existence of the glottalized variant of *k* leads us to expect sets for others; but it is possible that some signs could serve for both a plain consonant *and* its glottalized counterpart. For most consonants it has been possible to decipher signs for a consonant plus *a* (thus *ca*), but signs for *ci* are often used for *ce* and vice versa, just as signs for *cu* are often used for *co* and vice versa, occasionally with minor infixes apparently signaling the difference. Thus the syllabary seems to represent a three-vowel system, with precision at the five-vowel level furnished perhaps only in an early stage of development, or in the infixes.

Recent progress in decipherment has thus negated earlier claims that Maya writing would never be read in any detail. And in response to those who might complain that even these advances leave us with nothing but the most boring sort of history—lists of rulers and the formal events of their lives, all with associated dates—one might reflect how colorful this information must be to scholars who have long had to be content with hundreds of dates, each exact to the very day, but with none of the corresponding events ascertained at all. Even this limited sort of information can lead to discoveries important to historians and archaeologists. (The codices, too, offer us a fascinating insight into the spiritual life of the Post-classic Maya; would that the Spaniards had not thought to burn them all!)

It is often asked what percentage of the Mayan glyphs or inscriptions can be read, and to this question only the vaguest of answers can be given. Some texts are almost completely understood; others lie in relative obscurity in spite of progress. As examples of the amount and kind of information available to scholars from the best-understood records, Fig. 13.13 presents a decipherment of a page from the Postclassic Madrid Codex, and Fig. 13.14 a translation of a Late Classic text from Tikal Stela 22.

# 14

....

# ARCHITECTURE, SCULPTURE, AND PAINTING

It was then that they built temples in such numbers as are seen today on all sides, and in passing through the forests, there are seen in the midst of the woods the sites of houses and buildings of marvelous construction.
—*Landa's relación de las cosas de Yucatán* (Tozzer 1941: 40)

Our knowledge of ancient Maya society rests, in good measure, upon inferences derived from the physical remains of past activity, namely, the archaeological sites scattered across the Maya area. In this chapter we shall consider the principal fixed features of ancient Maya sites: architecture and its associated features, namely sculpture, stucco modeling, and painting.

## Architecture

The variations observable in the form of Classic Maya buildings have long suggested that each form served a particular function. The functions so posited have given rise to labels commonly applied by archaeologists to many structures, correctly or not, the most familiar being "temples," buildings elevated on high pyramidal platforms with restricted interior spaces and large free-standing façades called roof combs. There are also "palaces," elongated multi-room buildings usually situated on lower platforms, typically possessing benches, doorway niches ("curtain holders"), small windows, and other features that suggest a residential function. These (and similar) labels, though often justified by the available archaeological evidence, must be used with caution, for they often oversimplify the true functions of structures. Buildings in both categories undoubtedly hosted a variety of activities, and not all "temples," for instance, seem to have been used for the same purposes, and "palaces" probably were used for meetings, audiences, courts, and other functions beyond strictly residential activities. In addition, of course, there are other types of specialized Maya buildings, some of which are not easily subsumed under these or other functional categories. But for convenience these labels will be used here, together with other commonly used constructional designations, such as ball-courts, causeways (sacbeob), sweat baths, shrines, and the like (see Table 14.1).

Although some Maya buildings were built on level terrain, most were constructed on elevated surfaces. These ranged from the low earthen platforms that supported the simplest houses to the terraced masonry-faced "pyramids" crowned by the loftiest structures, at sites such as Tikal. Throughout the Maya area the remains of most domestic buildings indicate that they were constructed in the same manner as are contemporary Maya houses. Typically, a pole framework supports a thatched roof; walls are usually wattle and daub, a woven lattice of sticks plastered with a thick coating of adobe (mud mixed with straw or other binder). In the hottest regions, house walls are often unplastered, allowing the passage of cooling breezes. More substantial houses may have foundations of stone, or rough stone walls smoothed with plaster. These domestic structures, the oldest known form of Maya architecture, provide the basic design prototype for subsequent elaborations rendered in more durable stone and plaster.

Ancient building platforms in the southern Maya area were usually earthen-cored and faced with adobe plaster (typically mixed with volcanic ash, which is abundant in the southern area). Owing to the scarcity of suitable, easily worked building stone, even the largest and most elaborate southern Maya buildings were usually constructed of perishable materials, such as pole and thatch, wood, or adobe blocks. Stonework, when encountered, was usually used for pavements, steps, and occasional decorative elements. In a few cases, as at Asunción Mita in the southeastern highlands, the natural cleavage planes of the local stone provided masonry blocks of convenient sizes for structures.

The most durable and best-known examples of Maya architecture are the elaborate masonry structures found at most of the major centers in the southern, central, and northern lowlands. These regions are endowed with plentiful, easily obtained building materials from soft-limestone beds, materials that can be cut into blocks or reduced by burning to produce lime for plaster. Some regional variations occur; for instance, in the southeastern lowlands, sandstone, rhyolite, and marble were used as building stone at Quirigua, whereas trachyte was used at Copan. Masonry decorations, such as inset corner moldings, apron moldings, mosaic corner masks, and friezes, were often integrated with architecture.

From Preclassic times on, lime-based plaster was frequently used to pave level expanses ("plazas") between structures in the heavily built-up areas of most sites. Plaster almost invariably covered both exterior and interior masonry to provide a smooth finished surface. Surfaces of stairways, platforms, and building floors also received a thick coat of plaster. At many sites, three-dimensional modeled plaster decorations ("stucco reliefs") were used to adorn walls, building façades, and roof combs. The earliest examples are the monumental plaster masks that flank stairways on Preclassic platforms at many lowland sites (Uaxactun, Tikal, El Mirador,

632

TABLE 14.1

Functional Classification of Maya Architectural and Constructional Features, with Examples

(The numbers in parentheses refer to figure numbers in this book.)

| Features | Pacific plain and highlands | Maya area Southern and central lowlands | Northern lowlands |
|---|---|---|---|
| **BUILDINGS AND BUILDING ASSEMBLAGES** | | | |
| Pyramid temples | Awilix Temple, Utatlan (7.30) | Temple II, Tikal (4.11) | El Castillo, Chichen Itza (7.7) |
| Pyramid temples with tomb | Str. E-III-3, Kaminaljuyu (3.13) | Temple I, Tikal (4.13–4.16); Temple of the Inscriptions, Palenque (5.31, 5.32) | "High Priest's" Tomb, Chichen Itza (7.3) |
| Necropoli | Str. D6-1, Los Mangales | North Acropolis, Tikal (4.4) | |
| Palaces | Cawek Palace, Utatlan (7.29) | Central Acropolis, Tikal (4.5); Palace, Palenque (5.30) | Nunnery, Uxmal (6.16) |
| Ballcourts | Ballcourt, Utatlan (7.29) | Strs. 8 and 9, Copan (5.46) | Great Ball Court, Chichen Itza (7.9) |
| Sweat baths | Str. B-12, Los Cimientos-Chustum | Str. N-1, Piedras Negras | |
| Skull platforms (*tzompantli*) | Plaza A platforms, Iximche | | Chichen Itza (7.11) |
| Astronomical assemblages | | Group E, Uaxactun (4.27) | |
| Twin Pyramid groups | | Group 4E-4, Tikal (4.18) | |
| Council houses (*popol na*) | | Str. 10L-22A, Copan (5.61) | Governor's Palace, Uxmal (6.15) |
| **PUBLIC AREAS** | | | |
| Monument plazas | Monument Plaza, Izapa | Great Plazas at Copan and Quirigua (5.42, 5.54) | Terrace of the Monuments, Uxmal (6.12) |
| Elevated plaza-platforms | | Terrace of Temple IV, Tikal; Danta Platform, El Mirador | Terrace of the Governor's Palace, Uxmal |
| "Reviewing stands" | | Ballcourt Plaza, Quirigua (5.54) | |
| Market areas | Plaza C(?), Iximche | East Plaza, Tikal (?) | |

## COMMUNICATION AND DEFENSIVE FACILITIES

| | | | |
|---|---|---|---|
| Intrasite causeways | Entrance Causeway, Utatlan (7.29) | Tikal (4.5); Yaxha | Coba; Dzibilchaltun (6.6) |
| Intersite causeways | | El Mirador region | Coba-Yaxuna (6.11) |
| Bridges | | Pusilha | |
| Docking and landing areas | | Northwest side, Ballcourt Plaza, Quirigua | Tulum (7.19) |
| Harbors/ports | | | Isla Cerritos (7.1) |
| Gateway arches | | | Kabah (6.20); Labna (6.24) |
| Ditches and ramparts | | Becan (4.36); Tikal | |
| Encircling walls | | Dos Pilas (5.6); Muralla de León | Mayapan (7.16); Tulum (7.22) |
| Lookout posts | Atalaya (Utatlan) | Group A, Quirigua | Str. 45(?), Tulum (7.24) |

## RESOURCE-MANAGEMENT FACILITIES

| | | | |
|---|---|---|---|
| Aqueducts | | Palenque | |
| Reservoirs | | Tikal (4.5) | |
| Reservoirs with aqueducts | | | Edzna (8.4) |
| Wells | | | |
| Chultunes (Cisterns) | | Quirigua | Labna; Sayil |
| Quarries | | Tikal | |
| Field walls | | Calakmul (14.7) | |
| Agricultural terraces | | Río Bec region, Maya Mountains | Northwestern Yucatan |
| Raised fields and drainage canals | | Pulltrouser Swamp (8.6); Río Candelaria (8.8) | |
| Salt pans | | | Northern Yucatan coast (9.1) |

Lamanai, Cerros, to name the best known; see Figs. 3.26, 3.29, and 3.30). These and other conventions established in the Preclassic continue into the Classic and beyond. The most famous and most elaborate examples of Classic-period modeled-plaster decoration are the beautiful relief panels at Palenque (Fig. 14.25). These modeled scenes were once further embellished by painting. Plastered surfaces were either left an unpainted white to cream, or painted in one or more colors. Occasionally, as in the case of the red-painted Str. 5D-22 at Tikal, the evidence indicates that an entire building was covered by colored plaster (Fig. 4.7). Interior painted scenes or murals are rarely preserved, but a number of fragmentary examples have survived: from the Preclassic period at Tikal (Fig. 3.22), from the Classic period at several sites, including Uaxactun, and from the Postclassic period at Chichen Itza, Tulum, and several other northern sites (Figs. 7.18, 7.23). But the most spectacular examples are the Late Classic murals at Bonampak, as we shall see.

Although masonry styles vary throughout the Maya area, a core of traits is common to most or all lowland Classic Maya buildings. The supporting platforms were usually built up with rubble and earth and faced with cut-stone masonry. Summit access is often gained by a medial stairway. Most platforms surmounted by a single building have either a single frontal stairway or four medial stairways. At many sites, the substructural platforms support more than one building, and in some cases modifications and additions eventually unified separate platforms into a single mass. A large, complex multibuilding platform of this kind is usually termed an acropolis; a good example is the North Acropolis at Tikal (Figs. 4.3–4.5). Superimposed construction is a hallmark of Maya architecture; when one building had outlived its usefulness, it was often partially or totally covered by a new and larger structure.

The masonry buildings situated on these platforms usually have relatively little interior space in proportion to their bulk (Fig. 14.1). This feature follows from the predominant building technique of rubble-filled walls, cut-stone facings, and corbeled vaults (Fig. 14.2). Rather than solid masonry-block walls, most Maya wall surfaces consist of a single layer of masonry that serves as a facing for a rubble hearting. The result is a relatively thick wall, and to support the corbeled vaulting and roof a thick wall was necessary. The corbeled, or "false," arch, which typically takes the form of an inverted "V," is constructed of a vertical series of successively overlapping blocks, each of which projects farther inward until the intervening space between the two walls can be bridged by a single capstone (the capstone does not anchor the whole, as does the keystone of the true arch). The earliest vaults are of rough masonry, thickly plastered to provide a smoothed soffit, or slope to the ceiling. Later vaults achieved a finished soffit by using beveled vault stones. In a true arch, an architectural concept the Maya never used, each block (including the keystone) is supported by the adjacent blocks, so that the whole forms a strong, integrated unit. Corbeling is a form of cantilever, in which the only support is from the

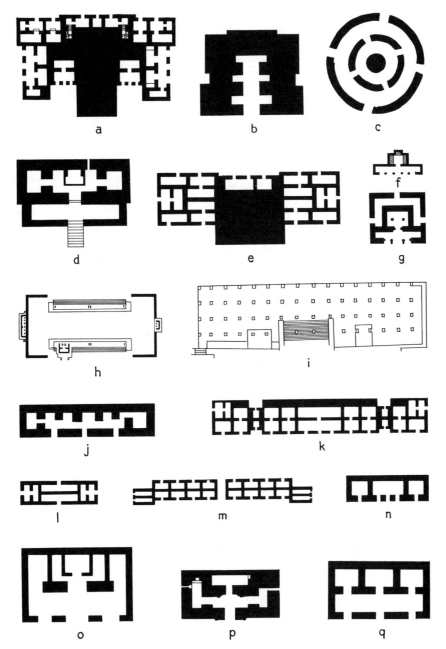

Fig. 14.1. Plans of various Maya structures: (*a*) Xtampak Palace; (*b*) Tikal Temple IV; (*c*) Chichen Itza Caracol; (*d*) Uaxactun Str. E-II; (*e*) Chichen Itza Akabtzib; (*f*) Chichen Itza Sweat Bath 2; (*g*) Chichen Itza El Castillo; (*h*) Chichen Itza Ballcourt; (*i*) Chichen Itza Northwest Colonnade; (*j*) Yaxchilan Str. 33; (*k*) Uxmal Governor's Palace; (*l*) Uxmal House of the Turtles; (*m*) Uxmal House of the Pigeons; (*n*) Yaxchilan Str. 21; (*o*) Palenque Temple of the Sun; (*p*) Copan Str. 10L-22; (*q*) Chichen Itza Red House.

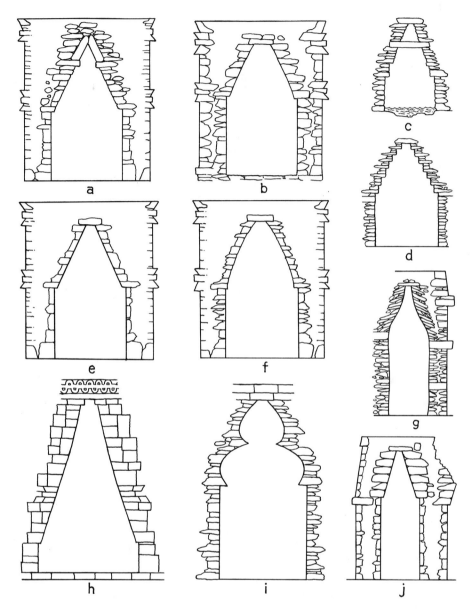

Fig. 14.2. Cross sections of Maya corbeled vaults: (*a*) Chichen Itza Monjas Annex; (*b*) typical Classic vault with irregular vault stones; (*c*) Palenque Viaduct; (*d*) Uaxactun Str. E-X; (*e*) typical Puuc vault with veneer vault stones, or (*f*) with "shoe-shaped" vault stones and curved soffit; (*g*) Uaxactun Str. A-V; (*h*) Uxmal Governor's Palace arcade; (*i*) Palenque Palace trefoil vault; (*j*) Chichen Itza Monjas, second story.

overlap with the block below, and each vault stone is counterbalanced by the weight of the hearting above that holds it in place. The corbeled arch is much weaker than a true arch, thus necessitating the thick walls typical of Maya buildings. In consequence, Maya corbel-vaulted rooms rarely exceed 3 m in width.

Because of the inherent limitations of corbeled vaulting, most Maya buildings are single-story, but by the use of massive walls and narrow vaults the Maya built two- and even three-story masonry buildings, as for example the Central Acropolis at Tikal (Fig. 4.17). In addition, the roofs of many Maya structures supported decorative elements, such as façades or roof combs. Roof combs are masonry backdrops for front-facing decorative elements, usually constructed of mosaic or stucco work, that add to the height of the building. Sometimes of solid masonry, they are often supported and lightened by narrow, one- or two-story corbeled vaults. Most roof combs rise above the midline of the building, but some are supported by the front wall, giving the building a false front, called a "flying façade."

The best exemplars of roof-comb architecture are the great temples at Tikal (Fig. 4.13). Serving as funerary monuments to that center's Late Classic rulers, each temple is capped by a huge roof comb bearing the mosaic-sculptured portrait of the commemorated personage. As such, Tikal's great temples culminate the lowland tradition of integrating platform, building, and roof comb into a single monumental structure, appropriately considered to be examples of Maya sacred mountains.

Despite these overall architectural similarities, considerable variation in style and even technique can be seen in Maya masonry buildings. Although it remains difficult to set temporal and spatial boundaries around architectural styles, by the Late Classic a series of broad regional styles can be defined. The most famous of these is undoubtedly the central Peten style, epitomized by Tikal's lofty, massive platforms each supporting a temple with a single doorway and roof comb. This style encompasses much of the central lowlands, at least to the modern Belize border on the east. The western extent is undefined, for we know relatively little about the western portion of the central lowlands (the large but uninvestigated site of El Perú may hold a key for this area). To the north, the central Peten style probably extends as far as Calakmul; and Coba, far to the north in eastern Yucatan, is often seen as an outlying representative.

The Usumacinta region is marked by another architectural style, although its definition and boundaries are even less well established. The site of Yaxchilan, with its three-doorwayed buildings set high on natural hills, is typical of this regional style, a style also seen at Piedras Negras, Bonampak, and, further to the southwest, Palenque. In some respects the style of Palenque's buildings represents a distinctive development, but the basic template is clearly related to that of the Usumacinta region. The temples at Palenque typically have two parallel vaulted rooms that are noticeably larger and more open than are most of their contemporaries (Figs. 5.31, 5.35). The upper façades, which elsewhere are vertical, here slope inward (forming what is called a mansard roof), generally following the angle of the interior vaulting. This reduced the weight borne by the exterior walls, and therefore allowed them to be less massive. As a result, the front wall could be opened by multiple doorways and the vaults made wider. A single transverse interior wall supports the bulk of the roof, which includes a reduced roof comb made lighter by being built as an open lattice rather than solid masonry. The vaults in the palace at Palenque display considerable variety in shape, including a doubly rounded soffit (Fig. 14.2*i*).

In the southeastern lowlands another distinctive style emerged, one defined almost exclusively by the architecture of Copan. Its most prominent features were the extensive use of elaborate modeled reliefs on building exteriors and large platforms and acropoli faced with monumental stairways ("reviewing stands"). Recent excavations reveal that the tradition of modeled reliefs on building façades extends back to the Early Classic, when the reliefs were rendered in painted plaster. In the Late Classic, modeled plaster was replaced by mosaic stone sculpture, as for example in the elaborate corner masks and doorways of the famous Str. 10L-22 at Copan (Fig. 5.43), although in this case the sculpture was originally coated with painted plaster. Quirigua, with its monumental reviewing stands, belongs to this stylistic tradition, but only remnants indicate that its buildings were once elaborately decorated with modeled plaster. The southeastern style probably extends farther north to sites such as Lubaantun and Nimli Punit in southern Belize, as well.

The elaborate façade mosaics of Copan may have been prototypes for similar features that developed in the northern lowlands, the setting for the Late Classic Chenes (Fig. 4.37) and Río Bec traditions (Fig. 4.38), and the Terminal Classic Puuc style. The latter, perhaps the most consistent and most pleasing variation in Maya architecture, developed in the Puuc region of the northwestern lowlands (Fig. 14.3). Although probably related to styles outside the Maya area (most explicitly, those of Mitla and similar sites in the Valley of Oaxaca), Puuc architecture retains many features of earlier Maya buildings. In the era between the World Wars, Puuc architecture was the principal inspiration for a minor episode in the history of American architecture, usually referred to as the Maya Revival. Associated primarily with theaters, office buildings, and residences, the style found its most famous exponent in Frank Lloyd Wright.

The hearting of Puuc buildings is a solidified lime-based concrete, which gives the structure considerable strength. The masonry consists of finely shaped limestone veneer blocks applied to the concrete hearting. As can be seen in the ruined Puuc buildings that have lost their veneer, the veneer masonry provides no structural support, and the concrete hearting usually continues to support the structure. Though the vaults of Puuc buildings retain the *form* of the corbeled arch (with either straight-sided or rounded soffits), they are not technically corbeled, since the vault stones, usually shoe-shaped to secure a better purchase in the hearting, are a veneer over the concrete that actually supports the vault (Fig. 14.2*f*).

Fig. 14.3. The Puuc style, defined by a decorated upper zone and a plain lower zone, is seen here on La Iglesia at Chichen Itza; the building to the left exhibits the Chenes style (see Fig. 7.4).

On the exterior, the lower façade of Puuc buildings is usually devoid of decoration (Figs. 14.3 and 6.16). Doorways were single or multiple, the multiple easily formed by using round or square columns to divide the openings. A variation on the Puuc style, generally found south of the Puuc region, has been traditionally treated as a separate architectural style, the Chenes style, which typically differs in having elaborately decorated lower façades, especially doorways incorporated into elaborate mosaic sculptures of monster masks (Fig. 7.4; see also Fig. 6.17). Another variation, the Río Bec style, adds false towers to the building façade (Fig. 4.38).

Upper façades often have a negative batter, that is, they slope slightly outward to compensate for distortions in visual perception. The upper façade of Puuc buildings is decorated with elaborate precut sculptured mosaics. Common motifs include X-shaped lattices, multiple columns (plain or banded "spools"), stepped frets, and the like (Figs. 14.3 and 14.4). Although curvilinear and naturalistic designs—serpents, masks, and other motifs typical of most Classic Maya building decorations—persist, it is this geometric mosaic style that most strongly recalls the architecture of Mitla and other Oaxacan sites. The use of plaster decoration appears to be rare or nonexistent on Puuc buildings. Frontal roof combs are typical, but their overall scale is reduced, and these roof ornaments are often completely absent.

The architectural florescence at Chichen Itza was marked by a synthesis of Maya and other Mesoamerican traditions. The result is a distinctive and innovative style, its principal feature being colonnaded buildings (see Chapter 7). This development provided the template for much of Postclassic architecture in the northern lowlands, but Chichen Itza's descendants at Mayapan, Tulum, and other late period sites did not approach the masonry skill apparent at Chichen Itza.

Fig. 14.4. Puuc-style building details on the Great Pyramid, Uxmal: (*left*) corner masks; (*upper right*) mask step; (*lower right*) mosaic façade.

## Stone Sculpture

Ancient Maya sculpture falls into two basic categories, free-standing monuments and actual architectural elements, although the two share the same technology and many of the same stylistic conventions. Architectural sculpture may be found on lintels, wall panels, doorjambs, steps, façades, and roof elements. These elements were often intended to be viewed closely only by the residents of these buildings—rulers, priests, and other members of the elite class. Free-standing monuments include upright stone shafts (stelae), flat, rounded or squared stones ("altars"), and, more rarely, boulder sculptures (such as the "zoomorphs" found at Quirigua). Monuments were almost always set in accessible plazas, indicating that they were intended to be seen and appreciated by everyone, elite and non-elite alike.

Recent decipherments indicate that the Maya referred to stelae as "stone trees" and altars as "throne stones." The former label might be a clue to the distant origin of the custom of erecting monuments. The phrase "throne stone" offers a clue to the function of these flat stones, which are usually found paired with stelae—the stones were not "altars" but seats probably used by rulers during public ceremonies conducted in the plazas where most were placed.

It has often been noted that ancient Maya sculpture tends to "abhor a vacuum": it allows very little free space, and most surface areas are filled with sculptural detail. The motifs of Maya sculpture are usually a combination of supernatural symbolism and portrayals of natural human and animal forms. The natural forms appear recognizable and "normal" to our eyes; the supernatural elements often seem grotesque and alien. But given what we know about Maya ideology (see Chapter 11), we can assume that the clear distinction we see between the natural and the grotesque was irrelevant to the ancient Maya.

Limestone, being the most plentiful, was the principal stone used in ancient Maya sculptures. A few sites, like Quirigua, Pusilha, Altar de Sacrificios, and Tonina, employed sandstone, the native rock in their localities, and Copan used trachyte, a volcanic tuff.

The tools of the Maya sculptors were principally of stone, although wooden mallets may also have been used. The principal tools were chisels and hammerstones. The chisels (Fig. 14.5) were 5–15 cm in length, with a single cutting edge, the handle end being rounded. The hammerstones, roughly spherical in shape, varied from 5 to 7 cm in diameter. The chipped-flint chisels so plentiful in some Maya sites were probably used for stone cuttings. The massive amounts of debris from ancient flint working that have been found in recent archaeological excavations at Colha, Belize, indicate that Colha was a major center for the manufacture of chipped-flint tools.

As it occurs in the ground, the native limestone is relatively soft, but it hardens after exposure. It was quarried with comparative facility and, while still fresh from the quarries, was easily carved. The sandstone of Quirigua, Tonina, and Pusilha was

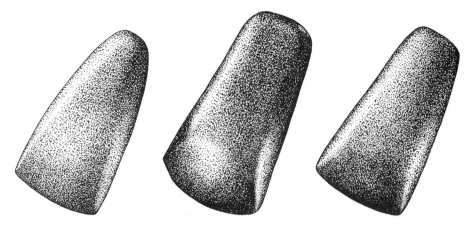

Fig. 14.5. Maya ground-stone celts, or chisels used to work stone.

also softer in its native state, but the trachyte used in Copan is of about the same hardness before and after quarrying. Trachyte is so fine-grained and even-textured that it is admirably adapted to carving. It has one serious drawback, however: it contains nodules of flint so hard that stone chisels could not have worked them. When such nodules were encountered they were either removed, leaving a depression in the face of the monument, or left protruding, often on the same monument. Sometimes, when the inclusion was too difficult to remove entirely, the projecting part was battered off. In the case of the human head in the Long Count introducing glyph on Stela 2 at Copan (Fig. 14.6), clever manipulations incorporated a stubborn nodule into the design itself. The heads represented in Maya inscriptions almost always face the observer's left, but this profile faces to the right. By thus reversing the direction, the sculptor put this flinty inclusion in the right position to serve as an earplug.

Maya sculpture was doubtless finished by abrasion and then painted, and most architectural surfaces, including carved elements, were covered with plaster. The color most often associated with both plastered building surfaces and carved monuments is a dark red. This pigment was probably made from an oxide of iron obtained from natural deposits or even from anthills, which abound in the forest. Blue

Fig. 14.6. Flint inclusion on Copan Stela 2, skillfully incorporated into the Long Count introductory glyph as a large, round ear ornament.

was the next most common color. The pigment materials were ground and probably mixed with copal (a resin), for in many places the paint still adheres to the stone with the tenacity of a good varnish. Although the colors have for the most part worn off, traces of the original paint can still be found where the relief is high and undercut.

In quarrying the shafts of stone from which the stelae were made, the Maya took advantage of natural cleavage planes in the rock; in some of the Quirigua stelae, to cite a good example, the cross sections are trapezoidal in shape, and no single corner makes a true right angle. The method of quarrying at Calakmul (Fig. 14.7) was to free the blocks from the surrounding limestone by digging down along their sides and ends, preparatory to prying them loose from the bedrock. Several of the Quirigua stelae still show "quarry stumps" on their plain, undressed butts (Fig. 14.8).

Drawings by the French artist Jean Charlot illustrate the principal steps in making a Maya stela: quarrying the shaft, transporting it, erecting it, and carving it (Fig. 14.9). The forests of the Peten abound in hardwood trees, sections of which would have served admirably for rollers, and fiber-yielding plants well suited to the mak-

Fig. 14.7. Two partially quarried stela shafts at Calakmul, Campeche, Mexico.

Fig. 14.8. Quarry stumps
on the butt of
Quirigua Monument 10.

ing of ropes and cable are equally common. Three sides of a masonry socket, to fit the butt of the shaft, were placed in the ground. Then, probably by means of a ramp and an A-frame of beams, the shaft was pulled upright into the socket and the fourth side of the socket was filled in. It is important to note that the shafts were brought from the quarries in an unfinished state and carved after being erected.

As we have already seen (Chapter 3), the earliest known Maya sculptures are concentrated in the southeastern Maya area. The monuments of Izapa, Abaj Takalik, Kaminaljuyu, and other sites in the southern area demonstrate that the custom of carving portraits of rulers and hieroglyphic inscriptions, including calendrical dates, on stone stelae and their companion altars was established there by the Late Preclassic. Fragmentary sculptures that date from the Late and Terminal Preclassic are also found at Nakbe, El Mirador, and other lowland sites. Thus far, however, the oldest examples of the sculptured-monument tradition with calendrical dates found in the lowlands are from the Early Classic era. Stela 29 at Tikal bears the earliest known Long Count calendrical date in the lowlands, A.D. 292. This monument and a series of slightly later Baktun 8 stelae from the core of the central lowlands belong to a sculptural tradition with direct affinities to the earlier southern Maya monuments. The human figures on these monuments are often shown in the same position—head, legs, and feet in profile; torso and arms in full front; and feet in tandem (Figs. 4.26, 14.10). A little later, before the close of Baktun 8 (A.D. 435), the position of human figures became a bit more natural: the toes of the back foot advanced slightly, overlapping the heel of the front foot, but the rest of the body remained unchanged. The profile presentation of the human figure per-

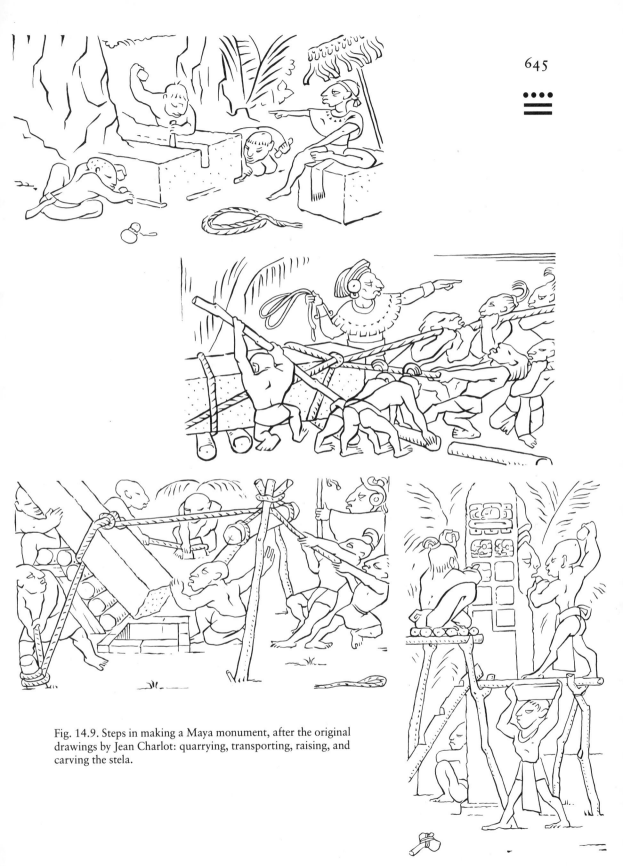

Fig. 14.9. Steps in making a Maya monument, after the original drawings by Jean Charlot: quarrying, transporting, raising, and carving the stela.

sisted throughout Maya history, and remained a common position in Maya art, but it ceased to be the dominant position portrayed.

The earliest dated lowland monument with a sculptured, fully frontal view of the human figure is Stela 4 at Tikal (Fig. 4.31). It records a calendar-round date corresponding to A.D. 378. On Stela 18, which portrays a seated full-front figure, the Long Count date is 396. Both of these monuments depict the Tikal ruler Curl Nose (see Chapter 4). Stela 26 at Uaxactun, dedicated in 9.0.10.0.0 (445), exhibits a similar frontal style. This monument was discovered beneath the floor of Shrine II in one of the earliest levels of Str. A-V. The figure on its front is badly eroded (Fig. 14.11), but the lower half of the face, the arms, and the feet can still be distinguished. The full-front view of the human figure, common at Tonina (Fig. 5.38), Copan, Quirigua, Piedras Negras, Palenque, Yaxchilan, Naachtun, and Seibal, reached its greatest expression at Copan and Quirigua; at the latter site frontal portraiture was established by 475 (see Fig. 5.53).

Fig. 14.10. Early Classic profile style on Tikal Stela 2 (ca. 9.3.10.0.0, or A.D. 504).

The front view of the human figure seated cross-legged is best expressed at Piedras Negras. Four Piedras Negras monuments (Fig. 5.23) depict the inaugurations of successive rulers (see Chapter 13), each of whom is seated cross-legged in a niche. The earliest of these four monuments, Stela 25, was dedicated in 9.8.15.0.0 (608); the portrait is within a niche too shallow to permit treatment of the figure in high relief. On Stela 6, dedicated in 9.12.15.0.0 (687), the niche is deeper, permitting the figure to be treated more successfully; the face is well done, but out of proportion to the rest of the body. By the time this composition was executed on Stela 11, which was dedicated in 9.15.0.0.0 (731), the niche had become so deep that the proportions of the seated figure are more lifelike, and the details are beautifully executed. Stela 14, dedicated in 9.16.10.0.0 (761), is a masterful combination of high- and low-relief carving, and perhaps the finest stela at this site. The niche is sufficiently deep to present the figure in the half round; the anatomical proportions are correct, and the details are exquisitely carved.

Fig. 14.11. Frontal portrait style detectable on the badly eroded Uaxactun Stela 26 (9.0.10.0.0, or A.D. 445).

The frontal presentation of the standing human figure was achieved brilliantly at Copan and Quirigua. The figures at Quirigua, carved in moderate relief (Fig. 5.60), are more restrained, and are probably more to modern taste. The famous Copan stelae include the finest examples of nearly full-round sculpture produced by the ancient Maya, and they are also among the most ornate (Fig. 5.51).

The last vestiges of the early style disappeared by the beginning of the Late Classic, from about 630 to 730, though in the provincial centers some sculptors did not follow the prevailing naturalistic trends of this era. For example, the figures on Stela 21 at Naachtun (Fig. 14.12), dedicated in 687, are misshapen for such a late date. The contrast between this monument and Stela A at Copan (Fig. 5.51), dedicated just 44 years later, in 731, is striking.

The century and a half from 731 to 889 of the Late Classic witnessed the most brilliant development of New World sculpture in pre-Columbian times. This period was in many ways the golden age of the Maya civilization, and its cultural expres-

Fig. 14.12. Eroded but poorly proportioned frontal portrait style on Naachtun Stela 21.

sion is perhaps best exemplified in its sculpture. By this time centuries of sculptural achievement lay behind the Maya, and the technical difficulties had long since been mastered; creativity was at last free to express itself, within the framework of its traditions and experience.

The very diversity of sculptures from the Late Classic makes it difficult to select any as typical. One of the most beautiful monuments at Piedras Negras, Stela 14, has already been illustrated (Fig. 5.23, right). Another, almost equally striking monument, Stela 12 (Fig. 14.13), dedicated in 9.18.5.0.0 (795), shows the profile presentation of the human figures, both ruler and his anguished captives. As we saw in Chapter 5, the distinctive style of this carving has led Mary Miller to suggest that it may have been rendered by sculptors taken prisoner from Pomona, to celebrate the victory of Piedras Negras over their city.

At Palenque, in the crypt below the Temple of the Inscriptions, the carving of the slab covering the sarcophagus (Chapter 5) is exceptional for its delicacy and

Fig. 14.13. The beautifully rendered figures on Piedras Negras Stela 12.

sureness of line (Fig. 5.34). The famous wall panels from Palenque are often considered among the best examples of skill and composition in Maya low-relief sculpture (Fig. 14.14).

One of the most beautiful Maya sculptures is Wall Panel 3 from Str. O-13 at Piedras Negras (Fig. 5.17), now in the Museo Nacional de Antropología in Guatemala City. This masterpiece of high and low relief was executed in 9.16.10.0.0 (761). In a number of places on the panel, arms and legs are sculptured in the full round. The composition represents the ruler seated on a throne, the back of which is a mask panel; he is flanked on each side by three standing figures. On the ground before the throne seven figures are seated cross-legged, facing an altar. The figure on the extreme right is the only one whose face is still preserved. M. Louise Baker has made an interesting restoration of this wall panel (Fig. 5.17), using the three-quarter view of figures, a stylistic device seldom seen in Maya art (see Chapter 5 for a discussion of the historical interpretation of this scene).

In Palace J-6 at Piedras Negras is a throne (Fig. 14.15) that is almost identical to the one represented on the wall panel, but whereas the two front supports of the throne on the wall panel are undecorated, those of the actual throne are covered on three sides with hieroglyphic inscriptions. The throne was dedicated in 9.17.15.0.0

Fig. 14.14. The beautifully carved figures and glyphs on the Palace Tablet, Palenque, Chiapas, Mexico.

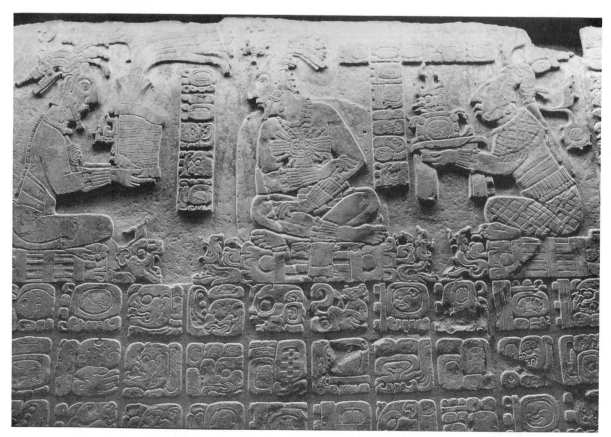

Fig. 14.15. Throne from Piedras Negras Str. J.-6, very similar to that depicted on Wall Panel 3 (Fig. 5.17); found smashed to pieces, its condition provoked theories of a violent end for this and other lowland sites, which are discussed in Chapter 6.

(785), 25 years later than the wall panel, and was so located in the principal hall of the palace that it could be seen from any point in the court below. Discovered by the University of Pennsylvania Museum, it also now resides in the Museo Nacional in Guatemala City.

At Yaxchilan, sculpture reached its highest level in the lintels of Str. 23, which was dedicated in 9.14.15.0.0 (726): Lintels 24, 25, and 26, the first two of which are now in the British Museum (Fig. 5.13). In its harmony of composition, balance of design, and brilliance of execution, Lintel 24 is the most outstanding example of sculptural art at Yaxchilan. The finest monuments at Yaxchilan—stelae 1, 3, 4, and 7—fall short of the lintels aesthetically, although most of them have experienced considerable erosion and may not convey their original quality.

There is more Late Classic sculpture at Copan than at any other Classic site. Copan is celebrated for its many fine monuments—stelae A (Fig. 5.51a), B, C, D, F, H (Fig. 5.51b), M, N, and 4, and Altars Q, R, S, and T—and for its assemblage of architectural sculpture on a series of spectacular constructions—strs. 11, 22, and

26, the Jaguar Stairway (Fig. 5.43), and the Reviewing Stand. Most of the monuments were carved during the reign of 18 Rabbit, who seems to have begun using the Great Plaza for his commemorative monuments (Chapter 5). The longest hieroglyphic inscription in the Maya area—the Hieroglyphic Stairway of Str. 26 (Fig. 5.45)—was dedicated in 9.16.5.0.0 (756), and the exquisite head and torso of the corn god (God E) illustrated in the frontispiece was also carved about this same time.

Quirigua, though a small site, erected 27 sculptured monuments. Stela E, from 771 (Fig. 5.60), and eight other stelae and zoomorphs were dedicated during the reign of Cauac Sky (Chapter 5). Zoomorph P (Fig. 5.57), perhaps the most massive stone monument in the Maya area, is completely covered with an intricate sculp-

Fig. 14.16. Finely executed carving at Quirigua: (*left*) Monument 6 (9.16.10.0.0, or A.D. 761); (*center*) Monument 4 (9.16.15.0.0, or A.D. 766); (*above*) detail of full-figure glyphs on Monument 4.

Fig. 14.17. Example of Terminal Classic
sculptural style of Xultun Stela 10.

tured design; it was dedicated in 9.18.5.0.0 (795). Perhaps the finest glyphs ever
carved on stone are to be found at Quirigua (Fig. 14.16), especially those on Stela
F, which was dedicated in 9.16.10.0.0 (761), and the rare full-figure glyphs on Stela
D, dedicated in 9.16.15.0.0 (766).

By the end of Baktun 9 (830), however, the wave had crested, and the later
sculpture in the Maya area never attained the standards set during the Late Classic.
Examples of Terminal Classic sculpture reflect the general decline in the fortunes of
the central and southern lowlands. Stela 10 at Xultun (Fig. 14.17), dedicated in
10.3.0.0.0 (889), is one of several monuments erected on this katun ending. The
loss in technical skill is evident, the figures are poorly proportioned, and a mass of
flamboyant detail clutters and all but obscures the design.

In Yucatan during the Late and Terminal Classic, distinctive local sculptural styles developed. There are sixteen sculptured stelae at Uxmal, but even the finest of them, Stela 7, is overly ornate by contrast with the sculptures of the central and southern lowlands. Architectural sculpture at Uxmal is represented by a well-executed human head, with tattooing on its right cheek, emerging from the jaws of a conventionalized serpent (Fig. 14.18). The head was originally attached to the façade of a range of chambers at the western base of the pyramid supporting the House of the Magician, and forms an element of the building's decoration. It is now in the Museo Nacional de Antropología in Mexico City.

During the Postclassic, carved monuments became rare, and sculpture was confined almost exclusively to the embellishment of architecture. At Chichen Itza no stelae are known after the Terminal Classic, but four other remarkable sculptural forms are in evidence. Most noteworthy are the famous Chacmool figures, reclining human figures (Fig. 14.19) whose heads are turned to the right or left, but there are also jaguar thrones, standard bearers, and Atlantean figures. At least a dozen Chacmools have been discovered at this site, and two of them still retain inset pieces of polished bone to represent the whites of the eyes and the fingernails and toenails. Each holds a stone plate clasped by the two hands and resting on the abdomen, suggesting that the Chacmool's function might have been to receive offerings.

Fig. 14.18. Terminal Classic architectural sculpture from the Uxmal Adivino.

Fig. 14.19. A chacmool: Terminal Classic / Early Postclassic sculpture from the Temple of the Warriors at Chichen Itza.

The jaguar thrones are life-sized figures of jaguars with flat backs serving as seats. Sculptured representations of them are found at Tikal, Piedras Negras, Palenque, and Xultun, but the actual thrones have been found only at Uxmal and Chichen Itza (Fig. 7.8). They also occur in the frescoes in the Temple of the Warriors at Chichen Itza.

The purpose of the standard bearers, which took the form of small human figures about a meter high (Fig. 14.20), was to support a staff, from the top of which hung a feather banner. The forearms are extended, and the hands form a hole through which the staff—none survive—passed. Another standard bearer found at Chichen Itza kneels on his left knee and grasps the staff in his right hand. The fourth group, the Atlantean figures, are anthropomorphic statues with arms raised above their heads. They were used to support daises or door lintels in buildings (Fig. 14.21).

Fig. 14.20. Standard bearers: Terminal Classic / Early Postclassic sculpture from Chichen Itza.

Fig. 14.21. Atlantean figure: Terminal Classic /
Early Postclassic sculpture from Chichen Itza.

## Wood Sculpture

As suggested earlier, the Maya name for stelae ("stone trees") might hark back to a time when monuments were carved from tree trunks, but if any once stood in the Maya area, none survives today. The few examples of wood carving that do survive are associated with architecture, though we can assume that many more have been lost to decay. The most famous and best preserved examples are the carved door lintels originally installed in the major temples at Tikal (Figs. 14.22, 14.23). Only the hardest species of wood have survived the damp climate of the Maya lowlands, and the only wooden objects that have been recovered had been in situations protected from the weather.

The Tikal lintels are each composed of from four to ten side-by-side beams of sapodilla wood with an overall length of 2–5.3 m. On one lintel (Fig. 14.22) is an elaborately decorated serpent, its body arching in the middle to form a central niche. The head is to the left, and issuing from its open mouth is the upper body of an ancestral figure, or *way* (see Chapter 13), perhaps the founder of the Tikal dynasty; the serpent's tail, at the right, terminates in two scrolls. A hieroglyphic inscription fills the upper left and right corners of the composition, and across the top, between the glyph panels, stretches a great bird with spreading wings, the sacred celestial bird of the Maya. In the niche formed by the upward curl of the serpent's body is the figure of Yax Kin, ruler of Tikal, seated on a throne. This lintel originally spanned one of the doorways of Temple IV (see also Fig. 4.20), which was dedicated in 9.16.0.0.0 (751). Another Classic-period lintel was found in Temple VII at Tzibanche, west of the southern end of Laguna de Bacalar. It bears an inscription of eight hieroglyphs but no figures, and probably dates from the early Late Classic, perhaps about 9.9.5.0.0 (618).

Occasionally the wooden poles spanning the vaults have also been carved. One of these was found at Tikal in a fourth-story rear chamber of the Palace of the Five Stories.

Carved wooden lintels have been found at Chichen Itza and Uxmal. The best-preserved at Chichen Itza spans the inner doorway of the Temple of the Jaguars, on top of the west wall of the ballcourt (Fig. 14.24). Each of the two beams forming this lintel bears the same design: the sun disk, a human figure inside it, and another human figure, outside the disk, enveloped in the coils of a feathered rattlesnake. Both figures face a centrally placed altar. The lintels in El Castillo at Chichen Itza were carved originally, but machetes have hacked off most of the low relief.

John Lloyd Stephens, the American diplomat and amateur archaeologist who visited Uxmal in 1840 and 1841, found in the Governor's Palace a sapodilla beam that he took to the United States when he left Yucatan. It was subsequently destroyed by a fire in New York—an irreparable loss. Stephens reported that it was the only beam at Uxmal that was carved, and its inscriptions might have dated the Governor's Palace, one of the most beautiful in pre-Columbian America.

Fig. 14.22. Carved wooden
Lintel 3 from Tikal Temple I
(Late Classic).

Other small objects of carved wood were taken from the Cenote of Sacrifice at Chichen Itza, among them the handle of a wooden sacrificial knife, carved in the likeness of two intertwined rattlesnakes (Fig. 11.13) and covered with a thin sheet of gold. The blade hafted to the handle is of chipped flint.

## Stucco Modeling

In the lowlands, from Middle Preclassic times on, stucco seems to have been used to face platforms (see Fig. 2.2). As mentioned earlier, by the Late Preclassic it was widely used in exterior decoration, especially for platform masks (Figs. 3.26, 3.30, 4.28), and it continued to be used on Classic buildings and, to a lesser extent, Postclassic façades. Modeled plaster was an important feature of the southeastern architectural style (see above). Stuccowork reached its highest development at Pa-

Fig. 14.23. Carved wooden Lintel 3 from Tikal Temple IV (Late Classic).

Fig. 14.24. Drawing of carved wooden lintels, Chichen Itza Temple of the Jaguars (Terminal Classic / Early Postclassic).

lenque, and the tablets and panels there (see Fig. 14.25) are the finest examples of this plastic art in the Maya area.

In the sealed crypt that Alberto Ruz Lhuillier discovered beneath the Temple of the Inscriptions, the walls are decorated with handsomely modeled reliefs of nine figures that may represent the Bolontiku, the Nine Gods of the Lower World. Two excellently modeled stucco heads beneath the sarcophagus itself illustrate the Classic Maya ideal of beauty (Fig. 14.26).

Even the provincial centers within the Palenque region displayed this mastery of the stucco technique. On three walls of a tomb found some years ago at Comalcalco, about 160 km northwest of Palenque, were representations of standing human figures in stucco, three to a wall; two, as restored, and three figures, as found, are shown in Fig. 14.27. Although less finely executed than the stucco figures at Palenque, these Comalcalco figures are of considerable merit. The best example of stuccowork in northern Yucatan is at Acanceh; on the upper half of a façade there

Fig. 14.25. Late Classic stucco reliefs from House D of the Palenque Palace.

are the remains of a handsome stucco panel of animals, birds, and serpents (Fig. 14.28). When it was uncovered, this Early Classic frieze still retained many traces of its original coloring, with a bright turquoise-blue predominating. Other fine examples of stucco decoration, in the form of recessed panels above the doors of buildings, can be seen in Postclassic Tulum.

## Painting

Among the ancient Maya, the art of painting was used to decorate the walls of important buildings. Like sculptured lintels and wall panels, these decorations were obviously intended for the elite residents of these buildings, and were inaccessible to the public. Few of these have survived the ravages of time, and only vestiges remain. Apart from frescoes used in wall decoration, painting was also used on portable objects such as ceramics and in illustrating the codices (see Chapters 13 and 15).

The Maya palette was extensive. There were several reds, ranging from an opaque purplish red to a brilliant orange. A coppery tan color was used extensively for preliminary outlining, and various mixtures of red with opaque white gave a number of pinks. The yellows ranged from a pale greenish to a dark yellow. A dark

Fig. 14.26. Late Classic stucco heads from the tomb of Pacal at Palenque.

Fig. 14.27. Late Classic stucco reliefs from the tomb at Comalcalco, Tabasco, Mexico: (*above*) restored figures and text; (*below*) stucco reliefs as originally found.

Fig. 14.28. Early Classic stucco reliefs from Acanceh, Yucatan, Mexico: (*above*) figure of a squirrel; (*below*) figures of a bat, a bird, and other animals.

brown resulted from mixing yellow and black. There seems to have been but a single blue; this was painted over an opaque ground to obtain a Prussian blue or laid directly on white plaster to achieve a bright cerulean blue. There are many greens, from olive to almost black. No basic green has been found, and the different shades probably resulted from varying mixtures of blue and yellow. A brilliant, lustrous black was used for final outlining, and an opaque white for mixing.

In many examples, the substance with which the colors were mixed seems to have been viscous. Chemical analyses of the pigments in the Chichen Itza frescoes show no trace of this carrying substance. It was probably organic and has disappeared with time. It may have been the resin of the *pom* tree, from which copal varnish is made today.

The colors themselves were of both vegetable and mineral origin. A number of trees in the Yucatan Peninsula yield excellent dyes. Analysis of Chichen Itza pigments shows that they were largely of mineral origin, but this finding may simply demonstrate that vegetable colors are more perishable. The reds were made from hematite, the yellows from ocherous earths and clays. Charcoal and other carbonized organic matter were the essential ingredients of the black pigment. The strong blue was inorganic, derived from a particular type of clay.

The brushes with which these pigments were applied have not been found, but the quality of the painting indicates their excellence. Some brushes were so delicately made that fine tapering lines could be drawn with them; coarser brushes filled in backgrounds and broader spaces. The materials used were probably fine feathers or hair. A brush in the hand of an artist is depicted on a fragmentary incised bone from Tikal (Fig. 14.29).

Fragments of wall paintings dating from the Late Preclassic have been discovered at Tikal (Fig. 3.22) and a few other central-lowland sites. These frescoes show stylistic similarities to the art of the southern Maya during this period. The fresco in Str. B-XIII at Uaxactun, excavated by the Carnegie Institution in 1937, dates from the Early Classic (Fig. 4.29). This building had undergone several changes in ancient times, and some of its chambers show beam-and-mortar roof construction. The fresco is colored black, red, orange, yellow, and gray and measures 3 m high. Twenty-six human figures are shown, arranged in two horizontal panels and interspersed with several panels of hieroglyphs.

A partially preserved Early Classic fresco panel with hieroglyphs painted in dark red has recently been found in a deeply buried building beneath Copan's acropolis. A series of designs and hieroglyphic inscriptions is painted on interior walls of the Late Classic palace at Palenque, but only fragments survive. The walls of the shrine in Str. 33 at Yaxchilan show traces of scrolls and figures in red and blue.

By far the most spectacular, as well as the most informative, Maya murals yet discovered are those at Bonampak, in Chiapas. These paintings, assigned the Late Classic date of 790 and discovered in 1946 by Giles Healey, cover the three vaulted chambers of a single small building (Fig. 5.19). When found, they were in excellent condition, preserved by the formation of a coat of stalactitic limestone deposited by the constant seepage of water over more than a thousand years.

The scenes (Figs. 5.20–5.22), proceeding room by room, show a series of activities that record the historical events surrounding the designation of an heir to the Bonampak throne. These were described in Chapter 5. Briefly, Room 1 shows the preparations, including the gathering of an orchestra, and the ruler, visitors, and elite assistants. Room 2 continues with a raid on a neighboring center, the taking of captives, and their "judgment" before their captors on the stairs of a temple or palace substructure (Figs. 14.30–14.32). Room 3 shows the culmination of these events in a ritual dance on the steps of a pyramid, the participants adorned in magnificent costumes, and in a bloodletting ceremony by the ruler and his family. A number of hieroglyphic texts in the murals date and explain the scenes and give the names and titles of the participants.

The Bonampak murals stand in sharp contrast to the sculpture of the stelae, where the principal figure remained stylized in attitude and accouterments for over five hundred years. The scenes are narrative, in a forthright yet sensitive style. Naturalism was held so important by the artist that the faces of certain of the participants in the murals can be recognized from room to room as they recur in parts of the story. The moods of the scenes vary: postures and facial expressions are relaxed during the preparations, ferocious in the raid, cold and forbidding during the judgment and sacrifice. Foreshortening and superposition give an effect of depth. The naturalism is stronger and the drafting more skillful than in any European art of the same period.

Initially, the observer is overpowered by the magnificence of costuming in the Bonampak murals. Headdresses of delicate featherwork nearly double the height of each principal figure, and the variety of materials used is dazzling—featherwork, cut stone, furs, intricate woven fabrics. One is struck next by the complete lack of self-consciousness in the performers. Each figure is portrayed in an attitude of conversation, and given a relaxed and individual posture. Such detailed information on the life of the Maya ruling class is nowhere else to be found, and that the wife and children of the ruler participated in the ceremonies is particularly interesting.

Fig. 14.29. Finely incised bone from the tomb of Ah Cacau, Tikal Temple I, showing a hand holding a scribe's or artist's brush.

Fig. 14.30. Interior of Bonampak Str. 1: (*above*) artist's rendering of Room 2 and its murals; (*below*) detail of the reconstructed mural, showing the judgment of the captives (see also Fig. 5.21).

Fig. 14.31. Bonampak Str. 1: detail of the original Room 2 murals, showing attendants and captives to the left of the ruler seen in Fig. 14.30.

Fig. 14.32. Bonampak Str. 1: detail of the original Room 2 murals, showing attendants to the right of the ruler seen in Fig. 14.30.

....
===

The central capstones in corbel-vaulted chambers were sometimes painted with designs of human figures and single rows of glyphs above and below the humans. These painted capstones, their remains confined exclusively to northern sites and probably dating to the Late and Terminal Classic periods (Fig. 14.33), are uncommon. Wall paintings are also more likely to have been preserved at northern centers than in the central area and have been found at Chichen Itza, Tancah, Tulum, Santa Rita Corozal, Chacmultun, and Xtampak.

The frescoes from the Temple of the Warriors, the Temple of the Jaguars, and the Monjas at Chichen Itza, all dating from the Terminal Classic and Early Postclassic, show Mexican influence, in keeping with their probable Putun Maya heritage (Chapters 6 and 7). Two scenes of human sacrifice are illustrated (Fig. 11.1e, f), and a painting of a coastal village, from a wall in the Temple of the Warriors, is

Fig. 14.33. Drawings of painted capstones at Chichen Itza: (left) from the Temple of the Owls; (right) from a tomb.

Fig. 14.34. Drawing of a mural in the Chichen Itza Temple of the Warriors, showing a coastal fishing village.

shown in Fig. 14.34. The sea occupies the lower third of this scene, and there are three canoes, each with an oarsman in the prow and two men fishing. A variety of marine life swarms in the water. On the shore at the right is a flat-roofed temple, a feathered serpent rising from the temple's inner chamber, and two worshipers kneeling in its outer chamber. There are several thatched houses of typical Maya design, interspersed with trees. A number of people go about their daily tasks, and the whole picture is peaceful and domestic.

Another mural from the Temple of the Jaguars portrays a vigorous assault on a village (Fig. 14.35). Only two of the attackers are to be seen, in the lower left corner; a serpent curling behind one of the attackers is apparently his patron deity. The defending warriors swarm out of their village, and behind them, among the thatched houses, are the women. The composition is full of action and there are no superfluous lines.

A mural from the Temple of the Warriors shows another battle. A temple stands in a lake in the upper left corner, and in the water are several fish, a snail, a crab, and a jaguar. Half a dozen nude captives, their bodies painted with stripes and their arms tied behind their backs, are being led off by warriors or priests. In the lower right corner, other warriors seem to be defending a temple (Fig. 14.36).

Fig. 14.35. Drawing of a mural in the Chichen Itza Temple of the Jaguars, showing a battle scene.

Several fragmentary murals have been discovered at Tancah (Fig. 14.37) on the east coast of Yucatan. These paintings, dating from the Late Postclassic, are stylistically related to the art of the Madrid Codex (Fig. 13.4). The wall paintings at Tulum (Figs. 7.20 and 7.23) and Santa Rita Corozal (Fig. 7.18) depict ceremonial and mythological scenes. Also dating from Late Postclassic times, they show such striking resemblances to Mixtec art as to assure connections between eastern Yucatan and Mexico during this period (see Chapter 7). ■

Fig. 14.36. Drawing of a mural in the Chichen Itza Temple of the Warriors, showing a battle scene and captives.

Fig. 14.37. Details of a Late Postclassic mural in Tancah Str. 44: (*above*) figure of a maize deity; (*below*) figure of a North Star deity.

# 15    ARTIFACTS

≡

The trades of the Indians were making pottery and carpentering. They earned a great deal by making idols out of clay and wood, with many fasts and observances.

—*Landa's relación de las cosas de Yucatán* (Tozzer 1941:94)

**T**he portable remains of past activities—artifacts, in archaeological terminology—provide many of the basic sources of information about chronology and behavior. In this chapter we will briefly describe some of the characteristics of the major categories of ancient Maya artifacts: ceramics, chipped stone, carved and polished stone, mosaics, and metalwork, along with the perishable media—painted books, textiles, basketry and matting, and featherwork.

## Ceramics and Archaeology

Ceramic remains have long been one of the most valuable evidences of past human society, around the world. Because of their durability, artifacts made of fired clay—pottery vessels, figurines, beads, and other items—usually survive long after most other human products have disappeared. The Maya area is no exception, and even in the humid lowland conditions that destroy most cultural remains, ceramic materials often survive. The most ubiquitous ceramic artifact is the potsherd. Even though ceramic materials resist decay, everyday experience testifies that pottery vessels are very fragile. Thus it is not surprising that a welter of potsherds litter most sites of ancient habitation.

Pottery remains have many uses for the archaeologist. The differences in vessels' size and shape are clues to their functions. Other clues are furnished by the identification of residues in vessels, and by painted glyphic texts that label a vessel as, for example, a chocolate pot (see Chapter 13). Ultimately, the determination of function leads to the reconstruction of ancient human activity. Thus if the remains of a structure are strewn with potsherds from a set of recognizable vessel shapes (storage jars, cook pots, griddles, and so forth), the structure was probably once a residence. Another building, littered with sherds from distinctly nondomestic pottery forms (incensarios, bowls for offerings, etc.), was probably the locus for ritual activity.

But the most traditional, and perhaps the most valuable, use of the potsherd has been as a marker of time. Because of the nature of pottery itself—a plastic medium sensitive to the subtle manipulations of the potter, but controlled by the prevailing traditions of vessel form and decoration, which gradually change and shift through time—a knowledgeable archaeologist can give a rather accurate date for most well-preserved ancient pottery fragments. Thus, the finding of potsherds during an archaeological excavation affords the investigator an immediate and convenient chronological check. In many cases, the archaeologist can quickly verify that an excavation has reached soil levels that date from, say, the Late Preclassic simply by examining the potsherds from that level.

Changes in pottery shapes and decorations through time are usually determined from the excavation of stratified archaeological deposits. As broken vessels are discarded, they may be swept or thrown, along with other trash, into refuse heaps, which archaeologists call middens. In some cases, a midden deposit may accumulate for hundreds or even thousands of years, the earliest material at the bottom of the deposit, the latest at the top. Each stratum or visibly distinct layer in the midden describes an interval of past time, an episode of trash deposition. These strata cluster the kinds of pottery and other surviving artifacts used at a particular time, and offer a key to overall changes in form and decoration through time.

Only a few long-term middens have been excavated in the Maya area, for the Maya were fond of recycling their own refuse. In refurbishing and expanding their centers, they found that both middens and demolished structures made excellent construction fill for new buildings. As a result, relatively few long-term accumulations seem to have survived undisturbed, and most that have been excavated were used for relatively short periods of time. Yet, by piecing together evidence from a series of such short-term middens, along with information from pottery found in construction fill and other places, Maya archaeologists have succeeded in defining pottery sequences at many sites. These sequences are composed of *ceramic complexes*, each complex marked by distinctive and relatively stable kinds of pottery made and used in a particular area during a particular period. Of course most shifts in the pottery inventory of a society do not occur suddenly but over time, so that ceramic complexes must be defined arbitrarily. Similarly, the convenient ordering of the eras of European history that we call the Dark Ages, the medieval period, and the Renaissance is not marked by sudden ruptures between eras.

The many local ceramic chronologies that have been worked out in the Maya area are relatively valid in reflecting the shifts in ancient pottery inventories through time (Table 15.1). Many have been cross-checked by radiocarbon analysis and other

TABLE 15.1

Ceramic Sequences at Selected Maya Sites

| General cultural eras | PERIOD | Pacific coast: Salinas la Blanca and Bilbao | Southern highlands: Chalchuapa | Southern highlands: Kaminaljuyu | Southern lowlands: Altar de Sacrificios | Uaxactun | Central lowlands: Barton Ramie and Cuello | Central lowlands: Becan | Northern lowlands: Dzibilchaltun | Northern lowlands: Mayapan | Date A.D. (Gregorian) |
|---|---|---|---|---|---|---|---|---|---|---|---|
| Late | POSTCLASSIC | Peor es Nada | Ahal | Chinautla | | | New Town | Lobo | Chechem | Chikinchel / Tases / Hocaba | 1400 |
| Early | POSTCLASSIC | Santa Lucia | Matzin / Payu | Ayumpuc / Pamplona | Jimba / Boca / Pasión | Tepeu 3 / Tepeu 2 / Tepeu 1 | Spanish Lookout / Tiger Run | Xcocom / Chintok / Bejuco | Zipche / Copo 2 / Copo 1 | Sotuta / Cehpech / Motul | 1200 / 1000 / 800 |
| Late | CLASSIC | Laguneta | Xocco | Amatle / Esperanza | Chixoy / Ayn / Salinas | Tzakol | Hermitage | Sabucan | Piim | Cochuah | 600 |
| Early | CLASSIC | Mejor es Algo | Vec | Aurora | | | Floral Park | Chacsik | Xculul | | 400 |
| Late | | | Caynac | Arenal | | Chicanel | Mount Hope | Paklum | | | 200 / 0 |

A.D.

Area

PRECLASSIC

B.C.

| 200 | 400 | 600 | 800 | 1000 | 1200 | 1400 | 1600 | 1800 | 2000 |
|---|---|---|---|---|---|---|---|---|---|

Tihosuco

Komchen — Nabanche

Acachen

Barton Creek — Jenney Creek — Swasey

Mamom

Plancha — San Felix — Xe

Miraflores (Verbena) — Providencia — Las Charcas

Chul — Kal — Colos — Tok

Crucero — 2 — Conchas — 1 — Jocotal — Cuadros — Ocos — Barra

Middle

Early

means of dating the past. Although these ceramic sequences are the most common and most complete time indicators available, they are not cultural chronologies; it is not valid to equate ceramic complexes with history, to say, in effect, that changes in traditions of pottery form and decoration reflect changes in political, social, religious, or other institutions of a past society. Profound social changes that affect nearly all aspects of society, such as military conquest, may in fact have a rather minor effect on the pottery of the conquered society. Still, ceramic studies have contributed priceless information about the origins and development of the early Maya, their trade networks, the development of social and occupational distinctions, ancient diet and culinary practices, religious beliefs and rituals, kinship relationships, funeral practices, and other aspects of the lives of both elite and commoner. And recent research to identify the sources of clay used in ancient Maya ceramics (based on neutron-activation and other analytic techniques) has begun to define major production centers and to clarify the patterns of pottery distribution and trade.

## A Chronological Review of Maya Pottery

The ancient Maya developed a remarkable ceramic tradition, one of the most varied and diverse of any known to the archaeological record anywhere in the world. An exhausting variety of pottery types, forms, and decorative techniques were produced during the roughly 3,500 years that span the time from the earliest origins of the Maya to the Spanish Conquest. Among the outstanding features of pre-Columbian Maya pottery are ceramics exhibiting deeply polished red and brown slips (surface coatings of clay), lustrous blacks, unusual resist-decorated wares, sensitive and grotesque modeling, delicate thin-walled creams and oranges, mass-produced molded vessels, and beautiful polychromes (multicolored vessels), including the exquisite portrait vases of the Late Classic era.

### Early Preclassic

As in the Old World, pottery first appeared in Mesoamerica with the emergence of settled village life. The technology of making containers of clay probably owes its ultimate origin to the human capacity for experimenting with and manipulating the environment. Learning to fire clay to produce the characteristic hardness and durability of pottery may well have been accidental. Whatever its origins, the earliest pottery in Mesoamerica probably imitated preexisting containers: globular, neckless jars (the *olla* of today) were modeled after containers made from gourds; and wide, flat-bottomed bowls (similar to the *sarten* of today) may have been fashioned after the form of pans made of wood or stone.

The technical excellence and variety of decorations of this early Mesoamerican pottery might indicate ultimate origins or influences from elsewhere. Indeed, the earliest pottery yet discovered in the New World is from South America (Brazil, Colombia, and Ecuador) and dates at least a thousand years earlier than any in Mesoamerica. Perhaps the first New World peoples to practice village life, by farming manioc and fishing in the coastal lagoons, arose to the south, and their new techniques of ceramic fabrication may then have spread north by means of migration and diffusion along the coasts of Central America (see Chapter 2).

The oldest known pottery from the Maya area (the Barra and Ocos ceramic complexes) has been found along the Pacific coast where the modern nations of Mexico and Guatemala meet. The remains of a series of early villages dating from the second and third millennia B.C. have been excavated in these areas. The earliest pottery thus far discovered in the highlands, apparently representing the first penetration of the highlands via the major valleys (such as the Río Paz), appeared soon thereafter. This movement was demonstrated by archaeological research at several sites, including Chalchuapa, just across the Guatemalan border in El Salvador, where occupation was established by 1200–900 B.C. Similarly early occupation is documented on the western flank of the Maya highlands, in the central depression of Chiapas, and the earliest occupation at the major highland site of Kaminaljuyu followed shortly.

This early pottery is generally well-fired, hard, and durable. Some wares are slipped and well-polished (black, red, and ivory wares dominate). Other, more utilitarian wares (storage and cooking vessels) are unslipped. Decoration (see Fig. 15.1) includes punctuations (impressed dots), in both rows and zones, appliques and modeling (heads and faces on jar shoulders), incising, fluting, differential firing effects (white-rim black ware), resist lines, and painting (red-rim neckless jars).

The ceramic inventory from this early period is well-developed; findings include many of the vessel forms used for basic subsistence functions throughout the pre-Columbian era. The large, neckless jar forms are well suited for the storage of water and perhaps food products. The general scarcity of smaller jars and suitable handles indicates that pottery vessels were not often used for the transport of water or other substances at this early date. A relative lack of external burning on some pottery has led investigators to conclude that cooking was probably done by placing hot stones inside the larger vessels to heat both liquids and solid foods (such as tamales).

Hand-modeled figurines, usually anthropomorphic (Fig. 15.2) but occasionally zoomorphic, first appear during this period. The earliest examples were usually modeled in a rather free, naturalistic style that is both individualistic and unstereotyped. The function of these fascinating clay effigies has never been satisfactorily explained. Some researchers suggest a religious function, as idols for a village-level, agricultural-fertility cult. Others propose more mundane explanations, such as toys or dolls for children. Whatever their ancient function, these figurines were distributed sporadically in both time and space, appearing rather commonly in several regions of Mesoamerica (including the southern Maya highlands) during the Pre-classic, then nearly disappearing in the Early Classic era, only to reappear and flourish during the Late Classic.

## Middle Preclassic

This era, characterized by the occupation of much of the Maya area, saw the beginnings of widespread settlement across the central lowlands, and the fairly rapid development of complex societies in both the lowlands and the southern area. The earliest pottery in the lowlands can be associated with two ceramic traditions, the more restricted Xe sphere in the western portion of southern lowlands, and the much more widespread Mamom sphere that extends from Yucatan to the highland transition (Chapter 3).

Many of the pottery traditions of the Early Preclassic not only were sustained but were elaborated during this period. New elements, especially prevalent in the highlands, include the first attempts at polychrome painting (black, white, red, and yellow paints applied after firing), the first bichrome slipping (for instance, red-on-cream and red-on-orange), and the beginnings of the Usulutan tradition of resist decoration. Red, black, orange, and streaky-brown slipped wares are typical; the streaky-brown pieces were often highly polished. Forms include necked jars (with handles on the neck or high on the shoulder), bowls with composite wall profiles, bowls with labial and medial flanges, bowls with vertical tubular spouts, and elaborately modeled, cylindrical incense burners (three-pronged incensarios; see Fig. 15.3). These incense burners constitute the earliest clear indication of specialized ritual pottery.

Fig. 15.1. Early Preclassic pottery. From the southern highlands: (*a*) red-rimmed tecomate; (*b*) red-painted incised brown bowl; (*c*) incised brown bowl; (*d*) resist-decorated gray bowl. Early Middle Preclassic pottery from the eastern lowlands: (*e*) red-rimmed bowl with chevron grooves; (*f*) red bowl with black paint; (*g*) incised buff bowl.

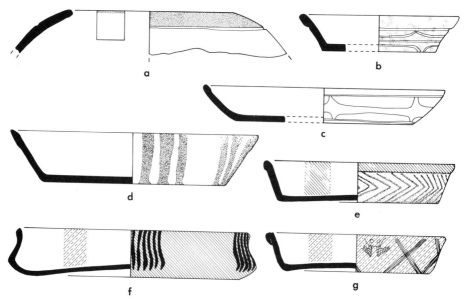

Fig. 15.2. Early Preclassic figurine heads from the southern highlands.

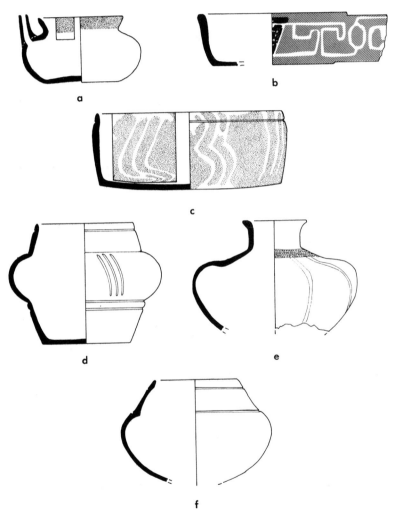

Fig. 15.3. Middle Preclassic pottery from the southern highlands: (*a*) red-rimmed spouted vessel; (*b*) polychrome stucco-painted bowl; (*c*) Usulutan decorated bowl; (*d*) incised gray bowl; (*e*) punctated-incised jar; (*f*) grooved orange bowl.

Other distinctive Middle Preclassic pottery includes shoe-shaped cooking pots, spouted vessels, bowls with grater bottoms, and peculiar cup-shaped vessels with long, tripod legs, which continued in use through all periods in some areas of Mesoamerica. Both cylindrical and flat clay seals, or stamps (probably used to decorate textiles), whistles in animal form, and hand-modeled figurines are also found. Clay figurines increased in popularity during this era, but lost their individualistic character, becoming stereotyped and uniform in style (Fig. 15.4).

### Late Preclassic and Protoclassic

The pottery of the Late Preclassic was dominated by two related and rather uniform ceramic traditions, the Providencia/Miraflores sphere in the highlands, and the Chicanel sphere in the lowlands. Both are outgrowths of Middle Preclassic traditions, but by now the ceramic inventory had become even more elaborate and innovative, in both forms and decorations (Figs. 15.5 and 15.6). Black-brown, lustrous-red, orange, and cream slipped wares predominate. The distinctive Usulutan decorated pottery, typified by a swirling pattern of parallel resist lines, was produced in the southeastern periphery of the Maya area and traded widely during this time. Usulutan decoration was apparently produced by the application of narrow bands of wax or pitch to the vessel surface. When fired, this substance melted away, leaving a lighter-colored surface in its wake. Other features of the vessels in-

Fig. 15.4. Middle and Late Preclassic figurine heads from the southern highlands: (*top row*) Middle Preclassic; (*bottom row*) Late Preclassic.

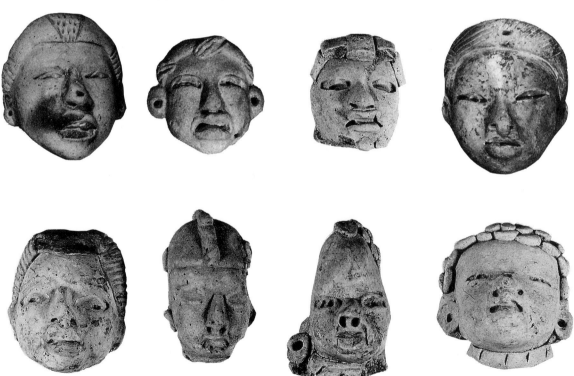

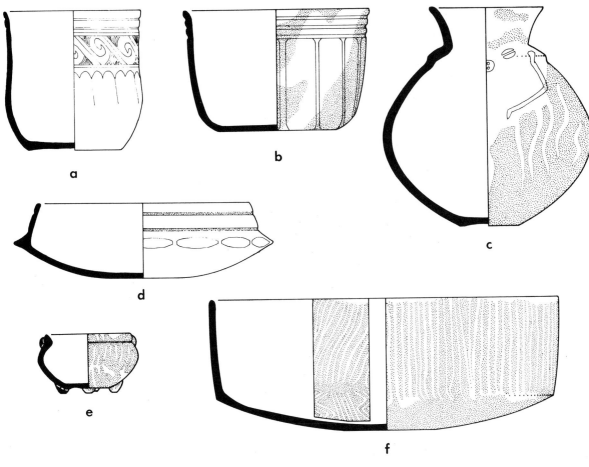

Fig. 15.5. Late Preclassic pottery from the southern highlands: (*a*) finely incised black-brown bowl; (*b*) fluted Usulutan bowl; (*c*) Usulutan jar; (*d*) fine red bowl with faceted shoulder and graphite-painted grooves; (*e*) miniature Usulutan bowl with tetrapod supports; (*f*) Usulutan bowl.

cluded supports (tripods and tetrapods, each conical support solid or hollow), shallow modeled decorations (for example, "toad effigies"), stucco, bichromes, and trichromes. Typical forms included necked jars (with handles on the jar shoulder), tall cylinders with flaring walls, bowls with grooved, everted rims, and bowls with covers. The incensario tradition was elaborated by modeling and polychrome painting often applied after firing. The pottery tradition of the southern and central lowlands, dominated by a distinctive type called Sierra Red, became unusually uniform from site to site during this period.

Certain highland pottery common in the Late Preclassic times, such as toad bowls and modeled mushrooms in both clay and stone, both associated with the ritual use of psychotropic substances by religious specialists, probably were associated with divinatory ceremonies. Since similar practices are documented in the ethnographic literature of Mesoamerica (as well as in other areas of the New

Fig. 15.6. Late Preclassic pottery from Tikal, central lowlands: (*above*) Usulutan bowl with tetra-pod supports; (*below*) spouted vessel with painted imitation Usulutan design.

World), these effigies may reflect the continuity of religious practices in the Maya area (see Chapter 11).

The pottery figurines of the Late Preclassic continued the trends of the previous era, generally appearing even less expressive and more uniform than before (Figs. 15.4 and 15.7).

At the close of the Preclassic, a series of new pottery elements appears to have spread over much of the eastern Maya lowlands. This Protoclassic assemblage (Chapter 3), probably originating in the southeastern periphery (eastern Guatemala and western El Salvador), includes the "mammiform tetrapod" bowl (bowls with four bulbous supports; Fig. 15.8) and painted Usulutans. In these areas the red finishes of the Chicanel pottery were replaced by orange slips, red-on-orange bichrome decoration, and the first orange polychromes (red and black on orange).

## Early Classic

The Classic period is noted for the development and spread of polychrome pottery, in both highland and lowland areas. The Early Classic Tzakol sphere in the lowlands marks several diagnostic shifts, including glossy surfaces that replace the "waxy" surfaces of Preclassic pottery, a prevailing orange slip that overwhelms the earlier red slips, and a tendency toward thinner vessel walls.

The widespread adoption of polychrome decoration is the traditional marker for the beginning of the Early Classic in much of the Maya area. Decoration is typically red and black painting on an orange or cream base, with painted motifs executed in bands, and repetitive geometric patterns. Both red-painted and red-and-

Fig. 15.7. Late Preclassic figurines from the central lowlands.

black-painted Usulutan pottery are diagnostic of this period in the highlands and southeastern lowlands. Monochrome slipped wares are dominated by polished black, cream, and orange pottery types. Stucco painting (postfiring) is common, often decorated with elaborate motifs rendered in bright colors. One distinctive highland utilitarian type is decorated with scraped slip (the slip is swirled with the fingers while still wet to produce an effect like finger painting).

Common and distinctive forms include ring-based bowls and basally flanged bowls. Later in this era several new forms enjoyed widespread distribution. These include tripod-supported cylindrical vessels and small pitchers emulating forms typical of those from Teotihuacan (see Figs. 15.9–15.11). In the Maya area, the cylindrical tripod was decorated with polychrome paint, stucco, and beautiful, gouged-incised relief motifs.

The near absence of pottery from the Early Classic in many areas of the Maya highlands may reflect the disruptions in this region mentioned in Chapter 4. Moreover, the pottery from many sites, including many in the lowlands, is characterized by a relative lack of development and elaboration.

In northern Yucatan the ceramics of the Classic period divided sharply into two traditions: the earlier (regional-stage) pottery is very similar to the Early Classic pottery of the central lowlands; the later (florescent-stage) pottery is a separate tradition developed in Late and Terminal Classic times. Regional pottery consisted largely of monochromes that are strikingly similar to those of the Peten; polychrome decoration was less frequently used. In Yucatan, however, we find one of the best-documented and most enduring ceramic sequences in the Maya area, spanning Preclassic and Classic times, not to mention impressive Middle and Late Preclassic architectural achievements. These accomplishments are the work of well-organized

Fig. 15.8. Protoclassic pottery: (*a*, *b*) Usulutan bowls with mammiform tetrapod supports, from the southern highlands; (*c*) polychrome bowl with mammiform tetrapod supports, from the central lowlands.

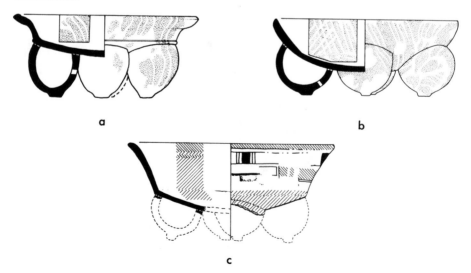

a                    b

c

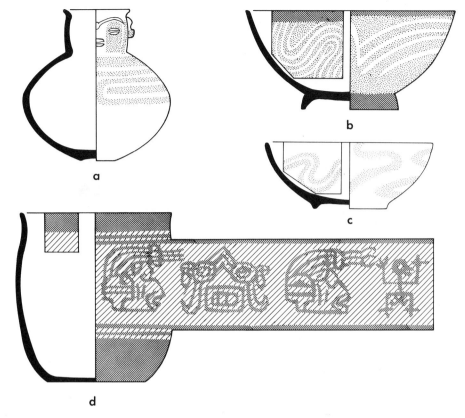

Fig. 15.9. Early Classic pottery from the southern highlands: (*a*) red-on-cream jar with effigy neck; (*b*) red-rimmed Usulutan bowl with ring base; (*c*) scraped-slip cream bowl with ring base; (*d*) red-on-orange painted bowl with Tlaloc-like motifs.

communities of considerable size. It is also notable that nearly every archaeological site sampled in the northern lowlands produced Late Preclassic ceramics.

With the onset of the Classic period the long tradition of clay figurines nearly vanished throughout most of the Maya area. The decline of this familiar Preclassic tradition has been equated with the suppression of the local village-agricultural cults by an increasingly powerful (and jealous) state-controlled elite religion. The figurines known from this period, such as the Teotihuacan-related cache from the lowland site of Becan (Fig. 15.11, lower illustration), are almost invariably associated with elite ritual contexts. These Mexican-influenced figurines were often molded, whereas those of the Preclassic tradition were hand-modeled.

## Late Classic

The Late Classic era is noted for its fine polychrome pottery. Although some of this pottery was poorly or incompletely fired, the painted scenes are justly noted for their artistic merit (Figs. 15.12 and 15.13). Motifs include both naturalistic and

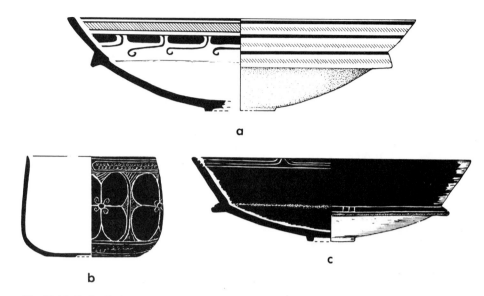

Fig. 15.10. Early Classic pottery from the central lowlands: (*a*) basal-flange polychrome bowl; (*b*) incised black bowl; (*c*) incised black bowl with a basal flange and ring base; (*below*) basal-flange polychrome bowl with ring base and effigy-handled cover, from Tikal.

Fig. 15.11. Early Classic pottery from the central lowlands: (*above left*) cylindrical tripod bowl with stucco-painted polychrome motifs and effigy-handled lid, from Tikal; (*above right*) cylindrical tripod orange bowl and lid with incised motifs, from Tikal; (*below*) cylindrical tripod black bowl with carved incised motifs, a Teotihuacan-style hollow figurine found inside, from Becan.

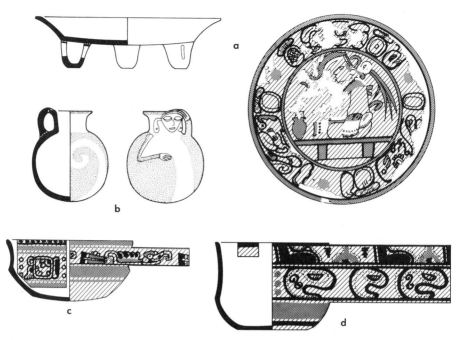

Fig. 15.12. Late Classic pottery from the southern highlands: (*a*) polychrome tripod vessel imported from the lowlands; (*b*) white-on-orange jar with modeled monkey figure; (*c*) Copador polychrome bowl; (*d*) purple polychrome bowl.

Fig. 15.13. Late Classic polychrome pottery from Tikal, central lowlands: (*above*) bowl with glyph band; (*right*) portrait vase.

geometric designs, glyphic texts, and individual portraits. The polychrome vases and dishes (on tripod supports) exhibit sophisticated painted and resist techniques in black, orange, red, white, and a variety of other colors. The most notable examples come from the lowlands, but significant centers of the art were located in the northern Maya highlands (see the Chama, Nebaj, and Ratinlinxul vases, Figs. 15.14–15.16) and along the southeastern periphery (the Copador polychrome produced at Copan; Fig. 15.12c).

Specialists divide the lowland Tepeu sphere into two periods. Tepeu 1 (ca. 550–700), marked by black and red on orange ware ("Saxche Orange Polychrome"), is associated with round-sided bowls and large tripod plates. Tepeu 2 (ca. 700–800) is marked by more elaborate decorations on brighter orange ("Palmar Orange Polychrome") and cream ("Zacatel Cream Polychrome") wares. Designs are painted on plates and flaring-wall bowls. But the culmination of ceramic portrait artistry is found on Tepeu 2 polychrome cylindrical vases (see Figs. 15.17–15.19 and the discussion of the Altar Vase below).

Ceramic art was also well expressed in the delicately modeled and painted Late Classic incensarios. Resist and negative-painted decoration, two other typical Late Classic characteristics, appeared on tall cylindrical vases, ring-stand vessels, and tripod-supported dishes. Generally speaking, there were two size ranges of slipped-ware jars: one large enough to carry a full backload of water, the other of 2- to 3-liter capacity. Hemispheroid basins are common, and low platters are found in some areas; both have thickened rims. Bowls are usually of two shapes: those with nearly flat bases and flaring sides, supported by either a ring or three legs; and hemispheroid bowls with either a small flattened base or a ring base. The unslipped,

Fig. 15.14. Late Classic polychrome pottery from the northern highlands: roll-out drawing of the Chama Vase, Chixoy valley, Guatemala.

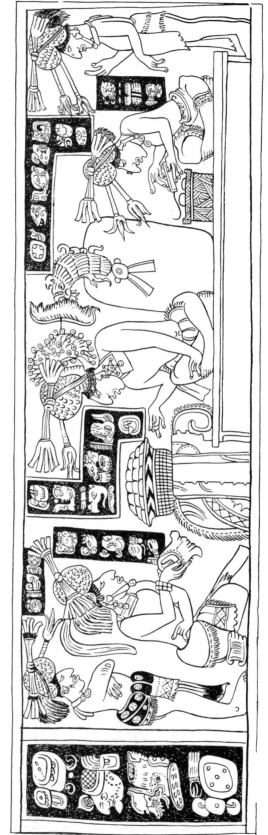

Fig. 15.15. Late Classic polychrome pottery from the northern highlands: roll-out drawing of the Nebaj Vase, Chixoy valley, Guatemala.

Fig. 15.16. Late Classic polychrome pottery from the northern highlands: roll-out drawing of the Ratinlinxul Vase, Chixoy valley, Guatemala.

Fig. 15.17. Late Classic polychrome pottery from the central lowlands: drawing of a plate with a portrait figure and glyph band, from the tomb in Uaxactun Str. A-I.

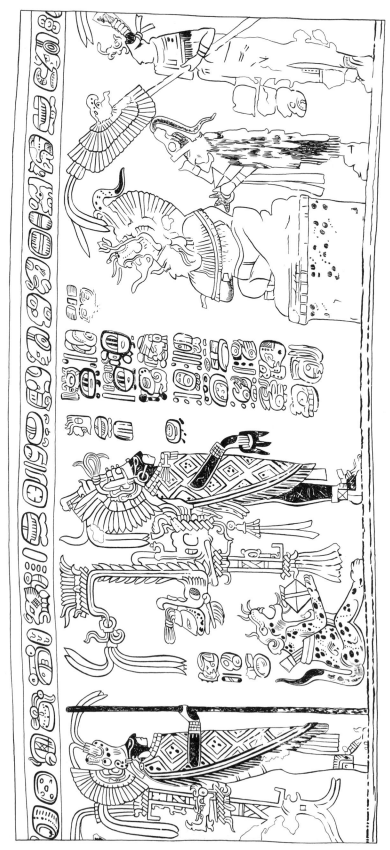

Fig. 15.18. Late Classic polychrome pottery from the central lowlands: roll-out drawing of a vase with a seated lord and attendants, from the tomb in Uaxactun Str. A-1 (see Fig. 10.6).

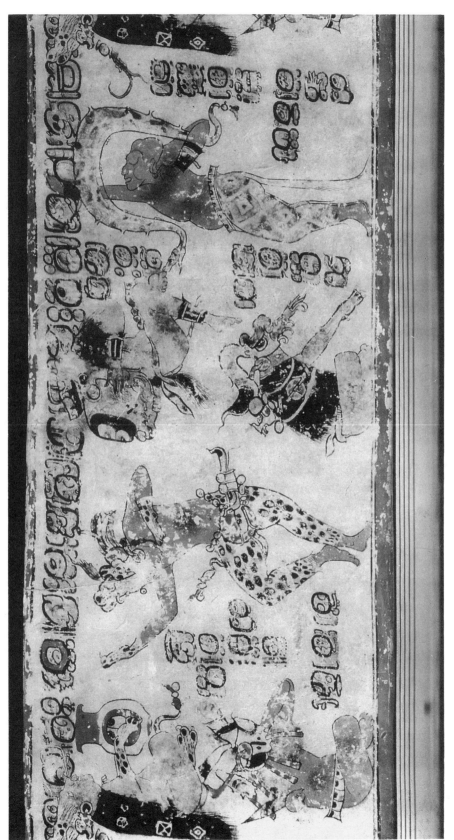

Fig. 15.19. Late Classic polychrome pottery from the southern lowlands: roll-out photograph of the Altar de Sacrificios Vase, found buried with the remains of a young woman—perhaps the woman depicted at the lower left, her throat cut and her hand clutching a leaf-shaped knife.

externally striated cooking pots continued the traditions begun in earlier times. Among the thin, finely made, and elaborately decorated vessels that were widely traded, the most common shape is cylindrical; some flare slightly, some are barrel-shaped.

Because the Late Classic is the most thoroughly studied era of Maya civilization, more data have been collected about the pottery of the Late Classic than about that of any other. Some of these studies have provided new and important insights not only into our knowledge of Maya ceramics, but also into the nature of Maya economic, social, and political organization (see Chapters 9 and 10). For example, studies of Late Classic pottery have delineated the localized pottery manufacture and distribution patterns at both Tikal and Palenque, including relationships with their surrounding dependencies.

One of the most beautiful examples of Classic lowland polychrome pottery, the Altar Vase (Fig. 15.19), was excavated by archaeologists at Altar de Sacrificios. Its painted scene, interpreted by R. E. W. Adams, provides a vivid portrayal of the ritual activity and customs of the Maya ruling elite. The Altar Vase depicts a funeral rite that occurred in A.D. 754. The subject of the funeral, a middle-aged woman of obvious importance, was probably from the ruling dynasty at Altar de Sacrificios. The scene on the vase depicts an elaborate ritual of dancing, singing, and sacrifice involving six figures, seemingly individuals and their spirit companions from the ruling dynasties of other centers: Tikal, Yaxchilan, and an unknown center in the Chama region of the northern Maya highlands. The offerings brought by these visitors (including several pottery vessels) were apparently placed in the woman's tomb. The vase also depicts the autosacrifice of a young female, possibly a member of the dead woman's family. The Altar Vase, together with the knife that was presumably the instrument of her death, was buried with the young sacrificial victim in a simple grave near the tomb.

Other finely painted vessels have been excavated from burials and tombs at Tikal, Holmul, Seibal, Tayasal, Altun Ha, and other sites. One of the finest assemblages of polychrome-painted pottery was found in a stone-lined tomb in Str. A-I at Uaxactun, the burial of a ruling personage, to judge from the magnificence of his burial offerings. The skeleton lay at full length, with the head pointing to the north and both hands clasped against the right shoulder (Fig. 10.6). At the head stood a painted vase; its extended design is shown in Fig. 15.18. The background is a brilliant orange-red; the figures are outlined in black and painted with black and several shades of yellow. Around the rim is a line of glyphs, and glyph panels are interspersed between the figures. The principal panel of sixteen glyphs records an incorrect Maya date, 7.5.0.0.0 8 Ahau 13 Kankin. The date intended may have been 8.5.0.0.0 12 Ahau 13 Kankin (A.D. 140), which would involve two simple changes in the original inscription. Nevertheless, the date must refer to a past event, since stylistically the vase dates about 600 years later.

The design shows a ruler or elite official seated on a throne, facing the central glyph panel. Behind him stands an attendant, painted black, holding a spiked implement (or "knuckle duster"; see Figs. 15.18 and 15.30: the latter shows this artifact rendered in chipped flint); another figure holds a feather canopy over the ruler's head. To the left of the glyph panel are three figures. The two standing figures, wearing elaborate cloaks, are also painted black; one carries another "knuckle duster" and the other holds a spear. Between them is the third figure, a seated jaguar offering two bowls, one inverted over the other, much like many cache vessels found archaeologically.

This tomb contained other polychrome vessels of equal beauty. There were eleven pieces of pottery, nine of them painted. A flat plate with three supports and an unpainted background (Fig. 15.17) bears a design outlined in black and painted in black and red. A dancer is poised on his toes, his right arm rests lightly on his hip and his left is turned outward in a graceful gesture. The sure sweep of line and the admirable fitting of the design to the circular space indicate mastery of the art. A small hole broken through the bottom of the plate is apparently a ceremonial "releasing of the spirit" of the vessel so that it might accompany the owner on his journey to the underworld.

The famous Chama, Nebaj, and Ratinlinxul vases, polychrome vessels from the adjacent northern Maya highlands, appear to depict the merchant elites that rose to power in the Late Classic, for their scenes often portray mercantile themes and symbols. On the Ratinlinxul Vase (Fig. 15.16), a "merchant prince" is borne in a palanquin carried by retainers; a dog stretches himself below. Five other retainers follow: the first carries a jaguar-cushioned throne, the next three carry what appear to be canoe paddles; and the last grasps a fold of cloth in his left hand. This scene may reflect the importance of the southern periphery of the Maya lowlands, an area of independent enclaves established and maintained by aggressively competitive merchant princes. Their power was seemingly based on control of the lucrative trade routes between the resource zones of the highlands and the markets in the lowlands.

The famous painted vase from Chama in the upper Chixoy valley in the northern highlands of Guatemala (Fig. 15.14) is painted in black, red, and brown on a background of pink. Seven figures, interspersed with as many glyph panels, are portrayed. The two principals, painted black, face each other; the one on the right wears a jaguar-skin cloak. The black body paint may symbolize associations with Ek Chuah (God M), patron of Maya merchants (Chapter 11). Three of the remaining figures carry fans. Because personal characteristics are so faithfully rendered, the figures are probably portraits.

A similar vase from Nebaj (Fig. 15.15) displays five human figures, five glyph panels, and four larger glyphs at the back of the design. Two figures sit on a dais, with a ruling personage occupying the central position.

During the Late Classic, figurines reappeared in the central Maya lowlands; their center of development seems to have been along the Bahía de Campeche in the states of Tabasco and Campeche. The finest figurines, which are usually found in graves, come from Isla de Jaina (Fig. 15.20), although good examples also come from the region of Palenque and Jonuta. The figurines, about 10–25 cm high, are made of a fine-textured orange clay and often bear a white wash with traces of paint in blue and other colors. These solid pieces were either hand-modeled or mold-made (Fig. 15.21). Mold-made specimens often contain pellets to make a rattle, or incorporate a whistle and stops to form an ocarina. The detailing on these figurines is extremely fine; tattooed designs show clearly on faces no larger than a thumbnail. Without question these are the most intricate and detailed ceramic work in pre-Columbian America. Figurines, small flutes, and other pottery objects, generally similar in style to the Jaina mold-made figurines, are found over a larger area, including the Peten, Puuc, and Gulf coast regions.

## Terminal Classic

This era saw the decline of most central and southern lowland centers, and the rapid acceleration of prosperity in the northern lowlands. Domestic pottery shows little change, but both the frequency of occurrence of polychrome ceramics and the skill manifested on them decrease, presumably due to the decline of the specialized, elite-sponsored workshops that produced these fine ceramics.

The most diagnostic marker of this era is Fine Orange ware, made from a fine-grained clay or paste. Fine Orange was produced in the western edge of the lowlands in Tabasco, the homeland of the Putun (Chontal) Maya (see Chapter 6). Standardization in both shape and mold-made decorations speak of commercial production for export, as part of the lucrative trading economy sponsored by the Putun Maya. The stereotyped scenes on Fine Orange pottery (Fig. 15.22) are often militaristic, and may even celebrate the conflicts that led to the takeovers of sites in several regions of the Maya area, including the Usumacinta drainage (Altar de Sacrificios and Seibal) and Yucatan (Chichen Itza; see Chapter 7). Fine Orange pottery was traded widely, and is found over much of the Maya area.

In Yucatan, the pottery of the Late and Terminal Classic is largely devoid of polychrome decoration, although there are exceptions (Fig. 15.23). The distinguishing and diagnostic remains are the slatewares, characterized by a waxy gray to brownish slip, occasionally covered with a pale, grayish paint. Despite their drab coloring, the characteristically fine, smooth finish, the careful forming, and the technical excellence evinced in this ware (Fig. 15.24) seem to derive from a competent, carefully organized group of craftsmen, whereas the Late Classic Peten polychromes are the creations of talented individual artists. Further evidence of the "industrialization" of Maya pottery is found in the use of the *k'abal* among modern

Fig. 15.20. Late Classic figurines from Isla de Jaina, Campeche, Mexico.

Fig. 15.21. Figurine shaped by a Late Classic mold, from the northern highlands.

Fig. 15.22. Terminal Classic pottery from the northern lowlands: Fine Orange vessels from (*a*) Uxmal; (*b, c*) Chichen Itza.

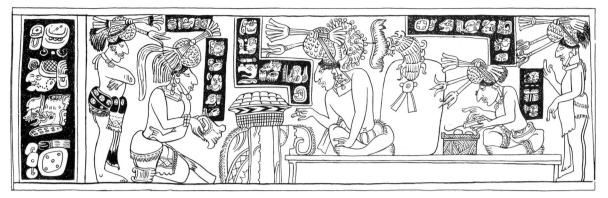

Fig. 15.23. Terminal Classic pottery from the northern lowlands: roll-out drawing of a polychrome vase from Yucatan.

Fig. 15.24. Terminal Classic pottery slateware from (*upper left*) Uxmal (central lowlands); (*lower left*) Dzan (northern lowlands); (*above*) provenience unknown; (*below*) near Tikal (central lowlands).

Yucatecans. The *k'abal* is a wooden disk that rests on a smooth board and is spun between the soles of the potter's feet, in a procedure very like the wheel-throwing used by Old World potters from as early as 3000 B.C. Although the true potter's wheel was never used by the Maya, vessels made on a *k'abal* have the even, elaborate contours characteristic of wheel-made pottery, and this feature characterizes much of the pre-Conquest Maya ceramics from the northern lowlands.

## Early Postclassic

At the close of the Classic new types of pottery began to appear throughout the Maya area. Hard, thin-walled, fine-pasted, and technologically superior, these remains (Figs. 15.22 and 15.24) include later types of Fine Orange ware and the Yucatecan slateware already discussed. The most distinctive Early Postclassic pottery is Plumbate ware (Fig. 15.25), the only true vitrified (glazed) pottery in pre-Columbian America, which was produced along the Pacific piedmont in southwestern Guatemala. An apparent production center for an early form of Plumbate pottery ("San Juan Plumbate") has been discovered on the Pacific coast. Pottery of this tradition was fired in enclosed pit kilns capable of reaching the high temperatures required for vitrification. Often, Plumbate pottery was elaborately decorated by molding or by a combination of modeling and carving, especially in "Tohil Plumbate," that characterized the Early Postclassic. Plumbate ceramics, which underwent several hundred years of development, were widely traded even beyond the Maya area, beginning in the Terminal Classic, and are hallmarks of the Early Postclassic.

Despite the technological excellence of these particular ceramics and the lingering of a simple polychrome tradition in the lowlands (Fig. 15.26), in other respects the pottery of the Early Postclassic demonstrates an overall decline in quality from that of earlier times.

## Late Postclassic

The pottery of the Late Postclassic has been found at a variety of sites, including the capitals of the independent, highland Maya "kingdoms" destroyed during the Conquest. Several investigators have also traced the Late Postclassic wares of Yucatan and the central Maya lowlands (the latter largely restricted to the areas around Lago Peten Itza, Lago Yaxha, and other lakes).

The Late Postclassic fostered the continued, widespread tradition of monochrome utilitarian pottery (Figs. 15.27 and 15.28). Paste variations probably reflect regional or local production centers. In the highlands, wares continued to be tempered with volcanic ash. Surfaces often appear to be unslipped and smoothed, but exterior surfaces are usually polished to a low gloss. Other examples have a thin, polished slip or wash. Red wares predominate, especially in the north and extending

Fig. 15.25. Terminal Classic and Early Postclassic pottery from the northern lowlands: Plumbate ware imported from the Pacific coastal plain.

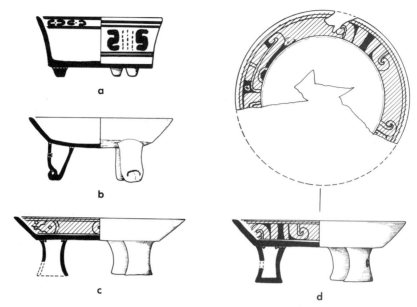

Fig. 15.26. Pottery from the central lowlands: (*a*) Terminal Classic polychrome bowl with solid tripod supports; (*b*) Early Postclassic red bowl with hollow-scroll tripod supports; (*c*, *d*) Early Postclassic polychrome bowls with hollow "trumpet" supports.

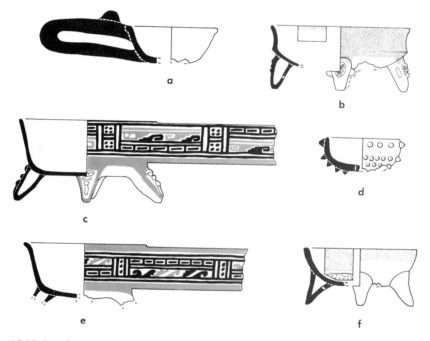

Fig. 15.27. Postclassic pottery from the southern highlands: (*a*) ladle incensario; (*b*) red-painted bowl with molded figure supports; (*c*, *e*) Chinautla polychrome bowls; (*d*) miniature bowl with appliqué spikes; (*f*) red-on-buff bowl with grater interior base.

Fig. 15.28. Late Postclassic pottery from the northern lowlands: (*above*) coarse red-ware tripod bowls: (*below*) effigy incensario from near Chichen Itza.

down the Caribbean coast well into Belize. Other colors range from tan or cinnamon to brown, depending on local clays and firing conditions. Common shapes include necked jars (*tinajas*), with two strap handles placed low on the jar body, and a variety of unsupported bowls similar to contemporary shapes. Bowls with plain or elaborately modeled tripod supports are also found.

Bichrome wares accompany the prevalent monochrome pottery, but now bear white painted motifs. The primarily geometric designs include bands, circles, dots, scrolls, frets, zigzags, triangles, diamonds, chevrons, and sunbursts, either singly or in combination, although some may represent stylized animals. Common shapes are water jars, with designs painted on the vessel shoulders and handles, and tripod-supported bowls with flaring walls, often painted white on both interior and exterior surfaces.

During the Late Postclassic, simple, polychrome-decorated pottery flourished, and a range of similar polychrome pottery was produced and exchanged over much of the highlands. This ware, generally defined by red and black motifs painted on a white or cream background, is usually referred to as Chinautla polychrome (Fig. 15.27c, e). In fact, on the basis of painting style this polychrome tradition can be divided into at least three categories. One of these, a "dull paint style," is generally associated with sites in the northern and western portions of the highlands (from Chiapas in Mexico to the Verapaz in Guatemala). It occurs at the Conquest-period sites of Zaculeu, Utatlan, Chuitinamit-Atitlan, and Iximche. Another style, the "bright paint style," appears to be distributed in the southern highlands and may be found at Mixcu Viejo, Chinautla Viejo, Chimaltenango, and Chalchuapa. Finally, a "black-outlined style" appears to be a companion to the bright-paint tradition, although on the Marihua red-on-buff type found in the southeastern highlands of El Salvador, there are similarities to Mexican motifs. The vessel forms of these southern polychrome traditions are generally similar: tripod-supported bowls and water jars displaying exterior-painted zones on the shoulder, handle, and neck.

Widely spread throughout the Maya highlands are vessels made of a highly "micaceous" paste. This distinctive specular (reflective) component in the clay has been identified as a form of talc, mined in the Baja Verapaz and used today in several pottery-production centers. Forms of this Late Postclassic ware include jars, a variety of bowl shapes, and, most typically, *comales*, or tortilla griddles. Vessels may be unslipped or, often in the case of *comales*, slipped on the interior with talc to provide a nonstick cooking surface.

In Yucatan there were changes in the method of preparing the pottery clay and later a change in the red slip color that is still used in the northern area (Fig. 15.28, upper illustration). Later still, the introduction of a new form of cooking pot might suggest the arrival of foreign women, and the introduction of figurine incensarios indicates a striking change in religious custom. Several categories of apparently ritual vessels, including mold-decorated ladle censers, flanged censers, and hourglass-shaped or pedestal-based vessels, were used during the Late Postclassic. Elaborate incensarios like these (Fig. 15.28, lower illustration) were often destroyed as heathen idols by the Spanish conquerors.

## Patterns of Household and Industrial Ceramic Production

During the pre-Conquest era, the Maya appear to have developed four related systems of pottery production, and by Postclassic times all four were probably in use. The earliest and most persistent pattern, inferred from the archaeological data for all time periods, can be described as nonspecialized household production. Under this system, households produced pottery for their own needs, perhaps producing an excess for consumption by local non-pottery-making households by selling vessels through a market or peddler distribution system. This kind of household activity was secondary to the primary function of subsistence farming. The second type, which appears to have developed by the Late Preclassic, can be described as semi-specialized household production, whereby households began to specialize in particular pottery forms or types—again, as a part-time activity.

By the Classic period, at least in the Maya lowlands, more specialized household production appears to have developed alongside continuing nonspecialized and semi-specialized production. In this mode, pottery production became the primary economic activity of the household unit, usually under the aegis of a family-member artisan, and these households probably no longer undertook subsistence farming. In addition, there appear to have been specialized workshops sponsored by the elite class for the production of the elaborately painted vessels produced in the Classic period.

The final development, during the Terminal Classic and Early Postclassic eras, saw the emergence of specialized industrial production. The production of certain pottery types now took place in a specialized facility, often incorporating mass-production methods such as the use of molds to impart standardized motifs to vessels. Plumbate pottery and, perhaps, effigy incensarios and certain polychrome-decorated vessels were mass-produced in these facilities for widespread distribution. Certainly the finding of such vessels throughout much of the Maya area supports this conclusion, but only a few technological studies designed to define actual production centers and patterns of trade have been conducted. Moreover, with the exception of Plumbate-vessel production, which reached its highest development with Tohil Plumbate, truly industrialized production remains unverified by archaeological excavation. The disappearance of Plumbate pottery by the Late Postclassic remains unexplained, but was doubtless related to a major shift in political and economic alliances associated with the emergence of the independent, highland Maya "kingdoms" during this period.

By the time these mass-production and firing procedures had declined, during the Late Postclassic, all pottery had come to be unvitrified, and low-temperature, open-firing methods may be inferred. One significant new development in the Late Postclassic highlands is the production of pottery using a high proportion of talc, both as a slip and as an ingredient in the pastes of vessels. This mineral, properly incorporated, imparts a nonstick surface to cooking vessels, and its use represents an important technological breakthrough.

## Lithics

The Maya used a variety of stone materials to make a range of artifacts, from utilitarian tools to beautifully fashioned status goods. Two basic technologies were employed, the chipping of flint or chert and obsidian (volcanic glass) by percussion or pressure and the pecking and grinding of basalts and other igneous stones. The first method produced sharper cutting and scraping tools, the most common being the obsidian blade, which was used for everything from domestic tasks to ritual bloodletting. The second method was used to make axes, for felling trees, and a variety of grinding or processing implements (Fig. 15.29), the most common being the mano and metate used (still today, in some regions) to produce flours from

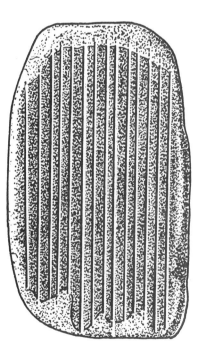

Fig. 15.29. A stone bark beater from Seibal, Guatemala, used to prepare bark paper.

maize or other seeds. Here we will briefly consider the most elaborated examples of the art of chipped stone, a variety of specialized forms usually associated with elite use, the so-called eccentric flints.

## Chipped-Stone Eccentrics

Elaborately chipped stone items were important ritual objects, and the manufacture of large sacrificial knives, scepters, and the like are among the finest examples of lithic technology ever produced by the Maya (Fig. 15.30). Caches of eccentric-shaped flints and blades are often found buried under Maya monuments and buildings. Perhaps the finest examples of this craft are the elaborate but delicately chipped staff heads excavated at El Palmar in Quintana Roo and at both Copan and Quirigua. Three human heads in profile are shown on the Quirigua piece (Fig. 15.30). A recently discovered cache found inside a buried Early Classic building at Copan ("Rosalila structure"; see Fig. 5.49) included an entire array of elaborate figures rendered in eccentrically chipped flint (Fig. 15.31).

## Jade and Similar Carved and Polished Stone

The finest examples of Maya lapidary art are carved jades, the earliest of which were made during Preclassic times. On the earliest dated piece—the Leyden Plaque, engraved in A.D. 320 (Fig. 4.24)—the carving is little more than incised. Another early piece, from Copan, dating perhaps two hundred years later, is carved in the round. This piece (Fig. 15.32, upper left), a pendant 7–8 cm long, shows a seated human figure in left profile. The hole for the suspension cord enters at the mouth of the figure and emerges at the back of the neck; the drilling was done from both sides, as with most examples.

A fine example of Early Classic carved jadeite was excavated at Kaminaljuyu, the important highland center on the outskirts of modern Guatemala City. This piece, 15 cm high, presents a standing human figure rather than a seated one, and the design is more elaborate. The body appears in front view, the head and headdress in left profile. The head has a typical Maya profile, and the headdress is formed by the head and foreleg of a crocodile. A large, waterworn boulder of unworked solid jade weighing slightly over 90 kilograms was discovered under the stairway of a platform at Kaminaljuyu. Many small pieces have apparently been sawed from it, perhaps to be made into ornaments.

The jadeite head shown in Fig. 15.32, although found at Chichen Itza, was probably carved at Piedras Negras. The historical (non-period-ending) date it presents, 9.12.2.0.16 (A.D. 674), appears nowhere else in the Maya area except at Piedras Negras. The pendant, measuring 9.5 cm long, is hollowed out behind. A jaguar head forms the headdress, and the inscription is incised on a flat edge surrounding the hollow at the back.

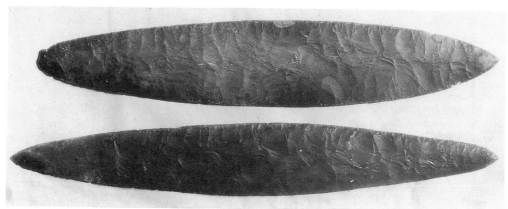

Fig. 15.30. Classic-period eccentric chipped flints: (*upper left*) "knuckle duster" from El Palmar, Quintana Roo, Mexico, like that held by the attendants in Fig. 15.18; (*upper right*) leaf-shaped blades and eccentrics from El Palmar; (*center*) leaf-shaped blades from Quirigua, Guatemala; (*lower left*) eccentric representing a profile figure with back ornament, from El Palmar; (*lower right*) eccentric representing a profile figure, from Quirigua (the lower eccentrics may be originally from manikin scepters or similar objects).

Fig. 15.31. Classic-period eccentric chipped flint representing a profile figure, from Rosalila Structure, Copan, Honduras (one of a cache of eccentric flints possibly originally from manikin scepters).

The wedge-shaped plaque shown in Fig. 15.33 also dates from late in the Classic period. It is perforated longitudinally near the top, and is about 10 cm high. A well-dressed ruler is seated on a throne, his body in front view and his head in left profile. The headdress consists of a serpent with opened jaws, from which emerges a small figure with a grotesque face. Another figure kneels before the throne, and an elaborate "speech scroll" issues from the ruler's mouth. This lovely blue-green piece is of Maya origin, and was probably traded to the great urban center of Teotihuacan, 40 km northeast of Mexico City, where it was found.

Several jadeite figurines have been found in the recent excavations at Copan (Fig. 15.32). A statuette of a human figure (Fig. 15.34) carved in the full round from fuchsite, a softer jadelike stone, was found under the stairway leading to Temple A-XVIII at Uaxactun. The eyes are rectangular and painted a brilliant red. A number of small holes were drilled in the figure, possibly so that ornaments might be attached. A similar figure (Fig. 15.35), carved from the same material though fitted with a jadeite nose, was excavated from a cache at El Portón, in the Salama Valley of the Maya highlands.

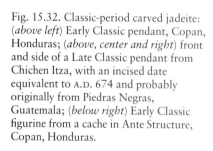

Fig. 15.32. Classic-period carved jadeite: (*above left*) Early Classic pendant, Copan, Honduras; (*above, center and right*) front and side of a Late Classic pendant from Chichen Itza, with an incised date equivalent to A.D. 674 and probably originally from Piedras Negras, Guatemala; (*below right*) Early Classic figurine from a cache in Ante Structure, Copan, Honduras.

Fig. 15.33. Late Classic carved jadeite plaque depicting a Maya lord, found at Teotihuacan, Valley of Mexico.

Fig. 15.34. Early Classic figurine from Uaxactun Str. A-XVIII, carved of fuchsite, a softer, jade-like stone.

Fig. 15.35. Late Preclassic fuchsite figurine with a jadeite nose, from the northern highlands (El Portón, Guatemala).

The largest jadeite sculpture known from the Maya area (Fig. 5.28) was discovered in the tomb of a ruler at Altun Ha, Belize. It portrays Kinich Ahau, the Maya sun god (God G). The tomb of Pacal at Palenque yielded a carved jade of excellent workmanship (Fig. 15.36, left). This figurine, which was found in the sarcophagus itself, also represents Kinich Ahau. A beautiful carved jade of a young jaguar was found in the tomb presumed to be that of the Tikal ruler Yax Kin (Fig. 15.36, right).

Artifacts of engraved jadeite from Chichen Itza (Fig. 15.37) represent the continued importance of these symbols of elite authority. The two largest examples were found in a stone box at the base of the stairway that leads to the early temple buried inside the El Castillo pyramid.

Natural deposits of jadeite have been found in the middle Motagua Valley of Guatemala, and pieces of jade were probably found in streams as waterworn pebbles or boulders ranging in weight from a few grams to several hundred kilograms. The shape and size of the original piece often influenced the design into which it was carved. A study of Mesoamerican jades by mineralogists of the Carnegie Institution of Washington has shown that Maya jades are jadeite, which differs in chemical composition from the most common Chinese jade, or nephrite. They thus differ somewhat in appearance from Chinese jades: Maya jade is slightly harder, less translucent, and more mottled. It varies from dark green to light blue-green, although all shades from near-black to white are known.

Jadeite is extremely hard—6.5 to 6.8 in the mineralogical scale (diamond is graded 10)—and when we consider that the ancient Maya did not use metal tools, their mastery of jade carving is a remarkable technical achievement. Pieces of jadeite were sawed by drawing cords back and forth through grooves, using hard stone particles and water as a cutting agent. Holes were bored from both ends with drills of bone or hardwood, again using finely crushed stone and water as the cutting agent, with the perforations meeting in the interior. Hollow bird bones were used for drilling circles. In the finer pieces a modeled effect was probably achieved by careful incising, followed by a deepening and smoothing of the grooves.

Fig. 15.36. Late Classic jadeite from royal tombs: (*left*) figurine from the Pacal Tomb at Palenque, Chiapas, Mexico; (*right*) reclining jaguar from presumed tomb of Yax Kin at Tikal, Guatemala.

## Mosaics

Few mosaics from either the Classic or Postclassic periods have survived. Mirrors made of fitted pieces of pyrite attached to backs of wood or stone have been found at Piedras Negras, Quirigua, Kaminaljuyu, and several highland sites. There are suggestions of jadeite mosaics in Classic-period reliefs, and a fine mask has been reconstructed from jadeite pieces found in the tomb of Pacal at Palenque. A spectacular life-sized mosaic mask of jadeite, shell, and pyrite was excavated from a tomb at Tikal (Fig. 15.38), and a miniature jade mosaic mask in the same style was found in an earlier cache at El Portón in the Salama Valley (Fig. 15.39). The apogee of Maya jadeite mosaic work is represented by two similar, cylindrical vessels found in two Late Classic rulers' tombs at Tikal (Fig. 15.40). Originally constructed on wooden backings, they have been reconstructed from the fragmentary states they were discovered in.

Examples of turquoise mosaic from the Postclassic are four disks found buried in ceremonial caches at Chichen Itza. These were not made in Yucatan, which lacks deposits of turquoise, but were brought from Central Mexico, where the technique

Fig. 15.37. Carved jadeite pendant from a cache under the El Castillo stairway, Chichen Itza.

Fig. 15.38. Early Classic life-sized mosaic mask of jadeite and other materials, from Burial 160 (9.4.13.0.0?, or ca. A.D. 527) at Tikal, Guatemala.

Fig. 15.39. Terminal Preclassic miniature mosaic mask of jadeite, from a cache in Str. J7-4, El Portón, Guatemala.

Fig. 15.40. Late Classic jadeite mosaic vessels from Tikal, Guatemala: (left) vessel from Burial 116, the tomb of Ah Cacau, bearing his presumed portrait on the lid; (right) vessel from Burial 196, the apparent tomb of his successor, Yax Kin, with his probable portrait on the lid.

was common in the fourteenth to sixteenth centuries. The first disk was found cached in a covered limestone vessel (Fig. 7.14) beneath the floor of the Temple of the Chacmool, which was later incorporated into the platform of the Temple of the Warriors (Chapter 7). The wood backing of this disk was almost rotted away, and the restored disk is in the Museo Nacional de Antropología, Mexico City. Three similar disks were later found in the buried temple under El Castillo at Chichen Itza—two in the same box with the carved jadeite illustrated in Fig. 15.37, and the third on the seat of the Red Jaguar Throne. One of the two disks found with the jadeite is in the Museo de Arqueología e Historia at Mérida; the third still rests on the seat of the Red Jaguar Throne (Fig. 7.8).

## Metalwork

Metal objects from Classic-period Maya centers are rare. A pair of legs belonging to a small, hollow figurine made of a gold-copper alloy (Fig. 15.41c) was found cached at Copan. Analysis of this alloy, and of the casting technique employed, suggests that it was made in lower Central America (Costa Rica or Panama). The legs were recovered from the dirt fill of the dedicatory cache vault under Stela H, which was dedicated in A.D. 782 (Fig. 5.51). The other parts of the figurine were not located, and the pieces recovered may have found their way into the vault some time later than the dedicatory date. Copper bells and ornaments dating from the Terminal Classic or Early Postclassic have been found at Quirigua.

Metal objects from the Postclassic are more common. The greatest number recovered have been dredged from the sacred Cenote of Sacrifice at Chichen Itza, though copper bells have been found elsewhere. Gold and copper objects from the Cenote include disks decorated with repoussé work, a cup and saucer, necklaces, bracelets, masks, pendants, rings, earplugs, bells, and beads (Figs. 15.41–15.43). The most common objects are small copper bells of the sleigh-bell type; these bells were a common ornament of the death god, Yum Cimil (God A), and are usually associated with him. The style and workmanship of many of the smaller objects indicate that they, too, were made in lower Central America.

Most of these metal objects probably reached Chichen Itza as articles of trade. Chemical analyses indicate that the metal alloys probably came from as far south as Colombia, Panama, Honduras, and Guatemala, and from as far west and north as Chiapas, Oaxaca, and the Valley of Mexico. The copper pieces that contain tin and arsenic came from Oaxaca and the Valley of Mexico; those containing only tin are from Honduras; and the purest copper came from Guatemala and Chiapas. These origins testify to the extent of the Postclassic trade networks of the Maya.

Not all metal objects that show casting are of foreign origin. A miscast copper bell found near Quirigua indicates probable local production. But the technique with which Maya goldsmiths were most skilled was the hammering for repoussé work (in which raised ornamentation is forced outward by hammering the reverse side of the metal sheet). The gold used in the objects made at Chichen Itza was probably obtained by reworking cast-gold objects of foreign origin. These local pieces are usually thin disks portraying scenes of battle. The scenes represent conflicts between Maya warriors and Mexicanized (Putun?) warriors (Fig. 15.44). The human figures are similar to those in the reliefs and frescoes of the Early Postclassic at Chichen Itza, and the disks probably date from that era.

## Painted Books

We open consideration of the most perishable of Maya artifacts with one of the most specialized and important items. Maya books or codices, discussed at length in Chapter 13, were made from bark paper or deerhide coated with a thin plaster wash and then painted with black and other pigments. These were used to record hieroglyphic texts and accompanying painted scenes. Only three or four pre-Columbian examples are known to have survived the Conquest.

Fig. 15.41. Examples of metalwork from the Maya area: (*a, b*) gold finger rings and (*d, e, f*) copper bells, all dredged from the Cenote of Sacrifice, Chichen Itza, Yucatan, Mexico; (*c*) a pair of gold figurine legs from a cruciform cache vault beneath Stela H, Copan, Honduras.

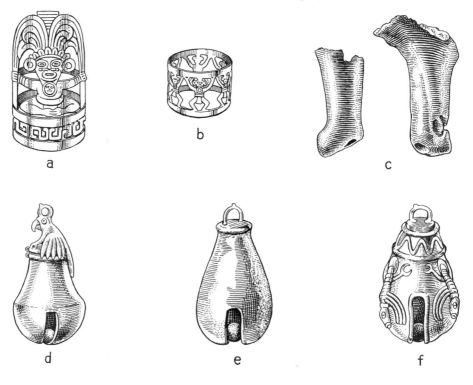

a

b

c

d

e

f

Fig. 15.42. Gold and copper objects from the Cenote of Sacrifice, Chichen Itza: (*a, d, e*) disks decorated in repoussé technique; (*b*) gold bracelet; (*c*) gold cup and saucer.

Among the codices, the brushwork of the Dresden Codex (Fig. 11.3) is of the highest quality; the lines are bold and fluid. The Paris Codex (Fig. 13.3) is not quite as well done, but the difference is slight. In the Madrid Codex (Figs. 13.4 and 13.13), however, both the human figures and the glyphs are less skillfully drawn. All these codices are suspected to be Postclassic copies of Classic-period originals.

Fig. 15.43. Goldwork from the Cenote of Sacrifice, Chichen Itza: (*right*) animal figure and bell; (*below*) eye and mouth elements from a perishable mask or shield.

## Textiles

Only a few examples of ancient Maya textiles have survived. Fragments of textiles were still wrapped around some of the eccentric flints found in the Rosalila cache mentioned previously. Fragments of white cotton cloth, thought to date from before the Conquest, are reported from Tenam in eastern Chiapas; the supposed Late Postclassic dating of this cloth is based on the associated pottery. Numerous small pieces of carbonized cloth were recovered from the Cenote of Sacrifice at Chichen Itza. They show many complicated weaves, and date from Late Postclassic times.

Fig. 15.44. Drawings of the central motifs from three repoussé-technique gold disks from the Cenote of Sacrifice, Chichen Itza, depicting warfare and capture scenes.

Classic-period sculptures indicate that the cotton fabrics of the period were of rich and complicated weave, and that elaborate embroidery was employed, at least for the elite. Representations of these textiles can be seen on carved monuments (Fig. 15.45, top row). Textiles from the Postclassic are known from wall paintings and pottery (Fig. 15.45, bottom row). The spectacular Bonampak murals portray a variety of Late Classic fabrics (Figs. 5.20–5.22).

Hand-woven cotton materials of fixed length and width (*patis*) were used as articles of trade in ancient times, and after the Conquest became the principal form of tribute exacted by the Spanish.

The Classic and Postclassic sculptures bear witness to the former abundance and variety of Maya weaving. The modern Maya of the highlands of Guatemala pursue a rich textile art that no doubt derives from their pre-Conquest ancestors. The craft disappeared in northern Yucatan only recently, but the Lacandon Maya of eastern Chiapas, whose technology closely resembles that of the ancient Maya, still spin cotton thread and weave a coarse cloth, using the same techniques as did their ancestors. Spinning and handloom weaving are done by the women. They gather the cotton and spin it into thread, using as a spindle a slender pointed stick about 24 cm long, weighted near the lower end with a disk of pottery. These disks, or spindle whorls, are all that has survived of ancient Maya spinning and weaving implements. They gave balance and weight to the spindle as it was twirled in the

Fig. 15.45. Textiles drawn from (*top row*) Classic monuments; (*bottom row*) Postclassic murals and pottery.

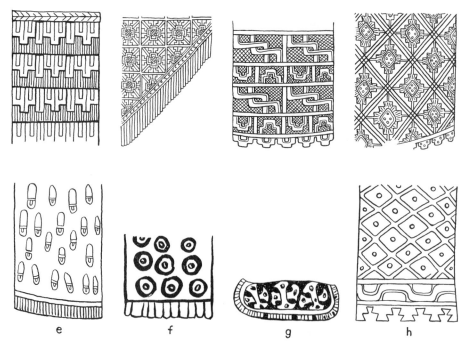

e          f          g          h

right hand, while the lower end of the spindle rested in a gourd on the ground; the unspun cotton was held in the left hand or thrown over the left shoulder (Fig. 15.46).

The Maya loom was of the same general type as those of modern American Indian groups. One wooden rod is fastened to each end of the warp to keep the cloth stretched to the desired width. A thick hemp cord (*yamal*), attached to each end of the lower rod, passes behind the weaver, permitting her to tighten the warp by leaning backward. The upper rod is attached to a tree or post. The strip of cloth produced may be as long as 2.4 m, and as it lengthens it is wound around the upper rod. The weaver sits as far back from the post as possible in order to hold the loom horizontally at the required tension (Fig. 15.46, right). The looms are about a meter wide, and when wider cloth is desired, two strips are sewn together. A Postclassic representation of this technique appears in the Madrid Codex (Fig. 15.47), where Ix Chebel Yax, patroness of weaving, is shown at work.

Many Maya communities in highland Guatemala are still characterized by the different kinds of cloth they weave and by their traditional designs. Although wool has been introduced since the Conquest, most native clothing is still made of hand-loomed cotton cloth. Today silk is generally used for embroidery, but in earlier times colored cotton threads and feathers were used. No two designs are ever identical, but the weavers of each village generally conform to a distinctive traditional pattern (Fig. 10.5, upper illustrations).

The color symbolism used in highland Guatemalan textile designs still bears some relation to that used by the ancient Maya. Black, the color of obsidian, represents weapons; yellow, the color of corn, symbolizes food; red represents blood;

Fig. 15.46. Lacandon Maya spinning cotton thread and weaving textiles, Chiapas, Mexico.

and blue means sacrifice. The royal color is green, because that is the color of the quetzal bird's plumage, which was reserved for the rulers.

In the coloring of textiles, the thread, rather than the finished fabric, is dyed. Although organic and mineral colors are now being replaced by aniline dyes, a few are still in use. Perhaps the most highly prized native dye was a deep purple obtained from a mollusk (*Purpura patula*) found along the Pacific coast, a large sea snail related to the Mediterranean mollusk that gave the Phoenicians the famous "royal purple of Tyre."

In Yucatan the type of embroidery used by the modern Maya is cross-stitch (*xoc bil chui*, or "threads that are counted"). The earlier designs may have been geometric, like those still used in central Quintana Roo, but geometric designs have now been generally displaced by floral motifs (Fig. 10.5, lower illustrations).

Today, native weaves and colors are everywhere giving way to machine-made fabrics and aniline dyes. Even in the highlands of Guatemala, the native textile art is rapidly disappearing.

Fig. 15.47. Deity identified as Ix Chebel Yax weaving; from the Madrid Codex, p. 79.

## Basketry and Matting

Baskets and matting must have been common among the ancient Maya, and the materials from which they were made occur in abundance throughout the area. No early Maya baskets have been discovered, but they are depicted in Classic-period graphic art. An elaborate basket appears on Lintel 24 at Yaxchilan (Fig. 15.48*a*). The upper half is worked in a twilled pattern, the middle section shows a design of stepped frets and small squares, and the bottom seems to be ornamented with featherwork. There are two representations of Late Classic baskets on the Nebaj Vase (Fig. 15.48*b*, *c*). A Postclassic basket from a wall painting in the Temple of the Jaguars at Chichen Itza (Fig. 15.48*d*) is more elaborate.

Modern Maya baskets are far less elaborate. Those woven from thin, tough vines are large and coarse, suitable for carrying corn. Split-cane baskets, smaller and more neatly woven, are used in the home.

Few pieces of ancient matting have survived, but imprints have been found on

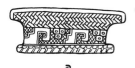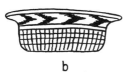

Fig. 15.48. Baskets drawn from monuments, murals, and pottery: (*a*) Lintel 24, Yaxchilan; (*b*, *c*) the Nebaj Vase; (*d*) mural in the Temple of the Jaguars, Chichen Itza.

pottery and plaster. A small heap of disintegrated material, apparently the remains of a palm-fiber mat, was found below the plaza floor at Uaxactun. The imprint of another piece was found in the temple beneath El Castillo at Chichen Itza; the Red Jaguar Throne had rested upon this matting. The weave of this Postclassic piece was identical to that of mats still made in nearby Mérida.

Mats played an important role in ancient Maya life. The sun symbol beside a piece of matting (Fig. 12.5*a*) is the hieroglyph for the first month of the ancient Maya year, Pop, which means "matting." Sitting on a mat was a mark of authority, and throughout *The Book of Chilam Balam of Chumayel* the words "mat" and "throne" appear interchangeably. The title *ahpop*, "he of the mat," was used by rulers. The sequence of the hieroglyphic inscription on the back of Stela J at Copan follows the weave of a mat pattern in the order of its readings, whereas the superficially similar designs on two other monuments do not (Fig. 15.49).

## Featherwork

A few examples of Mexica (Aztec) featherwork from Central Mexico have been preserved, but none of the ancient Maya work has survived. The graphic art of the Classic and Postclassic periods, such as the Bonampak murals (Figs. 5.20–5.22), shows how rich and highly developed it must have been, and early Spanish writers frequently allude to it.

The forests of the Peten teem with birds of gorgeous plumage, and the northern highlands of Guatemala are the habitat of the spectacularly beautiful quetzal. Feathers were used in making panaches (ornamental tufts on headdresses), crests, capes, and shields and in decorating canopies, fans, personal ornaments, and pendants for spears and scepters. Featherwork was also used in embroideries and fringes for cotton fabrics.

One of the loveliest examples is the panache of the headdress worn by a ruler on Wall Panel 3 at Piedras Negras (Fig. 5.17). Such long plumes must have been the tail feathers of the quetzal. On Stela 12 at Piedras Negras (Fig. 14.13), a similar headdress is worn by the ruler, who also wears a short feather cape. The graceful and slightly stylized treatment of the featherwork lends distinction to these fine reliefs. Some featherwork is shown on the wooden lintels from the Temple of the Jaguars at Chichen Itza (Fig. 14.24), and another example is from Xculoc, Campeche (Fig. 15.50).

Father Bernardino de Sahagún, our greatest authority on the Mexica, tells us that they had two kinds of featherwork: "They [the Mexica] make the devices which they wear on their backs in dancing, all the costumes of the dance, and the trappings [of feathers] with which they dance and they executed the craft and profession of feather-workers in two different ways: the first kind of work consists of fastening the feathers to the background with paste in order thus to finish the work; the second way consists in doing the work and finishing it with the help of thread and cord." In describing the second of these techniques Father Sahagún writes further: "There is another kind of work, the handicraft of thread and cord. In this way they make their fans out of the plumes of the quetzal, their feather brace-lets, the devices they wear on their backs and other things, their tunics blazoned with their arms etc.; and in addition pendants, panaches, balls, tassels of feathers, with all of which they adorn themselves and decorate their fans," adding that this art, especially the use of the brightly colored feathers of tropical birds, was relatively recent among the Mexica.

Fig. 15.49. Mat patterns on the backs of Classic monuments, at various scales: (*left*) Stela J, Co-pan, Honduras, the glyph sequence following the interwoven pattern of a mat; (*center*) Monument 7, Quirigua, Guatemala, the glyph sequence following a nonwoven diagonal pattern; (*right*) Stela 3, Cancuen, Guatemala, again, with a nonwoven diagonal sequence.

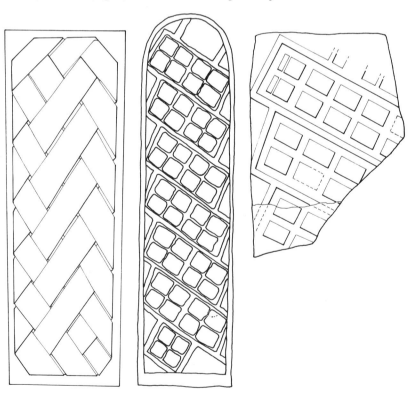

Fig. 15.50. Examples of feather headdresses carved on the doorjambs of Str. 2 at Xculoc, Campeche, Mexico.

Early Spanish writers relate the importance of this craft among the Quiche Maya of the Guatemala highlands, who had aviaries where birds were bred for their plumage. Fuentes y Guzmán, the seventeenth-century historian of Guatemala, says that the Quiche rulers at Utatlan had "places set apart for the breeding of ducks, for the sake of their plumage which they employed in weaving." Another early authority, describing the same place, states: "The throne of the king was notable because it had a canopy of very rich plumes and above this protection or covering, other coverings of different colors, in such a way as to give an effect of great majesty. The prince, or he who has to succeed, had three canopies and the other brothers or sons, two."

Besides weaving the feathers into their cotton fabrics, the Maya attached them to wood and wicker frames for headdresses. Father Morán, in his manuscript dictionary of Pokomam Mayan, defines the *mayut* as a "framework of wood adorned with plumage, which they wear on their backs in their dances." The Musées Royaux d'Art et d'Histoire du Cinquantenaire in Brussels display an ankle-length cape of macaw feathers built on a framework of wickerwork; this cape supposedly belonged to Moctezuma II, the Mexica ruler at the time of the Conquest. A quetzal-plume headdress, certainly belonging to the same ruler, is in the former Imperial Museum in Vienna.

Feathers, cotton fabrics, seashells, and semiprecious stones were used not only personally but for trade and for payment of legal penalties; in Postclassic times turquoise, copper, and gold were similarly used: "they exchanged manta [*patis*] of cotton for gold and for certain axes of copper, and gold for emeralds, turquoises and plumes. . . . At the end [the man who had committed the legal offense] was sentenced to pay a certain quantity of rich plumes, or mantas, or cacao, which went to the treasury."

The most highly prized feathers were of course the brilliant, iridescent-green tail plumes of the quetzal, which were reserved for royal use. According to Bartolomé de Las Casas, to kill or even to capture one was a capital offense: "in the province of Vera Paz [Guatemala], they punish with death him who killed the bird with the rich plumes, because it is not found in other places and these feathers were things of great value because they used them as money."

# EPILOGUE: THE SPANISH CONQUEST

11 Ahau was when the mighty men arrived from the east. They were the ones who first brought disease here to our land, the land of us who are Maya, in the year 1513.
—*Book of Chilam Balam of Chumayel* (Roys 1967: 138)

Forty-nine years have passed since the Castilians came to Xepit and Xetulul. On the day 1 Ganel the Quiches were destroyed by the Castilians. Tunatiuh Avilantaro, as he was called, conquered all the towns. Their countenances were previously unknown, and the people rendered homage to sticks and stones.
—*Annals of the Cakchiquels* (Brinton 1885: 177)

**T**ragically, contacts between alien societies often begin in peace and end in war. Such was the case in the sixteenth century when the expanding nations of Europe encountered the unexpected, a whole New World populated by an array of cultures isolated from the rest of the human race. The destructive consequences of this contact, now well known, represent one of the most catastrophic episodes in human history. In Mesoamerica and in the Andes, traditions of civilization thousands of years old were terminated by the Spanish Conquest. For the Maya, the Conquest was especially long and brutal, stretching over nearly two hundred years before the last stronghold of Maya independence was destroyed. (Most of the Maya region was subdued by the mid-sixteenth century, but it took the Spaniards another 150 years to crush the powerful Itza of the Peten; see Table E.1.) In many ways, the Maya were ill prepared for this assault, for on the eve of the Conquest the independent states of both Yucatan and the highlands were preoccupied with local conflicts that were to aid the cause of the invaders. The following account, it should be understood, is based on a heavily biased history of these events, for almost all of the records of the Spanish invasion and conquest were written by the winners in this conflict. If we did possess a thorough history of these events from the Maya perspective, there can be no doubt that what we would be relating would be not so much a tale of valorous deeds as an account of brutal subjugation—of both Maya independence and the Maya way of life.

## First Contacts, 1502–25

The first recorded contact between Europeans and the Maya occurred several decades before dreams of wealth and glory brought the armies of the conquista-

TABLE E.1

Summary of Events of the Spanish Conquest Period

| Date | Event |
|------|-------|
| 1502 | Maya trading canoe contacted in the Gulf of Honduras during Columbus's fourth voyage. |
| 1511 | Shipwrecked Spaniards captured on the east coast of Yucatan. |
| 1515 or 1516 | *Mayacimil*, "the easy death" epidemic of smallpox (?), spreads among the Maya of Yucatan. |
| 1517 | Córdoba expedition defeated in battle with the Maya after landing in Campeche. |
| 1518 | Grijalva expedition circumnavigates the Yucatan peninsula. |
| 1519 | Cortés expedition sails along the coast of Yucatan before landing on the Gulf coast to begin the conquest of Mexico. |
| 1519–21 | Cortés, aided by native forces, leads the conquest of the Mexica (Aztecs) and the destruction of their capital, Tenochtitlan. |
| 1523–24 | Alvarado, aided by Mexican and Cakchiquel Maya forces, leads the conquest of the Quiche Maya; the Quiche capital destroyed, and most Quiche leaders killed. |
| 1524 | Alvarado founds the first Spanish capital of Guatemala at Iximche, the former capital of the Cakchiquel Maya (July 25). |
| 1524–25 | Cortés expedition to Honduras passes through the Maya lowlands and discovers the independent city of Tayasal, capital of the Itza Maya. |
| 1527 | Second capital of Guatemala founded at Ciudad Vieja after a Cakchiquel-led revolt is subdued by Spanish forces. |
| 1527–28 | First unsuccessful attempt to conquer Yucatan led by Montejo the Elder. |
| 1531–35 | Second unsuccessful attempt to conquer Yucatan led by Montejo the Elder. |
| 1540–46 | Successful conquest of Yucatan led by Montejo the Younger; Spanish capital at Mérida founded January 6, 1542. |
| 1618 | Fathers Fuensalida and Orbita visit Tayasal (October). |
| 1697 | Tayasal, last capital of the Itza Maya, captured and destroyed by forces led by Martín de Ursua. |

dores to the shores of Mesoamerica: during the final voyage of Columbus, a Maya oceangoing trading canoe was contacted in the Gulf of Honduras (see Chapter 9). Subsequent voyages of exploration resulted in a series of contacts between the Spanish and Maya settlements along the coast of Yucatan.

By 1511 the Spanish had established several colonies in the Caribbean, with their capital at Havana, Cuba. In that year a Spanish official named Valdivia set out from Darien (part of present-day Panama) in a caravel for the island of Santo Domingo (present-day Haiti and Dominican Republic) to report to its governor about quarrels between Diego de Nicuesa and Vasco Nuñez de Balboa. Near Jamaica the caravel foundered and sank, but Valdivia and eighteen sailors escaped in a small boat, without sails and without food. The Yucatan Current carried the survivors westward for fourteen days, during which time seven men died. The survivors were cast upon the east coast of the Yucatan Peninsula, where further misfortunes were in store. They were seized by an unfriendly Maya lord, who sacrificed Valdivia and four companions and gave their bodies to his people for a feast. Gerónimo de Aguilar, Gonzalo de Guerrero, and five others were spared for the moment as being too thin for this cannibalistic ceremony. Says Aguilar, in describing their situation, "I together with six others remained in a coop, in order that for another festival that was approaching, being fatter, we might solemnize their banquet with our flesh."

But Aguilar and his companions escaped, and fled to the country of another lord, an enemy of the first chieftain. This second lord enslaved the Spaniards, and soon all of them except Aguilar and Guerrero died. Aguilar was serving still another Maya chieftain when Cortés reached Yucatan in 1519. Guerrero, in the meantime, had drifted farther south and entered the service of Nachan Can, the lord of Chetumal, whose daughter he married. Guerrero rose to a position of power in that province, and when Cortés's messengers offered to take him back to the Spaniards he declined, choosing to spend his life with his Maya family. Aguilar suggests that Guerrero was ashamed to rejoin his countrymen "because he has his nostrils, lips, and ears pierced and his face painted, and his hands tattooed . . . and on account of the vice he had committed with the woman and his love for his children."

The pestilence of 1515 or 1516, the *mayacimil* or "easy death," which was characterized by great pustules that "rotted their bodies with a great stench so that the limbs fell to pieces in four or five days," may have been smallpox, perhaps introduced among the Maya by survivors of the Valdivia expedition or transmitted overland from Darien by Indian traders.

## The Francisco Hernández de Córdoba Expedition, 1517

Early in 1517, Francisco Hernández de Córdoba sailed westward from Santiago de Cuba in search of slaves. It is not clear exactly where he first sighted the Yucatan mainland, but it is believed that he first landed at Isla de Mujeres, on the northeastern coast. After leaving this island, Córdoba turned northwest to Cabo Catoche and then, skirting along the north coast of the Peninsula, sailed southward as far as Bahía de Campeche, where he landed on February 23, 1517. At Campeche the Spaniards heard of a large town called Champoton, farther south along the coast, where they next landed. The lord of Champoton received the Spaniards with open hostility, and a fight ensued. In spite of the gunfire, which the Maya encountered for the first time in this battle, they fought bravely, inflicting heavy losses on the better-armed Spaniards. Córdoba himself received 33 wounds and "sadly returned to Cuba" to report the new land as very rich, a conclusion suggested to him by the gold trinkets he had found. Shortly after his return he died of his wounds.

## The Juan de Grijalva Expedition, 1518

Diego de Velásquez, governor of Cuba, was greatly excited by the reports of gold, and fitted out another expedition of four ships and two hundred men under the command of his nephew, Juan de Grijalva. Francisco de Montejo, the future conqueror of Yucatan, was also a member of this second expedition, which left Cuba in April 1518.

Grijalva's pilot was Anton de Alaminos, who had piloted the Córdoba expedition. The first landing was made at Isla de Cozumel, off the east coast, where the Maya fled at sight of the Spaniards. Grijalva continued southward along the coast, passing three large sites, one of which is described as follows:

We followed the shore day and night, and the next day toward sunset we perceived a city or town so large, that Seville would not have seemed more considerable nor better; one saw there a very large tower; on the shore was a great throng of Indians, who bore two standards which they raised and lowered to signal us to approach them; the commander [Grijalva] did not wish it. The same day we came to a beach near which was the highest tower we had seen. . . . We discovered a wide entrance lined with wooden piles set up by fishermen.

The largest of the sites seen by Grijalva was probably the archaeological site of Tulum, and the "highest tower" was almost certainly the Castillo of Tulum (Figs. 7.21 and 7.22). The large bay was Bahía de la Ascensión, so named because it was discovered on Ascension Thursday, 1518.

This was the southernmost point reached. From here Grijalva sailed north again and around the Peninsula to Campeche on the west coast. Continuing southward from Campeche, he discovered Laguna de Términos, named Río San Pablo and Río San Pedro, and entered Río Tabasco. In this region considerable treasure was obtained, including the first Mexica (Aztec) turquoise mosaic work the Spaniards had seen. Following the Gulf coast northward, Grijalva first heard of the Mexica nation, presumably somewhere on the Veracruz coast, and finally sailed as far north as Río Pánuco. On the return voyage to Cuba, the armada put in at Champoton to avenge the defeat of Córdoba, the year before. Here the Maya again attacked the Spaniards fiercely, killing one and wounding 50 others, including Grijalva. Thus frustrated, Grijalva returned to Havana, after having been away for five months.

### The Hernán Cortés Expedition, 1519

The voyage of Grijalva stirred tremendous excitement in Cuba. Yucatan was thought to be a land of gold and plenty, awaiting only the adventurous to seize its riches. A third expedition was fitted out, consisting of eleven ships, five hundred men, and some horses. Hernán Cortés was put in command of the armada, and with him went a number of other captains: Francisco de Montejo, Pedro de Alvarado, Diego de Ordaz, Gonzalo de Sandoval, Cristóbal de Olid, and Bernal Díaz del Castillo, most of them destined to win fame in the conquest of Mexico.

The armada first anchored off Isla de Cozumel, where Cortés spent several days. Idols in the temples were destroyed, and a cross was erected in one of them. While there, Cortés learned of the presence of "bearded men" on the mainland. These seemed to be Europeans, and Cortés sent messengers to summon them. In this manner Gerónimo de Aguilar was rescued, and later served Cortés well as interpreter.

Leaving Cozumel, the armada sailed around the north coast of the Peninsula and continued on to the Río Tabasco, which was renamed Río Grijalva in honor of its discoverer. In Tabasco, Cortés was given a beautiful young Maya girl named Marina. Her father, who had been a chief, seems to have died when she was young. She was given by her mother to people in Xicalango, who later gave her to others in Tabasco, and these gave her to Cortés. Marina spoke both Mayan and Nahuatl, and because Aguilar spoke Mayan and Spanish, the two of them thus supplied Cortés with a means of communicating in Nahuatl with the Mexica. They would play vital roles in the conquest of Mexico.

## The Cortés Expedition Through the Maya Lowlands, 1524–25

Hernán Cortés and his party were the first Europeans to pass through the central and southern Maya lowlands, when in 1524–25 they crossed this region on a march from Mexico to Honduras, only a few years after the conquest of the Mexica.

In 1524, Cortés sent one of his captains, Cristóbal de Olid, to subdue Honduras. Olid made the most of the opportunity, rebelling against his leader and setting himself up independently. When news of this defection reached Mexico, Cortés set out from Tenochtitlan (present-day Mexico City) on October 12, 1524, to march to Honduras, a six-month trip.

The undertaking proved to be one of the most formidable sustained efforts in military history. Because of the difficult character of the terrain, the attendant hardships and privations were almost beyond endurance, and the army was always just one step ahead of actual starvation. Cortés was accompanied by about 140 Spanish soldiers, 93 of them mounted, and by more than 3,000 warriors from Mexico, with 150 horses, a herd of pigs, artillery, munitions, and supplies. Because he dared not leave them behind, he also took Cuauhtemoc, Cohuanacox, and Tetlepanquetzal, the deposed rulers of Tenochtitlan, Texcoco, and Tlacopan. To transport such a large body of men across this wilderness would tax the strength and endurance of a well-organized modern army. When it is remembered that this expedition was undertaken in the early years of the sixteenth century, Cortés's determination and leadership are magnified to almost unbelievable proportions.

Cortés entered the Maya area in what is now central Tabasco and crossed the Río Usumacinta just below the modern town of Tenosique. Pushing eastward, he reached Acalan, ruled by a Chontal Maya lord named Paxbolon Acha, toward the close of February 1525. Somewhere near the western frontier of this province occurred the blackest deed of Cortés's career—the summary execution of the last Mexica emperor, Cuauhtemoc, and his fellow ruler, Tetlepanquetzal, lord of Tlacopan.

When these princes had surrendered at Tenochtitlan, Cortés had promised them their lives, but here in the wilds of Acalan he broke his promise. The two eye-witnesses to this tragedy who have left accounts of it are Cortés himself and one of his captains, Díaz del Castillo; both claimed that there was a conspiracy among the Mexica lords to fall upon the Spaniards and slay them. That this was no idle fear is confirmed by a recently discovered document in the files of the Archives of the Indies at Seville. This document, dated 1612, is a petition from the Chontal ruler of that day, a grandson of Paxbolon Acha. It appeals to the Crown of Spain for a pension for himself, because of his grandfather's services nearly a century earlier. The petitioner relates that Cuauhtemoc approached his grandfather and urged him to join the conspiracy against the Spaniards, pointing out how Cortés was abusing and robbing the Chontal. According to the testimony of his grandson, Paxbolon Acha was wary of these counsels and betrayed the conspiracy to the Spanish leader.

The danger was obviously great. The Spaniards were vastly outnumbered by their own native troops, and immediate action was imperative. Cortés arrested the two leaders and hanged them without delay. Pablo Paxbolon, however, says in his account of the affair that the lords were beheaded. A Mexica hieroglyphic manu-script dating from the middle sixteenth century seems to indicate that both ac-counts may be correct. This manuscript portrays Cuauhtemoc's headless body hanging by its feet from a tree. The body of the dead ruler is swathed in bandages—the Mexica symbol denoting death—and his name glyph, an eagle, is attached to his head.

Cortés, with 600 Chontal Maya as carriers, left Acalan on March 5, 1525, and reached the shores of a large lake eight days later. Here Canek, the Itza ruler, met Cortés, on the northern shore of the lake. Cortés had the Catholic priests with the expedition celebrate mass, which so impressed Canek that he promised to destroy his idols and replace them with the worship of the Cross. He invited Cortés to visit Tayasal, the Itza capital, and the invitation was accepted. Cortés took with him twenty Spanish soldiers, and the rest of the army proceeded around the lake and met him on the southern shore.

Leaving Tayasal, the army entered the rugged country on the western flanks of the Maya Mountains. Here they encountered a pass so tortuous it took the tired army twelve days to travel 32 km, and more than two-thirds of the horses were lost.

Emerging from this pass, the army reached a larger river swollen by the tor-rential rains that had never ceased falling. Turning upstream, they encountered a series of "terrifying and impetuous rapids." Today these same rapids are ironically known as "Gracias a Dios." It took the army two days to find its way over the rap-ids, and more horses were lost in the crossing. Beyond lay the village of Tenciz, which the crippled force reached on April 15, the Saturday before Easter, in 1525.

After leaving Tenciz, the army became lost in a wilderness of hills north of Lago de Izabal. The Indian guides deserted them here, and had it not been for the capture of a Maya boy, who finally led them out, they would all have died of starvation. But just beyond this point, Cortés heard definite news of the Spaniards he was seeking. To the delight of the exhausted army, it was learned that Nito, the object of their wanderings, lay only two days' journey ahead. In fact, three days passed before they finally emerged on the northwestern bank of the Río Dulce opposite Nito; here Cortés was met by Diego Nieto, representing the authorities of the settlement. Cortés and ten or twelve companions crossed immediately to the other side of the river and the rest of the army straggled in during the next five or six days.

On his march across the Maya area, Cortés visited the site of only one important Maya center, Tayasal, though he must have passed within a few miles of several others, notably Palenque, Laguna Perdida, Itsimte, Polol, Motul de San José, Ixkun, and Pusilha, ending his journey at Nito, not far from Quirigua.

## The Period of Conquest, 1524–1697

The conquest of both the Mexican and Maya peoples was facilitated by the superior arms of the Spanish, since they alone possessed firearms and cavalry. But other factors were just as important. In the first place, the Spanish could not have succeeded without the assistance of the Mexican and Maya warriors who joined their cause. For the native armies, the principal motive for these alliances was vengeance for past grievances. In Mexico, the Tlaxcalans joined Cortés to defeat their traditional enemy, the Mexica. In the Maya highlands, the Cakchiquel would join Alvarado for a time and help him vanquish their old enemies, the Quiche. Thus, in the conquest of the Maya the Spanish frequently took advantage of preexisting rivalries among the independent states of both Yucatan and the highlands.

A second factor contributing to the Spanish success cannot be overestimated. The Europeans brought with them a series of Old World diseases for which the Maya and other New World peoples had no immunities, and as a result, epidemics often decimated armies and entire populations even before the battle lines were drawn.

## The Subjugation of the Southern Maya by Pedro de Alvarado, 1524–27

After the fall of Tenochtitlan, the Mexica capital, in 1521, Cortés received representatives from various powers seeking to express their allegiance to the new masters of Mexico. Several accounts mention that one delegation came to Tenochtitlan from the Cakchiquel capital of Iximche, and another may have come from the Quiche capital of Utatlan.

In the following year, Cortés sent a small party of Mexican allies to reconnoiter the borders of the southern Maya area. In the province of Soconusco, on the Pacific coast of what is now Chiapas, the patrol met delegations from both Iximche and

Utatlan. Cortés later reported that, on that occasion, both highland Maya states declared their vassalage to the King of Spain. But according to his account, he learned later that the Cakchiquel and Quiche

have not kept faith, but are molesting the towns of Soconusco because they are our friends. On the other hand, the Christians [native allies in Soconusco] have written me that they [the highland Maya] constantly send messages to excuse themselves, saying that these things had been done by others, and that they had no part in it. So, to learn the truth of this, I dispatched Pedro de Alvarado with 80 horsemen and 200 foot soldiers, amongst whom were many crossbowmen and musketeers; he took four field pieces and artillery, and a great supply of ammunition and powder.

The departure of Alvarado's expedition was delayed. But by the time it was ready to leave, on December 6, 1523, Cortés had seen fit to strengthen his "fact-finding mission" to 120 cavalry (with 50 spare horses), 300 infantry, and an unspecified number of Mexican warriors, along with the four artillery pieces.

Throughout the trials of the conquest of Mexico, Alvarado had served as Cortés's principal captain. Díaz del Castillo had served with Alvarado, and described him in his *True History of the Conquest of New Spain*: "He was about thirty-four years old when he came here, of good size, and well proportioned, with a very cheerful countenance and a winning smile, and because he was so handsome the Mexicans gave him the name of *Tonatio*, which means the Sun." But Alvarado was also infamous for his cruelty and his inhuman treatment of his foes. While in temporary command of the Spanish army in Tenochtitlan he led a brutal massacre of the Mexica. And his conquest of Guatemala was punctuated by numerous reports of similar events. According to Bartolomé de Las Casas, Alvarado's Maya conquests were heinous: "He advanced killing, ravaging, burning, robbing, and destroying all the country wherever he came, under the pretext, namely, that the Indians should subject themselves to such inhuman, unjust and cruel men, in the name of the unknown King of Spain, of whom they had never heard and whom they considered to be much more unjust and cruel than his representatives."

Las Casas goes on to itemize the atrocities committed by Alvarado during the conquest of the southern Maya area. There is no reason to reject Las Casas's account, for Alvarado's own letters, which provide the best history of the conquest of Guatemala, allude to the terror tactics he employed against the defenseless populace: "And, after entering in the houses we struck down the people, and continued the pursuit as far as the market place and half a league beyond. . . . " In late 1523 Alvarado's force marched from Mexico to Soconusco, following the ancient trade route from Tehuantepec along the Pacific coast. No opposition appeared until the Spanish reached the Río Samala, in what is now western Guatemala. There, in the coastal province held by the Quiche, a native force tried and failed to block the army's progress. Once across the river, the invaders rampaged through the nearby settlements, hoping to strike terror into the Quiche who still resisted.

From this point, Alvarado turned north to attack the heartland of the Quiche state, crossing over the mountain pass and into the rich valley of Quetzaltenango. In the pass, Alvarado's contingent of Mexican warriors was driven back by the Quiche, but a charge by the Spanish cavalry won the day, for "as they had never seen horses they showed much fear, and we made a very good advance and scattered them and many of them died."

Alvarado's force was soon able to enter the deserted city of Xelahu, once the major center in the valley, called Quetzaltenango by Alvarado's Mexican allies (most place names in the southern Maya area today bear Nahuatl names, because the Mexicans, Nahuatl speakers, served as interpreters for the new masters of the lands).

Six days later a climactic battle was fought in the valley of Quetzaltenango, as the Quiche made yet another attempt to stop the invaders.

We commenced to crush them and scattered them in all directions and followed them in pursuit for two leagues and a half until all of them were routed and nobody was left in front of us. Later we returned against them, and our friends [the Mexican allies] and the infantry made the greatest destruction in the world at a river. They surrounded a bare mountain where they had taken refuge, and pursued them to the top, and took all that had gone up there. That day we killed and imprisoned many people, many of whom were captains and chiefs and people of importance.

One of the Quiche commanders that led the fight against the Spanish was Tecun Uman, a hero of his people. But Tecun Uman and many other leaders were killed in battle, and the Quiche resistance was nearly exhausted. The Quiche then sued for peace, offering tribute, and invited Alvarado to enter their capital, Gumarcaaj, known as Tecpan Utatlan in Nahuatl. The ever-suspicious Alvarado sensed a trap, believing that the Quiche "would lodge me there, and that when thus encamped, they would set fire to the town some night and burn us all in it, without the possibility of resistance." Nevertheless, Alvarado accepted the Quiche offer and ordered his force to proceed to Utatlan.

When the Spanish came to Utatlan (Fig. 7.29), Alvarado believed that his fears were well founded.

And in truth their evil plan would have come to pass but that God our Lord did not see good that these infidels should be victorious over us, for this city is very, very strong, and there are only two ways of entering it; one of over thirty steep stone steps and the other by a causeway. . . . And as we rode up and I could see how large the stronghold was, and that within it we could not avail ourselves of the horses because the streets were so narrow and walled in, I determined at once to clear out of it on to the plain . . . and outside the city there were many warriors, and as they saw me pass out on to the plain, they retreated, but not so much that I did not receive much harm from them. But I concealed it all so that I might capture the chiefs who were taking flight, and by the cunning with which I approached them, and through presents which I gave them, the better to carry out my plan, I took them captive and held them prisoners in my camp.

The chiefs Alvarado captured by his cunning were the highest officials of Utatlan, Oxib-Queh, the *ahpop* of the Quiche, and the *ahpop c'amha*, Beleheb-Tzy. "And I knew them to have such a bad disposition toward the service of His Majesty, and to insure the good and peace of this land, I burnt them, and sent to burn the town and destroy it. . . ."

With Utatlan destroyed and its rulers dead, Alvarado sent a delegation to Tecpan Quauhtemalan ("City of Guatemala," or Iximche), the Cakchiquel capital, asking them to join him in the final defeat of the Quiche. The Cakchiquel were, until the arrival of the Spanish, the paramount new power in the highlands, and the traditional enemy of the Quiche. According to Alvarado, they sent a force of four thousand warriors (although the *Annals of the Cakchiquels* mentions only four hundred) and joined the Spanish against the Quiche.

From Utatlan, Alvarado was received by his new Cakchiquel allies into their capital of Iximche. The Cakchiquel appear to have thought that they could use their new alliance to vanquish another of their enemies, the Tzutuhil. At the request of the Cakchiquel, Alvarado sent two messengers to the Tzutuhil capital, Tecpan Atitlan. And when the news arrived that they had been killed, the Spaniards and their Cakchiquel allies attacked the Tzutuhil. Following their defeat in a battle on the shores of Lago de Atitlan, the Tzutuhil offered tribute and allegiance to the King of Spain.

From the highlands, Alvarado launched a further expedition to the Pacific coast and eastward to conquer the Pipil province of Cuscatlan, in what is now El Salvador. He then returned to the Maya highlands, and on July 25, 1524, founded the first Spanish capital of the province of Guatemala, at Iximche. But the first capital was short-lived, for as related in the *Annals of the Cakchiquels*, the oppressive policies of the Spanish brought revolt from their former allies.

There was no fighting and Tunatiuh (Tonatio, "the Sun," as Alvarado was known) rejoiced when he entered Iximche. Thus did the Castilians enter of yore, o my children; but it was a fearful thing when they entered; their faces were strange, and the chiefs took them for gods. . . . Then Tunatiuh began to ask the chiefs for money. He wished that they should give him jars full of precious metals, and even their drinking cups and crowns. Not receiving anything, Tunatiuh became angry and said to the chiefs: "Why have you not given me the metal? If you do not bring me the precious metal in all your towns, choose then, for I shall burn you alive and hang you." Thus did he speak to the chiefs.

War soon broke out again, and the Spanish were driven from their new capital at Iximche. For the next several years the highland Maya, led by the Cakchiquel, fought a desperate campaign in an attempt to drive the Spanish from the highlands. But in the end the Maya were defeated. On November 22, 1527, a new Spanish capital, known today as Ciudad Vieja, was founded at the foot of Agua volcano. Fourteen years later it was devastated by a mudslide from the volcano, and the colonial capital was reestablished nearby in the city now known as Antigua Guatemala. With the highlands more or less subdued, the Spanish could turn their attention to the Maya of the north.

## The Subjugation of Yucatan by the Montejos, 1527–46

Francisco de Montejo was a member of both the Grijalva and the Cortés expeditions. He did not take part in the conquest of Mexico, however, having been sent to Spain in 1519 by Cortés, in charge of the King's share of the treasure that had been collected. At the same time, Montejo was to plead Cortés's cause at the Spanish court, for it seems that Cortés's unauthorized departure from Cuba had brought him into open conflict with Diego de Velásquez, the governor of Cuba.

During the seven years Montejo was at court, he did that and more—he applied to the King of Spain on his own behalf for permission to conquer Yucatan. In a royal decree, dated December 8, 1526, Montejo was granted the hereditary title of Adelantado, and the crown authorized him to raise an army for the conquest and colonization of the Peninsula. The conquest of Yucatan would consume twenty years.

### First Phase: An Attempt from the East, 1527–28

The Montejo armada, consisting of three ships and four hundred men, set sail from Spain in 1527, with Alonso d'Avila as second in command. A stop was made at Santo Domingo to pick up supplies and horses, and one ship was left behind to bring additional supplies later. The two other ships made Isla de Cozumel toward the end of September, where Ah Naum Pat, the lord of Cozumel, received them peaceably. After a brief stop, the ships sailed for the mainland, where Montejo took possession of the land in the name of God and the King of Castile, somewhere near the town of Xelha in Ekab.

To quell a mutiny among his troops, Montejo set fire to his two ships. Leaving 40 men at Xelha under the command of d'Avila, and another 20 at the nearby town of Pole, he set out with 125 men on a tour of the towns and villages in the northeastern corner of the Peninsula. None of the towns visited survives today, and even the location of most of them is unknown: Xamanha, Mochis, and Belma; the last may perhaps be identified with the modern settlement of El Meco. Here the chiefs of the surrounding towns were called together to swear allegiance to the Spanish crown.

From Belma the little army proceeded to Conil in Ekab, a settlement that is said to have been composed of five thousand houses; here the Spaniards rested for two months. They left Conil in the spring of 1528 for the capital of Chauaca, where the first serious encounter took place. The Maya, abandoning the town in the night, attacked vigorously the next morning, but were defeated.

From Chauaca the army moved to Ake, 16 km north of the modern town of Tizimin. There a great battle took place, in which more than 1,200 Maya were killed. In this action

the Indians appeared with all the arms which they use in the wars: quivers of arrows, poles with their tips hardened by fire, lances with points of sharp flints, two-handed swords of very strong woods inset with obsidian blades, whistles, and beating the shells of great turtles with deer horns, trumpets of large conch-shells of the sea; naked except for the shameful parts which were covered with a cloth, [their bodies] daubed with earth of divers colors, so they appeared as most ferocious devils; their noses and ears pierced with nose- and ear-plugs of bone and stones of varied colors.

Following this battle, all the neighboring Maya chiefs surrendered.

From Ake, the Spaniards went to Sisia and Loche, and then returned to Xelha by an inland route. But at Xelha, Montejo found his first settlement in desperate straits: of the 40 Spaniards he had left there, only twelve remained, and all twenty of those stationed at Pole had been massacred. Of the 125 Spaniards who had accompanied him on his journey, only 60 returned, and the entire force must now have numbered fewer than a hundred men.

Later, the third vessel of his flotilla having arrived from Santo Domingo, Montejo decided to continue his exploration of the coast to the south. D'Avila was sent overland, and Montejo, sailing southward, discovered a settlement called Chetumal on a good bay (Bahía de Chetumal, in modern Belize) and learned that Gonzalo de Guerrero, the Valdivia survivor, was in the vicinity. Montejo sent messengers to persuade him to rejoin his countrymen, but Guerrero again refused.

The Adelantado and d'Avila failed to meet in Chetumal, for the Maya had been purposely keeping them apart by false reports. D'Avila, after waiting some time, made his way back to Xelha and moved the Spanish settlement from this location to the nearby town of Xamanha. And Montejo, after waiting in vain for d'Avila to appear at Chetumal, continued southward to the Río Ulúa in Honduras and then turned back, rejoining his lieutenant at Xamanha. Late in 1528, leaving d'Avila at Xamanha as lieutenant governor, Montejo sailed around the northern coast of the Peninsula and returned to New Spain (Mexico), ending the first attempt to conquer Yucatan.

## First Interval, 1528–31

Montejo, having secured an appointment as *alcalde mayor* of the province of Tabasco, left Mexico City for Tabasco in 1529, taking with him his son, also named Francisco de Montejo. They succeeded in subduing the province and founded the town of Salamanca at Xicalango, near the north coast. D'Avila, recalled from the east coast of Yucatan, was sent to reduce Acalan south and east of Laguna de Términos.

Montejo did not long enjoy his new post in Tabasco, however; the former governor, regaining power there, threw him into prison. Later the Adelantado was allowed to rejoin his son at Xicalango, and both father and son went on to Champoton, in southwestern Yucatan, where d'Avila had preceded them.

## Second Phase: An Attempt from the West, 1531–35

From Champoton the Adelantado moved to Campeche. With this as his base of operations, he launched the second attempt to conquer Yucatan. D'Avila was dispatched to Chauaca in the east. On his way there he passed through Mani, where the Xiu gave him a friendly reception. Finally he reached Chetumal, far to the southeast, where he founded Villa Real, or "royal town." The natives here resisted so stubbornly that d'Avila had to abandon the newly founded town and to embark in canoes for Honduras. He got as far as Trujillo before turning back, after an absence of two years.

After the departure of d'Avila for the east in 1531, the Montejos withstood a strong attack at Campeche in which the elder Montejo nearly lost his life. The Spaniards prevailed, however, and accepted the surrender of Ah Canul, north of Campeche.

Montejo next sent his son to conquer the northern provinces, instructing him to divide among his followers the services of the Maya they encountered. The younger Montejo first went to the province of the Cupules, to the site of the former Itza capital at Chichen Itza, where he was received somewhat reluctantly by the Cupul ruler, Naabon Cupul. Montejo, finding the population submissive, founded the first Ciudad Real, or "royal city," at Chichen Itza and divided the towns and villages of the region among his soldiers, each Spaniard being allotted the services of two to three thousand Maya.

The Cupules soon became dissatisfied under Spanish rule. After six months of the foreign yoke, Naabon Cupul tried to kill Montejo, but lost his own life in the attempt. The death of their ruler so exacerbated their hatred for the Spaniards that about the middle of 1533 the Cupules blockaded the small Spanish garrison at Chichen Itza. Fortunately for the invaders, however, the Xiu, Chel, and Pech polities of the western peninsula remained loyal.

The younger Montejo, seeing the countryside roused against him, decided to abandon the royal city (which in fact was probably no more than a small military camp) and to rejoin his father in the west. To accomplish this maneuver, according to an early chronicler, he resorted to the following ruse:

. . . finally one night they abandoned the town, leaving a dog attached to the clapper of a bell, and a little bread placed at one side so that he could not reach it; and the same day they wearied the Indians with skirmishes, so that they should not follow them. The dog rang the bell in his efforts to reach the bread, which greatly astonished the Indians, who thought the

Spaniards wished to attack them; later, when they learned how they had been tricked, they resolved to look for the Spaniards in all directions as they did not know which road they had taken. And those who had taken the same road overtook the Spaniards, shouting loudly as at people who were running away, because of which six horsemen awaited them in an open place and speared many. One of the Indians seized a horse by the leg and felled it as though it were a sheep.

Young Montejo finally reached Dzilam in the polity of the Chels, where the young lord, Namux Chel, received him with friendship. Later in the spring of 1534 Montejo rejoined his father at Dzibikal in Chakan, near T'ho (the present Mérida).

Meanwhile, the Adelantado had advanced inland as far as Mani, and had visited the Xiu ruler there. Throughout the Conquest, the Xiu repeatedly showed their friendship for the Spaniards, and it was largely owing to their aid that Spanish authority was established permanently. The Montejos met at Dzibikal, and shortly afterward the Adelantado founded the second royal city, at Dzilam, where the Spaniards are said to have "suffered many privations and dangers."

When the Adelantado determined to return to Campeche, the friendly Namux Chel offered to conduct him there, accompanied by two of his cousins. The cousins were taken in chains, perhaps as hostages, though Namux Chel was provided with a horse for the long overland journey. Montejo left his son at Dzilam to carry on the work of conquest and pacification as best he might. The Adelantado was well received by the Maya around Campeche, where he was presently joined by d'Avila and shortly afterward by his son, who found his position at Dzilam no longer tenable.

At this point the conquest of Yucatan received a setback. News of the conquest of Peru and of the riches to be had there reached the disheartened followers of Montejo at Campeche. The Spaniards had been fighting through northern Yucatan for seven years, and had found no more gold than would fill a few helmets. They had begun to realize that there would be none of the rich rewards that the soldiers of Cortés had reaped in Mexico, or that the companions of Pizarro were now gaining in Peru, and the Adelantado could no longer hold his already depleted forces together. The little army dwindled until it became necessary to abandon the conquest of the Peninsula a second time. Late in 1534 or early in 1535, the Montejos withdrew from Campeche to Veracruz with the remnants of their army.

## Second Interval, 1535–40

Since he had first visited Honduras in 1528, the Adelantado had been petitioning the Spanish king for the governorship of that province. Combined with the *adelantazgo* of Yucatan and certain administrative rights in Tabasco and Chiapas, this would have given him jurisdiction over all of what is now southern Mexico and northern Central America. In answer to his petitions, Montejo was named governor and captain general of Honduras-Hibüeras in 1535, although notice of the appointment did not reach him until after he had left Yucatan for Tenochtitlan. He did not actually return to Honduras until 1537.

From the outset the Honduras episode was unsuccessful. Montejo found himself seriously embroiled with another Adelantado, Pedro de Alvarado, who had been named governor and captain general of Guatemala by royal appointment. But Alvarado claimed jurisdictional rights over Honduras as well as Guatemala, and in August 1539 Montejo was obliged to relinquish his interests in Honduras-Hibüeras to Alvarado. Montejo returned to Tabasco, where in his father's absence Montejo the younger had been acting as lieutenant governor and captain general.

In 1535 the Franciscan Brother Jacobo de Testera had gone to Champoton to subdue Yucatan by peaceful means. The Crown had promised him that all Spanish soldiers would be excluded from the country while he attempted to subjugate it by preaching. He was enjoying some success in this enterprise when Captain Lorenzo de Godoy appeared at Champoton with Spanish soldiers sent by Montejo the Younger to subdue the region. Trouble between Testera and Godoy broke out, and the priest was forced to return to Mexico.

Under Godoy, affairs at Champoton went from bad to worse. The Couohs of the surrounding region became more and more warlike until, in 1537, Montejo the Younger was obliged to send his cousin from Tabasco to take charge of the situation. The new Spanish leader, more politic than Godoy, persuaded the Couohs to a less hostile stance, but want and misery continued, and this last Spanish toehold in Yucatan became more and more precarious.

### Third Phase: Conquest Completed, 1540–46

The Adelantado was now about 67 years old and had been trying unsuccessfully for 13 years to conquer Yucatan. Weary, disillusioned, and impoverished, he resolved to entrust the conquest to his son. In 1540 he drew up a formal document turning over the conquest of Yucatan to his son and giving him elaborate instructions. Early in 1541 Montejo the younger left Tabasco for Champoton, where his cousin had already been stationed for more than two years. Shortly after his arrival, Montejo moved his headquarters to Campeche, which was the first permanent Spanish *cabildo*, or town government, to be set up in the northern Maya area. The army again numbered between three and four hundred soldier-colonists under the command of Montejo the son.

Early in 1541 Montejo summoned the Maya lords to Campeche to render submission to the Spanish crown. The Xiu ruler and a number of neighboring caciques obeyed the summons, but the polity of Ah Canul refused, whereupon Montejo dispatched his cousin to subdue the Ah Canules, while he remained behind to await the arrival of new recruits. His cousin met the Ah Canules in Chakan, near T'ho, and on the following January 6, 1542, he founded "The Very Noble and Very Loyal City of Mérida," setting up the second Spanish *cabildo* in Yucatan.

Seventeen days after the founding of Mérida, Spanish sentries stationed at the base of the pyramid where Montejo's army was encamped sighted a throng of warriors escorting a young Maya lord seated in a palanquin. From the deference shown him it was obvious that he was a person of high status. The Spaniards were terrified, fearing an immediate attack in force, but the lord made signs that he had come in peace, bringing with him food, which the Spaniards direly needed.

Through an interpreter, this personage indicated that he was the lord Tutul Xiu, supreme ruler of Mani, that he admired the bravery of the white men, and that he wanted to know them and see some of their religious ceremonies. Montejo ordered the chaplain of the army to celebrate "a solemn Adoration of the Holy Cross," in which all the Spanish soldiers took part. The Xiu ruler was deeply impressed, and said that he wished to become a Christian. He stayed at the Spanish camp for two months, during which time he was instructed in the Catholic faith and baptized Melchor.

The results of this visit were far-reaching. Since the fall of Mayapan a century earlier, the Xiu province of Mani had been the most powerful polity in northern Yucatan, and its peaceful submission to the Spaniards was followed by that of other western polities. Before leaving Mérida, Melchor promised to send ambassadors to the other Maya lords, urging them to give obedience to Montejo, and the pacification of the west was accomplished without further fighting. The east, however, remained unconquered.

Following the submission of the western polities, Montejo the younger sent his cousin to Chauaca. All of the eastern lords except the Cochua chieftains received him peacefully, and after a brief but bitterly contested campaign against the Cochua lords, Montejo defeated them.

Next the Cupules, incited by their priests, revolted and were subdued. Montejo finally reached the east coast at Pole, in Ekab, and tried to cross to Isla de Cozumel, but was prevented from doing so by stormy weather. In the attempt, however, nine Spaniards were drowned and a tenth was killed by the Maya. Exaggerated reports of these losses encouraged both the Cupules and the Cochuas to rebel again.

Landa describes the unrest among the eastern Maya: "The Indians received with sorrow the yoke of slavery, but the Spaniards had the towns of the country well divided into *repartimientos* [individual holdings]." The eastern polities—Cupul, Cochua, Sotuta, and Chetumal, and to a lesser degree the Tazes—managed to regain their independence, and it was obvious that further military action would be needed.

The conquest of Yucatan was drawing to a close, but one more rebellion was to occur before final Spanish victory. This revolt involved an alliance of almost all of the eastern polities, and the night of November 8, 1546, was chosen for the uprising. By way of friendly Maya, Mérida and Campeche had word of the impending revolt, but in the east the surprise was complete. Says a contemporary Spanish writer:

Late in the year of '46 the natives of all these provinces, of the Cupules, Tazes, and Chikin Cheles rose and rebelled against His Majesty, making a great massacre of the Spanish *encomenderos* [those among whom the Indians had been divided] of whom they killed eighteen Spaniards who were in their towns, where they sacrificed them . . . and besides more than four hundred Indian free-men who had served the Spaniards as servants, without leaving anything alive, if it was a thing that savoured of the Spanish, including the herds and other things, until help came from the city of Mérida in the same year and the natives became peaceful again, the culprits being punished.

When the revolt began, both of the younger Montejos were in Campeche, awaiting the arrival of the Adelantado from Chiapas. The Adelantado reached Mérida in December and raised additional troops from his plantations at Champoton and Campeche. After losing twenty Spaniards and several hundred of the loyal Maya allies, they defeated the coalition of the eastern Maya lords in a single engagement. With these victories, in 1546, the conquest of Yucatan was concluded.

## The Independent Itza, 1525–1696

With the conquest of Yucatan completed, there remained only one independent Maya group—the powerful Itza nation, centered in the lake region of the Peten. The Itza were able to resist the Spaniards and to maintain their political independence for another century and three-quarters.

Tayasal, the Itza capital, was situated on an island in Lago Peten Itza (Fig. 1.10), a long distance both from Mérida in northern Yucatan and from Antigua, the Spanish capital in the southern highlands. For nearly a century after Cortés had visited Tayasal in 1525, neither Yucatan nor Guatemala attempted to reduce the remote and hostile province of the Itza. Between 1550 and 1556, Franciscan missionaries had made evangelizing expeditions from Campeche into Acalan and had persuaded the Chontal Maya of that region to move nearer to Campeche, where they could be instructed in the Catholic faith, but the warlike Itza, farther to the southeast, were left alone.

In 1618 two Franciscans, Fathers Bartolomé de Fuensalida and Juan de Orbita, having secured permission to attempt to Christianize the Itza peaceably, set out from Mérida for Tayasal. They left Mérida in the spring of 1618, traveling by way of Laguna de Bacalar, and were accompanied by the *alcalde* of Bacalar and a number of Maya converts. With the delays incident to travel, the fathers did not reach Tayasal until nearly six months later. Canek, the Itza ruler, received them with friendliness.

They remained at Tayasal for some days, attempting to Christianize the Itza, but Canek, though interested in the services held by the missionaries, refused to renounce his own religion. He believed that the time had not yet arrived when, according to their ancient prophecies, the Itza were to accept a new faith.

The fathers were shown a large idol in the form of a horse, called Tzimin Chac, the "thunder horse." When Cortés had visited Tayasal, he left a lame horse with the Canek of that day, promising to return for it himself or to send for it. After Cortés's departure, the Itza treated the horse as a god, offering it fowl, other meats, and flowers, on which diet the horse died. The Itza later made a stone idol of the horse. When Father Orbita saw this image, the idolatry so enraged him that he smashed the image to bits. The Itza, outraged at such a sacrilege, tried to kill the missionaries, but Father Fuensalida seized the occasion to preach a sermon of such eloquence that the tumult subsided and the missionaries' lives were spared. When the fathers saw that they were making no progress in Christianizing the Itza, they took friendly farewell of Canek, who seems to have borne them no ill will for destroying the idol. Father Fuensalida reached Mérida on December 8, 1618, but Father Orbita remained at Tipu, a small settlement near Laguna de Bacalar.

In September of the following year, the fathers set out from Tipu for Tayasal a second time, accompanied by some Tipu guides and servants. They reached the Itza capital at the beginning of October and remained there for eighteen days. Although Canek was at first friendly, the Tipu Maya were suspicious of the Itza and deserted in a body (later, however, three of them came back to serve the fathers). The Itza priests were becoming jealous of the growing influence of the Catholic missionaries and persuaded Canek's wife to urge her husband to expel them. The fathers' house was surrounded by armed warriors, and the fathers themselves were hustled into a canoe with their Tipu servants and told never to return. The Itza wanted no more of their religion. Father Orbita offered some resistance, but a young Itza warrior seized the collar of his habit and twisted it so violently that Orbita fell to the ground senseless. The party was pushed off in a canoe without food or drink, the Itza hoping that they would die of hunger on the long trip back to Tipu.

The Tipu Maya, however, had managed to secrete a little food, and the five subsisted on this until they reached Tipu. The fathers rested there for only a few days before they returned to Mérida.

Three years later, in 1622, the governor of Yucatan authorized Captain Francisco de Mirones to conduct a military expedition against the Itza. On March 30 of that year, Mirones with 20 Spaniards and 140 Indians left Hopelchen in Campeche for the Itza country. A Franciscan missionary, Father Diego Delgado, joined the army later. At Sacalum, finding Mirones's treatment of the Maya inexcusably brutal, Father Delgado decided to leave the soldiers and go on without them. He left camp secretly and proceeded to Tayasal by way of Tipu, taking with him 80 converted Tipu Maya. Father Delgado and his converts were escorted to Tayasal by the Itza with a great show of friendship. But on reaching the town, all were seized and sacrificed to the Itza idols.

News of the death of Father Delgado reached Mérida slowly, but as soon as the authorities at the capital heard of it they sent word to Captain Mirones at Sacalum to be on his guard. But the news came too late. On February 2, 1624, the Spaniards at Sacalum were all in the village church, without arms, when the Itza fell upon them and slaughtered them.

These two massacres put a stop to all attempts either to Christianize the Itza or to conquer them. When, about twelve years later, the Tipu converts began to apostatize, and to return to idolatry, the last link of friendly contact between northern Yucatan and the province of the Itza was severed. And thus affairs remained for nearly three-quarters of a century. The Spanish continued to consolidate their positions in Yucatan and in Guatemala, but the territory between remained unconquered and un-Christianized, a continual irritation to both the military and the ecclesiastical authorities of the two provinces.

In June 1695, Martin de Ursua, governor of Yucatan, sent a contingent of Spanish soldiers and Maya workers to the village of Cauich in northern Campeche, to begin the construction of a road to the Peten. Toward the end of the month, the road builders reached a village called Nohthub in southern Campeche, where three Franciscans headed by Father Andres de Avendaño joined them. But disgusted by the Spanish captain's treatment of the Maya, the priests soon returned to Mérida.

On December 15, 1695, Father Avendaño again left Mérida for the province of the Itza, accompanied by two other Franciscans, four Maya singers from Yucatan, and three Maya guides. Instead of proceeding by way of Tipu, Father Avendaño followed the new road as far south as it had been built and then pushed on through the forests with his Maya guides.

They reached the lake on January 13, 1696, and were given a boisterous reception by the Chakan Itza living at the western end. The next day the ruler Canek met them there, having crossed from Tayasal with an escort of 80 canoes. The fathers returned to Tayasal with Canek and remained there for three and a half days, baptizing more than three hundred Itza children. Thus emboldened, Father Avendaño urged Canek and his councillors to surrender to the Crown of Spain and accept Christianity. The Itza council took this proposal under advisement, but again decided that the time had not yet arrived when their prophecies had foretold that they should abandon their old gods. They promised that if Governor Ursua would send the fathers back in another four months, the Itza would declare allegiance to the Spanish king and embrace Christianity.

Canek, learning of a plot among the Chakan Itza to waylay and kill the fathers on their return trip, persuaded Avendaño to return to Mérida by the longer though safer route through Tipu. On the night of January 17, 1696, having taken an affectionate farewell of Canek and his family, the three fathers and their guides embarked from Yucatan in a canoe.

From this point on, back luck and increasing hardships beset the fathers. The promised guides to Tipu were not forthcoming, and on January 20, after waiting two days, they set out on the long, dangerous return journey to northern Yucatan. At the end of five days the party came to a large stream, probably the Río Holmul, which they followed for another five days, becoming hopelessly lost. At this point they determined to strike west, hoping to reach the road that Ursua was having built from Cauich to the shores of the lake. They pushed on in this direction for fifteen days more, living on a meager diet of wild honey, green mammee, and palm nuts. On the fourth day of this exhausting trek Avendaño became so weak that the other two Franciscans, taking with them one of the four guides, pushed on in the hope of locating some frontier settlement and bringing back help and supplies.

After six more days of slow, painstaking progress, Father Avendaño came upon the ruins of an ancient city, which he describes as follows:

With so few comforts and so many hardships my strength was failing rapidly, which brought home to me the truth of the adage that the Biscayans, my countrymen, have, namely, that "the belly supports, or carries the legs, and not the legs, the belly."

Among these high mountains which we passed there are a number of ancient buildings; among them I recognized some as living places, and although they were very high and my strength very little, I climbed them, but with difficulty. They are in the form of a convent with small cloisters and many rooms for living, all roofed, surrounded by a terrace and whitened with lime inside, which latter abounds in these parts, because all the hills are of limestone; and these said buildings are of such form that they did not appear like those of this province [Yucatan] which latter are entirely of dressed stone put together without mortar, especially as to their arches, but these [in Peten] are of stone masonry plastered over with lime.

The archaeological site best answering this description is Tikal. Father Avendaño was perhaps the first European to see this greatest of all ancient Maya centers.

Avendaño traveled westward and northward for another three days until his strength gave out altogether. He ordered his Maya companions to leave him propped against a tree with a lighted fire and a gourd of water, and to push on for help. The next morning his companions returned with ten carriers. After leaving Avendaño the day before, they had come out on a trail that led them to Chuntuqui on the new road from Cauich. Here they found some Maya porters who agreed to return with them to rescue the father. The porters carried him in a hammock to Chuntuqui, where they arrived on February 19, 1696, after being lost for 31 days. At Chuntuqui he found the two other Franciscans, who had left him eighteen days before in search of help. After resting at Chuntuqui for a few days, Avendaño and his companions continued to Mérida, where they reported on their mission.

## The Subjugation of the Itza, 1696–97

Although the road from Cauich to the Peten had been opened for 80 km beyond Chuntuqui by September 1695, heavy rains prevented the movement of supplies along this route. The road gangs were in fact obliged to return to Zucthok, north of the present boundary between Mexico and Guatemala, until the rainy season was over.

An embassy from Canek, which reached Mérida in December 1695, convinced Ursua that the Itza were at last ready to submit to Spanish rule. He ordered Captain Paredes, who was still at work on the road, to proceed to Tayasal. Paredes, unable to comply with the order in person, sent Captain Pedro de Zubiaur, with 60 Spanish soldiers, some Maya warriors, and Father San Buenaventura, to take possession of the Itza lands.

By this time the road had advanced to within 32 km of the lake, and Zubiaur's command reached the shore on January 18, 1696. Zubiaur had expected a peaceful reception by the Itza, but as the Spaniards approached the lake, they saw a flotilla of canoes filled with armed warriors advancing toward them. Leaping ashore, the Itza attacked vigorously, seizing some of the Maya from Yucatan as prisoners. Father San Buenaventura, a lay Franciscan brother, and a Spanish soldier were also taken prisoner, and a fourth Spaniard was killed in the fight. The Itza numbered about two thousand.

Battle having been forced upon them, the Spaniards defended themselves bravely, but finding his force outnumbered, Zubiaur withdrew to the main camp of Captain Paredes. A day or so later, a second and larger Spanish force was dispatched to the lake. When it met with a similarly hostile reception, further attempts to press the attack were discontinued.

The news of the Chaken Itza's hostility to Father Avendaño and word of Zubiaur's defeat reached Ursua at the same time. It was evident that the Itza could be reduced only by military force, and Ursua ordered that one hundred extra soldiers, shipwrights, and carpenters be dispatched to build a dugout and a galley to navigate the lake, wherewith an armed force could dominate Tayasal and the other villages. The men were recruited in Mérida and sent to Paredes, with instructions to press forward the work of opening the road the remaining 32 km. But Ursua, at this time, became embroiled in a lawsuit with a political rival, and ordered Captain Paredes to retire to Campeche to await his coming with larger forces the next year.

The close of 1696 and the beginning of 1697 were spent in reassembling the army at Campeche. The reconstituted army consisted of 235 Spanish soldiers, 120 Maya muleteers and road workers, and a number of porters. The infantry, artillery, and supply trains were sent ahead under Paredes, with orders to Zubiaur to proceed to within 8 km of the lake with the ship carpenters and caulkers. They were to cut and trim sufficient timber for a galley and a dugout, and to await the arrival of the rest of the army. On January 14, 1697, Ursua left Campeche with the cavalry, his personal suite, and the rest of the supplies, and on March 1, the needed timber ready, the whole army moved forward to the shore of the lake, where a fortified camp was built.

For the next twelve days the Itza undertook hostile demonstrations against the Spanish camp. Flotillas of canoes maneuvered in front of the camp daily. Companies of painted warriors surrounded it on the landward side, beating their war drums and threatening the Spaniards with death and sacrifice. On March 10, a number of canoes were seen approaching the camp from the direction of Tayasal, the first canoe carrying a white flag. It was an embassy from Canek, consisting of the Itza high priest and other chiefs, who came to offer peace. Ursua received them in a friendly manner, and through them invited Canek to visit the Spanish camp the third day hence. The embassy was dismissed after being given a number of gifts, and the camp settled down to await the arrival of the Itza ruler.

On the appointed day, the Itza ruler did not appear. Instead, a great flotilla of canoes advanced across the lake toward the camp, while on shore companies of warriors threatened to attack. But as night fell, both the canoes and the land forces withdrew. Ursua accordingly called a council of war of all his officers, requesting of each his opinion on what should be done. All agreed that further efforts to reduce the Itza by peaceable means were useless and that the only course open to them was to conquer the Itza by force of arms. A decree was read to the army ordering the attack on Tayasal the following morning.

On March 13, before dawn, mass was celebrated, breakfast was eaten, and the soldiers selected for the attack embarked on the galley. Ursua took with him 108 Spanish soldiers, the vicar-general of the army, and a nephew of Canek, who had shown himself friendly to the Spanish cause. He left behind, as a garrison, 127 Spaniards and all the Maya bowmen, road workers, and servants.

The galley swept toward Tayasal at dawn. The order of the preceding day was read again aboard ship; the vicar-general urged all who had sinned to ask forgiveness, and granted a general absolution.

Soon those on the galley saw canoes putting out from the shore in two flanking squadrons, the occupants shouting and threatening with their weapons. Ursua ordered the oarsmen to row with all speed toward the town itself, which was now clearly seen in the morning light. The number of canoes grew so rapidly that, as the galley neared shore, they formed a crescent around it, cutting it off from the lake. The Spaniards were now close enough to see the fortifications that had been built against them. They saw, too, the multitude already under arms waiting to defend the town.

Having come within bowshot of the galley, the Itza in the canoes began to discharge a hail of arrows. In spite of this attack, Ursua held back, shouting above the tumult, "No one fire, for God is on our side and there is no cause for fear." The Itza pressed close, the arrows fell more thickly, and still Ursua held fire, shouting that no one was to discharge a shot, under pain of death. The Itza, mistaking this restraint for cowardice, mocked the Spaniards as not only already vanquished but killed and eaten.

Finally the Spanish general made one last appeal. The galley was slowed, and through an interpreter he told the Itza that the Spaniards came in peace and friendship. Unless the Itza laid down their arms, he said, they alone would be responsible for the slaughter that would follow. Although the Itza heard Ursua's plea, they again mistook his forbearance for weakness. Jeering at the Spaniards, they let fly more arrows. In spite of the congestion on the galley, only two Spaniards were wounded—Sergeant Juan González and a soldier named Bartolomé Durán.

Durán, infuriated, ignored Ursua's orders and discharged his harquebus at the Itza. The others followed his example, until firing from the galley became general. The Spaniards, not waiting for the galley to ground, leaped into the water, firing their guns. Even here Ursua showed mercy, for he prevented his men from discharging the artillery. Had this been brought into action, the slaughter would have been frightful, for the Itza were numerous and closely packed.

Having gained the shore, the Spaniards continued firing with such effect that the Itza were soon in full flight. Everyone who could took to the lake, swimming frantically for the opposite shore. The stretch of water that separated Tayasal from the mainland was soon so thick with people that swimming was almost impossible and many perished.

Ursua and the victorious Spaniards pressed up the hill, while the galley was rowed back and forth, the men shooting from its deck. The Itza in the canoes also sought to escape by hurling themselves into the lake and swimming for the mainland, so that soon the entire population of Tayasal was in the water.

Upon reaching the highest temple, Ursua planted the royal standard. From this temple, surrounded by his principal captains and the two Catholic priests, he gave thanks to God for their victory and for having preserved them from any loss of life. On every side there were congratulations; Ursua thanked his officers and men for their bravery and constancy, which had made possible the whole undertaking. The amenities being concluded, and finding themselves masters of the town, Ursua formally renamed Tayasal "Nuestra Señora de los Remedios y San Pablo de los Itzaes."

Ursua and the vicar-general made a tour of the temple, breaking the idols found in them as well as those in the dwellings of the Itza. So vast was the number of idols that their destruction took the entire Spanish force from nine in the morning to half past five in the afternoon. As the final act of the day, Ursua selected the principal temple, where human sacrifice had recently been offered to the Itza deities, to be the sanctuary of the Christian God. Thus, in the morning of a single day the power of the Itza was crushed, and the last independent Maya polity was brought under the domination of the Spanish crown.

The conquest of the Maya by the Spanish was a long and brutal process, a campaign that ultimately succeeded in destroying the last remnants of ancient Maya civilization. In succeeding so well, of course, the subjugation of the Maya also marked the beginning of a long period of European suppression that has shaped much of the world of the modern Maya people. But as is often said, that is another story indeed. ∎

# APPENDIX

## CONVERSION BETWEEN MAYA AND
## GREGORIAN CHRONOLOGIES

**W**hat follows is most usefully undertaken with the material in Chapter 12 on "The Calendar" already thoroughly understood.

The conversion of the Maya and Gregorian calendars, one to the other, is accomplished by the use of Julian Day Numbers (JDN's), a correlation constant, and a conversion between Julian and Gregorian dates. JDN's, based on the Julian calendar in use in Europe prior to the adoption of the modern Gregorian calendar, are a standard chronological reference used by astronomers and other scholars to count the days from a base date of January 1, 4712 B.C. The current Maya calendrical era counts the days from the Maya "zero" or base date of 4 Ahau 8 Cumku, 3114 B.C. Thus, subtracting the correlation constant from a given JDN yields the corresponding day number in Maya chronology. (Conversely, when the correlation constant is *added* to a given Maya day number, it yields the corresponding JDN.) All of this is explained below, using examples.

A variety of correlation constants has been proposed over the years, each corresponding to one of the proposed Maya calendrical correlations (see Chapter 12). The generally accepted correlation constant used here (by which the Short Count date of Katun 13 Ahau corresponds to the Long Count date of 11.16.0.0.0) is 584,283 (Thompson 1950). That constant corrects the figure of 584,285 (Thompson 1935), which in turn was a correction of the original constant of 584,280 (Goodman 1905).

The 584,283 correlation is preferred by many scholars, since it synchronizes the ancient Maya calendar with the surviving 260-day almanacs used in several highland Maya communities today. Other scholars prefer to use correlation constants a day or two different from that value, in which case the calculation of dates can be adjusted by the appropriate one or two days.

## Date-Conversion and Sky-Chart Computer Programs

There are a variety of computer programs for converting Maya dates to Western dates, using either the Gregorian or the Julian calendar. (Even if one is available to you, you may still wish to learn the conversion procedure below, for doing so will afford you a better appreciation of the workings of the Maya calendar.) There are also computer programs that allow the plotting of the positions of planets and other celestial objects on a given date. By using these sky-chart programs to plot the astronomical phenomena visible to the ancient Maya on dates given in their inscriptions, several interesting patterns have emerged. For instance, several people have noticed a number of correlations between the positions of the planet Venus and many of the events recorded at the site of Copan. But before beginning to compare Maya dates with astronomical phenomena, be sure to check whether your computer programs are based on the Gregorian calendar or the Julian calendar—many sky-chart programs use Julian dates. If you need to convert from Gregorian to Julian, to use a sky-chart program based on the Julian calendar, this is easily accomplished by using Table A.1, which was kindly provided by Tony Aveni. (Converting from Julian to Gregorian simply reverses the procedure; note that there are no Julian dates after 1582 A.D.)

## How to Convert Dates (the Old-Fashioned Way)

Calculating the Gregorian date for a given Maya Long Count date (or vice versa) can be done with a simple hand calculator. To convert a Maya Long Count date to the Gregorian system, begin by calculating its equivalent Julian Day Number (JDN). This is done by the use of the correlation constant, 584,283, for the 11.16.0.0.0 date (other correlations, discussed in Chapter 12, use 489,383 for the 12.9.0.0.0 date, and 679,183 for the 11.3.0.0.0 date). A given Long Count date,

TABLE A.1

Conversion from Gregorian to Julian Dates
Within the Pre-Columbian Era

(Subtract *x* days from a Gregorian date falling within the centuries given)

| Century | *x* | Century | *x* | Century | *x* |
|---------|-----|---------|-----|---------|-----|
| 1400 A.D. | −9 | 700 A.D. | −4 | 100 B.C. | +2 |
| 1300 | −8 | 600 | −3 | 200 | +3 |
| 1200 | −8 | 500 | −2 | 300 | +4 |
| 1100 | −7 | 400 | −2 | 400 | +4 |
| 1000 | −6 | 300 | −1 | 500 | +5 |
| 900 | −5 | 200 | 0 | 600 B.C. | +6 |
| 800 A.D. | −5 | 100 A.D. | +1 | | |

Julian Day Numbers (JDN's) for January 1 of the Gregorian-Calendar Years
A.D. 1–2000

| Year | JDN | Year | JDN | Year | JDN |
|------|-----|------|-----|------|-----|
| 1 | 1,721,060 | 700 | 1,976,730 | 1400 | 2,232,400 |
| 100 | 1,757,585 | 800 | 2,013,254 | 1500 | 2,268,924 |
| 200 | 1,794,109 | 900 | 2,049,779 | 1600 | 2,305,448 |
| 300 | 1,830,633 | 1000 | 2,086,303 | 1700 | 2,341,973 |
| 400 | 1,867,157 | 1100 | 2,122,827 | 1800 | 2,378,497 |
| 500 | 1,903,682 | 1200 | 2,159,351 | 1900 | 2,415,021 |
| 600 | 1,940,206 | 1300 | 2,195,876 | 2000 | 2,451,545 |

for example 9.15.6.14.6, is first converted into its Maya day number by multiplying out and then adding the numbers of days in its component units. In this case, $9 \times 144,000$ (baktuns) $+ 15 \times 7,200$ (katuns) $+ 6 \times 360$ (tuns) $+ 14 \times 20$ (uinals) $+ 6 \times 1$ (kins) $= 1,406,446$. This Maya day number is then added to the correlation constant $(1,406,446 + 584,283 = 1,990,729)$ to give its corresponding JDN. From this JDN, the nearest *smaller* JDN for which an equivalent Gregorian date is given in Table A.2 is then subtracted. Using our example and selecting the closest smaller JDN to 1,990,729 (in this case, that for A.D. 700), we see that the remainder of 13,999 days $(1,990,729 - 1,976,730)$ corresponds to 38 years, 129 days $(13,999 \div 365 = 38 +$ a remainder of 129). However, it must be remembered that in the Gregorian calendar (but not in the Maya calendar) every fourth year adds one leap day. If we then subtract the number of leap days between A.D. 700 and 738 (nine) from the 129-day remainder, we find that the Maya Long Count date 9.15.6.14.6 corresponds to day 120 of A.D. 738, or May 1. Leap *centuries* (see Chapter 12) are those that end in 00 and are divisible by 400 (A.D. 400, 800, 1200, 1600, etc.), and because 700 is therefore *not* a leap year, it does not add a tenth leap year to our total. (Use Table A.1 if you wish to convert May 1, 738, to a Julian date.)

To convert a Gregorian date to the Maya Long Count, the procedure is reversed, and a little more complex. As before, first convert a given Gregorian date, October 12, 1992, for example, to its equivalent JDN: $2,415,021 + (92 \times 365) + 28,621 + 1$ leap day $= 2,448,908$. The correlation constant is then subtracted to yield the Maya day number $(2,448,908 - 584,283 = 1,864,625)$. This Maya day number is next divided by the baktun, katun, tun, uinal, and kin values as follows:

$$1,864,625 \div 144,000 \quad = \quad 12 \text{ baktuns} \quad +136,625$$
$$136,625 \div 7,200 \quad = \quad 18 \text{ katuns} \quad +7,025$$
$$7,025 \div 360 \quad = \quad 19 \text{ tuns} \quad +185$$
$$185 \div 20 \quad = \quad 9 \text{ uinals} \quad +5$$
$$5 \div 1 \quad = \quad 5 \text{ kins}$$

This calculation produces the Long Count date 12.18.19.9.5.

To determine the calendar-round positions for this date, divide the Maya day number by 13, 20, and 365 (see Chapter 12) to yield the remainders for each:

$$1,864,625 \div 13: \quad \text{remainder of } 9$$
$$1,864,625 \div 20: \quad \text{remainder of } 5$$
$$1,864,625 \div 365: \quad \text{remainder of } 205$$

The *day number* in the 260-day almanac, the first component of the calendar-round date, is determined by adding the first remainder to 4 ($9 + 4 = 13$), and 13 is thus the day number. (If the result were to have exceeded 13, you would subtract 13 from this sum.) The corresponding *day name* in the 260-day almanac is found by using the value of the second remainder above (5) to determine the number of days after Ahau (see the legend for Fig. 12.4). These steps are necessary because the beginning of the current Maya calendrical era (which embraces all recorded Maya history) was on the calendar-round date 4 Ahau 8 Cumku. By counting five positions forward from Ahau (the twentieth day name) the day Chicchan is arrived at, so that the complete 260-day almanac date is 13 Chicchan.

The vague-year day and month position (Fig. 12.5) is determined by counting the number of days after 8 Cumku (again, we are working from the calendar-round date 4 Ahau 8 Cumku) that are equal to the third remainder calculated above (205). There are 17 days from 8 Cumku to 0 Pop, the beginning of a new vague year (12 days remaining in Cumku and 5 days in Uayeb), so that by subtracting 17 from 205, and counting forward the resulting number of days (188), the day 8 Yax is reached. Thus the complete Long Count date for October 12, 1992, is 12.18.19.9.5 13 Chicchan 8 Yax.

## Gregorian Equivalents for Katun and Half-Katun Endings

To assist the reader in correlating the two calendars, Table A.3 provides the conversions of Maya Long Count dates to their Gregorian equivalents for the katun and half-katun endings from 8.0.0.0.0 to 13.0.0.0.0, on the basis of the Goodman-Martinez-Thompson correlation and the 584,283 correlation constant (Thompson 1950).

TABLE A.3

Correlations Between Maya and Gregorian Chronologies
According to the Goodman-Martinez-Thompson (GMT) Correlation

| Long Count date | Katun or half-katun ending date in the Maya Long Count (Initial Series) | Katun ending date in the Maya Short Count (the *u kahlay katunob*) | Gregorian equivalent, A.D. (584,283 correlation constant) |
|---|---|---|---|
| 8.0.0.0.0 | 9 Ahau 3 Zip | Katun 9 Ahau | 41, September 5 |
| 8.0.10.0.0 | 8 Ahau 18 Cumku | | 51, July 15 |
| 8.1.0.0.0 | 7 Ahau 8 Pax | Katun 7 Ahau | 61, May 23 |
| 8.1.10.0.0 | 6 Ahau 18 Mac | | 71, April 1 |
| 8.2.0.0.0 | 5 Ahau 8 Zac | Katun 5 Ahau | 81, February 7 |
| 8.2.10.0.0 | 4 Ahau 18 Mol | | 90, December 17 |
| 8.3.0.0.0 | 3 Ahau 8 Xul | Katun 3 Ahau | 100, October 26 |
| 8.3.10.0.0 | 2 Ahau 18 Zip | | 110, September 4 |
| 8.4.0.0.0 | 1 Ahau 8 Pop | Katun 1 Ahau | 120, July 13 |
| 8.4.10.0.0 | 13 Ahau 3 Kayab | | 130, May 22 |
| 8.5.0.0.0 | 12 Ahau 13 Kankin | Katun 12 Ahau | 140, March 30 |
| 8.5.10.0.0 | 11 Ahau 3 Ceh | | 150, February 6 |
| 8.6.0.0.0 | 10 Ahau 13 Chen | Katun 10 Ahau | 159, December 15 |
| 8.6.10.0.0 | 9 Ahau 3 Yaxkin | | 169, October 24 |
| 8.7.0.0.0 | 8 Ahau 13 Zotz | Katun 8 Ahau | 179, September 2 |
| 8.7.10.0.0 | 7 Ahau 3 Uo | | 189, July 11 |
| 8.8.0.0.0 | 6 Ahau 18 Kayab | Katun 6 Ahau | 199, May 20 |
| 8.8.10.0.0 | 5 Ahau 8 Muan | | 209, March 29 |
| 8.9.0.0.0 | 4 Ahau 18 Ceh | Katun 4 Ahau | 219, February 5 |
| 8.9.10.0.0 | 3 Ahau 8 Yax | | 228, December 14 |
| 8.10.0.0.0 | 2 Ahau 18 Yaxkin | Katun 2 Ahau | 238, October 23 |
| 8.10.10.0.0 | 1 Ahau 8 Tzec | | 248, August 31 |
| 8.11.0.0.0 | 13 Ahau 18 Uo | Katun 13 Ahau | 258, July 10 |
| 8.11.10.0.0 | 12 Ahau 13 Cumku | | 268, May 18 |
| 8.12.0.0.0 | 11 Ahau 3 Pax | Katun 11 Ahau | 278, March 27 |
| 8.12.10.0.0 | 10 Ahau 13 Mac | | 288, February 3 |
| 8.13.0.0.0 | 9 Ahau 3 Zac | Katun 9 Ahau | 297, December 12 |
| 8.13.10.0.0 | 8 Ahau 13 Mol | | 307, October 22 |
| 8.14.0.0.0 | 7 Ahau 3 Xul | Katun 7 Ahau | 317, August 30 |
| 8.14.10.0.0 | 6 Ahau 13 Zip | | 327, July 9 |
| 8.15.0.0.0 | 5 Ahau 3 Pop | Katun 5 Ahau | 337, May 17 |
| 8.15.10.0.0 | 4 Ahau 18 Pax | | 347, March 26 |
| 8.16.0.0.0 | 3 Ahau 8 Kankin | Katun 3 Ahau | 357, Febuary 1 |
| 8.16.10.0.0 | 2 Ahau 18 Zac | | 366, December 11 |
| 8.17.0.0.0 | 1 Ahau 8 Chen | Katun 1 Ahau | 376, October 19 |
| 8.17.10.0.0 | 13 Ahau 18 Xul | | 386, August 28 |
| 8.18.0.0.0 | 12 Ahau 8 Zotz | Katun 12 Ahau | 396, July 6 |
| 8.18.10.0.0 | 11 Ahau 18 Pop | | 406, May 15 |
| 8.19.0.0.0 | 10 Ahau 13 Kayab | Katun 10 Ahau | 416, March 23 |
| 8.19.10.0.0 | 9 Ahau 3 Muan | | 426, January 30 |
| 9.0.0.0.0 | 8 Ahau 13 Ceh | Katun 8 Ahau | 435, December 6 |
| 9.0.10.0.0 | 7 Ahau 3 Yax | | 445, October 17 |
| 9.1.0.0.0 | 6 Ahau 13 Yaxkin | Katun 6 Ahau | 455, August 26 |
| 9.1.10.0.0 | 5 Ahau 3 Tzec | | 465, July 4 |
| 9.2.0.0.0 | 4 Ahau 13 Uo | Katun 4 Ahau | 475, May 13 |
| 9.2.10.0.0 | 3 Ahau 8 Cumku | | 485, March 21 |
| 9.3.0.0.0 | 2 Ahau 18 Muan | Katun 2 Ahau | 495, January 28 |
| 9.3.10.0.0 | 1 Ahau 8 Mac | | 504, December 7 |
| 9.4.0.0.0 | 13 Ahau 18 Yax | Katun 13 Ahau | 514, October 16 |

TABLE A.3 (*continued*)

| Long Count date | Katun or half-katun ending date in the Maya Long Count (Initial Series) | | Katun ending date in the Maya Short Count (the *u kahlay katunob*) | Gregorian equivalent, A.D. (584,283 correlation constant) |
|---|---|---|---|---|
| 9.4.10.0.0 | 12 Ahau | 8 Mol | | 524, August 24 |
| 9.5.0.0.0 | 11 Ahau | 18 Tzec | Katun  11 Ahau | 534, July 3 |
| 9.5.10.0.0 | 10 Ahau | 8 Zip | | 544, May 11 |
| 9.6.0.0.0 | 9 Ahau | 3 Uayeb | Katun  9 Ahau | 554, March 20 |
| 9.6.10.0.0 | 8 Ahau | 13 Pax | | 564, January 27 |
| 9.7.0.0.0 | 7 Ahau | 3 Kankin | Katun  7 Ahau | 573, December 5 |
| 9.7.10.0.0 | 6 Ahau | 13 Zac | | 583, October 14 |
| 9.8.0.0.0 | 5 Ahau | 3 Chen | Katun  5 Ahau | 593, August 22 |
| 9.8.10.0.0 | 4 Ahau | 13 Xul | | 603, July 2 |
| 9.9.0.0.0 | 3 Ahau | 3 Zotz | Katun  3 Ahau | 613, May 10 |
| 9.9.10.0.0 | 2 Ahau | 13 Pop | | 623, March 19 |
| 9.10.0.0.0 | 1 Ahau | 8 Kayab | Katun  1 Ahau | 633, January 25 |
| 9.10.10.0.0 | 13 Ahau | 18 Kankin | | 642, December 4 |
| 9.11.0.0.0 | 12 Ahau | 8 Ceh | Katun  12 Ahau | 652, October 12 |
| 9.11.10.0.0 | 11 Ahau | 18 Chen | | 662, August 21 |
| 9.12.0.0.0 | 10 Ahau | 8 Yaxkin | Katun  10 Ahau | 672, June 29 |
| 9.12.10.0.0 | 9 Ahau | 18 Zotz | | 682, May 8 |
| 9.13.0.0.0 | 8 Ahau | 8 Uo | Katun  8 Ahau | 692, March 16 |
| 9.13.10.0.0 | 7 Ahau | 3 Cumku | | 702, January 24 |
| 9.14.0.0.0 | 6 Ahau | 13 Muan | Katun  6 Ahau | 711, December 3 |
| 9.14.10.0.0 | 5 Ahau | 3 Mac | | 721, October 11 |
| 9.15.0.0.0 | 4 Ahau | 13 Yax | Katun  4 Ahau | 731, August 20 |
| 9.15.10.0.0 | 3 Ahau | 3 Mol | | 741, June 28 |
| 9.16.0.0.0 | 2 Ahau | 13 Tzec | Katun  2 Ahau | 751, May 7 |
| 9.16.10.0.0 | 1 Ahau | 3 Zip | | 761, March 15 |
| 9.17.0.0.0 | 13 Ahau | 18 Cumku | Katun  13 Ahau | 771, January 22 |
| 9.17.10.0.0 | 12 Ahau | 8 Pax | | 780, November 30 |
| 9.18.0.0.0 | 11 Ahau | 18 Mac | Katun  11 Ahau | 790, October 9 |
| 9.18.10.0.0 | 10 Ahau | 8 Zac | | 800, August 17 |
| 9.19.0.0.0 | 9 Ahau | 18 Mol | Katun  9 Ahau | 810, June 26 |
| 9.19.10.0.0 | 8 Ahau | 8 Xul | | 820, May 4 |
| 10.0.0.0.0 | 7 Ahau | 18 Zip | Katun  7 Ahau | 830, March 13 |
| 10.0.10.0.0 | 6 Ahau | 8 Pop | | 840, January 20 |
| 10.1.0.0.0 | 5 Ahau | 3 Kayab | Katun  5 Ahau | 849, November 28 |
| 10.1.10.0.0 | 4 Ahau | 13 Kankin | | 859, October 7 |
| 10.2.0.0.0 | 3 Ahau | 3 Ceh | Katun  3 Ahau | 869, August 15 |
| 10.2.10.0.0 | 2 Ahau | 13 Chen | | 879, June 24 |
| 10.3.0.0.0 | 1 Ahau | 3 Yaxkin | Katun  1 Ahau | 889, May 2 |
| 10.3.10.0.0 | 13 Ahau | 13 Zotz | | 899, March 11 |
| 10.4.0.0.0 | 12 Ahau | 3 Uo | Katun  12 Ahau | 909, January 18 |
| 10.4.10.0.0 | 11 Ahau | 18 Kayab | | 918, November 27 |
| 10.5.0.0.0 | 10 Ahau | 8 Muan | Katun  10 Ahau | 928, October 5 |
| 10.5.10.0.0 | 9 Ahau | 18 Ceh | | 938, August 14 |
| 10.6.0.0.0 | 8 Ahau | 8 Yax | Katun  8 Ahau | 948, June 22 |
| 10.6.10.0.0 | 7 Ahau | 18 Yaxkin | | 958, May 1 |
| 10.7.0.0.0 | 6 Ahau | 8 Tzec | Katun  6 Ahau | 968, March 9 |
| 10.7.10.0.0 | 5 Ahau | 18 Uo | | 978, January 16 |
| 10.8.0.0.0 | 4 Ahau | 13 Cumku | Katun  4 Ahau | 987, November 25 |
| 10.8.10.0.0 | 3 Ahau | 3 Pax | | 997, October 3 |
| 10.9.0.0.0 | 2 Ahau | 13 Mac | Katun  2 Ahau | 1007, August 13 |
| 10.9.10.0.0 | 1 Ahau | 3 Zac | | 1017, June 21 |
| 10.10.0.0.0 | 13 Ahau | 13 Mol | Katun  13 Ahau | 1027, April 30 |

TABLE A.3 (*continued*)

| Long Count date | Katun or half-katun ending date in the Maya Long Count (Initial Series) | | Katun ending date in the Maya Short Count (the *u kahlay katunob*) | Gregorian equivalent, A.D. (584,283 correlation constant) |
| --- | --- | --- | --- | --- |
| 10.10.10.0.0 | 12 Ahau | 3 Xul | | 1037, March 8 |
| 10.11.0.0.0 | 11 Ahau | 13 Zip | Katun 11 Ahau | 1047, January 15 |
| 10.11.10.0.0 | 10 Ahau | 3 Pop | | 1056, November 23 |
| 10.12.0.0.0 | 9 Ahau | 18 Pax | Katun 9 Ahau | 1066, October 2 |
| 10.12.10.0.0 | 8 Ahau | 8 Kankin | | 1076, August 10 |
| 10.13.0.0.0 | 7 Ahau | 18 Zac | Katun 7 Ahau | 1086, June 19 |
| 10.13.10.0.0 | 6 Ahau | 8 Chen | | 1096, April 27 |
| 10.14.0.0.0 | 5 Ahau | 18 Xul | Katun 5 Ahau | 1106, March 7 |
| 10.14.10.0.0 | 4 Ahau | 8 Zotz | | 1116, January 14 |
| 10.15.0.0.0 | 3 Ahau | 18 Pop | Katun 3 Ahau | 1125, November 22 |
| 10.15.10.0.0 | 2 Ahau | 13 Kayab | | 1135, October 1 |
| 10.16.0.0.0 | 1 Ahau | 3 Muan | Katun 1 Ahau | 1145, August 9 |
| 10.16.10.0.0 | 13 Ahau | 13 Ceh | | 1155, June 18 |
| 10.17.0.0.0 | 12 Ahau | 3 Yax | Katun 12 Ahau | 1165, April 26 |
| 10.17.10.0.0 | 11 Ahau | 13 Yaxkin | | 1175, March 5 |
| 10.18.0.0.0 | 10 Ahau | 3 Tzec | Katun 10 Ahau | 1185, January 11 |
| 10.18.10.0.0 | 9 Ahau | 13 Uo | | 1194, November 20 |
| 10.19.0.0.0 | 8 Ahau | 8 Cumku | Katun 8 Ahau | 1204, September 28 |
| 10.19.10.0.0 | 7 Ahau | 18 Muan | | 1214, August 7 |
| 11.0.0.0.0 | 6 Ahau | 8 Mac | Katun 6 Ahau | 1224, June 15 |
| 11.0.10.0.0 | 5 Ahau | 18 Yax | | 1234, April 24 |
| 11.1.0.0.0 | 4 Ahau | 8 Mol | Katun 4 Ahau | 1244, March 2 |
| 11.1.10.0.0 | 3 Ahau | 18 Tzec | | 1254, January 9 |
| 11.2.0.0.0 | 2 Ahau | 8 Zip | Katun 2 Ahau | 1263, November 18 |
| 11.2.10.0.0 | 1 Ahau | 3 Uayeb | | 1273, September 26 |
| 11.3.0.0.0 | 13 Ahau | 13 Pax | Katun 13 Ahau | 1283, August 5 |
| 11.3.10.0.0 | 12 Ahau | 3 Kankin | | 1293, June 13 |
| 11.4.0.0.0 | 11 Ahau | 13 Zac | Katun 11 Ahau | 1303, April 23 |
| 11.4.10.0.0 | 10 Ahau | 3 Chen | | 1313, March 1 |
| 11.5.0.0.0 | 9 Ahau | 13 Xul | Katun 9 Ahau | 1323, January 8 |
| 11.5.10.0.0 | 8 Ahau | 3 Zotz | | 1332, November 16 |
| 11.6.0.0.0 | 7 Ahau | 13 Pop | Katun 7 Ahau | 1342, September 25 |
| 11.6.10.0.0 | 6 Ahau | 8 Kayab | | 1352, August 3 |
| 11.7.0.0.0 | 5 Ahau | 18 Kankin | Katun 5 Ahau | 1362, June 12 |
| 11.7.10.0.0 | 4 Ahau | 8 Ceh | | 1372, April 20 |
| 11.8.0.0.0 | 3 Ahau | 18 Chen | Katun 3 Ahau | 1382, February 27 |
| 11.8.10.0.0 | 2 Ahau | 8 Yaxkin | | 1392, January 6 |
| 11.9.0.0.0 | 1 Ahau | 18 Zotz | Katun 1 Ahau | 1401, November 15 |
| 11.9.10.0.0 | 13 Ahau | 8 Uo | | 1411, September 24 |
| 11.10.0.0.0 | 12 Ahau | 3 Cumku | Katun 12 Ahau | 1421, August 2 |
| 11.10.10.0.0 | 11 Ahau | 13 Muan | | 1431, June 11 |
| 11.11.0.0.0 | 10 Ahau | 3 Mac | Katun 10 Ahau | 1441, April 19 |
| 11.11.10.0.0 | 9 Ahau | 13 Yax | | 1451, February 26 |
| 11.12.0.0.0 | 8 Ahau | 3 Mol | Katun 8 Ahau | 1461, January 4 |
| 11.12.10.0.0 | 7 Ahau | 13 Tzec | | 1470, November 13 |
| 11.13.0.0.0 | 6 Ahau | 3 Zip | Katun 6 Ahau | 1480, September 21 |
| 11.13.10.0.0 | 5 Ahau | 18 Cumku | | 1490, July 31 |
| 11.14.0.0.0 | 4 Ahau | 8 Pax | Katun 4 Ahau | 1500, June 9 |
| 11.14.10.0.0 | 3 Ahau | 18 Mac | | 1510, April 18 |
| 11.15.0.0.0 | 2 Ahau | 8 Zac | Katun 2 Ahau | 1520, February 25 |
| 11.15.10.0.0 | 1 Ahau | 18 Mol | | 1530, January 3 |
| 11.16.0.0.0 | 13 Ahau | 8 Xul | Katun 13 Ahau | 1539, November 12 |

TABLE A.3 (*continued*)

| Long Count date | Katun or half-katun ending date in the Maya Long Count (Initial Series) | Katun ending date in the Maya Short Count (the *u kahlay katunob*) | Gregorian equivalent, A.D. (584,283 correlation constant) |
|---|---|---|---|
| 11.16.10.0.0 | 12 Ahau  18 Zip | | 1549, September 20 |
| 11.17.0.0.0 | 11 Ahau  8 Pop | Katun  11 Ahau | 1559, July 30 |
| 11.17.10.0.0 | 10 Ahau  3 Kayab | | 1569, June 7 |
| 11.18.0.0.0 | 9 Ahau  13 Kankin | Katun  9 Ahau | 1579, April 16 |
| 11.18.10.0.0 | 8 Ahau  3 Ceh | | 1589, February 22 |
| 11.19.0.0.0 | 7 Ahau  13 Chen | Katun  7 Ahau | 1599, January 1 |
| 11.19.10.0.0 | 6 Ahau  3 Yaxkin | | 1608, November 9 |
| 12.0.0.0.0 | 5 Ahau  13 Zotz | Katun  5 Ahau | 1618, September 18 |
| 12.0.10.0.0 | 4 Ahau  3 Uo | | 1628, July 27 |
| 12.1.0.0.0 | 3 Ahau  18 Kayab | Katun  3 Ahau | 1638, June 5 |
| 12.1.10.0.0 | 2 Ahau  8 Muan | | 1648, April 13 |
| 12.2.0.0.0 | 1 Ahau  18 Ceh | Katun  1 Ahau | 1658, February 20 |
| 12.2.10.0.0 | 13 Ahau  8 Yax | | 1667, December 30 |
| 12.3.0.0.0 | 12 Ahau  18 Yaxkin | Katun  12 Ahau | 1677, November 7 |
| 12.3.10.0.0 | 11 Ahau  8 Tzec | | 1687, September 16 |
| 12.4.0.0.0 | 10 Ahau  18 Uo | Katun  10 Ahau | 1697, July 25 |
| 12.4.10.0.0 | 9 Ahau  13 Cumku | | 1707, June 4 |
| 12.5.0.0.0 | 8 Ahau  3 Pax | Katun  8 Ahau | 1717, April 12 |
| 12.5.10.0.0 | 7 Ahau  13 Mac | | 1727, February 19 |
| 12.6.0.0.0 | 6 Ahau  3 Zac | Katun  6 Ahau | 1736, December 28 |
| 12.6.10.0.0 | 5 Ahau  13 Mol | | 1746, November 6 |
| 12.7.0.0.0 | 4 Ahau  3 Xul | Katun  4 Ahau | 1756, September 14 |
| 12.7.10.0.0 | 3 Ahau  13 Zip | | 1766, July 24 |
| 12.8.0.0.0 | 2 Ahau  3 Pop | Katun  2 Ahau | 1776, June 1 |
| 12.8.10.0.0 | 1 Ahau  18 Pax | | 1786, April 10 |
| 12.9.0.0.0 | 13 Ahau  8 Kankin | Katun  13 Ahau | 1796, February 17 |
| 12.9.10.0.0 | 12 Ahau  18 Zac | | 1805, December 27 |
| 12.10.0.0.0 | 11 Ahau  8 Chen | Katun  11 Ahau | 1815, November 5 |
| 12.10.10.0.0 | 10 Ahau  18 Xul | | 1825, September 13 |
| 12.11.0.0.0 | 9 Ahau  8 Zotz | Katun  9 Ahau | 1835, July 23 |
| 12.11.10.0.0 | 8 Ahau  18 Pop | | 1845, May 31 |
| 12.12.0.0.0 | 7 Ahau  13 Kayab | Katun  7 Ahau | 1855, April 9 |
| 12.12.10.0.0 | 6 Ahau  3 Muan | | 1865, February 15 |
| 12.13.0.0.0 | 5 Ahau  13 Ceh | Katun  5 Ahau | 1874, December 25 |
| 12.13.10.0.0 | 4 Ahau  3 Yax | | 1884, November 2 |
| 12.14.0.0.0 | 3 Ahau  13 Yaxkin | Katun  3 Ahau | 1894, September 11 |
| 12.14.10.0.0 | 2 Ahau  3 Tzec | | 1904, July 21 |
| 12.15.0.0.0 | 1 Ahau  13 Uo | Katun  1 Ahau | 1914, May 30 |
| 12.15.10.0.0 | 13 Ahau  8 Cumku | | 1924, April 7 |
| 12.16.0.0.0 | 12 Ahau  18 Muan | Katun  12 Ahau | 1934, February 14 |
| 12.16.10.0.0 | 11 Ahau  8 Mac | | 1943, December 22 |
| 12.17.0.0.0 | 10 Ahau  18 Yax | Katun  10 Ahau | 1953, November 1 |
| 12.17.10.0.0 | 9 Ahau  8 Mol | | 1963, September 10 |
| 12.18.0.0.0 | 8 Ahau  18 Tzec | Katun  8 Ahau | 1973, July 19 |
| 12.18.10.0.0 | 7 Ahau  8 Zip | | 1983, May 28 |
| 12.19.0.0.0 | 6 Ahau  3 Uayeb | Katun  6 Ahau | 1993, April 5 |
| 12.19.10.0.0 | 5 Ahau  13 Pax | | 2003, February 12 |
| 13.0.0.0.0 | 4 Ahau  3 Kankin | Katun  4 Ahau | 2012, December 21 |

# REFERENCE MATERIAL

# BIBLIOGRAPHIC SUMMARIES

The study of the ancient Maya has led to a broad and varied literature about their society and culture. The rapid growth in works dealing with the Maya, ranging from the popular to the scholarly, has produced such a vast literature that it is clearly impossible to list all possible sources for any given topic. Therefore the citations given here, organized to follow the topics in the order in which the text presents them, are only a sample of the relevant sources. The sample attempts to represent some of the diversity of opinion about the topics under discussion, and at the same time to include both "classic" works and the more useful recent contributions; note that the bibliographies in most recent publications will provide the serious researcher with further sources. Full citations of the sources cited here, and of other works dealing with the Maya, are given in the Bibliography that follows these Summaries.

## Introduction

*Early explorers and theories:* Maler 1901, 1903, 1908a,b, 1911; Maudslay 1889–1902; Stephens 1841, 1843; G. Stuart 1989; Sullivan 1989; Tozzer 1907, 1911, 1913; Wauchope 1962, 1965.

*Classic works on Maya civilization:* Brainerd 1954; Gann & Thompson 1931; Morley 1946; Morley & Brainerd 1956; Spinden 1917, 1928; Thompson 1954a, 1966.

*Recent works on Maya civilization:* Benson 1977a; M. Coe 1987; Culbert 1974; Hammond 1982; Henderson 1981; Stuart & Stuart 1977.

*Post-Conquest histories:* Farriss 1984; Helms 1975; Jones 1989; Roys 1943, 1952; Scholes 1933; Scholes and Roys 1938; Wolf 1959.

*Ethnohistories and ethnographies:* G. Jones 1983; King 1974; LaFarge 1947; LaFarge & Byers 1931; McBryde 1947; Means 1917; Miles 1957; Oakes 1951; Redfield 1941;

Scholes & Roys 1948; Steggerda 1941; Sullivan 1989; Tedlock 1982; D. Thompson 1960; J. Thompson 1930; Tozzer 1907; Villa Rojas 1934; Vogt 1969, 1983.

*Destruction of ancient Maya archaeological remains:* Chase, Chase & Topsey 1988; Coggins 1972; Meyer 1977; Robertson 1972b; Saville 1893; Sheets 1973.

## CHAPTER 1: The Setting

*Mesoamerican culture area:* Helms 1975; Kirchhoff 1952; Wolf 1959; see also the *Handbook of Middle American Indians (HMAI)* and the more recent *Supplement*, vol 1.

*Languages and language divisions:* Campbell 1976; Greenberg 1987; Justeson et al. 1985; Kaufman 1964; McQuown 1956.

*Maya area, boundaries, and neighbors:* Andrews 1977; Boone & Willey 1988; Fox 1981; Longyear 1947; Lothrop 1939; Ochoa & Lee 1983; Robinson 1987; Schortman 1986; Sharer 1974, 1984; Thompson 1970; Urban & Schortman 1986, 1988.

### Natural and Cultural Subdivisions of the Maya Area

*Highland-lowland dichotomy:* Coe 1966: 19–27; Sanders 1973.

*Environmental diversity:* Harrison & Turner 1978; Sanders 1977.

*Geography:* Huntington 1912; Sapper 1896; Tamayo 1964; West 1964.

*Climate:* Dahlin 1983; Escoto 1964; Shattuck 1933.

*Flora:* Carnegie Institution of Washington 1935, 1940; Lundell 1937; Standley 1930; Wagner 1964.

*Fauna:* Griscom 1932; Murie 1935; Schmidt & Andrews 1936; L. Stuart 1964.

*Environmental studies:* Abrams & Rue 1988; Barrera Rubio 1985; Darch 1983; McAnany 1990; McBryde 1947; Voorhies 1982.

*Resources:* Coe & Flannery 1964; Foshag & Leslie 1955; Graham & Hester 1968; Hammond et al. 1977; Sheets 1975, 1976a; Voorhies 1982.

*Geology:* Pearse, Creaser & Hall 1936; Plafker 1976; Sheets 1979a, 1983; Siemens 1978; Ward, Weidie & Back 1985.

## CHAPTER 2: The Origins of Maya Civilization

### The Chronological Framework

Sabloff 1985, 1990; Willey & Phillips 1958.

### The Developmental Stages of Maya Civilization

Grove 1981a; Sabloff 1985, 1990; Sabloff & Henderson 1993; Sanders & Price 1968.

### The Origins of Highland and Coastal Cultural Traditions

*Oaxaca:* Flannery 1976; Flannery & Marcus 1983; Marcus 1989a.

*Tehuacan:* Byers 1967; Johnston 1972; MacNeish 1964a,b; MacNeish, Peterson & Flannery 1970.

*The Maya highlands:* Brown 1979, 1980; Brown & Majewski 1979; MacNeish & Peterson 1962; Sanders & Murdy 1982; Sedat & Sharer 1972; Sharer 1989b; Sharer & Sedat 1987; Shook 1971.

*The Maya lowlands:* Andrews V 1990; Andrews & Hammond 1990; Hammond et al. 1976; MacNeish, Wilkerson & Nelken-Terner 1980.

*Yucatan:* Brainerd 1958; Mercer 1975; Thompson 1897a; Velázquez Valadez 1980.

*The Pacific coast:* Bove 1989; Clark et al. 1987; Clewlow & Wells 1986; Coe 1961; Coe & Flannery 1967; Green & Lowe 1967; Lowe 1977; Shook 1971; Shook & Hatch 1979.

*South America:* Lathrap, Marcos & Zeidler 1977; Meggers, Evans, & Estrada 1965; Reichel-Dolmatoff 1965.

### Preclassic Antecedents and Contemporaries

*The Olmec (traditional views):* Bernal 1969; M. Coe 1965, 1968; Lowe 1989.

*The Olmec (revised views):* Drennan & Uribe 1987; Grove 1981b; Sharer & Grove 1989.

*La Venta:* Drucker 1952; Drucker, Heizer & Squier 1955; Heizer 1968; Heizer, Graham & Napton 1968; Rust & Sharer 1988.

*Monuments:* Clewlow 1974; Grove 1981b; Stirling 1965.

*Interaction within Mesoamerica:* Demarest 1989; Flannery 1968; Lowe 1977; Sharer & Grove 1989.

*San Lorenzo:* M. Coe 1970; Coe & Diehl 1980.

*Chalcatzingo:* Grove 1987; Grove et al. 1976.

*Oaxaca:* Flannery 1968; Flannery & Marcus 1983; Marcus 1992.

### The Prelude to Maya Civilization

*Ecological adaptation:* Adams 1980; Culbert, Levi & Cruz 1990; Darch 1983; Flannery 1982; Gann 1918; Harrison 1990; Netting 1977; Puleston & Puleston 1971; Rice 1978; Sanders 1973, 1977; Turner 1978b; Turner & Harrison 1983.

*Temporal and spatial diversity:* Adams & Smith 1981; Andrews V 1990; Carmack 1977; Freidel 1981b; Haviland 1985b; Lowe 1985; Marcus 1993; Mathews 1987, 1991; Sabloff 1990; Sharer 1991, 1993.

*The unity of the elite subculture:* Chase & Chase 1992; Culbert 1991b; Freidel & Schele 1988a; Schele & Mathews 1991; Schortman 1986; Sharer 1991; Yoffee 1991.

*Networks of interaction:* A. Andrews 1983, 1990b; Arnauld 1986; Clark & Lee 1984; Freidel 1978; Graham 1987; Hirth 1984; McKillop & Healy 1989; Sabloff 1986; Schortman & Urban 1987; Sharer 1989a; Sharer & Sedat 1987; Tourtellot & Sabloff 1972; Voorhies 1982, 1989.

*Competition and conflict:* Freidel 1986a; Freidel & Schele 1989a; Rice & Rice 1990; Sanders 1977; Sanders & Price 1968; Webster 1977.

*Ideology and cosmology:* Ashmore 1989; Aveni & Hartung 1986; Demarest 1987; Dütting 1985; Edmonsen 1986, 1988; Flannery & Marcus 1976; Freidel 1979b; Freidel & Schele 1988a,b; Loten 1990; Marcus 1989a; Tedlock 1985.

## CHAPTER 3 : The Preclassic Maya

### The Emergence of Complex Societies in the Maya Area

*The origins of Maya civilization (traditional views):* Adams 1972; M. Coe 1965, 1968; W. Coe 1965a; Meggers 1954.

*The origins of Maya civilization (revised views):* E. Andrews 1990; Boone & Willey 1988;

Demarest 1988; Robinson 1987; Sharer 1987, 1988a; Sharer & Sedat 1987; Urban & Schortman 1986; Willey 1987.

*Chiefdoms:* Drennan & Uribe 1987; Marcus 1989a; Service 1962, 1975; Turner 1990; Webster 1976a.

### The Pacific Coastal Plain in the Middle Preclassic

*Sites and monuments:* Boggs 1950; Bove 1989; Clewlow & Wells 1986; J. Graham 1979; Hatch 1989; Lowe 1977; Miles 1965; Navarrete 1960; Sharer 1978a, 1989a; Sorenson 1956; Thompson 1943a.

*Interaction and trade:* Cobean et al. 1971; Flannery 1968; Hatch 1989; Jackson & Love 1991; Lowe 1977; Sharer 1974, 1978a, 1989; Voorhies 1989.

*Proposed language correlations:* Campbell 1976; Campbell & Kaufman 1976; Greenberg 1987; Justeson et al. 1985; Justeson & Kaufman 1993.

### The Highlands in the Middle Preclassic

*Sites and regions:* Arnauld 1986; Borhegyi 1965a,b; Fash 1982; Sanders & Murdy 1982; Sharer 1989a, 1990a; A. Smith 1955.

THE SALAMA VALLEY: Sharer 1989a, 1990a; Sharer & Sedat 1973, 1987.

### The Lowlands in the Middle Preclassic

*Sites and regions:* Andrews V 1990; Ekholm 1973; Hammond 1977a, 1985a; Pring 1976; Ricketson & Ricketson 1937; Smith 1972; Voorhies 1982; Willey 1978a.

NAKBE: Graham 1967; Hansen 1987, 1989.

### Late Preclassic Maya Civilization and the Origins of Writing

Caso 1965; Freidel 1979a; Freidel & Schele 1988a; Hammond 1985a; Marcus 1980; Sharer 1988a; Sharer & Sedat 1973, 1987; Shook & Kidder 1952.

### The Late Preclassic Mixe-Zoquean Tradition

*Language and cultural affiliations:* Andrews V 1990; Campbell 1976; Campbell & Kaufman 1976; Greenberg 1987; Justeson et al. 1985; Lowe 1977; Ochoa & Lee 1983.

*Sites and monuments:* M. Coe 1965; J. Graham 1979; Justeson & Kaufman 1993; Miles 1965; Proskouriakoff 1971; Quirarte 1973, 1977; Stirling 1940; Winfield C. 1988.

IZAPA: Ekholm 1969; Lowe, Lee & Martínez 1982; Norman 1973, 1976.

### The Southern Maya in the Late Preclassic

*Monuments and ceramics:* Demarest & Sharer 1982a, 1986; Miles 1965; Parsons 1986; Proskouriakoff 1971; Sharer & Sedat 1987; Thompson 1943a.

KAMINALJUYU: Kidder 1961; Kidder, Jennings & Shook 1946; Maudslay 1889–1902; Sanders & Michels 1977; Sanders & Murdy 1982; Shook & Kidder 1952; Wetherington 1978.

CHALCHUAPA: Boggs 1950; Fowler 1984; Longyear 1944; Sharer 1978a, 1989a.

ABAJ TAKALIK: J. Graham 1977, 1979; Graham, Heizer & Shook 1978; Miles 1965; Parsons 1986; J. E. Thompson 1943a.

*Other Southern Maya Sites in the Late Preclassic*

*Monuments and writing:* Campbell, Justeson & Norman 1980; Demarest, Switsur & Berger 1982; J. Graham 1971, 1979; Graham & Porter 1989; Ichon 1977a; Prem 1971; Sharer 1990a.

*Sites and ceramics:* Bove 1989; Demarest 1986; Demarest & Sharer 1982a, 1986; Hatch 1989; Shook & Kidder 1952; Parsons 1967–69; Shook 1971; A. Smith 1955.

*Processes and links:* Demarest 1986, 1988; Demarest & Sharer 1986; Lowe 1977; Sedat & Sharer 1972; Sharer 1989a; Sharer & Sedat 1987.

*Highland-Lowland Interaction*

Adams 1972; Arnauld 1986; Kidder 1940; Miller 1983; Sedat & Sharer 1972; Sharer 1988a, 1989a; Sharer & Sedat 1987; A. Smith 1955; Voorhies 1982.

*The Central Lowlands in the Late Preclassic*

*Sites and interpretations:* Andrews V 1990; W. Coe 1965a, 1968, 1990; Freidel 1978, 1979a,b; Freidel & Schele 1988a; Hammond 1985a; Pendergast 1981; Ricketson & Ricketson 1937; Sharer 1988a, 1989b; Valdés 1986, 1988.

EL MIRADOR: Dahlin 1984; Demarest & Fowler 1984; Demarest & Sharer 1982b; Demarest et al. 1984; Forsyth 1989; Hansen 1984, 1991; Howell 1983; Matheny 1980, 1986, 1987.

CERROS: Cliff 1988; Freidel 1977, 1978; Freidel, Robertson & Cliff 1982; Freidel & Schele 1988a; Robertson & Freidel 1986; Scarborough 1991; Scarborough & Robertson 1986; Schele & Freidel 1990.

*The Style of Power in Late Preclassic Maya Civilization*

Freidel 1979a,b; Freidel & Schele 1988a; Freidel et al. 1991; Gibson, Shaw & Finamore 1986; Hammond 1985a; Justeson & Mathews 1983; Justeson, Norman & Hammond 1988; Schele 1985; Sharer 1988a, 1990a; Valdés 1988; Willey 1987.

*The Northern Lowlands in the Preclassic*

KOMCHEN: Andrews IV & Andrews V 1980; Andrews V et al. 1984; Ringle & Andrews 1988, 1990.

*The Protoclassic and the Decline of the Southern Maya*

Dahlin 1979; Dahlin, Quizar & Dahlin 1987; Hansen 1984; Sharer 1974; Sheets 1976b, 1979b; Willey 1977, 1987.

CHAPTER 4: The Early Classic and the Rise of Tikal

*The Emergence of States in the Maya Area*

*State systems:* Childe 1954; Jones & Kautz 1981; Marcus 1983b; Sanders et al. 1984; Service 1975.

*Maya hallmarks:* Berlin 1958; Freidel 1979a; Freidel & Schele 1988a; Lounsbury 1973; Marcus 1983a, 1992; Mathews 1986, 1991; Proskouriakoff 1961a; Pyburn n.d.; Riese 1984a; Sabloff 1985, 1990; Sharer 1988a; Stuart 1985a, 1988a; Stuart & Houston 1989; Willey 1982a, 1987, 1991.

*Competition and Warfare in the Maya Area*

Chase & Chase 1987; Demarest & Houston 1990; Freidel 1986a; Schele 1984; Sharer 1978b; Webster 1976b, 1977.

*The Protoclassic as Transition to the Classic*

*The highlands:* Borhegy 1965a; Sharer 1969, 1974, 1978a; Sheets 1971, 1979a; Shook & Proskouriakoff 1956.
*The lowlands:* W. Coe 1965a; Culbert 1977a; Dahlin 1984; Freidel 1990; Freidel & Schele 1988a, 1988b; Merwin & Vaillant 1932; Pring 1976.
*Interaction:* Dahlin 1979; Sharer 1978a; Sheets 1971; Willey 1977, 1987.

*The Southern Maya Area in the Classic*

*Sites:* Arnauld 1986; Kidder, Jennings & Shook 1946; Sanders & Michels 1977; Sanders & Murdy 1982; Sharer 1978a; Sharer & Sedat 1987; Shook & Hatch 1978.
*Teotihuacan connections:* Bove 1991; Kidder, Jennings & Shook 1946; Sanders & Murdy 1982; Sharer 1974.

*The Lowlands in the Early Classic*

Proskouriakoff 1993; Turner 1990; Willey & Mathews 1985.
TIKAL: Carr & Hazard 1961; W. Coe 1968, 1990; Coe & Haviland 1982; Coe & Larios 1988; Haviland 1970, 1985a, 1989; Jones & Satterthwaite 1982; Laporte 1988; Orrego & Larios 1983; Shook et al. 1958; Trik 1963.

*Tikal as a Major Power in the Early Classic*

Coggins 1975, 1990; Culbert 1991c; Culbert et al. 1990; Fahsen 1988; Jones 1991; Laporte & Fialko 1990; Laporte & Vega de Zea 1988; Mathews 1985; A. Miller 1986a; Schele 1986; Schele & Freidel 1990: 131–71.

*Some Neighboring Centers in the Central Lowlands*

Culbert 1991c; Willey & Mathews 1985.
UAXACTUN: I. Graham 1986; Ricketson & Ricketson 1937; A. Smith 1937, 1950; R. Smith 1937, 1955; Valdés 1986, 1988; Von Euw 1984; Wauchope 1934.

*Tikal Consolidates Its Position*

Coggins 1975; Jones 1991; Laporte & Vega de Zea 1988; Mathews 1985; A. Miller 1986a; Schele & Freidel 1990.
*Teotihuacan and other external ties:* Ashmore 1984a; Coggins 1975, 1976, 1980; Fialko 1988, Jones 1979, 1983a; Jones & Sharer 1986; Laporte 1988; Laporte & Fialko 1990.

*Some Other Centers in the Central Lowlands*

RÍO AZUL: Adams 1984, 1986, 1987, 1990.
YAXHA: Hellmuth 1971a,b, 1972; Maler 1908a.
NAKUM: Hellmuth n.d.; Tozzer 1913.
CALAKMUL: Folan 1985, 1988; Folan, Kintz & Fletcher 1983; Folan & May Hau 1984; Marcus 1976b, 1987; Ruppert & Denison 1943.

BECAN: Adams 1975; Andrews 1976; Andrews V & A. Andrews 1979; Ball 1974b, 1977b; Thomas 1980; Webster 1976b.

*The Successors of Stormy Sky at Tikal*

Coggins 1975, 1979; Jones 1991; Laporte & Vega de Zea 1988; Mathews 1985; Schele & Freidel 1990.

*The Basis of Tikal's Power in the Early Classic*

Culbert 1991c; Ford 1986; Jones 1977, 1979, 1991; Mathews 1985; Moholy-Nagy & Nelson 1990; Puleston & Callender 1967; Rice & Rice 1990.

*The Middle Classic "Hiatus" and the Decline of Tikal*

Coggins 1975; Proskouriakoff 1950; Shook et al. 1958; Willey 1974.

## CHAPTER 5: The Late Classic and the Expansion of the Lowland States

*The New Order in the Late Classic*

Culbert 1991b; Proskouriakoff 1993; Rice & Culbert 1990; Sabloff 1985, 1990; Sabloff & Henderson 1993; Turner 1990.

CARACOL: Anderson 1958; Beetz 1980; Beetz & Satterthwaite 1981; A. Chase 1991; Chase & Chase 1987; Chase, Chase & Haviland 1990; Satterthwaite 1950a, 1954; Willcox 1954.

*The Defeat of Tikal and the Rise of the New Polities*

A. Chase 1991; Chase & Chase 1987, 1989; Coggins 1975; Culbert 1991c; Culbert et al. 1990; Houston 1987; Jones 1977, 1991; Schele & Freidel 1990; Willey 1974.

*Further Caracol Conflicts*

Chase & Chase 1987, 1989; Houston 1987; Marcus 1976b; Schele & Freidel 1990.

*The Petexbatun Expansion*

Demarest 1989; Demarest & Houston 1990; Houston 1992; Houston & Mathews 1985; Johnson 1985; Mathews & Willey 1991; Schele & Freidel 1990.

*Resurgence in the Central Lowlands*

Coggins 1975; Culbert 1991c; Graham 1975, 1980; Houston & Mathews 1985; Marcus 1976b; Proskouriakoff 1961b; Schele & Freidel 1990.

*The Expansion of Polities on the Usumacinta*

ALTAR DE SACRIFICIOS: Adams 1971; J. Graham 1972; Houston 1986; Maler 1908b; Mathews & Willey 1991; Saul 1972; Smith 1972; Willey 1972, 1973; Willey & Smith 1963, 1969.

YAXCHILAN: Carrasco 1991; I. Graham 1979, 1982; Graham & Von Euw 1977; Maler 1903; Mathews 1988; Proskouriakoff 1963, 1964; Schele 1991a; Schele & Freidel 1990; Tate 1985, 1986, 1991, 1992.

BONAMPAK: Lounsbury 1982; M. Miller 1986; Ruppert, Thompson & Proskouriakoff 1955; Schele 1991a; Schele & Freidel 1990.

PIEDRAS NEGRAS: Coe 1959, Houston 1983; Maler 1901; Mason 1931, 1932; Proskouriakoff 1960, 1961a; Satterthwaite 1937a,b, 1943, 1944a,b, 1944/1954, 1952; Schele 1991a; Schele & Freidel 1990.

## The Revitalization of Tikal

Ashmore & Sharer 1975; Coggins 1975; Culbert 1991c; Jones 1969, 1977, 1991; A. Miller 1986a; M. Miller 1985; Schele & Freidel 1990; Trik 1963.

## Sites in the Eastern Lowlands

ALTUN HA: Pendergast 1965, 1969, 1971, 1979, 1982a, 1990a.

XUNANTUNICH: Mackie 1961; Maler 1908a; Satterthwaite 1950b.

LUBAANTUN: Gann 1904–5; Hammond 1975; Joyce, Clark & Thompson 1927; Leventhal 1990.

## The Expansion of Polities in the Southwest Lowlands

PALENQUE: Acosta 1977; Berlin 1963; Blom & LaFarge 1926–27; Dütting 1978; González 1993; Josserand 1991; Kelley 1985; Lounsbury 1974, 1976, 1985; Mathews & Schele 1974; Rands & Rands 1959, 1961; Robertson 1983, 1985a,b; Ruz L. 1973; Schele 1981, 1990a, 1991a,b.

## The Early Rulers of Palenque

Lounsbury 1974; Mathews & Robertson 1985; Schele 1991a; Schele & Freidel 1990.

## The Supernatural Basis of Power in the Maya Cosmology

Lounsbury 1976, 1985; Schele & Freidel 1990.

## The Late Rulers of Palenque

Lounsbury 1974; Ruz L. 1973; Schele 1991a; Schele & Freidel 1990.

TONINA: Becquelin 1979; Becquelin & Baudez 1975, 1979, 1982a,b; Becquelin & Taladoire 1991; Mathews 1983.

## Recovery and Decline at Palenque

Schele 1991a,b; Schele & Freidel 1990.

## The Expansion of Polities in the Southwest Lowlands

Boone & Willey 1988; Urban & Schortman 1986.

COPAN: Abrams 1987; Andrews & Fash 1992; Ashmore 1989; Baudez 1983; Cheek 1986; Fash 1982, 1983a,b, 1986, 1987, 1991a, 1991b; Fash & Sharer 1991; Fash et al. 1992; Gordon 1896; Hohman & Vogrin 1982; Miller 1988; Morley 1920, 1989; Rue, Freter & Ballinger 1989; Sanders 1986, 1990; Sharer, Miller & Traxler 1992; Stromsvik 1942, 1952; Trik 1939; Webster 1988; Webster & Freter 1990a,b; Willey & Leventhal 1979; Willey, Leventhal & Fash 1978.

*Archaeology and History at Copan*

Baudez 1986; Fash 1988, 1989, 1991b; Fash & Fash 1990; Fash & Sharer 1991; Fash & Stuart 1991; Riese 1984b, 1988; Schele 1986, 1988; Schele & Freidel 1990; D. Stuart 1987a, 1989; Stuart & Schele 1986; Stuart et al. 1989.

QUIRIGUA: Ashmore 1979, 1980a,b, 1984a,b, 1986, 1988, 1990, in press; Ashmore & Sharer 1978; Becker 1972; Hewett 1911, 1912, 1916; Jones 1983a,b; Jones & Sharer 1986; Morley 1935; Schortman 1986, 1993; Sharer 1978b, 1988b, 1990b, 1991.

*A Tale of Two Cities*

Ashmore 1984a; Fash 1986; Fash & Fash 1990; Fash & Stuart 1991; Kelley 1962b; Marcus 1976a; Proskouriakoff 1973; Riese 1984b, 1988; Schele & Freidel 1990; Sharer 1978b, 1988b, 1990, 1991.

*The Revitalization of Copan*

Ashmore 1989; Fash 1988, 1991b; Fash & Fash 1990; Fash & Sharer 1991; Fash & Stuart 1991; Robinson 1987; Schele & Freidel 1990; Schele & Grube 1987; Schortman et al. 1986; Sheets 1983; Webster 1989.

*The Last Days of Quirigua*

Ashmore 1984b, in press; Schortman 1986, 1993; Sharer 1978b, 1985b, 1990.

*The Development of the Maya Lowlands in the Late Classic*

Culbert 1991a; Culbert & Rice 1990; Marcus 1976b, 1992; Rice & Culbert 1990; Sabloff 1985, 1990; Schele & Mathews 1991; Turner 1990; Willey 1982a, 1987, 1991.

CHAPTER 6: The Terminal Classic

Culbert 1991a; Culbert & Rice 1990; Diehl & Berlo 1989; Fash 1988, 1989; Fash & Fash 1990; Fash & Stuart 1991; Freidel 1986b; R. Joyce 1986, 1988, 1991; Lowe 1985; Marcus 1983a, 1989b; Pendergast 1986; Rice 1988; Rue 1989; Sabloff 1990; Schele & Grube 1987; Sharer 1985b; Stuart 1993; Webster & Freter 1990a; Willey 1982a, 1987.

*The Decline of Dynastic Rule*

Fash 1991b; Schele & Freidel 1990.

*The Collapse Issue*

Culbert 1988; Erasmus 1968; Marcus 1983a; Sabloff 1990, in press; Sabloff & Andrews 1986; Sharer 1982, 1985b; Willey 1987; Yoffee & Cowgill 1988.

*Investigations into the Classic Decline*

*Internal factors:* Abrams & Rue 1988; Adams 1973a; Cook 1921; Cooke 1931; Cowgill 1979; Culbert 1973, 1974, 1977b; Deevey et al. 1979; Demarest 1989; Demarest & Houston 1990; Erasmus 1968; Hamblin & Pitcher 1980; Harrison 1977; Haviland 1967; Lowe 1985; Mackie 1961; Meggers 1954; Puleston 1979; Rathje 1971, 1973; Sabloff & Willey 1967; Sanders 1962, 1963, 1973; Satterthwaite 1937a, 1958; Saul

1973; Sharer 1982, 1985b; Shimkin 1973; Thompson 1954a, 1966; Turner & Harrison 1978.

*External factors:* Adams 1973b; Cowgill 1964; Jones 1979; Sabloff 1973a; Sabloff & Rathje 1975b; Sabloff & Willey 1967; Thompson 1970; Webb 1964, 1973; Willey 1974.

### The Emergence of New Power Brokers

A. Andrews 1990b; Andrews & Robles 1985; Andrews V 1979a,b; Ball 1974a, 1977a, 1986; Edmonsen 1982, 1986; McVicker 1985; Sabloff 1977, 1990, in press; Scholes & Roys 1948; Thompson 1966, 1970.

### Intervention in the Southern Lowlands

Ball 1974a, 1977a; A. Chase 1986; Coggins 1990; Miller 1977a; D. Rice 1986.

SEIBAL: Graham 1973; Maler 1908b; Mathews & Willey 1991; Sabloff 1973b; Sabloff & Willey 1967; Smith 1977; Tourtellot 1970, 1988b; Willey 1975, 1978a,b, 1982b, 1990.

### The Founding of Chichen Itza

Krochock 1989; Schele & Freidel 1991; Wren, Schmidt & Krochock 1989.

### Reconstructing the Classic Decline

Culbert 1988; Erasmus 1968; Lowe 1985; Sabloff 1990; Sharer 1982.

### The Rise of the Northern Polities

A. Andrews 1990b; Andrews & Robles 1985; Anon. 1988, 1989; Ball 1986; A. Chase 1986; Chase & Rice 1985; Kowalski 1985; Pollock 1980; D. Rice 1986; Rice & Andrews 1986; Sabloff 1990, in press.

DZIBILCHALTUN: Andrews IV 1975; Andrews V 1981; Andrews & Andrews 1980; Ball & Andrews 1975; Kurjack 1974; Stuart et al. 1979.

EDZNA: Andrews 1969; Forsyth 1983; Matheny 1976, 1987; Matheny et al. 1985.

COBA AND YAXUNA: Andrews & Robles 1985; Benavides C. 1977, 1979, 1981; Folan, Kintz & Fletcher 1983; Freidel et al. 1990; Thompson, Pollock & Charlot 1932; Villa Rojas 1934.

### The Puuc and Related Regional Traditions

G. Andrews 1975; Barrera Rubio 1980; Harrison 1985; Kubler 1962; Marquina 1951; McAnany 1990; Pollock 1980; Potter 1977; Ruppert & Denison 1943.

UXMAL: Barrera Rubio & Hutchin 1990; Blom 1930; Kowalski 1980, 1987; Morley 1910, 1970; Pollock 1980.

KABAH: Kowalski 1985; Pollock 1980.

SAYIL: Killion et al. 1989; Pollock 1980; Sabloff 1990; Tourtellot, Sabloff & Carmean 1989; Tourtellot, Sabloff & Smyth 1990.

LABNA: Pollock 1980; E. Thompson 1897b.

### The Emergence of a New Order in Yucatan

A. Andrews 1978, 1980a,b, 1990b; Blanton & Feinman 1984; Chase & Rice 1985; Erasmus 1968; Sabloff 1990; Sabloff & Andrews 1986; Sabloff & Rathje 1975a; Sharer 1982; Willey 1982a.

CHAPTER 7: The Postclassic

Andrews & Sabloff 1986; Brotherston 1979; Chase & Rice 1985; Edmonsen 1982, 1986; Kelley 1985; Robles & Andrews 1986; Roys 1933; Sabloff & Andrews 1986; Tozzer 1941; Willey & Phillips 1958.

*The Early Postclassic and the Dominance of Chichen Itza*

Andrews & Gallareta 1986; Andrews & Sabloff 1986; Andrews et al. 1989; Ball 1986; A. Chase 1986; Freidel & Schele 1989a; D. Rice 1986.
CHICHEN ITZA: Bolles 1977; Krochock 1989, 1991; Lincoln 1986; Lothrop 1952; Morris 1931; Morris, Charlot & Morris 1931; Pollock 1937; Proskouriakoff 1974; Ruppert 1931, 1935, 1943, 1952; Wren, Schmidt & Krochock 1989.

*The Organization of the Itza State*

Andrews & Robles 1986; Andrews V 1979a,b; Andrews & Sabloff 1986; Ball 1974a, 1977a, 1986; Freidel, Suhler & Krochock 1990; Kelley 1985; Marcus 1993; Miller 1977a; Ringle 1990; Roys 1943; Sabloff 1977; Schele & Freidel 1990; Scholes & Roys 1948; Thompson 1966, 1970; Tozzer 1941; Wren & Schmidt 1991; Wren, Schmidt & Krochock 1989.

*External Connections of the Itza State*

Abascal et al. 1976; Acosta 1956, 1960; A. Andrews 1990b; Ball 1974a; Blanton & Feinman 1984; Covarrubias 1954; Diehl & Burlo 1989; Fowler 1989; J. W. Fox 1980, 1987; Keleman 1943; Kubler 1961; Litvak-King 1972; McVicker 1985; Miller 1977a; Moreno 1959; Pasztory 1978; Pendergast 1986, 1990b; Sabloff 1973b; Sabloff & Willey 1967; A. Smith 1955; Thompson 1943b, 1948, 1970; Toscano 1944.

*The Late Postclassic and the Dominance of Mayapan*

A. Andrews 1990a; Andrews & Sabloff 1986; Freidel & Sabloff 1984; A. Miller 1986b; Roys 1943, 1965; Sabloff & Rathje 1975a; Tozzer 1941.
MAYAPAN: Bullard 1952; Jones 1952; Pollock 1954; Proskouriakoff 1954, 1955; Shook 1954; Shook & Irving 1955; P. Smith 1955; R. Smith 1954, 1971; Thompson 1954b.
TULUM: Barrera Rubio 1985; Lothrop 1924; Miller 1977b, 1982; Sanders 1960; Sullivan 1989.

*The Fall of Mayapan and the Rise of Petty States*

Andrews & Sabloff 1986; Barrera Vásquez & Morley 1949; Bullard 1970; Edmonsen 1982, 1986; Freidel & Sabloff 1984; Marcus 1993; Pendergast 1986, 1990b; D. Rice 1986; P. Rice 1986; Rice & Rice 1984, 1990; Roys 1943, 1965; Tozzer 1941; Turner 1990; Willey 1986.
SANTA RITA COROZAL: D. Chase 1981, 1985, 1986, 1990, 1991; Gann 1900, 1918.

*The Final Days of Maya Independence*

A. Chase 1979, 1990; Jones, Rice & Rice 1981; Roys 1943, 1965; Villagutierre 1983.

*The Southern Maya Area in the Postclassic*

Borhegyi 1965a,b; Brown 1980; Burkitt 1930b; Carmack 1968, 1973; Dillon 1978; Edmonsen 1971; Fowler 1989; J. W. Fox 1978, 1981, 1987; Gruhn & Bryan 1976; Guillemin 1965, 1967; Ichon 1975, 1977b; Ichon et al. 1980; Lehmann 1968; Lothrop 1933; Richardson 1940; Sanders & Murdy 1982; Sharer & Sedat 1987; Shook & Proskouriakoff 1956; Smith & Kidder 1951; Tedlock 1985; Wallace & Carmack 1977; Wauchope 1948, 1975; Weeks 1983; Woodbury & Trik 1953.

*Summary: The Evolution of Maya Civilization*

Henderson & Sabloff 1993; Marcus 1983a, 1993; Sabloff 1985, 1990; Willey 1991.

CHAPTER 8: Subsistence Systems

*The Traditional View*

Brainerd 1954; Carter 1969; Coe 1966; Cook 1921; U. Cowgill 1962; Dumond 1961; Hester 1954; Lundell 1933; Meggers 1954; Morley & Brainerd 1956; Reina 1967; Ricketson & Ricketson 1937; Sanders 1973; Stadelman 1940; Thompson 1931, 1954a, 1966; Tozzer 1941.
*Evidence from Ceren:* Sheets 1983; Sheets & McKee 1989; Sheets et al. 1990.

*Subsistence Systems Available to the Ancient Maya*

Bronson 1966; Flannery 1982; Hammond 1978b; Harris 1972, 1978; Harrison 1990; Siemens & Puleston 1972; Turner 1974, 1978a; Turner & Harrison 1978, 1983; Vlcek, González & Kurjack 1978; Wilkin 1971; Willey 1978c.
*Hunting and gathering:* Barrera Vásquez 1980; C.I.W. 1935, 1940; Gann 1918; Grisom 1932; Lange 1971; Lundell 1937, 1938; McKillop 1984; Pohl 1983; Puleston & Puleston 1971; D. Rice 1978; Roys 1931; Schmidt & Andrews 1936; L. Stuart 1964; Urban 1978; Wagner 1964.
*Animal husbandry:* Thompson 1974; Tozzer 1941; Turner & Harrison 1978.
*Agriculture:* Boserup 1965; Bronson 1966; Carneiro 1967, 1988; Netting 1977; Puleston 1968; D. Rice 1978; Sanders 1977; Turner & Harrison 1978, 1983.
*Fallow systems:* Netting 1977; Puleston 1978; Sheets & McKee 1989; Turner 1974, 1978b; Wiseman 1978.
*Intensive systems:* Armillas 1971; Culbert, Levi & Cruz 1990; Darch 1983; Denevan 1970; Eaton 1975; Gómez-Pompa, Flores & Fernández 1990; Harrison 1977, 1978, 1990; Healy 1983; Kirke 1980; Matheny 1976; Matheny et al. 1985; McAnany 1990; Netting 1977; Olsen et al. 1975; Puleston 1968, 1971, 1977, 1978; Scarborough 1983; Siemens & Puleston 1972; Turner 1974, 1978b; Wiseman 1978.

*Reconstructing the Patterns of Maya Subsistence*

Abrams & Rue 1988; Carneiro 1988; Dahlin & Litzinger 1986; Deevey et al. 1979; Harrison 1990; Pohl 1990; Puleston 1978; Puleston & Puleston 1971; D. Rice 1978; Rue 1989; Rust & Sharer 1988; Turner & Harrison 1978, 1983; Willey 1978c, 1987.

## CHAPTER 9: Trade and External Contact

*Prehistoric Trade in Mesoamerica*

Chapman 1957; Culbert 1977b; Demarest 1989; Dillon 1975; Duran 1965; Earle & Ericson 1977; Grove 1981a; Hirth 1984; Lee & Navarrete 1978; McBryde 1947; Rathje 1971; Rathje, Gregory & Wiseman 1978; Sabloff & Lamberg-Karlovsky 1975; Sahagún 1946; Sanders 1956; Sanders, Parsons & Santley 1979; Schortman & Urban 1987; Sharer 1977, 1984; Tourtellot & Sabloff 1972; Voorhies 1989.

*Goods and Mechanisms in Long-Distance Trade*

A. Andrews 1983, 1990b; Benzoni 1970; Bittman & Sullivan 1978; Blom 1932; Clark & Lee 1984; Cortés 1928; Díaz del Castillo 1963; Duran 1965; Feldman 1978; Freidel 1981b; Fuentes y Guzmán 1932–34; E. Graham 1987; Guderjan et al. 1989; Hester & Shafer 1984; Jones 1979; Las Casas 1909; Lee & Navarrete 1978; McKillop 1984; McKillop & Healy 1989; MacKinnon & Kepecs 1989; MacKinnon & May 1990; McAnany 1989; P. Rice 1984; Rice et al. 1985; Sabloff 1986; Sahagún 1946; Schortman 1986; Shafer & Hester 1983; Sharer & Sedat 1987; Thompson 1970; Tozzer 1941; Voorhies 1982.

*Preclassic Trade*

A. Andrews 1980a,b; Bishop 1984; Demarest & Sharer 1986; Freidel 1978, 1979a; Garber 1983; Hatch 1989; Jackson & Love 1991; Lowe 1977; Lowe, Lee & Martinez 1973; L. Parsons 1967–69; Rathje 1971; Sanders, Parsons & Santley 1979; Sharer 1974, 1978a, 1984, 1989a; Sharer & Sedat 1987; Sheets 1971, 1976b, 1979a; Voorhies 1982, 1989.

*Classic Trade*

A. Andrews 1980a; Andrews V 1977; Arnauld 1990; Ball 1977a; Bove 1991; Culbert 1991b; Freidel 1978; Hammond 1972; C. Jones 1977, 1979, 1991; R. Joyce 1986; Kidder, Jennings & Shook 1946; King & Potter 1989; Moholy-Nagy 1975, 1976; L. Parsons 1967–69; Pasztory 1978; Rathje 1977; Rathje, Gregory & Wiseman 1978; Sanders & Michels 1977; Sanders, Parsons & Santley 1979; Santley 1980; Schortman et al. 1986; Sidrys 1976; Stross et al. 1983; Tourtellot & Sabloff 1972; Webb 1973; Willey 1974.

*Postclassic Trade*

A. Andrews 1978, 1980a,b; A. Andrews et al. 1989; Andrews & Sabloff 1986; Chapman 1957; Freidel & Sabloff 1984; Fuentes y Guzmán 1932–34; G. Jones 1977; Las Casas 1957; Sabloff & Rathje 1975a,b; Scholes & Roys 1948; Thompson 1970.

## CHAPTER 10: The Organization of Maya Society

*A. Reconstructing the Social Landscape*

Ashmore 1981a; Chang 1972; Farriss 1984; Fash & Sharer 1991; Flannery 1976; Henderson & Sabloff 1993; Houston 1988; Lee & Hayden 1988; Montmollin 1989; Riese 1988; Sabloff 1990; Schele & Freidel 1990; Sharer 1985b, 1991, 1993; Ucko, Tringham & Dimbleby 1972; Willey 1953, 1956, 1982a, 1987.

### Evidence from Settlement Studies

Andrews IV 1965; Andrews & Andrews 1980; Ashmore 1981b, 1983, 1986, in press; Borhegyi 1965b; Bullard 1960; Fash 1983a; J. W. Fox 1978; Haviland 1966, 1968, 1985a, 1989; Montmollin 1989; Puleston 1983; Pyburn 1990; D. Rice 1976, 1986; Sanders 1960; Scarborough 1991; Tourtellot 1988b; Tozzer 1941; Turner & Harrison 1983; Willey & Bullard 1965.

### Population Reconstructions

Ashmore 1984a, 1990; D. Chase 1990; Culbert & Rice 1990; Culbert et al. 1990; Ford 1986; McAnany 1990; Rice & Culbert 1990; Rice & Rice 1990; Turner 1990; Webster & Freter 1990b.

### Settlement Units in the Maya Lowlands

Ashmore 1981a, 1986; Becker 1972, 1973; Bullard 1960; Dahlin & Litzinger 1986; Ford 1991; Haviland 1970, 1988; Manzanilla & Barba 1990; McAnany 1990; Puleston 1971; D. Rice 1988; Sheets 1983; Sheets et al. 1990; Tourtellot 1983, 1988a; Turner, Turner & Adams 1981; D. Wallace 1977; Webster & Gonlin 1988; Wilk 1988; Wilk & Ashmore 1988.

### The Individual in Maya Society

Fowler 1984; Haviland 1968; Rathje 1970; Rice & Culbert 1990; Ruz 1965; Thompson 1954a, 1966; Tozzer 1941.

*Marriage and the family:* Haviland 1967, 1968, 1977; Marcus 1983a, 1987; Molloy & Rathje 1974; Roys 1943, 1965; Scholes & Roys 1948; Tozzer 1907, 1941; Wilk & Ashmore 1988.

### Descent Groups

Carmack 1977; Haviland 1968, 1977, 1985b; Marcus 1976b, 1983a; Mathews & Schele 1974; Proskouriakoff 1961b; Roys 1943, 1965; Scholes & Roys 1948; Sharer 1993; Tozzer 1941.

### Social Stratification

Carmack 1977; Chase & Chase 1992; Hammond 1991; Haviland 1968, 1985a,b; Jones & Kautz 1981; Marcus 1983a, 1987, 1992; Rathje 1970; Roys 1943, 1965; Sharer 1991, 1993; Tozzer 1941; Webster & Gonlin 1988; Wilk & Ashmore 1988; Yoffee 1991.

### B. Reconstructing the Political Landscape

Benson 1986; Bey & Ringle 1989; Culbert 1991a,b; Fash 1988, 1991a; Fash & Fash 1990; Freidel 1981b; Freidel & Schele 1988a, 1989a; Hammond 1991; Henderson & Sabloff 1993; Justeson & Mathews 1983; Laporte & Fialko 1990; Marcus 1976b, 1983a, 1993; Pyburn n.d.; Sabloff 1986, 1990; Schele & Mathews 1991; Sharer 1988a, 1989b; Webster 1976a; Wren & Schmidt 1991.

### Location and Power

*Economic factors:* Adams, Brown & Culbert 1981; A. Andrews 1983, 1990b; Arnauld 1990; Ashmore in press; Blanton & Feinman 1984; Garber 1983; E. Graham 1987; Hester & Shafer 1984; Hirth 1984; Jones 1979, 1991; Lee & Navarrete 1978; Sanders 1977; Sanders & Murdy 1982; Schortman 1986, 1993; Sharer 1978b.

*Ideological factors:* Ashmore 1983, 1986, 1989, in press; Aveni & Hartung 1986; Barthel 1968; Coggins 1980, 1985, 1990; Gillespie 1989; Leventhal 1983; Marcus 1976b, 1983a; Miller 1977b, 1982; Schele 1981.

## Size and Power

Adams & Jones 1981; Andrews & Robles 1985; Benavides 1977, 1981; Dahlin 1984; Marcus 1976b, 1993; Sabloff 1990; Sharer 1978b.

## The Number and Size of Lowland Polities

Adams & Jones 1981; Culbert 1991b,c; Culbert & Rice 1990; Demarest & Houston 1989; Freidel 1983; Hammond 1974a, 1991; Johnson 1985; Jones 1991; Marcus 1973, 1976b, 1993; Mathews 1987, 1991; Sabloff 1990; Sharer 1991; Thompson 1954a.

## Evidence From Ethnohistorical Studies

Carmack 1973; D. Chase 1986; Cline 1972–75; Edmonsen 1971, 1982, 1986; Farriss 1984; J. W. Fox 1981, 1987; Gillespie 1989; Marcus 1993; Recinos 1950; Roys 1943, 1965; Sanders 1981; Scholes & Roys 1948; Tedlock 1982; Tozzer 1941; Wallace & Carmack 1977.

## The Evolution of Social Systems

Abrams 1987; Adams 1970; Adams & Smith 1981; Ashmore 1981b; Becker 1973, 1979; Brainerd 1954; Bullard 1964; Carmack 1977; Chase, Chase & Haviland 1990; Drennan & Uribe 1987; Haviland 1968, 1970, 1977; Marcus 1983a,b, 1989b, 1993; Morley & Brainerd 1956; Sabloff 1985, 1990; Sanders & Price 1968; Sanders & Webster 1989; Sanders et al. 1984; Sharer 1993; Thompson 1954a, 1966; Vogt 1961, 1964b, 1983; Willey 1991.

## The Lowland Maya as Galactic Polities

Adams & Jones 1981; Demarest 1987; Demarest & Houston 1989; Freidel 1981b; Sabloff 1986, 1990.

## CHAPTER 11: Ideology and Cosmology

## The Origins of Maya Ideology

Brotherson 1979; Demarest 1987; Freidel 1990; Freidel & Schele 1988a,b; Houston & Stuart 1989; Marcus 1989a; A. Miller 1986a; Sharer 1988a; Thompson 1970; Tozzer 1907, 1941; Watanabe 1983.

## Transformations by Outsiders

Chamberlain 1948; Edmonsen 1960; Farriss 1984; Fowler 1984; Herrera 1726–30; Kelley 1984; McVicker 1985; Redfield & Villa Rojas 1934; Reed 1964; Roys 1943, 1965; Scholes & Roys 1938, 1948; Sullivan 1989; Tedlock 1982; Thompson 1952, 1970; Tozzer 1941.

*Cosmology*

Coggins 1975; Freidel 1979b; Roys 1943, 1965; Schele & Freidel 1990; Scholes & Roys 1938; Thompson 1970; Tozzer 1941; Watanabe 1983.

*The creation myth:* Berlin 1963; Edmonsen 1971; Kelley 1985; Lounsbury 1976, 1985; Recinos 1950; Schele & Freidel 1990; Taube 1989a; Tedlock 1985.

*The Maya universe:* Ashmore 1983, 1986, 1989, in press; Aveni & Hartung 1986; Bricker 1983; Coggins 1976, 1980, 1990; Harrison 1985; Miller 1985, 1988; Schele 1981; Schele & Freidel 1990.

*The afterlife:* Ashmore 1989; Coe 1988; Fash 1991a; Freidel & Schele 1989b; Schele & Freidel 1990, 1991; Thompson 1970; Tozzer 1941.

*The Maya Deities*

M. Coe 1973, 1975a; Coggins 1979; Edmonsen 1986; Kelley 1976; Ringle 1988; Schellhas 1904; Seler 1902–23; Stone 1985a,b; Stuart 1986; Taube 1985, 1987, 1989a; Thompson 1934, 1939b, 1970; Zimmermann 1956.

*Rituals and Ceremonies*

D. Chase 1991; Fahsen 1987; Herrera 1726–30; Love 1987; Pohl 1983; Schele 1985, 1990a; Schele & Miller 1986; Stone 1985c; D. Stuart 1988a; Thompson 1970; Tozzer 1941.

*Divination and Altered Consciousness*

Borhegyi 1961; Furst 1976; Furst & Coe 1977; Robertson 1972a; Robicsek 1978; Thompson 1946, 1958, 1970; Tozzer 1941.

*Human Sacrifice*

Adams 1971; Benson & Boone 1984; Kowalski & Fash 1991; Orrego & Larios 1983; Proskouriakoff 1974; Schele 1984; Schele & Freidel 1990, 1991.

*The Thirteen Katun Endings, New Year Ceremonies, and Celebrations of the Nineteen Months*

Chase 1985; Coggins 1979, 1990; Taube 1988; Tozzer 1941.

CHAPTER 12: Arithmetic, Calendrics, and Astronomy

*Arithmetic*

Lambert, Ownbey-McLaughlin & McLaughlin 1980; Lounsbury 1978; Morley 1915; Satterthwaite 1947; Thompson 1942, 1950, 1971.

*The Calendar*

Aveni & Hartung 1986; Edmonsen 1988; Justeson & Mathews 1983; Kelley 1976; Lounsbury 1976, 1978; Morley 1915; Thompson 1950, 1971; Tozzer 1941.

*The almanac, the vague year, and the calendar round:* Berendt 1957; Brown 1987; Earle & Snow 1985; Kelley 1976; Lounsbury 1978; Morley 1915; Satterthwaite 1965; Thompson 1971.

*The Long Count and distance-number and period-ending dates:* Andrews IV 1951; Beyer 1936; Linden 1986; Maudslay 1889–1902; Morley 1915, 1916, 1925; Satterthwaite 1965; Spinden 1924, 1930; Taube 1988; Teeple 1931; Thompson 1929, 1950, 1971; Tozzer 1941.

*Correlating the Maya and European calendars:* Andrews IV 1940; Beyer 1935; A. Chase 1986; Goodman 1905; Kelley 1983; Palacios 1932; Satterthwaite & Ralph 1960; Spinden 1924; Thompson 1927, 1935, 1950; Vaillant 1935.

## Astronomy

Aveni 1975a,b, 1979, 1982; Aveni, Gibbs & Hartung 1975; Bricker & Bricker 1983; M. Coe 1975b; Dütting 1985; Fox & Justeson 1978; Hartung 1975; Kelley 1975, 1976; Kelley & Kerr 1973; Lounsbury 1978, 1982; Ricketson & Ricketson 1937; Tate 1986; Teeple 1926, 1931; Thompson 1972b.

## CHAPTER 13 : Language and Writing

Campbell et al. 1978; J. A. Fox 1978; Greenberg 1987; Kaufman 1974; McQuown 1967.

### History of the Mayan Languages

Campbell 1977; Diebold 1960; J. A. Fox 1978; Greenberg 1987; Haas 1969; Kaufman 1964, 1969, 1974; McQuown 1964, 1976; Sapir 1916; Sapper 1897; Swadesh 1967.

*Mixe-Zoquean studies:* Andrews V 1990; Brown & Witkowski 1979; Campbell 1977; Campbell, Justeson & Norman 1980; Campbell & Kaufman 1980; Fox 1979; Josserand 1975; Kaufman 1973, 1976; N. Thomas 1974; Witkowski & Brown 1978.

*Cholan studies:* Charencey 1872; Gates 1920; Kaufman & Norman 1984; Sapper 1897; Thompson 1938.

### The Structure of Mayan Languages

Andrade 1955; Attinasi 1973; Berlin 1968; Blair 1964; Fisher 1973; Fought 1967; J. A. Fox 1978; Keller 1959; McClaran 1973; McQuown 1967; Moran 1935; Smailus 1975a; Thompson 1950; Tozzer 1921.

*Dictionaries and terminology:* Alvarez 1980; Aulie & Aulie 1978; Barrera Vásquez 1980; Berlin, Breedlove & Raven 1974; Berlin & Kay 1969; Eggan 1934; Fox & Justeson 1980; Hunn 1977; Laughlin 1975; Marcus 1982; Martínez-Hernandez 1930; Miles 1957; Moran 1935; Roys 1931.

*Mayan discourse:* Andrade 1971; Bricker 1973; Bruce 1975; Du Bois 1978; Fought 1972, in press; Furbee 1976; Furbee-Losee 1979, 1980; J. Haviland 1977; Josserand 1991; Laughlin 1976, 1977; Schele 1989; Smailus 1975b.

### Maya Documents of the Colonial Period

Coe 1973; Craine & Reindorp 1979; Edmonsen 1971, 1982, 1986; Makemson 1951; Norman 1973; Recinos 1950; Roys 1933; Tedlock 1985.

### Ancient Maya Writing

Ascher & Ascher 1981; Benson 1973; Berlin 1977; Childe 1954; Goodman 1897; Kelley 1976; Justeson 1978; Justeson & Campbell 1984; Marcus 1980; Morgan 1877; Morley

1915, 1946; Smith 1973; Spinden 1917; Stephens 1841; Teeple 1926; Thompson 1950, 1972a.

### Pre-Columbian Maya Texts

*Codices:* Anders 1967, 1968, 1975; Bricker 1983; Coe 1973; Dresden Codex 1880, 1892, 1962; Glass 1975; Glass & Robertson 1975; Kingsborough 1831–48; Knorozov 1982; Lee 1985; Madrid Codex 1869–70, 1892, 1930; A. Miller 1982; Paris Codex 1887, 1909; Stuart 1986; Thompson 1972b; Tozzer 1941; Villacorta & Villacorta 1933; Von Hagen 1944; Zimmermann 1956.

*Other media:* Catherwood 1844; M. Coe 1973, 1975a; CMHI (various dates); Graham 1972; Greene, Rands & Graham 1972; Maler 1901, 1903, 1908a,b, 1911; Maudslay 1889–1902; Mayer 1978; Morley 1920, 1937–38.

### Deciphering Maya Writing

M. Coe 1992; Houston 1986, 1988; Justeson 1978; Kelley 1976; Kubler 1973; Mathews 1986, 1987, 1991; Riese 1971; Schele 1989, 1990b; Schele & Freidel 1990; Stuart & Houston 1989; G. Stuart 1988, 1989; Thompson 1950, 1972a.

*Early work:* Bowditch 1901; Förstemann 1904, 1906; Goodman 1897; Morley 1915; Schellhas 1904; Seler 1904; Teeple 1926, 1931; C. Thomas 1882, 1893; Tozzer 1941; Tozzer & Allen 1910; Whorf 1933, 1942.

*Breakthroughs:* Berlin 1958; Kelley 1976; Knorozov 1958, 1967; Mathews & Schele 1974; Proskouriakoff 1960, 1961a, 1963, 1964; Thompson 1950, 1953, 1971.

*Recent progress:* Bricker 1986, 1987; Closs 1987; Fahsen 1987, 1990; Fox & Justeson 1980, 1984; Hopkins 1991; Houston 1986, 1988; Houston & Stuart 1989; Houston & Taube 1987; Knorozov 1982; Justeson & Campbell 1984; Lounsbury 1973, 1976, 1984; Love 1987; MacLeod 1984; Mathews 1991; Riese 1984a; Schele 1982, 1986, 1989, 1990a,b; Schele, Mathews & Lounsbury n.d.; D. Stuart 1985a,b,c, 1987a,b, 1988b, 1990a, 1993.

### The Mayan Syllabary

Fox & Justeson 1984; Kelley 1976; Knorozov 1958, 1967; Lounsbury 1973; Schele 1990b; Stuart 1987b.

### The Origins of Maya Writing

Coe 1976; Gibson, Shaw & Finamore 1986; J. Graham 1979; Graham, Heizer & Shook 1978; Graham & Porter 1989; Hansen 1991; Justeson 1986; Justeson et al. 1985; Justeson, Norman & Hammond 1988; Kelley 1976; Marcus 1976a; Sharer 1989c; Sharer & Sedat 1973; Winfield C. 1988.

### The Status of Decipherment

Coe 1973, 1992; Culbert 1991b; Fox & Justeson 1984; Hanks & Rice 1989; W. Haviland 1977; Houston 1988; C. Jones 1977; Josserand 1991; Justeson & Campbell 1984; Marcus 1976b, 1992; Schele 1986, 1990a; Sharer 1978b; Stuart 1993; Stuart & Houston 1989.

CHAPTER 14: Architecture, Sculpture, and Painting

*Architecture*

Abrams 1987; G. Andrews 1975; Coe 1990; Garza T. & Kurjack 1980; Hohmann & Vogrin 1982; Ingle 1984; Kowalski 1987; Kubler 1962; Laporte 1988; Marquina 1951; Pollock 1965, 1980; Potter 1977; Proskouriakoff 1946; Smith 1965; Taladoire 1981; Totten 1926; Valdés 1986; Wauchope 1938.

*Architecture and cosmology:* Ashmore 1983, 1986, 1989, in press; Aveni 1982, Aveni & Hartung 1986; Freidel & Schele 1989b; Kowlaski & Fash 1991; Leach 1983; Marcus 1976b; Miller 1985, 1988; Schele 1981, 1990a; Schele & Freidel 1991; Vogt 1964a.

*Stone and Wood Sculpture*

Catherwood 1844; Clancy 1985, 1990; CMHI (various dates); Covarrubias 1954; Greene 1967; Greene, Rands & Graham 1972; Hansen 1991; Jones & Satterthwaite 1982; Keleman 1943; Kubler 1962, 1971; Marcus 1987; Mathews 1985; Maudslay 1889–1902; Miles 1965; Morley 1920, 1937–38; Proskouriakoff 1950, 1965, 1971; M. Robertson 1983, 1985a,b; Sharer 1990b; Shook 1960; Spinden 1913; Stone 1985a; Stromsvik 1942.

*Sculpture and cosmology:* Freidel & Schele 1988a; D. Stuart 1987a, 1989.

*Stucco Modeling*

Blom & LaFarge 1926–27; Maudslay 1889–1902; M. Robertson 1977, 1983, 1985a,b; Sharer, Miller & Traxler 1992; Valdés 1988.

*Painting*

Arnold & Bohor 1975; Barrera Rubio 1980; M. Coe 1973, 1975a; Quirarte 1976, 1979; Coggins 1975; Gordon & Mason 1925–43; Jones 1975; Littmann 1980; Miller 1982; M. Miller 1986; M. Robertson 1985a; Ruppert, Thompson & Proskouriakoff 1955; Shepard 1971; Smith 1950; Thompson 1973b.

CHAPTER 15: Artifacts

*Ceramics and Archaeology*

Gifford 1976; Grube 1991; Hall et al. 1990; Matson 1956; Reents-Budet 1987; Rice & Sharer 1987; Shepard 1948, 1971; D. Stuart 1988b; J. E. Thompson 1970; R. Thompson 1958.

*A Chronological Review of Maya Pottery*

Adams 1971; Andrews V 1990; Andrews & Hammond 1990; Arnauld 1986; Ball 1977b, 1993; Ball & Andrews 1975; Brainerd 1958; Bullard 1970; Coe & Flannery 1967; Culbert 1963; Demarest 1986; Demarest & Sharer 1982a,b, 1986; Ekholm 1969; Forsyth 1983; Fry & Cox 1974; Gifford 1976; Gordon & Mason 1925–43; Green & Lowe 1967; Kidder 1961; Lincoln 1985; Lowe 1977; Parsons 1967–69; Rands & Smith 1965; P. Rice 1987; R. Robertson 1983; Sabloff 1975; Sharer 1978a; Sharer & Sedat 1987; Smith & Gifford 1965; Warren 1961; Wauchope 1970; Wetherington 1978; Willey et al. 1980; Willey, Culbert & Adams 1967.

*Figurines:* Ball 1974b; Borhegyi 1950; Dahlin 1978; Kidder 1965; Lee 1969; R. Rands 1965b; R. Rands & B. Rands 1965.

### Patterns of Household and Industrial Ceramic Production

Ball 1983, 1993; Beaudry 1987; Bishop 1984; D. Chase 1988; Reents-Budet 1987; Reina & Hill 1978; Rice & Sharer 1987; R. Thompson 1958.

### Lithics

*Chipped-stone eccentrics:* Hester & Hammond 1976; Hester & Shafer 1984; Lee 1969; McAnany 1989; Moholy-Nagy & Nelson 1990; Morley 1935; P. Rice 1984; Shafer & Hester 1983; Sheets 1972, 1975, 1976a; Stromsvik 1942; Stross et al. 1983; Willey 1978a.

*Jade and similar carved and polished stone:* Digby 1972; Easby 1961; Foshag & Leslie 1955; Hammond et al. 1977; Kidder 1951; Morley & Morley 1939; Pendergast 1969; Proskouriakoff 1974; Rands 1965a; Woodbury 1965.

### Mosaics

W. Coe 1975; Morris, Charlot & Morris 1931; Rands 1965a; Ruz L. 1973; Sharer & Sedat 1987.

### Metalwork

Bray 1977; Pendergast 1962, 1982b; Stromsvik 1942; Lothrop 1952.

### Textiles, Basketry, and Featherwork

Barrera Vásquez 1939; Fuentes y Guzmán 1932–34; Las Casas 1909; Lounsbury 1973; Mahler 1965; M. Miller 1986; Osborne 1935, 1965; Robicsek 1975; Sahagún 1946; Tozzer 1907.

## Epilogue: The Spanish Conquest

### First Contacts and the Period of Conquest, 1502–1697

Díaz del Castillo 1963; Farriss 1984; G. Jones 1977, 1989; Sahagún 1946.

### The Subjugation of the Southern Maya by Pedro de Alvarado, 1524–27

Alvarado 1924; Edmonsen 1971; Fuentes y Guzmán 1932–34; Las Casas 1909; Recinos 1950; Recinos & Goetz 1953; Tedlock 1985; Ximenez 1929–31.

### The Subjugation of Yucatan by the Montejos, 1527–46

Ancona 1889; Blom 1936; Carrillo y Ancona 1937; Chamberlain 1948; Farriss 1984; G. Jones 1983, 1989; Lizana 1893; Means 1917; Roys 1952; Scholes et al. 1936.

### The Independent Itza and the Subjugation of the Itza, 1525–1697

A. Chase 1979, 1990; Jones, Kautz & Graham 1986; Jones, Rice & Rice 1981; Roys 1943, 1965; Villagutierre 1933, 1983.

# BIBLIOGRAPHY

The following abbreviations are used for frequently cited publications and institutions:

| | |
|---|---|
| A | *Archaeology* |
| AA | *American Anthropologist* |
| AAnt | *American Antiquity* |
| AM | *Ancient Mesoamerica* |
| APA | *Archaeoastronomy in Precolumbian America*, A. F. Aveni, ed. Austin: University of Texas Press, 1975 |
| BAE | Bureau of American Ethnology, Smithsonian Institution |
| BAR | British Archaeological Reports International Series, Oxford |
| CARUTS | Center for Archaeological Research, University of Texas at San Antonio |
| CCM | *Cerámica de Cultura Maya* |
| CEMCA | Centre D'Etudes Mexicaines et Centramericaines, Mexico City |
| CIW | Carnegie Institution of Washington (*NMA: Notes on Middle American Archaeology and Ethnology*) |
| CMHI | Corpus of Maya Hieroglyphic Inscriptions, Peabody Museum, Harvard University |
| CN | Copán Notes, Copán Mosaics Project and the Instituto Hondureño de Antropología e Historia, Copán, Honduras |
| CNRSIE | Centre National de la Recherche Scientifique, Institut d'Ethnologie, Paris |
| DO | Dumbarton Oaks, Trustees for Harvard University, Washington, D.C. |
| ECAUY | Escuela de Ciencias Antropologicas de la Universidad de Yucatán |
| ECM | *Estudios de Cultura Maya* |
| FMAS | Field Museum of Natural History, Anthropological Series, Chicago |
| HMAI | *Handbook of Middle American Indians*, R. Wauchope, general ed. 15 vols. Austin: University of Texas Press, 1964–75 |
| ICA | International Congress of Americanists |
| IJAL | *International Journal of American Linguistics* |

IMS        Institute for Mesoamerican Studies, State University of New York, Albany
INAH       Instituto Nacional de Antropología e Historia, Mexico City
*JFA*        *Journal of Field Archaeology*
*LAA*        *Latin American Antiquity*
MARI       Middle American Research Institute, Tulane University, New Orleans
MCM        Microfilm Collection of Manuscripts on Middle American Cultural
           Anthropology, Regenstein Library, University of Chicago
NWAF       New World Archaeological Foundation, Brigham Young University, Provo,
           Utah
PARI       Pre-Columbian Art Research Institute, San Francisco
PMAE       Peabody Museum of Archaeology and Ethnology, Harvard University,
           Cambridge, Mass.
PRTS       Palenque Round Table Series:
           Parts I–II: 1974. M. G. Robertson, ed. Pebble Beach, Calif.: The Robert
           Louis Stevenson School
           Part III: 1976. M. G. Robertson, ed. Pebble Beach, Calif.: The Robert
           Louis Stevenson School
           Vol. 4: 1978. M. G. Robertson and D. C. Jeffers, eds. Palenque: Pre-
           Columbian Art Research Center
           Vol. 5: 1980. M. G. Robertson, ed. Austin: University of Texas Press
           Vol. 6: 1985. E. P. Benson, ed. San Francisco: PARI
           Vol. 7: 1985. V. M. Fields, ed. San Francisco: PARI
           Vol. 8: 1991. M. G. Robertson, ed. Norman: University of Oklahoma
           Press
RRAMW      Research Reports on Ancient Maya Writing, Center for Maya Research,
           Washington, D.C.
*SA*         *Scientific American*
SAR        School of American Research, Advanced Seminar Series, Santa Fe, N.M.
*SHMAI*      *Supplement to Handbook of Middle American Indians*, Vol. 1. J. A. Sabloff,
           ed. Austin: University of Texas Press, 1981
*SWJA*       *Southwestern Journal of Anthropology*
UCARF      University of California Archaeological Research Facility, University of
           California, Berkeley
UM         University Museum, University of Pennsylvania, Philadelphia
*WA*         *World Archaeology*

Abascal, R., P. Davila, P. J. Schmidt, and D. Z. Davila. 1976. *La arqueología del sur-oeste de Tlaxcala*. Primera Parte. Suplemento, Comunicaciones Proyecto Puebla-Tlaxcala. Puebla, Mexico: Fundación Alemana para la Investigación Científica.

Abrams, E. M. 1987. Economic Specialization and Construction Personnel in Classic Period Copan, Honduras. *AAnt* 52: 485–99.

Abrams, E. M., and D. Rue. 1988. The Causes and Consequences of Deforestation Among the Prehistoric Maya. *Human Ecology* 16: 377–95.

Acosta, J. R. 1956. Exploraciones arqueológicas en Tula, Hidalgo, Temporadas VI, VII, y VIII. *INAH Anales* 8: 37–115.

————. 1960. Las exploraciones arqueológicas en Tula, Hidalgo, durante la XI temporada, 1955. *INAH Anales* 11: 39–72.

————. 1977. Excavations at Palenque, 1967–1973. In Hammond 1977b: 265–85.

Adams, R. E. W. 1970. Suggested Classic-Period Occupational Specialization in the Southern Maya Lowlands. PMAE Papers 61: 489–502.

————. 1971. *The Ceramics of Altar de Sacrificios.* PMAE Papers 63 (1).

————. 1972. Maya Highland Prehistory: New Data and Implications. UCARF Contribution 16: 1–21.

————. 1973a. The Collapse of Maya Civilization: A Review of Previous Theories. In Culbert 1973: 21–34.

————. 1973b. Maya Collapse: Transformation and Termination in the Ceramic Sequence at Altar de Sacrificios. In Culbert 1973: 133–63.

————, comp. 1975. Preliminary Reports on Archaeological Investigations in the Río Bec Area, Campeche, Mexico. MARI Publication 31: 103–46.

————, ed. 1977. *The Origins of Maya Civilization.* SAR. Albuquerque: University of New Mexico Press.

————. 1980. Swamps, Canals, and the Locations of Ancient Maya Cities. *Antiquity* 54: 206–14.

————. 1981. Settlement Patterns of the Central Yucatan and Southern Campeche Regions. In Ashmore 1981b: 211–57.

————, ed. 1984. *Río Azul Reports, No. 1: The 1983 Season.* CARUTS.

————, ed. 1986. *Río Azul Reports, No. 2: The 1984 Season.* CARUTS.

————, ed. 1987. *Río Azul Reports, No. 3: The 1985 Season.* CARUTS.

————. 1990. Archaeological Research at the Lowland Maya Site of Río Azul. *LAA* 1: 23–41.

Adams, R. E. W., and R. C. Aldrich. 1980. A Reevaluation of the Bonampak Murals: A Preliminary Statement on the Paintings and Texts. PRTS 5: 45–59.

Adams, R. E. W., V. L. Broman, W. R. Coe, W. A. Haviland, R. E. Reina, L. Satterthwaite, E. M. Shook, and A. S. Trik. 1961. Tikal Report Nos. 5–10. UM Monograph 20.

Adams, R. E. W., W. E. Brown, and T. P. Culbert, 1981. Radar Mapping, Archaeology, and Ancient Maya Land Use. *Science* 213: 1457–63.

Adams, R. E. W., and R. C. Jones. 1981. Spatial Patterns and Regional Growth Among Maya Cities. *AAnt* 46: 301–22.

Adams, R. E. W., and W. D. Smith. 1977. Apocalyptic Visions: The Maya Collapse and Mediaeval Europe. *A* 30: 292–301.

————. 1981. Feudal Models for Classic Maya Civilization. In Ashmore 1981b: 335–49.

Adams, R. E. W., and A. S. Trik. 1961. Temple I (Str. 5D-1): Post-constructional Activities. Tikal Report 7. UM Monograph 20: 113–47.

Adams, R. M. 1958. On the Environmental Limitations of Maya Cultural Development. *SWJA* 14: 189–98.

Alvarado, P. de. 1924. *An Account of the Conquest of Guatemala in 1524.* Trans. S. J. Mackie. New York: Cortés Society.

Alvarez, C. 1980. *Diccionario etnolingüístico del idioma Maya Yucateco colonial.* Vol. 1: *Mundo físico.* Mexico City: Universidad Nacional Autónoma de México.

Amram, D. W. 1942. The Lacandon, Last of the Maya. *El México Antiguo* 6: 15–26.

Ancona, E. 1889. *Historia de Yucatán*. 2d ed. 4 vols. Barcelona: Raviratta.

Anders, F., ed. 1967. *Codex Tro-Cortesianus (Codex Madrid), Museo de América, Madrid*. Graz: Akademische Druck- und Verlagsanstalt.

———, ed. 1968. *Codex Peresianus (Codex Paris), Bibliothèque Nationale, Paris*. Graz: Akademische Druck- und Verlagsanstalt.

———, ed. 1975. *Codex Dresdensis, Sächsische Landesbibliothek Dresden*. Graz: Akademische Druck- und Verlagsanstalt.

Anderson, A. H. 1958. More Discoveries at Caracol, British Honduras. 33rd ICA *Actas* 2: 211–18.

Anderson, D. 1978. Monuments. In Sharer 1978a: 155–80.

Andrade, M. J. 1955. A Grammar of Modern Yucatec. MCM, No. 41.

———. 1971. Yucatec Maya Texts. MCM, No. 108.

Andrews, A. P. 1978. Puertos costeros del Postclasico Temprano en el norte de Yucatán. *ECM* 11: 75–93.

———. 1980a. The Salt Trade of the Ancient Maya. *A* 33 (4): 24–33.

———. 1980b. Salt-Making, Merchants and Markets: The Role of a Critical Resource in the Development of Maya Civilization. Ph.D. diss., University of Arizona.

———. 1983. *Maya Salt Production and Trade*. Tucson: University of Arizona Press.

———. 1990a. The Fall of Chichen Itza: A Preliminary Hypothesis. *LAA* 1: 258–67.

———. 1990b. The Role of Trading Ports in Maya Civilization. In Clancy and Harrison 1990: 159–67.

Andrews, A. P., F. Asaro, H. V. Michel, F. H. Stross, and P. Cervera R. 1989. The Obsidian Trade at Isla Cerritos, Yucatan, Mexico. *JFA* 16: 355–63.

Andrews, A. P., and T. Gallareta N. 1986. The Isla Cerritos Archaeological Project, Yucatan, Mexico. *Mexicon* 8 (3): 44–48.

Andrews, A. P., and F. Robles C. 1985. Chichen Itza and Coba: An Itza-Maya Standoff in Early Postclassic Yucatan. In Chase and Rice 1985: 62–72.

Andrews, E. W., IV. 1940. Chronology and Astronomy in the Maya Area. In *The Maya and Their Neighbors*, C. L. Hay et al., eds.: 150–61. New York: Appleton Century.

———. 1951. The Maya Supplementary Series. 29th ICA *Selected Papers* 1: 123–41.

———. 1965. Archaeology and Prehistory in the Northern Maya Lowlands: An Introduction. In *HMAI* 2: 288–330.

———. 1975. Progress Report on the 1960–1964 Field Seasons NGS-Tulane University Dzibilchaltun Program. MARI Publication 31: 23–67.

Andrews, E. W., IV, and E. W. Andrews V. 1980. *Excavations at Dzibilchaltun, Yucatan, Mexico*. MARI Publication 48.

Andrews, E. W., V, and B. W. Fash. 1992. Continuity and Change in a Royal Maya Residential Complex at Copan. *AM* 3: 63–88.

Andrews, E. W., V. 1977. The Southeastern Periphery of Mesoamerica: A View from Eastern El Salvador. In Hammond 1977b: 113–34.

———. 1979a. Some Comments on Puuc Architecture of the Northern Yucatan Peninsula. In *The Puuc: New Perspectives*, L. Mills, ed.: 1–17. Pella, Iowa: Central College Press.

———. 1979b. Early Central Mexican Architectural Traits at Dzibilchaltun, Yucatan. 42nd ICA *Actas* 8: 237–49.

———. 1981. Dzibilchaltun. In *HMAI Supplement 1*, J. A. Sabloff, ed.: 313–41. Austin: University of Texas Press.

———, ed. 1986. *Research and Reflections in Archaeology and History: Essays in Honor of Doris Stone*. MARI Publication 57.

———. 1990. The Early Ceramic History of the Lowland Maya. In Clancy and Harrison 1990: 1–19.

Andrews, E. W., V, and A. P. Andrews. 1979. NGS-Tulane University Program of Archaeological Research in the Yucatan Peninsula, Mexico. *National Geographic Society Research Reports*, 1970 Projects: 7–22.

Andrews, E. W., V, and N. Hammond. 1990. Redefinition of the Swasey Phase at Cuello, Belize. *AAnt* 55: 570–84.

Andrews, E. W., V, W. M. Ringle, P. J. Barnes, A. Barrera R., and T. Gallareta N. 1984. Komchen, an Early Maya Community in Northwest Yucatan. In *Investigaciones recientes en el área maya* 1: 73–92. Mexico City: XVII Mesa Redonda, Sociedad Mexicana de Antropología.

Andrews, E. W., V, and J. A. Sabloff. 1986. Classic to Postclassic: A Summary Discussion. In Sabloff and Andrews 1986: 433–56.

Andrews, G. F. 1969. *Edzna, Campeche, Mexico: Settlement Patterns and Monumental Architecture*. Eugene: University of Oregon.

———. 1975. *Maya Cities: Placemaking and Urbanization*. Norman: University of Oklahoma Press.

Andrews, G. F., D. Hardesty, C. Kerr, F. E. Miller, and R. Mogul. 1967. *Comalcalco, Tabasco, Mexico: An Architectonic Survey*. Eugene: University of Oregon.

Andrews, J. M. 1976. Reconnaissance and Archaeological Excavations in the Río Bec Area of the Maya Lowlands. *National Geographic Society Research Reports*, 1968 Projects: 19–27.

Anon. 1988. *Oxkintok 1*. Madrid: Misión Arqueológica de España en México.

———. 1989. *Oxkintok 2*. Madrid: Misión Arqueológica de España en México.

Armillas, P. 1971. Gardens on Swamps. *Science* 174: 653–61.

Arnauld, M. C. 1986. *Archéologie de l'Alta Verapaz, Guatemala: habitat et société*. CEMCA.

———. 1990. El comercio clásico de obsidiana: rutas entre tierras altas y tierras bajas en el area maya. *LAA* 1: 347–67.

Arnold, D. E., and B. F. Bohor. 1975. Attapulgite and Maya Blue. *A* 28: 23–29.

Arqueta, J. G. 1979. Introducción al patron de asentamiento del sitio de Cobá, Quintana Roo. Thesis, Escuela Nacional de Antropología e Historia, Mexico City.

Ascher, M., and R. Ascher. 1969. Code of Ancient Peruvian Knotted Cords (Quipus). *Nature* 222: 529–53.

———. 1981. *Code of the Quipu*. Ann Arbor: University of Michigan Press.

Ashmore, W. A., ed. 1979. *Quirigua Reports I*. UM.

———. 1980a. The Classic Maya Settlement at Quirigua. *Expedition* 23 (1): 20–27.

———. 1980b. Discovering Early Classic Quirigua. *Expedition* 23 (1): 35–44.

———. 1981a. Some Issues of Method and Theory in Lowland Maya Settlement Archaeology. In Ashmore 1981b: 37–70.

———, ed. 1981b. *Lowland Maya Settlement Patterns*. SAR. Albuquerque: University of New Mexico Press.

———. 1983. Ideological Structure in Ancient Maya Settlement Patterns. Paper presented at the 82nd Annual Meeting of the American Anthropological Association, Chicago.

———. 1984a. Quirigua Archaeology and History Revisited. *JFA* 11: 365–86.

———. 1984b. Classic Maya Wells at Quirigua, Guatemala: Household Facilities in a Water-rich Setting. *AAnt* 49: 147–53.

———. 1986. Peten Cosmology in the Maya Southeast: An Analysis of Architecture and Settlement Patterns at Classic Quirigua. In Urban and Schortman 1986: 35–49.

———. 1988. Household and Community at Classic Quirigua. In Wilk and Ashmore 1988: 153–69.

———. 1989. El Proyecto Copán Cosmología: Concepts of Directionality Among the Ancient Maya. Paper presented at the V Seminario de Arqueología Hondureña, Copán, Honduras.

———. 1990. Ode to a Dragline: Demographic Reconstructions at Classic Quirigua. In Culbert and Rice 1990: 63–82.

———. In press. *Quirigua Reports IV. Settlement Archaeology at Quirigua, Guatemala: Ecological, Social, and Ideological Aspects of a Precolumbian Landscape.* University Museum Monographs. UM.

Ashmore, W. A., E. M. Schortman, and R. J. Sharer. 1983. The Quirigua Project: 1979 Season. In *Quirigua Reports II*, E. M. Schortman and P. A. Urban, eds. UM.

Ashmore, W. A., and R. J. Sharer. 1975. A Revitalization Movement at Late Classic Tikal. Paper presented at the Area Seminar in Ongoing Research, West Chester State College.

———. 1978. Excavations at Quirigua, Guatemala: The Ascent of an Elite Maya Center. *A* 31 (6): 10–19.

Ashmore, W. A., and G. R. Willey. 1981. An Historical Introduction to the Study of Lowland Maya Settlement Patterns. In Ashmore 1981b: 3–18.

Attinasi, J. J. 1973. Lak T'an: A Grammar of the Chol (Mayan) Word. Ph.D. diss., University of Chicago.

Aulie, H. W., and E. W. Aulie. 1978. *Diccionario Ch'ol-Español, Español-Ch'ol.* Serie de Vocabularios y Diccionarios Indígenas Mariano Silva y Aceves, No. 21. Mexico City: Instituto Lingüístico de Verano.

Aveni, A. F. 1975a. Possible Astronomical Orientations in Ancient Mesoamerica. In Aveni 1975b: 163–90.

———, ed. 1975b. *Archaeoastronomy in Precolumbian America.* Austin: University of Texas Press.

———. 1979. Venus and the Maya. *American Scientist* 67: 274–85.

———, ed. 1982. *Archaeoastronomy in the New World.* Cambridge, Eng.: Cambridge University Press.

Aveni, A. F., S. L. Gibbs, and H. Hartung. 1975. The Caracol Tower at Chichen Itza: An Ancient Astronomical Observatory? *Science* 188: 977–85.

Aveni, A. F., and H. Hartung. 1986. Maya City Planning and the Calendar. *Transactions of the American Philosophical Society* 76 (7). Philadelphia.

Ball, J. W. 1974a. A Coordinate Approach to Northern Maya Prehistory: A.D. 700–1200. *AAnt* 39: 85–93.

———. 1974b. A Teotihuacan-Style Cache from the Maya Lowlands. *A* 27 (1): 2–9.

———. 1977a. An Hypothetical Outline of Coastal Maya Prehistory: 300 B.C.–A.D. 1200. In Hammond 1977b: 167–96.

———. 1977b. *The Archaeological Ceramics of Becan, Campeche, Mexico.* MARI Publication 43.

————. 1978. Archaeological Pottery of the Yucatan-Campeche Coast. MARI Publication 46: 76–146.

————. 1979. Southern Campeche and the Mexican Plateau: Early Classic Contact Situation. 42nd ICA *Actas* 8: 271–80.

————. 1980. Ceramics and Central Mexican Highland–Maya Lowland Classic-Period Social Interaction: A Theoretical Perspective. Paper presented at the DO Symposium on Mesoamerican Highland-Lowland Interaction, Washington, D.C.

————. 1983. Teotihuacan, the Maya, and Ceramic Interchange: A Contextual Perspective. In A. G. Miller 1983: 126–46.

————. 1986. Campeche, the Itza, and the Postclassic: A Study in Ethnohistorical Archaeology. In Sabloff and Andrews 1986: 379–408.

————. 1993. Ceramics of the Lowlands. In Sabloff and Henderson 1993.

Ball, J. W., and E. W. Andrews V. 1975. The Polychrome Pottery of Dzibilchaltun, Yucatan, Mexico: Typology and Archaeological Context. MARI Publication 31: 227–47.

Barrera Rubio, A. 1978. Settlement Patterns in the Uxmal Area, Yucatan, Mexico. Paper presented at the 43rd Annual Meeting of the Society for American Archaeology, Tucson.

————. 1980. Mural Paintings of the Puuc Region in Yucatan. PRTS 5: 173–82.

————. 1985. Littoral-Marine Economy at Tulum, Quintana Roo, Mexico. In Chase and Rice 1985: 50–61.

Barrera Rubio, A., and J. Hutchin H. 1990. *Architectural Restoration at Uxmal, 1986–1987.* University of Pittsburgh Latin American Archaeology Reports No. 1. Pittsburgh.

Barrera Vásquez, A. 1939. Algunos datos acerca del arte plumaria entre los Mayas. *Cuadernos Mayas* 1. Mérida.

————. 1980. *Diccionario Maya Cordemex, Maya-Español, Español-Maya.* Mérida: Ediciones Cordemex.

Barrera Vásquez, A., and S. G. Morley. 1949. *The Maya Chronicles.* CIW Publication 585.

Barthel, T. 1968. El complejo "emblema." *ECM* 7: 159–93.

Baudez, C. F., ed. 1983. *Introducción a la arqueología de Copán, Honduras.* 3 vols. Tegucigalpa: Secretaría de Estado en el Despacho de Cultura y Turismo, y Instituto Hondureño de Antropología e Historia.

————. 1986. Iconography and History at Copán. In Urban and Schortman 1986: 17–26.

Beaudry, M. P. 1987. Southeast Maya Polychrome Pottery: Production, Distribution, and Style. In Rice and Sharer 1987: 503–23.

Becker, M. J. 1972. Plaza Plans at Quirigua, Guatemala. *Katunob* 8 (2): 47–62.

————. 1973. Archaeological Evidence for Occupational Specialization Among the Classic-Period Maya at Tikal, Guatemala. *AAnt* 38: 396–406.

————. 1979. Priests, Peasants and Ceremonial Centers: The Intellectual History of a Model. In Hammond and Willey 1979: 3–20.

————. 1988. Caches as Burial, Burials as Caches: The Meaning of Ritual Deposits Among the Classic Period Lowland Maya. In *Recent Studies in Pre-Columbian Archaeology,* N. J. Saunders and O. de Montmollin, eds. BAR 421: 117–42.

Becquelin, P. 1969. *Archéologie de la region de Nebaj (Guatemala).* Memoires de l'Institut d'Ethnologie No. 2. Paris.

————. 1979. Tonina: A City State of the Western Maya Periphery. Paper presented at the 43rd ICA, Vancouver.

Becquelin, P., and C. Baudez, eds. 1975. Architecture et sculpture à Tonina, Chiapas, Mexique. 41st ICA *Actas* 1: 433–35.

———, eds. 1979. *Tonina, une cité Maya du Chiapas, Tome I.* CEMCA.

———, eds. 1982a. *Tonina, une cité Maya du Chiapas, Tome II.* CEMCA.

———, eds. 1982b. *Tonina, une cité Maya du Chiapas, Tome III.* CEMCA.

Becquelin, P., and E. Taladoire. 1991. *Tonina, une cité Maya du Chiapas, Tome IV.* CEMCA.

Beetz, C. P. 1980. Caracol Thirty Years Later: A Preliminary Account of Two Rulers. *Expedition* 22 (3): 4–11.

Beetz, C. P., and L. Satterthwaite. 1981. *The Monuments and Inscriptions of Caracol, Belize.* University Museum Monograph 45. UM.

Benevides Castillo, A. 1976. El sistema prehispánico de comunicaciones terrestres en la región de Cobá, Quintana Roo, y sus inplicaciones sociales. Thesis, Universidad Nacional Autónoma de México.

———. 1977. Los caminos prehispánicos de Cobá. *XV Mesa Redonda de la Sociedad Mexicana de Antropología* 2: 215–25.

———. 1979. Cobá y Tulum: adaptación al medio ambiente y control del medio social. Paper presented at the 43rd ICA, Vancouver.

———. 1981. Cobá: *una ciudad prehispánica de Quintana Roo.* Mexico City: INAH Centro Regional de Sureste.

Benson, E. P., ed. 1968. *Dumbarton Oaks Conference on the Olmec.* DO.

———, ed. 1973. *Mesoamerican Writing Systems.* DO.

———. 1977a. *The Maya World.* Rev. ed. New York: Crowell.

———, ed. 1977b. *The Sea in the Pre-Columbian World.* DO.

———, ed. 1987. *City States of the Maya: Art and Architecture.* Denver: Rocky Mountain Institute for Pre-Columbian Studies.

Benson, E. P., and E. H. Boone, eds. 1984. *Ritual Human Sacrifice in Mesoamerica.* DO.

Benson, E. P., and G. G. Griffin, eds. 1988. *Maya Iconography.* Princeton: Princeton University Press.

Benzoni, G. 1970. *History of the New World.* Trans. W. H. Smith. New York: Lenox Hill.

Berdan, F. F. 1978. Ports of Trade in Mesoamerica: A Reappraisal. In Lee and Navarrete 1978: 187–98.

Berendt, C. H. 1957. Calendario cakchiquel de los indios de Guatemala, 1685. *Antropología e Historia de Guatemala* 9 (2): 17–29.

Berlin, B. 1968. *Tzeltal Numeral Classifiers: A Study in Ethnographic Semantics.* The Hague: Mouton.

Berlin, B., D. E. Breedlove, and P. H. Raven. 1974. *Principles of Tzeltal Plant Classification.* New York: Academic Press.

Berlin, B., and P. Kay. 1969. *Basic Color Terms: Their Universality and Evolution.* Berkeley: University of California Press.

Berlin, H. 1958. El glifo "emblema" en las inscripciones mayas. *Journal de la Société des Américanistes* 47: 111–19.

———. 1959. Glifos nominales en el sarcófago de Palenque. *Humanidades* 2 (10): 1–8.

———. 1963. The Palenque Triad. *Journal de la Société des Américanistes* 52: 91–99.

———. 1965. The Inscription of the Temple of the Cross at Palenque. *AAnt* 30: 330–42.

———. 1970. The Tablet of the 96 Glyphs at Palenque, Chiapas, Mexico. MARI Publication 26: 137–49.

———. 1977. *Signos y significados en las inscripciones mayas*. Guatemala: Instituto Nacional del Patrimonio Cultural de Guatemala.

Bernal, I. 1969. *The Olmec World*. Trans. from the Spanish by D. Heyden and F. Horcasitas. Berkeley: University of California Press.

Bey, G. J., and W. M. Ringle. 1989. The Myth of the Center: Political Integration at Ek Balam, Yucatan, Mexico. Paper presented at the 54th Annual Meeting of the Society for American Archaeology, Atlanta.

Beyer, H. 1931. The Analysis of the Maya Hieroglyphs. *Internationales Archiv für Ethnographie* 31: 1–20.

———. 1935. On the Correlation Between Maya and Christian Chronology. *Maya Research* 2 (1): 64–72.

———. 1936. The True Zero Date of the Maya. *Maya Research* 3: 202–4.

———. 1937. *Studies on the Inscriptions at Chichen Itza*. CIW Publication 483.

Bishop, R. L. 1984. Análisis por activación de neutrones de la cerámica de El Mirador. *Mesoamerica* 5 (7): 103–11.

Bittman, B., and T. D. Sullivan. 1978. The Pochteca. In NWAF Paper 40: 211–18.

Blair, R. W. 1964. Yucatec Maya Noun and Verb Morphology. Ph.D. diss., Indiana University. Also in MCM, No. 109.

Blanton, R., and G. Feinman. 1984. The Mesoamerican World System. *AA* 86: 673–82.

Blom, F. 1930. Uxmal: The Great Capital of the Xiu Dynasty of the Maya. *Art and Archaeology* 30: 198–209.

———. 1932. *Commerce, Trade and Monetary Units of the Maya*. MARI Publication 4.

———. 1936. *The Conquest of the Yucatan*. Boston: Houghton Mifflin.

Blom, F., and O. La Farge. 1926–27. *Tribes and Temples*. MARI Publications 1 and 2.

Boggs, S. H. 1950. Olmec Pictographs in the Las Victorias Group, Chalchuapa Archaeological Zone, El Salvador. CIW *NMA* 99.

Bolles, J. S. 1977. *Las Monjas: A Major Pre-Mexican Architectural Complex at Chichen Itza*. Norman: University of Oklahoma Press.

Boone, E. H., and G. R. Willey, eds. 1988. *The Southeast Maya Zone*. DO.

Borhegyi, S. F. 1950. A Group of Jointed Figurines in the Guatemala National Museum. CIW *NMA* 100.

———. 1961. Miniature Mushroom Stones from Guatemala. *AAnt* 26: 498–504.

———. 1965a. Archaeological Synthesis of the Guatemalan Highlands. In *HMAI* 2: 3–58.

———. 1965b. Settlement Patterns of the Guatemalan Highlands. In *HMAI* 2: 59–75.

Boserup, E. 1965. *The Conditions of Agricultural Growth: The Economics of Agrarian Change Under Population Pressure*. Chicago: Aldine.

Bove, F. J., ed. 1989. *New Frontiers in the Archaeology of the Pacific Coast of Southern Mesoamerica*. Arizona State University Anthropological Research Papers No. 39. Tempe.

———. 1991. The Teotihuacan-Kaminaljuyu-Tikal Connection: A View from the South Coast of Guatemala. PRTS 8: 135–42.

Bowditch, C. P. 1901. *Notes on the Report of Teobert Maler in Memoirs of the Peabody Museum* 2 (1). PMAE.

———. 1910. *The Numeration, Calendar Systems and Astronomical Knowledge of the Mayas*. Cambridge, Mass: University Press.

Brainerd, G. W. 1954. *The Maya Civilization*. Los Angeles: Southwest Museum.

————. 1958. *The Archaeological Ceramics of Yucatan.* Anthropological Records, No. 19. University of California, Berkeley.

Brasseur de Bourbourg, C. E. 1866. *Palenque et autres ruines de l'ancienne civilisation du Mexique.* Paris: Bertrand.

Bray, W. 1977. Maya Metalwork and Its External Connections. In Hammond 1977b: 365–403.

Bricker, H. M., and V. R. Bricker. 1983. Classic Maya Prediction of Solar Eclipses. *Current Anthropology* 24: 1–24.

Bricker, V. R. 1973. *Ritual Humor in Highland Chiapas.* Austin: University of Texas Press.

————. 1983. Directional Glyphs in Maya Inscriptions and Codices. *AAnt* 48: 347–53.

————. 1986. *A Grammar of Mayan Hieroglyphs.* MARI Publication 56.

————. 1987. Noun and Verb Morphology in the Maya Script. Paper presented at the 86th Annual Meeting of the American Anthropological Association, Chicago.

Brinton, D. G. 1882. *The Maya Chronicles.* Brinton's Library of Aboriginal American Literature, No. 1. Philadelphia.

————. 1885. *The Annals of the Cakchiquels.* Brinton's Library of Aboriginal American Literature, No. 6. Philadelphia.

————. 1895. *A Primer of Mayan Hieroglyphs.* University of Pennsylvania Series in Philology, Literature and Archaeology 3 (2). Philadelphia.

Bronson, B. 1966. Roots and the Subsistence of the Ancient Maya. *SWJA* 22: 251–59.

Brotherston, G. 1979. Continuity in Maya Writing: New Readings of Two Passages in the Book of Chilam Balam of Chumayel. In Hammond and Willey 1979: 241–58.

Brown, C., and S. Witkowski. 1979. Aspects of the Phonological History of Mayan-Zoquean. *IJAL* 45: 34–47.

Brown, C. H. 1987. The Linguistic History of Mayan Year (*ha?ab'). *Anthropological Linguistics* 29: 362–88.

Brown, K. L. 1977. The Valley of Guatemala: A Highland Port of Trade. In Sanders and Michels 1977: 205–395.

————. 1979. Ecology and Settlement Systems in the Guatemalan Highlands. Paper presented at the 44th Annual Meeting of the Society for American Archaeology, Vancouver.

————. 1980. A Brief Report on Paleo-Indian-Archaic Occupation in the Quiche Basin, Guatemala. *AAnt* 45: 313–24.

Brown, K. L., and T. Majewski. 1979. Culture History of the Central Quiche Area. Paper presented at the Popol Vuh Conference, Santa Cruz del Quiche, Guatemala.

Bruce, R. D. 1975. *Lacandon Dream Symbolism: Dream Symbolism and Interpretation Among the Lacandon Maya of Chiapas, Mexico.* Mexico City: Ediciones Euro-Americanas Klaus Thiele.

Bullard, M. R., and R. J. Sharer. n.d. *The Pottery of Quirigua, Guatemala.* Quirigua Reports. UM Monograph.

Bullard, W. R., Jr. 1952. *Residential Property Walls at Mayapan.* CIW Current Reports, Department of Archaeology, No. 3.

————. 1960. Maya Settlement Pattern in Northeastern Peten, Guatemala. *AAnt* 25: 355–72.

————. 1964. Settlement Pattern and Social Structure in the Southern Maya Lowlands During the Classic Period. Paper presented at the 35th ICA, Mexico City.

————. 1970. Topoxte, A Postclassic Site in Peten, Guatemala. In PMAE Papers 61: 245–307.

Bunzel, R. 1952. *Chichicastenango, a Guatemalan Village*. American Ethnological Society Publication 22. Locust Valley, N.Y.

Burkitt, R. 1930a. Excavations at Chocola. *UM Journal* 15: 115–44.

————. 1930b. Explorations in the Highlands of Western Guatemala. *UM Journal* 21: 41–72.

Byers, D. S., ed. 1967. *The Prehistory of the Tehuacan Valley*. Vol. 1: *Environment and Subsistence*. Austin: University of Texas Press.

Campbell, L. R. 1976. The Linguistic Prehistory of the Southern Mesoamerican Periphery. *XIV Mesa Redonda, Sociedad Mexicana de Antropología* 1: 157–83.

————. 1977. *Quichean Linguistic Prehistory*. University of California Publications in Linguistics, No. 81. Berkeley: University of California Press.

———— (with P. Ventur, R. Stewart, and B. Gardner). 1978. *Bibliography of Mayan Languages and Linguistics*. IMS Publication No. 3.

Campbell, L. R., J. S. Justeson, and W. C. Norman. 1980. Foreign influence on Lowland Mayan Language and Script. Paper presented at the DO Symposium on Mesoamerican Highland-Lowland Interaction, Washington, D.C.

Campbell, L. R., and T. S. Kaufman. 1976. A Linguistic Look at the Olmecs. *AAnt* 41: 80–89.

————. 1980. On Mesoamerican Linguistics. *AA* 82: 850–57.

————. 1984. The implications of Mayan Historical Linguistics for Glyphic Research. In Justeson and Campbell 1984: 1–16.

Carlson, J. B. 1980. On Classic Maya Monumental Recorded History. PRTS 5: 199–203.

Carmack, R. M. 1968. Toltec Influences on the Postclassic Culture History of Highland Guatemala. MARI Publication 26: 49–92.

————. 1973. *Quichean Civilization*. Berkeley: University of California Press.

————. 1977. Ethnohistory of the Central Quiche: The Community of Utatlan. In Wallace and Carmack 1977: 1–19.

————. 1981. *The Quiche Mayas of Utatlan*. Norman: University of Oklahoma Press.

Carmack, R. M., and J. M. Weeks. 1981. The Archaeology and Ethnohistory of Utatlan: A Conjunctive Approach. *AAnt* 46: 323–41.

Carnegie Institution of Washington, 1935. *Botany of the Maya Area*. CIW Publication 461.

————. 1940. *Botany of the Maya Area*. CIW Publication 522.

Carneiro, R. L. 1967. On the Relationship Between Size of Population and Complexity of Social Organization. *SWJA* 23: 234–43.

————. 1970. A Theory of the Origin of the State. *Science* 169: 733–38.

————. 1988. The Circumscription Theory. *American Behavioral Scientist* 31: 497–511.

Carr, R. F., and J. E. Hazard. 1961. *Map of the Ruins of Tikal, El Peten, Guatemala*. Tikal Report No. 11, UM Monograph 21.

Carrasco V. R. 1991. The Structure 8 Tablet and the Development of the Great Plaza at Yaxchilan. PRTS 8: 110–17.

Carrillo y Ancona, C. 1937. *Historia antigua de Yucatán*, Mérida: Tipográfica Yucateca.

Carter, W. E. 1969. *New Lands and Old Traditions: Kekchi Cultivators in the Guatemalan Lowlands*. Latin American Monograph No. 6 Gainesville: University of Florida Press.

Caso, A. 1936. *La religión de los Aztecas*. Mexico City: Imprenta Mundial.

———. 1965. Sculpture and Mural Painting of Oaxaca. In *HMAI* 3: 849–70.

Catherwood, F. 1844. *Views of Ancient Monuments in Central America, Chiapas, and Yucatan*. New York: Barlett and Welford.

Chamberlain, R. S. 1948. *The Conquest and Colonization of Yucatan*, 1517–1550. CIW Publication 582.

Chang, K. C. 1972. *Settlement Patterns in Archaeology*. Reading, Mass.: Addison-Wesley Modules in Anthropology, No. 24.

Chapman, A. M. 1957. Port of Trade Enclaves in Aztec and Maya Civilizations. In *Trade and Market in the Early Empires*, K. Polanyi, C. Arensberg, and H. Pearson, eds. Glencoe, Ill.: Free Press.

Charencey, H. de. 1872. Recherches sur les lois phonétiques dans les idiomes de la famille Mame-Huastèque. *Revue de Linguistique et de Philologie Comparée* 5: 129–67.

Chase, A. F. 1976. Topoxte and Tayasal: Ethnohistory in Archaeology. *AAnt* 41: 154–67.

———. 1979. Regional Development in the Tayasal-Paxcaman Zone, El Peten, Guatemala: A Preliminary Statement. *CCM* 11: 87–119.

———. 1986. Time Depth of Vacuum: The 11.3.0.0.0 Correlation and the Lowland Maya Postclassic. In Sabloff and Andrews 1986: 99–140.

———. 1990. Maya Archaeology and Population Estimates in the Tayasal-Paxcaman Zone, Peten, Guatemala. In Culbert and Rice 1990: 149–65.

———. 1991. Cycles of Time: Caracol in the Maya Realm. PRTS 8: 32–42.

Chase, A. F., and D. Z. Chase, 1987. *Investigations at the Classic Maya City of Caracol, Belize: 1985–1987*. PARI Monograph 3.

———. 1989. The Investigation of Classic Period Maya Warfare at Caracol, Belize. *Mayab* 5: 5–18.

———, eds. 1992. *Mesoamerican Elites: An Archaeological Assessment*. Norman: University of Oklahoma Press.

Chase, A. F., D. Z. Chase, and H. W. Topsey. 1988. Archaeology and the Ethics of Collecting. *A* 41 (1): 56–60, 87.

Chase, A. F., N. Grube, and D. Z. Chase. 1991. Three Terminal Classic Monuments from Caracol, Belize. RRAMW 36.

Chase, A. F., and P. M. Rice, eds. 1985. *The Lowland Maya Postclassic*. Austin: University of Texas Press.

Chase, D. Z. 1981. The Maya Postclassic at Santa Rita Corozal. *A* 34 (1): 25–33.

———. 1985. Ganned but Not Forgotten: Late Postclassic Archaeology and Ritual at Santa Rita Corozal, Belize. In Chase and Rice 1985: 104–25.

———. 1986. Social and Political Organization in the Land of Cacao and Honey: Correlating the Archaeology and Ethnohistory of the Postclassic Lowland Maya. In Sabloff and Andrews 1986: 347–77.

———. 1988. Caches and Censerwares: Meaning from Maya Pottery. In *A Pot for All Reasons*, C. C. Kolb and M. Kirkpatrick, eds.: 81–104. Philadelphia: Cerámica de Cultura Maya (Special Publication).

———. 1990. The Invisible Maya: Population History and Archaeology at Santa Rita Corozal. In Culbert and Rice 1990: 199–213.

———. 1991. Lifeline to the Gods: Ritual Bloodletting at Santa Rita Corozal. PRTS 8: 89–96.

Chase, D. Z., A. F. Chase, and W. A. Haviland. 1990. The Classic Maya City: Reconsidering "The Mesoamerican Urban Tradition." *AA* 92: 499–506.

Cheek, C. D. 1977a. Excavations at the Palangana and the Acropolis, Kaminaljuyu. In Sanders and Michels 1977: 1–204.

———. 1977b. Teotihuacan Influence at Kaminaljuyu. In Sanders and Michels 1977: 441–52.

———. 1980. The Developmental Sequence in the Plaza, the Main Group, Copan, Honduras. Paper presented at the 44th Annual Meeting of the Society for American Archaeology, Philadelphia.

———. 1986. Construction Activity as a Measurement of Change at Copán, Honduras. In Urban and Schortman 1986: 50–71.

Childe, V. G. 1954. *What Happened in History*. Harmondsworth, Eng.: Penguin.

Clancy, F. S. 1985. Maya Sculpture. In Gallenkamp and Johnson 1985: 58–70.

———. 1990. A Genealogy for Freestanding Maya Monuments. In Clancy and Harrison 1990: 21–32.

Clancy, F. S., and P. D. Harrison, eds. 1990. *Vision and Revision in Maya Studies*. Albuquerque: University of New Mexico Press.

Clark, J. E., M. Blake, P. Guzzy, M. Cuevas, and T. Salcedo. 1987. *Early Preclassic Pacific Coastal Project*. Final report submitted to INAH, Mexico City.

Clark, J. E., and T. A. Lee. 1984. Formative Obsidian Exchange and the Emergence of Public Economies in Chiapas, Mexico. In Hirth 1984: 235–74.

Clewlow, C. W. 1974. *A Stylistic and Chronological Study of Olmec Monumental Sculpture*. UCARF Contribution 18.

Clewlow, C. W., and H. F. Wells. 1986. El Balsamo: A Middle Preclassic Complex on the South Coast of Guatemala. In Pahl 1986: 27–40.

Cliff, M. B. 1988. Domestic Architecture and the Origins of Complex Society at Cerros. In Wilk and Ashmore 1988: 199–225.

Cline, H. F. 1944. Lore and Deities of the Lacandon Indians, Chiapas, Mexico. *Journal of American Folklore* 57: 107–15.

———, ed. 1972–75. Guide to Ethnohistorical Sources. In *HMAI* 12–15.

Closs, M. P. 1985. The Dynastic History of Naranjo: The Middle Period. PRTS 7: 65–77.

———. 1987. Bilingual Glyphs. RRAMW No. 12.

———. 1988. The Hieroglyphic Text of Stela 9, Lamanai, Belize. RRAMW No. 21.

Cobean, R., M. Coe, E. Perry, K. Turekian, and D. Kharkar. 1971. Obsidian Trade at San Lorenzo Tenochtitlan, Mexico. *Science* 174: 666–71.

Coe, M. D. 1961. *La Victoria: An Early Site on the Pacific Coast of Guatemala*. PMAE Papers 53.

———. 1965. The Olmec Style and Its Distribution. In *HMAI* 3: 739–75.

———. 1966. *The Maya*. New York: Praeger.

———. 1968. *America's First Civilization*. New York: American Heritage.

———. 1970. The Archaeological Sequence at San Lorenzo Tenochtitlan, Veracruz, Mexico. UCARF Contribution 8: 21–34.

———. 1973. *The Maya Scribe and His World*. New York: Grolier Club.

———. 1975a. *Classic Maya Pottery at Dumbarton Oaks*. DO.

———. 1975b. Native Astronomy in Mesoamerica. In Aveni 1975b: 3–31.

———. 1976. Early Steps in the Evolution of Maya Writing. In *Origins of Religious Art and Iconography in Preclassic Mesoamerica*, H. B. Nicholson, ed.: 107–22. Los Angeles: UCLA Latin American Center Publications/Ethnic Arts Council of Los Angeles.

———. 1977. Olmec and Maya: A Study in Relationships. In Adams 1977: 183–95.

———. 1980. *The Maya*. Rev. and enlarged ed. New York: Thames and Hudson.

———. 1987. *The Maya*. 4th ed. New York: Thames and Hudson.

———. 1988. Ideology of the Maya Tomb. In Benson and Griffin 1988: 222–35.

———. 1989. The Royal Fifth: Earliest Notices of Maya Writing. RRAMA No. 28.

———. 1992. *Breaking the Code*. New York: Thames and Hudson.

Coe, M. D., and R. A. Diehl. 1980. *In the Land of the Olmec*. 2 vols. Austin: University of Texas Press.

Coe, M. D., and K. V. Flannery. 1964. The Pre-Columbian Obsidian Industry of El Chayal, Guatemala. *AAnt* 30: 43–49.

———. 1967. *Early Cultures and Human Ecology in South Coastal Guatemala*. Smithsonian Contributions to Anthropology 3. Washington, D.C.: Smithsonian Institution.

Coe, W. R. 1959. *Piedras Negras Archaeology: Artifacts, Caches and Burials*. UM Monograph 18.

———. 1962. A Summary of Excavation and Research at Tikal, Guatemala: 1956–61. *AAnt* 27: 479–507.

———. 1965a. Tikal, Guatemala, and Emergent Maya Civilization. *Science* 147: 1401–19.

———. 1965b. Tikal: Ten Years of Study of a Maya Ruin in the Lowlands of Guatemala. *Expedition* 8 (1): 5–56.

———. 1968. Tikal: In Search of the Mayan Past. In *The World Book Yearbook*: 160–90. Chicago: Field Educational Enterprises.

———. 1975. Resurrecting the Grandeur of Tikal. *National Geographic* 148 (6): 792–95.

———. 1990. *Excavations in the Great Plaza, North Terrace and North Acropolis of Tikal*. 6 vols. Tikal Report No. 14. UM.

Coe, W. R., and W. A. Haviland. 1982. *Introduction to the Archaeology of Tikal, Guatemala*. Tikal Report No. 12. UM.

Coe, W. R., and R. Larios V. 1988. *Tikal: A Handbook of the Ancient Maya Ruins*. 2d ed. Guatemala: UM and Asociación Tikal.

Coggins, C. C. 1972. Archaeology and the Art Market. *Science* 175: 263–66.

———. 1975. Painting and Drawing Styles at Tikal: An Historical and Iconographic Reconstruction. Ph.D. diss., Harvard University.

———. 1976. Teotihuacan at Tikal in the Early Classic Period. 42nd ICA *Actas* 8: 251–69.

———. 1979. A New Order and the Role of the Calendar: Some Characteristics of the Middle Classic Period at Tikal. In Hammond and Willey 1979: 38–50.

———. 1980. The Shape of Time: Some Political Implications of a Four-part Figure. *AAnt* 45: 729–39.

———. 1985. Maya Iconography. In Gallenkamp and Johnson 1985: 47–57.

———. 1990. The Birth of the Baktun at Tikal and Seibal. In Clancy and Harrison 1990: 79–97.

Cohodas, M. 1978. *The Great Ball Court at Chichen Itza, Yucatan, Mexico*. New York: Garland.

Cook, O. F. 1921. Milpa Agriculture: A Primitive Tropical System. In *Annual Report of the Smithsonian Institution, 1919*: 307–26. Washington, D.C.

Cooke, C. W. 1931. Why the Mayan Cities of the Peten District, Guatemala, Were Abandoned. *Journal of the Washington Academy of Sciences* 21 (13): 283–87.

Cortés, Hernán. 1928. *Five Letters of Cortés to the Emperor (1519–1526)*. Trans. J. B. Morris. New York: Norton.

Covarrubias, M. A. 1954. *The Eagle, the Jaguar, and the Serpent: Indian Art of the Americas.* New York: Knopf.

Cowgill, G. L. 1964. The End of the Classic Maya Culture: A Review of Recent Evidence. *SWJA* 20: 145–59.

———. 1979. Teotihuacan, Internal Militaristic Competition, and the Fall of the Classic Maya. In Hammond and Willey 1979: 51–62.

Cowgill, U. M. 1962. An Agricultural Study of the Southern Maya Lowlands. *AA* 64: 273–86.

Cowgill, U. M., and G. E. Hutchinson. 1963. El Bajo de Santa Fe. *Transactions of the American Philosophical Society* 53 (7). Philadelphia.

Craine, E. R., and R. C. Reindorp, eds. and trans. 1979. *The Codex Pérez and the Book of Chilam Balam of Maní*. Norman: University of Oklahoma Press.

Culbert, T. P. 1963. Ceramic Research at Tikal, Guatemala. *CCM* 1: 34–42.

———, ed. 1973. *The Classic Maya Collapse*. SAR. Albuquerque: University of New Mexico Press.

———. 1974. *The Lost Civilization: The Story of the Classic Maya*. New York: Harper and Row.

———. 1977a. Early Maya Development at Tikal, Guatemala. In Adams 1977: 27–43.

———. 1977b. Maya Development and Collapse: An Economic Perspective. In Hammond 1974b: 509–30.

———. 1985. Maya Ceramics. In Gallenkamp and Johnson 1985: 71–83.

———. 1988. The Collapse of Classic Maya Civilization. In Yoffee and Cowgill 1988: 69–101.

———, ed. 1991a. *Classic Maya Political History*. SAR. Cambridge: Cambridge University Press.

———. 1991b. Maya Political History and Elite Interaction: A Summary View. In Culbert 1991a: 311–46.

———. 1991c. Polities in the Northeast Peten, Guatemala. In Culbert 1991a: 128–46.

Culbert, T. P., L. J. Kosakowsky, R. E. Fry, and W. A. Haviland. 1990. The Population of Tikal, Guatemala. In Culbert and Rice 1990: 103–21.

Culbert, T. P., L. J. Levi, and L. Cruz. 1990. Lowland Maya Wetland Agriculture. In Clancy and Harrison 1990: 115–24.

Culbert, T. P., and D. S. Rice, eds. 1990. *Precolumbian Population History in the Maya Lowlands*. Albuquerque: University of New Mexico Press.

Dahlin, B. H. 1976. An Anthropologist Looks at the Pyramids: A Late Classic Revitalization Movement at Tikal, Guatemala. Ph.D. diss., Temple University.

———. 1978. Figurines. In Sharer 1978a: 134–211.

———. 1979. Cropping Cash in the Protoclassic: A Cultural Impact Statement. In Hammond and Willey 1979: 21–37.

———. 1983. Climate and Prehistory on the Northern Yucatan Peninsula. *Climate Change* 5: 245–63.

————. 1984. A Colossus in Guatemala: The Preclassic City of El Mirador. *A* 37 (5): 18–25.

Dahlin, B. H., and W. J. Litzinger. 1986. Old Bottle, New Wine: The Function of Chultuns in the Maya Lowlands. *AAnt* 51: 721–36.

Dahlin, B. H., R. Quizar, and A. Dahlin. 1987. Linguistic Divergence and the Collapse of Preclassic Maya Civilization. *AAnt* 52: 367–82.

Darch, J. P., ed. 1983. *Drained Field Agriculture in Central and South America.* BAR 189.

Dávalos Hurtado, E., and A. Romano Pacheco. 1973. Estudio preliminar de los restos osteológicos encontrados en la tumba del Templo de las Inscripciones, Palenque. In Ruz Lhuillier 1973: 253–54.

Deevey, E. S., D. S. Rice, P. M. Rice, H. H. Vaughan, M. Brenner, and M. S. Flannery. 1979. Maya Urbanism: Impact on a Tropical Karst Environment. *Science* 206: 298–306.

del Rio, A. 1822. *Description of the Ruins of an Ancient City Discovered near Palenque, in the Kingdom of Guatemala, in Spanish America.* Trans. from the Spanish. London: Berthoud and Suttaby, Evance and Fox.

Demarest, A. A. 1981. Santa Leticia and the Development of Complex Society in Southeastern Mesoamerica. Ph.D. diss., Harvard University.

————. 1986. *The Archaeology of Santa Leticia and the Rise of Maya Civilization.* MARI Publication 52.

————. 1987. Ideology in Ancient Maya Cultural Evolution: The Dynamics of Galactic Polities. Paper prepared for the SAR Advanced Seminar, "Ideology and Cultural Evolution in the New World," Santa Fe.

————. 1988. Political Evolution in the Maya Borderlands. In Boone and Willey 1988: 335–94.

————. 1989. The Olmec and the Rise of Civilization in Eastern Mesoamerica. In Sharer and Grove 1989: 303–44.

Demarest, A. A., and J. Conrad. 1983. Ideological Adaptation and the Rise of the Aztec and Inca Empires. In Leventhal and Kolata 1983: 345–400.

Demarest, A. A., and W. R. Fowler, eds. 1984. Proyecto El Mirador de la Harvard University, 1982–1983. *Mesoamérica* 5 (7): 1–160.

Demarest, A. A., and S. D. Houston. 1989. The Dynamism and Heterogeneity of Ancient Maya States. Paper presented at the 54th Annual Meeting of the Society for American Archaeology, Atlanta.

————, eds. 1990. Proyecto Arqueologico Regional Petexbatun. Informe Preliminar No. 2, Segunda Temporada 1990. A Report presented to the Instituto de Antropología e Historia de Guatemala.

Demarest, A. A., and R. J. Sharer. 1982a. The Origins and Evolution of Usulutan Ceramics. *AAnt* 47: 810–22.

————. 1982b. The 1982 Ceramic Excavation Program at El Mirador, Guatemala. Paper presented at the 44th International Congress of Americanists, Manchester, England.

————. 1986. Interregional Patterns in the Late Preclassic of Southeastern Mesoamerica: A Definition of Highland Ceramic Spheres. In Urban and Schortman 1986: 194–223.

Demarest, A. A., R. J. Sharer, W. L. Fowler, E. King, and J. Fowler. 1984. Las excavaciones. In *Proyecto El Mirador de la Harvard University, 1982–1983*, A. A. Demarest and W. R. Fowler, eds. *Mesoamerica* 5 (7): 14–52.

Demarest, A. A., R. Switsur, and R. Berger. 1982. The Dating and Cultural Associations of the "Potbellied" Sculptural Style: New Evidence from Western El Salvador. *AAnt* 47: 557–71.

Denevan, W. M. 1970. Aboriginal Drained-Field Cultivation in the Americas. *Science* 169: 647–54.

Díaz del Castillo, B. 1963. *The Conquest of New Spain*. Trans. and introduction by J. M. Cohen. Baltimore: Penguin.

Diebold, A. R., Jr. 1960. Determining the Centers of Dispersal of Language Groups. *IJAL* 26: 1–10.

Diehl, R. A., and J. C. Berlo, eds. 1989. *Mesoamerica After the Decline of Teotihuacan, A.D. 700–900*. DO.

Digby, A. 1972. *Maya Jades*. London: Trustees of the British Museum.

Dillon, B. D. 1975. Notes on Trade in Ancient Mesoamerica. UCARF Contribution 24: 80–135.

———. 1977. *Salinas de los Nueve Cerros, Guatemala*. Socorro, N.M.: Ballena Press.

———. 1978. A Tenth-Cycle Sculpture from Alta Verapaz, Guatemala. UCARF Contribution 36: 39–46.

Dobkin de Rios, M. 1974. The Influence of Psychotropic Flora and Fauna on Maya Religion. *Current Anthropology* 15: 147–64.

Drennan, R. D., and C. A. Uribe, eds. 1987. *Chiefdoms in the Americas*. Lanham, Md.: University Press of America.

Dresden Codex. 1880. *Die Maya-Handschrift der Königlichen Bibliothek zu Dresden*. Ed. E. Förstemann. Leipzig: Röder. 2d ed., 1892, reprinted as *Codex Dresdensis: Die Maya-Handschrift in der Sächsischen Landesbibliothek Dresden*. Foreword by E. Lips. Berlin: Akademie-Verlag, 1962. (See also Anders 1975; Kingsborough 1831–48; Thompson 1972b; Villacorta and Villacorta 1933.)

Drucker, P. 1952. *La Venta, Tabasco: A Study of Olmec Ceramic and Art*. BAE Bulletin 153.

Drucker, P., R. F. Heizer, and R. J. Squier. 1955. *Excavations at La Venta, Tabasco, 1955*. BAE Bulletin 170.

Du Bois, J. W. 1978. Mayan Sign Language: An Ethnography of Non-Verbal Communication. Paper presented at the 77th Annual Meeting of the American Anthropological Association, Los Angeles.

Dumond, D. E. 1961. Swidden Agriculture and the Rise of Maya Civilization. *SWJA* 17: 301–16.

Dunham, P. S., T. R. Jameson, and R. M. Leventhal. 1989. Secondary Development and Settlement Economics: The Classic Maya of Southern Belize. *Research in Economic Anthropology*, Supplement 4: 255–92.

Durán, D. 1965. *Historia de las Indias de Nueva España y islas de tierra firme*. Mexico City: Editoria Nacional.

Dütting, D. 1978. Birth, Inauguration and Death in the Inscriptions of Palenque, Chiapas, Mexico. PRTS 4: 183–214.

———. 1985. On the Astronomical Background of Mayan Historical Events. PRTS 7: 261–74.

Earle, D. M., and D. R. Snow. 1985. The Origin of the 260-day Calendar: The Gestation Hypothesis Reconsidered in Light of Its Use Among the Quiche Maya. PRTS 7: 241–44.

Earle, T. K., and J. E. Ericson, eds. 1977. *Exchange Systems in Prehistory*. New York: Academic Press.

Easby, E. 1961. The Squier Jades from Tonina, Chiapas. In *Essays in Pre-Columbian Art and Archaeology*, S. K. Lothrop et al., eds. 60–80. Cambridge, Mass.: Harvard University Press.

Eaton, J. D. 1975. Ancient Agricultural Farmsteads in the Río Bec Region of Yucatan. UCARF Contribution 27: 56–82.

——. 1978. Archaeological Survey of the Yucatan–Campeche Coast. MARI Publication 46: 1–67.

Edmonson, M. S. 1960. Nativism, Syncretism and Anthropological Science. MARI Publication 19: 181–203.

——. 1967. Classical Quiche. In *HMAI* 5: 249–67.

——. 1971. *The Book of Counsel: The Popol Vuh of the Quiche Maya of Guatemala*. MARI Publication 35.

——, ed. and trans. 1982. *The Ancient Future of the Itza: The Book of Chilam Balam of Tizimin*. Austin: University of Texas Press.

——. 1986. *Heaven Born Merida and Its Destiny: The Book of Chilam Balam of Chumayel*. Austin: University of Texas Press.

——. 1988. *The Book of the Year: Middle American Calendrical Systems*. Salt Lake City: University of Utah Press.

Edwards, E. R. 1978. Precolumbian Maritime Trade in Mesoamerica. In Lee and Navarrete 1978: 199–209.

Eggan, F. 1934. The Maya Kinship System and Cross-Cousin Marriage. *AA* 36: 188–202.

Ekholm, S. M. 1969. *Mound 30a and the Early Preclassic Ceramic Sequence of Izapa, Chiapas, Mexico*. NWAF Paper 25.

——. 1973. *The Olmec Rock Carving at Xoc, Chiapas, Mexico*. NWAF Paper 32.

Erasmus, C. J. 1968. Thoughts on Upward Collapse: An Essay on Explanation in Anthropology. *SWJA* 24: 170–94.

Escoto, J. A. 1964. Weather and Climate of Mexico and Central America. In *HMAI* 1: 187–215.

Fahsen, F. 1987. A Glyph for Self-Sacrifice in Several Maya Inscriptions. RRAMW No. 11.

——. 1988. A New Early Classic Text from Tikal. RRAMW No. 17.

——. 1990. A Logograph in Maya Writing for the Verb "To Record." *AM* 1: 91–98.

Farriss, N. M. 1984. *Maya Society Under Colonial Rule: The Collective Enterprise of Survival*. Princeton: Princeton University Press.

Fash, W. L. 1982. A Middle Formative Cemetery from Copán, Honduras. Paper presented at the 81st Annual Meeting of the American Anthropological Association, Washington, D.C.

——. 1983a. Deducing Social Organization from Classic Maya Settlement Patterns: A Case Study from the Copan Valley. In Leventhal and Kolata 1983: 261–88.

——. 1983b. Maya State Formation: A Case Study and Its Implications. Ph.D. diss., Harvard University.

——. 1986. History and Characteristics of Settlement in the Copán Valley, and Some Comparisons with Quirigua. In Urban and Schortman 1986: 72–93.

——. 1987. EI PECEMCO: Orígenes, metas y alcances. Paper presented at the IV Seminario de Arqueología Hondureña, La Ceiba, Honduras.

——. 1988. A New Look at Maya Statecraft from Copan, Honduras. *Antiquity* 62: 157–59.

———. 1989. Politics, Patronage, and Polity in the Evolution of Dynastic Power at Copan, Honduras. Paper presented at the 54th Annual Meeting of the Society for American Archaeology, Atlanta.

———. 1991a. Lineage Patrons and Ancestor Worship Among the Classic Maya Nobility: The Case of Copan Structure 9N-82. *PRTS* 8: 68–80.

———. 1991b. *Scribes, Warriors and Kings: The City of Copan and the Ancient Maya.* New York: Thames and Hudson.

Fash, W. L., and B. Fash. 1990. Scribes, Warriors, and Kings. *A* 45 (3): 26–35.

Fash, W. L., and R. J. Sharer. 1991. Sociopolitical Developments and Methodological Issues at Copan, Honduras: A Conjunctive Perspective. *LAA* 2: 166–87.

Fash, W. L., and D. Stuart. 1991. Dynastic History and Cultural Evolution at Copan, Honduras. In Culbert 1991a: 147–79.

Fash, W. L., R. V. Williamson, C. R. Larios, and J. Palka. 1992. The Hieroglyphic Stairway and Its Ancestors: Investigations of Copan Structure 10L-26. *AM* 3: 105–16.

Feldman, L. H. 1978. Moving Merchandise in Protohistoric Central Quauhtemallan. NWAF Paper 40: 7–17.

Fernández, M. A., and H. Berlin. 1954. Drawing of Glyphs and Structure XVIII, Palenque. CIW *NMA* 119.

Fettweis-Vienot, M. 1980. Las pinturas murales de Coba. ECAUY *Boletin* 7 (40): 2–50.

Fialko, V. 1988. Mundo perdido, Tikal: un ejemplo de complejos de conmemoración astronómica. *Mayab* 4: 13–21.

Fisher, W. M. 1973. Towards the Reconstruction of Proto-Yucatec. Ph.D. diss., University of Chicago.

Flannery, K. V. 1968. The Olmec and the Valley of Oaxaca: A Model for Interregional Interaction in Formative Times. In Benson 1968: 79–117.

———, ed. 1976. *The Early Mesoamerican Village.* New York: Academic Press.

———, ed. 1982. *Maya Subsistence: Studies in Memory of Dennis E. Puleston.* New York: Academic Press.

Flannery, K. V., and J. Marcus. 1976. Formative Oaxaca and the Zapotec Cosmos. *American Scientist* 64: 374–83.

———, eds. 1983. *The Cloud People: Divergent Evolution of the Zapotec and Mixtec Civilizations.* New York: Academic Press.

Folan, W. J. 1985. Calakmul, Campeche: un centro urbano, estado y región en relación al concepto del resto de la Gran Mesoamérica. *Información* 9: 161–85.

———. 1988. Calakmul, Campeche: el nacimiento de la tradición clásica en la Gran Mesoamérica. *Información* 13: 122–90.

Folan, W. J., E. R. Kintz, and L. A. Fletcher. 1983. *Coba: A Maya Metropolis.* New York: Academic Press.

Folan, W. J., and J. May Hau. 1984. Proyecto Calakmul 1982–1984: el mapa. *Información* 8: 1–14.

Folan, W. J., G. E. Stuart, L. A. Fletcher, and E. R. Kintz. 1977. El proyecto cartográfico arqueológico de Cobá, Quintana Roo. ECAUY *Boletín* 4 (22, 23): 14–18.

Follett, P. H. F. 1932. *War and Weapons of the Maya.* MARI Publication 4.

Foncerrada de Molina, M. 1980. Mural Painting in Cacaxtla and Teotihuacan Cosmopolitism. PRTS 5: 183–98.

Ford, A. 1986. *Population Growth and Social Complexity: An Examination of Settlement and Environment in the Central Maya Lowlands*. Arizona State University Anthropological Research Papers No. 35. Tempe.

———. 1990. Maya Settlement in the Belize River Area: Variations in Residence Patterns of the Central Maya Lowlands. In Culbert and Rice 1990: 167–81.

———. 1991. Economic Variation of Ancient Maya Residential Settlement in the Upper Belize River Area. *AM* 2: 35–46.

Ford, J. A. 1962. *A Quantitative Method for Deriving Cultural Chronology*. Technical Manual 1. Washington, D.C.: Department of Social Affairs, Pan American Union.

Förstemann, E. W. 1904. Translations of Various Papers. BAE Bulletin 28: 393–590.

———. 1906. *Commentary on the Maya Manuscript in the Royal Public Library of Dresden*. PMAE Papers 4 (2).

Forsyth, D. W. 1983. *Investigations at Edzna, Campeche, Mexico*. Vol. 2: *Ceramics*. NWAF Publication 46.

———. 1989. *The Ceramics of El Mirador, Petén, Guatemala*. NWAF Publication 63.

Foshag, W. F., and R. Leslie. 1955. Jade from Manzanal, Guatemala. *AAnt* 21: 81–82.

Fought, J. G. 1967. Chorti (Mayan): Phonology, Morphophonemics, and Morphology. Ph.D. diss., Yale University.

———. 1972. *Chorti (Mayan) Texts*. Philadelphia: University of Pennsylvania Press.

———. In press. Cyclical Patterns in Chorti (Mayan) Literature. In *HMAI Supplement 2*, M. S. Edmonsen, ed. Austin: University of Texas Press.

Fowler, W. R. 1984. Late Preclassic Mortuary Patterns and Evidence for Human Sacrifice at Chalchuapa, El Salvador. *AAnt* 49: 603–18.

———. 1989. *The Cultural Evolution of Ancient Nahua Civilizations: The Pipil-Nacarao of Central America*. Norman: University of Oklahoma Press.

Fox, J. A. 1978. Proto-Mayan Accent, Morpheme Structure Condition, and Velar Innovations. Ph.D. diss., University of Chicago.

———. 1979. The Etymology of Quichean *Kumats* "Snake" and the Linguistic Affiliation of the Olmecs. In *Proceedings of the Annual Symposium of the Deseret Language and Linguistic Society*, J. S. Robertson, ed. Provo, Utah: Brigham Young University Press.

———. 1980. Review of *Corpus of Maya Hieroglyphic Inscriptions*. *AAnt* 45: 210–11.

Fox, J. A., and J. S. Justeson. 1978. A Mayan Planetary Observation. UCARF Contribution 36: 55–59.

———. 1980. Maya Hieroglyphs as Linguistic Evidence. PRTS 5: 204–16.

———. 1984. Polyvalence in Mayan Hieroglyphic Writing. In Justeson and Campbell 1984: 17–76.

Fox, J. W. 1978. *Quiche Conquest: Centralism and Regionalism in Highland Guatemalan State Development*. Albuquerque: University of New Mexico Press.

———. 1980. Lowland to Highland Mexicanization Processes in Southern Mesoamerica. *AAnt* 45: 43–54.

———. 1981. The Late Postclassic Eastern Frontier of Mesoamerica: Cultural Innovation Along the Periphery. *Current Anthropology* 22: 321–46.

———. 1987. *Maya Postclassic State Formation*. Cambridge, Eng.: Cambridge University Press.

Freidel, D. A. 1977. A Late Preclassic Monumental Mayan Mask at Cerros, Northern Belize. *JFA* 4: 488–91.

———. 1978. Maritime Adaptation and the Rise of Maya Civilization: A View from Cerros, Belize. In Stark and Voorhies 1978: 239–65.

———. 1979a. Culture Areas and Interaction Spheres: Contrasting Approaches to the Emergence of Civilization in the Maya Lowlands. *AAnt* 44: 36–54.

———. 1979b. World Image and World View: The Structural Foundations of Lowland Maya Civilization. Paper presented at the 43rd ICA, Vancouver.

———. 1981a. Continuity and Disjunction: Late Postclassic Settlement Patterns in Northern Yucatan. In Ashmore 1981b: 311–32.

———. 1981b. The Political Economics of Residential Dispersion Among the Lowland Maya. In Ashmore 1981b: 371–82.

———. 1983. Political Systems in Lowland Yucatan: Dynamics and Structure in Maya Settlement. In Vogt and Leventhal 1983: 375–86.

———. 1986a. Maya Warfare: An Example of Peer Polity Interaction. In *Peer Polity Interaction and Socio-Political Change*, C. Renfrew and J. F. Cherry, eds.: 93–108. Cambridge, Eng.: Cambridge University Press.

———. 1986b. Terminal Classic Lowland Maya: Successes, Failures, and Aftermaths. In Sabloff and Andrews 1986: 409–30.

———. 1990. The Jester God: The Beginning and End of a Maya Royal Symbol. In Clancy and Harrison 1990: 67–78.

Freidel, D. A., M. Masucci, S. Jaeger, and R. A. Robertson. 1991. The Bearer, the Burden, and the Burnt: The Stacking Principle in the Iconography of the Late Preclassic Maya Lowlands. PRTS 8: 175–83.

Freidel, D. A., R. Robertson, and M. B. Cliff. 1982. The Maya City of Cerros. *A* 35 (4): 12–21.

Freidel, D. A., and J. A. Sabloff. 1984. *Cozumel: Late Maya Settlement Patterns.* New York: Academic Press.

Freidel, D. A., and L. Schele. 1988a. Kingship in the Late Preclassic Maya Lowlands: The Instruments and Places of Ritual Power. *AA* 90: 547–67.

———. 1988b. Symbol and Power: A History of the Lowland Maya Cosmogram. In Benson and Griffin 1988: 44–93.

———. 1989a. Tlaloc-Venus Warfare and the Triumph of the Confederacy at Chichen Itza. Paper presented at the 54th Annual Meeting of the Society for American Archaeology, Atlanta.

———. 1989b. Dead Kings and Living Mountains: Dedication and Termination Rituals of the Lowland Maya. In Hanks and Rice 1989.

Freidel, D. A., C. Suhler, and R. Krochock. 1990. *Yaxuná Archaeological Survey: A Report of the 1989 Field Season and Final Report on Phase One.* Dallas: Department of Anthropology, Southern Methodist University.

Fry, R. E. 1979. Nativistic Movements Among the Postclassic Lowland Maya. Paper presented at the 78th Annual Meeting of the American Anthropological Association, Cincinnati.

Fry, R. E., and S. C. Cox. 1974. The Structure of Ceramic Exchange at Tikal, Guatemala. *JFA* 1: 209–25.

Fuentas y Guzmán, F. A. 1932–34. *Historia de Guatemala o recordación florida.* Guatemala: Biblioteca Goathemala.

Furbee, L., ed. 1976. *Mayan Texts I. IJAL*, Native American Texts Series 1 (1). Chicago: University of Chicago Press.

Furbee-Losee, L., ed. 1979. *Mayan Texts II. IJAL*, Native American Texts Series, Monograph No. 3. Chicago: University of Chicago Press.

———, ed. 1980. *Mayan Texts III. IJAL*, Native American Texts Series, Monograph No. 5. Chicago: University of Chicago Press.

Furst, P. T. 1976. *Hallucinogens and Culture*. San Francisco: Chandler and Sharp.

Furst, P. T., and M. D. Coe. 1977. Ritual Enemas. *Natural History* 86 (3): 88–91.

Gallenkamp, C., and R. E. Johnson, eds. 1985. *Maya: Treasures of an Ancient Civilization*. New York: Harry N. Abrams.

Gann, T. W. F. 1900. Mounds in Northern Honduras. *BAE Annual Report* 19 (2): 655–92.

———. 1904–5. Report of a Visit to the Ruins on the Columbia Branch of the Río Grande in British Honduras. *Proceedings of the Society of Antiquaries of London* 20: 27–32.

———. 1918. *The Maya Indians of Southern Yucatan and Northern British Honduras*. BAE Bulletin 64.

———. 1927. *Maya Cities: A Record of Exploration and Adventure in Middle America*. London: Duckworth.

Gann, T. W. F., and J. E. S. Thompson. 1931. *The History of the Maya from the Earliest Time to the Present Day*. New York: Scribner's.

Garber, J. F. 1983. Patterns of Jade Consumption and Dispersal at Cerros, Northern Belize. *AAnt* 48: 800–807.

———. 1986. The Artifacts. In Robertson and Freidel 1986: 117–26.

Garza Tarzana de González, S. G., and E. B. Kurjack. 1980. *Atlas arqueológico de estado de Yucatán*. 2 vols. Mexico City: INAH Centro Regional del Sureste.

Gates, W. 1920. The Distribution of the Several Branches of the Mayance Linguistic Stock. In Morley 1920: Appendix 12.

———, trans. and notes. 1937. *Yucatan Before and After the Conquest, by Friar Diego de Landa, with Other Related Documents*. Maya Society Publication No. 20. Baltimore.

———. 1938. *A Grammar of Maya*. Maya Society Publication No. 13. Baltimore.

Gibson, E. C., L. C. Shaw, and D. R. Finamore. 1986. *Early Evidence of Maya Hieroglyphic Writing at Kichpanha, Belize*. Working Papers in Archaeology No. 2. CARUTS.

Gifford, J. C. 1976. *Prehistoric Pottery Analysis and the Ceramics of Barton Ramie in the Belize Valley*. Comp. C. A. Gifford. PMAE Memoirs 18.

Gillespie, S. D. 1989. *The Aztec Kings: The Construction of Rulership in Mexica History*. Tucson: University of Arizona Press.

Glass, J. B. 1975. A Survey of Native Middle American Pictorial Manuscripts. In *HMAI* 14: 3–80.

Glass, J. B., and D. Robertson. 1975. A Census of Native Middle American Pictorial Manuscripts. In *HMAI* 14: 81–280.

Gómez-Pompa, A., J. S. Flores, and M. A. Fernández. 1990. The Sacred Cacao Groves of the Maya. *LAA* 1: 247–57.

González, A. 1993. El Templo de la Cruz. *Arqueología Mexicana* 1 (2): 39–41.

Goodman, J. T. 1897. The Archaic Maya Inscriptions. Appendix to Maudslay 1889–1902.

———. 1905. Maya Dates. *AA* 7: 642–47.

Gordon, G. B. 1896. *Prehistoric Ruins of Copan, Honduras*. PMAE Memoirs 1 (1).

Gordon, G. B., and J. A. Mason. 1925–43. *Examples of Maya Pottery in the Museum and in Other Collections*. 3 vols. UM.

Graham, E. 1987. Resource Diversity in Belize and Its Implications for Models of Lowland Trade. *AAnt* 52: 753–67.

Graham, E., and D. M. Pendergast. 1989. Excavations at the Marco Gonzalez Site, Ambergris Cay, Belize, 1986. *JFA* 16: 1–16.

Graham, I. 1967. *Archaeological Explorations in El Peten, Guatemala*. MARI Publication 33.

———. 1975. *Corpus of Maya Hieroglyphic Inscriptions*. Vol. 1: *Introduction*. PMAE.

———. 1978. *Corpus of Maya Hieroglyphic Inscriptions*. Vol. 2, Part 2: *Naranjo, Chunhuitz, Xunantunich*. PMAE.

———. 1979. *Corpus of Maya Hieroglyphic Inscriptions*. Vol. 3, Part 2: *Yaxchilan*. PMAE.

———. 1980. *Corpus of Maya Hieroglyphic Inscriptions*. Vol. 2, Part 3: *Ixkun, Ucanal, Ixtutz, Naranjo*. PMAE.

———. 1982. *Corpus of Maya Hieroglyphic Inscriptions*. Vol. 3, Part 3: *Yaxchilan*. PMAE.

———. 1986. *Corpus of Maya Hieroglyphic Inscriptions*. Vol. 5, Part 3: *Uaxactun*. PMAE.

Graham, I., and E. Von Euw. 1975. *Corpus of Maya Hieroglyphic Inscriptions*. Vol. 2, Part 1: *Naranjo*. PMAE.

———. 1977. *Corpus of Maya Hieroglyphic Inscriptions*. Vol. 3, Part 1: *Yaxchilan*. PMAE.

Graham, J. A. 1971. Commentary on Calendrics and Writing. UCARF Contribution 11: 133–40.

———. 1972. *The Hieroglyphic Inscriptions and Monumental Art of Altar de Sacrificios*. PMAE Papers, 64 (2).

———. 1973. Aspects of Non-Classic Presences in the Inscriptions and Sculptural Art of Seibal. In Culbert 1973: 207–17.

———. 1977. Discoveries at Abaj Takalik, Guatemala. *A* 30: 196–97.

———. 1979. Maya, Olmecs and Izapans at Abaj Takalik. 42nd ICA *Actas* 8: 179–88.

Graham, J. A., R. F. Heizer, and E. M. Shook. 1978. Abaj Takalik 1976: Exploratory Investigations. UCARF Contribution 36: 85–110.

Graham, J. A., and R. Hester. 1968. Notes on the Papalhuapa Site, Guatemala. UCARF Contribution 5: 101–25.

Graham, J. A., and J. Porter. 1989. A Cycle 6 Initial Series? A Maya Boulder Inscription of the First Millennium B.C. from Abaj Takalik. *Mexicon* 11: 46–49.

Green, D. F., and G. W. Lowe. 1967. *Altamira and Padre Piedra, Early Preclassic Sites in Chiapas, Mexico*. NWAF Paper 20.

Greenberg, J. H. 1987. *Language in the Americas*. Stanford, Calif.: Stanford University Press.

Greene, M. 1967. *Ancient Maya Relief Sculpture*. New York: Museum of Primitive Art.

Greene, M., R. L. Rands, and J. A. Graham. 1972. *Maya Sculpture from the Southern Lowlands, the Highlands, and Pacific Piedmont Guatemala, Mexico, Honduras*. Berkeley, Calif.: Lederer, Street and Zeus.

Griscom, L. 1932. *The Distribution of Birdlife in Guatemala*. American Museum of Natural History Bulletin 64. New York.

Grove, D. C. 1981a. The Formative Period and the Evolution of Complex Culture. *SHMAI* 1: 373–91.

————. 1981b. Olmec Monuments: Mutilation as a Clue to Meaning. In *The Olmec and Their Neighbors*, E. P. Benson, ed.: 49–68.

————, ed. 1987. *Ancient Chalcatzingo*. Austin: University of Texas Press.

Grove, D. C., K. G. Hirth, D. E. Bugé, and A. M. Cyphers. 1976. Settlement and Cultural Development at Chalcatzingo. *Science* 192: 1203–10.

Grube, N. 1991. An Investigation of the Primary Standard Sequence on Classic Maya Ceramics. PRTS 8: 223–32.

Gruhn, R., and A. L. Bryan. 1976. An Archaeological Survey of the Chichicastenango Area of Highland Guatemala. *CCM* 9: 75–119.

Guderjan, T. H., J. F. Garber, H. A. Smith, F. Stross, H. V. Michel, and F. Asaro. 1989. Maya Maritime Trade and Sources of Obsidian at San Juan, Ambergris Cay, Belize. *JFA* 16: 363–79.

Guillemin, J. F. 1965. *Iximche: capital del antiguo reino Cakchiquel*. Guatemala: Instituto de Antropología e Historia.

————. 1967. The Ancient Cakchiquel Capital of Iximche. *Expedition* 9 (2): 22–35.

Guthe, C. E. 1932. The Maya Lunar Count. *Science* 75: 271–77.

Haas, M. L. 1969. *The Prehistory of Languages*. The Hague: Mouton.

Hall, G. D., S. M. Tarka, W. J. Hurst, D. Stuart, and R. E. W. Adams. 1990. Cacao Residues in Ancient Maya Vessels from Rio Azul, Guatemala. *AAnt* 55: 138–43.

Hamblin, R. L., and B. L. Pitcher. 1980. The Classic Maya Collapse: Testing Class Conflict Hypotheses. *AAnt* 45: 246–67.

Hammond, N. 1972. Obsidian Trade Routes in the Mayan Area. *Science* 178: 1092–93.

————. 1974a. The Distribution of Late Classic Maya Major Ceremonial Centres in the Central Area. In Hammond 1974b: 313–34.

————, ed. 1974b. *Mesoamerican Archaeology: New Approaches*. Austin: University of Texas Press.

————. 1975. *Lubaantun, a Classic Maya Realm*. PMAE Monograph 2.

————. 1977a. The Earliest Maya. *SA* 236 (3): 116–33.

————, ed. 1977b. *Social Process in Maya Prehistory, Essays in Honour of Sir J. Eric S. Thompson*. New York: Academic Press.

————. 1978a. *Cuello Project 1978 Interim Report*. Archaeological Research Program, Douglas College, Rutgers University, Publication 1. New Brunswick, N.J.

————. 1978b. The Myth of the Milpa: Agricultural Expansion in the Maya Lowlands. In Harrison and Turner 1978: 23–24.

————. 1980. Early Maya Ceremonial at Cuello, Belize. *Antiquity* 54: 176–90.

————. 1981. Settlement Patterns in Belize. In Ashmore 1981b: 157–86.

————. 1982. *Ancient Maya Civilization*. New Brunswick, N.J.: Rutgers University Press.

————. 1983. Nohmul, Belize: 1982 Investigations. *JFA* 10: 245–54.

————. 1985a. The Emergence of Maya Civilization. *SA* 255 (2): 106–15.

————, ed. 1985b. *Nohmul: A Prehistoric Maya Community in Belize*. BAR 250.

————. 1991. Inside the Black Box: Defining Maya Polity. In Culbert 1991a: 253–84.

Hammond, N., and W. A. Ashmore. 1981. Lowland Maya Settlement: Geographical and Chronological Frameworks. In Ashmore 1981b: 19–36.

Hammond, N., A. Aspinall, S. Feather, J. Hazelden, T. Gazard, and S. Agrell. 1977. Maya

Jade: Source Location and Analysis. In *Exchange Systems in Prehistory*, T. K. Earle and J. E. Ericson, eds. 35–67. New York: Academic Press.

Hammond, N., C. Clark, M. Horton, M. Hodges, L. McNatt, L. J. Kosakowsky, and A. Pyburn. 1985. Excavations at Nohmul, Belize, 1983. *JFA* 12: 177–200.

Hammond, N., S. Donaghey, C. Gleason, J. C. Staneko, D. Van Tuerenhout, and L. J. Kosakowsky. 1987. Excavations at Nohmul, Belize, 1985. *JFA* 14: 257–82.

Hammond, N., D. Pring, R. Berger, V. Switsur, and A. Ward. 1976. Radiocarbon Chronology for Early Maya Occupation at Cuello, Belize. *Nature* 260: 579–81.

Hammond, N., K. A. Pyburn, J. Rose, J. C. Staneko, and D. Muyskens. 1988. Excavation and Survey at Nohmul, Belize, 1986. *JFA* 15: 1–16.

Hammond, N., and G. R. Willey, eds. 1979. *Maya Archaeology and Ethnohistory*. Austin: University of Texas Press.

Hanks, W. F., and D. S. Rice, eds. 1989. *Word and Image in Maya Culture: Explorations in Language, Writing and Representation*. Salt Lake City: University of Utah Press.

Hansen, R. D. 1984. Excavation on Structure 34 and the Tigre Area, El Mirador, Petén, Guatemala: A New Look at the Preclassic Lowland Maya. Master's thesis, Brigham Young University.

———. 1987. *Informe preliminar de los estudios realizados en el sitio arquelógico Nakbe, Peten, Guatemala*. Guatemala: Instituto de Antropología e Historia.

———. 1989. *Las investigaciones del sitio arqueológico Nakbe, Peten, Guatemala: Temporada 1989*. A report presented to the Instituto de Antropología e Historia de Guatemala.

———. 1991. An Early Maya Text from El Mirador, Guatemala. RRAMW 37.

Hansen, R. D., and D. W. Forsyth. 1987. Late Preclassic Development of Unslipped Pottery in the Maya Lowlands: The Evidence from El Mirador. In Rice and Sharer 1987: 439–68.

Harris, D. R. 1972. Swidden Systems and Settlement. In Ucko, Tringham, and Dimbleby 1972: 245–62.

———. 1978. The Agricultural Foundations of Lowland Maya Civilization. In Harrison and Turner 1978: 301–23.

Harrison, P. D. 1977. The Rise of the Bajos and the Fall of the Maya. In Hammond 1977b: 469–508.

———. 1978. Bajos Revisited: Visual Evidence for One System of Agriculture. In Harrison and Turner 1978: 247–53.

———. 1981. Some Aspects of Preconquest Settlement in Southern Quintana Roo, Mexico. In Ashmore 1981b: 259–86.

———. 1985. Ancient Maya Architecture. In Gallenkamp and Johnson 1985: 84–96.

———. 1990. The Revolution in Ancient Maya Subsistence. In Clancy and Harrison 1990: 99–113.

Harrison, P. D., and B. L. Turner, eds. 1978. *Pre-Hispanic Maya Agriculture*. Austin: University of Texas Press.

Hartung, H. 1975. A Scheme of Probable Astronomical Projections in Mesoamerican Architecture. In Aveni 1975: 191–204.

Hassig, R. 1988. *Aztec Warfare: Imperial Expansion and Political Control*. Norman: University of Oklahoma Press.

Hatch, M. 1989. Observaciones sobre el desarollo cultural prehispánico en la costa sur de Guatemala. In Whitley and Beaudry 1989: 4–37.

Haviland, J. B. 1977. *Gossip, Reputation and Knowledge in Zinacantan*. Chicago: University of Chicago Press.

Haviland, W. A. 1966. Maya Settlement Patterns: A Critical Review. MARI Publication 26: 21–47.

———. 1967. Stature at Tikal, Guatemala: Implications for Ancient Maya Demography and Social Organization. *AAnt* 32: 316–25.

———. 1968. Ancient Lowland Maya Social Organization. MARI Publication 26: 93–117.

———. 1970. Tikal, Guatemala, and Mesoamerican Urbanism. *WA* 2: 186–98.

———. 1977. Dynastic Genealogies from Tikal, Guatemala: Implications for Descent and Political Organization. *AAnt* 42: 61–67.

———. 1981. Dower Houses and Minor Centers at Tikal, Guatemala: An Investigation into the Identification of Valid Units in Settlement Hierarchies. In Ashmore 1981b: 89–117.

———. 1985a. *Excavations in Small Residential Groups of Tikal: Groups 4F-1 and 4F-2*. Tikal Reports No. 19. UM.

———. 1985b. Population and Social Dynamics: The Dynasties and Social Structure of Tikal. *Expedition* 27 (3): 34–41.

———. 1988. Musical Hammocks at Tikal: Problems with Reconstructing Household Composition. In Wilk and Ashmore 1988: 121–34.

———. 1989. *Excavations in Residential Areas of Tikal: Non-Elite Groups Without Shrines*. Tikal Reports No. 20. UM.

Hay, C. L., R. L. Linton, S. K. Lothrop, H. L. Shapiro, and G. C. Vaillant, eds. 1982. *The Maya and Their Neighbors: Essays on Middle American Anthropology and Archaeology*. Reprint of the original 1940 edition. Salt Lake City: University of Utah Press.

Healy, P. F. 1983. An Ancient Maya Dam in the Cayo District, Belize. *JFA* 10: 147–54.

———. 1990. Excavations at Pacbitun, Belize: Preliminary Report on the 1986 and 1987 Investigations. *JFA* 17: 247–62.

Healy, P. F., J. D. H. Lambert, J. T. Arnason, and R. J. Hebda. 1983. Caracol, Belize: Evidence of Ancient Maya Agricultural Terraces. *JFA* 10: 397–410.

Heizer, R. F. 1968. New Observations on La Venta. In Benson 1968: 9–40.

Heizer, R. F., J. A. Graham, and L. K. Napton. 1968. The 1968 Investigations at La Venta. UCARF Contribution 5: 127–54.

Hellmuth, N. M. 1971a. Possible Streets at a Maya Site in Guatemala. Mimeo.

———. 1971b. Preliminary Report on Second-Season Excavations at Yaxha, Guatemala. Mimeo.

———. 1972. Excavations Begin at Maya Site in Guatemala. *A* 25: 148–49.

———. n.d. Nakum, Guatemala: A New Sketch Map of the Classic Maya Ruins.

Helms, M. W. 1975. *Middle America: A Cultural History of Heartland and Frontiers*. Englewood Cliffs, N.J.: Prentice-Hall.

Henderson, J. S. 1979. *Atopula, Guerrero and Olmec Horizons in Mesoamerica*. Yale University Publications in Anthropology, No. 77. New Haven.

———. 1981. *The World of the Ancient Maya*. Ithaca, N.Y.: Cornell University Press.

Henderson, J. S., and J. A. Sabloff. 1993. Re-Conceptualizing the Maya Cultural Tradition: Programmatic Comments. In Sabloff and Henderson 1993.

Henderson, J. S., I. Sterns, A. Wonderly, and P. A. Urban. 1979. Archaeological Investigations in the Valle de Naco, Northwestern Honduras: A Preliminary Report. *JFA* 6: 169–92.

Herrera, A. 1726–30. *Historia general de los hechos de los Castillanos en las islas i tierra firme del mar oceano.* 5 vols. Madrid: Imprenta Real de Nicolas Rodríguez Franco.

Hester, J. A., Jr. 1954. Natural and Cultural Bases of Ancient Maya Subsistence Economy. Ph.D. diss., University of California, Los Angeles.

Hester, T. R., ed. 1979. *The Colha Project: A Collection of Interim Papers.* CARUTS.

Hester, T. R., and N. Hammond, eds. 1976. *Maya Lithic Studies: Papers from the 1976 Belize Field Symposium.* CARUTS

Hester, T. R., and H. J. Shafer. 1984. Exploitation of Chert Resources by the Ancient Maya of Northern Belize. *WA* 16 (2): 157–73.

Hester, T. R., H. J. Shafer, and J. D. Eaton. 1982. *Archaeology at Colha, Belize: The 1981 Interim Report.* CARUTS.

Hewett, E. L. 1911. Two Seasons' Work in Guatemala. *Bulletin of the Archaeological Institute of America* 2: 117–34.

———. 1912. The Excavations at Quirigua in 1912. *Bulletin of the Archaeological Institute of America* 3: 163–71.

———. 1916. Latest Work of the School of American Archaeology at Quirigua. In *Holmes Anniversary Volume: Anthropological Essays*, F. W. Hodge, ed.: 157–62. Washington, D.C.

Hirth, K. G., ed. 1984. *Trade and Exchange in Early Mesoamerica.* Albuquerque: University of New Mexico Press.

Hodder, I., ed. 1987. *The Archaeology of Contextual Meanings.* Cambridge, Eng.: Cambridge University Press.

Hohmann, H., and A. Vogrin. 1982. *Die Archutektur von Copan.* Graz: Akademische Druck Verlagsanstalt.

Holmes, W. H. 1895–97. *Archaeological Studies Among the Ancient Cities of Mexico.* Part 1: *Monuments of Yucatan.* Part 2: *Monuments of Chiapas, Oaxaca and the Valley of Mexico.* Field Columbian Museum, Anthropological Series 1. Chicago.

Hopkins, N. A. 1985. On the History of the Chol Language. PRTS 7: 1–5.

———. 1987. The Lexicon of Maya Hieroglyphic Inscriptions. Paper presented at the 86th Annual Meeting of the American Anthropological Association, Chicago.

———. 1991. Classic and Modern Relationship Terms and the "Child of Mother" Glyph. PRTS 8: 255–65.

Houston, S. D. 1983. On "Ruler 6" at Piedras Negras, Guatemala. *Mexicon* 5: 84–86.

———. 1986. Problematic Emblem Glyphs: Examples from Altar de Sacrificios, El Chorro, Río Azul, and Xultun. RRAMW No. 3.

———. 1987. Notes on Caracol Epigraphy and Its Significance. In Chase and Chase 1987: 85–100.

———. 1988. Political History and the Decipherment of Maya Glyphs. *Antiquity* 62: 135–52.

———. 1989. Archaeology and Maya Writing. *Journal of World Prehistory* 3: 1–32.

———. 1992. *Hieroglyphs and History at Dos Pilas: Dynastic Politics of the Classic Maya.* Austin: University of Texas Press.

Houston, S. D., and P. Mathews. 1985. *The Dynastic Sequence of Dos Pilas, Guatemala.* PARI Monograph 1.

Houston, S. D., and D. Stuart. 1989. The Way Glyph: Evidence for "Co-essences" Among the Classic Maya. RRAMW No. 30.

Houston, S. D., and K. A. Taube. 1987. "Name-Tagging" in Classic Mayan Script. *Mexicon* 9: 38–41.

Howell, W. K. 1983. Excavations in the Danta Complex, El Mirador, Petén, Guatemala. Master's thesis, Brigham Young University.

Hunn, E. 1977. *Tzeltal Folk Zoology: The Classification of Discontinuities in Nature.* New York: Academic Press.

Huntington, E. 1912. The Peninsula of Yucatan. *Bulletin of the American Geographical Society* 44: 801–22.

Ichon, A. 1975. *Organización de un centro Quiché protohistórico: Pueblo Viejo Chichaj.* Instituto de Antropología e Historia Publicación Especial No. 9. Guatemala.

———. 1977a. *Les sculptures de la Lagunita, El Quiche, Guatemala.* Paris: Centre National de la Recherche Scientifique.

———. 1977b. A Late Postclassic Sweathouse in the Highlands of Guatemala. *AAnt* 42: 203–9.

———. 1979. *Rescate arqueológico en la cuenca del Río Chixoy.* Guatemala: Informe Preliminar, Misión Científica Franco-Guatemalteca.

———. In press. *Evolution regional de la ceramique dans la zone nord des hautes terres du Guatemala.* CNRSIE.

Ichon, A., M. F. Fauvet-Berthelot, C. Plocieniak, R. Hill, R. González L., and M. A. Bailey. 1980. *Archéologie de sauvetage dans la vallé du Río Chixoy 2: Cauinal.* CNRSIE. Guatemala: Editorial Piedra Santa.

Ichon, A., and R. Grignon. 1981. *Archéologie de sauvetage dans la vallé du Río Chixoy 3: El Jocote.* CNRSIE. Guatemala: Editorial Piedra Santa.

Ichon, A., and R. Grignon-Cheesman. 1983. *Archéologie de sauvetage dans la vallé du Río Chixoy 5: les sites classiques de la vallée moyenne du Chixoy.* CNRSIE. Guatemala: Editorial Piedra Santa.

Ichon, A., and M. Hatch. 1982. *Archéologie de sauvetage dans la vallé du Río Chixoy 4: los encuentros.* CNRSIE. Guatemala: Editorial Piedra Santa.

Ingle, M. I. 1984. *The Mayan Revival Style.* Albuquerque: University of New Mexico Press.

Jackson, T. L., and M. W. Love. 1991. Blade Running: Middle Preclassic Obsidian Exchange and the Introduction of Prismatic Blades at La Blanca, Guatemala. *AM* 2: 47–59.

Johnson, K. 1985. Maya Dynastic Territorial Expansion: Glyphic Evidence for Classic Centers of the Pasion River, Guatemala. PRTS 7: 49–56.

Johnston, F. 1972. *Chronology and Irrigation.* Ed. R. S. MacNeish. Vol. 4: *The Prehistory of the Tehuacan Valley.* Austin: University of Texas Press.

Jones, C. 1969. The Twin Pyramid Group Pattern: A Classic Maya Architectural Assemblage at Tikal, Guatemala. Ph.D. diss., University of Pennsylvania.

———. 1975. A Painted Capstone from the Maya Area. UCARF Contribution 27: 83–110.

———. 1977. Inauguration Dates of Three Late Classic Rulers of Tikal, Guatemala. *AAnt* 42: 28–60.

———. 1979. Tikal as a Trading Center. Paper presented at the 43rd ICA, Vancouver.

———. 1983a. Monument 26, Quiriguá, Guatemala. In Schortman and Urban 1983: Paper No. 13.

———. 1983b. New Drawings of Monuments 23 and 24, Quiriguá, Guatemala. In Schortman and Urban 1983: Paper No. 15.

———. 1991. Cycles of Growth at Tikal. In Culbert 1991a: 102–27.

Jones, C., and L. Satterthwaite. 1982. *The Monuments and Inscriptions of Tikal: The Carved Monuments*. Tikal Report No. 33A. UM.

Jones, C., and R. J. Sharer. 1986. Archaeological Investigations in the Site Core of Quirigua, Guatemala. In Urban and Schortman 1986: 27–34.

Jones, G. D., ed. 1977. *Anthropology and History in Yucatan*. Austin: University of Texas Press.

———. 1983. The Last Maya Frontiers of Colonial Yucatan. In MacLeod and Wasserstrom 1983: 64–91.

———. 1989. *Maya Resistance to Spanish Rule: Time and History on a Colonial Frontier*. Albuquerque: University of New Mexico Press.

Jones, G. D., and R. R. Kautz, eds. 1981. *The Transition to Statehood in the New World*. Cambridge, Eng.: Cambridge University Press.

Jones, G. D., R. R. Kautz, and E. A. Graham. 1986. Tipu: A Maya Town on the Spanish Colonial Frontier. *A* 39 (1): 40–47.

Jones, G. D., D. S. Rice, and P. M. Rice. 1981. The Location of Tayasal: A Reconsideration in Light of Peten Maya Ethnohistory and Archaeology. *AAnt* 46: 530–47.

Jones, M. R. 1952. *Map of the Ruins of Mayapan, Yucatan, Mexico*. CIW Current Reports, Department of Archaeology, No. 1.

Josserand, J. K. 1975. Archaeological and Linguistic Correlations for Mayan Prehistory. 41st ICA *Proceedings* 1: 501–10.

———. 1991. The Narrative Structure of Hieroglyphic Texts at Palenque. PRTS 8: 12–31.

Joyce, R. A. 1986. Terminal Classic Interaction on the Southeastern Maya Periphery. *AAnt* 51: 313–29.

———. 1988. The Ulua Valley and the Central Maya Lowlands: The View from Cerro Palenque. In Boone and Willey 1988: 269–95.

———. 1991. *Cerro Palenque: Power and Identity on the Maya Periphery*. Austin: University of Texas Press.

Joyce, T. A., J. C. Clark, and J. E. S. Thompson. 1927. Report on the British Museum Expedition to British Honduras. *Journal of the Royal Anthropological Institute* 57: 295–323.

Justeson, J. S. 1978. Mayan Scribal Practice in the Classic Period: A Test-Case of an Explanatory Approach to the Study of Writing Systems. Ph.D. diss., Stanford University.

———. 1986. The Origin of Writing Systems: Preclassic Mesoamerica. *WA* 17: 437–58.

Justeson, J. S., and L. R. Campbell, eds. 1984. *Phoneticism in Mayan Hieroglyphic Writing*. IMS Publication No. 9.

Justeson, J. S., and T. Kaufman. 1993. A Decipherment of Epi-Olmec Hieroglyphic Writing. *Science* 259: 1665–79.

Justeson, J. S., and P. Mathews. 1983. The Seating of the Tun: Further Evidence Concerning a Late Preclassic Lowland Maya Stela Cult. *AAnt* 48: 586–93.

Justeson, J. S., W. M. Norman, L. Campbell, and T. Kaufman. 1985. *The Foreign Impact on Lowland Mayan Language and Script*. MARI Publication 53.

Justeson, J. S., W. M. Norman, and N. Hammond. 1988. The Pomona Jade Flare: A Preclassic Mayan Hieroglyphic Text. In Benson and Griffin 1988: 94–151.

Kaufman, T. S. 1964. Materiales lingüísticos para el estudio del las relaciones internas y externas de la familia de idiomas Mayanos. In *Desarrollo cultural de los Mayas*, E. Z. Vogt and A. Ruz L., eds.: 86–136. Mexico City: Universidad Nacional Autónoma de México.

———. 1969. *Some Recent Hypotheses on Mayan Diversification*. Language Behavior Research Laboratory, Working Paper No. 26. Berkeley: University of California.

———. 1973. Areal Linguistics in Middle America. In *Current Trends in Linguistics* 11, T. A. Sebeok, ed.: 459–83. The Hague: Mouton.

———. 1974. Mesoamerican Indian Languages. *Encyclopaedia Britannica* (15th ed.) 11: 959–63.

———. 1976. Archaeological and Linguistic Correlations in Mayaland and Associated Areas of Mesoamerica. *WA* 8: 101–18.

Kaufman, T. S., and W. M. Norman. 1984. An Outline of Proto-Cholan Phonology and Morphology. In Justeson and Campbell 1984.

Keleman, P. 1943. *Medieval American Art*. 2 vols. New York: Macmillan.

Keller, K. C. 1959. The Phonemes of Chontal. *IJAL* 25: 44–53.

Kelley, D. H. 1962a. A History of the Decipherment of Maya Script. *Anthropological Linguistics* 4 (8): 1–48.

———. 1962b. Glyphic Evidence for a Dynastic Sequence at Quirigua, Guatemala. *AAnt* 27: 323–35.

———. 1975. Planetary Data on Caracol Stela 3. In Aveni 1975b: 257–62.

———. 1976. *Deciphering the Maya Script*. Austin: University of Texas Press.

———. 1983. The Maya Calendar Correlation Problem. In Leventhal and Kolata 1983: 157–208.

———. 1984. The Toltec Empire in Yucatan. *Quarterly Review of Archaeology* 5: 12–13.

———. 1985. The Lords of Palenque and the Lords of Heaven. PRTS 7: 235–39.

Kelley, D. H., and K. A. Kerr. 1973. Mayan Astronomy and Astronomical Glyphs. In Benson 1973: 179–215.

Kidder, A. V. 1937. *Notes on the Ruins of San Agustin Acasaguastian, Guatemala*. CIW Publication 456.

———. 1940. Archaeological Problems of the Highland Maya. In Hay et al. 1982 (original 1940): 117–25.

———. 1947. *The Artifacts of Uaxactun, Guatemala*. CIW Publication 576.

———. 1951. Artifacts. In *Excavations at Nebaj, Guatemala*. CIW Publication 594: 32–76.

———. 1961. Archaeological Investigations at Kaminaljuyu, Guatemala. *American Philosophical Society Proceedings* 105: 559–70.

———. 1965. Preclassic Pottery Figurines of the Guatemala Highlands. In *HMAI* 2: 146–55.

Kidder, A. V., J. D. Jennings, and E. M. Shook. 1946. *Excavations at Kaminaljuyu, Guatemala*. CIW Publication 501: 493–510.

Killion, T. W., J. A. Sabloff, G. Tourtellot, and N. P. Dunning. 1989. Intensive Surface Collection of Residential Clusters at Terminal Classic Sayil, Yucatan, Mexico. *JFA* 16: 273–94.

King, A. 1974. *Copan and the Verapaz: History and Culture Process in Northern Guatemala*. MARI Publication 37.

King, E., and D. Potter. 1989. Small Sites in Prehistoric Maya Socioeconomic Organization: A Perspective from Colha, Belize. Paper presented at the 54th Annual Meeting of the Society for American Archaeology, Atlanta.

Kingsborough, E. K. 1831–48. *Antiquities of Mexico*. 9 vols. London: Aglio.

Kirchoff, P. 1952. Mesoamerica. In *Heritage of Conquest*, S. Tax, ed. 17–30. Glencoe., Ill.: Free Press.

Kirke, C. M. 1980. Prehistoric Agriculture in the Belize River Valley. *WA* 11: 281–87.

Knorozov, Y. V. 1958. The Problem of the Study of the Maya Hieroglyphic Writing. *AAnt* 23: 284–91.

———. 1967. *The Writing of the Maya Indians*. English trans. by S. Coe of Chapters 1, 6, 7, and 9 of *Pis'menost Indeitsev Maiia*. Moscow-Leningrad: Academy of Sciences. PMAE Russian Translation Series, No. 4.

———. 1982. *Maya Hieroglyphic Codices*. Trans. S. Coe. IMS.

Kowalski, J. K. 1980. A Historical Interpretation of the Inscriptions of Uxmal. Paper presented at the 4th Mesa Redonda, Palenque, Mexico.

———. 1985. Lords of the Northern Maya: Dynastic History in the Inscriptions. *Expedition* 27 (3): 50–60.

———. 1987. *The House of the Governor: A Maya Palace of Uxmal, Yucatan, Mexico*. Norman: University of Oklahoma Press.

Kowalski, J. K., and W. L. Fash. 1991. Symbolism of the Maya Ball Game at Copan: Synthesis and New Aspects. PRTS 8: 59–67.

Krochock, R. 1989. Hieroglyphic Inscriptions at Chichen Itza, Yucatan, Mexico: The Temples of the Initial Series, the One Lintel, the Three Lintels, and the Four Lintels. RRAMW No. 23.

———. 1991. Dedication Ceremonies at Chichen Itza: The Glyphic Evidence. PRTS 8: 43–50.

Kubler, G. 1961. Chichen Itza y Tula. *ECM* 1: 47–80.

———. 1962. *The Art and Architecture of Ancient America: The Mexican, Maya, and Andean Peoples*. Baltimore: Pelican History of Art.

———. 1971. Commentary on Early Architecture and Sculpture in Mesoamerica. UCARF Contribution 11: 157–68.

———. 1973. The Clauses of Classic Maya Inscriptions. In Benson 1973: 145–64.

Kudlek, M. 1977. *Computer Printout of Dated Maya Monuments by Ceremonial Center*. Hamburg: University of Hamburg.

Kurjack, E. B. 1974. *Prehistoric Lowland Maya Community and Social Organization: A Case Study at Dzibilchaltun*. MARI Publication 38.

Kurjack, E. B., and E. W. Andrews V. 1976. Early Boundary Maintenance in Northwest Yucatan, Mexico. *AAnt* 41: 318–25.

Kurjack, E. B., and S. Garza T. 1981. Precolumbian Community Form and Distribution in the Northern Maya Area. In Ashmore 1981b: 287–310.

La Farge, O. 1927. Adaptations of Christianity Among the Jacalteca Indians of Guatemala. *Thought* (Dec.): 1–20.

————. 1947. *Santa Eulalia*. Chicago: University of Chicago Press.

La Farge, O., and D. Byers. 1931. *The Year Bearer's People*. MARI Publication 3.

Lambert, J. B., B. Ownbey-McLaughlin, and C. D. McLaughlin. 1980. Maya Arithmetic. *American Scientist* 68: 249–55.

Landa, D. de. 1938. *Relación de las cosas de Yucatán*. Mérida: Edición Yucateca.

Lange, F. W. 1971. Marine Resources: A Viable Subsistence Alternative for the Prehistoric Lowland Maya. *AA* 73: 619–39.

Laporte, J. P. 1988. Alternativas del clásico temprano en la relación Tikal-Teotihuacan: Grupo 6C-XVI, Tikal, Petén, Guatemala. Ph.D. diss., Universidad Nacional Autónoma de México.

Laporte, J. P., and V. Fialko C. 1990. New Perspectives on Old Problems: Dynastic References for the Early Classic at Tikal. In Clancy and Harrison 1990: 33–66.

Laporte, J. P., and R. Torres. 1987. Los señores del sureste de Petén. *Mayab* 3: 7–23.

Laporte, J. P., R. Torres, and B. Hermes. 1988. Ixtontón: evolución de un asentamiento en el alto Río Mopan, Petén, Guatemala. Paper presented at the Segundo Simposio Sobre Arqueología Guatemalteca, Guatemala.

Laporte, J. P., R. Torres, B. Hermes, E. Pinto, R. Acevedo, and R. M. Flores. 1988. Proyecto Sureste de Petén, Guatemala: Segunda Temporada. *Mexicon* 9: 49–56.

Laporte, J. P., and L. Vega de Zea. 1988. Aspectos dinásticos para el clásico temprano de Mundo Perdido. In *Primer simposio mundial sobre epigrafía maya*: 127–41. Guatemala: Asociación Tikal.

Las Casas, B. de. 1909. *Apologética historia de las Indias*. 2 vols. Madrid: Serrano y Ganz.

————. 1957. *Historia de las Indias*. Madrid: Ediciones Atlas.

Lathrap, D. W., J. G. Marcos, and J. Zeidler. 1977. Real Alto: An Ancient Ceremonial Center. *A* 30 (1): 2–13.

Laughlin, R. M. 1975. *The Great Tzotzil Dictionary of San Lorenzo Zinacantan*. Smithsonian Contributions to Anthropology, No. 19. Washington, D.C.: Smithsonian Institution Press.

————. 1976. *Of Wonders Wild and New: Dreams from Zinacantan*. Smithsonian Contributions to Anthropology, No. 22. Washington, D.C.: Smithsonian Institution Press.

————. 1977. *Of Cabbages and Kings: Tales from Zinacantan*. Smithsonian Contributions to Anthropology, No. 23. Washington, D.C.: Smithsonian Institution Press.

Leach, E. R. 1983. The Gatekeepers of Heaven: Anthropological Aspects of Grandiose Architecture. *Journal of Anthropological Research* 29: 243–64.

Lee, T. A. 1969. *The Artifacts of Chiapa de Corzo, Chiapas, Mexico*. NWAF Paper 26.

————. 1985. *Los códices mayas: introducción y bibliografía*. San Cristóbal de las Casas: Universidad Autónoma de Chiapas.

Lee, T. A., and B. Hayden, eds. 1988. *Ethnoarchaeology Among the Highland Maya of Chiapas, Mexico*. NWAF Paper 56.

Lee, T. A., and C. Navarrete, eds. 1978. *Mesoamerican Communication Routes and Cultural Contacts*. NWAF Paper 40.

Lehmann, H. 1968. *Mixco Viejo: guía de las ruinas de la plaza fuerte Pokoman*. Guatemala: Tipografía Nacional.

Leventhal, R. M. 1979. Settlement Patterns at Copan, Honduras. Ph.D. diss., Harvard University.

———. 1981. Settlement Patterns in the Southeast Maya Area. In Ashmore 1981b: 187–210.

———. 1983. Household Groups and Classic Maya Religion. In Vogt and Leventhal 1983: 55–76.

———. 1990. Southern Belize: An Ancient Maya Region. In Clancy and Harrison 1990: 125–41.

Leventhal, R. M., and K. H. Baxter. 1988. The Use of Ceramics to Identify the Function of Copan Structures. In Wilk and Ashmore 1988: 51–71.

Leventhal, R. M., and A. L. Kolata. 1983. *Civilization in the Ancient Americas: Essays in Honor of Gordon R. Willey.* PMAE and University of New Mexico Press.

Leventhal, R. M., G. R. Willey, and A. A. Demarest. 1987. The Cultural and Social Components of Copan. In *Polities and Partitions: Human Boundaries and the Growth of Complex Societies,* K. Trinkhaus, ed. Arizona State University Anthropological Research Papers No. 37. Tempe.

Lincoln, C. E. 1980. A Preliminary Assessment of Izamal, Yucatan, Mexico. Senior honors thesis, Tulane University.

———. 1985. Ceramics and Ceramic Chronology. In Willey and Mathews 1985: 55–94.

———. 1986. The Chronology of Chichen Itza: A Review of the Literature. In Sabloff and Andrews 1986: 141–96.

Linden, J. H. 1986. Glyph X of the Maya Lunar Series: An Eighteen-Month Lunar Synodic Calendar. *AAnt* 51: 122–36.

Littmann, E. R. 1980. Maya Blue: A New Perspective. *AAnt* 45: 87–100.

Litvak-King, J. 1972. Las relaciones externas de Xochicalco: una evaluación de su significado. *Anales de Antropología* 9: 53–76.

Lizana, B. de. 1893. *Historia de Yucatan. Devocionario de Nuestra Señora de Izmal y conquista espiritual impresa en 1633.* 2d ed. Mexico City: Museo Nacional de México.

Longacre, R. 1967. Systematic Reconstruction and Comparison. In *HMAI* 5: 117–59.

Longyear, J. M. 1944. *Archaeological Investigations in El Salvador.* PMAE Memoirs 9 (2).

———. 1947. *Cultures and Peoples of the Southeastern Maya Frontier.* CIW Theoretical Approaches to Problems, No. 3.

———. 1952. *Copan Ceramics: A Study of Southeastern Maya Pottery.* CIW Publication 597.

López, D., and D. Molina. 1976. Los Murales de Cacaxtla. *INAH Boletín* 16 (2): 3–8.

Loten, H. S. 1990. Monumentality: Power and Dwelling in the Maya Lowlands. Paper presented at the 89th Annual Meeting of the American Anthropological Association, New Orleans.

Lothrop, S. K. 1924. *Tulum: An Archaeological Study of the East Coast of Yucatan.* CIW Publication 335.

———. 1933. *Atitlan: An Archaeological Study of the Ancient Remains on the Borders of Lake Atitlan, Guatemala.* CIW Publication 444.

———. 1939. The Southeastern Frontier of the Maya. *AA* 41: 42–54.

———. 1952. *Metals from the Cenote of Sacrifice, Chichen Itza, Yucatan.* PMAE Memoirs 10 (2).

Lounsbury, F. G. 1973. On the Derivation and Reading of the "Ben-Ich" Prefix. In Benson 1973: 99–143.

————. 1974. The Inscription of the Sarcophagus Lid at Palenque. PRTS 2: 5–19.

————. 1976. A Rationale for the Initial Date of the Temple of the Cross at Palenque. PRTS 3: 211–24.

————. 1978. Maya Numeration, Computation, and Calendrical Astronomy. In *Dictionary of Scientific Biography*, C. C. Gillispie, ed.: 759–818.

————. 1982. Astronomical Knowledge and Its Uses at Bonampak, Mexico. In Aveni 1982: 143–68.

————. 1984. Glyphic Substitutions: Homophonic and Synonymic. In Justeson and Campbell 1984: 167–84.

————. 1985. The Identities of the Mythological Figures in the Cross Group Inscriptions of Palenque. PRTS 6: 45–58.

Love, B. 1987. Glyph T93 and Maya "Hand-scattering" Events. RRAMW No. 5.

————. 1989. The Hieroglyphic Lintels of Yula, Yucatan, Mexico. RRAMW No. 24.

Lowe, G. W. 1962. *Mound 5 and Minor Excavations, Chiapa de Corzo, Chiapas, Mexico*. NWAF Paper 12.

————. 1976. A Rationale for the Initial Date of the Temple of the Cross at Palenque. PRTS 3: 211–24.

————. 1977. The Mixe-Zoque as Competing Neighbors of the Early Lowland Maya. In Adams 1977: 197–248.

————. 1989. The Heartland Olmec: Evolution of Material Culture. In Sharer and Grove 1989: 33–67.

Lowe, G. W., P. Agrinier, J. A. Mason, F. Hicks, and C. E. Rozaire. 1960. *Excavations at Chiapa de Corzo, Chiapas, Mexico*. NWAF Papers 8–11 (issued as Publication No. 7).

Lowe, G. W., T. A. Lee, and E. Martínez E. 1982. *Izapa: An Introduction to the Ruins and Monuments*. NWAF Paper 31.

Lowe, J. G. W. 1985. *The Dynamics of Apocalypse: A Systems Simulation of the Classic Maya Collapse*. Albuquerque: University of New Mexico Press.

Lundell, C. L. 1933. The Agriculture of the Maya. *Southwest Review* 19: 65–77.

————. 1937. *The Vegetation of Peten*. CIW Publication 478.

————. 1938. Plants Probably Utilized by the Old Empire Maya of Peten and Adjacent Lowlands. *Papers of the Michigan Academy of Science, Arts, and Letters* 24: 37–56.

Mackie, E. W. 1961. New Light on the End of the Classic Maya Culture at Benque Viejo, British Honduras. *AAnt* 27 (2): 216–24.

MacKinnon, J. J., and S. M. Kepecs. 1989. Prehispanic Saltmaking in Belize: New Evidence. *AAnt* 54: 522–33.

MacKinnon, J. J., and E. M. May. 1990. Small-scale Maya Lime Making in Belize. *AM* 1: 197–203.

MacLeod, B. 1984. Cholan and Yucatecan Verb Morphology and Glyphic Verbal Affixes in the Inscriptions. In Justeson and Campbell 1984.

MacLeod, M. J., and R. Wasserstrom, eds. 1983. *Spaniards and Indians in Southeastern Mesoamerica: Essays on the History of Ethnic Relations*. Lincoln: University of Nebraska Press.

MacNeish, R. S. 1964a. Ancient Mesoamerican Civilization. *Science* 143: 531–37.

————. 1964b. The Origins of New World Civilization. *SA* 211 (5): 29–37.

MacNeish, R. S., and F. A. Peterson. 1962. *The Santa Marta Rock Shelter, Ocozocoantla, Chiapas, Mexico*. NWAF Paper 14.

MacNeish, R. S., F. A. Peterson, and K. V. Flannery. 1970. *The Prehistory of the Tehuacan Valley.* Vol. 3: *Ceramics.* Austin: University of Texas Press.

MacNeish, R. S., S. J. K. Wilkerson, and A. Nelken-Terner. 1980. *First Annual Report of the Belize Archaeological Reconnaissance.* Andover, Mass.: Robert F. Peabody Foundation for Archaeology, Phillips Academy.

Madeira, P. C. 1931. An Aerial Expedition to Central America. *UM Journal* 22 (2).

Madrid Codex. 1869–70. *Manuscrit Troano: études sur le système graphique et la langue des mayas* [Tro Fragment]. Comp. C. E. Brasseur de Bourbourg. Paris: Imprimerie Impériale.

———. 1892. *Códice Maya denominado cortesiano que se conserva en el Museo Arqueológico Nacional* (Cortés Fragment). Madrid: Hecha y publicada bajo la dirección de Dios y Delgado y López de Ayala y del Hierro.

———. 1930. Facsimile of combined fragments issued by Artes e Industrias Gráficas. Madrid: Matev. (See also Anders 1967; Villacorta and Villacorta 1933.)

Madsen, W. 1960. Christo-Paganism. MARI Publication 19: 105–79.

Mahadevan, I. 1977. *The Indus Script.* Memoirs of the Archaeological Survey of India, No. 77. New Delhi: Tata Press.

Mahler, J. 1965. Garments and Textiles of the Maya Lowlands. In *HMAI* 3: 581–93.

Makemson, M. W. 1951. *The Book of the Jaguar Priest: A Translation of the Book of Chilam Balam of Tizimin.* New York: Schuman.

Maler, T. 1901. *Researches in the Central Portion of the Usumatsintla Valley: Report of Explorations for the Museum, 1898–1900.* PMAE Memoirs 2 (1).

———. 1903. *Researches in the Central Portions of the Usumatsintla Valley: Reports of Explorations for the Museum.* PMAE Memoirs 2 (2).

———. 1908a. *Explorations in the Department of Peten, Guatemala, and Adjacent Region: Topoxte; Yaxha; Benque Viejo; Naranjo.* PMAE Memoirs 4 (2).

———. 1908b. *Explorations of the Upper Usumatsintla and Adjacent Region: Altar de Sacrificios; Seibal; Itsimté-Sácluk; Cankuen.* PMAE Memoirs 4 (1).

———. 1911. *Explorations in the Department of Peten, Guatemala: Tikal.* PMAE Memoirs 5 (1).

Manzanilla, L., and L. Barba. 1990. The Study of Activities in Classic Households: Two Case Studies from Coba and Teotihuacan. *AM* 1: 41–50.

Marcus, J. 1973. Territorial Organization of the Lowland Classic Maya. *Science* 180: 911–16.

———. 1974. The Iconography of Power Among the Classic Maya. *WA* 6: 83–94.

———. 1976a. The Origin of Mesoamerican Writing. *Annual Review of Anthropology* 5: 35–67.

———. 1976b. *Emblem and State in the Classic Maya Lowlands.* DO.

———. 1980. Zapotec Writing. *SA* 242 (2): 50–64.

———. 1982. The Plant World of the Sixteenth- and Seventeenth-Century Lowland Maya. In *Maya Subsistence: Studies in Memory of Dennis E. Puleston,* K. V. Flannery, ed.: 239–73. New York: Academic Press.

———. 1983a. Lowland Maya Archaeology at the Crossroads. *AAnt* 48: 454–88.

———. 1983b. On the Nature of the Mesoamerican City. In Vogt and Leventhal 1983: 195–242.

———. 1987. *The Inscriptions of Calakmul: Royal Marriage at a Maya City in Campeche,*

*Mexico*. University of Michigan, Museum of Anthropology, Technical Report 21. Ann Arbor.

———. 1989a. Zapotec Chiefdoms and the Nature of Formative Religions. In Sharer and Grove 1989: 148–97.

———. 1989b. From Centralized Systems to City States: Possible Models for the Epiclassic. In Diehl and Berlo 1989: 201–8.

———. 1992. Royal Families, Royal Texts: Examples from the Zapotec and Maya. In Chase and Chase 1992.

———. 1993. Ancient Maya Political Organization. In Sabloff and Henderson 1993.

Marquina, I. 1951. *Arquitectura prehispánica*. Mexico City: Instituto Nacional de Antropología e Historia.

Martínez-Hernández, J. H., ed. 1930. *Diccionario de Motul, Maya Español, atribuido a Fray Antonio de Ciudad Real, y arte de lengua maya por Fray Juan Coronel*. Mérida: Talleres de la Compañía Tipográfica Yucateca.

Mason, J. A. 1931. A Maya Carved Stone Lintel from Guatemala. *UM Bulletin* 3 (1): 5–7.

———. 1932. Excavations at Piedras Negras. *UM Bulletin* 3 (6): 178–79.

Matheny, R. T. 1976. Maya Lowland Hydraulic Systems. *Science* 193: 639–46.

———. 1979. El Mirador, Peten, Guatemala: Report of the 1979 Season. Paper presented at the 43rd ICA, Vancouver.

———, ed. 1980. *El Mirador, Peten, Guatemala, an Interim Report*. NWAF Paper 45.

———. 1986. Investigations at El Mirador, Petén, Guatemala. *National Geographic Research* 2: 322–53.

———. 1987. Early States in the Maya Lowlands During the Late Preclassic Period: Edzna and El Mirador. In Benson 1987: 1–44.

Matheny, R. T., D. L. Gurr, D. Forsyth, and F. R. Hauck. 1985. *Investigations at Edzna, Campeche, Mexico*. Vol. 1, Part 1: *The Hydraulic System*. NWAF Paper 46.

Mathews, P. 1980. Notes on the Dynastic Sequence of Bonampak. Part 1. PRTS 5: 60–73.

———. 1983. *Corpus of Maya Hieroglyphic Inscriptions*. Vol. 6, Part 1: *Tonina*. PMAE.

———. 1985. Maya Early Classic Monuments and Inscriptions. In Willey and Mathews 1985: 5–54.

———. 1986. Classic Maya Site Interaction. Paper presented at the symposium, "Maya Art and Civilization: The New Dynamics," Fort Worth.

———. 1987. Thoughts on Classic Maya Political Geography. Paper presented at the University Museum Centennial Symposium, "The Use of Written Texts and Archaeological Material in the Reconstruction of Ancient Cultures," Philadelphia.

———. 1988. The Sculptures of Yaxchilan. Ph.D. diss., Yale University.

———. 1991. Classic Maya Emblem Glyphs. In Culbert 1991a: 19–29.

Mathews, P., and D. M. Pendergast. 1979. The Altun Ha Jade Plaque: Deciphering the Inscription. UCARF Contribution 41: 197–214.

Mathews, P., and M. G. Robertson. 1985. Notes on the Olvidado, Palenque Chiapas, Mexico. PRTS 7: 7–17.

Mathews, P., and L. Schele. 1974. Lords of Palenque—The Glyphic Evidence. PRTS 1: 63–75.

Mathews, P., and G. R. Willey. 1991. Prehistoric Polities of the Pasion Region: Hieroglyphic Texts and their Archaeological Settings. In Culbert 1991a: 30–71.

Matson, F. R. 1956. *Ceramics and Man*. Chicago: Aldine.

Maudslay, A. P. 1889–1902. *Biología Centrali-Americana: Archaeology*. 5 vols. London: R. H. Porter and Dulau and Co.

Maudslay, A. P., and A. C. Maudslay. 1889. *A Glimpse at Guatemala, and Some Notes on the Ancient Monuments of Central America*. London: Murray.

Mayer, K. H. 1978. *Maya Monuments: Sculptures of Unknown Provenance in Europe*. Trans. S. L. Brizee. Ramona, Calif.: Acoma.

———. 1984. *Maya Monuments: Sculptures of Unknown Provenance in Middle America*. Berlin: Verlag Karl-Friedrich von Flemming.

———. 1989. *Maya Monuments: Sculptures of Unknown Provenance*. Supplement 2. Berlin: Verlag Karl-Friedrich von Flemming.

McAnany, P. A. 1989. Stone-Tool Production and Exchange in the Eastern Lowlands: The Consumer Perspective from Pulltrouser Swamp, Belize. *AAnt* 54: 332–46.

———. 1990. Water Storage in the Puuc Region of the Northern Maya Lowlands: A Key to Population Estimates and Architectural Variability. In Culbert and Rice 1990: 263–84.

McBryde, F. W. 1947. *Cultural and Historical Geography of Southwest Guatemala*. Institute of Social Anthropology Publication 4. Washington, D.C.: Smithsonian Institution.

McClaran, M. 1973. Lexical and Syntactic Structures in Yucatec Maya. Ph.D. diss., Harvard University.

McKillop, H. 1984. Prehistoric Maya Reliance on Marine Resources: Analysis of a Midden from Moho Cay, Belize. *JFA* 11: 25–36.

McKillop, H., and P. F. Healy, eds. 1989. *Coastal Maya Trade*. Occasional Papers in Anthropology No. 8. Peterborough, Eng.: Trent University.

McQuown, N. 1955. The Indigenous Languages of Latin America. *AA* 47: 501–70.

———. 1956. The Classification of Maya Languages. *IJAL* 22: 191–95.

———. 1964. Los orígenes y la diferenciación de los Mayas según se infiere del estudio comparativo de las lenguas mayanas. In *Desarrollo cultural de los Mayas*, E. Z. Vogt and A. Ruz L., eds.: 49–80. Mexico City: Universidad Nacional Autónoma de México.

———. 1967. Classical Yucatec (Maya) In *HMAI* 5: 201–47.

———. 1976. American Indian Linguistics in New Spain. In *American Indian Languages and American Linguistics: Papers of the Second Golden Anniversary Symposium of the Linguistic Society of America*, W. Chafe, ed. Lisse, Belgium: Peter de Ridder Press.

McVicker, D. 1985. The Mayanized Mexicans. *AAnt* 50: 82–101.

Means, P. A. 1917. *History of the Spanish Conquest of Yucatan and of the Itzas*. PMAE Papers 7.

Meggers, B. J. 1954. Environmental Limitation on the Development of Culture. *AA* 56: 801–24.

Meggers, B. J., C. Evans, and E. Estrada. 1965. *Early Formative Period of Coastal Ecuador: The Valdevia and Machalilla Phases*. Smithsonian Contributions to Anthropology 1. Washington, D.C.: Smithsonian Institution.

Mercer, H. C. 1975. *The Hill-Caves of Yucatan*. Reprint of 1896 ed., with an introduction by J. E. S. Thompson. Norman: University of Oklahoma Press.

Merwin, R. E., and G. C. Vaillant. 1932. *The Ruins of Holmul, Guatemala*. PMAE Memoirs 3 (2).

Meyer, K. E. 1977. *The Plundered Past*. New York: Atheneum.

Michels, J. W., ed. 1979. *Settlement Pattern Excavations at Kaminaljuyu, Guatemala*. Pennsylvania State University Press Monograph Series of Kaminaljuyu. University Park.

Miles, S. W. 1957. The Sixteenth-Century Pokom Maya: A Documentary Analysis of Social Structure and Archaeological Setting. *Transactions of the American Philosophical Society* 47: 731–81.

———. 1965. Sculpture of the Guatemala-Chiapas Highlands and Pacific Slopes and Associated Hieroglyphs. In *HMAI* 2: 237–75.

Miller, A. G. 1977a. "Captains of the Itza": Unpublished Mural Evidence from Chichen Itza. In Hammond 1977b: 197–225.

———. 1977b. The Maya and the Sea: Trade and Cult at Tancah and Tulum. In Benson 1977b: 97–225.

———. 1978. A Brief Outline of the Artistic Evidence for Classic-Period Culture Contact Between Maya Lowlands and Central Mexican Highlands. In Pasztory 1978: 63–70.

———. 1980. Art Historical Implications of Quirigua Sculpture. Paper presented at the 45th Annual Meeting of the Society for American Archaeology, Philadelphia.

———. 1982. *On the Edge of the Sea: Mural Painting at Tancah-Tulum, Quintana Roo, Mexico*. DO.

———, ed. 1983. *Highland-Lowland Interaction in Mesoamerica: Interdisciplinary Approaches*. DO.

———. 1986a. *Maya Rulers of Time*. UM.

———. 1986b. From the Maya Margins: Images of Postclassic Politics. In Sabloff and Andrews 1986: 199–222.

Miller, M. E. 1985. Tikal, Guatemala: A Rationale for the Placement of the Funerary Pyramids. *Expedition* 27 (3): 6–15.

———. 1986. *The Murals of Bonampak*. Princeton: Princeton University Press.

———. 1988. The Meaning and Function of the Main Acropolis, Copan. In Boone and Willey 1988: 149–94.

Millon, R., ed. 1973. *Urbanization at Teotihuacan, Mexico*. Vol. 1: *The Teotihuacan Map*. Austin: University of Texas Press.

Moholy-Nagy, H. 1975. Obsidian at Tikal, Guatemala. 41st ICA *Actas* 1: 511–18.

———. 1976. Spatial Distribution of Flint and Obsidian Artifacts at Tikal, Guatemala. In Hester and Hammond 1976: 91–108.

Moholy-Nagy, H., and F. W. Nelson. 1990. New Data on Sources of Obsidian Artifacts from Tikal, Guatemala. *AM* 1: 71–80.

Molloy, J. P., and W. L. Rathje. 1974. Sexploitation Among the Late Classic Maya. In Hammond 1974b: 431–44.

Montmollin, O. de. 1988. Tenam Riosario—A Political Microcosm. *AAnt* 53: 351–70.

———. 1989. *The Archaeology of Political Structure: Settlement Analysis in a Classic Maya Polity*. Cambridge, Eng.: Cambridge University Press.

Morán, F. 1935. *Arte y Diccionario en Lengua Cholti: A Manuscript Copied from the Libro Grande of Fray Pedro Moran of About 1625*. Baltimore: Maya Society Publication No. 9.

Moreno, W. J. 1959. Síntesis de la historia pretolteca de mesoamérica. In *Esplendor del México antiguo*, C. Cook de Leonard, ed.: 1019–1108. Mexico City: Centro Investigaciones Antropológicas.

Morgan, L. H. 1877. *Ancient Society*. New York: Holt.

Morley, S. G. 1910. Uxmal—A Group of Related Structures. *American Journal of Archaeology*, ser. 2, 14: 1–18.

———. 1911. The Historical Value of the Books of Chilam Balam. *American Journal of Archaeology*, ser. 2, 15: 195–214.

———. 1915. *An Introduction to the Study of the Maya Hieroglyphs*. BAE Bulletin 57.

———. 1916. The Supplementary Series in the Maya Inscriptions. In *Holmes Anniversary Volume: Anthropological Essays*, F. W. Hodge, ed.: 366–96. Washington, D.C.: n.p.

———. 1920. *The Inscriptions at Copan*. CIW Publication 219.

———. 1925. The Earliest Mayan Dates. *Compte-Rendu of the 21st ICA* 2: 655–67.

———. 1935. *Guide Book to the Ruins of Quirigua*. CIW Supplemental Publication 16.

———. 1937–38. *The Inscriptions of the Peten*. 5 vols. CIW Publication 437.

———. 1946. *The Ancient Maya*. Stanford, Calif.: Stanford University Press. [2d ed. 1947.]

———. 1953. *La civilización maya*. Trans. A. Recinos. 2d ed. Mexico City: Fondo de Cultura Económica.

———. 1970. The Stela Platform at Uxmal, Yucatan, Mexico. Ed. and annotated by H. E. D. Pollock. MARI Publication 26: 151–80.

Morley, S. G., and G. W. Brainerd. 1956. *The Ancient Maya*. 3d ed. Stanford, Calif.: Stanford University Press.

Morley, S. G., and F. R. Morley. 1939. *The Age and Provenance of the Leyden Plate*. CIW Publication 509.

Morris, A. A. 1931. *Digging in Yucatan*. New York: Doubleday, Doran.

Morris, E. H., J. Charlot, and A. A. Morris. 1931. *The Temple of the Warriors at Chichen Itza, Yucatan*. CIW Publication 406.

Muntsch, A. 1943. Some Magico-Religious Observations of the Present-Day Maya Indians of British Honduras and Yucatan. *Primitive Man* 16 (1): 31–44.

Murie, A. 1935. Mammals from Guatemala and British Honduras. University of Michigan Museum of Zoology, Miscellaneous Publications 26: 7–30. Ann Arbor.

Navarrete, C. 1960. *Archaeological Explorations in the Region of the Frailesca, Chiapas, Mexico*. NWAF Paper 7.

———. 1976. Algunas influencias mexicanas en el area maya meridional durante el postclásico tardío. *Estudios de Cultura Nahuatl* 14: 345–82.

Netting, R. M. 1977. Maya Subsistence: Mythologies, Analogies, Possibilities. In Adams 1977: 299–333.

Neugebauer, B. 1983. Watershed Management by the Maya Civilization of Central Yucatan, Mexico. *Vierteljahresberichte* 94: 395–409.

Norman, V. G. 1973. *Izapa Sculpture*. Part 1: *Album*. NWAF Paper 30.

———. 1976. *Izapa Sculpture*. Part 2: *Text*. NWAF Paper 30.

Nuñez Chinchilla, J. 1963. *Copan Ruins*. Publications of the Banco Central de Honduras. Tegucigalpa.

Oakes, M. 1951. *The Two Crosses of Todos Santos*. New York: Pantheon.

Ochoa, L. 1983. El medio Usumacinta: un eslabón en los antecedentes olmecs de los Mayas. In Ochoa and Lee 1983: 147–74.

Ochoa, L., and T. A. Lee, eds. 1983. *Antropología e historia de los Mixe-Zoques y Mayas: un homenaje a Frans Blom*. Mexico City: Centro de Estudios Mayas, Universidad Nacional Autónoma de México and Brigham Young University.

Olsen, G. W., A. H. Siemens, D. E. Puleston, G. Cal, and D. Jenkins. 1975. Ridged Fields in British Honduras. *Soil Survey Horizons* 16: 9–12.

Orrego C., M., and R. Larios V. 1983. *Investigaciones arqueológicas en el Grupo 5E-11, Tikal.* Guatemala: Instituto de Antropología e Historia.

Osborne, L. de Jongh. 1935. *Guatemala Textiles.* MARI Publication 6.

———. 1965. *Indian Crafts of Guatemala and El Salvador.* Norman: University of Oklahoma Press.

Pahl, G. W. 1976. The Maya Hieroglyphic Inscriptions of Copan: A Catalog and Historical Commentary. Ph.D. diss., University of California, Los Angeles.

———. 1977. The Inscriptions of Río Amarillo and Los Higos: Secondary Centers of the Southeastern Maya Frontier. *Journal of Latin American Lore* 3: 133–54.

———, ed. 1986. *The Periphery of the Southeastern Classic Maya Realm.* Los Angeles: UCLA Latin America Center Publications.

Paillés, H. M. 1978. The Process of Transformation at Paijón: A Preclassic Society Located in an Estuary in Chiapas, Mexico. In Stark and Voorhies 1978: 81–95.

Palacios, E. J. 1932. Maya-Christian Synchronology or Calendrical Correlation. In MARI Publication 4: 147–80.

———. 1933. *El calendario y los jeroglíficos cronográficos mayas.* Mexico City: Editorial Cultura.

Paris Codex. 1887. *Manuscrit hiératique des anciens Indiens de l'Amérique centrale conservé à la Bibliothèque Nationale de Paris; avec une introduction par Leon de Rosny.* 2d ed. Paris: Maisonneuve et cie., Libraires de la Société Ethnographie. Reissued "under the care of William E. Gates, 1909." (See also Anders 1968; Villacorta and Villacorta 1933.)

Parsons, J. R. 1972. Archaeological Settlement Patterns. *Annual Review of Anthropology* 1: 127–50.

Parsons, L. A. 1967–69. *Bilbao, Guatemala.* 2 vols. Milwaukee Public Museum Publications in Anthropology, Nos. 11 and 12.

———. 1986. *The Origins of Maya Art: Monumental Stone Sculpture of Kaminaljuyu, Guatemala, and the Southern Pacific Coast.* DO.

Pasztory, E., ed. 1978. *Middle Classic Mesoamerica.* New York: Columbia University Press.

Pearse, A. S., E. P. Creaser, and F. G. Hall. 1936. *The Cenotes of Yucatan, a Zoological and Hydrographic Survey.* CIW Publication 457.

Pendergast, D. M. 1962. Metal Artifacts in Prehispanic Mesoamerica. *AAnt* 27: 520–45.

———. 1965. Maya Tombs at Altun Ha. *A* 18 (3): 210–17.

———. 1969. *Altun Ha, British Honduras (Belize): The Sun God's Tomb.* Royal Ontario Museum Art and Archaeology Occasional Paper 19. Toronto.

———. 1971. Evidence of Early Teotihuacan–Lowland Maya Contact at Altun Ha. *AAnt* 36: 455–60.

———. 1979. *Excavations at Altun Ha, Belize, 1964–1970.* Vol. 1. Toronto: Royal Ontario Museum.

———. 1981. Lamanai, Belize: Summary of Excavation Results, 1974–1980. *JFA* 8: 29–53.

———. 1982a. *Excavations at Altun Ha, Belize, 1964–1970.* Vol. 2. Toronto: Royal Ontario Museum.

———. 1982b. Ancient Maya Mercury. *Science* 217: 533–535.

————. 1986. Stability Through Change: Lamanai, Belize, from the Ninth to the Seventeenth Century. In Sabloff and Andrews 1986: 223–49.

————. 1988. Lamanai Stela 9: The Archaeological Context. RRAMW No. 20.

————. 1990a. *Excavations at Altun Ha, Belize, 1964–1970.* Vol. 3. Toronto: Royal Ontario Museum.

————. 1990b. Up from the Dust: The Central Lowlands Postclassic as Seen from Lamanai and Marco Gonzalez, Belize. In Clancy and Harrison 1990: 169–77.

Plafker, G. 1976. Tectonic Aspects of the Guatemala Earthquake of 4 February 1976. *Science* 193: 1201–8.

Pohl, M. D. 1983. Maya Ritual Faunas: Vertebrate Remains from Burials, Caches, Caves, and Cenotes in the Maya Lowlands. In Leventhal and Kolata 1983: 55–103.

————, ed. 1990. *Ancient Maya Wetland Agriculture: Excavations on Albion Island, Northern Belize.* Boulder, Colo.: Westview Press.

Pollock, H. E. D. 1937. *The Casa Redonda at Chichen Itza, Yucatan.* CIW Publication 456.

————. 1954. Department of Archaeology. *CIW Yearbook* 53: 263–67.

————. 1965. Architecture of the Maya Lowlands. In *HMAI* 2: 378–440.

————. 1980. *The Puuc, an Archaeological Survey of the Hill Country of Yucatan and Northern Campeche, Mexico.* PMAE Memoirs 19.

Pollock, H. E. D., R. L. Roys, T. Proskouriakoff, and A. L. Smith. 1962. *Mayapan, Yucatan, Mexico.* CIW Publication 619.

Potter, D. F. 1977. *Maya Architecture of the Central Yucatan Peninsula, Mexico.* MARI Publication 44.

Prem, H. J. 1971. Calendrics and Writing in Mesoamerica. UCARF Contribution 41: 215–29.

Pring, D. C. 1976. Outline of the Northern Belize Ceramic Sequence. *CCM* 9: 11–51.

Proskouriakoff, T. 1946. *An Album of Maya Architecture.* CIW Publication 558. Reprinted by the University of Oklahoma Press, 1963.

————. 1950. *A Study of Classic Maya Sculpture.* CIW Publication 593.

————. 1954. Mayapan, Last Stronghold of a Civilization. *A* 7 (2): 96–103.

————. 1955. The Death of a Civilization. *SA* 192 (5): 82–88.

————. 1960. Historical Implications of a Pattern of Dates at Piedras Negras. *AAnt* 25: 454–75.

————. 1961a. The Lords of the Maya Realm. *Expedition* 4 (1): 14–21.

————. 1961b. Portraits of Women in Maya Art. In *Essays in Pre-Columbian Art and Archaeology,* S. K. Lothrop et al., eds.: 81–99. Cambridge, Mass.: Harvard University Press.

————. 1963. Historical Data in the Inscriptions of Yaxchilan (Part I). *ECM* 3: 149–67.

————. 1964. Historical Data in the Inscriptions of Yaxchilan (Part II). *ECM* 4: 177–202.

————. 1965. Sculpture and Major Arts of the Maya Lowlands. In *HMAI* 2: 469–97.

————. 1971. Early Architecture and Sculpture in Mesoamerica. UCARF Contribution 11: 141–56.

————. 1973. The Hand-Grasping-Fish and Associated Glyphs on Classic Maya Monuments. In Benson 1973: 165–73.

————. 1974. *Jades from the Cenote of Sacrifice, Chichen Itza, Mexico.* PMAE Memoirs 10 (1).

———. 1993. *Maya History*. Ed. R. A. Joyce. Austin: University of Texas Press.

Puleston, D. E. 1968. *Brosimum alicastrum* as a Subsistence Alternative for the Classic Maya of the Central Southern Lowlands. Master's thesis, University of Pennsylvania.

———. 1971. An Experimental Approach to the Function of Classic Maya Chultuns. *AAnt* 36: 322–35.

———. 1974. Intersite Areas in the Vicinity of Tikal and Uaxactun. In Hammond 1974b: 303–11.

———. 1977. The Art and Archaeology of Hydraulic Agriculture in the Maya Lowlands. In Hammond 1977b: 449–67.

———. 1978. Terracing, Raised Fields, and Tree Cropping in the Maya Lowlands: A New Perspective on the Geography of Power. In Harrison and Turner 1978: 225–45.

———. 1979. An Epistemological Pathology and the Collapse, or Why the Maya Kept the Short Count. In Hammond and Willey 1979: 63–74.

———. 1983. *The Settlement Survey of Tikal*. Tikal Reports No. 13. UM.

Puleston, D. E., and D. W. Callender, Jr. 1967. Defensive Earthworks at Tikal. *Expedition* 9 (3): 40–48.

Puleston, D. E., and O. S. Puleston. 1971. An Ecological Approach to the Origins of Maya Civilization. *A* 24 (4): 330–37.

Pyburn, K. A. 1990. Settlement Patterns at Nohmul: Preliminary Results of Four Excavation Seasons. In Culbert and Rice 1990: 183–97.

———. n.d. Prehispanic Maya States: The Evidence for Absence. Ms.

Quirarte, J. 1973. *Izapa-Style Art: A Study of Its Form and Meaning*. Studies in Pre-Columbian Art and Archaeology, No. 10. DO.

———. 1976. The Underworld Jaguar in Maya Vase Painting: An Iconographic Study. *New Mexico Studies in the Fine Arts* 1: 20–25.

———. 1977. Early Art Styles of Mesoamerica and Early Classic Maya Art. In Adams 1977: 249–83.

———. 1979. The Representation of Underworld Processions in Maya Vase Painting: An Iconographic Study. In Hammond and Willey 1979: 117–48.

Rands, B. C., and R. L. Rands. 1961. Excavations in a Cemetery at Palenque. *ECM* 1: 87–106.

Rands, R. L. 1965a. Jades of the Maya Lowlands. In *HMAI* 3: 561–80.

———. 1965b. Classic and Postclassic Pottery Figurines of the Guatemalan Highlands. In *HMAI* 2: 156–62.

Rands, R. L., and B. C. Rands. 1959. The Incensario Complex of Palenque, Chiapas, Mexico. *AAnt* 25: 225–36.

———. 1965. Pottery Figurines of the Maya Lowlands. In *HMAI* 2: 535–60.

Rands, R. L., and R. E. Smith. 1965. Pottery of the Guatemalan Highlands. In *HMAI* 2: 95–145.

Rathje, W. L. 1970. Socio-Political Implications of Lowland Maya Burials: Methodology and Tentative Hypotheses. *WA* 1: 359–74.

———. 1971. The Origin and Development of Classic Maya Civilization. *AAnt* 36: 275–85.

———. 1973. Classic Maya Development and Denouement: A Research Design. In Culbert 1973: 405–56.

———. 1977. The Tikal Connection. In Adams 1977: 373–82.

Rathje, W. L., D. A. Gregory, and F. M. Wiseman. 1978. Trade Models and Archaeological Problems: Classic Maya Examples. NWAF Paper 40: 147–75.

Rau, C. 1879. *The Palenque Tablet in the United States National Museum, Washington, D.C.* Smithsonian Contributions to Knowledge 22 (5). Washington, D.C.: Smithsonian Institution.

Recinos, A. 1950. *Popol Vuh: The Sacred Book of the Ancient Quiche Maya.* English transl. by S. G. Morley and D. Goetz. Norman: University of Oklahoma Press.

Recinos, A., and D. Goetz. 1953. *The Annals of the Cakchiquels.* Norman: University of Oklahoma Press.

Redfield, R. 1941. *The Folk Culture of Yucatan.* Chicago: University of Chicago Press.

———. 1956. *The Little Community.* Chicago: University of Chicago Press.

Redfield, R., and A. Villa Rojas. 1934. *Chan Kom: A Maya Village.* CIW Publication 448.

Reed, N. 1964. *The Caste War of Yucatan.* Stanford, Calif.: Stanford University Press.

Reents-Budet, D. J. 1987. The Discovery of a Ceramic Artist and Royal Patron Among the Classic Maya. *Mexicon* 9: 123–26.

———. 1988. The Iconography of Lamanai Stela 9. RRAMW No. 22.

Reichel-Dolmatoff, G. 1965. *Excavaciones arqueológicas en Puerto Hormiga, Departamento de Bolivar.* Publicaciones de la Universidad de los Andes, Antropología 2. Bogotá.

Reina, R. E. 1962. The Ritual of the Skull of Peten, Guatemala. *Expedition* 4 (4): 26–36.

———. 1966. *The Law of the Saints: A Pokomam Pueblo and Its Community Culture.* Indianapolis, Ind.: Bobbs-Merrill.

———. 1967. Milpas and Milperos: Implications for Prehistoric Times. *AA* 69: 1–20.

Reina, R. E., and R. M. Hill II. 1978. *The Traditional Pottery of Guatemala.* Austin: University of Texas Press.

———. 1980. Lowland Maya Subsistence: Notes from Ethnohistory and Ethnography. *AAnt* 45: 74–79.

Rice, D. S. 1976. Middle Preclassic Maya Settlement in the Central Maya Lowlands. *JFA* 3: 425–45.

———. 1978. Population Growth and Subsistence Alternatives in a Tropical Lacustrine Environment. In Harrison and Turner 1978: 35–61.

———. 1986. The Peten Postclassic: A Settlement Perspective. In Sabloff and Andrews 1986: 301–44.

———. 1988. Classic to Postclassic Maya Household Transitions in the Central Peten, Guatemala. In Wilk and Ashmore 1988: 227–47.

Rice, D. S., and T. P. Culbert. 1990. Historical Contexts for Population Reconstruction in the Maya Lowlands. In Culbert and Rice 1990: 1–36.

Rice, D. S., and D. E. Puleston. 1981. Ancient Maya Settlement Patterns in the Peten, Guatemala. In Ashmore 1981b: 121–56.

Rice, D. S., and P. M. Rice. 1979. Introductory Archaeological Survey of the Central Peten, Savanna, Guatemala. UCARF Contribution 41: 231–77.

———. 1981. Muralla de León: A Lowland Maya Fortification. *JFA* 8: 271–88.

———. 1984. Collapse to Contact: Postclassic Archaeology of the Peten Maya. *A* 37 (2): 46–51.

———. 1990. Population Size and Population Change in the Central Peten Lakes Region, Guatemala. In Culbert and Rice 1990: 123–48.

Rice, P. M. 1979. Ceramic and Nonceramic Artifacts of Lakes Yaxha-Sacnab, El Peten, Guatemala. *CCM* 11: 1–85.

———. 1984. Obsidian Procurement in the Central Peten Lakes Region, Guatemala. *JFA* 11: 181–94.

———. 1986. The Peten Postclassic: Perspectives from the Central Peten Lakes. In Sabloff and Andrews 1986: 251–99.

———. 1987. *Macanche Island, El Peten, Guatemala: Excavations, Pottery, and Artifacts.* Gainesville: University of Florida Press.

Rice, P. M., H. V. Michel, F. Asaro, and F. Stross. 1985. Provenience Analysis of Obsidians from the Peten Central Lakes Region, Guatemala. *AAnt* 50: 591–604.

Rice, P. M., and D. S. Rice. 1979. Home on the Range: Aboriginal Maya Settlement in the Central Peten Savannas. *A* 32 (6): 16–25.

Rice, P. M., and R. J. Sharer, eds. 1987. *Maya Ceramics: Papers from the 1985 Maya Ceramic Conference.* 2 vols. BAR 345.

Richardson, F. B. 1940. Non-Maya Monumental Sculpture of Central America. In *The Maya and Their Neighbors*, C. L. Hay et al., eds.: 395–416. New York: Appleton Century.

Ricketson, O. G. 1931. *Excavations at Baking Pot, British Honduras.* CIW Supplemental Publication 6: 1–15.

Ricketson, O. G., and E. B. Ricketson. 1937. *Uaxactun, Guatemala, Group E, 1926–1937.* CIW Publication 477.

Riese, B. 1971. *Grundlagen zur Entzifferung der Mayahieroglyphen, Dargestellt an den Inschriften von Copan.* Beiträge zur mittelamerikanischen Völkerkunde 11. Hamburgisches Museum für Völkerkunde und Vorgeschichte. Munich: Kommissionsverlag Klaus Renner.

———. 1980. Late Classic Relationships Between Copan and Quirigua: Some Epigraphic Evidence. Paper presented at the 45th Annual Meeting of the Society for American Archaeology, Philadelphia.

———. 1984a. Hel Hieroglyphs. In Justeson and Campbell 1984: 263–86.

———. 1984b. Relaciones clásico-tardías entre Copán y Quiriguá: algunas evidencias epigráficas. *Yaxkin* 7 (1): 23–30.

———. 1988. Epigraphy of the Southeast Zone in Relation to Other Parts of Mesoamerica. In Boone and Willey 1988: 67–94.

Ringle, W. M. 1988. Of Mice and Monkeys: The Value and Meaning of T1016, the God C Hieroglyph. RRAMW No. 18.

———. 1990. Who Was Who in Ninth-Century Chichen Itza. *AM* 1: 233–43.

Ringle, W. M., and E. W. Andrews V. 1988. Formative Residences at Komchen, Yucatan, Mexico. In Wilk and Ashmore 1988: 171–97.

———. 1990. The Demography of Komchen, An Early Maya Town in Northern Yucatan. In Culbert and Rice 1990: 215–43.

Rivet, P. 1954. *Cités maya.* 4th ed. Paris: Guillot.

Robertson, M. G. 1972a. The Ritual Bundles of Yaxchilan. Paper presented at the Tulane University Symposium on the Art of Latin America, New Orleans.

———. 1972b. Monument Thievery in Mesoamerica. *AAnt* 37: 147–55.

———. 1977. Painting Practices and Their Change Through Time of the Palenque Stucco Sculptors. In Hammond 1977b: 297–326.

————, ed. 1980. *Third Palenque Round Table, Part 2.* Vol. 5. Austin: University of Texas Press.

————. 1983. *The Temple of the Inscriptions.* Vol. 1 of *The Sculpture of Palenque.* Princeton: Princeton University Press.

————. 1985a. *The Early Buildings of the Palace and the Wall Paintings.* Vol. 2 of *The Sculpture of Palenque.* Princeton: Princeton University Press.

————. 1985b. *The Late Buildings of the Palace.* Vol. 3 of *The Sculpture of Palenque.* Princeton: Princeton University Press.

Robertson, R. A. 1983. Functional Analysis and Social Process in Ceramics: The Pottery from Cerros, Belize. In Leventhal and Kolata 1983: 105–42.

Robertson, R. A., and D. A. Freidel, eds. 1986. *Archaeology at Cerros, Belize, Central America.* Vol. 1. Dallas: Southern Methodist University Press.

Robicsek, F. 1972. *Copan: Home of the Mayan Gods.* New York: Museum of the American Indian, Heye Foundation.

————. 1975. *A Study in Maya Art and History: The Mat Symbol.* New York: Museum of the American Indian, Heye Foundation.

————. 1978. *The Smoking Gods.* Norman: University of Oklahoma Press.

Robinson, E. J., ed. 1987. *Interaction on the Southeast Mesoamerican Periphery: Prehistoric and Historic Honduras and El Salvador.* BAR 327.

Robles Castella, J. F. 1980. La secuencia cerámica de la región de Cobá, Quintana Roo. Thesis, Escuela Nacional de Antropología e Historia, México.

Robles Castella, J. F., and A. P. Andrews. 1986. A Review and Synthesis of Recent Postclassic Archaeology in Northern Yucatan. In Sabloff and Andrews 1986: 53–98.

Rosny, L. de. 1875. *L'interpretation des anciens textes mayas.* Paris: Société Américaine de France.

Roys, R. L. 1931. *The Ethno-Botany of the Maya.* MARI Publication 2.

————. 1933. *The Book of Chilam Balam of Chumayel.* CIW Publication 438.

————. 1943. *The Indian Background of Colonial Yucatan.* CIW Publication 548. Reprinted by the University of Oklahoma Press, 1972.

————. 1952. *Conquest Sites and the Subsequent Destruction of Maya Architecture in the Interior of Northern Yucatan.* CIW Publication 596.

————. 1965. Lowland Maya Society at Spanish Contact. In *HMAI* 3: 659–78.

————. 1967. *The Book of Chilam Balam of Chumayel.* Introduction by J. E. S. Thompson. Reprint of the original CIW edition (1933). Norman: University of Oklahoma Press.

Rue, D. J. 1987. Early Agriculture and Early Postclassic Maya Occupation in Western Honduras. *Nature* 326: 6110.

————. 1989. Archaic Middle American Agriculture and Settlement: Recent Pollen Data from Honduras. *JFA* 16: 177–84.

Rue, D. J., A. C. Freter, and D. A. Ballinger. 1989. The Caverns of Copan Revisited: Preclassic Sites in the Sesesmil River Valley, Copan, Honduras. *JFA* 16: 395–404.

Ruppert, K. J. 1931. *Temple of the Wall Panels.* CIW Publication 403.

————. 1935. *The Caracol at Chichen Itza, Yucatan, Mexico.* CIW Publication 454.

————. 1943. *The Mercado, Chichen Itza, Yucatan, Mexico.* CIW Publication 546.

————. 1952. *Chichen Itza: Architectural Notes and Plans.* CIW Publication 595.

Ruppert, K. J., and J. H. Denison. 1943. *Archaeological Reconnaissance in Campeche, Quintana Roo, and Peten.* CIW Publication 543.

Ruppert, K. J., E. M. Shook, A. L. Smith, and R. E. Smith. 1954. Chichen Itza, Dzibiac, and Balam Canche, Yucatan. *CIW Yearbook* 53: 286–89.

Ruppert, K. J., J. E. S. Thompson, and T. Proskouriakoff. 1955. *Bonampak, Chiapas, Mexico*. CIW Publication 602.

Rust, W. F., and R. J. Sharer. 1988. Olmec Settlement Data from La Venta, Tabasco, Mexico. *Science* 242: 102–4.

Ruz Lhuillier, A. 1952a. Exploraciones en Palenque: 1950. *INAH Anales* 5: 25–45.

———. 1952b. Exploraciones en Palenque: 1951. *INAH Anales* 5: 47–66.

———. 1954. La Pirámide-tumba de Palenque. *Cuadernos Americanos* 74: 141–59.

———. 1955. Exploraciones en Palenque: 1952. *INAH Anales* 6: 79–110.

———. 1958a. Exploraciones arqueológicas en Palenque: 1953. *INAH Anales* 10: 69–116.

———. 1958b. Exploraciones arqueológicas en Palenque: 1954. *INAH Anales* 10: 117–84.

———. 1958c. Exploraciones arqueológicas en Palenque: 1955. *INAH Anales* 10: 185–240.

———. 1958d. Exploraciones arqueológicas en Palenque: 1956. *INAH Anales* 10: 241–99.

———. 1962. Exploraciones arqueológicas en Palenque: 1957. *INAH Anales* 14: 35–90.

———. 1965. Tombs and Funerary Practices in the Maya Lowlands. In *HMAI* 2: 441–61.

———, ed. 1973. *El Templo de las Inscripciones*. Mexico City: INAH.

———. 1977. Gerontocracy at Palenque? In Hammond 1977b: 287–95.

Sabloff, J. A. 1973a. Major Themes in the Past Hypotheses of the Maya Collapse. In Culbert 1973: 35–40.

———. 1973b. Continuity and Disruption During Terminal Late Classic Times at Seibal: Ceramic and Other Evidence. In Culbert 1973: 107–33.

———. 1975. *Excavations at Seibal, Department of the Peten, Guatemala: The Ceramics*. PMAE Memoirs 13 (2).

———. 1977. Old Myths, New Myths: The Role of Sea Traders in the Development of Ancient Maya Civilization. In Benson 1977b: 67–88.

———. 1983. Classic Maya Settlement Pattern Studies: Past Problems and Future Prospects. In Vogt and Leventhal 1983: 413–22.

———. 1985. Ancient Maya Civilization: An Overview. In Gallenkamp and Johnson 1985: 34–46.

———. 1986. Interaction Among Maya Polities: A Preliminary Examination. In *Peer Polity Interaction and Socio-Political Change*, C. Renfrew and J. F. Cherry, eds.: 109–16. Cambridge, Eng.: Cambridge University Press.

———. 1990. *The New Archaeology and the Ancient Maya*. New York: W. H. Freeman.

———. In press. Interpreting the Collapse of Classic Maya Civilization: A Case Study of Changing Archaeological Perspectives. In *Meta-Archaeology*, L. Embree, ed. Boston: Kluwer Academic Publishers.

Sabloff, J. A., and E. W. Andrews V, eds. 1986. *Late Lowland Maya Civilization: Classic to Postclassic*. Albuquerque: University of New Mexico Press.

Sabloff, J. A., and D. A. Freidel. 1975. A Model of a PreColumbian Trading Center. In Sabloff and Lamberg-Karlovsky 1975: 369–408.

Sabloff, J. A., and J. S. Henderson, eds. 1993. *Lowland Maya Civilization in the Eighth Century A.D.: A Symposium at Dumbarton Oaks 7th and 8th October, 1989.* DO.

Sabloff, J. A., and C. C. Lamberg-Karlovsky, eds. 1975. *Ancient Civilization and Trade.* SAR.

Sabloff, J. A., and W. R. Rathje, eds. 1975a. *A Study of Changing PreColumbian Commercial Systems.* PMAE Monograph 3.

———. 1975b. The Rise of a Maya Merchant Class. *SA* 233 (4): 72–82.

Sabloff, J. A., and G. R. Willey. 1967. The Collapse of Maya Civilization in the Southern Lowlands: A Consideration of History and Process. *SWJA* 23: 311–36.

Saenz, C. A. 1975. Cerámica de Uxmal, Yucatán. *Anales del INAH* 7: 171–86.

Sahagún, B. de. 1946. *Historia general de las cosas de la Nueva España.* Mexico City: Editoria Nueva España. 2d ed., with numeration, notes, and appendixes by A. M. Garibay K., 1969. Mexico City: Biblioteca Porrúa.

Sanders, W. T. 1956. The Central Mexican Symbiotic Region. In Willey 1956a: 115–27.

———. 1960. *Prehistoric Ceramics and Settlement Patterns in Quintana Roo, Mexico.* CIW Publication 606.

———. 1962. Cultural Ecology of the Maya Lowlands I. *ECM* 2: 79–121.

———. 1963. Cultural Ecology of the Maya Lowlands II. *ECM* 3: 203–41.

———. 1973. The Cultural Ecology of the Lowland Maya: A Re-Evaluation. In Culbert 1973: 325–65.

———. 1977. Environmental Heterogeneity and the Evolution of Lowland Maya Civilization. In Adams 1977: 287–97.

———. 1981. Classic Maya Settlement Patterns and Ethnographic Analogy. In Ashmore 1981b: 351–69.

———, ed. 1986. *Excavaciones en el area urbana de Copán, Tomo I.* Tegucigalpa: Secretaría de Cultura y Turismo y Instituto Hondureño de Anthropología e Historia.

———, ed. 1990. *Excavaciones en el area urbana de Copán, Tomo II.* Tegucigalpa: Secretaría de Cultura y Turismo y Instituto Hondureño de Anthropología e Historia.

Sanders, W. T., and J. W. Michels, eds. 1977. *Teotihuacan and Kaminaljuyu: A Study in Prehistoric Cultural Contact.* Pennsylvania State University Press Monograph Series on Kaminaljuyu. University Park.

Sanders, W. T., and C. N. Murdy. 1982. Cultural Evolution and Ecological Succession in the Valley of Guatemala: 1500 B.C.–A.D. 1524. In Flannery 1982: 19–63.

Sanders, W. T., J. R. Parsons, and R. S. Santley. 1979. *The Basin of Mexico.* New York: Academic Press.

Sanders, W. T., and B. J. Price. 1968. *Mesoamerica: The Evolution of a Civilization.* New York: Random House.

Sanders, W. T., and D. Webster. 1989. The Mesoamerican Urban Tradition. *AA* 90: 521–46.

Sanders, W. T., H. Wright, R. McC. Adams, and T. Earle, eds. 1984. *On the Evolution of Complex Societies: Essays in Honor of Harry Hoijer.* Malibu, Calif.: Undena Publications.

Santley, R. S. 1980. Obsidian Trade and Teotihuacan Influence in Mesoamerica. Paper presented at the DO Symposium on Mesoamerican Highland-Lowland Interaction, Washington, D.C.

Sapir, E. 1916. *Time Perspective in Aboriginal American Indian Culture: A Study in Method*. Canada, Department of Mines, Geological Survey, Memoir 90, Anthropological Series No. 13. Ottawa: Government Printing Bureau. Reprinted in *Selected Writings of Edward Sapir in Language, Culture, Personality*, D. Mandelbaum, ed.: 389–462. Berkeley and Los Angeles: University of California Press, 1968.

Sapper, K. 1896. *Sobre la geografía física y la geología de la península de Yucatán*. Instituto Geología No. 3. Mexico City.

———. 1897. *Das Nördliche Mittel-Amerika Nebst einem Ausflug nach dem Hochland von Anahuac: Reisen und Studien aus den Jahren 1888–1895*. Braunschweig: F. Vieweg und Sohn.

Satterthwaite, L. 1937a. Thrones at Piedras Negras. *UM Bulletin* 7 (1): 18–23.

———. 1937b. Identification of Maya Temple Buildings at Piedras Negras. *Publications of the Philadelphia Anthropological Society* 1: 161–77.

———. 1943. *Piedras Negras: Architecture. Part 1: Introduction*. UM.

———. 1944a. *Piedras Negras Archaeology: Architecture. Part 2: Temples*. UM.

———. 1944b. *Piedras Negras Archaeology: Architecture. Part 4: Ball Courts*. UM.

———. 1944/1954. *Piedras Negras Archaeology: Architecture. Part 6: Unclassified Buildings and Substructures*. UM.

———. 1947. *Concepts and Structures of Maya Calendrical Arithmetic*. Joint Publications, Museum of the University of Pennsylvania and the Philadelphia Anthropological Society, No. 3.

———. 1950a. Reconnaissance in British Honduras. *UM Bulletin* 16 (1): 21–37.

———. 1950b. Plastic Art of a Maya Palace. *A* 3: 215–22.

———. 1952. *Piedras Negras Archaeology: Architecture. Part 5: Sweathouses*. UM.

———. 1954. Sculptured Monuments from Caracol, British Honduras. *UM Bulletin* 18 (1–2): 1–45.

———. 1958. The Problem of Abnormal Stela Placements at Tikal and Elsewhere. Tikal Report No. 3. UM Monograph 15: 61–83.

———. 1965. Calendrics of the Maya Lowlands. In *HMAI* 3: 603–31.

Satterthwaite, L., and E. K. Ralph. 1960. New Radiocarbon Dates and the Maya Correlation Problem. *AAnt* 26: 165–84.

Saul, F. P. 1972. *The Human Skeletal Remains of Altar de Sacrificios: An Osteobiographic Analysis*. PMAE Papers 63 (2).

———. 1973. Disease in the Maya Area: The Precolumbian Evidence. In Culbert 1973: 301–24.

Saville, M. 1893. Vandalism Among the Antiquities of Yucatan and Central America. *Archaeologist* 1: 91–93.

———. 1921. *Reports on the Maya Indians of Yucatan*. Indian Notes and Monographs 9 (3). New York: Heye Foundation.

Scarborough, V. L. 1983. A Preclassic Maya Water System. *AAnt* 48: 720–44.

———. 1991. *Archaeology at Cerros, Belize, Central America*. Vol. 3: *The Settlement System in a Late Preclassic Maya Community*. Dallas: Southern Methodist University Press.

Scarborough, V. L. and G. G. Gallopin. 1991. A Water Storage Adaptation in the Maya Lowlands. *Science* 251: 658–62.

Scarborough, V. L., and R. A. Robertson. 1986. Civic and Residential Settlement at a Late Classic Maya Center. *JFA* 13: 155–76.

Schele, L. 1978. Genealogical Documentation on the Tri-Figure Panels at Palenque. PRTS 4: 41–70.

———. 1980. Verb Morphology and Syntax of the Maya Hieroglyphic Writing System. Ph.D. diss., University of Texas.

———. 1981. Sacred Site and World-View at Palenque. In *Mesoamerican Sites and World-Views*, E. P. Benson, ed.: 87–117. DO.

———. 1982. *Maya Glyphs: The Verbs*. Austin: University of Texas Press.

———. 1984. Human Sacrifice Among the Classic Maya. In Benson and Boone 1984: 6–48.

———. 1985. The Hauberg Stela: Bloodletting and the Mythos of Maya Rulership. PRTS 7: 135–49.

———. 1986. *The Founders of Lineages at Copan and Other Maya Sites*. CN 8.

———. 1988. *Revisions to the Dynastic Chronology of Copan*. CN 45.

———. 1989. *Notebook for the XIII Maya Hieroglyphic Workshop at Texas*. Transcribed by Phil Wanyerka. Austin: Department of Art, University of Texas.

———. 1990a. House Names and Dedication Rituals at Palenque. In Clancy and Harrison 1990: 143–57.

———. 1990b. *The Proceedings of the Maya Hieroglyphic Workshop, 1990*. Transcribed by Phil Wanyerka. Austin: Department of Art, University of Texas.

———. 1990c. *Early Quirigua and the Kings of Copan*. CN 75.

———. 1991a. An Epigraphic History of the Western Maya Region. In Culbert 1991a: 72–101.

———. 1991b. The Demotion of Chac-Zutz: Lineage Compounds and Subsidiary Lords at Palenque. PRTS 8: 6–11.

Schele, L., and D. A. Freidel. 1990. *A Forest of Kings*. New York: W. Morrow & Co.

———. 1991. The Courts of Creation: Ballcourts, Ballgames, and Portals to the Maya Otherworld. In *The Mesoamerican Ballgame*, D. Wilcox and V. Scarborough, eds. Tucson: University of Arizona Press.

Schele, L., and N. Grube. 1987. *U Cit Tok, the Last King of Copan*. CN 21.

Schele, L., and P. Mathews. 1979. *The Bodega of Palenque, Chiapas, Mexico*. DO.

———. 1991. Royal Visits and Other Intersite Relationships Among the Classic Maya. In Culbert 1991a: 226–52.

Schele, L., P. Mathews, and F. Lounsbury. n.d. Parentage and Spouse Expressions from Classic Maya Inscriptions.

Schele, L., and J. H. Miller. 1983. *The Mirror, the Rabbit, and the Bundle: "Accession" Expressions from the Classic Maya Inscriptions*. DO.

Schele, L., and M. E. Miller. 1986. *The Blood of Kings*. New York: George Braziller.

Schellhas, P. 1904. *Representations of Deities of the Maya Manuscripts*. PMAE Papers 4 (1): 1–47.

Schmidt, K. P., and E. W. Andrews IV. 1936. Notes on Snakes from Yucatan. Field Museum of Natural History Zoological Series 20 (18): 167–87. Chicago.

Scholes, F. V. 1933. The Beginnings of Hispano-Indian Society in Yucatan. *Scientific Monthly* 44: 530–38.

Scholes, F. V., C. R. Menéndez, J. I. Rubio M., and E. Adams, eds. 1936. *Documentos para la historia de Yucatán. Tomo I. 1550–1561.* Mérida: Tipográfia Yucateca.

Scholes, F. V., and R. L. Roys. 1938. *Fray Diego de Landa and the Problem of Idolatry in Yucatan.* Cooperation in Research CIW Publication 501.

———. 1948. *The Maya Chontal Indians of Acalan-Tixchel.* CIW Publication 560.

Schortman, E. M. 1980. Archaeological Investigations in the Lower Motagua Valley. *Expedition* 23 (1): 28–34.

———. 1986. Interaction Between the Maya and Non-Maya Along the Late Classic Southeast Maya Periphery: The View from the Lower Motagua Valley, Guatemala. In Urban and Schortman 1986: 114–37.

———. 1993. *Quirigua Reports III: Archaeological Investigations in the Lower Motagua Valley, Izabal, Guatemala.* University Museum Monographs. UM.

Schortman, E. M., and P. A. Urban, eds. 1983. *Quirigua Reports* II, R. J. Sharer, general ed., Papers 6–14. University Museum Monograph 49. UM.

———. 1987. Modeling Interregional Interaction in Prehistory. *Advances in Archaeological Method and Theory* 11: 37–95.

Schortman, E. M., P. A. Urban, W. Ashmore, and J. Benyo. 1986. Interregional Interaction in the SE Maya Periphery: The Santa Barbara Archaeological Project, 1983–1984 Seasons. *JFA* 13: 259–72.

Sedat, D. W., and R. J. Sharer. 1972. Archaeological Investigations in the Northern Maya Highlands: New Data on the Maya Preclassic. UCARF Contribution 16: 23–35.

Seler, E. 1902–23. *Gesammelte Abhandlungen zur Amerikanischen Sprach und Alterthumskunde.* 5 vols. Berlin: Ascher, Behrend.

———. 1904. English translations of nine of Seler's articles. BAE Bulletin 28: 353–91.

Service, E. 1962. *Primitive Social Organization.* New York: Random House.

———. 1975. *Origins of the State and Civilization.* New York: Norton.

Shafer, H. J., and T. R. Hester. 1983. Ancient Maya Chert Workshops in Northern Belize, Central America. *AAnt* 48: 519–43.

Sharer, R. J. 1969. Chalchuapa: Investigations at a Highland Maya Ceremonial Center. *Expedition* 11 (2): 36–38.

———. 1974. The Prehistory of the Southeastern Maya Periphery. *Current Anthropology* 15 (2): 165–87.

———. 1975. The Southeastern Periphery of the Maya Area: A Prehistoric Perspective. Paper presented at the 74th Annual Meeting of the American Anthropological Association, San Francisco.

———. 1977. The Maya Collapse Revisited: Internal and External Perspectives. In Hammond 1977b: 532–52.

———, ed. 1978a. *The Prehistory of Chalchuapa, El Salvador.* 3 vols. UM Monograph 36. Philadelphia: University of Pennsylvania Press.

———. 1978b. Archaeology and History at Quirigua, Guatemala. *JFA* (1): 51–70.

———. 1980. The Quirigua Project, 1974–79. *Expedition* 23 (1): 5–10.

———. 1982. Did the Maya Collapse? A New World Perspective on the Demise of Harappan Civilization. In *Harappan Civilization: A Contemporary Perspective*, G. A. Possehl, ed. American Institute of Indian Studies. New Delhi: Oxford and IBH.

———. 1984. Lower Central America as Seen from Mesoamerica. In *Central American Archaeology*, F. Lange and D. Stone, eds. Albuquerque: University of New Mexico Press.

———.

———. 1985a. Terminal Events in the Southeastern Lowlands: A View from Quiriguá. In Chase and Rice 1985: 245–53.

———. 1985b. Archaeology and Epigraphy Revisited. *Expedition* 27 (3): 16–19.

———. 1987. Nuevas perspectivas sobre los orígenes de la civilización maya. *Yaxkin* 10 (2): 81–88.

———. 1988a. Early Maya Kingship and Polities. Paper presented at the 4th Texas Symposium, University of Texas, Austin.

———. 1988b. Quirigua as a Classic Maya Center. In Boone and Willey 1988: 31–65.

———. 1989a. The Olmec and the Southeast Periphery of Mesoamerica. In Sharer and Grove 1989: 247–71.

———. 1989b. Preclassic Foundations of Classic Maya Political Systems. Paper presented at the 54th Annual Meeting of the Society for American Archaeology, Atlanta.

———. 1989c. Preclassic Origins of Maya Writing: A Highland Perspective. In Hanks and Rice 1989.

———. 1990. *Quirigua: A Classic Maya Center and Its Sculptures*. Durham, N.C.: Carolina Academic Press.

———. 1991. Diversity and Continuity in Maya Civilization: Quirigua as a Case Study. In Culbert 1991a: 180–98.

Sharer, R. J., and D. C. Grove, eds. 1989. *Regional Perspectives on the Olmec*. SAR. Cambridge: Cambridge University Press.

Sharer, R. J., J. C. Miller, L. P. Traxler. 1992. Evolution of Classic Period Architecture in the Eastern Acropolis, Copan, Honduras. *AM* 3: 145–60.

Sharer, R. J., and D. W. Sedat. 1973. Monument 1, El Porton, Guatemala, and the Development of Maya Calendrical and Writing Systems. UCARF Contribution 18: 177–94.

———. 1987. *Archaeological Investigations in the Northern Maya Highlands, Guatemala: Interaction and the Development of Maya Civilization*. University Museum Monograph 59. UM.

Shattuck, G. C. 1933. *The Peninsula of Yucatan, Medical, Biological, Meteorological and Sociological Studies*. CIW Publication 431.

Sheehy, J. J. 1991. Structure and Change in a Late Classic Maya Domestic Group at Copan, Honduras. *AM* 2: 1–19.

Sheets, P. D. 1971. An Ancient Natural Disaster. *Expedition* 13 (1): 24–31.

———. 1972. A Model of Mesoamerican Obsidian Technology Based on Preclassic Workshop Debris in El Salvador. *CCM* 8: 17–33.

———. 1973. The Pillage of Prehistory. *AAnt* 38: 317–20.

———. 1975. A Reassessment of the Precolumbian Obsidian Industry of El Chayal, Guatemala. *AAnt* 40: 98–103.

———. 1976a. Islands of Lithic Knowledge and Seas of Ignorance in the Maya Area. In Hester and Hammond 1976: 1–9.

———. 1976b. The Terminal Preclassic Lithic Industry of the Southeast Maya Highlands: A Component of the Protoclassic Site-Unit Intrusions in the Lowlands. In Hester and Hammond 1976: 55–69.

———. 1979a. Maya Recovery from Volcanic Disasters, Ilopango and Ceren. *A* 32 (3): 32–42.

———. 1979b. Environmental and Cultural Effects of the Ilopango Eruption in Central

America. In *Volcanic Activity and Human Ecology*, P. D. Sheets and D. K. Grayson, eds.: 525–64. New York: Academic Press.

———, ed. 1983. *Archaeology and Volcanism in Central America: The Zapotitlan Valley of El Salvador*. Austin: University of Texas Press.

Sheets, P. D., H. F. Beaubien, M. Beaudry, A. Gerstle, M. McKee, C. D. Miller, H. Spetzler, and D. B. Tucker. 1990. Household Archaeology at Cerén, El Salvador. *AM* 1: 81–90.

Sheets, P. D., and B. R. McKee, eds. 1989. Archaeological Investigations at the Ceren Site, El Salvador: A Preliminary Report. Boulder: Department of Anthropology, University of Colorado.

Shepard, A. O. 1948. *Plumbate: A Mesoamerican Trade Ware*. CIW Publication 573.

———. 1971. *Ceramics for the Archaeologist*. CIW Publication 609.

Shimkin, D. B. 1973. Models for the Downfall: Some Ecological and Cultural-Historical Considerations. In Culbert 1973: 269–99.

Shook, E. M. 1954. *The Temple of Kukulcan at Mayapan*. CIW Current Reports, No. 20.

———. 1960. Tikal Stela 29. *Expedition* 2 (2): 29–35.

———. 1965. Archaeological Survey of the Pacific Coast of Guatemala. In *HMAI* 2: 180–94.

———. 1971. Inventory of Some Preclassic Traits in the Highlands and Pacific Guatemala and Adjacent Areas. UCARF Contribution 11: 70–77.

Shook, E. M., W. R. Coe, V. L. Broman, and L. Satterthwaite. 1958. *Tikal Report* 1–4. UM Monograph 15.

Shook, E. M., and M. P. Hatch. 1978. The Ruins of El Balsamo, Department of Escuintla, Guatemala. *Journal of New World Archaeology* 3 (1): 1–38.

———. 1979. The Early Preclassic Sequence in the Ocos-Salinas La Blanca Area, South Coast of Guatemala. UCARF Contribution 41: 143–95.

Shook, E. M., M. P. Hatch, and J. K. Donaldson. 1979. Ruins of Semetabaj, Dept. Solola, Guatemala. UCARF Contribution 41: 7–142.

Shook, E. M., and W. Irving. 1955. *Colonnaded Buildings at Mayapan*. CIW Current Reports, No. 20.

Shook, E. M., and A. V. Kidder. 1952. *Mound E-III-3, Kaminaljuyu, Guatemala*. CIW Publication 596.

Shook, E. M., and T. Proskouriakoff. 1956. Settlement Patterns in Mesoamerica and the Sequence in the Guatemalan Highlands. In Willey 1956a: 93–100.

Sidrys, R. V. 1976. Classic Maya Obsidian Trade. *AAnt* 41: 449–64.

Sidrys, R. V., C. M. Krowne, and H. B. Nicholson. 1975. A Lowland Maya Long Count/Gregorian Conversion Computer Program. *AAnt* 40: 337–44.

Siegel, M. 1941. Religion in Western Guatemala: A Product of Acculturation. *AA* 43: 62–76.

Siemens, A. H. 1978. Karst and the Pre-Hispanic Maya in the Southern Lowlands. In Harrison and Turner 1978: 117–43.

Siemens, A. H., and D. E. Puleston. 1972. Ridged Fields and Associated Features in Southern Campeche: New Perspectives on the Lowland Maya. *AAnt* 37: 228–39.

Smailus, O. 1975a. *El Maya-Chontal de Acalan: análisis lingüístico de un documento de los años 1610–12*. Centro de Estudios Mayas, Cuaderno 9. Mexico City: Universidad Nacional Autónoma de México.

——. 1975b. *Textos mayas de Belice y Quintana Roo: fuentes para una dialectología del Maya Yucateco.* Indiana 3. Beiträge zur Völker un Sprachenkunde, Archäologie und Anthropologie des Indianischen Amerika. Berlin: Gebr. Mann Verlag.

Smith, A. L. 1934. *Two Recent Ceramic Finds at Uaxactun.* CIW Publication 436.

——. 1937. *Structure A-XVIII, Uaxactun.* CIW Publication 483.

——. 1950. *Uxactun, Guatemala: Excavations of 1931–37.* CIW Publication 588.

——. 1955. *Archaeological Reconnaissance in Central Guatemala.* CIW Publication 608.

——. 1965. Architecture of the Maya Highlands. In *HMAI* 2: 76–94.

——. 1972. *Excavations at Altar de Sacrificios, Architecture, Settlement, Burials and Caches.* PMAE Papers 62 (2).

——. 1977. Patolli at the Ruins of Seibal, Peten, Guatemala. In Hammond 1977b: 349–63.

Smith, A. L., and A. V. Kidder. 1943. *Explorations in the Motagua Valley, Guatemala.* CIW Publication 546.

——. 1951. *Excavations at Nebaj, Guatemala.* CIW Publication 594.

Smith, M. E. 1973. *Picture Writing from Ancient Southern Mexico: Mixtec Place Signs and Maps.* Norman: University of Oklahoma Press.

Smith, P. E. 1955. *Excavations in Three Ceremonial Structures at Mayapan.* CIW Current Reports, No. 21.

Smith, R. E. 1937. *A Study of Structure A-1 Complex at Uaxactun.* CIW Publication 456.

——. 1954. *Explorations on the Outskirts of Mayapán.* CIW Current Reports, No. 18.

——. 1955. *Ceramic Sequence at Uaxactun, Guatemala.* 2 vols. MARI Publication 20.

——. 1971. *The Pottery of Mayapan.* 2 vols. PMAE Papers 66.

Smith, R. E., and J. C. Gifford. 1965. Pottery of the Maya Lowlands. In *HMAI* 2: 498–543.

Smithsonian Institution. 1904. *Mexican and Central American Antiquities, Calendar Systems, and History.* Twenty-four papers by E. Seler, E. Förstemann, P. Schellhas, C. Sapper, and E. P. Dieseldorff, translated from the German under the supervision of C. P. Bowditch. BAE Bulletin 28.

Smyth, M. P. 1990. Maize Storage Among the Puuc Maya: The Development of an Archaeological Method. *AM* 1: 51–70.

Sorenson, J. L. 1956. An Archaeological Reconnaissance of West-Central Chiapas, Mexico. NWAF Paper 1: 7–19.

Spinden, H. J. 1913. *A Study of Maya Art.* PMAE Memoirs 6.

——. 1917. *The Ancient Civilizations of Mexico and Central America.* American Museum of Natural History Handbook Series, No. 3. New York.

——. 1924. *The Reduction of Maya Dates.* PMAE Papers 6 (4).

——. 1928. *The Ancient Civilizations of Mexico and Central America.* 3d ed., rev.

——. 1930. *Maya Dates and What They Reveal.* Brooklyn Institute of Arts and Sciences 4 (1). New York.

Stadelman, R. 1940. *Maize Cultivation in Northwestern Guatemala.* CIW Publication 523.

Standley, P. C. 1930. *Flora of Yucatan.* Field Museum of Natural History Publication 279, Botanical Series 3 (3). Chicago.

Stark, B. L., and B. Voorhies, eds. 1978. *Prehistoric Coastal Adaptations: The Economy and Ecology of Maritime Middle America.* New York: Academic Press.

Steggerda, M. 1941. *Maya Indians of Yucatan*. CIW Publication 531.

Stephens, J. L. 1841. *Incidents of Travel in Central America, Chiapas, and Yucatan*. 2 vols. New York: Harper. Reprinted by Dover, 1962.

———. 1843. *Incidents of Travel in Yucatan*. 2 vols. New York: Harper. Reprinted by Dover, 1963.

Stewart, R. 1977. Classic to Postclassic Period Settlement Trends in the Region of Santa Cruz del Quiche. In Wallace and Carmack 1977: 68–81.

Stirling, M. W. 1940. *An Initial Series from Tres Zapotes, Vera Cruz, Mexico*. National Geographic Society Mexican Archaeology Series 1 (1).

———. 1965. Monumental Sculpture of Southern Veracruz and Tabasco. In *HMAI* 3: 716–38.

Stone, A. 1985a. Variety and Transformation in the Cosmic Monster Theme at Quirigua, Guatemala. PRTS 7: 39–48.

———. 1985b. The Moon Goddess at Naj Tunich. *Mexicon* 7: 23–30.

———. 1985c. Sacrifice and Sexuality: Metaphorical Relationships in Classic Maya Art. Paper presented at the 45th International Congress of Americanists, Bogotá.

Stone, A., D. Reents, and R. Coffman. 1985. Genealogical Documentation of the Middle Classic Dynasty of Caracol, El Cayo, Belize. PRTS 6: 267–76.

Stone, D. Z. 1984. Cacao and the Maya Traders. In *Central American Archaeology*, F. Lange and D. Stone, eds. Albuquerque: University of New Mexico Press.

Strecker, M. 1987. Representaciones sexuales en el arte rupestre de la región maya. *Mexicon* 9: 34–37.

Stromsvik, G. 1942. *Substela Caches and Stela Foundations at Copan and Quirigua*. CIW Publication 528.

———. 1952. *The Ball Courts of Copan, with Notes on Courts at La Union, Quirigua, San Pedro Pinula and Asunción Mita*. CIW Publication 596.

Stross, B. 1983. The Language of Zuyua. *American Ethnologist* 10: 150–64.

Stross, F. H., P. D. Sheets, F. Asaro, and H. V. Michel. 1983. Precise Characterization of Guatemalan Obsidian Sources, and Source Determination of Artifacts from Quirigua. *AAnt* 48: 316–22.

Stuart, D. 1985a. The Yaxha Emblem Glyph at Yax-ha. RRAMW No. 1.

———. 1985b. A New Child-Father Relationship Glyph. RRAMW No. 2.

———. 1985c. The "Count of Captives" Epithet in Classic Maya Writing. PRTS 7: 97–101.

———. 1987a. Nuevas interpretaciones de la historia dinástica de Copán. Paper presented at the 4th Seminario de Arqueología Hondureña, La Ceiba, Honduras.

———. 1987b. Ten Phonetic Syllables. RRAMW No. 14.

———. 1988a. Blood Symbolism in Maya Iconography. In Benson and Griffin 1988: 175–221.

———. 1988b. The Río Azul Cacao Pot: Epigraphic Observations on the Function of a Maya Ceramic Vessel. *Antiquity* 62: 153–57.

———. 1989. *The "First Ruler" on Stela 24*. CN 7.

———. 1990a. The Decipherment of "Directional Count Glyphs" in Maya Inscriptions. *AM* 1: 213–24.

———. 1990b. A New Carved Panel from the Palenque Area. RRAMW No. 32.

———. 1993. Historical Inscriptions and the Classic Maya Collapse. In Sabloff and Henderson, 1993.

Stuart, D., N. Grube, L. Schele, and F. Lounsbury. 1989. *Stela 63, a New Monument from Copan.* CN 56.

Stuart, D., and S. D. Houston. 1989. Maya Writing. *SA* 261 (2): 82–89.

Stuart, D., and L. Schele. 1986. *Yax-K'uk-Mo', the Founder of the Lineage of Copán.* CN 6.

Stuart, G. E. 1986. Los códices maya. *Archaeoastronomy* 9: 164–76.

———. 1988. Glyph Drawings from Landa's Relación: A Caveat to the Investigator. RRAMW No. 19.

———. 1989. The Beginnings of Maya Hieroglyphic Study: Contributions of Constantine S. Rafinesque and James H. McCulloh, Jr. RRAMW No. 29.

Stuart, G. E., J. C. Scheffler, E. B. Kurjack, and J. W. Cottler. 1979. *Map of the Ruins of Dzibilchaltun, Yucatan, Mexico.* MARI Publication 47.

Stuart, G. E., and G. S. Stuart. 1977. *The Mysterious Maya.* Washington, D.C.: National Geographic Society.

Stuart, L. C. 1964. Fauna of Middle America. In *HMAI* 1: 316–62.

Sullivan, P. 1989. *Unfinished Conversations: Mayas and Foreigners Between Two Wars.* New York: Alfred A. Knopf.

Swadesh, M. 1961. *Interrelaciones de las lenguas mayenses. INAH Anales* 13: 231–67.

———. 1967. Lexicostatistic Classification. In *HMAI* 5: 79–115.

Taladoire, E. 1981. *Les terrains de jeu de balle.* Mexico City: Mission Archéologique et Ethnologique Française au Mexico.

Tamayo, J. L. 1964. The Hydrography of Middle America. In *HMAI* 1: 84–121.

Tate, C. 1985. Summer Solstice Ceremonies Performed by Bird Jaguar III of Yaxchilan, Chiapas, Mexico. *Estudios de Cultura Maya* 16: 85–112.

———. 1986. Maya Astronomical Rituals Recorded on Yaxchilan Structure 32. *Rutgers Art Review* 7: 1–20.

———. 1991. The Period Ending Stelae of Yaxchilan, PRTS 8: 102–9.

———. 1992. *Yaxchilan: The Design of a Maya Ceremonial City.* Austin: University of Texas Press.

Taube, K. 1985. The Maya Maize God: A Reappraisal. PRTS 7: 171–81.

———. 1987. A Representation of the Principal Bird Deity in the Paris Codex. RRAMW No. 6.

———. 1988. A Prehispanic Maya Katun Wheel. *Journal of Anthropological Research* 44: 183–203.

———. 1989a. Itzam Cab Ain: Caimans, Cosmology, and Calendrics in Postclassic Yucatan. RRAMW No. 26.

———. 1989b. The Maize Tamale in Classic Maya Diet, Epigraphy, and Art. *AAnt* 54: 31–51.

Tedlock, B. 1982. *Time and the Highland Maya.* Albuquerque: University of New Mexico Press.

Tedlock, D. 1985. *Popol Vuh: The Mayan Book of the Dawn of Life.* New York: Simon and Schuster.

Teeple, J. E. 1926. Maya Inscriptions: The Venus Calendar and Another Correlation. *AA* 28: 402–8.

———. 1931. *Maya Astronomy.* CIW Publication 403.

Thomas, C. 1882. A Study of the Manuscript Troano. In U.S. Department of the Interior, *Contributions to North American Ethnology* 5: 1–237.

———. 1893. Are the Maya Hieroglyphs Phonetic? *AA* (o.s.) 6: 241–70.

Thomas, N. D. 1974. *The Linguistic, Geographic, and Demographic Position of the Zoque of Southern Mexico.* NWAF Paper 36.

Thomas, P. M., Jr. 1974. Prehistoric Settlement at Becan: A Preliminary Report. MARI Publication 31: 139–46.

———. 1980. *Prehistoric Maya Settlement Patterns at Becan, Campeche, Mexico.* MARI Publication 45.

Thompson, D. E. 1960. Maya Paganism and Christianity. MARI Publication 19: 1–35.

Thompson, E. H. 1897a. Cave of Loltun, Yucatan. PMAE Memoirs 1 (2): 49–72.

———. 1897b. *The Chultunes of Labna.* PMAE Memoirs 1 (3).

Thompson, J. E. S. 1927. A Correlation of the Mayan and European Calendars. FMAS 17 (1): 1–22.

———. 1929. Maya Chronology: Glyph G of the Lunar Series. *AA* 31: 223–31.

———. 1930. *Ethnology of the Maya of Southern and Central British Honduras.* FMAS 17 (2).

———. 1931. *Archaeological Investigations in the Southern Cayo District, British Honduras.* FMAS 17 (2).

———. 1932. The Solar Year of the Mayas at Quirigua, Guatemala. FMAS 17 (4): 365–421.

———. 1934. *Sky-Bearers: Colors and Directions in Maya and Mexican Religion.* CIW Publication 436.

———. 1935. *Maya Chronology: The Correlation Question.* CIW Publication 456.

———. 1938. Sixteenth- and Seventeenth-Century Reports on the Chol Mayas. *AA* 40: 584–604.

———. 1939a. *Excavations at San Jose, British Honduras.* CIW Publication 506.

———. 1939b. *The Moon Goddess in Middle America.* CIW Publication 509.

———. 1941. *Dating of Certain Inscriptions of Non-Maya Origin.* CIW Theoretical Approaches to Problems, No. 1.

———. 1942. *Maya Arithmetic.* CIW Publication 528.

———. 1943a. Some Sculptures from Southeastern Quetzaltenango, Guatemala. CIW *NMA* No. 17.

———. 1943b. A Trial Survey of the Southern Maya Area. *AAnt* 9: 106–34.

———. 1944. *The Fish as a Maya Symbol for Counting and Further Discussion of Directional Glyphs.* CIW Theoretical Approaches to Problems, No. 2.

———. 1945. A Survey of the Northern Maya Area. *AAnt* 11: 2–24.

———. 1946. Some Uses of Tobacco Among the Maya. CIW *NMA* No. 61.

———. 1948. *An Archaeological Reconnaissance in the Cotzumalhuapa Region, Escuintla, Guatemala.* CIW Publication 574.

———. 1950. *Maya Hieroglyphic Writing: An Introduction.* CIW Publication 589. Reprinted by the University of Oklahoma Press, 1960 and 1971.

———. 1952. Waxen Idols and a Sacrificial Rite of the Lacandon. CIW *NMA* No. 109.

———. 1953. Review of *La antigua escritura de los pueblos de América Central* by Y. V. Knorozov. *Yan: Ciencias Antropológicas* 2: 174–78. Mexico City: Centro de Investigaciones Antropológicas de México.

————. 1954a. *The Rise and Fall of Maya Civilization*. Norman: University of Oklahoma Press.

————. 1954b. *A Presumed Residence of Nobility at Mayapan*. CIW Current Reports, No. 19.

————. 1958. *Thomas Gage's Travels in the New World*. Edited with an introduction by J. E. S. Thompson. Norman: University of Oklahoma Press.

————. 1959. Systems of Hieroglyphic Writing in Middle America and Methods of Deciphering Them. *AAnt* 24: 349–64.

————. 1962. *A Catalog of Maya Hieroglyphs*. Norman: University of Oklahoma Press.

————. 1965a. Archaeological Synthesis of the Southern Maya Lowlands. In *HMAI* 2: 331–59.

————. 1965b. Maya Hieroglyphic Writing. In *HMAI* 3: 632–58.

————. 1966. *The Rise and Fall of Maya Civilization*. 2d ed., rev. Norman: University of Oklahoma Press.

————. 1970. *Maya History and Religion*. Norman: University of Oklahoma Press.

————. 1971. *Maya Hieroglyphic Writing: Introduction*. 3d ed. Norman: University of Oklahoma Press.

————. 1972a. *Maya Hieroglyphs Without Tears*. London: Trustees of the British Museum.

————. 1972b. *A Commentary on the Dresden Codex*. American Philosophical Society Memoir 93.

————. 1973a. Maya Rulers of the Classic Period and the Divine Right of Kings. In *The Iconography of Middle American Sculpture*. New York: Metropolitan Museum of Art.

————. 1973b. The Painted Capstone at Sacnicte, Yucatan, and Two Others at Uxmal. *Indiana* 1: 59–63.

————. 1974. "Canals" of the Río Candelaria Basin, Campeche, Mexico. In Hammond 1974b: 297–302.

————. 1975. The Grolier Codex. UCARF Contribution 27: 1–9.

Thompson, J. E. S, H. E. D. Pollock, and J. Charlot. 1932. *A Preliminary Study of the Ruins of Coba, Quintana Roo, Mexico*. CIW Publication 424.

Thompson, R. H. 1958. *Modern Yucatecan Maya Pottery Making*. Memoirs of the Society for American Archaeology, No. 15. Salt Lake City.

Toscano, S. 1944. *Arte precolumbino de México y de la América Central*. Mexico City: Universidad Nacional Autónoma de México.

Totten, G. O. 1926. *Maya Architecture*. Washington, D.C.: Maya Press.

Tourtellot, G. 1970. The Peripheries of Seibal: An Interim Report. PMAE Papers 61: 405–21.

————. 1983. An Assessment of Classic Maya Household Composition. In Vogt and Leventhal 1983: 35–54.

————. 1988a. Developmental Cycles of Households and Houses at Seibal. In Wilk and Ashmore 1988: 97–120.

————. 1988b. *Peripheral Survey and Excavation Settlement and Community Patterns. Excavations at Seibal, Department of Peten, Guatemala*, G. R. Willey, ed. PMAE Memoirs 16.

————. 1990. Population Estimates for Preclassic and Classic Seibal, Peten. In Culbert and Rice 1990: 83–102.

Tourtellot, G., and J. A. Sabloff. 1972. Exchange Systems Among the Ancient Maya. *AA* 37: 126–35.

Tourtellot, G., J. A. Sabloff, and K. Carmean. 1989. Progress Report on the 1987 and 1988 Field Seasons at Sayil, Yucatan, Mexico. *Mexicon 9*: 12–15.

Tourtellot, G., J. A. Sabloff, and M. P. Smyth. 1990. Room Counts and Population Estimation for Terminal Classic Sayil in the Puuc Region, Yucatan, Mexico. In Culbert and Rice 1990: 245–61.

Tozzer, A. M. 1907. *A Comparative Study of the Mayas and the Lacandones.* Archaeological Institute of America. New York: Macmillan.

———. 1911. *A Preliminary Study of the Prehistoric Ruins of Tikal, Guatemala: A Report of the Peabody Museum Expedition, 1909–1910.* PMAE Memoirs 5 (2).

———. 1912. The Value of Ancient Mexican Manuscripts in the Study of the General Development of Writing. *Smithsonian Institution Annual Report, 1911*: 493–506.

———. 1913. *A Preliminary Study of the Prehistoric Ruins of Nakum, Guatemala.* PMAE Memoirs 5 (3).

———. 1921. *A Maya Grammar with Bibliography and Appraisement of the Works Noted.* PMAE Papers 9.

———. 1941. *Landa's relación de las cosas de Yucatán.* PMAE Papers 28.

———. 1957. *Chichen Itza and Its Cenote of Sacrifice.* PMAE Memoirs 11 and 12.

Tozzer, A. M., and G. M. Allen. 1910. *Animal Figures in the Maya Codices.* PMAE Papers 4 (3).

Trik, A. S. 1939. *Temple XXXII at Copan.* CIW Publication 509.

———. 1963. The Splendid Tomb of Temple I, Tikal, Guatemala. *Expedition* 6 (1): 2–18.

Trik, H., and M. E. Kampen. 1983. *The Graffiti of Tikal.* Tikal Report No. 33. UM.

Turner, B. L. 1974. Prehistoric Intensive Agriculture in the Maya Lowlands. *Science* 185: 118–24.

———. 1978a. The Development and Demise of the Swidden Thesis. In Harrison and Turner 1978: 13–22.

———. 1978b. Ancient Agricultural Land Use in the Central Maya Lowlands. In Harrison and Turner 1978: 163–83.

———. 1990. Population Reconstruction of the Central Maya Lowlands: 1000 B.C. to A.D. 1500. In Culbert and Rice 1990: 301–24.

Turner, B. L., and P. D. Harrison. 1978. Implications from Agriculture for Maya Prehistory. In Harrison and Turner 1978: 337–73.

———, eds. 1983. *Pulltrouser Swamp: Ancient Maya Habitat, Agriculture, and Settlement in Northern Belize.* Austin: University of Texas Press.

Turner, E. S., N. I. Turner, and R. E. W. Adams. 1981. Volumetric Assessment, Rank Ordering and Maya Civic Centers. In Ashmore 1981b: 71–88.

Ucko, P. J., R. Tringham, and G. W. Dimbleby, eds. 1972. *Man, Settlement and Urbanism.* London: Duckworth.

Urban, P. A. 1978. An Analysis of Mammalian Fauna from Tikal, El Peten, Guatemala. Master's thesis, University of Pennsylvania.

Urban, P. A., and E. M. Schortman, eds. 1986. *The Southeast Maya Periphery.* Austin: University of Texas Press.

———. 1988. The Southeast Zone Viewed from the East: Lower Motagua-Naco Valleys. In Boone and Willey 1988: 223–67.

Vaillant, G. C. 1935. Chronology and Stratigraphy in the Maya Area. *Maya Research* 2: 119–43.

———. 1944. *The Aztecs of Mexico: Origin, Rise and Fall of the Aztec Nation*. New York: Doubleday. Reprinted by Pelican, 1950.

Valdés, J. A. 1986. Uaxactun: recientes investigaciones. *Mexicon* 7 (6): 125–28.

———. 1988. Los mascarones preclásicos de Uaxactún: el caso del Grupo H. In *Primer Simposio Mundial Sobre Epigrafía Maya*: 165–81. Guatemala: Associación Tikal.

Velázquez Valadez, R. 1980. Recent Discoveries in the Caves of Loltun, Yucatan, Mexico. *Mexicon* 2: 53–55.

Villacorta, J. A., and C. A. Villacorta. 1927. *Arqueología guatemalteca*. Guatemala: Tipografía Nacional.

———. 1933. *Códices mayas reproducidos y desarrollados*. Guatemala: Tipografía Nacional.

Villagra, A. 1949. Bonampak, la ciudad de los muros pintados. *INAH Anales* 3 (Supplement).

Villagutierre Soto-Mayor, J. de. 1933. *Historia de la conquista de la provincia de el Itzá*. Guatemala: Biblioteca Goathemala.

———. 1983. *History of the Conquest of the Province of the Itzas*. Trans. R. D. Wood. Ed. F. E. Comparato. Culver City, Calif.: Labyrinthos.

Villa Rojas, A. 1934. *The Yaxuna-Coba Causeway*. CIW Publication 436.

Vlcek, D. T. 1978. Muros de delimitación residencial en Chunchucmil. ECAUY *Boletín 5* (28): 55–64.

Vlcek, D. T., and W. L. Fash. 1986. Survey in the Outlying Areas of the Copán Region, and the Copan-Quirigua "Connection." In Urban and Schortman 1986: 102–13.

Vlcek, D. T., S. García de González, and E. B. Kurjack. 1978. Contemporary Farming and Ancient Maya Settlements: Some Disconcerting Evidence. In Harrison and Turner 1978: 211-23.

Vogt, E. Z. 1961. Some Aspects of Zinacantan Settlement Patterns and Ceremonial Organization. *ECM* 1: 131–45.

———. 1964a. Ancient Maya and Contemporary Tzotzil Cosmology: A Comment on Some Methodological Problems. *AAnt* 30: 192–95.

———. 1964b. Some Implications of Zinacantan Social Structure for the Study of the Ancient Maya. 35th ICA *Actas* 1: 307–19.

———. 1969. *Zinacantan: A Maya Community in the Highlands of Chiapas*. Cambridge, Mass.: Harvard University Press.

———. 1983. Ancient and Contemporary Maya Settlement Patterns: A New Look from the Chiapas Highlands. In Vogt and Leventhal 1983: 89–114.

Vogt, E. Z., and R. M. Leventhal, eds. 1983. *Prehistoric Settlement Patterns: Essays in Honor of Gordon R. Willey*. Cambridge, Mass.: PMAE and University of New Mexico Press.

Von Euw, E. 1977. *Corpus of Maya Hieroglyphic Inscriptions*. Vol. 4, Part 1: *Itzimte, Pixoy, Tzum*. PMAE.

———. 1978. *Corpus of Maya Hieroglyphic Inscriptions*. Vol. 5, Part 1: *Xultun*. PMAE.

———. 1984. *Corpus of Maya Hieroglyphic Inscriptions*. Vol. 5, Part 2: *Xultun, La Honradez, Uaxactun*. PMAE.

Von Hagen, V. 1944. *The Aztec and Maya Papermakers*. New York: Augustin.

Voorhies, B. 1978. Previous Research on Nearshore Coastal Adaptations in Middle America. In Stark and Voorhies 1978: 5–21.

———. 1982. An Ecological Model of the Early Maya of the Central Lowlands. In Flannery 1982: 65–95.

———, ed. 1989. *Ancient Trade and Tribute: Economies of the Soconusco Region of Mesoamerica*. Salt Lake City: University of Utah Press.

Wagley, C. 1949. *The Social and Religious Life of a Guatemalan Village*. AA Memoir No. 71.

Wagner, P. L. 1964. Natural Vegetation of Middle America. In *HMAI* 1: 216–64.

Wallace, A. F. C. 1956. Revitalization Movements. *AA* 58: 264–82.

Wallace, D. T. 1977. An Intra-Site Locational Analysis of Utatlan: The Structure of an Urban Site. In Wallace and Carmack 1977: 20–54.

Wallace, D. T., and R. M. Carmack, eds. 1977. *Archaeology and Ethnohistory of the Central Quiche*. IMS Publication No. 1.

Walters, G. R. 1980. A Summary of the Preliminary Results of the 1979 San Augustin Acasaguastlan Archaeological Project. *Mexicon* 2: 55–56.

Ward, W. C., A. E. Weidie, and W. Back. 1985. *Geology and Hydrogeology of the Yucatan and Quaternary Geology of Northeastern Yucatan Peninsula*. New Orleans: New Orleans Geological Society.

Warren, B. W. 1961. The Archaeological Sequence at Chiapa de Corzo. In *Los Mayas del sur y sus relaciones con los Nahuas meridionales*. Mexico City: Sociedad Mexicana de Antropología.

Watanabe, J. M. 1983. In the World of the Sun: A Cognitive Model of Mayan Cosmology. *Man* 18: 710–28.

Wauchope, R. 1934. *House Mounds of Uaxactun, Guatemala*. CIW Publication 436.

———. 1938. *Modern Maya Houses*. CIW Publication 502.

———. 1948. *Excavations at Zacualpa, Guatemala*. MARI Publication 14.

———. 1949. Las edades de Utatlán e Iximché. *Antropología e Historia de Guatemala* 1: 10–22.

———. 1962. *Lost Tribes and Sunken Continents*. Chicago: University of Chicago Press.

———, ed. 1964–76. *Handbook of Middle American Indians*. Vols. 1–16. Austin: University of Texas Press.

———. 1965. *They Found the Buried Cities*. Chicago: University of Chicago Press.

———. 1970. Protohistoric Pottery of the Guatemalan Highlands. PMAE Papers 61: 89–244.

———. 1975. *Zacualpa, El Quiche, Guatemala. An Ancient Provincial Center of the Highland Maya*. MARI Publication 39.

Wauchope, R., and M. N. Bond. 1989. *Archaeological Investigations in the Department of Jutiapa, Guatemala*. MARI Publication 55.

Webb, M. 1964. The Postclassic Decline of the Peten Maya: An Interpretation in Light of a General Theory of State Society. Ph.D., University of Michigan.

———. 1973. The Peten Maya Decline Viewed in the Perspective of State Formation. In Culbert 1973: 367–404.

Webster, D., 1976a. On Theocracies. *AA* 76: 812–28.

———. 1976b. *Defensive Earthworks at Becan, Campeche, Mexico*. MARI Publication 41.

———. 1977. Warfare and the Evolution of Maya Civilization. In Adams 1977: 335–72.

——. 1979. Three Walled Sites of the Northern Maya Lowlands. *JFA* 5: 375–90.

——. 1988. Copan as a Classic Maya Center. In Boone and Willey 1988: 5–30.

——, ed. 1989. *The House of the Bacabs, Copan, Honduras.* DO.

Webster, D., and E. M. Abrams. 1983. An Elite Compound at Copan, Honduras. *JFA* 10: 285–296.

Webster, D., and A. C. Freter. 1990a. Settlement History and the Classic Collapse at Copan: A Redefined Chronological Perspective. *LAA* 1: 66–85.

——. 1990b. The Demography of Late Classic Copan. In Culbert and Rice 1990: 37–61.

Webster, D., and N. Gonlin. 1988. Household Remains of the Humblest Maya. *JFA* 15: 169–90.

Weeks, J. M. 1983. *Chisalin: A Late Postclassic Maya Settlement in Highland Guatemala.* BAR 169.

——. 1988. Residential and Local Group Organization in the Maya Lowlands of Southwestern Campeche, Mexico: The Early Seventeenth Century. In Wilk and Ashmore 1988: 73–96.

West, R. C. 1964. Surface Configuration and Associated Geology of Middle America. In *HMAI* 1: 33–83.

Wetherington, R. K., ed. 1978. *The Ceramics of Kaminaljuyu, Guatemala.* Pennsylvania State University Press Monograph Series on Kaminaljuyu. University Park.

Wheaton, T. R. 1976. La cerámica clásica del área de Huejotzingo, Puebla. *Proyecto Puebla-Tlaxcala Comunicaciones* 13: 25–31.

Whitley, D. S., and M. P. Beaudry, eds. 1989. *Investigaciones arqueológicas en la costa sur de Guatemala.* Los Angeles: UCLA Institute of Archaeology Monograph 31.

Whorf, B. J. 1933. *The Phonetic Value of Certain Characters in Maya Writing.* PMAE Papers 13 (2).

——. 1942. Decipherment of the Linguistic Portion of the Maya Hieroglyphs. *Smithsonian Institution Annual Report, 1941:* 479–502.

Wilk, R. R. 1988. Maya Household Organization: Evidence and Analogies. In Wilk and Ashmore 1988: 135–51.

Wilk, R. R., and W. Ashmore, eds. 1988. *Household and Community in the Mesoamerican Past.* Albuquerque: University of New Mexico Press.

Wilkin, G. C. 1971. Food Producing Systems Available to the Ancient Maya. *AAnt* 36: 432–48.

Willcox, H. 1954. Removal and Restoration of the Monuments of Caracol. *UM Bulletin* 18 (1–2): 46–72.

Willey, G. R. 1953. *Prehistoric Settlement Patterns in the Virú Valley, Peru.* BAE Bulletin 155.

——, ed. 1956a. *Prehistoric Settlement Patterns in the New World.* Viking Fund Publications in Anthropology, No. 23. New York.

——. 1956b. The Structure of Ancient Maya Society: Evidence from the Southern Lowlands. *AA* 58: 777–82.

——. 1972. *The Artifacts of Altar de Sacrificios.* PMAE Papers 64 (1).

——. 1973. *The Altar de Sacrificios Excavation, General Summary and Conclusions.* PMAE Papers 64 (3).

——. 1974. The Classic Maya Hiatus: A Rehearsal for the Collapse? In Hammond 1974b: 417–44.

————, ed. 1975. *Excavations at Seibal, Department of Peten, Guatemala*. PMAE Memoirs 13 (1, 2).

————. 1977. The Rise of Maya Civilization: A Summary View. In Adams 1977: 383–423.

————. 1978a. Artifacts. In *Excavations at Seibal*. PMAE Memoirs 14 (1): 1–189.

————, ed. 1978b. *Excavations at Seibal, Department of Peten Guatemala*. PMAE Memoirs 14 (1–3).

————. 1978c. Pre-Hispanic Maya Agriculture: A Contemporary Summation. In Harrison and Turner 1978: 325–35.

————. 1980. Towards a Holistic View of Ancient Maya Civilization. *Man* 15: 249–66.

————. 1981. Maya Lowland Settlement Patterns: A Summary Review. In Ashmore 1981b: 385–415.

————. 1982a. Maya Archaeology. *Science* 215: 260–67.

————, ed. 1982b. *Excavations at Seibal, Department of Peten, Guatemala*. PMAE Memoirs 15 (1, 2).

————. 1986. The Postclassic of the Maya Lowlands: A Preliminary Overview. In Sabloff and Andrews 1986: 17–51.

————. 1987. Changing Conceptions of Lowland Maya Culture History. In *Essays in Maya Archaeology*, by G. R. Willey: 189–207. Albuquerque: University of New Mexico Press.

————, ed. 1990. *Excavations at Seibal, Department of Peten, Guatemala*. PMAE Memoirs 17 (1–4).

————. 1991. Horizontal Integration and Regional Diversity: An Alternating Process in the Rise of Civilizations. *AAnt* 56: 197–215.

Willey, G. R., and W. R. Bullard, Jr. 1965. Prehistoric Settlement Patterns in the Maya Lowlands. In *HMAI* 2: 360–77.

Willey, G. R., W. R. Bullard, Jr., J. B. Glass, and J. C. Gifford. 1965. *Prehistoric Maya Settlements in the Belize Valley*. PMAE Papers 54.

Willey, G. R., T. P. Culbert, and R. E. W. Adams. 1967. Maya Lowland Ceramics: A Report from the 1965 Guatemala City Conference. *AAnt* 32: 289–315.

Willey, G. R., and J. C. Gifford. 1961. Pottery of the Holmul I Style from Barton Ramie, British Honduras. In *Essays in Pre-Columbian Art and Archaeology*, S. K. Lothrop et al., eds.: 152–70. Cambridge, Mass.: Harvard University Press.

Willey, G. R., and R. M. Leventhal. 1979. Prehistoric Settlement at Copan. In Hammond and Willey 1979: 75–102.

Willey, G. R., R. M. Leventhal, and W. L. Fash, Jr. 1978. Maya Settlement in the Copan Valley. *A* 31: 32–43.

Willey, G. R., and P. Mathews, eds. 1985. *A Consideration of the Early Classic Period in the Maya Lowlands*. IMS Publication 10.

Willey, G. R., and P. Phillips. 1958. *Method and Theory in American Archaeology*. Chicago: University of Chicago Press.

Willey, G. R., and J. A. Sabloff. 1974. *A History of American Archaeology*. San Francisco: Freeman.

Willey, G. R., R. J. Sharer, R. Viel, A. A. Demarest, R. M. Leventhal, and E. M. Schortman. 1980. A Study of Ceramic Interaction in the Southeastern Maya Periphery. Paper presented at the 45th Annual Meeting of the Society for American Archaeology, Philadelphia.

Willey, G. R., and D. B. Shimkin. 1973. The Maya Collapse: A Summary View. In Culbert 1973: 457–502.

Willey, G. R., and A. L. Smith. 1963. New Discoveries at Altar de Sacrificios. *A* 16 (2): 83–89.

———. 1969. *The Ruins of Altar de Sacrificios, Department of Peten, Guatemala: An Introduction*. PMAE Papers 62 (1).

Willson, R. W. 1924. *Astronomical Notes on the Maya Codices*. PMAE Papers 6 (3).

———. 1950. Materials on the Chorti Language. MCM, No. 28.

Winfield Capitaine, F. 1988. *La Estela 1 de La Mojarra, Veracruz, México*. RRAMW No. 16.

Wiseman, F. M. 1978. Agricultural and Historical Ecology of the Maya Lowlands. In Harrison and Turner 1978: 63–115.

Witkowski, S. R., and C. H. Brown. 1978. Mesoamerican: A Proposed Language Phylum. *AA* 80: 942–44.

Wolf, E. R., ed. 1959. *Sons of the Shaking Earth*. Chicago: University of Chicago Press.

———, ed. 1976. *The Valley of Mexico*. SAR.

Woodbury, R. B. 1965. Artifacts of the Guatemalan Highlands. In *HMAI* 2: 163–79.

Woodbury, R. B., and A. S. Trik. 1953. *The Ruins of Zaculeu, Guatemala*. 2 vols. Richmond, Va.: William Byrd Press.

Wren, L. H., and P. Schmidt. 1991. Elite Interaction During the Terminal Classic Period: New Evidence from Chichen Itza. In Culbert 1991a: 199–225.

Wren, L. H., P. Schmidt, and R. Krochock. 1989. The Great Ball Court Stone of Chichen Itza. RRAMW No. 25.

Ximénez, F. 1929–31. *Historia de la provincia de San Vicente de Chiapa y Guatemala*. 3 vols. Guatemala: Sociedad de Geografía e Historia de Guatemala.

Yanez-Barnuevo, G., and A. Ciudad Ruiz, eds. 1990. *Los Mayas: el esplendor de una civilización*. Madrid: Turner Libros, S.A.

Yoffee, N. 1991. Maya Elite Interaction: Through a Glass, Sideways. In Culbert 1991a: 285–310.

Yoffee, N., and G. L. Cowgill, eds. 1988. *The Collapse of Ancient States and Civilizations*. Tucson: University of Arizona Press.

Zeitlin, R. N. 1978. Long-Distance Exchange and the Growth of a Regional Center on the Southern Isthmus of Tehuantepec, Mexico. In Stark and Voorhies 1978: 183–210.

Zimmermann, G. 1956. *Die Hieroglyphen der Maya Handschriften*. Hamburg: Cram, de Gruter.

# ILLUSTRATION CREDITS

Sources cited by author and date are given in the Bibliography. The following abbreviations are used for frequently cited sources:

CIW    Carnegie Institution of Washington, Washington, D.C.

EC    Estudio Cámara, Mérida, Yucatán, México

FG    Fotografía Guerra, Mérida, Yucatán, México

INAH    Instituto Nacional de Antropología e Historia, México, D.F.

MARI    Middle American Research Institute, Tulane University, New Orleans

NGS    National Geographic Society, Washington, D.C.

PM    Peabody Museum of Archaeology and Ethnology, Harvard University, Cambridge, Mass.

TAM    *The Ancient Maya*, 3rd edition (Morley & Brainerd, 1956)

TP    Tikal Project, UM

UM    The University Museum of Archaeology and Anthropology, University of Pennsylvania, Philadelphia

FRONTISPIECE: American Museum of Natural History.

INTRODUCTION

P. 2: R. J. Sharer. P. 4: (above) TP; (below) O. Imboden, courtesy of G. E. Stuart, NGS. Pp. 8, 9: R. J. Sharer. P. 11: G. G. Healey. P. 12: F. R. Morley. P. 13: (top four) F. R. Morley; (lower left) R. J. Sharer. P. 14: B. Reyes. P. 15: J. Hairs. P. 16: (above) TP; (below) J. Hairs.

CHAPTER I

1.1–1.4: maps drawn by C. P. Beetz. 1.5: W. Ashmore. 1.6: R. Eichenberger. 1.7: P. D. Sheets, Proyecto Ceren. 1.8: R. J. Sharer, Verapaz Project. 1.9: CIW. 1.10: *TAM*. 1.11: C. O. Lundell. 1.12: W. R. Coe, TP. 1.13: R. A. Hedlund. 1.14: E. Palma Losa. 1.15: EC.

CHAPTER 2

2.1: A. A. Demarest, Proyecto El Mesak. 2.2: N. Hammond, Corozal Project. 2.3: W. R. Rust, Proyecto La Venta. 2.4: R. J. Sharer, Chalchuapa Project. 2.5: courtesy J. Marcus.

CHAPTER 3

3.1: J. A. Graham, Abaj Takalik Project. 3.2: D. W. Sedat, Verapaz Project. 3.3: R. J. Sharer, Verapaz Project. 3.4–3.5: R. D. Hansen, Regional Archeological Investigation of the North Peten, Guatemala (UCLA). 3.6: G. E. Stuart, NGS. 3.7: Smithsonian Institution. 3.8: NGS. 3.9: after Fig. 1, Lowe, Lee & Martínez 1982; by permission of the New World Archaeological Foundation. 3.10: after Plate 202, Greene, Rands & Graham 1972; by permission. 3.11: R. J. Sharer; first published as Fig. 5.4, p. 152, in *Fundamentals of Archaeology* (Menlo Park, Calif.: Benjamin Cummings, 1979); by permission. 3.12: drawing by J. A. Porter, by permission. 3.13: after Fig. 15, Shook & Kidder 1952; by permission of CIW. 3.14: drawing by W. R. Coe, Chalchuapa Project. 3.15–3.16: J. A. Graham, Abaj Takalik Project. 3.17: UM. 3.18: PM. 3.19: drawing by C. P. Beetz, Verapaz Project. 3.20: (above) UM; (right) J. A. Graham, Abaj Takalik Project; (below) W. R. Coe, TP. 3.21: D. M. Pendergast, Lamanai Project. 3.22: W. R. Coe, TP. 3.23: R. Velazquez V., Proyecto Loltun. 3.24, 3.26: R. T. Matheny, El Mirador Project. 3.25, 3.27: R. D. Hansen, Regional Archeological Investigation of the North Peten, Guatemala (UCLA). 3.28–3.29: D. A. Freidel, Cerros Project. 3.30–3.31: CIW. 3.32: (left) after Fig. 1, Gibson, Shaw & Finamore 1986; (right) after Fig. 3.1, Justeson, Norman & Hammond 1988; by permission of Princeton University Press. 3.33: drawing by L. Schele, after Fig. 2.13, L. Schele and D. A. Freidel 1990; by permission of W. Morrow & Co. 3.34–3.36. E. Wyllys Andrews, MARI. 3.37–3.38: R. J. Sharer.

CHAPTER 4

4.1–4.2: after Figs. 1.7 and 1.8, Marcus 1976b; by permission of Dumbarton Oaks, Washington, D.C. 4.3–4.4: W. R. Coe, TP. 4.5: TP. 4.6: O. Imboden, courtesy of G. E. Stuart, NGS. 4.7: W. R. Coe, TP. 4.8: (drawings) after Jones & Satterthwaite 1982, by permission of UM; (photos) W. R. Coe, TP. 4.9: TP. 4.10: (drawings) after Jones & Satterthwaite 1982, by permission of UM; (photo) W. R. Coe, TP. 4.11: TP. 4.12: after Jones & Satterthwaite 1982; by permission of UM. 4.13: G. Holton, TP. 4.14: after Jones & Satterthwaite 1982; by permission of UM. 4.15: W. R. Coe, TP. 4.16–4.19: TP. 4.20–4.21: after Jones & Satterthwaite 1982; by permission of UM. 4.22: TP. 4.23: after Jones & Satterthwaite 1982; by permission of UM. 4.24: CIW. 4.25: courtesy of J. P. Laporte, Proyecto Mundo Perdido (Tikal). 4.26: CIW. 4.27: *TAM.* 4.28: after Valdés 1988. 4.29: *TAM.* 4.30: CIW. 4.31: (photo) TP; (drawings) after Jones & Satterthwaite 1982, by permission of UM. 4.32–4.33: Rio Azul Project, courtesy R. E. W. Adams. 4.34–4.35: courtesy J. C. Marcus & W. J. Folan. 4.36–4.37: Becan Project, courtesy J. W. Ball. 4.38: after Proskouriakoff 1946, p. 53; by permission of CIW. 4.39–4.42: after Jones & Satterthwaite 1982; by permission of UM.

CHAPTER 5

5.1–5.2: Caracol Project, courtesy A. F. Chase and D. Z. Chase. 5.3: drawing by S. D. Houston, Caracol Project, courtesy A. F. Chase and D. Z. Chase. 5.4–5.10: Proyecto Petexbatun, courtesy A. A. Demarest. 5.11: after figs. on pp. 2: 63, 2: 55, I. Graham 1978 (copyright 1978 by the President and Fellows of Harvard College; by permission). 5.12–5.13: after figs. on pp. 3: 6–7, 3: 53, 3: 55, 3: 57, I. Graham 1979 (copyright 1979 by the President and Fellows of Harvard College; by permission). 5.14: PM. 5.15–5.16: after figs. on pp. 3:13, 3:15, 3:17, 3:27, I. Graham 1979 (copyright 1979 by the President and Fellows of Harvard College; by permission). 5.17: UM. 5.18–5.22: after figs. 1, 3, 27, 28, 29, Ruppert, Thompson & Proskouriakoff 1955; by permission of CIW. 5.23: (upper and lower left, right) UM; (center) Museo Nacional de Guatemala. 5.24: after Jones & Satterthwaite 1982; by permission of UM. 5.25: W. R. Coe, TP. 5.26–5.29: D. M. Pendergast, Altun Ha Project. 5.30: O. Imboden; courtesy G. E. Stuart, NGS. 5.31: S. Greco.

5.32–5.33: A. Ruz L. 5.34: rubbing by M. Greene Robertson. 5.35: Maudslay 1889–1902, vol. I, plate 27, vol. II, plate 22. 5.36–5.38: Museo Nacional de Antropología, Mexico. 5.39: courtesy of P. Mathews. 5.40: B. Edgerton. 5.41: PM. 5.42: Proyecto Arqueológico Copán. 5.43: R. J. Sharer, Early Copan Acropolis Program. 5.44: M. J. Becker, Proyecto Arqueológico Copán. 5.45–5.48: R. J. Sharer, Early Copan Acropolis Program. 5.49: (top) C. Klein, NGS; (bottom) B. Fash, Proyecto Arqueológico Acópolis Copán, courtesy R. Agurcia F. 5.50–5.51: R. J. Sharer, Early Copan Acropolis Program. 5.52: UM, Quirigua Project. 5.53: C. P. Beetz, Quirigua Project. 5.54: UM, Quirigua Project. 5.55–5.56: R. J. Sharer, Quirigua Project. 5.57: School of American Research, Santa Fe, N. M. 5.58: Jones 1983b (W. R. Coe, Quirigua Project). 5.59: R. J. Sharer, Quirigua Project. 5.60: CIW. 5.61–5.62: R. J. Sharer, Early Copan Acropolis Program.

CHAPTER 6

6.1: after Fig. 2, Willey 1978b (copyright 1978 by the President and Fellows of Harvard College; by permission). 6.2: G. R. Willey, Seibal Project. 6.3: PM. 6.4: CIW. 6.5: after Fig. 272, G. Andrews 1975; by permission of Oklahoma University Press. 6.6–6.7: E. W. Andrews V, MARI. 6.8: R. J. Sharer. 6.9: UM. 6.10: R. J. Sharer. 6.11: CIW. 6.12–6.13: *TAM*. 6.14: UM and Fairchild Aerial Surveys. 6.15: R. J. Sharer. 6.16–6.17: CIW. 6.18: EC. 6.19: CIW. 6.20: EC. 6.21–6.23: Sayil Project, courtesy J. A. Sabloff. 6.24: R. J. Sharer.

CHAPTER 7

7.1: Isla Cerritos Project, courtesy A. P. Andrews. 7.2: UM and Fairchild Aerial Surveys. 7.3: *TAM*. 7.4: R. J. Sharer. 7.5: CIW. 7.6: *TAM*. 7.7: FG. 7.8: EC. 7.9: (above) FG; (below) EC. 7.10–7.11: INAH. 7.12: (above) CIW; (below) FG. 7.13: EC. 7.14: CIW. 7.15: EC. 7.16: after map in Jones 1952. 7.17: W. Ashmore. 7.18–7.20: A. G. Miller, Tancah Project. 7.21: UM Library. 7.22–7.24: A. G. Miller, Tancah Project. 7.25: A. F. Chase, Tayasal Project. 7.26: after Plate 189, Greene, Rands & Graham 1972; by permission. 7.27–7.28: R. J. Sharer. 7.29: D. T. Wallace, after Wallace & Carmack 1977. 7.30–7.31: R. J. Sharer.

CHAPTER 8

8.1: *TAM*. 8.2: G. G. Healey. 8.3: P. D. Sheets, Proyecto Ceren. 8.4: R. T. Matheny, Edzna Project. 8.5–8.7: B. L. Turner, Pulltrouser Swamp Project (Fig. 8.7 courtesy of the Royal Air Force). 8.8: A. H. Siemens, from Fig. 4, Siemens & Pulston 1972; by permission of the Society for American Archaeology.

CHAPTER 9

9.1: A. P. Andrews.

CHAPTER 10

10.1: after Fig. 4, Eaton 1975; by permission. 10.2: W. A. Ashmore. 10.3–10.4: *TAM*. 10.5: (upper two) A. Galindo; (lower two) CIW. 10.6: *TAM*. 10.7: after Fig. 43, Hammond 1975 (copyright 1975 by the President and Fellows of Harvard College; by permission). 10.8: after Figs. 2.5, 2.6, Mathews 1991; by permission of Cambridge University Press. 10.9: MARI. 10.10: PM.

CHAPTER 11

11.1: *TAM*. 11.2: G. G. Healey. 11.3–11.4: *TAM*. 11.5: from Jones 1983b (drawing by W. R. Coe). 11.6: drawing by W. R. Coe. 11.7–11.14: *TAM*.

CHAPTER 12

12.1–12.5: *TAM*. 12.6: drawing by C. P. Beetz. 12.7–12.12: *TAM*.

CHAPTER 13

13.1: map drawn by C. P. Beetz, after Fox 1978. 13.2: classification follows that in Fox 1978. 13.3: *TAM*. 13.4: Museum Library, UM. 13.5–13.7: drawings by C. P. Beetz, after originals by J. A. Fox. 13.8: from Tozzer 1941; by permission of PM. 13.9–13.10: drawings by C. P. Beetz, after originals by J. A. Fox. 13.11: *TAM*. 13.12: after glyphs on pp. 316, 326, 330, 336, 340, 343, 350, Thompson 1962; by permission of University of Oklahoma Press. 13.13: Museum Library, UM; decipherment by J. A. Fox. 13.14: C. Jones, TP.

CHAPTER 14

14.1–14.2: *TAM*. 14.3: F. R. Morley. 14.4: CIW. 14.5–14.6: *TAM*. 14.7–14.8: CIW. 14.9: *TAM*. 14.10: PM. 14.11–14.12: CIW. 14.13: UM. 14.14: R. J. Sharer. 14.15: UM. 14.16: (left, center) School of American Research, Santa Fe, N. M.; (right) R. J. Sharer. 14.17: *TAM*. 14.18–14.19: INAH. 14.20: (left) INAH; (right) EC. 14.21: FG. 14.22–14.23: Museum für Völkerkunde, Basel. 14.24: *TAM*. 14.25: Maudslay 1889–1902, vol. IV, Plate 33. 14.26: A. Ruz L. 14.27: MARI. 14.28: PM. 14.29: W. R. Coe, TP. 14.30–14.32: G. G. Healey. 14.33–14.36: *TAM*. 14.37: A. G. Miller, Tancah-Tulum Project.

CHAPTER 15

15.1: (a–d) after Sharer 1978a, by permission; (e–g) after Pring 1976, by permission. 15.2: after Dahlin 1978, by permission. 15.3: (a–e) after Sharer 1978a, by permission; (f) after Fig. 27p, Gifford 1976 (copyright 1976 by the President and Fellows of Harvard College; by permission). 15.4: after Dahlin 1978, by permission. 15.5: after Sharer 1978a, by permission. 15.6–15.7: W. R. Coe, TP. 15.8: (a, b) after Sharer 1978a, by permission; (c) after Fig. 72a, Gifford 1976 (copyright 1976 by the President and Fellows of Harvard College; by permission). 15.9: after Sharer 1978a, by permission. 15.10: (a–c) after Figs. 96i, 88o, 88a, Gifford 1976 (copyright 1976 by the President and Fellows of Harvard College; by permission); (below) W. R. Coe, TP. 15.11: (upper photos) W. R. Coe, TP; (below) J. W. Ball, Becan Project. 15.12: after Sharer 1978a, by permission. 15.13: W. R. Coe, TP. 15.14–15.18: *TAM*. 15.19: G. E. Stuart, NGS. 15.20: Museo Arqueológico, Etnográfico e Histórico, Campeche, México. 15.21: PM. 15.22–15.23: *TAM*. 15.24–15.25: CIW. 15.26: after Figs. 171g, 192v, 196a,b, Gifford 1976 (copyright 1976 by the President and Fellows of Harvard College; by permission). 15.27: after Sharer 1978a, by permission. 15.28: (above) PM; (below) CIW. 15.29: after Fig. 77, Willey 1978a (copyright 1978 by the President and Fellows of Harvard College; by permission). 15.30: CIW. 15.31: Proyecto Arqueológico Acrópolis Copán, courtesy R. Agurcia F. 15.32: (upper left) S. Stubbs; (upper center, right) MARI; (below) R. J. Sharer, Early Copan Acropolis Program. 15.33: Secretaría de Agricultura y Fomento, México. 15.34: CIW. 15.35: R. J. Sharer, Verapaz Project. 15.36: (left) A. Ruz L.; (right) W. R. Coe, TP. 15.37: Museo de Arqueología e Historia, Mérida, Yucatán, México. 15.38: W. R. Coe, TP. 15.39: R. J. Sharer, Verapaz Project. 15.40: W. R. Coe, TP. 15.41–15.42: *TAM*. 15.43: (upper photos) Museo Nacional de Antropología, México; (below) PM. 15.44–15.45: *TAM*. 15.46: PM. 15.47–15.48: *TAM*. 15.49: C. Jones, Quirigua Project. 15.50: Museo Arqueológico, Etnográfico e Histórico, Campeche, México.

# INDEX

In this index "f" after a number indicates a separate reference on the next page, and "ff" indicates separate references on the next two to three pages. A continuous discussion over two or more pages is indicated by a span of numbers. *Passim* is used for a cluster of references in close but not consecutive sequence.

breaking objects, 58, 106, 697; burning, 515, 519, 522, 539–42 passim, 550–55 passim; prayer, 513, 519, 539, 541, 552ff; sacrifices, 246, 515–16, 522ff, 534, 539–40, 541–42, 543–46, 696, 732; scattering, 248, 534, 542. See also Ceremonies; Divination
Roman numerals, 557–58, 572f
Rome, 1
Roof combs, see under Architecture
Rosetta Stone, 616
Rosny, León de, 600, 608
Royal Ontario Museum, 272
Roys, Ralph, 44, 138, 338, 384, 404, 498, 595, 731
Rubber, 33, 394, 455f, 540, 550
Ruler A, 264. See also Ah Cacau
Ruler B, 270. See also Yax Kin Caan Chac
Ruler C, 271. See also Chitam
Ruler 1 (Petexbatun), 200, 225–29. See also Flint Sky
Ruler 1 (Piedras Negras), 262f
Ruler 1 (Tonina), 294
Ruler 2 (Petexbatun), 229. See also Shield God K
Ruler 2 (Piedras Negras), 262
Ruler 2 (Tonina), 295
Ruler 3 (Petexbatun), 229, 350
Ruler 3 (Piedras Negras), 262–64
Ruler 3 (Tonina), 294, 295–96
Ruler 4 (Petexbatun), 229–31, 350
Ruler 5 (Petexbatun), 231
Ruler 7 (Calakmul), 198–200
Ruler 21 (Tikal), 265
Ruler 22 (Tikal), 216, 265
Ruler 28 (Tikal), 265, 271
Rulers, 57ff, 86f, 92–98 passim, 110, 120–28, 139–47 passim, 155–80, 183, 185–91, 195, 196–200, 203–9, 211, 215–20, 225–36, 237–71, 275–76, 289–97, 302–17, 327–37, 338–39, 345–46, 349f, 356, 359, 368f, 403ff, 415, 424, 431ff, 453ff, 461f, 477, 479, 488–91 passim, 498–510, 596, 598, 610, 617f, 627f, 637, 641, 647, 657, 666–67, 696f, 711, 714, 726–36 passim, 740ff, 753; and ideology, 69–70, 105–6, 135f, 276, 284–93 passim, 515–16, 524–32 passim, 539–40, 543; and prestige, 66–70 passim, 105, 140, 143–44, 176, 180, 512; as war leaders, 7, 68, 106, 124, 512; basis of power, 45, 57,

66–70 passim, 108–9, 134–36, 140, 143, 176, 180, 287–88, 292–93, 510ff, 515–16, 540, 556, 559; inauguration of, 143, 163, 175f, 188, 190, 216, 225, 233, 236, 245–47, 265, 270, 287ff, 296, 308, 313, 325ff, 331, 543, 612f. See also Political organization; Women rulers
Rulers A–C (Petexbatun), 225
Rulers 1–6, 8, and 9 (Calakmul), 200
Rulers 4 and 5 (Piedras Negras), 263f
Rulers 4–10 (Tonina), 296
Rulers 6 and 7 (Piedras Negras), 264
Rulers 15–18 (Tikal), 175, 265
Rulers 23 and 24 (Tikal), 216, 264f
Ruling houses, 233, 252, 294, 353, 422. See also Political organization
Ruppert, Karl, 200
Ruz Lhuillier, Alberto, 277–80 passim, 294, 296, 661

Sabacil than (ceremony), 549, 555
Sabloff, Jeremy A., 49, 64, 433
Sacapultec Mayan, 583, 585
Sacbeob, see Causeways
Sachsische Landesbibliothek (Dresden), 600
Sacred almanac, see under Calendar
Sacrifice, 59, 541–42, 552ff; animal, 105, 109, 185, 229, 239–40, 245, 255, 288, 515–16, 539–40; blood, 105, 109, 183, 185, 229, 239–40, 245, 255, 288f, 421–22, 453, 515–16, 539–40, 599, 666; human, 5, 77, 80, 96, 105, 124f, 143–44, 166, 176–78, 180, 187, 192, 216f, 225–31 passim, 245–46, 255, 268, 280, 287, 289, 294f, 308, 317, 328–33 passim, 396f, 402ff, 432, 478f, 501–2, 503, 507, 515ff, 522ff, 529, 534f, 539–46 passim, 550, 670, 696, 732, 748, 752f. See also Maya religion; Rituals
Sacrificial knives, 544f, 659
Saculum, 748f
Sac U Uayeb (deity), 549, 551
Sac Xib Chac (deity), 531
Sahagún, Bernardino de, 728
Sahal, 255, 491. See also Cahal
Saiyam uincob (adjusters), 520
Sakajut, 107
Sakic (lineage), 507f
Salama Valley, 31, 33, 77–80, 101ff, 108, 711, 716
Salinas de los Nueve Cerros, 453, 492

Library of Congress Cataloging-in-Publication Data

Morley, Sylvanus Griswold, 1883–1948.
    The ancient Maya / [edited by] Robert J. Sharer. — 5th ed.
        p.    cm.
Includes bibliographical references and index.
ISBN 0-8047-2130-0 (cl.)
ISBN 0-8047-2310-9 (pbk.)
1. Mayas.   2. Mayas—Antiquities.   3. Mexico—Antiquities.
4. Central America—Antiquities.   I. Title.
F1435.M75    1994
972.81'016—dc20    93-13566    CIP

⊖ This book is printed on acid-free paper.
It was typeset by Wilsted & Taylor in 10/12.5 Sabon.